COMPARATIVE CONSTITUTIONAL REASONING

To what extent is the language of judicial opinions responsive to the political and social context in which constitutional courts operate? Courts are reason-giving institutions with argumentation playing a central role in constitutional adjudication. However, a cursory look at just a handful of constitutional systems suggests important differences in the practices of constitutional judges whether in matters of form, style or language.

Focusing on independently verified leading cases globally, a combination of qualitative and quantitative analysis offers the most comprehensive and systematic account of constitutional reasoning to date. This analysis is supported by the examination of eighteen legal systems around the world, including the European Court of Human Rights and the European Court of Justice. Universally common aspects of constitutional reasoning are identified in this book, and contributors also examine whether common law countries differ from civil law countries in this respect.

ANDRÁS JAKAB is Director of the Institute for Legal Studies at the Centre for Social Sciences of the Hungarian Academy of Sciences. He is also Professor of Constitutional and European Law at the Catholic University Pázmány Péter in Budapest.

ARTHUR DYEVRE is Associate Professor of Empirical Jurisprudence at the KU Leuven Faculty of Law, Belgium.

GIULIO ITZCOVICH is Associate Professor of Philosophy of Law in the Department of Legal Science at the University of Brescia, Italy. He is also a permanent fellow of the Tarello Institute for Legal Philosophy at the University of Genoa.

COMPARATIVE CONSTITUTIONAL REASONING

Edited by

ANDRÁS JAKAB

Hungarian Academy of Sciences / Pázmány Péter Catholic University

ARTHUR DYEVRE

KU Leuven Faculty of Law

GIULIO ITZCOVICH

University of Brescia

CAMBRIDGE
UNIVERSITY PRESS

CAMBRIDGE
UNIVERSITY PRESS

University Printing House, Cambridge CB2 8BS, United Kingdom

One Liberty Plaza, 20th Floor, New York, NY 10006, USA

477 Williamstown Road, Port Melbourne, VIC 3207, Australia

314-321, 3rd Floor, Plot 3, Splendor Forum, Jasola District Centre, New Delhi - 110025, India

79 Anson Road, #06-04/06, Singapore 079906

Cambridge University Press is part of the University of Cambridge.

It furthers the University's mission by disseminating knowledge in the pursuit of education, learning and research at the highest international levels of excellence.

www.cambridge.org
Information on this title: www.cambridge.org/9781107449763
DOI: 10.1017/9781316084281

First published 2017
First paperback edition 2018

A catalogue record for this publication is available from the British Library

ISBN 978-1-107-08558-9 Hardback
ISBN 978-1-107-44976-3 Paperback

CONTENTS

CONTRIBUTORS

MARIAN AHUMADA RUIZ, Professor of Constitutional Law, Faculty of Law, Autonomous University of Madrid.

JENNIFER L. BROOKHART, Researcher, University of Wisconsin–Madison.

EOIN CAROLAN, Senior Lecturer, School of Law, University College Dublin.

WEN-CHEN CHANG, Professor, National Taiwan University College of Law, Taiwan.

HUGO CYR, Dean, Faculty of Political Science and Law, Université du Québec à Montréal.

ARTHUR DYEVRE, Associate Professor, KU Leuven Faculty of Law.

LOURENS DU PLESSIS, Extraordinary Professor, North-West University (Potchefstroom), South Africa.

JOHANNA FRÖHLICH, associate researcher and professor of comparative constitutional law, Law School, University San Francisco de Quito, Quito; doctoral candidate, Faculty of Law and Political Sciences, Pázmány Péter Catholic University, Budapest.

JANNEKE GERARDS, Professor of Fundamental Rights Law, Utrecht University, the Netherlands.

TANIA GROPPI, Full Professor of Public Law, University of Siena.

TAMAS GYORFI, Senior Lecturer, University of Aberdeen, School of Law.

MICHAELA HAILBRONNER, Senior Research Fellow, University of Münster.

CONRADO HÜBNER MENDES, Professor Doctor of Constitutional Law at the University of São Paulo.

GIULIO ITZCOVICH, Associate Professor in Philosophy of Law, University of Brescia, Italy.

ANDRÁS JAKAB, Director of the Institute for Legal Studies, Hungarian Academy of Sciences, Centre for Social Sciences, Budapest; Professor of Constitutional and European Law at the Catholic University Pázmány Péter in Budapest.

ZDENEK KÜHN, Associate Professor of Jurisprudence at Charles University Law School and Judge at the Supreme Administrative Court of the Czech Republic.

KONRAD LACHMAYER, Research Chair, Institute for Legal Studies, Hungarian Academy of Sciences, Centre for Social Sciences, Budapest; Research Fellow at the Durham Law School (UK), ERC Project on "Neo-Federalism".

STEFAN MARTINI, Walther Schücking Institute for International Law, Kiel University.

SUZIE NAVOT, Professor of Law, The Striks School of Law, The College of Management Academic Studies, Rishon Lezion (Israel).

MONICA POPESCU, Assistant Professor, Faculty of Law, Université Laval.

CHRISTA RAUTENBACH, Professor of Law, North-West University (Potchefstroom), South Africa and Ambassador Scientist, Alexander von Humboldt Foundation, Germany.

CHERYL SAUNDERS, Laureate Professor Emeritus, Melbourne Law School.

HOWARD SCHWEBER, Professor of Political Science and Legal Studies, University of Wisconsin–Madison.

IRENE SPIGNO, Professor of Constitutional Law, Universidad Autonoma de Coahuila (Mexico) and Director of the Centre of Comparative Constitutional Studies, Inter-American Academy of Human Rights (Mexico).

ADRIENNE STONE, Kathleen Fitzpatrick Australian Laureate Fellow, Professor Director, Centre for Comparative Constitutional Studies, Melbourne Law School.

PREFACE

This volume is the result of a research project which lasted almost five years. Since September 2011, the CONREASON project has generously been funded by the VolkswagenStiftung in the form of a Schumpeter Fellowship at the Max Planck Institute for Comparative Public Law and International Law in Heidelberg. The Max Planck Institute provided us with the perfect research environment, for which we have to thank its director, Armin von Bogdandy. The VolkswagenStiftung was very flexible on several occasions in order to fit our newly emerging costs into the original budget; we thank Hagen Hof, Silke Bertram and Nataliya Moor for this. We are also grateful to the Hungarian Academy of Sciences, which financially supported both the statistical analysis and one of our workshops. In the publication of the preparatory (theoretical) results of our research, the *German Law Journal* was open for fruitful cooperation, the result of which was a special issue in August 2013. We thank Russell Miller, *German Law Journal* editor-in-chief, for his openness to our original proposal.

In organising our first workshop in Heidelberg (15 February 2013), Margit Dagli helped us in every little detail, whereas in our second workshop in Budapest (7–8 February 2014), Mónika Ganczer proved to be of invaluable assistance. At these two workshops, we could enjoy helpful feedback not only from all the authors, but also from some further colleagues who took up the difficult task of commenting the draft versions of several chapters: Aileen Kavanagh, Zoltán Szente, Stefan Martini and Konrad Lachmayer (the latter two are also authors). We received statistical help from László Göndör, Ádám Telek, Eszter Vay-Farkas, Borbála Greskovits and Zsófia Papp.

The project has been presented in different stages at different events where we received numerous useful remarks and suggestions. We are grateful to the participants of the *Dienstagsrunde* at Max Planck Institute for Comparative Public Law and International Law of 15 November 2011 (especially to Matthias Goldmann, Simon Hentrei, Nele Yang, Carlino

Antpöhler, Johanna Dickschen, Stephan Hinghofer-Szalkay, Stephan Schill, Mateja Steinbrück Platise and Armin von Bogdandy), to the participants of the Bielefeld workshop on "Index Building in Socio-Legal Scholarship" on 10 June 2014 (especially to Tom Ginsburg, Mirjam Künkler, Asli Bali, Dawood Ahmed, Moamen Gouda, Tamir Moustafa, Mila Versteeg and Zachary Elkins), to the audience of the *Rechtskulturen* lecture on the CONREASON project at the Humboldt University Berlin on 20 November 2013 (especially to Christoph Möllers and Maximilian Steinbeis) and to all colleagues present at the first presentation of our concluding chapter on 23 January in Budapest at the Hungarian Academy of Sciences. For interesting discussions on the concept of leading cases, we are grateful to Nele Yang and Rainer Grote.

Cambridge University Press and especially Elizabeth Spicer helped us throughout the project with a constructive and positive approach in order to find the final form of this publication.

We would like to thank all of them.

Budapest / Leuven / Brescia, 1 September 2016

NOTE ON ONLINE MATERIALS

The full dataset which underlies the analysis in this book is available for download at www.cambridge/9781107085589. It is our hope that other scholars may make use of the data we have collected in their own research.

Accompanying the dataset is, for every court surveyed, a sample judgment in English from the high and a case note which explaining its significance. We hope that students and legal scholars may find these informative.

Finally, the data recording the responses of the experts who verified our authors' choice of cases examined is also available for download.

Introduction

Comparing Constitutional Reasoning with Quantitative and Qualitative Methods

ANDRÁS JAKAB, ARTHUR DYEVRE AND GIULIO ITZCOVICH

The past thirty years have witnessed a dramatic rise in the power wielded by judicial institutions.[1] Uneven as the judicial push may have been, it has been real and, despite regional variations, truly global in scope.[2] Not only have judges been playing an increasingly larger role in defining the direction, shape and content of public policies in an increasingly larger number of countries; from abortion and health care provision to party funding and same-sex marriage, there is hardly any facet of public or private life that can claim to have been left untouched by the judges' steadily expanding reach. Accompanying the rapid diffusion of judicial review across the world, constitutional judges have been at the forefront of this remarkable evolution. Their growing influence has spurred an explosion in constitutional litigation, with the result that constitutional modes of argumentation have become a pervasive feature of public discourse. And so, just as they have witnessed the creeping constitutionalisation of much of executive and legislative politics,[3] citizens have grown accustomed to the spectacle of constitutional courts setting aside democratically enacted laws in the name of constitutional rights.

[1] For critical remarks on the introductory and concluding chapters we are grateful to Mónika Ambrus, Lídia Balogh, Mátyás Bencze, Nóra Chronowski, Péter Cserne, György Gajduschek, Katalin Kelemen, Viktor Lőrincz, Margit Mészáros-Kiss, András László Pap, Zsófia Papp, Kálmán Pócza, Miklós Sebők, Jørn Øyrehagen Sunde, Miklós Szabó, Zoltán Szente, Michel Troper and Zsolt Ződi, in addition to the authors of the present volume.

[2] See C. Neal Tate and Torbjorn Vallinder (eds), *The Global Expansion of Judicial Power* (New York University Press 1995).

[3] Alec Stone, *The Birth of Judicial Politics in France: The Constitutional Council in Comparative Perspective* (Oxford University Press 1992); Alec Stone Sweet, *Governing with Judges: Constitutional Politics in Europe* (Oxford University Press 2000).

Some regard the constitutional judges' newfound assertiveness as nothing short of judicial usurpation.[4] Others, on the contrary, hail it as the triumph of the rule of law and human rights.[5] But one need not have a horse in this race to wonder how constitutional judges manage to justify and communicate their rulings when these so often touch on deeply divisive societal issues. Like legislators, constitutional judges are public decision makers. However, to the extent that they are not elected and cannot be voted out of office, they lack democratic credentials. This raises one of the central puzzles of constitutional law in democratic regimes. How do unelected judges explain their decision to the litigants who happen to wind up on the losing side of a constitutional dispute? How do judges justify the decision to disapply a law passed by legislators who have themselves been chosen in free and fair elections? Constitutional reasoning, understood as the reasons constitutional judges publicly adduce for their decisions, is thus crucial to understanding constitutional adjudication.[6] As non-majoritarian institutions, constitutional tribunals cannot hope to achieve social and political acceptance but by demonstrating that their rulings are based on sound justifications.

The present book undertakes to explore what these justifications are and how they vary across constitutional orders of the world. On the following pages, we first show how empirical methods are slowly gaining popularity in comparative constitutional scholarship in general (Section I), then we define what we mean by 'constitutional reasoning' in this volume

[4] See Ran Hirschl, *Towards Juristocracy: The Origins and Consequences of the New Constitutionalism* (Harvard University Press 2004).

[5] See e.g. András Jakab, 'Application of the EU Charter by National Courts in Purely Domestic Cases' in András Jakab and Dimitry Kochenov (eds), *The Enforcement of EU Law and Values: Ensuring Member States' Compliance* (Oxford University Press 2017) 252–62.

[6] On the legitimacy-building role of judicial reasoning in general, see Aulis Aarnio, *The Rational and the Reasonable: A Treatise on Legal Justification* (Reidel 1987); Jürgen Habermas, *Faktizität und Geltung. Beiträge zur Diskurstheorie des Rechts und des demokratischen Rechtsstaats* (Suhrkamp 1992); Uwe Kischel, *Die Begründung* (Mohr Siebeck 2003); Manuel Atienza, *El Derecho como argumentación* (Ariel 2006). On the different mechanisms of how legitimacy is created by constitutional courts, including *inter alia* their reasoning, see André Brodocz, 'Constitutional Courts and Their Power of Interpretation' in Antonia Geisler, Michael Hein and Siri Hummel (eds), *Law, Politics, and the Constitution. New Perspectives from Legal and Political Theory* (Peter Lang 2014) 15–29; Hans Vorländer, 'Deutungsmacht – Die Macht der Verfassungsgerichtsbarkeit' in Hans Vorländer (ed), *Die Deutungsmacht der Verfassungsgerichtsbarkeit* (VS Verlag 2006) 9–33; Christian Boulanger, 'Vergleichende Verfassungsgerichtsforschung: Konjunkturen verfassungsgerichtlicher Autorität am Beispiel Bundesverfassungsgericht und ungarisches Verfassungsgericht' in Robert Christian van Ooyen – Martin HW Möllers (eds), *Handbuch Bundesverfassungsgericht im politischen System* (2nd edn, Springer 2015) 911–926.

(Section II), we review the most important descriptive (i.e., not normative) theories of constitutional reasoning (Section III), and we explain the research design and the types of questions that we hoped to answer with our project (Section IV). Because we considered our research partly as a mapping exercise, and partly as following the general idea behind grounded theories, we wanted to avoid a narrow focus on very specific research questions.[7]

I The Emergence of Empirical Methods in Comparative Constitutional Scholarship

Of course, this book is not the first to deal with constitutional reasoning. The subject has spawned a vast literature. A glance at the bookshelves of a good law library will reveal a wealth of contributions on legal argumentation and constitutional interpretation in many different languages. Legal scholars and constitutional theorists alike have been engaged in endless debates about the merits of various approaches to constitutional interpretation.[8] In the United States, the debate, in a somewhat simplified manner, is often summed up as one pitting "originalists" against proponents of the "living constitution". Originalism is commonly associated with the view that judges should stick to the original meaning of the constitutional text or to the intentions of its framers when deciding cases. Theories of constitutional interpretation based on the idea of the "living constitution", by contrast, are supposed to emphasize the need to interpret and "update" the text in light of contemporary moral values. Echoes of the US discussion can be found in other jurisdictions, from Malaysia to the European Convention of Human Rights.[9] Elsewhere, as in the European Union, for example, critics have focused on the European Court of Justice

[7] In traditional (positivist) social science, for a research design we need a theory, a specific research question (in the form of a hypothesis) embedded into that theory and then the testing of the hypothesis. In contrast to this, grounded theory (or the "discovery of theory from data") is an inductive method where you start with a conceptual frame but without very specific hypotheses, you then analyse your material empirically and you try to build your theory based on the data you acquired. Cf. Barney Glaser and Anselm Strauss, *The Discovery of Grounded Theory* (Aldine 1967); Antony Bryant and Kathy Charmaz (eds), *The SAGE Handbook of Grounded Theory* (SAGE 2007).

[8] See the different discourses in each chapter of the present volume.

[9] Jeffrey Goldsworthy, 'Originalism in Constitutional Interpretation' (1997) 25 *Federal Law Review* 1; Yvonne Tew, 'Originalism at Home and Abroad' (2013) 52 *Columbia Journal of Transnational Law* 780; Danny Nicol, 'Original Intent and the European Convention on Human Rights' (2005) *Public Law* 152.

and its reliance on "teleological" interpretation as a means to expand the remit of EU legislation.[10] The discussion has, of course, touched upon various other questions, such as whether constitutional judges should be encouraged or prohibited to consider foreign legal materials; whether balancing and means-end tests like proportionality represent a legitimate way to adjudicate constitutional disputes;[11] whether judges should make consequentialist or strategic considerations explicit in their opinions, etc.

Poring over the countless monographs, edited volumes and law review articles, what strikes the reader is the overly normative focus of the discussion. Legal scholars, generally, have been focussing almost exclusively on how judges ought to arrive at their decisions.[12] Assuredly, if we conceive of law as a practical discipline continuous with the activity of legal practitioners, this normative focus appears entirely warranted. Aside from providing judges with normative guidance, this scholarship furnishes legal counsels with rhetorical ammunitions in the battle for persuasion that drives courtroom proceedings. Generally missing from this literature, though, is a systematic account of how constitutional judges

[10] Gerard Conway, *The Limits of Legal Reasoning and the European Court of Justice* (Cambridge University Press 2012).

[11] Short explanation for non-lawyers: judicial balancing (*Abwägung, ponderación, mise en balance/conciliation, bilanciamento/ponderazione, mérlegelés*) refers to explicit weighing of competing principles or interests to determine the outcome of a legal case. A distinct kind of balancing judgment is the proportionality test, which occurs when the adjudicator, faced with a law or other measure that impinges on a constitutional right, evaluates (a) whether the aim of the measure is legitimate, (b) whether the measure is suitable to achieve the legitimate aim, (c) whether the measure does not go beyond what is necessary to achieve the aim, and (d) whether the benefit of the measure is not outweighed by the harm caused to the constitutional right (so called "proportionality in the strict sense", which implies a balancing judgment). In the extensive literature on balancing and proportionality, recent contributions include Alec Stone Sweet and Jud Mathews, 'Proportionality Balancing and Global Constitutionalism' (2008) 47 *Columbia Journal of Transnational Law* 73; Grégoire CN Webber, *The Negotiable Constitution. On the Limitation of Rights* (Cambridge University Press 2009); Aharon Barak, *Proportionality. Constitutional Rights and Their Limitations* (Cambridge University Press 2012); Kai Möller, *The Global Model of Constitutional Rights* (Oxford University Press 2012); Moshe Cohen Eliya and Iddo Porat, *Proportionality and Constitutional Culture* (Cambridge University Press 2013); Jacco Bomhoff, *Balancing Constitutional Rights: The Origins and Meanings of Postwar Legal Discourse* (Cambridge University Press 2013); Liora Lazarus, Christopher McCrudden and Niegel Bowles (eds), *Reasoning Rights: Comparative Judicial Engagement* (Hart 2014); Grant Huscroft, Bradley W Miller and Grégoire Webber (eds), *Proportionality and the Rule of Law: Rights, Justification, Reasoning* (Cambridge University Press 2014).

[12] A remarkable contribution to this particular genre, resting its normative claims largely on comparative considerations, is Vicki C. Jackson, 'Multi-Valenced Constitutional Interpretation and Constitutional Comparisons: An Essay in Honor of Mark Tushnet' (2008) 26 *Quinnipiac Law Review* 599–670.

do actually justify their decisions. In fact, precisely because of its normative focus, constitutional law scholarship is easily enmeshed in domestic judicial politics. And so the discussion over constitutional reasoning tends to reflect the degree of political polarisation within the legal academy, along with the law professors' ideological predilections and attitudes towards the courts. The result is a literature that is almost as parochial as it is plethoric. Looking only at English-language contributions, we see new normative theories of constitutional interpretation continually adding to an already massive stock.[13] So numerous are the theories spawned by the normative discussion that it may not be entirely exaggerated to say that whatever decision she reaches, a constitutional judge will always find some normative theory to back it. Also, tailored as they are to the expectations and beliefs of their particular domestic audiences, these theories tend to reflect the degree of sophistication of public discourse in the jurisdiction under consideration as well as the controversies surrounding particular local rulings. Sensitivity to local concerns and politics means that the literature differs greatly in diversity, breadth and sophistication from one country to the next, with the consequence that issues regarded as central in one setting are comprehensively ignored in others.[14] A corollary of this state of affairs is that one is unlikely to get a reliable sense of how reasoning practices differ across constitutional systems by simply juxtaposing scholarly contributions from distinct jurisdictions.

Standing in sharp contrast to this cornucopia of normative arguments about constitutional reasoning is the relative paucity of research on the judges' actual reasoning practices. Traditionally, the discipline of comparative law has a more descriptive outlook. Detached, at least in appearance, from the inward-looking and often ideology-driven discussion unfolding in the domestic legal context, comparativists usually take the description of "foreign" law – rather than the advocacy or criticism of specific doctrines – as their primary concern. Early judicial comparativism was especially preoccupied with differences between the Common and Civil Law traditions and how these affected the style, tone and loquaciousness of court opinions. They contrasted the brevity and oracular style of French supreme court opinions with the more discursive approach practiced by

[13] For overviews of normative theories see e.g., Giulio Itzcovich, 'On the Legal Enforcement of Values. The Importance of the Institutional Context' in Jakab and Kochenov (n 5); Stephen M Griffin, *American Constitutionalism: From Theory to Politics* (Princeton University Press 1996) 140–191; Cesare Pinelli, 'Il dibattito sull'interpretazione costituzionale tra teoria e giurisprudenza' in *Scritti in memoria di L. Paladin* (Jovene 2004) III, 1671.

[14] For an overview of different national theories of constitutional interpretation, see Marie-Claire Ponthoreau, *Droit(s) constitutionnel(s) comparé(s)* (Economica 2010) 295–314.

US judges.[15] Among the most important contributions to this strand of literature in recent years is the work of the American comparativist Mitchell Lasser.[16] Comparing judicial reasoning of the French *Cour de cassation*, the US Supreme Court and the European Court of Justice, his analysis seeks to cast a wider light on the broader discursive setting in which these judges announce their decisions. He insists that, unlike US Supreme Court opinions, both French supreme court opinions and ECJ decisions are not self-contained documents. Far from standing alone, the opinions issued by these courts are embedded in a larger, less formal discourse developed by reporting judges, advocate generals and legal scholars. Based on careful documentation, his argument challenges the crude opposition between a reputedly rigidly formalist Civil Law style and a Common Law approach supposedly more candid and open to policy considerations – a perspective that long represented the received view within the discipline. While Lasser casts his argument as one about "judicial deliberations" and rests his analysis on mostly non-constitutional cases, his analysis does have implications for our comparative understanding of constitutional argumentation. Not only is the claim that judicial argumentation differs in constitutional cases nowhere to be found in his writing, but he explicitly suggests that what he says about the argumentative practices of the *Cour de cassation* holds in equal measure for the Constitutional Council.[17]

Lasser, to be sure, has not been alone in seeking to cast a wider light on the points of convergence and divergence among legal cultures when it comes to the justification of judicial outcomes. Similar to Lasser, comparative legal scholarship has addressed constitutional reasoning under the more general heading of "reasoning" or "legal reasoning".[18] But fresh

[15] See John Philip Dawson, *The Oracles of the Law* (University of Michigan Law School 1968); Gino Gorla, *Lo stile delle sentenze, ricerca storico-comparativa e testi commentati* (Foro italiano 1968).

[16] Mitchel de S Lasser, *Judicial Deliberations: A Comparative Analysis of Judicial Transparency and Legitimacy* (Oxford University Press 2004). For a thorough analysis of the conceptual frame and method applied by Lasser, see Nick Huls et al. (eds), *The Legitimacy of Highest Courts' Rulings – Judicial Deliberations and Beyond* (Springer 2009). For earlier carefully designed, but non-quantitative projects on comparative legal reasoning see Neil MacCormick and Robert S Summers (eds), *Interpreting Statutes. A Comparative Study* (Aldershot 1991) and *Interpreting Precedents. A Comparative Analysis* (Ashgate 1997).

[17] Lasser (n 16) 287. On the differences between the styles of the *Cour de cassation* and the *Conseil constitutionnel*, see John Bell, *French Legal Cultures* (Cambridge University Press 2008) 219.

[18] Jaap Hage, 'Legal Reasoning' in Jan Smits (ed), *Elgar Encyclopedia of Comparative Law* (2nd edn, Edward Elgar 2012) 521–537; Michal Bobek, *Comparative Reasoning in European Supreme Courts* (Oxford University Press 2013); PS Atiyah and Robert S Summers, *Form*

research has begun to look specifically at how constitutional reasoning differs across constitutional systems.[19]

Yet, however rich and insightful, the comparative studies that have come out of this line of research present important limitations. Such studies typically consist of loosely assembled country reports looking at half a dozen or more jurisdictions or, alternatively, of tightly-knit narratives but with a characteristically narrow geographical scope. Such an approach is certainly appropriate in the early, exploratory stage of a new field of inquiry when researchers have little clue as to which variables will emerge as important from the comparative study of legal systems that are, by definition, unfamiliar. Rather than devising a detailed questionnaire or an elaborate analytical matrix ex ante, it is then often preferable to allow the important issues to emerge freely from a discussion unimpaired by preconceived ideas. In that regard, it is probably in highlighting the most important unknown unknowns – i.e., the features of a legal system that we may not even anticipate to be relevant – that this early-stage scholarship on constitutional reasoning makes its greatest controbution. Yet, from this baseline, taking the research further requires a methodological upgrade. Argumentative practices can vary significantly across constitutional cases and tend to evolve over time. But variations of this sort are easily overlooked when sweeping claims about the reasoning style of a particular court are based on the analysis of a handful of opinions selected without any explicit methodology. So, there can be little hope of constructing a more accurate picture of the diversity of constitutional reasoning practices throughout the world unless scholars develop a more systematic approach to the comparative study of constitutional opinions.

Some scholars have already begun to take up the methodological challenge. In a pattern that is now familiar in legal scholarship, the first to embrace empirical methods were those with a foot in the social sciences. American political science has a long tradition of empirical research on law and courts.[20] Until recently, though, their work was more or less exclusively concerned with the courts' decisions on the merits and paid

and Substance in Anglo-American Law: A Comparative Study of Legal Reasoning, Legal Theory, and Legal Institutions (Clarendon 1991); Mario Bessone and Riccardo Guastini (eds), *Materiali per un corso di analisi della giurisprudenza* (Cedam 1994) 361–479.

19 See e.g. Jeffrey Goldsworthy, *Interpreting Constitutions: A Comparative Study* (Oxford University Press 2006).

20 Cf. John Henry Schlegel, *American Legal Realism and Empirical Social Science* (University of North Carolina Press 1995); Herbert M Kritzer, 'Empirical Legal Studies before 1940: A Bibliographic Essay' (2009) 6 *Journal of Empirical Legal Studies* 925.

little attention to judicial reasoning. But things have started to change, and the exclusive focus on case disposition has been gradually displaced by a more comprehensive approach to judicial decision making. There is now a rapidly expanding body of empirical work that seek to map, document and explain (but not justify) the content of judicial opinions. This research has brought a battery of new methods to the study of judicial reasoning. Some political scientists have used game theory to model opinion-writing dynamics on collegial courts[21] and to identify the conditions under which judges are more likely to write vague opinions.[22] Others have applied a technique called "network analysis" to explore patterns of citations to precedents.[23] Yet others have looked at the decision records of federal courts to identify the factors that influence the length of opinions.[24] Still others have gone on to manually code hundreds of US Supreme Court opinions to investigate temporal changes in interpretive regimes.[25] More recent research has deployed computer-based techniques to analyse characteristics such as the use of open-ended language.[26] Political scientists have even made use of plagiarism software to determine the extent to which Supreme Court opinions borrow arguments from the parties' briefs[27] or crib from the text of lower court decisions.[28] While much empirical work has concentrated on US courts, political scientists have begun to look at courts in other regions of the world. Erik Voeten, for one, has analysed citations of previous decisions in the decisions of the European Court of Human Rights.[29] Among other interesting findings,

21 Jeffrey R Lax and Charles M Cameron, 'Bargaining and Opinion Assignment on the US Supreme Court' (2007) 23 *Journal of Law, Economics, and Organization* 276.

22 Jeffrey K Staton and Georg Vanberg, 'The Value of Vagueness: Delegation, Defiance, and Judicial Opinions' (2008) 52 *American Journal of Political Science* 504.

23 James H Fowler et al. 'Network Analysis and the Law: Measuring the Legal Importance of Precedents at the U.S. Supreme Court' (2007) 15 *Political Analysis* 324; Yonatan Lupu and Erik Voeten, 'Precedents in International Courts: A Network Analysis of Case Citations by the European Court of Human Rights' (2012) *British Journal of Political Science* 413.

24 Lee Epstein, William M Landes and Richard A Posner, 'Why (And When) Judges Dissent: A Theoretical and Empirical Analysis' (2011) 3 *Journal of Legal Analysis* 101.

25 Nancy Staudt et al. 'Judging Statutes: Interpretive Regimes' (2004) 38 *Loyola of Los Angeles Law Review* 1909.

26 Rachael K Hinkle et al. 'A Positive Theory and Empirical Analysis of Strategic Word Choice in District Court Opinions' (2012) 4 *Journal of Legal Analysis* 407.

27 Pamela C Corley, 'The Supreme Court and Opinion Content. The Influence of Parties' Briefs' (2008) 61 *Political Research Quarterly* 468.

28 Pamela C Corley, Paul M Collins and Bryan Calvin, 'Lower Court Influence on U.S. Supreme Court Opinion Content' (2011) 73 *The Journal of Politics* 31.

29 Yonatan Lupu and Erik Voeten, 'Precedent in International Courts: A Network Analysis of Case Citations by the European Court of Human Rights' (2012) 42 *British Journal of Political Science* 413.

his study shows that when a case comes from a Common Law jurisdiction (such as the UK or Ireland), the Court takes extra care to embed its decisions in prior case law, with case citations going up by 30 per cent on average. Studies applying similar methods to the European Court of Justice have also started to appear in the pages of European law reviews.[30]

Recently, comparative legal scholars, too, have come to realize that their discipline badly needs a methodological update. In that regard, the volume edited by Tania Groppi and Marie-Claire Ponthoreau on the use of foreign precedents by constitutional judges represents an important contribution to the comparative study of constitutional reasoning.[31] In a spirit very similar to that followed in the present book, their research design mixes qualitative and quantitative approaches to compare citations to foreign judicial decisions across 16 courts. Along with a qualitative, highly contextualized account of judicial practices regarding the use of foreign law, each country report includes results on the number of foreign cases cited. The aggregate figures offer a measure of how prevalent references to foreign cases are in constitutional adjudication. Broken down by jurisdiction cited, they also provide a sense of which courts get the most citations and command the most authority abroad. (These would seem to be, in order of decreasing influence: the US Supreme Court, the Supreme Court of Canada, the South African Constitutional Court and the German Constitutional Court.) The authors use this evidence to discuss a number of hypotheses about the factors – such as a shared language or legal tradition – that appear to either drive or impede citations to foreign case law. Thus, while qualitative analysis remains essential in providing the necessary background information to allow understanding and interpretation of the quantitative indicators, the book demonstrates the potential of quantitative measures to enhance comparability.

Our project follows in these footsteps. More generally, though, we see it as part of a wider empirical shift that is enriching comparative constitutional scholarship. The last few years have seen the emergence of several large-scale research projects that, we are convinced, will forever change the study of constitutional systems. By systematically coding the content of all human rights catalogues enacted since WWII worldwide, Mila Versteeg and David Law have been able to shed light on fascinating trends in the evolution of global constitutionalism. These trends include

30 Urska Sadl and Sigrid Hink, 'Precedent in the Sui Generis Legal Order: A Mine Run Approach' (2013) 20 *European Law Journal* 544.

31 Tania Groppi and Marie-Claire Ponthoreau (eds), *The Use of Foreign Precedents by Constitutional Judges* (Hart 2013).

the phenomenon of "rights creep" – the fact that an ever larger number of constitutions enshrine an ever larger number of rights – and the rise of "generic" human rights provisions – i.e., standardized rights provisions that now appear in most constitutional charters of the world.[32] More impressive still, the Comparative Constitutions Project has undertaken to assemble data on all constitutions and constitutional amendments since 1789. The result is an incredibly rich database, compiling information on more than 500 indicators over more than two centuries. These data have already served to test a wide range of hypotheses, whether it is the global spread of judicial review, the longevity of constitutions[33] or the incorporation of international law into domestic legal orders.[34] This new scholarship, we believe, points the way to an exciting future for comparative constitutional law. Of course, the emergence of empirical methods will not make the normative (e.g., doctrinal-legal) debates redundant. Questions that are fundamentally normative in nature cannot, by definition, be reduced to empirical ones. Still, empirical approaches potentially represent a great enrichment of the normative discussion. By sharpening our understanding of how constitutional law operates in its global diversity, studies based on empirical social science methods promise to foster a more informed and, we believe, more interesting normative debate.

II What Is Constitutional Reasoning?

This book presupposes that we can identify and compare constitutional reasoning across disparate legal contexts. Such an enterprise is bound to raise, at some point, a problem of definition. What do we mean exactly by "constitutional reasoning"? Does it mean the same in the United States as in Taiwan? In Germany as in the United Kingdom? To start with, we can contrast two senses of the word "reasoning".[35] In a first sense, reasoning refers to the motives and mental processes that lead a decision maker to

[32] David S Law and Mila Versteeg, 'The Evolution and Ideology of Global Constitutionalism' (2011) 99 *California Law Review* 1163.

[33] Zachary Elkins, Tom Ginsburg and James Melton, *The Endurance of National Constitutions* (Cambridge University Press 2009).

[34] Tom Ginsburg, Svitlana Chernykh and Zachary Elkins, 'Commitment and Diffusion: How and Why National Constitutions Incorporate International Law' (2008) 1 *University of Illinois Law Review* 201.

[35] For more details on this, with further references to the literature, see the foreword to the Special Issue of *German Law Journal* which served as a prelude to the present project, Arthur Dyevre and András Jakab, 'Foreword: Understanding Constitutional Reasoning' (2013) 14 *German Law Journal* 983.

choose a particular course of action. In a second sense, though, reasoning refers to the justifications that the decision maker may publicly adduce for her elected course of action. The first sense may be said to denote the decision maker's "motivating reasons", whereas the second points to her "justificatory reasons". Related distinctions that have gained currency in the theoretical literature contrast "actions" and "justifications" for action, "explanatory" and "justificatory" reasons or "context of discovery" and "context of justification". Thus defined, motivating and justificatory reasons are independent from one another. Provided her motives are honourable enough, a decision maker may publicly offer them as justification for her course of action. But it need not always be so. Occasionally, a decision maker will refrain from revealing her true motives and will, instead, put forth reasons that she believes others are more likely to regard as valid and legitimate. The distinction applies to public decision makers – legislators, judges, bureaucrats – as well as to ordinary human beings in the most ordinary situations of every-day life (from courting a potential spouse to reviewing a colleague's work). We do not always say what we believe, nor do we always believe what we say. In the present book, the emphasis is on the second, justificatory sense of reasoning. Our primary interest is with the reasons judges publicly set forth for their determinations. What we seek to document and analyse are the justifications constitutional judges publicly invoke for their rulings. Having said this, however, we do not believe that a satisfactory account of constitutional reasoning can afford to ignore the judges' motivating reasons altogether. In many circumstances, it is impossible to establish what induces judicial actors to favour a particular mode of justification over another without elaborating, to some degree, on the judges' motivating reasons.

So much for the definition of reasoning.[36] But what makes reasoning specifically "constitutional"? Does constitutional reasoning exist solely where there is a formal, large-c constitution?[37] Or does it denote reasoning about any issue viewed as sufficiently important to deserve the label

[36] In the present volume we use the expressions 'reasoning' and 'argumentation' as synonymous, whereas 'argument' means an identifiable unit within a reasoning.

[37] On the distinction between small-c and large-c constitution (roughly equivalent to the distinction between substantive and formal constitutional law in continental European scholarship) see David S Law, 'Constitutions' in Peter Cane and Herbert M Kritzer (eds), *The Oxford Handbook of Empirical Legal Research* (Oxford University Press 2010) 376. A similar distinction (between a thin and a thick sense of 'constitution') is made by Joseph Raz, 'On the Authority and Interpretation of Constitutions: Some Preliminaries', in Larry Alexander (ed), *Constitutionalism. Philosophical Foundations* (Cambridge University Press 1998) 153.

"constitutional", irrespective of the existence of a formal, written constitution? It is useful to note that constitutional reason-giving can be defined in a capacious manner as encompassing every instance where a public or private decision maker invokes norms or values that are either formally or substantively constitutional. In that broad sense, the executive and legislative branches regularly need to engage in constitutional reasoning, as they, too, must apply and specify what the values and commands enshrined in the constitutional text require in concrete fact situations. Even in countries without a formal large-c constitution (like the United Kingdom), legislators regularly debate questions viewed as substantively constitutional, such as the configuration of checks and balances or the scope of fundamental rights.[38] Legal scholars, however, habitually employ the term constitutional reasoning in a narrower sense, as referring solely to the discursive practices of judges in the context of cases brought on formally constitutional grounds or at least on grounds that are commonly viewed as constitutional. While constitutional reasoning by non-judicial actors represents a fascinating subject in its own right, the definition adopted in the present book follows this narrower sense of the adjective constitutional. We focus on constitutional reasoning by judicial actors, and more specifically on constitutional reasoning by constitutional courts.[39] By constitutional court we mean a judicial institution explicitly erected as "constitutional court" or "constitutional tribunal" or the topmost court of the legal order with the power to review legal rules on constitutional grounds, irrespective of its name or title.[40] By constitution, we mean the rule or body of rules enjoying the highest rank in a legal order in the sense of having priority over other legal rules of the system.[41] We asked the contributors to the present volume to follow this formal definition of constitution whenever possible. Only when this definition did not apply (as in the case of the UK) did we instruct them to employ a substantive, or small-c, definition of constitution; in that case we recommended that they adopt the most widely accepted definition in their legal community and provide adequate explanation at the beginning of their report. Finally, we

[38] This is a point stressed in the context of the normative discussion by Jeremy Waldron and Richard Bellamy; see Jeremy Waldron, *Law and Disagreement* (Clarendon 1999); Richard Bellamy, *Political Constitutionalism* (Cambridge University Press 2007).

[39] This is but one of several possible approaches to the study of constitutional reasoning; see Dyevre and Jakab (n 35) with further references.

[40] András Jakab, 'Constitutional Reasoning. A European Perspective on Judicial Reasoning in Constitutional Courts' (2013) 8 *German Law Journal* 1215, 1217.

[41] Ibid 1216.

also take our definition to include reasoning by international courts that have come to assume the function of quasi-constitutional courts, such as the Court of Justice of the European Union[42] and the European Court of Human Rights.[43]

III Descriptive Theories of Comparative Constitutional Reasoning

The normative focus of constitutional law scholarship and the corresponding relative paucity of descriptive (i.e., not normative, or, to use social science terminology: positive) research explain why comparative constitutional reasoning remains a relatively under-theorized field of inquiry. Why do some courts invoke some argument forms more frequently than do tribunals in other places? Why is the repertoire of interpretive canons and modes of constitutional argumentation broad in some places and narrow in others? Why do some constitutional judges write longer opinions than their peers in other jurisdictions? What forces may spur changes in the judges' argumentative practices? How are these practices likely to evolve over time? Are constitutional judges around the world converging towards a generic argumentation template or is the global trend one of increasingly diverging practices? While recent contributions have discussed the impact of globalisation on constitutional structures and rights protection,[44] there have been relatively few efforts to theorize the mechanisms that shape constitutional reasoning across the

[42] On the constitutional character of the Court of Justice see Francis G Jacobs, 'Is the Court of Justice of the European Communities a Constitutional Court?' in DM Curtin, D O'Keeffe (eds), *Constitutional Adjudication in European Community and National Law* (Butterworth 1992) 25–32; Anthony Arnull, 'A Constitutional Court for Europe?' (2003–4) 6 *Cambridge Yearbook of European Legal Studies* 1–34; Loïc Azoulai, 'Le rôle constitutionnel de la Cour de Justice des Communautés européennes tel qu'il se dégage de sa jurisprudence' (2008) 44 *Revue trimestrielle de droit européen* 29, and the chapter by Giulio Itzcovich in the present volume.

[43] On the constitutional character of the Strasbourg Court see Wojciech Sadurski, 'Partnering with Strasbourg: Constitutionalisation of the European Court of Human Rights, the Accession of Central and East European States to the Council of Europe, and the Idea of Pilot Judgments' (2009) 9 *Human Rights Law Review* 397 and the chapter by Janneke Gerards in the present volume.

[44] See Mark Tushnet, 'The Inevitable Globalization of Constitutional Law' (2008) 49 *Virginia Journal of International Law* 985; David S Law, 'Generic Constitutional Law' (2004) 89 *Minnesota Law Review* 652; David S Law, 'Globalization and the Future of Constitutional Rights' (2008) 102 *Northwestern University Law Review* 1277; Rosalind Dixon and Eric A Posner, 'The Limits of Constitutional Convergence' (2010) 11 *Chicago Journal of International Law* 399; Law and Versteeg (n 32); Moshe Cohen-Eliya and Iddo Porat, *Proportionality and Constitutional Culture* (Cambridge University Press 2013).

world. In any case, one would look in vain for a theory of comparative constitutional reasoning sufficiently comprehensive and fine-grained to account for all these facets of judicial discourse.

Any attempt to explicate commonalities and discrepancies in the argumentative style practiced by constitutional judges must ultimately rest on some understanding of the motives and constraints that orient judicial decision making. The picture of judging implicitly assumed in much public discourse on and around constitutional adjudication corresponds to the formalist or legalist model of judicial decision making. In a nutshell, this model posits that judges are essentially, if not exclusively, preoccupied with the correct application of legal rules and doctrines.[45] This theory entails that the sole business of constitutional judges consists in enforcing pre-existing constitutional rules. If we accept this conception of judicial decision making and assume that judges say what they do and do what they say, then the implications for the comparative analysis of constitutional argumentation are straightforward. In this view, if judicial practices converge it is because constitutional judges must apply similar rules; and if they diverge it is because the rules they are in charge of applying differ. Formalism may, at some level, appear to make good sense of what is arguably one of the best-documented facts of comparative judicial research: the fact – also observed at the level of constitutional adjudication[46] – that Common Law courts tend to cite more precedents than do courts in Civil Law countries. From a formalist standpoint, it is easy to relate this difference to differences in the system of legal sources. Precedents, after all, constitute a valid, explicit source of law in the Common Law tradition but not in Civil Law systems. A variant of this view contrasts the "inductive" nature of Common Law legal reasoning with the deductive character of constitutional argumentation in Civil Law countries.[47] Echoing this alleged difference between Common Law and Civil Law jurisdictions is the view that formalism is not a universal phenomenon but more closely associated with the Civil Law tradition. Influenced by the writings of early American comparativists[48] and thinkers like Roscoe Pound,[49]

[45] On formalism as the 'denial of choice', see Frederick Schauer, 'Formalism' (1988) 97 *Yale Law Journal* 509, esp. 511–520.

[46] Groppi and Ponthoreau (n 31) 412. [47] Ibid 413.

[48] See Dawson (n 15); John Henry Merryman, *The Civil Law Tradition* (Stanford University Press 1970).

[49] Roscoe Pound, *The Spirit of the Common Law* (Marshall Jones 1921) 170, and 'What Is the Common Law' (1937) 4 *University of Chicago Law Review* 176, 186.

Gustav Radbruch[50] and Friedrich Hayek,[51] this view casts Civil Law judges as slaves to the codes mechanically enforcing written legislation but equates the Common Law with judge-made law.[52] Superficially at least, this differentiated account of judicial behaviour seems consistent with the general perception that Common Law constitutional opinions deploy a more discursive style which is also characterized by a greater openness to policy arguments.[53]

Most constitutional comparativists know better and repudiate, if not explicitly, at least implicitly, the picture of judicial decision making associated with formalism. In seeking to chart and predict the global trajectory of constitutional law, they have discussed the role played by economic and social mechanisms as well as the influence of inherited legal structures. Some scholars have emphasised converging trends and highlighted the effects of various globalisation processes as the great flattening force in the evolution of judicial practices. They variously point to the spread of human rights norms and the role played by global NGOs in promoting rights adjudication;[54] the felt necessity to adapt constitutional law arising from global economic competition;[55] the pressure to conform to the edicts of transnational treaty bodies or to the values endorsed by economically or politically dominant states;[56] along with judicial learning and judicial borrowing spurred by the need to address similar problems[57] and facilitated by the emergence of cross-national judicial networks.[58] Other scholars have stressed divergence, drawing attention to patterns of indigenous resistance to the adoption of foreign doctrines and practices. Lorraine Weinrib has contrasted the post-war paradigm of comprehensive rights protection, proportionality and balancing embraced by Canadian

50 Gustav Radbruch, *Der Geist des englischen Rechts* (Rausch 1946).

51 Friedrich August Hayek, *Law, Legislation and Liberty: A New Statement of the Liberal Principles of Justice and Political Economy* (University of Chicago Press 1973) 94.

52 This view seems common among economists as well as among law and economics scholars; see Thorsten Beck, Asli Demirgüç-Kunt and Ross Levine, 'Law and Finance: Why Does Legal Origin Matter?' (2003) 31 *Journal of Comparative Economics* 653; Paul G Mahoney, 'The Common Law and Economic Growth: Hayek Might Be Right' (2001) 30 *The Journal of Legal Studies* 503.

53 Groppi and Ponthoreau (n 31) 413; Lasser (n 16); Christian Kirchner, 'The Difficult Reception of Law and Economics in Germany' (1991) 11 *International Review of Law and Economics* 277, 282.

54 Tushnet (n 44) 989.

55 Law, 'Globalization and the Future of Constitutional Rights' (n 37).

56 Tushnet (n 44) 990; Dixon and Posner (n 44) 414.

57 Law, 'Generic Constitutional Law' (n 44).

58 Anne-Marie Slaughter, *A New World Order* (Princeton University Press 2005).

and European constitutional judges with the indigenous, historically fixed and textually circumscribed brand of constitutionalism championed by the conservative wing of the US Supreme Court.[59] Mark Tushnet has singled out Australia and the United States as the two nations with the strongest commitment to exceptionalism: Australia because it lacks a judicially enforceable bill of rights, and the United States because its constitutional judges resist references to non-US constitutional law. Tushnet sees the roots of Australian exceptionalism in a deep commitment to legislative supremacy as the best expression of democratic self-governance and relates American exceptionalism to an ingrained suspicion towards the expansive conception of the judicial role associated with the post-war paradigm.[60] Rosalind Dixon and Eric Posner, meanwhile, have argued that special conditions are required for constitutional convergence to occur. In practice, they insist, such conditions are rarely obtained, which greatly reduces the prospect of convergence, both at the structural and at the doctrinal level.[61]

Most of these theoretical contributions address the evolution of constitutional systems at a high level of abstraction and do not draw specific implications for constitutional opinion-writing and the incidence of particular modes of argumentation. Exceptions, though, include citations to foreign law and the spread of proportionality, which have both been linked to the emergence of transjudicial networks,[62] and originalist approaches to constitutional interpretation, whose popularity among judges has been linked to the historical process (revolutionary vs reorganisational) of constitutional ratification.[63] On the other hand, many of the more specific arguments advanced by legal comparativists for observed or alleged disparities in judicial practices tend to be under-theorized. It has been suggested that variations in judicial reasoning may arise from the judges' differing career backgrounds (academics vs career judges)[64]; the configuration of judicial review (diffuse vs centralized);[65] and the role played by litigants in setting the courts' agenda.[66] Yet these tentative explanations do not specify the mechanisms through which these factors

[59] Lorraine Weinrib, 'The Postwar Paradigm and American Exceptionalism' in Sujit Choudhry (ed), *The Migration of Constitutional Ideas* (Cambridge University Press 2007) 83.

[60] Tushnet (n 44) 986. [61] Dixon and Posner (n 44).

[62] Slaughter (n 58); Alec Stone Sweet and Jud Mathews, 'Proportionality Balancing and Global Constitutionalism' (2008) 47 *Columbia Journal of Transnational Law* 73.

[63] David Fontana, 'Comparative Originalism' (2009) 88 *Texas Law Review* 189.

[64] Groppi and Ponthoreau (n 31) 414. [65] Ibid 413. [66] Ibid.

influence the judges' writing behaviour. Moreover, these hypotheses are typically formulated without much sense of what actually drives judicial behaviour.

The approach we take in the present book draws on a realist account of judicial decision-making informed by recent advances in judicial behaviour research.[67] We take our cue from Oliver Wendell Holmes. "The life of the law", Holmes said in his oft-quoted quip, "has not been logic" but "experience".[68] Emphasizing the similarities between judges and other public decision makers, Holmes went on to argue that, far more than by syllogism, judicial decision making is determined by considerations that are not purely legal, such as the "felt necessities of the time, the prevalent moral and political theories, intuitions of public policy, avowed or unconscious, and even the prejudices which judges share with their fellow-men".[69] While we believe that constitutional language and doctrines may place important constraints on judges, we believe that these do not represent the only influence on judicial conduct. Empirical research has shown that constitutional adjudication is influenced by the policy preferences of the individual judge[70] as well as by institutional and strategic constraints which cannot be straightforwardly characterized as "legal".

Schematically, constitutional judges issue decisions that normally comprise two distinct parts: (1) the case disposition, and (2) the opinion (of which, in the jurisdictions where separate opinions are permitted, there might be more than one). The case disposition – or decision on the merits – settles the dispute at hand, thereby determining which party prevails and which loses (in case of abstract judicial review where a law is struck down, even if there is no concrete winner, the state can be

[67] See Arthur Dyevre, 'Unifying the Field of Comparative Judicial Politics: Towards a General Theory of Judicial Behaviour' (2010) 2 *European Political Science Review* 297; Lee Epstein, William M Landes and Richard A Posner, *The Behavior of Federal Judges: A Theoretical and Empirical Study of Rational Choice* (Harvard University Press 2013); Chris Guthrie, Jeffrey J Rachlinski and Andrew J Wistrich, 'Blinking on the Bench: How Judges Decide Cases' (2007) 93 *Cornell Law Review* 1; Matthew C Stephenson, 'Legal Realism for Economists' (2009) 23 *The Journal of Economic Perspectives* 191.

[68] Oliver Wendell Holmes, 'The Path of the Law' (1896) 10 *Harvard Law Review* 457.

[69] Ibid.

[70] See Chris Hanretty, 'Dissent in Iberia: The Ideal Points of Justices on the Spanish and Portuguese Constitutional Tribunals' (2012) 51 *European Journal of Political Research* 671; Erik Voeten, 'The Politics of International Judicial Appointments: Evidence from the European Court of Human Rights' (2007) 61 *International Organization* 669; Jeffrey Segal and Harold Spaeth, *The Supreme Court and the Attitudinal Model Revisited* (Cambridge University Press 2002); Epstein, Landes and Posner (n 67).

conceptualised as the loser). As distinct from the dispositive part of the decision, the opinion then serves two basic functions. The first and most obvious one is to provide a rationale for the case disposition. As such it is supposed to set forth the reasons which, according to the judges, determined the outcome of the particular case. Besides this justificatory function, constitutional opinions also perform a policy-making function. Even in Civil Law countries with no explicit doctrine of *stare decisis*,[71] the grounds set forth to justify the decision on the merits are typically interpreted as indicative of how the court intends to handle similar cases in the future. The expectation that like cases will be treated alike thus effectively enables constitutional judges to make rules – or "doctrines" in legal jargon – in the course of settling disputes, even when such disputes have a purely individual character. This policy-making function explains why the impact of a constitutional ruling often goes well beyond the cases actually adjudicated by the courts. It also explains why legal commentators habitually pay so much attention to the opinion of the court while the decision on the merits of the case is usually given short shrift. As the American comparativist Martin Shapiro observed for US courts, the "opinions themselves, not who won or lost, are the crucial form of political behaviour by the appellate courts, since it is the opinions which provide the constraining directions to the public and private decision makers who determine 99 per cent of the conduct that never reaches the courts".[72]

We conceptualise constitutional reasoning as an exercise in persuasion, and we suggest that the opinion writing practices of constitutional judges is basically determined by the interaction of three factors: (1) the judges' values and preferences over policy and case disposition, including their conception of the appropriate role of judicial officials; (2) the views and

[71] Short explanation for non-lawyers: *stare decisis* (lat. "to stand by things decided") is the doctrine that courts are under the obligation to follow their own previous decisions ("horizontal" *stare decisis*) as well as the decisions of courts exercising superior jurisdiction ("vertical" *stare decisis*): the rules and principles of law upon which a court has justified a past decision (the rationale for the court's decision – so called *ratio decidendi*) are binding in all future cases in which the facts are substantially identical. For more detailed information see e.g., N. MacCormick and R. S. Summers (eds), *Interpreting Precedents: A Comparative Study* (Aldershot 1997); Frederick Schauer, *Thinking Like a Lawyer* (Harvard University Press 2009), 36–60; Neil Duxbury, *The Nature and Authority of Precedent* (Cambridge University Press 2009); Grant Lamond, 'Precedent and Analogy in Legal Reasoning' in Edward N. Zalta (ed), The Stanford Encyclopedia of *Philosophy* (Spring 2014 Edition), http://plato.stanford.edu/archives/spr2014/entries/legal-reas-prec.

[72] Martin M Shapiro, *The Supreme Court and Administrative Agencies* (vol. 2, Free Press 1968) 39.

representation of the judicial role held by the judges' audiences, and (3) the judges' skills and creativity in crafting arguments that reflect their own preferences while remaining attuned to the beliefs and expectations of their audience(s). In other words, constitutional opinion-writers are rhetoricians who seek to persuade one or more audiences to accept a certain message (the judges' favoured policy and case disposition). While the term "rhetoric" may convey negative connotations, we do not mean to suggest any of these connotations and our focus is, instead, on the descriptive meaning of the word.[73] Nor is our characterisation of judicial opinion-writing intended to imply that constitutional judges are simply politicians or, worse, demagogues in robes. Constitutional judges may be motivated by a variety of policy goals and institutional interests rather than by the sole desire to follow the rules laid down in the constitution. But this does not mean that constitutional judges can do whatever pleases them.[74] The judges' audiences, in particular, can be a major source of constraints.[75] As opposed to other branches, constitutional judges do not have directly either the sword or the purse. Instead, they are forced to rely on cooperation with the other branches. So it is crucial that their rulings inspire authority in their audiences. To be sure, social acceptance is a necessity that is not per se specific to constitutional judges or even to the judicial branch in general, but one that holds for all public decision makers in a democratic regime. The executive and legislative branches, too, must persuade the public that their decisions are sound. In fact, it appears to be something to which they devote a great deal of resources and energy, as testified by the number of spin-doctors and PR gurus who make a living out of marketing political messages. Where judges face specific constraints, though, is in their need to conform to prevalent conceptions of what constitutes acceptable judicial behaviour. Judges must sound like judges rather than like legislators or cabinet members. In sum, there are not only evident similarities but also distinct differences between reason-giving by judges and reason-giving by other public decision makers. To

[73] A similar use of 'rhetoric' can be found in Chaïm Perelman, *Logique juridique. Nouvelle rhétorique* (Dalloz 1976). For an overview of rhetorical theories of legal reasoning, see Neil MacCormick, *Rhetoric and the Rule of Law. A Theory of Legal Reasoning* (Oxford University Press 2005) 17–20.

[74] On the constraints of legal interpretation, see Michel Troper, Véronique Champeil-Desplats and Christophe Grzegorczyk (eds), *Théorie des contraintes juridiques* (Bruylant-LGDJ 2005); Michel Troper, 'Une théorie réaliste de l'interprétation', in *La théorie du droit, le droit, l'Etat* (PUF 2001) 69–84.

[75] See Nuno Garoupa and Tom Ginsburg, *Judicial Reputation. A Comparative Theory* (University of Chicago Press 2015).

the extent that it strives to present a public decision in the "best light", a judicial opinion is rather like a government press release or even a party manifesto. But it also typically differs from these documents in its effort to provide justificatory reasons that are consonant with the criteria by which the court's audiences specifically assess the conduct of judicial actors.

Similarities in the way citizens perceive and understand the function of constitutional judges may account for some broad resemblances in constitutional discourse. Opinion surveys show that respondents who are more favourably oriented towards the judiciary are also more likely to subscribe to the belief, traditionally associated with formalism, that judges are neutral and objective servants of the law.[76] Of course, the extent to which formalism shapes the common perception of the judicial function may vary somewhat from one country to the next. In the United States, the influence of the legal realist movement together with the accumulated evidence of several decades of empirical research on the federal courts have certainly contributed to the erosion of formalism on the way lawyers and academics view the judicial branch. Outside the United States, lawyers and legal scholars are usually more reluctant to admit that considerations other than black letter law can play a role in adjudication. Yet, even in the United States, formalism remains firmly ingrained in the popular culture. It continues to serve as the official model of judicial decision making. Accordingly, nominees to the US Supreme Court insist that the job of a Supreme Court Justice, similar to that of an "umpire", is to "apply" not to "make" the law.[77] David Law argues that because constitutional judges are all confronted with the "counter-majoritarian difficulty" – the need to reconcile the apparent contradiction between democracy and judicial review – they will often develop similar solutions. One way to address the counter-majoritarian difficulty is to deny that judges are actually deciding anything, however bold the decision may in fact be:

> [J]udges go to considerable lengths to tether their efforts to their respective constitutions. If they are fortunate, they may have available to them some slender snippet of vague but actual text, such as "due process," from which

[76] James L Gibson, Gregory A Caldeira and Vanessa A Baird, 'On the Legitimacy of National High Courts' (1998) 92 *The American Political Science Review* 343.

[77] Paradoxically, the politicians who are quick to lament the courts' "activism" and lambaste constitutional judges for acting as a "*gouvernement des juges*" or an "*Ersatzregierung*" only contribute to reinforce this vision of the judicial function. Implicit in these tirades against the people in robes is the assumption that adjudication, including constitutional adjudication, can and should exclusively consist in the mechanical application of pre-defined rules.

> entire vistas of possibility unfold; if they have the nerve, they may even liken what they do to scientific inquiry. Elsewhere, judges may have to make do with "unwritten constitutional principles," or the "basic structure" of the constitution or the "governmental framework." From such unpromising materials, the audacious may find a way to strike down constitutional amendments. Those truly favored may even have the opportunity to reject an entire *constitution* on constitutional grounds. The more extreme the case, the clearer it becomes that judges do not obey or interpret constitutions as they *make* constitutions – then attempt to obscure what they are doing.[78]

Judges, evidently, know that the public looks at them through the normative lens of formalism, and this gives them a strong incentive to justify their decisions in terms that are consonant with the formalist model of adjudication. So this leads us to the paradox that a realist, anti-formalist theory of constitutional reasoning predicts that formalism is precisely the theory of adjudication constitutional judges will be keenest to invoke:

> [Legal reasoning] functions both as mask and shield. It hides and protects the promotion of one particular set of political objectives against contending objectives in the purely political sphere. In specifying this dual relationship between law and politics, we also uncover a striking paradox. Law can only perform this dual political function to the extent it is accepted as law. A "legal" decision that is transparently "political", in the sense that it departs too far from the methods and principles of the law, will invite direct political attack. It will thus fail as both mask and shield.[79]

At any rate, we should not be surprised to see constitutional judges emphasizing "legal" reasons over other reasons such as policy arguments or evidence from social scientific research in their opinions.

If we believe that judges are keen both to expand their influence over policy-making and to maintain the impression that they are only applying the law, we should expect constitutional courts to show a predilection for using the language of rights. Legal scholars associate the activism of the US Supreme Court under Chief Justice Earl Warren with the civil rights movement that swept the United States during the same period. More generally, there appears to exist a strong correlation between the global diffusion and intensification of rights discourse and the global expansion of judicial power. Judicial predilection for rights discourse and sympathy for rights litigants is, of course, only one aspect of a more

[78] Law, 'Generic Constitutional Law' (n 44) 684 (emphasis in the original).

[79] Anne-Marie Burley and Walter Mattli, 'Europe Before the Court: A Political Theory of Legal Integration' (1993) 47 *International Organization* 41.

complex story. Rights revolutions cannot be brought about by judges alone but require a support structure of NGOs and advocacy groups with enough resources to make effective use of the litigation process,[80] along with an advanced level of secularisation, a degree of suspicion towards nationalist ideas, and measure of social mobility and individualism.[81] Still, where such background conditions are met, adopting a jurisprudence emphasizing rights presents several advantages for constitutional judges desirous to expand their influence. First, the indeterminacy of rights provisions affords judges great flexibility and makes it easy to tether a particular policy determination, controversial as it may be, to a piece of constitutional language. No less alluring in the language of rights, though, is its normative appeal and the rhetorical force it lends to the judges' pronouncements.[82] The normative appeal of the rhetoric of rights stems precisely from the fact that public opinion is favourably prejudiced towards rights. Constant exposure to rights-legitimizing messages entails that many citizens spontaneously associate something positive with the label "right" and assume that the more "rights" the better. Aside from bolstering public support for the judicial cause, the rhetoric of rights makes the task of the courts' critics considerably more difficult. In the narrative evoked by the language of rights, courts and judges are the heroes championing the cause of liberty against oppressive politicians. For that reason, whoever ventures to criticize a ruling affirming a fundamental right risks being viewed as an enemy of rights and freedom.

In the same vein, flexibility and normative appeal suggest that constitutional judges may often resort to loose but normatively alluring standards such as "rule of law", "democracy", "equality" and even "human dignity" to justify judicial interventions in the policy-making process.[83] The same reasons predict that constitutional judges will be keen to embrace balancing tests such as proportionality. Not only does balancing allow judges to set the level of generality at which they define judge-made rules, or even to dispense with rule-making altogether to adjudicate constitutional

[80] See Charles R Epp, *The Rights Revolution: Lawyers, Activists, and Supreme Courts in Comparative Perspective* (University of Chicago Press 1998).

[81] On these phenomena and how they influenced our constitutional language, see András Jakab, *European Constitutional Language* (Cambridge University Press forthcoming).

[82] See e.g. the discourse on the "rights" of future generations, András Jakab, 'Sustainability in European Constitutional Law' available at http://ssrn.com/abstract=2593371 15–17. For a more general and rather critical account see Mary Ann Glandon, *Rights Talk. The Impoverishment of Political Discourse* (Free Press 1991).

[83] See Law, 'Generic Constitutional Law' (n 44) 672.

disputes on a case-by-case basis, but the degree of discretion it provides also makes it easier for judges to navigate the strategic constraints of their political environment.[84]

Conceptualising constitutional reasoning as a rhetorical exercise also helps in understanding how changes in the court's audience may affect judicial argumentation. Persuasion depends on the ability of the rhetorician to tailor her message to the beliefs of her audience. Because she normally cannot change all these beliefs at once, she usually does best by treating them as given. Applying the same idea to constitutional reasoning implies that opinion writers must take the definition of legitimate judicial conduct prevalent in the community as exogenously given. A corollary of this idea is that major shifts in writing practices will only occur when a change of commensurate magnitude affects the judges' audience. A dramatic audience change occurs when the geographic boundaries of a court's jurisdiction are redrawn.

Yet the normative expectations of a court's audience may also evolve in a more gradual fashion. This perhaps is what happened with the diffusion of rights discourse. As alluded to earlier, greater public sensitivity for human rights seems to have played an important part in the late twentieth-century surge in judicial power. As their constituencies grew more rights-conscious, judges were able to mobilize the rhetorical power of rights discourse to expand their influence. The creeping popularity of rights discourse in turn suggests that the beliefs entertained by their audience may not be entirely exogenous to the judges' actions. Indeed, what the court states in its opinions may itself contribute to shape public views on judicial behaviour. In the United States, the "Brandeis brief" is sometimes offered as an illustration of how policy arguments became acceptable in the context of constitutional adjudication, after the US Supreme Court endorsed the use of social-scientific information in the brief filed by then counsel Louis D. Brandeis.[85] More generally, by legitimizing them through repeated use, constitutional judges may turn arguments and considerations once deemed inacceptable in their legal community into accepted figures of constitutional discourse. This is what, in part, permits judges to take an active part in the global diffusion of constitutional ideas

[84] Cohen-Eliya and Porat (n 44) 104.

[85] *Muller v. Oregon*, 208 U.S. 412 (1908). See Thomas Lundmark, *Charting the Divide Between Common and Civil Law* (Oxford University Press 2012) 107. Some scholars, though, argue that the use of policy arguments in US courts predate the Brandeis brief; see Noga Morag-Levine, 'Facts, Formalism, and the Brandeis Brief: The Origins of a Myth' (2013) 2013 *University of Illinois Law Review* 59.

and borrow precedents and doctrines developed elsewhere as suits their agenda and domestic constraints.

When drafting their opinions, judges (and their clerks) have an audience in mind which on many occasions is likely to be plural. Indeed, a constitutional ruling is often addressed to various audiences: litigants, other judges, the legal community or the general public. But specific constraints may arise as a consequence of whom the constitutional judges regard as their primary audience. For instance, where the legal academia enjoys prestige and respect, a judge, especially if he is himself an academic, may compose his opinions in the hope of winning the esteem of law professors. He may have the inclination, therefore, to write long and complex opinions with frequent references to scholarly work. Where, by contrast, judges care little about academia and are more concerned with the reception of their opinions by journalists and members of the general public, the judge may ditch doctrinal jargon and strive, instead, for clarity and simplicity.

We sometimes equate rhetoric with flowery prose and verbal extravagance. But it need not always be so. In the constitutional sphere as in other domains, persuasion and social acceptance are often best achieved through discretion and depersonalized communication. Epstein et al. note that "The most effective public relations strategy for a court might well be dignified silence (and no dissents!), projecting a mystique of detachment, disinterested wisdom, consensus, and esoteric technical knowledge."[86]

However, while this may be the most effective public relations strategy for the institution, it may not always be the optimal strategy for the individual judge to pursue.[87] Bans on dissenting opinions are commonly justified on the grounds that it is what best serves the institution's interest. Such bans, though, are obviously not in the interest of the individual judge who wishes to vent his disagreement on a hotly disputed issue. One way to think of the variations in style and general form we observe across courts is as reflecting varying degrees of institutionalisation of the manner in which courts communicate with the outside world. At one end of the spectrum are the courts whose communication is subject to a high degree of institutionalisation. Opinion-writing on these courts is supposed to conform to a very rigid, stereotypical template with many do's (e.g., observe a specific structure, stick to an impersonal style, be

[86] Epstein, Landes and Posner (n 67) 315. [87] Ibid.

brief) and don'ts (no reference to prior decisions, no mention of scholarly work, no separate opinion). These requirements may result from explicit formal rules, as bans on separate opinions usually do, or established practices which judges keep following out of fear that a departure from the accepted norm of judicial communication be viewed as political usurpation. Such a formal rigidity has implications for the content as well as the evolution of judicial opinion-writing. First, it may considerably slow down the evolution of judicial practices by inhibiting constitutional borrowing from other jurisdictions. Second, it may significantly reduce the amount of argumentative variability and diversity across opinions. Third, the argumentative straightjacket which judicial communication is forced to fit leaves very little space for the eloquence and argumentative creativity of the individual opinion writer to shine through. Then, at the other end of the spectrum are the courts whose verbal behaviour is governed by a much more flexible template that imposes far fewer formal and stylistic requirements on opinion writers. Greater flexibility permits judges to deploy a broader and more diverse repertoire of argument forms and to borrow arguments and ideas developed elsewhere. Precisely because the pool of arguments from which opinion writers can potentially draw is larger, flexibility may also make for more cherry-picking, as judges choose the arguments that best suit the result they want to reach in the case at hand. As a result, we may see the same court stressing a different approach to constitutional interpretation from one case to the next. The overall picture will be one of much greater variability across cases. Such a context also gives the individual judge more opportunities to make her own, distinct voice heard, especially if the court allows separate opinions. Between these two extremes, many variations in the degree of rigidity and standardisation imposed by the received template are, of course, conceivable.

IV Research Design: Constitutional Reasoning in Leading Cases

Is it possible to map judicial practices and ascertain (either in this research or, based on the database that we offer, in future researches) whether these are consistent with the hypotheses and theories just outlined? At first, the sheer amount of constitutional decisions might seem to pose a daunting challenge. A constitutional court may issue several hundred decisions a year. Many of these come with an opinion spreading over dozens of pages and sometimes far more. Multiply this by the number of judicial bodies holding the power to make pronouncements on the application of constitutional norms across the planet, and it becomes readily apparent that no single book or research project may reasonably be expected to survey each and every aspect of constitutional reasoning for all constitutional systems currently in existence. So, even for a large research project like ours involving more than 20 scholars and researchers, choices had to be made.[88]

We eventually settled for a research design that, we believe, strikes a fair balance between depth and coverage. As for the jurisdictions covered, we assembled a team of comparative scholars to report on the practices of the following 18 courts: the High Court of Australia, the Austrian Constitutional Court, the Supreme Federal Tribunal of Brazil, the Supreme Court of Canada, the Czech Constitutional Court, the French Constitutional Council, the German Federal Constitutional Court, the Hungarian Constitutional Court, the Irish Supreme Court, the Supreme Court of Israel, the Italian Constitutional Court, the Spanish Constitutional Tribunal, the Constitutional Court of South Africa, the Constitutional Court of Taiwan, the Supreme Court of the United Kingdom, the Supreme Court of the United States, the Court of Justice of the European Union and the European Court of Human Rights.

While the overrepresentation of Europe reveals our initial impulse to focus on constitutional reasoning within the EU, we believe that this set of courts fairly reflects the diversity of constitutional traditions in the democratic world. In addition to featuring courts from all five continents, it achieves a remarkable balance between Common Law and Civil Law jurisdictions. Similarly, our nine specialized constitutional courts are matched by an almost equal number (eight) of generalist apex courts. By including the European Court of Justice and the European Court of Human Rights, our study further reflects the rise of supranational courts as quasi-constitutional tribunals. In Europe, the decisions rendered by these two institutions have become an integral part of domestic constitutional discourse. To be sure, we do not claim that these 18 judicial bodies are representative, in the statistical or probabilistic sense of the

[88] For more details on country selection, case selection (esp. the lack of determination of a time-frame, randomised samples, stratified samples, samples based on citation either in the literature or by courts), methodological dilemmas and a history of dead-ends in the project, see András Jakab, Arthur Dyevre and Giulio Itzcovich, 'CONREASON – The Comparative Constitutional Reasoning Project. Methodological Dilemmas and Project Design' (2015) 9 *MTA Law Working Papers*. http://jog.tk.mta.hu/uploads/files/mtalwp/2015_09_jakab.pdf. In order to keep this introduction more accessible, we did not include most of these details in the present text.

word, of the world's larger population of constitutional courts. Yet we are confident that we could greatly advance our comparative understanding of constitutional argumentation by looking at the decisions of the courts that are the most typical of their kind and the most influential outside their borders.

A similar philosophy guided our choice of cases. Ideally, we would have wanted our authors to collect, read and analyse all the decisions. But even for 18 courts, this was not a realistic option. There were simply too many decisions. Nor was, owing to the array of judicial practices we wanted to address, random sampling a plausible alternative.[89] Instead, we decided that each report would document the opinion-writing practices of a court on the basis of a systematic and thorough analysis of its 40 leading cases. By "leading cases" we meant the rulings deemed the most important in the legal community of the court under consideration. And 40 was chosen as the appropriate compromise to enable a thorough examination of every judgment while still providing a meaningful basis for comparison.

Why chose to focus on great cases rather than on routine decisions whose study may perhaps more easily lend itself to generalisations about a court's typical mode of argumentation? Oliver Wendell Holmes, for one, was wary of the distorting effect that great cases may have on legal thinking: "Great cases like hard cases make bad law. For great cases are called great, not by reason of their importance... but because of some accident of immediate overwhelming interest which appeals to the feelings and distorts the judgment."[90] The risk exists, indeed, that a fixation on landmark decisions distorts our picture of constitutional reasoning. Yet landmark judgments tend to set the tone of a court's jurisprudence, as they often provide the lens through which court watchers recognize the defining traits of a court's approach to constitutional argumentation. For the same reason, they probably exert more influence on the practices of other judges, both at home and abroad, than do less salient decisions.

[89] We would have needed samples of several hundred cases from every legal system that we analysed to arrive at generalisable conclusions. A goal still beyond the reach of our research team. For smaller samples to be representative of the whole population of judgments, we would have needed either more homogenous populations (which was not the case), or more information on the structure of the whole population concerning aspects which are relevant to reasoning (we did not have this information).

[90] *Northern Securities Co. v. United States*, 193 U.S. 197, 400 (1904) (Holmes, dissenting). For a recent work taking issue with Holmes' claim in US case-law see Lackland H. Bloom, Jr., *Do Great Cases Make Bad Law?* (Oxford University Press 2014).

Fair enough, but how can one possibly go about selecting constitutional opinions on the sole basis that they somehow represent "great", "important", or "leading" judgments?[91] How does this not constitute an irreducibly subjective criterion? We were fully aware of this problem. However, we assumed that, in any legal community, a relative consensus usually exists as to what decisions constitute leading judgments.[92] We asked the author(s) of each court report to draw up a list of 40 leading cases list according to his or her assessment of the scholarly consensus, or what German legal scholars call the *herrschende Meinung*. We expected the list to include the landmark constitutional cases law students commonly encounter in a standard constitutional law course at law school. We did more than just assume the existence of a consensus, however. Indeed, once her 40-cases list had been established, each author was required to designate five mainstream legal experts (preferably constitutional law scholars) to review her choice of opinions.[93] These experts were separately requested to indicate the extent to which they agreed with the

[91] Throughout this volume, the word "leading" is used interchangeably with "landmark", "important" and "great", and the word "case" with "judgment", "opinion", "ruling" and "decision", unless otherwise indicated or obvious from the context.

[92] This raises the question as to *why* a decision comes to be regarded as canonical by the scholarly community. For some tentative explanations see, e.g., Pascale Gonod, 'À propos des grands arrêts de la jurisprudence administrative' in *Mélanges en l'honneur de Daniel Labetoulle* (Dalloz 2007) 441–458 (arguing that leading cases provide a simplified summary of a more complex body of case law and encapsulate the values supposed to inspire judicial decision making); Jakab (n 5) (arguing that leading cases are often *contra legem* at the time they are decided but typically consonant with the present or upcoming social and political *Zeitgeist*); Jean-Claude Venezia, 'Petite note sur les Grands arrêts' in *Mélanges en l'honneur de Louis Dubois* (Dalloz 2002) 221–228 (suggesting that what makes a case canonical is the significance of the jurisprudential developments with which it coincides and the extent to which it is indicative of the direction of legal change). As for the question whether the landmark character of a case primarily derives from its legal significance, or arises mainly from its social and historical relevance, see Rt Hon Sir Ivor Richardson, 'What Makes a "Leading" Case' (2010) 41 *Victoria University Wellington Law Review* 317 (arguing for the latter). By defining canonicity in terms of the relative scholarly consensus, our approach avoids the pitfalls associated with substantive definitions relying on essentialist criteria of leading-ness. Cf. J. M. Balkin and Sanford Levinson, 'The Canons of Constitutional Law' (1997–1998) 111 *Harvard Law Review* 963, 979: 'Canonicity is not simply a matter of what one thinks important; it is also a matter of what one thinks *others* think important.'

[93] The names and the answers of all the experts are downloadable at the website of the Research Documentation Centre of the Centre for Social Sciences of the Hungarian Academy of Sciences (http://openarchive.tk.mta.hu/369/). We are aware that the selection method of experts is necessarily biased to a certain degree, but as outsiders, we would have been simply unable to establish who are the 'mainstream constitutional scholars' in a number of legal systems; thus we were compelled to leave the selection to the authors.

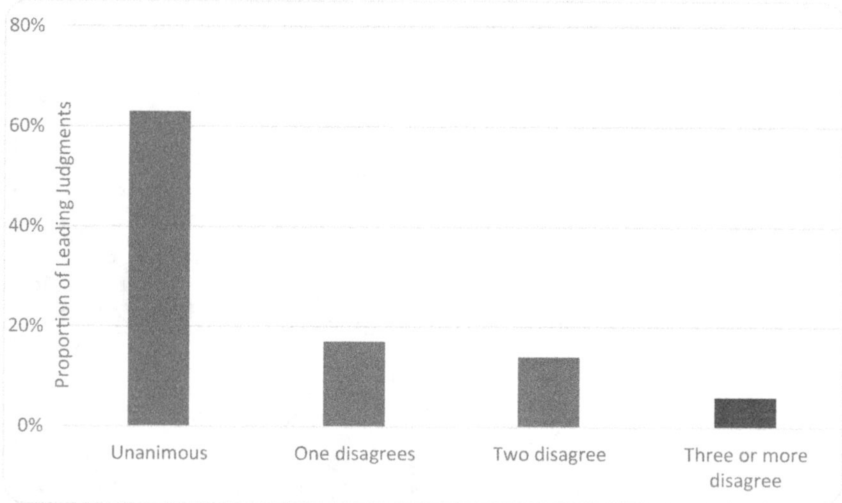

Figure 0.1 Degree of Expert Agreement on Case Selection

choice made. We did not expect perfect agreement among the experts. But we believed a consensus would exist over at least a subset of these 40 decisions.

Figure 0.1 shows that nearly 63 per cent of all judgments were unanimously ratified by all the experts. In 17 per cent of the cases, one expert disagreed and in 14 per cent two. In only 6 per cent of the cases did three or more experts opine that a judgment should not figure on the list. To be sure, such a procedure cannot guarantee absolute reliability. We cannot rule out the presence of a framing effect.[94] Had the experts been presented with a different initial list or had we gone for different set of experts, we might well have arrived at different results. Still, a list of the 40 most influential US Supreme Court cases would look very odd if did not include *Marbury v. Madison, Brown v. Board of Education* or *Roe v. Wade.* So too would a list of the top ECJ decisions that failed to mention *Van Gend en Loos* and *Costa v. ENEL.* Equally incomplete would be a list of the most important German constitutional cases without the *Lüth* judgment. In that regard, and to the extent that authors and experts all agreed on the inclusion of these cases, the resulting selection makes good sense. There

[94] On the effect of framing on decision making see Amos Tversky and Daniel Kahneman, 'The Framing of Decisions and the Psychology of Choice' (1981) 211 *Science* 453.

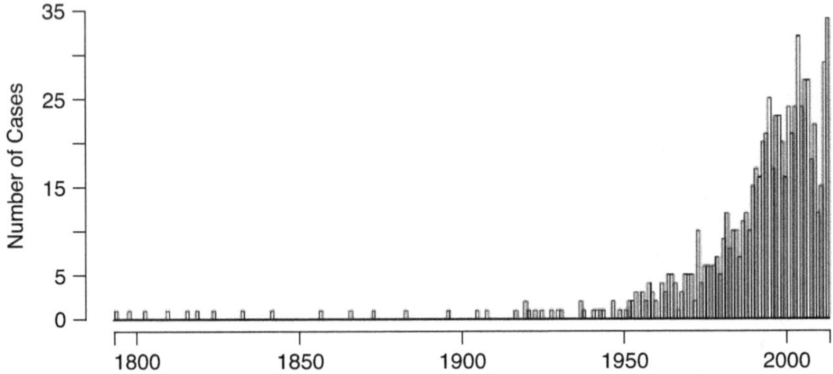

Figure 0.2 Leading Cases by Year of Issuance

is an intersubjective consensus over the relative importance of constitutional cases that the results of our procedure does seem to capture. At a minimum, it gives us a sense of how confident we can be about the extent of this consensus, even if there is some minor disagreement about the relative importance of certain constitutional cases.

Due to the dramatic changes in the competences, rules of standing, personnel and general political context that affected the Hungarian Constitutional Court after 2010 – events that culminated in the adoption of a new Basic Law in 2011 – the initial report on Hungary had largely become legal history.[95] The authors of the Hungarian report, therefore, conducted a second analysis on the basis of a distinct set of leading cases for the period corresponding to the new constitutional regime. The results were attached, as epilogue, to the initial report. This means that the present book is based on the investigation of $(18 + 1) \times 40 = 760$ leading judgments. As we decided to consider landmark rulings independently of the year in which they were rendered, the 18 reports assembled in this book cover periods of disparate lengths. Figure 0.2 plots the 760 leading judgments by year of issuance.

The first ruling in our corpus goes as far back as 1793 (US Supreme Court decision in *Chisolm v. Georgia*). Most leading judgments, though, were handed down after WWII. The skewed distribution suggests that

[95] Pál Sonnevend, Lóránt Csink and András Jakab, 'The Constitution as an Instrument of Everyday Party Politics: The Basic Law of Hungary' in Armin von Bogdandy and Pál Sonnevend (eds), *Constitutional Crisis in the European Constitutional Area* (Hart 2015) 33–109.

landmark constitutional cases tend to be relatively recent rulings. In part, this may reflect the predisposition of constitutional scholars to evaluate the importance of a constitutional ruling in light of current societal debates and policy preoccupations. As more recent rulings are more likely to speak to current policy preoccupations, constitutional scholars are also more likely to regard them as important. Evidently, there are structural causes, too, of the bulge in the temporal distribution of leading judgments. Before WWII, constitutional review was an essentially American institution (although we do find some Australian and British constitutional cases in the first half of the twentieth century). In fact, most of the courts considered in this book were set up after WWII, while some (the Spanish Constitutional Tribunal, the Brazilian Federal Supreme Court, the Czech Constitutional Court and the Hungarian Constitutional Court) were only established in their current form in the 1980s or 1990s after their countries embraced democracy.

To analyse and compare argumentation patterns in these leading judgments, we developed a detailed questionnaire (see Appendix at the end of the book). Our goal was to ensure maximum comparability across a broad array of constitutional practices. Designed to serve as guidelines for the authors of the court reports, the questionnaire embraced 12 sections covering not only the court's style of reasoning but also its institutional configuration and broader political environment. The questions directly addressing the court's argumentation style fell in three broad categories (for the detailed codebook, see the Questionnaire in the Appendix):

(1) *The dominant topical and argumentative structure of constitutional opinions.* Questions in this category included the weight of rights discourse and separation of powers discourse in judicial argumentation: are leading judgments more likely to be framed as raising a rights issue or a separation of powers issue? Another important question pertained to the basic structure of judicial reasoning and how sequences of arguments appearing in opinions fit together. For this purpose, we distinguished three basic argumentation structures: (a) "chain-like" – or, more technically, "one-line conclusive" – reasoning, when a conclusion is supported by a single argument; (b) what we initially called "legs-of-chair" reasoning but later renamed, for the sake of precision, "parallel conclusive" argumentation, when a conclusion is supported by separate sets of premises with each individually presented as conclusive; and (c) "dialogical" reasoning,

also called "parallel inconclusive but together conclusive" argument, when various considerations are presented neither as necessary nor as sufficient to entail the conclusion, but as elements bearing, at least, some relevance for the issue at hand. These questions came with others relating to the candour, or lack thereof, of judicial communication and the frequency of dissenting opinions.

(2) *The sources of constitutional law and the repertoire of interpretive methods.* These encompassed questions regarding the status of putatively constitutional texts, the justiciability of constitutional issues and the use of precedent-based arguments. We asked our contributors to report the incidence of various canons of constitutional construction: plain meaning, original intent (teleological-historical interpretation), purposive interpretation (teleological-textual interpretation), analogy, coherence (conciliation of conflicting constitutional requirements) and interpretation in light of international law. In this category figured further questions on the frequency of non-legal arguments, reference to scholarship and the use of foreign legal materials.

(3) *Key concepts and generic constitutional doctrines.* The third and final category included questions on the use of generic concepts such as "democracy", "sovereignty", the "rule of law" and "human dignity". Also included were questions regarding the propensity of opinions to rely on rights-based standards like equality and privacy. Finally, we asked our contributors to report the extent to which constitutional opinions consider means-end tests such as proportionality. We were fully aware that they key concepts and the different tests can have different meanings in different legal systems (cf. the endless debate about the relationship between *Rechtsstaat* and the rule of law), so we asked our authors to reflect on these conceptual issues in their respective reports.

Each author was to write a detailed account of her court's argumentative practices describing how these categories are instantiated in judicial discourse. The resulting court reports make up the 18 chapters of this book.

We made three further methodological choices when designing the project. First, we chose one single court from every legal system. While we are aware that both lower courts and non-judicial organs are sometimes employing constitutional reasoning to justify their decisions, we wanted to stay focused on a narrower question, and we also realised that specific institutional (esp. procedural) rules can very much influence the reasoning which might be relevant when explaining the different results. Second, we decided to code separate (dissenting or parallel) opinions together with the majority opinions. This means that we did not make a difference between cases when a certain argument appeared in the majority opinion as opposed to cases when that argument came up in a dissenting opinion. While we could have collected some additional information about the differences between typical 'winning' and 'losing' arguments, the additional effort and the considerably higher complexity of such a design made us not to choose this path. And third, we did not count the number of appearances of arguments: we only coded whether an argument was present in the case or not (1 or 0). While counting the number of arguments might sound appealing, it would have seriously endangered the reliability of our data:[96] whether the same type of argument is just a repetition of the very same argument, whether it is a better explained version of a former argument or whether it is already a new one are questions which are endlessly debatable and many times also conceptually artificial. Thus also here, we opted for the simpler design which does not show the absolute numbers, but which shows the pervasiveness of certain arguments along judgments.[97] An additional bonus of this choice was that we did not have to deal with outliers where one single judgment contains a high number of one specific type or argument distorting data on absolute numbers: for us, it was still a simple "1", and our authors could mention such cases in the qualitative part of their report (i.e., in the following chapters of this volume) if they found specific cases noteworthy. For similar reasons, we did not code the weight of arguments, but the treatment of this issue was left to the qualitative part of the reports.

While adherence to a detailed and comprehensive questionnaire promised to enhance comparability across the reports, we did not stop there. Indeed, we instructed each contributor to encode in a spreadsheet information on nearly 40 opinion characteristics covering the three categories above.[98] Each author had to repeat this for every single opinion

[96] On reliability as replicability see Lee Epstein and Andrew D Martin, *An Introduction to Empirical Legal Research* (Oxford University Press 2014) 48–49.

[97] Cf. on the different canons of acceptable arguments in different legal systems, changing also in time, AM Honoré, 'Legal Reasoning in Rome and Today' (1974) 91 *South African Law Journal* 84, esp. 92.

[98] Because of the very high level of expertise that was necessary to answer the questionnaire, we could not ask a second set of coders to control (or to do simultaneously) the coding

in her set of 40 cases. Thanks to the extra effort of our contributors, we were able to assemble a novel dataset, the CONREASON Dataset, summarizing the argumentative characteristics of 760 landmark constitutional decisions. Herein lies probably one of the principal and most original contributions of the present book. As the aggregate results presented in the concluding section demonstrate, our research design and the dataset we have constructed greatly facilitate the identification of argumentation patterns across judicial institutions as well as across time.

To be sure, the application of the questionnaire and the completion of the CONREASON Dataset, not unlike the application of a constitution, raised delicate interpretive questions. Yet again, our primary goal was to maximize comparability across the jurisdictions investigated. So we strived to ensure uniform operationalisation of our conceptual framework across the reports and compiled data. One of us developed a conceptual map fleshing out the abovementioned argumentative categories.[99] This comprehensive typology of constitutional arguments served as a reference point, which our authors were instructed to follow. On top of this, the entire international research team met physically on two occasions: the first time in Heidelberg in January 2012 to introduce the questionnaire and coding scheme; and the second time in Budapest in February 2013 to address conceptual issues and take stock of the progress made. Last but not least, as editors and team leaders, we kept constant contact with the contributors throughout the drafting and data collection process. The present volume is the end-product of this unprecedented collective effort.

Each of the 18 chapters of this book reports the argumentation practices of a constitutional court on the basis of its 40 leading judgments. To enhance comparability, each chapter follows the same structure. It

decisions that were made by the contributors (a method which is otherwise often applied in social sciences, and normally executed by research assistants).

[99] András Jakab, 'Constitutional Reasoning. A European Perspective on Judicial Reasoning in Constitutional Courts' (2013) 8 *German Law Journal* 1215. When building our conceptual frame we heavily drew on the pre-existing theoretical literature on legal reasoning, especially on MacCormick and Summers (n 16); MacCormick and Summers (n 71); Theodor Viehweg, *Topik und Jurisprudenz* (Beck 1953); Robert Alexy, *Theorie der juristischen Argumentation: Die Theorie des rationalen Diskurses als Theorie der juristischen Begründung* (Suhrkamp 1978); Chaïm Perelman, *Logique juridique: nouvelle réthorique* (2nd edn, Dalloz 1999) [1979]; Giovanni Tarello, *L'interpretazione della legge* (Giuffrè, 1980); Aleksander Peczenik, *Grundlagen der juristischen Argumentation* (Springer 1983); Aulis Aarnio, *The Rational as Reasonable: A Treatise on Legal Justification* (Reidel 1987); Jerzy Wróblewski, *The Judicial Application of Law* (Kluwer 1992); Neil MacCormick, *Legal Reasoning and Legal Theory* (Clarendon 1994); Riccardo Guastini, *Interpretare e argomentare* (Giuffrè 2011).

begins by setting out the broader cultural and political backdrop of constitutional reasoning: the court's political environment, its institutional make-up, the outlook and origin of its judges and its rapport with the law professoriate. Each chapter then moves on to discuss the court's general opinion-writing style before dissecting the content of its 40 leading judgments. Each chapter also includes a comparative section reflecting on what are perceived to be the principal differences and commonalities between the court and its counterparts in other jurisdictions. The book concludes by pulling together the results of the qualitative court reports along with those from the quantitative analysis of the CONREASON Dataset.[100]

[100] Our aim was also to create a multi-user dataset which can now be downloaded both from the Research Documentation Centre of the Centre for Social Sciences of the Hungarian Academy of Sciences (http://openarchive.tk.mta.hu/369/) and the Cambridge University Press companion website. The latter also contains one leading case from every court that we analysed in this volume (in English): we hope that not only postgraduate university courses on comparative constitutional law or on constitutional reasoning can make use of this resource, but also legal scholars might find it a useful addition to the present volume.

1

The High Court of Australia

CHERYL SAUNDERS AND ADRIENNE STONE

A Legal, Political, Institutional and Academic Context

1 Legal and Political Culture as Context for Constitutional Reasoning

The Australian Constitution is a written constitution that came into force in 1901 as the culmination of a decade-long process.[1] The drafting was undertaken principally by the elected members of a series of Constitutional Conventions held over the 1890s. It took place, however, with the approval of, and subject to the occasional intervention by, the government of the United Kingdom, where the Constitution ultimately was given legal effect.[2]

The Constitution continues to reflect this British heritage. Formally, the Constitution is contained within an Act of the Parliament at Westminster,[3] but it came into force only following its adoption at referenda held in each of the Australian colonies. The framers of the Australian Constitution, while seeking to federate the colonies, were not seeking full independence from the United Kingdom. Despite the role of the Australian 'people' (or a segment of them) in the Constitution's drafting, the accepted view remained that Australia was not a fully independent nation, but part of

[1] It is this Constitution and the reasoning of courts that implement it that is the focus of this chapter. We should note at the outset, however, that 'Australian constitutional law' can also be understood to include the constitutions of the Australian states and a body of unwritten law that is often thought as having constitutional status including principles of statutory interpretation. See, for instance, Anne Twomey, *The Constitution of New South Wales* (Federation Press 2004); Gerard Carney, *The Constitutional Systems of the Australian States* (Cambridge University Press 2006).

[2] For an historical account, see JA LaNauze, *The Making of the Australian Constitution* (Melbourne University Press 1972).

[3] *Commonwealth of Australia Constitution Act 1900* (UK).

the British Empire. Australia is now fully independent, but independence was achieved gradually, over a considerable period of time.[4]

The continuing influence of the British model, however, is still seen in the maintenance of constitutional monarchy, a parliamentary system of government and the common law. Moreover, under the influence of the nineteenth-century British model, the Australian Constitution contains little in the way of constitutional rights. Rights were to be protected by the common law and the electoral process, while the Constitution was to be concerned with establishing the Commonwealth – or national – government and dividing power between the Commonwealth and the other constituent parts of the federation, which were termed States.[5] The absence of constitutional rights was also a feature in other former British colonies for much of the twentieth century. However, unlike many other members of the British Commonwealth, Australia has still not adopted a charter of rights, and the absence of rights is now a distinctive feature of its Constitution.

The other dominant influence on the Australian Constitution was the United States.[6] The influence of that system is seen especially clearly in the federal structure. The Commonwealth Parliament, for instance, has listed (or 'enumerated powers') with the residual powers remaining with the States. Moreover, the subject matter of the Parliament's powers resembles the powers of Congress.[7] The influence of the US model is seen also in the separation of powers. In a mirror image of Articles I, II and III of the US Constitution, chapters I, II and III of the Australian Constitution are devoted to the Parliament, the Executive and the Judiciary, respectively. In this case in particular, however, the influence of the US model is mitigated by the Australian Constitution's British heritage. Thus, the separation of Executive and Legislative power is affected by principles of responsible government derived from the Westminster parliamentary tradition. The separation of judicial power resembles the US model more closely but

[4] See George Winterton, 'The Acquisition of Independence' in Robert French, Geoffrey Lindell and Cheryl Saunders (eds), *Reflections on the Australian Constitution* (Federation Press 2003) 41.

[5] *Australian Capital Television v Commonwealth* (1992) 177 CLR 106, 182 (Dawson J): '[the Constitution] does not seek to establish personal liberty . . . The choice was deliberate and based on a faith in the democratic process to protect Australian citizens'.

[6] Sir Owen Dixon, *Jesting Pilate: And Other Papers and Addresses* (Law Book Co 1965) 44.

[7] Though subsequent interpretation has erased much of the similarity.

has, as will be discussed, its own features that are in some cases unique to the Australian system.

2 *The Court and Constitutional Litigation*

The Constitution preserved the pre-existing colonial courts as courts of the new Australian States.[8] It established the High Court of Australia ('HCA') to serve as a final court of appeal from all other Australian courts.[9] The HCA has jurisdiction to hear appeals from all State, territory and federal courts on matters of State and federal law including the common law. It is therefore an important unifying force in Australian law. Its decisions were originally subject to appeal to the Privy Council, though the jurisdiction of the latter was always qualified in constitutional cases[10] and has in any event been abolished.[11]

Most matters come to the HCA by way of appeal from lower courts. The HCA has discretion to admit cases on appeal[12] and conduct preliminary hearings (or in some cases, review of papers) to determine which appeals will be subject to a full hearing.[13] In addition, it has original jurisdiction over specified matters, including constitutional matters.[14]

The power of the HCA to invalidate laws for lack of compliance with the Constitution has always been accepted,[15] though it is not explicitly granted by the Constitution. This power is shared with the State courts and lower federal courts. However, a decision of a State or lower federal court to invalidate a Commonwealth law would almost inevitably be subject to appeal and eventual resolution by the HCA.

However, the HCA's power (and the power of all federal courts) has been limited by the constitutional concept of 'judicial power of the Commonwealth', which, in the Australian context, means that the HCA cannot deliver advisory opinions nor engage in 'ex ante' review.[16] Additionally, the jurisdiction conferred by the Constitution is understood to be limited

[8] Constitution s 106. [9] Ibid. s 71. [10] Ibid. s 74.

[11] *Australia Act 1986* (Cth) and *Australia Act 1986* (UK).

[12] *Judiciary Act 1903* (Cth) ss 34, 35, 35AA, 35A.

[13] David Jackson, 'Leave to Appeal' in Tony Blackshield, Michael Coper and George Williams (eds), *The Oxford Companion to the High Court of Australia* (Oxford University Press 2001) 426.

[14] Constitution ss 75 and 76.

[15] *Australian Communist Party v Commonwealth* (1951) 83 CLR 1, 262 (Fullagar J).

[16] See *In re Judiciary and Navigation Acts* (1921) 29 CLR 257; Leslie Zines, 'Advisory Opinions and Declaratory Judgments at the Suit of Governments' (2010) 22.3 *Bond Law Review* 156–68.

to 'matters', a requirement that mimics, but is not entirely congruent with, the US conception of a 'case and controversy'.

Proceedings before the HCA always involve oral argument (with the exception of some preliminary hearings). Proceedings are adversarial and fairly lengthy. Most hearings last one or two days, and in the past they were frequently even longer.

The High Court's most recent annual report states that between 1 July 2015 and 30 June 2016 795 matters were filed at the Court, up from 698 in the previous year. Most are dismissed either without any hearing at all or immediately after a short hearing before one or two Justices. Of the 795 matters filed in 2015–16, 455 – nearly two thirds – were special leave applications. The special leave mechanism involves a preliminary determination about whether an appeal from a State, territory or federal court should be heard by the Full Bench. Of those 458 applications, only 45 – less than 10 per cent – went on to be heard by the Full Court. A total of 168 matters were brought in the original jurisdiction of the Court, though as with special leave applications, many of these do not proceed to a hearing before the Full Court: in 2015–16, the Full Court delivered judgments in 7 original jurisdiction cases.[17] Since 2006, the Court has usually delivered approximately 50 to 60 judgments per year.

3 *The Judges*

The HCA consists of seven judges, who are appointed until age 70, subject to removal only by a parliamentary procedure.[18] The profile of the HCA is notably homogenous. Overwhelmingly judges of the High Court have been drawn from other superior courts or from the practising bar, broadly conceived to include the position of Solicitor-General. There have been a number of politicians appointed to the High Court (13 members of the High Court have served in State legislatures or the Commonwealth Parliament), though no such appointment has been made since 1975.[19] Culturally, High Court Judges have been drawn from the Anglo-Celtic population (in particular, there have been no judges drawn from the large

[17] High Court of Australia, *Annual Report 2015–16*: http://www.hcourt.gov.au/assets/corporate/annual-reports/HCA_Annual_Report_2015-16.pdf. The remaining 16 matters are listed as 'Other'.

[18] Constitution s 72(ii).

[19] With the appointment of the Hon. Justice Lionel Murphy. See John Williams and Lionel Keith Murphy in Blackshield et al. (n 13) 484.

post-war immigrant communities of non-Anglo European[20] or Asian descent, nor has there been a judge from the Indigenous population). Most judges have also been drawn from the most populous States,[21] and almost all appointees to the bench have been men. Only four women have served on the HCA bench, three of whom are currently serving. No HCA judge has ever been appointed from the Academy though many HCA judges have, as practitioners or lower court judges, been part-time teachers in Universities.[22]

4 *Legal Scholarship and the Context for Constitutional Reasoning*

Constitutional reasoning is the subject of close study by Australian constitutional scholars, is routinely the subject of academic work of all kinds (journal articles, scholarly monographs, conferences and symposia) and is a central topic in the teaching of constitutional law in Australia's law schools.

Although High Court judges are not drawn from the ranks of the Academy, there is a relatively close and mutually respectful relationship between the higher judiciary and the Academy, reflected in, among other things, the members of judiciary publishing in academic journals, sometimes jointly with professors; conferences featuring academics and judges; and judges holding adjunct positions at law schools. It is also common for HCA judges to hold adjunct academic appointments of various kinds after their retirement. More generally, members of the higher judiciary actively support the activities of law schools and there is significant academic collaboration and interaction between judges and senior scholars.[23] Relevantly for the present purposes, much Australian legal scholarship deals with case law and in particular with decisions of the HCA. Academic writing is frequently used in argument and is cited by judges in their reasoning, generally in support of a position already reached but sometimes as a source of insight. The parties themselves may raise the arguments

[20] Though some judges have been of partly non-Anglo-European descent. See Francesca Dominallo and Eddy Neuman, 'Background of Justices' in Blackshield et al. (n 13) 48–52, 50.

[21] Ibid. [22] Ibid.

[23] See, e.g., Robert French, Geoffrey Lindell and Cheryl Saunders (eds), *Reflections on the Australian Constitution* (Federation Press 2003). (The Hon. Robert French, the former Chief Justice of Australia, was at this time a Judge of the Federal Court.)

of scholars and, in this case, these will be dealt with by the judges in the same way.

Scholars are most often cited as authorities on matters of constitutional law in the sense that their reasoning is appealed to for support. Leslie Zines and Cheryl Saunders are among the scholars whose work is cited by the Court in this way.[24] In some cases, although not many, a judge may engage directly with legal scholarship and consider scholarly criticism of the Court's reasoning. In one unusual example, in *Coleman v Power*, McHugh J, canvassed Adrienne Stone's work on the Australian equivalent of the proportionality test at some length.[25] Also rarely, the Court may engage with writings by foreign scholars or scholars from other disciplines. To provide another instance, in *Australian Capital Television*[26] Mason CJ quoted both the House of Lords and Archibald Cox in developing his point about the importance of 'public participation in political discussion' in a representative democracy. In *Lange v Australian Broadcasting Corporation*, the High Court referred to the work of (political scientist) AH Birch.[27]

In addition to its explicit use, academic writing constitutes an important part of the climate of opinion within which the HCA works. In terms of style, critical analysis of judicial decisions is common, often in comparative perspective, and overt deference is rare. Most analysis takes place within broadly shared boundaries, however. Most scholars accept the validity of the institution of judicial review, but they also assume that it has a relatively limited scope, given the dominance of Australian legalism as the mode of interpretation. Legalism offers greater flexibility than formalism, but reflects the inclination of the Court to confine its reasoning to legal resources, so far as possible.[28] Academic criticism tends to be confined to judicial reasoning or other aspects of judicial method, reach and particular conclusions. However, especially in the last 20 years, the High Court has been subject to more robust criticism aimed at its interpretive methods. One strand of criticism has focussed on the implied freedom of

[24] See, e.g., *Williams v Commonwealth* (2012) 248 CLR 156, which includes numerous citations to both Zines and Saunders.

[25] *Coleman v Power* (2004) 220 CLR 1, 46–7 [83]–[85] (McHugh J). Her work on this issue has been canvassed by the Court again more recently: *McCloy v New South Wales* (2015) 89 ALJR 857, 885 [141], Gageler J.

[26] See below (n 46) and accompanying text.

[27] See below (nn 40 and 41).

[28] Jeffrey Goldsworthy identifies it as the most positivist of the courts in his six-country comparative survey. See Jeffrey Goldsworthy, 'Conclusions' in Jeffrey Goldsworthy (ed) *Interpreting Constitutions: A Comparative Study* (Oxford University Press 2006), 321, 329.

political communication cases[29] and another on the Court's expansion of Commonwealth powers.[30]

In addition to scholarly work on constitutional law, it is likely that the HCA is influenced by more general trends in legal thought, particularly by theories of adjudication. It is has been much speculated that the work of legal realist Professor Julius Stone during the latter half of the twentieth century was highly influential on his students at the University of Sydney, including a number who later became Justices of the HCA.[31]

The relative prestige of judges and the academy in Australia is similar to that in other Anglo-Saxon jurisdictions. In both social and economic terms, judges of superior courts enjoy higher prestige than constitutional law professors. This is reflected also in their salaries. At July 2013, the salary of a High Court Justice was $486,480 AUD (Chief Justice, $536,070 AUD). At the same time, a regular professorial salary was $165,922 AUD (without loading).

Rule of Law

Australian legal and political culture still bears traces of its origins in the British common law parliamentary tradition, now modified by over 100 years of Australian development as a distinct constitutional polity, during which its independence from Britain was gradually acquired.[32] Perhaps paramount among these is a commitment to the rule of law. The independence of the judiciary and other key institutions (including the Australian Electoral Commission) is broadly respected. Law is understood to include both legislation and the common law. The latter comprises decisions of judges given effect through the doctrine of precedent.

On the other hand, Australian legalism has meant that the proper role of the courts is assumed to be to interpret and apply the law, using common law techniques, as understood through the lens of legalism. This ostensibly limited role is now reinforced by judicial understanding of the

[29] See, e.g., Jeffrey Goldsworthy, 'Constitutional Implications Revisited' (2011) 30.1 *University of Queensland Law Journal*, 9–34.

[30] See, e.g., Nicholas Aroney, 'Constitutional Choices in the *Work Choices Case*, or What Exactly Is Wrong with the Reserved Powers Doctrine?' (2008) 30.1 *Melbourne University Law Review*, 1–43.

[31] See Haigh Patapan, *Judging Democracy: The New Politics of the High Court of Australia* (Cambridge University Press 2000); AJ Brown, *Michael Kirby: Paradoxes and Principles* (Federation Press 2011).

[32] Anne Twomey, '*Sue v Hill* – The Evolution of Australian Independence' in Adrienne Stone and George Williams (eds), *The High Court at the Crossroads: Essays in Constitutional Law* (Federation Press 2000), 77–108.

constitutional separation of powers in the Commonwealth sphere as constraining courts to the resolution of questions of law, precluding consideration of the 'merits' of a case according to other non-legal criteria.[33]

While judicial review is widely accepted, there is a palpable tension between federalism, understood to require an entrenched Constitution limiting the authority of both spheres of government, and parliamentary government, imbued with the expectations and practices of parliamentary supremacy.

Nonetheless, the decisions of courts are invariably given effect by the elected branches even when politically inconvenient to the government of the day and even if considered more 'activist' than usual. Amongst the cases discussed below, *Wakim* was notably inconvenient for all Australian governments[34] and *Australian Capital Television v Commonwealth* was considered by its critics to be highly activist.[35] Even so, these decisions were given effect without question. Overt political criticism of individual decisions is also rare, though not unknown; it was especially marked during the mid-1990s, a period in which the High Court was highly innovative, by Australian standards.[36] Despite these caveats, however, and even in the face of criticism, compliance with judicial decisions and respect for judicial independence are attributes of the Australian rule of law that are secure.

Fundamental Values

In terms of political philosophical presuppositions, there is no conception of the existence of a pre-legal state or of human rights as natural rights. On the contrary, the idea of 'deep' common law rights that the Parliament cannot alter has been explicitly rejected by the Court, though accepted by some judges in other common law systems.[37]

While the point is somewhat different, since the decision in *Mabo v Queensland [No 2]*,[38] it has been accepted that indigenous societies with

[33] See especially the judgment of McHugh J in *Al-Kateb v Godwin* (2004) 219 CLR 562.

[34] *Re Wakim; Ex parte McNally* (1999) 198 CLR 511.

[35] See, e.g., Jeffrey Goldsworthy, 'Implications in Language, Law and the Constitution' in Geoffrey Lindell (ed), *Future Directions in Australian Constitutional Law: Essays in Honour of Professor Leslie Zines* (Federation Press 1994), 150–84; Jeffrey Goldsworthy, 'Constitutional Implications Revisited' (2011) *University of Queensland Law Journal*, 9–34.

[36] Jason L. Pierce, *Inside the Mason Court Revolution: The High Court of Australia Transformed* (Carolina Academic Press 2006).

[37] *Durham Holdings Pty Ltd v New South Wales* (2001) 205 CLR 399.

[38] (1992) 175 CLR 1.

their own systems of law and social organisation preceded European settlement. It is also accepted that the common law that developed in England from the thirteenth century, including common law rights historically developed by legislatures or courts, provides the basis for Australian law, which now has been adapted and refashioned as the Australian common law. The Australian common law gives some priority to common law rights through common law principles of statutory interpretation, including the principle of legality, which also draws justification from the rule of law.[39]

But beyond this commitment to rights through the common law, Australia's legal culture has been rather less ready to embrace constitutional rights than other constitutional democracies. Doubtless this attitude is partly traceable to expectations of parliamentary supremacy derived from Australia's British heritage, but some scholars trace this 'reluctance' to the dominance of utilitarianism in Australian political culture.[40]

There is little explicit discussion in Australia about the purpose of political community. It is assumed to take the form of a federal democratic polity based on equal citizenship, all of which is taken for granted in a somewhat complacent way, born of relative prosperity and distance. Even though the Constitution remains in form an Act of the British Parliament, it was drawn up and approved by referendum in Australia and has been acknowledged by the HCA as an exercise of popular sovereignty.[41]

This last point offers a key to Australia's constitutional culture more generally. One striking feature is the relatively muted social role of the Constitution. It is not generally thought that the Australian Constitution provides an expression of political values to which Australians aspire or to which they are jointly committed. Nor is it much associated with the establishment of a distinctive national identity.[42]

39 *Plaintiff S157/2002 v Commonwealth* (2003) 211 CLR 476; *Al-Kateb v Godwin* (2004) 219 CLR 562.

40 Jeffrey Goldsworthy, 'The Constitutional Protection of Rights in Australia' in Gregory Craven (ed), *Australian Federation Towards the Second Century* (Melbourne University Press 1992), 151; Hilary Charlesworth, 'The Australian Reluctance about Rights' (1993) 31.1 *Osgoode Hall Law Journal* 195.

41 See for example *Australian Capital Television v Commonwealth* (1992) 177 CLR 106, 138; *Theophanous v Herald & Weekly Times* (1994) 182 CLR 104, 171; *McGinty v Western Australia* (1996) 186 CLR 140, 230.

42 The Hon. Patrick Keane, 'In Celebration of the Constitution', http://www.naa.gov.au/collection/publications/papers-and-podcasts/australian-constitution/keane.aspx.

There are signs however that this aspect of Australia's legal and constitutional culture is changing. Over the last 15 years two movements for constitutional change have gained significant social support: a movement for the removal of the monarchy and the replacement of the Queen with an Australian Head of State; and a movement to recognise Aboriginal and Torres Strait Islander peoples in the Constitution. At the heart of both these movements is a belief that the Constitution should reflect Australian values more closely and, in the case of indigenous recognition especially, that constitutional change (even if largely symbolic) is a significant step towards justice.[43]

The HCA is the apex court in Australia, which administers Australian law as a whole, including the Commonwealth Constitution. There are no distinctions between its reasoning methodology and that of other courts, apart from those attributable to its position in the judicial hierarchy. As noted earlier, there is broad similarity in interpretive method used for the Constitution and the statutes. The nature of the Constitution is acknowledged as a factor that should be taken into account in interpretation, however. The particular characteristics of the Constitution on which emphasis is placed for this purpose include its longevity and the generality of its terms. The Australian Constitution in fact has proved very difficult to change, but this is rarely used by the HCA to explain its interpretive method. Decisions of the HCA are binding on other Australian courts and are invariably followed by them.

B Arguments in Constitutional Reasoning

Among these basic facts about the Australian Constitution and the tradition of argument in the HCA, it is especially important to note at the outset the continuing influence of the common law legal method. Through the doctrine of precedent, the HCA's decisions are themselves a source of law which are subject to close reading and which greatly influence future cases. Common law assumptions and methods infuse constitutional reasoning.[44] Australian constitutional law is in very large part an incrementally developing body of judge-made law.

[43] Elisa Arcioni and Adrienne Stone, 'Australian Constitutional Culture and the Social Role of the Constitution' (forthcoming).

[44] Leslie Zines, 'The Common Law in Australia: Its Nature and Constitutional Significance' (2004) 32.3 *Federal Law Review* 337–355.

5 *The Structure of Constitutional Arguments*

The Dominance of One-Line Conclusive Arguments

Turning to the structure of argument in the HCA, it is immediately striking that the one-line conclusive argument is overwhelmingly dominant in the 40 selected cases.

The rarity of parallel conclusive arguments ('legs of a chair') is traceable to the influence of common law methods of reasoning. In all cases, including constitutional cases, the HCA will generally decide only as much as is necessary to resolve the controversy and will usually decline to decide questions that are unnecessary for the resolution of the case.[45] The opposite is true of the arguments put to the Court: counsel appearing before the Court will frequently offer multiple arguments that assist their case. However, the Court will usually resolve only those it decides are necessary to reach a conclusion.

Constitutional cases in the HCA will typically turn on two kinds of questions: powers (competences) and limitations. When it comes to the question of competence, the Commonwealth government will commonly advance several arguments in support of its conclusion. Thus, in the *Tasmanian Dam*[46] case, the Court considered whether legislation providing 'World Heritage' protection to a Tasmanian wilderness area was within the legislative competence of the Commonwealth Parliament. Four legislative heads of power were advanced: the power over 'external affairs', 'corporations', 'special laws' for the people of any race (here, aboriginal people) and a putative power over matters pertaining to 'nationhood'. Different aspects of the law were found by the majority to be valid on the basis of the first three of these powers, but these arguments formed together one conclusive argument. For this reason, the judges found it unnecessary to resolve the arguments put on the basis of the more contentious 'nationhood' power.

Similarly, where multiple arguments are put on the basis of limitations, the Court will decide only as much as is necessary to resolve the case. So in *Australian Capital Television v Commonwealth*,[47] the Court by majority held that the impugned law infringed an implied guarantee of political communication and was therefore invalid. For this reason most judges did not deal with a second limitation argument, that the laws

[45] This practice is usually but not invariably adhered to. See below n 48 and accompanying text.

[46] *Commonwealth v Tasmania* (1983) 158 CLR 1 (*Tasmanian Dam Case*).

[47] (1992) 177 CLR 106.

impermissibly interfered with the operation of the governmental functions of the States.[48]

However, the tendency to decide only as much as is necessary to decide a case is not universally adhered to and on occasion, the Court (or particular members of it) may advance multiple arguments, each of which is sufficient for its conclusion. Of the 40 selected cases *Wakim* most clearly demonstrates the parallel conclusive arguments ('legs of a chair'). In that case the HCA held invalid a federal law pursuant to which federal courts were permitted to exercise the jurisdiction of State courts. The Court held that the law exceeded the competence of the Commonwealth Parliament, which had neither the power to invest federal courts with State jurisdiction nor the power to consent to such action being taken by the States.

The absence of parallel, individually inconclusive, but together conclusive arguments (dialogic structure) is perhaps even more fundamental. To put the point bluntly: if a competence has been exceeded or a limitation infringed, that fact is always conclusive of invalidity; if no such excess of power or infringement of a limitation can be identified, then a challenge conclusively fails. Excess of power or infringement of a limitation is never simply one factor in such a conclusion. So, for instance, the question of whether a federal law is validly made by the Commonwealth parliament turns on identifying a source of Commonwealth legislative power rather than identifying a range of factors that together provide a source of power. To return to the *Tasmanian Dam* case, the question of whether the Commonwealth parliament could validly enact a law protecting the Tasmanian wilderness area depended on a precise identification of a source of power for each operative element of the law. While several sources of power were relied upon to support discrete elements of the law, these supported the law as one-line conclusive arguments ('links of a chain') rather than through their combined weight. Similarly, a law that violates the separation of judicial power or another limitation on power (such as a constitutional 'right') is invalid for that reason alone.

Lowering the Level of Generality

The dominance of the one-line conclusive arguments method of reasoning is clear when considering the structure of argument at this high level of generality. However, if we focus more narrowly other structures of argument are evident. For instance, where it is argued that the separation

48 But see ibid. 167 (Brennan J), 241–5 (McHugh J).

of powers principle has been infringed, that question is resolved as part of one-line conclusive arguments ('chain structure'): a breach of the separation of powers is a conclusive argument for constitutional invalidity. However, in resolving the sub-questions raised by this aspect of constitutional law the analysis may employ parallel, individually inconclusive, but together conclusive arguments ('dialogical structure'). To determine whether the separation of judicial power has been breached, a court will consider the nature of 'judicial power'. The constitutional conception of judicial power is only vaguely defined, and the case law is replete with warnings that no definitive statement is possible and that no single characteristic can be said to be determinative one way or the other.[49] On the contrary, there are various 'indicia' of judicial power and these are considered by the court as part of an all-things-considered judgment made in the context of each case. Of the selected 40 cases, *Brandy's Case*[50] is representative of this kind of argument. In that case, the HCA held that the Human Rights and Equal Opportunity Commission's powers to mediate discrimination claims were in effect an impermissible exercise of judicial power. This determination depended upon a contextual judgment that took account of nature of the Commission's powers and the context in which they were exercised. The Court accepted that the Commission's powers of mediation considered in isolation were not judicial. Powers of mediation, where the focus is on finding a solution acceptable to all parties, have traditionally been distinguished from the judicial power to make determinations according to law. However, the provisions that governed the enforcement of the Commission's decisions changed the analysis. Determinations of the Commission were registered in the Federal Court and a determination, from the moment of registration, had effect 'as if it were an order made by the Federal Court', leading the Court to conclude that the Commission was invalidly invested with judicial power.

Another instance of parallel, individually inconclusive, but together conclusive arguments ('dialogical structure') is provided by the case law on the meaning of 'excise duty' (a form of tax on goods that only the Commonwealth parliament may levy). For some decades the HCA had recognised an anomalous exception pursuant to which States were able to

[49] *R v Davison* (1954) 90 CLR 353, 366 (Dixon CJ and McTiernan J); *R v Trade Practices Tribunal; Ex Parte Tasmanian Breweries Pty Ltd* (1970) 123 CLR 361, 394 (Windeyer J); *Precision Data Holdings v Wills* (1991) 173 CLR 167, 188–9.

[50] *Brandy v Human Rights and Equal Opportunity Commission* (1995) 183 *CLR* 245 (*Brandy's Case*).

levy duties on goods provided they took the form of a license fee calculated by reference to the value of goods sold over a period prior to the period of the license.[51] As the doctrine developed, the 'prior-period licence fee' exception was exploited by the States who posed higher and higher taxes and manipulated the licence fee exception so that these taxes closely mirrored the nature of excises. In a series of decisions culminating in *Ha*[52] the Court effectively precluded the States' reliance on this exception. It did so by indicating various factors that militate in favour of a conclusion that a 'prior period licence fee' is in reality an excise. In a dialogical fashion, the Court will consider the size of the levy, the length of the licence period and its proximity to the period for which the licence is granted.[53]

Thus the structure of constitutional argument in the HCA is layered. Its overall structure tends to consist of arguments that are themselves conclusive links in a 'chain' but within each 'link' other forms of argument proliferate.

6 *Types of Arguments in Constitutional Reasoning and Their Weight*

The Core Methods: Text, Precedent and Structural Inference

Reasoning in Australian constitutional cases is dominated by four key methods: text, history, precedent and inferences from 'text and structure'. Of these, textual analysis (which encompasses, but is not confined to, the *ordinary meaning of words* method) has, at least nominally, the most prominence.

The identity of the relevant text is well established (it is found in the *Constitution of the Commonwealth of Australia*, which in turn is part of the *Commonwealth of Australia Constitution Act* 1900 (Imp)). For this reason we found no cases which involved *debating or establishing the text* of the Australian Constitution.

The centrality of textual argument was settled early in Australia's constitutional history in one of the most important constitutional cases, *Amalgamated Society of Engineers v Adelaide Steamship Company* ('the *Engineers' Case*').[54] The substantive issue in that case concerned the extent to which federal laws could bind State governments (specifically, whether the Commonwealth Parliament could make laws for the resolution of

[51] Dating to *Dennis Hotels Pty Ltd v Victoria* (1960) 104 CLR 529.
[52] *Ha v New South Wales* (1997) 189 CLR 465.
[53] Ibid. 501–2. [54] (1920) 28 CLR 129.

industrial disputes that were binding on State governments). The decision greatly increased the Commonwealth Parliament's power to do so. Hence, the case is recognised as beginning the long trend towards the centralisation of legislative power in the Australian federation.[55]

For our purposes, however, it is significant because it also marked a turn towards 'textualism'[56] in interpretation. The means by which the Court abandoned its State-centered approach for one that favoured stronger Commonwealth powers was not an overtly 'centrist' approach. Rather, the Court insisted on reading the text according to its 'natural sense' and adopted an approach that precluded arguments based on an unwritten assumption that in certain respects the States were immune from Commonwealth legislative power or that certain areas of activity were to be reserved to the States. The following passage is indicative of the Court's approach:

> [T]he only safe course is to read the language of the statute in what seems to be its natural sense . . . The established Courts of Justice, when a question arises whether the prescribed limits have been exceeded, must of necessity determine that question; and the only way in which they can properly do so, is by looking to the terms of the instrument by which, affirmatively, the legislative powers were created, and by which, negatively, they are restricted.[57]

The turn to textualism in *Engineers' Case* remains a touchstone for constitutional argument. Hence argument from the ordinary meaning of words features in a clear majority (23) of the 40 selected cases. Scholars debate whether this turn was a deliberate attempt to increase Commonwealth powers or whether it is a good faith adoption of an interpretive strategy,[58] and the turn to textualism has been attributed to a preference for the English tradition of statutory interpretation over more overtly teleological American approaches.[59]

[55] See the judgment of Windeyer J in *Victoria v Commonwealth* (1971) 122 CLR 353 (*Payroll Tax Case*).

[56] In the Australian literature more often described as 'textualism'. See Greg Craven, 'The Crisis of Constitutional Literalism in Australia' in HP Lee and George Winterton (eds), *Australian Constitutional Perspectives* (Law Book Co 1992), 1.

[57] (1920) 28 CLR 129, 149, quoting, respectively, *Vacher and Sons Ltd v London Society of Compositors* [1913] AC 107, 113 (Lord Haldane LC) and *R v Burah* (1878) 3 App Case 889, 904 (Lord Selborne).

[58] Jeffrey Goldsworthy, 'Justice Windeyer on the Engineers' Case' (2009) 37.3 *Federal Law Review* 363–374.

[59] Ibid.

For well-rehearsed reasons, the text read according to its ordinary or natural meaning cannot resolve all, or even very many, questions of constitutional interpretation,[60] and therefore it is not surprising that, even in the face of the HCA's insistence on the primacy of the constitutional text, other arguments are almost always present.

Text, Purpose and History

Before leaving a discussion of text, however, it is necessary to note that in Australian constitutional law text is often considered according to its purpose, and thus both *teleological textual arguments* and *teleological historical arguments* feature strongly.

To start with the latter, the historical meaning of the text is often considered important, featuring in over half of the 40 selected cases. Historical argument includes reference to the records of the debates at the framing conventions and legal texts written at the time of the framing as well as other historical material. The use of history in Australia is often a form of *purposive argument referring to the purpose of the Constitution-maker.* Among the 40 selected cases, it is especially vividly illustrated in *Cole v Whitfield*, a case interpreting s 92 of the Constitution which guarantees freedom of interstate trade.[61] After a long series of cases failed satisfactorily to resolve the meaning of this provision, the HCA, in a rare unanimous judgment, revised the law radically following a careful historical analysis of the framers' intentions and understandings of the free trade principle.

The case is a particularly prominent example of this historical method, but the method is well-established.[62] However, this use of historical method does not amount to a full-blown commitment to 'originalism'[63] in constitutional interpretation. Most members of the Court have been clear that the Constitution's meaning changes over time and that its 'original meaning' may not govern the present.[64] Moreover, there is some

[60] These reasons are reviewed in Adrienne Stone, 'Judicial Review without Rights' (2008) 28.1 *Oxford Journal of Legal Studies* 8–11.

[61] (1988) 165 CLR 360.

[62] Jeffrey Goldsworthy, 'Originalism in Constitutional Interpretation' (1997) 25 *Federal Law Review* 1–50, 12.

[63] But see Goldsworthy, ibid.

[64] See for instance, *New South Wales v Commonwealth* (2006) 229 CLR 1 (*Work Choices Case*), 97 [120] (Gleeson CJ, Gummow, Hayne, Heydon and Crennan JJ); Cheryl Saunders, 'Interpreting the Constitution' (2004) 15.4 *Public Law Review* 289, 291. For an account of one Justice's (Justice Heydon) thorough-going originalist views, see Lael K

disagreement about the precise uses to which history is put. While historical material may be used as evidence of the intention of the *framers* on some occasions, it is used in other ways: to identify the historical understanding of the text at the time of its drafting (a separate idea from the framers' intention) or to identify historical practices that inform the meaning of the Constitution.[65]

A teleological argument that turns on the purpose of the text is also common, reflecting an overall view that the Constitution implements a coherent system of law. This method may supplement teleological/historical interpretations of the text. So, for instance, in *Street v Queensland Bar Association*,[66] which transformed the interpretation of the prohibition on discrimination on grounds of State residence, the reasons identified the purpose of this section (as securing equal treatment and promoting national unity). That purpose was identified both by historical analysis as well as by reference to the purpose of the text itself.[67]

Beyond the Text: Precedent and Structural Inference

Despite the nominal importance of textual analysis, the method of constitutional reasoning that is most important in practice is the use of precedent. Indeed, this method is the only one that appears in all 40 of the selected cases. The prominence of precedential argument reflects, of course, Australia's common law heritage. Incrementally and on a case-by-case basis, the text of the Australian Constitution is elaborated in cases that are themselves as much part of constitutional law as the text of the Constitution. In most cases, therefore, earlier decisions are at the centre of the analysis.

Precedential reasoning is so central to constitutional reasoning in a common law system like Australia that there is little overt discussion of its weight. Such discussion does occur occasionally when unusual

Weis, 'What Comparativism Tells Us about Originalism' (2013) 11.4 *International Journal of Constitutional Law* 842–69.

[65] See for instance, *Roach v Electoral Commissioner* (2007) 233 CLR 162, 188–9 [53] (Gummow, Kirby and Crennan JJ) and see generally Michael Coper, 'The Place of History in Constitutional Interpretation' in Gregory Craven (ed), *The Convention Debates 1891–1898: Commentaries, Indices and Guide* (Legal Books 1986), 5.

[66] (1989) 168 CLR 460.

[67] Indeed, one Justice relied *only* on the purpose of the text without reference to its historically understood purposes: Ibid. 570–1 (Gaudron J).

circumstances arise, most notably where the HCA overrules (or declines an argument for overruling) previous cases.[68]

Precedential reasoning in Australian Constitutional law encompasses a number of other forms of reasoning. It is through precedential reasoning that Australian constitutional law includes a significant measure of *doctrinal analysis of legal concepts.* The case law is replete with legal concepts – either drawn from the text or developed in the case law – that can only be properly understood by reference to their elaborations in precedent. Concepts like 'tax', 'excise', 'trade', 'trading and financial corporation' and 'marriage'[69] have their distinct constitutional meanings accessible only on a detailed reading of the case law.[70]

In this way, precedential reasoning provides the context for discussion of *concepts and principles not mentioned in the text.* For instance, the free-trade requirement of s 92 is not primarily resolved by reference to the text of the Constitution[71] but by reference to the concept of 'a discriminatory burden of a protectionist kind' first articulated in *Cole v Whitfield*[72] and elaborated in the subsequent case law. Another important concept is 'reasonably appropriate and adapted', a principle that is used to test the relationship between laws and legislative powers as well as to determine whether limitations on power have been exceeded.[73] By operation of the doctrine of precedent, these concepts themselves become part of constitutional law and are then invoked again and again (and sometimes revised) in subsequent cases.

Lastly, precedential reasoning is itself a form of *analogy.* Determining the applicability of precedent in a given case involves close comparison of the facts and analogical arguments as to their similarity. This is the principal context in which analogy is used in Australian constitutional law. However, analogy is also a sub-category of another kind of reasoning – domestic harmonising – and so we turn to that form of argument before making further comment.

[68] As in *Victoria v Commonwealth* (1957) 99 CLR 575 (*Second Uniform Tax Case*), 610–11, in which Chief Justice Dixon followed an earlier case that he considered to be wrong.

[69] See, respectively, Constitution ss 51(ii), 90, 92, 51(i), 51(xx) and 51(xxi).

[70] Among the 40 selected cases see *Australian Tape Manufacturers v Commonwealth* (1993) 176 CLR 480 ('tax'); *Ha v New South Wales* (1997) 189 CLR 465 ('excise').

[71] Which provides, in s 92, that 'On the imposition of uniform duties of customs, trade, commerce, and intercourse among the States, whether by means of internal carriage or ocean navigation, shall be absolutely free'.

[72] (1988) 165 CLR 360.

[73] In some contexts at least it is the conceptual equivalent of 'proportionality'.

Domestic harmonising arguments are extremely important in Australian constitutional law, second only to textual and precedential argument. The prevalence of harmonising arguments (seen in all but four of the 40 selected cases) reflects an underlying assumption that the Constitution should be read in a manner that makes sense of it as a whole. Particularly significant in Australia is a form of argument known as 'implications from text and structure'. There are three important instances of these 'implications': the implication protecting 'essential functions' of the States, which gives rise to principles protecting the States from some federal laws;[74] the implication from representative and responsible government, which gives rise to gives rise to a right of freedom of political communication (a limited kind of free speech right)[75] and, perhaps, to rights of freedom of movement and association;[76] and the implication of a separation of judicial power, which gives rise to a range of more specific rules, including a rules that the Parliament cannot enact a bill of attainder;[77] that the Parliament cannot order detention (at least of a punitive nature) without the intervention of a court;[78] and requiring that courts act consistently with judicial process.[79]

The form of these arguments is to reason from specific provisions (for instance those provisions preserving the colonies as States after federation), to a more general principle (namely a prohibition on interference with 'essential State functions'),[80] to a more specific set of rules (such

[74] *Melbourne Corporation v Commonwealth* (1947) 74 CLR 31.

[75] *Lange v Australian Broadcasting Commission* (1997) 189 CLR 520.

[76] The freedoms of movement and association have not determined any case but have received some judicial recognition. *Kruger v Commonwealth* (1997) 190 CLR 1, 91 (Toohey J), 116 (Gaudron J), 142 (McHugh J); *R v Smithers; Ex parte Benson* (1912) 16 CLR 99, 109–110; *Higgins v Commonwealth* (1998) 79 FCR 528, 535. On the constitutional right of freedom of association see *Australian Capital Television v Commonwealth* (1992) 177 CLR 106, 232 (McHugh J); *Kruger v Commonwealth* (1997) 190 CLR 1, 91 (Toohey J), 142 (Gaudron J); *Mulholland v Australian Electoral Commission* (2004) 220 CLR 181, 225–6 [113]–[116] (McHugh J), 234 [148] (Gummow and Hayne JJ, with whom Heydon J agreed), 277–8 [284]–[286] (Kirby J) cf 297 [334]–[335] (Callinan J).

[77] *Polyukhovich v Commonwealth* (1991) 172 CLR 501, 536.

[78] *Chu Kheng Lim v Minister for Immigration* (1992) 176 CLR 1, 27–28. Those limitations do not, however, preclude the Parliament authorizing indefinite administrative detention: *Al-Kateb v Goodwin* (2004) 219 CLR 562. Moreover, conditions of immigration detention are not relevant to the validity of that detention: *Behrooz v Secretary of the Department of Immigration and Multicultural and Indigenous Affairs* (2004) 219 CLR 486.

[79] Fiona Wheeler, 'The Doctrine of Separation of Powers and Constitutionally Entrenched Due Process in Australia' (1997) 23.2 *Monash University Law Review* 248–84.

[80] *Melbourne Corporation v Commonwealth* (1947) 74 CLR 31.

as those that govern federal regulation of State employees).[81] These are harmonising arguments because they do not concentrate on the text of a legal provision in isolation but look at it in the context of other legal provisions in order to determine meaning. Moreover, like harmonising arguments, implications from text and structure are designed to give effect to fundamental underlying principles.

This form of argument also includes *arguments from silence*. That is, there are cases in which the HCA responds to silence in the Constitution. But silence is considered in the overall context of the Constitution and is used as part of an overall harmonising argument that seeks to create a coherent whole from the constitutional text. For instance, the Constitution is silent on the question of whether state legislatures can confer State jurisdiction on federal courts and whether the Commonwealth could validly consent to such a conferral. The Constitution nominates the subjects of federal jurisdiction but is not explicit as to whether these listed subjects are exhaustive or not.[82] The Constitution also explicitly provides for the reverse situation: that is, it explicitly provides that the Commonwealth Parliament may confer federal jurisdiction on State courts.[83] In *Wakim*[84] the HCA settled the issue by finding that federal courts could not exercise State jurisdiction. In reaching this conclusion, the Court compared the explicit provision permitting the exercise of federal jurisdiction by State courts with the silence on the question of whether federal courts can exercise State jurisdiction.

Implication from text and structure, a form of domestic harmonising, is thus a central form of reasoning in Australian constitutional law. Two final points are worth noting. First, the centrality of this form of argument is in marked contrast to the use of 'international harmonising' arguments. That form of argument is present in only three of the 40 selected cases. One of these concerned the Commonwealth Parliament's power over the continental shelf and thus had a natural relationship to international law (from which the concept of territorial waters derives).[85] Beyond circumstances of this kind, there is no widespread acceptance that the Constitution should be 'harmonised' with international law. One judge – Justice Kirby – has advanced strong views that ambiguities in constitutional meaning should be resolved consistently with Australia's

[81] *Re Australian Education Union; Ex parte Victoria* (1995) 184 CLR 188.
[82] Constitution ss 73, 75, 76 and 77. [83] Ibid. s 77(iii).
[84] *Re Wakim; Ex parte McNally* (1999) 198 CLR 511.
[85] *New South Wales v Commonwealth* (1975) 135 CLR 337 (*Seas and Submerged Lands Case*).

obligations at international law (a view seen in the remaining two selected cases, *Kartinyeri v Commonwealth*[86] and *Al-Kateb v Godwin*).[87] Justice Kirby's views have not been adopted by other members of the Court and were subject to criticism in *Al-Kateb v Godwin*.[88]

Second, the proliferation of implication as a form of domestic harmonising argument has raised tensions between its use and the long commitment to the primacy of the text. Critics of implication – including judges within the Court[89] – have criticised the liberal use of this method as inconsistent with textual analysis.[90] Especially criticised has been the implied freedom of political communication (a limited free speech right derived by implication from those provisions of the Constitution governing election of the Parliament). In a move that reaffirms the nominal primacy of text, the HCA in its landmark 1997 decision in *Lange v Australian Broadcasting Commission* sought to ensure that implications are closely tied to the text of the Constitution.[91] Whether this attempt has been, or could be, successful is still a matter for debate among Australian constitutionalists.[92]

Analogy

These structural implications are an especially important form of domestic harmonising argument because they provide the precedential and doctrinal foundation for large bodies of law. However, another form of domestic harmonising occurs when the Court compares directly individual provisions of the Constitution. These are domestic harmonising arguments because judges draw the comparison in order to demonstrate the rationality and coherence of its view. But these arguments turn upon the identification of relevant similarities and differences and are also forms of reasoning by analogy.

One particularly prominent form of this analogical, harmonising form of argument occurs in relation to the legislative powers of the Commonwealth Parliament. Some of the listed powers include an internal limit (for instance the power over 'banking, other than State banking').[93] The

86 (1998) 195 CLR 337. 87 (2004) 219 CLR 562. 88 Ibid. 594–5 (McHugh J).

89 *McGinty v Western Australia* (1996) 186 CLR 140, 171 (Brennan CJ), 180–3 (Dawson J), 233 (McHugh J), 281–3 (Gummow J).

90 Nicholas Aroney, 'A Seductive Plausibility: Freedom of Speech in the Constitution' (1995) 12.2 *University of Queensland Law Journal*, 249–74.

91 (1997) 189 CLR 520.

92 Adrienne Stone, 'The Limits of Constitutional Text and Structure' (1999) 23 *Melbourne University Law Review* 668.

93 Constitution s 51(iii).

question has arisen whether the limitation applies to other listed heads of power. In other words, could the power over 'corporations' be used to make laws with respect to State banking carried on by corporations and thus avoid the limitation found in the banking power? In a series of decisions the Court has distinguished between internal limits that constrain other powers (including the 'other than State banking' proviso[94] and the limitation that acquisition of property must take place on 'just terms'[95]) and those that do not (such as the limitation of federal industrial relations power to certain kinds of laws governing 'disputes extending beyond the limits of any one State').[96] The reasoning is both harmonising and analogical. It seeks to create a coherent scheme of constitutional powers, and it relies on careful comparison of the relevant provisions both according to their text and according to their purpose or place in the Constitution.

The use of analogy is extensive in Australian constitutional law, but it should not be thought of as a necessarily unprincipled method of reasoning. It can be understood as an 'incomplete theorizing'[97] that allows judges to postpone the identification of the guiding principles either because of uncertainty or because of disagreement in a multi-member court.[98] The identification of an underlying principle very often is a task for later courts reviewing the series of decisions in the course of precedential reasoning.

Non-legal (Moral, Sociological and Economic) Arguments

The methods just discussed are the most important in Australian constitutional reasoning. Collectively, they comprise Australian legalism, the roots of which go back at least to the *Engineers' Case* in 1920. Legalism is a strong theme in the HCA's modern implications cases as well.

Nonetheless, non-legal arguments are sometimes explicitly invoked. Among the cases we identified, the most common 'non-legal' argument involved reference to history. In many cases, as noted earlier, the use of history merges with teleological analysis of text. In these cases history informs legal meaning. However, in other circumstances history is invoked not as a means of determining original meaning but because history is otherwise thought to be relevant. In the course of determining

94 *Bourke v State Bank of New South Wales* (1990) 170 CLR 276.

95 *Attorney-General (Cth) v Schmidt* (1961) 105 CLR 361, 371–2.

96 *New South Wales v Commonwealth* (2006) 229 CLR 1 (*Work Choices Case*).

97 Cass R Sunstein, *Legal Reasoning and Political Conflict* (Oxford University Press 1996).

98 See Adrienne Stone, 'Incomplete Theorizing in the High Court' (1998) 26.1 *Federal Law Review* 195–205.

the extent of the right to vote, the HCA has put significant emphasis on established legislative practice. In one of the majority opinions in *Roach v Electoral Commission*[99] (concerning prisoner voting rights), there is a long historical analysis of voting laws before and after federation that is directed to understanding legislative practices, which in turn inform constitutional meaning.[100]

Putting history to one side, other non-legal arguments tend to be about the practical circumstances in which the constitution operates. Thus in the *Second Uniform Tax Case*,[101] the conclusion of World War II was taken to be relevant to the extent of the power to make laws with respect to defence. In other cases, there are references to 'expediency', 'common sense' or 'practicality' that suggest the Court is willing to consider the practical effects of its decisions, including any inconvenience that its decisions might cause.[102]

Thus in determining the extent of the Commonwealth power to regulate aviation as a form of 'interstate trade', the particular features of airline travel – its speed, the dangers posed, the need for aviation in modern life and the great distances of Australia – were thought relevant to the analysis.[103] Because of the 'sui generis' status of airline travel, the Court extended Commonwealth powers further in this field than in relation to other forms of travel.[104] But at the same time a note of caution was sounded:

> The Court is entrusted with the preservation of constitutional distinctions, and it fails in its task and exceeds its authority if it discards them, however out of touch with practical conceptions or with modern conditions they may appear to be.[105]

This warning was put into effect in *Wakim*. The laws challenged in that case involved a co-operative scheme enacted by all Australian governments (federal, State and territory) in order to solve the administrative inconvenience posed by the parallel system of State and federal courts. That governments had agreed that the scheme was a convenient solution

[99] (2007) 233 CLR 162. [100] Ibid 192 (Gummow, Kirby and Crennan JJ).

[101] *Victoria v Commonwealth* (1957) 99 CLR 575.

[102] *Abebe v Commonwealth* (1999) 197 CLR 510, 532; *Re Governor, Goulbourn Correctional Centre; Ex parte Eastman* (1999) 200 CLR 322, 332; *Airservices Australia v Canadian Airlines* (2000) 202 CLR 133, 177–8, 237–9.

[103] *Airlines of New South Wales Pty Ltd v New South Wales (No 2)* (1965) 113 CLR 54.

[104] Ibid 115. [105] Ibid 116.

to a common problem was not enough, however, to save the law from challenge. The 'convenience' of government could not be used in a manner that overcame substantive limitations to the capacity of the Parliament to authorise the conferral of State jurisdiction on federal courts. Justice McHugh acknowledged that this course might lead to greater convenience but denied that it lay within the authority of the courts to 'give effect to what judges think is in the public interest'.[106]

Thus, as *Wakim* shows, extra-legal considerations can be raised negatively, to deny their relevance to judicial determination and therefore their impact on the outcome of the case. *Al-Kateb v Godwin*[107] provides another illustration. In that case, in confirming the validity of the law authorising the continuing detention of a stateless asylum-seeker, McHugh J expressly repudiated the relevance of the 'justice or wisdom of the course taken by Parliament' or the question whether it was 'contrary to basic human rights'.[108]

7 *Judicial Candour and Judicial Rhetoric*

The foregoing review of the cases demonstrates that the HCA has, for the most part, a strong commitment to resolving cases by reference to legal materials and has typically eschewed reference to non-legal materials, especially non-legal considerations of morality. This approach to judicial reasoning, including reasoning in constitutional cases is known as Australian legalism.[109] At the core of this admittedly fluid methodology is an insistence that courts resolve legal questions by reference to standards drawn from the body of existing law and not to standards that are subjective or personal to the judge. This commitment accounts for the dominance of legal methods of interpretation including its insistence that the implications method be grounded in the text[110] so far as is possible, and its general reticence with respect to non-legal considerations. Therefore, as a general rule, value judgments, in the sense of extra-legal considerations that affect the outcome of cases, are not explicitly acknowledged in opinions, though the influence of such values may be surmised from the reasoning.

106 (1999) 198 CLR 511, 549. 107 (2004) 219 CLR 562. 108 Ibid. 595.

109 Jeffrey Goldsworthy, 'Australia: Devotion to Legalism' in Jeffrey Goldsworthy (ed), *Interpreting Constitutions: A Comparative Study* (Oxford University Press 2006), 106.

110 Stone (n 92), 668.

This relative lack of candour is especially evident in relation to value judgments as to the wisdom of a challenged law. There is a long tradition of aversion to such judgments that strongly infuses Australian constitutional reasoning. *Wakim*[111] (just discussed) provides one instance, but to give another, the HCA's traditional approach to determining the extent of Commonwealth legislative competence is deferential to the Commonwealth Parliament and explicitly eschews the question of the justice or wisdom of the law. This sentiment was also evident in *R v Barger*, the first of the 40 selected cases, which stresses the irrelevance of 'the motive which actuates the legislature, and the ultimate end desired to be attained'.[112] There are of course exceptions to this rule. Justice Murphy (who sat on the Court from 1975 to 1986) was especially frank about the value judgments that motivated his decision-making and consequently was a very controversial judge.[113]

Although judicial opinions of the HCA are not candid as to their underlying ideology, they are long and comprehensive (and there is no correlation between length and judicial candour). The length is partly attributable to a commitment, derived from a concept of fairness, to give detailed reasons.[114] The adversary system, as practised in Australia, requires judges to take account of the arguments of the parties, and they frequently do so explicitly in their reasons for judgment.[115] It is rare for judges to explicitly deal with points that were not raised in argument in any way, although the court may place pressure on parties to argue a particular point. If an argument is substantial, the assumption in Australian practice is that fairness requires parties to be given the opportunity to express a view.

The HCA's judgments also reflect an inevitable element of technicality. The terminology used in judicial reasoning is not necessarily technical, but the Constitution includes technical legal concepts (the remedies of prohibition and mandamus are examples).[116] Moreover, the manner in which judicial reasoning is constructed is often highly technical. Some judges write more clearly and concisely than others and most have taken steps in recent years to make their reasons more accessible by, for

[111] (1999) 198 CLR 511. [112] *R v Barger* (1908) 6 CLR 41, 67.

[113] AR Blackshield et al. (eds), *The Judgments of Justice Lionel Murphy* (Primavera Press 1986).

[114] Stephen Gageler, 'Why Write Judgments?' (2014) 36.2 *Sydney Law Review* 189–203; Sir Frank Kitto, 'Why Write Judgments?' (1992) 66.12 *Australian Law Journal* 787–99.

[115] Gerard Brennan, 'Decision-making Process' in Blackshield et al. (n 13) 197.

[116] Constitution s 75(v).

example, the use of headings, tables of contents and summaries of the conclusions reached. Nonetheless, coupled with the length of many judicial opinions, the result is to make constitutional decisions very difficult for non-specialists to understand.

The technicality of the judgments reflects in part the audience for decisions of the HCA.[117] Although the most important audience for judicial reasons is the parties to the proceeding, other target audiences, in probable order of importance, are the Australian courts for whom the reasons constitute precedent and Australian lawyers, including legal advisers to the government. Precisely because other Courts and lawyers will rely on opinions as a source of law, the HCA needs to provide a detailed and comprehensive legal argument that goes beyond what may be of interest to the parties.

The media and the public are important secondary audiences and in recent years techniques have been adopted to assist lay understanding of reasons for decision through, for example, public 'judgment summaries', which are distinct from the Court's reasons and have no authority in their own right. Neither law students nor academics are significant distinct audiences separate from the body of Australian lawyers as a whole. There is no sign that the HCA regards foreign or international courts as relevant audiences for its reasons, although no doubt it assumes that major decisions will be read elsewhere, just as it refers to foreign reasons.

The sense of obligation to give reasons that prevails in the Australian judicial decision means that all opinions will address the particular legal questions before the court. As discussed above, any reasons for judgment are relatively narrowly confined to these arguments (leaving some lines of argument unexplored). Relatedly, this method can mean that the general framework is not entirely clear. Thus, in the recent decision of *Williams v Commonwealth*,[118] to take only one example, the Court held that the particular contract in issue in the case could not be made without legislative authority, but it did not clearly identify where the line might be drawn between contracts of this kind and those that could be made in the exercise of executive power alone.

This approach is not consistently applied, however. Just as the Court occasionally decides a matter that it is not strictly necessary to rule on,

[117] On the audience for judges, see Susan Kiefel, 'Reasons for Judgment: Objects and Observations' (Speech delivered at Sir Harry Gibbs Law Dinner, University of Queensland, 18 May 2012). Copy held at the National Library of Australia.

[118] (2012) 248 CLR 156.

it also occasionally articulates principles in terms broader than strictly necessary to decide the case. Thus, in the *Boilermakers' Case*[119] the Court made it clear that, subject to relatively confined exceptions, non-judicial power could never validly be conferred on federal courts, thus pre-empting undecided issues. Similarly in the more recent case of *Kirk* the Court laid down a broad principle that precludes State Parliaments from ousting the jurisdiction of State courts to deal with jurisdictional error in resolving the particular case before it.[120] The drawing of implications, extensively discussed above, almost inevitably involves the identification of a general conceptual frame. Implications are general principles – that government is to be chosen by the people, that the States are to be protected and that judicial power is separated – taken to be inferred from more specific provisions.

Thus HCA opinions consist of a mix of reasons directed to specific issues and reasons directed to the developments of a general conceptual frame. The precise balance of the mix varies from time to time and from judge to judge and can be somewhat difficult to predict. The inclusion of the more general form of reasoning reflects the HCA's role as an apex court, the decisions of which are binding on all other Australian courts. It is inevitable, therefore, that the HCA will pay attention to the delimitation of principles by which other courts must be guided and that, where it fails to do so clearly, others will seek to extract such principles from its reasoning.

Finally, when it comes to questions of tone and degree of rhetoric, the Court is relatively restrained. In general, there is little political and/or emotive language in the reasons of justices of the HCA. Of course, what is perceived as rhetorical in judicial reasoning depends to a degree on legal and constitutional tradition. However, the preference for legalist methods of reasoning contributes to an overall restrained tone. Disagreements and dissent are generally expressed 'respectfully' and judges largely avoid commenting on the justice of the outcome.

Interestingly, however,there have been notable exceptions, most especially when judges feel bound to reach a conclusion that they find personally troubling. In *Al-Kateb v Godwin*, Justice McHugh upheld the detention of a stateless asylum seeker though the result was, in his view, 'tragic'.[121] Most recently, Justice Heydon found a law criminalising the

[119] *R v Kirby; Ex parte Boilermakers' Society of Australia* (1956) 94 CLR 254.

[120] *Kirk v Industrial Court of New South Wales* (2010) 239 CLR 531.

[121] *Al-Kateb v Godwin* (2004) 219 CLR 562, 581 (McHugh J).

sending of offensive letters invalid but wrote passionately about the hurt caused by the letters (which were sent to the relatives of Australian soldiers killed in wars in Iraq and Afghanistan).[122]

8 *Length, Dissenting and Concurring Opinions*

There is no direct correlation between the topic area of a case before the HCA and the length of the resulting opinions. More complex legal disputes may engage a wider range of arguments, however, making the opinions longer in order to deal with them. There were some very long cases in the first half-century of the existence of the HCA: *Melbourne Corporation v Commonwealth*[123] and *Australian Communist Party v Commonwealth*[124] are examples. In general, however, the collective reasons for decision seem to be getting longer. To the extent that this is correct, it is attributable to the styles of both legal argument and judicial writing. There are no other factors that would persuasively account for a development of this kind.

Both dissenting and concurring opinions are common in the HCA and in other Australian superior courts. In contrast to apex courts in some other jurisdictions, in HCA practice, there is no single set of reasons that necessarily represents those of a majority of the Court. Of the 40 significant Australian cases selected for the purposes of this project, all but four had dissenting or concurring opinions or both. A single set of reasons in which all Justices join may reflect the relative ease of the decision from the perspective of participating judges. Ironically, it may also reflect the critical nature of a decision that is novel or needed to resolve uncertainty about the law. Of the four cases in the examples for this project, *Air Caledonie*[125] and *Cheatle*[126] fall into the first category and *Cole v Whitfield*[127] and *Lange*[128] into the second. The frequency of dissenting and concurring opinions reflects the Australian view that each judge is obliged to determine a case as he or she thinks best, in accordance with the judicial oath to 'do right to all manner of people according to law'. Nevertheless, there are factors that may make it more likely that judges who agree on an outcome will deliver joint reasons, all else being equal. These include interpersonal relations between the

[122] *Monis v The Queen* (2013) 249 CLR 92, 179–80.
[123] (1947) 74 CLR 31, 101. [124] (1951) 83 CLR 1, 285.
[125] *Air Caledonie International v Commonwealth* (1988) 165 CLR 462.
[126] *Cheatle v The Queen* (1993) 177 CLR 541. [127] (1988) 165 CLR 360.
[128] *Lange v Australian Broadcasting Corporation* (1997) 189 CLR 520.

judges, the persuasiveness of the reasoning of some judges, management of workload and consideration of the intelligibility of the reasons of the court as a whole.

9 *Framing of Constitutional Issues*

At a general level, decisions of the HCA involving the Constitution are likely to fall into one of three categories: federalism, separation of powers, or constitutional rights. Cases dealing with the constitutionality of actions by an Australian State might be assigned to a fourth category, whether they engage the Commonwealth Constitution, the State Constitution or both. The boundary between these categories is often indistinct: for some time, for example, the doctrine of separation of judicial power was rationalised in part by reference to the obligations of courts in a federal system,[129] and some rights provisions in the Constitution also have a federalism rationale.[130] Within each of the three main categories of cases there are further sub-divisions. By way of example, cases dealing with separation of powers divide between the separation of judicial power and the boundaries of legislative and executive power. Sub-categories for federalism cases include questions about the federal division of legislative power and other structural federal issues, including the scope and application of intergovernmental immunities.

There have been some shifts over time in the way in which constitutional decisions are conceptualised. These are attributable partly to changes in the nature of the issues that come before the Court and partly to developments in the Court's own jurisprudence. Thus, both the range and frequency of cases dealing with aspects of the separation of powers have increased over time, and the use of separation of powers as a generic label for such cases has become more familiar. More obviously still, it is only in the last two decades[131] that the HCA has clearly accepted that rights might be implied from the institutional arrangements for which the Constitution provides, substantially increasing the number and variety of matters that can be categorised as rights cases. In yet another example, in recent decades the Court has accepted a wider range of ways in which the Commonwealth Constitution constrains State institutions, in effect creating a new category or sub-category of constitutional cases.

[129] *R v Kirby; Ex parte Boilermakers' Society of Australia* (1956) 94 CLR 254.

[130] See especially Constitution s 117, prohibiting discrimination on grounds of state residence.

[131] Dating to *Australian Capital Television v Commonwealth* (1992) 177 CLR 106.

10 Key Concepts

Turning to the key concepts of Australian constitutional law, four concepts stand out: federalism,[132] the separation of powers,[133] nation[134] and democracy.[135] That federalism would be a key concept seems obvious given that federating the Australian colonies was a key motivation for the Constitution's framers. Federalism concepts form part of the reasoning in most of the cases concerning federal legislative power.

The High Court's articulation of federal principles is complicated by the interpretive commitments adopted in the *Engineers' Case* discussed above.[136] To recall, the High Court's commitment in that case is to a literal approach to the interpretation of federal legislative power. In other words, because federal legislative power is to be given as broad a reading as its language will permit, its breadth is determined without regard to the idea of powers 'reserved' to the States.

However, federalism remains a central concept in many cases. Although the *Engineers'* approach has broadly prevailed, its precise meaning is hotly disputed and there are notable dissenting judgments in key cases that strongly argue for narrower federal powers (and correspondingly broader State powers). These arguments implicitly invoke the notion of a federal balance, which, as a result, receives corresponding attention in the majority judgments.[137] Moreover, federalism is a central concept in the reasoning in other kinds of cases: those concerning 'intergovernmental immunity', that is the (limited) immunity each level of government enjoys from the laws of the other;[138] the representation of (non-State) territories in the Commonwealth Parliament;[139] the prohibition on State-based

132 An element of the reasoning in 16 of the 40 selected cases.

133 Of the 40 selected cases, 10 concern federal judicial power, judicial review or state Supreme Courts, all of which centrally concern the separation of judicial power; in addition 4 more (*Victorian Stevedoring and General Contracting Co Pty Ltd and Meakes v Dignan* (1931) 46 CLR 73; *Victoria v Commonwealth* (1974) 134 CLR 81 (*PMA Case*); *Al-Kateb v Godwin* (2004) 219 CLR 562; and *Williams v Commonwealth* (2012) 248 CLR 156) concern the powers of Parliament and/or the federal Executive

134 An element of the reasoning in 14 of the 40 selected cases.

135 An element of the reasoning in 6 of the 40 selected cases.

136 Above n 54.

137 The two modern cases that best exemplify this debate are *Commonwealth v Tasmania* (1983) 153 CLR 1 (*Tasmanian Dams Case*) and *New South Wales v Commonwealth* (2006) 229 CLR 1 (*Work Choices Case*).

138 *Melbourne Corporation v Commonwealth* (1947) 74 CLR 31.

139 *Western Australia v Commonwealth* (1975) 134 CLR 201.

discrimination;[140] the respective powers of federal and State courts; and as well as the scope of federal executive power.[141]

Much of the High Court's attention to federalism is thus conditioned by underlying questions about interpretation and the primacy of text. No such anxiety attends its attention to questions of separation of powers, at least when it comes to the separation of judicial power. That principle requires that only courts formed under the Constitution may exercise 'the judicial power of the Commonwealth' and that those courts shall exercise only that form of power.[142] Therefore, federal courts cannot exercise either non-judicial power or the judicial power of the States.[143] The separation of powers therefore has arisen for consideration principally in those cases concerning federal judicial power and, increasingly, the judicial power of State Courts over which the High Court has extended a degree of constitutional scrutiny since 1996.

The Australian conception of the separation of powers has a distinctive cast. First, the principle is most often invoked in the context of the separation of judicial power. The relationship between legislative and executive power is governed by principles derived from British political conceptions and thus does not implement a strict separation of powers. Even more distinctive to the Australian context are the values that the separation of powers is taken to serve. Although it clearly serves some rule of law values by protecting the independence of the judiciary and ensuring compliance with fundamental norms of the judicial process, its foundation lies in federalism, which requires an independent judiciary for the 'maintenance and enforcement of the boundaries within which governmental power might be exercised'.[144]

By contrast, the rule of law is rarely invoked directly as the ground for a decision in Australian constitutional law. Of the cases where the concept features explicitly, the most significant is the opinion of Justice Dixon in *Australian Communist Party v Commonwealth*[145] in which the principle was invoked as a fundamental assumption of the Constitution. Even as an assumption, however, there is little doubt of its importance. Indeed, precisely because of the HCA's invocation of the rule of law, the *Communist Party Case* is regarded as perhaps the most important case

[140] *Street v Queensland Bar Association* (1989) 168 CLR 461.

[141] *Williams v Commonwealth* (2012) 248 CLR 156.

[142] *R v Kirby; Ex parte Boilermakers' Society of Australia* (1956) 94 CLR 254.

[143] *Re Wakim; Ex parte McNally* (1999) 198 CLR 511.

[144] *R v Kirby; Ex parte Boilermakers' Society of Australia* (1956) 94 CLR 254, 276.

[145] *Australian Communist Party v Commonwealth* (1951) 83 CLR 1.

in Australia's constitutional history.[146] The rule of law features incidentally in a range of cases, including those dealing with the jurisdiction, powers and procedures of the courts. Moreover, as discussed below, rule of law ideals are central to the Court's approach to constitutional law in general[147] and ground, in particular, the High Court's approach to constitutional interpretation.[148] This concept of the rule of law is, however, rather thin and procedural and does not include ideas like 'moral justice' or – overtly at least – 'access to justice'.[149]

Alongside these concepts, democracy and nation are also prominent. 'Nation' or 'nationhood' is in one sense a counterpart to federalism. Those judges who have defended strong Commonwealth powers have done so by reference to the idea that the Commonwealth government needs powers that allow it to function as a nation. This idea was especially acute during war[150] but has also been important in developing the Commonwealth's power over 'external affairs',[151] its power to respond to crises like the 2008 global financial crisis[152] and, recently, in protecting competition in national markets.[153] Indeed the very evolution of Australian independence, its emergence as a nation, is traceable through its case law.[154] The independence of the Australian nation explains the absence of reference to the monarchy in the Court's constitutional reasoning. Although the Constitution retains the monarchy, its role is almost entirely symbolic.

Related to the concept of 'nation' is 'democracy'. The High Court also pays attention to the democratic nature of the Australian Constitution, though it prefers the term 'representative government' to 'democracy'. This concept has been especially prominent in the last 20 years over which the High Court has developed an unwritten right of freedom of political communication as an 'implication' drawn from representative government[155] and has also enabled the High Court to protect the breadth

[146] George Winterton, 'The Significance of the *Communist Party Case*' (1992) 18.3 *Melbourne University Law Review*, 630–58.

[147] See below (nn 155–62) and accompanying text.

[148] Stone (n 92).

[149] Though the separation of powers principles requires that the courts act consistently with 'judicial process'.

[150] *South Australia v Commonwealth* (1942) 65 CLR 373 (*First Uniform Tax Case*); *Australian Communist Party v Commonwealth* (1951) 83 CLR 1.

[151] *Commonwealth v Tasmania* (1983) 153 CLR 1.

[152] *Pape v Commissioner of Taxation* (2009) 238 CLR 1.

[153] *Betfair v Western Australia* (2008) 234 CLR 418.

[154] *Sue v Hill* (1999) 199 CLR 462.

[155] *Australian Capital Television v Commonwealth* (1992) 177 CLR 106; *Lange v Australian Broadcasting Corporation* (1997) 189 CLR 520.

of the franchise for federal elections.[156] The concept is principally relevant to the federal system of government but can also protect freedom of political communication about State politics.[157] (Its application to local government is largely untested though local governments act under the auspices of State law.)[158] The Court also draws upon the concept of 'responsible government', derived from Australia's British heritage, pursuant to which the Executive is both drawn from and accountable to the legislature.[159]

Just as revealing as these key concepts are those that are not evident in Australian constitutional reasoning: the near total absence of concepts like privacy, dignity, secularism and equality reflect the absence of constitutional rights. In the main, such concepts find expression only where derived from the key concepts discussed above: thus the separation of powers gives rise to rights akin to due process rights, the concepts of representative and responsible government give rise to a limited right of freedom of political communication, and equality and non-discrimination principles arise principally[160] in the context of federal-State relations[161] and the creation of freedom of interstate trade.[162]

This last feature of Australian constitutional law has isolated it to some extent from the development of constitutional law in many other countries. So, for instance, the concept of proportionality has a distinctive place and more limited application in Australia. There has been some discomfort with the concept, especially as it might be used in determining the extent of Commonwealth legislative power, which for the most part is not regarded as purposive.[163] This reluctance to embrace proportionality is traceable to the High Court's long commitment to textualist interpretation and legalist reasoning. The proportionality inquiry – and in particular the 'balancing' element – seems to the High Court to depart from this method, raising concerns about the separation of judicial power.

[156] *Roach v Electoral Commissioner* (2007) 233 CLR 162; *Rowe v Australian Electoral Commission* (2010) 243 CLR 1.

[157] *Coleman v Power* (2004) 220 CLR 1.

[158] *Attorney-General (SA) v Corporation of the City of Adelaide* (2013) 249 CLR 1.

[159] *Australian Capital Television v Commonwealth* (1992) 177 CLR 106.

[160] Although not exclusively. In an innovative judgment in *Kartinyeri v Commonwealth* (1998) 195 CLR 337 Justice Gaudron invoked the conception of (non)discrimination in determining the limits of Commonwealth's power to make laws affecting aboriginal peoples.

[161] Constitution s 99. [162] *Cole v Whitfield* (1988) 165 CLR 360.

[163] *Leask v Commonwealth* (1996) 187 CLR 579.

However, the Court has embraced proportionality in the context of limitations on power – including freedom of political communication.[164]

For similar reasons – as well as its British rather than European heritage – the High Court has not used the concept of '*Wesensgehalt*', expressed in that way. However, the concept of the 'core' of a legislative power (or competence) is found in Australian constitutional law. It was especially prevalent during the first sixty years of the twentieth century in the context of developing the federal power over 'trade and commerce with other countries, and among the States (which was strictly understood to have a 'core' area and an 'incidental' operation).[165] Incidental power exists to give effect to expressly conferred powers.[166] The concept of the incidental power is akin to, though perhaps not equivalent to, the 'necessary and proper' clause in the US Constitution.[167] For some time the High Court drew a clear distinction between the 'core' aspect of the trade and commerce power (which allowed federal regulation of interstate trading and commerce, but which also was subject to the protection of free trade in s 92) and its 'incidental' aspect which allows federal regulation of matters like production or even intrastate trade in certain circumstances.

C Comparative Perspective

A comparative perspective on constitutional reasoning in the HCA not only reveals Australian constitutional reasoning as stubbornly idiosyncratic in some respects but also reveals notable points of commonality.

Its distinctiveness derives in part from its unusual scope. Because the Constitution does not contain comprehensive fundamental rights, the content of Australian constitutional law is distinctive. For this reason many concepts that commonly feature in other constitutional systems are not evident in Australian constitutional law – the concepts of dignity, equality and secularism among them. Thus the High Court of Australia is to some extent isolated from the transnational judicial 'conversation' about these concepts.

164 *Lange v Australian Broadcasting Corporation* (1997) 189 CLR 520; *Monis v The Queen* (2013) 249 CLR 92.

165 Constitution s 51(i).

166 Incidental power may be implied (i.e. unexpressed but derived as a matter of necessity). In addition s 51(xxxviii) of the Constitution expressly confers on the Parliament a power over 'matters incidental to the execution of any power vested by this Constitution'.

167 Constitution of the United States art I, § 8, cl 18.

The other notably distinctive aspect of the reasoning of the HCA is its devotion to 'legalism', including the emphasis on the text of the Constitution and the comparatively non-activist judicial role. In this respect, Australia provides a significant counter-example for the hypothesis that the older the Constitution is and the more difficult it is to amend it, the more likely the judges are to use purposive arguments instead of literal arguments. (The Australian Constitution, at over 100 years old, is – in world terms – very old and is relatively difficult to amend.) The dominance of literalist arguments is doubtless partly due to the status of the Australian Constitution as a statute of the British Parliament (albeit a statute of a special kind).[168] Though the significance of this feature has since been challenged,[169] it has meant that traditional methods of statutory interpretation – including an emphasis on the plain meaning of the text – have great influence. In addition, and paradoxically, the literalist tradition is traceable in part to the Constitution's age: its interpretive culture was formed during the early part of the twentieth century before the rise of intellectual movements like legal realism, which might have challenged 'legalism', including its reliance on text.

Despite these distinctive features, the HCA shares much with other courts in this comparative study. Although somewhat isolated from transnational judicial conversation about rights, reference to foreign law is common and has always been part of HCA practice. The practice can be explained in a variety of ways: the historical connections of Australia with the United Kingdom and other former Dominions of the British Empire, which also refer freely to other common law jurisdictions, and to the influence of the Constitution of the United States on the Australian Constitution and in particular on the key concepts of federalism and separation of powers. These connections have mitigated any isolation of Australian constitutional reasoning from transnational judicial practice. More recently, notably, 'proportionality' has made its way into Australian constitutional law, though the concept is often deployed interchangeably with a related and older conception of a 'reasonably appropriate and adapted' law that is distinctive to Australia.[170]

The Australian High Court also shares much in common with other courts in the common law world in its style of reasoning. In particular, the long, detailed reasons and frequent use of concurrences is typical of

[168] See above (n 3) and accompanying text.

[169] By judges who locate the authority of the Constitution in popular sovereignty.

[170] See above (nn 163 and 164) and accompanying text.

the common law tradition. Indeed in this respect the HCA is a somewhat extreme example, giving longer judgments and more frequent use of concurrences than other common law jurisdictions. The length and detail of HCA opinions is likely attributable to a strong commitment to the giving of reasons and provides a counter-example to the hypothesis that long, detailed reasons correlate with the presence of academics on a court.

In conclusion, constitutional reasoning in the HCA has at least four key defining features: its focus on structure (federalism, separation of powers, nationhood and democracy) as opposed to rights, reflecting the distinctive place of rights in the Australian constitutional order; legalism in constitutional interpretation, which has its origins in early twentieth-century theories of statutory interpretation but is now reinforced by the Australian conception of the separation of judicial power; the weight placed on the rule of law, which, though unexpressed, undergirds much of the HCA's approach to the Constitution; and the significance of Australia's common law heritage, which informs the meaning of the Constitution and shapes the Court's style of analysis and method of reasoning.

D Evaluation, Pathology and Criticism

Constitutional reasoning in the HCA is susceptible to two main lines of criticism. The first is directed at Australian legalism.[171]

Within the rubric of legalism, however, there is room for considerable variation of style and approach. At one end of the spectrum is a tendency towards formalism, placing emphasis on text, modified to a greater or lesser degree by considerations of context, which may be broadly understood. At the other, legalism is said to accommodate 'fundamental . . . settled legal principles' including, for example, common law rights and interpretive approaches developed by the judges themselves. In this mode, at least, legalism lends itself to the development of the law within boundaries that may be relatively generous, although typically without the acknowledgement of choices that are consciously or unconsciously made. Legalism does not preclude the explicit overturning of precedent, although this is relatively rare and it accommodates the avoidance of unwelcome precedent through familiar common law techniques of

[171] On 'legalism' and its critics, see Michael Coper, 'Concern about Judicial Method' (2006) 30.2 Melbourne University Law Review 554–575.

reasoning. Nor does Australian legalism preclude reference to foreign law, although the HCA does not draw directly on international law.[172]

Nonetheless, the challenges to Australian legalism include the following. First, it is not clear precisely what practices it encompasses. Thus, the Court's repeated insistence that the nature of the Constitution as an 'instrument of government meant to endure'[173] must be taken into account in the interpretive process and might be understood either as drawing on context or as endorsement of the idea of a living constitution.

Secondly, and relatedly, critics have observed that in the constitutional context some of the touchstones used by the court in judicial reasoning cannot be justified solely by reference to constitutional text and structure and are inevitably extrinsic in that sense.[174] Examples include the conceptions of federalism, representative government or democracy and separation of powers, all of which play major roles in the reasoning of the court. At one point in its history the HCA seemed somewhat more prepared to acknowledge the relevance of extrinsic considerations in its reasoning, to the point where some described its approach as a brand of judicial realism.[175] While the reasoning of the Court was somewhat more transparent over this period, however, the development should not be overstated. Even at this point the reasoning was cast largely in terms of existing legal sources. And the phase did not last long. The methodology of the current HCA is typified by a focus on text, structure and context in both constitutional and statutory interpretation. The HCA's insistence on a largely legalistic method in the face of the inevitability of value judgment means that legalism often serves to conceal judicial choices that in fact are made. Therefore, value judgments that are in fact contestable and contingent are presented as politically neutral and inevitable.

Finally, the absence of a constitutional bill of rights, coupled with the limitations of Australian judicial method, constrain the capacity of courts to overcome problems purely by reference to justice. Nevertheless, it is possible to identify decisions of the HCA in which constitutional authority arguably has been stretched to deal with injustice, unfairness or a threat to underlying constitutional principles. Typically, these are rationalised by reference to existing law and ultimately accepted on that basis. One

[172] See Stephen Gageler, 'Legalism' in Blackshield et al. (n 13), 429–30.

[173] *Australian National Airways Pty Ltd v Commonwealth* (1945) 71 CLR 29, 81.

[174] Stone (n 92); Aroney (n 90).

[175] Haigh Patapan, *Judging Democracy: The New Politics of the High Court of Australia* (Cambridge University Press 2000).

example is the *Communist Party Case*, in which the HCA invalidated a law outlawing membership of the Communist Party of Australia on federalism grounds, in the absence of a right to freedom of association. Equally, however, there are cases where manifest injustice is not resolved by the court, which explicitly identifies the Parliament as the only source of redress. *Al-Kateb v Godwin*, in which a majority of the HCA upheld the validity of legislation precluding the release from detention of a stateless but unsuccessful asylum seeker, is an example of this kind.

Appendix: 40 Leading Cases

1. *R v Barger* (1908) 6 CLR 41
2. *Amalgamated Society of Engineers v Adelaide Steamship Company* (1920) 28 CLR 129 (*Engineer's Case*)
3. *Re Judiciary & Navigation Acts* (1921) 29 CLR 257
4. *Ex Parte McLean* (1930) 43 CLR 472
5. *Victorian Stevedoring and General Contracting Co Pty Ltd and Meakes v Dignan* (1931) 6 CLR 73
6. *South Australia v The Commonwealth* (1942) 65 CLR 373 (*First Uniform Tax Case*)
7. *Melbourne Corporation v the Commonwealth* (1947) 74 CLR 31
8. *Australian Communist Party v The Commonwealth* (1951) 83 CLR 1
9. *R v Kirby and Others; Ex parte Boilermakers' Society of Australia* (1956) 94 CLR 254 (*Boilermakers Case*)
10. *Victoria v The Commonwealth* (1957) 99 CLR 575 (*Second Uniform Tax Case*)
11. *Victoria v The Commonwealth* (1975) 134 CLR 81 (*PMA Case*)
12. *Western Australia v the Commonwealth* (1975) 134 CLR 201 *(First Territory Senators' Case)* (1975) 134 CLR 201
13. *New South Wales v Commonwealth of Australia* (1975) 135 CLR 337 (*Seas and Submerged Lands Case*)
14. *Murphyores Inc Pty Ltd v Commonwealth* (1976) 136 CLR 1
15. *Attorney-General (WA); Ex rel Ansett Transport Industries (Operations) Pty Ltd v Australian National Airlines Commission* (1976) 138 CLR 492
16. *Attorney-General (Vic); Ex Rel Black v Commonwealth* (1981) 146 CLR 559 (*DOGS Case*)
17. *Commonwealth v Tasmania* (1983) 158 CLR 1 (*Tasmanian Dams Case*)
18. *Cole v Whitfield* (1988) 165 CLR 360
19. *Air Caledonie v Commonwealth* (1988) 165 CLR 462

20. *Davis v The Commonwealth* (1988) 166 CLR 79
21. *Street v Queensland Bar Association* (1989) 168 CLR 461
22. *New South Wales v The Commonwealth* (1990) 169 CLR 482 (*Incorporation Case*)
23. *Chu Kheng Lim v Minister for Immigration Local Government & Ethnic Affairs* (1992) 176 CLR 1
24. *Australian Tape Manufacturers Association Ltd v Commonwealth* (1993) 176 CLR 480
25. *Australian Capital Television v Commonwealth* (1992) 177 CLR 106
26. *Cheatle v The Queen* (1993) 177 CLR 541
27. *Brandy v Human Rights & Equal Opportunity Commission* (1995) 183 CLR 245 (*Brandy's Case*)
28. *Kable v Director of Public Prosecutions for NSW* (1996) 189 CLR 51
29. *Ha v New South Wales* (1997) 189 CLR 465
30. *Lange v Australian Broadcasting Corporation* (1997) 189 CLR 520
31. *Residential Tenancies Tribunal of NSW v Henderson; Ex parte Defence Housing Authority* (1997) 190 CLR 410
32. *Kartinyeri v The Commonwealth* (1998) 195 CLR 337
33. *Re Wakim; Ex parte McNally* (1999) 198 CLR 511
34. *Sue v Hill* (1999) 199 CLR 462
35. *Plaintiff S157 /2002 v The Commonwealth* (2003) 211 CLR 476
36. *Al-Kateb v Godwin* (2004) 219 CLR 562
37. *New South Wales v The Commonwealth* (2006) 229 CLR 1 (*Work Choices Case*)
38. *Roach v Electoral Commissioner* (2007) 233 CLR 162
39. *Kirk v Industrial Court of New South Wales* (2010) 239 CLR 531
40. *Williams v The Commonwealth* (2012) 248 CLR 156

2

The Austrian Constitutional Court

KONRAD LACHMAYER

> The case law of the Austrian Constitutional Court is nowadays characterized by an apparent unsystematic coexistence of different methods of legal interpretation[1]

A Legal, Political, Institutional and Academic Context

1 *Legal and Political Culture as Context for Constitutional Reasoning*

The Historical Context

The Austrian Constitution dates back to the year 1920 in the aftermath of the World War I.[2] The Austrian Constitution of 1920 reflects the process of constitutionalisation and democratisation since 1848, the end of the Austro-Hungarian monarchy and the political struggle of the conservative and socialist parties in this new republic. Moreover, the Constitution of 1920 is deeply related with the person of Hans Kelsen not only as a world-famous scholar of jurisprudence[3] but also as founding father of the Austrian Constitution.[4] His masterpiece in drafting the Austrian Constitution was the concept of the Austrian Constitutional Court as a centralized court exclusively dealing with constitutional matters. Kelsen's legacy is still part of the Austrian constitutional narrative.[5]

[1] Excerpt from one of the most important Austrian constitutional law textbooks, Theo Öhlinger and Harald Eberhard, *Verfassungsrecht* (10th edn facultas Verlag 2014) 38: "Die Entscheidungspraxis des VfGH ist heute gekennzeichnet durch ein anscheinend systemloses Nebeneinander unterschiedlichster Auslegungsmethoden . . . ".

[2] See in general on the Austrian Constitution Manfred Stelzer, *The Constitution of the Republic of Austria. A Contextual Analysis* (Hart 2011).

[3] See Hans Kelsen, *Pure Theory of Law* (Max Knight tr, U of California P 1967).

[4] See Felix Ermacora, *Die Entstehung der Bundesverfassung 1920: Die Sammlung der Entwürfe zur Staats- und Bundesverfassung* (Braumüller 1990) 62.

[5] See the analysis of Andras Jakab, 'Two Opposing Paradigms of Continental European Constitutional Thinking: Austria and Germany' (2009) 58 *International and Comparative*

In the nearly 100 years since 1920, many developments have had an impact on the Austrian Constitution and the culture of constitutional thinking. The Constitution of 1920 did not include a catalogue of the allocation of powers between the Federation and the States, which changed with a constitutional amendment in 1925 as a result of international pressure to make the Austrian state organisation more efficient.[6] It remained an unsatisfying compromise, which was not resolved.[7] The second amendment in the First Republic (1929) has to be seen as the forerunner of an authoritarian shift, which introduced a strong presidential system in the Austrian Constitution but was never realized politically. The time of Austro-fascism from 1933 to 1938 not only invalidated the Austrian Constitution but also destroyed democracy and rule of law in Austria. These developments resulted in Austria becoming part of the Nazi regime and World War II.[8]

In the year 1945 the (old) Constitution of 1920 (as amended in 1925 and 1929) was once again in force. The prohibition of national-socialist activities became part of Austrian constitutional law. The change of political culture, however, to deal with the Austrian Nazi past took more than 40 years.[9] In the Second Republic the Austrian constitution was amended nearly 100 times adapting to political and international developments. Most prominently, it must be mentioned that Austria acceded to the European Convention on Human Rights (ECHR) in 1958 and, in 1964,

Law Quarterly 933 and 58 *Comparative Law Quarterly* 933 and see the leading scholar of the contemporary Austrian narrative on Kelsen Ewald Wiederin, 'Denken vom Recht her. Über den modus austriacus in der Staatsrechtslehre' in Helmuth Schulze-Fielitz, *Staatsrechtslehre als Wissenschaft. Die Verwaltung Beiheft 7* (Duncker&Humblot 2007) 293–317.

6 An economic crisis at the beginning of the 1920s created huge economic pressure on the country, which could only be overcome by international money provided by the League of Nations (Geneva Protocols) and structural reform of the administration; see Klaus Berchtold, *Verfassungsgeschichte der Republic Österreich I: 1918–1933* (Springer 1998) 289–368.

7 The allocation of powers is strictly separated between the Federation and the States. There are no shared powers. Thus, it is necessary to qualify if a certain competence shall be addressed by the Federation or the States. Over the last 90 years the catalogue of powers of the Federation became more and more detailed and casuistic. See Stelzer (n 2) 153–64.

8 See Stelzer (n 2) 10–12.

9 After the Waldheim scandal and the rise of Jörg Haider and the Freedom Party in the 1980s, awareness with regard to the Austrian Nazi past increased and led to certain measures by the state (including the establishment of a "historian committee" and certain in rem restitutions). See Josef Aicher, Erich Kussbach and August Reinisch (eds.), *Decisions of the Arbitration Panel for In Rem Restitution Vol. I–5* (facultas 2008–12).

declared it as a formal part of the Austrian Constitution (retroactively to 1958). Moreover, Austria's accession to the European Union in 1995 was considered a total revision of the Austrian Constitution.[10] In accordance with the formal proceedings in Art. 44 para. 3 of the Austrian Constitution a referendum was held, in which 66 per cent of the (voting) Austrians agreed to revise the Austrian Constitution in its basic principles and to accede to the EU. Finally, the attempts to rewrite the Austrian Constitution in a constitution-making process by the establishment of a so-called "Austrian Convention" (2003–2005)[11] failed.[12] The attempts to reform Austrian Constitution, however, resulted in significant amendments in 2008[13] as well as in 2012.[14]

The Constitutional Context

From a formal perspective the Austrian Constitution can be understood as fragmented and multi-layered.[15] Both elements are quite particular and important for understanding Austrian constitutional thinking. The Austrian Constitution is fragmented as there exist – besides the core document of the Austrian Constitution (Federal Constitutional Act 1920) – several other constitutional acts as well as so-called constitutional provisions, which are singular provisions in ordinary statutes but with constitutional rank. Thus, Austrian constitutional law can be found in many different forms. Moreover, the Austrian Constitution is multi-layered. With regard

[10] Stelzer (n 2) 33.

[11] All materials are available (in German): www.konvent.gv.at.

[12] The intention of the Austrian Convention was (inspired by the European Convention to establish a European Constitutional Treaty) to revise the Austrian Constitution formally and substantially. The basic structural and substantial problems would be resolved to create a modern constitution, which could serve as foundation for a professional and efficient administration. However, the initiative for a new constitution did not reflect any political constitutional "momentum" in Austria. Finally, after two years of intense discussions and substantially valuable work, politicians of the two major parties (conservative, social democrats) on the one hand and the politicians of the *Bund* and the *Länder* on the other hand were not able to agree on a new constitution.

[13] See Harald Eberhard and Konrad Lachmayer, 'Constitutional Reform 2008 in Austria' (2008) 2 *ICL-Journal* 112. The amendment was primarily concerned with the formal situation of the Austrian Constitution. Around 1.000 constitutional provisions were abolished. However, the Austrian Constitution remained complex with various constitutional acts and provisions (in ordinary statutes).

[14] The major amendment of 2012 introduced administrative courts of first instance to the Austrian Constitution, which had not existed earlier.

[15] See Jakab (n 5).

to the concept of hierarchical structure of law (*Stufenbau*), Austrian constitution law distinguishes between two different levels of constitutional law: ordinary constitutional law and the basic principles of constitutional law.

The distinction relates to the formal procedure for constitutional amendment. Amendment of the Austrian Constitution always requires a two-thirds majority in both houses of the parliament and in certain (very limited) cases approval of a majority of the States.[16] With regard to the total revision of the Constitution, a popular referendum is also needed.[17] A total revision of the Austrian Constitution exists, when the basic principles of Austrian constitutional law (including democracy, federalism, rule of law and human rights) are affected significantly. These basic principles are understood as higher ranked constitutional law and distinguished from ordinary constitutional law.[18] This hierarchy of constitutional law gives the Constitutional Court the possibility to review constitutional law on the basis of the basic principles of the Constitution.

The Austrian Constitution is known to be easily amendable. This, however, does not refer to the legal requirements but rather to the political will to amend the constitution, especially to create exceptions from certain constitutional rules. For a long period of time the government (a grand coalition government of the two grand parties) had a two-thirds majority. The legislator was very generous about amending constitutional law. The fragmented structure of the Constitution was promoted by this development. The Constitutional Court took notice of the development when the constitutional legislator started to overrule judgments of the Constitutional Court, in which the court declared a certain statutory provision as violating human rights, by enacting the same provision as (ordinary) constitutional law. The Constitutional Court developed the doctrine of a "creeping total revision" of the Austrian Constitution (*Schleichende Gesamtänderung der Bundesverfassung*). This case law finally led to a decision in 2001, when the Constitutional Court declared – for the first and so far only time – a constitutional provision to be unconstitutional.[19]

[16] See Manfred Stelzer, 'Constitutional change in Austria' in Xenophon Contiades (ed.), *Engineering Constitutional Change. A Comparative Perspective on Europe, Canada and the USA* (Routledge 2013) 7–34 (15–6).

[17] Stelzer (n 2) 32–7.

[18] The basic principles are, however, not explicitly mentioned in the Austrian Constitution, but the result of interpretation of the Austrian Constitutional Court.

[19] Official Collection of the Judgments of the Austrian Constitutional Court (VfSlg) 16.327/2001. See Eberhard and Lachmayer (n 13) 117: 'According to the Court, a constitutional provision in the Federal Public Procurement Act was in contradiction to the basic constitutional principle of democracy as well as of that of the Rechtsstaat (rule of law).'

From a substantive perspective on Austrian constitutional law, it is worth mentioning that Austria is a federal state with nine States (*Bundesländer*). The constitutional concept provides a strong Federation, whereas the political culture supports strong State governors. The Austrian human-rights situation is – like the Constitution in general – also fragmented. The various catalogues of rights in the Austrian Constitution focus on liberal rights. Moreover, the principle of equality plays a crucial part in the case law of the Constitutional Court.[20] A social state principle (like that in Germany) is missing as well as a catalogue on social rights.[21] Certain rights of children were introduced to the Austrian Constitution in 2011.[22] Austria is a parliamentary republic with a directly elected Federal President, who in the political realm has mainly representative functions.[23] A strict understanding of the principle of legality is supplemented by a not fully comprehensive legal protection.

The existing challenges to the Austrian constitutional system refer to the missing coherent domestic concept of human rights, to the complicated and out-dated allocation of powers between the Federation and the States and to certain deficits of legal protection with regard to a formalistic approach to the rule of law and access to the courts. The political debate does not primarily concern these deficits of constitutionalism in Austria. The strengthening of elements of direct democracy and the emerging of a broader spectrum of political parties are more dominant in public debates.[24] In recent years, the re-occurring grand coalition has no longer had a constitutional majority. This new situation gave opposition parties a stronger position in negotiating with the government, as the government often needs to change constitutional provisions.[25] These

[20] See below.

[21] Although Austria has a very comprehensive system of social welfare, it was not possible (for ideological reasons) to integrate social rights into the Austrian Constitution. The conservative People´s Party prohibited in the Austrian Convention 2003–2005 that social rights (as a socialist concept) should be included in the Constitution. Stelzer (n 2) 215.

[22] Official Federal Gazette I 2011/4; see also Claudia Fuchs, 'Kinderrechte in der Verfassung: Das BVG über die Rechte von Kindern' in Georg Lienbacher and Gerhart Wielinger (eds.), *Jahrbuch Öffentliches Recht 2011* (Neuer wissenschaftlicher Verlag 2011) 91–110.

[23] Stelzer (n 2) 111–120.

[24] See e.g. Theo Öhlinger and Klaus Poier (eds.), *Direkte Demokratie und Parlamentarismus: Wie kommen wir zu den besten Entscheidungen?* (Böhlau 2015).

[25] As the government changed the constitutional provisions so many times in recent decades, there are many constitutional provisions that limiting the legislator to regulating certain subject matter. The government needs in many cases to amend the Constitution when changing ordinary statutes. Without a Constitution-changing majority, the government becomes more dependent on the opposition parties.

developments also foster the political importance of the Constitutional Court.[26]

The function of the Austrian Constitutional Court is, however, changing within the EU's network of constitutional law and the European system of human rights protection. The Austrian Constitution can be considered as an open constitution with regard to European developments. The ECHR has been a part of Austrian constitutional law since 1964, the Austrian Constitution was totally revised within the accession procedure to the European Union in 1995, and in 2012, the Constitutional Court declared the EU Charter of Fundamental Rights (EUCFR) as the basis of the court's review on human rights with regard to Austrian administrative decisions.[27]

The Court System

The Austrian court system distinguishes between ordinary courts and administrative courts. While ordinary courts deal with civil and criminal matters, the administrative courts deal with administrative matters including penal administrative law. These administrative courts of first instance were only established in the year 2014. They replace independent administrative tribunals, which fulfilled the criteria of a court according to Art. 6 ECHR and Art. 267 TFEU, but could not be considered as fully fledged courts in the Austrian constitutional concept. The constitutional amendment of 2012 introduced this major reform of Austrian state organization mainly based on the accession to the European Union and the case law of the European Court of Human Rights (ECtHR) as well as for efficiency reasons.[28]

The Austrian Constitution provides three supreme courts which in theory are equal, but functionally distinguishable from each other: the Constitutional Court, the Administrative Court and the Supreme Court.[29] The Constitutional Court deals with abstract and concrete judicial review of statutes and all other kinds of constitutional question. The

[26] As the constitution cannot be changed that easily, the Constitutional Court becomes more important to review the constitutionality of statutes. Since 2015, the Constitutional Court by constitutional amendment (Federal Law Gazette I 2014/101) has had the power to decide procedural conflicts between political parties in parliamentary committees of inquiry (see Art. 138b Austrian Constitution).

[27] VfSlg 19.632/2012.

[28] More than 120 independent tribunals were dissolved and substituted by these administrative courts.

[29] Stelzer (n 2) 190–205.

Administrative Court considers the conformity of administrative acts with regard to the statutory provisions[30] and the Supreme Court is the highest court of appeal within the system of ordinary courts. The equality among the courts is expressed by the lack of an individual constitution complaint (*Verfassungsbeschwerde*).[31] An individual cannot file a complaint against the decisions of the Administrative Court or the Supreme Court at the Constitutional Court.[32]

The Constitutional Court is of particular importance. First, the Constitutional Court has to decide with regard to the conflict of competences between the different courts. Second, the court is the only court to review statutes with regard to their constitutionality; thus, the other courts have to file a complaint at the constitutional court, if they want a statute to be reviewed. However, all supreme courts have the possibility to interpret the constitution and other of legal acts in the light of the constitution (*verfassungskonforme Interpretation*). This can even lead to different results in constitutional interpretation.

The Austrian Court system has to be seen in the light of the Court of Justice of the European Union (CJEU) and the European Court of Human Rights. The Austrian Constitutional Court engaged in EU law from the very beginning of the Austrian EU membership in 1995, and it has had very open attitude towards EU law.[33] This includes the willingness to refer questions to the CJEU for a preliminary ruling[34] and the above-mentioned case of the Constitutional Court to include EUCFR into the human rights review procedure.

30 See Stelzer (n 2) 192–7.

31 A 2015 constitutional amendment introduced ithe possibility of individuals filing a constitutional complaint against the judgment of ordinary courts of first instance. The individuals, however, can only complain that the statute, which builds the foundation of the judgment, is unconstitutional; the Constitutional Court cannot review the judgment itself.

32 The detailed interrelation between the different supreme courts is very complex: The Administrative Court and the Supreme Court can start a "preliminary procedure" at the Constitutional Court to review the constitutionality of a statute. If an individual files a complaint at the Constitutional Court, the Court can state that there are no relevant constitutional questions and can pass the case on to the Administrative Court to check the legality of the administrative questions. See Stelzer (n 2) 177.

33 VfSlg 14.390/1995; VfSlg 14.863/1997; VfSlg 14.886/1997; VfSlg 15.427/2000; VfSlg 17.967/2006; VfSlg 19.499/2011; VfSlg 19.632/2012.

34 See the recent decision taken by the Constitutional Court on 28 November 2012, G-47/12 et al. (questions for a preliminary ruling with regard to the data retention directive) – see in English: http://www.vfgh.gv.at/cms/vfgh-site/attachments/1/4/5/CH0007/CMS1363699922389/vorlage_vorratsdatenspeicherung_english.pdf.

2 *The Court and Constitutional Litigation*

Competences

The Austrian Constitutional Court has a broad variety of competences, which have increased over the decades.[35] The most important competences are the review of acts of parliament (Art. 140 Austrian Constitution) and the review of judgments of the administrative courts of first instance with regard to human rights violations (Art. 144 Austrian Constitution). Further competences include deciding power in competence conflicts (Art. 138 Austrian Constitution), rulings in financial conflicts with the Federation or State entities, review of legality of administrative ordinances, review of elections, deciding the constitutional responsibility of highest authorities of the state and judgments regarding international treaties.

The main idea at the beginning, more than 90 years ago, was that the Constitutional Court reviews statutes regarding their constitutionality on the one hand and administrative action with regard to the principle of legality on the other hand.[36] Another function from the very beginning was conflict resolution between the Federation and the States. Although the Court has made important judgments with regard to federalism in Austria and especially developed a particular constitutional reasoning in the field of federalism, it has developed more and more towards a human rights court in recent decades. The competence to review fundamental rights violations at the beginning and human rights violations after the accession to the ECHR with regard to administrative decisions became the most relevant competence of the court. In the 1980s the effects of its human rights function finally changed the approach to constitutional reasoning.[37]

The core function of the Constitutional Court is the review of statutes (*Normenkontrolle*). The abstract judicial review is made possible by a complaint of e.g. one-third of members of a parliamentary chamber or as a direct complaint from an individual (if certain restrictive requirements

[35] See Ronald Faber, 'The Austrian Constitutional Court – An Overview' (2008) 2 *ICL-Journal* 49; Christoph Bezemek, 'A Kelsenian Model of Constitutional Adjudication. The Austrian Constitutional Court' (2012) 67 *Zeitschrift für Öffentliches Recht* 115; Stelzer (n 2) 197.

[36] Ewald Wiederin, 'Grundlagen und Grundzüge staatlichen Verfassungsrechts: Österreich' in Armin von Bogdandy, Pedro Cruz Villalón and Peter M Huber (eds.), *Handbuch Ius Publicum Europaeum Vol. I* (C.F. Müller 2007) 389, 400.

[37] See below.

are fulfilled). The concrete judicial review can be based on concerns of the Constitutional Court itself, the administrative courts (including the Administrative Court) and ordinary courts (including the Supreme Court).[38] The Constitutional Court can declare a statute as unconstitutional and void. The effect of the Constitutional Court judgment is usually *ex nunc*, but the court has the discretion to annul the provision *ex tunc* or prolong the validity of the relevant provision for a certain time period (up to 18 months).[39]

The workload of the court increased steadily. The annual report of the Constitutional Court also includes the number of court decisions (including formal decisions of the Court). Whereas in 1981 the Constitutional Court decided in 694 cases, in 2012 it decided in 4574 cases.[40] In recent years the Constitutional Court has had to deal with especially many asylum cases with regard to a constitutional amendment in the year 2008, which restricted the access of asylum seekers to the Administrative Court. With the establishment of the administrative court of first instance in 2014, the extraordinary high workload should be reduced – at least to a certain extent. The 4574 decisions of the year 2012 include 201 positive judgments, 117 rejecting judgments, 203 refusals on formal grounds, 1531 dismissals (because no constitutional question was concerned), and 2522 further decisions (regarding legal aid, further dismissals, etc.).[41] With regard to the different competences of the Constitutional Court, the review of human rights violations concerned 4304 cases, and the judicial review of statutes referred to 126 (including administrative ordinances, 216) cases. The number of conflict of competence cases was very small (11 cases).[42]

The Procedure

The procedure of the Constitutional Court is laid down in the Constitutional Court Act (*Verfassungsgerichtshofsgesetz*). It is remarkable that the Civil Procedural Code is applied subsidiary, if the Constitutional Court

[38] Further possibilities will be introduced in form of a constitutional complaint against ordinary court "rulings" (excluding the Supreme Court).

[39] See Konrad Lachmayer, 'Austria. Constitutional Court as Positive Legislators' in Allan R. Brewer-Carias (ed.), *Constitutional Courts as Positive Legislators. A Comparative Law Study* (Cambridge University Press 2011) 251, 257.

[40] See 'Bericht des Verfassungsgerichtshofs über seine Tätigkeit im Jahr 2012', 43–4 – available at www.vfgh.gv.at.

[41] Ibid, 17. [42] Ibid 58.

Act does not provide any provision.[43] Parties must be represented by a lawyer, but can apply for legal aid if they can prove that they cannot afford the procedure. The State is represented by public officers of the ministries or the state authorities. The Federation is usually represented by public officers of the Constitutional Service (*Verfassungsdienst*) of the Federal Chancellery.[44] One judge is appointed as reporter of the case. Although public hearings should legally be the rule, the exemptions are formulated broadly, and in fact a public hearing very seldom takes place.[45] The deliberations of the Court are not public.[46] The Court decides with a definite majority. At least a chairman (usually the President) and eight further judges must participate in the voting. In many minor cases only the presence of the chairman and four further judges is required.[47] Interestingly enough, the President as chairman of the deliberations is not allowed to vote. Only if an opinion is shared by half of the members can the chairman elevate the opinion to a decision by majority. If there is no majority voting, the deliberations must be continued.[48]

The Constitutional Court still holds its sessions only four times a year for three weeks. In this session, the Court decides on the cases. The rest of the year is used for preparing the cases and issuing the judgments. The Court can hold short in-between sessions, which actually only happened some years ago when the caseload was very high with regard to asylum cases.

Finally, the judgments typically have the following structure: headnote, dictum and reasoning. The reasoning first introduces the facts of the case, including the previous (usually administrative) procedures. After the facts, the relevant statutory provisions are mentioned. In a next step, the Court summarizes the arguments of the complaint and the counter-arguments, which are usually presented by the government (represented by the Constitutional Service of the Federal Chancellery). In a final step, the Constitutional Court takes its own position considering the formal admissibility first and then analysing the substance of the case, which is

[43] See Art. 35 para. 1 Constitutional Court Act.

[44] Ewald Wiederin, 'Verfassungsinterpretation in Österreich' in Georg Lienbacher (ed.), *Verfassungsinterpretation in Europa* (Jan Sramek 2011) 81, 97.

[45] The annual report of the Constitutional Court does not provide any statistics to public hearings. However, it is possible to calculate the number with regard to the press releases of the Court, which announce the public hearings of each session. In 2014 there had been only seven public hearings; in 2013 there had been nine hearings.

[46] See Art. 30 Constitutional Court Act.

[47] See Art. 7 Constitutional Court Act.

[48] See Art. 31 Constitutional Court Act.

concluded by a final statement regarding the constitutionality/legality of the statutory/administrative/judicial act concerned.

The Constitutional Court and the Media

In the last 10 years the Constitutional Court developed its own media strategy. The Court provides its own website (www.vfgh.gv.at). On the website, the Court not only introduces its members, it publishes upcoming oral hearings, upcoming topical cases, summaries of recent judgments and an annual report of the Court. It provides legal texts, gives information on the procedure of court and answers frequently asked questions, including legal aid. The Court started its own blog in 2009;[49] in 2014 the press spokesman of the Court officially joined Twitter.[50] Moreover, all judgments of the Constitutional Court are available in German on the website of the Austrian Legal Informatics System (*Rechtsinformationssystem*).[51] Interestingly, the Court does not broadly provide English translation. Only in two cases with significant European relevance has the Court translated the judgment into English.

The Court has its own media representative. After important judgments the President of the Constitutional Court presents the case and the result to the media. As mentioned, media summaries of important judgments are provided on the website. Finally, the President gives interviews to the media on a regular basis and takes certain points of view with regard to constitutional developments in the country.[52]

3 *The Judges*

The Austrian Constitutional Court consists of a president, a vice-president and a further 12 judges.[53] Moreover, six substitute members are appointed.[54] All judges are appointed by the Federal President of Austria. In making his appointment,[55] he is bound by the proposals of different actors. The president, the vice-president and six members of the Court are proposed by the federal government. The appointment of the

[49] https://www.vfgh.gv.at/cms/vfgh-site/blog/index.html.

[50] https://twitter.com/VfGHSprecher.

[51] See www.ris.bka.gv.at/vfgh.

[52] See in 2014 regarding the NSA revelations http://derstandard.at/1389860549764/NSA-Affaere–VfGH-Praesident-fand-harte-Worte-fuer-USA.

[53] Art. 147 para. 1 Austrian Constitution.

[54] See the biographies of all judges since 1945 in Kurt Heller, *Der Verfassungsgerichtshof* (Verlag Österreich 2010) 623–56.

[55] So far, a woman has never served as Federal President of the Republic of Austria.

other six members is based on proposal of the parliament (three of each chamber).[56]

The members of the Constitutional Court must have "completed their legal studies or studies in law and political science and for at least ten years have held a professional appointment which prescribes the completion of these studies."[57] The members proposed by the Federal Government must be judges, administrative officials or lawyers. Moreover, three members must have their center of living outside Vienna. This constitutional provision guarantees the federal structure of the court. The judges are appointed for a flexible period of time until they reach the age of 70.[58]

The current 12 members represent the administration (4), the courts (1), the universities (4) and the solicitors (3). Moreover, one member has worked in rather political positions. There is incompatibility between the function of a judge at the Constitutional Court and the membership in parliament and any other elected general representative body as well as membership in the government. Persons who are employed by political parties cannot be members of the Constitutional Court.[59] This, however, does not mean that a judge at the Constitutional Court cannot be a member of a political party.

Regarding diversity, the Austrian Constitutional Court is still male dominated. Since the year 2003, the Constitutional Court has had its first female Vice President.[60] At the moment, four (of 12) judges at the Court are female. The first female judge was appointed in 1994. There has never been a female President of the Court; however, the current Vice-President is female (appointed in 2003). Although the judges represent different political philosophies, they do not represent any minorities or other specific groups of Austrian society.

It is important to know that – besides the position of the President and the Vice-President – membership at the Constitutional Court is primarily understood as an additional occupation. Thus, the primary employment can still be exercised. This concept dates back to the times when the Constitutional Court did not have a heavy work load. Nowadays, most of the judges have the position of a permanent referent, which means that they

[56] The first chamber is the National Council (*Nationalrat*), the second (federal) chamber is the Federal Council (*Bundesrat*). The political importance of the second chamber is very low in Austria.

[57] Art. 147 para. 3 Austrian Constitution.

[58] Art. 147 para. 6 Austrian Constitution.

[59] Art. 147 para. 4 Austrian Constitution.

[60] http://www.vfgh.gv.at/cms/vfgh-site/richter/bierlein.html.

hold a full-time position at the Court. This does not mean that they are obliged to terminate other employments. Only those appointed members who have been administrative officials are exempted from all their activities. The lawyers usually continue – at least to a certain extent – with legal representation. The university professors also keep their positions at universities. Although judges must declare themselves partial if they are involved in certain cases, this concept still creates inappropriate situations before the court and certainly reduces its independence and impartiality. In 2013, there was public discussion about the several side jobs of the Constitutional Court judges, including the situation that law professors, who are judges at the Constitutional Court, provide (paid) legal opinions.[61] Since 2015, the judges have to make public other occupations and positions on boards of directors or similar management positions. There are still no rules of incompatibility regarding positions in economy or transparency with regard to legal advice given to private companies by the judges of the Constitutional Court.

4 *Legal Scholarship and Constitutional Reasoning*

Legal scholarship and the Constitutional Court are closely related to each other.[62] One third of the present judges come from academia. This situation has not changed over recent decades. At one point, the President of the Court was also a university professor before his appointment. As mentioned previously, it is possible for a judge at the Constitutional Court to hold a position at a university; even the Constitution refers to law professors as potential members of the Court. The Court and the university have been interrelated from the very beginning. Hans Kelsen was not only a member of the Constitutional Court but also professor of law at the University of Vienna.

In Austria, only five law faculties exist, and there are about 40 law professors in constitutional law. The whole constitutional law community is very small and includes about 150 persons. The interaction between the court and legal scholarship is an important part of the development of Austrian constitutional law. Thus, the impact of legal scholarship on

61 http://derstandard.at/1358304938734/Ein-bisschen-Transparenz-im-Hoechstgericht; http://kurier.at/politik/inland/gruene-verfassungsrichter-sollen-nebenjobs-offenlegen/2.914.959.

62 See also Anna Gamper, 'Austria: Non-cosmopolitan, but Europe-friendly – The Constitutional Court's Comparative Approach' in Tania Groppi and Marie-Claire Ponthoreau (eds.), *The Use of Foreign Precedents by Constitutional Judges* (Hart 2013) 213, 219.

the Constitutional Court is high. Most judgments contain references to scholarly work. The judges not only read but also participate in scholarly debates. Moreover, the legal scholarship in constitutional law analyses the case law of the Constitutional Court intensively. The developments of new concepts and principles in Austrian constitutional law are often fruitful co-productions of the constitutional scholarship and the Constitutional Court. Finally, informal personal relationships between the judges and the legal scholars are very common. The relationships are not only promoted by conferences but also by the fact that the Constitutional Court judges are supported by the scientific staff of the Constitutional Court. This staff is usually recruited from postdoctoral members of the law faculties. Some of these staff members return to university after some years and follow their own academic career. Some of these law professors finally become judges of the Constitutional Court. Other law professors not only publish articles on case law of the Constitutional Court, but also provide legal opinions in constitutional cases, which are brought forward by lawyers in Constitutional Court proceedings.

The prestige of a constitutional law professor in Austria is generally high. Law professors contribute to media discussion on constitutional law; they co-operate with the government, with law firms and other institutions; they give legal opinions and contribute to legislation; and they may hold several other important positions in authorities, institutions and NGOs. The prestige of a judge at the Constitutional Court, however, is much higher, as the authority which the office includes is one of the highest in Austria. The salary of the constitutional judge is at least equal to the salary of the (average) law professor.[63] The actual salary still depends on the side jobs of the judge and the law professor. It also occurs – as mentioned earlier – that a Constitutional Court judge is also a law professor and combines both salaries.

B Arguments in Constitutional Reasoning

Introduction: The Change of Constitutional Reasoning

Each textbook of constitutional law in Austria contains a chapter on the particularities of the Austrian interpretation of constitutional

[63] The basic annual salary of constitutional court judge is €110.000; however, further remunerations and reimbursements are possible. The annual salary of an average law professor is between €90.000 and €150.000. It is telling that Sec. 5i Constitutional Court Act clarifies that the annual salary which a constitutional court judge earn by her income as judge and all other jobs (which are financed by the state, e.g. law professorship) shall not exceed the income of a minister of the Federal government, which is €240.000.

law.[64] The approach to constitutional reasoning as applied by the Austrian Constitutional Court is distinguished by two time periods: the old style of constitutional interpretation and the new style.[65] Both styles of interpretation can be found in constitutional reasoning nowadays. However, the new style of interpretation has significantly overlaid the old style of interpretation in most cases.

The old style of constitutional reasoning refers to the beginning of Austrian constitutional law in the 1920s (the First Republic) and from the 1950s to the 1970s (the Second Republic). The old style is characterized by a very formalistic approach towards constitutional law by the Constitutional Court. A strict interpretation based on the meaning of the wording of the Constitution and a certain form of historical interpretation are associated with this form of constitutional reasoning. The Court followed an approach of judicial self-restraint. The objective protection of the Constitution, the hierarchy of norms (*Stufenbau der Rechtsordnung*) and principle of legality characterized the main forms of constitutional reasoning. The Constitution was understood as a document free of political programs, which should only include basic procedural rules to run a state in a democratic manner. Such a form of formal and reductionist constitutional reasoning of the Court led to short judgments based on the meaning of the words.

The petrification theory (*Versteinerungstheorie*) as a method of interpreting constitutional law is usually mentioned as an expression of this kind of constitutional reasoning.[66] "This means that, as a general rule, the words describing the division of competences between the federal and the state level have to be interpreted according to the meaning they had in the statutes then in force, at the time they were incorporated into the text of the constitution. Later changes of definitions in statutes, or at an even

[64] See Öhlinger and Eberhard (n 1) 35.

[65] See further Austrian literature Bernd-Christian Funk, 'Abbildungs- und Steuerungsleistungen der Rechtswissenschaft', *Liber Amicorum Adamovich* (Verlag Österreich 2002) 111; Anna Gamper, *Regeln der Verfassungsinterpretation* (Verlag Österreich 2012); Michael Holoubek, 'Gedanken zur Auslegungslehre', *Liber Amicorum Mayer* (Manz Verlag 2011) 139; *Korinek*, 'Zur Interpretation von Verfassungsrecht', *Liber Amicorum Walter* (Manz Verlag 1991) 363; Konrad Lachmayer, 'System und systematische Interpretation im Kontext des Verfassungsrechts', *Liber Amicorum Funk* (Springer Verlag 2003) 287; Heinz Schäffer, *Verfassungsinterpretation in Österreich* (Springer Verlag 1971); Somek, 'Wissenschaft vom Verfassungsrecht', in Armin v Bogdandy et al. (eds), *Handbuch Ius Publicum Europaeum Vol. II* (C. F. Müller 2008) 637; Ewald Wiederin, 'Verfassungsinterpretation in Österreich' in Georg Lienbacher (ed.), *Verfassungsinterpretation in Europa* (Jan Sramek Verlag 2011) 81; Norbert Wimmer, *Materiales Verfassungsverständnis* (Springer Verlag 1971).

[66] See a comparison of the petrification theory to US originalism Greg Taylor, *Characterisation in federations: six countries compared* (Springer 2006).

lower level, are not relevant to the interpretation."[67] The petrification theory is still relevant with regard to the division of powers in the constitutional reasoning of the Constitutional Court, but it has been further developed and rendered more flexible.[68]

The change in the approaches of the Constitutional Court is usually associated with the 1980s. However, slight shifts of the Constitutional Court can be observed from the 1950s, e.g. with regard to Rule of Law principle (*Rechtsstaatsprinzip*) or the Principle of Reasonability (*allgemeines Sachlichkeitsgebot*).[69] The changes in the judgments of the Constitutional Court were supported by important amendments of the Austrian Constitution. As already mentioned, the accession to the ECHR and the domestic elevation of the ECHR to formal constitutional law in the 1960s changed the importance of human rights law in Austria. Further improvements of access to constitutional justice and the improvement of legal protection in the 1970s further strengthened the position of the Constitutional Court. Finally, the 1980s led to a series of changes in the case law of the Constitutional Court, which is understood as the 'new style' of constitutional reasoning.[70]

The new style is mainly influenced by constitutional reasoning regarding human rights. The interpretation of human rights is based on the proportionality principle and cannot be limited to the wording of a certain right. The purpose has to be considered and thus, the teleological interpretation is more relevant. Human rights consider not only the principle of legality but also the possibilities of effective legal protection and certain basic procedural rights. Human rights understood as principles for the legislator are also value-based and not only procedural rules of the legislative procedure. Finally, rights-based reasoning led to the extension of the scope of rights and the judicial development of new (elements of) rights.

The constitutional reasoning shifted towards more judicial activism by the Court. Inspired by the German Constitutional Court and its constitutional reasoning, the Austrian Constitutional Court used the

[67] András Jakab, 'Judicial Reasoning in Constitutional Courts: A European Perspective' (2013) 14 *German Law Journal* 1215 (1234–5).

[68] See e.g. VfSlg 15.552/1999.

[69] On the *Rechtsstaatsprinzip* see VfSlg 2455/1952, on the *allgemeines Sachlichkeitsgebot* see VfSlg 5318/1966. On further developments of these concepts see in more detail below.

[70] See e.g. VfSlg 9950/1984; VfSlg 10.043/1984; VfSlg 10.179/1984; VfSlg 10.292/1984; VfSlg 11.196/1986; VfSlg 11.309/1987; VfSlg 11.403/1987; VfSlg 11.500/1987; VfSlg 11.567/1987; VfSlg 12.420/1990.

concept of rights to develop its own possibilities of substantive review.[71] The most prominent case law refers to the right to equality, which was used as a constitutional basis for the judicial establishment of a principle of reasonability[72] or the principle of the protection of legitimate expectations.[73]

The function and the self-understanding of the Court have changed. This, however, does not mean that the Court abandoned the old approach completely. On the contrary, the Court developed its own mix of judicial restraint, focusing on the meaning of words and historical approach, with rights-based judicial activism promoting legal protection and teleological reasoning. The Austrian Constitutional Court, in comparison to the German Constitutional Court, still follows an unemotional, prosaic style with relatively short reasoning. As the Austrian approach does not focus on the concept of state sovereignty in the same manner as the German Constitutional Court does, the Court could approach the EU accession quite differently. Although inspired by the German approach towards EU law, the Austrian Constitutional Court developed an open-minded attitude towards EU law, trying to implement the EU's legal thinking in Austrian constitutional law. The past 20 years mainly reflect the adaptation of the Constitutional Court to EU constitutional law.[74] This development – combined with an increasing following of the case law of the ECtHR in Strasbourg – led to further strengthening of a rights- and principle-based approach towards constitutional law. In the 1990s the Austrian Constitutional Court began to base its constitutional reasoning on the rule of law principle and the democratic principle.[75] This again leads to an opening in the understanding of the Austrian Constitution not only regarding human rights but also concerning state organization. The introduction of administrative courts of first instance in 2014 is an

[71] See Konrad Lachmayer, 'Eine Sprache, zwei Rechtskulturen: deutsches und österreichisches Verfassungsrechtsdenken' in Uwe Kischel (ed.), *Der Einfluss des deutschen Verfassungsrechtsdenkens in der Welt: Bedeutung, Grenzen, Zukunftsperspektiven* (Mohr Siebeck Verlag 2014) 65–91.

[72] VfSlg 10.043/1984. [73] VfSlg 11.309/1987.

[74] VfSlg 14.390/1995; VfSlg 14.863/1997; VfSlg 14.886/1997; VfSlg 15.427/2000; VfSlg 17.967/2006; VfSlg 19.499/2011; VfSlg 19.632/2012.

[75] See e.g. Martin Hiesel, 'Die Rechtsstaatsjudikatur des Verfassungsgerichtshofes' (1999) *Österreichische Juristenzeitung* 522; Martin Hiesel, 'Die Entfaltung der Rechtsstaatsjudikatur des Verfassungsgerichtshofs' (2009) *Österreichische Juristenzeitung* 111; see also Harald Eberhard and Konrad Lachmayer, 'Rule of Law in Austria' in *Understandings of the Rule of Law in Various Legal Orders of the World*, Rule of Law Wiki 2011, http://wikis.fu-berlin.de/display/SBprojectrol/Austria.

impressive result of these changes in the Austrian Constitution and the constitutional reasoning of the Constitutional Court. Not only has the Court changed its reasoning, but also the constitutional text is changing permanently. Austrian constitutional law can hardly be compared to the Austrian Constitution in 1920. It superficial resemblance cannot hide the normative situation that constitutional law, constitutional thinking and constitutional reasoning are different at their very core.

The following analysis focuses on the new style of constitutional reasoning of the last 30 years. It does, however, consider the old style as far as it is necessary and is still relevant for current constitutional reasoning.

5 *The Structure of Constitutional Arguments*

Usually the Court tries to deploy one-line conclusive arguments. As already mentioned, the Court gives only a brief reasoning, often just a few paragraphs. In recent years the constitutional reasoning and thus the engagement with arguments brought before the Court (by an individual or the government) have become longer. An important element of constitutional reasoning can be identified in the procedure of judicial review of statutes. In certain cases of concrete review, the Court, while dealing with a complaint regarding human rights violations by administrative decisions, identifies constitutional concerns regarding the applicable statutory provisions. In such a case the Court can stop the proceeding regarding the review of the human rights violation by the administrative act and can, by a separate review decision (*Prüfbeschluss*), commence the judicial review of the underlying statutory provision. In this review decision, the Court already summarizes its concerns about the unconstitutionality of the statutory provision. In most cases when the Court decides to interrupt the proceedings because of constitutional concerns, the Court in the end declares the provision unconstitutional. However, in a significant number of cases, the Court reconsiders its primary ideas and concludes that the provision is nevertheless constitutional. The reasons for the Court to change its mind can be explained by the majority principle in the Court. Although judges tend to start a review procedure more easily, they will then get into more involved discussion and deliberation about the constitutional reasoning, and during this deliberation, the majority might change. The effect on the constitutional reasoning of the *Prüfbeschluss*is that the Court does not start its reasoning from scratch, but refers back to that decision. Thus, the Court not only cites its own review decision extensively, but also discusses why the Court's preliminary arguments were correct and the statutory provision unconstitutional, or why the Court changed its mind – for good reasons –and held the statutory provision as constitutional. In such a case the "one-line conclusive arguments" are often split in two parts: the part of the review decision and the part of the final judgment.

The reasons for "parallel conclusive arguments" (a 'legs of a chair' structure) can be found in the constitutional complaints of the party, which refers to several constitutional problems in the administrative decisions or the statutory provision. Although the Constitutional Court often refers to only one argument, which suffices to declare the act or the provision as unconstitutional, the Court often has to deal with cumulative-parallel arguments because of party complaints. This kind of argumentation is not found that often. Finally, the 'parallel, individually inconclusive, but together conclusive arguments' can only be found in very rare cases ('dialogic structure').

The overall conclusion with regard to the structure of the constitutional arguments is that, especially in leading cases, the structure is becoming more complex, involving different lines of argumentation.[76] It is therefore questionable whether the arguments are as conclusive as they might have been. Too-short judgments in the early period tended to be too apodictic, because often they did not lay out the argument. Some of the recent judgments tend to deploy more than one conclusive argument.

6 *Types of Arguments in Constitutional Reasoning*

Formal Approaches

While the "meaning of the words" argument is highly emphasized in the literature,[77] the relevance of this kind of argument in analysed case law is lower than one might assume. Moreover, Austrian constitutional scholarship tries to suppress the case law of the Court in which the Court overrules the meaning of the words (e.g. in the context of the so-called correcting interpretation of the Court).[78] The historical intentions of the constitution maker (including the travaux préparatoires) did not play an important role in this formal approach.

[76] See VfSlg 19.750/2013.

[77] Ewald Wiederin, 'Verfassungsinterpretation in Österreich' in Georg Lienbacher (ed.), *Verfassungsinterpretation in Europa* (Jan Sramek Verlag 2011) 81 (82–3).

[78] See an analysis of Anna Gamper, *Regeln der Verfassungsinterpretation* (Verlag Österreich 2012) 151–66.

The formal approach to constitutional reasoning has effects with regard to certain forms of legal reasoning. The concept of analogies[79] is regularly neglected by the Court.[80] The Court finds other ways of extending the scope of constitutional provisions.[81] The adoption procedure of the constitution does not play a role in Court case law. The positivistic approach prohibited moral reasoning by the Court and the application of natural law as well as of the general concept of justice in constitutional reasoning.[82] The primacy of EU law raised questions concerning the applicability of constitutional law. However, the Constitutional Court made it quite clear that it follows the position that EU law supersedes national law, including constitutional law.[83] Arguments from silence have been important with regard to certain topics such as self-government but have also lost their relevance with the ongoing amendments of Austrian constitutional law: e.g. the non-territorial self-government was included in Art. 120 a-c in the text of the Austrian Constitution in 2008.[84]

References

The most consistent elements of the constitutional reasoning of the Constitutional Court are certain forms of references. First of all, the Constitutional Court in nearly every case refers to its own case law. As the Austrian Constitutional system is not built on precedents, the Court is formally not bound by its own case law, which only serves the purpose of deciding a single particular case. However, the Court always tries to include its judgments in the more or less coherent body of case law that it has developed over the decades. The Court's strategy to create consistency also includes the establishment of certain formulae, which are identically repeated in similar judgments. With regard to the application of human rights (especially but not only in the context of proportionality), the Court developed certain tests for each human right, which are regularly repeated in the case law of the Court.

As already mentioned, the Constitutional Court is actively engaged in the scholarly debate on constitutional law, not only citing supporting

[79] See Jakab (n 67) 1220–2.

[80] See Anna Gamper, *Regeln der Verfassungsinterpretation* (Verlag Österreich 2012) 168.

[81] See Konrad Lachmayer, 'System und systematische Interpretation im Kontext des Verfassungsrechts', *Liber Amicorum Funk* (Springer Verlag 2003) 287.

[82] See principle of reasonability. [83] See VfSlg 15.427/2000.

[84] See Ulrich Zellenberg, 'Self-government and Democratic Legitimacy' (2009) 3 *Vienna Journal on International Constitutional Law* 123; Harald Eberhard, 'Self-government in Austria' (2009) 3 *Vienna Journal on International Constitutional Law* 120.

scholarship, but also opposing literature. The Court, however, focuses on Austrian legal doctrine. The development of a constitutional argument often refers to a scholarly concept.[85]

The reference to foreign, comparative material by the Austrian Constitutional Court has been analysed in detail by Austrian scholarship in recent years.[86] The Austrian Constitutional Court refers extensively to European sources, especially the case law of the ECtHR and the CJEU. If one excludes the ECtHR and CJEU, the results of this analysis change.[87] The Austrian Constitutional Court refers to foreign sources in only a minority of cases. Moreover, the reference is usually to the case law of the judgments of the German Constitutional Court.[88] Given the small number of explicit legal references to foreign case law, the implicit influence of German case law is much higher. In particular, the human rights turn in the 1980s and further concepts developed in the 1990s were inspired by German case law.[89] The missing references to the case law of other courts might be explained simply by the tradition of not referring to foreign courts and a lack of constitutional knowledge on the part of the Constitutional Court judges. It, finally, reflects the relatively small scholarly debate on comparative constitutional law in Austria in general, which mostly limits itself to the treatment of German constitutional developments. The explanation for the lack of references to foreign law cannot be found in the formalistic approach of the Court, because the Court is well aware of the non-binding character of such references; it is much more a result of the legal culture.

Substantive Approaches

The most important substantive approaches in constitutional reasoning refer to systematic and harmonising arguments. Especially in the last

[85] It is, however, remarkable to observe that in certain leading cases the Court did not refer to legal scholarship.

[86] See e.g. Anna Gamper, Austria: Non-cosmopolitan, but Europe-friendly – The Constitutional Court's Comparative Approach, in Tania Groppi and Marie-Claire Ponthoreau (eds.), *The Use of Foreign Precedents by Constitutional Judges* ([Hart 2013] 213; [Humblot 2008] 85 ff); Harald Eberhard, 'Funktionalität und Bedeutung der Rechtsvergleichung in der Judikatur des VfGH' in Anna Gamper and Bea Verschraegen (eds.), *Rechtsvergleichung als juristische Auslegungsmethode* (Jan Sramek Verlag 2013) 141; Claudia Fuchs, 'Verfassungsvergleichung durch den Verfassungsgerichtshof', *Journal für Rechtspolitik [Journal of Law and Politics]* 2010, 176.

[87] See Lachmayer (n 71) 65–91.

[88] In the 60 cases (out of 20.000), in which the Austrian Constitutional Court refers to foreign cases, the Court referred to Germany in 81,7 per cent. See the details in Gamper (n 86) 213 (221–23).

[89] Ibid, 224–6.

20 years, the Constitutional Court has identified and developed different concepts, principles and systems based on domestic harmonising arguments regarding different parts of the constitution. The meaning of the words as an approach to constitutional reasoning could be overcome by reading different provisions together and, from them, developing independent concepts and principles of constitutional law. This kind of argument is combined with 'interpreting of the Constitution in the light of doctrinal concepts and principles' and certain key concepts of the Constitution. Finally, teleological/purposive arguments referring to the purpose of the constitutional text can be part of such an argumentation strategy.

The most important example of this case law refers to an extension of the right to equality regarding the development of the principle of reasonability (*Allgemeines Sachlichkeitsgebot*) and the protection of legitimate expectations. Interestingly, the extension of the right to equality led to the opening of the constitutional reasoning of the Court to non-legal, especially economic, arguments. Besides the right to equality, the Constitutional Court discovered the rule of law (*Rechtsstaatlichkeit)* as a principle for various concepts (such as the principle of effective legal protection or the constitutional limitation of independent authorities). The system of representative parliamentary democracy was understood by the Court as a limitation to direct democracy.[90]

Besides the domestic harmonizing arguments, the international harmonizing arguments play a crucial role in the constitutional reasoning of the Constitutional Court. The relevance of the ECHR as domestic constitutional law as well as international human rights law led to a certain approach by the Court to use its reasoning to harmonize the fragmented structure of fundamental rights in the Austrian Constitution. The Court explicitly "reads the different provisions together" (*zusammenlesen*) to identify the relevant human right.[91] This method of constitutional reasoning enables the Court to apply all existing domestic and international provisions in the relevant case.[92]

Regarding EU law, from the very beginning of the Austrian accession to the European Union the Court began to harmonize Austrian (constitutional) law with European law. Taking a very active, pro-European attitude, the Court implemented European legal reasoning and tried to

[90] VfSlg 13.500/1993; VfSlg 16.327/2001.

[91] See e.g. in the context of freedom of religion VfSlg 15.592/1999, 19.349/2011.

[92] The Court even extended its approach towards the EU Charter of Fundamental Rights VfSlg 19.632/2012.

harmonize it with Austrian constitutional reasoning.[93] In co-operation with Austrian legal scholarship and inspired by German constitutional doctrine, the Austrian Constitutional Court developed concepts to deal with EU law.[94]

The Constitutional Court developed different forms of constitutional reasoning in certain areas of constitutional law. As mentioned previously, the Court developed a very particular form of constitutional reasoning with regard to federalism, especially the division of powers. The Court, however, did not stop at developing the petrification theory but went on to supplement the theory by introducing further theories, including the so-called intra-systematic development of the existing interpretation and the principle of mutual consideration. The flexibility of theories in principles with regard to the allocation of powers gives the Court the possibility for extensive reasoning in deciding which argument should carry more weight in the concrete case.

With regard to human rights, the Court followed the German concept of the principle of proportionality, which also plays an important role in the case law of the ECtHR. The dynamic interpretation of human rights in accordance with the case law of the ECtHR describes the Court's approach to human rights.

In the last 20 years, the Austrian Constitutional Court developed a set of principles with regard to state organization, including democratic legitimation, the rule of law understood as effective legal protection, reasonability and efficiency, by using systematic, domestic harmonizing interpretation as well as teleological arguments. EU law promotes these principles to a certain extent; if, however, EU law contradicted these constitutional requirements, they would not have to be considered because EU law – as European harmonizing argument – supersedes domestic constitutional law.

7 *The Weight of Arguments*

The Constitutional Court usually follows one-line conclusive arguments. This kind of argumentation does not support the idea of giving specific weights to different types of arguments. The Court in general tries to avoid

[93] See Öhlinger and Eberhard (n 1).

[94] Gerhard Baumgartner, 'Verfassungsgerichtliche Normenkontrolle und EU-Recht' (2010) *Zeitschrift für Öffentliches Recht* 295; Magdalena *Pöschl*, 'Verfassungsgerichtsbarkeit nach Lissabon' (2012) *Zeitschrift für Öffentliches Recht* 587.

giving more argumentation than necessary and follows a restricted form of reasoning. If one kind of argumentation is sufficient to underpin the unconstitutionality of a statute, the Court will not go on to extend its reasoning. Thus, it is not possible to categorise certain arguments as auxiliary or secondary arguments. However, references to foreign court decisions, which are not often included in the judgments, can be understood as auxiliary forms of argumentation. If the Court refers to the case law of the CJEU or the ECtHR, this is usually part of its primary argumentation and cannot be understood as just secondary.

In certain subject matter, specific doctrine plays a specific role, which gives a certain kind of argument a particular importance. With regard to the allocation of powers, the Court developed different doctrines on the interpretation of the relevant provisions of the Constitution. Most important is the petrification theory, which relates to the understanding of the constitutional wording at the time it was enacted. This kind of interpretation does not, however, refer to the preparatory works of the Constitution, but to the statutes that were in force at that time. It encourages an interpretation of the Constitution with regard to the statutes that were in place historically.[95] The interpretation of the allocation of powers, however, is furthermore based on a certain form of intrasystematic interpretation, a principle of mutual consideration, a principle of adhesion and so on. The Constitutional Court created a complex structure of argumentation, which gives certain arguments a greater weight than others.[96]

In the field of human rights, the principle of proportionality and its line of argumentation are of extraordinary importance.[97] The Court, however, prefers in many cases the principle of equality and the principle of reasonability.[98] Arguments referring to human dignity, which is not explicitly part of the Austrian human rights catalogues, would not be considered by the court in the same manner.[99]

8 *Judicial Candour and Judicial Rhetoric*

Before focusing on judicial candour and rhetoric, it is necessary to make a preliminary note regarding the decision-making of the court in order to understand the context of this question. The Austrian Constitution does not allow any kind of dissenting or concurring opinions. The concrete

[95] Stelzer (n 2) 160. [96] Ibid, 162–4. [97] Somek (n 65) 637.
[98] Stelzer (n 2) 242–4. [99] Öhlinger and Eberhard (n 1) 330.

case is prepared by one judge as rapporteur of the case, but the discussion and decision-making take place in the plenary session of the Court. If the majority of the members of the Court agree, the rapporteur can finalize the judgment on the basis of her proposed draft. In politically sensitive or constitutionally relevant cases, there is usually an intensive debate going on between the judges. The rapporteur has to finalize the judgment on the basis of the result that was decided in the plenary session. The name of the rapporteur is not mentioned in the judgment explicitly, but the names of all the judges who participated in the plenary session are mentioned.[100] In very important cases it is also possible that two judges are working on the case, so it can also happen that the rapporteur is changing within the ongoing procedure of the decision-making of the court.[101]

This framework of the decision-making process has significant impact on the judgment. Although it is possible in some judgments to trace the opinion of one judge, in general the judgment does not reflect the opinion of one judge but the opinion of the Court. The inner controversies usually remain hidden; the judgment primarily serves to develop reasoning with regard to the arguments of the parties, but not to develop a general discourse on the issue concerned.

The reasoning of the judgment is usually very short (between 2 and 10 pages). The judgments remain technical and are not argued in political or emotional language. The target audience is not the general public, which would usually not be able to understand the reasoning of the judgment.[102] The language, however, is quite clear and precise. The target audience is usually lawyers, including the judges of the courts and the advocates of the parties involved in the proceedings. The reasoning of the Court regularly deals with possible counter-arguments, which were brought forward by the parties and/or the government, which is defending the parliamentary statute in question. The court usually sticks to the topic and exercises self-restraint with regard to *obiter dicta.* Especially in the last 30 years, the development of certain constitutional standards of reasoning can be observed. In these cases the Court usually develops a general conceptual framework, or principles, which are relevant for future cases. The court then refers to its own concepts or standing forms.

[100] In the group of constitutional lawyers in Austria, it is usually possible to learn the name of the rapporteur in advance.

[101] E.g. because the rapporteur is not able to find a majority within the court and another judge wants to take over his/her role.

[102] The language is rather technical, using legalistic terminology and form of argumentation.

Moreover, the Court also involves itself in academic discussions of the topic. It regularly cites Austrian academic literature[103] which supports or opposes its own opinion. As about half of its members have an academic background and are still working at universities, the academic debate is relevant for the Court. Even if the Court does not cite the relevant scholarly literature, it is aware of and sometime implicitly reacts to academic debate.

The Austrian Constitutional Court traditionally did not engage in transnational judicial dialogue with foreign courts. Although there are rare citations, especially of the German Constitutional Court,[104] the Austrian Constitutional Court has changed its approach to a limited extent in the last five years. Two judgments of the Austrian Constitutional Court have been translated into English (one on the application of the EU's Charter of Fundamental Rights in 2012,[105] and the other on the Austrian reaction to the preliminary ruling of the CJEU with regard to the Data Retention Directive in 2014[106]). Although both judgments refer to European decision making, it has become obvious that the Court wanted to address not only the European courts but also all other domestic constitutional and supreme courts in the EU. With regard to the two European courts, the ECtHR and the CJEU, the Austrian Constitutional Court often addresses these courts and refers to their judgments to engage in transnational judicial dialogue.[107]

9 *Length, Dissenting and Concurring Opinions*

The length of the judgments varies between 5 and 50 pages. The opinion of the Court is usually very limited (2–10 pages). Thus, the reasoning of the Court is quite short. If one looks at the developments of the last 50 years, the judgments of the Court as well as its opinions have become

[103] The Court usually focuses on the Austrian academic debate. Only in certain cases does the Court refer to foreign literature, and then usually to German Literature. See e.g. in the context of poker and gambling references by the Court to the following articles: Dedonno/Detterman, 'Poker Is a Skill', *Gaming Law Review* 2008/1, 31; Fiedler/Rock, 'Quantifying Skill in Games – Theory and Empirical Evidence for Poker', *Gaming Law Review* 2009/1, 50; Glöckner/Towfigh, Geschicktes Glücksspiel, JZ 2010, 1033 (VfSlg 19.767/2013).

[104] Claudia Fuchs, 'Verfassungsvergleichung durch den Verfassungsgerichtshof' (2010) 18.4 *Journal für Rechtspolitik* 176.

[105] VfSlg 19.632/2012; see https://www.vfgh.gv.at/cms/vfgh-site/attachments/9/6/0/CH0006/CMS1353421369433/grundrechtecharta˙english˙u466–11.pdf.

[106] VfGH 27.06.2014, G 47/2012; see https://www.vfgh.gv.at/cms/vfgh-site/attachments/1/5/8/CH0006/CMS1409900579500/erwaegungeneng28082014.pdf.

[107] Gamper (n 86) 213.

longer.[108] Although there are still very short judgments of high relevance, the average judgments are three times longer than 30 years ago. However, the overall length of the judgments is still short.

As already mentioned, the Austrian Constitutional Court delivers only a single opinion in every case. There are no dissenting or concurring opinions. Although the Court decides on majority, the disagreeing judges do not have the opportunity to express their opinions. This represents the Austrian approach to the Constitutional Court. It is intended to underscore the authority of the Court, but it also limits its transparency and has a significant impact on the subsequent public debate, which is not informed of the constitutional counter-arguments made by the judges of the Constitutional Court.

10 *Framing of Constitutional Issues*

In the concept of the Constitution from 1920, the Austrian Constitutional Court was first of all a court that was meant to deal with conflict of competences and the objective control of statutes. Constitutional issues were framed in a formal way with regard to the compliance of the Constitution. After the Second World War, the situation slowly began to change towards a more substantive approach while formalism still played a significant role.[109]

In 1964 the Austrian parliament declared the ECHR, to which Austria acceded in 1958, as part of Austrian constitutional law. Especially since the 1970s, a shift can be observed in the framing of constitutional issues. Human and fundamental rights have become more and more relevant in the jurisdiction of the Constitutional Court, which has developed the principle of equality in a significant way. Since then the principle of equality has had outstanding importance in the constitutional reasoning of the Court. Various kinds of rule-of-law issues were framed, not by the rule of law principle, but by the principle of equality (including e.g. the prohibition of arbitrariness, the principle of reasonability or the principle of legitimate expectations).[110]

In the 1990s the Court further developed the principles of democracy and the rule of law, especially with regard to institutional issues of the

[108] The average reasoning of the judgment was between 1 and 4 pages.

[109] See Ewald Wiederin, 'Denken vom Recht her. Über den modus austriacus in der Staatsrechtslehre', Helmuth Schulze-Fielitz (ed.), *Staatsrechtslehre als Wissenschaft, Die Verwaltung* 2007, Suppl. 7, 293, 314.

[110] See Magdalena Pöschl, *Gleicheit vor dem Gesetz* (Springer 2007); Stelzer (n 2) 242–4.

Court. Certain key judgments in the last 20 years include the concepts of democratic legitimacy or the rule of law.[111] However, human and fundamental rights remain the most important framework for the reasoning of the Constitutional Court. Besides the overwhelming importance of the right to equality, the Court refers especially to rights regarding personal liberty (e.g. privacy), procedural rights (e.g. fair trial) and economic rights (e.g. the right to own property or freedom to carry on a business). The court usually does not frame constitutional issues as political rights or social rights.

11 Key Concepts

Fundamental Principles of the Austrian Constitution

Art. 44 para. 3 of the Austrian Constitution requires a referendum in case of a total revision of the Austrian Constitution. The Austrian Constitutional Court and the doctrine have developed a specific interpretation of this provision.[112] A total revision is interpreted as interference with the so-called fundamental principles of the Constitution. These principles are not explicitly stated as such in the Constitution, but are the result of a systematic interpretation of the Constitution. Over decades the Constitutional Court derived the following principles from the Austrian Constitution: the democratic principle, the republican principle, the federal principle, the rule of law principle, the separation of powers principle and the liberal principle. A substantive and significant interference with these principles demands a popular referendum. Moreover, the Court argued that they build a higher ranking kind of constitutional law. Thus, the Constitutional Court is able to review "ordinary" constitutional law based on these fundamental principles. In 2001, based on this concept, the Court declared a constitutional provision to be unconstitutional.[113] In the constitutional reasoning of the Court, the democratic principle and the rule of law principle play significant roles.

Nation State, Sovereignty and Secularism

The Austrian Constitution was drafted by Hans Kelsen[114] and is understood as a Kelsenian Constitution, which is not built upon constitutional

[111] See e.g. 15.427/2000; 16.327/2001; 17.967/2006; 18.614/2008; 19.499/2011.

[112] See Stelzer (n 2) 32–36.

[113] See Anna Gamper, 'Introduction to the Study of the Law of the Austrian Federal Constitution' (2008) 2 *Vienna Journal on International Constitutional Law* 92, 97.

[114] See Felix Ermacora, *Die Entstehung der Bundesverfassung 1920: Die Sammlung der Entwürfe zur Staats- und Bundesverfassung* (Braumüller 1990).

patriotism or substantive constitutional values.[115] Certainly the Austrian Constitution does not include much solemnity regarding the nation state. The concept of the nation state, which was obviously the underlying concept of the Austrian Constitution, is not explicitly mentioned there. The concept of the nation or the sovereignty of the country is not a crucial part of the Austrian understanding of the Constitution. The reason for this form of constitutional thinking might be found in the post-WWI situation, that the Austrian Republic is somehow a leftover from an old monarchic empire without a defined identity.[116]

The constitutional reasoning of the Austrian Constitutional Court does not apply the concept of nation or sovereignty explicitly. However, in certain cases one might find an indirect application of such ideas. An example in the case law refers to the privatization of sovereign powers. The Constitutional Court developed an understanding of core functions ("Kernaufgaben") of the state, which the Court derives from certain provisions of the Constitution as well as the democratic and rule of law principle.[117] This concept represents a certain understanding of a sovereign state, which must fulfil certain basic functions. The concept of a nation can be found disguised as citizenship issues. The possibility of voting in general elections is interpreted by the Austrian Constitutional Court quite narrowly, based on the concept of citizenship and the principle of democracy.[118] In conclusion, one might argue that Austrian constitutional thinking cannot abandon concepts of nation state and sovereignty, but the way that these concepts are applied is not analysed properly and reflected by the community of constitutional lawyers in Austria.

The Austrian Constitution does not contain an explicit principle of secularism. Although a certain separation of state and church can be argued by looking at the Austrian Constitution[119], there are still *de facto*

[115] Ewald Wiederin, 'Verfassungsinterpretation in Österreich' in Georg Lienbacher (ed.), *Verfassungsinterpretation in Europa* (Jan Sramek 2011) 88–92.

[116] The Austrian situation after the First World War was not a constitutional moment of nation building. On the contrary, the state was built out of the leftovers of the Austro-Hungarian monarchy (see Ewald Wiederin, 'Grundlagen und Grundzüge staatlichen Verfassungsrechts: Österreich' in *von Bogdandy, Cruz Villalón and Huber* (n 36) Vol. I 389, 393–7. However, the constitutional moment after the First World War can be understood with regard to democracy (abolition of the monarchy, voting rights for women) and the rule of law (principle of legality, new constitutional court).

[117] See Harald Eberhard, 'Limits of Outsourcing Core Functions of the States' (2010) 4 *Vienna Journal of International Constitutional Law* 217.

[118] See Michaela Salamun, 'Suffrage for Aliens (Other than Union Citizens) at Borough Level in Vienna Unconstitutional' (2012) 6 *Vienna Journal of International Constitutional Law* 133.

[119] Öhlinger and Eberhard (n 1) 59.

and *de jure* links between the state and especially the Roman Catholic Church,[120] which date back not only to Austro-Hungarian monarchy but also to the period of Austrian fascism in the 1930s. The Austrian Constitutional Court, however, remains ambivalent about secularism. In two recent judgments the Court defended certain links: in one case the Court argued that crosses in kindergartens represent Austrian culture (instead of addressing the issue of separation of state and church);[121] in another case the court defended tax privileges of individuals regarding church contributions (*Kirchenbeitrag*).[122] Certain kinds of religious pluralism can also be identified.[123]

State Form, Form of Government and Federalism

State form and form of government are determined quite clearly by the Austrian Constitution, but are not usually applied in constitutional reasoning by the Constitutional Court. The state form is only relevant in cases referring to the abolition of the nobility.[124]

Federalism is interpreted as a fundamental principle of the Austrian Constitution, which can only be abolished with a constitutional referendum.[125] The role of federalism as a concept in the reasoning of the Austrian Constitutional Court mainly refers to questions of the allocation of powers between the Federation and the States.[126] The Court developed a sophisticated model of constitutional reasoning (including different kinds of interpretations, e.g. a petrification theory, an intrasystematic interpretation and a principle of mutual consideration).[127] The allocation of powers is one of the biggest structural problems of the Austrian Constitution; thus the Court has to decide time and again on certain issues. Although these cases are quite relevant substantially, the number of these cases is – in relation to human rights cases – not significant.

[120] Stelzer (n 2) 44–5.

[121] See Valerie Trofaier-Leskovar, 'Crucifix in the Kindergarten' 6 (2011) *Vienna Journal of International Constitutional Law* 246.

[122] See VfGH 07.10.2014, B 905/2013.

[123] See Markus Vasek, 'Ritual Slaughter and the Freedom of Religion Constitutional Developments in Austria' (2011) 3 *Vienna Journal of International Constitutional Law* 228.

[124] See on recent case law Thomas Kröll, 'European Court of Justice, a Guardian (Hüter) of the Republican Principle of the Austrian Federal Constitution – Case Note on C-208/09, Sayn-Wittgenstein' (2012) 6 *Vienna Journal of International Constitutional Law* 110.

[125] Anna Gamper, 'Introduction to the Study of the Law of the Austrian Federal Constitution' 2 (2008) *Vienna Journal on International Constitutional Law* 92, 99.

[126] See Art. 138 Austrian Constitution.

[127] Stelzer (n 2) 160–4.

Democracy and the Rule of Law Principle

With regard to the rule of law principle, from its very beginnings in the 1920s the Court extensively recurred to the principle of legality, which is explicitly mentioned in the Austrian Constitution.[128] It was the starting point towards a rule of law understanding of the Constitution. The rule of law principle itself was first mentioned in the 1950s and was further elaborated in the following decades.

In the 1990s, the Constitutional Court began to use the rule of law principle and the democratic principle more often as foundations of its constitutional reasoning. The Court did not necessarily refer to these principles as fundamental principles, but as part of the system of constitutional provisions. The Court discovered the rule of law principle to derive certain concrete (sub)principles. One example is the principle of effective legal protection, which was not only established but regularly used by the Court.[129] The same development could be observed in a similar manner regarding the principle of democracy. The Austrian Constitutional Court developed a (sub)principle of representative democracy, opposing certain developments of direct democracy.[130]

The most important case law regarding the principles of democracy and the rule of law refers to independent administrative authorities[131] (which were mainly established after the accession to the EU and in the context of European law). The court established certain constitutional limits to these developments based on the principles of democracy and the rule of law. The highlight, however, was the case in which the Constitutional Court declared a constitutional provision as null and void in 2001, because it contradicted the principles of democracy and the rule of law as fundamental principles of the Austrian Constitution.[132]

Human Rights, Wesensgehalt and Proportionality test

As mentioned earlier, human rights in general build a key concept of the Austrian Constitutional Court. The fragmented structure of the Austrian human rights system in the Constitution provides many different sources

[128] See Art. 18 Austrian Constitution.

[129] Anke Sembacher, 'Effective Remedies' (2011) 5 *Vienna Journal on International Constitutional Law* 423.

[130] See Öhlinger and Eberhard (n 1) 158–9.

[131] Bernhard Painz, 'Administrative Regulations by Independent Bodies' (2011) 5 *Vienna Journal on International Constitutional Law* 236; Konrad Lachmayer, 'Regulatory Constitutional Law' (2014) 4 *European Networks Law & Regulation Quarterly* 297.

[132] See VfSlg 16.327/2001.

for the Constitutional Court. The Constitutional Court uses a fundamental rights catalogue from 1867,[133] various post-war treaties (St. Germain 1919, Vienna 1955),[134] the ECHR and other international treaties,[135] further constitutional provisions (e.g. data protection)[136] and finally, since 2012, the EU Charter of Fundamental Rights.[137] These broad possibilities of the Court are substantively only limited with regard to social rights, which play a tiny role in the Austrian system of human rights.[138] While the concept of *Wesensgehalt* had a certain importance in the 1970s and 1980s,[139] the principle of proportionality is presently the crucial concept of rights reasoning. The application of the proportionality test is the most important step when the Austrian Constitutional Court deals with human rights questions. However, one should be aware of certain areas in which the proportionality test is not applied, including the principle of equality and procedural rights.

Principle of Equality and Human Dignity

The most important fundamental right in the case law of the Constitutional Court is the principle of equality.[140] The Court used this principle in particular to develop new principles and rights. Thus, it plays a major role in the constitutional reasoning of the Austrian Constitutional Court. The core of the principle of equality refers to the right to equal treatment before the law (Art. 7 Austrian Constitution). The Austrian Constitutional Court has derived a whole set of principles and rights from Art. 7 Austrian Constitution since the 1970s. This includes principles of non-discrimination, of prohibition of arbitrariness, of reasonability, of the protection of legitimate expectations, of tax capacity (ability-to-pay principle), of equal treatment of men and women, of system coherence etc. These developments can be linked to the Court's change towards being more substantive, value-based and active.

Although the principle of equality has developed in many directions and has somewhat loosened constitutional reasoning, the Austrian

133 Stelzer (n 2) 209. 134 Ibid, 211–12.

135 See e.g. the International Convention on the Elimination of All Forms of Racial Discrimination, adopted and opened for signature and ratification by General Assembly resolution 2106 (XX) of 21 December 1965 entry into force 4 January 1969.

136 See Art. 1 Data Protection Act. 137 See VfSlg 19.632/2012.

138 Öhlinger and Eberhard (n 1) 307.

139 Somek (n 65) 637; Ewald Wiederin, 'Verfassungsinterpretation in Österreich' in Georg Lienbacher (ed.), *Verfassungsinterpretation in Europa* (Jan Sramek Verlag 2011) 637, 656.

140 Stelzer (n 2) 242–4.

Constitutional Court limits its interpretation of the right to equal treatment in a remarkable way. Art. 7 Austrian Constitution is considered to be a fundamental right, which refers only to all citizens (not to all human beings). The Austrian Constitutional Court still argues that Art. 7 Austrian Constitution cannot be invoked by foreigners. However, two important disclaimers have to be made: first, in the scope of EU law, Union citizens are also protected by Art. 7 Austrian Constitution; second, the International Convention on the Elimination of All Forms of Racial Discrimination[141] was implemented in the Austrian Constitution, which the court uses to argue for the existence of a principle of equal treatment of foreigners. However, this formalistic approach of the Court remains odd, as so many other substantive principles are derived from this provision.

While the principle of equality plays an extraordinary role in the constitutional reasoning of the court, the concept of human dignity plays a limited role. The Austrian Constitution does not explicitly refer to human dignity, and the Austrian Constitutional Court uses the concept of human dignity primarily in the context of torture (Art. 3 ECHR), asylum cases ('non-refoulement', Art. 3, 8 ECHR) and media law cases (Art 10 ECHR).[142] Human dignity cannot be understood as a key concept of the Austrian Constitutional Court.

Procedural Rights and Economic Rights

The Austrian Constitutional Court regularly uses procedural rights such as the right to fair trial (Art. 6 ECHR) and the right to one's lawful judge (Art. 83 para. 2 Austrian Constitution) to address structural and procedural questions of administrative law and procedure. The prohibition of arbitrariness as part of the principle of equality also plays an important role with regard to procedural rights. Between 2008 and 2014 the Constitutional Court was challenged in particular to apply procedural rights, because a complaint against a judgment of the Asylum Court, established in the year 2008, was allowed only to the Constitutional Court and not to the Administrative Court.[143] As a result, the Constitutional Court was

[141] Öhlinger and Eberhard (n 1) 336.

[142] See Benjamin Kneihs, 'Schutz von Leib und Leben sowie Achtung der Menschenwürde' in Detlef Merten and Hans-Jürgen Papier (eds.), *Handbuch der Grundrechte in Deutschland und Europa*, Vol. VII/1, *Grundrechte in Österreich* (C. F. Müller 2009) 137–74.

[143] See Cornelia Wiesböck, 'Establishment of the Asylum Court' (2009) 3 *Vienna Journal of International Constitutional Law* 303; Iris Golden, 'Case Law of the Constitutional Court Related to the Establishment of the Asylum Court' 3 (2009) *Vienna Journal of International Constitutional Law* 299.

flooded with asylum cases, which often had procedural problems.[144] The Court could not refer to Art. 6 ECHR, which does not include asylum cases, but extended its jurisdiction on arbitrariness. However, the Court did not activate the rule of law principle to broaden procedural rights regarding asylum cases. Finally, the Court opened the EU Charter of Fundamental Rights as standard of constitutional review in 2012 in an asylum case with regard to Art. 47 CFR (right to fair trial). Since 2012, the full scope of Art 47 CFR resp. Art. 6 ECHR could be used in asylum cases. Meanwhile (since 2014), the Asylum Court was replaced by a new system of administrative courts of first instance, which again opens up the possibility to review by the Administrative Court. The possibilities of effective legal protection in asylum cases are thus broadened.

The Constitutional Court used the freedom to carry on a business in the last 30 years to liberalize certain Austrian limitations in commercial law. The Court, moreover, broadened its case law regarding the right to property. Thus, economic rights are regularly used by the Court to establish and uphold the liberal market and to limit state interference. Certain restrictions, such as the prohibition of opening shops on Sundays, are upheld.

Conclusion

Since the Second World War, the Austrian Constitutional Court has developed more and more active key concepts in its constitutional reasoning. This strategy gave the Court the possibility not only to leave its limited and formalistic approach behind, but also to widen its own scope of review substantially. Nowadays, the Court has a very elaborate tool-kit of key concepts, which the Court can use in its reasoning. Step by step, the case law is growing and the key concepts are deepened and widened. The Court is using key concepts as principles to review the legislator, administration and judiciary in general (e.g. principle of reasonability, prohibition of arbitrariness, rule of law principle) or to focus on very specific questions. The court, however, does not follow a rights-creation strategy like the German Constitutional Court,[145] but regularly develops new principles

144 The Austrian Constitution does not provide a constitutional right to asylum. Thus, asylum seekers could not file a complaint at the Constitutional Court based on the right to asylum, but in most cases they referred to procedural questions. Art. 8 ECHR also played a crucial role in these cases.

145 A reason for that might be that the Austrian constitutional legislator has introduced certain rights in the last 50 years (e.g. the right to data protection in the 1970s or the rights of children in 2010). Thus, the Court's possibilities are broadened in the constitution, and it is not necessary for the court to develop certain rights in the same way.

to open up its scope of jurisdiction. The Court's strategy to establish the EUCFR as a standard of constitutional review might open up completely new rights, which so far have not been found in the Austrian Constitution (e.g. right to good administration).

C Comparative Perspective

The following comparative perspective on the Court is based on a short summary of relevant elements of the Austrian Constitutional Court. This summary focuses on elements which are of particular importance for the comparative perspective.

Implied Presuppositions

Austrian Constitutional Court cases are usually framed as human rights, rule of law or federalism cases. The court decides on majority decision, but the voting of the judges is not made public. No dissenting opinions are allowed, which not only makes the judgment opaque, but also presents only the compromise between the majority of judges. Thus, judgments are quite short and deal in a precise way at least with certain arguments of the complainant. The judges are usually equally divided between academics and practitioners. Although the Austrian Constitution is famous for its Kelsenian roots, the court primarily deals with human rights cases, which are mainly based on the case law of the ECtHR. Since the 1970s and 1980s the Court has developed a substantive, principle-based approach in its reasoning, which – since the Austrian accession to the EU in 1995 – is also pro-European. In its legal theoretical basis, the influence of Kelsen can be observed in certain formalistic approaches, which emerge only from time to time, and in refusing arguments based on nation, sovereignty or human dignity. However, these elements can be traced in the case law of the courts by using other terminology.

From a political perspective, the Court is liberal in different ways: first, by defending civil liberties, such as freedom of expression, privacy and personal liberty; second, by an economic understanding following an agenda of liberalizing economy and third, in the last 15 years based on the case law of the ECtHR, also regarding social integration of homosexuals and LGBT rights.[146] The Court has, however, been reluctant to develop

[146] See most recently a judgment of the Austrian Constitutional Court, which states that prohibiting homosexuals from adopting children is an unconstitutional discrimination (unequal treatment); see VfGH 14.01.2015, G 119/2014.

further social rights guarantees. Finally, one might argue that the Court also follows the pragmatic strategy of being a stabilizing factor in the political landscape. Although it has become more active in the last 30 years, it is still possible to argue that the Court sticks to a certain case law which is characterised by judicial self-restraint. Key judgments, such as the extension of constitutional review regarding the EUCFR,[147] show the court's ability to overcome at certain times structural deficits of the Austrian constitution with judicial activism.

Key Concepts

With regard to key concepts, constitutional reasoning follows its own unique approach. Although some concepts are certainly borrowed and adopted from other countries,[148] the final usage is deeply rooted in the unique constitutional setting. The opening of the Austrian Constitutional Court towards the rule of law principle (e.g. effective legal protection) is certainly influenced by European developments (EU, ECHR). The application of the proportionality principle regarding human rights has its roots in the ECHR and the German Constitutional Court. The dynamic understanding of the right to private life relates to the judgments of the ECtHR.

Besides these examples, which could be extended further, some key concepts are uniquely developed by the Austrian Constitutional Court, e.g. its approach towards the principle of equality. The unique way of interpreting the allocation of powers is another example of the Austrian approach towards constitutional reasoning. Finally, its own method of principle-based, pro-European reasoning makes the court unique.

Procedural Aspects

The Austrian Constitution gives the Austrian Constitutional Court a relatively big leeway in accepting or rejecting cases. The access to constitutional justice is further limited by certain formal elements. Thus, the Court can – based on the complaints – pick and choose its cases. However, if the Court decides to review an act of legislation in a concrete review

[147] Valerie Trofaier-Leskovar, 'The Charter of Fundamental Rights of the European Union in the Austrian Constitutional Court's Case Law' (2013) 7 *Vienna Journal on International Constitutional Law* 71.

[148] Most influential is the German Constitutional Court; see Lachmayer (n 71) 65–91.

in administrative matters by the Court itself, the inner dynamics of the Court play an important role. The Court has the possibility to start a review procedure if the majority of judges doubt the constitutionality of a certain provision. The discussions of the judgment, however, which are not public, can turn things around, and may result in the Court finally confirming the constitutionality of the statute. The constitutional reasoning is deeply rooted in the fact that the reporting judge is able to convince the majority of judges by her arguments. The reasoning, however, also must be changed, if the majority decides differently on a formal or substantive level. The constitutional reasoning, thus, could be revised and must follow the decision of the judges.

Hypothesis

The following hypothesis cannot be confirmed by looking at the Austrian example:

1. 'Without a full posterior constitutional review and a great number of cases, the conceptual sophistication in constitutional law (*Verfassungsdogmatik*) remains underdeveloped.'

The Austrian Constitutional Court has a very broad posterior constitutional review and at least the potential for a great number of cases. The conceptual sophistication, however, depends much more on the interrelation between the scholars who are working as constitutional judges. The development of case law over recent decades and the integration of international concepts are much more relevant for the conceptual sophistication than the number of cases per year.

2. 'The larger and/or economically stronger the country, the more likely foreign law is to be rejected.'

Austria is a relatively small country. Although the GDP is high, it is not economically strong in comparison to global players such as the US, China, Germany or Japan. Interestingly enough, Austria uses international law (EU, ECHR) quite openly, but it does not refer to the law of other countries very often. If foreign law is understood as foreign domestic constitutional law, the Austrian Constitutional Court does not rely heavily on foreign law.

3. 'The older the Constitution is and the more difficult it is to amend, the more likely the judges are to use purposive arguments instead of literal arguments.'

The Austrian Constitution dates back to 1920, but has often been amended in recent decades. The shift from literal to purposive arguments, however, did not depend on these facts. It was much more a change in the attitude of the Court itself in the 1970s and 1980s to change from a formalistic to a substantive approach in constitutional reasoning. The Court was influenced to a certain extent by the ECHR system of human rights protection and by the German Constitutional Court approach towards human rights.

4. 'The more academics are sitting in a court, the longer and more detailed the judgments / the more abstract the judgments / the more references to academic literature.'

More or less half of the members of the Austrian Constitutional Court are academics. The judgments of the court are still quite short and are related to the case. The reason for this approach is linked to the impossibility of including dissenting opinions. The judgment represents the opinion of the court and leaves out the internal discussions. It is somehow the minimal consent of the judges. The hypothesis that more references to academic literature are based on the fact that academics are working at the court, however, seems convincing from the Austrian perspective.

D Evaluation, Pathology and Criticism

Since its establishment in 1920, the Austrian Constitutional Court has changed a great deal. Although until the 1960s the reasoning of the Austrian Constitutional Court was formalistic and exercised self-restraint, the influence of the ECHR as constitutional law in Austria and the human rights approach of the German Constitutional Court have been significant. The Austrian Constitutional Court started to open up towards a human rights based and substantive approach. The 1990s and the accession to the EU intensified these developments towards a more active and open court. The reasoning of the court advanced from a literal text-based understanding towards a more sophisticated approach, which is principle-based and builds upon a systematic understanding of the Austrian Constitution and its interrelation with European legal developments. As time goes by, the decisions of the court have gotten longer, although the reasoning is still quite short (up to 10 pages) and follows a stringent and clear structure.

There still exist certain challenges to the Austrian Constitutional Court externally and internally. From an external perspective, the Austrian Constitutional Court must find its position within the European and Austrian supreme courts. While the Court found an open approach towards the European Courts, the Constitutional Court in Austria is in a struggle with both the Administrative Court and the Supreme Court. The EUCFR implementation as a standard of constitutional review by the Austrian Constitutional Court can be understood as a strategic move in the struggle for primacy among the three supreme courts in Austria. The Austrian Supreme Court actively prohibited a constitutional amendment which should have introduced a constitutional complaint against its judgments. The Constitutional Amendment 2015 gives individuals only the possibility to apply to the Constitutional Court after a judgment of an ordinary court of first instance regarding the unconstitutionality of a statutory provision, which was applied by the ordinary court. A constitutional complaint against decisions of the Supreme Court is still not possible.

Another external challenge refers to the still existing limits for an individual to file a complaint against administrative actions or omissions. The Constitutional Court is step by step broadening the possibilities of the individual, which however are still restricted. The right to access constitutional justice regarding the administration is not fully guaranteed.

Finally, the Court remains non-transparent internally. Dissenting or concurring opinions are not allowed. Although the Court argues with the authority and importance of the Court not to disclose details of its internal debate and voting, it remains a lack in the democratic dimension of the Court not to disclose its internal struggles towards constitutional reasoning to the public. This situation contradicts the rise of the Court's importance in political struggles by a newly introduced competence of the Court in 2015 to decide legal struggles between different political parties in the parliamentary investigation committee.

Appendix: 40 Leading Cases

1. VfSlg 176/1923
2. VfSlg 1123/1928
3. VfSlg 2455/1952
4. VfSlg 2778/1954
5. VfSlg 3666/1959
6. VfSlg 5318/1966
7. VfSlg 8009/1977

8. VfSlg 8136/1977
9. VfSlg 8215/1977
10. VfSlg 9581/1982
11. VfSlg 9950/1984
12. VfSlg 10.043/1984
13. VfSlg 10.179/1984
14. VfSlg 10.292/1984
15. VfSlg 11.196/1986
16. VfSlg 11.309/1987
17. VfSlg 11.403/1987
18. VfSlg 11.500/1987
19. VfSlg 11.567/1987
20. VfSlg 12.420/1990
21. VfSlg 13.500/1993
22. VfSlg 13.836/1994
23. VfSlg 14.390/1995
24. VfSlg 14.473/1996
25. VfSlg 14.863/1997
26. VfSlg 14.886/1997
27. VfSlg 15.129/1998
28. VfSlg 15.394/1998
29. VfSlg 15.552/1999
30. VfSlg 15.427/2000
31. VfSlg 16.241/2001
32. VfSlg 16.327/2001
33. VfSlg 16.404/2001
34. VfSlg 16.565/2002
35. VfSlg 17.023/2003
36. VfSlg 17.264/2004
37. VfSlg 17.967/2006
38. VfSlg 18.614/2008
39. VfSlg 19.499/2011
40. VfSlg 19.632/2012

3

The Supreme Federal Tribunal of Brazil

CONRADO HÜBNER MENDES*

Introduction

The Brazilian eighth Constitution, a major political symbol of democratic transition, is almost 30 years old.[1] The Brazilian *Supremo Tribunal Federal* (STF), the apex court of the country's judiciary, is a century older. Despite having deeply remodelled the system of constitutionality control and the overall outlook of the STF, the 1988 Constitution had conducted that regime shift without breaking the institutional continuity of the old court. Such continuity, occasional tensions notwithstanding, has been the general tendency of political transitions in the country's history. The STF, thus, with the same old members and legal ethos inherited from the military dictatorship, took quite some time to renovate, to gain the political traction envisioned by the new Constitution, to acquire a refreshed

* I would like to thank András Jakab, Arthur Dyevre and Giulio Itzcovich for the opportunity to participate in the Conreason Project. I owe a special thanks to Konrad Lachmayer for his thoughtful comments on a first draft of this paper and to all the colleagues who have been fellow participants in the project. I would like to thank Virgílio Afonso da Silva (University of São Paulo – USP), Antonio Maués (Federal University of Pará – UFPA), Daniel Sarmento (Rio de Janeiro State University – UERJ), Juliano Benvindo (University of Brasília – UnB) and Vera Karam Chueiri (Federal University of Paraná – UFPR), constitutional law experts who generously agreed to review my list of 40 cases of the Brazilian Supreme Court. I am also grateful to our dedicated group of post-graduate students at the University of São Paulo, Faculty of Law, for probing criticism and suggestions.

[1] The eight constitutions of Brazilian political history, which repeatedly marked regime transitions, are the following. In 1824, after the country achieved independence from Portugal in 1822, the first was called the *Brazilian Constitution of the Empire of Brazil*, a monarchic and centralising constitution. In 1891, after the proclamation of the Republic in 1889, the second was called *Constitution of the Republic of the United States of Brazil.* In 1934, the third constitution received the same name, and in 1937, the fourth was called *Constitution of the United States of Brazil*, and embodied the "Estado Novo" dictatorship. In 1946, after redemocratization, a fifth constitution was promulgated. After the military coup of 1964, in 1967, the sixth constitution was called *Constitution of Brazil.* In 1969, the military dictatorship promulgated the seventh constitution, named *Constitution of the Federative Republic of Brazil.* The 1988 democratic Constitution, currently in force, has the same name.

self-perception of its role and to credibly respond to the aspirational blueprint of that constitutional landmark.[2]

Thirty years on, the STF has come to be recognised as an activist court, a court that apparently does not hesitate to fill the legislative void, to implement a strong conception of fundamental rights and to stretch the compass of constitutional scrutiny. A court that has arguably come to terms, at last, with its transformative mandate. This is the collective perception, one that has become a commonplace in journalistic rhetoric and has aggrandised judicial self-image. Reality, though, is surrounded by shades. The diagnosis of activism itself, rather than being based on a comprehensive analysis, remains conceptually hasty and empirically impressionistic, if not myopic.

In 2014, the STF was probably at the height of its popularity and public exposure. This feat of self-legitimation is largely due to a small set of progressive decisions in fundamental rights over the last 15 years. It is also, to a non-negligible extent, a result of an overheated criminal judgment that came forth in 2012 and occupied the centre of the court's agenda for many months afterwards – the famous "Mensalão case".[3] This case dealt with a corruption charge levelled against the federal government's party members and collaborators who allegedly paid for parliamentary support during the first years of Lula's government. It was the most inflamed and watched case in the history of the STF. The court's punitive attitude towards the indicted politicians was celebrated as a moralising cleanse of the Brazilian political regime.

On the other hand, that decision was also attacked by political adversaries as ideologically-driven and persecutory. An ordinary criminal case on the merits, Mensalão was a political dynamite in its context and a fitting stage for judges to inflate the court's popularity – and to some extent, to inflate their own, too. The STF sentence, which has sent many indictees to prison, has largely echoed public opinion and taken advantage of that momentum. The "Mensalão case" is an instance of why one cannot accurately depict the volatile political stature of the STF as a constitutional court if its several supplementary roles – as an appeals court and as an ordinary court for some special legal issues and political actors – are not brought into the picture. The court's performance under all such

[2] The Brazilian military dictatorship was triggered by a military coup on April 1, 1964, and finished in January 15, 1985, with the indirect election of a President from the opposition party – Tancredo Neves.

[3] AP 470. The "Mensalão case" is a criminal case which, for that reason, was not included within the list of 40 decisions that are examined in this chapter.

roles plays a significant part in building its delicate political capital. The political salience of its docket is not always related to the constitutional nature of cases.

The STF is possibly at the pinnacle of its reasoning vices. Unsurprisingly, this is not widespread conventional wisdom in Brazilian constitutional scholarship, let alone among judges and practitioners, but has recently gained some hold. Construing the court's constitutional jurisprudence is an arduous, if attainable, exercise. Both institutional and methodological reasons account for that practical hurdle. This chapter provides some initial grounding for that claim and attempts to synthesise the institutional features and argumentative mannerisms of the STF.

A Legal, Political, Institutional and Academic Context

1 *Legal and Political Culture as Context for Constitutional Reasoning*

The *Supremo Tribunal Federal* has been portrayed as one of the responsible actors, if not the foremost, for the main achievements in fundamental rights by Brazilian democracy since the beginning of the 2000s. Paradigmatic decisions taken during this period include the permission of marriage for same-sex couples,[4] the confirmation of affirmative action programmes,[5] the authorization of the abortion of anencephalic foetuses,[6] the validation of stem-cell research,[7] intervention in health rights policies,[8] and public officials' right to strike,[9] to mention but a few. Constitutional issues that are unlikely to progress in parliament necessarily end up in the STF. Politically divisive issues that are actually dealt with by parliamentary legislation end up there, too, and political struggle goes on. When it comes to public morality and rights, for example, the religious conservatism voiced by political parties that integrate the government coalition has been playing a gradually increasing role in blocking progressive liberal agendas such as women's reproductive rights and gay rights.

Despite the diagnosis of activism, inspired by an outdated conception of the separation of powers and by a vulgar text-based approach to constitutional interpretation, the STF has not faced any consistent and vigorous political resistance during the 3 decades of the 1988 Constitution. That diagnosis is itself based on a handful of intrusive decisions that the court has indeed taken in areas like the regulation of democratic elections or public finance, apart from the stereotypically contested cases in fundamental rights. Plausible though the diagnosis of activism might sound, it

[4] ADPF 132, 2011. [5] ADI 3330, 2012. [6] ADPF 54, 2012. [7] ADI 3510, 2008.
[8] Pet 1246, 1997 (among many other cases related to health rights). [9] MI 670, 2007.

is still far from taking full account of the immense docket of the court, part of which is subject to strategic procrastination in view of the political voltage of each case or of the powerful economic interests that each case may challenge. The court decides intrusively as much as it decides not to decide, depending on contextual variables that are still hard to grasp and generalize. A set of procedural devices help it to postpone judgment and back off from confrontation. Underneath the vocal activism, there seems to lie a deliberately disguised and selective passivism, yet to be duly acknowledged, quantified and appraised.

Despite the ambiguous posture of the court, the crude image of activism has not failed to trigger some parliamentary backlash by the government's political party in Congress. Legislators had put forward a constitutional amendment bill that would raise the STF's quorum for any declaration of unconstitutionality (from simple majority to a three-fourths majority) and allow for a popular consultation, to be initiated by the parliament, in cases where the STF declares a constitutional amendment unconstitutional.[10] That putative backlash was not, therefore, a proper threat of noncompliance, but rather a reform bill that would mitigate, relocate and recalibrate the power of the STF. In the context of the "Mensalão case", which reportedly harmed the image of the governing party, it was immediately understood as political revenge against the court.

Aside from the mostly respectful yet occasionally irritable political milieu in which the STF treads, the 1988 Constitution marks a pivotal stage of a gradual shift in the country's interpretative and argumentative practices. Constitutional reasoning has become pervasive in Brazilian legal culture since 1988. Constitutional adjudication, too. Such a shift is surely attributable to the novel institutional arrangements and all-encompassing substantive provisions that were brought about by that constitutional text. But that is not the whole story. One should not ignore, on the one hand, the anti-formalist "legal software" that began to operate and to grow in Brazilian lawyers' hearts and minds, and on the other, the new democratic moment, pregnant with expectations of social and political change attached to the implementation of rights.

Nowadays, one can barely say that the Brazilian culture of legal reasoning is a predominantly formalistic one, if one understands by the formalist quality a literal attachment to the normative text and a concern with strictly deductive, non-creative and value-free reasoning. Neither is it formalist in the sense of a general avoidance to engage with extralegal arguments that may bear upon the legal question at hand. Zooming out,

[10] The amendment bill is PEC 33/2011.

this cultural reversal is the culmination of a handful of anti-formalist critiques to law that were put forward in the 1970s and '80s. Those anti-formalist movements have encountered fertile soil in the domain of constitutional law in a moment of constitutional makeover. That moment put a lot of hope in the project of social development through law, especially through constitutional law. The concern with the effectiveness of the generous catalogue of rights enshrined in the 1988 Constitution, and the question of what and how much could be judicialised, was the crucial inquiry that constitutional dogmatics asked itself in those first years. It still grapples to stabilise an answer, but the most influential one has been to recommend a full-blown judicial application of rights. That is the language and the institutional forum lawyers feel comfortable with. The dogmatics of constitutional law has not fallen short of demanding judges and courts to intervene.

It is in this general atmosphere that constitutional lawyers have started to talk about "emancipatory constitutional reasoning", a "new constitutional interpretation" and "neoconstitutionalism".[11] This evocative jargon consisted in a mode of constitutional thinking, theorizing and reasoning that has called itself, somewhat enigmatically and uninspiredly, "post-positivistic". It celebrated, in the eloquent words of a famous constitutional lawyer, the "tardy triumph of constitutional law".[12]

This thriving trend tends to be more eager to reason from abstract constitutional principles with low normative density than from a diligent rule-based or statutory interpretation. The basic theoretical tenets of "neoconstitutionalism", as flagged by its proponents, are the defense of the normativity of principles, alongside rules, and the openness to the moral embeddedness of constitutional language, which would be ultimately inspired by the towering ideal of human dignity. It advocates the horizontal effect of fundamental rights (or their application to private legal relationships) and the immediate normative force of the constitution, regardless of supplementary legislation. That is, the constitution is taken as either the self-sufficient platform for both political and legal claims, or the main grounding for judicial justification. It is a free-standing

[11] See Miguel Carbonell, *Neoconstitucionalismo(s)* (Trotta 2003). As Eros Grau, a former judge of the STF, has tellingly stated in a public speech: "Yesterday, the legal codes; today, the constitutions. The revenge of Greece against Rome". ("Discurso de Agradecimento pela Medalha Teixeira de Freitas", *Revista da Faculdade de Direito*, Universidade de São Paulo, v. 98, at 667, 2003).

[12] As expressed by a current judge of the STF, Luís Roberto Barroso, in his manuscript "Neo-constitucionalismo e constitucionalização do direito", available at http://georgemlima.xpg.uol.com.br/barroso.pdf

shortcut for legal justification, not only an interpretative starting point to be necessarily complemented by legislation.

This sort of "constitutional turn" to legal reasoning has effectuated a widespread dissemination of arguments based on open-ended principles (sometimes connected with fundamental rights, sometimes not) in judicial cases. Running parallel to that fashionable approach to hermeneutics, the renovated system of constitutional adjudication has been invigorated by that way of thinking.

Critics have recently started to point out the lack of rigour, the superficiality, the capriciousness and arbitrariness of this widely entrenched and consolidated argumentative practice, at least in its most unrefined version.[13] This intellectual trait has been informing constitutional dogmatics and jurisprudence for several years and ended up contributing, according to these critics, to less accountable and more fiat-like judicial decision-making. Free-floating judicial will would be camouflaged under a veneer of fancy abstract principles. That, however, remains an incipient academic denunciation that has not yet affected practice. In fact, if that portrait is indeed accurate, the criticised practice remains alive and kicking.

2 *The Court and Constitutional Litigation*

The present system of Brazilian judicial review mixes the two reputedly matrix-models of the history of western constitutionalism: on the one hand, the diffuse and concrete control created by Marshall's Supreme Court in the beginning of the nineteenth century, and, on the other, the abstract and concentrated control conceived by Kelsen a century later and adopted in several European countries. This has been the stock point of departure to locate the Brazilian system within the canonical taxonomic schemes of comparative constitutional law. Since it is not possible to insert this particular system into either of the "pure" historical types, comparative common sense has included it in the heterogeneous group of "hybrid" systems. Whether that remains an enlightening standpoint to classify and compare diverse systems of constitutional review, and whether there are still any pure types out there, are matters of debate.

[13] For critical insights on the Brazilian practice, see Virgílio Afonso da Silva, 'Ponderação e objetividade na interpretação constitucional' in Ronaldo Porto Macedo et al. (eds), *Direito e Interpretação* (Saraiva 2011); Marcelo Neves, *Entre Hidra e Hercules* (Martins Fontes 2013); Carlos Ari Sundfeld, 'Princípio é Preguiça?', in *Direito Administrativo para Céticos* (Malheiros 2014).

The current features of the Brazilian model derive from the combination of historical episodes that, one by one, successively brought new institutional details and resilient layers of complexity. The system currently in force is the final product of a chain of constituent, legislative and judicial decisions, not a model built on the basis of a single overarching institutional calculus, or of one architectural *fiat* by a single author located in time and space.

This historical evolution has at least three main milestones: (i) in 1891, the first republican constitution, heavily inspired by the US Constitution, created the STF and the diffuse control of constitutionality;[14] (ii) in 1965, through an amendment of the constitution of 1946, a modest form of abstract review was added to the system, an instrument that could only be prompted by the Attorney General (a procedural feature that made it a tool at the service of the federal government, not the other way round); (iii) and the Constitution of 1988, which brought many crucial and democratizing changes: it multiplied the number of legitimate actors that have standing to trigger the concentrated control (for the first time, different social and political actors were granted that procedural right);[15] it instituted a much more complex repertoire for the abstract control alongside the diffuse control; it increased and sophisticated the declaration of rights and magnified the material scope of the constitutional text. The 1988 text, thus, rather than being a mere incremental step, implements a qualitative overhaul of the Brazilian system. An empowered and more accessible court coupled with a multi-thematic and open-ended text: this was the new institutional and argumentative backdrop for the disputes upon constitutional meaning.

Neither the above historical moments, nor the authoritarian shake-ups that the STF has suffered along the way,[16] display the gradual logic of the

[14] To be more accurate, the STF was officially instituted by the Decree 510, in 1890, a document that marks the beginning of the constituent process that would culminate in 1891's republican constitution. This is the second constitution of Brazilian history, which replaced the independence and imperial constitution of 1824.

[15] 1988 Constitution, art. 103: "The following may file direct actions of unconstitutionality and declaratory actions of constitutionality: I – the President of the Republic; II – the directing board of the Federal Senate; III – the directing board of the Chamber of Deputies; iv – the directing board of a state legislative assembly or of the federal District Legislative Chamber; V – a State Governor or the Federal District Governor; VI – the Attorney-General of the Republic; VII – the Federal Council of the Brazilian Bar Association; VIII – a political party represented in the National Congress; IX – a confederation of labour unions or a professional association of a nationwide nature."

[16] The years of 1937, with the advent of the authoritarian constitution of Getulio Vargas, and 1968, with the promulgation of the Institutional Act n. 5 by the military dictatorship, had a profound effect on the STF's political place and status.

construction of the Brazilian model, which was born as purely diffuse, and went the progressive route of concentration without suppressing that original diffuse element. Two amendments to the 1988 Constitution (n. 3, in 1993, and n. 45, in 2004) have also considerably impacted the current system, as we shall see below. Moreover, apart from the constitutional text and the amendments themselves, the Brazilian system of constitutional review is moulded by three additional normative sources: the legislation, the internal regulations of the STF and the STF's own jurisprudence on procedural matters, which mostly shape variables of institutional design "writ small".

Concentrated and Abstract Control

The abstract model comprises three kinds of action: the direct action of unconstitutionality (DAU);[17] the declaratory action of constitutionality (DAC);[18] and the claim of noncompliance with a fundamental precept (CNFP).[19] The three actions can be launched by the same list of actors (art. 103), but have slightly different purposes and admissibility requirements.

The DAU and DAC are the actions for the abstract constitutionality analysis of both federal and state normative acts with inverted aims: whereas the former can be filed in order to obtain a declaration of unconstitutionality, the latter intends to reinforce the constitutionality of legislation (and therefore to domesticate the diffuse review power of the rest of the judiciary, which becomes, thus, powerless to check the constitutional validity of laws that have already been ratified by the STF through a DAC, hence attenuating legal instability).[20]

Furthermore, the DAU can be proposed not only on the basis of legislative action, but also on the basis of a legislative inaction or omission, in cases where the constitution has mandated the legislator to flesh out a more concrete regulatory content to some constitutional provisions through ordinary legislation.[21] In the context of a transformative constitution that imposes several duties on the legislator, the STF is in charge of tackling legislative inertia.

The CNFP is a subsidiary instrument of abstract control and may be applied only when the two other actions, for some procedural or substantive reason, could not be resorted to.[22] It is, accordingly, an action

[17] 1988 Constitution, art. 102, I, a; and art. 102, § 2.

[18] 1988 Constitution, art. 102, I, a; and art. 102, § 2.

[19] 1988 Constitution, art. 102, §1; and Lei n. 9882/99.

[20] Lei 9868/99, art. 24.

[21] 1988 Constitution, art. 102, § 2.

[22] Lei 9882/99, art. 4, § 1.

that involves a previous "subsidiarity judgment".[23] Apart from that, this action also has two distinct features in relation to the others: the notion of a "fundamental precept", which restricts the judicial scrutiny to those constitutional provisions that are qualified as "fundamental" by the jurisprudence; and also the notion of "acts of the public power", which expands the spectrum of abstract constitutional jurisdiction to acts other than the exclusively normative ones of the federal and state levels (and hence including municipal legislation, legislation promulgated before 1988 and infralegislative norms).

In relation to their effects, decisions taken in the course of these actions have *erga omnes* and a binding effect on the rest of the judiciary and the public administration. There is a subtle distinction to be noted: whereas the *erga omnes* effect is granted to the dispositive part of the decision, the binding effect would also comprise the "determinant groundings", in Brazilian parlance, or the holding of the decision, although this is still a matter of jurisprudential dispute.

This vertical bindingness of constitutional precedents is also complemented by, but is distinct from, the instrument of "binding summary", or "summulas" (a succinct normative statement derived from a set of converging decisions in diffuse control, as explained below).[24] Despite sharing the role of authoritative rule-making in a vertical perspective, the latter does not allow much space for argumentative engagement or distinguishing. It is a short and straightforward normative statement or, more technically, a rule.

From a hierarchical point of view, thus, one can rightly contend that constitutional jurisprudence formed in abstract control enjoys absolute supremacy over the other branches. Since the STF has the power to control not only the constitutionality of infra-constitutional normative acts, like legislation, but also of constitutional amendments (in the light of open-ended yet specified eternity clauses[25]), it has the opportunity of emitting the last word in the decisional circuit of the separation of powers, no matter how defeasible that last word might prove to be in the long run.

[23] See ADPF 1, ADPF 17 and ADPF 54. [24] 1988 Constitution, art. 103-A.

[25] 1988 Constitution, art. 69, § 4: "No proposal of amendment shall be considered which is aimed at abolishing: I – the federative form of State; II – the direct, secret, universal and periodic vote; III – the separation of the Government Powers; IV – individual rights and guarantees." For some, judicial review of constitutional amendments in Brazil was a product of an act of self-empowerment by the STF, since the constitutional text, despite its eternity clauses, is not explicit about that particular judicial power. See ADI n. 939 (1993).

The Diffuse and Concrete Control

Constitutionality control can be exercised by any single judge, in any type of judicial action. By way of "extraordinary appeal" (EA), the question may ultimately achieve the STF, the court of last resort for constitutional matters. The STF, since the promulgation of a constitutional amendment of 2004, has discretionary power to delimit its docket on diffuse control and select those cases which have "general repercussion".[26] The decisions on extraordinary appeals that pass the discretionary test of "general repercussion", a complex procedure that combines quantitative and qualitative scrutiny, have binding effect on all other instances of the judiciary.

The decisions taken by the STF in the course of incidental control, thus, generate effects not only between the respective parties of the lawsuit (*inter partes*), as it had always been until the 2004 reform, but do bind other similar judicial cases. Nevertheless, those decisions still do not invalidate the respective statute. When there is such a recognition of the unconstitutionality of a statute, the Senate has the discretionary competence to annul that legislative provision.[27] This particular invention of Brazilian constitutionalism – the Senate power to invalidate laws deemed unconstitutional by the STF – was brought about by the 1934 Constitution with the purpose of filling one alleged gap of the original system: in the absence of a mechanism of binding precedent (*stare decisis*), the decisions of the STF produced effects only in specific cases and would thus generate legal uncertainty. Such a mechanism – the Senate discretionary power of invalidation whenever it agrees with the court's position – was a way of giving a parliamentary pedigree to the more intrusive act of overruling. This Senate power, for many constitutional lawyers, did not seem to make much procedural sense after the advent of abstract control (in which the court already has the power of invalidation with *erga omnes* effects), and more so after the advent of the "general repercussion" mechanism.[28] It still survives, it is believed, by the default inertia of the Brazilian constitutional tradition in that respect, although that claim remains empirically untested.

Apart from the ordinary actions that might raise constitutional issues and reach the STF by way of extraordinary appeal, it is relevant to mention a set of actions related to the so-called "constitutional jurisdiction of

[26] 1988 Constitution, art. 102, § 3.

[27] 1988 Constitution, art. 52, X. The discretionary character of that competence is under fierce debate in Brazilian constitutional debate.

[28] See ADI n. 3345. See also Marcos Paulo Veríssimo, 'A Constituição de 1988, 20 anos depois: Suprema Corte e ativismo judicial 'à brasileira'', (2008) 4.2 *Revista Direito GV* 430.

fundamental rights".[29] This category includes the "habeas corpus"; the "writ of mandamus" (individual or collective), which empowers any individual or group of individuals to challenge abuses of power not covered by habeas corpus; the "habeas data" and, finally, the "writ of injunction",[30] which complements the abstract control of the omissions of the parliament. This last instrument applies to concrete cases in which the lack of legislative provision impedes the individual enjoyment of some constitutional right.

The procedural palette of the Brazilian system of constitutional review is, therefore, broad and complex. It passes over the whole judiciary, combines autonomous actions and procedural incidents in ordinary actions, concrete and abstract judgments, district judges and the Supreme Court, original (first instance) and appeal competences. Such a mixed character has sparked constant criticism. Alongside a concentrated control which produces a binding and *erga omnes* effect, there is a diffuse system that, even after a decision by the STF at an appeal level, does not settle the matter beyond the respective parties, unless the apex court decides to issue a "binding summary". For the critics, that leads to instability. For the advocates, such arrangement instils bottom-up experimentalism and ventilation.

The history of the Brazilian system of constitutional review from 1988 onwards is a history of reforms in order to domesticate and stabilise (but not exactly to suppress) the diffuse control. The tension between centralisation and decentralisation has always been tipped in favour of the former. The direction of this century-long timeline goes from diffuse to concentrated and from restricted to broad (yet not universal) channels of access to the STF. It is a system built through successive steps, through the accumulation of layers brought by each new constitution, legislation or jurisprudential innovation. Instead of a single mastermind, it is the product of institutional accretion.

The maximalist and all-encompassing character of the 1988 constitutional text has also engendered a notable impact on the role of the judiciary and of the STF in particular. Rather than simply specifying the rules of the political game, the constitution took over the normative status of a substantive anchor of the legal order, and "irradiates" (a common metaphor

[29] 1988 Constitution, art. 5, LXVIII; LXIX; LXX; LXXI; LXXII.

[30] 1988 Constitution, art. 5, LXXI: "a writ of injunction shall be granted whenever the absence of a regulatory provision disables the exercise of constitutional rights and liberties, as well as the prerogatives inherent to nationality, sovereignty and citizenship."

of the aforementioned "neoconstitutionalism" conceptual framework) its normative magnetism on most legal subjects. There is hardly a legal claim that does not allow for or rather demand constitutional grounding.

Finally, one should also note that the STF has a multiplicity of competences (constitutionally ascribed powers) that go well beyond the so-called constitutional jurisdiction. Apart from being a "constitutional court" (which is an adequate qualification as far as its power of constitutional review is concerned), the STF is an ordinary appeals court of last resort, and also an ordinary court of first instance in specified issues. This triple face needs to be well assimilated in order to understand the court routines, its general inclinations and its legal identity, if there is one.

The Caseload

For the numerous reasons sketched above, the *Supremo Tribunal Federal* is an overloaded court and has developed a gamut of institutional techniques for a massive production of decisions. After a peak in 2007, the number of judgments handed down has been slowly decreasing. An overpowering magnitude, however, still persists. This table gives an idea of the sheer size of its yearly docket in the past decade:

Year	Filed Suits	Judgments Handed Down
2013	72.070	**78.437**
2012	72.148	87.784
2011	64.018	97.380
2010	71.670	103.869
2009	84.369	95.524
2008	100.781	130.747
2007	119.324	**159.522**
2006	127.535	110.284
2005	95.212	103.700
2004	83.667	101.690

Source: STF official statistics

Such awe-inspiring numbers cannot go unnoticed and call for an explanation. After all, one can't help but wonder how a court with 11 judges can cope with such quantities and produce, for example, almost 160000 decisions in a single year, or almost 80000 decisions in 2013, its lowest record in the decade, while the majority of constitutional courts around the world supply just a few hundred per year. Even if the 11 judges could split their work among themselves and decide individually, it would still require handing down several cases per hour to get to so many thousands.

A comprehensive explanatory account of this quantitative problem would entail delving into deeper sociological considerations than this article allows. However, cultural explanations aside, there are patent institutional reasons for such an overwhelming docket and corresponding decision-making techniques that enable the court to handle, for better or worse, such a docket.

If one breaks these numbers down, one understands that, in the first place, so many cases can be filed at the STF because the procedural system allows for a numerous range of entry points. In other words, too many types of actions and appeals may require the STF's judgment in any of its triple faces: the constitutional court, the appeals court and the ordinary court.

What's more, the STF has very little discretion as to what cases and types of actions it has to handle. In spite of the "general repercussion" filter recently created by constitutional amendment in order to enable the court to select the extraordinary appeals it deems relevant, it still lacks additional instruments to protect itself against that overload with respect to the other entry points.[31]

But how does it manage, after all, to deliver so much? Although there is still empirical work to be done in order to precisely decipher the role and weight of each factor, one can safely point to a set of elements that make such a gigantic docket workable. First, it is essential to realise that, on average, almost 90 per cent of the cases correspond to liminal decisions taken by one single judge with regard to procedural matters (liminal decisions that, oftentimes, terminate the matter). That is, the STF remains, most of the time, a monocratic court, or rather 11 monocratic courts dealing with interlocutory appeals. More seriously, the collegiate may sometimes become exposed to monocratic manoeuvres that remain unaccountable and mostly unregulated.[32]

The STF, in addition to its monocratic side, has three collegiate internal bodies: the plenum and two panels. The plenum, which has the core competence for constitutional review, decides less than 1 per cent of all

[31] See Joaquim Falcão, Pablo de Camargo Cerdeira and Diego Werneck Arguelhes, '*1° Relatório Supremo em Números: O Múltiplo Supremo*' (Research report, FGV Direito Rio, 2011).

[32] See Joaquim Falcão, Ivar Hartman and Vitor Chaves, '3° Relatório Supremo em Números: O Supremo e o Tempo', (Research report, FGV Direito Rio, 2014).

the docket, and the panels decide around 10 per cent.[33] Although the STF is a remarkably individualist court, with a special fondness for *seriatim* decisions, this general cultural rule does not apply so easily to less salient cases, in which the panels do not shy away from going the *per curiam* style and following the *rapporteur*.

Finally, in order to explain those vast numbers, it is also critical to note that, time and again, blocks of similar cases are decided in one go. That is a technique mainly applied by the liminal monocratic decisions and by both panels when deciding low-profile procedural matters. Putting all these factors together, one realises that the STF is a collegiate constitutional court that deals with high-profile substantive constitutional issues in only a tiny minority of cases, quantitatively speaking. However that may be, it is safe to contend that, overall, the STF is still held hostage to the procedural demands it needs to respond to in peripheral cases. And such cases drain part of the institutional time and energy that could be dedicated to its high-profile constitutional issues. That flood does not entail that the STF submerges in minor questions and loses political centrality, but it undoubtedly has a bearing on the substantive and argumentative quality of its decisions. The hardest lingering puzzle, then, is to understand how, under such extraordinary decisional workload, the court still allows itself to write strikingly extensive *seriatim* decisions on those high-profile cases. As I describe below, the average length of the 40 canonical cases here selected revolves around 200 pages.

3 *The Judges*

The membership of the STF consists of 11 judges appointed by the President and subsequently ratified after a Senate hearing. Every two years, the collegiate body elects one of the members to the presidency of the court, a practice that informally respects an order of seniority. No judge becomes the court's president more than once, and the one who has been in the bench for the longest time among those who have not yet been president invariably gets elected, according to that internal convention. The second in the line of seniority becomes the vice-president (who will be, *mutatis mutandis*, the next president two years later). This post has crucial political and administrative tasks, apart from holding a vital discretionary agenda-setting power of the court. This biannual rotation through internal election is believed to be one cornerstone of the court's independence

[33] See Marcos Paulo Veríssimo, 'A Constituição de 1988, 20 anos depois: Suprema Corte e ativismo judicial 'à brasileira'', (2008) 4.2 *Revista Direito GV* 407.

vis-à-vis the other branches, and also a promoter of a non-hierarchical environment among judges. After all, there is no permanent president: the most senior judges have already been president once, and younger judges will likely be president in the not too distant future, a custom that avoids giving one single judge a protagonist role for too long.

The judges of the STF usually come from slightly similar socioeconomic and academic backgrounds. There is very little race and gender plurality, and slight diversity in terms of geographical origin.[34] In terms of previous professional and political background, there is a mixture of politically powerful career judges, public advocates and private lawyers.[35] Regardless of the political coalition in charge of the federal government, and regardless of the President's political party, one can hardly pinpoint a partisan leaning in the way that judges conduct their decisional biography in the court. On the contrary, it is quite unsurprising for judges nominated by one particular President to vote against that government's or party's interests.

Legal academics do not have, by virtue of that condition, a special status and leverage at the appointment process. Several judges, though, are part-time law professors, since teaching law at a reputed law school is a way of acquiring a measure of prestige and rank in legal practice. This promiscuous connection between legal scholarship and high rank legal practice is not recognised as a problem for the integrity of the former. It is rather a boost for the prestige of the latter. There has never been a full-time legal scholar at the STF, and, to my knowledge, one has never been considered as a strong candidate for such a public post. To be sure, the very institution of a full-time legal scholar is a far from general practice in Brazilian legal education; it is rather a relatively recent and still nascent phenomenon.[36]

[34] In October 2000, President Fernando Henrique Cardoso appointed the first woman in the history of the STF: Ellen Gracie Northfleet. In June 2003, President Lula appointed the first black man to the court: Joaquim Barbosa (although Pedro Lessa, a STF judge from the beginning of the twentieth century, also had African ancestry). After that, two other women were also appointed to the court.

[35] The best source for getting such biographical information on all the judges who have been sitting at the STF is the court's own website: http://www.stf.jus.br/portal/ministro/.

[36] The demographic profile of legal education in Brazil today can be summarised as follows: there are almost 1200 law schools spread all over the country, and 85 per cent of such schools are private institutions. The great majority of law professors do not have a doctoral degree and are part-time academics. The immense expansion of private institutions is a phenomenon of the last 15 years, and the private sector has, in overall, with the exception of some traditional private universities, a strikingly low level in comparison to public law schools. Only 15 per cent of law graduates, on average, manage to pass the bar exam. See José Garcez Ghirardi et al. (eds). "Quem é o professor de direito no Brasil?", research report, Observatório do Ensino de Direito (Direito GV 2013).

Finally, unlike in the histories of other democratic transitions, the STF did not have an "inaugural generation" of democratic judges with the advent of the 1988 Constitution. There was a basically seamless continuity of those who had already been sitting on the bench. That fact, to some observers, partly explains the initially reluctant and conservative attitude of the STF towards the exercise of the more robust powers, with broader substantive reach, that the court was granted by the new constitutional text and spirit.

The table below offers a summary of the central institutional design variables:

1. System of constitutional review	"Mixed": combines abstract and concrete; concentrated and diffuse (source: Constitution)
2. Institutional location	Non-specialist, generalist court: combines constitutional and ordinary jurisdiction (source: Constitution)
3. Name of the top court	Supremo Tribunal Federal (STF)
4. Number of judges	11 (source: Constitution, art. 101) Only the plenum can decide on constitutionality issues (source: Constitution, art. 98)
5. Mode of appointment	American type: nomination by the President + confirmation by a Senate hearing (source: Constitution, art. 101, §1)
6. Character of judges	"citizens over thirty-five and under sixty-five years of age, with notable legal knowledge and immaculate reputation" (source: Constitution, art. 101) In practice: there is very little diversity in terms of gender, race etc.
7. Tenure	Life tenure, compulsory retirement at 70 (source: Const., art. 40)
8. Docket-forming	a) Diffuse: discretionary (source: Constitution, art. 102, §3) b) Concentrated: mandatory (source: Constitution, art. 102)
9. Timing of judgments	Discretionary (source: internal rules) In practice: the court developed several mechanisms to prioritise or postpone cases, but is neither accountable nor does it reveal the criteria that orient such choices
10. Average number of cases judged per year	Diffuse: tens of thousands Concentrated: around 150 (source: STF's website)

11. Character of litigants/rules of standing	a) Diffuse: any litigant can reach the STF at an appeal stage b) Concentrated: a list of 9 actors can initiate direct control – 8 public authorities and 1 from civil society (source: Constitution, art. 103) Other mechanisms: *amicus curiae* is accepted, and public consultations may be summoned with them
12. Mode of interaction between judges and litigants	Formally, through written and oral mechanisms: the litigants present written petitions and have one public hearing (source: legislation and internal rules). In practice: the hearing sessions are not interactive and the lawyers have 15 minutes to summarize their arguments
13. Mode of interaction between judges themselves	Public and broadcasted (source: internal rules). In practice, there is very little dialogical interaction among judges. Sessions consist of the reading of individual opinions in public. Reportedly, there is no secret meeting between judges
14. Standard of decisiveness	Simple majority rule (source: legislation)
15. Public display of internal division	Seriatim (source: internal rules)
16. Decision-drafting	With respect to high profile constitutional agenda, every judge writes her own vote most of the time, unless she concurs, which is uncommon, perceived as a lack of "judicial craftsmanship"
17. Communicating	The court publishes summaries of the decisions ("ementas") and newsletters. It also broadcasts public sessions on TV
18. Cataloguing	All full decisions are available on the court's website

4 Legal Scholarship and Constitutional Reasoning

Traditional doctrinal work in Brazilian constitutional law has, curiously enough, not dealt with constitutional case-law. Decisions of the STF were, at best, cited as examples of particular constitutional issues in footnotes of textbooks. "Doctrinalists" usually postulate their constitutional interpretations *ex cathedra*, in the form of legal opinions. They do not critically engage with constitutional case law. Textbooks written by practitioners/professors have been the mainstream vehicles for the dissemination of the knowledge of constitutional law.

In the last 10 years, though, this academic scenario has been slightly changing in the most important post-graduate departments in the country. There is an emerging, though yet quite marginal, practice of "constitutional jurisprudence studies" that attempts to develop the categories and the empirical methods for analysing the STF's and other courts' decisions.[37]

Sometimes, the STF is criticised in journalistic articles written by scholars, but rarely by legal scholars, who are plunged in legal practice and are neither used nor trained nor predisposed to tackle judicial decisions in a critical and analytically thorough fashion. Advocacy movements in fundamental rights cases have been another major actor in pressing and scrutinising those decisions that are perceived to be non-progressive.

These innovative intellectual movements, however, are still not at all representative of the bulk of constitutional law publications in the country. Constitutional discourse is majorly framed by a miscellanea of cursory textbooks and reasoning canons imported from prestigious European or North-American authors, which get recycled and incorporated in local idiom, no matter how adaptable they are or incoherently syncretic that combination might become.

In overall, decisions of the STF are taken as authoritative definitions of constitutional meaning on the respective matter. There is not much attempt by the legal community to examine the arguments, detect inconsistencies, identify and reconstruct a *ratio decidendi* that may transcend as guidance for future cases and so on. Strategically construing the meaning of a STF decision is a more frequent intellectual exercise than challenging the very consistency and correctness of that decision. The traditional posture still looms large.

B Arguments in Constitutional Reasoning

5 The Structure of Constitutional Arguments

Before I analyse the structure of arguments, I would draw attention to four methodological caveats.

[37] One can point out the research endeavours of institutions like the *Sociedade Brasileira de Direito Público* (SBDP), the *Centro Brasileiro de Análise e Planejamento* (CEBRAP), the law schools of *Fundação Getulio Vargas* (FGV) both in São Paulo and Rio de Janeiro, the law school at the *Universidade de Brasília* (UnB) and the recently created *Rede de Pesquisa Empírica em Direito* (REED).

Selecting the 40 Cases

Thanks to the all-encompassing character of the Brazilian constitutional text (which includes quite specific provisions of tax law, administrative law, welfare law, and law on particular public policies and public finance), and also due to the fashionable practice of raising constitutional arguments on the basis of open-ended and morally-laden principles, the constitutional docket of the STF is not only characterised by *quantitative gigantism* (as seen above), but also by *substantive maximalism.* Again, there is hardly a legal claim that cannot be phrased in the light of a more or less precise constitutional provision.

In a way, the constitutional text is not only an object of concern to constitutional lawyers, usually trained to interpret and develop the concepts of the political core of the constitution (its structural provisions and rights protection), but to almost every other legal expert – tax lawyers, private lawyers and so on. This is not only due to the fact that abstract principles on rights can reverberate in subjects as varied as procedural law, criminal law or economic law, but to the additional fact that not-so-abstract provisions regulating these legal spheres were also constitutionalised.

Therefore, the broad material compass of the constitutional text reflects the equally vast range of constitutional topics and reasons that permeate Brazilian argumentative practices. Still, perhaps for a disciplinary propensity of a constitutional lawyer, the 40 cases here selected tend to deal with traditional themes of constitutional law: that is, they mostly include cases related to fundamental rights and to separation of powers questions. This represents a possible indicator of biased selection and may perhaps overlook vital cases in subjects that are not typically familiar to a constitutional lawyer (such as public finance law). However that may be, such a potential bias has the advantage of hopefully facilitating comparison across jurisdictions, since the chosen topics tend to be more universal and less parochial. More importantly, for the purpose of getting a sense of the reasoning peculiarities of the STF, the patterns identified in this short list are very much replicated in other issues. The reasoning and rhetorical styles, from a formal point of view, do not significantly vary across distinct cases or legal subjects.

Secondly, one should note that Brazilian legal culture does not have a solid tradition of appointing generally agreed "leading cases", a concept that, although not wholly alien, has a hard time gaining traction in a decisional environment that does not have a stable use of precedents. This tradition of constitutional law primarily attempts to derive concepts and conclusions syllogistically from the constitutional text, rather than inspecting the structure of the former judicial decisions themselves. When cases are cited, therefore, it is more by way of illustration than argumentative engagement. Not rarely, this happens just for embellishing or enhancing the authority of the decision at stake in a sort of confirmatory citation. Generally agreed lists of cases or more or less convergent casebooks practically do not exist in the Brazilian constitutional law literature. Nonetheless, surprisingly enough, the five Brazilian constitutional law experts who were asked to validate the list here assembled have agreed with about 80 per cent of the cases.[38]

The list includes a majority of abstract control actions (mainly DAU), but also comprises a few cases in diffuse control at the extraordinary appeal stage. In a temporal perspective, they range from 1991 to 2012, 21 years of the 1988 Constitution jurisprudence. In terms of their subject-matter, 29 cases are mainly related to fundamental rights, 2 cases are more closely connected to state organization, and the other 9 comprise a slight variety of topics such as economic regulation, international arbitration and party loyalty. Almost all decisions had a large degree of public exposure and expectation when they were decided, and are also recognised, by the STF itself, as central achievements of its institutional history and as legal innovations in its jurisprudence.

Reading and Understanding Decisions of a Soloist Court

Another major difficulty faced by any research on Brazilian constitutional case law, apart from the obvious quantitative challenges one faces, is the atomistic and non-dialogical *seriatim* format of written decisions. Although one cannot say that such a written style comprises the entire docket of the STF (or its constitutional docket), this strikingly individualist and aggregative approach to constitutional decision-making and drafting is very much a rule when it comes to minimally salient cases (a political quality that applies to almost the whole list of 40 cases).

[38] That may sound contradictory to the claim that the Brazilian legal community has no tradition of filtering "leading cases". I believe, though, that there is an important difference between, on the one hand, the large consensus of the legal community with regard to the set of cases that were legally remarkable and, on the other, the alleged lack of truly "leading cases" in a more technical sense: whereas that consensus is based on a perception of the legal impact on a particular subject-matter, I conceive of a "leading case" as a more demanding notion, which applies to a case that is important not only for the innovation it brought to the legal system, but for the network of reasons that irradiates the case-law, acquiring an authority of its own, and, to a minimal extent, straying from the particular factual situation of that original case. If one adopts this more taxing notion, one will hardly find a leading case in Brazilian constitutional jurisprudence.

This lack of collegiality or sense of co-authorship turns the search for a *ratio decidendi* into a self-deceptive endeavour. The very intelligibility of the justificatory part of the decision becomes deeply compromised. It becomes far-fetched to claim that there is any such thing as a set of "reasons of the court". Likewise, it may also be far-fetched and methodologically overhasty, on the basis of individual opinions and individual styles, to generalise types of reasons as instances of constitutional arguments adopted by "the court". As a general rule, the reasons for each individual opinion do not even engage with the other individual opinions.

This means that, apart from the dispositive part of the decision, to which the judges inevitably have to agree in order to settle any issue in one direction or another, the STF has a technical and practical impediment to setting genuine precedents. The supra-individual reason-giver "the court", in almost all salient cases, does not exist apart from the 11 individual judges. No matter whether the legal community, inadvertently (or rhetorically), takes the part for the whole (that is, the isolated opinion of one judge for the "opinion of the court"), more rigorous research is able to detect such incongruence.

Nonetheless, in spite of those features, precedent-based reasoning is ubiquitous through a mostly rhetorical construction of putative "reasons of the court", which, as has been said, do actually turn out to be the reasons of one of the individual opinions that might get more influential amid the messy concatenation of arguments. The idea of the STF's "constitutional jurisprudence", under such institutional conditions of reason-giving, cannot but be a sort of doctrinal mythmaking. It is hardly possible to say, thus, that there is anything like a "culture of precedents". If there is one, it is shallow and fuzzy, hence susceptible to wilful mishmash. "The precedent" turns out to be in the eyes of the beholder. However a sceptic could claim that this statement applies to every legal tradition that deals with precedential reasoning, the singularities of the Brazilian case should be well detected for meaningful comparison.

Classifying the Argumentative Structure of Judicial Decisions

The coordinators of the Conreason project asked the authors to classify the structure of arguments according to a general trichotomy: (i) a "chain structure", or "one-line conclusive arguments", which would entail, in their words, a self-standing and interdependent sequence of premises and inferences that compose an argument; (ii) a "cumulative parallel structure", or "parallel conclusive arguments", which imply a sum of separate self-sufficient considerations that more or less lead to the same conclusion;

and (iii) a "dialogical structure", or "parallel, individually inconclusive, but together conclusive arguments", which indicate that "the various considerations brought up by the opinion are neither presented as necessary nor as sufficient to entail the conclusion, but as elements bearing, at least, some relevance for the issue at hand."[39]

Regardless of the blurred lines between the three types of argumentative structure, and the inevitable controversy that may arise when one tries to operationalise this classification, applying it to the STF becomes distinctly tricky because of some special features of this court. Despite the individualistic and non-deliberative style of the STF, one should note that, quite frequently, the argumentative structure that comes up in each separate opinion, more often than not, approximates the "parallel-conclusive arguments" type.[40] This is a common trait of a prolix legal culture with constant display of encyclopaedia-like erudition.

For that reason, too, one single *seriatim* decision might display individual opinions that adopt different types of argumentative structure. To face such methodological difficulty, I classified the decisions according to the structure that is predominant in most individual votes. For the purpose of generalisation, that caveat must be kept in mind. Since classifying vote by vote would increase complexity and somewhat impair comparison with other countries, pinpointing the "predominant structure" across votes is probably the best one can do here. Following such procedure, of the 40 cases, 19 were classified as adopting a "cumulative parallel structure", 11 as "one-line conclusive arguments" and 10 as "dialogic" (parallel, individually inconclusive, but together conclusive reasoning).

Classifying and Quantifying the Types of Arguments

The methodological implication of the prolix culture and the soloist institutional trait of the STF is that, in every decision, many types of argument will be detected, irrespective of the weight they have. Even when one

[39] These quotes derive from the general guidelines of the Conreason project.

[40] An expressive example of such cumulative culture is the application of the three-tiered "proportionality test" in fundamental rights jurisprudence: As it was conceived and structured in many constitutional courts around the world, each subsequent analytical step of the test is only necessary if the right's limitation under scrutiny passes the previous step. There is, thus, an element of subsidiarity, and, for example, if a right's limitation fails to meet the requirement of the first step, one does not have to go through the subsequent steps. Quite often, though, one can find individual opinions of the STF that do exactly that: they exhaust each and every step regardless of the nonnecessity and illogicality of the exercise.

individual opinion does not adopt such a diverse range of arguments, the chances are so high that, after dissecting the several opinions that each *seriatim* decision might have, a large amount of that argumentative typology will be used. In a closer scrutiny, thus, the argumentative plurality could be measured not only on a case-by-case basis, but also on an opinion-by-opinion basis within each case.

The understandable methodological choice of not quantifying the number of times each argument is used in each case, and of just box-ticking whether that type of argument is used at least once, runs the risk, in the particular case of the STF, of overlooking important differences of the court's argumentative practices (not to mention the important differences among the judges' styles). Such a procedure, therefore, is not able to capture whether one argument, for example, was used once in one individual opinion, or came up in most individual opinions of that case. By not quantifying, the result of the coding might be misleading and unable to differentiate how truly ingrained that kind of argument is in the reasoning practices of the STF. These practices and formal features of the STF's judgments turn this court, in this specific sense, not only reader-unfriendly, but also research-unfriendly.

6 *Types of Arguments in Constitutional Reasoning*

When it comes to expert constitutional discourse, there is no such thing as a mainstream official philosophy or method of constitutional interpretation in Brazilian constitutionalism. Despite the general acceptance of anti-formalist modes of reasoning and interpretation, as explained above, it is difficult to single out anything like an orthodoxy. On the contrary, the reasoning practices of the STF are quite eclectic and reverential to a mixture of influential interpretative trends that permeate Brazilian legal culture.[41]

The individualist collegiate behaviour and the non-dialogical *seriatim* decisions magnify the argumentative cacophony that emerges from STF case law. Besides cacophony, there is usually a lack of methodological consistency (i) across different judges, (ii) across opinions of the same judge over time or, every so often, and more problematically, (iii) within single opinions of an individual judge.

[41] Virgílio Afonso da Silva, "Interpretação constitucional e sincretismo metodológico" in Virgílio Afonso da Silva (ed), *Interpretação constitucional* (*Malheiros* 2005).

Analogies

Although straightforward analogies were not common in the 40 cases, I could find 8 decisions in which such arguments were somewhat implied. For example, the constitutionality of the legal requirement of a graduate diploma for the exercise of journalism was construed, to some extent, by analogising this profession, and respective legal regimes, with a variety of other professions.[42]

Establishing/Debating the Text of the Constitution

There is no instance of any argument that considers what counts as a constitutional text in the 40 decisions examined. This is an alien question to a fully documental and maximalist type of constitution. The 1988 Constitution is the primary legal grounding of virtually 100 per cent of all the decisions taken by the STF, which does not take issue with the constitutional character of the text.[43]

Applicability of the Constitution

Although a certain doctrine on the justiciability of constitutional norms was quite influential in the first decade of 1988 Constitution jurisprudence, in order to ground the non-enforcement or modest enforcement of several rights provisions due to their "programmatic" character, such doctrines have been gradually losing prestige and collapsing.[44] Thus, despite the absence of a "political question-like" doctrine, the conception of different degrees of efficacy doctrinally enabled the court not to pursue a strong judicialization of rights that would escalate in the following years.

The constitutional applicability debate, in any event, came up only three times in the 40 cases. The main instance of such occurrence has to do with the possibility of judicializing the right to health and intervening in health policy.[45] The other instance refers to the question of whether controlling the constitutionality of constitutional amendments was admissible.[46]

[42] RE 511961

[43] Joaquim Falcão, Pablo Cerdeira and Diego Werneck Arguelhes, 'O Supremo Tribunal Federal Processual' in Ives Gandra Martins, Patrícia Rosset and Antonio Carlos Rodrigues do Amaral (eds), *Estudos: Direito Público* (Lex Magister 2013).

[44] José Afonso da Silva, in an influential book, imported Vezio Crisafulli's doctrine (*Le Costituzione e le sue disposizioni di principio*, Giuffrè 1952) on the applicability of constitutional norms. He postulated three kinds of constitutional norms in the light of their respective efficacy: norms of full efficacy, norms of limited efficacy and norms of contained efficacy.

[45] STA 91.

[46] ADI 939 and ADI 3128.

Ordinary Meaning of the Words of the Constitution or References to the 'Wording of the Constitution' in General

This is a type of argument that has come up in seven decisions of the list, and hence one cannot claim this to be a dominant type of argument. The decision that recognised the right of same-sex couples to have stable unions, for example, has considered the everyday meaning and the legal technical meaning of the constitutional terms "family" and "marriage".[47] Likewise, in a case that examined the constitutionality of the external control of the judiciary in the light of the separation and independence of powers, the literal dimension of the concept was also taken into account.[48]

Harmonising Arguments

The domestic harmonizing argument is a quite common way of interpreting the constitution (the so-called systematic interpretation). That is a way of making sense of how each constitutional provision fits in the overall structure of the text. This sort of argument has come up in 29 decisions.

Arguments that attempted to harmonise constitutional interpretation with international law requirements were, in turn, seen in four instances. The STF aired this kind of argument, for example, by way of examining the validity conditions of international arbitration report,[49] of checking whether it was possible to harmonise the environmental provisions of the 1988 Constitution with WTO decisions with respect to the importation of used tyres,[50] and of pondering whether the constitutionality of the Brazilian amnesty law could also be considered in light of the Interamerican System of Human Rights.[51]

Precedents (Former Own Cases)

Precedents were mentioned in 36 cases and are a permanent justificatory source of the STF reasoning practice. Some qualifications, though, are in order, because the individualistic pattern sketched above produces momentous implications for precedent-based reasoning.

As claimed earlier, an individualist decision-making culture has a limitation on producing precedents conceived as collegially shared justification that devises an intelligible *ratio decidendi*. A non-dialogical *seriatim* decision will usually have as much *ratio decidendis* as there are individual

[47] ADPF 132. [48] ADI 3367. [49] SE 5206. [50] ADPF 101. [51] ADPF 153.

opinions on that decision (or, in other words, will not have a *ratio decidendi* at all). Precedents that are cited, in that sense, end up corresponding to the individual opinion of a single judge.

Furthermore, since the concept of precedent, as practiced by the STF, entails any previous decision taken on that subject, without any additional substantive qualification or filter, and since a gigantic docket, by way of consequence, produces an equally gigantic body of precedents, it is quite common that each judge will have her own canon of cherished precedents (her own set of esteemed individual opinions within the previous cases, sometimes her own). Also because of that, it looks like there is almost never a "case of first impression".

The way a precedent gets cited or plays an argumentative role is also quite disparate and erratic. Precedents are usually mentioned in a non-analytical or argumentative way, that is, by merely alluding to the official number of the previous case that the judge deems to be a precedent. At most, a decision may quote the precedent's summary or a particular insightful passage. There is hardly a more substantive indication of why that would be a relevant precedent for that case, or of how the identity between the precedent and the current case was constructed. Such inferences are by no means self-evident.

Sometimes precedents are cited to ground *obiter dicta* of the respective individual opinion, not only the apparent *ratio decidendi*. Sometimes, rather than citing a precedent, the judge simply quotes an interesting or expressive passage that a particular judge wrote in a previous decision, as a sort of aphorism of legal wisdom that gains literary and moral authority in the jurisprudence, no matter how detached from the *ratio decidendi* that might be. The argumentative aid, in this case, has less to do with the fact and value of precedent, and more to do with the inspirational flair of the quoted passage.

Finally, strategic cherry-picking, which is common in other traditions, seems to be an almost inevitable feature in such a decisional context and hard-wired in its operational mode. In the absence of a more demanding "culture of precedent" in the legal community, this patchy way of dealing with and arguing through precedents undermines the emergence of meaningful and rational accountability. The retrospective construction of precedent, thus, is not so much based on the actual scrutiny of the reasons that were invoked, but on capturing bits and pieces of arguments and conceptual analysis that may receive precedential authority.

Doctrinal Analysis of Legal Concepts or Principles

This sort of argumentative recourse is present in 10 decisions. Richer conceptual analysis has come up, for example, in cases that addressed technical arguments about the legal character and limits of tax categories,[52] the meaning of the separation of powers according to the Brazilian constitutional tradition,[53] the applicability of the consumer code to financial institutions,[54] or the legal regime of heinous crime law.[55]

Linguistic-logic Formulae Based on Silence

This sort of argument was spotted in two cases on the list. The first concerned the marriage of same-sex couples and pointed out that, although the constitutional text was explicit in defining marriage as the union between a man and a woman, it did not necessarily exclude or prohibit the marriage of same-sex couples: that is, in the light of the right to equality, the constitutional provision should be read as accepting a semantic expansion.[56] The second referred to the abortion of anencephalic foetuses: the court considered that the legislation did not actually criminalise the abortion of anencephalic foetuses because, in that particular case, there was no actual life at stake and hence it could not be technically classified as abortion.[57]

Teleological/purposive Arguments Referring to the Purpose of the Text

Teleological arguments, together with precedent-based arguments, scholarly works and harmonising (systematic) interpretations, are the most common argumentative type used by the STF. It could be identified in 26 cases. Quite often, this argument inhabits a high level of abstraction and generality, as in the interpretative remarks made about the general purpose of "democracy".

Teleological/purposive Arguments Referring to the Purpose of the Constitution-Maker

In Brazilian constitutional discourse, not much importance has been given, so far, to the intent of the Constitution-maker, although, thanks to its symbolic value in the democratic transition, there is a modicum of reverence for the founding moment of 1988 (nothing remotely compared

[52] ADI 939 and ADI 3128. [53] ADI 3367. [54] ADI 2591.
[55] HC 82959. [56] ADPF 132. [57] ADPF 54.

to general US culture, which grants the constitution the status of a foundational myth). This sort of argument came up in only one case, which briefly considered, in conjunction with other types of argument, whether the intent of the constituent power was to restrict marriage to the union between a man and a woman.[58]

Non-legal (Moral, Sociological, Economic) Arguments

Non-legal arguments or, as this project has defined it, explicit references to other sciences in order to interpret the constitution, have appeared in 24 decisions, a relatively high score. The STF does not have misgivings about addressing non-legal questions in cases that clearly reflect such knowledge. No matter how dilettantish that might usually be, decisions have already dealt with the social sciences or the natural sciences, have made use of historical and economic arguments and so on.

References to Scholarly Works

Reference to legal scholarly works, both domestic and foreign (i.e. European and, to a lesser extent, North American) is usual in STF case law. It has come up in no fewer than 35 cases. Reference to non-legal scholarly works is less frequent, though also significant mainly in fundamental rights cases. There is no hesitation or any sort of legitimacy unease connected to relying on them. There is rather an underlying cultural encouragement to display such erudition. A variety of genres of scholarly works are cited: textbooks, monographs, law commentaries, academic journal articles or non-legal monographs.

References to Foreign (National) Law

Reference to foreign law is quite frequent in complex fundamental rights cases and has come up in 20 cases. That does not mean that the STF has a clear comparative curiosity, or an open compass to learn from the similar legal experiences of other countries. References to foreign law, oftentimes, are limited to a set of canonical constitutional courts.

Other Methods/Arguments

I was able to detect only two instances of another sort of argument, which, to my mind, would not perfectly fit any other category of the comprehensive list here conventionalised. The argument relates to the social and economic impact of the decision. That was an important consideration in

[58] ADPF 132.

the a case about the compulsory character of a university degree in journalism for the practice of the profession, and in the case of the applicability of the consumer code to financial institutions.[59]

General Results

Former Brazilian constitutional texts have never established an explicit methodological standard for their own interpretation, and neither did the 1988 Constitution. Arguments and methods, thus, are chosen according to the case and its respective constitutional provisions, to the judge's individual persuasion and to academic fashions. Although the numbers here presented are related to a specific set of 40 cases which are deemed, more or less consensually, as ground-breaking in the STF's contemporary jurisprudence, the results do probably capture core characteristics of the overall jurisprudence of the court.

7 *The Weight of Arguments*

The weight of arguments is usually hard to grasp in each individual opinion, and practically impossible to gauge in a standard *seriatim* opinion. It is also safe to say that the quantity or the regularity of arguments do not tell much about their overall weight. This conclusion, however, cannot be entirely generalised, and it hinges upon the argumentative intricacy of each case. In order to have a more reliable qualitative portrait, one would have to delve into each individual vote of each of the 40 cases and check whether, among the several opinions, there is a type of reason (or set of reasons) that stands out in each case, and if that type of reason is also prominent, to some degree and in comparison to the other types, in the full list of cases.

To be fair, it is sometimes possible to note, in an individual opinion, a leading thread of argument, a set of reasons that are central and others that are auxiliary or supplementary to the core argument. Feasible though that analysis might be within the domain of a single opinion, it is less clear whether that reason should transcend the individual votes and integrate some sort of holding or *ratio decidendi* of the court.

At least as important as understanding the variety of argument types voiced by the STF is to grasp a certain mode of putting them forward, of articulating them through a discursive written text and making sense of a legal position. In other words, one has to devise what the

[59] RE 511961 and ADI 2591, respectively.

court's argumentative style looks like. The following section elaborates on that.

8 *Judicial Candour and Judicial Rhetoric*

The STF's argumentative style, if there is a general one beyond individual styles, does not shy away from acknowledging, on the surface, the creative aspect of constitutional judgments. That methodological stance holds true at least for most current judges, and at least at the level of explicit hermeneutical affiliation. The STF as an institution does not have an attachment, strategic or otherwise, to a text-positivistic discourse, neither does it show any hint of embarrassment to affirm the non-mechanical character of legal interpretation. So much so, that this open recognition is sometimes conceived as an indicator of "activism", and not in a disapproving way. At least, again, at the level of articulated premises, the court does not face notable resistance from the legal community.

A slightly different question, yet worthy of serious attention, is whether the doctrinal or value judgments of the STF are transparent and, to a plausible degree, logically complete, or whether its style is rather a cryptic one. Textualist or formalist constitutional reasoning might be a road for judicial obfuscation. One could expect from its antipode, then, a measure of judicial candour. The anti-formalist strand, however, does not necessarily entail sincere and thorough engagement with the open-ended dimensions of constitutional disputes. I postulate this is probably a more accurate depiction of the STF's predominant style, laudable exceptions notwithstanding.

If one gazes at the comparative landscape of constitutional adjudication, one may find diverse modes of obfuscation. A typical one strives to wrap the opinions in legalistic parlance that eclipse inescapable volitional choices and constructive engagement with constitutional meaning. There are a few examples of such a mode in this book (the French being the prototypical reference). Another one, which can have either formalist or anti-formalist undertones, works through abstruse leaps between premises and conclusions, a sudden jump between mostly uncontroversial statements of principle and a particular solution. That is, an apodictic style that conceals deeper motivations and ends up in non sequiturs, or, more bluntly, in decisional *fiat*. This is not at all incompatible with a non-formalist approach to interpretation, but is rather a typical instance of its manipulation.

Most decisions within the set of 40 cases are closer to this second mode. The expository structure usually starts with an announcement of which rules and principles are at stake and of what their abstract meanings are, followed by a messy bricolage of citations (which mainly include precedents and scholarly works, both national and international) and the final conclusion. There is scant effort, along this argumentative path, to address counter-arguments and rebuke them; even less so, to engage with others judges' opinions.

The STF barks confidently, invoking abstract constitutional platitudes and commonplace slogans (like "human dignity is at the core of our constitutional project", "respecting rights against majority will is the price of democracy", or "rights are not absolute"). In spite of the noisy barking, though, the STF bites selectively and uses a set of procedural instruments for postponing or avoiding case disposition. The political sensitivity of its docket, thus, may well have some bearing upon this selectivity, the patterns of which still need to be accounted for.

The target audiences that appear to be relevant to the STF's decisional rhetoric and style comprise, at the very least, the two other political branches, the legal community in general, and the informal public sphere. Since the advent of televised judgments, the informal public sphere has been increasingly taken into account. Although this is a swift generalisation, which certainly may overlook the variety of further interest groups that are more involved in each case, these three audiences are certainly at stake in most decisions.

9 *Length, Dissenting and Concurring Opinions*

The average length of the 40 chosen cases is 180 pages, which means that the whole list amounts to somewhat more than 7200 pages. The longest decision deals with stem-cell research and has 526 pages.[60] That decision is closely followed by a case on freedom of expression and anti-Semitism, which has 488 pages,[61] and a case regarding the right to abortion of anencephalic foetus, which reached 433 pages. The shortest is a monocratic liminal decision pertaining to the right to health and the free delivery of drugs, with 2 pages.[62] Most of the decisions, in sum, range way above 200 pages, and only eight are below 50 pages.

This non-trivial average extension is not necessarily the rule for the whole STF docket, but is certainly the most common practice in salient cases in which the *seriatim* format commands. The main feature of a non-dialogical *seriatim*, as already claimed, is the virtual impossibility of crafting, or deriving, an "opinion of the court". Likewise, in virtue of this

[60] ADI 3510 [61] HC 82424 [62] STA 91

facet, it is not conceptually accurate to classify split opinions as dissenting or concurring. Because individual opinions tend not to clearly dissent from or concur with any other, because of the lack of argumentative engagement among them, one can only identify majority and minority opinions. Or, in other words, the court can only have opinions which end up winning and ones which end up being defeated.[63]

With regard to the degree of collegiate division in the current group of 40 cases, there are only 6 unanimous decisions (15 per cent), one of them being the monocratic decision just mentioned. Even in unanimity cases, the prevailing format remains the standard *seriatim*. Finally, of the 40 decisions, there was case disposition (acceptance of the constitutionality claim) in 23, but this variable does not apparently bear, with respect to these cases, any correlation with either decisional length or the adoption of a *seriatim* format.

10 *Framing of Constitutional Issues*

The leading frame of the 40 cases is the fundamental rights language. This definitely does not mean that most constitutional cases of the STF are related to rights. As already said, in the context of such a multi-thematic and comprehensive text, and of a culture of constitutional interpretation that feels comfortable granting full normative effect to abstract principles alone, framing the constitutional argument, or giving to a legal argument a constitutional character, is not exactly a controversial task.

11 *Key Concepts*

The chief constitutional concepts invoked by the 40 cases were, unsurprisingly, democracy, human dignity and equality, as the table below indicates. These terms do certainly inhabit a primary place of the court's rhetoric under the spirit of the 1988 Constitution. Such expressive signifiers not infrequently inspire an apodictic style of argumentation, which economizes on logical steps and makes large leaps from major premises to specific conclusions. In conjunction with these primary terms, of course, the STF adopts a widespread language of rights and principle-based interpretation that has come up in the majority of cases as well.

[63] See Virgílio Afonso da Silva, 'Deciding Without Deliberating', (2013) 11(3) *International Journal of Constitutional Law*, 583.

A methodological caveat is in order here: the mere fact that a term was spotted more or less frequently in the group of 40 cases does not correlate to a more or less thorough conceptual elaboration of its meaning. On the contrary, the three leading terms are more prone to quick rhetorical use rather than theorisation or careful legal analysis. These numbers, thus, are not capable of measuring whether or how the respective word shapes an argument to a meaningful degree, or whether it is constitutive of jurisprudence on that matter. This would involve a more subtle interpretive issue, not always amenable to hard-and-fast box-ticking.

C Comparative Perspective

From a comparative standpoint, the STF style is located at a long distance from courts that display unity and conciseness as do, in their own ways, the French and the Italian courts. One should also be wary not to mistake it for other kinds of plural opinions. The kind of *seriatim* decision it tends to produce in most salient cases cannot be equated, for example, with the way the US Supreme Court takes plural decisions either. That is because it does not provide a unified majority opinion as the "opinion of the Court". That comparison would be yet less plausible in relation to the German Constitutional Court, which is open to dissenting opinions in quite exceptional circumstances, when the dissenting judge has the collegial burden of justifying it. Finally, one should not be too quick to approximate the STF *seriatim* to the way that the Australian court, shaped by the British tradition of judicial reasoning, also delivers divided opinions. A closer empirical inspection could reveal to what extent the Brazilian non-dialogical *seriatim* impedes the search of a holding or *ratio decidendi*. When votes talk past each other, it becomes more difficult to construe shared reasons. Comparative law has yet to supply a sensitive enough taxonomy to capture the differences of this under-conceptualized dimension of constitutional adjudication.

D Evaluation and Criticism

The particular working mode of the STF strays from some general patterns one might find in the contemporary landscape of constitutional review. Not only is it an individualistic court in the markedly cumbersome way portrayed above,[64] but it is a court where judges are granted important

[64] See also Virgílio Afonso da Silva, who contends: "The Brazilian Supreme Court is an extremely uncooperative and individualistic court." Ibid 29)

competences of liminal monocratic decision-making. Monocratic decisions sometimes consummate heavy concrete effects, such as preventively suspending the efficacy of legislation until the plenum delivers the final decision. That decision may take several years (unless the case becomes moot due to some supervening event, which is not uncommon). Judges do also have an almost unbridled power to obstruct the court's agenda, and they do not face any meaningful argumentative burden or institutional constraint as to when it is justified to postpone a judgment. This *de facto* individual power engendered a unique mode of internal filibuster.[65]

The predilection for *individual authorship* in every prominent case, instead of *institutional authorship*, generates severe hurdles to the potential functioning of the system itself, especially in its intent of seeking predictability and intra-judiciary coordination through the authority of precedents. Furthermore, the judges' distinct voices within a decision do not properly and frankly communicate, which turns plurality (a feature that is present in other courts) into cacophony.

Research in the reasoning practices of the STF under such conditions becomes a thorny exercise. Most importantly, holding such reasoning practices to account is a challenge that Brazilian constitutionalism has not yet managed to meet. The court's deliberative practices are enmeshed in powerful centripetal forces. To be sure, it is not a court in search of unity, but comfortably accommodated to atomistic reason-giving. One cannot rigorously speak about "the court" because, as already contended, that collective agent does not exist as far as public reasoning is concerned.

A court with a prevalent aggregative character and low degree of collegiality has deep trouble in consolidating consequential precedents. That pattern might work as a fitting strategy for, consciously or not, keeping itself free from stricter standards of accountability. Legal scholarship has not been an effective account-holder. It does not even recognise itself as in charge of such a political role.

The STF has turned itself into an overwhelmingly visible court. Some judges have become public personas and do not hesitate to maintain a

[65] The procedural tool for obstruction is called "vista", a right of every judge to interrupt the judgment when her or his turn to declare the individual opinion arrives. Its rationale is to provide additional time for the judge to think through. The session is suspended and the judgment is resumed only after that judge is convinced on what stand to take on the matter and delivers her or his "voto-vista". Despite internal regulations providing for a time limit of two weeks, there is a conventional non-enforcement of that rule and the case might be kept on hold for years. It has been used by judges to postpone decisions on arguably sensitive issues.

close and ceaseless relation with the media (criticising public policies, criticising their own colleagues, sometimes even anticipating their opinions on public matters that sooner or later might reach the court). Such visibility was magnified by the practice of broadcasting the deliberative sessions of the court. Such communication policy has been overly celebrated, both by the court and the public, on the left and on the right of the ideological spectrum, as a unique democratic feature of the STF and as a valuable indicator of its transparency.

A minority of scholars, myself included, raise the hypothesis that such surface transparency conceals a deep obscurantism in the way the STF behaves and articulates its decisions. Public sessions turn out to be rigid and extremely ritualised meetings for the purpose of reading precooked and prêt-à-porter individual votes that were drafted without any meaningful interpersonal interaction in the secrecy of the judge's office. Such "reading sessions" have a very strict order of "readers", beginning with the rapporteur and then following from the youngest to the most senior judge. That stiff sequence turns out, in a somewhat nonsensical way, to reduce the importance of the most senior judges in deliberations, since they are the last ones to vocalize their votes, a moment in which majority is very likely to have already been formed (except, of course, in a handful of cases in which they become the swing vote).[66] And once the vote is given, it would be more than an extraordinary fact for a judge to change it in light of a later argument voiced by another judge.

One might also suspect that the length of written judgments was magnified by the practice of broadcasting. The TV would have, some advocates claim, beyond the alleged transparency, an educative effect as an additional positive externality. That misguided notion of transparency, however, may ossify a strikingly arcane way of reasoning and decision-making. If one believes that argumentative quality is a more significant dimension of the accountability of non-elected bodies, this unnoticed obscurantism should be a strong source of concern. TV broadcasting brings up a pride of transparency that echoes Brandeis's oft-repeated maxim: "sunlight is said to be the best of disinfectants", a chief motto of transparency movements. Such self-congratulatory enthusiasm underestimates, perhaps, that too much or misdirected sunlight can also blind.

These institutional features express and reinforce themselves through, among others things, the broad publicity and the inflexible ritual of the deliberative sessions. This type of public session and the STF's *seriatim*

[66] I thank Virgílio Afonso da Silva for that remark.

format are mutually implicated. Such dynamics undermines the possibility, for example, of the emergence of truly "dissenting opinions", that is, an opinion which converses with majoritarian votes by way of arguments and counter-arguments.[67] Final decisions end up being a patchwork of individual votes which, after contrast with each other, are classified as part of the majority or minority block, a place the author of each opinion could not know while drafting it.[68]

The public sessions of the STF suggest a certain inclination to what Hirschman has called, in another context, the "overproduction of opinionated opinions".[69] For him, the remedy against that individual or institutional habit would be to instil, on top of the "delights of winning an argument", "the pleasures of being good listeners".[70] The predominant individualism that exists in the STF's institutional culture, however, does not have much to do with "winning an argument". To win or to lose, in the court's environment, matter less than to publicly state an individual opinion, especially in salient cases.

The STF cultivates and pays tribute to the emission of "strong opinions", those which resist, as a matter of principle and character, the counter-argument in order to avoid any sign or moral or intellectual weakness.[71] The STF would be, to evoke a recurrent musical metaphor that illustrates cooperative endeavours: not an "orchestra", where the whole is bigger than the sum of its parts, but rather a "court of soloists", in which individual virtuosity and brilliance prevails, rather than being subordinate to, the ideal of a concert.

[67] Silva describes that feature: "Therefore, just as there is no real (oral) deliberation, there is no dialogue, no exchange of arguments among the written opinions. In other words, in a 6 to 5 decision, the written opinions of the five justices who do not share the opinion of the majority are not dissenting opinions, at least not in the sense that this term is used in the debate on judicial decision-making. They are mere defeated opinions." (Ibid. 36–37)

[68] Silva also elaborates on the lawyerly reasoning style of STF's votes, a style that ignores contrary evidences, precedents and arguments: "Just as lawyers often cite only academic works and judicial precedents that corroborate their interests, the justices in the Brazilian Supreme Court frequently do the same." (Ibid. 28)

[69] Albert Hirschman, 'Having Opinions – One of the Elements of Well-being?' (1989) 79.2 *The American Economic Review* 77.

[70] In the complete passage: "The most straightforward way of avoiding this overproduction would be for individuals to change the value system under which they operate: might they learn to value both having opinions and keeping an open mind, to mix the delights of winning an argument with the pleasures of being good listeners?" (Ibid. 77–78)

[71] The culture of strong opinions would be, according to Gambetta, a fundamental feature of "discursive machismo". Diego Gambetta, "'Claro!' An Essay on Discursive Machismo", in Jon Elster (ed.), *Deliberative Democracy* (Cambridge University Press 1998) 20.

The soloist and anti-deliberative mentality produces, it seems to me, institutional damages that should be more meticulously diagnosed. From the formal point of view, again, such pathology significantly restricts the STF's capacity to craft precedents upon which constitutional jurisprudence can be built. The meaning of the Brazilian constitution remains fragmented and unstable. It is captured by each judge's vagaries and idiosyncrasies. When decisions are ultimately nothing but the sum of their individual pieces, constitutional meaning remains up for grabs. The court is held hostage to the ritualistic conventions it does not dare to challenge and to the irrationalities it does not dare to candidly recognise.

Cultural inclinations and procedural variables account for these features. Turning the public judgment into a rigid and televised reading session certainly explains part of this story and has a bearing on the debatable quality of decisions. Furthermore, the distinction between salient and non-salient cases (with all nuances in between) does also correlate to the degree of argumentative multiplicity and divisiveness one might find in a decision. The bricolage of arguments may be found not only across different votes, but also inside an individual vote.

A foreign lawyer may well find it difficult to understand the intricacies and argumentative traits of this court. Constitutional talk has pervaded Brazilian legal discourse across the board in most legal subjects in the last 30 years. These subjects are influenced not only by constitutional abstract principles framed by the language of rights and political ideals, but also by more precise constitutional rules. However, the decision-making habits and procedures described above, among other things, still make it hard for constitutional dogmatics to flourish.

Arguments, in this sense, do not have a high currency in the Brazilian jurisprudential dynamics. Not, at least, in the wholesale, by way of facilitating the construction of a well-knit case law with workable gravitational force. This is not necessarily because judges do not take them seriously or lack the competence and occasion to put forward well-crafted arguments, but simply because those arguments do not find a way to receive the institutional imprimatur. They remain crude individual opinions, mere hints or *obiter dicta* at what judges think about an issue. The aggregate effect is that individual opinions remain just that: a quotable passage with doubtful jurisprudential import. Hence, institutional arguments with which the public sphere could engage do not take root.

Where reasons are cheap and persevere unchallenged, casuistry is doomed to ensue at the cost of sound constitutional dogmatics. The practice of intermittent 'reason-dropping' is still pervasive, and Brazilian constitutional jurisprudence remains a case-by-case matter, less in Cass Sunstein's sense of judicial minimalism,[72] more in the rudimentary sense of "*ad hocism*" and unpatterned decision-making. Deliberately bereft of an argumentative web, decisions are taken with neither the constraints of the past, nor those of the future. What really matters is the case at hand and its circumstances: perhaps a wise approach when stakes are high, but a disenchanting fact for those who bet on the promises of the "constitutional rule of law" enterprise.

Appendix: 40 Leading Judgments

1) ADI 4, 1991 (interest rates)
2) ADI 466, 1991 (death penalty and preventive constitutionality control)
3) ADI 534, 1992 (Collor economic plan)
4) ADI 939, 1993 (tax law and constitutionality control of amendment)
5) HC 71373, 1994 (paternity DNA investigation)
6) DI 1439 MC, 1996 (minimum wage)
7) RE 153531, 1997 (cultural rights and environment – "Farra do Boi")
8) Pet 1246, 1997 (right to health)
9) ADI 1480 MC, 1997 (international treaties, WLO and unfair dismissal)
10) ADI/MC 1949, 1999 (regulatory agencies)
11) RE 226855, 2000 (economic plans and FGTS)
12) SE 5206, 2001 (constitutionality of arbitration)
13) HC 82424, 2003 (freedom of expression and anti-Semitism)
14) ADI 3128, 2004 (tax law and pensioners)
15) RE 201819, 2005 (horizontal effects of fundamental rights)
16) ADI 3367, 2005 (external control of the judiciary)
17) ADI 2591, 2006 (application of consumer code to financial institutions)
18) RE 407688, 2006 (right to housing)
19) ADI 1351, 2006 (barrier clause for political parties)
20) HC 82959, 2006 (legal regimes of heinous crimes)
21) MI 670, 2007 (right to strike of public officials)
22) STA 91, 2007 (right to health)
23) ADI 3112, 2007 (disarmament statute)

[72] Cass Sunstein, *One Case at a Time: Judicial Minimalism on the Supreme Court* (Harvard University Press 2001).

24) ADI 3999, 2008 (party fidelity)
25) ADI 3510, 2008 (stem-cell research)
26) RE 397762, 2008 (right to pension and the concubine)
27) RE 466343, 2008 (unfaithful trustee, human rights treaties and supra-legality)
28) RE 511961, 2009 (journalism university degree)
29) ADPF 46, 2009 (monopoly of postal services – "Correio")
30) ADPF 101, 2009 (import of second-hand tyres)
31) ADPF 130, 2009 (media law)
32) RE 389808, 2010 (bank secrecy)
33) ADPF 153, 2010 (amnesty law)
34) ADC 9, 2011 ("Apagão")
35) ADI 4274, 2011 (right to protest – "Marijuana march")
36) ADPF 132, 2011 (same-sex marriage)
37) ADPF 54, 2012 (abortion of anencephalic foetus)
38) ADI 3330, 2012 (affirmative action – "Pro-Uni")
39) ADI 4029, 2012 ("Instituto Chico Mendes")
40) ADC 29, 2012 (corruption and electoral laws – "Ficha Limpa")

4

The Supreme Court of Canada

HUGO CYR AND MONICA POPESCU

A Legal, Political, Institutional and Academic Context

1 *Legal and Political Culture as Context for Constitutional Reasoning*

In 1867, three British colonies of North America (the Province of Canada, Nova Scotia and New Brunswick) were federalised to form the Dominion of Canada.[1] The Dominion was initially composed of four provinces: Ontario, Québec, Nova Scotia and New Brunswick.[2] Over time, other provinces and territories joined the Federation through a wide variety of constitutional instruments.[3] Canada is now composed of ten provinces and three territories. Unlike other former colonies that accomplished a clean break from their imperial masters through revolution, Canada acquired its autonomy so gradually that we cannot pinpoint the exact moment when it became independent from the British Empire. At the end of the 1926 Imperial Conference, the *Balfour Declaration* confirmed that no autonomous Dominion could be bound by commitments incurred by the Imperial Government except with the consent of the Dominion concerned.[4] The *Statute of Westminster* gave, in large parts, legal effect to that declaration in 1931.[5] While the process leading to independence

[1] We would like to thank Aileen Kavanagh for commenting so generously on a previous draft presented in Budapest. We would also like to thank all participants of the Heidelberg and Budapest meetings for their comments and suggestions. Finally, we would like to thank Adam Dodek, Peter Hogg, Jean Leclair, Dwight Newman and Maxime St-Hilaire for having reviewed our proposed list of leading constitutional cases decided by the Supreme Court and for having suggested their own alternative lists (for the latter, see Cambridge University Press companion website).

[2] *Constitution Act, 1867* (UK), 30 & 31 Vict, c 3, ss 56 and 90, reprinted in RSC 1985, App II, No 5 [*CA 1867*].

[3] See the list at *Constitution Act, 1982*, being Schedule B to the *Canada Act 1982* (U.K.), 1982, c. 11, Schedule of the Constitution Act, 1982 [*CA 1982*].

[4] U.K., Inter-Imperial Relations Committee, *Proceedings and Memoranda (Balfour Declaration)*, E (I.R./26) Series at 2. See also Maurice Olliver, ed., *The Colonial and Imperial Conferences from 1887 to 1937* (Queen's Printer 1954) 3 146.

[5] *Statute of Westminster*, 1931, (U.K.), 22 & 23 Geo. V, c 4, s 4 [*Statute of Westminster*].

seems to have been mainly achieved by the end of the 1930s, when Canada entered World War II with a formal declaration of war issued separately from the United Kingdom's, the process was not completely over. Canada had gained its international autonomy, but it had not yet completely gained its formal independence from the United Kingdom. For example, and mostly because of the lack of agreement between the federal government and the provinces on an appropriate amending formula, it did not yet enjoy the full powers to modify its own formal Constitution.[6] In 1947, the King issued new Letters Patent to the Governor General devolving his remaining executive powers in relation to "Canada".[7] In 1949, the possibility of appeal to the Judicial Committee of the Privy Council was terminated.[8] The federal government, after concluding an agreement with nine of the ten provinces in 1981, asked the British Parliament to finally "patriate" the remaining powers over the Canadian Constitution. The government of Québec, the second largest province and the only one populated by a majority of francophones, opposed the deal. The British Parliament adopted the *Canada Act*, which contains in its Schedule B[9] the *Constitution Act, 1982* that had been drafted by Canadians.[10] The country is now considered fully independent from the United Kingdom.[11] The *Constitution Act, 1982* does not substantially modify the division of legislative powers between the Parliament and the provincial Legislatures,[12] but it contains, besides a full amending formula, among other things, a recognition of existing aboriginal and treaty rights and an entrenched *Canadian Charter of Rights and Freedoms*. The Québec government, while

[6] *Statute of Westminster*, *Ibid.*, s. 7.

[7] *Letters Patent Constituting the Office of the Governor General of Canada*, reproduced at R.S.C. 1985, Appendix II, No. 31 [*Letters Patent Constituting the Office of the Governor General of Canada*].

[8] *Act to Amend the Supreme Court Act*, S.C. 1949 (2nd Sess.), c. 37, s. 3.

[9] *Canada Act 1982*, 1982 c.11 (U.K.). [10] CA 1982.

[11] However, the recent adoption of the *Succession to the Throne Act, 2013*, S.C. 2013, c. 6 seems to put into question that full independence. Indeed, the federal government supposes that it only needs to "assent" to alteration in the law touching the succession to the Throne set out in a statute of the Parliament of the United Kingdom for the changes to be effective for Canada as well. A fully independent country may assent out of courtesy or comity to the changes proposed by another country, but it seems that it would also have to adopt the same changes for its own purposes for such changes to be effective in both legal systems. For an illuminating analysis of such problems, see Paul Benoit and Garry Toffoli, 'More is Needed to Change the Rules of Succession for Canada' (2013) 36 *Canadian Parliamentary Review* 10.

[12] The term "Parliament" with a capital "P" refers to the federal legislative organ, while the term "Legislature" with a capital "L" refers to the legislative institution of the Provinces.

bound by the *Constitution Act, 1982*,[13] never gave its assent to this important constitutional modification. The failed *Meech Lake Accord* (1987) was an attempt to address Québec's grievances, but its ultimate rejection by the Province of Newfoundland derailed the process.[14] The following *Charlottetown Accord* (1992) was a second attempt at meeting Québec's grievances, but it also aimed at responding to other complaints voiced elsewhere in Canada. The latter accord was rejected in referenda by a majority both in Québec, and in the rest of Canada. Following such failures to bring back Québec into the constitutional fold "in honour and enthusiasm",[15] a Québec government led by an independentist party called a referendum on Québec's secession from Canada. The results of the 1995 Referendum were 50,58 per cent against the proposal to 49,42 per cent in favour (93,52 per cent participation rate). Since then, both the federalist and the independentist camps have not made concrete attempts to settle the issue once and for all.

What does that brief overview of Canadian constitutional history tell us about the prevailing legal and political culture, including traditional conceptions of the nature of the constitution, law and the proper role of courts? Eight points must be highlighted for our purposes.

First, the Canadian constitutional tradition owes a lot to the British one.[16] Canadians use the term "constitution" to refer to what Continental jurists call the "material constitution"[17] (or "constitution" with a lower-case "c"), that is, the set of rules, principles and practices that *constitute* and give shape to the primary powers of government. What makes those elements "constitutional" is not their rank in a normative hierarchy, but rather their subject-matter. In fact, some "practices" may count as being part of the constitutional make-up of Canada without even having a normative aspect. This means that some judicial decisions forming the

[13] *Re: Objection by Quebec to a Resolution to amend the Constitution*, [1982] 2 S.C.R. 793 [*Reference re Quebec veto*].

[14] Now called the Province of Newfoundland and Labrador (*Constitution Amendment, 2001 (Newfoundland and Labrador)*, SI/2001–117).

[15] That was the promise made by Prime Minister Brian Mulroney (Progressive-Conservative) – successor to Pierre-Elliott Trudeau (Liberal) who had patriated the Constitution in 1982 without Quebec's consent.

[16] The preamble of the *Constitution Act, 1867* states explicitly: "Whereas the Provinces of Canada, Nova Scotia, and New Brunswick have expressed their Desire to be federally united into One Dominion under the Crown of the United Kingdom of Great Britain and Ireland, with a Constitution similar in Principle to that of the United Kingdom".

[17] H. Cyr, 'L'absurdité du critère scriptural pour qualifier la Constitution' (2011) 6 *Revue de droit parlementaire et politique* 293.

Canadian constitutional canon may be about rules, principles or practices that are not formally entrenched. Also, whereas many constitutional rules, in the material sense, may be legal in nature, many are simply intergovernmental agreements or "constitutional conventions".[18] Constitutional conventions are non-legal constitutional rules that are taken to be binding by the relevant political agents in part by reason of their antiquity, but mostly because of the reasons that underlie them.[19] They are not to be taken lightly as they often override, in practice, the legally binding constitutional norms. For example, the Governor General, despite having the legal right to refuse to assent to bills passed by both Houses of Parliament,[20] or to disallow a provincial statute that has been adopted in the last two years,[21] would be said to have acted *unconstitutionally* if he were to exercise this right because of clear "constitutional conventions" prohibiting such actions. Moreover, constitutional conventions are somewhat like the constitutional flesh to the constitutional bone. For example, the office of "Prime Minister" does not appear in the *Constitution Act, 1867*, and is merely mentioned, but not defined, in certain sections of the *Constitution Act, 1982*. None of the 28 federal statutes to ever mention it defined its functions or how the position is to be filled.[22] The Prime Minister is a creation of constitutional conventions, and no one would be capable of understanding how the Canadian political system works without knowing her/his roles. But constitutional conventions, no matter how powerful they are in practice, are not fully justiciable; courts may confirm their existence, but they will not sanction their violation.[23] Therefore, such an important set of constitutional norms (and the way that they are interpreted) will mostly escape our attention here as the common project's goal is focused on examining how *courts* reason about constitutional norms.[24]

Second, Canada being originally a British colony, its legislatures and governments expected, right from the start, that their powers were limited

18 See, for example, the agreement at issue in the *Reference Re Canada Assistance Plan (B.C.)*, [1991] 2 S.C.R. 525 [*Canada Assistance Plan*].

19 *Re: Resolution to amend the Constitution*, [1981] 1 S.C.R. 753, at 888ff [*Patriation Reference*].

20 *CA 1867*, s. 55.

21 *Ibid*, ss 56 and 90.

22 See H. Cyr, 'De la formation du gouvernement' (2013) 43 *Revue générale de droit* 381, fn 39.

23 *Patriation Reference, supra* n 19, at 880 (majority) and 853 (minority).

24 There are two notable exceptions in our list of cases forming the canon where constitutional conventions played a crucial role: *Patriation Reference, supra* n 19 and *Reference re Quebec veto, supra* n 13.

by the Imperial laws that had created them. So, for Canadians, the term "constitution" *also* means the set of rules and principles that are supreme within a legal system – i.e. the term may refer to what Continental jurists call the "formal constitution" (or "Constitution" with a capital "C").[25] Colonial powers being limited, there had to be an agent to ensure that the limits were respected. Constitutional review, therefore, has a long tradition in Canada. While it must be noted that constitutional review was often exercised by the Governor General through its powers to refuse to sanction federal bills, to reserve Bills for the signification of Her Majesty's pleasure and to disallow provincial statutes recognized by ss. 55–57 of the *Constitution Act, 1867*, constitutional review of legislation was, by the end of the nineteenth century, exercised by the judiciary.[26]

Third, Canadian appeals to the Judicial Committee of the Privy Council being only abolished in 1949, a large part of the Canadian constitutional law canon was actually produced by British jurists. Indeed, until those appeals were abolished, major Supreme Court of Canada cases tended to end up being appealed in London and were only studied in Canada as preliminary decisions leading to the Privy Council's final opinion. Thus, the major cases establishing the foundations of the Canadian federal system were ultimately the product of the Privy Council. Because the common guidelines of this project require that we focus only on the top domestic constitutional jurisdiction, our presentation of the canon of Canadian constitutional law will necessarily be significantly truncated.

Fourth, while Canada was slowly gaining its autonomy, judicial review remained *legally* justified by old Imperial instruments. However, politically, the institution reached a point where it had to be justified in terms

[25] Such rules and principles, however, do not all find their explicit expression in written constitutional instruments. Apart from Imperial laws, certain federal statutes (e.g. the statutes that created the Provinces of Manitoba, Alberta and Saskatchewan) and constitutional instruments adopted according to the current constitutional modification procedures, the Constitution also contains implied constitutional principles. The Supreme Court has previously identified, among others, "judicial independence", "federalism", "democracy", "the rule of law and constitutionalism" and the "protection of minorities" as constitutional principles. The Supreme Court described such principles in the *Reference re Secession of Quebec*, [1998] 2 S.C.R. 217 paras 49, 51–54 [*Reference re Secession of Quebec*].

[26] B.L. Strayer, *Judicial Review of Legislation in Canada* (University of Toronto Press 1968) 3. Gordon Bale, however, demonstrates that the first case of *judicial* review post-*Constitution Act, 1867* was met with significant resistance by the provincial legislature. There were indeed debates as to who should control the validity of laws: the Governor General or courts? See Gordon Bale, 'The New Brunswick Origin of Canadian Judicial Review' (1991) 40 *U.N.B. L.J.* 100.

of a Constitution that *belongs* to Canadians. That is what the 1982 Constitution was meant to achieve. While the formal Constitution of Canada no longer consists of Imperial rules towering over domestic statutes, s. 52(1) of the *Constitution Act, 1982* maintains that "[t]he Constitution of Canada is the supreme law of Canada, and any law that is inconsistent with the provisions of the Constitution is, to the extent of the inconsistency, of no force or effect." Constitutional review is now justified on the basis that the Constitution is the supreme law of the land. The text of the Constitution does not expressly mention that *courts* ought to be in charge of constitutional review. However, judges having long claimed to be the "guardians of legality" and see themselves as being entrusted by the People with the duty to ensure that they only apply rules consistent with the constitutional standards adopted by the democratically elected representatives.[27] This comes with one *caveat*: the *Canadian Charter* innovated by allowing Parliament and legislatures to override for a renewable five years certain constitutional rights through express declaration to that effect.[28] However, the "notwithstanding clause" has rarely been used by provinces and has never been used by the Parliament.

Fifth, the Canadian constitutional tradition being one of slow but gradual transformation, it values continuity over rupture. The general narrative that sustains the Canadian constitutional culture is that the constitution is an "unfinished" business.[29] Canadians cannot look back in time to find a Golden Age of constitution-making when "We the People" came together, on their own, to adopt their basic law. The constitutional Holy Grail for Canadians – to the extent they think that it may exist – is perceived as being somewhere in the distant future. A famous Canadian constitutional scholar summarised the Canadian constitutional predicament with the title of one of his books: *Constitutional Odyssey: Can Canadians Become a Sovereign People?*[30]

Constitutional interpretation is seen as part of a collective quest towards ever better constitutional arrangements. Canadians expect their Constitution to "evolve" over time. The dominant metaphor comes from an opinion of Lord Sankey of the British Judicial Committee of the Privy Council writing, in 1929, that "[the *Constitution Act, 1867*] planted in

27 See *Re B.C. Motor Vehicle Act*, [1985] 2 S.C.R. 486 at para. 16 [*Re B.C. Motor Vehicle Act*].

28 *CA 1982*, s. 33.

29 See generally H. Cyr, 'Conceptual Metaphors for an Unfinished Constitution' (2014) 19 *Rev. Const. St.* 1.

30 Peter H. Russell, *Constitutional Odyssey: Can Canadians Become a Sovereign People?*, 3d ed. (University of Toronto Press 2004).

Canada *a living tree capable of growth and expansion within its natural limits*".[31] Apart from some discrete sectors of Canadian constitutional law,[32] purely textual or originalist arguments tend to have little purchase in constitutional litigation. To be taken seriously, they must be cast in teleological terms. This means, for example, that courts may not consider what the framers meant by the use of a specific expression, but they will be interested in the function the rule was meant to serve, the general type of problem it was meant to solve and how such issues are instantiated in the contemporary world. The Supreme Court maintains that "[a] large and liberal, or progressive, interpretation ensures the continued relevance and, indeed, legitimacy of Canada's constituting document."[33]

Sixth, the *Constitution Act, 1982* provoked a change of focus in Canadian constitutional discourse. Previously, constitutional law was mostly about *powers*: Imperial powers as opposed to domestic ones, and the internal division of powers between the central government and the provinces. The adoption of the *Canadian Charter of Rights and Freedoms* created a shift towards a discourse about *rights*. In a sense, the issue was no longer who could commit the injustice, but which injustices would no longer be permitted . . . Commitment to progressive interpretativism means that constitutional rights are not presented as entrenching rights dictated by "the Law of Nature", but as representing the evolving product of the history, values, cultures and social philosophies of the country. Human rights entrenched in the *Charter* are mainly interpreted according to a "purposive" approach.[34] In defining the scope and purpose of *Charter* rights, the Supreme Court writes that it "must be guided by the values and principles essential to a free and democratic society which I believe to embody, to name but a few, respect for the inherent dignity of the human

[31] *Edwards v Attorney General for Canada*, [1930] AC 124 at 136 [emphasis added].

[32] See discussion, *infra* in section B.7.

[33] *Reference re Same-Sex Marriage*, [2004] 3 S.C.R. 698, para. 23 [*Reference re Same-Sex Marriage*]. However, in one of the early *Charter* cases, Justice McIntyre, writing for himself only, warned that while a "liberal and not overly legalistic approach should be taken to constitutional interpretation, the *Charter* should not be regarded as an empty vessel to be filled with whatever meaning we might wish from time to time. The interpretation of the *Charter*, as of all constitutional documents, is constrained by the language, structure, and history of the constitutional text, by constitutional tradition, and by the history, traditions, and underlying philosophies of our society" (*Reference Re Public Service Employee Relations Act (Alta.)*, [1987] 1 S.C.R. 313 at 394 [*Reference Re Public Service Employee Relations Act*]).

[34] The *locus classicus* for *Charter* rights interpretation is *R. v. Big M Drug Mart Ltd.*, [1985] 1 SCR 295 at paras 116–117 (Chief Justice Dickson, for the majority) [*Big M Drug Mart*].

person, commitment to social justice and equality, accommodation of a wide variety of beliefs, respect for cultural and group identity, and faith in social and political institutions which enhance the participation of individuals and groups in society".[35] In short, "[i]t is well accepted that the *Charter* should be given a generous and expansive interpretation and not a narrow, technical, or legalistic one."[36] This purposive interpretation is not limited to the rights in themselves; it is also used to ensure that "a full, effective and meaningful remedy for Charter violations"[37] will be available through courts.

This "Rights revolution", combined with the dominant progressive ethos of constitutional interpretation, have allowed judges a significant amount of leeway in crafting solutions to constitutional problems. The most extreme case of creative constitutional development by the Court is probably to be found in *Reference re Remuneration of Judges of the Provincial Court (P.E.I.)*[38] where the Court used a combination of the right for a person charged with an offense to a "fair and public hearing by an independent and impartial tribunal" and a statement in the preamble of the *Constitution Act, 1867* that is "similar in Principle to that of the United Kingdom" to flesh out a full principle of judicial independence.[39] From that principle, the Court concluded that governments could not unilaterally reduce the financial treatment of judges as part of a general budget deficit reduction plan that applies to the entire public sector without affecting judicial independence. In fact, governments could not freeze salaries of the entire judiciary if there is inflation as this would amount to a pay cut. The Court then devised a new constitutionally mandatory system whereby Parliament and Legislatures must, in principle, act upon recommendations on judges' remuneration given by specially created "independent, objective and effective" committees. Such committees are effectively pure creations of the Court. If Parliament and Legislatures disagree with the recommendations of the committees, they may set salaries for the judiciary on their own, but such salaries will be subject to judicial

[35] *R. v. Oakes*, [1986] 1 S.C.R. 103 at 136 [*Oakes*].

[36] *Doucet-Boudreau v. Nova Scotia (Minister of Education)*, [2003] 3 SCR 3, para. 23 [*Doucet-Boudreau*]. In support of this proposition, the majority of the Court refers to a series of classic cases: *Hunter v. Southam Inc.*, [1984] 2 S.C.R. 145; *Big M Drug Mart, supra* n 34; *Re B.C. Motor Vehicle Act, supra* n 27; *Reference re Prov. Electoral Boundaries (Sask.)*, [1991] 2 S.C.R. 158 and *Vriend v. Alberta*, [1998] 1 S.C.R. 493 [*Vriend*].

[37] *R. v. 974649 Ontario Inc.*, [2001] 3 S.C.R. 575, 2001 SCC 81, para. 19.

[38] Reference re Remuneration of Judges of the Provincial Court (P.E.I.), [1998] 2 S.C.R. 443 [Reference re Remuneration of Judges of the Provincial Court (P.E.I.)].

[39] *Charter*, s. 11(d).

scrutiny according to a "rationality" standard. What is most astonishing about this episode is probably the fact that, seven years earlier, Chief Justice Lamer, who wrote the Court's majority opinion in the *Reference*, had asked then Justice Minister Kim Campbell to include provisions protecting judicial independence in what would become the failed *Charlottetown Agreement* (1992).[40] However, no such provision had been included in the final draft of the Accord.

Seventh, constitutional interpretation is not understood, in Canada, to differ significantly from statutory interpretation. Of course, the terms of the Constitution may be broad and abstract, but so are the terms used in quasi-constitutional statutes dealing with human rights. Canadian courts have long adopted a flexible "contextual" approach to statutory interpretation that allows for an eclectic mix of interpretative arguments to be used.[41] That being said, this flexibility was to a large extent the product of the adoption of the *Constitution Act, 1982*. Prior to its adoption, judges were much more timid in protecting rights guaranteed in human rights statutes.[42] The entrenchment of the *Charter* definitely sent a signal to the judiciary that they benefited from more leeway in crafting appropriate remedies.[43]

Eighth, all the constitutional instruments adopted by the British Parliament up until 1982 have been written in English. Only the English version of such documents is authoritative. The *Constitution Act, 1982*, has been adopted in the two official languages of Canada (English and French) and, therefore, requires to be interpreted following a method that reconciles both versions.[44]

[40] Letter dated October 21, 1991 from Chief Justice Antonio Lamer to the Justice Minister Kim Campbell. See M.L. Friedland, *Une place à part: l'indépendance et la responsabilité de la magistrature au Canada* (Canadian Judicial Council 1995) 27–8.

[41] This approach is summarized in this quote – first cited by the Supreme Court in *Vachon v. Canada Employment and Immigration Commission*, [1985] 2 S.C.R. 417, (Beetz J. for an unanimous Court) has since been repeated 46 times – of E. A. Driedger, *The Construction of Statutes*, 2nd (Butterworth 1983) 87: "Today there is only one principle or approach, namely, the words of an Act are to be read in their entire context and in their grammatical and ordinary sense harmoniously with the scheme of the Act, the object of the Act, and the intention of Parliament.".

[42] E.g. *Attorney General of Canada v. Lavell*, [1974] S.C.R. 1349; *Miller et al. v. The Queen*, [1977] 2 S.C.R. 680; *Bliss v. Attorney General of Canada*, [1979] 1 S.C.R. 183.

[43] S. 24 (1) of the *Charter* is quite explicit: "Anyone whose rights or freedoms, as guaranteed by this Charter, have been infringed or denied may apply to a court of competent jurisdiction to obtain such remedy as the court considers appropriate and just in the circumstances."

[44] See *infra* nn 125-133 and accompanying text.

2 *The Court and Constitutional Litigation*

In Canada, constitutional review fits to a large extent the so-called American model of judicial review.[45] No institution has an exclusive jurisdiction over constitutional review; all courts and administrative tribunals have the power to review the constitutionality of statutes and governmental actions. Constitutional law cases usually reach the Supreme Court after being granted a leave to appeal by the Supreme Court,[46] or because they fall under one of the exceptional criminal law cases that come with an automatic right of appeal to the highest tribunal.[47] Constitutional review is mostly an *in concreto* and *a posteriori* process that is conducted in the course of regular legal proceedings. For example, an accused may raise the constitutionality of the statute that created the offense with which he is charged, a private litigant may challenge the constitutionality of a statute that restricts his freedom of expression, a divorced parent may seek to have part of a child custody statute struck down because it violates one of her *Charter* rights, etc.

The Supreme Court may declare a statute of no force or effect – or "inoperable" – by reason of its inconsistency with the Constitution, but it may also decide to invalidate only the problematic portions of the statute in question. But these are not the only remedies available when a legal rule violates the Constitution.[48] An impugned legal rule may also be "read down" to conform to the Constitution – i.e. otherwise open-ended terms in a legal rule are read in a restrictive way in order to limit the scope of the rule to constitutionally valid applications.[49] The Supreme Court may also extend the scope of statutory provisions through the process of "reading in" elements that were unconstitutionally excluded from the

[45] For a very powerful and convincing critique of the artificial opposition between the so-called "American model" and the "European model" of constitutional review, see Guillaume Tusseau, *Contre les "modèles" de justice constitutionnelle: essai de critique méthodologique – Modelli di giustizia costituzionale: saggio di critica metodologica* (Bononia University Press 2009).

[46] *Supreme Court Act*, R.S.C., 1985, c. S-26, ss 37–43 [*Supreme Court Act*].

[47] See *Criminal Code*, R.S.C. 1985, c. C-46, ss 691–693.

[48] A list of the possible remedies and the criteria to be used to select the appropriate ones in a specific cases are examined at length in *Schachter v. Canada*, [1992] 2 S.C.R. 679 [*Schachter*].

[49] For example, in *McKay v. The Queen*, [1965] S.C.R. 798, the Court held that a general municipal ordinance prohibiting the erection of unauthorized signs on private properties had to be "read down" in order to avoid encroaching on federal competence over federal elections. The general prohibition on posting signs on one's lawn was thus read as not intended to be applicable to federal election signs.

challenged legal rule. For example, in *Vriend v. Alberta*,[50] the Supreme Court of Canada "read in" "sexual orientation" as a prohibited ground of discrimination in an otherwise exhaustive list contained in an anti-discrimination statute from the Province of Alberta. The Court may also suspend its declaration of unconstitutionality for a certain period of time to allow Parliament or Legislatures to rectify the situation.[51]

In principle, the effects of the decision are only between the parties to the litigation. However, through the common law principle of precedent, the effects of a judicial decision may extend to other cases as well. The Supreme Court decisions bind all the courts below, but the decisions of Courts of Appeal are strictly binding only within their respective provinces, and they are considered pertinent and persuasive elsewhere.

The constitutional review process in Canada sometimes departs from the *in concreto* model. Indeed, through the "reference" mechanism, the executive may ask courts for advisory opinions on important questions of law or fact.[52] The reference mechanism may be used to test the constitutionality of statutes *a posteriori* of their adoption, but it may also be used *a priori* to verify the validity of a bill prior to its adoption[53] or to check the constitutionality of a proposed course of action by the executive.[54] The Court enjoys a certain degree of discretion in deciding to answer reference questions and may refuse to answer such questions if they are "purely" political.[55] While there are no apparent constitutional impediments for the federal government (the "Governor in Council") to referring such questions to Courts of Appeal (either the provincial courts or the Federal Court of Appeal), the current statute directs its references questions to the Supreme Court of Canada. Provincial governments may also refer such questions to their respective Courts of Appeal. The latter's opinions may then be appealed to the Supreme Court of Canada.[56] Judicial opinions given as a result of a reference are often said by the

50 *Vriend, supra* n 36.

51 See e.g. *Reference re Manitoba Language Rights*, [1985] 1 SCR 721 [*Reference re Manitoba Language Rights*] or *M. v. H.*, [1999] 2 S.C.R. 3.

52 The Senate and the House of Commons also enjoy a limited statutory right to seek the opinion of the Supreme Court, or two of its judges, on private bills (or petition for a private bill), but this mechanism is very rarely – if it ever has been – used. See *Supreme Court Act, supra* n 46, s. 54.

53 See e.g. *Reference re Same-Sex Marriage, supra* n 33.

54 See e.g. *Re: Authority of Parliament in relation to the Upper House*, [1980] 1 S.C.R. 54 [*Senate Reference (1980)*] and *Patriation Reference, supra* n 19.

55 *Reference re Secession of Quebec, supra* n 25 at para 28.

56 *Supreme Court Act, supra* n 46, s. 36.

Supreme Court not to be technically subject to the rule of precedent; however, such proposition is debatable in light of the Supreme Court's own practices.[57]

Apart from leaves to appeal and some procedural issues, the Supreme Court does not decide cases simply based on written records; there are always hearings before a decision is delivered on the merits. Litigants may present both their written submissions and their oral arguments in either of the two official languages (English and French). The Court may sometimes decide not to hear the respondent in a case when, after hearing the appellant, it is satisfied that the latter has not demonstrated that a mistake was made by the appellate jurisdiction. The Court may then deliver an oral judgment from the bench. However, most of the time, the Court reserves its judgments for later.

The Court rather liberally grants permission to intervene to other parties who have an interest in the issues being debated. The advent of polycentric cases under the *Charter* where rights and interests of multiple groups and individuals are at play has increased such opportunities.[58] When permitted to participate in an appeal, the interveners must accept the record as it has been defined by the main parties.[59] The federal government as well as provinces will often intervene in constitutional cases to ensure that their interests are protected. The Supreme Court also has discretion to appoint *amici curiae* "to argue the case with respect to any interest that is affected and with respect to which counsel does not appear".[60]

The regular rules of evidence generally apply to constitutional cases. However, courts will also consider a wider range of social and legislative facts based on complex social science evidence.[61] Trial judges' findings on these matters are entitled to deference, "absent a palpable and overriding error".[62] While the general standard of proof in constitutional cases is

[57] See the precedent-like effects of *Reference re Manitoba Language Rights, supra* n 51 on *Bilodeau v. Manitoba (Attorney General)*, [1986] 1 S.C.R. 449. For an illuminating analysis of references in Canada and their concrete effects, see F. Chevrette and G.Webber, 'L'utilisation de la procédure de l'avis consultatif devant la Cour suprême du Canada: Essai de typologie' (2003) 82 Can. Bar Rev. 757.

[58] *McKinney v. University of Guelph*, [1990] 3 S.C.R. 229, at p. 304.

[59] *R. v. Marshall*, [1999] 3 SCR 533, para. 9.

[60] *Supreme Court Act, supra* n 46, s. 53 (7).

[61] This practice tended to be frowned upon until the Supreme Court allowed parties to present evidence in relation to the gravity of the inflationary situation in *Re: Anti-Inflation Act*, [1976] 2 S.C.R. 373 [*Re: Anti-Inflation Act*]. The practice of referring to "legislative facts" became more widespread with the advent of the *Charter*.

[62] *Canada (Attorney General) v. Bedford*, 2013 SCC 72, para. 48.

the preponderance of probability,[63] Parliament and the Legislatures are "afforded a margin of appreciation to form legitimate objectives based on somewhat inconclusive social science evidence" when attempting to justify infringements upon *Charter* rights.[64] In fact, the Supreme Court recognized that in the absence of solid social science evidence, "a reasonable apprehension of harm" could be sufficient to ground an argument on the first stage of analysis of s. 1, the saving proviso, of the *Charter*.[65] Also, in Aboriginal rights cases, the Supreme Court has relaxed the admissibility threshold of what would otherwise be qualified as hearsay to allow traditional songs and legends to be adduced as valid evidence of historical occupation of land.[66]

An amendment to the *Supreme Court Act* adopted in 1975 eliminated most cases with an automatic right to appeal to the Court,[67] thus empowering the institution with a significant amount of control over its own docket.[68] The Supreme Court of Canada has received, on average, 541 complete applications for leave to appeal per year between 2002 and 2012.[69] Leave to appeal has been granted every year to about 12 per cent of those applications.[70] On average, 14 notices of appeal as of right have been filed every year during the same period.[71] This means that the Supreme Court heard about 75 cases per year during that period.[72] This is a marked decline from the previous decade.[73] In 2012, only 17 per cent of the appeals heard by the Supreme Court dealt with constitutional and

63 See especially *Oakes*, *supra* n 35 at para. 67 on s. 1 of the *Charter*.

64 *Irwin Toy Ltd. v. Quebec (Attorney General)*, [1989] 1 S.C.R. 927, at 990.

65 *R. v. Butler*, [1992] 1 S.C.R. 452, at p. 503; *R. v. Keegstra*, [1990] 3 S.C.R. 697, at 768, 776 [*Keegstra*]; *RJR-MacDonald Inc. v. Canada (Attorney General)*, [1995] 3 S.C.R. 199, at para. 137; *Thomson Newspapers Co. v. Canada (Attorney General)*, [1998] 1 S.C.R. 877 at paras 104–7; *R. v. Sharpe*, [2001] 1 S.C.R. 45, 2001 SCC 2; *Harper v. Canada (Attorney General)*, [2004] 1 S.C.R. 827, 2004 SCC 33, para. 77–79; *R. v. Bryan*, [2007] 1 S.C.R. 527, 2007 SCC 12, para. 20.

66 *Delgamuukw v. British Columbia*, [1997] 3 S.C.R. 1010, at para. 93–101 [*Delgamuukw*].

67 S.C. 1974–75–76, c. 18, s. 5 amending the then *Supreme Court Act*, R.C.S. 1970, c. S-19, now *Supreme Court Act*, *supra* n 46.

68 *Supreme Court Act*, *supra* n 46, s. 40 (1).

69 Supreme Court of Canada, *Statistics 2002 to 2012. Summary*, internet: http://www.scc-csc.gc.ca/case-dossier/stat/sum-som-eng.aspx [*Statistics 2002 to 2012. Summary*].

70 Ibid. 71 Ibid. 72 Ibid.

73 Between 1987 and 1997, the Court heard, on average, 120 decisions per year. 1997 started a trend downwards with only 104 decision heard. While this larger caseload of the Court may be explained in part by the fact that many more "as of rights" cases reached the Supreme Court during that period (47 cases on average per year), the Court also was more generous in granting leave to appeal (on average 77 cases per year between 1987 and 1996). (Supreme Court of Canada, *Statistiques 1987 à 1997: Bulletin des procédures:*

human rights matters.[74] On average, 72 per cent of the decisions were unanimous between 2002 and 2012[75] and appeals were allowed in 37 per cent of cases.[76] While 20 decisions were delivered from the bench in 2002, this fell to only 2 in 2007 and 2009.[77] All decisions – even those delivered from the bench – are published in both English and French.

There is no commonly accepted typology of judgments *specific* to constitutional cases. The Supreme Court, for example, may issue declaratory judgments, it may rule on the admissibility of evidence obtained in contravention of the *Charter*, it may advise the government on the existence and application of certain constitutional imperatives in the course of references, it may strike down statutes that violate the division of legislative powers between Parliament and Legislatures, etc.

3 *The Judges*

The Supreme Court of Canada is composed of the Chief Justice of Canada and eight puisne judges.[78] All judges must have been members in good standing for 10 years at the bar of a province.[79] Three seats are constitutionally reserved for judges appointed directly from the Superior Court, from the Court of Appeal of Québec, or from the current members of the Québec bar, to ensure the protection of the distinct civil law tradition of the province.[80] By convention, the remaining six judges have the following connections: one judge is from British Columbia, one from the Prairies (the provinces of Alberta, Saskatchewan and Manitoba), three from Ontario and one from Atlantic Canada (New Brunswick, Nova Scotia, Prince Edward Island and Newfoundland and Labrador). Judges "hold office during good behaviour"[81] and they serve until they reach the age of 75.[82]

édition special (Supreme Court of Canada 1998) (available at https://web.archive.org/web/19980626114315/ http://www.scc-csc.gc.ca/statistics/fcourt.pdf).

74 Supreme Court of Canada, *Statistics 2002 to 2012. Category 3: Appeals Heard*, internet: http://www.scc-csc.gc.ca/case-dossier/stat/cat3-eng.aspx. [*Statistics 2002 to 2012 Category 3: Appeals Heard*].

75 *Statistics 2002 to 2012. Summary*, *supra* n 69.

76 *Statistics 2002 to 2012 Category 3: Appeals Heard*, *supra* n 74.

77 *Statistics 2002 to 2012. Summary*, *supra* n 69.

78 *Supreme Court Act*, *supra* n 46, s. 4(1).

79 Ibid, s. 5.

80 Ibid, s. 6. See *Reference re Supreme Court Act, ss. 5 and 6*, 2014 SCC 21 [*Reference re Supreme Court Act, ss. 5 and 6*].

81 Ibid, s. 9 (1). No Supreme Court judge has ever been removed from office on this basis.

82 Ibid., s. 9(2).

Technically, judges are appointed by the Governor in Council by letters patent under the Great Seal of Canada,[83] but in practice, this means that the Prime Minister of Canada ultimately decides whom she or he will appoint. The appointment is the end result of a process that is still in flux, as there have been several attempts in the last decade to find an appropriate set of consultation mechanisms. Between 2006 and 2016, appointments were the product of a non-binding consultation led by the Minister of Justice and Attorney General of Canada with the Attorneys General of the relevant provinces,[84] the Chief Justice of such provinces, the Chief Justice of the relevant provincial Superior Courts, the Chief Justice of the Federal Court of Appeal and the Chief Justice of the Federal Court, as well as representatives of prominent legal organizations, including the relevant provincial bars and the Canadian Bar Association. A long-list of qualified candidates was then sent to a selection panel for review. The selection panel is composed of five Members of Parliament: three members were taken from the Government caucus and the others were selected by the two officially recognised Opposition caucuses. The selection panel provided to the Prime Minister and the Minister of Justice an unranked list of three qualified and recommended candidates. Deliberations of the selection panel were entirely confidential. However, there are clearly no indications that the recommendations made by the committee were unanimous; members of the Government caucus, having a majority of votes, could thus safely ensure that the Government's preferred candidate would make the final list. The Prime Minister then selected a candidate from the short-list and the nominee appeared at a public hearing of an *ad hoc* committee of the Parliament to answer tightly controlled questions; the hearing was more in the nature of a public presentation of the nominee, rather than a vetting process. The nominee was then sworn in.[85]

In 2016, the newly elected government put in place a new informal appointment process whereby an independent and non-partisan advisory board composed of seven members (four of whom are selected by independent professional organisations) is tasked with reviewing applications. The advisory board must submit a short-list of three to

[83] Ibid, s. 4 (2).

[84] The failed *Meech Lake Accord*, s. 101C, would have provided that the Federal government would not only consult the relevant provinces, but that it would only appoint qualified candidates submitted by such provinces.

[85] On the appointment process and the recent *Reference re Supreme Court Act, ss. 5 and 6, supra* n 80 see generally, H. Cyr, 'The Bungling of Justice Nadon's Appointment to the Supreme Court of Canada' (2014) 67 *Sup Ct L. Rev.* 73.

five candidates for consideration to the Prime Minister. The assessment criteria used by the advisory board, the questionnaire filled by applicants and the answers given to that questionnaire by the eventual nominee are made public. Once the Prime Minister has made his selection known, the Minister of Justice and the chair of the advisory board appear before Parliament to discuss the appointment process and answer questions as to the qualifications of the nominee. An informal public session of "questions and answers", led by an academic, is then held with a number of parliamentarians from all federal parties and the nominee before his or her appointment to the Supreme Court.

Up until the mid-1950s, the federal government often appointed former politicians to the Supreme Court. However, this practice gave way in favour of a certain "professionalization" of the magistrates. Now, a strong majority of the appointees are former Court of Appeal judges, and sometimes Superior Court justices[86] or exemplary legal practitioners.[87] In recent decades, there have been two or three former academics on the bench at all times, but they were first appointed to a Court of Appeal and only subsequently called to the Supreme Court.

4 *Legal Scholarship and Constitutional Reasoning*

If being a full professor ("professeur titulaire"), or if holding a Chair in constitutional law is prestigious in Canadian society, it simply does not compare to the status of a Supreme Court judge. Being appointed to the Supreme Court is considered the pinnacle of a legal career. This is reflected in the income expected by law professors and Supreme Court judges. Whereas law professors' entry salaries may range from about $70 000 to $110 000, probably fewer than 10 professors in the entire country will earn salaries higher than $270 000, and such high salaries usually come with significant administrative duties such as those of a deanship. The yearly salary of the Chief Justice of the Supreme Court, however, is $370 000 and the other eight justices earn $342 000 each.[88]

Although black-letter law scholarship is still present in Canadian law schools, it is no longer dominant as it used to be. Legal scholarship is widely varied. Scholars engage in a wide range of interdisciplinary projects

[86] See e.g. Justice Charles D. Gonthier (1989–2003).

[87] See e.g. Justice Ian C. Binnie (1998–2011). For a short profile of his career, see http://www.scc-csc.gc.ca/court-cour/judges-juges/bio-eng.aspx?id=william-ian-corneil-binnie

[88] *Judges Act*, R.S.C., 1985, c. J-1, s. 9 (1) and 9 (2).

(e.g. "sociology of law", "law and economics", "law and literature", or "law and psychology"). Those who work on legal doctrine tend to maintain a healthy critical distance from the Court's opinions. Courts are not impervious to scholarly criticisms and doctrinal developments; they frequently refer with approval – or disapproval – to academic works. For example, Peter Hogg's book *Constitutional Law of Canada* is the second most often cited piece of academic writing by the Supreme Court.[89] Another good illustration of this practice is the Supreme Court's frequent reference to Peter Hogg and Allison A. Bushell's article entitled "The *Charter* Dialogue between Courts and Legislatures"[90] in which the authors proposed a theory aiming at reconciling judicial review and the democratic roles of legislatures in Canada.

B Arguments in Constitutional Reasoning

5 *The Structure of Constitutional Arguments*

Constitutional law cases are rarely simple enough to be solved through mere "one-line conclusive" arguments.[91] Rather, constitutional arguments have more traditionally been constructed around the "legs of a chair" structure consisting of cumulative-parallel arguments, each being sufficient on its own. However, with the advent of *Charter* litigation and polycentric constitutional issues, the so-called dialogic structure based on a range of relevant considerations – none of which alone is conclusive – appears to be also common[92].

[89] As of January 17th, 2014, the search in the Supreme Court of Canada' judgments database for "Côté" and "interpretation des loi" yielded 209 results (http://scc-csc.lexum.com/decisia-scc-csc/scc-csc/fr/d/s/index.do?cont=côté+and+%22interprétation+des+lois%22&ref=&d1=&d2=&p=&col=1&su=0). The search for "Constitutional Law of Canada" and "Hogg" returned 165 cases (http://scc-csc.lexum.com/decisia-scc-csc/scc-csc/en/d/s/index.do?cont=%22constitutional+law+of+canada%22+and+hogg&ref=&d1=&d2=&p=&col=1&su=0). "Driedger" and "*Construction of Statutes*" is a close third with 164 cases.

[90] Peter W. Hogg and Allison A. Bushell, 'The *Charter* Dialogue Between Courts and Legislatures' (1997) 35 Osgoode Hall L.J. 75. This article has been cited 6 times between 1998 and 2002.

[91] For further details about the present terminology see András Jakab, 'Constitutional Reasoning. A European Perspective on Judicial Reasoning in Constitutional Courts' (2013) 14 *German Law Journal*, available at http://www.germanlawjournal.com/index.php?pageID=11&artID=1553 [Jakab, "Constitutional Reasoning"].

[92] See for example the Court's analysis of the requirements of "fundamental justice" under s. 7 of the *Charter* in *United States v. Burns*, 2001 SCC 7, [2001] 1 S.C.R. 283 [*Burns*].

6 *Types of Arguments in Constitutional Reasoning*

Nowhere do the Canadian constitutional instruments declare what types of arguments are valid ones when engaging in constitutional review. Eclecticism now rules the day in constitutional interpretation![93] Courts rely, among other things, on:

- textual arguments, both in the narrow textualist sense of examining the meaning of the specific words used in the constitutional text (in both English and French), as well as in the wider sense of interpreting the meaning of a proposition in light of the rest of the constitutional texts (systemic approach);
- *historical arguments*, including references to the putative intentions of the framers of the Constitution;
- *authority-based arguments*, including binding precedents, relevant and persuasive international and foreign legal norms, and convenient scholarly works;
- *teleological arguments*, including arguments about (a) institutional functions, (b) value-based finalities and (c) implied constitutional principles that sustain the Constitution;
- *pragmatic arguments based on institutional practices and interpretative presumptions*, including arguments based on assumptions concerning the normal functioning of institutions and interpretative heuristics (such as the "argument from silence");
- *social context arguments*, including arguments about the specific political, economical, sociological, historical, psychological, etc. contexts in which a constitutional norm is to be applied.

This explains why most of the types of arguments identified by the working group are found at one point or another in Canadian jurisprudence. Here are more precise comments on the different types of arguments as they are found in the Canadian canon of constitutional law.

Establishing the Existence of an Applicable Constitutional Norm

i Filling Gaps through Analogies In order to ensure a common vocabulary among all the studies in this project, we do *not* use the term "analogy"

[93] See H. Cyr, 'L'interprétation constitutionnelle, un exemple de postpluralisme' (1998) 43 *McGill L.J.* 565 at 569–80 for an analysis and for illustrations of the eclectic uses of interpretative methods in Canadian constitutional law.

to refer to the simple extension of a precedent by analogy – which is done in almost all Constitutional cases of importance in Canada. Instead, the term is reserved here to cases where there may be an apparent *lacuna* in the *express texts of the entrenched constitutional instruments*, and this gap is filled through the identification of a norm by means of a comparison with already established norms that are applicable in similar situations.

Constitutional decisions by means of *analogia legis*[94] is rather rare (if it ever happens). However, *analogia iuris*[95] has been rather common since the late 1990s. This is the case because the Supreme Court has started to explicitly invoke implied constitutional principles in major cases such as *New Brunswick Broadcasting Co. v. Nova Scotia (Speaker of the House of Assembly)*,[96] *Reference re Remuneration of Judges of the Provincial Court (P.E.I.)*[97] and *Reference re Secession of Quebec*[98].

While the expression is foreign to Canadian constitutional scholarship, the reality of "teleological reduction" (*teleologische Reduktion*) may not be. András Jakab describes such method in the following terms: "a norm which covers the case is not applied, as it would contradict a general principle, the objective *ratio legis* or the subjective intention of the constitution-maker."[99] A most striking Canadian example of the overriding powers of principles over a regular norm can certainly be found in the *Reference re Manitoba Language Rights*[100] where the principle of the rule of law was applied by Supreme Court to temporarily suspend its declaration of invalidity of all the Manitoba statutes that had been adopted solely in English, in direct violation of the constitutionally mandated bilingual requirement.[101]

ii Establishing/Debating the Text of the Constitution This section is not about establishing or debating the *meaning* of the Constitution, but rather whether or not a certain "text" is contained in the entrenched

[94] In case of a situation not covered by an existing norm (lacuna), a positive norm not directly applicable to the case, but which nonetheless covers situations relevantly similar, is applied to fill the gap.

[95] In case of a situation not covered by an existing norm (lacuna), a norm is inferred from general principles not explicitly codified and fills the gap.

[96] *New Brunswick Broadcasting Co. v. Nova Scotia (Speaker of the House of Assembly)*, [1993] 1 SCR 319 [*New Brunswick Broadcasting*].

[97] *Reference re Remuneration of Judges of the Provincial Court (P.E.I.)*, *supra* n 38.

[98] *Reference re Secession of Quebec*, *supra* n 25.

[99] Jakab, 'Constitutional Reasoning', *supra* n 91.

[100] *Reference re Manitoba Language Rights*, *supra* n 51.

[101] See discussion, *infra* in section B.6.iii.

Constitution. This issue may arise in certain constitutional systems where, for example, it is unclear whether or not a specific constitutional modification was successful. No explicit attempt at formal constitutional amendment has ever been successfully challenged as of June 2013. However, because s. 35 of the *Constitution Act, 1982* entrenched Aboriginal treaties and because, historically, such agreements did not necessarily follow specific procedures, there are debates as to whether a specific agreement between the Crown and members of a First Nation was a treaty. Also, modern agreements between the government and First Nations may be subject of such debates.

iii Applicability of the Constitution in the Context The Constitution of Canada is the supreme law of the land and no other norm may displace its applicability in Canadian courts. However politically sensitive a question is, as long as there is a legal component to it, courts may tackle it. In other words, the so-called political question doctrine has little traction in Canada. For example, the exercise of the Crown prerogatives over national defence, including the decision to allow a foreign power to conduct cruise missile testing in Canada,[102] or the existence of a provincial right to secede from Canada[103] were both deemed appropriate subjects of constitutional scrutiny by the Supreme Court.

Things appear slightly more complicated in a state of emergency. Courts have developed what is known as the "national emergency" doctrine to allow for Parliament to temporarily legislate in matters that would normally fall within the legislative jurisdiction of provinces.[104] While an early case decided by the Judicial Committee of the Privy Council suggested that the state of emergency actually suspends the application of the division of powers on the basis of an implicit power given to

[102] *Operation Dismantle v. The Queen*, [1985] 1 S.C.R. 441. On the power of the courts to review the existence of Crown prerogatives and the exercise of such prerogatives over foreign affairs, see also, among others, *Burns*, *supra* n 92 (extraditing an accused towards a country where he may face the death penalty violates his *Charter* rights) and *Canada (Prime Minister) v. Khadr*, [2010] SCR 3, 1 SCR 44 (participation of Canadian officials in the illegal process and deprivation of Khadr's liberty and security while being held captive in Guantanamo).

[103] *Reference re Secession of Quebec*, *supra* n 25.

[104] *Fort Frances Pulp & Power Co. v. Manitoba Free Press Co.*, [1923] A.C. 695 [*Fort Frances Pulp & Power*]; *Co-operative Committee on Japanese Canadians v. Attorney-General of Canada*, [1947] A.C. 87; *Reference as to the Validity of the Wartime Leasehold Regulations*, [1950] S.C.R. 124 [*Reference as to the Validity of the Wartime Leasehold Regulations*]; *Re: Anti-Inflation Act*, supra n 61.

Parliament by the Constitution,[105] the Supreme Court later held that such power was found in the explicit jurisdiction given to Parliament to legislate for "peace, order and good government" under s. 91 *Constitution Act, 1867*.[106] The doctrine was last used in 1976 to validate a temporary statute adopted by the Parliament to fight what was perceived as an exceptional economic crisis caused by inflation.[107] Whereas the "national emergency" doctrine has been developed in the context of federalism issues, the Supreme Court has never had to deal directly with states of emergency with regard to *Charter* rights.

A close cousin of the notion of the "state of emergency" is found in the doctrine of "necessity". According to the Supreme Court, such doctrine elaborated in foreign jurisdictions "provides a justification for otherwise illegal conduct of a government during a public emergency" allowing the Courts to "recognize as valid the constitutionally invalid Acts of the Legislature."[108] The doctrine "is not used in these cases to support some law which is above the Constitution; it is, instead used to ensure the unwritten but inherent principle of rule of law which must provide the foundation of any constitution."[109] After going over the foreign cases dealing with the principle of necessity, the Court in the *Reference re Manitoba Language Rights*[110] argued that the situation at hand was different; the emergency would not be caused by a direct act of the Legislature or the executive, but rather by the Court if it were to declare immediately all the statutes invalid. The Court then shifted away from discussing the notion of necessity, to focus on the importance of maintaining the rule of law. But the Court made a bold – and ironical – move by redefining the latter principle as meaning at least two things: first, that "law is supreme over officials of the government as well as private individuals",[111] and second, "the rule of law requires the creation and maintenance of an actual order of positive laws which preserves and embodies the more general principle of normative order."[112] In other words, the meaning given by the Court to the rule of law entails that the existence of a concrete order could, in certain exceptional circumstances, trump the respect for actual legal rules. This sounds more like a simple "principle of order" than "the rule of law". At any rate, this intellectual contortion allowed the Court to claim

[105] *Fort Frances Pulp & Power*, Ibid.

[106] *Re: Anti-Inflation Act, supra* n 61, at 408 (Laskin C.J. and Judson, Spence and Dickson JJ.).

[107] Ibid.

[108] *Reference re Manitoba Language Rights, supra* n 51, para. 85.

[109] Ibid, para. 105.

[110] Ibid.

[111] Ibid, para. 59.

[112] Ibid, para. 60.

that it was not suspending the Constitution in itself – it was not the same thing as a Schmittian case of "exception"[113] – but that the protection of the rule of law required that the Court suspend temporarily the applicability of their judgment declaring the invalidity of the quasi-totality of Manitoba statutes during the minimum period necessary for correcting the situation.

In the *Reference re Secession of Quebec*[114] where the federal government asked the Supreme Court to declare whether or not Quebec had a unilateral right to secede – either under Canadian constitutional law, or according to public international law – the Court was invited by the *amicus curiae*[115] to consider the "principle of effectivity". According to such a principle, an illegal act, such as a revolution or an illegal secession, could eventually gain a legal status if, as a matter of empirical fact, revolutionaries or secessionists effectively control the territory subject to the illegal act and the international community recognizes the resulting political entity.[116] The Court stated that the principle of effectivity does not have the effect of *retroactively* giving legal validity to the illegal acts committed. Whereas it may be the source of a new legal system, it has no impact on the legal content of the previous one. While the special meaning given to the principle of the rule of law and the principle of effectivity may both appear to allow for legality to adapt to extreme social circumstances, the Supreme Court was of the opinion that the two situations differ fundamentally, as the rule of law rationale was not used to validate what was otherwise invalid; it was rather used to justify postponing the consequences of declaring invalid certain state actions to allow for correctives to take place.[117]

Interpreting the Applicable Constitutional Norm

i Wording and "Ordinary Meaning" of the Words of the Constitution When interpreting provisions of specific constitutional instruments adopted by the "framers", the actual words used matter.

[113] C. Schmitt, *Politische Theologie. Vier Kapitel zur Lehre von der Souveränität* (Duncker & Humblot 1922).

[114] *Reference re Secession of Quebec, supra* n 25.

[115] The Quebec government refused to intervene, claiming that it was exclusively a political matter and not an issue to be decided by the Supreme Court.

[116] *Reference re Secession of Quebec, supra* n 25, paras 106–108, 140–146.

[117] Ibid, para. 145. Suspended declarations are now a very common remedy used by the Supreme Court. See *Schachter, supra* n 48.

Even though textualism is not usually taken to be determinative, textual arguments are nonetheless part of the Court's toolkit. For example, the majority in *Rodriguez v. British Columbia (Attorney General)*[118] concluded, among other reasons to sustain the validity of a criminal prohibition on giving assistance to commit suicide, that such a prohibition did not violate the *Charter* provision that offers protection against being "*subjected to* any cruel and unusual *treatment*".[119] The majority claimed that to hold the prohibition, "without the [person seeking assistance to commit suicide] being in any subject to the state administrative or justice system, falls within the bounds of s. 12 stretches the ordinary meaning of being 'subjected to . . . treatment' by the state".[120] The use of "ordinary meaning" arguments is not limited to the interpretation of constitutional instruments; it may also be used to interpret the meaning of constitutional standards elaborated by previous constitutional decisions.[121]

However, it appears that the Court perceives such textualist arguments as not being entirely convincing. Indeed, in another case, the Court came to the conclusion that the meaning of another constitutional provision (*Constitution Act*, 1867, s. 133) *had to be stretched to accomplish its purpose!*[122]

And yet, the Court went in the exact opposite interpretative direction in concluding that text of the *Constitution Act, 1867* granting Parliament exclusive legislative power over "trade and commerce" had to be read in a *narrower sense* than the ordinary meaning of the words used.[123] This was deemed necessary to protect the exclusive legislative powers reserved to provinces over "Property and Civil Rights in the Province" (*Constitution Act, 1867*, s. 92 (13)). The fear was that a literal reading of the terms "trade and commerce" would have emptied to a large extent s. 92 (13) powers. That explains why, despite being written in wider terms that the American version of the commerce clause, the scope of the federal powers over "trade and commerce" is tremendously narrower.

It is probably because textualist arguments tend to have such a flexible character in Canada that the Supreme Court mostly uses them in a mere

[118] *Rodriguez v. British Columbia (Attorney General)*, [1993] 3 S.C.R. 519 [*Rodriguez*].
[119] *Charter*, s. 12. [120] *Rodriguez, supra* n 118, at 612.
[121] See e.g. *Canadian Western Bank v. Alberta*, [2007] 2 S.C.R. 3, 2007 SCC 22 at para. 51 [*Canadian Western Bank*].
[122] *Attorney General of Quebec v. Blaikie*, [1981] 1 S.C.R. 312, at 328.
[123] *General Motors of Canada Ltd. v. City National Leasing*, [1989] 1 S.C.R. 641 at 655–656.

supportive role; they buttress teleological arguments that are perceived as being more persuasive.[124]

ii Harmonising Arguments Harmonising arguments take several forms. We distinguish three forms for our purposes: (1) harmonisation of the linguistic versions of the constitutional texts; (2) harmonisation of distinct provisions of the Constitution; (3) harmonisation of the Constitution with public international law norms.

(1) Although prior to 1982 constitutional instruments were mostly officially adopted only in English (governments later produced French versions that are not authoritative),[125] the *Constitution Act, 1982* and all subsequent constitutional amendments to the "Constitution of Canada"[126] are authoritative in both official languages[127].

There are rules applicable to solve tensions between the two authoritative linguistic versions of constitutional texts. First, when one version is ambiguous on a certain point, and the other version is clear, the ambiguity could be solved in favour of the clearer version.[128] Second, the version of the text that *best protects the right* in question has been sometimes favoured.[129] Third, the leniency rule of statutory interpretation – i.e. an

[124] See e.g. *Doucet-Boudreau, supra* n 36 at para. 45.

[125] There are exceptions, such as *Manitoba Act, 1870*, R.S.C. 1970, App. II, No. 8, ratified by the *Constitution Act, 1871*, R.S.C. 1970, App. II, No. 11. The *CA 1982*, s. 55 provides that a French version of the portions of the Constitution of Canada not yet adopted in both official languages ought to be prepared and submitted for adoption. However, for fear of failing to meet the requirements of the relevant amending procedures, the drafted translations have never been submitted for approval to the provinces.

[126] We must distinguish the expression "Constitution of Canada" that contains the constitutional rules of the Federation as a whole, as well as the constitutional rules of its central institutions, from the "Constitution" of the Provinces that only cover provincial institutions. Certain rules of the provincial constitutions are part of the "Constitution of Canada" – such as the Office of the Lieutenant Governor – but not all constitutional rules of provinces belong to the "Constitution of Canada". That explains why unilingual provinces may possess provincial constitutional rules in English only.

[127] *Constitution Act*, 1982, ss. 56–57.

[128] *R. v. Rahey*, [1987] 1 S.C.R. 588, para. 93–94 (McIntyre and La Forest JJ.); *R. v. Conway*, [1989] 1 S.C.R. 1659, 1706–07 (Sopinka J., dissenting) [*Conway*]; *Mahe v. Alberta*, [1990] 1 S.C.R. 342, at p. 370); *Harvey v. New Brunswick (Attorney General)*, [1996] 2 S.C.R. 876 at para 28. However, see *R. v. Kapp*, [2008] 2 S.C.R. 483, 2008 SCC 41, para. 87–88 [*Kapp*], where Bastarache J., despite finding that the French version of s. 25 of the *Charter* was clearer than the English version, did "not believe that the difference in wording [was] decisive."

[129] *R. v. Collins*, [1987] 1 S.C.R. 265, at 287; *R. v. Burlingham*, [1995] 2 S.C.R. 206, at para. 70.

accused may benefit from the more liberal of two or more equally authoritative versions of a norm – has also been used to interpret the *Charter*.[130] It may be tempting to conflate the second and the third rule, but it is possible that a purposeful interpretation of a specific right may actually lead to a lesser protection of that right than an interpretation guided by the imperative to ensure its maximal protection.[131] Fourth, it is sometimes said that the proper interpretation is the one compatible with both linguistic versions.[132] Fifth, the interpretation that gives better effect to the *purpose* of the right should be preferred.[133] Those rules may not always be compatible with one another, but the Supreme Court has yet to unify its interpretative approach.

(2) When harmonising distinct *provisions* of the Constitution, the Court may sometimes have recourse to a form of linguistic harmonising analysis or, more frequently, to teleological arguments.[134] At any rate, the Supreme Court maintains that "[a] hierarchical approach to rights, which places some over others, must be avoided"[135] and "rather than giving one right priority over the other, the Court must engage in a balancing exercise that takes into account the salutary and deleterious effects of the measure and any alternatives."[136]

Another complicated issue arises from the fact that the *Charter* may have curtailed the exercise of certain powers provided by the Constitution, but it is deemed not to have implicitly abrogated such powers. This leads to the necessity of distinguishing between a "constitutional power" and the "exercise of a constitutional power"; if applying a constitutional norm in a

130 *Conway, supra* n 128.

131 The Court refused to rule in favour of the more generous French version of s. 12 of the *Charter* in *Burns, supra* n 92, para. 50–57. Whereas the English version of s. 12 appears to guarantee a mere negative right ("the right *not to be subjected* to any cruel and unusual treatment or punishment"), the French version suggests that a positive obligation of *protection against* cruel and unusual treatment or punishment falls to the state.

132 *R. v. Kapp, supra* n 128, para. 87 (Bastarache J.).

133 *R. v. Turpin*, [1989] 1 S.C.R. 1296, at 1314.

134 For a prime example of such exegetical method, see *Law Society of Upper Canada v. Skapinker*, [1984] 1 S.C.R. 357, 377–80.

135 *Dagenais v. Canadian Broadcasting Corp*, [1994] 3 S.C.R. 835 at 877. However, certain sections of the *Charter* anticipate the possibility of certain conflict and expressly settle them: see *Charter*, ss. 25 and 29.

136 *Toronto Star Newspapers Ltd. v. Canada*, 2010 SCC 21, [2010] 1 S.C.R. 721, para. 15. However, there are some exceptional circumstances where the Court attempted to reconcile the rights at the definitional stage, rather than at the stage where justification for the infringement is usually examined: see *R. v. O'Connor*, [1995] 4 S.C.R. 411 and *R. v. Mills*, [1999] 3 S.C.R. 668.

certain context would amount to "negating or removing a constitutional power",[137] that norm is inapplicable.

(3) International legal norms, within the Canadian domestic legal system, are not considered superior to the Constitution. Canada could be said to be a "qualified dualist" country when it comes to the interplay between domestic law and international law.[138] International law rules – whether customary or conventional in nature – do not bind the judiciary in interpreting the Constitution; they are rather considered "relevant and persuasive".[139] This means that it is not a binding subsidiary source that has to be used to fill in possible gaps in the Constitution.

Nonetheless, international legal norms are used as an important interpretative tool to determine whether or not a constitutionally guaranteed right has been violated.[140] Recently, the Supreme Court has strengthened the role of international law by declaring that the *Charter* "should be presumed to provide at least as great a level of protection as is found in the international human rights documents that Canada has ratified".[141] And this presumption was turned into an injunction to the Courts: "in interpreting the scope of application of the *Charter*, the courts should seek to ensure compliance with Canada's binding obligations under international law *where the express words are capable of supporting such a construction*".[142] While the Court appears to create a strong presumption in favour of compliance of *Charter* rights to international law, its actual record has been somewhat chequered[143] – especially in the first years after the adoption of

[137] *New Brunswick Broadcasting, supra* n 96 at 390–393 (McLachlin J. (as she then was) with L'Heureux-Dubé, Gonthier and Iacobucci JJ.).

[138] The rules guiding such *rapport* are not the same for constitutional as opposed to infra-constitutional norms. On such rules, see H. Cyr, *Canadian Federalism and Treaty Powers: Organic Constitutionalism at Work* (PIE Peter Lang 2009) 137–59.

[139] *Reference Re Public Service Employee Relations Act, supra* n 33 at 348–350 (Dickson C.J. and Wilson J.) (dissenting on the result but not on this point). This is cited with approval by the Court in *Burns, supra* n 92 at para. 80.

[140] See e.g. *Slaight Communications Inc. v. Davidson*, [1989] 1 S.C.R. 1038 [*Slaight Communications*]; *Keegstra, supra* n 65 at 750; *Burns*, Ibid at paras 82–92.

[141] *Health Services and Support – Facilities Subsector Bargaining Assn. v. British Columbia*, 2007 SCC 27, [2007] 2 S.C.R. 391, para. 70, confirming a statement previously made by C. J. Dickson in *Reference Re Public Service Employee Relations Act, supra* n 33 at 349.

[142] *R. v. Hape*, [2007] 2 S.C.R. 292 at para. 56 (emphasis added).

[143] Former Supreme Court Justice Louise Arbour and Prof. Fannie Lafontaine wrote "[R]eferences to international law in Supreme Court's judgements are on the rise, and a growing awareness of the relevance and usefulness of international law is palpable in the entire legal profession. However, the methodological framework for international law,

the *Charter* – and the use of international norms in the Court's opinions may often appear to serve little more than a supportive function.

iii Precedents In the common law tradition, a precedent is not so much a "rule" laid down by a previous judicial decision as it is an example of the right decision in the circumstances. Indeed, according to this rhetoric, judicial decisions are not making law, they are merely declaratory of existing law. The decision-maker thus had to come to similar conclusions in similar cases because previous decisions were presumed to reflect the correct set of legal reasons. In that sense, the use of precedents in the common law tradition was necessarily analogical. However, this understanding of precedents is eroding and common lawyers now tend to see precedents as instantiations of more general rules to be applied in subsequent cases. Therefore, while traditional common law reasoning tended to be analogical in nature, it now often takes the form of a double movement composed of (a) an induction or abduction of a general norm based on existing precedents, and (b) a deduction through the application of the inducted, abducted general norm to the facts at hand. This contemporary form of common law reasoning can thus be described as only "indirectly analogical". We do not have the space to go over the history of this shift, nor can we quantify here precisely the prevalence of this shift in the current practice of Canadian courts.

That being said, precedents are crucial to Canadian constitutional reasoning. One could not understand most of the Constitution without referring to past judicial decisions. For example, the text of the *Constitution Act, 1867* casts the image of a quasi-unitary State, but the succeeding jurisprudence – especially the early decisions of the Privy Council – clearly established a Federation.[144] The ever-growing body of case law incrementally shapes and reshapes the Constitution through its interpretations and reinterpretations. The Constitution grows "organically" through this mechanism.

While the Canadian constitutional tradition favours gradual transformation through piecemeal additions to the body of law, sometimes a

at present, is imperfect at best and improvised at worst" (L. Arbour and F. Lafontaine, "Beyond Self-Congratulation: The Charter At 25 in an International Perspective" [2007] 45 *Osgoode Hall L.J.* 239 at 252. For a disheartening list of references to public international law by Canadian courts – including the Supreme Court – containing basic errors, see A. F. Bayesfky, 'International Human Rights Law in Canadian Courts' in B. Conforti and Francesco Francioni, ed., *Enforcing International Human Rights in Domestic Courts* (Martinus Nijhoff Publishers 1997) 295, 325–7.

144 See *Reference re Secession of Quebec*, *supra* n 25, paras 55–57.

single case may have a tremendous impact on large sectors of the Constitution. The prime example of this is most certainly *R. v. Oakes*,[145] where the Supreme Court went far beyond what was necessary to decide the case at hand by expounding a full set of criteria[146] to determine whether an infringement to a *Charter* right may be accepted as a "reasonable limits prescribed by law as can be demonstrably justified in a free and democratic society".[147] Only one of those criteria could fairly be said to flow directly from the wording of s. 1. Recognizing this law-making role, Justice Binnie wrote for the Court that, departing from the established common law rule, the authority of a case may, in the post-*Charter* period, go beyond what that case actually decides.[148]

Nonetheless, precedents are not straitjackets; the Supreme Court uses different techniques to circumvent past decisions that it considers no longer adapted without reversing such decisions. For example, the Court may interpret narrowly what previous cases stand for, it may distinguish them by pointing out factual differences or it may claim, when the precedents established criteria to consider, that the weight to be given to each criterion must be reassessed in light of changes of circumstances.[149] These techniques are favoured by the Court because they allow for change while maintaining continuity; they avoid the rupture from the past that straight reversals of precedents entail. But the Court may also depart from precedent if it has "compelling reasons to do so"[150] and the "Court has made it clear that constitutional decisions are not immutable, even in the absence of constitutional amendment".[151]

iv Doctrinal Analysis of Legal Concepts or Principles (Verfassungsdogmatik) Both the Courts and legal scholars engage in extensive doctrinal analysis of legal concepts and principles. In fact, it is a criticism often

[145] *Oakes*, *supra* n 35. [146] Ibid., paras 69–70. [147] *Charter*, s. 1.

[148] *R v Henry*, 2005 SCC 76, [2005] 3 SCR 609 at para 53 [*Henry*].

[149] For an example of the latter technique, see *Burns*, *supra* n 92 where the criteria used to determine if the State action in question would amount to an infringement of s. 7 remained the same as those used a decade earlier (Kindler v. Canada (Minister of Justice), [1991] 2 S.C.R. 779; *Reference re Ng Extradition (Can.)*, [1991] 2 S.C.R. 858), but where a change in the weight given to each criterion led to the exact opposite results. The Court later admitted that *Burns*, ibid, "effectively overturned the result (if not the reasoning)" of the two previous cases (*Henry*, ibid, at para. 44).

[150] *Henry*, ibid, at para. 44; *R. v. Salituro*, [1991] 3 S.C.R. 654; *R. v. Chaulk*, [1990] 3 S.C.R. 1303; *R. v. B. (K.G.)*, [1993] 1 S.C.R. 740, at pp. 777–83; and *R. v. Robinson*, [1996] 1 S.C.R. 683, at paras. 16–46.

[151] *Clark v. Canadian National Railway Co.*, [1988] 2 S.C.R. 680, at 704, cited with approval *Henry*, ibid, para. 44.

heard – especially amongst legal practitioners – that the Court's judgments are now too long because the Court spends a considerable amount of energy reviewing the history and evolution of legal concepts and principles, often both in Canada and in a comparative perspective.

v **Arguments from Silence** Arguments based on the absence of particular textual references are sometimes considered by the Court when interpreting the Constitution. For instance, the Court found in the lack of any reference to situations of national emergency in the enumeration of the classes of subjects reserved to the provinces under s. 92 of the *Constitution Act, 1867* an indication that such cases were to be dealt with under the general federal power to legislate for the "peace, order and good government" of Canada – power conferred upon the Parliament by the introductory clause of s. 91 of the act.[152] Likewise, the Court reasoned that the *Charter* does not apply to judicial decisions since no mention of the judicial branch appears in the text of s. 32 of the *Charter* which specifies to whom it applies.[153]

vi **Teleological/Purposive Arguments Referring to the Purpose of the Text** We have only found four cases in the entire Supreme Court jurisprudence before 1984 that used the expression "purposive" – none using it in the context of constitutional interpretation. We have found no occurrence of the term "teleological" before 1984 in the entire body of Supreme Court cases. However, between 1984 and 2013, 172 constitutional law cases decided by the Supreme Court used the expression "purposive" – 10 of which are included in our canon. Almost all of them either dealt with *Charter* rights, or were about Aboriginal and Treaty rights – all 10 of the cases in the canon fall in one of those two categories.

That is the case because Canadian constitutional reasoning is not always guided by purposive arguments related to a *text*. Not all constitutional norms are the result of a purposive positing of norms.[154] More importantly, many fields of Constitutional law have evolved – explicitly or not – in ways that reflect teleological concerns that go beyond the mere purpose that one could ascribe to a specific text and refer to the general purposes

152 *Re: Anti-Inflation Act*, *supra* n 61, at p 141.

153 *RWDSU v. Dolphin Delivery Ltd.*, [1986] 2 SCR 573 at paras 33ff.

154 Some of Her Majesty's prerogatives may be interpreted purposively to the extent that they are understood as having been purposively *restricted or constrained*. Otherwise, the boundaries of the prerogatives are drawn with an eye to what such powers have covered in the past, and not with their potential purpose in mind.

of the different *institutions* in the political ecology of the Federation. In other words, the *telos* that will often matter more to the result may not be the one of the words used in the text,[155] but rather the *telos* of the institutions at play. That probably explains why the expression "purposive interpretation" is so rarely used in federalism cases.[156] As a consequence, for example, the Court refuses to give precise content to many heads of legislative powers in order to ensure, over time, that both Parliament and the Legislatures will be able to fulfil their democratic functions.[157]

vii Teleological/Purposive Arguments Referring to the Purpose of the Constitution-Maker (Including Travaux Préparatoires) Evidence intended to demonstrate the actual intention of the Constituent powers is admissible,[158] but it carries only "minimal weight".[159] The "framers" are considered in the abstract in a way to avoid freezing the meaning of the Constitution at one point in time.

viii Non-legal (Moral, Sociological, Economic) Arguments Constitutional review by courts in Canada is not directed towards evaluating the "merits or wisdom of enactments" or State actions.[160] Nonetheless, moral, sociological, economic, etc. arguments are integrated in the Court's reasoning in many different ways. For example, as we have seen earlier,[161] economic arguments, presented as representing the factual situation, were used to justify invoking the "national emergency" doctrine. Sociological arguments are used, for example, to contextualise the interpretation to be given to ancient Aboriginal treaties. To take a last example, moral arguments related to "fairness" – and not simply "justice" –, "generosity" and "honour" – are also invoked to orient the way judges should go about interpret different parts of the Constitution. The tendency, however, is not to portray concepts such as "principles of fundamental justice"[162] as having a subjective meaning, but rather to try to link them to established

[155] *Canadian Western Bank, supra* n 121. See, *infra*, ns 187 and 188 and accompanying text.

[156] *Consolidated Fastfrate Inc. v. Western Canada Council of Teamsters*, 2009 SCC 53, [2009] 3 S.C.R. 407, para. 90 (Binnie J. for McLachlin CJ and Fish J., dissenting); *Westcoast Energy Inc. v. Canada (National Energy Board)*, [1998] 1 S.C.R. 322 (McLachlin J (as she then was) (dissenting). Moreover, we have not found a single Supreme Court case dealing with federalism where the words "interpretation" and "object" (and their cognates) appear in the same sentence.

[157] *Canadian Western Bank, supra* n 121, at para 43.

[158] *Senate Reference (1980), supra* n 54 at 66.

[159] *Re B.C. Motor Vehicle Act, supra* n 27 at para. 52. See generally paras 49–53.

[160] Ibid, para. 19.

[161] See *supra* n 107 and accompanying text.

[162] *Charter*, s. 7.

(but often wide) legal principles.[163] Judges are not presented as being *phronimos*, but rather as responsible, highly skilled legal technicians.

ix References to Scholarly Works In the early 1950s, Chief Justice Rinfret refused to permit a lawyer, during the argument in the *Reference as to the Validity of the Wartime Leasehold Regulations*,[164] to refer to an article in the *Canadian Bar Review* because he considered that it was "not an authority in [the] Court".[165] Only dead authors – who obviously could not change their mind – were then considered "authorities". Things have changed significantly since then. Two authors have shown that during the first years of *Charter*-based litigation, 54,9 per cent of *Charter* cases referred to academic writings, with an average of 8,5 cites per case.[166] This is now a well-established practice.

x References to Foreign (National) Law Canada being a former British colony, references to decisions from the United Kingdom and from former colonies such as Australia abound. Those decisions guide in the interpretation of Canada's basic political structure (e.g. Crown law, parliamentary privileges[167], and federalism). The Supreme Court also often refers to foreign national law and decisions by regional human rights institutions, both to interpret the scope of guaranteed rights and to help determine what may be justifiable in a "free and democratic society".[168] It also used to refer to the American Constitution[169] – often to contrast the differences in the way the guaranteed rights are protected under the two Constitutions[170] – but it has lately turned its gaze mostly elsewhere. This

[163] See for example in *Burns*, *supra* n 92.

[164] *Reference as to the Validity of the Wartime Leasehold Regulations*, *supra* n 104.

[165] See Ian Bushnell, *The Captive Court: A Study of the Supreme Court of Canada* (McGill-Queen's 1992) 282.

[166] Vaughan Black and Nicholas Richter, "Citation of Academic Authority by the Supreme Court of Canada 1985–1990" [1993] 16 Dalhousie L.J. 377 at 389. This is a marked departure from past practices. The authors have perused the *Supreme Court Reports* for 1957, 1967 and 1977 and the respective rate of cases citing secondary materials during those years was 15 per cent, 13,3 per cent and 21,6 per cent (see p. 383).

[167] *New Brunswick Broadcasting*, *supra* n 96.

[168] *Charter*, s.1.

[169] Between 2014 and 2004, the Supreme Court used the expression "Constitution of the United States" in only one case (Quebec *(Attorney General) v. Lacombe*, 2010 SCC 38, [2010] 2 SCR 453), while it did use the same expression in 40 cases between 2004 and 1984. The expression "U.S. Constitution" was used in 3 cases between 2014 and 2004, but 19 times between 2004 and 1984. The last time the expression "American Constitution" was used was in 2005, and it referred to the title of Lawrence Tribe's book.

[170] See e.g. *R. v. Wholesale Travel Group Inc.*, [1991] 3 SCR 154 at 251.

is in part due to the fact that Canada (like Germany, South Africa and Israel) has adopted a different two-stage model of constitutional review in relation to *Charter* rights.[171]

7 The Weight of Arguments

All those arguments – even if they may be in tension with one another – may appear in a constitutional decision and none can be said, *a priori*, to be consistently decisive. In other words, each type of argument is not ranked according to a predetermined weight. Rather, the whole appears to be brought together when a "reflective equilibrium" is reached – and inconvenient arguments are either discarded or downplayed. It is true that the Supreme Court stated in the *Reference re Secession of Quebec*[172] that explicit rules found in an entrenched constitutional text should not be displaced by implicit "constitutional principles",[173] but the Court seems to have done precisely the opposite with the implied constitutional principle of "judicial independence";[174] it used that principle to invalidate statutes adopted by legislatures in the course of exercising their explicitly granted powers over "the Constitution, Maintenance, and Organization of Provincial Courts, both of Civil and of Criminal Jurisdiction".[175] Neither is it true that social context arguments tend to be used as supporting arguments only. Evidence of an economic emergency was determinant in deciding to suspend the normal rules of the division of powers between Parliament and Legislatures.[176] This should not be entirely surprising in light of the eclectic nature of the sources of Canadian constitutional law that include both will-based (e.g. entrenched constitutional texts) and "authorless" (e.g. implied constitutional principles) norms.[177]

That being said, there is a general tendency towards privileging evolving "progressive" constitutional interpretations. As we have seen earlier this is especially true of *Charter* cases, but it is not limited to that sector of constitutional law.

[171] The first stage of the inquiry seeks to determine if a guaranteed right has been infringed upon, and the second stage aims at determining if the infringement is constitutionally justified.

[172] Ibid. [173] Ibid.

[174] See *Reference re Remuneration of Judges of the Provincial Court (P.E.I.), supra* n 38. For an enlightening analysis of this case and, more generally, the uses of implied constitutional principles, see Jean Leclair, 'Canada's Unfathomable Unwritten Constitutional Principles' (2002), 27 *Queen's L.J.* 389.

[175] *CA 1867*, s. 92 (14). [176] *Re: Anti-Inflation Act, supra* n 61.

[177] *Reference re Secession of Quebec, supra* n 25.

The meanings of entrenched Aboriginal and treaty rights are not "frozen" in time; such rights may be interpreted in ways that make them meaningful in the modern world.[178] This means that such rights may cover modern practices that are "reasonably incidental"[179] to the right in the contemporary context.[180] Aboriginal and treaty rights are community-specific and are interpreted as such.[181] While historical Aboriginal treaty rights may tend to be liberally interpreted by taking into consideration the linguistic and cultural differences of the parties involved,[182] the text of modern-day treaties that have been drafted with the help of legal counsels may be the object of stricter scrutiny to determine the common intentions of the parties.[183] There are a series of interpretative principles meant to favour a generous interpretation of treaty rights,[184] but one that also applies to Aboriginal rights has to be highlighted in particular: it is the principle of *the honour of the Crown*. The Supreme Court declared that "[i]nterpretations of treaties and statutory provisions which have an impact upon treaty or aboriginal rights must be approached in a manner which maintains the integrity of the Crown. It is always assumed that the Crown intends to fulfil its promises. No appearance of 'sharp dealing' will be sanctioned".[185] Again, the overall principle is that constitutional interpretation should not be static.

This is also generally true of contemporary federalism cases[186]. In fact, to ensure that the respective heads of legislative competence of Parliament and Legislatures do not fossilise under the weight of precedent, the Supreme Court states that "the very functioning of Canada's federal system must continually be reassessed in light of the fundamental values it was designed to serve."[187] Therefore, as we have seen, the Court opposes

[178] *Lax Kw'alaams Indian Band v. Canada (Attorney General)*, 2011 SCC 56, [2011] 3 S.C.R. 53, para. 49. In relation to treaty rights, see *R. v. Van der Peet*, [1996] 2 S.C.R. 507 [*Van der Peet*] and *R. v. Sundown*, [1999] 1 S.C.R. 393, para. 32 [*Sundown*].

[179] *Simon v. The Queen*, [1985] 2 S.C.R. 387, at 402 and *Sundown*, ibid, at para. 27–30.

[180] *R. v. Marshall*, [1999] 3 S.C.R. 456, para. 78 (McLachlin J., as she then was, dissenting, but not on this point).

[181] *Van der Peet, supra* n 178, para. 69.

[182] *R. v. Badger*, [1996] 1 S.C.R. 771, para. 52 [*Badger*].

[183] See, for example, *Quebec (Attorney General) v. Moses*, 2010 SCC 17, [2010] 1 S.C.R. 557.

[184] *Badger, supra* n 182, para. 41.

[185] *R. v. Badger*, ibid. See also: *Province of Ontario v. Dominion of Canada and Province of Quebec; In re Indian Claims* (1895) 25 S.C.R. 434, at pp. 511–12 (Gwynne J., dissenting) and *Ontario Mining Co. v. Seybold* (1901), 32 S.C.R. 1, at p. 2.

[186] See e.g. *Reference re Employment Insurance*, [2005] 2 S.C.R. 669, 2005 SCC 56 [Reference re Employment Insurance].

[187] *Canadian Western Bank, supra* n 121, para. 23.

an interpretative method that would require judges to define a "core" for each legislative head of power; it has traditionally "refrained from trying to define the possible scope of such powers in advance and for all time" as it favours an incremental approach.[188]

However, when the constitutional rules in question are perceived as being the product of an essential initial compromise without which the Federation would not have been born, such as those involving the composition and functions of the Senate[189] and certain religious and educational rights,[190] the Court will be careful to avoid upsetting the initial bargain.[191] In those cases, the Court may draw more heavily on historical accounts to determine the purpose of the relevant sections of the constitutional texts.

8 *Judicial Candour and Judicial Rhetoric*

Over time, as its role has changed from being a Court of error to being a judicial policy institution, the rhetoric of the Supreme Court has evolved. No longer writing primarily for the individual parties involved in the litigation, it now writes for several audiences at the same time. Obviously, the Court writes for judges to guide them in applying the law and for lawyers to help them counsel their clients. It also engages with academia by examining arguments developed in scholarly works, and it often provides extensive genealogies of rules and principles that are very useful to help law students understand where certain legal concepts come from. And it

188 Ibid, para. 43. 189 *Senate Reference (1980), supra* n 54.

190 *Adler v. Ontario*, [1996] 3 S.C.R. 609; *Reference re Education Act (Que.)*, [1993] 2 S.C.R. 511; *Greater Montreal Protestant School Board v. Quebec (Attorney General)*, [1989] 1 S.C.R. 377; *Reference Re Bill 30, An Act to amend the Education Act (Ont.)*, [1987] 1 S.C.R. 1148; *Reference re Adoption Act*, [1938] S.C.R. 398, at p. 402 (Duff J.). This also used to be the case also with the protection of the two official languages (see *Société des Acadiens du Nouveau-Brunswick Inc. v. Association of Parents for Fairness in Education*, [1986] 1 S.C.R. 549, at p. 578)., but recent case law has turned the tide towards a more generous and purposive approach (see *R. v. Beaulac*, [1999] 1 S.C.R. 768 para. 24–25).

191 *British Columbia (Attorney General) v. Canada (Attorney General); An Act respecting the Vancouver Island Railway* (Re), [1994] 2 S.C.R. 41, at p. 88., the Court raised doubts about the applicability of the "living tree" doctrine to the Terms of Union that made possible the entry of British Columbia in the Canadian Federation: "In passing, I would not wish to be taken as having decided whether the other broad principles established in the *Edwards* case apply to specific agreements like Terms of Union, which were intended to settle specific problems." See also *Reference re Employment Insurance, supra* n 186, para. 10, that "[a] progressive interpretation cannot . . . be used to justify Parliament in encroaching on a field of provincial jurisdiction." (para. 10) and that "[t]he evolution of the scope of a constitutional head of power cannot result in encroachment on a power assigned to another level of government." (para. 87.)

is clearly involved in a global judicial dialogue with other Constitutional or Supreme Courts throughout the world.[192]

But its new policy role has brought the Court to also address itself more squarely to politicians. It presents itself as being engaged in a "dialogue"[193] with Parliament and Legislatures over the interpretation of the *Charter*. This means that it will often refrain from completely putting an end to a controversial issue, leaving the work to be done by elected officials. In the *Reference re Same-Sex Marriage*[194], for instance, the federal government asked the Court whether its proposed bill extending capacity to marry to persons of the same sex was constitutionally valid, but it also asked whether or not the traditional rule that had been previously invalidated by three provincial Courts of Appeal was consistent with the Constitution. The latter question was meant to deflect political criticisms away from the Parliament and to lay responsibility for adoption of the same-sex marriage statute at the feet of the judiciary; politicians wanted to be able to take cover by saying that they had no choice but to obey the Constitution – or, more precisely, the "unelected judges on the bench of the Supreme Court". The Court refused to play; it gave a generally positive answer to the question of the validity of the bill, extolling its virtues in implementing the equality rights guaranteed in the *Charter*, but it stopped short of declaring it constitutionally necessary. Indeed, it refused to answer the question as to the validity of the traditional marital rule that was declared unconstitutional by different Courts of Appeal, thus leaving to Parliament the responsibility of adopting the statute based on its own merits. The Supreme Court often uses similar "incomplete decision" tactics when facing politically charged debates that would be better settled through principled negotiations rather than judicial fiat; the Court's reasons will put in place a matrix of negotiations that incentivises all parties to come to an agreement instead of simply pulling the rug in one direction.[195]

The new role of the Court also means that it is addressing itself to the press and the general public. The editors of the Supreme Court Report –

[192] Almost every year, the Canadian Supreme Court sends one of its judges to the Yale Law School "Global Constitutionalism Seminar" that brings together, for both open and closed sessions over several days, supreme court and constitutional judges from around the world to discuss selected themes. Justice L'Heureux-Dubé once told one of us, around 1997, that she was in constant contact through an email distribution list with judicial colleagues from around the world, and that they frequently discussed how each of them solved different constitutional matters in their own jurisdiction.

[193] See *supra* n 90 and accompanying text.

[194] *Reference re Same-Sex Marriage, supra* n 33.

[195] See e.g. *Reference re Secession of Quebec, supra* n 25 and *Delgamuukw, supra* n 66.

the official printer of the Court – prepare headnotes for each case that are approved by the judges. Void of any legal value, they offer nevertheless a useful summary of the facts and the Court's reasoning. However, the Court became keenly aware that this was not sufficient to inform the public in simple terms with respect to what the cases were about – and what they *were not* about. An officer of the Court now meets with the press a few minutes before the decisions are delivered to offer explanations about the case. Also, since the late 1990s, the Court has formed the habit of writing a short introduction in lay terms to explain what the case is about, how the Court decided and what it left to be decided in the future.[196]

9 *Length, Dissenting and Concurring Opinions*

On average, between 2010 and 2012, cases were about 33 pages long. The shorter decisions, where the Court basically states that the appeal is dismissed for the reasons given by such and such judges of the Court of Appeal, obviously bring the numbers down. Important constitutional cases will range from 40 pages[197] to over 200 pages.[198]

The length of decisions grew significantly between the early 1970s and the end of the 1980s. These changes cannot be solely attributed to the adoption of the *Constitution Act, 1982* because this trend started earlier. One institutional element that could surely contribute to explaining this transformation is the gradual integration of "law clerks" into the workings of the Court.[199] The clerkship program effectively started in 1968 with judges being able to hire one law clerk each. With the increase of the expected workload flowing from the adoption of the *Constitution Act, 1982*, the program was expended in 1983 to three law clerks per judge.[200] Law clerks are chosen from among the top finishing law students from across Canada, and they are hired to work for a single judge during one

[196] See e.g. *Burns, supra* n 92, para 1–8.

[197] See e.g. *Oakes, supra* n 35 takes 41 pages of the Supreme Court Report.

[198] See e.g. *Reference re Remuneration of Judges of the Provincial Court (P.E.I.), supra* n 38, takes 209 pages of the Supreme Court Report. The *Patriation Reference, supra* n 19 is about 160 pages long.

[199] See, in general: L. Sossin, "The Sounds of Silence: Law Clerks, Policy Making and the Supreme Court of Canada" (1996) 30 *U.B.C. L.Rev.* 279; M. McInnes, J. Bolton and N. Derzko, "Clerking at the Supreme Court of Canada" (1994) 33 *Alberta L.R.* 58 [McInnes, J. Bolton and N. Derzko]; J. Herman, "Law Clerking at the Supreme Court of Canada" (1975) 13 *Osgoode Hall L.J.* 279. See also J. G. Snell and F. Vaughan, *The Supreme Court of Canada: The History of the Institution* (McGill-Queen's Press 1992).

[200] McInnes, J. Bolton and N. Derzko, ibid, at p. 61.

year.[201] This is the most prestigious internship that any graduating law student can obtain out of law school. A great many former law clerks have become judges themselves, law school deans and professors, senior officials, lawyers in major law firms, etc. For example, Justice Louise Arbour was among the first Supreme Court law clerks at the beginning of the program. Having 27 highly motivated, academically minded law school graduates – most having obtained university degrees in other subjects before entering law and often already having graduate degrees in law – working on appeal memos, doing research and giving a helping hand in preparing draft opinions surely increases the quantitative output of the institution. And as three previous clerks have noted, "the use of clerks represents a move away from a conception of the judicial function as one of simply resolving a dispute between parties. By increasing the Court's capacity, and by providing perspectives not represented by litigants, clerks contribute to the larger, policy-making role assumed by the Court in recent years."[202] Thus, the Court's decisions are longer nowadays not only because it can count on more human resources, but because the institutional setting favours scholarly presentations, and the Court's new role as an unelected policy-maker requires more complex and nuanced justifications.

On average, between 2002 and 2012, the Court was split over the disposition of cases 27,5 per cent of the time.[203] A judge may agree with the ultimate disposition of the case proposed by another colleague, but not with his or her reasoning. In such cases, the judge may nonetheless join the opinion of that other judge, or he or she may decide to write concurring reasons. Dissenting judges will also write their own reasons – alone or with colleagues concurring in their dissent.

10 Framing of Constitutional Issues

Prior to the adoption of the *Charter of Rights and Freedoms* in 1982, most constitutional law cases were distribution of powers cases. Even

[201] For a brief period, Quebec judges retained the services of the same individual for 2 years (McInnes, J. Bolton and N. Derzko, ibid, at p. 61). Nowadays, it may happen that a judge will offer on an ad hoc basis an extension of a few months to a clerk in order to finish some important project.

[202] McInnes, J. Bolton and N. Derzko, ibid, at p. 62.

[203] Calculated on the basis of the statistics available at Supreme Court of Canada, *Statistics 2002 to 2012. Category 4: Appeal Judgments*, internet: http://www.scc-csc.gc.ca/case-dossier/stat/cat4-eng.aspx.

equality-rights-based arguments were sometimes crafted to suit the division of powers frame.[204] However, with the advent of the *Charter*, human rights issues have become an important part of the Supreme Court's constitutional caseload.

11 *Key Concepts*

A list of key concepts invoked and relied upon by the Court include concepts such as the "Crown", "federalism", "democracy", "the rule of law and constitutionalism", "protection of minorities", "judicial independence", "responsible government", "sovereignty of Parliament", "equality" and "human dignity". These concepts may sometimes carry multiple meanings. The principle of the rule of law, for instance, is understood both in a formal and a substantive sense. In the former, it postulates that the acts of both public officials and private persons are subject to the law[205] and that "the exercise of all public power must find its ultimate source in a legal rule".[206] In the latter, it provides that certain principles of "natural justice" (e.g. the principle of non-retroactivity, the rules *audi alteram partem* or *nemo judex in re sua*) are applicable in all circumstances if they are not expressly set aside by the legislator.[207] The Court also found that, from a more general perspective, a substantive conception of the rule of law "requires the creation and maintenance of an actual order of positive laws which preserves and embodies the more general principle of normative order".[208]

Key concepts may equally stand in tension vis-à-vis one another. The Court, for instance, strongly asserts constitutionalism – that is, the supremacy of the Constitution over any law enacted by the legislator – as one of Canada's "foundational constitutional principles"[209] while also relying, at least rhetorically, on the principle of the "sovereignty of Parliament".[210]

[204] See e.g. *Union Colliery Co. of British Columbia c. Bryden*, [1899] A.C. 580.

[205] *Roncarelli v. Duplessis*, [1959] S.C.R. 121, at p. 142.

[206] *Reference re Remuneration of Judges of the Provincial Court (P.E.I.), supra* n 38 at para. 10.

[207] See e.g. *Alliance des Professeurs Catholiques de Montréal v. Quebec Labour Relations Board*, [1953] 2 S.C.R. 140 at pp. 154, 157, 166.

[208] *Reference re Manitoba Language Rights, supra* n 51, at p. 749. See also *Reference re Secession of Quebec, supra* n 25 at para 70.

[209] *Reference re Secession of Quebec*, ibid, paras 49, 76ff.

[210] *Canada Assistance Plan, supra* n 18; *Patriation Reference, supra* n 19, *Hape*, supra n 142 at paras 39, 53, 68.

Such key concepts are often interwoven. Take, for example, how the concepts of "democracy", "federalism" and "constitutionalism" are interrelated. According to the Court, it is a "grave mistake" to simply equate democracy with a process-oriented majority rule;[211] democracy has, on the contrary, a substantive meaning which covers a robust set of values and principles.[212] Most importantly, it promotes self-government, which has to be construed consistently with other constitutional values, such as federalism, constitutionalism and the rule of law and the protection of minorities.[213] The interplay between democracy and federalism means that "there may be different and equally legitimate majorities in different provinces and territories and at the federal level. No one majority is more or less 'legitimate' than the others as an expression of democratic opinion".[214] Accordingly, democracy implies a continuous process of discussion, negotiation, deliberation and compromise where dissenting opinions are taken into consideration and fairly addressed.[215] The Court thus found that inherent in the democratic principle lay a specific duty to negotiate constitutional changes incumbent upon all the participants to the Federation when one initiates such changes.[216]

Finally, it is of interest to mention that the concept of "human dignity" played an unexpected role in the antidiscrimination jurisprudence of the Court. While the concept was initially introduced to break away from a formalist conception of equality protection in favour of "substantive equality",[217] "human dignity" ended up serving more as a barrier than as a gateway to equality claimants. Indeed, the Court came to conclude that in order to be successful, a claimant must demonstrate that her dignity is impaired by the burden imposed or the benefit withheld.[218] For instance, the Court found that reducing welfare benefits for individuals under 30 years old was not age discrimination since it was designed "to promote the self-sufficiency and autonomy of young welfare recipients through their integration into the productive workforce" and, thus, it was tantamount to fostering human dignity rather than an encroachment upon it.[219]

211 *Reference re Secession of Quebec*, *supra* n 25 at para 67.

212 See quote from *Oakes*, *supra* n 35, reproduced in the text.

213 *Reference re Secession of Quebec*, *supra* n 25, para 64–67.

214 Ibid, para. 66. 215 Ibid, para 68. 216 Ibid, para 69.

217 *Egan v. Canada*, [1995] 2 SCR 513, 543–47, 556 (*per* L'Heureux-Dubé J., dissenting), 584, 593, 599, 603–604 (*per* Cory and Iacobucci JJ., dissenting) and *Vriend*, *supra* n 36, para. 67–86, 104.

218 *Law v. Canada (Minister of Employment and Immigration)*, [1999] 1 S.C.R. 497.

219 *Gosselin v. Quebec (Attorney General)*, [2002] 4 S.C.R. 429, 2002 SCC 84 at para 65.

The Court recently concluded that equality claimants no longer need to demonstrate an infringement upon their dignity to succeed.[220]

C Comparative Perspective

Canadian constitutional law is the product of a mixture of different legal and political traditions. Not only is it rooted in the British tradition emphasising the importance of informal constitutional conventions and "organic growth", it also shares a colonial past with other common law countries that have long been in the habit of having their local authorities constrained by higher laws. While the Canadian Constitution is no longer seen as a colonial constraint on the federal Parliament and the provincial legislatures, it nonetheless constrains their powers. The British influence on Canadian constitutional reasoning is sustained, among other things, by the fact that many Canadian constitutional scholars have conducted their graduate studies in the United Kingdom. For example, in the 1980s, five members of the Supreme Court had studied at Oxford on Rhodes Scholarships. But many others have also done graduate work in the United States (Justice La Forest [1985–97] had studied in Oxford as a Rhodes Scholar, and had obtained a LL.M. and a J.S.D. at the Yale Law School).[221] While Canadian courts had not paid much attention to American federalism jurisprudence, the American constitutional experience with entrenched rights obviously loomed large in the judicial discourse in the aftermath of the adoption of the *Charter of Rights and Freedoms* in 1982. As we have

[220] *R. v. Kapp*, *supra* n 128; *Withler v. Canada (Attorney General)*, 2011 SCC 12, [2011] 1 S.C.R. 396; *Quebec (Attorney General) v. A*, 2013 SCC 5 (*per* Abella J. dissenting but not on this issue).

[221] Justice La Forest, whom we mentioned has having been educated both in the United Kingdom and in the United States, wrote in *R. v. Rahey*, [1987] 1 S.C.R. 588, para. 108: "Why we should follow American precedents, when these have led judges to avoid redressing unreasonable delay and scholars to scurry to find ways of limiting the application of the only remedy there, I fail to understand, particularly when the Charter expressly provides a flexible remedy to avoid these consequences. While it is natural and even desirable for Canadian courts to refer to American constitutional jurisprudence in seeking to elucidate the meaning of Charter guarantees that have counterparts in the United States Constitution, they should be wary of drawing too ready a parallel between constitutions born to different countries in different ages and in very different circumstances, particularly given the substantive implications of both s. 1 and s. 24(1) of the Charter. Canadian legal thought has at many points in the past deferred to that of the British; the Charter will be no sign of our national maturity if it simply becomes an excuse for adopting another intellectual mentor. American jurisprudence, like the British, must be viewed as a tool, not as a master."

seen earlier, while the Courts referred to the different standards developed in the United States to operationalize what are otherwise vague terms defining rights, the Supreme Court often used American case law as counterexamples. The nation-building endeavour behind the so-called Patriation of 1982 also meant that Canada had to be independent from its Southern neighbours. And since the drafting of the *Charter* had been influenced by more recent human right instruments devised in Europe and by international organisations, it made sense for the Supreme Court to seek guidance in the case law of other countries and international institutions to give meaning to its new constitutional provisions. This means that, contrary to other constitutional systems, key concepts of Canadian constitutional law and modes of reasoning have developed in large part through dialectic references to other constitutional systems. While Canada is a large and economically secure country, it does not hesitate to refer to foreign law. Canadian constitutional cosmopolitanism is not perceived as a sign of internal weakness, it is rather portrayed as the expression of a confident legal system that seeks to improve itself through useful comparisons.

The Supreme Court of Canada, being also a general court of appeal, is understood as a true "jurisdiction" and not a hybrid political body where jurists and politicians (or other public figures) are asked to pass judgment on a proposed course of action. While Supreme Court decisions obviously have political impacts, they remain framed in legal terms. Thus, decisions are not presented as mere syllogisms, nor are they couched in political terms. Rather, they are expected to be fully explained in terms that fit the accepted canon of legal reasoning. Such legal reasoning is not understood as being the sole product of the will of a *pouvoir constituant* or of a lawmaker; rather, it is understood to be flowing from a tradition that has its own immanent logic. Thus, judges, as "guardians of legality", are not called upon to make "political decisions", but are expected to ensure the "development" of the Constitution in accordance with its internal logic.

The Canadian practice of judicial review reveals that one does not need a great number of cases to achieve a high level of conceptual sophistication in constitutional law (*Verfassungsdogmatik*). Rather, the level of conceptual sophistication, in the Canadian case, appears to be the product of open channels of communication between scholars and the Supreme Court bar, the multiplicity of actors arguing a particular case (the opposing parties and the multiple interveners), the limited number of cases decided every year, the expectation that judges will fully explain the reasoning that justifies their decisions and the role played by law clerks in the production of the Supreme Court opinions. Focussing entirely on judges when describing constitutional reasoning of different courts may lead us to miss significant processes at work. For example, some may have thought that, as a general rule, the more academics are sitting in a court, the longer and more detailed the judgments are, and the more references to academic literature one is likely to find buried in them. But this is to forget the role of law clerks in the work of Supreme Courts. As we have seen earlier, they are practically in-house scholars assisting judges in the preparation of their opinions. In such circumstances, the relative length of opinions and the amount of academic literature that finds its way in the decisions is less a matter of the nature of the ultimate decision-maker as it is of the type of assistance he or she gets in preparing his or her judgment.

One may be tempted to test the hypothesis, in a comparative setting, that the older the Constitution is and the more difficult it is to amend it, the more likely the judges are to use purposive arguments instead of literal arguments. The Canadian case seems to suggest that there is some truth to that. However, the full truth appears more complicated. As we have seen, the Supreme Court of Canada favours a purposive interpretation of the newer *Charter* of rights, but it may sometimes be more willing to stick to some original meaning or purpose when doing otherwise would disrupt an initial bargain that made possible the unification of the different parts of Canada.

When comparing different forms of constitutional decisions, one gets a sense of the respective audience of each of them. Supreme Court decisions are oriented to several readerships simultaneously: not only the parties and interveners (including the governments), but also the legal professions (lawyers and legal scholars), the media and the general population. Judgments have taken the form they have in order to better reach each of those audiences, in both official linguistic communities. This explains, for example, why there often is a short narrative at the beginning of recent Supreme Court decisions explaining what the "story" is (and is not) about before actually starting to examine the case at hand; the goal is to frame the issues for the journalists covering the Court. While constitutional reasoning in the Supreme Court remains independent from whatever popular views may be expressed by the public, judges remain sensitive to the way they convey their decisions to Canadians. The fact that their decisions are addressed to a series of distinct audiences forces judges to write in a way that highlights their impartiality and their seriousness; their legitimacy depends on it.

D Evaluation, Pathology and Criticism

This report has mostly presented constitutional reasoning in the Canadian Supreme Court in a synchronic fashion. We have briefly highlighted how the adoption of the *Constitution Act, 1982* had provoked certain changes in the way the Court tackles constitutional issues, but a fuller understanding of the Court's reasoning would require a more comprehensive diachronic approach. Indeed, the Court's interpretative strategies have evolved over time, and so did our understanding of what was involved in the hermeneutical task. Interpretative approaches may also vary according to circumstances. For instance, "war jurisprudence" may reflect more the practical imperatives of the moment rather than the sober decisions made in time of peace. Also, as we have seen, certain interpretative strategies are domain-specific.[222]

It is therefore tricky to come to general conclusions as to the overall performance of the Court. That being said, the Supreme Court of Canada appears well-adjusted overall to Canadians' expectations. The fact that it is often criticised by conservatives for being too "activist" and by progressives for being too conservative is probably a sign that it strikes a healthy middle ground.

There are four general criticisms that we could level against the Supreme Court's constitutional reasoning. First, its use of international law sources generally appears unprincipled and merely rhetorical – except when violation of the international norm in question may entail concrete retaliation. Second, three decades after the adoption of the *Charter*, the key elements that equality claimants have to demonstrate remain in flux. Three, the length and multiplicity of the Court's opinions often constitute an obstacle to the access to justice. Only those with significant financial resources can afford the research necessary to adequately present their case. Fourth, the length and multiplicity of the Court's opinions also make it harder for judges – and their successive law clerks – to remain consistent with previous decisions and their detailed doctrinal developments. Federalism cases have been particularly prone to this problem.

However, despite these shortcomings, the Court must be commended for its overall performance on reference questions. Judges have generally demonstrated great statesmanship when answering the most politically

[222] See e.g., *supra* ns 189 and 190 and accompanying text.

charged questions.[223] They did not hide behind a formalist approach that would have inflamed the situation, nor did they appear to enforce their own policy preferences. Indeed, the Court not only managed to answer the reference questions in a principled manner, but it was also able to create incentives for politicians to assume responsibility and cooperate to find adequate solutions.

Appendix: 40 Leading Cases[224]

1 *Alliance des Professeurs Catholiques de Montréal v. Quebec Labour Relations Board*, [1953] 2 S.C.R. 140
2 *Roncarelli v. Duplessis*, [1959] S.C.R. 121
3 *R. c. Drybones*, [1970] S.C.R. 282
4 *Calder et al. v. Attorney-General of British Columbia*, [1973] S.C.R. 313
5 *Attorney General of Canada v. Lavell*, [1974] S.C.R. 1349
6 *Re: Anti-Inflation Act*, [1976] 2 S.C.R. 373
7 *Re: Authority of Parliament in relation to the Upper House*, [1980] 1 S.C.R. 54
8 *Re: Resolution to amend the Constitution*, [1981] 1 S.C.R. 753
9 *Re: Objection by Quebec to a Resolution to amend the Constitution*, [1982] 2 S.C.R. 793
10 *Reference re Upper Churchill Water Rights Reversion Act*, [1984] 1 S.C.R. 297
11 *Singh v. Minister of Employment and Immigration*, [1985] 1 S.C.R. 177
12 *R. v. Big M. Drug Mart Ltd.*, [1985] 1 S.C.R. 295
13 *Operation Dismantle v. The Queen*, [1985] 1 S.C.R. 441
14 *Re B.C. Motor Vehicle Act*, [1985] 2 S.C.R. 486
15 *R. v. Oakes*, [1986] 1 S.C.R. 103
16 *RWDSU v. Dolphin Delivery Ltd.*, [1986] 2 S.C.R. 573
17 *Ford v. Quebec (Attorney General)*, [1988] 2 S.C.R. 712
18 *R. v. Morgentaler*, [1988] 1 S.C.R. 30
19 *R. v. Crown Zellerbach Canada Ltd.*, [1988] 1 S.C.R. 401

[223] See e.g. *Senate Reference (1980)*, *supra* n 54; *Patriation Reference*, *supra* n 19; *Reference re Secession of Quebec*, *supra* n 25; *Reference re Same-Sex Marriage*, *supra* n 33; *Reference re Supreme Court Act, ss. 5 and 6*, *supra* n 80; *Reference re Senate Reform* [2014] SCC 32.

[224] For the sake of uniformity across country reports, ground-breaking cases decided after June 2013 are not included within our canon of 40 leading cases, but may be included in this report.

20 *Slaight Communications Inc. v. Davidson*, [1989] 1 S.C.R. 1038
21 *Irwin Toy Ltd. v. Quebec (Attorney General)*, [1989] 1 S.C.R. 927
22 *Andrews v. Law Society of British Columbia*, [1989] 1 S.C.R. 143
23 *R. v. Keegstra*, [1990] 3 S.C.R. 69
24 *Reference Re Canada Assistance Plan* (B.C.), [1991] 2 S.C.R. 525
25 *Reference re Manitoba Language Rights*, [1992] 1 S.C.R. 212
26 *Schachter v. Canada*, [1992] 2 S.C.R. 679
27 *New Brunswick Broadcasting Co. v. Nova Scotia (Speaker of the House of Assembly)*, [1993] 1 S.C.R. 319
28 *Rodriguez v. British Columbia (Attorney General)*, [1993] 3 S.C.R. 519
29 *R v. Sparrow*, [1990] 1 S.C.R. 10751 S.C.R. 311
30 *Reference re Secession of Quebec*, [1998] 2 S.C.R. 217
31 *Vriend v. Alberta*, [1998] 1 S.C.R. 493
32 *Reference re Remuneration of Judges of the Provincial Court (P.E.I.)*, [1998] 2 S.C.R. 443
33 *Baker v. Canada (Minister of Citizenship and Immigration)*, [1999] 2 S.C.R. 817
34 *United States v. Burns*, [2001] 1 S.C.R. 283, 2001 SCC 7
35 *Gosselin v. Quebec (Attorney General)*, [2002] 4 S.C.R. 429, 2002 SCC 84
36 *Doucet Boudreau v. Nova Scotia (Minister of Education)*, [2003] 3 S.C.R. 3, 2003 SCC 62
37 *Reference re Same-Sex Marriage*, [2004] 3 S.C.R. 698, 2004 SCC 79
38 *Chaoulli v. Quebec (Attorney General)*, [2005] 1 S.C.R. 791, 2005 SCC 35
39 *Canadian Western Bank v. Alberta*, [2007] 2 S.C.R. 3, 2007 SCC 22
40 *Quebec (Attorney General) v. A*, [2013] SCC 5

5

The Constitutional Court of the Czech Republic

ZDENĚK KÜHN

A Legal, Political, Institutional and Academic Context

1 Legal and Political Culture as Context for Constitutional Reasoning

A new development in the Czech legal system began after 1989, when the Czechoslovak communist system collapsed. Within three years, the Czechoslovak federation was gone as well (1992), and a new judicial system began to take shape in the two successor states.

With the exception of the constitutional courts, the majority of Czech courts continued in their formalist reading of the law, inherited from the final era of the communist system. Legal academia also attempted to approach new laws in an utterly textualist way. Thus, the simplified version of textual positivism, inherited from communist times, was able to survive. To some extent, formalism might have worked well in a society with simplified life, where the judiciary usually faces only easy cases and complex cases are channeled through mediators other than the courts.

In post-Communist countries, such an approach became untenable, however, as literally overnight the level of societal life became much more complex and the courts were faced with a transition – in which they had to solve completely new legal issues, such as commercial cases, privatization and new types of business practices – and had to cope with an increased caseload. Many of the new laws, especially in earlier phases of the transition, were of poor quality; some of them, however – and increasingly as time passed – were laws that in content were fully comparable with their Western counterparts. Yet, even the best laws cannot accomplish anything unless they are permanently improved through judicial practice and supported by a strong public demand for that.

The deepest layers of the old legal culture, although without a direct connection to the former official political ideology, are often clothed in new legal vocabulary, thereby influencing legal thought insidiously. Lawyers and ordinary judges used to argue (and some still do) that the application of statutory law is an essentially textualist enterprise; teleological argumentation is a domain reserved for the Constitutional Court. This is allegedly because the Constitution is loaded with open-ended and general concepts and principles. Linked to this has been the unwillingness of many ordinary judges to apply general provisions of their codes which are functionally similar to open-ended constitutional provisions. A gradual disintegration of the old concepts and ideologies of law application after 1993 is connected with the all-pervading activity of the Constitutional Court.

The development of Czech law in the first 10 years of the independent Czech Republic (1993–2003) are characterized by a clash between formalist and self-restrained general courts, on the one hand, and an activist and resolutely anti-formalist Constitutional Court (CCC), on the other. The CCC was the most important element in the legal paradigm shift in the Czech Republic. The second decade (2003–13) saw a gradual change in the general judiciary, which has started to take the Constitution and constitutional reasoning very seriously.

The idea that statutory interpretation is in some way different from constitutional interpretation is supported by the CCC itself. Some of its judgments refer to statutory interpretation as interpreting "simple" law, as opposed to constitutional reasoning, which is not "simple".[1] The champion of this thesis is Professor Pavel Holländer, judge at the Court for two terms (1993–2013). He has written an entire book defending the idea that there is a difference between constitutional and statutory reasoning.[2] Although the CCC does not explain this view clearly, it is clear that the notion of simple law rests on the alleged differences between constitutional and non-constitutional law. The former implies balancing and difficult evaluative reasoning, which is not the case in the latter.

It does not mean that the CCC claims a monopoly on constitutional reasoning. What it demands is rather a final say. The ordinary courts have to use constitutional reasoning while applying the statutes if fundamental rights are at stake. The CCC made a systematic attempt at transplanting into the national legal order major German constitutional

[1] See for instance III. ÚS 224/98 of 8 July 1999. Like many other concepts and terms, this has also been taken over from German dogmatics. See, e.g., BVerfGE 18, 85, *passim* (1964) or BVerfGE 80, 137, at 155 (1989), referring to ordinary non-constitutional law as "*einfaches Recht*", literally translated as "simple" law.

[2] Cf. generally Pavel Holländer, *Ústavněprávní argumentace. Ohlédnutí po deseti letech Ústavního soudu ([Constitutional Argumentation: A Look Back at the Constitutional Court's First Ten Years]* Linde 2003).

doctrines, including the doctrine of the "radiation" of constitutional law throughout the legal system ("*Ausstrahlungswirkung*"),[3] which characterizes mainstream German tendencies in respect of the third-party effect of basic rights.[4] The radiation of basic rights throughout the legal system means that many cases, though governed *prima facie* by "simple" (non-constitutional) law only, have constitutional dimensions, so that in order to decide them properly, the provisions of "simple law" must be interpreted and applied in a manner that takes into account and balances conflicting constitutional rights. For instance, when applying the provisions of the Civil Code concerning defamation and slander, judges must take into account the freedom of speech and counterbalance it against the rights of personal honor. To ignore this constitutional dimension of the application of ordinary law, i.e., the conflict of basic rights in horizontal relations, would lead to one-sided jurisprudence, completely undermining free speech by private means. The CCC directed ordinary courts that

> one of the functions of the Constitution, and especially of the constitutional system of basic rights and freedoms, is its "radiation" throughout the legal order. The sense of the Constitution rests not only in ordering basic rights and freedoms, as well as institutional mechanism and process of making legitimate state decisions, not only in a direct effect of the Constitution and its position as the source of law, but also in a duty of state and public bodies to interpret and apply law considering the protection of basic rights and freedoms. In this case it means the duty of the law courts to interpret particular provisions of the civil procedure code from the viewpoint of the sense and purpose of constitutionally guaranteed basic rights and freedoms.[5]

2 *The Court and Constitutional Litigation*

After the fall of authoritarian or totalitarian regimes, in many countries the deep distrust in the old conception of state and law led to the creation of a constitutional court, which ensures adherence to the state's basic law

[3] Cf. e.g. BVerfGE 7, 198 (206), "*Lüth*" and its Czech counterpart, decision III. ÚS 139/98 of 24 September 1998.

[4] In English see Robert Alexy, *A Theory of Constitutional Rights* (J. Rivers tr, Oxford University Press 2002) 350ff. (at 350, explaining the "substantive fundamentality" of the constitution in this way: "constitutional rights and constitutional rights norms are substantively fundamental, because they incorporate decisions about the basic normative structure of state and society").

[5] III. ÚS 139/98 of 24 September 1998.

through its counter-majoritarian functions.[6] The Czech Republic fits this trend perfectly. There is a tradition of constitutional review which goes back almost 100 years in former Czechoslovakia. This was the first country which incorporated in its Constitution provisions for a constitutional court.[7] The Constitutional Court created in 1920 was the result of the revolutionary atmosphere after World War I. Although the Court was not entirely insignificant, it suffered from serious setbacks. The initial impetus to review a statute had to be given by either chamber of the Parliament, or the Supreme Court, or the Supreme Administrative Court. The high courts, however, did not have this power in relation to a pending case; rather, only *in abstracto*, through the court acting *en banc*.[8] Another major problem was that the statute could not be reviewed if it had been promulgated more than three years before.[9] In addition, after the terms of the justices, who had been appointed in 1921, expired in 1931, the legislature delayed seven years before appointing new justices. The reason for that was the distaste of the legislature to appoint the body which would exercise the control over the legislature's own job. The new justices were appointed only a few months before the collapse of Czechoslovakia and thus did not have time to finish work on important cases pending before the court. After the Constitutional Court ceased to exist with the Nazi occupation in 1939, it took more than five decades to create this institution again. In 1992 a new federal Constitutional Court was established. Because of the dissolution of the Czechoslovak Federation, the Court existed for only 11 months. Both republics which emerged established their own constitutional courts in 1993.

Typology of Decision-Making and the Overall Trends

The Czech Constitutional Court is equipped with virtually all the powers one can give to a constitutional tribunal. It deals with the constitutionality of international treaties prior to their ratification (this has happened only twice, both times with respect to the Lisbon Treaty), the impeachment

[6] Cf., on the counter-majoritarian function of constitutional review, Michel Troper, 'The Logic of Justification of Judicial Review' (2003) 1 *International Journal of Constitutional Law* 99.

[7] Stanley L. Paulson, 'On Hans Kelsen's Role in the Formation of the Austrian Constitution' in Werner Krawietz, Robert S. Summers, Ota Weinberger, Georg Henrik von Wright, et al., *The Reasonable as Rational? On Legal Argumentation and Justification. Festschrift for Aulius Aarnio* (Duncker & Humblot 2000) 385–395, at 390.

[8] See the decision of the Supreme Administrative Court, Boh.adm. 1097/22, 1757/22.

[9] Art. 12 of the Act on the Constitutional Court of 1920.

of the president (the Court dealt with this issue at the beginning of 2013, relating to President Klaus, but it discontinued its proceedings on procedural grounds) and competence disputes between state bodies and bodies of self-governing regions. It has also some other powers, but so far they have never been exercised.

The most important powers are the review of the constitutionality of laws (both acts enacted by parliament and laws made by the executive branch) and constitutional complaints against decisions of state authorities including courts.

The Court sitting as a whole can annul an act of parliament for being unconstitutional based on the proposal of the President or a group of at least 41 deputies (out of all 200) or of at least 17 senators (out of 81). A general court adjudicating the case might also ask the CCC to annul the law if it considers that the law applied is unconstitutional. The panel of the CCC which reviews constitutional complaints can also make a proposal to annul the law which is applicable to the case. Last but not least, a complainant might combine a constitutional complaint with a proposal to annul the law which has been applied.

The CCC has the exclusive competence to annul an act of parliament for being unconstitutional. This applies also to a law which has been abolished by the parliament but is still applied by the general courts because of temporal rules. The general court cannot proclaim such a law unconstitutional. Instead, it must ask the CCC to *declare* its unconstitutionality (annulment is obviously impossible as the law has already been abolished).[10]

This does not mean, however, that a general court does not deal with the constitutionality of an act of parliament in any way. Quite the contrary – it must always consider its constitutionality. If a party argues that the law is unconstitutional, and if the court finds it constitutional, the court must justify its opinion. If it finds the law unconstitutional, it must interrupt proceedings and refer the issue to the CCC. As a rule, it will justify its referral.

The situation is different with respect to all other laws enacted by the executive branch or local self-governments. General courts must always judge their constitutionality, and if they find them unconstitutional, they

[10] The Constitution itself is silent with respect to laws which have been abolished. The CCC basically took this competence without the firm support in the text of the law. See the decision Pl. ÚS 33/2000 of 10 January 2001, in which majority argued in favor of this power against a very strong minority vote.

are not to be applied. The law remains valid but is not applied by the court in a pending case. If the high court decides that such a law is not applicable, lower courts will usually follow such an opinion. A general court cannot ask the CCC to annul such a law; if it does so, the CCC will reject such a proposal. Still, other actors could ask the CCC to annul a law. This includes the government; a group of at least 25 deputies (out of a total number of 200) or a group of at least 10 senators (out of 81); the representative body of a region; or the Ombudsman. Similarly to the annulment of general laws, the panel of the CCC that reviews a constitutional complaint, or a complainant, can also make a proposal to annul the law.

The second most important power of the CCC is the power to review constitutional complaints against individual decisions of state authorities, including judgments of general courts. This follows the German model of constitutional tribunal and eventually makes the CCC the supreme court of the land.[11] In order to gain the right to make a constitutional complaint, one must first exhaust all remedies available. In practice, if not in theory, this power makes the Constitutional Court a super supreme court.[12]

When we see the number of litigations relating to both the review of laws and the review of individual decisions, we can see that especially the latter has multiplied within the past 20 years of the Court's existence.

On the one hand, the number of cases relating to the constitutional review of legislation remains stable. On average, the number of petitions made by deputies or senators has been approximately five annually between 1993 and 2013. In addition, President Havel (1993–2003) was very active in making proposals to the Court. He made 10 petitions in total, and he succeeded at least partly in eight of them. His successor, President Klaus (2003–13), was an outspoken critic of judicial activism, and that is why he used his power with regard to the CCC only once.[13] Third President Zeman (2013–) seems to share Klaus' skepticism, so within the first four years of his term he used this presidential power just once.

[11] See § 13 para. 8a of the law on Federal Constitutional Court, Art. 93 para. 1(4a) and (4b) of the Basic Law.

[12] Procházka rightly noted that the CCC, because of its review of judicial decisions, is the most "judicial" constitutional tribunal in Central Europe. Radoslav Procházka, *Mission Accomplished. On Founding Constitutional Adjudication in Central Europe* (CEU Press 2002) at 166.

[13] It was case Pl. ÚS 17/07, which has been discontinued by the Court because the lawmaker amended the law at stake.

Last but not least, I shall mention the power of general courts to initiate proceedings relating to control of legislation before the CCC. The general courts initiated more than 250 proceedings until the end of 2013, almost half of them decided by the CCC on merits. The rest were rejected for procedural reasons or for being manifestly unfounded. The general courts have been much more active with regard to the CCC in the second decade than in first 10 years of the Court's existence. This also shows the level of internalization of the constitutional tribunal by other legal actors of the judicial system.

There has been a visible rise and now even a flood of constitutional complaints. In the very first year, in 1993, the number of constitutional complaints was less than 500. The complainants and their lawyers had yet to learn the possibilities of this new institution. But they soon found their way. Within two years (by 1995) the number of complaints reached 1200 per year. It took an additional three years to get the number over 2000, and only two years then to get it over 3000. In 2011 the number reached almost 4000 complaints, and in 2013 almost 5000. The CCC actually goes to the merits of a tiny portion of those cases. It deals with about 5 per cent of constitutional complaints, whereas the rest are rejected, usually because the complaint is manifestly unfounded (see below).

As seen from these numbers, the CCC regularly decides on the constitutionality of ordinary court decisions and, therefore, has substantial potential to influence the post-Communist ideology of judicial decision-making. During the first 10 years of its existence (1993–2003), the CCC repeatedly emphasized the anti-formalist nature of the judicial interpretation of law and repeatedly criticized the excessive textual positivism deeply embedded in the post-Communist perception of the judicial application of law and judicial self-understanding. It has provided a major impetus for a more open public discourse on textual positivism in the Czech Republic. From the perspective of the ordinary judiciary, however, it was a very unpleasant intrusion upon their relatively private and otherwise not publicly discussed activities.[14]

Proceedings before the Court

The Court sits either in a full court or in four panels composed of three justices. All cases relating to the review of laws are decided in a full court. In contrast, most constitutional complaints are decided in one of the

[14] See in detail Zdeněk Kühn, *The Judiciary in Central and Eastern Europe. Mechanical Jurisprudence in Transformation?* (Brill 2011).

four panels. It does not matter whether the complaint brings a novel question or whether it is a type of case that has been adjudicated many times. The only exceptions are a few cases, typically those which challenge a decision of the grand chamber of the high court. This system causes many inconsistencies in adjudicating constitutional complaints.

The parties to the procedure of control of laws are the petitioner(s) and the legislature (or another lawmaker, if another law is challenged). The government and the ombudsman have the right to enter any proceedings relating to the review of laws. However, if the referral has been made by the general court, the parties to the original case have no voice before the CCC. In the proceedings relating to constitutional complaints, the complainant and courts (or other state bodies) whose decisions are challenged are the parties; other parties of proceedings before the general courts could also make their arguments before the CCC.

In cases of control of laws, the Court frequently asks other state bodies for their opinion; exceptionally, this is also applied in constitutional complaints. Sometimes opinions of other interveners (*amici curiae*) are allowed as well, though the practice is far from settled.

Proceedings before the Court are based on paperwork. With respect to constitutional complaints the Court can order oral hearings at will, but it almost never does so. Although it is different in cases of the constitutional review of laws, and the hearing as a rule takes place (unless all parties agree to withhold oral arguments), the actual importance of oral hearings is very low. The hearing is usually just a show for the media – the Court has almost always deliberated already, and the votes of the justices have been cast. This proves the different nature of civil law proceedings, where judges tend to decide issues of law *in camera* and lawyers are not used to persuade judges face to face during hearings. On the other hand, written submissions to the Court have become more and more professional in the course of time.

The Court technically has no power to select its cases. In reality, this rule applies to some extent only to the review of laws. The majority of petitions challenging constitutionality of laws, especially those brought by parliamentarians, are decided on merits. Only exceptionally does it happen that the Court rejects the proposal as "manifestly unfounded". The Court is not equipped with any political question doctrine, so it is obliged to decide all cases brought by actors who have standing. However, sometimes the Court refrains from answering some questions because of their political nature and its own self-restraint.[15]

[15] This happened, for instance, in both judgments relating to the Lisbon Treaty. When petitioners tried to press the Court to list all powers which could not be transferred to the

On the contrary, the enormous number of constitutional complaints has forced the Court to apply a sort of selection of cases to be decided on merits. As I have already mentioned, only about 5 per cent of constitutional complaints are decided by the Court on merits, whereas the rest is rejected for being "manifestly unfounded". The latter means that the Court has not reviewed the case in detail and has explained (usually only in a few sentences) that the case did not touch any issue of a constitutional nature. Since 2013, the Court has had the power to not justify those decisions. In reality, those decisions continue to be briefly justified (one might guess that this is also due to the need for other justices than the author of the draft to know what they are deciding). The precedential value of those decisions is very low. One might also notice that some judges' rapporteurs are much more reluctant to decide a constitutional complaint on merits than some others. This indicates that proceedings in thousands of constitutional complaints are controlled by judges' rapporteurs and their law clerks, with only occasional contribution by two remaining judges.

The Court Adopts Three Basic Types of Decisions

First, there are judgments on the merits in the constitutional review of laws. Those judgments can either reject the proposal or annul the law. The Court determines the moment when the law will be annulled: it sometimes happens at the moment of the publication of the judgment, but sometimes the effects of the judgment are delayed. The latter happens routinely if the Court wants to give a chance to the lawmaker to enact new legislation. The effects of laws which have been found unconstitutional but not yet annulled are questionable. The most recent case law of the CCC seems to give such a law all its effects until the annulment comes into effect. All decisions relating to such proceedings are published in both the official *Collection of Laws* and the official *Reports of Constitutional Court's Judgments*. In the former, judgments are published (including the court's reasoning), but dissenting or concurring opinions are omitted; in the latter separate opinions are published as well. In principle, the judgment goes into effect when it is published in the *Collection of Laws*. Similarly, it applies also to judgments relating to the preliminary review of international treaties.

Second, there are judgments on merits relating to constitutional complaints. In this type of judgment, the Court either rejects the constitutional complaint or quashes the decision of public authority. The judgment is

European Union, the Court rebuffed it, arguing that this is essentially a political question. See Pl. ÚS 29/09 of 3 November 2009 (*Lisbon Treaty II*).

published only in the official *Reports of Constitutional Court's Judgments*; dissenting or concurring opinions are included. The Court can also decide to publish such a decision in the *Collection of Laws*, if the decision is very important for the legal system as a whole.

Third, there are decisions on admissibility. The Court can dismiss or reject any complaint and any proposal, if it was made after the deadline for such a proposal, if the complainant is not represented by an attorney, if the complaint is incomprehensible, etc. The most frequent case is when the petition is manifestly unfounded. Those decisions are usually only lightly justified, and they are not published in any official publication. Since 2006, however, they have been published online at the Court's website. A few of those decisions are published in the *Reports of Constitutional Court's Judgments* if the judge-rapporteur recommends this and if the majority of judges agree.

3 *The Judges*

The Court is composed of 15 justices, including the Chief Justice and two deputies. Justices, unlike career judges, are political appointees with a visible professional and sometimes political past behind them. The American model of appointments is followed, where justices are appointed by the President with the approval of the Senate. The term of each justice is 10 years, and unlike in almost all European countries, it is renewable.

The strategies and the nature of presidential appointments have differed. President Havel appointed all justices within several months (in 1993 and two in 1994), having little trouble persuading parliamentarians to approve his nominees. President Klaus' strategy was different; some of his nominees were awkward, to say the least, and a very painful process followed, when the Court had a number of vacancies and for some time was even unable to sit in full court.[16] Yet another scenario is that of President Zeman. Thanks to his friendly relations with Chief Justice Rychetský, the President consulted on all nominations in advance with the Chief Justice. It appears that many appointed justices in 2013 and 2014 have been the choices of the Chief Justice rather than the President.

Because there was no initial preliminary period, the first justices were appointed after the Court's creation in 1993 by first president Havel. All

[16] In English see Zdeněk Kühn, Jan Kysela, "Nomination of Constitutional Justices in Post-Communist Countries: Trial, Error, Conflict in the Czech Republic" (2006) 2 *European Constitutional Law Review* 183.

terms were about to expire in 2003 or early 2004. With few exceptions (deaths, resignations) the Court continues to operate in 10-year periods (1993/4–2003/4, 2003/04–2013/14, and so on). That is why every president is able to model the Court according to his own taste. In fall 2014, when this paper was finished, the majority of the Court was composed of justices appointed by the third president Zeman. A sort of continuity has been achieved, however, through repeated appointments of former justices: President Klaus reappointed three "Havel" justices, and Zeman until 2014 reappointed two "Klaus" justices including Chief Justice Rychetský (appointed in 2003, reappointed in 2013). Two other reappointed justices were rejected by the Senate, apparently for political reasons and because of senators' distaste over their decision making.

The Court has been getting its justices from academia, the ordinary judiciary, and attorneys. Exceptionally, former politicians have been appointed to the bench. Initially, the number of academics was lower than in other Central European countries. This perhaps reflects the difficulty of finding academics not compromised by the Czechoslovak communist regime. In spring 2003, at the end of the existence of the first "Havel Court", only one-third of the bench was composed of law professors (5 of 15). The number declined in the second Court appointed by Klaus – only three academics were sitting on the bench. The number rose again in the Court appointed by Zeman – six academics were at the Court in 2014. The number of ordinary judges on the bench seems to be more stable (usually around five).

In its first decade (1993–2003), the composition of the Court was interesting indeed. We could find there outstanding figures able to give the Court's reasoning moral legitimacy as well as appropriate direction toward more sophisticated adjudication. An important role was also played by charismatic lawyers exiled during the communist rule or subject to persecution.[17] Such exceptional figures were necessary if we consider the very nature of the activity of the new courts, especially in its first 10 years: to introduce new conceptions of constitutionalism in a society governed by very different ideals. The leading figures of the CCC were scholars who had a background in Western doctrine.[18]

Generally, justices of the first Court were rightist and resolutely anticommunist. This reflected the atmosphere shortly after the fall of the

[17] Such as Vladimír Klokočka (1993–2003) or Eliška Wagnerová (from 2002).

[18] For instance, Pavel Holländer, a legal philosopher, was reappointed for his second term in 2003 (on the bench 1993–2013).

communist regime. Thereby one can also see a relatively small number of dissenting opinions in that era (only 73 judgments with separate opinions between 1993 and 2003). In the years 2003 and 2004, with the flood of President Klaus' appointees, the Court became more diverse, with some robust leftist justices joining the bench. Since then, the number of dissenting opinions has doubled (more than 140 judgments with separate opinions between 2004 and 2013).[19] After the election of the leftist President Zeman in 2013, the Court seems to be moving considerably leftwards, at least considering the professional background of some justices appointed in 2013 and 2014.

Each justice could hire three law clerks; some justices employ more part-time law clerks. Much of the drafting is actually performed by law clerks, who cannot, however, be present at judicial deliberations. Law clerks are paid a good salary, so the job is attractive even for more experienced lawyers. Some law clerks are law professors, others are recent law school graduates. Interestingly, one former justice remained at the court after 2003 in the position of law clerk. Since the 2000s the Court has been equipped with a comparative law research body, composed mostly of young lawyers. It is noteworthy that three current justices spent some time as law clerks in the 1990s (Sládeček, Šimíček and Šimáčková).

4 *Legal Scholarship and Constitutional Reasoning*

The collaboration between scholars and judges, so typical of Continental legal culture, was seriously hampered during the Communist regime. On the one hand, case notes and critical analyses of case law have mostly disappeared. Clearly this is a legacy not only of the Communist era, but also of the lack of resources and low salaries in legal academia, where academics do not have time to analyze and criticize their own courts' case law. Moreover, Central and Eastern Europe consists primarily of small countries which have a small number of law schools and few academics. The Czech Republic, a nation of 10 million, has only four law schools. There are only two professors of constitutional law in the country, one of them sitting on the bench since 2013. Taking into account the parochial

[19] For more detail, see Zdenek Kühn, "Ústavní soud České republiky: proměny instituce v průběhu dvou desetiletí" ([Constitutional Court of the Czech Republic: transformation of the institution in two decades], in: *20 let Ústavy České republiky. Ohlédnutí zpět a pohled vpřed [20 years of the Czech Constitution. A glance at the past and considerations for the future]* Aleš Čeněk 2013), 246 ff.

attitude of local academia, it should come as no surprise that the situation in countries where all scholars and high court judges know each other personally is not conducive to an atmosphere of open and critical discourse.

The situation is slowly improving. Case notes have appeared since the 2000s, and the most important judgments of the Court are analyzed and sometimes criticized. Most judges of the Court take those comments into account and, exceptionally, address them in their judgments as well (see below). Still, scholarship is mostly deferential towards the Court, and academics often restrain themselves to just repeating what the Court said.

The position of constitutional judge is considered the most prestigious among law professions in the country. Since the early 2000s, their salary has been repeatedly reduced, however. The salary was still better than that of a typical law school professor but a bit lower than that of supreme court judges. This was because the Court repeatedly annulled laws lowering the wages of ordinary judges, whereas constitutional judges themselves suffered repeated cuts in their income. This issue was remedied in summer 2014 when the pay of the CCC's justices was increased considerably. Now they are again the best-paid state legal profession, their pay being approximately 10 per cent above that of supreme court judges.

B Arguments in Constitutional Reasoning

5 *Structure of Constitutional Arguments*

My selection of 40 cases is representative over time. Of those 40 cases, almost half were produced by the Court in its first decade (1993–2003), and 21 were decided by the Court in its second decade (2003–2013). The Court's methodology and style have been developing through the work of charismatic and influential legal thinkers, such as professors Klokočka (1929–2009, on the bench 1993–2003), Čermák (1929–2004, 1993–2003) and especially Holländer (1953, 1993–2013). Both Klokočka and Holländer have written several books on constitutional interpretation.[20] Holländer, perhaps the most intelligent judge of the first 20 years, enjoyed the opportunity to model the Court's style within his two terms. In fact, of

[20] V. Klokočka, *Ústavní zřízení evropských států (srovnávací studie)* ([*Constitutional systems of European states (comparative study)*] Linde 1996); P. Holländer, *Ústavněprávní argumentace – ohlédnutí po deseti letech Ústavního soudu* ([*Constitutional reasoning – a glance at ten years of the Constitutional Court*] Linde 2003), published also in German as *Verfassungsrechtliche Argumentation – zwischen dem Optimismus und der Skepsis* (Duncker & Humblot 2007).

the 40 judgments I selected for this study, 3 have been written by Klokočka and 8 by Holländer. Last but not least, one should not forget the name of Eliška Wagnerová, the most activist judge of the second term (2003–2013). She has written six judgments selected for my study. So almost half of the judgments in this study were written by three people.

Usually, the judgment starts with a short description of the case, followed by the arguments of the parties. Then a more precise description of the facts of the case follows (with respect to constitutional complaints). This makes judgment rather chaotic. The argumentation proper follows, usually divided into sections.

Even though some judges of the Court, especially Holländer, struggled to imitate the German style (as summarized in the term *Verfassungsdogmatik*[21]), the Court's judgments have never had one single face. Over time, the style of judgments has become even more diverse than it used to be in the 1990s. One reason for this might be the ever-growing caseload of the Court and the gradual delegation of writing to the law clerks. So the style of some weaker judges differs from case to case, depending on who actually did the writing.

Within the 40 cases under study, one can see especially chain-structure arguments ("one-line conclusive arguments": 9 cases) or "legs of a chair" argumentation ("parallel conclusive arguments": 25 cases). In the 2000s the latter seems to have prevailed over the former. Between 1993 and 1998, of 7 cases, 5 were one-line conclusive arguments. Since 1999, I have been able to identify only 4 other cases of this kind, out of remaining 33. It would be difficult to say which of those two models is considered superior. I personally think that this answer cannot be generalized and that it depends on the case. In routine constitutional cases one-line conclusive argument seems to be preferred. However, the harder the case, the more likely the use of the "legs of a chair" model. By bringing more arguments, the judges do all they can to persuade their readers that their decision is correct and lawful.

An enlightening example is the *European Arrest Warrant* case.[22] Here the Court used several independent lines of argumentation to justify why it is not unconstitutional to surrender a Czech national under European Arrest Warrant despite the wording of the Czech Bill of Rights, which seemed to prohibit extradition. Another example is the *Vondráčková v.*

[21] A. Jakab, 'Judicial Reasoning in Constitutional Courts. A European Perspective' (2013) 14 *German Law Journal*, at 38–40.

[22] Pl. ÚS 66/04 of 3 May 2006.

Rejžek case, a leading case relating to the freedom of expression. The Court used a first line of argumentation criticizing ordinary courts for not balancing freedom of speech and privacy, and then it used an independent line of arguments demonstrating that the criticized person was a public figure, which would itself cause a lower level of privacy protection.[23]

The result of my study might be tricky, however. The selection of 40 cases brings mostly hard cases. Judges reason here more than in routine constitutional cases. If we have studied all judgments on merits (between 1993 and 2013, almost 4000), a typical pattern of reasoning would be perhaps a chain structure. After all, it relates to syllogism, which is considered an ideal model for all legal reasoning, including constitutional law.

The dialogic model ("parallel, individually inconclusive, but together conclusive arguments") occurs rarely. In our set of 40 cases, it has been used in just a few. One leading example is the decision relating to the constitutionality of post–World War II presidential decrees that deprived Czechoslovak Germans and Hungarians of their nationality and effectively meant their expulsion and loss of property. Addressing a constitutional complaint of one German who tried to annul decrees and get back his property, the Court wrote a lengthy judgment through which it tried to evaluate history. The judgment is far from a typical legal writing; instead its passionate arguments are closer to a historical defense of the actions of the Czechoslovak government after World War II.[24] A legal formalist would have tried to avoid this hot historical potato by escaping on jurisdictional grounds.[25] In other cases, the dialogic model seems to be a byproduct of the inability of the writer to produce a coherent set of arguments which would fit either the chain structure model or the legs of a chair argumentation.

6 *Types of Arguments in Constitutional Reasoning*

The Constitution does have some rules as to how it should be interpreted. One has to mention above all Bill of Rights Art. 4(3), according to which "[a]ny statutory limitation upon the fundamental rights and freedoms must apply in the same way to all cases which meet the specified

[23] I. ÚS 367/03 of 15 March 2005 (*Vondráčková v. Rejžek*)

[24] Pl. ÚS 14/94 of 9 March 1995.

[25] It is hard to say why judges jumped into this heated debate instead of simply saying that the presidential decrees produced their results fifty years earlier and so the Court cannot review legislation which is no longer applied. One answer might be that the first Court was composed of many personal witnesses of the atrocities of World War II.

conditions" (generality of constitutional interpretation) and the often applied Art. 4(4), which refers to the core content of fundamental rights ("When employing the provisions concerning limitations upon the fundamental rights and freedoms, the essence and significance of these rights and freedoms must be preserved. Such limitations shall not be misused for purposes other than those for which they were enacted"). With respect to social rights, Art. 41 states that one can call for protection only within the scope of laws which implement social rights. However, Art. 41 remains controversial, as can be seen from those cases where it has been applied.[26]

Analogies

The number of decisions dealing with analogies is very low. The argument of analogy is considered a regular legal argument. However, the CCC seems to delegate it to dealing with ordinary ("simple") law. I have been able to identify only four cases which address analogy. Usually, analogy is referred to when the CCC deals with competences of state bodies, competence conflicts, etc. Here, it deals with enumeration of competences within the Constitution which sometimes contains gaps.

It seems that justices do not view analogy to be noble enough. A good example is the case where analogy was discussed by both the Court and a concurring judge. The case was about the power of the President to veto the law within 15 days of receiving it. The Constitution does not explicitly say what happens if the President vetoes a law, but his veto was delivered to the House of Representatives on the 16th or 17th day because the 15th day was Saturday or Sunday. The Court rejected the textualist argument that the President simply missed the deadline. Instead, it construed general principles of law, allegedly dating back to Roman law, which filled the gap in the constitutional text. One judge concurred with the verdict but noted that what the Court really did was a simple analogy. There was no need for a noble justification through principles of law if analogy was at hand, in judge's view. However, this was obviously not the opinion of the remaining 14 justices who simply did not consider analogy to fit a "high" constitutional rhetoric.[27]

Establishing/Debating the Text of the Constitution

Five cases have been identified as either establishing or discussing what counts as the text of the Constitution. Taking into account the fact that the

[26] Pl. ÚS 1/08 of 20 May 2008 (*Health Care Fees*).

[27] Pl. ÚS 33/97 of 17 December 1997.

most important cases have been selected, I doubt one would find more cases of this type in the Court's case law.

Into the first type of cases which fit into this category belong "transitional" cases, discussing the conflict of the communist and democratic systems after 1989. The very first judgment of the Court, dealing with the constitutionality of the act on the lawlessness of the communist regime, is a primary example of that. The Court compared the old and the new Constitution and explicitly rejected the argument that the law proclaiming the old regime as criminal was unconstitutional. The Court argued that this was a new Constitution which was applicable and denounced the protection of the legal certainty of those who referred to the protection of values under the old Constitution.[28]

In the second type, the CCC discusses what counts as a constitution, and by so doing it expands its own powers. For instance, the Court rejected the constitutional amendment which classified international human rights treaties as not being part of the Constitution. Against the wording of the constitutional amendment, the CCC expanded the concept of the Constitution and added human rights treaties as part of the Constitution.[29] Because those treaties are sometimes difficult to identify (are they human rights treaties, thereby being parts of the Constitution, or are they regular treaties, thereby not being parts of the Constitution?) the Court ironically decides what the Constitution is.[30]

Another example is the (in)famous *Melčák* case, where the Court annulled the constitutional law for being unconstitutional. The constitutional law shortened the term of the House of Representatives elected in 2006 from four to three years. Because this happened through the special constitutional law rather than through the procedure envisaged by the Constitution, the Court concluded that the constitutional law breached the requirement of the generality of the laws. The Court declared its power to determine the constitutionality of constitutional laws (whether they are not in conflict with the unalterable core of the Constitution).[31]

Last but not least, I shall mention a less problematic judgment, relating to a competence conflict between the President and the Prime Minister over the countersignature of the appointment of the governor of the National Bank. The text of the Constitution implied that the

[28] Pl. ÚS 19/93 of 21 December 1993 (*lawlessness of the communist regime*).

[29] Pl. ÚS 36/01 of 25 June 2002.

[30] That is why the judgment has been severely criticized by many scholars, including myself.

[31] Pl. ÚS 27/09 of 10 September 2009

countersignature of the Prime Minister is necessary; however, the practice between 1993 and 2000 was that President Havel appointed governors and vice-governors without any approval or interference from any Prime Minister. The Court was debating to what extent constitutional conventions could amend the text of the Constitution. The Court ended divided about the length and strength of the practice. A majority of justices, however, wrote that constitutional practices could overwrite the text of the Constitution.[32]

Applicability of the Constitution

Five cases discuss to what extent the Constitution or some of its provisions are applicable. Most frequently this happens in EU law–related cases where the Court had to discuss to what extent the Constitution is applicable to EU laws.[33]

Another case discussed to what extent social rights could be invoked against the legislature, which, according to petitioners, violated the constitutional right to free medical services by imposing fees for every time a patient visits her physician or has a medicine prescribed by her physician (fee approximately 1 euro). The Court interpreting the text of the Bill of Rights agreed that social rights could be referred to, but the legislature enjoys a substantial margin of appreciation untouched by constitutional review.[34]

The last group is close to what is known in the USA as *political question doctrine.* In my set of cases, this is the case where the Court to some extent insulated the political campaign from judicial intervention. The Court annulled the judgment of the Supreme Administrative Court (SAC), which had annulled the results of the elections of one senator. The SAC annulled the elections because the elected senator violated the rules of political campaign. The Court harshly criticized the SAC for interfering with political competition. Even though the Court agreed that some parts of the campaign were not fair, the courts still respect the insulation of a political campaign from judicial review unless it has been proved that the unfairness has been in direct relation to the actual result of elections. The term *political question doctrine* is not technically used, but the Court

[32] Pl. ÚS 14/01 of 20 June 2001

[33] A good example of that is European Arrest Warrant case, Pl. ÚS 66/04 of 3 May 2006.

[34] Pl. ÚS 1/08 of 20 May 2008. *Health Care Fees* case, going against clear wording of the constitutional right to free medical care, has become one of the most controversial cases the Court has ever decided.

made it clear that a political campaign shall be, save extreme instances, subject to the final verdict of voters, not courts.[35]

Ordinary Meaning of the Words of the Constitution

One obvious difference from statutory interpretation is the fact that the Court quite often does not deal with the textual interpretation of the Constitution at all (in 19 cases under my review the Court did not mention textual interpretation). Especially in cases of fundamental rights, the Court does not even recite the actual wording of the provision interpreted; instead it follows previous case law on that particular issue. The connection between the text of the provision and the result of interpretation is usually very indirect and distant.

The most often invoked provision in constitutional complaints is Art. 36(1) of the Bill of Rights, which says that "[e]veryone may assert, through the prescribed procedure, her rights before an independent and impartial court or, in specified cases, before another body". In the absence of another provision to use, one would simply refer to Art. 36(1). The Court uses this fundamental right for both procedural and substantive law errors before the ordinary courts. The Court calls this fundamental right the "fundamental right to due [or fair] process", and further it added some substantive meaning (similar to "substantive due process" in the US). As the link between the text of the Constitution, which says nothing about fairness or due process, and the meaning attributed to it by the Court is close to zero, the Court simply avoids any textual interpretation whatsoever.[36]

Exceptions to this rule are the judgments which refer to more concrete fundamental rights. A notable example is the *European Arrest Warrant*. A group of Euro-skeptic parliamentarians challenged the law which implemented EU framework decision on Arrest Warrant, claiming that it is in conflict with Art. 14(4) of the Bill of Rights which says that no citizen may be forced to leave his homeland. Before going into both teleological arguments the Court first emphasized that the text of Art. 14(4) does not itself, without further arguments, unambiguously resolve the issue, although a linguistic interpretation of the phrase "forced to leave one's

[35] Pl. ÚS 73/04 of 26 January 2005.

[36] In my set of 40 cases, this is the example of the judgment of III. ÚS 258/03 of 6 May 2004. Here the right to (substantive) due process enabled the Court to interfere with the interpretation of contracts as made by ordinary courts.

homeland" might include even such a relatively brief surrender of a citizen to a foreign state for a criminal proceeding.[37]

Decisions which routinely start by considering the ordinary wording of the Constitution are usually those dealing with institutional design and competences. The best example is the case about the power of the President to veto the law within 15 days of receiving it, discussed earlier (in the *Analogies* section). Let us just remember that the Constitution does not explicitly state what happens if the 15th day is Saturday or Sunday and the veto is returned on Monday. Textually, it means the veto has been returned late. This was also the position of the Parliament. The Court denounced such a textual reading of the Constitution. First, it emphasized that the textual reading of the law has been abused by totalitarian regimes of the twentieth century. In the view of the Court, the judiciary has been manipulated by such textualist approaches. Then the Court concluded:

> The Court cannot accept if someone relies only on textual interpretation. Textual (linguistic) interpretation represents only the first step in understanding the law. It is only an exposure to understanding the rationale and meaning of the law (that is why other steps must be used, such as logical and systemic interpretation, interpretation *e ratione legis* [i.e. teleological or purposive method] etc.). Mechanical application of the law, whether disregarding the rationale and meaning of the legal norm intentionally or by ignorance, makes from the law an instrument of alienation and absurdity.[38]

This paragraph has become perhaps the most often quoted from the entire Court's jurisprudence. Although the Court used it first for the interpretation of the Constitution, in its later case law the Court has been using it for both constitutional and statutory interpretation without any distinction.[39] And so did a plethora of decisions of ordinary courts. We will see this again when teleological interpretation is discussed later.

Harmonising Arguments

The Court is using several arguments which will harmonize the meaning of the interpreted provision with other constitutional provisions or with international or EU law. Some kind of harmonizing arguments were found in the majority of the cases. Domestic harmonization has been found

[37] Pl. ÚS 66/04 of 3 May 2006, paras 64 – 65.

[38] Pl. ÚS 33/97 of 17 December 1997. The judge-rapporteur Pavel Holländer, who is familiar with German jurisprudence, took his inspiration from the German Constitutional Court, cf. BVerfGE 35, 263 (278 ff.).

[39] See, e.g., III. ÚS 258/03 of 6 May 2004, where the Court applies it for statutory interpretation. The author of this judgment, by the way, is also Holländer.

in 31 cases, transnational harmonization (international or EU-friendly construction) in 22 cases. In many cases both types of harmonization are used.

On a domestic level, both (originally German) concepts of the unity of the constitution and *praktische Konkordanz* are used.[40] The Court faces conflicts of fundamental rights in both abstract review and constitutional complaints cases. The Court prefers to find a compromise in those conflicts rather than approaching them in an "all-or-nothing" fashion. The influence of contemporary doctrines on principles and their weighing, especially Alexy and Dworkin, is visible in much of the Court's case law. Sometimes those scholars are even quoted in the judgment. On the other hand, one must keep in mind that the balancing approach puts the final word into the Constitutional Court, which can always say that balancing has been done incorrectly. So those doctrines effectively empower the CCC as the ultimate guardian of the Constitution.

On a transnational level, both EU and international law–friendly meta-rules are applied. They were summarized in the European Arrest Warrant case. It referred to the general principle expressed in Art. 1(2) of the Constitution, according to which the Czech Republic shall obey its obligations resulting from international law. Because the Constitution itself proclaims the value of being open towards international law,[41] in principle the Constitution shall be construed so as to be in harmony with international law. Since the entry of the Czech Republic into the EU, Art. 1(2)

> took on new significance in relation to the observance of duties which arise for the Czech Republic from its membership in the EU. As the Czech Republic has already emphasized in its case-law, European law is founded on fundamental values, common to all EU Member States. The Constitutional Court thus declared the Czech Republic's allegiance to the European legal culture and to its constitutional traditions. The Constitutional Court also interprets constitutional acts, above all the Bill of Rights, in light of the general principle of law existing in all Member States of the Union . . . [Thereby it] follows a constitutional principle according to which national legal enactments, including the Constitution, should whenever possible be interpreted in conformity with the process of European integration and the cooperation between European and Member State organs.[42]

40 Pl. ÚS 4/94 of 12 October 1994 (*Anonymous Witness*) is the first example of this line of cases.

41 Here I refer to the judgment Pl. US 31/03 of 11 February 2004 (*Protection of Secret Information*), also contained in my list of judgments.

42 Pl. ÚS 66/04 of 3 May 2006 (*European Arrest Warrant*), paras 80 and 81.

Precedents

Today it is hard to find a judgment which does not refer to the Court's previous case law. Even in novel cases of the first impression, without any guiding precedent, it is considered necessary to legitimize the judgment by quoting some case law, no matter how distant its relation to the current issue. Indeed, I have been able to identify only four cases without any reference to the Court's earlier case law (not surprisingly, all belong to the first three years of the Court's existence). Interestingly, the very first judgment of the Court (that on constitutionality of the act on lawlessness of the communist regime), facing the total absence of any Court case law, referred at least to one German case.[43] Since late 1996, I have always found at least one quotation of earlier case law. My rough estimate is that in the 2010s an average judgment refers to 10 earlier cases.

The Court is technically bound by its previous case law. It does not matter whether case law is composed of a line of cases or one single judgment. The Court can freely deviate only from those cases which have not been decided on merits. However, if the case has been decided on merits, whether through the entire Court or the panel of three judges (judgments on constitutional complaints), the Court is obliged to follow the *ratio* of the decided case unless the plenum overrules the precedent by a majority of at least 9 judges out of 15.

Formal overruling through the Court sitting *en banc* happens rarely. Between 1993 and 2013 it happened just 26 times. Considering thousands of cases decided meanwhile, it is a rather rare procedure. The Court rather tries to avoid overruling its case law, making various distinctions.

In *Melčák* (unconstitutionality of constitutional law case) the Court indicated that it makes a difference between holding (*ratio*) and *dicta*:

> In this regard, democratic constitutional law theory agrees that it is relevant to the binding nature of a precedent to distinguish the importance of *ratio decidendi* and *obiter dicta*: "the written opinion of the precedent-setting court is not binding in its entirety; only the grounds for the decision, the *ratio decidendi*, are binding."[44]

Doctrinal Analysis of Legal Concepts and Principles

The Court often develops various constitutional concepts which are not expressly mentioned in the Constitution. Those concepts include legal certainty, protection of legitimate expectations, the untouchable

[43] Pl. ÚS 19/93 of 21 December 1993 (*lawlessness of the communist regime*).

[44] Pl. ÚS 27/09 of 10 September 2009.

core of social rights (which are otherwise within free discretion of the legislature),[45] democracy capable of defending itself,[46] etc. The Court enjoys a rather large space for its arguments, which are constrained, though to some extent only, by a consensus of constitutional scholarship. Because legal scholarship usually refers to its case law, "doctrinal" analysis by the Court often becomes self-referential. The strong position of law professors at the Court multiplies this problem. Some judgments look like a piece of scholarship. Some judges write their judgments and then support their doctrinal works by quoting those judgments (or vice versa, but this happens usually without quoting the original article or book[47]). Effectively, the only restraint on this kind of argumentation is the earlier case law of the Court.

I have been able to identify this sort of argumentation in at least 15 cases. In the overall number of judgments the frequency would be lower, however. The doctrinal analysis is limited to really hard cases.

Arguments from Silence

Arguments from silence are well known in Czech law, but their use in constitutional interpretation remains limited. The reason for this seems to be similar to what I have already explained with respect to analogy. To put it simply, arguments such as *a contrario*, *a fortiori*, etc., do not seem to be noble enough for constitutional litigation. Another reason why they are rarely used is the fact that the use of those (for the Court too formalistic) arguments might undermine the domination of teleological arguments in the Court's reasoning.

The arguments were considered in only four cases, and in three of those cases the results brought by this sort of argument were ultimately rejected. The only exception was the case relating to the dismissal of the Supreme Court Chief Justice by President Klaus, where the Court noted that the Constitution gives the President the power to appoint a Chief Justice, not to dismiss her. Still, this argument was far from being controlling. What decided the case in favor of the Chief Justice were arguments by the purpose of the Constitution.[48] Therefore, unlike ordinary statutory

[45] Pl. ÚS 1/08 of 20 May 2008 (*Health Care Fees*).

[46] Cf. for instance, Pl. ÚS 9/01 of 5 December 2001 (*Lustration*).

[47] The example of this is Pl. ÚS 27/09 of 10 September 2009 (*Melčák* case) which declared a constitutional act as being unconstitutional. The judgment in many parts follows, word for word, an article published by judge rapporteur Professor Holländer five years earlier.

[48] Pl. ÚS 18/06 of 11 July 2006 (*dismissal of Supreme Court Chief Justice*).

interpretation, the arguments from silence of the Constitution might be supplementary, at most.

Teleological (Purposive) Arguments Referring to the Purpose of the Text

This type of argument dominates the Court's reasoning, at least in hard cases. In all cases under my review some sort of (objective) teleology has always been used. The Court often does not deal with the constitutional text; however, it always considers the purpose behind the constitutional text. The exceptions are the cases which just follow what has been decided earlier where the result is justified by the Court's own case law (those cases are not part of my list of "Top 40").

The move towards objective teleological interpretation was part of the transformative function of the Court in the 1990s and early 2000s. The Court here acted as a principal contender to post-Communist legal culture, dominated by formalist legal reasoning and simplified textualism. Following the Communist legacy, post-Communist lawyers (including academics) overestimated the possibilities of the literal reading of the law, viewing teleological arguments as a rather unimportant tool to be employed only in very exceptional situations.[49] Many decisions of the CCC have performed the function which should have been, under normal conditions, exercised above all by legal scholars. The CCC, inspired by foreign case law, has tried to teach the ordinary courts that they are not

> absolutely bound by the literal wording of a legal provision, as they can and must deviate therefrom if such a deviation is demanded by serious reasons of the law's purpose, the history of its adoption, systematic reasons or any principle deriving from the constitutionally conforming legal order . . . In doing so, it is necessary to avoid arbitrariness; the court decisions must be based on a rational argumentation.[50]

The Court has argued in favor of purposive (teleological) argumentation from the very beginning of its existence. In doing so, it acted indiscriminately whether this was the case of constitutional or statutory

[49] See, e.g., views about interpretation, as made in a prominent Czech textbook on legal theory, according to which the basic methods of interpretation are grammatical, logical and systemic, whereas historical and teleological are exceptional and rather unimportant. The textbook presents interpretation as a rather mechanical activity, so it takes up only five pages out of 350. See J. Boguszak, J. Čapek, A. Gerloch, *Teorie práva* ([Legal Theory], 2nd ed., Eurolex Bohemia 2004,), 182–187.

[50] Pl. ÚS 21/96 of 4 February 1997. This case is not part of my selection of the "Top 40", but the quotation above has been repeated many times since it was included in our list of cases. Cf. III. ÚS 258/03 of 6 May 2004 (*Interpretation of contracts*).

interpretation. Justice Holländer has argued that the move towards purposive (teleological) argumentation is a necessary shift which must be completed in Central European legal doctrine.[51] Similarly, the CCC argued that the purpose and meaning of the law is to be found not only in the letter of the law, because "legal enactments do, and must always, include within themselves the principles recognized as part of the democratic states governed by the rule of law".[52]

Teleological (Purposive) Arguments Referring to the Purpose of the Constitution-Maker

Unlike objective teleological arguments, the impact of the purpose of the constitution-maker is much smaller. In fact, the CCC refers to the history of the constitution rarely. In our list of 40 cases it happened only six times.

The unwillingness of the Court to refer to legislative history is caused by two factors. First, the Constitution and especially the Bill of Rights have got very poor travaux préparatoires. Also other sources of legislative history (speeches of parliamentarians while enacting the constitution) are very brief, if they exist at all.

Second, it is generally accepted that objective teleological argumentation, found by the interpreter, is superior to subjective teleological argumentation of the constitution-maker. It has been mentioned in the *European Arrest Warrant* case. The Court had to interpret whether the constitutional ban on "forcing a national to leave his homeland" also covers the prohibition against extraditing a national. The Court agreed with all parties to the proceedings that the experience of the crimes of the Communist regime played a critical role in drafting this provision. This was especially the operation of the secret police in the early 1980s, whose aim was to force troublesome dissidents to leave Czechoslovakia. Subjective teleology thus attested to the fact that the ban was never concerned with extradition.[53] This finding was not, however, conclusive:

> The intention of the constitutional framers is not alone a decisive argument, where it is based on historical experience, particularly in the circumstance where historical memory fades and cannot be passed on to future generations, because they are bound up with the experience of their own times.[54]

[51] Cf. generally Pavel Holländer, *Ústavněprávní argumentace. Ohlédnutí po deseti letech Ústavního soudu* ([*Constitutional Argumentation: A Look Back at the Constitutional Court's First Ten Years*] Linde 2003).

[52] IV. ÚS 275/96 of 15 October 1996 (1996 Senate elections, unconstitutionality of banning some candidates to run).

[53] Pl. ÚS 66/04 of 3 May 2006 (*European Arrest Warrant*), para 66.

[54] Para 67.

For this reason, the Court sought the objective meaning of the provision, which must be gauged against contemporary life and institutions at the start of the twenty-first century. If Czech citizens enjoy certain advantages connected with the status of EU citizenship, then it is natural in this context that a certain degree of responsibility must be accepted along with these advantages. The investigation and suppression of criminality in the EU cannot be successfully accomplished within the framework of individual Member States, but requires extensive international cooperation. The objective meaning of the Constitution has been interpreted against these considerations.[55]

Non-legal (Moral, Sociological, Economic) Arguments

The CCC uses "non-legal" arguments much more often than any other court in the Czech legal system. One of the first judgments of the Court, dealing with post–World War II presidential decrees and the expulsion of Sudeten Germans, was loaded with historical and moral justifications, better resembling a popular historical treatise than the work of lawyers.[56]

In other cases, non-legal arguments are less important but still visible. The champion of non-legal argumentation has been Eliška Wagnerová, who did not hesitate to quote, for instance, from the Bible.[57] However, other judges were ready to quote some non-legal arguments as well, such as the Code of Hammurabi while deciding whether medical fees are consistent with the Constitution.[58] The actual importance of those arguments is small; quite often they are just there to show off, to catch the reader's attention. An interesting example of a non-legal argument is the judgment proclaiming a decision of the European Court of Justice *ultra vires*. The Court criticized the ECJ for not understanding European history and the uniqueness of the dissolution of Czechoslovakia.[59]

It depends, however, on the taste of judges. Some more positivistic judges would never quote arguments like that, without any explicit link

[55] Paras 71 and 72.

[56] Pl. ÚS 14/94 of 8 March 1995 (Constitutionality of Post WW 2 Decrees – Expulsion of Czechoslovak Germans).

[57] A person's honor and good name are values that belong to the cultural heritage of our civilization, with its roots in Christianity and Judaism ("A good name is to be chosen rather than great riches, loving favor rather than silver and gold" Proverbs 22:1). See I. ÚS 453/03 of 11 November 2005 (Free speech of politicians, protection of privacy).

[58] Pl. ÚS 1/08 of 20 May 2008 (*Constitutionality of Health Care Fees*). Dissenting judges noted that they do not understand what the Code of Hammurabi has in common with modern-era social rights.

[59] Pl.ÚS 5/12 of 31 January 2012 (*Slovak Pensions*).

to the law. After all, teleological arguments are broad enough to encompass virtually any argument relating to the law's purpose.

References to Scholarly Work

The first visible feature of the CCC, which can be found by even a cursory review of its judgments in the course of the 1990s, is the lack of citation of legal writings. The Court openly preferred citations of foreign (mostly German) sources and ignored domestic writings. We must remember that the main lines of its jurisprudence were in tension with domestic theory. Furthermore, mainstream domestic legal theory, at least as viewed by some law professors on the bench, was quite weak. This lack of interaction further alienated domestic scholarship.

The situation is changing, however. Out of the first 15 judgments in my list of cases (1993–2002), the Court referred to scholarly work just twice (the very first citation was of German scholarship, though). Out of the remaining 25 judgments (2002–12) the Court quoted scholarship 19 times. Returning to Germanic legal tradition, the Court in the second decade of its existence refers to legal scholarship much more often. Currently references to legal scholarship are becoming more and more usual in case law.

References to Foreign Law

The frequency of comparative law arguments is striking. In my list of top 40 judgments, only seven do not consider foreign and transnational law. The Court used comparative and international law to a great extent and in fact developed its new case law and its style of decision-making by adhering to the foreign Western models. Through the use of Western constitutional case law and scholarship, the Court could internalize the shift which has occurred in Western legal culture since World War II. Let us remember that some judges have experience from abroad, either having been in exile or having studied there.

Besides these cognitive gaps of the new legal systems, i.e., the almost complete absence of constitutional conventions, doctrines and case law,[60] there was also a legitimacy gap, which could be felt by many actors of those new systems.[61] "In countries beginning their experience with

[60] For plenty of colorful illustrations, see Eric Stein, *Czecho/Slovakia, Ethnic Conflict, Constitutional Fissure, Negotiated Breakup* (University of Michigan Press 1997).

[61] Cf. Juliane Kokott, "From Reception and Transplantation to Convergence of Constitutional Models in the Age of Globalization – with Special Reference to the German Basic

constitutional judicial review, the use of comparative law makes normal what would otherwise appear revolutionary and dramatically new."[62]

Comparative arguments thus often serve as "distancing devices"[63] with a considerable force. The Court uses its arguments often in a very strong, principled style. Distancing devices are frequently observed in a value-based approach. The judges can prove through these arguments that they do not arbitrarily choose and formulate rules. Quite the contrary: the rule applied by them is considered to be generally recognized within established democracies, or among nations which are comparable for some specific purpose – for example having experienced the same problem, such as transition from communism to democracy.

"Distancing devices" seem to have a higher force than simple supportive arguments; in fact, they are arguments having real normative force of their own. They have played an extremely important role in the justification of a disputed legal issue; they are one of the key reasons used in interpretation of domestic law. In addition to the German Federal Constitutional Court, whose influence seems to be overwhelming,[64] quotations include the US Supreme Court, the *Conseil Constitutionnel* of France, the Spanish Constitutional Tribunal, the Swiss Federal Supreme Court, the Portuguese Constitutional Court and the Belgian Arbitration Court. The most prominent example of distancing devices is, however, the jurisprudence of the ECHR in Strasbourg. It has a vast impact on the Court's case law; the character of its arguments is authoritative and sometimes, from the court's rhetoric, might seem close to being binding.

Among the 40 cases, some bizarre examples of comparative law argumentation might be found as well. For instance, the 2001 *Lustration* case

Law" in Christian Starck (ed.), *Constitutionalism, Universalism and Democracy – a Comparative Analysis* (Nomos 1999), 71 ff, at 78 (arguing that "[t]he reception of a concept common in another jurisdiction may lend this concept the appearance of a general principle discovered, and not invented, by the judges.").

62 That is Choudhry's view of the South African Constitutional Court. Sujit Choudhry, "Globalization in Search of Justification: Toward a Theory of Comparative Constitutional Interpretation" (1999) 74 *Ind. L. J.* 819, at 845.

63 Proposed by Christopher McCrudden, "A Common Law of Human Rights? Transnational Judicial Conversations on Constitutional Rights" in Katherine O'Donovan, Gerry R. Rubin (eds) *Human Rights and Legal History, Essays in Honour of Brian Simpson* (Oxford University Press 2000) 29, at 32 (citing Raz).

64 Cf. Pl. ÚS 50/04 of 8 March 2006, *Sugar Quotas III*, which has taken over German model of the relation between EU law and the national constitution. Or I. ÚS 367/03 of 15 March 2005 (*Vondráčková v. Rejžek*) which is heavily based on the German conception of balancing free speech and privacy. Both judgments quote several German cases.

dealing with the treatment of the agents of the communist secret police and high-ranking communist party functionaries refers to a US Supreme Court precedent from the 1950s McCarthy era.[65]

7 *The Weight of Arguments*

The Court avoids construing any hierarchy of the methods used in constitutional reasoning. There are some exceptions, though, which I have already mentioned and will summarize as follows. First, in the case of the conflict between the purpose of the constitution as envisaged by the interpreter (objective teleological interpretation) and the intention of the constitution-maker (subjective teleological interpretation), the former always prevails.[66] Second, the wording of the Constitution is not decisive (save easy cases which are rarely adjudicated by the Court), but its purpose is usually controlling. Third, wording is more important in institutional cases, relating to competences of constitutional actors (competence disputes between president, parliament, etc.). In human rights cases the actual wording of the Bill of Rights matters less. Fourth, foreign law arguments and references to scholarly work are always of supplemental value. Teleological and systemic arguments are decisive. This theoretical claim, however, might be misleading. If there is a strong consensus on some particular issue among foreign constitutional courts or the ECHR, foreign law argument is close to a binding source of law.

8 *Judicial Candour and Judicial Rhetoric*

The Court or at least some of its influential judges strive to follow the German dogmatic style of reasoning. This is natural because modern

[65] Pl. ÚS 9/01 of 5 December 2001. The judgment quoted the decision of the US Supreme Court *Adler v. Board of Education* (without dating this decision). Yet, the undated precedent cited by the CCC is the decision made in the era of McCarthyism of the early 1950s, 342 U.S. 485 (1952) (the law challenged in *Adler* disqualified from the civil service and from the educational system all members of the US Communist Party). The Supreme Court in *Keyishian v. Board of Regents of University of State of N.Y.* 385 U.S. 589 (1967) overruled in part and distinguished in part *Adler*, criticizing Adler for its premise "that public employment, including academic employment, may be conditioned upon the surrender of constitutional rights which could not be abridged by direct government action." *Keyishian*, 385 U.S. at 605.

[66] See my explanation in the section on teleological arguments referring to the purpose of the constitution-maker.

Czech legal culture can be traced back to the Austrian legal heritage, including its professorial reasoning. The side effect of this style is highly technical language. It can be incomprehensible not only to lay people, but also to the majority of lawyers.[67] The dogmatic language of the Court thus makes constitutional arguments an exclusive arena for a small minority of lawyers used to that language. Another side effect is that this language insulates the Court from external criticism.[68] Although it is not rare that the Court communicates relatively simple ideas, which by their very nature are close to common sense, they are hidden under a veil of technical language. To put it bluntly, the language makes judges look smarter than they really are.[69] Value judgments are lost under the surface of legal technicalities.

Most opinions try to address counterarguments, but usually only those brought by parties to the proceedings. So the Court would typically deal with an opposing scholarly argument if some party will argue by it. In contrast, if the argument fits the Court's conclusion it will use it even without being urged to do so.

German constitutional dogmatics is not used in all judgments. Some judgments do resemble collage-type writings. To be precise, they resemble notes prepared by a law clerk for a judge-rapporteur which the judge forgot to edit. In our typology it corresponds to a dialogical type of argumentation. From the point of view of the Czech legal system this style is deficient – as I already mentioned, the dialogical model seems to be a byproduct of the inability of the writer to produce a coherent set of arguments which would fit either the one-line conclusive model or legs of a chair argumentation.[70] Those judgments are lengthy, but their length does not automatically mean that they disclose more about the value choices made by the Court's judges. Rather, they are less accessible to the reader.

Some other judgments try to avoid "scientific" arguments and use instead arguments which are more accessible to normal lawyers (I do

[67] I remember that I myself – then a fourth-year law school student – had serious problems understanding some of the Court's judgments.

[68] One would wonder whether it also insulates the author of the judgment from internal criticism of his/her fellow judges – I doubt that all of them understand what is being said in the very difficult language of the Court.

[69] So I agree fully with Jakab (n 21), 8.

[70] The best example among our top 40 cases is Pl. ÚS 50/04 of 8 March 2006 (*Sugar Quota case III*, relation of the national constitution and EU law), which is full of arguments, but one would have serious trouble recognizing which one really matters.

not say normal people, as I do not expect laymen would read those judgments).[71]

Which brings us to the issue of target audience. Generally, the parties and their lawyers take part in the proceedings. In cases of constitutional complaints, we shall add also ordinary courts which are bound by the Court's judgments. In more important cases the audience is broader and can include politicians and the general public (or, to be more precise, journalists who interpret judgments to the general public – so a good press release might matter more than the judgment itself[72]). Exceptionally the Court aims at an international audience as well – for instance the judgment proclaiming ECJ judgment *ultra vires* has been translated into both English and German, and the English press release was available at the Court's website on the day the judgment was announced. About 200 judgments of the Court have been translated into English, and those translations are freely available at the Court's website.[73]

While the opinions of common law judges have traditionally functioned as the main communicators of law to students, in continental law the traditional medium between courts and law students has not been a judicial decision but rather a textbook.[74] However, this situation is changing and judicial opinions – above all, constitutional court opinions – are increasingly studied throughout Czech law schools. So the ambition of some judges might also be to write a judgment which would be studied by law students.

The Court usually decides in a general way and tries to cover as many cases as possible. Only exceptionally is its scope narrower, usually in those cases which are meant to be distinguished from earlier precedents.

The rhetoric is usually detached and impartial. Judgments are written in the neutral third person; it is the court which decides, not "us" judges. Political or emotional arguments are usually missing, save some exceptional situations such as the decision on constitutionality of post–World

[71] The example is Pl. ÚS 14/94 of 8 March 1995, relating to the constitutionality of presidential decrees after World War II and expulsion of Sudeten German. Writing is essentially non-legal and is accessible to anyone interested in modern European history.

[72] Recently the Court has begun to issue press releases, although it seems that some judges are more active in doing so than others.

[73] http://www.usoud.cz/en/decisions/ Considering that the Czech Republic is a small country which is not particularly influential in legal thought, one should not overestimate the influence of the CCC's reasoning abroad.

[74] Cf. René David, John E. C. Brierley, *Major Legal Systems in the World Today* (3rd ed., Stevens & Son 1985), at 378.

War II decrees. Here the CCC argued passionately, fiercely defending the actions of the Czechoslovak government 50 years before and condemning the German atrocities.[75] Passionate rhetoric can be occasionally found in some concurring or dissenting opinions.

9 *Length, Dissenting and Concurring Opinions*

The length of judgments has been growing over time. This growth has become more visible since 2000. The reasons for this trend are multiple. Judges are more open about the fact that their decisions include choices among more interpretations. That is why they try to bring more arguments in favor of the particular solutions they voted for. This trend is not limited to the CCC but is rather a sign of the general development throughout the entire judicial system.

The fact that judicial opinions are slowly becoming longer is yet another sign of the gradual erosion of the formalist conception of limited law. Judges are increasingly coming to feel that – in order to reason and justify their decisions – it is not sufficient merely to recite the relevant legal provision and then employ a simple legal syllogism. Some further arguments are needed to explain their decision. When the text provides no sufficient solution, other arguments and standards must come into play.

There might be other factors contributing to this trend. The use of text editors and copy/paste functions also contributes to writing longer judgments. Last but not least, the fact that the number of law clerks has multiplied within the last 20 years (one judge now employs three law clerks). This has effectively resulted in the majority of judgments today being written by law clerks, who usually tend to write longer texts. If the judge rapporteur is not able to edit what has been brought to him by law clerks, the size of the judgment might become unbearable. Therefore, longer judgments are sometimes more chaotic, and it is impossible to find any rationale.

The actual size of an average judgment on constitutional review of legislation is about 100 paragraphs. In the past it used to be about 30 paragraphs. Judgments dealing with constitutional complaints are shorter – usually they do not exceed 40 reasoned paragraphs.

Concurring and dissenting opinions have been available since the very beginning of the Court. In my list of 40 judgments, dissenting or concurring opinions have been written in half of them. This shows the

[75] Pl. ÚS 14/94 of 8 March 1995.

importance of those cases. In total, there were over 200 judgments with separate opinions between 1993 and 2013 (73 judgments between 1993 and 2003; more than 140 judgments between 2004 and 2013), which is approximately 5 per cent. The increasing number of dissenting opinions is caused by the fact that the judges have become more diverse, representing political left, right, or conservative values.[76]

Some opinions are written in a legalistic fashion, basically competing to become the opinion of the Court. Some of those separate opinions were originally draft judgments produced by a judge rapporteur who found himself in a minority during deliberation. There are also passionate and non-legal separate opinions. In my list of cases, for instance, judge Balík produced a dissenting opinion in *European Arrest Warrant* which describes one day in the life of an imagined Czech inmate imprisoned in changing European countries; the opinion uses many European tongues and shows the confused inmate who does not understand Hungarian, Greek, Latvian, Spanish etc.[77] With respect to some dissenting opinions one might wonder what the dissenting judge wanted to say and what it meant to the Court's majority.[78]

10 *Framing of Constitutional Issues*

The CCC by its very nature deals mostly with fundamental rights (after all, most of its cases come as constitutional complaints). Competence conflicts are very rare, but if they appear, they are very important. Therefore, the typical framing of constitutional issues rests with fundamental rights, which is also the best avenue for the parliamentarians to urge the Court to consider their complaint in an abstract review of laws.

11 *Key Concepts*

The rule of law (*právní stát* in Czech, which is basically the German *Rechtstaat*) is one of the most often used concepts in the Court's reasoning (in my list of cases it has been invoked as an argument 29 times out of 40). This concept is expressly used in Article 1 of the Constitution. The court inferred from this concept the principles of legitimate expectations, legal

[76] On the development of the Court, see section 3 above.

[77] Pl. ÚS 66/04 of 3 May 2006.

[78] In another judgment (II. ÚS 773/07 of 23 August 2012), which is not in my list, the same judge Balík wrote a dissenting opinion in which he used one position in a chess game. The legal meaning of this, if any, is very difficult to find out.

certainty, the ban on retroactivity, and so on. This provision serves as a default rule for the Court's reasoning if no concrete rule can be applied.

The Court refers to the rule of law in a morally loaded way. In its very first judgment the Court highlighted that the rule of law is not based on any formal notion. Instead, it has a strong substantive meaning that stands in sharp contrast with socialist legality and similar conceptions of the previous regime:

> Our new Constitution is not founded on neutrality with regard to values, it is not simply a mere demarcation of institutions and processes, rather it incorporates into its text also certain governing ideas, expressing the fundamental, inviolable values of a democratic society. The Czech Constitution accepts and respects the principle of legality as a part of the overall basic outline of the rule of law; positive law does not, however, bind it merely to formal legality, rather the interpretation and application of legal norms are subordinated to their substantive purpose, law is qualified by respect for the basic enacted values of a democratic society... This conception of the constitutional state rejects the formal-rational legitimacy of a regime and the formal rule of law.[79]

The second most used conception is the right to fair trial (due process). It has a dual nature – usually it is only about procedure, but in some cases it has substantive meaning as well (typically the ban on excessive formalism in general courts). It is applied as a default rule for the cases of constitutional complaints, if no specific provision can be found. The use of this concept far outnumbers any other argument in constitutional complaints proceedings.

Democracy or the sovereignty of the people is used rarely, usually in the most important cases (such as the systemic conflict of two political regimes). International sovereignty is invoked in cases relating to EU law. Similarly, in those cases one might find some indications relating to federalism. Given the secular character of the Czechs, it is not surprising that religious issues are rarely adjudicated by the Court.

The proportionality test is applied in both abstract review of legislation and constitutional complaints. The test has German origins; the very first case on proportionality is basically a translation of the German test (without expressly quoting to the source).[80]

[79] Pl. ÚS 19/93 of 21 December 1993 (*Constitutionality of the Act on Lawlessness of the Communist Regime*).

[80] Pl. ÚS 4/94 of 12 October 1994 (*Unconstitutionality of Anonymous Witnesses in Criminal Proceedings*).

The Court construed the Constitution's untouchable core. By using this conception the Court made one of its most controversial judgments when it annulled the constitutional act on shortening the term of the House of Representatives for being unconstitutional.[81]

C Comparative Perspective

The CCC in its first two decades is a typical example of the constitutional court in a country in transition. The Court has neither a settled methodology nor the ideal of what is a good style of reasoning. It can be fairly said that the Court's methodology is still under development. Some cases are influenced by American style of legal argumentation; most of them, however, follow the German pattern of constitutional dogmatics. The key in this is often the personality and experience of judges (or their law clerks). The frequent use of comparative and foreign law seems to be directly linked to the fact that the Czech legal culture does not view itself in paternalistic fashion – quite the contrary; the CCC is willing to listen to foreign models and take from them useful inspiration. Sometimes the influence of German constitutional jurisprudence is so overwhelming that the Court simply follows its German archetype (e.g., in EU law issues).

Some courts equipped with only abstract review use a very abstract and tedious style. In contrast the Czech methodology is livelier. This seems to be the case because the CCC is more attached to real-life cases through very frequent constitutional complaints. This eventually affects also the cases of abstract review, which are often far from a rigorous, didactic style.

D Evaluation, Pathology and Criticism

The CCC – composed of many justices not bound by the old-fashioned concepts of law – started reshaping the outdated Czech legal culture in the 1990s. Its significance is far-reaching, touching even long-standing legal conceptions, judicial decision-making, etc.[82] New and, from the perspective of traditional scholarship, revolutionary ideas have shaken lawyers' ideology on the proper methods of legal interpretation.

[81] Pl. ÚS 27/09 of 10 September 2009

[82] M. Taruffo has mentioned that this character of constitutional courts is in fact a worldwide phenomenon. Cf. "Institutional Factors Influencing Precedents" in D. Neil MacCormick and Robert S. Summers (eds) *Interpreting precedents: a comparative study* (Dartmouth 1997), 437, at 450).

Constitutional courts in Central Europe after 1989 are often characterized as further incarnations of the Kelsenian model of constitutional review. However, one should be aware that this formally Kelsenian model of centralized constitutional review is applied in a substantively non-Kelsenian way. Hans Kelsen did not call for activist constitutional courts, such as those which appeared in Europe after World War II. His model was based on the constitutional court as the guardian of the constitution in cases where a breach of constitutional provisions was clear and evident. Kelsen was opposed to the constitutional tribunal which would intrude into individual cases and deal with fundamental rights; those cases were within the competence of ordinary judges, and constitutional courts were empowered solely to determine the constitutionality of general norms – not of individual judicial decisions.[83] However, post–World War II constitutional courts, most notably the German Federal Constitutional Court, engaged in highly activist decision-making.

Needless to say, not the Kelsenian but rather the German "anti-Kelsenian" constitutional court became the archetype of the Czech constitutional adjudication. A strict positivist approach to interpretation was not appropriate for the post-Communist democracies. The CCC often has based its reasoning on abstract clauses such as the rule-of-law state, due process which entails both procedural and substantive features, etc. This has created a complex set of dynamic constitutional propositions which has extended far beyond the strict reading of the constitutional texts.

The Court, originally self-restrained vis-à-vis the legislature in the 1990s, has become much more activist in its second decade, especially in the judgments which found a constitutional act unconstitutional (2009) or declared the judgment of the ECJ *ultra vires* (2012). Reasoning in both judgments suffers from many deficits. Last but not least, frequent Court interference with ordinary courts' case law creates uncertainties and conflicts within the legal system.

For all those reasons, at the end of the second decade of its existence, criticism of the Court has increased from both political and academic circles. Some outspoken critics of the Court's activism have been appointed to the bench (2013/14). So, one might expect that the Court would be more self-restrained in its third decade. Judicial self-restraint is likely

[83] On the description of Kelsen's model of constitutional judiciary, as implemented in 1920 in Austria and Czechoslovakia, see in English Hans Kelsen, 'Judicial Review of Legislation. A Comparative Study of the Austrian and the American Constitution' (1942) 4 *The Journal of Politics* 183.

to replace activism until the next wave of different political and legal atmospheres changes the situation again.

Appendix: 40 Leading Cases

1. nález sp. zn. Pl. ÚS 19/93 ze dne 21. 12. 1993 (N 1/1 SbNU 1; 14/1994 Sb.)
2. nález sp. zn. Pl. ÚS 4/94 ze dne 12. 10. 1994 (N 46/2 SbNU 57; 214/1994 Sb.)
3. nález sp. zn. Pl. ÚS 14/94 ze dne 8. 3. 1995 (N 14/3 SbNU 73; 55/1995 Sb.)
4. nález sp. zn. IV. ÚS 81/95 ze dne 18. 9. 1995 (N 50/4 SbNU 41; 32/1997 Sb.)
5. nález sp. zn. IV. ÚS 275/96 ze dne 15. 10. 1996 (N 104/6 SbNU 249)
6. nález sp. zn. Pl. ÚS 33/97 ze dne 17. 12. 1997 (N 163/9 SbNU 399; 30/1998 Sb.)
7. nález sp. zn. III. ÚS 425/97 ze dne 2. 4. 1998 (N 42/10 SbNU 285)
8. nález sp. zn. I. ÚS 526/98 ze dne 18. 2. 1999 (N 27/13 SbNU 203; 70/1999 Sb.)
9. nález sp. zn. Pl. ÚS 30/98 ze dne 13. 10. 1999 (N 137/16 SbNU 27; 243/1999 Sb.)
10. nález sp. zn. Pl. ÚS 42/2000 ze dne 24. 1. 2001 (N 16/21 SbNU 113; 64/2001 Sb.)
11. nález sp. zn. Pl. ÚS 14/01 ze dne 20. 6. 2001 (N 91/22 SbNU 267; 285/2001 Sb.)
12. nález sp. zn. Pl. ÚS 16/99 ze dne 27. 6. 2001 (N 96/22 SbNU 329; 276/2001 Sb.)
13. nález sp. zn. Pl. ÚS 9/01 ze dne 5. 12. 2001 (N 192/24 SbNU 419; 35/2002 Sb.)
14. nález sp. zn. III. ÚS 256/01 ze dne 21. 3. 2002 (N 37/25 SbNU 287)
15. nález sp. zn. Pl. ÚS 7/02 ze dne 18. 6. 2002 (N 78/26 SbNU 273; 349/2002 Sb.)
16. nález sp. zn. Pl. ÚS 36/01 ze dne 25. 6. 2002 (N 80/26 SbNU 317; 403/2002 Sb.)
17. nález sp. zn. Pl. ÚS 6/02 ze dne 27. 11. 2002 (N 146/28 SbNU 295; 4/2003 Sb.)
18. nález sp. zn. Pl. ÚS 3/02 ze dne 13. 8. 2002 (N 105/27 SbNU 177; 405/2002 Sb.)
19. nález sp. zn. Pl. ÚS 11/02 ze dne 11. 6. 2003 (N 87/30 SbNU 309; 198/2003 Sb.)

20. nález sp. zn. Pl. ÚS 44/02 ze dne 24. 6. 2003 (N 98/30 SbNU 417; 210/2003 Sb.)
21. nález sp. zn. Pl. ÚS 41/02 ze dne 28. 1. 2004 (N 10/32 SbNU 61; 98/2004 Sb.)
22. nález sp. zn. Pl. ÚS 1/03 ze dne 11. 2. 2004 (N 15/32 SbNU 131; 153/2004 Sb.)
23. nález sp. zn. Pl. ÚS 31/03 ze dne 11. 2. 2004 (N 16/32 SbNU 143; 105/2004 Sb.)
24. nález sp. zn. III. ÚS 258/03 ze dne 6. 5. 2004 (N 66/33 SbNU 155)
25. nález sp. zn. I. ÚS 167/04 ze dne 12. 5. 2004 (N 70/33 SbNU 197)
26. nález sp. zn. III. ÚS 459/03 ze dne 20. 8. 2004 (N 117/34 SbNU 223)
27. nález sp. zn. Pl. ÚS 73/04 ze dne 26. 1. 2005 (N 17/36 SbNU 185; 140/2005 Sb.)
28. nález sp. zn. I. ÚS 367/03 ze dne 15. 3. 2005 (N 57/36 SbNU 605)
29. nález sp. zn. Pl. ÚS 11/04 ze dne 26. 4. 2005 (N 89/37 SbNU 207; 220/2005 Sb.)
30. nález sp. zn. I. ÚS 453/03 ze dne 11. 11. 2005 (N 209/39 SbNU 215)
31. nález sp. zn. Pl. ÚS 20/05 ze dne 28. 2. 2006 (N 47/40 SbNU 389; 252/2006 Sb.)
32. nález sp. zn. Pl. ÚS 50/04 ze dne 8. 3. 2006 (N 50/40 SbNU 443; 154/2006 Sb.)
33. nález sp. zn. Pl. ÚS 37/04 ze dne 26. 4. 2006 (N 92/41 SbNU 173; 419/2006 Sb.)
34. nález sp. zn. Pl. ÚS 66/04 ze dne 3. 5. 2006 (N 93/41 SbNU 195; 434/2006 Sb.)
35. nález sp. zn. Pl. ÚS 18/06 ze dne 11. 7. 2006 (N 130/42 SbNU 13; 397/2006 Sb.)
36. nález sp. zn. Pl. ÚS 77/06 ze dne 15. 2. 2007 (N 30/44 SbNU 349; 37/2007 Sb.)
37. nález sp. zn. Pl. ÚS 25/07 ze dne 13. 3. 2008 (N 56/48 SbNU 791; 160/2008 Sb.)
38. nález sp. zn. Pl. ÚS 1/08 ze dne 20. 5. 2008 (N 91/49 SbNU 273; 251/2008 Sb.)
39. nález sp. zn. Pl. ÚS 27/09 ze dne 10. 9. 2009 (N 199/54 SbNU 445; 318/2009 Sb.)
40. nález sp.zn. Pl.ÚS 5/12 ze dne 31. 1. 2012 (N 24/64 SbNU 237)

6

The European Court of Human Rights

JANNEKE GERARDS

A Legal, Political, Institutional and Academic Context

1 Legal and Political Culture as Context for Constitutional Reasoning

Background

The context in which the European Court of Human Rights (ECtHR or Court) has to do its work is different from that of most national constitutional courts. Its 'legal system' is created by an international treaty, the European Convention of Human Rights (ECHR or Convention) and the ECtHR originally really is an international court, which was intended to function as an 'early warning' system on a supranational level when it was drafted in the 1940s.[1] For the first 20 years of its existence, the ECHR-system, which then still consisted of a non-permanent Court supported by a filtering body (the European Commission of Human Rights (EComHR)), had little practical importance.[2] Only a few applications were lodged, and by far the most cases were dealt with by the EComHR, so the Court had little opportunity to develop any argumentative principles and methods. In the 1970s, however, individuals discovered the potential of protection of their rights through the ECHR system and ever more applications were forwarded to the Court to be decided on their merits.[3] Many of these pertained to principled fundamental rights issues,

[1] E. Bates, 'The Birth of the European Convention on Human Rights – and the European Court of Human Rights' in J. Christoffersen and M. R. Madsen (eds.) *The European Court of Human Rights between Law and Politics* (Oxford University Press 2011) 17–42, at 21 and 25.

[2] Cf. Bates n 1, at 32 and 33; also S. Greer, 'What's Wrong with the European Convention of Human Rights?', (2008) 30 *Human Rights Quarterly* 680 at 682; R. Ryssdal, 'The coming of age of the European Convention on Human Rights' (1996) 1 *European Human Rights Law Review* 18 at 18.

[3] E. Bates, *The Evolution of the European Convention on Human Rights – From its Inception to the Creation of a Permanent Court of Human Rights* (Oxford University Press 2010). See also Ryssdal n 2, at 20.

which allowed the Court to develop a general philosophy of Convention interpretation and a set of interpretive principles and doctrines which are still relevant today. These cases and judgments helped the Court to firmly establish its authority as final arbiter in human rights cases.[4] Gradually it came to be accepted throughout Europe that it is the ECtHR which determines the appropriate level of protection of fundamental rights and which has the final say in interpreting the terms and notions contained in the Convention. Given that the Court also provides for authoritative general interpretations of fundamental rights matters, many even came to regard the Court as a constitutional court for Europe.[5]

In the 1990s a new era started for the Court. A large number of Central and Eastern European states acceded to the Convention, having recently escaped from communist dictatorship. Turkey recognised the right of individual application and states such as Russia, Moldova, Georgia and Azerbaijan became parties to the Convention. By the end of the millennium the Court's jurisdiction covered almost all of geographical Europe, with a potential of more than 800 million individual applicants. At the same time the ECHR system underwent an important change as a result of the entry into force of Protocol No. 9 to the Convention.[6] This new Protocol enabled individual applicants to bring their complaints to the Court, while formerly only the States and the Commission had been competent to do so. These developments brought about important changes for the Court.[7] First of all, there was an enormous increase in the number of applications being brought directly to the Court. Where the Court from 1959 (when it received its first case) until 1998 had to deal with about 45,000 complaints in total, currently more than 60,000 applications are made each year.[8] In turn, this has led to important institutional and procedural change. Already in the 1990s the states realised that the steep increase of cases could not be handled by the 'old-fashioned' system of the non-permanent Court and the EComHR. With the entry into force of Protocol No. 11 in 1998, the EComHR was abolished and the Court

4 Cf. L.R. Helfer and A.-M. Slaughter, 'Toward a Theory of Effective Supranational Adjudication' (1997) 107 *Yale Law Review* 273.

5 See further e.g. S. Greer and L. Wildhaber, 'Revisiting the Debate about 'constitutionalising' the European Court of Human Rights' (2012) 12 *Human Rights Law Review* 655.

6 ETS No. 140, see http://conventions.coe.int.

7 For further analysis, see e.g. Ryssdal n 2; N.-L. Arold, *The Legal Culture of the European Court of Human Rights* (Martinus Nijhoff Publishers 2007) 24ff; R. Harmsen, 'The European Convention on Human Rights after Enlargement' (2001) 5 *International Journal of Human Rights* 18.

8 See www.echr.coe.int > statistical data.

was transformed into a permanent court with obligatory jurisdiction for all Convention States. Although this marked an important moment in the development of the Court, it did not provide a real solution to the case-load problem, which continued to increase. Since 1998, the Court has been continually 'under construction' to help it meet the demands made on its capacity.

The enlargement of the Council of Europe in the 1990s also had significant consequences for the substance of the Court's work. Many of the acceding states were newly established democracies in a situation of transition, or they were disunited as a result of internal conflicts. Individual applicants from these states started to bring other types of complaints than the Court was used to so far, such as applications stemming from systemic problems related to the transition to a rule of law-based democratic system, or complaints about enforced disappearances during internal armed conflicts. These fundamental rights problems constitute an important challenge for the ECHR system, which was not originally built to deal with such systemic and transitional human rights problems. Indeed, since the 1990s the Court has struggled to find an adequate response to this.[9]

Currently, the ECtHR faces the challenges of having to deal with a wide range of fundamental rights cases in a situation where its position and legitimacy are not undisputed, where it is confronted with constant changes in its procedural and institutional structure and where it is seriously overburdened by its case-load. It will be seen in this chapter that many of the Court's argumentative techniques are actually informed by the need to meet one or more of these challenges.

The Dual Nature of the ECtHR – the ECtHR as a Constitutional Court

The Court's main task is that of the supervision of the compliance by the states with their obligations under the Convention.[10] The concomitant task to provide for individual protection against human rights violations by the state is generally regarded as the cornerstone of the Convention system.[11] The Court itself sees it as its primary role to assess all individual cases on their merits, looking at the particular circumstances of

[9] See e.g. the sources mentioned in n 7. [10] Article 19 ECHR.

[11] See e.g. Report of the Committee of Minister's Steering Committee for Human Rights (CDDH) on measures requiring amendment of the European Convention on Human Rights (Strasbourg, February 2012, CDDH(2012)R74 Addendum I).

the case and evaluating the reasonableness of restrictions on a case-by-case basis.[12] For a long time, however, the Court has accepted that it also has a 'constitutional' function.[13] The Court has an essential role to play in standard-setting and creating a minimum level of fundamental rights protection for all European states.[14] Indeed, already in 1979, the Court emphasised that its task is 'not only to decide those cases brought before the Court but, more generally, to elucidate, safeguard and develop the rules instituted by the Convention'.[15] For this reason the Court can be regarded as a 'constitutional' court, even though it lacks some of the classical features of such national constitutional courts.[16]

The duality of the Court's role has an important impact on its argumentative approach. In particular, the Court is confronted with many cases in which it needs to exercise both its constitutional and its individual protection roles, and it has sought to find answers to the argumentative questions this combination raises. These are discussed in more detail in section 4.

Subsidiarity of the Supervisory System

Although the Court is commonly regarded as a constitutional court for Europe, it is still an international court which has to deal with individual complaints against otherwise sovereign states. According to Article 1 of the Convention, the national authorities bear the primary responsibility to guarantee the Convention rights and protect them at a level at least equal to that provided by the ECtHR. The national authorities are generally regarded as being better placed than the Court to make policy choices and protect fundamental rights in a way that fits well with national law and national constitutional traditions.[17] In turn, the fundamental principle of

[12] See already *Sunday Times* v. *UK*, ECtHR 26 April 1979, no. 6538/74, para. 65.

[13] Cf. S. Greer and L. Wildhaber, 'Revisiting the Debate about "Constitutionalising" the European Court of Human Rights' (2012) 12 *Human Rights Law Review* 655; see also e.g. F. De Londras, 'Dual Functionality and the Persistent Frailty of the European Court of Human Rights' (2013) *European Human Rights Law Review* 38.

[14] E.g. *Rantsev* v. *Cyprus and Russia*, ECtHR 7 January 2010, no. 25965/04, para. 197; see also A. Stone Sweet, 'The European Convention on Human Rights and National Constitutional Reordering', (2012) 33 *Cardozo Law Review* 1859.

[15] E.g. *Ireland* v. *UK*, ECtHR 18 January 1978, no. 5310/71, para. 154.

[16] Cf. e.g. Stone Sweet n 14; E.A. Alkema, 'The European Convention as a Constitution and its Court as a Constitutional Court' in: P. Mahoney et al. (eds) *Protecting Human Rights: The European Perspective* (Carl Heymans 2000) 41–63.

[17] See already *Handyside* v. *UK*, ECtHR 7 December 1976, no. 5493/72, para. 48.

'primarity' and the 'better placed argument' define the Court's own task as being subsidiary and supervisory.[18]

The Court has always acknowledged its subsidiary position,[19] which has had great impact on its argumentation methods. It has developed a set of distinctive notions and doctrines related to the subsidiarity principle, such as the famous 'margin of appreciation doctrine'. This doctrine entails that the Court leaves the national authorities a certain leeway to decide how to comply with their Convention obligations, which can be wider or narrower depending on the circumstances of the case.[20] The amount of leeway left to the states subsequently determines the intensity of the Court's scrutiny of national measures, which in many cases is very deferential, but at times may be very strict.

Such doctrines notwithstanding, the Court has been criticised for interfering too strongly with national policy choices. Resistance to the Court's interventions in areas such as voting rights[21] and immigration policy[22] has even led the European government leaders to adopt a new Protocol (No. 15) to the Convention in 2013, in which the principle of subsidiarity and the margin of appreciation doctrine are codified.[23] The government leaders have also expressly invited the Court to not too easily overturn national judicial decisions.[24] Since these developments are relatively new, it is difficult to predict their impact on the Court's argumentation.[25]

18 See e.g. *Demopoulos and others* v. *Turkey*, ECtHR (GC) 1 March 2010 (dec.), nos. 46113/99 et al., para. 69. On the principle of 'primarity', see J. Christoffersen, *Fair Balance: Proportionality, Subsidiarity and Primarity in the European Convention on Human Rights* (Martinus Nijhoff Publishers 2009).

19 *Belgian Linguistics Case*, ECtHR 23 July 1968, no. 1474/62, para. I.B.10. See also Christoffersen n 18, at 248.

20 See in more detail below, section 4.

21 See in particular the British criticism of the Court's judgments; e.g. D. Davids, 'Britain Must Defy the European Court of Human Rights on Prisoner Voting as Strasbourg Is Exceeding Its Authority' in S. Flogaitis, T. Zwart and J. Fraser (eds) *The European Court of Human Rights and Its Discontents: Turning Criticism into Strength* (Edward Elgar 2013) 65.

22 See e.g. M. Bossuyt, 'Judges on Thin Ice: The European Court of Human Rights and the Treatment of Asylum Seekers' 3.1–2. (2010) *Inter-American and European Human Rights Journal* 47.

23 ETS No. 213.

24 High-level conference on the future of the European Court of Human Rights, Brighton, 18–20 April 2012, CDDH(2012)007.

25 See J. H. Gerards, 'The European Court of Human Rights and the National Courts – Giving Shape to the notion of "Shared Responsibility"' in J. H. Gerards and J. W. A. Fleuren (eds) *Implementation of the European Convention on Human Rights and of the Judgments of the ECtHR in National Case Law. A Comparative Analysis* (Intersentia 2014, forthcoming).

2. *The Court and Constitutional Litigation*

Individual Applications and Their Admissibility

Both individuals and states have the right to bring complaints about violations of the Convention before the ECtHR.[26] This chapter focuses on individual applications, however, since inter-state conflicts are rare and the rules of procedure and the Court's argumentative approach are similar. The Court can receive individual applications if the applicant claims to be a victim of a violation of one of the rights protected by the Convention.[27] The 'victim requirement' entails that there is no possibility for *actiones populares*: the applicant must have suffered individual and concrete harm as a result of the alleged violation.[28] If the direct victim has died, however, an application may be brought by his family members.[29] Also, if the cause of an infringement is the existence *in abstracto* of legislation, the Court may admit an application even if the legislation has not yet been applied in the concrete case or it is not known if it has (as in the case of secret surveillance).[30] In addition, it is accepted that, next to natural persons, legal persons and NGOs can submit applications, as long as they meet the requirement of being a direct victim of a violation.[31]

Another important requirement for admissibility is that the applicant must have exhausted all domestic remedies.[32] This requirement is related to the subsidiary character of the Convention system and the primary responsibility of the states to protect the Convention rights. If an individual alleges a fundamental rights violation, the state must be given the opportunity to correct eventual mistakes and offer redress.[33] One of the consequences of this is that the Court is usually confronted with cases that have been fully and completely tried on the national level and in

[26] Articles 33 and 34 ECHR. [27] Article 34 ECHR.

[28] See e.g. *Michaud* v. *France*, ECtHR 6 December 2012, no. 12323/11, para. 51. See elaborately the Court's *Practical Guide on Admissibility Criteria*, http://www.echr.coe.int/Documents/Admissibility_guide_ENG.pdf, section B.

[29] For references to case-law, see *Admissibility Guide* n 28, paras. 10 and 30–31.

[30] See in particular *Dudgeon* v. *United Kingdom*, ECtHR 22 October 1981, no. 7525/76, para. 41 and *Klass and Others* v. *Germany*, ECtHR 6 September 1978, no. 5029/71, paras. 33–38. Also *Admissibility Guide* n 28, paras. 26–27.

[31] *Admissibility Guide* n 28, para. 9. [32] Article 35(1) ECHR.

[33] See e.g. *Scoppola* v. *Italy (No. 2)*, ECtHR (GC) 17 September 2009, no. 10249/03, para. 68. See also *Admissibility Guide* n 28, para. 47.

which the relevant fundamental rights issues have already been thoroughly addressed.[34]

Fact-Finding, Communication and Hearings

Given its subsidiary role, the Court has consistently held that it is not its task to act as a 'court of first instance'.[35] In principle the Court will not re-establish the facts, it will not re-assess any evidence and it will not deal with the interpretation of national law given by the national courts.[36] The Court on these points has still accepted a supervisory task, however, and it will ascertain that the states have respected the Convention rights and obligations.[37] If there is any cause for doubt regarding the establishment of the facts of the case, or if the assessment of evidence by the national courts appears to have been faulty, the Court will intervene.[38] The Court is empowered by the Convention to do so by means of, inter alia, hearing the parties to the case, asking them to provide information and even organising on-the-spot fact-finding missions.[39]

As a rule, the Court refers applications it wants to examine on their merits to the respondent government to ask for its opinion on the matter ('communication').[40] In its communication it may ask specific procedural and substantive questions and it may request certain documents to be delivered.[41] According to Article 38 of the Convention it is obligatory to furnish such information and a lack of co-operation may lead the Court to find a violation of this provision.[42]

[34] This may be different if the remedy offered at the national level was not effective or flawed; in those cases further fact-finding and re-assessment of evidence may be necessary (but also extremely difficult); see e.g. *Nizomkhon Dzhurayev* v. *Russia*, ECtHR 3 October 2013, no. 31890/11.

[35] E.g. *Giuliani and Gaggio* v. *Italy*, ECtHR (GC) 24 March 2011, no. 23458/02, para. 180.

[36] *Idem*. See also *Kononov* v. *Latvia*, ECtHR 24 July 2008, no. 36376/04, para. 108.

[37] E.g. *Nizomkhon Dzhurayev* v. *Russia*, ECtHR 3 October 2013, no. 31890/11, para. 86.

[38] *Idem*.

[39] See Articles 38 and 40 ECHR and the Rules of Court, in particular also the Annex concerning investigations. See further P. Leach, C. Paraskeva and G. Uzelac, *International Human Rights & Fact Finding – An Analysis of the Fact-Finding Missions Conducted by the European Commission and Court of Human Rights* (London Metropolitan University 2009).

[40] See Rule 54(2)(b) Rules of Court.

[41] See further P. Leach, *Taking a Case to the European Court of Human Rights* (3rd edn Oxford University Press 2011) para. 2.91.

[42] See e.g. *Janowiec and Others v. Russia*, ECtHR (GC) 21 October 2013, nos. 55508/07 and 29520/09.

The Court may further invite any State that is not a party to the proceedings or any other person or organisation to intervene in the case and submit written comments.[43] Especially in high-profile cases such interventions often occur and they provide the Court with a rich source of information.[44]

The Court may also decide to hear the parties.[45] Hearings are almost standard in proceedings before the Court's largest and most important formation (the Grand Chamber, further discussed hereafter), but they are exceptional in proceedings before the Court's smaller formations (Committees and Chambers) and excluded in proceedings before a single judge.[46] Only if the President of a Chamber considers a hearing to be of real added value will the parties be invited to travel to Strasbourg.[47] A hearing typically is a rather formal occasion where the parties plead their case and the judges of the Chamber ask some (usually not that many) questions. In practice, the written part of the proceedings is much more important in providing the basis for the Court's decisions and judgments.

Discretionary Power to Select Cases

(1) The need for filtering – single judges and the 'Filtering Section'

The Court has no formal discretionary powers to select the cases coming before it.[48] This is one of the consequences of its function as a supervisory organ offering redress to individual victims of human rights violations. On average, the Court receives about 60,000 individual applications every year and in recent years there has been a relatively stable increase of about 10 per cent of incoming applications each year.[49] For a long time the Court was hardly able to cope with the influx of cases, mainly because the system was not designed to deal with such a heavy case-load.[50] In recent years, the caseload has decreased, but it is still alarmingly high.[51]

43 Article 36 ECHR; Rule 44 Rules of Court.

44 For one example out of many, see *D.H. and Others* v. *Czech Republic*, ECtHR (GC) 13 November 2007, no. 57325/00. See further Leach, *supra* n 41, paras. 2.118ff.

45 The basis for hearings is Article 40(1) ECHR; see Leach n 41, para. 2.204. There is also a possibility for hearings in relation to fact-finding missions, but these are rare. See further the Annex to the Rules of Court on investigations.

46 Cf. Leach n 41, paras. 2.110.

47 Rule 54(5) Rules of Court; see also Leach n 41, para. 2.204.

48 Cf. R. A. White and I. Boussiakou, 'Separate Opinions in the European Court of Human Rights', 9 *Human Rights Law Review* (2009) pp. 37–60 at p. 38.

49 See www.echr.coe.int > statistical data.

50 See section 1.

51 31 December 2016: 79,750 cases pending (www.echr.coe.int > statistical data).

The awareness of the case-load problem and the concomitant risk of ineffectiveness or even collapse of the Court have resulted in a series of reforms of the procedure before the Court. In 2010, the entry into force of Protocol No. 14 has provided for a number of efficiency-increasing measures, such as the introduction of a single judge formation to deal with simple cases.[52] It also enabled the Court to develop a new, streamlined system to dispose of such simple cases more quickly.[53] The new 'filtering system' starts from the given that about 97 per cent of all applications are inadmissible, either because they manifestly do not comply with the criteria mentioned above or because they do not disclose any apparent violation of the Convention. The 'filtering section' within the Court's Registry is burdened with the task of assessing all incoming applications for their admissibility.[54] If there is some merit in the case, the application is forwarded to one of the Court's judicial Sections to be decided by a Committee of three judges or (in more difficult cases) a Chamber of seven judges. If the case is clearly inadmissible, it is placed before a single judge, who usually just rubber-stamps the Registry's proposal for an inadmissibility decision.

The new filtering procedure has proved to be very effective and has resulted in a steep decrease in pending cases.[55] Moreover, it means that a small and implicit element of discretion is introduced in the procedure: only possibly meritorious cases or cases raising important fundamental rights issues are actually decided by the Court's larger formations and looked at on their merits.

(2) Discretion and the constitutional role of the Grand Chamber

An element of discretion that is important from the perspective of constitutional adjudication can be found in the role of the Court's Grand Chamber. The Grand Chamber, being the Court's 'heaviest' formation, consists of 17 judges, including the President, the Vice-Presidents and the Chamber Presidents.[56] It only comes into play in two instances. Firstly, if a Chamber deals with a case it finds to raise serious questions of

[52] ETS-No. 194. See for an evaluation of the consequences CDDH, *Report containing elements to contribute to the evaluation of the effects of Protocol No. 14 to the Convention and the implementation of the Interlaken and Izmir Declarations on the Court's Situation* (Strasbourg, 30 November 2012), CDDH(2012)R76 Addendum II, paras. 18ff.

[53] See further the CDDH evaluation report n 52, paras. 11 and 21.

[54] See CDDH evaluation report n 52, paras. 20–21 and http://echr.coe.int/Documents/Filtering_Section_ENG.pdf.

[55] CDDH Evaluation report n 52.

[56] Article 26(5) ECHR.

interpretation or to lead to inconsistencies in the case-law, it may decide to relinquish jurisdiction in favour of the Grand Chamber.[57] Secondly, if a Chamber has pronounced judgment, but one of the parties objects to it, the party may request for the case to be referred to the Grand Chamber for review.[58] However, the Grand Chamber will review such a case only if a panel of five judges has decided that it raises a serious question affecting the interpretation or application of the Convention or a serious issue of general importance.[59] In practice, only a relatively small number of cases are decided on by the Grand Chamber each year.[60]

Since the cases to be decided by the Grand Chamber are selected for the importance of the interpretative questions they raise, there is an element of discretion and selection as regards the cases to be placed before the Court's most important formation. In turn this means the Grand Chamber can play an essential role in exercising the Court's constitutional function.[61] Especially through relinquishment it may consider yet unanswered interpretative questions, while in its review judgments it may harmonise lines of case-law created by the Chambers and Committees, confirm or correct interpretations previously given, or further develop or refine general standards and criteria.[62]

[57] Article 30 ECHR. It may only do so if both parties to the case agree, which is not always the case. Since this may form an impediment to the potential constitutional function of this procedural possibility, the Court has suggested removing the requirement of consent (*Preliminary opinion of the Court in preparation for the Brighton Conference*, adopted by the Plenary Court on 20 February 2012, v2-#3841140). This suggestion is adopted by the states, as is apparent from Article 3 of Protocol No. 15 (ETS No. 213).

[58] Article 43 ECHR. [59] Article 43(2) ECHR; Rule 73(1) Rules of Court.

[60] In more detail, see J. H. Gerards, 'Artikel 30. Afstand van rechtsmacht' [Article 30. Relinquishment of jurisdiction] in J. H. Gerards et al. (eds) *Sdu Commentaar EVRM. Deel 2 – procedurele bepalingen* [ECHR Commentary – Part 2. Procedural provisions] (Sdu 2014); L. Wildhaber, 'La Grande Chambre de la Court Européenne des Droits de l'Homme' [The Grand Chamber of the ECtHR], in: *La conscience des droits* [The conscience of rights] (Paris: Dalloz 2011) pp. 687–702; A. Mowbray, 'An Examination of the Work of the Grand Chamber of the European Court of Human Rights' (2007) *Public Law* 507; J.-P. Costa, 'Les arrêts de la Grande Chambre rendus après renvoi' [The judgments of the Grand Chamber after referral] in L. Caflisch et al. (eds) *Human Rights – Strasbourg Views. Liber Amicorum Luzius Wildhaber* (N. P. Engel 2007) 133–144 at p. 136. This may be different if Protocol No. 15 enters into force – see n 57.

[61] Chambers may also give important findings of a more general and abstract nature. Some of the most important interpretative cases were decided by Chambers rather than by the Grand Chamber. An example is *Pretty* v. *United Kingdom*, ECtHR 29 April 2002, no. 2346/02.

[62] Cf. also Gerards n 60.

Competences: Declaratory Judgments, Suggestions and Force of Interpretation

Besides the competence to award just satisfaction to the individual if it has found a violation,[63] the Court only has the power to issue declaratory judgments.[64] In line with its primarily international character, it may not declare national legislation null and void.[65] Nevertheless, the Court's declaratory judgments are binding on the parties to the case.[66] This means the respondent state must provide for *restitutio in integrum* by ending any violation found and offering effective redress.[67] The states are granted much discretion in making choices in this respect.[68] The Committee of Ministers of the Council of Europe supervises the execution of the judgments of the Court, but it only has political pressure and 'naming and shaming' as its weapons if a state refuses to do so.[69]

Although the Court's powers seem relatively limited, two important developments have increased the impact of its judgments. Firstly, on the express invitation of the States,[70] the Court has started to define more clearly what effect the state must give to the judgment in order to remedy the violation.[71] The Court now regularly indicates how individual redress should be offered,[72] but it may also suggest taking general measures to prevent similar violations from taking place in the future.[73] If such

[63] Article 41 ECHR.

[64] See e.g. *Papamichalopoulos and Others* v. *Greece*, ECtHR 31 October 1995 (Article 50), no. 14556/89, para. 34 and, more expressly, *Assanidze* v. *Georgia*, ECtHR (GC) 8 April 2004, no. 71503/01, para. 202.

[65] Cf. Leach n 41, para. 3.20. [66] Article 46(1) ECHR.

[67] *Papamichalopoulos* n 64, para. 34; *Scozzari and Giunta* v. *Italy*, ECtHR (GC) 13 July 2007, nos. 39221/98 and 41963/98, para. 249.

[68] *Idem.*

[69] Article 46(2); Leach n 41, paras. 3.67ff; for more detail: E. Lambert Abdelgawad, *The Execution of Judgments of the European Court of Human Rights* (Council of Europe 2008). See also E. Voeten, 'The Politics of International Judicial Appointments: Evidence from the European Court of Human Rights (2007) 61 *International Organization* 669 at p. 674.

[70] Resolution Res (2004)3 on judgments revealing an underlying systemic problem, 114th Session of the Committee of Ministers, 12 May 2004.

[71] See further e.g. V. Colandrea, 'On the Power of the European Court of Human Rights to Order Specific Non-Monetary Measures: Some Remarks in Light of the *Assanidze*, *Broniowski* and *Sejdovic* Cases', (2007) 7 *Human Rights Law Review* 396.

[72] E.g. *Oleksandr Volkov* v. *Ukraine*, ECtHR 9 January 2013, no. 21722/11; *Del Río Prada* v. *Spain*, ECtHR (GC) 21 October 2013, no. 42750/09.

[73] There are many examples of this, in particular in the special form of pilot judgments. See further on this e.g. J. H. Gerards, 'The Pilot Judgment Procedure before the European Court of Human Rights as an Instrument for Dialogue' in M. Claes et al. (eds.), *Constitutional*

suggestions find their way into the operative part of the judgment, they are binding on the respondent state and their execution will be supervised by the Committee of Ministers.

Secondly, although the declaratory judgments of the Court have no *erga omnes* effect,[74] it has come to be accepted that the Court's interpretations have *res interpretata* or 'force of interpretation'. Through its judgments the Court elucidates the meaning of the various Convention terms and concepts, as follows from the express definition of its competences in Article 32 ECHR,[75] and the states have committed themselves to 'taking into account the Court's developing case-law, also with a view to considering the conclusions drawn from a judgment finding a violation of the Convention by another State, where the same problem exists within their own legal system'.[76] The acceptance of this *res interpretata* both explains and enhances the importance of the Court's constitutional role and the interpretative judgments of the Grand Chamber.[77]

Judgments and Decisions

(1) Decisions by single judges

By far the most applications received by the Court are dealt with by single judges, who are only competent to render decisions of inadmissibility.[78] These decisions are extremely succinctly reasoned: they

Conversations in Europe (Intersentia 2012) pp. 371–97; L. Wildhaber, 'Pilot Judgments in Cases of Structural or Systemic Problems on the National Level' in R. Wolfrum and U. Deutsch (eds) *The European Court of Human Rights Overwhelmed by Applications* (Springer 2009); E. Lambert Abdelgawad, *The Execution of Judgments of the European Court of Human Rights* (2nd ed. Council of Europe Publishing 2008). For one example out of many, see *Glykantzi* v. *Greece*, ECtHR 30 October 2012, no. 40150/09.

[74] Cf. E. Klein, 'Should the Binding Effect of the Judgments of the European Court of Human Rights Be Extended?' in P. Mahoney (ed) *Protecting Human Rights: the European Perspective* (Heymanns 2000) 705–13 at p. 706; G. Ress, 'The Effect of Decisions and Judgments of the European Court of Human Rights in the Domestic Legal Order' (2005) 40 *Texas International Law Journal* 359 at p. 374.

[75] See e.g. Gerards n 25, section 3.2 and M. Marmo, 'The Execution of Judgments of the European Court of Human Rights – A Political Battle', (2008) 15 *Maastricht Journal of European and Comparative Law* 235 at 242–3.

[76] High Level Conference on the Future of the European Court of Human Rights, Interlaken Declaration, 19 February 2010 – Action plan, para. B.4.c. See earlier already PACE Resolution 1226/2000, *Execution of judgments of the European Court of Human Rights*, 28 September 2000 (30th Sitting), para. 3.

[77] See further J. H. Gerards and J. W. A. Fleuren (eds) *Implementation of the European Convention on Human Rights and of the judgments of the ECtHR in National Case Law. A Comparative Analysis* (Intersentia 2014).

[78] See *supra*, section 2, dealing with the Court's filtering system.

typically take the form of a one-page letter in which only the main ground for inadmissibility is mentioned.[79] Single-judge decisions are not published through the internet database of the Court (HUDOC), nor are they made available to the public in any other way.[80] In a very large percentage of all applications (about 80 to 90 per cent), the Court's decisions thus remain inscrutable for the general public.[81] The Court is sometimes criticised for this reason, but its practice can be explained by the need for efficiency and the lack of principled fundamental rights issues at stake in these cases.[82]

(2) Reasoning and publication of decisions and judgments; separate opinions

Admissibility decisions and final judgments of the Committees, Chambers and Grand Chamber are always published.[83] As a rule, and in accordance with Article 45 ECHR, Chamber and Grand Chamber decisions and judgments are extensively reasoned.[84] They include a detailed account of the procedure followed and the relevant facts, as well as the applicable national legislation.[85] They also often contain overviews of relevant international and foreign materials. These accounts are followed by an extensive part in which the observations by the parties and third party interveners are summarised and the arguments underpinning the Court's judgment are set out.[86] The actual reasoning part of the judgment, which is typically structured according to the different ECHR rights invoked, usually consists of a general discussion of the general principles arising from the Court's previous case-law, followed by a separate part in which these principles are applied to the case at hand. After attention has been paid to any costs and just satisfaction claims,[87] the judgment or decision

79 Leach n 41, at pp. 41 and 586; in more detail, see J. H. Gerards, 'Inadmissibility Decisions by the European Court of Human Rights – A Critique of the lack of Reasoning', 14 *Human Rights Law Review* 2014 (1).

80 According to Rule 33 (4) Rules of Court, only general information about the single-judge formations' work is periodically made accessible to the public.

81 It appears from the statistics for 2012, for example, that of a total of 87,879 applications decided by the Court, 81,764 cases were disposed of by a single judge, which is about 93 per cent. In 2016, this was about 80 per cent.

82 See further Gerards n 79.

83 Cf. Article 44 (3) and Rule 78 (for final judgments of Chambers and the Grand Chamber) and Articles 28 (2), 42 and Rule 33 (4) (for decisions of Committees and Chambers).

84 There is little difference between the amount of reasoning of (Grand) Chamber decisions and judgments; cf. *Admissibility Guide* n 28, para. 370.

85 Cf. Rule 74 (1).

86 Rule 74 (1)(h).

87 Cf. Rule 74 (1)(j), Article 41 ECHR and the Practice Directions on just satisfaction annexed to the Rules of Court.

is concluded by an operative part.[88] In this part the Chamber or Grand Chamber summarise their findings for each applicable Convention claim, as well as its findings as regards costs and just satisfaction. The operative part also specifies, for inadmissibility decisions, whether the decision is reached unanimously or by a majority,[89] and, for judgments, how many judges constituted the majority.[90]

When a Chamber or the Grand Chamber renders a judgment, any judge is entitled to deliver a separate opinion, either a concurring or (partly) dissenting opinion, either alone or jointly with other judges.[91] Especially on the level of the Grand Chamber, it hardly ever occurs that judges who do not agree with the opinion of the majority leave the possibility to state the reasons for their disagreement unused.[92]

Judgments and decisions of Committees of three judges have the same elements as Chamber judgments, but their reasoning is typically terse. Moreover, since Committees may only make decisions by unanimity, there is no possibility for separate opinions accompanying their decisions or judgments.[93]

(3) Decisions versus judgments

Up until the 2000s, decisions on the admissibility of cases were usually rendered separately, but nowadays it is standard practice to hand down a single judgment addressing both admissibility issues and the merits of the case.[94] Importantly, however, there are many inadmissibility decisions in which the Court declares the case to be 'manifestly ill-founded'.[95] In practice it may be difficult to tell the difference between such 'manifestly ill-founded' decisions and judgments on the merits where the Court finds no violation.[96] Many cases resulting in decisions are far from straightforward and easy and they frequently concern important legal issues.[97] Hence, inadmissibility decisions may be just as important for understanding the Court's case-law and reasoning as judgments are.[98]

[88] Rule 74 (1)(i). [89] Rule 56 (1). [90] Rule 74 (1)(k).

[91] Article 45 (2) and Rule 74 (2).

[92] For further analysis, see e.g. Arold 2007 n 7, pp. 94ff and White and Boussiakou n 48. See also further section 4.

[93] Article 27 (1) and Rule 53.

[94] Cf. Article 29 (1) and Rule 54A. See also Leach n 41, para. 2.115. [95] Article 35 (3)(a).

[96] Cf. Gerards n 79; see also *Admissibility Guide* n 28, para. 370.

[97] To give just one example: *Neij and Kunde Kolmisoppi* v. *Sweden*, ECtHR 19 February 2013 (dec.), no 40397/12.

[98] The procedural differences between decisions and judgments are nevertheless considerable; see further Gerards n 79.

(4) Importance of Chamber and Grand Chamber judgments

Grand Chamber judgments are usually the most important from a perspective of development of Convention interpretation, but judgments of the Chambers may also have an important constitutional function. In fact, several Chamber judgments have turned out to be leading cases with the same authority as judgments of the Grand Chamber.[99] It is difficult to predict which judgments will have such impact, as this depends not only on the judgment but also on the way it is perceived by the audience. Nevertheless, a good way to tell the impact the Court expects a judgment to have is to look at the 'importance level' granted to the judgments by the Registry, although it should be noted that this is not a formal classification system and it does not in any way bind the Court.[100] If a case is classified as 'level 3', it has 'low importance', meaning that it is of little legal interest and simply applies existing case law. Level 2 means 'medium importance' and is accorded if a judgment or decision may not make a significant contribution to the case-law, but nevertheless goes beyond merely applying existing case-law. Finally, importance level 1 means 'high importance' and is reserved for judgments and decisions which make a significant contribution to the development, clarification or modification of the case-law, either generally or in relation to a particular State.[101]

3 *The Judges*

Procedure for Election

The ECtHR has 47 judges, one for each of the State Parties to the Convention.[102] They are elected by the Parliamentary Assembly of the Council of Europe (PACE) from a list of three candidates nominated by the States Parties.[103] The procedure to draw up a list of candidates is determined by each state individually, although the Committee of Ministers

[99] For an important example, see *Pretty* v. *United Kingdom*, ECtHR 29 April 2002, no. 2346/02.

[100] The 'importance level' system is explained in the Court's HUDOC database, http://hudoc.echr.coe.int; see also e.g. Annual Report 2012, *Short Survey of the main judgments and decisions delivered by the Court in 2012*, http://echr.coe.int/Documents/Short_Survey_2012_ENG.pdf, footnote 2.

[101] Indeed, these judgments are usually considered for publication in the official Reports of Judgments and Decisions of the Court.

[102] Article 20.

[103] Article 22; see further e.g. A. Drzemczewski, 'Election of judges to the Strasbourg Court: an overview', 2010 (4) *European Human Rights Law Review* 377.

(CM) has drafted guidelines for these procedures.[104] The candidates must fulfil the criteria for office of Article 21 ECHR, which means they have to be of high moral character and must either possess the qualifications required for appointment to high judicial office or be jurisconsults of recognised competence. Additional requirements have been defined by the PACE and the CM, in particular as regards the command of the two official languages of the Court (French and English).[105] Moreover, the PACE requires the list of candidates to demonstrate gender balance.[106] The lists have to be made up in alphabetical order so as to avoid the State expressing any preferences for one of the candidates.[107] Since 2010, the States have had to present their lists of candidates to an advisory panel of the CM before the lists are sent to the PACE.[108] This is an additional check to safeguard the quality, independence and impartiality of the candidates. Once the list has arrived at the PACE, a sub-committee interviews the candidates and draws up an advice to the PACE, which will finally take votes to select the preferred candidate.[109]

Impartiality and Independence Guarantees

Judges are appointed in the ECtHR for a period of nine years, without possibility of re-election.[110] Their terms of office expire if they reach the age of 70,[111] although this requirement will be deleted from the Convention upon the entry into force of Protocol No. 15.[112] Judges may not

[104] Guidelines of the Committee of Ministers on the selection of candidates for the post of judge at the European Court of Human Rights, CM(2012)40 final, 29 March 2012; for more information, see also the preparatory document: CDDH(2012)R74 Addendum IV.

[105] Report of the PACE Committee on Legal Affairs and Human Rights concerning Resolution 1366, 7 October 2003, Doc. 9963; Guidelines of the Committee of Ministers on the selection of candidates for the post of judge at the European Court of Human Rights, CM(2012)40 final, 29 March 2012.

[106] PACE Resolution 1627 (2008); see also PACE Committee on Legal Affairs and Human Rights, *Procedure for electing judges to the European Court of Human Rights*, Information document prepared by the Secretariat, AS/Jur/Inf (2012) 02 rev4, 7 December 2012.

[107] PACE Resolution 1646 (2009), para. 4.3.

[108] Resolution CM/Res(2010)26 on the establishment of an Advisory Panel of Experts on Candidates for Election as Judge to the European Court of Human Rights, 10 November 2010.

[109] PACE Committee on Legal Affairs and Human Rights, *Procedure for electing judges to the European Court of Human Rights*, Information document prepared by the Secretariat, AS/Jur/Inf (2012) 02 rev4, 7 December 2012; see also Drzemczewski n 103.

[110] Article 23 (1). [111] Article 23 (2).

[112] Article 2 Protocol No. 15, ETS No. 213. See further on this the Preliminary Opinion of the Court in preparation for the Brighton Conference, adopted by the Plenary Court on 20 February 2012, para. 29.

engage in activities incompatible with their independence, impartiality and the demands of a full-time office.[113] These requirements are further elaborated and detailed in the Court's Resolution of Judicial Ethics.[114]

Selection of Judges and Their Backgrounds

The PACE selects candidates primarily for their expected qualities as judges. There is no particular preference for a certain background, e.g. as judge, practitioner or scholar, although judicial experience is welcome[115] and the desire sometimes has been expressed that the Court would represent 'the different worlds of the legal profession'.[116] In practice, scholarly or judicial backgrounds appear to prevail.[117]

Composition of Formations; Taking Account of Geographical and Gender Balance

Given the special character of the Court as a supranational court and its composition of judges of very different origins and backgrounds, the composition of the formations in which the Court sits in deciding certain cases is extremely important.[118] The smaller formations are drawn from the five Sections of the Court, which need to be geographically and gender balanced and must reflect the different legal systems among the States Parties.[119] Factors such as background (scholar, judge) and legal specialisations are also taken into account in composing the Sections (as well as the formations selected from these Sections).[120]

The Grand Chamber is composed of the President, the two Vice-Presidents, the five Section Presidents and the judge elected for the respondent state. These are supplemented by either the judges who were in the

[113] Article 21 (3), further detailed in Rule 4 Rules of Court.

[114] http://www.echr.coe.int/Documents/Resolution_Judicial_Ethics_ENG.pdf.

[115] Drzemczewski n 103, p. 382.

[116] H. C. Krüger, 'Selecting Judges for the New European Court of Human Rights', 17 *Human Rights Law Journal* (1996) p. 404.

[117] Arold n 7, p. 52. Voeten has found that there are also candidates with a political background (n 69, p. 676), but this may have changed over the past few years as a result of the introduction of new elements and guarantees for impartiality in the election procedure.

[118] For the effects of the backgrounds (historical-political, professional, ideological) of the judges on the Court's decision-making, see Arold n 7, pp. 69ff.

[119] Rule 25(2).

[120] Cf. A. Drzemczewski, 'The Internal Organization of the European Court of Human Rights: the Composition of Chambers and the Grand Chamber' (2000) 3 *European Human Rights Law Review* 233 at p. 237.

Chamber which relinquished judgment or, in case of referral, judges who did not sit on the Chamber which rendered the judgment.[121]

An important aspect in the composition of both the Chambers and the Grand Chamber is that the judge for the respondent state should always sit on the case.[122] The reason for this is mainly that the national judge has valuable knowledge of the state's legal system. The element of expertise is considered so important that if the national judge is unable to sit on a case, the President of the Court will appoint an *ad hoc* judge based on a list of candidates drawn up by the state.[123] The 'national judge' does not represent the state in any way, however, as this would conflict with the requirement that judges sit on the Court in their individual capacity and should be entirely independent and impartial.[124]

4 *Legal Scholarship and Constitutional Reasoning*

Response by the ECtHR to Scholarly Work

The Court's 'constitutional' jurisprudence generally seems to be favourably received by legal scholarship, but certain judgments, and sometimes the Court's work more generally, also have been met with scepticism.[125] Recent studies have disclosed that the Court takes this kind of criticism very seriously, especially if it concerns specific judgments or interpretations.[126] Although the Court never refers to scholarly literature in its judgments, interviews with judges reveal that they assess any critique for its reasonableness and where necessary take account of it in its case-law.[127] Judges with a scholarly or relatively political background generally seem to be the most inclined to respond to national criticism.[128]

[121] Article 26 (1) and (5) and Rule 24; see also Explanatory Memorandum to Protocol No. 11, ETS No. 155, paras. 73 and 74.

[122] For Committees there is a special rule; see Article 28 (3). For the Chambers and the Grand Chamber, see Article 26 (4).

[123] Article 26 (4) and Rule 29. [124] Article 21 (2).

[125] See further e.g. Gerards and Fleuren n 77; L. R. Helfer, 'Redesigning the European Court of Human Rights: Embeddedness as a Deep Structural Principle of the European Human Rights Regime' 19 (2008) *European Journal of International Law* 125; N. Krisch, 'The Open Architecture of European Human Rights Law', (2008) 71 *Modern Law Review* 183 at pp. 184 and 197; L. Caflisch, 'The Reform of the European Court of Human Rights: Protocol No. 14 and Beyond', (2006) 6 *Human Rights Law Review* 403 at p. 411; E. Lambert Abdelgawad, 'The Execution of the Judgments of the European Court of Human Rights: Towards a Non-coercive and Participatory Model' (2009) 69 *Zeitschrift für ausländisches und öffentliches Recht und Völkerrecht* 471 at p. 499.

[126] In particular Gerards and Fleuren n 77. [127] Gerards n 25, sections 6.2 and 6.3.

[128] Arold n 7, 73.

In turn, the case-law of the ECtHR has been shown to be extremely influential for legal scholarship and the development of fundamental rights doctrine throughout Europe.[129] National fundamental rights discourse in Europe is increasingly framed in the terminology as it is developed and refined in the Court's case-law.[130] Indeed, typical Convention notions such as the 'margin of appreciation doctrine', 'positive obligations' and 'evolutive interpretation' in many states appear to be as easily used by national courts and scholars as by European judges.[131]

Basic Principles of Constitutional Reasoning

(1) The Convention as a 'living instrument' – evolutive/dynamic and consensus interpretation

The Court has recognised that the understanding of fundamental rights is continually evolving as a result of societal and technological developments and changes in views on fundamental rights.[132] The Court expressly relies on the notion that the Convention is a 'living instrument', 'which must be interpreted in the light of present-day conditions'. It has also stated time and again that it must take account 'of evolving norms of national and international law in its interpretation of Convention provisions'.[133] Indeed, taking a different approach would mean the Convention would quickly get out of step with the developments in national fundamental rights law and policy, and the Court would have great difficulty in performing its task to provide for a pan-European minimum level of protection of fundamental rights.

[129] See sources mentioned in n 125.

[130] See sources mentioned in n 125. See also H. Keller and A. Stone Sweet (eds), *A Europe of Rights. The Impact of the ECHR on National Legal Systems* (Oxford University Press 2008); Stone Sweet n 14; G. Martinico and O. Pollicino (eds), *The National Judicial Treatment of the ECHR and EU Laws. A Comparative Constitutional Perspective* (European Law Publishing 2010).

[131] See sources mentioned in ns 125 and 130.

[132] See further J. Mahoney, *The Challenge of Human Rights. Origin, Development and Significance* (Blackwell 2007) p. 97 and A. Mowbray, 'Between the Will of the Contracting Parties and the Needs of Today: Extending the Scope of Convention Rights and Freedoms beyond What Could Have Been Foreseen by the Drafters of the ECHR' in E. Brems and J.H. Gerards (eds), *Shaping Rights in the ECHR. The Role of the European Court of Human Rights in Determining the Scope of Human Rights* (Cambridge University Press 2013), ch. 2.

[133] *Demir and Baykara* v. *Turkey*, ECtHR (GC) 12 November 2008, no. 34503/97, para. 68; see already *Tyrer* v. *United Kingdom*, ECtHR 25 April 1978, no. 5856/72, para. 31.

To adapt its interpretations to present-day societal and legal views and opinions, the Court uses a special interpretative technique, i.e., 'common ground' or 'consensus' interpretation.[134] This method implies that the Court will usually accept a novel (mostly wider) interpretation of the Convention if there is a sufficiently clear European consensus supporting such an interpretation.[135] To discover if there is such a consensus, or rather, convergence of legal views in Europe, the Court generally looks at comparative studies (produced by one of the intervening parties or, especially in Grand Chamber cases, by the Court's registry),[136] international treaties,[137] reports of international organisations,[138] and EU law.[139]

(2) Effectiveness principle; meta-teleological interpretation

According to the Court's case-law, the Convention's central objective is to guarantee fundamental rights to individuals in a practical and effective manner.[140] The Court gives shape to this by giving a reading to the Convention rights that respects the fundamental principles underlying the Convention as a whole, such as respect for human dignity, personal autonomy, democracy, the rule of law, and pluralism.[141] It does so mainly by means of 'meta-teleological interpretation'.[142] This means that in interpreting the terms and notions of the Convention, the Court does not refer so much to the concrete aim of certain provisions of the Convention (as would be the case with classic teleological interpretation) as to the overall objectives and underlying principles of the Convention.[143]

[134] On this method, see *in extenso* (and with many references) H. C. K. Senden, *Interpretation of Fundamental Rights in a Multilevel Legal System. An analysis of the European Court of Human Rights and the Court of Justice of the European Union* (Intersentia 2011).

[135] Cf. *Christine Goodwin* v. *United Kingdom*, ECtHR (GC) 11 July 2002, no. 28957/95, para. 74.

[136] *Idem.*

[137] E.g. *Mamatkulov and Askarov* v. *Turkey*, ECtHR (GC) 4 February 2005, nos. 46827/99 & 46951/99; *Demir and Baykara* v. *Turkey*, ECtHR (GC) 12 November 2008, no. 34503/97.

[138] E.g. *D.H. and Others* v. *Czech Republic*, ECtHR (GC) 13 November 2007, no. 57325/00.

[139] E.g. *Scoppola (No. 2)* v. *Italy*, ECtHR (GC) 17 September 2009, no. 10249/03.

[140] See already *Airey* v. *Ireland*, ECtHR 9 October 1979, no. 6289/73, para. 24 and, more recently, *Mamatkulov & Askarov* v. *Turkey*, ECtHR (GC) 4 February 2005, nos. 46827/99 and 46951/99. See more extensively Senden, n 134, at p. 73.

[141] Cf. O. De Schutter and F. Tulkens, 'Rights in Conflict: the European Court of Human Rights as a Pragmatic Institution', in E. Brems, ed., *Conflicts between Fundamental Rights* (Antwerp/Oxford/Portland, Intersentia 2008) pp. 169 at p. 214; Senden n 134, at p. 199. See further below, section 11.

[142] M. Lasser, *Judicial Deliberations. A Comparative Analysis of Judicial Transparency and Legitimacy* (Oxford University Press 2004); Gerards n 25, section 4.2.2.

[143] Cf. Senden n 134, at p. 204; Gerards n 25, section 4.2.2.

(3) Primarity, subsidiarity, the 'better placed' argument and the margin of appreciation doctrine

As discussed in the first section of this chapter, the Court acknowledges that the States have the primary responsibility to safeguard the Convention rights and that, for that reason, the Court itself exercises only a 'subsidiary' or supervisory role. Another reason for the Court to keep some distance from national acts and measures is expressed in the 'better placed argument'.[144] In the Court's view, the domestic authorities know most about the national circumstances and traditions, they have better means than the Court does to gauge public and political support for decisions in delicate socioeconomic fields, and they can better appraise the pertinent individual and general interests. This finds clear expression in the Court's famous margin of appreciation doctrine.[145] In theory, this doctrine functions as a yardstick for the intensity of the Court's scrutiny of national arguments advanced in justification of an interference.[146] In practice, however, the margin of appreciation has slowly developed into a rhetorical formula, which is mainly used to express that some leeway is left to the States.[147] Nevertheless, the European government leaders have stressed the importance of the margin of appreciation and decided in the 2012 Brighton Declaration that the doctrine should be codified in the Convention.[148] Since October 2013, a new Protocol (No. 15) has been opened for signature and ratification, which adds a new recital to the preamble referring to the principle of subsidiarity and the margin of appreciation doctrine.[149]

[144] See section 1.

[145] The doctrine and its effect have been analysed and discussed extensively; for a recent overview with many references to the most important contributions, see J. H. Gerards, 'Diverging Fundamental Rights Standards and the Role of the European Court of Human Rights' in M. Claes and M. De Visser (eds), *Constructing European Constitutional Law* (Hart, forthcoming), http://ssrn.com/abstract=2344626.

[146] However, some scholars have rightly stated that the determination of the scope of the margin of appreciation is sometimes presented as an outcome of substantive assessment of a justification, rather than as a tool to determine the intensity of review in a preliminary stage; e.g. G. Letsas, 'Two Concepts of the Margin of Appreciation' (2006) 26 *Oxford Journal of Legal Studies* 705; J. Kratochvíl, 'The Inflation of the Margin of Appreciation by the European Court of Human Rights' (2011) 29 *Netherlands Quarterly of Human Rights* 324; Gerards n 145.

[147] See in particular Kratochvíl n 146; Gerards n 145.

[148] Brighton Declaration, adopted at the High-Level Conference on the future of the European Court of Human Rights, 18–20 April 2012, CDDH(2012)007, paras. 11 and 12.

[149] ETS No. 213, Article 1.

(4) Autonomous interpretation

The Convention contains many notions and concepts which are also used in national constitutions and legislation, such as 'privacy', 'property' or 'court', and of which the precise legal meaning can differ for each legal system.[150] When interpreting or defining the Convention terms, the Court must choose between respecting the national meaning of such a term, and adopting a European definition. The Court has stressed that a European, *autonomous* definition should usually prevail.[151] This is understandable from the perspective that the Convention should guarantee an equal level of protection for all states.[152]

(5) Case-based reasoning and incrementalism

The Court usually refrains from directly providing for abstract, wide and deeply morally reasoned interpretations and strongly on case-based reasoning.[153] The Court decides most cases by comparing the facts of the case before it to the facts of cases decided previously, looking for analogies, similarities and differences. In some cases, it finds the similarities sufficiently clear as to justify extending a certain line of case-law or a certain interpretation to a new, slightly different set of facts. In other cases, it may find reason to distinguish the facts of the case, stopping the case-law from developing in a certain direction.[154]

Characteristic of the Court's case-law is also that the Court (especially its Grand Chamber) every now and then distils the common elements

[150] Cf. R. Bernhardt, 'Thoughts on the Interpretation of Human Rights Treaties', in R.St.J. Macdonald et al. (eds), *The European System for the Protection of Human Rights* (Martinus Nijhoff 1993) 65–71 at p. 67.

[151] Cf. F. Sudre, 'Le recours aux "notions autonomes"', in F. Sudre, ed., *L'interprétation de la Convention européenne des droits de l'homme* (Bruylant 1998) 93 at p. 117; see also elaborately Senden n 134, at 177.

[152] F. Matscher, 'Methods of Interpretation of the Convention', in R. St. J. Macdonald et al. n 150, at 73; Sudre n 151, at 94; Senden n 134, at 294–5; Gerards n 25, section 4.4.4.

[153] See J. H. Gerards, 'The Prism of Fundamental Rights', (2012) 8.2 *European Constitutional Law Review* 173; Gerards n 25, section 5.3.3; Gerards n 145. See also Y. Lupu and E. Voeten, 'Precedent on International Courts: A Network Analysis of Case Citations by the European Court of Human Rights', APSA 2010 Annual Meeting Paper, http://ssrn.com/abstract=1643839.

[154] See e.g. *Vajnai* v. *Hungary*, ECtHR 8 July 2008, no. 33629/06, para. 49), where the Court distinguished the case from a previous case on limitations of freedom of expression in Hungary (*Rekvényi* v. *Hungary*, ECtHR 20 May 1999, no. 25390/94), holding that in the current case and after 20 years of democracy, it was no longer necessary to allow Hungary additional leeway to combat the danger to democracy that might be constituted by certain forms of speech.

and criteria that it has used to decide a series of individual cases, re-shaping them into a set of 'general principles derived from the Court's case-law'.[155] Thus the Court may use previous case-law as a basis to draw up authoritative lists of general criteria which may subsequently be used to determine the applicability of the Convention or the review of a justification for interference.[156] These principles and criteria may serve as standards to be applied by the Court as well as national authorities, doing justice to the Court's task to 'elucidate, safeguard and develop the rules instituted by the Convention'.[157]

B Arguments in Constitutional Reasoning

5 *The Structure of Constitutional Arguments*

In most of the judgments and decisions analysed for the purposes of the current study, the Court first provides for an account of the general principles it derives from earlier decisions on a similar topic and it then applies these to the case at hand, as was explained in section 4. In such judgments the line of reasoning is usually relatively linear in nature ('chain structure'). In other cases, however, it concludes that these principles are not sufficiently clear and that it needs to arrive at a new or adapted interpretation. Looking at the 40 leading cases, it seems that the Court most often employs one-line conclusive argumentation.[158] Although the Court may refer to a myriad different principles, arguments and methods, they are typically presented as pointing in the same direction, one argument reinforcing the other. In a few judgments, the argumentation has a parallel conclusive argumentative structure.[159] In particular, in several judgments the Court defines a set of 'topoi' or relevant factors to be taken into account when assessing an alleged violation of a fundamental right, without indicating the relative weight of the various factors. In these cases it is up to the national courts and, eventually, the ECtHR to apply these

155 Cf. Ress n 74, at p. 726.

156 See e.g. *Kotov* v. *Russia*, ECtHR (GC) 3 April 2012, no. 54522/00, paras. 92–107.

157 See e.g. *Konstantin Markin* v. *Russia*, ECtHR (GC) 22 March 2012, no. 30078/06, para. 89.

158 28 of 40 cases.

159 In only one case was there a relatively clear 'legs of a chair' structure (parallel conclusive arguments), where it seems that different arguments of similar value supported the final outcome – see *Hirst (No. 2)* v. *United Kingdom*, ECtHR (GC) 6 October 2005, no. 74025/01. It may be, however, that some the judgments classified as discursive should rather be seen as containing 'legs of a chair' argumentation, especially the judgments in which lists of 'topoi' are developed and applied.

factors to the facts of the case and decide how they interrelate.[160] In yet other cases the Court's reasoning is clearly discursive in nature, in the sense that the Court presents pros and contras of a certain interpretation and balances these in order to arrive at a specific outcome.[161]

Generally, the most apt description of the Court's argumentative approach might be that of the search for a 'reflective equilibrium'.[162] This characterisation does justice to the Court's practice of 'going back and forth' between principles and concrete circumstances, by first setting out its general principles and lists of topoi; then, via a host of arguments arriving at a more general understanding of certain Convention notions; and subsequently refining these notions by applying them to the facts of the case at hand and by discussing elaborately the case's particularities, the arguments of the parties and the way the general principles should be understood.[163]

6 *Types of Arguments in Constitutional Reasoning*

Incrementalism, Analogical Reasoning and References to Previous Judgments

The analysis of the 40 leading cases confirms the expectation expressed in section 4 that most of the ECtHR's judgments are inspired by its core interpretative principles. First and foremost, the Court thereby uses a strongly case-based and incrementalist approach. Arguments based on precedent and analogical reasoning are therefore apparent in virtually all the judgments analysed.[164] With the exception of its very first judgment,[165]

[160] A very clear example of such a catalogue of topoi is *Üner* v. *the Netherlands*, ECtHR (GC) 18 October 2006, no. 46410/99. In case-law on the freedom of expression, similar (though less clearly defined) catalogues can be found; see e.g. *Féret* v. *Belgium*, ECtHR 16 July 2009, no. 15615/07.

[161] This was found for 11 of 40 cases, yet it could be that some must be regarded as containing 'legs of a chair' argumentation. For a clear example of a discursive approach, see e.g. *Gäfgen* v. *Germany*, ECtHR (GC) 1 June 2010, no. 22978/05, in particular in relation to the complaint about Article 6 ECHR.

[162] Cf. J. Rawls, *A Theory of Justice* (Belknap 1971) 20; the Court's approach then seem to match well with Rawls' own reference to Goodwin's rather circular theory of justification; see N. Goodman, *Fact, Fiction and Forecast* (4th ed, Belknap 1983) 63 and Putman's introduction to the book by Goodman, p. ix. Others have termed this the 'unfolding narrative approach'; see F. M. J. den Houdijker, *Afweging van grondrechten in een veellagig rechtssysteem* [Balancing fundamental rights in a multilayered legal system] (WLP 2012) 623ff.

[163] For a typical example, see *Féret* v. *Belgium*, ECtHR 16 July 2009, no. 15615/07.

[164] Precedent-based reasoning is apparent in 38 of 40 cases.

[165] In the *Belgian Linguistics* case the Court could not yet rely on earlier case-law as such case-law simply was not available (ECtHR 23 July 1968, nos. 1474/62 et al).

in all cases studied the Court thereby distils general principles and rules from its own judgments, formulating them as foundations for decision-making in subsequent cases and then refining them by applying them to the facts of the concrete case.

Every now and then, however, the Court considers that the incremental development of general principles is heading in the wrong direction.[166] In particular in those cases it employs additional arguments to underpin the new interpretation to be given to a certain Convention notion, which will be discussed hereafter.

Reliance on General Principles, International Law and Consensus

When searching for arguments to be used in formulating 'new' general principles to steer its interpretation of the Convention, the Court often relies on notions of effectiveness and evolutive interpretation, which it considers to be central to the Convention system. Either or both of these notions are referred to in more than half the cases analysed.[167] Moreover, the Court often mentions that its interpretation must be 'autonomous', which means that Convention terms like 'property' or 'family life' are given a meaning that is independent from the meaning given to these notions in national law.[168] To establish such new or autonomous interpretations, the Court frequently refers to international and European instruments (both binding and non-binding)[169] and to national or comparative materials disclosing divergent or converging national standards.[170] The existence of or tendency towards international or European consensus (or, by contrast, the lack thereof) may provide important support for adopting a certain interpretation.[171] In rare cases, and for different reasons, the Court also refers to non-European, foreign case-law.[172] In some cases these references

166 For some examples, see, *Kudła* v. *Poland*, ECtHR (GC) 26 October 2000, no. 30210/96; *Stec* v. *United Kingdom*, ECtHR (GC) 6 July 2005 (dec.), nos. 65731/01 and 65900/01; *Üner* v. *the Netherlands*, ECtHR (GC) 28 October 2006, no. 46410/99; *Jussila* v. *Finland*, ECtHR (GC) 23 November 2006, no. 73053/01; *Vilho Eskelinen* v. *Finland*, ECtHR (GC) 19 April 2007, no. 63235/00.

167 24 of 40 cases.

168 Autonomous interpretation was expressly mentioned in 5 of 40 cases.

169 In 24 of 40 cases, references to European or international materials were found. For an example, see *Scoppola (No. 2)* v. *Italy*, ECtHR (GC) 17 September 2009, no. 10249/03.

170 In 16 of 40 cases, the Court referred to national law, comparative law, European consensus or foreign judgments.

171 Two examples are *Christine Goodwin* v. *United Kingdom*, ECtHR (GC) 11 July 2002, no. 28957/95 and *Demir and Baykara* v. *Turkey*, ECtHR (GC) 12 November 2008, no. 34503/97.

172 In 4 of 40 cases.

are used to clarify the meaning or importance a certain notion in the national law. An example is a case about the common law notion of 'hearsay evidence', where the Court referred to the meaning given to a similar notion in other common law systems.[173] In other cases the Court mainly seems to use such references as support for a certain interpretation, which it finds in the recognition of this interpretation in other legal systems.[174]

In addition, the Court often uses arguments based on the general principles underlying the Convention as a whole, such as 'rule of law',[175] 'democracy',[176] 'pluralism'[177] and 'human dignity' or 'personal autonomy'.[178] In many cases these general notions are invoked to support a new or slightly different interpretation of Convention principles and their application in concrete cases, as is further discussed in section 11. In all 40 judgments studied, the Court consistently connected these general principles to the text and structure of the Convention, the Convention's aim and purpose (sometimes also mentioning the views of the drafters), or its own precedents (in which it has recognised a certain principle for the first time). Thus, the Court's approach cannot to be regarded as interpretation based on 'extra-constitutional' principles: the Court always takes great care to ground its general principles (and any tests and criteria following from them) in the Convention.

Subsidiarity

The Court's argumentation is strongly inspired by its special position as a supranational court. In all 40 judgments analysed, the Court makes express mention of one of the notions related to this position, such as subsidiarity, the margin of appreciation doctrine or the better placed argument. The translation of these notions into the actual argumentation of the Court shows much variation. In many cases there is a relationship between subsidiarity and the application of consensus interpretation. The Court then refers to a growing convergence of European opinions to support a new interpretation which may not be in line with the views in

[173] As in *Al- Khawaja and Tahery* v. *United Kingdom*, ECtHR (GC) 15 December 2011, nos. 26766/05 and 22228/06.

[174] As in *Christine Goodwin* v. *United Kingdom*, ECtHR (GC) 11 July 2002, no. 28957/95.

[175] 13 of 40 cases. [176] 17 of 40 cases. [177] 2 of 40 cases.

[178] Either human dignity or personal autonomy was expressly referred to in 9 of 40 cases; the Court thereby clearly favours 'personal autonomy' over 'human dignity', referring to the former notion more often.

the respondent state.[179] In other cases, subsidiarity does not much affect the meaning given to the wording of the Convention provisions, but it determines the application of general principles (such as the proportionality requirement) to the case at hand.[180] Hence, subsidiarity may have an impact on both interpretation and application of the Convention.

'Classic' Methods: Textual Interpretation, Travaux Préparatoires, Harmonising Arguments

It is often thought that 'classic' interpretation methods, such as textual and historical methods, are less relevant for the interpretation of the Convention. Indeed, the Court has expressly stated that the *travaux* may not be the best point of reference in determining the present-day meaning of the Convention rights.[181] Nevertheless, in the 40 leading cases quite a few references to explanatory texts can be found,[182] as well as references to the text of the Convention.[183] These arguments are seldom decisive, however. This is only different in rare cases where the applicant has requested an interpretation that is clearly contrary to the ordinary meaning of the text of the Convention. An example is the case of *Pretty* v. *United Kingdom*, where the Court refused to follow the applicant's request to read the right to life as including a right to die.[184]

The Court further relatively frequently employs internal harmonising arguments or 'systematic' interpretation.[185] It may find, for example, that an interpretation that has been given to a notion in one particular Convention provision, such as the notion of 'criminal charge' in Article 6 (right to a fair trial), must also be followed in relation to other articles to which this notion is relevant, such as Articles 5 and 7 (habeas corpus and the *nulla poena* principle).[186]

[179] See e.g. *Christine Goodwin* v. *United Kingdom*, ECtHR (GC) 11 July 2002, no. 28957/95; *Stec* v. *United Kingdom*, ECtHR (GC) 6 July 2005 (dec.), nos. 65731/01 and 65900/01; *Demir and Baykara* v. *Turkey*, ECtHR (GC) 12 November 2008, no. 34503/97.

[180] For extensive case-law studies in this field, see the sources mentioned in n 145.

[181] *Loizidou* v. *Turkey* (ECtHR 23 March 1995, no. 15318/89, para. 71. See also e.g. F. Ost, 'The Original Canons of Interpretation of the European Court of Human Rights', in M. Delmas-Marty (ed), *The European Convention for the Protection of Human Rights. International Protection versus National Restrictions* (Kluwer 1992) 290.

[182] 7 of 40 cases. [183] 19 of 40 cases.

[184] ECtHR 29 April 2002, no. 2346/02. [185] 18 of 40 cases.

[186] See e.g. *Pretty* v. *United Kingdom*, ECtHR 29 April 2002, no. 2346/02; *Kudła* v. *Poland*, ECtHR (GC) 26 October 2000, no. 30210/96; *Gäfgen* v. *Germany*, ECtHR (GC) 1 June 2010, no. 22978/05; *Zolotukhin* v. *Russia*, ECtHR (GC) 10 February 2009, no. 14939/03; *Othman (Abu Qatada)* v. *United Kingdom*, ECtHR 7 January 2012, no. 8139/09.

Moral Arguments and Other Sources

The Court hardly ever expressly relies on moral arguments, i.e., arguments which are not directly or indirectly derived from the meta-principles underlying the Convention, or arguments of a social or economic nature.[187] A few notable exceptions may be mentioned here, but even in these examples it seems clear that there is some relationship to underlying legal principles such as human dignity and democracy. In the case of *Pretty*, for example, which concerned assisted suicide, the Court stressed the reasonableness of an individual's concern about having to be in a state of decrepitude.[188] In the *Refah Partisi* case, concerning the dissolution of a political party, the Court referred to notions such as the need to protect vulnerable groups and the need to fight against the risk of the imposition of a theocratic regime.[189] Equally rare are the judgments in which the Court relied on other types of non-legal arguments, such as statistical data, historical evidence or medical reports.[190]

Scholarly sources are never expressly mentioned in the judgments of the ECtHR. Usually the Court bases its argumentation purely on what it considers to follow from the states' acceptance of the Convention and its underlying principles.

7 The Weight of Arguments

Arguments from effectiveness, the living instrument character of the Convention and meta-teleological arguments play a key role in the Court's case-law. In many cases, however, arguments such as respect for subsidiarity and national diversity in the end appear to prevail. This is the result of the Court's tendency to first establish a general interpretation and only then apply this interpretation to the facts of the case. A case in point is the *Pretty* case, in which the Court established on the basis of

[187] Such arguments have been found (often only implicitly) in 9 of 40 cases.

[188] *Pretty* v. *United Kingdom*, ECtHR 29 April 2002, no. 2346/02.

[189] *Refah Partisi (Welfare Party) and Others* v. *Turkey*, ECtHR (GC) 13 February 2003, nos. 41340/98 et al.

[190] It did do so in several cases, although some are difficult to qualify, as the Court sometimes only refers to general sources such as 'experience shows'. See e.g. *Kudła* v. *Poland*, ECtHR (GC) 26 October 2000, no. 30210/96; *Christine Goodwin* v. *United Kingdom*, ECtHR (GC) 11 July 2002, no. 28957/95; *Hatton and Others* v. *United Kingdom*, ECtHR 8 July 2003, no. 36022/97; *D.H. and Others* v. *Czech Republic*, ECtHR (GC) 13 November 2007, no. 57325/00; *Al-Khawaja and Tahery* v. *United Kingdom*, ECtHR (GC) 15 December 2011, nos. 26766/05 and 22228/06.

meta-teleological arguments that it could not be excluded that assisted suicide was covered by the right to respect for one's private life. Subsequently, however, it left a wide margin of appreciation to the states to decide whether and to what extent this right could be exercised.[191] In the end, the argument of subsidiarity thereby prevailed over the meta-teleological argument. Hence, the Court's reasoning is determined not so much by the importance and weight of certain arguments in an absolute sense, as by a process of the balancing of varying arguments and a continuous interaction between general principles and case-based reasoning.

Moreover, the Court's case-law discloses some contradictions as to the weight it attaches to certain arguments. This was already shown with respect to the use of the *travaux préparatoires*, of which in some judgments the Court has expressly nuanced the importance, whilst in other cases it has ostensibly relied on these documents. Especially in relation to the application of consensus-based arguments, the Court is sometimes even accused of 'cherry picking'.[192] Indeed, the cases studied for this volume confirm that the Court does not always give similar weight to arguments derived from (the lack of) convergence. In particular it sometimes looks at different 'levels' of consensus (either on a rather specific aspect of a right or more generally on a certain issue) to find out if there is convergence or not.[193]

8 *Judicial Candour and Judicial Rhetoric*

Dialogue

Most of the Court's judgments are candid and open as to the reasons and considerations underlying the outcome of the case. In some judgments the Court explicitly discusses different possible readings, explaining their advantages and problems and only then settling on a certain interpretation.[194] Sometimes the Court even expresses its appreciation of the problems a state may experience in dealing with a certain matter. In

[191] ECtHR 29 April 2002, no. 2346/02.

[192] See further on this in particular Senden n 134, with further references.

[193] E.g. *Vo* v. *France*, ECtHR (GC) 8 July 2004, no. 53924/00 and *Lautsi* v. *Italy*, ECtHR (GC) 18 March 2011, no. 30814/06.

[194] This is especially visible in the cases disclosing a dialogical approach rather than a 'chain' structure, as explained in section 6. For an example, see *Gäfgen* v. *Germany*, ECtHR (GC) 1 June 2010, no. 22978/05, in particular in relation to the complaint about Article 6 ECHR.

Al-Khawaja and Tahery v. *United Kingdom*, for example, the Court engaged in an express dialogue with the British courts, which had responded very critically to the previous Chamber judgment in the case.[195] The Court addressed the national courts' objections to the Chamber's approach one by one, providing for clarity where it was asked for. Moreover, it slightly (yet ostensibly) adapted its approach in response to one of the concerns expressed by the British Supreme Court. More generally, it can be seen from the Court's argumentation that in each leading case, it essentially endeavours to persuade the reader by presenting a plethora of relevant reasons and arguments and by referring to the underlying principles of the Convention.[196]

Composition of the Reasoning

As explained in section 2, the reasoning component of the judgments usually consists of two different parts.[197] In the first part, the Court reiterates and further develops, adds to or changes the principles that can be derived from its previous case-law. In the second part, the general principles are applied to the case at hand. The first part of the judgment usually is the most interesting from a constitutional perspective, as it is in this part that the Court formulates the guiding principles, based on references to previous case-law and a variety of principles and methods of interpretation. This is not to say that the application in the concrete case cannot be interesting from the perspective of interpretation and constitutional development. The application of general principles to the facts immediately provides for refinement and nuance, specifying the interpretation of the Convention and thereby sowing the seeds for further development of the Court's case-law in subsequent cases. The continuous interplay in the Court's judgments between developing and distilling general principles and highly case-based application is characteristic of the Court's style of reasoning.

Objective Style

The Court appears to aim at deriving conclusions from earlier cases or the underlying principles of the Convention in a neutral, objective

[195] *Al-Khawaja and Tahery* v. *United Kingdom*, ECtHR (GC) 15 December 2011, nos. 26766/05 and 22228/06.

[196] For an extensive analysis of the dialogic character of the Court's argumentation, see Gerards n 25.

[197] This bifurcated approach is visible in almost all cases studied here, although it is less apparent in the Court's early judgments.

and logical fashion. Only rarely does the Court articulate its express disapproval of certain behaviour, such as the consistent and unjustified refusal of a government to present essential documents to the Court, and even then, the Court seems to strive towards keeping the wording of the judgment objective.[198] Nonetheless, the Court's judgments sometimes contain references to arguments or doctrines which do not play any role in the actual review of the case. For example, the Court often refers to the margin of appreciation doctrine without actually determining the scope of the margin and without indicating the effects of the margin for its assessment of the case.[199] Such references seem to be aimed at creating a certain image with the Court's audience (e.g., the image of a Court not meddling with national affairs) rather than contributing to substantive reasoning towards a certain interpretation or application of the Convention.

Audience

The audience of the Court's judgments is rather difficult to establish. On the one hand, the applicant party will often not be able to read the judgment because it is rendered in either French or English.[200] It is, therefore, not to be expected that the Court should write its judgments to be read by the individual applicants. On the other hand, it is evident from the 40 leading cases that the Court endeavours to frame its judgments in understandable and transparent language, making the judgments readable even to non-lawyers. Moreover, in some of its judgments the Court relatively directly addresses the government or the applicant, e.g. by expressing that it can understand the position of the parties to the case or it values the efforts made by the authorities to protect certain fundamental rights.[201]

198 This is not apparent in the 40 landmark cases discussed here, but it can be seen, for example, in a case like *Janowiec and Others* v. *Russia*, ECtHR (GC) 21 October 2013, nos. 55508/07 and 29520/09.

199 For a further analysis of this tendency, see e.g. Gerards 2014 and Kratochvíl, both n 145. For an example, see *Nada* v. *Switzerland*, ECtHR (GC) 12 September 2012, no. 10593/08, para 184.

200 Rule 76. There is a trend to have judgments translated into different languages, and such translations are made available through the ECtHR's database HUDOC; the Court does not have its own budget for doing so and the translations are non-official versions of the judgments. See on the translation policy www.echr.coe.int > case-law > case-law translations.

201 Some recent examples are *M.S.* v. *United Kingdom*, ECtHR 3 May 2012, no. 24527/08 and *Redfearn* v. *United Kingdom*, ECtHR 6 November 2012, no. 47335/06.

Thus the judgments at least partly do seem to be written for the parties to the case.

At the same time, it seems that the Court more generally uses its argumentation to convince national authorities (including the authorities of states other than the respondent state) of the need and desirability of implementing the judgment in their national law. It does so not only by framing interpretations in autonomous and general terms, but also by referring to the limitations of its own task, the primary role played by the national authorities, the margin of appreciation, the subsidiarity principle, and so on.[202] There would be no need for such language if the Court would not expect the critical authorities (government officials, parliamentarians) and relevant stakeholders in states other than those of the respondent state to actually read its judgments.

Finally, it appears from recent studies that the Court highly values its partnership with national courts.[203] The Court regards the national courts as being best able to understand and implement its judgments and apply the criteria and standards it develops in its case-law.[204] National courts therefore are an important audience for the Court's judgments, and the Court often directly gives attention to them in its judgments. In some of the 40 leading cases studied for this volume, the Court even responds explicitly and directly to arguments made in a certain cases by the national courts, as was discussed in section 8.[205]

9 *Length, Dissenting and Concurring Opinions*

The average judgment in the 40 analysed cases counts about 50 pages, including summaries of the facts and relevant international and comparative materials, as well as separate opinions. If only the number of pages is counted in which the Court provides its substantive argumentation, the judgments on average contain about 20 pages of reasoning.[206]

202 For an extensive analysis of the Court's argumentation from this perspective, see Gerards n 25; this is also apparent from the frequent references to notions of subsidiarity, the margin of appreciation doctrine, the better placed-argument and so on; on that, see section 7.

203 Gerards n 25.

204 This is clear from several studies into the implementation of the ECHR in national law; see the references in n 130 and see Gerards and Fleuren n 77.

205 See e.g. *Al-Khawaja and Tahery* v. *United Kingdom*, ECtHR (GC) 15 December 2011, nos. 26766/05 and 22228/06 and *Von Hannover (No. 2)* v. *Germany*, ECtHR (GC) 7 December 2012, nos. 40660/08 and 60641/08.

206 Including the statements of the parties, but excluding the procedure, the facts, accounts of national and international law, the dictum and separate opinions.

Politically sensitive or legally complex topics have always given rise to controversy within the Court and, accordingly, they have led to many separate opinions being written.[207] Of the 40 leading cases and decisions studied here, only 4 were not accompanied by either concurring or dissenting opinions.[208]

Separate opinions to the Court's judgments generally make for interesting reading, as they disclose the hard issues on which the opinions within the Court differed. As a consequence, they may clarify interpretative issues and they may help to predict the direction of the case-law's future development.

Over the 60 years of the Court's existence, the form, style and number of separate opinions of the Court have remained remarkably stable.[209] At the same time, the separate opinions are as different as the judges writing them.[210] Some opinions are brief and articulate only one special objection; others are lengthy, detailed and full of footnotes. Some reflect an attitude of judicial activism, others plead in favour of judicial restraint.[211] Some dissents clearly stem from the practical backgrounds of certain judges, others are intricate pieces of scholarly work.[212] As a result of these differences and variations, it has proved to be difficult to find clear tendencies and correlations between separate opinions and, for example, professional background or geographical origin of the judges.[213]

10 Framing of Constitutional Issues

According to Article 32, the ECtHR's competence extends 'to all matters concerning the interpretation and application of the Convention and the

[207] Cf. Arold n 7, pp. 103ff.

[208] This is in line with a previous study conducted by White and Boussiakou, who found in a much larger sample of cases that about 80 per cent of the cases decided were non-unanimous and that in most of these cases separate opinions were included; see White and Boussiakou n 48, 50.

[209] That is true, at least, for the cases studied here; empirical research based on a much larger set of cases is needed to demonstrate this. See further Arold n 7, pp. 97ff and Voeten n 69, p. 697.

[210] This also appears to be the findings of Arold n 7, p. 154, Voeten n 69, p. 670 and White and Boussiakou n 48, p. 52ff. The latter arrive at the 'key conclusion' that 'it is judicial temperament which determines the extent to which a judge appends his or her own individual voice to the judgment of the Court' (at p. 59).

[211] For a further analysis of separate opinions along these lines, see Voeten n 69, p. 685ff. One of the best-known examples of a separate opinion in favour of judicial restraint is Judge Sir Fitzmaurice's dissenting opinion to *Marckx* v. *Belgium*, ECtHR 13 June 1979, no. 6833/74.

[212] Voeten n 69, p. 696, found a slight difference as to professional background.

[213] See further in particular Arold n 7, Voeten n 69, and White and Boussiakou n 48.

Protocols thereto'. The issue of 'framing' a case coming before it as either a fundamental rights case or as another constitutional issue is therefore not very relevant to this Court. For that reason, this matter is not further discussed in this chapter.

11 Key Concepts

Rule of Law, Democracy, Pluralism, Secularism and State Neutrality

As explained in sections 4 and 6, the Court often relies on 'meta-teleological interpretation', finding support for its interpretations in the general notions and principles underlying the Convention. In particular the Court frequently refers to the notions of rule of law, democracy and pluralism.[214] The 40 judgments confirm that the Court considers these principles of great importance for the interpretation of a variety of fundamental rights, such as freedom of expression, freedom of religion, freedom of demonstration and the right to vote.[215] The notions of rule of law, democracy and pluralism thereby appear to be closely connected and the Court does not always clearly distinguish between them.[216] Nevertheless, in some of the judgments it has endeavoured to clarify their interrelationship, for example, by mentioning that concepts such as 'separation of powers' and 'pluralism' are inherent to both the 'rule of law' and 'democracy'.[217] The concept of pluralism as such is mainly used to refer to the need for respect for and tolerance of a certain diversity of opinions, beliefs and convictions in a modern society.[218]

[214] See section 6. [215] See further the references in the table of cases.

[216] See further Committee on Legal Affairs and Human Rights of the Parliamentary Assembly of the Council of Europe, *The Principle of the Rule of Law*, Draft Report by E. Jurgens, AS/Jur (2007) 28, 3 May 2007, para. 12 and Appendix.

[217] Cf. H. M. ten Napel, 'The European Court of Human Rights and Political Rights: The Need for More Guidance', (2009) 5 *European Constitutional Law Review* 464 at p. 465; for separation of powers, see e.g. (although rather implicitly) *Broniowski* v. *Poland*, ECtHR (GC) 22 June 2004, no. 31443/96 and *Scoppola (No. 2)* v. *Italy*, ECtHR (GC) 17 September 2009, no. 10249/03; see further D. Kosař, 'Policing Separation of Powers: A New Role for the European Court of Human Rights?' (2012) 8 *European Constitutional Law Review* 33.

[218] See in particular *Kokkinakis* v. *Greece*, ECtHR 25 May 1993, no. 14307/88, *Refah Partisi and Others* v. *Turkey*, ECtHR (GC) 13 February 2003, nos. 41340/98 et al., *Leyla Şahin* v. *Turkey*, ECtHR (GC) 10 November 2005, no. 44774/98, *Lautsi* v. *Italy*, ECtHR (GC) 18 March 2011, no. 30814/06. See also A.J. Nieuwenhuis, 'The Concept of Pluralism in the Case-Law of the European Court of Human Rights' (2007) 5 *European Constitutional Law Review* 367 at p. 384.

The Court also sometimes refers to notions of secularism and state neutrality in its freedom of religion case-law.[219] The Court has continually stressed that state neutrality should be a governing principle in cases related to freedom of religion and it has always embraced arguments based on secularism. Nevertheless, it has not expressly promoted a purely secular state in its case-law, nor has it listed secularism as one of the underlying Convention principles.[220]

Human Dignity and Personal Autonomy

Next to the group of 'democracy and pluralism'-related principles, the Court has recognised human dignity, human freedom, personal autonomy and personal development as of primary importance to the Convention.[221] Without providing any clear definition of these principles, it frequently refers to these notions in interpreting, in particular, the right to privacy, the right to marry and the rights related to bodily and mental integrity (right to life, prohibition of torture).[222]

Procedural Fairness and Effective Remedies

Mainly as part of the overall principle of effectiveness, the Court has attached much weight to procedural fairness, accessibility of judicial remedies and, overall, procedural rights.[223] The Court has often linked such procedural rights and obligations to the rule of law and the importance of

219 Much has been written on this, in particular after the cases of *Leyla Şahin* v. *Turkey*, ECtHR (GC) 10 November 2005, no. 44774/98 and *Lautsi* v. *Italy*, ECtHR (GC) 18 March 2011, no. 30814/06. See e.g. H. van Ooijen, *Religious Symbols in Public Functions – Unveiling State Neutrality* (Intersentia 2012) ch. 5 and J. Temperman (ed), *The Lautsi Papers: Multidisciplinary Reflections on Religious Symbols in the Public School Classroom* (Martinus Nijhoff Publishers 2012).

220 See the sources mentioned in n 219; see also e.g. D. Kyristis and S. Tsatsyrakis, 'Neutrality in the Classroom' (2013) 11 *International Journal of Constitutional Law* 200.

221 In 9 of 40 cases notions of human dignity and personal autonomy are expressly mentioned.

222 For some examples in the cases studied here, see e.g. *Pretty* v. *United Kingdom*, ECtHR 29 April 2002, no. 2346/02 and *Christine Goodwin* v. *United Kingdom*, ECtHR (GC) 11 July 2002, no. 28957/95. For an extensive analysis (in Dutch) see J. H. Gerards, N. R. Koffeman and A. C. Hendriks, 'Zelfbeschikking in het recht van de Raad van Europa' [Personal autonomy in the law of the Council of Europe], in *Achtergrondstudies Zelfbeschikking in the zorg* [Background Studies of Autonomy in Care] (ZonMW 2013), www.zonmw.nl/publicaties, ch. 2; see more generally also Ch. McCrudden, 'Human Dignity and Judicial Interpretation of Human Rights', (2008) 19 *European Journal of International Law* 655.

223 Procedural rights or aspects of procedural fairness are mentioned in 20 of 40 cases. See elaborately e.g. *Bosphorus* v. *Ireland*, ECtHR (GC) 30 June 2005, no. 45036/98.

a fair trial in a democracy.[224] This finds expression in the development of procedural positive obligations as an inherent part of almost all Convention rights. In its *Šilih* judgment, the Court even decided that the positive obligation for the state to investigate suspicious deaths and provide for sufficient judicial remedies should be regarded as a separate, detachable aspect of the right to life, which can be invoked independently.[225]

Proportionality and Fair Balance

Many Convention provisions expressly refer to elements of proportionality, necessity and balancing. In this regard, it is not surprising that the Court has remarked that 'inherent in the whole of the Convention is a search for a fair balance between the demands of the general interest of the community and the requirements of the protection of the individual's fundamental rights'.[226] Unsurprisingly, therefore, balancing and proportionality language can be found throughout the Court's case law.[227] This is different only for non-derogable rights such as the prohibition of torture, where the Court has emphasised there is no room for proportionality review.[228] Even in respect of such 'absolute' rights, however, the Court appears to be sensitive to the ideas of balancing and necessity and it often (implicitly) includes elements of proportionality review in its argumentation.[229]

Core Rights

In many of its judgments the Court employs a core rights approach, but it does so in a variety of ways. Firstly, the more closely the set of facts presented is related to one of the guiding principles mentioned above, the sooner the Court will recognise it as being covered by a certain fundamental right.[230] The 40 leading cases disclose, however, that this

224 E.g. *Šilih* v. *Slovenia*, ECtHR (GC) 9 April 2009, no. 71463/01 and *Gäfgen* v. *Germany*, ECtHR (GC) 1 June 2010, no. 22978/05.

225 *Šilih* v. *Slovenia*, ECtHR (GC) 9 April 2009, no. 71463/01.

226 *Soering* v. *United Kingdom*, ECtHR 7 July 1989, no. 14038/88, para. 89.

227 25 of 40 cases. 228 *Gäfgen* v. *Germany*, ECtHR (GC) 1 June 2010, no. 22978/05.

229 No such cases were analysed for the current study, but see extensively e.g. S. Smet, 'The "Absolute" Prohibition of Torture and Inhuman or Degrading treatment in Article 3 ECHR: Truly a Question of Scope Only?' in E. Brems and J. H. Gerards (eds), *Shaping Rights in the ECHR. The Role of the European Court of Human Rights in Determining the Scope of Human Rights* (Cambridge University Press 2013) 273, with many further references.

230 See e.g. (but rather implicitly) *Von Hannover (No. 2)* v. *Germany*, ECtHR (GC) 7 February 2012, nos. 40660/08 and 60641/08, paras. 95–96 and see *Golder* v. *United Kingdom*, ECtHR 21 February 1975, no. 4451/70.

variant of core reasoning does not have much impact. The Court's 'core reasoning' is often rather implicit, and the Court usually quickly accepts applicability of the Convention rights anyway.

More important is the use of core rights reasoning in the assessment of the reasonableness of an interference with fundamental rights. Generally the Court very strictly scrutinises interferences with rights related to the very core of one's private life or the rule of law; it then leaves hardly any or even no margin of appreciation to the states.[231] In these cases, thus, the core rights doctrine is used to heighten the intensity of the Court's review.[232]

Finally, the closeness of an individual right to the core of the principles underlying the Convention may determine its weight in a balancing exercise. The more a fundamental right goes to the heart of the Convention, the weightier it will be and the more compelling the government's justification must be to override it.[233] Related to this, the Court sometimes mentions that limitations of fundamental rights are not acceptable if they affect 'the very core' or 'essence' of a right.[234] This formulation should not be read as implying that there is an absolute limit to restrictions in the shape of an inviolable core. Instead, the Court uses the 'core rights' phrasing to refer to the outcome of a classic balancing or proportionality test, indicating that the core of the right is affected because the case discloses a lack of fair balance between general and individual interests.[235]

C Comparative Perspective

The ECtHR's reasoning discloses a number of special characteristics, which are mainly related to its role as a supranational court supervising the compliance with fundamental rights by 47 sovereign states. Even more than national constitutional courts, this means the Court has to be very much aware of its position in relation to its 'constitutional' counterparts. This awareness is reflected in the Court's use of a variety of

[231] E.g. *Dudgeon* v. *United Kingdom*, ECtHR 22 October 1981, no. 7525/76 and *(Welfare Party) and Others* v. *Turkey*, ECtHR (GC) 13 February 2003, nos. 41340/98 et al.

[232] More detail and examples can be found in various studies on the margin of appreciation doctrine; see sources in n 145.

[233] For an application, albeit relatively implicit, see *Von Hannover (No. 2) v. Germany*, ECtHR (GC) 7 December 2012, nos. 40660/08 and 60641/08.

[234] See expressly e.g. *Demir and Baykara* v. *Turkey*, ECtHR (GC) 12 November 2008, no. 34503/97.

[235] See more elaborately e.g. J. Rivers, 'Proportionality and Variable Intensity of Review' (2006) 65 *Cambridge Law Journal* 174 at p. 185.

argumentative techniques and principles, such as the principle of subsidiarity and the margin of appreciation doctrine. At the same time, the Court has always stressed that it needs to safeguard the effective protection of fundamental rights and to guarantee a minimum level of protection throughout the Council of Europe. This particular objective also has resulted in the development of a number of special methods and techniques, such as autonomous and evolutive interpretation, consensus interpretation, meta-teleological interpretation and proportionality review.

Surely the use of a 'margin of appreciation doctrine' and references to subsidiarity are not uncommon in constitutional reasoning generally. National constitutional courts likewise vary the intensity of their review, for example by applying tests with different 'tiers' as in the United States or by giving various expressions to notions of 'deference'. Similarly, the comparison with national constitutional courts shows that meta-teleological interpretation, proportionality-based review and evolutive ('living tree') interpretation are less extraordinary than many ECHR scholars have made it appear. Even the ECtHR's use of 'consensus interpretation', which implies that it sometimes bases its judgments on comparisons between the laws of the 47 States of the Council of Europe, is not really unique. Not only has this method been used frequently by the Court of Justice of the European Union, but it can also be seen (albeit rarely) in the case-law of a court such as the United States Supreme Court. Although judges of the US Supreme Court hardly ever refer to foreign legal material, they do sometimes take account of the existence or lack of 'internal' consensus within the United States, by finding out whether there is sufficient support for a certain interpretation on the federal level within the 50 states.

Perhaps most special for the ECtHR, and only shared by the other supranational court under study, the CJEU, is its use of 'autonomous interpretation', which means that, as a rule, it will provide for 'European' definitions of Convention notions, which may have a diversity of meanings in the national laws of the Contracting Parties, such as 'possessions' or 'law'. Indeed, the rarity of this approach can be explained by the lack of a need for such an autonomous approach in national constitutional systems.

Finally, it has been stressed in this chapter that the ECtHR's case-law is characterised by an incremental approach which inclines towards a 'reflective equilibrium'. Based on an individual use of the aforementioned techniques in individual cases, the Court at some point may decide to induce some general principles and standards from these and express them in a judgment. These general principles and standards are then further refined and developed by application in further cases, up until the moment the Court sees that inconsistencies or incoherence have arisen. This may then result in reformulation of the relevant principles and standards, which then re-starts the process of individual application and further development. This process of going to and fro between general principles and individual cases and arriving at a reasonable and intuitively fair outcome is not unique, as it is also visible in the constitutional approach in many other constitutional courts, especially Canada. It is special, however, to the extent that the Court clearly expresses the distinction between general principles and their application by using separate headings for them in its judgments.

All in all, thus, it can be concluded that, although in terms of the use of argumentative techniques, methods and overall style of reasoning the ECtHR stands out because of its supranational role and position and its incremental approach, the analysis in this chapter reveals more similarities than differences with national constitutional reasoning.

Appendix: 40 Leading Cases

1. Case relating to certain aspects of the laws on the use of languages in education in Belgium v. Belgium (Merits), Appl. Nos. 1474/62, 1677/62, 1691/62, 1769/63, 1994/63, 2126/64
2. Golder v. the United Kingdom, Appl. No. 4451/70
3. Handyside v. the United Kingdom, Appl. No. 5493/72
4. Klass and Others v. Germany, Appl. No. 5029/71
5. Marckx v. Belgium, Appl. No. 6833/74
6. Airey v. the United Kingdom, Appl. No. 6289/73
7. Winterwerp v. the Netherlands, Appl. No. 6301/73
8. Dudgeon v. the United Kingdom, Appl. No. 7525/76
9. Soering v. the United Kingdom, Appl. No. 14038/88
10. Kokkinakis v. Greece, Appl. No. 14307/88
11. Papamichalopoulos and Others v. Greece (Article 50), Appl. No. 14556/89
12. Osman v. the United Kingdom, Appl. No. 23452/94
13. Kudła v. Poland, Appl. No. 30210/96
14. Pretty v. the United Kingdom, Appl. No. 2346/02
15. Christine Goodwin v. the United Kingdom, Appl. No. 28957/95
16. Refah Partisi (the Welfare Parti) and Others v. Turkey, Appl. Nos. 41340/98, 41343/98 and 41344/98

17. Hatton and Others v. the United Kingdom, Appl. No. 36022/97
18. Broniowski v. Poland, Appl. No. 31443/96
19. Vo v. France, Appl. No. 53924/00
20. Öneryildiz v. Turkey, Appl. No. 48939/99
21. Mamatkulov and Askarov v. Turkey, Appl. Nos. 46827/99 and 46951/99
22. Bosphorus Hava Yolları Turizm ve Ticaret Anonim Şirketi v. Ireland, Appl. No. 45036/98
23. Stec and Others v. the United Kingdom (admissibility decision), Appl. Nos. 65731/01 and 65900/01
24. Hirst v. the United Kingdom (No. 2), Appl. No. 74025/01
25. Leyla Şahin v. Turkey, Appl. No. 44774/98
26. Üner v. the Netherlands, Appl. No. 46410/99
27. Jussila v. Finland, Appl. No. 73053/01
28. Vilho Eskelinen and Others v. Finland, Appl. No. 63235/00
29. Agim Behrami and Bekir Behrami v. France, Appl. No. 71412/01 and Ruzhdi Saramati v. France, Germany and Norway, Appl. No. 78166/01
30. D.H. and Others v. the Czech Republic, Appl. No. 57325/00
31. Demir and Baykara v. Turkey, Appl. No. 34503/97
32. Sergey Zolotukhin v. Russia, Appl. No. 14939/03
33. Šilih v. Slovenia, Appl. No. 71463/01
34. Féret v. Belgium, Appl. No. 15615/07
35. Scoppola v. Italy (No. 2), Appl. No. 10249/03
36. Gäfgen v. Germany, Appl. No. 22978/05
37. Al-Khawaja and Tahery v. the United Kingdom, Appl. Nos. 26766/05 and 2228/06
38. Lautsi and Others v. Italy, Appl. No. 30814/06
39. Othman (Abu Qatada) v. the United Kingdom, Appl. No. 8139/09
40. Von Hannover v. Germany (No. 2), Appl. Nos. 40660/08 and 60641/0

7

The European Court of Justice

GIULIO ITZCOVICH

A Legal, Political, Institutional and Academic Context

1 *The Court and Constitutional Litigation*

A 'Sui Generis' Court

Determining whether the Court of Justice of the European Union is a constitutional court or not is not a straightforward matter of course.[1] To qualify it in such a way requires some introductory terminological and conceptual considerations. Following the negative results of the 2005 French and Dutch referenda on the Treaty establishing a Constitution for Europe, the European Council expressly decided that the new European Treaties 'will not have a constitutional character. The terminology used throughout the Treaties will reflect this change: the term "Constitution" will not be used'.[2] However, the main reason why the constitutional status of the Court of Justice can be contested does not relate to the contingent political vicissitudes of the EU, but to one of its most salient features: what the legal doctrine constantly refers to as its *sui generis* nature. The *sui generis* nature is the result and the synthetic formulation of several institutional novelties that have characterised the European Communities since the beginning, such as directly applicable regulations, majority voting in the Council, independency of the Commission, and – last but not least – the jurisdiction of the Court of Justice. Since the establishment of the European Coal and Steel Community in 1951, legal scholarship has always qualified the Community institutions as *sui generis* entities in order to express the fact (and to endorse the project) that they lie (and

[1] See e.g. L. Azoulai, 'Le rôle constitutionnel de la Cour de Justice des Communautés européennes tel qu'il se dégage de sa jurisprudence' (2008) 44 *Revue trimestrielle de droit européen* 29; E. Sharpston and G. De Baere, 'The Court of Justice as a Constitutional Adjudicator' in A. Arnull et al. (eds), *A Constitutional Order of States? Essays in EU Law in Honour of Alan Dashwood* (Hart 2011), 123–50.

[2] Council of the EU, *IGC 2007 Mandate*, document 11218/07, 26 June 2007, at 3.

should lie) somewhere in between international law and constitutional law, and between interstate organisation and federal construction.[3]

True enough, the *sui generis* nature has never been, so to say, a brute fact – a state of things capable of being simply observed and described in a detached and objective manner. It is a complex institutional fact or, to put it differently, a 'narrative' with notable consequences for several legal issues of European integration. In any case, the institutional self-understanding and the political project expressed by the *sui generis* formula have deeply affected the semantics of European law. As a consequence of the *sui generis* nature of the Community, several fundamental concepts of public law, once they are applied to the European institutions, have undergone significant transformation and adaptation.[4] And the concepts of 'constitution' and 'constitutional' are no exceptions in this regard.

The Court of Justice is a particularly salient example for illustrating this point. First of all, the Court of Justice of the European Union is at present composed of two judicial organs: the Court of Justice properly called, whose legal reasoning is the subject of our inquiry, and the General Court, formerly Court of First Instance (the Civil Service Tribunal was dissolved on 1 September 2016).

Secondly, and most importantly, the heads of jurisdiction of the Court of Justice are so diverse and miscellaneous that the court has no analogues in national and international law. The Court ensures 'that in the interpretation and application of the Treaties the law is observed' (Article 19 TEU), and in performing this task it is competent, among other things, to review the acts, or failure to act, of the European institutions (actions for annulment and failure to act), to interpret European law at the request of the national courts and to rule on its validity (references for a preliminary ruling), to rule on actions against Member States for failure to fulfil their obligations under the Treaty (infringement procedure), to give binding opinions on the lawfulness of the international agreements concluded by the EU, to hear claims for compensation for damage based on the non-contractual liability of the EU and to hear appeals on points of law against decisions of the General Court. Thus, the Court resembles

[3] Paradigmatic in this regard is R. Schuman, 'Préface' in P. Reuter, *La Communauté Européenne de Charbon et de l'Acier* (LGDJ 1953), at 7.

[4] On the 'problems of translation' of the concepts of constitutionalism from the state to the European Union setting, see N. Walker, 'Postnational Constitutionalism and the Problem of Translation' in J. H. H. Weiler and M. Wind (eds), *European Constitutionalism Beyond the State* (Cambridge University Press 2003), 27–54.

an administrative tribunal when it reviews the legality of the acts of the EU, it resembles an international tribunal when it declares that a Member State has failed to comply with the Treaty,[5] and resembles a highest court of appeal (a *cour de cassation*) when it ensures the exact observance and the uniform application of European law throughout the EU.

Is the Court of Justice a 'constitutional court' and, if so, in what sense? The Court is by all means a constitutional court – let's call it a *sensu stricto* constitutional court of the EU legal system – if we adopt the Kelsen-inspired concept of constitution proposed by Jakab and stipulate that a constitution is 'a norm or a group of norms which are of the highest rank in a legal order in the sense that the validity of all other norms is measured on them'.[6] If we adopt this concept of constitution, the Court wears its constitutional hat mainly in annulment proceedings. The action can be brought by the Member States, by the European institutions and by any natural or legal person against acts that address them or that directly and individually concern them (Article 263(4) TFEU). Moreover, the Court of Justice serves as a constitutional court when it gives a preliminary ruling on the validity of European law: when a question on the validity of acts of the EU is raised before a national court, that court may (or must, if it is a court of last instance) request the Court of Justice to give a ruling thereon (Article 267(1)(b) TFEU). With regard to actions for annulment and references for a preliminary ruling on the validity of European law, the Court of Justice is undoubtedly the highest court of the EU legal order. It has the task of adjudicating on the validity of all norms of that legal order by reference to a highest law – the Treaties. Its jurisdiction is exclusive, as no other court (except the General Court, which is subject to review by the Court of Justice) has the competence to annul EU legislation.[7]

However, according to a widespread and well-grounded opinion, it is not in annulment proceedings that the Court has acquired its constitutional status, nor is it in preliminary ruling proceedings concerning the validity of European law. The Court has become a *sensu lato* constitutional

[5] The Member States have rarely used their power to bring a case against other Member States (one rare recent example is Case C-364/10, *Hungary v Slovakia* [2012] on the ban of Hungarian President László Sólyom from Slovakia in August 2009 – case dismissed). In practice, all infringement proceedings are initiated by the Commission.

[6] A. Jakab, 'Constitutional Reasoning. A European Perspective on Judicial Reasoning in Constitutional Courts' (2013) 14 *German Law Journal* 1215, at 1216.

[7] *Foto-Frost* (1985), para. 15. The decisions that are included in the list of 40 leading cases analysed by the research will be quoted in shortened form; the decisions that are not included in the list will be quoted in the usual complete form.

court – a *sui generis* constitutional court – mainly thanks to the powers it exercises in preliminary ruling proceedings on the interpretation of European law. According to Article 267(1)(a) TFEU, when a national court has any doubt about the meaning of European law, it may (or must, if it is a court of last instance) initiate a preliminary ruling proceeding referring the question of interpretation to the Court of Justice.

There is no doubt that the Court of Justice's power to give a preliminary ruling on the interpretation of European law when requested by a national court is the most important head of its jurisdiction. The Court has given the majority of its landmark judgments under this head of jurisdiction. It is revealing in this regard that in the 40 leading cases analysed by the research, 32 are preliminary rulings on the interpretation of European law, two are preliminary rulings on its validity, one is a preliminary ruling on both the interpretation and the validity of European law, three are decisions on annulment proceedings, one is an opinion and one is an appellate decision. No judgment was rendered in an infringement procedure.

The preliminary ruling procedure is the central instrument of the EU for judicial control. This procedural channel between the Court of Justice and the national judges is vital in order to achieve the uniform application of European law over all of Europe. Moreover, the viability of the preliminary ruling procedure transforms all citizens into potential guardians of compliance with European law, therefore contributing not only to the uniformity but also to the effectiveness of European law enforcement.

By means of preliminary rulings, the Court has been able to develop a constructive and mutual relationship (a 'dialogue', as it has become customary to say) with the national courts, which means that the European and the national courts have collaborated in shaping the content of European law 'in action' without establishing a formal hierarchical relationship between themselves; the Court of Justice has initiated a process of 'constitutionalisation' of the European Treaties making it acceptable to the national courts.[8] Thus, thanks to the preliminary ruling proceedings, the Court has gradually laid the basis of, and eventually established, its most authentic and significant constitutional status.

[8] On the constitutionalisation process, see e.g. A.-M. Slaughter, A. Stone Sweet, and J. H. H. Weiler (eds), *The European Court and National Courts – Doctrine and Jurisprudence: Legal Change in Its Social Context* (Hart 1998).

Note that when we speak here of the constitutional status of the Court of Justice in the preliminary interpretative rulings, the word 'constitutional' is not employed in its non-technical sense – the Court as a 'very important' judge – but in its technical meaning, and the legal order whose norms are evaluated against the constitution is no longer limited to the legal order of the EU strictly conceived, as it happens in annulment proceedings, but is inclusive of the legal order of the Member States. In fact, once the national courts in principle accepted the doctrines of direct effect and supremacy of European law, the Court of Justice became *de facto* empowered to assess, by means of the preliminary ruling proceedings, not only the validity of European law but also the conformity to European law of Member States' legislation and practices.[9]

While it is true that in preliminary ruling proceedings the Court is not competent to assess the validity of national legislation, nonetheless by interpreting European law it can indirectly but unequivocally rule on Member States' compliance. Thanks to the enduring cooperation of the national courts, their willingness to refer questions for preliminary rulings and their acceptance of supremacy of European law, the Court evaluates the 'European validity' of national legislation and practises: its interpretative judgments can render national law inapplicable in the case at hand and, indirectly, *erga omnes*. Therefore, the Court is not only the constitutional court of the EU, but is the constitutional court – or, to say it better, *a* constitutional court: one among many – of the European 'legal space'; a legal space that is comprehensive both of the EU legal order and of the legal orders of the Member States, and that is not hierarchically structured.

The *sensu lato* constitutional jurisdiction of the Court is not exclusive, because the competence to annul national legislation belongs primarily to national courts. Moreover, national courts are also generally competent, if not to annul EU legislation, at least to suspend its applicability when it is deemed to be incompatible with fundamental domestic constitutional provisions or with the national legislators' explicit decision to withdraw from their European obligations. In its capacity as *sensu lato* constitutional

[9] 'Direct effect' is the obligation of a court or another authority to apply the relevant provision of European law, either as a norm which governs the case or as a standard legal review, and 'supremacy' is the capacity of European law to take precedence over inconsistent norms of national law: S. Prechal, 'Direct Effect, Indirect Effect, Supremacy and the Evolving Constitution of the European Union', in C. Barnard (ed), *The Fundamental of EU Law Revisited* (Oxford University Press 2007), 35–69, at 37–8.

court of the European legal space, the Court of Justice is not alone but shares its responsibility with other courts – with the constitutional courts of the Member States and, indirectly, with the European Court of Human Rights. It is not the highest court of the legal order, but it is one of several high courts of justice of the European constitutional space. To put it in the usual irreplaceable way, it is a *sui generis* constitutional court.

Access to the Court and Workload, Procedure and Evidence

The Court of Justice does not have the discretionary power to refuse to review a case and must rule on all the cases lodged with its registry. As a consequence, the Court has a very limited capability to determine its workload autonomously.[10] Following the constant expansion of EU competences and the successive enlargements of the EU, the judicial activity of the Court has steadily increased over time. In the 1950s the Court had fewer than 50 new cases each year; in the 1970s usually between 100 and 200 new cases each year; in the 1990s between 300 and 500 cases and since 2001 there have been between 400 and 600 new cases each year (713 in 2015).[11] This increase has had an adverse effect on the Court of Justice's ability to deliver its judgments within a short timeframe. In 1975 it took the Court of Justice an average of six months to deal with preliminary references, and in 1983 12 months; in 2003 the average period reached a peak of 25.5 months and then it started to decrease to 15.3 months in 2015.[12] Preliminary references represent by far the greatest source of the caseload of the Court: in the five years from 2011 to 2015, 61.15 per cent of the proceedings before the Court of Justice were references for a preliminary ruling.

In order to respond to the increasing workload, the Court has benefited from the autonomy it enjoys in devising its own rule of procedure and in organising and managing the cases. In recent years the statute of the Court and its rules of procedure have been amended several times in order to secure greater organisational autonomy, flexibility and efficiency. Without going into much detail, it is worth mentioning that the use of chambers

[10] P. Craig, 'The Jurisdiction of the Community Courts Reconsidered' in G. de Búrca, J. H. H. Weiler (eds), *The European Court of Justice* (Oxford University Press 2001), 177–214, examining the mechanisms possessed by the Court for controlling the number of cases brought before it.

[11] Detailed statistics concerning the judicial activity of the Court of Justice are available on the website of the Court. See the CJEU, *Annual Report 2015*, Luxembourg, 2016, at http://curia.europa.eu/jcms/jcms/Jo2_7000/en/.

[12] CJEU, *Annual Report 2015*.

has evolved considerably and has been gradually extended to the current situation in which cases are assigned to the Full Court or to the Grand Chamber only exceptionally. At present, the Court of Justice is divided into ten chambers consisting of either three or five judges, and cases are assigned to chambers 'so far as the difficulty or importance of the case or particular circumstances are not such as to require that it should be assigned to the Grand Chamber' (now Article 60(1) Rules of Procedure).

The procedure followed by the Court is essentially written and inquisitorial, and from the viewpoint of a jurist accustomed to the proceedings before the national courts it is marked by great flexibility and informality. The Court of Justice may require the parties, the Member States' governments and the EU institutions to produce all documents and to supply all information the Court considers necessary, and at any time it may entrust individuals or organisations it chooses with the task of giving an expert opinion. The judge-rapporteur can chair informal preparatory meetings with the parties, and the Court can decide to dispense with the oral part of the procedure.

The language of the case is chosen by the applicant among the official languages of the EU, except where the defendant is a Member State, in which case the language of the case is the official language of that State. In preliminary ruling proceedings the language of the case is the language of the referring court. The internal working language of the Court, however, is French: it is the language in which the judges deliberate and the language in which preliminary reports and judgments are drafted.

2 *The Judges*

Composition and Independence

A response to the growing workload of the Court of Justice was the increase in the number of the members of the Court of Justice. Following several incremental enlargements, today's Court of Justice of the EU is composed of the Court of Justice's 28 judges and 11 Advocates General, and of the General Court's 44 judges, all appointed by the common accord of the governments of the Member States for a renewable term of six years.

With regard to appointments of the judges, the basic rule is 'one State, one judge': the Court of Justice consists of one judge from each Member State. Each judge is proposed by their country of origin, and in practice the choice made by the national government is never disputed by other national governments. To a limited extent, therefore, the Court of Justice is a representative jurisdiction whose members have always been appointed by common accord of the Member States without any formal assessment of their appropriateness at European level. 'It is in the muffled atmosphere of ministerial cabinets and diplomatic meetings, sheltered from the public gaze, that the members of the Court of Justice are appointed'.[13] As the mandate of the judges is renewable, the system of appointment gives national authorities a means of applying pressure on the Court, and this raises concerns for its independence.

In order to meet these concerns, the Lisbon Treaty modified the appointment procedure and required the Member States to consult a panel before appointing the members of the Court of Justice and the General Court so as to obtain a non-binding opinion on candidates' suitability for office.[14] The strongest guarantee of the Court's independence, however, lies in the fact that decisions are taken collegiately and that judges' deliberations remain secret. Judgments contain no indications of the votes taken nor do they contain any dissenting opinion. Obviously, if the judges' votes and opinions were published, the governments would be able to check and control their nominees. In addition, it seems that a guarantee is provided by the strong group identity and institutional culture that the Court has been able to develop and consolidate over the course of time,[15] which hinders – although it cannot fully prevent – the risk of a judge acting as a docile instrument of his or her government of origin.

Little information exists, however, about how Member States select their members for the Court of Justice; no thorough study has ever been conducted on who the judges of the Court of Justice are, their social backgrounds, and their political preferences.[16] We know that the judges of

[13] R. Dehousse, *The European Court of Justice: The Politics of Judicial Integration* (Macmillan 1998) at 14.

[14] On the effects of the establishment of the advisory panel, see T. Dumbrovský, B. Petkova and M. Van Der Sluis, 'Judicial Appointments: The Article 255 TFEU Advisory Panel and Selection Procedures in the Member States' (2014) 51 *Common Market Law Review* 455.

[15] D. Chalmers, 'Judicial Preferences and the Community Legal Order' (1999) 5 *Columbia Journal of European Law* 101, at 168; D. Edwards, 'How the Court of Justice Works' (1995) 20 *European Law Review* 539, at 556 ff.; J. Bell, 'European Perspectives on a Judicial Appointments Commission' (2003–4) 6 *Cambridge Yearbook of European Legal Studies* 35.

[16] Noteworthy exceptions are S.J. Kenney, 'The Members of the Court of Justice of the European Communities' (1999) 5 *Columbia Journal of European Law* 101; H. Rasmussen, *On Law and Policy in the European Court of Justice: A Comparative Study* (Martinus Nijhoff 1986). Recent legal history has started to investigate the first Court of Justice: see e.g. A. Cohen, 'Constitutionalism without Constitution: Transnational Elites between

the Court of Justice are chiefly professors, often of community, comparative or international law; most of them have previous judicial experience in their Member State of origin, often as judges of the supreme courts or constitutional courts; not infrequently they have professional backgrounds as higher civil servants, politicians and lawyers. We also know that while the very first Court of Justice included members who lacked any prior judicial experience (e.g. a trade unionist and an economist) and low-profile and soon-to-retire jurists, today the technical expertise of the members of the Court is generally high, with a predominance of the academic component. The prestige of the judges of the Court is generally superior to that of the European law professors, and their annual salary is approximately € 250,000.

About the judges of the Court of Justice we do not know much more. Notwithstanding the 'contextual' and political-science inspired approach of many of today's legal studies on the EU, their tendency to abandon a purely legal-dogmatic approach to their subject, the mainstream legal doctrine has been largely unresponsive to Martin Shapiro's call for 'exposing . . . the human flesh of its [the Court of Justice's] judges'.[17]

The Advocates General

Eleven Advocates General assist the Court of Justice. Their presence is an original feature of the Court of Justice inspired by the *Commissionaires du government* who appear before the French *Conseil d'Etat*. They do not directly take part in the Court's deliberations, but are subject to the same conditions of recruitment and are appointed by means of the same process as the judges, are subject to the same duties of impartiality and independence, receive the same salary and, according to the Court of Justice, 'have the same status as the Judges, particularly so far as concerns immunity and the grounds on which they may be deprived of their office'.[18] They act as a kind of institutionalised *amicus curiae* – an *amicus curiae* which is internal to the Court – and deliver a written opinion after the hearing and before the judgment. In the opinion, the Advocate General reviews

Political Mobilization and Legal Expertise in the Making of a Constitution for Europe (1940s–1960s)' (2007) 32 *Law & Social Inquiry* 109; issue 14/2 of the *Journal of European Integration History* (2008), co-ordinated by N. P. Ludlow.

[17] M. Shapiro, 'Comparative Law and Comparative Politics' (1980) 53 *Southern California Law Review* 537, at 540.

[18] Case C-17/98, *Emesa Sugar* [2000] ECR I-665, para. 11. See also Article 6 Rules of Procedure: 'Judges and Advocates General shall rank equally in precedence according to their seniority in office'.

the facts of the case, evaluates the arguments of the parties, reports the existing law and case law and finally expresses a view on how the Court should decide.

Although it is difficult to assess the overall influence of the Advocates Generals' opinions on the deliberations of the Court,[19] their importance for its legal reasoning is beyond question. As shown by the analysis of the 40 leading cases, the arguments of the Advocates General are often upheld and reiterated by the Court using formulas such as 'as the Advocate General correctly observed/noted/pointed out at paragraph . . . of her/his opinion'.[20] Most importantly, the opinions are indispensable for understanding what arguments might have influenced the Court without being explicitly endorsed in the final judgment and what arguments have been implicitly rejected. The judgments of the Court of Justice should be self-sufficient texts, but if we want to fully grasp their meaning we must make reference to the opinions of the Advocates General. Their legal reasoning is much more open and candid than that of the Court, and it often takes into account factors such as budgetary and economic considerations, pragmatic concerns, policy issues, arguments based on equity, foreign judgments and doctrinal articles that might exercise a persuasive force upon the Court's deliberations without being explicitly endorsed in the final judgment. We cannot appreciate the specific features of the Court's legal reasoning without taking into consideration what Mitchel Lasser calls its 'bifurcated structure'.[21]

3 *Legal Scholarship and Constitutional Reasoning*

The attitude of legal scholarship towards the Court of Justice changed over the course of time. As Joseph Weiler noted, until the publication in

[19] For an assessment, see T. Tridimas, 'The Role of the Advocate General in the Development of Community Law: Some Reflections' (1997) 34 *Common Market Law Review* 1349; C. Ritter, 'A New Look at the Role and Impact of Advocates-General – Collectively and Individually' (2006) 12 *Columbia Journal of European Law* 751.

[20] 13 references in eight judgments: *Antonissen* [1991], para. 20; *Brasserie du Pêcheur* [1996], para. 34; *Bosman* [1995], para. 53, 99 and 110; *Schmidberger* [2003], para. 66; *Omega* [2004], para. 27 and 34; *Köbler* [2003], para. 48; *Pupino* [2005], para. 42 and 48; *Mangold* [2005], para. 53 and 73.

[21] M. de S.-O.-L'E. Lasser, *Judicial Deliberations: A Comparative Analysis of Judicial Transparency and Legitimacy* (Oxford University Press 2004), at 141: 'the Court of Justice produces two argumentative modes. In the sphere of the Court of Justice's official judicial decision operates the discourse of the magisterial and deductive application of EU law . . . In the sphere of the [Advocates Generals'] Opinions . . . operates the discourse of the personal and subjective construction of purposive judicial solutions'.

1986 of Hjalte Rasmussen's *On Law and Policy in the European Court of Justice*, in virtually all books on the Court of Justice 'the underlying ethos [was] one of praise and admiration' and criticism of the Court was 'muted and on most occasions confined to specific cases or areas of jurisprudence and not the overall posture of the court'.[22] The legal doctrine surrounding the Court was highly supportive of its constitutionalising efforts. All the landmark decisions of the Court in the 1960s and 1970s were welcomed by the enthusiastic support of a 'comprehensive transnational network of European minded jurists':[23] a relatively small group of scholars, often professionally involved in the European institutions, who were very active in terms of publications as well as very homogeneous in terms of professional ethos and value choices. Dissenting voices were usually confined to the few writings of the traditional academic jurists, who were more prestigious in terms of cultural legitimacy but ultimately un-influential on the developments of the case law.[24]

Following the Maastricht Treaty (1992), legal doctrine started to change fast.[25] As the political relevance of the European institutions significantly increased, academic interest and the quantitative dimension of the EU legal scholarship grew enormously. The composition of EU legal scholarship changed and became more internally differentiated both with regard to the methodological perspectives (traditional expository jurisprudence and legal dogmatics were now joined by the new 'law in context'

[22] J. H. H. Weiler, 'The Court of Justice on Trial' (1987) 24 *Common Market Law Review* 555, at 555 f.

[23] M. Rasmussen, 'From Costa v ENEL to the Treaties of Rome: A Brief History of a Legal Revolution' in M. Maduro and L. Azoulai (eds), *The Past and Future of EU Law: The Classics of EU Law Revisited on the 50th Anniversary of the Rome Treaty* (Oxford University Press 2010) 69–85, 78; H. Schepel and R. Wesseling, 'The Legal Community: Judges, Lawyers, Officials and Clerks in the Writing of Europe', (1997) 3 *European Law Journal* 165; G. Itzcovich, *Teorie e ideologie del diritto comunitario* (Giappichelli 2006), 276–307; A. Vauchez, 'The Transnational Politics of Judicialization. *Van Gend en Loos* and the Making of EU Polity' (2010) 16 *European Law Journal* 1.

[24] Itzcovich, *Teorie e ideologie* (n 23) 307–14 and 324–82.

[25] Among the critics of the Court, standard references include Rasmussen, *On Law and Policy* (n 16); Sir Patrick Neill, *The European Court of Justice. A Case Study in Judicial Activism* (European Policy Forum 1995); T. C. Hartley, *The Foundations of European Community Law* (4th ed. Oxford University Press 1998); Id., 'The European Court, Judicial Objectivity and the Constitution of the European Union' (1996) 112 *Law Quarterly Review* 95. See more recently R. Herzog and L. Gerken, 'Stoppt den Europäischen Gerichtshof' in *Frankfurter Allgemeine Zeitung*, 8 September 2008, English translation at http://euobserver.com/opinion/26714: the Court of Justice 'deliberately and systematically ignores fundamental principles of the Western interpretation of law . . . its decisions are based on sloppy argumentation'.

tendencies of a legal scholarship informed by political science, by the new constitutionalist and 'principled' approaches characteristic of a normatively oriented jurisprudence and by cultural and critical legal studies) and with regard to normative assessments of the Court of Justice's role and case law.[26] Today's legal doctrine is far less deferential towards the Court than it used to be. Indeed, it seems fair to say that almost every piece of legal doctrine dealing with the Court must now contain, in order to be appealing and publishable, a normative (better, critical) assessment of certain aspects of its case law.

4 *Political Culture as Context for Constitutional Reasoning*

In the 1990s, political science and international relations theory engaged in a debate on the degree of responsiveness of the Court of Justice to perceived national interests and to other environmental factors. Theorists inspired by realism (or intergovernmentalism) opposed a neo-functionalist interpretation of the Court's role in European integration according to which the driving forces of the constitutionalisation process successfully initiated by the Court in the 1960s and 1970s were to be traced not in the national interests but in the inputs coming from private litigants (mainly private companies and professional associations) and from lower-ranked national courts.[27] While the debate did not reach any firm conclusions, it is undeniable that the Court exercised its most active and creative role after the 'Empty Chair Crisis' (1965–6), which provoked the end of any ambition of political protagonism by the Commission (until the Delors presidency in 1985–94), a long-lasting legislative gridlock at a European level and the so-called 'Eurosclerosis' – the perceived stagnation of the Community project. According to a famous interpretation by Joseph Weiler, the end of the 'institutional supranationalism' determined by the Empty Chair Crisis triggered the Court to strengthen 'normative

[26] F. Snyder, 'New Directions in European Community Law' (1987) 14 *Journal of Law and Society* 167; A. von Bogdandy, 'A Bird's Eye View on the Science of European Law' (2000) 6 *European Law Journal* 208; J. Shaw, 'The European Union: Discipline Building Meets Polity Building' in P. Cane and M. Tushnet (eds) *Oxford Handbook of Legal Studies* (Oxford University Press 2003), 325–52; N. Walker, 'Legal Theory and the European Union: A 25th Anniversary Essay', (2005) 25 *Oxford Journal of Legal Studies* 581; P. Dann, 'Thoughts on a Methodology of European Constitutional Law' (2006) 6 *German Law Journal* 1453.

[27] Cfr. A.-M. Burley and W. Mattli, 'Europe before the Court: A Political Theory of Legal Integration' (1993) 47 *International Organization* 41; G. Garrett, 'The Politics of Legal Integration in the European Union' (1995) 49 *International Organization* 171.

supranationalism' by pursuing the politics of the judicial constitutionalisation of the Treaties.[28] In turn, following the Maastricht Treaty and the beginning of the 'semi-permanent Treaty revision process',[29] the approach of the Court changed significantly: it became more cautious and sometimes committed to self-restraint.[30] The closer scrutiny on the Court exercised by an enlarged and not always friendly legal community is likely to have had an influence on the changing attitude of the Court.

B Arguments in Constitutional Reasoning

'Constitutional Reasoning' at the Court of Justice

For the reasons outlined above, there are two possible ways in which the expression 'constitutional reasoning' can be understood.[31] First, the Court of Justice engages in constitutional reasoning when it interprets the Treaties in order to rule on the validity of EU secondary legislation. In annulment proceedings and in preliminary proceedings on the validity of European law, the Court of Justice is the *sensu stricto* constitutional court of the EU, at least according to the definition of 'constitution' here adopted, and the Treaties are, as the same Court of Justice solemnly declared, the 'basic constitutional charter of a Community based on the rule of law'.[32] In that context, the expression 'constitutional reasoning'

[28] J. H. H. Weiler, 'The Community System: the Dual Character of Supranationalism' (1981) 1 *Yearbook of European Law* 267.

[29] B. De Witte Bruno, 'The Closest Thing to a Constitutional Conversation in Europe: The Semi-Permanent Treaty Revision Process' in P. Beaumont et al. (eds), *Convergence and Divergence in European Public Law* (Hart 2002) 39–57.

[30] On the reasons for this change of attitude, see N. Mancini, 'Attivismo e autocontrollo nella giurisprudenza della Corte di Giustizia' (1990) 30 *Rivista di diritto europeo* 229, at 236–40.

[31] On the legal reasoning of the Court of Justice, broad references to the existing literature in G. Itzcovich, 'The Interpretation of Community Law by the European Court of Justice' (2009) 10 *German Law Journal* http://www.germanlawjournal.com/article.php?id=1106. See moreover E. Paunio and S. Lindroos-Hovinheimo, 'Taking Language Seriously: An Analysis of Linguistic Reasoning and Its Implications in EU Law' (2010) 16 *European Law Journal* 395; U. Neergaard, R. Nielsen, 'Where Did the Spirit and Its Friends Go?' in U. Neergaard, R. Nielsen and L. Roseberry (eds), *European Legal Method* (DJØF 2011) 95–184; G. Conway, *The Limits of Legal Reasoning and the European Court of Justice* (Cambridge University Press 2012); G. Beck, *The Legal Reasoning of the Court of Justice of the EU* (Hart 2012); S. Sankari, *European Court of Justice Legal Reasoning in Context* (Europa Law Publishing 2013).

[32] *Les Verts* [1986], para. 23; Opinion 1/91 [1991], para. 21; *Kadi* [2008], para. 281.

could refer exclusively to the reasoning that is based on the text of the Treaties or that is intended to expound and develop its meaning.

Secondly, the Court of Justice engages in *sensu lato* constitutional reasoning when it evaluates the 'European validity' of national legislation and practises in preliminary ruling proceedings on the interpretation of European law. Here the object of interpretation is not limited to the Treaties but comprises the whole body of European law. As already mentioned, this kind of constitutional jurisdiction of the Court is not exclusive, nor supreme, nor direct – the intervention of national courts is necessary for removing the conflict between national law and European law.

The indirect nature of the review exercised by the Court of Justice has one significant consequence for our research. In almost every preliminary ruling of the Court, it can be dubious whether it is exercising its *sensu lato* constitutional jurisdiction by indirectly controlling the compliance of Member States with European law, or is simply doing what it says it is doing, that is, interpreting European law in order to answer the questions referred by the national court. Thus, for the purposes of this study the *sensu lato* concept of constitutional reasoning is definitely too broad, as for every case analysed by the research the difficult question would be open: 'Is this really a case of constitutional reasoning or is it just ordinary interpretation of the EU legislation?'. The answers to that question cannot be anything but speculative and controversial.

Therefore, this study did not take into consideration the arguments adopted by the Court of Justice for interpreting EU secondary legislation and analysed only the arguments adopted by the Court of Justice for interpreting the Treaties: what can be called *sensu stricto* constitutional reasoning, although it is a kind of reasoning that can be employed not only in case of action for annulment and preliminary questions on the validity of European law but also in every other kind of judicial proceeding before the Court.[33]

[33] It is doubtful whether the methods adopted for interpreting the Treaties are different from the those adopted for interpreting secondary law. Although K. Lenaerts, 'Interpretation and the Court of Justice: A Basis for Comparative Reflection' (2007) 41 *The International Lawyer* 1011, denies the existence of any significant difference, it seems that references to precedents play a more prominent role in the interpretation of primary law than they do in the interpretation of secondary law, as the latter is more easily amended by the legislator (P. Dann, 'Methodology of European Constitutional Law' n 26, at 1462 f). Moreover, for the reasons explained below, subjective teleological arguments are likely to be less common in the interpretation of the Treaties than they are in the interpretation of secondary legislation.

5 The Structure of Constitutional Arguments

We found that the majority of the judgments (16) have a cumulative parallel structure, in which distinct, autonomous considerations lead to the same conclusion; a robust minority (14) exhibits one-line conclusive arguments – a self-standing structure, in which every premise is presented as a necessary component of the argument; 10 judgments contain parallel, individually inconclusive, but together conclusive arguments. It is worth noting that often the one-line conclusive arguments consist in one single argument, or even in no argument at all, when the Court limits itself to straightforwardly stating the interpretative conclusion of its (implicit) reasoning.[34]

Often the judgments do not make clear if the arguments they employ are *per se* sufficient to sustain the conclusion of the reasoning. However, in some cases the distinction between conclusive and inconclusive arguments is relatively easy, either because there is some textual basis available – e.g., the Court states that a conclusion 'is confirmed' by another argument, which presumably would not have been self-sufficient, and that an interpretation is 'reinforced' by a certain consideration[35] – or because the content and nature of the argument put forward by the Court makes it clear that it is not self-sufficient but merely reinforces other arguments.

It must be stressed that parallel, individually inconclusive but together conclusive arguments do not imply that the judgment is 'dialogical' in the sense of adopting a discursive style of reasoning. By all means the style of the Court of Justice is not discursive; at times, however, the Court considers it appropriate to reinforce its line of reasoning by adding some further considerations in support of the conclusion. Thus, a decision such

[34] E.g. *Stauder* [1969]: the Court provides several arguments of non-constitutional interpretation directed to showing that 'interpreted in this way the provision at issue contains nothing capable of prejudicing the fundamental human rights', but with regard to the interpretation of the Treaties it limits itself to stating that 'fundamental human rights [are] enshrined in the general principles of Community law' (para. 7) without providing arguments.

[35] E.g. *CILFIT* [1982], para. 21 ('In the light of all those considerations, the answer to the question . . . must be that . . . '); *Foto-Frost* [1987], para. 18 ('It must also be emphasized that . . . '); *Factortame* [1990], para. 22 ('That interpretation is reinforced by the system established by Article 177'); *Francovich* [1991], para. 36 ('A further basis for the obligation . . . is to be found in . . . '); Opinion 1/91 [1991], para. 35 ('This exclusive jurisdiction of the Court of Justice is confirmed by . . . '); *Köbler* [2003], para. 49 ('It may also be noted that, in the same connection . . . '); *Pupino* [2005], para. 43 ('In the light of all the above considerations, the Court concludes that . . . '); *Advocaten voor de Wereld* [2007], para. 39 ('The interpretation . . . is corroborated by . . . ').

as *Van Gend en Loos* (1963) that is renowned not only for its importance in the development of European law but also for the laconic and magisterial tone, exhibits parallel, individually inconclusiv, but together conclusive arguments:

> This view is confirmed by the Preamble . . . It is also confirmed more specifically by the establishment of institutions endowed with sovereign rights . . . Furthermore, it must be noted that the nationals of the states . . . are called upon to cooperate in the functioning of this community.[36]

6 *Types of Arguments in Constitutional Reasoning*

Analogies

We have found seven judgments in which the Court had recourse to analogical reasoning, and in one case the Court dismisses the argument by analogy as irrelevant for the case.[37] In the majority of cases the Court simply makes reference to a precedent of its case law that can be applied to the case at hand only 'by way of analogy': there is no identity between the prior decision and the issue of the case, but still there are some similarities that suggest that the prior decision should be extended to cover the new case.[38]

Establishing/Debating the Text of the Treaties

We have not found any arguments dealing with this kind of issue.

Applicability of the Treaties

It is not surprising that no less than one-quarter of our leading cases (11 judgments precisely) deals with the applicability of the Treaties to the case. The competences of the EU are governed by the principle of conferral and the EU legal order is a sectional legal order that does not claim to be complete in the sense of providing a solution for every possible controversy: certain matters fall outside the scope of European law. Therefore, the issue of the applicability of the Treaties is quite common

36 *Van Gend en Loos* [1963], 12.
37 *Bosman* [1995], para. 78.
38 *Francovich* [1991], para. 21 and 43; *Omega* [2004], para. 30; *Advocaten voor de Wereld* [2007], para. 59; *Laval* [2007], para. 87; *Viking* [2007], para. 34 and 40; *Kadi* [2008], para. 224. One interesting case of analogical reasoning not based on precedents is *Brasserie du Pêcheur* [1996], para. 34 and 42.

in European law litigation. On the one hand, the so-called vertical distribution of competences between the EU and the Member States is an object of frequent controversies upon which the Court may be called to adjudicate; on the other hand, in almost every legal proceeding before the Court of Justice the referring court, the private parties or the intervening Member States may find it appropriate to raise the question of whether the matter falls within the province of European law and challenge the jurisdiction of the Court or the competence of the EU.

In all cases except one, the Court ruled that the issue of the case did not fall outside the scope of European law.[39] The arguments supporting that conclusion do not share any structural features and can be very diverse among themselves – teleological considerations, harmonisation arguments, implicit principles, and so on. However, in the case law of the Court there is one peculiar way of supporting the decision favourable to the applicability of the Treaties, a traditional argument that Loïc Azoulai calls 'retained powers formula' and that is virtually capable of eliminating or overcoming every positive limit to the applicability of European law.[40] While the classical formulation of this doctrine can be found in the *Schumacker* case (1995) and in the 'British fishing vessels' case of 1991[41] and its origins can be traced back to *Steenkolenmijnen* (1961) and *Casagrande* (1974)[42] (decisions not included in the list of 40 leading cases), our study found it in *Viking* (2007):

> even if, in the areas which fall outside the scope of the Community's competence, the Member States are still free, in principle, to lay down the conditions governing the existence and exercise of the rights in question, the fact remains that, when exercising that competence, the Member States must nevertheless comply with Community law.[43]

Ordinary Meaning of the Words

We found only six judgments in which reference to the wording of the Treaty is made in order to provide an argument in favour or against a

[39] The exception is *Grogan* [1991], para. 27.

[40] L. Azoulai, 'The "Retained Powers" Formula in the Case Law of the European Court of Justice: EU Law as Total Law?' (2011) 4 *European Journal of Legal Studies* 192.

[41] Case C-279/93, *Schumacker* [1995] ECR I-225, para. 21; Case C-246/89, *Commission* v. *United Kingdom* [1991], ECR I-04585, para. 12 ('the powers retained by the Member States must nevertheless be exercised consistently with Community law').

[42] Case C-30/59, *Steenkolenmijnen* [1961] ECR 3, 24; Case 9/74, *Casagrande* [1974] ECR 773, para. 12. See also Joined Cases C-6 and C-11/69 *Commission* v. *France* [1969] ECR 523, para. 17.

[43] *Viking* [2007], para. 40.

certain interpretation of the Treaty, and in three the literal argument is taken into consideration and ultimately rejected by the Court on the basis of prevailing teleological and harmonising considerations.[44]

According to many scholars and critics of the Court, the relative unimportance of text-based arguments is a remarkable feature of its legal reasoning. A 'double advice' from Judge Pierre Pescatore confirms this view: 'never employ the literal argument if you have not preliminarily checked every other linguistic version of the text – that is a Sisyphean task – or simply base your arguments not on the wording but on the content, the system or the purpose of the text'.[45]

However, given the nature of the cases analysed by the research, the significance of this finding cannot be over-emphasised. We selected the 40 leading cases because of their impact on the legal culture of the Member States, their contribution to the completion of the common market, and their influence on the development of European law: thus, the fact that literal arguments are almost absent cannot be regarded as indicative of a general feature of the Court's legal reasoning.

Domestic Harmonising Arguments

This argument is quite common in the 40 leading cases: we found 19 judgments that contain it.

Actually, this category comprises more than one argument, as it identifies a family of arguments that share the structural feature of supporting a certain interpretation by referring to other norms or groups of norms. Thus, under the heading 'harmonising arguments' we grouped, first of all, the cases in which the Court makes some generic reference to the 'spirit of the Treaty', 'the whole scheme of the Treaty', the 'system' established by the Treaty, without specifying which are the provisions that articulate the system and embody the spirit.[46] Secondly, we grouped the cases in which the Court clarifies the relationships between different provisions of the

[44] *Defrenne II* [1976], para. 27 ('the terms of article 119 cannot be relied on to invalidate this conclusion'); *Antonissen* [1991], para. 9 ff, rejecting the interpretation based on 'the strict wording of Article 48'; Opinion 1/91 [1991], para. 14. The argument was adopted by the Court in *Van Gend en Loos* [1963], 13; *Costa* [1964], 597; *Pupino* [2005], para. 33–34; *Kadi* [2008], para. 166 ff. and 199 ff.

[45] P. Pescatore, *Vade-mecum. Recueil de formules et de conseils pratiques à l'usage des rédacteurs d'arrêts* (3rd ed. Bruylant 2007), at 43 f.

[46] The case law of the Court is not short of generic references of this kind. E.g. *Costa* [1964], 593; 'ERTA' [1971], para. 15; *Defrenne II* [1976], para. 7.

Treaty and constructs the rule of the case by reading a plurality of provisions 'in conjunction' with one another. For example, the Court states that a certain interpretation of the Treaty is 'confirmed' or 'supported' by other provisions of the Treaty, it declares to be following considerations dictated by 'the necessary coherence' of the Treaty, and it reads one provision in the light of some 'fundamental principle' of European law in order to avoid internal conflicts and inconsistencies.[47] Here the Court does not limit itself to evoking the scheme of the Treaty but concretely constructs it by reading together a group of Treaty provisions. Finally, we considered instances of harmonising arguments as those arguments that refer to the *sedes materie*, that is, arguments based on the internal systematic structure of the Treaties, as designed by the legislator.[48]

Moreover, we grouped under the heading 'harmonising arguments' those cases in which the Court adopts a certain interpretation in order not to 'render meaningless' other principles of European law by depriving them of their 'essential effectiveness' and by compromising the achievement of the objectives set out in the Treaties.[49] These cases differ from the former ones in that they assess the 'external' effects of the proposed interpretation: they do not look solely to the consequences of the proposed interpretation of the system of the Treaties, but they consider also the practical consequences of the achievement of the objectives set out by the Treaties. Thus, this kind of harmonising argument is mixed in nature and must also be regarded as an instance of teleological argumentation: it is a teleological argument in which the Court declares that it intends to prevent a conflict with the objectives pursued by the Treaties.

Harmonising with International Law

We have found 14 cases in which the Court refers to international law sources in order to support the interpretation of the Treaty. The vast

[47] E.g., *Costa* [1964]; 'ERTA' [1971], para. 22; *Defrenne II* [1976], para. 63; *CILFIT* [1982], para. 10; *Foto-Frost* [1987], parr. 16 and 17; Opinion 1/91 [1991], par. 71; *Kadi* [2008], par. 309.

[48] E.g., 'ERTA' [1971], para. 14 ('this provision, placed at the head of part six of the Treaty, devoted to "general and final provisions", means that . . . '); *Defrenne II* [1976], para. 15 ('since article 119 appears in the context of the harmonization of working conditions . . . '); *Van Gend en Loos* [1963], 12 ('This provision is found at the beginning of the part of the Treaty . . . '); *Costa* [1964], 595 ('This article, placed in the chapter devoted to the "approximation of laws", is designed to . . . ').

[49] E.g. *Costa* [1964], 594; *Grad* [1970], para. 5; *Simmenthal* [1978], para. 18; *Traghetti del Mediterraneo* [2006], para. 36; *Advocaten voor de Wereld* [2007], para. 42; *Laval* [2007], para. 98.

majority of references consist of a literal or almost literal quote from the *Nold* formula:

> international treaties for the protection of human rights on which the Member States have collaborated or of which they are signatories can supply guidelines which should be followed within the framework of Community law.[50]

In six cases the Court makes reference to the European Convention on Human Rights[51] and in four cases it refers to the case law of the European Court of Human Rights.[52] Moreover, we found references to International Labour Organisation conventions[53] and to general principles of international law and customary international law.[54]

Precedents

The Court has made reference to its previous case law since the very beginning of its activity: the first example can be found as early as in a case of 1955,[55] and in 1956 the Court quoted a precedent as authority for the proposition that certain provisions of the ECSC Treaty were of a 'fundamental character'.[56] References to its case law became increasingly frequent in the 1970s and especially in the 1980s. Today the practice of relying on precedents is firmly established. Almost every decision of the Court contains extensive references to the case law.

Such evolution is reflected in the analysis of the 40 important judgments that we have undertaken. The first argument based on precedents that we have found is a generic and unnamed reference to the previous case law in *Defrenne* (1976),[57] and the first explicit reference is in *Ratti* (1979).[58] From *Ratti* onwards we found only two judgments in which the Court does not make explicit reference to its case law[59] while all other cases contain detailed references to previous rulings and copy-and-paste quotations

[50] Case C-4/73, *Nold* [1974] ECR 491, para. 13. See, e.g., *Hauer* [1979], para. 15; *Wachauf* [1989], para. 17; *ERT* [1991], para. 41; *Viking* [2007], para. 43; *Laval* [2007], para. 90; *Kadi* [2008], para. 283.

[51] *Hauer* [1979], para. 17; *ERT* [1991], para. 41; *Bosman* [1995], para. 79; *Pupino* [2005], para. 58; *Advocaten voor de Wereld* [2007], para. 45 and 49; *Viking* [2007], para. 43.

[52] *Köbler* [2003], para. 49; *Pupino* [2005], para. 60; *Advocaten voor de Wereld* [2007], para. 50; *Kadi* [2008], para. 256 and 311.

[53] *Defrenne II* [1976], para. 20; *Viking* [2007], para. 43; *Laval* [2007], para. 90.

[54] *Van Duyn* [1974], para. 22; *Brasserie du Pêcheur* [1996], para. 34; *Köbler* [2003], para. 32.

[55] Case C-4/54, *Industrie Siderurgiche Associate* [1955] ECR 91.

[56] Joined Cases C-7 and C-9/54, *Groupement des industries* [1956] ECR 175.

[57] *Defrenne II* [1976], para. 31 ('as the court has already found in other contexts').

[58] *Ratti* [1979], para. 19.

[59] *Foglia* [1980]; *Antonissen* [1991].

from earlier judgments. In one case the Court (almost) explicitly overruled a previous decision.[60] Overall we have found 27 judgments in which the Court employs the argument from precedents.

Implicit Concepts and Principles

We have found 20 judgments invoking concepts and principles not mentioned in the text of the Treaties as operative arguments supporting a certain constitutional interpretation. Such concepts and principles are the outcome of doctrinal construction on the part of the Court: they are not the product of the interpretation of the Treaty (they are not expressed in any given provision) but result from a heterogeneous set of (often implicit) non-interpretative argumentations. Some such concepts and principles constitute the 'living constitutional law' of the EU and the reason why the EU is often thought of as being international in origin but constitutional in nature.

Thus, the Court famously established that '[b]y contrast with ordinary international treaties, the EEC Treaty has created its own legal system'[61] and that 'fundamental human rights [are] enshrined in the general principles of Community law and protected by the Court'.[62] The Court invented the principles of 'uniformity and efficacy of Community law', it held that 'the law stemming from the Treaty, an independent source of law, cannot because of its very nature be overridden by rules of national law',[63] and that 'the right to reparation is the necessary corollary of the direct effect'.[64] It laid down the keystone of the common market – the principle of mutual recognition[65] – and theorised the existence of an 'institutional balance' among the different Community institutions – a balance that the Court is entitled to maintain by reviewing the observance of the various institutions' prerogatives.[66]

Moreover, since the beginning of its activity the Court has created a value-laden ('axiological') hierarchy between some of the provisions of the Treaty, qualifying as 'fundamental' the corresponding right or principle (e.g. the principle of equal pay for men and women, free movement of workers, free movement of goods, and so on); then, based on such a hierarchy, the Court has ruled that fundamental principles must be

[60] 'Chernobyl' [1990], para. 16. [61] *Costa* [1964], 593.

[62] *Stauder* [1969] para. 7. See also *Internationale Handelsgesellschaft* [1970] para. 4.

[63] *Internationale Handelsgesellschaft* [1970] para. 3; see also *Simmenthal* [1978], para. 17 ('principle of the precedence of Community law').

[64] *Brasserie du Pêcheur* [1996], para. 22. [65] 'Cassis de Dijon' [1979], para. 14.

[66] 'Chernobyl' [1990], para. 21.

interpreted broadly while exceptions and derogations must be interpreted strictly.[67]

Linguistic-Logical Formulae Based on Silence

As is well known,[68] the Court of Justice is very reluctant to adopt *a contrario* reasoning and in some of its earliest judgments it even theorised this attitude explicitly: 'an argument in reverse is only admissible when no other interpretation appears appropriate and compatible with the provision and its context and with the purpose of the same'.[69]

We found five judgments employing the *argumentum a contrario*, and in four of them the argument was explicitly rejected. The Court held, for instance, that the existence of the infringement procedure does not exclude that individuals can plead the violation of European law before the national courts,[70] and that it does not follow from the fact that according to Article 189 EEC regulations are directly applicable that 'other categories of legal measures mentioned in that article can never produce similar effects'.[71]

Teleological Arguments Referring to the Purpose of the Text

In the 40 judgments analysed by the research the teleological argument is used in no fewer than 27 cases, thus emerging as the most frequently employed argument.

This finding is hardly surprising. Although in European law there is no commonly accepted doctrine on the relative weight of arguments, teleological interpretation enjoys a distinguished record and a particularly strong standing before the Court of Justice. It is indicative in this regard that the 'spirit', that is, teleological argumentation, comes first in the list of interpretative methods formulated in *Van Gend en Loos* ('it is necessary to consider the spirit, the general scheme and the wording

[67] *Van Duyn* [1974], para. 18; *Defrenne II* [1976], para. 12–14; *Antonissen* [1991], para. 11; *Schmidberger* [2003], para. 60; *Omega* [2004], para. 30.

[68] E.g., H. G. Schermers and D. F. Waelbroeck, *Judicial Protection in the European Union* (6th ed. Kluwer Law International 2001), at 12; Beck, *The Legal Reasoning* (n 31), at 221–2.

[69] Case C-9/56, *Meroni* [1958], ECR 133, 140; Case C-8/55, *Fédération Charbonnière de Belgique* [1956], ECR 293, 300: 'Such an argument is, in fact, acceptable only in the last resort when no other interpretation appears to be adequate or compatible with the text, the context and their objectives'.

[70] *Van Gend en Loos* [1963], 13.

[71] *Grad* [1970], para. 5; *Van Duyn* [1974], para. 12; *Ratti* [1979], para. 19. The only case analysed by the research in which the argument was actually adopted by the Court is *Faccini Dori* [1994], para. 24,

of those provisions'[72]). The Court of Justice is well-known for having adopted the teleological method, and the hallmark of the Court is to interpret the Treaties in the way that best fits their overall objectives. While it may be true that in the everyday activities of the Court recourse to teleological interpretation is less common than we are accustomed to think, nonetheless it cannot be denied that teleological interpretation is of decisive importance in those judgments that 'have "famous status" and are continuously referred to in the literature'.[73] Several judges of the Court have explained and justified that method in writings and journal articles in which they claim that the most appropriate way of fulfilling their office is to contribute to the achievement of the goals of the Community by bearing them in mind when interpreting the open-ended Treaties' provisions.[74]

Particularly in the case of the Treaties, it is often impossible to sharply distinguish between teleological argumentation and systematic interpretation ('domestic harmonising arguments'). The Treaties are imbued with teleology from top to bottom, as they are functional to a project of transformation of the legal orders of the Member States ('an ever closer union among the peoples of Europe', as is stated in the Preamble of the Treaty on European Union); they are 'designed along functional lines' and are 'structured with a view to the Community's achievement of the various objectives' they establish.[75] Systematic interpretation is meant to achieve coherence and consistency between the rules of the system; if these rules set forth goals and policy objectives, then systematic interpretation implies and includes teleological argumentation.

[72] *Van Gend en Loos* [1963], 12.

[73] U. Neergaard and R. Nielsen, 'Where Did the Spirit and Its Friends Go? On the European Legal Method(s) and the Interpretational Style of the Court of Justice of the European Union' in U. Neergaard et al. (eds), *European Legal Method. Paradoxes and Revitalisation* (DJØF 2011), 95–184, at 122.

[74] P. Pescatore, 'Les objectifs de la Communauté européenne comme principes d'interprétation dans la jurisprudence de la Cour de Justice' in *Miscellanea W. J. Ganshof van der Meersch*, Vol. II (Bruylant-LGDJ 1972), 325–63; H. Kutscher, 'Alcune tesi sui metodi d'interpretazione del diritto comunitario dal punto di vista d'un giudice', *Rivista di diritto europeo* (1976), 283–314 and (1977), 3–24; R. Lecourt, *L'Europe des juges* (Bruylant 1976), 235 f.; G. F. Mancini and D. T. Keeling, 'Democracy and the European Court of Justice' (1994) 57 *Modern Law Review* 175, at 186; M. P. Maduro, 'Interpreting European Law: Judicial Adjudication in a Context of Constitutional Pluralism' (2007) *European Journal of Legal Studies*, http://www.ejls.eu/2/25UK.pdf

[75] K. Lenaerts, 'Interpretation and the Court of Justice: A Basis for Comparative Reflection', (2007) 41 *The International Lawyer* 1011. For extensive references to the first European legal scholarship, see G. Itzcovich, *Teorie e ideologie* (n 23), 93 ff. and 97 ff.

Thus, the distinction between teleological argumentation and systematic interpretation is blurred when the Court takes into consideration the practical consequences of the interpretive decision, which in turn it assesses in light of the objectives of the Union and of the principles of effectiveness and uniform application of European law. This is a special kind of teleological interpretation: the guiding goal is the effectiveness of the provision the Court is about to interpret, or of other provisions of the Treaty, and the Court examines the foreseeable extra-systematic consequences of the decision.

For instance the Court maintained that '[t]he executive force of Community law cannot vary from one State to another in deference to subsequent domestic laws, without jeopardizing the attainment of the objectives of the Treaty'.[76] It held that

> [p]articularly in cases where . . . the Community authorities by means of a decision have imposed an obligation . . . to act in a certain way, the effectiveness ('l'effet utile') of such a measure would be weakened if the nationals of that state could not invoke it in the courts and the national courts could not take it into consideration as part of Community law.[77]

The goals that the teleological argument may take into account can vary from being more or less determinate objectives set out in given Treaty provisions or groups of provisions to more abstract and indeterminate general principles such as the 'social purpose of the Community', the effectiveness of European law, its uniform application, the goal of securing effective judicial protection, and so on. Sometimes, the goal that guides the teleological reasoning of the Court is totally indeterminate and unnamed: 'the spirit of the Treaty', 'the objectives of the Treaty', 'the obligations undertaken under the Treaty', 'the framework of the structure and objectives of the Community'.

Teleological Arguments Referring to the Purpose of the Treaty-Maker

We found only one case in which it is possible to sustain that the Court is referring to the subjective intentions of the framers of the Treaty, although the point is uncertain and open to different qualifications.[78] In fact,

[76] *Costa* [1964], 594.

[77] *Grad* [1970], para. 5. Other examples can be found in *Simmenthal* [1978], para. 18; *Carpenter* [2002], para. 39.

[78] *Pupino* [2005], para. 36. The argument could also be qualified as a harmonising interpretation and/or objective teleological reasoning: 'Irrespective of the degree of integration envisaged by the Treaty of Amsterdam . . . , it is perfectly comprehensible that the authors of the Treaty on European Union should have considered it useful to make provision . . . for

some early rulings by the Court resolutely denied any binding or even persuasive force to the original intentions of the (representatives of) the Contracting Parties, and this view was further articulated by some of the most authoritative judges of the Court in public speeches and journal articles.[79] The reason publicly given is that the Court cannot rely on documents which have not been published and which are not, therefore, accessible to the general public.[80] It is likely, however, that the guiding consideration is that the Court does not want to tie the future developments of European law to the past intentions of the representatives of the Contracting Parties. Besides, international treaties are not usually interpreted in this way, by having recourse to the original intentions of the States' representatives. The Vienna Convention on the Law of Treaties establishes a different criterion of subjective interpretation (Article 31.3), which the Court of Justice, however, does not follow: the Court does not refer to the subsequent agreements between the parties or to their subsequent practice in the application of the treaty.

Thus, subjective criteria of treaty interpretation are almost entirely absent from the legal reasoning of the Court. Because of the increasingly frequent revisions to the Treaties in recent years, things are likely to change in the near future – after all, starting from the Single European Act of 1987, the *travaux préparatoires* of the European treaties have been regularly and extensively made available to the public. However, the Court is still reluctant to use preparatory materials:[81] for the time being, we can conclude that the Treaties are interpreted like a constitution with no framers, or like an international treaty with no parties.

Non-legal Arguments

We have not found any non-legal (moral, sociological, economic) arguments. We have, however, found some cases in which the Court dismissed

recourse to legal instruments [framework decisions] with effects similar to those provided for by the EC Treaty, in order to contribute effectively to the pursuit of the Union's objectives'.

[79] See L. N. Brown and T. Kennedy, *The Court of Justice of the European Communities* (Sweet & Maxwell 2000) 330 ff., for references to Pescatore, Lecourt and to Case C-6/60, *Humblet* [1960] 559, 575: 'The opinions of the governments put forward during the parliamentary debates on the ECSC Treaty do not touch on this question'.

[80] This rationale can be inferred from cases that dealt with secondary legislation: Case C-15/60, *Simon* 1961 ECR 225; *Antonissen* [1991], para. 18. See also Joined Cases C-283/94, C-291/94 and C-292/94, *Denkavit* 1996 ECR I-5063.

[81] See, however, Case C-370/12, *Pringle* [2012], para. 135: 'It is apparent from the preparatory work relating to the Treaty of Maastricht that the aim of Article 125 TFEU is to ensure that the Member States follow a sound budgetary policy.'

a non-legal argument not on the basis that it was unfounded and substantially wrong – which would count as a (negative) instantiation of non-legal argumentation and as such would have been recorded by the research – but because it was non-pertinent to the case or *per se* irrelevant. In *Grogan*, for instance, the Court held that

> Whatever the merits of those arguments [against abortion] on the moral plane, they cannot influence the answer to the national court's first question. It is not for the Court to substitute its assessment for that of the legislature in those Member States where the activities in question are practised legally.[82]

Moreover, on several occasions the Court of Justice made explicit profession of legal positivism and referred to a doctrine that might be called *dura lex sed lex*. In *Defrenne*, in *Bosman* and in other cases the Court held that

> [al]though the practical consequences of any judicial decision must be carefully taken into account, it would be impossible to go so far as to diminish the objectivity of the law and compromise its future application on the ground of the possible repercussions which might result, as regards the past, from such a judicial decision.[83]

In other cases not included in the list of 40 leading cases the same point is expressed even more clearly:

> although . . . [the issue of the case] is a very sensitive social issue in many Member States, marked by their multiple traditions and value systems, the Court is not called upon . . . to broach questions of a medical or ethical nature, but must restrict itself to a legal interpretation of the relevant provisions.[84]

It is interesting to note that the Court insists on the *dura lex sed lex* principle not only when it wants to reject arguments based on moral,

[82] *Grogan* [1991], para. 20.

[83] *Defrenne II* [1976], para. 71; *Bosman* [1995], para. 77. Further references include Case C-69/80, *Worringham* [1981], ECR 767, para. 31; Case 24/86, *Blaizot* [1988] ECR 379, para. 30; Case C-163/90, *Legros* [1992] ECR I-4625, para. 30; Case C-437/97, *EKW* [2000] ECR I-1157, para. 57; Joined cases C-177 and C-181/99, *Ampafrance and Sanofi* [2000], ECR I-7013, para. 66; Case C-228/05, *Stradasfalti* [2006], ECR I-8391, para. 72.

[84] Case C-506/06, *Mayr* [2008], ECR I-1017, para. 38; Case C-34/10, *Brüstle v Greenpeace* [2011], ECR I-9821, para. 30. See also Case C-1/96, *Compassion in World Farming* [1998] ECR I-1251, para. 67; Case C-92/71, *Interfood GmbH v Hauptzollamt Hamburg Ericus* [1972] ECR 231, para. 5: 'No matter how unsatisfactory it is in practice . . . it is not for the Court to remedy this situation, by modifying, by way of interpretation, the content of the provisions applicable to one or other case'.

economic or pragmatic considerations, but also when it actually wants to accept such non-legal arguments by introducing an exception to a legal rule, such as a limitation of the temporal effect of its ruling. So, in *Defrenne*, in *Bosman* as well as in *Barber* and in other cases the Court adds to the *dura lex sed lex* formula that it

> may, by way of exception, taking account of the serious difficulties which its judgment may create as regards events in the past, be moved to restrict the possibility for all persons concerned of relying on the interpretation which the Court, in proceedings on a reference to it for a preliminary ruling, gives to a provision.[85]

However, in this kind of case, when the Court limits the temporal effects of its decisions on account of the practical consequences that they would have, the Court always mentions the principle of legal certainty – which is by all means a legal principle – as the determining ground of that limitation.[86] Thus, it is debatable whether at present the legal reasoning practised by the Court leaves any room for arguments that are explicitly non-legal in nature.

References to Scholarly Works

Although references to scholarly works are quite common in the opinions of the Advocates General, they are absent from the rulings of the Court.

References to Foreign Law

In the context of the legal reasoning of the Court of Justice, 'foreign law' is mainly the law of the Member States. However, since *Internationale Handelsgesellschaft* (1970), 'respect for fundamental rights forms an integral part of the general principles of law protected by the Court', and 'the protection of such rights [is] inspired by the constitutional traditions common to the Member States'.[87] Thus, on closer inspection it might be argued that the law of the Member States is not foreign at all: it is a constitutive part of European law, which lives in an osmotic relationship with the constitutional traditions of the Member States – and the Court of Justice is the 'guardian' of that osmosis.

[85] *Barber* [1990], para. 41. Analogous expressions in *Defrenne II* [1976], para. 72; *Bosman* [1995], para. 142.

[86] *Defrenne II* [1976], para. 74. See analogously *Barber* [1990], para. 44, and *Bosman* [1995], para. 144 ('overriding considerations of legal certainty').

[87] *Internationale Handelsgesellschaft* [1970], para. 4.

In any case, we found 13 references to the law of the Member States. The vast majority of the references were mechanical quotes from the *Internationale Handelsgesellschaft* formula. Thanks to the bridge provided by the common constitutional traditions, in our 40 leading cases the Court has accepted as general principles of European law the social function of the right to property,[88] freedom of expression,[89] freedom of assembly,[90] human dignity,[91] the principle of the non-contractual liability of the Community and of the Member States for loss and damage caused to individuals,[92] the right to a fair trial,[93] the principle of non-discrimination on grounds of age,[94] the principle *nullum crimen, nulla poena sine lege*,[95] the right to take collective action,[96] the right to be heard and the right to effective judicial review.[97]

However, we have found only two cases in which the Court did not limit itself to declare that a certain rule results from the common constitutional traditions but engaged in an explicit comparison between the laws of the Member States.[98]

7 *The Weight of Arguments*

In the *Cilfit* case (1982) the Court clarified the concept of 'reasonable [interpretative] doubt' for the purposes of the preliminary ruling procedure by proposing a set of criteria for interpreting European law.[99]

The Court recommended the adoption, first of all, of linguistic criteria that derive legal arguments from the semantic and syntactic features of the language in which legal provisions are expressed. In interpreting European law, the judge should bear in mind that 'Community legislation is drafted in several languages' and that 'Community law uses terminology which is peculiar to it'. Secondly, the Court recommended the adoption of systemic criteria of interpretation ('harmonising arguments'). According to the Court, 'every provision of Community law must be placed in

[88] *Hauer* [1979], para. 20. With regard to the right to property, see also *Wachauf* [1989], para. 17–18.
[89] *ERT* [1991], para. 41; *Schmidberger* [2003] para. 71.
[90] *Schmidberger* [2003] para. 71.
[91] *Omega* [2004], para. 33–34.
[92] *Brasserie du Pêcheur* [1996], para. 27–32; *Köbler* [2003], para. 48.
[93] *Pupino* [2005], para. 58–59.
[94] *Mangold* [2005], para. 74–75.
[95] *Advocaten voor de Wereld* [2007], para. 49.
[96] *Viking* [2007], para. 43.
[97] *Kadi* [2008], para. 283.
[98] *Hauer* [1979], para. 20, on the social function of the right to property, and *Köbler* [2003], para. 48, on state liability for judicial decisions.
[99] Case C-283/81, *CILFIT v Ministry of Health* [1982] ECR 3415.

its context and interpreted in the light of the provisions of Community law as a whole'. Finally, the Court recommended the adoption of purposive criteria of interpretation: 'every provision of Community law must be... interpreted in the light of... the objectives [of Community law] and to its state of evolution at the date on which the provision in question is to be applied'.[100]

These last criteria are certainly the most characteristic of the constitutional reasoning of the Court of Justice. It is probably not by chance that teleological arguments come first in the famous list of interpretative methods formulated in *Van Gend en Loos* (1963): in interpreting European law 'it is necessary to consider the spirit, the general scheme and the wording' of the Treaty (the *telos* of the Treaties is their 'spirit').[101] Some precedents of the Court explicitly suggest that the ordinary meaning must be disregarded if it is inconsistent with the objectives set by the legislator.[102] The Court may sometimes disregard the plain meaning of words in order to give effect to what it conceives as the aims and objectives of the Treaties. Many of our 40 leading cases are characterised by bold construction and apparent lack of interest in literal interpretation.

However, on other occasions the Court has also declared that it 'is not entitled to assume the role of the Community legislature and interpret a provision in a manner contrary to its express wording'[103] and that the principle of legal certainty precludes the Court from departing from the ordinary meaning of the provision.[104] Recently Advocate General Trstenjak has denied that purposive criteria of interpretation have precedence, as 'the starting-point of any interpretation, and also its boundary, is always the wording of a provision',[105] and Advocate General Léger has maintained that '[c]areful examination of the case-law shows that purposive interpretation is used only where the provision in question is open to

[100] Ibid., para. 18–20. On the distinction between linguistic, systematic and purposive criteria of interpretation, see J. Bengoetxea, *The Legal Reasoning of the European Court of Justice: Towards a European Jurisprudence* (Clarendon 1993) 218 ff.; G. Itzcovich, 'The Interpretation of Community Law (n 31) 549; G. Beck, *The Legal Reasoning of the Court of Justice* (n 31), 187.

[101] *Van Gend en Loos* [1963], 12.

[102] Case C-9/70, *Franz Grad v Finanzamt Traunstein* [1970] ECR 825, para 12–14; Case C-118/79 *Gebrüder Knauf Westdeutsche Gipswerke* [1980] ECR 1183, para 5; Case C-173/88, *Skatteministeriet v Morten Henriksen* [1989] ECR 2763, para. 11.

[103] Joined Cases C-310/98 and C-406/98 *Met-Trans and Sagpol* [2000] ECR I-1797, para. 32.

[104] Case C-361/06, *Feinchemie Schwebda* [2008] ECR I- 3865, para. 50; Case C-161/06, *Skoma-Lux* [2007] ECR I-10841, para. 36 and 38.

[105] Opinion in Case C-482/09, *Budějovický Budvar* [2011], para. 68.

several interpretations' and that 'teleological interpretation is not used where . . . the text in question is absolutely clear and unambiguous'.[106]

As the case law is inconsistent and the practice is variable, we can conclude that before the Court of Justice there is no fixed hierarchy between different methods of interpretation: when they lead to different conclusions, the Court is essentially free to choose among text-based, harmonising and teleological arguments.

8 *Judicial Candour and Judicial Rhetoric*

The general style of the Court's legal reasoning seems to depend on a series of factors which will be presented in the next paragraphs: the collegiate nature of the judgments, their subject matter, the declining but persisting influence of the French model, the need for translation and informatisation, the extensive use of precedents and literal self-quotations, and the contradictory and unsettled status of the Court as *sensu lato* constitutional court of the European legal space (*supra* section 1.).

With the exception of this last one, none of these factors is peculiar to the Court of Justice, but they have a mutually reinforcing effect and their coming together gives rise to a constitutional reasoning that is remarkable for its lack of colour, character and individuality: a style of legal argumentation that stands out for its abstractness, uniformity, homogeneity and impersonality.

9 *Length, Dissenting and Concurring Opinions*

The first factor affecting the style of the Court's legal reasoning consists in the committee decision-making procedure adopted by the Court, which is typical of European civil law jurisdictions. The collegiate nature of the judgment implies that dissenting opinions are not allowed and the decision is the outcome of the collective work of the whole collegium. Moreover, within the Court an attempt is usually made to achieve the broadest possible consensus. This affects the quality of the legal reasoning developed by the Court: in the words of one of its judges, Pierre Pescatore,

> the system of collegiate deliberation adopted by the Statute of the Court has the consequence of 'laminating' the grounds of the judgment up to the point that they lose every relief. We are far away from the colour of the judgments of the English judges.[107]

[106] Opinion in Case C-350/03 *Schulte* [2005] ECR I-9215, para. 85 and 88.

[107] P. Pescatore (n 45) at 292.

Especially to common law eyes, the Court seems to confirm the old saying that a camel is a horse designed by a committee.[108] As another judge of the Court once noted, the 'need to render judgments that are acceptable to all the signatories' frequently forces the Court to adopt an 'oracular tone' and to express 'stunted reasoning'.[109] Thus, when there are two lines of reasoning leading to the same conclusion and there is disagreement within the Court as to what are the best arguments for the case, the Court often adopts a middle-ground solution that might be unsatisfactory for both sides.[110]

The average length of the Court's decisions has increased in the course of time: from the laconic brevity of its first judgments it reached the 380 paragraphs and 29,000 words of the *Kadi* judgment of 2008.[111] This tendency is indicative of the declining influence of the French model (see below).

The Influence of the French Model

The traditional understatement of the Court and its tendency to avoid constitutional rhetoric and bold political statements are certainly linked to the diminishing but still present influence of the French model.

At the beginning of its activity the Court of Justice adopted a style of legal reasoning based on that of the French courts: 'formal, terse, and abstract';[112] 'a terse and opaque summary of the outcome and the reasons for it', expressed in a 'strictly deductive form'.[113] The French version of the judgments was written according to the typical French and syllogistic model of the *attendus que*. As a result, the Court reached 'a

[108] Edwards, 'How the Court of Justice Works' (n 15) 557: 'some judgments of the Court of Justice are camels'.

[109] G. F. Mancini and D. T. Keeling, 'Language, Culture and Politics in the Life of the European Court of Justice' (1994–1995) 1 *Columbia Journal of European Law* 397, at 398.

[110] Hartley, *The Foundations* (n 25), 75.

[111] The length of *Kadi* [2008] is certainly due to the nature of the proceeding (appeal against a judgment of the General Court) and to the importance of the case (the 'findings of the Court' cover para. 158 to para. 376), but is not at all unprecedented: see the 632 paragraphs of Joined Cases C-40/73 et al., *Suiker Unie* v *Commission* [1975] ECR 1663 (partial annulment of a Commission decision concerning concerted practices in the sugar market).

[112] Hartley, *The Foundations* (n 25), 74.

[113] M. Wells, 'French and American Judicial Opinions' (1994) 19 *Yale Journal of International Law* 85, 92 and 94; U. Everling, 'Reflections on the Reasoning in the Judgments of the Court of Justice of the European Communities' in J. Rosenløv et al. (eds), *Festskrift til Ole Due* (Kbh 1994), 55–74, 59: 'strict, disciplined form and apodictic brevity'.

stern, authoritarian style, expressed in a single-sentenced statement in which shines a single subject (the Court)'.[114]

In 1979 the Court abandoned the model of the *attendus* in order to favour a more discursive style of argumentation, but its judgments remained strongly structured and somewhat rigid. Arguments are introduced with standard phrases such as 'it must be observed that', 'it must be pointed out that', 'it is clear that' and 'it follows from the foregoing that'. According to their critics, the decisions of the Court still tend to be 'short, terse, and magisterial decisions that demonstrate tremendous interpretative confidence and suggest a certain logical compulsion'.[115]

However, the importance of this factor affecting the general style of the Court of Justice's legal reasoning should not be overemphasised. The influence of the French model has gradually declined and the judgments of the Court have started to deal with possible counter-arguments raised by the parties to the proceedings as a matter of course.[116] The change has been rightly described as a 'stylistic earthquake' that occurred when the Court, in order to communicate more effectively with the national judges through the vehicle of the preliminary ruling procedure, embraced a more dialogical style of legal argumentation, 'testing its reasons with a more thoughtful motivation and exposing itself to the controversial debate of scholarship'.[117]

Impersonality: Translation, Informatisation and the Use of Precedents

Written in French, the judgments of the Court of Justice are designed to be translated into every official language of the EU.[118] This has significant consequences for the kind of prose that the Court is able to employ:

[114] G. Gorla, *Lo stile delle sentenze* (Soc. ed. Foro Italiano 1968), Vol. I, 16.

[115] Lasser (n 21) 112.

[116] According to some authors, however, the tendency towards better argumentation has recently turned into an opposite trend: see J. Komárek, '"In the Court(s) We Trust?" On the Need for Hierarchy and Differentiation in the Preliminary Ruling Procedure' (2007) 32 *European Law Review* 467, 482; M. Bobek, 'Learning to Talk: Preliminary Rulings, the Courts of the New Member States and the Court of Justice' (2008) 45 *Common Market Law Review* 1611, 1639.

[117] G. Martinico, 'Reading the Others: American Legal Scholars and the Unfolding European Integration' 11 (2009) *European Journal of Law Reform* 35, at 37; G. Davies, 'Abstractness and Concreteness in the Preliminary Reference Procedure' in N. Nic Shuibhne (ed), *Regulating the Internal Market* (Elgar 2006), 210–44, at 213.

[118] On the consequences of multilingualism in European law, see J. Bengoetxea, 'Multilingual and Multicultural Legal Reasoning' in A. L. Kjær and S. Adamo (eds), *Linguistic Diversity and European Union* (Ashgate 2011), 97–122 (maintaining that the preference for French hinders the development of a genuinely multilingual form of legal reasoning).

'Write simple and uncluttered sentences, use the simplest possible vocabulary, avoid abstract and learned terms',[119] recommends the *Vade-mecum* that Pierre Pescatore wrote for his colleagues at the Court of Justice. His suggestion has been generally followed by the practice. The Court of Justice tends to avoid rhetorically shaped, ornate language and elegant and brilliant prose, as well as abstract conceptualism and academic thoughtfulness. It prefers plain terms, a simple and compact style and, above all, impersonality.[120]

Even if it were true that 'over the years, the Court of Justice has developed not just its own style, but undoubtedly a unique way of looking at and interpreting Union law',[121] the style of the Court would be unique but certainly not characteristic. Even from the viewpoint of a civil law lawyer, let alone from the viewpoint of a common law lawyer, one of its striking aspects is the high degree of impersonality that it strives for and is able to achieve in its judgments.

Impersonality is a consequence of the need for translation as much as of the need for informatisation. The *rationes decidendi* of the Court of Justice's rulings tend to be standardised in order to be stored and retrieved using database queries so as to be easily quoted by subsequent judgments. Already in the 1980s the Court of Justice began to show ICT awareness, recognised the need for informatisation and begun to draft its judgments accordingly, taking into consideration the requirement for information retrieval: according to Pescatore's *Vade-mecum*, 'legal reasoning, even when it is complicated, should eventually be reduced . . . to simple options that are compatible with the work of the machine'.[122]

Another remarkable feature of the legal reasoning of the Court of Justice is the extensive use of copy-and-paste quotations from the previous case law ('building blocks', as Gunnar Beck calls them[123]). The Court wants to avoid originality at all costs. The reason for this is not mainly economic in nature – it is not only a matter of preventing waste of time or the hard intellectual labour of thinking anew about the best

[119] Pescatore, *Vade-mecum*, cit., at 46.

[120] Possibly the only exception to the rule of impersonality is due to a translation inaccuracy: in Joined Cases C-202/08 P and C-208/08 P, *American Clothing Associates NV* [2009], ECR I-6933, para. 47, the impersonal French phrase 'il convient tout d'abord de relever que' becomes a highly unusual 'let me start by observing that'.

[121] M. Horspool, 'Over the Rainbow: Languages and Law in the European Union', in Arnull et al. (eds.), *A Constitutional Order of States* (n 1) 99–120, at 113.

[122] Pescatore, *Vade-mecum* (n 45) 28.

[123] Beck, *The Legal Reasoning* (n 31) at 245 ff., with a convincing analysis of the differences between the use of precedents by the Court of Justice, the practice of precedent in civil law jurisdictions and the English model of precedent.

arguments for the case. Copy-and-paste quotations create (an appearance of) consistency in the case law or – to put it in a more precise way – they create redundancy:[124] they show that the decision of the case is deeply embedded in a long line of decisions repeating the same legal principle. By doing so, copy-and-paste quotations provide legitimacy for the judgment and the Court and, at the same time, they provide flexibility in adjudication because, in the absence of a doctrine of precedent, the Court is basically free to choose whatever quotation it deems appropriate for the case at hand from the body of its previous case law. Thus, the extensive use of precedents, literal self-quotations and typical formulas by the Court of Justice has much to do with the need for standardisation and self-legitimation of a court that operates in a pluralistic legal space and that is actively engaged in a constitutionalisation process. While providing reasonable room for manoeuvre for the Court, redundant self-quotations create the perception of stable reference points in a highly uncertain legal and political environment.

In any case, copy-and-paste quotations tend to eliminate any personal or idiosyncratic elements in the justification of the judgment. As noted by Loïc Azoulai, it is as if the judgments of the Court were 'the result of a complex kind of "collage" of judicial formulas', i.e. of doctrines and *rationes decidendi* formulated in the landmark decisions of the Court of Justice: 'This collage effect is typical for Community case law – to such an extent that in some cases it may seem as if it is the formulas which are speaking, instead of the Court and the preferences of its members'.[125]

10 Framing of Constitutional Issues

The Subject Matter of the Judgments and Their Non-constitutional Tone

Another element affecting the general style of the judgments of the Court is their subject matter. The majority of the Court's judgments deal with the daily management of the internal market and thus with detailed and highly technical regulations. The judgments that present a constitutional tone are quite rare. In turn, it is not unusual to find judgments that are concerned with interpretative questions such as

[124] M. Shapiro, 'Toward a Theory of "Stare Decisis"' (1972) 1 *Journal of Legal Studies* 125.

[125] L. Azoulai, 'The Court of Justice and the Social Market Economy: The Emergence of an Ideal and the Conditions for Its Realization' (2008) 45 *Common Market Law Review* 1335, 1339.

> whether the words 'emballés séparément' (packaged separately) refer to 'morceaux désossés' (boned or boneless cuts) or whether they refer on the contrary to the exception made for les 'joues, les abats, le flanchet et le jarret' (the chaps, the offals, the thin flanks and the shin).[126]

The Court has ruled on the distinctive features of slide fasteners[127] and has carefully reconstructed the manufacturing process of xanthan gum.[128] On more than one occasion it has been called to expound on the concept of pyjamas.[129]

True enough, the case law of the Court is not short of decisions of the greatest importance. All of the 40 leading cases we analysed are of the utmost constitutional significance. However, generally speaking, the grounds that the Court employs in order to decide the constitutional issues are characterised by a certain understatement.

Framing the Constitutional Issues as Non-constitutional Issues

Of our 40 leading cases, 14 dealt with fundamental rights issues, 4 dealt with issues relating to the organisation of the EC/EU and in particular to the 'horizontal' division of competences between the European institutions, and 24 dealt with other issues such as the system of sources and the legal effects of European legal acts, the interpretative duties incumbent upon national judges, the civil liability for the violation of European law and the governing principles of the common market.

The significance of the relatively high number of important judgments that deal with or mention fundamental rights can easily be misunderstood. European legal scholarship tends to consider as more important those judgments that exhibit and refine some sort of doctrine of fundamental rights and principles. The frequency of important judgments on fundamental rights should be regarded as much more revealing of the prevailing constitutionalist tendencies of the European legal scholarship than it is of the features of the legal reasoning usually adopted by the Court. In fact, from the 1960s onwards there has been an increasing doctrinal and institutional pressure on the Court for it to embrace

126 Case C-803/79, *Roudolff* [1980], ECR 2015, para.7.

127 Case C-34/78, *Yoshida* [1979] ECR 115, para. 10.

128 Case C-160/80, *Smuling-de Leeuw* [1981] ECR 1767, para. 10.

129 Case C-395/93, *Neckermann* [1994] ECR I-4027, para. 7. See also Case C-338/95, *Wiener* [1997] ECR I-6495 (on the concept of 'nightdress') and the Opinion of AG Jacobs: 'The present case is a perfect example of a case where it may be questioned whether it is appropriate for this Court to be involved'.

what might be called – no irony is meant – 'constitutional rhetoric': a narrative style of reasoning and argumentative form that resembles that of other constitutional courts and rights-based jurisdictions such as the US Supreme Court, the German Constitutional Court and the European Court of Human Rights.

The institutional pressure on the Court results from a series of initiatives that can be traced back to the 'Declaration on the European Identity' of 1973, which created the notion of the 'special rights' of European citizens, and which became increasingly important in the European constitutional debate following the Maastricht Treaty. The Maastricht Treaty and the subsequent amendments to the Treaties adopted at Nice, Amsterdam and Lisbon solemnly entrenched certain constitutional principles as founding principles of the EU and eventually led to the adoption of the Charter of Fundamental Rights of the EU. In the long run, the adoption of the Charter and of the language of rights is likely to have an increasing effect on the way in which the Court constructs the cases upon which it is called to decide.[130]

The legal culture and the political environment surrounding the Court generally endorse these tendencies by urging it to adopt a different and more principled style of legal argumentation. As the Community has evolved from a market organisation into a more comprehensive form of constitutional entity – so the reasoning goes – the Court should stop being the promoter of an integration process entirely based on market freedoms and start to 'take (other) rights seriously'.[131]

The criticism of the rather uninspiring style of legal argumentation adopted by the Court is often based on the theory of deliberative democracy – democracy as a form of government that allows for open, public and principled argumentation leading to rational consensus – and/or on the adoption of an ideal of constitutional patriotism, according to which constitutional discourse can be crucial for fostering a sense of civic identity.[132]

[130] This is the opinion of the majority of the Advocate Generals interviewed by S. Morano-Foadi and S. Andreadakis, 'Reflections on the Architecture of the EU after the Treaty of Lisbon: The European Judicial Approach to Fundamental Rights' (2011) 17 *European Law Journal* 595, at 599: 'the language of the common market is being more and more replaced by the new language of the human rights standards'.

[131] See, e.g., M. Cartabia, 'Europe and Rights: Taking Dialogue Seriously', (2009) 5 *European Constitutional Law Review* 5, at 31: 'the European Court, especially when acting as a constitutional court or a court of fundamental rights, should seriously consider moving away from the old-style telegraphic judgments'.

[132] J. Habermas, *The Postnational Constellation: Political Essays* (MIT Press 2001).

Thus, according to the critics of the Court, 'the cryptic, Cartesian style which still characterizes many of its decisions' and 'its pretence of logical legal reasoning and inevitability of results' may not be 'conducive to a good conversation with national courts'.[133] By eschewing constitutional rhetoric the Court falls short of its role of *sensu lato* constitutional court of the European legal space. In contrast, in order to broaden and deepen the constitutional dialogue with the national courts, the Court should attempt as much as possible to identify and develop the general principles of a common European legal culture.

Those who require legal culture to contribute to the forging of 'We, the Europeans' expect the Court to expound, if not the ethical foundations of the Union as the common constitutional home of the Europeans, at least the substantive reasons for its decisions. The adoption of the language of rights is seen as a necessary step towards the construction of a feeling of shared identity and the development of a common 'constitutional conversation' with the other courts of Europe.[134] Moreover, the language of fundamental rights is often recommended for its alleged ability to foster the legitimacy of the legal system (and of the Court). The strictly technical approach of the Court may have its drawbacks in terms of legitimacy, as it can easily be interpreted as a lack of constitutional awareness or sensibility. In its characteristic role of promoter and guardian of the internal market, the Court may well appear to disregard the constitutional traditions of the Member States and, more generally, any non-market-based legal principles.

The strong idea underlying these doctrinal criticisms is that the content of the Court's decisions may sometimes be less important than the communication that precedes and follows those decisions: the legal reasoning and the public discourses that they promote.

However, especially when litigation revolves around national measures impinging on the principles of free movement, the Court has generally resisted such tendencies. Although it is true that the Court has accepted

[133] J. H. H. Weiler, 'Epilogue: The Judicial Après Nice' in G. de Búrca and J. H. H. Weiler (eds), *The European Court of Justice* (Oxford University Press 2001), 225 and 219 ('the style of judicial decisions is outmoded, does not reflect the dialogical nature of European Constitutionalism'); A. Arnull, *The European Union and Its Court of Justice* (2nd ed. Oxford University Press 2006), 12.

[134] Weiler, 'Epilogue: The Judicial Après Nice' (n 154) 219 and 225; recently D. Robertson, *The Judge as Political Theorist: Contemporary Constitutional Review* (Princeton University Press 2010), at 345.

that the protection of fundamental rights may occasionally take priority over market freedoms,[135] its case law on human rights is at least cautious – according to the critics of the Court, it is symbolic, insufficient or merely instrumental.[136] In terms of the number of cases decided by the Court, its role in the field of fundamental rights protection is more limited by far than that of a national constitutional court.[137] Generally speaking, the Court still strives to eschew constitutional rhetoric and resists the call to become another fully fledged human rights jurisdiction alongside the constitutional courts of the Member States and the European Court of Human Rights.

Thus, the Court might well be one of the many constitutional courts of the European legal space (*supra* section 1), but it tends to conceal its status as far as possible. Occasionally in the judgments of the Court it is possible to find declamatory political statements such as the often-cited *dictum* in *Grzelczyk* ('Union citizenship is *destined* to be the fundamental status of nationals of the Member States'[138]), but in principle the Court sticks to a legalistic and unpretentious understanding of the way in which its reasoning ought to be framed.

The traditional understatement of the Court might well be due to pragmatic reasons. As the authority of the Court depends on the continuing collaboration of the national courts, it is understandable that, in order to avoid offending their constitutional (national) sensibilities, the Court might be willing to keep a low profile, highlight the strictly technical grounding of its rulings and eschew constitutional rhetoric. After all, in preliminary ruling proceedings concerning the interpretation of European law the Court of Justice is a constitutional court only *sensu lato* and its rulings enjoy a supremacy that is conditional and negotiated.

135 E.g., *Schmidberger* [2003] and *Omega* [2004].

136 See e.g. J. Coppel and A. O'Neill, 'The European Court of Justice: Taking Rights Seriously?' (1992) 29 *Common Market Law Review* 669.

137 B. de Witte, 'The Past and Future Role of the European Court of Justice in the Protection of Human Rights', in P. Alston (ed), *The EU and Human Rights* (Oxford University Press 1999), 859, 869. Rightly B.-O. Bryde, 'The ECJ's Fundamental Rights Jurisprudence – A Milestone in Transnational Constitutionalism', in Maduro, Azoulai (eds), *The Past and Future of EU Law* (n 23) 119–29, 125, notes that this depends upon the fact that the Court of Justice is not a specialised constitutional court, but a court of general jurisdiction in European law and that European law remains limited to mainly socio-economic functions.

138 Case C-184/99 *Grzelczyk* [2001] ECR I-6193, para. 31. See lastly Case C-503/09, *Stewart* [2011], ECR I-6497, para. 80.

11 Key Concepts

Among the key concepts taken into consideration by the analysis of the 40 important judgments of the Court of Justice, the rule of law occupies the dominant position. No fewer than 14 judgments invoke the concept either explicitly or implicitly by having recourse to notions such as legal certainty, legality, non-retroactivity and – particularly important in the context of the EU – uniform application of European law and autonomy of its legal order.

This comes as no surprise: the rule of law was the first classical constitutional principle to be claimed for European law, and today it is commonly regarded as one of the foundational principles legitimating the constitutional order of the EU.[139] The principle plays a crucial role in strengthening the authority of the EU institutions, and in particular the authority of the Court of Justice, vis-à-vis the Member States, as clearly expressed in the often-quoted maxim from *Les Verts*:

> the European Economic Community is a Community based on the rule of law, inasmuch as neither its Member States nor its institutions can avoid a review of the question whether the measures adopted by them are in conformity with the basic constitutional charter, the Treaty. In particular . . . the Treaty established a complete system of legal remedies and procedures designed to permit the Court of Justice to review the legality of measures adopted by the institutions.[140]

According to the Court, respect for the principle of the rule of law implies that European law cannot be overridden by domestic legal provisions,[141] and 'imposes upon all persons subject to Community law the obligation to acknowledge that regulations are fully effective so long as they have not been declared to be invalid by a competent court'.[142] The validity of European law can only be judged in light of the Treaties and cannot be affected by its alleged incompatibility with domestic

139 A. von Bogdandy, 'Founding Principles' in A. von Bogdandy, J. Bast (eds), *Principles of European Constitutional Law* (2nd ed. Hart and Beck 2009), 11–54, at 28; L. Pech, 'A Union Founded on the Rule of Law: Meaning and Reality of the Rule of Law as a Constitutional Principle of EU Law' (2010) 6 *European Constitutional Law Review* 359, at 362.

140 *Les Verts* [1986], para. 23. See also *Foto-Frost* [1987], para. 16; *Kadi* [2008], para. 281. See also *Advocaten voor de Wereld* [2007], para. 45 for a similar formulation.

141 *Costa* [1964], 593 f.

142 Case C-101/78, *Granaria* [1979] ECR 623, para. 5.

constitutional rights[143] or with domestic rules as to the division of powers between constitutional authorities.[144] The national courts do not have the power to declare acts of the European institutions invalid:[145] only the Court of Justice can do so and, when needed, it can also limit the temporal effects of its judgments, taking into account 'overriding considerations of legal certainty'.[146]

In this respect, the principle of the rule of law seems to undergo a significant transformation once it is applied to the European institutions. While, in the national setting, the rule of law is generally conceived as a principle that limits the pre-existing coercive powers of the state, at the EU level it appears to be a principle that constitutes and justifies the authority of the supranational institutions.

Analogously, in our 40 leading cases the Court makes relatively frequent references to the principle of equality and to basic procedural rights (10 and 5, respectively) not only for ensuring respect for individual rights, but also for affirming certain structural principles of European law such as direct effect and supremacy.[147] In the legal reasoning of the Court, fundamental rights discourse exhibits certain remarkable features. Fundamental rights stop being thought of as indefeasible rules that work as 'trumps' against any illegitimate exercise of public authority. As shown by the relatively high number of cases that dealt with proportionality[148] and with the *Wesengehalt* of fundamental rights,[149] fundamental rights come to resemble generic and defeasible reasons that the Court of Justice, in the same way as every other authority, should take into consideration when adjudicating on public policy issues.

On the other hand, although we are not short of references to concepts that relate to the EU as an autonomous legal order based on the rule of law, legal certainty and respect for fundamental rights, in our 40 leading cases we did not find concepts that refer to the EU as a political

143 *Internationale Handelsgesellschaft* [1970], para. 3

144 *Brasserie du Pêcheur* [1996], para. 33.

145 *Foto-Frost* [1987], para. 15.

146 *Barber* [1990], para. 44; *Bosman* [1995], para. 144. See also *Defrenne II* [1976], para. 74.

147 *Van Gend en Loos* [1963], 13; *Costa* [1964], 594; *Bosman* [1995], para. 84; *Köbler* [2003], para. 33; *Viking* [2007], para. 54.

148 *Internationale Handelsgesellschaft* [1970] para. 12 and 16; 'Cassis de Dijon' [1979], para. 8; *Hauer* [1979], para. 23; *Wachauf* [1989], para. 18; *Bosman* [1995], para. 104; *Schmidberger* [2003] para. 79; *Omega* [2004] para. 36; *Mangold* [2005], para. 65; *Viking* [2007], para. 46 and 75; *Kadi* [2008], para. 355.

149 *Hauer* [1979], para. 23; *Wachauf* [1989], para. 18; *Kadi* [2008], para. 335. For a reference to the 'essential part' of the Community competences, see Opinion 1/91 [1991], para. 41.

community in its own right – concepts that in political theory and in legal scholarship are intended to express some distinctive features of the EU, or some normative expectations relating to the EU, such as 'supranational', 'constitutional pluralism', 'mixed constitution', 'multilevel governance', 'association of states', or even the evergreen notion of the *sui generis* nature of the Community.

Probably this is due to the fact that, in the context of an 'essentially contested', evolutive and open-ended political community such as the EU, concepts that refer to the EU as a political authority are likely to have a divisive effect: they would add little to the justification of the decision reached by the Court and would certainly stir up a harsh theoretical and ideological controversy among the scholars.

This applies *a fortiori* to the concepts of (political) sovereignty and nation.

With regard to sovereignty, it can be safely said that the Court is very conscious of the political environment in which it operates and often takes into consideration the political dimension of the sovereignty of Member States – the salience of national interests and identities involved in the controversies before the Court and the autonomy of the national political authorities. Even before the Treaties of Maastricht and Lisbon introduced the obligation of the Union to respect the national identities of the Member States (Article 4(2) TEU), deference to national sovereignty has made its way into the explicit legal reasoning of the Court by means of a (rather rudimentary, in comparison with the case law of the European Court of Human Rights) margin of appreciation doctrine.[150] The Court employed the concept of *marge d'appréciation* in order to show respect for the political sovereignty of the Member States in areas such as public policy,[151] public morality,[152] public health,[153] and fundamental rights protection.[154] Moreover, the Court has acknowledged that 'the preservation of the Member States' national identities is a legitimate aim respected

[150] See e.g. Case C-83/94, *Leifer* [1995] ECR I-3231, para. 35; Case C-273/97, *Sirdar* [1999] ECR 7403, para. 27; Case C-285/98, *Tanja Kreil* [2000] ECR I-69, para. 24.

[151] *Van Duyn* [1974], para. 18; Case C-30/77, *R* v *Pierre Bouchereau* [1977] ECR 1999, para. 34; *Omega* [2004], para. 31.

[152] Case C-34/79, *R* v *Henn & Darby* [1979] ECR 3795, para. 15.

[153] Case C-141/07 *Commission* v *Germany* [2008] ECR I-6935, para. 51; Case C-84/11, *Susisalo* [2012], para. 28. For this line of reasoning, see already Case C-322/01 *Deutscher Apothekerverband* [2003] ECR I-14887, para. 103.

[154] *Schmidberger* [2003], para. 82 and 89.

by the Community legal order',[155] although it has made reference to that concept only on a few occasions and always in passing.[156]

However, the concept of sovereignty as such does not play a decisive role in the legal reasoning of the Court, as demonstrated by the fact that we were able to find only three references to this concept in the 40 leading cases we selected. This probably depends on the intrinsically polemical nature of the concept: the question 'who is (still) sovereign in the EU?' has produced a growing body of scholarship, but it is not the kind of question that can be easily addressed and solved *ex cathedra* within the confines of the legal process. For the Court of Justice to declare the sovereign nature of the Community would be as pointless and counterproductive as declaring the definitive abandonment of Member States' sovereignty. Declarations of this sort would provoke critical reactions and certainly could not contribute to the persuasive force of the judgment.

Thus, the discourse on the limitation of Member States' sovereignty appears in a few foundational judgments of the 1960s and early 1970s,[157] and soon tended to disappear from the case law of the Court. In the 40 leading cases we found it solely in *Van Gend en Loos* (1963), in *Costa* (1964) and in Opinion 1/91 on the incompatibility with Community law of the EEA: 'the Community constitutes a new legal order of international law for the benefit of which the states have limited their sovereign rights'.[158] Even in these judgments, however, it is clear that the Court is using the word 'sovereignty' in quite a broad and generic sense, as synonymous with a bundle of competences and powers that the States are free to limit and transfer to the Community.

When the Court intended to establish the principle that Community law does not derive its binding force from the law of the Member States and is not subordinate to their constitutions and statutes – which can be called the legal concept of sovereignty, as opposed to the political concept – it

[155] Case C-473/93, *Commission v Luxembourg* [1996] ECR I-3207, para. 35. See also Case C-208/09, *Sayn-Wittgenstein* [2010] ECR I-13693, para. 80, for a reference to the need to balance the legitimate goal of preserving Austrian constitutional identity on the one side, and the freedom of movement of persons on the other.

[156] See A. von Bogdandy and S. Schill, 'Overcoming Absolute Primacy: Respect for National Identity Under the Lisbon Treaty' (2011) 48 *Common Market Law Review* 1417, 1422 ff.

[157] *Van Gend en Loos* [1963], 12; *Costa* [1964], 593. See also Case C-17/67, *Neumann* [1967] ECR 441, 453; Case C-28/67, *Molkerei* [1968] ECR 143, 152; Case C-48/71, *Commission* v *Italy* [1972], ECR 529, para. 9.

[158] *Van Gend en Loos* [1963], 12; *Costa* [1964], 593; Opinion 1/91 [1991], para. 21. See also Opinion 1/09 [2011] ECR I-1137, para. 65. The concept of limitation of sovereignty is occasionally employed by the General Court.

reasoned in terms of *primauté* (primacy, supremacy) of Community law and autonomy of the Community legal order, and carefully avoided the lexicon of sovereignty. Therefore, we have considered these concepts as being corollaries of the concept of rule of law rather than instances of the concept of sovereignty: maintaining that *Kadi* revolves around the sovereignty of the EU would be overly emphatic, bizarre and confusing, while it is fair to say that the issue at stake under the label of 'autonomy of Community law' was the respect for the rule of law.

Similar considerations apply to the concept of 'nation' and to the characteristically European neologism of 'supranational'. Given their potentially divisive nature, these concepts are not frequently used in the legal reasoning of the Court.[159] They are not mentioned in the judgments analysed in the research, with the sole exception of *Bosman* (1995): here the Court dismisses the argument that the 'nationality clauses' (rules restricting the extent to which foreign players can be fielded in a match) are justified on non-economic grounds by arguing that there is nothing qualitatively distinct about the kind of belongingness conveyed by the concept of nationality in comparison with other kinds of links, such as locality, town and region.[160]

C Comparative Analysis

According to the reading here proposed, this modest and, so to say, 'unconstitutional' approach or style of the Court of Justice depends not only on the history of the Court – the declining influence of the French model – and its institutional features – the subject matter of the judgments, their collegiate nature and the need to preserve the independency of the Court – but also on a structural feature of this *sui generis* jurisdiction, that is, its 'less-than-constitutional' standing vis-à-vis the national courts – what we have called the *sensu lato* constitutional nature of the Court. As the authority of the Court is a matter of dialogue and negotiation with the national courts, the Court may avoid fully-fledged constitutional rhetoric in order not to offend their constitutional identities and escape the rush

[159] A judgment dealing with the concept of national identity ex Article 4(2) TEU is Case C-208/09, *Sayn-Wittgenstein* [2010] ECR I-13693, para. 83. See also Case C-473/93 *Commission* v *Luxembourg* [1996] ECR I-3207, para. 35; Case C-51/08, *Commission* v *Luxembourg* [2011] ECR I-4231, para. 124; Case C-202/11, Las [2013], para. 26–27 (preservation of national identity as a legitimate aim of national policy).

[160] *Bosman* [1995], para. 131.

for the monopoly of constitutional adjudication in the European legal space.

Things might change, of course, and in many respects have already.[161] The *Kadi* case (2008) provides a major example of the new tendency, and also *Les Verts* (1986) and the Opinion 1/91 can be mentioned as cases of self-conscious constitutional language in the area of institutional organisation. The terse and laconic style of the first judgments of the Court of Justice has largely been abandoned, and since the 1980s the judgments have become considerably longer. Today nobody would argue that they stick strictly to the French model of administrative jurisdiction. The adoption of the Charter of Fundamental Rights and the move of the EU into policy areas such as police and judicial co-operation in criminal matters are likely to strongly affect the legal reasoning of the Court. The Court will have to address fundamental rights issues more openly.

For the time being, however, the Court has continued to avoid, as far as possible, the language of fundamental rights and constitutional principles: it speaks 'strict legalese' and stays away from political rhetoric and vibrant moral calls. Its judgments seem to strive for 'a simple and direct style',[162] not for brightness and depth, and they run the risk of being dry and boring, not emphatic and pompous.

Appendix: 40 Leading Cases

1. Case 26/62, NV Algemene Transporten Expeditie Onderneming van Gend en Loos v Nederlandse Administratis der Belastingen [1963] ECR 1
2. Case C-6/64, Flaminio Costa v E.N.E.L. [1964] ECR 585
3. Case C-29/69, Erich Stauder v City of Ulm – Sozialamt [1969] ECR 419
4. Case C-9/70, Franz Grad v Finanzamt Traunstein [1970] ECR 825
5. Case C-11/70, Internationale Handelsgesellschaft mbH v Einfuhr- und Vorratsstelle für Getreide und Futtermittel [1970] ECR 1125
6. Case C-22/70, Commission of the European Communities v Council of the European Communities [1971] ECR 263 ("ERTA")
7. Case C-8/74, Procureur du Roi v Benoît and Gustave Dassonville [1974] ECR 8377

[161] See U. Haltern, 'On Finality' in Bogdandy and Bast (eds), *Principles of European Constitutional Law* (n 107) 222 ff., which analyses the case law on European citizenship in order to show how the Court entered 'into what might be called "political rhetoric"'.

[162] Pescatore, *Vade-mecum* (n 45) 24.

8. Case C-41/74, Yvonne van Duyn v Home Office [1974] ECR 1337
9. Case C-43/75, Gabrielle Defrenne v Société anonyme belge de navigation aérienne Sabena [1976] ECR 455
10. Case C-106/77, Amministrazione delle Finanze dello Stato v Simmenthal SpA [1978] ECR 629
11. Case C-120/78, Rewe-Zentrale [1979] ECR 649 ("Cassis de Dijon")
12. Case C-148/78, Tullio Ratti [1979] ECR 1629
13. Case C-44/79, Liselotte Hauer v Land Rheinland-Pfalz [1979] ECR 3727
14. Case C-104/79, Pasquale Foglia v Mariella Novello [1980] ECR 745
15. Case C-283/81, Srl CILFIT and Lanificio di Gavardo SpA v Ministry of Health [1982] ECR 3415
16. Case C-294/83, Parti écologiste "Les Verts" v European Parliament [1986] ECR 1339
17. Case C-314/85, Foto-Frost v Hauptzollamt Lübeck-Ost [1987] ECR 4199
18. Case C-5/88, Hubert Wachauf v Bundesamt für Ernährung und Forstwirtschaft [1989] ECR 2609
19. Case C-70/88, European Parliament v Council of the European Communities [1990] ECR I-2041
20. Case C-262/88, Douglas Harvey Barber v Guardian Royal Exchange Assurance Group [1990] ECR I-1889
21. Case-C-106/89, Marleasing SA v La Comercial Internacional de Alimentacion SA [1990] ECR I-4135
22. Case C-213/89, The Queen v Secretary of State for Transport, ex parte: Factortame Ltd and other [1990] ECR I-2433
23. Case C-260/89, Elliniki Radiophonia Tiléorassi AE and Panellinia Omospondia Syllogon Prossopikou v Dimotiki Etairia Pliroforissis and Sotirios Kouvelas and Nicolaos Avdellas and others (ERT) [1991] ECR I-2925
24. Case C-292/89, The Queen v Immigration Appeal Tribunal, ex parte Gustaff Desiderius Antonissen [1991] ECR I-745
25. Joined Cases C-6/90 and 9/90, Andrea Francovich and Danila Bonifaci and others v Italian Republic [1991] ECR I-05357
26. Case C-159/90, The Society for the Protection of Unborn Children Ireland Ltd v Stephen Grogan and others [1991] ECR I-4685
27. Opinion 1/91 [1991] ECR I-6079
28. Case C-91/92, Paola Faccini Dori v Recreb Srl. [1994] ECR I-3325
29. Case C-415/93, Union royale belge des sociétés de football association ASBL v Jean-Marc Bosman, Royal club liégeois SA v Jean-Marc

Bosman and others and Union des associations européennes de football (UEFA) v Jean-Marc Bosman [1995] ECR I-4921

30. Joined Cases C-46/93 and C-48/93, Brasserie du Pêcheur SA and Factortame [1996] ECR I-1029
31. Case C-85/96, María Martínez Sala v Freistaat Bayern [1998] ECR I-2691
32. Case C-60/00, Mary Carpenter v Secretary of State for the Home Department [2002] ECR I-06279
33. Case C-112/00, Eugen Schmidberger, Internationale Transporte und Planzüge v Republik Österreich [2003] ECR I-05659
34. Case C-224/01, Gerhard Köbler v Republik Österreich [2003] ECR I-10239
35. Case C-36/02, Omega Spielhallen- und Automatenaufstellungs-GmbH v Oberbürgermeisterin der Bundesstadt Bonn [2004] ECR I-09609
36. Case C-144/04, Werner Mangold v Rüdiger Helm [2005] ECR I-9981
37. Case C-105/03, Maria Pupino [2005] ECR I-5285
38. Case C-303/05, Advocaten voor de Wereld VZW v Leden van de Ministerraad [2007] ECR I-3633
39. Case C-438/05, International Transport Workers' Federation and Finnish Seamen's Union v Viking Line ABP and OÜ Viking Line Eesti [2007] ECR I-10779
40. Joined Cases C-402/05 P and C-415/05 P, Kadi [2008] ECR I-6351

8

The French Constitutional Council

ARTHUR DYEVRE

A Legal, Political, Institutional and Academic Context

1 Legal and Political Culture as Context for Constitutional Reasoning

The French political culture was long hostile to judicial power. Distrust towards judges and things judicial was in large part a reaction of revolutionary France against the influence held by the robed magistrates of the *Ancien Régime.* This anti-judicial philosophy found an echo in Article 5 of the Civil Code, which barred courts from making "pronouncements by means of general and regulatory provisions on the cases submitted to them."[1] By the early twentieth century, the *Ancien Régime* had receded into distant memory and hostility towards the judiciary began to wane. Academics soon started debating the introduction of the judicial review of statutes, with some speaking approvingly of the American model.[2] The scholarly discussion, though, was cut short by the publication, in 1921, of Edouard Lambert's *Le gouvernement des juges et la lutte contre la législation sociale aux Etats-Unis* (literally: *The Governement of Judges and the Struggle Against Social Legislation in the United States*).[3] Documenting the US Supreme Court's *Lochner* era jurisprudence, the book warned that, due to

[1] Article 1351 added that "the authority of the matter adjudicated only relates to that which has been the object of the judgment." Needless to say, although these provisions still figure in the Code, the reality of judicial policy-making flies in the face of what they command.

[2] Gaston Jèze, 'Notions sur le contrôle des délibérations des assemblées délibérantes' (1895) *Revue générale d'administration* 401; Léon Duguit, *Traité de droit constitutionnel* (E de Boccard 1921) 721 <http://gallica.bnf.fr/ark:/12148/bpt6k932649r> accessed 13 November 2014. For a general account of this pre- and interwar debate see Marc Milet, 'La Controverse de 1925 sur l'exception d'inconstitutionnalité. Genèse d'un débat: L'affaire Ratier' (1999) 49 *Revue française de science politique* 783; Alec Stone Sweet, 'Why Europe Rejected American Judicial Review and Why It May Not Matter' (2003) 101 *Michigan Law Review* 201.

[3] Édouard Lambert, *Le gouvernement des juges et la lutte contre la législation sociale aux États-Unis* (M Giard 1921) <http://bibdig.biblioteca.unesp.br/handle/10/6661> accessed 14 November 2014.

the conservative slant of the French judiciary, bringing in judicial review in France would jeopardize progressive legislation. The book's impact on the collective perception of judicial review proved dramatic. Not only did it introduce the expression "*gouvernement des juges*" into the French political lexicon, but it also made a durable impression on the political class.[4] The founding fathers of the Fifth Republic had misgivings about judicial review that were in no small measure the product of Lambert's continuing influence. They did not intend to establish a constitutional court on the model of the German and Italian constitutional tribunals. True to their choice of words, they did not design the Constitutional "Council" to act as a court, but as a cannon aimed at Parliament. As such, the Council's function was not to protect the rights and freedoms of individual citizens but to secure the new constitutional prerogatives of the executive against legislative encroachments. Tellingly, the framers ruled out granting the Council the power to review legislation for its conformity with the 1789 Declaration of the Rights of Man on the explicit grounds that doing so would lead to a "*gouvernement des juges*".[5]

Such was the hostility towards judicial power that the transformation of the Constitutional Council, from an obscure proto-judicial body overseeing parliamentary proceedings into a mighty constitutional court wielding vast law-making powers, took no less than what has been described as a judicial "*coup d'Etat*".[6] By turning the Preamble of the 1958 Constitution's into hard law, and with it the Declaration of the Rights of Man, the Council's 1971 *Freedom of Association* decision effectively subverted the framers' original intent (see below n 6). At the same time though, the legacy of the Revolution, along with Lambert's enduring influence, meant the Council had to tread political controversies carefully. This was especially true in the periods that followed legislative elections when these were won by the opposition, as in 1981, 1986 and 1993.

The desire to ward off the charge of *gouvernement des juges*, while vetoing legislative bills at an increasing rate, gave the Council members a strong incentive to communicate in a way that would reinforce the image that their institution was a "court" rather than a political outfit. This explains the Council's strict adherence to the distinctive, laconic opinion-writing

4 See Stone Sweet (n 2) 2758.

5 Comité Consultatif Constitutionnel, *Documents pour servir à l'histoire de l'élaboration de la constitution du 4 octobre 1958: Des origines de la loi constitutionnelle du 3 juin 1958 a l'avant-projet du 29 juillet 1958* (La Documentation Française 1987) 388, 425.

6 Alec Stone Sweet, 'The Juridical Coup d'État and the Problem of Authority' (2007) 8 *German Law Journal* 915.

style of French high courts in its early years. Constitutional opinions were to be modelled on that of the two French supreme courts, the *Cour de cassation* and the *Conseil d'Etat.* Yet, as it became clear that adherence to the French form in its canonical variant would not always suffice to silence the critics, the Council showed it was willing to adjust its rhetorical strategy. Opinions, especially after 1980, became longer and the reasoning grew in doctrinal sophistication. Whereas the Council frequently resorted to an ever-expanding list of "Fundamental Principles Recognized by the Laws of the Republic" (FPRLR) to strike down legislation in the 1970s and early 1980s, it began to switch to "equality" as the new catch-all constitutional standard. In the same spirit, the Council has sought to counter the accusation that it is usurping legislative prerogatives by continuously repeating that it "does not have a general power of appreciation and decision identical to that of Parliament".[7,8]

By the turn of the millennium the Constitutional Council had already grown into a more established institution. Its authority and legitimacy were now widely accepted by the political class. Because the centre-right held sway over the Presidency, the legislature and the appointment process for many of the years between 1995 and 2012, the charge that the Council was a creature of the opposition did not assume the same degree of vehemence it had in 1981–2 and 1993. What is more, even politicians on the left have seemingly come to find it convenient to have the Council veto campaign pledges they no longer wish to fulfill once in power.[9]

[7] John Philip Dawson, *The Oracles of the Law* (University of Michigan Law School 1968).

[8] See Decision No. 74–54 DC, 15 January 1975 (cons. 1), Rec. 19; 80–127 DC, 20 January 1981 (cons. 12), Rec. 15; 84–176 DC, 25 July 1984 (cons. 10), Rec. 55; 86–218 DC, 18 November 1986 (cons. 10), Rec. 167; 93–331 DC, 13 January 1994 (cons. 4), Rec. 17; 90–280 DC, 6 December 199 (cons. 26), Rec. 84; 94–343/344 DC, 27 July 1994 (cons. 6 7 and 9–10), Rec. 100; 98–402 DC, 25 June 1998 (cons. 17), Rec. 269; 98–407 DC, 14 January 1999 (cons. 2–4, Rec. 21; 2000–433 DC, 27 July 2000 (cons. 41), Rec. 121; 2001–444 DC, 9 May 2001 (cons. 3), Rec. 59; 2001–446 DC, 27 June 2001 (cons. 4), Rec. 74; 2003–468 DC, 3 April 2003 (cons. 42), Rec. 325; 2005–529 DC, 15 December 2005 (cons. 5), Rec. 165; 2005–530 DC, 29 December 2005 (cons. 20), Rec. 168; 2006–535 DC, 30 March 2006 (cons. 20), Rec. 50; 2007–550 DC, 27 February 2007 (cons. 5), Rec. 81; 2007–555 DC, 16 August 2007 (cons. 8), Rec. 310; 2007–559 DC, 6 December 2007 (cons. 14), Rec. 439; 2008–564 DC, 19 June 2008 (cons. 34), Rec. p. 313; 2008–568 DC, 7 August 2008 (cons. 5), Rec. 352; 2009–585 DC, 6 August 2009 (cons. 7), Rec. 159; 2010–603 DC, 11 February 2010 (cons. 13); 2010–602 DC, 18 February 2010 (cons. 20); 2010–14/22 QPC, 30 July 2010 (cons. 30); 2010–32 QPC, 22 September 2010 (cons. 9); 2011–625 DC, 10 March 2011 (cons. 7).

[9] See post Arthur Dyevre, '75 per cent Millionaire Tax Rate Ruled Unconstitutional: Are Good Judges Bad for Democracy?' <http://www.iconnectblog.com/2013/01/75-millionaire-tax-rate-ruled-unconstitutional-are-good-judges-bad-for-democracy/> accessed 22 January 2014.

Gone were the days when, in the early years of the Fifth Republic, socialist opposition leader Francois Mitterrand derided the Constitutional Council as President de Gaulle's "errand boy" and as a "Supreme Court from a waxwork museum".[10] The 2008 constitutional revision has contributed to consolidate the Council's status as central actor in the political system of the Fifth Republic. Indubitably, by introducing a form of concrete review in the French constitutional system, the reform has greatly expanded the Council's influence over the legal system.[11] But the debates surrounding its adoption and implementation also revealed broad partisan consensus over the place the Council has come to occupy in policy-making.[12] All in all, the Council now operates in a much more favourable environment than it did in the first decades of the Fifth Republic.

2 The Court and Constitutional Litigation

The French model of judicial review initially owed its peculiarity to three characteristics. First, because the founding fathers of the Fifth Republic essentially viewed the Council as a means to rein in the excesses of the elected assemblies so as to strengthen the executive, judicial review of legislation was initially restricted to statutes awaiting promulgation. Second, the Council was conceived as an institution entirely detached from the rest of the court system – again, it was a "council" not a "court". There was no mechanism by which the ordinary courts could submit constitutional questions to the Council. Only politicians had standing to challenge the constitutionality of legislative bills. Prior to 1974, when it was extended to opposition MPs, this meant only the President, the Prime Minister, and the speakers of the two chambers. Finally, the Constitution of the Fifth Republic did not include a catalogue of fundamental rights. The framers' chief preoccupation was to create the conditions of political stability, not to protect civil liberties. Accordingly, the primary task of the Council was to ensure that Parliament did not encroach upon the prerogatives of the executive branch. The reference to the Declaration of the Rights of Man and to the Preamble of the 1946 Constitution in the Preamble of the new

[10] Such were the words of then opposition leader François Mitterrand, see Bastien François, 'La perception du Conseil constitutionnel par la classe politique, les médias et l'opinion' (2003) 105 *Pouvoirs* 133, 137.

[11] See Arthur Dyevre, 'Filtered Constitutional Review and the Reconfiguration of Inter-Judicial Relations' (2013) 61 *American Journal of Comparative Law* 729.

[12] Ibid.

Constitution was thought of as a reverential homage carrying no legal weight. As said above, it took what has been characterised as a "legal revolution" or more provocatively as a "juridical coup d'Etat"[13] to turn it into something resembling a catalogue of binding rights.

The restrictive access rules had the effect of severely limiting the number of legislative bills annually referred to the Council. The Council's jurisdiction over constitutional matters extended to international treaties awaiting ratification, and it was also charged with overseeing legislative and presidential elections.[14] Still, its caseload remained fairly small in its first 15 years of existence. Only a dozen or so cases a year addressed constitutional issues. Of those, fewer than five, on average, were brought against legislative bills. By allowing any group of 60 deputies or senators to refer bills to the Council, and thereby allowing the parliamentary opposition to use constitutional litigation as a weapon against the ruling majority, the 1974 constitutional reform almost immediately led to a significant increase in the number of referrals. Meanwhile, starting with its landmark 1971 *Freedom of Association* decision, the Council had begun to evolve fundamental rights jurisprudence out of the 1946 Preamble, the 1789 Declaration of the Rights of Man and the indefinite FPRLR. It thereby provided the opposition with an additional incentive to initiate referrals.[15] Further boost to the Council's activity came in 1981 with the victory of the Socialist Party in presidential and legislative elections, which marked the first alternation in power in the history of the regime. By then, all Council members had been appointed by the centre-right. Now in the opposition, centre-right parliamentarians quickly realized that the Council could serve as an effective means to thwart the radical programme of social and economic reforms of the new left-wing government. As of the early 1980s, the figures for decisions on legislative bills (which are all published in the *Journal officiel*) rose to between 10 and 20 per year. That this was still a modest caseload would seem to explain why the Council did not care to develop standing doctrines or admissibility criteria that would have enabled it to pick and choose among the cases brought by

[13] Stone Sweet (n 6).

[14] While legislative elections generate a large caseload, lawsuits brought under the Council's election disputes jurisdiction seldom give rise to constitutional issues.

[15] Decision No. 70–39 DC, 19 June 1970, Rec. 15 (mentioning the Preamble as relevant constitutional norm); 71–44 DC, 16 July 1971 (cons. 2), Rec. 29 (holding that the freedom of association constitutes a FPRLR); 73–51 DC, 27 December 1973 (cons. 2), Rec. 25 (applying the Declaration of the Rights of Man).

politicians. In what remains a mandatory docket system, the Council's priority has been to attract cases rather than to try to filter them. Differently put, relative case scarcity meant it could not really afford to be picky. The Council has, though, arrogated to itself the right to raise constitutional issues *sua sponte* when the litigants elect to challenge only a fraction of the provisions contained in a referred bill.[16] This self-arrogated right entails that the Council may choose from the menu of unchallenged provisions the one it will effectively review.

Then came the 2008 constitutional revision, which significantly enlarged the Council's review powers. The revision introduced a system of preliminary referral which has brought the French model closer to the institutional configuration of other European constitutional courts. The new "*question prioritaire de constitutionnalité*", which became effective on 1 March 2010, is best characterised as "filtered concrete review".[17] In other constitutional arrangements, concrete review usually means that any judge whatsoever can refer a constitutional issue directly to the constitutional tribunal. By contrast, in the new French referral mechanism the two supreme courts, the *Conseil d'Etat* and the *Cour de Cassation*, operate as filters. That is, they have not only the duty, but also the power, to decide whether questions raised in proceedings before the lower courts are worth sending to the Constitutional Council.[18] On the face of things, the addition of such a filter would seem to be a concession to the two supreme courts. Looking only at the wording of the constitutional provision, it seemed reasonable to expect that constitutional referrals would be few and far between and that, in any case, the new procedure would not upset the operations of the two judicial hierarchies. Yet the reality has proved quite different. In just three years, the procedure has already generated 255 Council decisions (by 1 March 2013 count).[19] It might be too early to predict long-term trends. But the "*QPC*", as the new preliminary referral mechanism is known in France, appears to be well on its way to becoming the main procedural route to the Council.

[16] Thierry Di Manno, *Le Conseil constitutionnel et les moyens et conclusions souleves d'office* (Economica 1994).

[17] See Dyevre (n 11).

[18] Ibid 743; see also Gerald L. Neuman, 'Anti-Ashwander: Constitutional Litigation as a First Resort in France' (2010) 43 *New York University Journal of International Law and Politics* 15.

[19] See the data analysis in Dyevre (n 11) 731.

3 *The Judges*

While bringing the Council closer to the mainstream of European constitutionalism, the introduction of concrete review has also served to boost its credentials as a "true" constitutional court. In terms of public perception, though, the Council's composition remains a recurring issue. Inasmuch as the authority of a judicial institution rests on its ability to preserve a myth – the myth that judges are neutral and impartial expounders of the law – the appointment process and, to some extent, the appointment results, continue to be the Council's Achilles heel. Just as the institution's name betrays its origins as agent of the executive branch, those who sit on the Council are not "*juges*" but "*membres*". Now, members fall into two categories. The nine ordinary members are appointed for a nine-year non-renewable term. Three are appointed by the President of the Republic, who also decides which of them will sit as President of the Council. A further three are appointed by the speaker of the National Assembly; and the other three by the speaker of the upper chamber, the Senate. The typical ordinary member is a former minister or MP, usually in the twilight of her political career, rewarded with a stable and well-paid job for her loyalty to the appointing authority. Judges from the ordinary courts also feature regularly in appointees lists. Academics, on the other hand, are rarely invited to sit on the Council. Notable exceptions were Jean-Claude Colliard (professor of public law), Georges Vedel (professor of public law), Alain Lancelot (political scientist) and Dominique Schnapper (sociologist).

Beside the ordinary members, the other category is the "*membres de droit*" (members as of right). The Constitution stipulates that all former presidents of the Republic are *membres de droit*. Two former presidents from the defunct Fourth Republic, Vincent Auriol and René Coty, briefly sat on the Council in its early days. For most of the Fifth Republic, however, the provision seemed essentially a dead letter. It remained so until Valéry Giscard d'Estaing, by then in the twilight of his political career, decided to sit on the Council in the early 2000s. He was later joined by his old political rival Jacques Chirac, who moved to the *Palais Royal* – the Parisian palace housing the Constitutional Council – soon after the end of his presidency. More recently, Nicolas Sarkozy followed suit. Not surprisingly, the presence of the former heads of state has aroused suspicions of politicization. What is more surprising is that, despite the presence of the three former presidents and the climate of patronage and cronyism that usually surrounds the appointment of ordinary members, the media coverage attracted by the Council is overwhelmingly favourable. To the general public, Council members are known as "*les sages*" (the sages). This, in turn, tends to make those who dare criticize them look unwise.

4 Legal Scholarship and Constitutional Reasoning

In the battle for public support, the constitutional law professoriate is often a precious ally of the Council. Mainstream French constitutional scholarship rarely finds faults with the outcome of constitutional cases or, for that matter, with the argumentation deployed by the Council. In fact, when the Council comes under attack in the media, constitutional law professors often go out of their way to defend the institution and its members, penning features articles in *Le Monde*, speaking on the radio, or making the odd television appearance. In many respects, French constitutionalists are even more beholden to "their" constitutional court than the German *Staatsrechtslehrer* Bernhard Schlink scolded for acting as subservient followers of the *Bundesverfassungsgericht.*[20] Several factors explain the markedly deferential attitude of French constitutional scholars towards the Council. One is that constitutional law was long regarded as a rather obscure, marginal discipline. The near-irrelevance that characterised the Constitutional Council's institutional position in the early years of the Fifth Republic was only matched by the moribund state of constitutional law scholarship. Within the field of public law (*droit public*), administrative law still reigned supreme. The supreme administrative court, the *Conseil d'Etat*, was *the* judicial body dealing with public law matters. So the leading scholarly figures of the time were primarily specialists in the *Conseil d'Etat*'s jurisprudence. What rescued constitutional law scholarship from irrelevance was the rapid transformation of the Council from impotent creature of the executive into powerful legislative veto-player. Constitutional lawyers now had their own judicial body, and the Council's newly-found activism is what ultimately spurred the revival that constitutional scholarship experienced in the 1970s. This suggests that French constitutional scholars are heavily indebted to the Council in the sense that their discipline largely owes its contemporary social

[20] See Bernhard Schlink, 'Die Entthronung Der Staatsrechtswissenschaft Durch Die Verfassungsgerichtsbarkeit' (1989) 28 *Der Staat* 161; Bernhard Schlink, 'German Constitutional Culture in Transition' (1992) 14 *Cardozo Law Review* 711.

significance to the Council's jurisprudence. Assuredly, without the Council's activist turn, early academic expounders of its jurisprudence, such as Louis Favoreu, would hardly have been able to gain name-recognition by writing, as they did, almost exclusively about constitutional issues.

Moreover, the French constitutional law professoriate makes up a highly cohesive group whose interests are closely aligned with those of the Constitutional Council. The French legal academy is eminently specialised. Constitutional law professors hardly ever venture beyond their sub-discipline to write about other areas of public law (whether EU law, international public law or administrative law) or other courts, unless this appears of direct relevance to the Council's jurisprudence. So, because their discipline is congruent with the Council's jurisdiction and its significance is proportionate to the Council's influence, French constitutional law professors have a strong interest in supporting the Council and in advocating the expansion of its remit. In that respect, the debate around the introduction and implementation of concrete review provides a perfect illustration of the constitutionalists' role as the pro-Council academic lobby.[21] Before the reform, the absence of concrete review meant that the Council was completely detached from the rest of the judiciary. This, in turn, had the consequence that arguments grounded in constitutional law had little traction, and thus barely featured at all in litigation before the ordinary courts. So French constitutional scholars could only glance with envy at Italy and Germany, where no lawyer could afford to ignore constitutional law. Thus, when the reform actually came into effect, the sudden surge in constitutional litigation not only raised the profile of constitutional scholars; it also created a demand for expertise on the Council's case law, which for some established professors translated into juicy consultancy fees.[22] In short, the reform represented an unmitigated boon for the constitutional law professoriate. Accordingly, they actively promoted the new procedure while denouncing everything – including a recalcitrant *Cour de Cassation* – that threatened to come in the way of the announced and visibly hoped-for "legal revolution".[23]

Finally, the Council itself has a policy of cultivating and encouraging scholarly support. One of the most prominent constitutional law journals, the *Cahier du Conseil constitutionel*, is edited by the Council. Also, every year, the Council awards prizes for monographs and doctoral

[21] Dyevre (n 11).

[22] See Guillaume Tusseau, 'La Fin D'une Exception Française?' (2011) 137 *Pouvoirs* 5.

[23] Dyevre (n 11).

dissertations on constitutional law. One might think it should take more to cajole academic lawyers into supporting constitutional judges. But the fact is French law professors continue to suffer from relatively low social prestige. Indeed, while they are frequently dismissed, outside academia, as a mindless, out-of-touch sort, their fixed remuneration (monthly gross pay in the €2100–6100 range) remains well below that of a Council member (in the €12,000–14,000 range).

In any case, the ethos that dominates the legal scholarship on the Council is one of praise and respect. To be sure, many characteristics of the scholarly literature addressing the Council and its decisions are attributes of French legal scholarship at large. French legal academics in general have little taste for theoretical issues or for interdisciplinary approaches. Especially striking is the paucity of literature on constitutional interpretation.[24] Some French legal theorists, most notably Otto Pfersmann and Michel Troper, have written extensively on the subject.[25] But their insights have not really trickled down to the mainstream scholarship. In fact, most constitutional law textbooks do not have a chapter or section on interpretation and the word does not even come up in the index.[26] Moreover, the exegesis of a constitutional clause rarely goes beyond vague references

[24] To the work of Michel Troper and Otto Pfersmann (see note below), a comprehensive overview would only need to add the work of François Luchaire, 'De La Méthode En Droit Constitutionnel' [1981] Revue du Droit Public 294; Yann Aguila, 'Cinq Questions Sur L'interprétation Constitutionnelle' [1995] Revue française de droit constitutionnel 9 together with the contributions inclued in the volume edited by; Ferdinand Mélin-Soucramanien (ed), *L'interprétation Constitutionnelle* (Dalloz 2005).

[25] See Michel Troper, 'Une théorie réaliste de l'interprétation' in Éric Millard and Olivier Jouanjan (eds), *Théories réalistes du droit* (Presses universitaires de Strasbourg 2001); Michel Troper, 'L'interprétation Constitutionnelle' in Mélin-Soucramanien (ed), *L'interprétation de la constitution* (2005); Otto Pfersmann, 'Le Sophisme Onomastique: Changer Au Lieu de Connaître' in Ferdinand Mélin-Soucramanien (ed), *L'interprétation constitutionnelle* (Dalloz 2005); Otto Pfersmann, 'Contre le néo-réalisme juridique. Pour un débat sur l'interprétation' (2002) 52 *Revue française de droit constitutionnel* 789; Otto Pfersmann, 'De L'impossibilité Du Changement de Sens de La Constitution', *Mélanges Pierre Pactet* (Dalloz 2003).

[26] See Philippe Ardant, *Droit constitutionnel et institutions politiques* (LGDJ / Montchrestien 1997); Pierre Pactet, *Institutions politiques – Droit constitutionnel* (Armand Colin 1997); Jean Gicquel and Jean-Eric Gicquel, *Droit constitutionnel et institutions politiques* (Montchrestien 2005); Dominique Turpin, *Droit constitutionnel* (Presses Universitaires de France – PUF 2003); Michel Verpeaux and Bertrand Mathieu, *Droit constitutionnel* (Presses Universitaires de France – PUF 2004); Dimitri Georges Lavroff, *Droit constitutionnel de la 5e République* (3rd edn, Dalloz 1999); Bernard Chantebout, *droit constitutionnel* (Dalloz 2006).

to its "letter" and "spirit".[27] Besides textbooks compiling lines of cases, much of constitutional law scholarship consists of case notes and short essays published in journals that cater to a professional rather than to an academic (not to say "scientific") audience. Often written in pompous, pedantic prose – with the odd, somewhat corny metaphor serving as a substitute for theoretical sophistication – the mainstream literature treats the Council's constitutional pronouncements as if they somehow revealed the true, and until then hidden, meaning of the Constitution. Of the 1971 *Freedom of Association* ruling, Louis Favoreu, for one, says that it definitely "settles the doctrinal debate on the constitutional status of the Preamble",[28] as if the Council had finally cast light on a hitherto invisible constitutional provision. In similar fashion, Favoreu's views on the meaning of the phrase "fundamental principles recognized by the laws of the Republic" in the Preamble to the 1946 Constitution changed many times, closely following the evolution of the Council's jurisprudence. Initially, he saw the FPRLR as a very broad category,[29] but he later revised his position, observing that the Council's subsequent rulings had proved his initial views "wrong".[30] Nor did he find fault with the way the Council derived the principle of human dignity from the Preamble to the 1946 Constitution.[31] On the contrary, he held it as a perfectly legitimate reading of the Preamble.[32] Favoreu's unwavering faith in the Constitutional Council could also be seen in his attempts to refute the attacks leveled at the institution. To prove that it did not encroach upon the prerogatives of Parliament, for example, he cited the Council's

[27] Pactet (n 26) 509; Louis Favoreu and Loïc Philip, *Les Grandes Décisions Du Conseil Constitutionnel* (Dalloz 2003) 101, 311, 316, 318; Guy Carcassonne, *La Constitution* (Seuil 2000) 204.

[28] Louis Favoreu and others, *Droit Constitutionnel* (Dalloz 2005) 117.

[29] See Louis Favoreu, '1977, Année charnière, le développement de la saisine parlementaire relative aux droits et libertés fondamentaux' (1978) *Revue du Droit Public* 801.

[30] Louis Favoreu, 'Les Principes Fondamentaux Reconnus Par Les Lois de La République' in Bertrand Mathieu and Michel Verpeaux (eds), *La République en droit français* (Economica 1996). Another prominent French constitutional scholar, Georges Vedel, took an even sharper U-turn in his interpretation of the phrase. In his 1949 textbook, he argued that an expression such as "fundamental principles recognized by the laws of the Republic" was so vague that it could not possibly be taken as spelling out a binding constitutional command; see Georges Vedel, *Manuel élémentaire de Droit Constitutionnel* (Sirey 1949) 324. After serving on the Council himself, however, he changed his mind, wondering how the clause could conceivably be denied full constitutional status; see Georges Vedel, 'Neuf ans au conseil constitutionnel' (1989) 55 *Le débat* 54.

[31] See *infra*.

[32] Favoreu and others (n 28) 795.

own declaration to the effect that it does not have powers identical to Parliament's.[33]

B Arguments in Constitutional Reasoning

5 *The Structure of Constitutional Arguments*

Much has been said and written about the peculiar style of French judicial opinions. They typically strike foreign lawyers as short, formal, and opaque to the point of obfuscation. As a comparative law scholar notes: "Rather than a reasoned and candid essay, an opinion in the highest courts is a terse and opaque summary of the outcome and the reasons for it."[34] About the differences between American and French opinion writing, he further observes:

> The differences are not merely stylistic. They reflect a fundamental difference in the way French and American judges conceive of the judicial decision. For many Americans, the opinion is a vehicle for setting forth the judges' views of the substantive considerations bearing on the outcomes of cases, as well as the interplay between policy concerns and such formal constraints as precedent and rules. French judges begin from a radically different premise. In their view, the role of the opinion is to apply settled law to the facts, or rather, to create the appearance that the court is merely applying law to the fact. French judges treat application as a matter of mere deductive logic.[35]

The French form has, of course, received its fair share of criticism. Foreign commentators, occasionally joined by the odd French jurist, have disparaged the lack of candour and the sketchiness with which the judges treat factual considerations along with the terse justifications they set forth for their case and policy determinations. Common lawyers have usually figured among those most at pains to find merits in the cryptic style of French opinions: "Propositions of law are drafted with utmost care and precision but they hang suspended in space, for no effort is made to reconcile them with different propositions asserted in other, nearly related

[33] Louis Favoreu, *La Politique saisie par le droit: alternances, cohabitation et Conseil constitutionnel* (Économica 1988) 15, 73. On the role played by Louis Favoreu in French debates on the legitimacy of constitutional review see Alec Stone Sweet, 'The Politics of Constitutional Review in France and Europe' (2007) 5 *International Journal of Constitutional Law* 69.

[34] Michael Wells, 'French and American Judicial Opinions' (1994) 19 *Yale Journal of International Law* 81, 92.

[35] Ibid.

cases or to explain why they would not apply if the facts of the case were somewhat different."[36]

Some scholars, though, have begun to challenge this picture of French judicial discourse as over-simplistic. Most prominent among them has been Mitchel Lasser.[37] Against the view prevailing in the Anglophone scholarship, the American comparativist has argued that in the French legal culture judicial opinions are only the most formal and most visible facet of a broader discursive sphere. There exist not just one but two parallel portraits of decision-making in France. The official portrait is the one expressed in the laconic, rigidly formalistic opinion of the court, which is meant, as the received view has it, to depict the court as the mere mouth of the law.[38] But, according to Lasser, the pronouncements made by French judges are not meant to stand alone but form part of and are embedded in a richer and less formal legal discourse developed by advocates general, reporting judges, and academics. So, besides the official formalist self-portrait there exists a second, non-official portrait, which offers a much more realistic picture of adjudication. Considerations of policy, consequentialist reasoning and the repercussions of past, present and future decisions routinely feature in this non-official portrait. Instead of presenting the application of legal rules as mechanical and univocal, this parallel discourse fully acknowledges interpretive uncertainty and the fact of judicial discretion. Whereas judicial discourse in the Common Law context goes out of its way to combine both formalist and policy discourse in one and the same document – the supreme court opinion – the French judicial system is characterized by what Lasser calls "radical bifurcation".[39]

Assuredly, Lasser's analysis cannot obviate the fact that, as most addressees of the law will never get beyond the official portrait, the official portrait is all there will be to their perception of the judicial branch. But Lasser is also right to suggest that the received view in American comparative law scholarship exaggerates the vices and distinctiveness of the French tradition. As highlighted by other contributions in the present book, the detractors of the French form seem to set it against standards of judicial candour and clarity that in practice seldom obtain in any jurisdiction whatsoever, Common Law included. They idealize the system implicitly

[36] Dawson (n 7) 414.

[37] Mitchel de S Lasser, *Judicial Deliberations: A Comparative Analysis of Judicial Transparency and Legitimacy* (Oxford University Press 2004).

[38] Ibid 37. [39] Lasser (n 37).

assumed as yardstick, which leads them to overstate the singularity of French courts in matters of reasoning. As Lasser points out and as this book makes plain, French courts are by no means alone in their emphasis on formalism.[40]

What is more, this literature may easily distort our perception of the Constitutional Council's argumentative practices. When discussing the style of French judicial opinions, the comparative literature tends to lump the Constitutional Council together with the *Cour de cassation* and the *Conseil d'Etat*.[41] The suggestion is that there are no major differences among the three tribunals when it comes to matters of reasoning and opinion-writing. Although his study explicitly focuses on the *Cour de cassation* – the supreme court which in France has jurisdiction over civil and criminal law matters – even Mitchell Lasser claims that Council decisions show "all the earmarks of French judicial discourse".[42] This view, though, does not appear to be entirely warranted. True, there is an undeniable family resemblance in terms of style and general structure in the opinions issued by the three courts. This family resemblance is manifest in the one-sentence, (pseudo-)syllogistic scheme that Council decisions continue to follow. Yet Council opinions – a fact also reflected in the 40 leading judgments set – diverge from those handed down by the two French supreme courts in a number of ways. As we shall see, this applies for textual characteristics such as loquaciousness. But there are also major differences regarding the institutional setup in which opinions are formulated. One such difference, discussed *infra*, is the absence in proceedings before the Council of a figure comparable to the advocate general or *rapporteur public*.

The (Pseudo-)Syllogistic Form

All Council opinions, including the 40 opinions in the leading cases sample, follow the same basic structure:

The Constitutional Council,

(a) Given [numerical citations of constitutional provisions and other legal texts] . . . ;
(b) Whereas [holding] . . . ;
(c) Decides, [case disposition].

[40] Ibid 72 (noting that in US Supreme Court opinions large doses of vehemently anti-formalist rhetoric coexist with a large measure of equally vehement anti-policy rhetoric).

[41] Wells (n 34) 112.

[42] Lasser (n 37) 278 (citing the Council 1975 abortion decision as example).

In this pseudo-syllogism, part (a), the constitutional provisions under consideration, is supposed to provide the major premise; part (b), the act or piece of legislation under review, is supposed to constitute the minor premise; and part (c), the decision on the merits, is supposed to follow as the logical conclusion. The whole thing is supposed to be composed as a single sentence. A Council opinion thus features one single, lonely period! In practice, part (a), the major premise, presents itself as a list of constitutional and other legal texts. It is usually very short, although more recent decisions, and decisions on the ratifications of international and European treaties in particular, tend to include longer lists of texts. Part (b), meanwhile, is invariably structured as a string of "whereas" clauses (*considérants*), each of which forms a quasi-paragraph. These clauses are sometimes numbered in the published decisions, and commentators mostly refer to passages in Council opinions by specifying the corresponding whereas-clause number.

The syllogistic, single-sentence structure along with the legalese ("*considérant...*") perpetuate the image of constitutional judges as neutral, technical expounders of the law while giving the decision on the merits (c) a sense of logical inevitability. Council reasoning, however, has merely the semblance of a syllogism. In moving from part (a), the major, to part (b), the minor, the Council skips the steps in which it does, in fact, introduce additional premises. It does not take a very perspicacious reader to note that no conclusion follows by simply juxtaposing constitutional and statutory language. The premises (particularly the major premise) are too indeterminate to yield a valid conclusion. In strict logical terms, we would be dealing with a *non sequitur*. So what the Council does is that it uses part (b) of its opinion to redefine the constitutional norms listed in part (a) so as to generate the desired conclusion. To put it differently, the Council redefines the major term of the syllogism as it goes along, yet without ever acknowledging its doing so.

French Supreme Court Opinions vs. Constitutional Council Opinions

The single-sentence, pseudo-syllogistic scheme is a central, defining feature of the French form, which Council opinions share with those of the *Conseil d'Etat* and the *Cour de cassation*. From the *Conseil d'Etat*, which is housed in the same Parisian palace, the Council borrowed the "*considérant*" phraseology. (Clauses in *Cour de cassation* opinions begin not with "*considérant*" but with the phrase "*attendu que*", which has similar meaning.) At any rate, as far as form is concerned, the early decisions in the leading cases set closely follow the style characteristic of the two French supreme courts. Yet there is a sense in which the Council's practice has always differed from that of the two other top French judicial bodies. As hinted above, an important difference with the two supreme courts usually overlooked by the comparative literature is the absence in the case of the Council of a figure comparable to the advocate general or *commissaire du gouvernement*. The absence of a functional equivalent meant, at least during the first 20 years of the Council's existence, that there was even less discursive context to make sense of its opinions, which even constitutional scholars were at times at pains to understand. Council decisions are now accompanied by a press release and a quasi-official commentary is immediately available on its website. Because these documents are penned in more accessible legal prose than the official decision, they usually constitute the first stop for journalists and laypeople trying to make sense of the Council's pronouncements. So, to borrow Lasser's terminology, the Council has witnessed a gradual institutionalization of a more limited form of bifurcation. Compared to the official portrait emerging from the official decision, the quasi-official portrait is less cryptic and more readable, but it remains one that refuses to acknowledge the fact of interpretive indeterminacy and judicial discretion.

Prevalence of the Chain Structure (One-Line Conclusive Reasoning)

The univocal, anti-deliberative character of the French form entails that no answer to objections, arguments raised in public debate or alternative readings of a particular constitutional provision are ever considered even implicitly. Unsurprisingly, no decision in our sample features anything that might be adequately characterized as a "dialogical" (parallel, individually inconclusive but together conclusive) argument according to the definition given to that expression within the conceptual framework followed by the present book. Instead, Council opinions typically exhibit a chain structure (one-line conclusive reasoning). A holding on a particular issue is thus backed by a single, free-standing argument, with no room for additional, supplementary or auxiliary considerations.

In our sample, the 1962 decision on the constitutional referendum is the sole decision that departs from the chain structure.[43] The issue at hand

[43] Decision No. 62–20 DC, 6 November 1962, Rec. 27.

was a deeply controversial one. And the outcome was one that the Council was seemingly at pains to justify, which may explain the unusual legs-of-a-chair – or, more technically, parallel conclusive – structure displayed by the opinion. Under the original 1958 Constitution, the French President was designated not by a direct, democratic ballot, but by an electoral college. In 1962, having put an end to the Algerian crisis, General de Gaulle sought to reassert his authority by making the President directly elected. Yet Article 89 of the Constitution required a parliamentary approval before a constitutional amendment could be put to a referendum. Owing to widespread opposition to the reform among MPs, de Gaulle thus seemed in an unlikely position to have it passed by normal, constitutional means. However, brushing aside constitutional objections, de Gaulle went on to use Article 11 of the Constitution – which only provided for referendum on statutory matters – to bypass parliamentary opposition and submit the matter directly to the electorate. Extra-constitutional though it manifestly was, the amendment was approved by a large margin on the day of the referendum. Before it could be promulgated, though, the president of the Senate referred it to the Council. Yet, to the dismay of de Gaulle's political opponents, the Council refused to rule on the amendment's constitutionality. The Council held that it had no authority to review laws adopted through a plebiscite. In support of this outcome, it advanced three distinct arguments. The first was that it resulted from the "spirit of the Constitution"[44] that the Council was charged with overseeing the decisions of public authorities and not those which had to be regarded as the "direct expression of national sovereignty".[45] The Council then added that this interpretation also resulted from various constitutional provisions and notably Articles 60 and 11, as these did not foresee further proceedings between the adoption of legislation in a referendum and its promulgation.[46] Finally, the Council mentioned a third, independent reason pertaining to the organic law on the Constitutional Council. The organic law, the Council insisted, referred to the laws reviewed as the laws "adopted by Parliament" or as the laws, which after a Council decision, the President could decide to "resubmit to the chambers".[47]

[44] This is the only instance in our sample where the Council refers to the "spirit" of the Constitution. Note that in the Table this passage of the decision has been classified as instantiating a teleological-textual argument.

[45] See *supra* n 43 (cons. 2). [46] *Id.* (cons. 3). [47] *Id.* (cons. 4).

6 *Types of Arguments in Constitutional Reasoning*

The decisions in our leading cases set span six decades (1962–2013). The bulk of those (over 87 per cent) were rendered after 1980, reflecting the marginal role played by the Council prior to the 1974 constitutional reform and the rise in the number of referrals brought about by the Socialist Party's assumption of power in 1981. The experts solicited for this book largely ratified the list submitted to them.[48] Of the cases, 85 per cent were approved by four experts or more, while our experts were unanimous on 60 per cent of the cases included in the list. No case was approved by fewer than two experts.

Looking at the distribution of arguments across time and cases, what first strikes the observer is their paucity. Council decisions rely on a very limited repertoire of argument forms. When we carefully comb through the opinions equipped with our typology of constitutional arguments, we find that many argument forms are never instantiated. Moreover, to the extent that a decision does feature an argument from our typology, it is usually the only such argument used in the decision. Yet a thorough analysis of our leading cases set also reveals some unexpected patterns and trends. As we shall see, and as counterintuitive as it might seem at first glance, we do find opinions where the Council explicitly refer to earlier decisions. In the same way, more recent rulings highlight a movement towards greater doctrinal sophistication which should guard us against embracing an overly stylized picture of French constitutional reasoning.

Absent Arguments

The paucity of reasoning that is taken to constitute one of the hallmarks of French constitutional opinions suggests that the most effective way to describe the range of arguments used by the Council in the leading cases is to start by enumerating those that are never considered.

Taking this approach, we could not find any opinion arguments based on analogy or citations of scholarly works. Equally absent from the leading cases set are arguments discussing or problematizing particular words or phrases occurring in the constitutional provisions under consideration. Nor could we find anything resembling an attempt to

[48] Six French academics, all specialising in constitutional law, responded to our questionnaire. One expert agreed with all decisions included in the list, but suggested an additional decision, thereby violating our protocol that any addition to the list had to be matched by a deletion.

construe the constitutional text in light of international law norms. Ditto for foreign legal materials. Officially, the Council does not consider decisions by foreign or supranational courts. The same holds for non-legal arguments. While it could be argued that the reference to "*intérêt général*" (public interest) in its 2007 *Tax Rebate* decision[49] exemplifies the use of a non-legal argument by the Council, the opinion does not adduce "*intérêt général*" as a consideration external to constitutional law. On the contrary, the Council suggests that the requirement that a tax rebate for new home-owners be conform to public interest is one deriving directly from the Constitution.

As with other French courts, the Council never makes general statement about canons of interpretation and the method by which constitutional provisions are to be construed. The only explicit reference to something akin to a maxim of interpretation is in the aforementioned decision on the 1962 referendum, where the Council invokes the "spirit" of the constitutional clauses defining its review powers to dismiss the referral. Aside from this appeal to the spirit of the Constitution, we encountered one phrase that can plausibly be said to qualify as a teleological-historical argument.[50] Beyond these two cases there is precious little to say about the use of interpretive methods by the Council.

Not that the doctrinal-conceptual apparatus deployed by the Council is much richer. Although more recent rulings, as we will see below, point to a trend towards greater sophistication, many concepts that routinely feature in constitutional reasoning elsewhere in the world never come up in Council decisions. That a concept such as federalism does not show up makes intuitive sense, since France remains a unitary state. But it is telling that when reviewing alleged violations of legislative procedures the Council does not take the pain to elaborate on the nature of parliamentary democracy. Nor do the decisions where the Council specifies the scope of its authority or the need to defer to the determinations of the legislature give rise to reflections on the concept of democracy and government by the people. The rule of law (which translates as "*État de droit*" in French) is similarly absent from the Council's conceptual repertoire. So too is

[49] See Decision No. 2007–555 DC, 16 August 2007.

[50] Decision No. 81–132, 16 January 1982, (cons. 14) Rec. 19. (Arguing that the socio-economic rights of the 1946 Preamble could not supersede the right to property enshrined in the Declaration of the Rights of Man because in May 1946 the French people had rejected a previous draft constitution that would have effectively repealed the 1789 Declaration.)

the notion that fundamental rights have an inviolable core.[51] The same applies for considerations relating to state or government form, as these categories have been operationalized in the present book.

Establishing the Text of the Constitution

Even more than the restricted range of argument forms, what lends Council opinions their anti-deliberative, univocal character is the way in which they treat the major premise, i.e. part (a), of the pseudo-syllogism. On no occasion does Council problematize the constitutional character of the texts to which its decisions ascribe this quality. Nor does it take the trouble to explain how it derives meaning from the texts assumed to possess constitutional nature. Instead, decisions proceed as if constitutional language were always straightforward, as if every constitutional provision were self-explaining and as if the status of the constitutional texts it invokes were never controversial.

Two decisions in our leading cases list illustrate how indifferent Council's reasoning is to interpretive debates and controversies surrounding the documents included in the constitutional canon. The first is the 1971 *Freedom of Association* decision. Following the adoption of the 1958 Constitution, a robust scholarly debate over the legal character of its Preamble unfolded.[52] In its original wording, the second sentence of the Preamble read: "The French people solemnly proclaim their attachment to the Rights of Man and the principles of national sovereignty as defined by the Declaration of 1789, confirmed and complemented by the Preamble to the Constitution of 1946." Arguably, the language suggested a solemn homage rather than a legal command. On that score the Preamble stood in stark contrast to the language of the rest of the Constitution and notably to that of the immediately following Article 1, whose wording relied on more standard French legal terminology. Moreover, following a more explicitly originalist variant of the textualist approach, contemporary dictionaries implied that a "preamble" was not, at the time of the Constitution's adoption and promulgation, supposed to spell out anything resembling

[51] The doctrine that international treaties deemed to affect the "conditions essential to the exercise of national sovereignty" may not be ratified without a prior constitutional revision might seem to come close to doctrine of core legislative competence. Yet, even though the Council invokes this doctrine to flag certain transfer of authority to supranational organisation, it does not frame these essential conditions in terms of legislative competences.

[52] See Robert Pelloux, 'Quelques Réflexions Sur Le Préambule de La Constitution Française de 1958', *Mélanges Basdevant* (Pédone 1960).

a binding legal rule.[53] To this, we must add the fact that neither the 1789 Declaration nor the Preamble to the 1946 Constitution were annexed to the text of the new Constitution when it was put to referendum on 28 September 1958 and when it was published in the Law Report (*Journal officiel*) on 5 October 1958.[54] Hence, for want of an explicit statement in the Constitution to the effect that the Council had power to review legislation on Preamble grounds, it was linguistically impossible to construe the new Constitution as introducing a practice that would have constituted such a conspicuous break with the then still entrenched tradition of parliamentary sovereignty. A historical-intentional approach offered the Council no more basis for turning the Preamble into hard law. If anything, the *travaux préparatoires* indicated that the framers did not see the Preamble and the texts it referred to as spelling out binding constitutional principles.[55] All the same, in its 1971 decision the Council merely asserted "Given the Constitution and notably its Preamble".[56] As we observed in the introductory section, this is the decision that did most to change the face of French constitutional law. Because they entailed that the Council would now regard the Declaration of the Rights of Man along with the Preamble of the 1946 Constitution as spelling out binding constitutional norms, these four little words amounted to a revolution. Yet the opinion does not offer any justification – whether in the form of reference to legislative materials, textual exegesis or doctrinal analysis – for this momentous assertion of judicial power.

As illustrated by the 1994 *Bioethics* decision,[57] French constitutional judges make no more effort to refute potential objections when it comes to deriving new principles from texts already pronounced constitutional. The Preamble to the 1946 Constitution opens with the following sentence:

[53] See *Dictionnaire de l'Académie française* (8th ed.) 1935; *Larousse de poche* édition 1954.

[54] *Journal officiel*, 5 October 1958, 9151.

[55] The record of the discussion between the government's spokesman Raymond Janot and the MP Dejean before the Advisory Committee on the Constitution on 7 August 1958 is the best evidence that the framers did not intend the Preamble to be binding constitutional law:

> M. Dejean: *I had asked whether the preamble has constitutional force?*
>
> M. Janot: *No. Do you think that the rules enacted in 1789 still have normative value in the Twentieth century, that they relate to the structure of today's society?*
>
> Dejean: *For the authors of the pre draft, the preamble, therefore, does not have constitutional force?*
>
> M. Janot: *No, certainly not.*
>
> *Travaux préparatoires de la constitution du 4 octobre 1958: avis et débats du comité consultatif constitutionnel* (la documentation Française 1960) 101 (translation is mine).

[56] See Decision No. 71–44 DC. [57] No. 94–343/344 DC, 27 July 1994, Rec. 100.

"In the morrow of the victory achieved by the free peoples over the regimes that had sought to enslave and degrade humanity, the people of France proclaim anew that each human being, without distinction of race, religion or creed, possesses sacred and inalienable rights." Elementary linguistic maxims of interpretation would suggest that the "inalienable and sacred rights" referred to are those enumerated in the remainder of the Preamble. At any rate, the text makes no mention of human dignity. However, the Council, no doubt influenced by the public debate over the ethics of biomedical research which had done much to make the ill-defined concept fashionable, ruled that this meant legislators had to uphold the principle of "human dignity".[58] Again, one will search the opinion in vain for anything resembling a justification for this unlikely construction of the 1946 Preamble.[59]

Reference to Previous Decisions

More surprising is that, while the Council does not normally cite its own rulings or those of other domestic or foreign courts, our sample contains three exceptions. The first is in a 1962 decision in which the Council dismissed the referral initiated by the Prime Minister on the grounds that it had already ruled on the issue in a decision rendered a year earlier.[60] The Council held that under Article 62 of the Constitution its decision had authority *erga omnes* and that this authority did not solely apply to the case disposition but extended to the *ratio decidendi*.[61] What seemed to motivate the reference to this previous decision was not the adherence to some sort of doctrine of stare decisis, but the desire to expand the effects of its rulings beyond the cases it actually reviewed. The second reference to a previous ruling appears in the *Lisbon* decision.[62] The opinion points out that, in holding that nothing in the EU Charter of Fundamental Rights contravenes the French Constitution, it is merely repeating what it had already said in its ruling on the Constitutional Treaty.[63] A more intriguing reference is in the *Online Gambling* decision, where the Council explicitly cites the decision of the *Cour de cassation* to seek a preliminary ruling from the European Court of Justice on the conformity of the new priority referral mechanism – the *QPC* – to EU law.[64] The exceptional

[58] *Id.* (cons. 2).

[59] Reference to the Preamble of the Constitution and the invocation of human dignity were both classified as reference to concepts or principles not found in the text of the constitution (Q15).

[60] No. 62–20 DC, 6 November 1962.

[61] *Id.* (cons. 2).

[62] Decision No. 2007–560 DC, 20 December 2007, Rec. 459.

[63] *Id.* (cons. 12).

[64] Decision No. 2010–605 DC, 12 May 2010.

character of this reference must be appreciated against the backdrop of the controversy surrounding the *Cour de cassation*'s move, which was widely perceived – and certainly portrayed by the Council and its allies – as an attempt to instrumentalize EU law to derail a popular constitutional reform.[65] The reference was in fact a message destined for the European Court in a bid to prevent an adverse ruling. The Council wanted to bring it to the Luxembourg judges' attention that the reading set forth by the *Cour de cassation* in its request for a preliminary ruling was not the only possible construction of the legislation implementing the new procedure. So the opinion went on to articulate an alternative reading, which basically relaxed the "priority" imperative in the new constitutional procedure.[66] So, again, this was a case in which the Council had little choice but to cite the *Cour de cassation*'s request for a preliminary ruling, as it would have otherwise faced the risk that its peace offer would not be recognized as such by the European Court.

7 *The Weight of Arguments*

As one would expect given the enduring influence of the French form on the opinion-writing style of the Council, the dominant argument form in our sample is best described as circular, para-textual, pseudo-syllogistic argumentation. By para-textual I mean that the major premise in the pseudo-syllogism is habitually a written constitutional provision but that no effort is actually made to explain how the language of the provision in question can be construed to apply to the case at hand. Para-textualism then combines with circularity to give the opinion its oracular character. Why should the Declaration of the Rights of Man and the Preamble to the 1946 Constitution be regarded as part of constitutional law? Because they should. Why should due process rights, such as the right to the assistance of a counsel in criminal proceedings, be regarded as a FPRLR? Because they should. Why should the first paragraph of the 1946 Preamble be understood as protecting human dignity? Because it should. French constitutional discourse builds on a succession of similar question-begging assertions.

As noticed above, this broad picture comes with nuances that have become more marked in recent years. Just as they tend to be significantly longer, the more recent opinions in our sample generally deploy a more diverse and more sophisticated set of doctrines. Not only are they more

[65] See Dyevre (n 11). [66] Ibid.

likely to invoke equality,[67] but they are also more likely to mention proportionality as a means-end test[68] or to acknowledge the need to balance and reconcile conflicting constitutional commands.[69]

8 *Judicial Candour and Judicial Rhetoric*

French constitutional opinions are, if anything, the opposite of candour. They are written to hide rather than acknowledge the interpretive and policy choices made by the judges. The single-sentence, pseudo-deductive structure on which they rely not only lends the decision a sense of inevitability, but by inhibiting clarity, this structure also masks many important steps in the reasoning. We have already seen how part (a) invariably presents constitutional provisions as if they constituted a set of mathematical axioms. But a systematic examination of part (b), the minor premise in the pseudo-syllogism, reveals that this part too serves to obfuscate the choices that are being made.

To illustrate this point, the aforementioned *Freedom of Association* is as good as any other in our sample. Remarkable, as seen above, for the long-term constitutional transformation it brought about, the decision also represented the first high-profile fundamental rights case ever heard by the Council. At issue was a legislative bill that purported to introduce a new mechanism for the incorporation of private non-profit associations. Repealing parts of the landmark 1901 law on non-profit associations, the legislative bill subjected incorporation to a regime of prior administrative approval, which gave state officials the power to deny incorporation to criminal or violent groupings. Seized by the president of the Senate, the Council ended up striking down the bill on the grounds that it unduly restricted the freedom of association. Yet the 1958 Constitution made no mention whatsoever of anything akin to "freedom of association". Nor did the Preamble and the texts it referred to – the Declaration of the Rights of Man and the Preamble to the 1946 Constitution, which the

[67] In our sample, equality is considered in 14 of the last 20 rulings (covering the period 1992–2013), whereas it appears only 6 times in the first 20 (1962–91).

[68] See Decision No. 93–321 DC, 20 July 1993; No. 93–325 DC, 13 August 1993; Decision No. 2007–555 DC, 16 August 2007; Decision No. 2008–564 DC, 19 June 2008; Decision No. 2009–599 DC, 29 December 2009; Decision No. 2012–647 DC, 28 February 2012.

[69] Decision No. 82–141 DC, 27 July 1982; Decision No. 85–187 DC, 25 January 1985; Decision No. 93–325 DC, 13 August 1993; Decision No. 94–343/344 DC, 27 July 1994; Decision No. 99–412 DC, 15 June 1999; Decision No. 2007–557 DC, 15 November 2007; Decision No. 2010–605 DC, 12 May 2010; Decision No. 2010–14/22 QPC, 30 July 2010.

Council had elevated to constitutional status – make any allusion to such a right. So, knowing only the major (the Preamble) and minor premise (the legislative bill), it was positively impossible to predict what the direction of the decision would be. In fact, the Council took the reference to the "fundamental principles recognized by the laws of the Republic" in the Preamble to the 1946 Constitution to include the 1901 law on non-profit associations: the very law the statute under review was meant to modify. In other words, the Council leapfrogged from the Preamble to the 1958 Constitution to that of the 1946 Constitution and from there to the FPRLR, thereby transforming a piece of ordinary legislation into a constitutional principle binding upon the legislature. What made the 1901 law so special and fundamental that it deserved to be called a FPRLR? Was the legislature now barred from making any change to the old statute? The Council did not bother to say. Nor did it take the pain to justify why the new incorporation procedure, which was commonly applied in other rights-sensitive areas, fell afoul of the newly discovered principle.

This example makes plain that Council opinions, as observed above, have only the semblance of a syllogism. The Council redefines the major term and shifts the goalposts as it goes along, although without ever acknowledging its doing so. In any case, the appearance of syllogistic reasoning that Council opinions seek to maintain is not there to help the reader make sense of the successive steps leading to the argument's conclusion. In fact, the opinion is designed to achieve the opposite, hiding the choices made behind a smokescreen of cryptic legalese. To that extent, and despite the evolution its reasoning practices have witnessed, it is not unfair to say that Council opinions remain somewhat more of an exercise in judicial obfuscation than in judicial candour.

9 *Length, Dissenting and Concurring Opinions*

Plotted in Figure 8.1 is the evolution of the length of Council opinions in abstract review and (from 2010 onwards) concrete review cases, as measured by the number of whereas-clauses. As the chart makes plain, council opinions become significantly longer over time. Early opinions had few whereas-clauses and were extremely brief. But average opinion length increased sharply in the early 1980s and then again in the 1990s. Upsurges in loquaciousness have frequently coincided with elections and partisan alternation in power. This strongly suggests that Council members feel the need to invest more time and effort in justifying their decisions when the political environment turns less supportive. Compared to

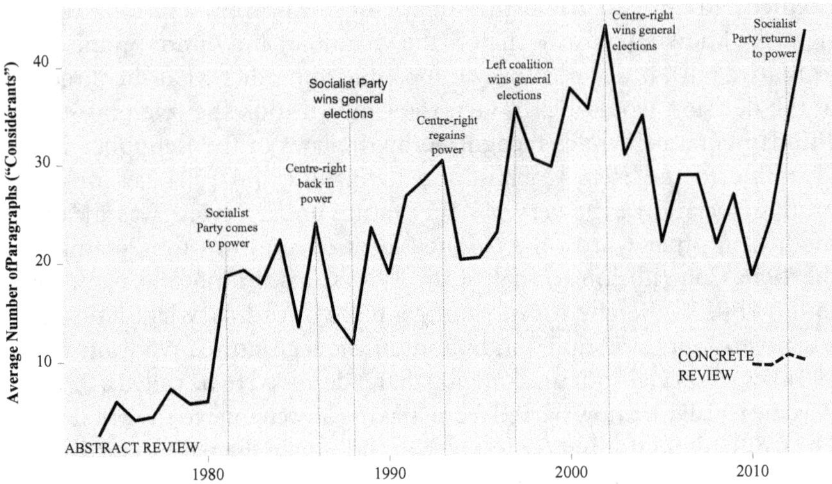

Figure 8.1 Constitutional Council, Overall Evolution of Opinion Length

abstract review decisions, though, the decisions issued by the Council in concrete review cases look relatively succinct. This may owe to the fact that concrete review cases tend to address less hotly contested pieces of legislation that have long been in the statute book and over which partisan tensions may have had time to cool off. Another explanation, though, follows from the need to process a considerably larger caseload. As indicated above, the new referral mechanism has resulted in a considerably greater workload for the Council. Yet the number of judges has remained constant. Brevity may have thus become a convenient strategy to make up for scarcer judicial resources.

The opinions in the leading judgments set are consistent with the overall evolution of constitutional reasoning in abstract review cases. The first four opinions have between 4 and 10 whereas-clauses, with each opinion barely filling up a single page. Subsequent decisions, though, tend to come out as substantially longer, especially when the Council ends up annulling the statutory provisions under review. The more recent constitutional opinions come across as more reader-friendly, too. Headings have been added to indicate sections where a specific question is dealt with.[70] The arguments raised by those who referred the statute are explicitly mentioned, and the Council takes the trouble to briefly summarize them. On the whole, and despite the 'whereas' formula, the more recent

[70] See e.g. Decision No. 2009–600 DC, 29 December 2009, Rec. 238.

opinions develop a language that appears less cryptic and more easily intelligible to the layperson. This does not mean that these opinions, even the more recent ones, do not retain many of the defining characteristics of the French form. The decisions are still written so as to convey a sense of inevitability. They continue to treat the meaning of constitutional provisions as self-explaining, and they still fail to acknowledge the choice made among competing constructions and methods of interpretation. Yet, while far from being radical or revolutionary in nature, the evolution is undeniable.

Aside from the enduring constraints of the French form, the evolution of the Council's reasoning is certainly affected by the ban on separate opinions. As scholars have now been granted access to the minutes of the Council's deliberations for all rulings older than 25 years, there is now ample evidence that Council members do, at times, disagree[71] – a fact also acknowledged by retiring members of the institution.[72] Nevertheless, whatever internal divergence there might be, there is little that transpires in the Council's official communication. We can easily imagine that Council opinions would look different were it not for the ban on dissents. This is, of course, a counterfactual argument. But it seems reasonable to believe that by threatening to expose the limitations of the majority opinion, potential dissenters would put pressure on the majority to beef up its argumentation. Had French constitutional judges been allowed to dissent, Council opinions would quite possibly be longer and would probably instantiate a broader and more diverse range of arguments.

10 Framing of Constitutional Issues

While indubitably more cryptic than those of other constitutional tribunals, the Council leading decisions are less original in the accent they put on fundamental rights. In our Great Cases set, fundamental rights are clearly the dominant frame. Of the 40 cases, 31 are either partly or exclusively framed as fundamental rights issues. The pervasiveness of fundamental rights discourse is also manifest in the key concepts that occur in the opinions: equality, due process rights (*droits de la défense*), freedom of expression, privacy rights, proportionality and human dignity.

[71] Bertrand Mathieu and others, *Les Grandes Délibérations Du Conseil Constitutionnel 1958–1983* (Dalloz-Sirey 2009).

[72] Pierre Joxe, *Cas de conscience* (Labor et Fides 2010) 159.

Not all constitutional issues are wrapped in a fundamental rights frame, however. In our sample, issues pertaining to the procedures and standing orders of the parliamentary assemblies as well as matters relating to European integration and international organizations are not cast as fundamental rights questions. The Council has developed a complex and sophisticated case law regarding the assemblies' standing orders, the right of parliamentarians to amend bills tabled by the executive, the delegation of legislative powers to the government, etc.[73] In fact, many opinions (13 of them to be exact) begin by considering procedural challenges to the bill under review before moving on to fundamental rights matters. The importance of this area reflects the exclusively *ex ante* character that judicial review assumed before the 2010 reform. Most decisions in our sample pertain to bills freshly passed by the chambers, where the opposition initiated a referral after losing the vote on the parliamentary floor. In such circumstances, the Council operates as a sort of third chamber, giving opposition MPs a natural incentive to cry foul in legislative proceedings. Intriguingly, though, the Council does not subsume this area of litigation under any single, overarching constitutional concept. The passages where the Council deals with parliamentary procedure typically draw on a language that is more technical than emotional. They feature little in the way of appeal to values or broad constitutional principles.

Opinions addressing international and EU treaties, meanwhile, have a less technical streak. Here the concept that looms largest in constitutional discourse is indubitably "sovereignty". In its *Maastricht*, *Amsterdam*, *Rome Statute* and *Lisbon* decisions, the Council declares the treaty provisions under review compatible or incompatible with the Constitution, depending on whether these are deemed to affect "conditions essential to the exercise of national sovereignty".[74] Also in our sample is the 2012 *Online Gambling* decision, in which the Council was concerned, among other things, with the limits of the constitutional duty to transpose EU directives. Borrowing a phraseology first used by the German and Italian constitutional courts, the Council held that such a duty found its limit

[73] See e.g. Decision No. 85–191 DC, 10 July 1985, Rec. 46; 88–251 DC, 12 January 1989 (cons. 6), Rec. 10; 94–338 DC, 10 March 1994 (cons. 2), Rec. p. 71; 94–338 DC, 10 March 1994 (cons. 2), Rec. 71; 98–402 DC, 25 June 1998 (cons. 2–3), Rec. 269; 98–403 DC, 29 July 1998 (cons. 50–51), Rec. 276.

[74] See Decision No. 92–308 DC, 9 April 1992 (cons. 9–14), Rec. 55; 97–394 DC, 31 December 1997 (cons. 1–7), Rec. 344; 98–408 DC, 22 January 1999 (cons. 32), Rec. 29; 2007–560 DC, 20 December 2007 (cons. 3–10), Rec. 459.

in the "the rules and principles inherent to the constitutional identity of France".[75]

11 *Key Concepts*

In line with the general doctrinal sparsity of French constitutional reasoning, most generic constitutional doctrines, phrases and expressions identified as "key concepts" for the purpose of the present book are either not instantiated in the leading judgments set or, when they are, appear only in a couple of opinions. As noted earlier, we could not find any language in the 40 opinions alluding to "democracy" or the "rule of law". Nor could we find a reference to something akin to a doctrine of core institutional rights or core competences, although it may be argued that the reference to the "rules and principles inherent to the constitutional identity of France" in the *Online Gambling* decision come close. While the absence of reference to "federalism" is hardly surprising given that France regards itself as a unitary state, we could not find any elaboration on the country's state form or the government form created by its constitution.

Of the generic constitutional doctrines that do appear in the 40 landmark rulings, we find mention of "privacy" ("*respect de la vie privée*") in one decision; "human dignity" ("*dignité humaine*") in three; "secularism" ("*principe de laïcité*") in four; "procedural rights" ("*droits de la défense*") and "freedom of expression" ("*liberté d'expression*") in five; "sovereignty" ("*souveraineté*") in seven; and "proportionality" ("*proportionnalité*") in six. The last is sometimes explicitly developed as a three-prong test requiring that a measure restricting the exercise of a right be suitable, necessary and reasonable.[76] Ubiquitous, by contrast, is the principle of "equality", which appears in half the leading judgments. Equality considerations are especially common in more recent decisions. We find mention of the principle in 14 of the 17 most recent leading judgments.

C Comparative Perspective

Standing Alone?

Some of the main differences and commonalities with constitutional reasoning in other countries should already be plain from the foregoing analysis. The terse, magisterial style of constitutional opinions remains,

[75] Decision No. 2010–605 DC, 12 May 2010 (cons. 17–19).
[76] Decision No. 2012–647 DC, 28 February 2012 (cons. 5).

despite the evolution it has undergone, the most peculiar characteristic of constitutional discourse in France. One anecdote sometimes heard among comparativists tells the story of an American academic coming to Paris to study the Constitutional Council but complaining that he could not manage to get hold of the full text of a single decision. All he could find, the American professor lamented, were summaries, not realizing that these were in fact the full, unabridged opinions.

Now, it is true that a constitutional opinion along the lines of the German Federal Constitutional Court's *Lisbon* ruling, recounting the history of European integration in textbook-like fashion and replete with references to academic works, the whole thing over more than 100 pages, is still inconceivable. So too is the kind of idiosyncratic, flowery rhetoric often employed in US Supreme Court opinions. Seen from the French perspective, Justice Scalia's sarcastic – when not outright insulting – tone is not just foreign, but outlandish. Equally remote from the norms and expectations of constitutional reasoning in France is the free-flowing story-telling sometimes encountered in opinions of the Supreme Court of Israel.

As some foreign commentators have noticed,[77] though, French judicial exceptionalism is easily overstated. Judicial candor is by no means the rule in other systems. Judges know that the public at large tend to evaluate the legitimacy of judicial decision-making through the lens of the formalist model.[78] Because citizens continue to believe that a good judge is one who mechanically applies the law to the cases brought before her without adding to or subtracting from it, the formalist model remains the official portrait of the judicial function, even though it is painted using different colours and techniques depending on the place and time. Even in Common Law countries, judges tend to hide their value judgments behind standards such as "reasonableness" or "balancing". For all the talk about the influence of Legal Realists on American legal thinking, formalism continues to permeate opinion writing on the US Supreme Court.[79] In his comparative analysis, Mitchell Lasser points to the tension between formalism and realism in US Supreme Court opinions.[80] In many ways, US Supreme Court judges are just as reluctant to acknowledge that they

[77] Wells (n 34) 121.

[78] See James L. Gibson, Gregory A. Caldeira and Vanessa A. Baird, 'On the Legitimacy of National High Courts' (1998) 92 *The American Political Science Review* 343.

[79] Erwin Chemerinsky, 'The Rhetoric of Constitutional Law' (2002) 100 *Michigan Law Review* 2008.

[80] Lasser (n 37) 63.

engage in policy-making as are members of the Constitutional Council. As remote as his opinions may be from the standards governing judicial opinion-writing in France, Justice Scalia is a champion of formalism who denies that constitutional rules leave any discretion to the judges enforcing them.

In terms of tone, French constitutional reasoning bears a distinct though somewhat distant family resemblance to the style of other continental European courts. German, Italian, Spanish or Hungarian constitutional courts' decisions are usually considerably longer than those of their French counterparts. But they tend to be similarly impersonal and magisterial in their overall tone. Not unlike Constitutional Council opinions, they are written in legal jargon with an audience of lawyers rather than laypeople in mind. They also strive to hide the judges' policy-making role and seldom acknowledge interpretive uncertainty.

Owing to the influence of French judicial practices on the European Court of Justice's original setup, scholars have pointed out similarities with the French form in its argumentation style. As Mitchell Lasser writes: "ECJ decisions are rather short, terse, and magisterial decisions that offer condensed factual descriptions, impersonally clipped and collegial legal reasoning and ritualized stylistic forms."[81] Lasser casts the European Court's discursive style as a milder version of the French form.[82] Unlike the Council, the Court of Justice is characterized by thoroughly institutionalized discursive bifurcation. Next to the Court's more univocal, magisterial reasoning style runs a parallel legal discourse embodied in the opinions of the Advocates General with their more open-ended argumentation mode. Yet, regardless of this institutional difference, Council decisions are certainly closer to the decision making style of the Court of Justice than to that of the US Supreme Court or even the German Constitutional Court. Interestingly, the European Court's opinion-writing practices have themselves undergone a significant evolution, and it may prefigure how the Council's approach to reasoning could evolve in a more distant future.

Conclusion: Long-Term Convergence?

The foregoing analysis suggests that French constitutional discourse retains many of its idiosyncratic traits. At the same time, though, it has undergone a remarkable evolution, bringing it closer to the mainstream

[81] Ibid 104. [82] Ibid 203.

of European constitutionalism. One question is whether this evolution is likely to go on in the future, ultimately forcing the Council to ditch the French form in favour of a more deliberative style.

With the recent opening of Sciences Po Law School, which offers courses in English as well as in French and vies to compete with the best international law schools abroad, French legal academy may be on the cusp of radical change.[83] By opening up new recruitment paths, and thus possibilities to overcome the traditional barriers to entry established by the law professoriate, these institutional changes may help foster a new generation of scholars keener to challenge the Constitutional Council and to shake up the cosy conservatism of the French legal academy.

More plausibly, though, the prod to change is likely to come, as it has in the past, from politics. As political parties alternate in power and counter-majoritarian tensions re-emerge, the chance is the Council will be even more desirous to look like other European constitutional courts, which in turn will lead it to update the official judicial self-portrait. But this remains to be seen.

Appendix: 40 Leading Cases

1. Décision n° 62–18 L du 16 janvier 1962
2. Décision n° 62–20 DC du 06 novembre 1962
3. Décision n° 62–20 DC du 06 novembre 1962
4. Décision n° 73–51 DC du 27 décembre 1973
5. Décision n° 74–54 DC du 15 janvier 1975
6. Décision n° 80–127 DC du 20 janvier 1981
7. Décision n° 81–132 DC du 16 janvier 1982
8. Décision n° 82–141 DC du 27 juillet 1982
9. Décision n° 82–143 DC du 30 juillet 1982
10. Décision n° 82–146 DC du 18 novembre 1982
11. Décision n° 83–165 DC du 20 janvier 1984
12. Décision n° 85–187 DC du 25 janvier 1985
13. Décision n° 85–198 DC du 13 décembre 1985
14. Décision n° 86–207 DC du 26 juin 1986
15. Décision n° 86–210 DC du 29 juillet 1986
16. Décision n° 86–224 DC du 23 janvier 1987

[83] See Christophe Jamin and Mikhail Xifaras, 'De la vocation des facultés de droit (françaises) de notre temps pour la science et l'enseignement' (2014) Volume 72 *Revue interdisciplinaire d'études juridiques* 107.

17. Décision n° 91–290 DC du 09 mai 1991
18. Décision n° 92–308 DC du 09 avril 1992
19. Décision n° 92–312 DC du 02 septembre 1992
20. Décision n° 93–321 DC du 20 juillet 1993
21. Décision n° 93–325 DC du 13 août 1993
22. Décision n° 93–329 DC du 13 janvier 1994
23. Décision n° 94–343/344 DC du 27 juillet 1994
24. Décision n° 97–394 DC du 31 décembre 1997
25. Décision n° 98–404 DC du 18 décembre 1998
26. Décision n° 98–408 DC du 22 janvier 1999
27. Décision n° 99–412 DC du 15 juin 1999
28. Décision n° 2003–469 DC du 226 mars 2003
29. Décision n° 2004–496 DC du 10 juin 2004
30. Décision n° 2006–203 L du 31 janvier 2006
31. Décision n° 2007–555 DC du 16 août 2007
32. Décision n° 2007–557 DC du 15 novembre 2007
33. Décision n° 2007–560 DC du 20 décembre 2007
34. Décision n° 2008–564 DC du 19 juin 2008
35. Décision n° 2009–599 DC du 29 décembre 2009
36. Décision n° 2010–605 DC du 12 mai 2010
37. Décision n° 2010–14/22 QPC du 30 juillet 2010
38. Décision n° 2012–647 DC du 28 février 2012
39. Décision n° 2012–662 DC du 29 décembre 2012
40. Décision n° 2013–314P QPC du 04 avril 2013

9

The German Federal Constitutional Court

MICHAELA HAILBRONNER AND STEFAN MARTINI

A Legal, Political, Institutional, and Academic Context

1 *Legal and Political Culture as Context for Constitutional Reasoning*

When the Allies handed over the *Frankfurter Dokumente* to the West German states, mandating them to write a new constitution for a Western German state, this was – unlike in other transitions – little cause for joy and optimism. Many West Germans disliked the idea of adopting a new constitution considering that Germany was still divided into two parts and would have preferred to wait for reunification.[1] To indicate the transitory character of the new document they were drafting, they therefore called their new constitution a "Basic Law" rather than a "Constitution". Nor was the Basic Law a particularly inspiring document; it lacked, as one commentator lamented, "lighthearted fresh ideas" and the "forward-looking spirit of enterprise",[2] seeking instead to preserve those parts of the German legal tradition that had – so it now seemed – been forgotten and neglected during the years of National Socialist rule.

For the framers this implied, first and foremost, the need to resurrect the German *Rechtsstaat* as it had been established over the course of the nineteenth and early twentieth centuries.[3] In doing so, they made sure to take their lessons from the more recent past into account, most importantly the "take-over" of the Weimar democracy by the National Socialists. These past experiences influenced particularly the institutional design and ordering of the new Western German state. Geared to ensure that non-democratic forces would never again be able to do away with democracy and rights, the framers chose to establish what Karl Loewenstein has called

[1] Michael Stolleis, *Geschichte des öffentlichen Rechts in Deutschland: Staats-und Verwaltungsrechtswissenschaft in West und Ost, 1945–1990* (Beck 2012) 125.

[2] Werner Weber, *Weimarer Verfassung und Bonner Grundgesetz* (Karl-Friedrich Fleischer 1949) 12.

[3] Stolleis (n 1) 211 ff.

a "militant democracy".[4] To this purpose, they included in the Basic Law rules providing for the prohibition of unconstitutional parties and super-entrenched key principles such as democracy, the *Rechtsstaat*, federalism and human dignity against any later constitutional amendments (Art. 79 BL[5]). In order to avoid the mistakes of Weimar, they were, moreover, careful to establish a system of checks and balances that would guard against future concentrations of power, in particular within the executive branch and the office of the president, who was now reduced to the position of a mere figurehead without real political powers.[6] Another consequence of the framers' cautious approach was their mistrust of participatory forms of democracy at the federal level.[7] The German political system and its political culture hence center around a particularly strong federal parliament.

Part of this attempt to constrain state power was the establishment of a new institution, the *Bundesverfassungsgericht* (federal constitutional court). Though the *Bundesverfassungsgericht* did not feature much in the framers' debates,[8] it was early on accorded a wide range of powers, including the competence to declare parliamentary statutes unconstitutional if they violated either the Basic Law's organizational or rights provisions, mentioned upfront in the Basic Law in conscious contrast to the Weimar Constitution. With this, the framers went beyond the classical model of a constitutional court as it had been developed by the famous positivist scholar Hans Kelsen and set up in Austria. To ensure that individual rights would indeed be considered justiciable – and not as in the Weimar Republic be set aside as mere directive principles ("*Programmsätze*") – the framers included only those traditional liberal rights that had a considerable historical pedigree.[9] Socio-economic rights in contrast, which the

[4] Karl Loewenstein, "Militant Democracy and Fundamental Rights" in András Sajó (ed), *Militant Democracy* (Eleven International 2004) 231 ff.

[5] For an English translation of the Basic Law see http://www.gesetze-im-internet.de/englisch_gg/englisch_gg.html.

[6] Stolleis (n 1) 124 f.

[7] Christoph Möllers, "'We Are (Afraid of) the People'": Constituent Power in German Constitutionalism" in Martin Loughlin and Neil Walker (eds), *The Paradox of Constitutionalism: Constituent Power and Constitutional Form* (Oxford University Press 2007) 87–105, 101.

[8] Michaela Hailbronner, "Rethinking the Rise of the German Constitutional Court: From Anti-Nazism to Value Formalism" (2014) 12.3 *International Journal of Constitutional Law* 626.

[9] Deutscher Bundestag und Bundesarchiv under guidance from Rubert Schick und Friedrich Kahlenberg (eds), *Der Parlamentarische Rat 1948–1949. Akten und Protokolle. Band 5: Ausschuss für Grundsatzfragen* (1993) 1, 33 ff., 43.

Weimar Constitution had included, were left mostly out of the picture. And the framers did follow the Kelsenian model in other respects, most importantly by choosing to charge one particular court with the task of constitutional review rather than leaving constitutional questions to be decided by the judiciary at large as suggested by the model of the US judiciary.

Though itself a new institution, the new Court could build on a considerable tradition of constitutional thought. German legal and political culture integrates elements of nineteenth-century legal positivism, idealistic philosophy and, as is commonly argued, a conception of constitutionalism primarily as a means to constrain first royal and then state power more generally.[10] The major schools of constitutional thought – the positivist Kelsenian, anti-positivist integrationist Smendian and statist Schmittian – that had dominated the famous Weimar debate on methodology (*Weimarer Methodenstreit*) still influenced German postwar legal thinking.[11] While the influence of the emigrated Kelsen and Pure Theory thinking was primarily felt intellectually,[12] insofar as it shaped the idea of constitutional supremacy (following the hierarchical structure of pure theory law systems) and the evolving separation of law and politics, the two other schools managed to attract "disciples" who sometimes even found their way to the *Bundesverfassungsgericht*, most famously among them Konrad Hesse (representing the Smend school) and Ernst-Wolfgang Böckenförde (a follower of the Schmittian tradition). (Smendian) integrationist and (Schmittian) statist elements thus continued to shape the reasoning of the *Bundesverfassungsgericht*. In particular, the idea of the Basic Law as an "objective order of values" as the Court developed it in the Lüth case built on Smend's integrationist theory;[13] in later years, this approach became increasingly oriented towards more pluralist

[10] See Christoph Möllers, "Pouvoir constituant-Constitution-Constitutionalism" in Armin v. Bogdandy and Jürgen Bast (eds), *Principles of European Union Law* (Hart 2011) 169 ff.; similarly Oliver Lepsius, "Rezension von: Frieder Günther: Denken vom Staat her. Die bundesdeutsche Staatsrechtslehre zwischen Dezision und Integration 1949–1970" (2004) *sehepunkte* 4, 5. For a somewhat different account of the GFCC's jurisprudence see Michaela Hailbronner, *Traditions and Transformations. The Rise of German Constitutionalism* (Oxford University Press 2015).

[11] See Arthur J. Jacobson and Bernhard Schlink (eds), *Weimar. A Jurisprudence of Crisis* (University of California Press 2000); also Frieder Günther, *Denken vom Staat her* (Oldenbourg 2004).

[12] Möllers (n 7) 98.

[13] Siehe Lüth – BVerfGE 7, 198, and Dominik Rennert, "Die verdrängte Werttheorie und ihre Historisierung" (2014) 53 *Der Staat* 31.

conceptions under the influence of Smend's famous disciple Peter Häberle.[14] At the same time, the tradition of statist and nation-centered thought (or in Frieder Günther's words: "Denken vom Staat her") could still be felt in a number of other decisions, conceptualizing the state as a nation (only) of German citizens (denying foreigners voting rights in municipal elections)[15] or in emphasizing the relative homogeneity of the German people (as compared to the European Union, for example).[16]

In other respects, however, the Constitutional Court broke new ground. Though it had initially been conceived by many as a successor to the *Staatsgerichtshof* of the Weimar Republic that would mainly guard the functional and organizational divisions between the different governmental branches and institutions,[17] the Court eventually became famous for its rights jurisprudence. This development, however, took some time. In its first years of operation, the Court saw itself mainly confronted with a number of cases involving organizational issues of high political importance such as the integration of two states into one (Baden-Württemberg[18]) and the debate on German rearmament which brought the Court into sharp conflict with Adenauer's government[19]. In resisting manipulations by the government to make sure that "its own" senate, i.e. the second senate with a majority of CDU (the Christian Democratic party) nominees, would deal with the question of German rearmament, the Court succeeded in publicly asserting its judicial independence. In doing so, it attracted sharp

[14] See for one of many citations of his work, BVerfGE 128, 326, 369, 370 (2011) – preventive custody. His influence (Grundrechte im Leistungsstaat, 30 (1972) VVDStRL, 43, 114: "Der Zugangsanspruch zu den Hochschulen ist ein 'Maßgaberecht' (Art. 12, 5 III, 1 I, 3, 20 I GG), d. h. es steht von vornherein unter dem – verfassungskonformen – Vorbehalt des Leistungsstaats, seiner Möglichkeiten zur Effektivierung dieses Rechts." [The right to be admitted to university is a measured right, i.e. it is – constitutionally so – only conditionally granted in the Beneficial State, dependent on his possibilities to put it into effect.] (footnotes omitted), on BVerfGE 33, 303, 333 ("if at all possible") is often acclaimed.

[15] BVerfGE 83, 37, 51 (1990) – foreigners' suffrage.

[16] BVerfGE 89, 155, 186 (1993) – Maastricht. Ingolf Pernice, Carl Schmitt, Rudolf Smend und die europäische Integration 120 (1995) Archiv des öffentlichen Rechts, 100; Joseph W. Weiler, "The state 'über alles' Demos, Telos and the German Maastricht Decision", Jean Monnet Working Paper 6/95, http://www.jeanmonnetprogram.org/archive/papers/95/9506ind.html. See also more broadly Christoph Möllers, *Staat als Argument* (C. H. Beck 2001).

[17] Heinz Laufer, *Verfassungsgerichtsbarkeit und politischer Prozess: Studien zum Bundesverfassungsgericht der Bundesrepublik Deutschland* (J. C. B. Mohr 1968) 54 f.

[18] See BVerfGE 1, 14.

[19] Richard Häußler, *Der Konflikt zwischen Bundesverfassungsgericht und politischer Führung* (Duncker & Humblot 1994) 28 ff.

criticism from Thomas Dehler, the then-Minister of Justice, but received support from the press and wider public, which eventually forced the government and Dehler to back down. Around the same time, the Court self-consciously asserted its independence in a different, institutional sense by claiming financial and administrative authority over its own staff and budget, which had so far been part of the Ministry of Justice's general budget, and oversight of the judiciary at large.[20] The Court ultimately succeeded in its quest, gaining recognition as a constitutional organ in its own right as it had called for in the so-called *Status-Denkschrift*.[21] The government's defeat and the recognition attained by the Court set the trend for the court's later high public admiration and approval.

It was not its role as an arbiter in institutional conflicts, however, that earned the Constitutional Court its later public approval, which is second only to the trust Germans place in the police,[22] but its role as a rights tribunal. And this was also where it was at its most transformative.[23] Though Smend's theory of integration provided the basis for the Court's concept of the Basic Law as an "objective order of values", the Court in *Lüth* went further than many of Smend's own disciples would have preferred.[24] In developing the indirect horizontal effect of constitutional rights together with the expansion of its jurisdiction by reading Art. 2 GG as a broad residual right to liberty (*Elfes*)[25] and the development of proportionality analysis[26], the Court turned to a much more positive and activist approach to constitutional law than the standard negative liberal paradigm encouraged[27] and laid the ground for the later comprehensive constitutionalization of German law. From the late 1950s and early 1960s onwards, the Court gradually expanded its rights jurisprudence, entrenching and formalizing its newly created constitutional concepts and tools.

But while initially perhaps the most progressive institution, the Court increasingly came into conflict with the Social Democrat government in the 1970s under Willy Brandt, many of whose reform proposals the Court declared wholly or in parts unconstitutional.[28] Another wave of public

[20] Häußler, 24 ff. [21] Id. [22] http://prreport.de/home/gpra-vertrauensindex/.
[23] For a fuller argument see Hailbronner (n 10) Chapter 2.
[24] Günther (n 11) 171. [25] BVerfGE 6, 32.
[26] As first developed in the Pharmacies Decision (Apothekenurteil), BVerfGE 7, 377.
[27] Hailbronner (n 10) Chapter 2.
[28] See e.g. its judgments on abortion (BVerfGE 39, 1), also Häußler (n 20) 52 ff and for a more comprehensive account of the Court's history generally Justin Collings, *Democracy's Guardians: A History of the German Federal Constitutional Court 1951–2001* (Oxford University Press 2015).

resentment swept the Court in the 1990s – now once more from the conservative spectrum for its liberal decisions on free speech (protecting e.g. the statement "soldiers are murderers") and freedom of religion (challenging the placing of crosses in Bavarian classrooms).[29] More recently, the Court has received criticism for its decisions on European electoral law, European integration and the financial crisis, but overall criticism has been comparatively restrained after the 1990s.[30] And although politicians at times try to evade decisions by the court,[31] more often they abide by the judgments and even turn to the court to settle disputes and unsolved political problems. It would be virtually unthinkable today to openly tinker with the competencies of the court.

2 *The Court and Constitutional Litigation*

The Court's different competences and procedures are regulated in a general statute, the *Bundesverfassungsgerichtsgesetz* (BVerfGG[32]), and complemented by the Court's own rules of procedure (*Geschäftsordnung*). The Justices are aided by four judicial clerks each, the majority of whom are recruited from the ranks of the judiciary, though some of them are also young scholars, sometimes working as research assistants at the academic chair of one of the current Justices.[33]

Unlike the US Supreme Court, the German Court is not generally free to accept or refuse particular cases but must accept a case if it fulfills the statutory requirements. Nevertheless, unlike other constitutional proceedings, individual complaints require an explicit admission decision of the Court (sitting in chambers of three Justices) over which it enjoys significant discretion.[34] Though statute (the BVerfGG) stipulates that the Court must admit an individual complaint if the issue is of fundamental constitutional importance or is necessary to realize the plaintiff's constitutional rights in the sense that she would otherwise suffer severe disadvantages, this leaves the Justices de facto considerable discretion about which cases to pick. In individual complaints and some other cases, the Court is also free to charge the plaintiff a fee of up to €2.600 if her

[29] Oliver W. Lembcke, *Über das Ansehen des Bundesverfassungsgerichts. Ansichten und Meinungen in der Öffentlichkeit 1951–2001* (Berliner Wissenschafts-Verlag 2006) 19.

[30] Id.

[31] E.g. the Bavarian government after the crucifix decision, see Georg Vanberg, *The Politics of Constitutional Review in Germany* (Cambridge University Press 2005) 4.

[32] For an English translation see http://www.iuscomp.org/gla/statutes/BVerfGG.htm.

[33] Klaus Schlaich/Stefan Korioth, *Das Bundesverfassungsgericht*, 10th ed (Beck 2015) para. 48.

[34] Schlaich/Korioth (n 33) paras. 258 ff.

or his request is so ludicrous and obviously unfounded that it constitutes abuse (§ 34 BVerfGG), especially if it is brought by a lawyer, which is, however, no requirement (except if there is a public hearing in which case the plaintiff must have legal advice by a lawyer or a law professor).

The Court has in the past 60 years encountered a wide range of subject matters and plaintiffs. Political parties, ordinary citizens and civil society organizations have brought many cases to the Court whose jurisprudence contributed much to the liberalization of German society, especially during the 1950s and the 1960s.[35] The Justices are generally well aware of the political impact of their decisions,[36] but have nevertheless mostly managed to stay outside the fray of party politics.[37] Whether or not they have exceeded their powers remains contested among German scholars – the question is fraught with methodological difficulties since there is no objective measure of when the Court overreaches. Its record of annulments (approximately 10 per year) is in any case comparatively high.[38]

Jurisdiction

The Constitutional Court was from the start equipped with a wide array of powers. Ironically, however, the individual complaint mechanism was initially not listed in the Basic Law itself,[39] even though today more than 95 per cent of its docket consists of individual complaints.[40] Conservatives had feared that the introduction of such a mechanism would endanger the sovereignty of the German state because it would encourage troublemakers to challenge the state on their own accord.[41] Nevertheless, individual complaints were provided for from the start on a statutory basis; a constitutional amendment would follow only in 1969. Another

[35] Christoph Schönberger, "Verwaltungsrecht als konkretisiertes Verfassungsrecht" in Michael Stolleis (ed), *Das Bonner Grundgesetz: altes Recht und neue Verfassung in den ersten Jahrzehnten der Bundesrepublik Deutschland (1949–1969)* (Berliner Wissenschafts-Verlag 2006) 53, 69 ff.

[36] Uwe Kranenpohl, *Hinter dem Schleier des Beratungsgeheimnisses. Der Willensbildungs- und Entscheidungsprozess des Bundesverfassungsgerichts* (VS Verlag für Sozialwissenschaften 2010, 367 ff.

[37] Ibid., 410 ff.

[38] Sascha Kneip, "Rolle und Einfluss des Bundesverfassungsgerichts in international vergleichender Perspektive" (2013) *Zeitschrift für Politik,* 72, 81 S. http://www.bundesverfassungsgericht.de/DE/Verfahren/Jahresstatistiken/2015/gb2015/A-VI.pdf.

[39] Stolleis (n 1) 212.

[40] See official Court statistics for the years 1951–2015, http://www.bundesverfassungsgericht.de/DE/Verfahren/Jahresstatistiken/2015/gb2015/A-I-1.pdf.

[41] Laufer (n 17) 118.

notable if less important feature of Court's jurisdiction is that it allows for abstract review, thus enabling particular office-holders and institutions to challenge the constitutionality of a law independent of a concrete case or controversy. Though this possibility enables political actors to litigate their political differences in the Constitutional Court, in Germany this mechanism has generally been less important than elsewhere (e.g. in France)[42] – possibly as a result of the Court's broad reading of liberty and other rights that enable plaintiffs to claim violations of their rights quite easily.

The Court's jurisdiction is set out in Art. 93 of the Basic Law and complemented by § 13 BVerfGG. According to these, the Court is mainly competent to decide

1. conflicts between the Bund (federation) and the individual states about their respective competences,
2. cases where different constitutional organs disagree about their respective functions and competences,
3. cases where specifically mandated institutions challenge the constitutionality of a norm independent of its concrete application (abstract review),
4. cases where "ordinary" courts believe that a statute that is relevant to the outcome in a particular case is unconstitutional (concrete review),
5. on individual complaints where individuals complain that a particular act or omission of the state (including judicial decisions) violates their constitutional rights,
6. on the prohibition of political parties or the impeachment of the president or Justices,
7. and finally, the validity of previous elections and the loss and acquisition of parliamentary seats.[43]

Case Load and Litigation

The Court's case load is considerable and has steadily risen from around 1.000 cases a year in its first decade to roughly 6.000 new cases a year today.[44] Suggestions to curtail this case load and make it more manageable are frequent, but so far none of these suggestions have resulted in a significant decrease in the number of cases brought. This may have at

[42] See also for a French-German comparison Alec Stone Sweet, *Governing with Judges. Constitutional Politics in Europe* (Oxford University Press 2000) 63.

[43] For details see Schlaich/Korioth (n 33) Part IV, paras. 79 ff.

[44] Schlaich/Korioth (n 33) para. 78.

least partly to do with the fact that the Court is often perceived by the public as a friend of the ordinary citizen,[45] a reputation that might suffer if it declined more cases, most of which would inevitably be individual complaints. Nevertheless, only about 2 per cent of all constitutional complaints are successful; most of them are rejected because they are manifestly unfounded or otherwise inadmissible. This is why only a fraction of the over 200.000 cases[46] are actually published in the Court's official case selection (BVerfGE). It is mainly cases that are argued in full court (the two senates) which bring new developments or constellations/configurations of German constitutional law and therefore merit publication. Important chamber decisions are published in law journals and in a rather new but already closed official case selection (BVerfGK).

Contrary to § 25 BVerfGG, oral argument takes place in only a minority of cases; in individual complaint proceedings, participating constitutional organs but not individual plaintiffs can demand an oral argument.[47] According to its own rules of procedure, the Court may ask other individuals or entities such as experts, municipalities, non-governmental and governmental organizations or state governments to provide expertise and input. Especially in complex cases, the Court often attempts to hear many different voices.[48] It is moreover competent to hear evidence (§ 26 BVerfGG) but rarely does – except where it functions as a court of first instance such as when dealing with the prohibition of a political party.[49] Another difference between constitutional and ordinary litigation is the more flexible handling of remedies. This is a hallmark of many constitutional jurisdictions and while the German Constitutional Court has not perhaps gone as far as jurisdictions such as India or South Africa, it has often granted the legislature time to remedy certain problems within a given period and sometimes gives advice as to the potential remedies the legislature might choose[50] or declares that a statute does not

[45] Werner Patzelt, "Warum verachten die Deutschen ihr Parlament und lieben ihr Verfassungsgericht? – Ergebnisse einer vergleichenden demoskopischen Studie" (2005) 36 *Zeitschrift für Parlamentsfragen* 521.

[46] http://www.bundesverfassungsgericht.de/DE/Verfahren/Jahresstatistiken/2015/gb2015/A-I-1.pdf.

[47] Schlaich/Korioth (n 33) para. 69.

[48] Schlaich/Korioth (n 33) para. 63 ff.

[49] Stefan Brink, "Tatsachengrundlagen verfassungsgerichtlicher Judikate" in Hartmut Rensen and Stefan Brink (eds), *Linien der Rechtsprechung des Bundesverfassungsgerichts* (Walter de Gruyter 2009) 3–33.

[50] E.g., BVerfGE 33, 303, 348, 358; BVerfGE 39, 1, 44; BVerfGE 78, 249 (1988); BVerfGE 123, 267, 433 ff.; BVerfGE 125, 175, 258 ff.

yet violate the constitution, but nevertheless calls on the legislature to remedy the situation, etc.[51]

3 *The Judges*

The Constitutional Court sits in two separate chambers, called senates, each staffed with eight Justices.[52] Initially, the first senate was charged to deal with fundamental rights issues and the second with questions of organizational constitutional law. As more and more individual complaints and thus typically fundamental rights cases started to fill the Court's docket, however, this division of labour was no longer sustainable and the second senate also took over some fundamental rights cases.

Half of the Justices are elected by the Bundestag (federal parliament), the other half by the Bundesrat, the federal chamber. Each appointment must be supported by two-thirds of those voting.[53] Candidates must have formal legal training, German nationality and be 40 years or older.[54] The Justices are appointed for a single, non-renewable term of 12 years and retirement is mandatory after their 68th birthday.[55] Three of the eight seats in each senate are reserved for members of the federal bench (even though all candidates must be qualified to be Justices in terms of their legal training).[56] Currently, in neither senate is the number of previous Justices on the constitutional bench higher than required (three). Most of the current Justices are former professors of (public) law, and it has become rare that Justices are recruited among former politicians, with Peter Müller, a former prime minister of the state Saarland, as the main current exception. Practicing lawyers or other legal practitioners are only in rare cases appointed to the Court.

Generally, the selection process is not particularly transparent. Candidates are typically picked in negotiations behind closed doors. Because of the two-thirds requirement for appointment, however, the two major parties need to agree on their respective candidates. Parties that are not represented in the Bundestag with at least a third of the vote are therefore not able to claim their own seats unless one of the large parties agrees

[51] Schlaich/Korioth (n 33) paras. 370 ff.; Thomas Gawron and Ralf Rogowski, "Implementation of German Federal Constitutional Court Decisions. Judicial Orders and the Federal Legislature" in id. (eds) *Constitutional Courts in Comparison. The U.S. Supreme Court and the German Federal Constitutional Court* (Berghahn 2002) 239 ff.

[52] § 2 BVerfGG. [53] Art. 94 sec. 1 BL, §§ 5, 6 BVerfGG.

[54] § 3 BVerfGG. [55] § 4 BVerfGG. [56] § 2 sec. 3 BVerfGG.

to yield one of its seats to them, which typically happens when there is a coalition government. The need for agreement generally encourages the selection of centrist candidates who do not hold extreme political views.[57] Public debates on the appointees are rare but can happen, as in the case of a previous appointee (Horst Dreier) who had attracted public criticism for his less than absolutist views on the protection of human dignity which were thought to be both too liberal for those worrying about stem cell research etc. and too conservative for some who worried (unfairly) about his stance on torture. His candidature was eventually withdrawn. Generally, however, no public debate takes place, and even though since very recently the entire Bundestag rather than just a committee elects half the candidates, a plenary discussion about the candidates will not take place; instead candidates have closed-door meetings, about which they are not allowed to talk in public, with the different parties in the Bundestag to present themselves to the parliamentarians.

4 *Legal Scholarship and Constitutional Reasoning*

Legal scholarship has been key to the development of German constitutional law. As we note below, judicial decisions frequently refer to and engage with academic literature; sometimes, the Court even adopts constitutional doctrines and concepts developed in the literature.[58] This relevance of German academic writing to the actual development of constitutional jurisprudence has much to do with the doctrinal (*dogmatische*) orientation of German legal scholarship, which is mostly practice-oriented rather than engaging with subjects more removed from judicial practice such as constitutional theory or history. However, while legal scholars seemed to be leading the development of public law in the nineteenth century and during the Weimar Republic, with the courts following, this relationship has been turned upside down in post-war Germany. It has now primarily been the Court that has set the fundamental structures and tests and scholars have largely followed its jurisprudence and filled in the gaps and details – famously prompting Bernard Schlink's critique of German constitutional scholarship as "constitutional court positivism".[59]

57 Schlaich/Korioth (n 33) para. 43.

58 E.g., BVerfGE 67, 100, 138.

59 Bernhard Schlink, "Die Entthronung der Staatsrechtswissenschaft durch die Verfassungsgerichtsbarkeit" (1989) 28 *Der Staat* 161, 163.

B Arguments in Constitutional Reasoning

Unlike some more recent constitutions, such as the South African, the Basic Law does not establish guidelines for its own interpretation. This leaves the Constitutional Court great methodological freedom, which it has been known to use to its advantage. The style of reasoning it has developed over time reflects its own authority as a judicial institution with a broad vision of constitutional law as a roadmap for politics. Its decisions are deductive and technical and yet operate at the same time with broad concepts and open, purposive analysis.[60] The Court's early cases, of course, read somewhat differently. Their reasoning often appears more imprecise and the lack of fully worked out doctrinal structures makes their analysis appear less technical. This is no accident as the Court had only just developed many of the basic doctrinal concepts of German constitutional law in these early decisions: its broad reading of liberty as a residual right,[61] the indirect horizontal effect of constitutional law based on an idea of the Basic Law as an "objective order of values"[62] and last but not least proportionality analysis.[63] Especially the latter two doctrines have since become export models, adopted by many later constitutions and constitutional courts.[64]

Later judgments tend to be longer and more technical as a rule – partly perhaps in response to the technical nature of issues arising in any (post-) industrial society.[65] Moreover, the Court can draw on a much larger reservoir of previous jurisprudence and academic doctrine in setting out the standards to be applied in a given case (the "*Massstäbe*"[66]). By developing these overall standards, as Oliver Lepsius has pointed out, the Court steers and guides legislative action beyond the particular case at hand.[67] It sets out general guidelines that public officials and legislators will typically take into account in framing future statutes and decrees. The Court, however, does not confine itself to the development of these abstract standards, but also often engages in great detail and depth with the regulatory regimes in

60 See Hailbronner (n 10) for a more detailed analysis of the Court's style of jurisprudence (called Value Formalism).

61 BVerfGE 6, 32. 62 BVerfGE 7, 198. 63 BVerfGE 7, 377.

64 See more below in the comparative section.

65 For the complex nature of modern legislation see Hans Schneider, *Gesetzgebung* (3rd ed, C. F. Müller 2002) 273, also mentioning the influence of European law since the 1970s.

66 Oliver Lepsius, "Die maßstabsetzende Gewalt" in Oliver Lepsius, Matthias Jestaedt, Christoph Möllers, and Christoph Schönberger (eds), *Das entgrenzte Gericht. Eine kritische Bilanz nach sechzig Jahren Bundesverfassungsgericht* (Suhrkamp 2011) 157–278.

67 Id.

place, i.e. with ordinary statutory law, and even legislative history. Though the Court has developed particular doctrines that address the scope of the scrutiny of judicial decisions (they must violate specific constitutional law which is typically the case if the courts either completely overlook the constitutional dimension of a case, or misapply constitutional law in a fundamental way),[68] their practical application is a different matter, often leaving little interpretive room to other courts. It is striking then that beyond some conflicts with the Supreme Court in its early years,[69] the Court's relationship with the rest of the judiciary has overall been quite harmonious.

5 *The Structure of Constitutional Arguments*

Following classical nineteenth-century German legal tradition, the Court has generally adopted a syllogistic style of argument. In deductive fashion, it first identifies the relevant norms and construes their meaning and content based on previous scholarship and jurisprudence. These are the so-called *Massstäbe*, the standards to be applied in the following.[70] At the second stage, the Court then applies these standards to the case at hand by comparing the existing rationale of the previous judgment or statute with the standards set out. Within this stage, too, the Court typically proceeds in a strictly deductive fashion where clearing one constitutional hurdle leads to the next. Only rarely, in 5 of our 40 cases, does the Court offer multiple reasons at this most general level of argument. One such case is the famous Aviation Security Act decision[71] (involving the shooting down of an airplane in a 9/11 situation) where the Court did not end its inquiry after finding the statute in question unconstitutional on competence grounds, but proceeded to declare it in addition unconstitutional for its violation of the right to life and human dignity. One reason for this way of proceeding may be that the violation of dignity could not be remedied by constitutional amendment, which was a real option for the coalition government between SPD (social democratic party) and CDU at the time. On a lower level of abstraction the Court engages more frequently in parallel, more discursive arguments – this is especially true

[68] BVerfGE 18, 85, 93 (1964).

[69] These conflicts mostly concerned the disagreement between the Supreme Court and the Constitutional Court about the legal status of civil servants employed during the Nazi Era; see Collings (n 28) for a historical account, see also BVerfGE 3, 58.

[70] See above, in particular Lepsius (n 66).

[71] BVerfGE 115, 118.

within the last step of proportionality analysis (the actual balancing test) where the Court often weighs multiple considerations against the aims pursued.

6 *Types of Arguments in Constitutional Reasoning*

Concurrences and Dissents

Like German courts more broadly, the German Constitutional Court was initially not allowed to publish dissenting and concurring votes. Based on lobbying by the Justices themselves as well as the legal community at large, this changed in 1970; since then the Constitutional Court has been the only German court that may publish dissenting and concurring votes.[72] Even before the formal introduction of separate votes, however, the Justices had started not only to publish the voting patterns within the Court (a contested measure as a matter of law), but also to publish dissenting opinions in two previous cases where the Justices had been equally split (4–4) about the results.[73] In the case on acoustic surveillance, a dissenting vote was retroactively added, since the law providing for separate opinions had been signed just after the decision had been taken.[74] But in spite of the eventual introduction of dissenting and concurring votes, the Justices only rarely publish their opinions separately, i.e. in only 7 per cent of all cases published in the official selection between 1971 and 2015, according to the official court statistics.[75] Most of these votes are dissenting votes; concurring votes are permissible but extremely rare.[76] Perhaps unsurprisingly, among our sample of 40 cases, the percentage of those that come with dissenting or concurring votes are higher than the average with 11 of 34 decisions, hence nearly a third, suggesting that the Justices disagree more often in those cases that are important and hence make new law. Nevertheless, it remains contested among academics and the Justices themselves whether separate votes should be allowed, and

[72] Schlaich/Korioth (n 33) paras. 51 ff.

[73] Hans Spanner, "Zur Praxis des Sondervotums beim Bundesverfassungsgericht" in Gerhard Leibholz et al. (eds), *Menschenwürde und freiheitliche Grundordnung, Festschrift Willi Geiger* (J. C. B. Mohr 1974) 891, 893.

[74] Id., 893 f.

[75] http://www.bundesverfassungsgericht.de/DE/Verfahren/Jahresstatistiken/2015/gb2015/A-I-7.pdf.

[76] Hans J. Lietzmann, "Kontingenz und Geheimnis. Die Veröffentlichung der Sondervoten beim Bundesverfassungsgericht" in Robert Chr. van Ooyen and Martin H. W. Möllers (eds), *Das Bundesverfassungsgericht im politischen System* (VS Verlag für Sozialwissenschaften 2006) 269–82.

they are certainly not encouraged in the Court's practice. However, unlike other courts that strive for unanimous opinions by saying very little (hence following a minimalist approach), the German Court seems at least in its more recent cases (e.g. the decision on the Lisbon treaty[77] or in its *Wunsiedel* decision on Nazi speech[78]) to follow the opposite strategy of saying many, partly inconsistent things.

Disposition

The Court's general record of annulments is, at approximately 10 norms per year, comparatively high, even though less than half of all norms challenged are actually invalidated.[79] For our 40 important cases, the number of invalidations is quite high with 25 of 39 cases invalidating at least part of a law, administrative decree or judicial decision. In addition, like other courts the German Court sometimes follows the established *Marbury v. Madison* pattern of pronouncing broad, ground-breaking principles while still upholding the measure in question. Perhaps the most famous example in this regard is the *Elfes* case[80] where the Court developed its broad reading of Art. 2 of the Basic Law as a residual right of liberty, thus significantly expanding its own jurisdiction in future cases, but did not invalidate the government's travel ban against the German politician Elfes who sought to speak out against Adenauer's policy of integration with Western Europe and the US (*Westintegration*) at an international conference.

General Topic

More than 95 per cent of the Court's current docket represents constitutional complaints and thus typically concerns claims involving the violation of individual rights. Once again, however, among our 40 "leading judgments" the percentage of those concerning organizational divisions and institutional competences is much higher and half of them have at least an organizational law component – unsurprisingly again, since the more important cases are more likely to touch on fundamental questions of state organization. Nevertheless, it has been pointed out by German

[77] BVerfGE 123, 267, see for an excellent analysis Franz Mayer, "Rashomon in Karlsruhe: A reflection on democracy and identity in the European Union: The German Constitutional Court's Lisbon decision and the changing landscape of European constitutionalism" (2011) 9 *International Journal of Constitutional Law* 757–85.

[78] BVerfGE 124, 300.

[79] Kneip (n 38) 81. See, http://www.bundesverfassungsgericht.de/DE/Verfahren/Jahresstatistiken/2015/gb2015/A-VI.pdf.

[80] BVerfGE 6, 32.

scholars that organizational law remains comparatively under-theorized in German legal doctrine, compared to rights.[81]

Concrete Issue

Previous cases have involved all kinds of issues, from the most intimate questions (involving homosexuality or incest) and the most banal ones (horse riding in a forest) to highly technical subjects (surveillance) and high politics including foreign policy and military affairs (the relationship with Eastern Germany in the Basic Treaty case or the role of the federal parliament in German military engagements).

Establishing or Discussing Text

The constitutional text as such is not typically at issue in the Court's decision. The German Basic Law is, like most current constitutions, laid down in one written document. It does, however, in its Art. 140, incorporate five provisions of the Weimar Constitution, dealing with the relationship between state and church. But apart from an abstract reference to human rights in Art. 1 BL, it does not – unlike the French Constitution with its broad reference to the Declaration of the Rights of Man and the Citizen – refer more broadly to other documents. Indeed, it even regulates its own amendment and even replacement. Questions as to which norms enjoy constitutional rank therefore do not typically arise. In our sample, there is only one exception to this general rule: In its decision on life-long imprisonment the Court tried to determine whether the German framers had considered life-long imprisonment constitutional and found that the fact that they had included in the early Basic Law an article providing for life-long imprisonment in cases of treason suggested that they did. In passing, the Court mentioned that it could remain an open question whether this early constitutional provision enjoyed constitutional rank, considering that it was abandoned two years later and had mostly been inserted to provide for criminal sanctions in cases of treason while a new criminal code was still being worked out.[82]

Applicability Discussed

Whether constitutional law is applicable to the case at hand – rather than the issue being a question of politics or ordinary statutory law – is often a hard question. Is every discussion about legislative room for manoeuvre

[81] See esp. Lepsius (n 10). [82] BVerfGE 45, 187.

already one about the applicability of constitutional law? If the answer is yes, the German Court engages frequently with the issue, but if we do not count such discussions, but only more explicit ones about whether constitutional law is applicable at all (rather than how far it reaches), the answer will be different. In our quantitative analysis, we have chosen the narrower standard and accordingly only five out of our 40 cases qualify in this category. Moreover, in only one of those cases (the decision on the Basic Treaty, which put West Germany's relationship with the GDR on a new legal basis) did the Court explicitly consider the non-applicability of constitutional law as a matter of whether the issue at hand was political rather than legal (concluding that it was not).[83] In all four other cases, the Court debates the applicability of constitutional law vis-à-vis other bodies of law, twice with respect to European law,[84] once with respect to ordinary private law (in *Lüth*)[85] and finally with respect to GDR law (as part of the question of whether West German law could be applied in the case).[86]

If we were to take a broader approach to the question of applicability, as engaging with the question of legislative discretion more broadly, our analysis would yield many more cases, especially in our sample of important cases. Almost standardly, the Court emphasizes in many cases that the legislature enjoys broad discretion. It is, however, doubtful how seriously we can take the Court's own pronouncements in this regard – given that it emphasized discretion even in some of its most expansive decisions, such as its decision on the Basic Treaty[87] or the welfare grants (in *Hartz IV*).[88] Nevertheless, other cases suggest that the Court treats politically sensitive issues, such as foreign and economic policy, with particular caution.[89] In particular, the Court has replaced substantive with more procedural forms of constitutional scrutiny in some of these areas,[90] though it remains contested whether this is less intrusive. Unfortunately, evaluating the Court's jurisprudence in this regard is impossible, as a matter of sound methodology, because there are no objective standards to determine whether or not the Court accorded the legislature appropriate discretion.

[83] BVerfGE 36, 1. [84] BVerfGE 123, 267; BVerfGE 89, 155. [85] BVerfGE 7, 198.
[86] BVerfGE 95, 96. [87] BVerfGE 36, 1. [88] BVerfGE 125, 175.
[89] Ingwer Ebsen, *Das Bundesverfassungsgericht als Element gesellschaftlicher Selbstregulierung* (Duncker & Humblot 1985).
[90] See e.g. BVerfGE 129, 124, 183 (2011) – European financial stability; BVerfGE 132, 195, 242, 247 (2012) – European stability mechanism.

Analogies

Explicit analogical reasoning is probably rarer in German constitutional jurisprudence than in other jurisdictions. In our case sample, we have only identified six cases where the Court engages in analogical reasoning. The reasons for this are probably twofold: First, the German Basic Law is still among the more recent constitutions that have tended to regulate more issues than previous ones. Secondly, the Court's broad teleological style of argument often makes analogical reasoning superfluous because the constitutional purpose can already be constructed in a sufficiently broad manner.

Ordinary Meaning of Words of the Constitution or References to the "Wording of the Constitution" in General

Very often the starting point of the Court's interpretive journeys is the specific wording or ordinary meaning of the particular provision or concept, but it is never the end of it.

Harmonizing Arguments – Domestic Law

Since constitutional norms and concepts are often both broad and vague, the Court frequently has to grapple with conflicts that arise between them in their application in individual cases. Such conflicts between different constitutional concepts are often dealt with in proportionality analysis, but they are not confined to it. According to standard constitutional doctrine, developed by Konrad Hesse and building on Smend's integrationist understanding of constitutional law, conflicts between constitutional norms must be reconciled in a process called "practical concordance" which means that both concepts must be realized to the fullest extent possible.[91] Whatever the success of this strategy in any particular case, it is notable that proportionality and "practical concordance" enable the Court to address the diverging public and private interests at play. This at least sometimes seems to enable both parties to a case to reconcile themselves with the Court's reasoning and to enhance the Court's legitimacy as an independent arbiter and its ability to pacify social conflicts by finding constitutional middle ground.[92]

[91] Konrad Hesse, *Grundzüge des Verfassungsrechts der Bundesrepublik Deutschland* (20th ed, C. F. Müller 1999) para 72.

[92] Whether the Court has in fact contributed to the integration of German society must, however, remain unclear; see Ulrich Herbert, "Integration der jungen Republik durch Verfassungsrecht?" in Michael Stolleis (ed), *Das Bonner Grundgesetz. Altes Recht und neue*

Harmonizing Arguments – International Law

Perhaps surprisingly, international law plays a smaller role in the Constitutional Court's jurisprudence than many foreign observers would expect based on the generally good compliance of German institutions with the requirements of international law.[93] Broadly, German law follows a dualist approach that requires incorporation of norms of international law and does not generally accord them constitutional rank, but rather one alongside ordinary statutes (see Art. 59 sec. 2 BL). However, despite their official rank within the German legal hierarchy, international human rights and the jurisprudence of international courts de facto influence the interpretation of German fundamental rights considerably – following the jurisprudence of the Constitutional Court.[94]

Since the 1970s, the law of the European Union and the European Convention on Human Rights have gained particular importance in German constitutional jurisprudence. The relationship with European Union law follows the Court's famous *Solange II*-approach that held that the Court would not subject Union law to the standards of German constitutional rights as long as Union institutions would guarantee a roughly equivalent standard of rights protection.[95] This line of jurisprudence has further been elaborated in a number of contested subsequent decisions (*Maastricht*,[96] *Honeywell*[97]). In *Honeywell*, the Court stated that it will only exercise its own powers of scrutiny if "European institutions have violated their competences in a sufficiently qualified way"; it has also announced to control for violations of Germany's constitutional identity (more below). This requires that the violation of competences should be obvious and the act in question should lead to a structurally significant shift in the competence between European Union and the Member States (BVerfGE 125, 286). Thus, typically, the Court defers to European jurisprudence,[98] and even to international jurisprudence.[99] Nevertheless, more recently

Verfassung in den ersten Jahrzehnten der Bundesrepublik Deutschland (1949–1969) (Berliner Wissenschafts-Verlag 2006) 85–102.

93 For the relative – given the size of its population – low number of pending applications before the European Court of Human Rights, see the latter's Annual Report 2013, 192, http://www.echr.coe.int/Documents/Annual_report_2015_ENG.pdf.

94 Developed in BVerfGE 74, 358 (1987) – presumption of innocence.

95 BVerfGE 73, 339 (1986).

96 BVerfGE 89, 155.

97 BVerfGE 126, 286 (2011).

98 BVerfGE 125, 286 (2011) – Honeywell.

99 BVerfGE 128, 326 (2011) – preventive custody; BVerfGE 120, 180 (2008) – Caroline of Monaco III.

it submitted for the first time a question to the ECJ for a preliminary ruling (Art. 267 TFEU), threatening not to follow the ECJ if its interpretation diverges too far from its own understanding.[100] It has not followed through, however, ultimately accepting the ECJ's interpretation, albeit narrowly.[101]

With regard to the ECtHR, the German Court has taken slightly longer to accept its decisions as binding for German courts – obliging them initially only to take the ECtHR's decisions into account. More recently, however, the Court made it clear that even though courts are not strictly bound to follow the ECtHR's jurisprudence, its decisions nevertheless should weigh heavily in the interpretation of rights and may even justify overturning a previous line of jurisprudence.[102]

Precedents

Though German law does not recognize any formal *stare decisis* rule, the Court's decisions are binding on other courts as a matter of law (§ 31 BVerfGG). It is a more difficult question whether they are binding on the Constitutional Court itself. The majority of commentators, however, answer that question in the negative.[103] Whatever the correct answer, the Court is, in any case, subject to the general constraints of academic scrutiny and public opinion. Moreover, the high regard for legal consistency and certainty in German legal culture means that the Court will seek to avoid openly changing its jurisprudence and will frequently refer to its own previous jurisprudence to bolster its credibility. It is therefore not surprising that every single one of our 40 cases refers to previous jurisprudence. Together with doctrinal writings, precedents have played a major role in shaping the frequently broad constitutional terms and tests such as the proportionality analysis. Precedents structure such tests by providing sub-questions and sub-standards, giving content to hitherto vague concepts and principles. In contrast to common law reasoning, though, precedents are usually not discussed in any detail, neither on points of law nor on the comparability of facts. Instead, the Court typically refers only briefly to complete or abbreviated lines of its own jurisprudence to either demonstrate consistency or spare itself the effort of restating its previously developed standards.

[100] BVerfG, 2 BvR 2728/13, 14.1.2014 – ESM.

[101] BVerfG, 2 BvR 2728/13, 21.6.2016 – ESM.

[102] BVerfGE 128, 326.

[103] See only Schlaich/Korioth (n 33) para 482.

Concept or Principle Not Mentioned in the Text

Over half of the decisions in our sample (26) refer to concepts or principles not mentioned in the text itself. In this, we excluded, however, cases that only apply the most important concept, i.e. proportionality analysis, since we deal with proportionality in a separate section below (even though it technically qualifies here). The remaining high number of decisions mentioning principles or concepts not mentioned in the text is not surprising – the Court's broad teleological style of reasoning lends itself to the development of new rights and principles that are based on reading multiple provisions in the Basic Law together. Similarly to the US in this regard, the German right to privacy represents the classical example of such a penumbral right that builds on the right to liberty and human dignity. The German Court has further developed this right to reflect changing technical and social developments, creating a right to dispose of one's data[104] and a right to the confidentiality and integrity of (one's) communication technology against threats from digital technology.[105] Similarly, the rule of law principle, read together with Art. 2 BL, has been the source of new procedural rights (see below). Other examples are concepts such as openness/comity towards international and European law[106] or the requirement of parliamentary consent in case of military operations.[107]

Arguments from Silence

Arguments from silence are more rare in the Court's jurisprudence, though occasionally they, too, can be found. Nevertheless, they are of no specific significance.

Teleological/Purposive Arguments Referring to the Purpose of a Textual Provision

Teleological/purposive arguments are at the core of German-style constitutional reasoning. Though teleological reasoning is not always explicit, the Court nearly constantly expounds the meaning of particular constitutional provisions in a way that can only be considered to reflect teleological interpretation. Typically, the Court will develop the content of a particular fundamental right with respect to its meaning for individuals and their happiness and freedom or for the working of democracy (e.g. free speech).

[104] BVerfGE 65, 1. [105] BVerfGE 120, 274.

[106] BVerfGE 111, 307, 123, 267. [107] BVerfGE 90, 286.

Teleological/Purposive Arguments Referring to the Purpose of the Constitution-Maker

Historical purposive interpretation is a standard tool of German constitutional jurisprudence, without, however, holding any special status in relation to other methods. Thus, references to the constitutional framers' intentions are typically just arguments among others. Nevertheless, 25 of our 40 decisions engage (mostly extensively) with drafting history. Sometimes, such arguments are hidden within a longer and broader section on historical developments going back sometimes even beyond the Weimar Republic and mentioning the founders of the Basic Law only as part of a larger argument in order to better understand the underlying context and purpose of a particular provision (we counted such broader historical references going beyond the framing of the Basic Law as other types of arguments, however).

Non-legal Arguments

German legal culture emphasizes legal autonomy and courts typically try to stay within the confines of legal argumentation; nevertheless, boundaries may be crossed from time to time. Of course, identifying arguments as non-legal is an enterprise fraught with strong methodological difficulties: it would be easy to disagree about almost any of the cases identified. We have applied here a comparatively high threshold for what counts as a non-legal argument to include only the kind of arguments where the Court does not attempt to link its argument to any established legal principles or methodology. A relatively clear case in this regard is the Court's decision upholding the criminal convictions of former Eastern German politicians responsible for killings at the German Wall, where the Court refers to the "demands of substantive justice" as one reason for its decision.[108] Based on similar considerations, the Constitutional Court denied certain Nazi decisions their legal recognition as such because they deviated from fundamental demands of justice in an extreme manner.[109] Many other cases, however, are much less clear: We have not, for example, considered any broad teleological or historical argument such as references to National Socialism as non-legal, in contrast to some other contributors to this volume. The German purposive style of argumentation, with its use of broad legal concepts such as proportionality, often makes explicit recourse to non legal arguments unnecessary, since most

[108] BVerfGE 95, 96.

[109] BVerfGE 23, 98, 106 (1968) – denaturalization. See also 6, 132, 198 (1957) – Gestapo.

considerations can be framed in terms of constitutional law.[110] We have, however, taken the explicit creation of new fundamental rights in the Court's jurisprudence, such as a right to privacy in BVerfGE 65, 1 and a more specific right to the privacy and integrity of information technology in BVerfGE 120, 274 as an indication for non-legal argumentation. That the number of non-legal arguments altogether remains comparatively high in our sample, with eight cases, no doubt reflects selection-bias again, since more important cases typically involve newer social and political problems where recourse to not strictly legal arguments may be more often helpful.

References to Scholarly Work

German decisions standardly refer to academic work, though they do not always deeply engage with it and sometimes merely use it to bolster their authority. In our sample, we found references to scholarly work in 37 of our 40 cases. Once again, this should not surprise us in the light of the tradition of continental law, of which Germans are part, which views law as a science that can only be dealt with by those with scientific education and professional training. In addition, scholars focus in their work traditionally on doctrinal topics with potential application in the Court's practice. From 2000 on, references to scholarship in the Court's jurisprudence increase dramatically.[111] This rise might on the one hand be a late reaction to the increase of academic positions at university and in scholarly writings, and on the other hand to the fact that an increasing number of Constitutional Court Justices have been recruited from academic ranks in recent years.

References to Foreign Legal Material

Even though more than a third of all decisions in our sample included some sort of reference to foreign legal material, the Court almost never

[110] Bernhard Schlink, "Hercules in Germany?" (2003) 1 *International Journal of Constitutional Law* 610, 615. See, e.g., BVerfGE 45, 187, 246 (1977) – life penalty, for the concept of the substantial rule of law; BVerfGE 33, 303, 334 ff., for the notion of social justice in equality arguments. But see also BVerfGE 123, 267, 344 (2009) – Lissabon, where the court recognizes a "universal foundation" of the Basic Law in the so called eternity clause (Art. 79 sec. 3 BL) that may not be touched upon by positive law. The court also stresses the specific openness of the constitution and its provisions, BVerfGE 62, 1, 39, 45 (1982) – dissolution of parliament; BVerfGE 74, 51, 57 (1986) – grounds of persecution after flight.

[111] 1950s: appr. 3; 1960s: appr. 2; 1970s: appr. 3; 1980s: appr. 4; 1990s: appr. 3; 2000s: appr. 11 references per decision in the official case selection (the numbers are based on Stefan Martini's PhD research, data is on file with the authors).

engages with any of this material in any detail or depth. Instead, it merely mentions the foreign legal source in passing without drawing on it substantively for its own argument. There are a few exceptions, though: In the first abortion law case of 1975 the majority rejected liberal decisions by other highest courts (e.g., *Roe v. Wade*) on the same subject by alluding to the singularity of Germany's Nazi past forbidding a liberal approach on prenatal life. The dissenting opinion by Rupp-v. Brünneck and Simon in turn sharply argued against the majority, drawing not only on those foreign decisions, but also more broadly the experience of other states. Sometimes, the Court takes into consideration how similar regulation had fared in other countries: In the pharmacies judgment, for example, it stated that it could not ignore the fact that the unrestricted establishment of pharmacies in comparable states did not lead to detrimental health consequences.[112] The foreign law argument is – as elsewhere – never controlling. Yet, its use shows that, mostly in important cases, the Court's decisions are based on a broad set of information and arguments. The ratio of decisions referring to foreign law in our sample is much higher than in the official case selection, where only roughly 5 per cent of all decisions include some sort of comparative references.[113] Compared to jurisdictions like Namibia, South Africa or Australia, these numbers are low.[114] The relative lack of engagement with foreign sources by the German Federal Constitutional Court may partly stem from the fact that German legal doctrine often provides quite a comprehensive framework of analysis that has few entry points for comparative reasoning. Nevertheless, one can see that since 2000 the numbers have risen significantly – probably due to stronger links between (especially European) legal orders and the more open attitudes of a new generation of Justices.

Other Methods/Arguments

Unsurprisingly, the Court does not take its decisions in isolation from reality. In particular, it takes the implementation of statutes and the effects of its jurisprudence into consideration.[115] A number of other standard

112 BVerfGE 7, 377, 415.

113 Stefan Martini, Vergleichende Verfassungsrechtsprechung (dissertation, Kiel University, to be published 2017).

114 Tania Groppi and Marie-Claire Ponthoreau, "Conclusion. The Use of Foreign Precedents by Constitutional Justices: A Limited Practice, an Uncertain Future" in id. (eds), *The Use of Foreign Precedents by Constitutional Justices* (Hart 2013) 411 ff.

115 See the famous dissent of Grimm in BVerfGE 80, 137, 168 ff. (1989) – Horse Riding in the Woods. From our sample BVerfGE 33, 303, 356; 47, 46, 76; 118, 277, 381; BVerfGE 132, 1, para. 87.

argumentative patterns surface regularly in the Court's jurisprudence. Perhaps the most notable one is the frequent analysis of constitutional tradition, i.e. constitutional history before 1933. Rarely, the Court will also refer to current political practice (*Verfassungspraxis*) for interpretive guidance,[116] though it has stressed that such practice must itself be in accordance with the constitution as determined by the Court.[117] Decisions also frequently refer to broader principles distilled from a holistic analysis of the Basic Law; beyond those mentioned below (under key concepts), the Court invokes, for example, the idea of humanity (*Menschenbild*) incorporated in the Basic Law, stressing in particular that human beings do not exist in isolation from one another.[118]

7 *The Weight of Arguments*

In general, teleological arguments represent probably the most widely used type of argument. Important other types of arguments are particularly those from history and the framers' intent, as well as systematic arguments that set out to harmonize different constitutional provisions. This reflects that German Justices and legal scholars do not usually pick one particular method as more appropriate than others – rather, there is common agreement that all these methods are important to determine the right result in a given case, but one cannot determine independently of the facts at hand which method should carry more weight in a given case.

8 *Judicial Candour and Judicial Rhetoric*

Unlike some of its counterparts in Common Law countries and in spite of its tendency towards broad purposive arguments, German constitutional jurisprudence still makes for a comparatively dry and technical read. The Court's style of reasoning emphasizes the scientific aspect of legal interpretation as distinct from political speech. Judicial opinions hence typically do not contain any "subjective" or openly rhetorical elements such as emotional appeals. This only changes sometimes in dissenting votes where the Justices feel freer to express their personal views.

[116] See e.g. BVerfGE 62, 1; BVerfGE 65, 1. [117] BVerfGE 91, 148.

[118] BVerfGE 33, 303, 334 ff. Seminal BVerfGE 4, 7, 15 ff. (1954). Christian Bumke, 'Der gesellschaftliche Grundkonsens im Spiegel der Rechtsprechung des Bundesverfassungsgerichts' in Gunnar Folke Schuppert and Christian Bumke (eds), *Bundesverfassungsgericht und gesellschaftlicher Grundkonsens* (Nomos 2000) 197.

How candid the Justices are in their jurisprudence remains unclear. Though there have been studies of the Court's internal workings, which have involved interviews with the Justices,[119] the question has not really been researched in a more systematic fashion. The available literature suggests that the Justices are mostly aware of the political context they operate in and take public and elite opinions into account in their decision-making practice,[120] even though this kind of consideration is not usually apparent in the Court's writings. This may be partly because the Justices would think such considerations improper to admit, but partly also because established doctrine lends itself even less to this kind of argument than elsewhere. Since the Court only very rarely engages in explicit discussions of its own role vis-à-vis the political branches, Justices who seek to account for political and cultural trends by now have a hard time framing this kind of argument.[121] When it comes to assessing the weight of the Justices' own political beliefs for the Court's jurisprudence, the issue seems contested. Especially those Justices who come from a more political background have often sought to ensure that their colleagues perceive them as impartial arbiters, frequently taking decisions against the interests of their own parties. In the press, talk about a "black" (majority CDU nominees) and a "red" (majority SPD nominees) senate has largely faded since the 1960s.[122] Nevertheless, there have also been more recent studies that link Justices' voting pattern to their political background.[123]

9 *Length, Dissenting and Concurring Opinions*

German decisions are generally of medium length, falling somewhere between their Indian colleagues with hundreds of pages and the French *Conseil Constitutionnel.* In the official case selection of the Court, the average length rises slowly from 10 to 20 pages between the 1950s and the 1990s. From 2000 on, decisions have become considerably longer with an average length of over 30 pages.[124] Unsurprisingly, in our sample, the average length is significantly higher, at 68 pages. The longest opinions in our sample seem to be those that concern basic principles and concepts of

[119] Especially Kranenpohl (n 36). [120] Id.

[121] Hailbronner (n 10). [122] Collings (n 28) 48.

[123] Christoph Hönnige, "The Electoral Connection: How the Selection of the Pivotal Judge Affects Oppositional Success at European Constitutional Courts" (2009) 35.2 *West European Politics* 963.

[124] 1950s: 11,77; 1960s: 10,78; 1970s: 15,18; 1980s: 16,99; 1990s: 19,45; 2001–2011: 31,92 (numbers until volume 129). One page comprises approximately 2.000 characters.

the German state such as the prohibition of the Communist party in 1956, which is sometimes considered one of the best short introductions to the history of the socialist and communist movements and thought available in German. Another long judgment is the court's nearly 200-page-long decision on the Lisbon treaty, which goes into great detail about the basic principles and structures of German statehood and democracy.[125] Especially in these longer cases, considerable parts of the Court's reasoning will not be relevant to the outcome of the case. Scholars have therefore sometimes criticized the Court's tendency to superfluous conceptual reasoning.[126] Indeed, decisions frequently engage with political theory and abstract principles in the style of a textbook on constitutional law.[127] In a number of cases, the Court includes obiter dicta in which the Court tries to make broader points, which it considers to be of general importance.[128] As noted previously, about a third of our sample cases come with dissenting opinions, which is considerably more than the average rate of 7 per cent.

10 Framing of Constitutional Issues

Most cases will be framed in terms of individual rights. This is primarily a consequence of (1) the breadth of German fundamental rights doctrine and (2) the fact that it allows institutional and organizational constitutional questions to be addressed within the rights analysis itself. German rights analysis first sets out to determine the scope of a right in relation to the asserted violation, then, secondly, investigates whether the right can be limited and has been limited in the case in question and finally whether this limitation can be justified. Because the hard questions are typically dealt with in the justification analysis (i.e. in the last step), the Court has been able to take a generous approach to the earlier stages of the inquiry, i.e. when determining the scope of constitutional rights. A good example for this generous approach has been its jurisprudence on voting rights in the context of European integration where it argued that the right to vote entails a right to vote for someone who retains sufficient

125 BVerfGE 123, 267 (2009) – Lisbon.

126 Lepsius (n 66).

127 BVerfGE 123, 267 (2009) – Lisbon.

128 E.g., recently BVerfGE 128, 226, 248, criticized by Schluckebier dissenting, id., 275. Indirectly, through citing an Israeli Supreme Court judgment BVerfGE 130, 76, 121 (2012). The qualification as obiter can be difficult, see the controversy between BVerfGE 96, 375, 404, and BVerfGE 96, 409.

policy-making power to make the vote meaningful.[129] Violations of the prescribed law-making process or competences can then be raised in the justifications analysis since rights infringements are only justified if they have a sufficient *constitutional* basis in law. This in turn triggers a review of the formal constitutionality of the legal basis in question, including procedural and competence requirements. Moreover, not only are rights generally broadly defined in their scope, but the Court has also read the Basic Law's Art. 2 as a residual right of liberty, entailing the freedom to do or not to do whatever one pleases.[130] Nearly all state action will, therefore, qualify as a potential infringement of Art. 2 GG and thus open the door to a justifications analysis that includes review of procedural and competence requirements.

11 Key Concepts

Rule of Law

The German concept of the *Rechtsstaat* is somewhat distinct from the rule of law, which is often used in a broader sense to differentiate, for example, law and politics (see e.g. US report). In German constitutional jurisprudence, the *Rechtsstaat* is typically employed as a basis for procedural rights and safeguards and as a foundation for a number of sub-concepts that apply mostly to the legislative process, such as the requirement that statutes be sufficiently clear or that the legislature itself take decisions on "essential" issues rather than delegating them to the administration (*Wesentlichkeitsgebot*).[131] Especially the non-delegation doctrine, which also rests on the concept of democracy, has proved important in a number of constitutional decisions. Moreover, the *Rechtstaat* principle together with fundamental rights is understood to provide the doctrinal basis for the Court's jurisdiction when ordinary courts apply international law, even though there is no explicit basis for this in the Basic Law.[132]

Democracy

Democracy features as a regular theme in 26 of our 40 cases, dealing with both organizational questions and individual rights. Like the *Rechtsstaat*, democracy provides an important background concept that is often

[129] See e.g. BVerfGE 123, 267; 89, 155. [130] See above, Elfes, BVerfGE 6, 32.

[131] Katharina Sobota, *Das Prinzip Rechtsstaat. Verfassungs- und verwaltungsrechtliche Aspekte* (Mohr Siebeck 1997); Philip Kunig, *Das Rechtsstaatsprinzip* (Mohr Siebeck 1986).

[132] BVerfGE 111, 307.

mentioned but is rarely itself the controlling standard at hand. Instead, the Court typically draws on democracy to underline the importance of more specific rights such as freedom of speech, freedom of assembly or parliamentary competences. In such cases, drawing on the broad notion of democracy increases the Court's interpretive discretion even further. This can be seen, for example, in its decision on European integration where the Court argued that five core areas of policy-making could not be transferred to the European Union, based on the argument that voting rights served to protect national self-determination, resting in turn on democracy.[133] More generally, the Court has taken to portraying itself as the guardian of rather strictly and conservatively understood minimum democratic requirements (see more below).[134]

Sovereignty

Sovereignty – largely understood as self-preservation of statehood and self-determination of the national collectivity in German constitutional thinking – mainly only plays a role with regard to foreign relations and in particular when the government binds itself in treaties with other nations. As such, sovereignty places limits on what the government may promise others – in the Basic Treaty decision it ensured that the government would not accept the division of Germany into two separate states as a matter of law, and in the decision on European integration it limited the transfer of policy competence to the European Union (see above).[135] In both cases, the loss of sovereignty is a legal interest protected by the Court. As such, it is in the European cases closely related to and conflicting with conceptions of (open) statehood pervasive in its jurisprudence.

One can increasingly notice a semantic supplement in the jurisprudence of the court, though, introducing the concept of constitutional identity.[136] It comprises the core contents of the Basic Law that may not be dismissed either by constitutional amendments or by measures of transnational integration, thus fleshing out the limits of sovereign statehood. This signals a slight shift in constitutional thinking as the – typically German –

[133] BVerfGE 123, 267, 359. [134] BVerfGE 130, 76, 123 ff.

[135] BVerfGE 36, 1; 89, 155; 123, 267.

[136] Most prominently in the Lisbon judgment of 2009, BVerfGE 123, 267, 344; more limited and less explicit already in Solange I of 1974, BVerfGE 37, 271, 280. Cf. Monika Polzin, "Irrungen und Wirrungen um den Pouvoir Constituant. Die Entwicklung des Konzepts der Verfassungsidentität im deutschen Verfassungsrecht seit 1871" (2014) 53 *Der Staat* 61, for traces of this concept in preceding German scholarship.

concentration on pre-constitutional statehood is mitigated with the help of additional discrete, though unwritten, constitutional principles.[137]

State Form (Republic, Monarchy)

Germany's state form as a republic does not feature in the Court's jurisprudence – this is not surprising since Germany's identity as a republic is mainly seen as a negative identity: preventing the reestablishment of monarchy.[138]

Government Form (Parliamentary, Presidential)

The Court regularly invokes government form in its jurisprudence in passing (in 14 of 40 decisions), though usually not as a decisive argument. Nevertheless, the Court quite often refers to the German model of representative parliamentary democracy to back up other arguments.[139] Parliamentary democracy may serve as a supporting argument (together with the rule of law) for strengthening parliamentary powers vis-à-vis the government[140] as well of the rights and functions of individual MPs.[141] It also serves as a basis for the non-delegation doctrine (see above).[142]

Secularism (Separation of Church and State)

The Court has developed a subtle and liberal doctrine on religious issues and the neutrality of the state in religious matters; in our sample only four cases deal with secularism, in two of which secularism was the central issue. The German separation of church and state is not absolute – the state for example collects tax on behalf of certain officially recognized religious communities, but it has to refrain from unequal treatment.[143]

Nation

Although the Court regularly mentions the concept of "nation", "people" or "state nation" (10 times in our sample), its doctrinal value as an

[137] But see Polzin (n 135) 92, 94, who locates the background of the concept, the concept of pouvoir constituant, somewhat beyond the constitution.

[138] See BVerfG, Neue Juristische Wochenschrift 2004, 2008, 2011.

[139] In the Lisbon treaty decision, presidential systems are also included in the comparative discussion of basic legitimacy requirements of representative democratic political systems, BVerfGE 123, 267, 342 f., 366 f. (2009) – Lisbon.

[140] BVerfGE 49, 89, 126; 67, 100, 130, 136, 144; 90, 286, 378.

[141] BVerfGE 118, 277, 324, 326, 353. [142] BVerfGE 33, 303, 346.

[143] BVerfGE 93, 1, 17; 108, 282, 299 f. Stephan Mückl, "Relationship between State and Church – Church Law versus Religious Constitutional Law" in Pünder et al. (eds), *Debates in German Public Law* (Bloomsbury 2014) 159–80.

argument beyond Art. 116 BL regulating German citizenship/nationality is limited. Only rarely does it serve as an autonomous argument. In the decision on the Basic Treaty between the Federal Republic of Germany and the German Democratic Republic, the Court emphasized that the concept of citizenship in the Basic Law was not confined to the people within the boundaries of West Germany.[144] Most often, nation or nationality is mentioned in the context of democratic legitimacy: In particular, the Court has linked the concept of "the people" as the democratic sovereign (Art. 20 sec. 2 BL) to German nationality,[145] thus blocking state attempts to grant foreigners voting rights in municipal elections.[146] Apart from that, the Court draws on "the people" to question the legitimacy of the European institutions as a matter both of only remote direct legitimation and the supposed lack of a "European people".

Federalism

Federalism represents a key feature of German statehood that is deeply entrenched against amendments by Art. 79 BL. Conflicts involving federalism typically arise when states and the federal government disagree about the allocation of competences between them.[147] Moreover, even when the federal government is competent to legislate, the German Bundesrat, the representation of states, may still have to participate and consent. In our sample of cases, issues involving federalism appear in 25 per cent of all cases. This number is perhaps lower than one might expect – it is due to the primacy of federal law (see only Art. 31 BL), and the wide scope of federal fundamental rights that control state matters as well. Furthermore, the guarantee of federalism in Art. 20 sec. 1 BL has only limited legal effect, mostly procedural in nature,[148] such as a duty of federal comity (*Bundestreue*) that commits both the federal state and the individual states to cooperate in fulfilling their tasks.[149] The states (*Länder*) moreover owe each other and the federation limited financial solidarity, compelling a certain degree of financial redistribution between them.[150]

144 BVerfGE 36, 1, 30 ff. 145 BVerfGE 83, 37, 50 ff.

146 Art. 28 sec. 1 BL resolved this issue (only) for EU citizens.

147 BVerfGE 12, 205; BVerfGE 108, 282, 302; BVerfGE 115, 118; 132, 1, overturning the former.

148 Grzeszick, in: Maunz/Dürig, GG (December 2014), Art. 20 margin no. 88 ff.

149 See BVerfGE 12, 205. For the context of European integration see BVerfGE 131, 152 (2012). Christian Waldhoff, "Federalism – Cooperative Federalism versus Competitive Federalism" in Pünder et al. (n 143) 117–30.

150 BVerfGE 1, 117 (1952); BVerfGE 72, 330 (1986); 86, 148 (1991); 101, 158 (1999); 116, 327 (2006).

Proportionality (or Means-and-Ends)

Proportionality is nearly omnipresent in German rights' jurisprudence. In spite of recurring criticism by some German scholars, most German lawyers treat it – unlike their US counterparts – as just another legal concept.[151]

Proportionality is part of the last step of rights analysis that asks if the infringement can be justified. Justification requires that both the legal basis for the infringement and its potential application are themselves constitutional and therefore that they only limit rights in a proportional manner. German proportionality analysis proceeds in four consecutive steps that are, at least analytically, clearly distinct. If a limitation fails one of the first hurdles, the analysis is not continued, i.e. there is no general free-floating balancing where all considerations are considered simultaneously as constitutional arguments as for example in South Africa. German proportionality is quite rigorous in this respect.

The first step involves asking whether the limitation of a right serves a "legitimate purpose", which depends on the limitations provided for in the text of the Basic Law itself, but is generally interpreted generously by the Court. The second step requires the court to determine if the measure prescribed by the parliament or taken by the administration is at all "suitable" to reach its goal. Again, as one may imagine, most laws or administrative acts will pass this threshold, which does not yet include a comparison between different means. The third step then contains the least-restrictive means test. The question is thus whether the end pursued could with the same efficiency have been achieved by a more lenient, i.e. less rights-infringing method. Finally, in a last step called balancing or proportionality in the narrow sense, the test requires the court to balance the overall weight of the right's violation with the good achieved by it and determine if it is, on the whole, proportional. Though the two last steps have both proved to have considerable bite in the Court's practice, it is the balancing analysis itself that leads to the most invalidations.[152] Once again, this is from a comparative perspective perhaps surprising since it is the last balancing stage that seems elsewhere to be thought the most problematic due to its "political" aspect (e.g., in Canada whose Supreme Court has – though without acknowledging it – adopted German proportionality analysis).[153]

151 Or Bassok, "The Supreme Court's New Source of Legitimacy" (2013) 16 *University of Pennsylvania Journal of Constitutional Law* 153, 174.

152 Dieter Grimm, "Proportionality in Canadian and German Constitutional Jurisprudence" (2007) 57 *University of Toronto Law Journal* 383, 389.

153 Id.

Wesensgehalt, or Core of Constitutional Rights or Competences?

The Basic Law's requirement that rights limitations may not violate the *Wesensgehalt*/core of a constitutional right (Art. 19 sec. 2 BL) does not play a large role in the Court's jurisprudence. While decisions sometimes invoke this clause, the Court has only once found a violation of this inner core.[154] Nevertheless, the principle is mentioned a number of times in our sample. In the first abortion decision, the Court even took the core of the right to life into account as a supporting argument when it decided on the principled priority of the right of the foetus over the personality rights of the mother.[155] In only 2 of the 40 decisions, however, is the core guarantee actually used as an independent test.[156] Moreover, the concept is invoked in some way in a surprisingly large total of 13 of 40, considering that the concept is considered by academic commentators to be of little practical relevance.[157] If it is almost never raised successfully, this stems from the fact that proportionality analysis requires basically the same kind of consideration, making the core guarantee superfluous: Disproportionate rights limitations are already unconstitutional and end the justifications analysis, so the core guarantee does not matter anymore; if limitations are in contrast proportional, Art. 19 sec. 2 BL cannot be violated.[158] At times, the Court nevertheless mentions that it is ready and able to guard the core of constitutional rights.[159]

In its jurisprudence on European integration, the Court has moreover read Art. 79 sec. 3 BL to protect a core of constitutional identity against transfers of competences to the European Union.[160] Though it is unclear where this core begins and ends, it has never prevented any loss or gain of competencies to date. Finally, the Court accepted in another case that preliminary stages of deliberation within the cabinet may remain confidential, protecting a "core of executive responsibility".[161]

Human Dignity

The Court frequently mentions human dignity, but the concept only rarely has any purchase of its own. Typically it serves as a supporting

[154] BVerfGE 22, 180, 219, Barbara Remmert, in Maunz/Dürig, Grundgesetz (May 2008), Art. 19 Abs. 2, margin no. 38; Horst Dreier, in id. (ed), Grundgesetz. Kommentar (3rd ed, Mohr Siebeck 2013), Art. 19 II margin no. 8 fn. 29.

[155] BVerfGE 39, 1, 43 – first abortion case.

[156] BVerfGE 45, 187, 270; 115, 118, 165.

[157] Remmert (n 154) Art. 19 Abs. 2, margin no. 47.

[158] BVerfGE 58, 300, 348.

[159] BVerfGE 89, 155, 174 f. (1993) – Maastricht. See also BVerfGE 7, 377, 411; 33, 303, 353.

[160] BVerfGE 123, 267.

[161] BVerfGE 67, 100. Cf. also BVerfGE 131, 152 (2012).

argument in the balancing of other individual rights, which are linked to dignity in order to emphasize their importance in the balancing process. In this vein, though it was from a doctrinal stance superfluous, the Court mentioned in the Lisbon judgment that dignity provides the basis for the right to vote.[162] Nevertheless, there are a number of decisions where human dignity plays a more important role – these are the decision on life imprisonment,[163] on abortion,[164] on the Aviation Security Act[165] and last but not least on welfare grants.[166] Dignity moreover serves as a motor for creating new privacy rights such as the right to self-determination over one's private data (see above).

Equality

Equality arguments feature regularly in our case selection (15 of 40). Considering the breadth of all equality clauses in the Basic Law and the (unresolved) complexity of doctrinal sub-concepts under the heading of equality, this number nevertheless does not convey the significance of equality in the Court's jurisprudence, e.g., in tax law requirements. The jurisprudence of the Court step by step heightened the standards for justification of unequal treatment, from an arbitrariness test (close to Wednesbury reasonableness) to what resembles a proportionality test,[167] leading to a convergence of liberties and equality rights.

The Court moreover emphasizes that political parties must enjoy broadly equal opportunity to participate in elections and win votes[168] and that votes must count equally within the German mixed electoral system, putting a heavy onus on election thresholds.[169]

Basic Procedural Rights

The Federal Constitutional Court frequently invokes basic procedural rights (in 15 of the 40 selected cases), but decisions rarely center on them. Partly, this reflects the considerable work done by the Court in the past in enforcing such rights strictly (especially the right to be heard, Art. 103

[162] BVerfGE 123, 267, 341 (2009). One consequence, nevertheless, of this doctrinal statement is its twofolded protection from Europeanization (one in Art. 20, one in Art. 1 BL – through Art. 23 sec. 1, 79 sec. 3).

[163] BVerfGE 45, 187.

[164] BVerfGE 39, 1; 88, 203.

[165] BVerfGE 115, 118.

[166] E.g. BVerfGE 125, 175; BVerfGE 132, 134.

[167] See the critique on general rationality requirements of legislation inside the court in this specific decision BVerfGE 121, 317, 378 ff. (2008) – ban on smoking.

[168] See, e.g., BVerfGE 20, 56.

[169] See, e.g. for EU elections BVerfGE 129, 300.

sec. 1 BL). By now, the Court has knitted a tight web of constitutional procedural requirements safeguarding procedural rights. In addition to the existing rights, it has created additional procedural rights such as a right to a fair trial[170] and a principle of legitimate expectations.[171] Furthermore, the Court argues that the state's obligation to protect fundamental rights often entails a duty to guarantee certain procedural and organizational requirements for the exercise of such rights.[172]

Freedom of Expression

Roughly a third of our selected decisions mention freedom of expression, making it an important strand in the Court's human rights jurisprudence. The Court has especially stressed the function of freedom of expression for the political process and the formation of public opinion[173] and has overall taken a robust approach to its protection.[174] This liberal approach also characterizes many of the Court's decisions in related areas such as freedom of artistic expression and freedom of assembly – in one case, for example, the Court asked a lower court to reconsider the criminal conviction of an artist who had produced a collage showing a man urinating on the German flag.[175] Although the Court has upheld the criminalization of certain kinds of Nazi speech as in the *Wunsiedel* case,[176] it is important to point out that these exceptions generally have to be read narrowly.

Privacy Rights

Privacy rights are another important prong in the Court's human rights jurisprudence. Lacking an explicit textual basis for a right to privacy, the Court has been especially expansive in this field, developing a number of different strong privacy rights. This jurisprudence starts from the protection of an individual's private sphere (including her reputation) against encroachments from third parties such as the media[177] as well as the state itself. It has moreover been further developed to reflect new threats based on technological innovations, such as a right against online searches –

[170] BVerfGE 57, 250, 274 f. (1981). [171] BVerfGE 13, 261, 271 (1961).

[172] BVerfGE 35, 202 (1973); 53, 30 (1979).

[173] BVerfGE 5, 85, 134 f.; 7, 198, 208; 12, 205, 260. Recently BVerfGE 123, 267, 341 f. Links to institutions such as free press, radio, television etc. are also established, see BVerfGE 35, 202, 221 f.

[174] See BVerfGE 132, 1, Gaier dissenting (para 85): "In the shadow of a military arsenal, free speech cannot prosper." ("Im Schatten eines Arsenals militärischer Waffen kann freie Meinungsäußerung schwerlich gedeihen.")

[175] BVerfGE 81, 278. [176] BVerfGE 124, 300. [177] BVerfGE 6, 32; 34, 269.

always striving to balance individual interests with the state's need to acquire information for multiple purposes.[178]

Further Fundamental Rights

Another important right in the Court's jurisprudence has been the freedom of assembly.[179] The Court emphasizes that especially in strict representative systems, the freedom of assembly is important to enable citizens to participate in the formation of public opinion.[180] Other important rights are personal freedom,[181] the protection of property[182] and what Oliver Lepsius has called *the* German paradigm right, the freedom of profession.[183]

C Comparative Perspective

As previously noted, a number of the key concepts of German constitutionalism have been exported to other jurisdictions. Especially human dignity and proportionality analysis have been adopted in a wide range of jurisdictions, from Europe to Canada to South Africa and elsewhere. As is inevitable with constitutional borrowing, these concepts are elsewhere often applied and understood in quite a different way.[184] This reflects, of course, no more than the fact that these concepts are not universal in their application and must be fitted within the very different political and cultural environments they are exported to. If there is something remarkable about the German way of doing things, it might be first and foremost the level of analysis that has gone into the theorization and application of some of these concepts in recent decades. Though some scholars question the ability of these concepts to actually constrain constitutional interpretation (see especially the recurring criticism of proportionality analysis),[185] the quality of the reasoning in German decisions is still

178 BVerfGE 65, 1; 109, 279; 120, 274. 179 BVerfGE 69, 315, 344 ff.

180 BVerfGE 69, 315, 347. 181 BVerfGE 45, 187. 182 BVerfGE 58, 300.

183 BVerfGE 7, 377; Oliver Lepsius, "Die Religionsfreiheit als Minderheitenrecht in Deutschland, Frankreich und den USA" (2006) 34.3 *Leviathan* 321.

184 See e.g. with respect to proportionality Grimm (n 152) for Canada and for South Africa Kevin Iles, "A Fresh Look at Limitations: Unpacking Section 36 A" (2007) *South African Journal on Human Rights* 23; for the many meanings of dignity see e.g. Christopher McCrudden, "Human Dignity and Judicial Interpretation of Human Rights" (2008) 19 *European Journal of International Law* 655.

185 For many see Bernhard Schlink, *Abwägung im Verfassungsrecht* (Duncker & Humblot 1976) or more recently Benjamin Rusteberg, *Der grundrechtliche Gewährleistungsgehalt*, Mohr Siebeck 2009).

comparatively high – decisions are typically complex and nuanced and rarely reek of direct party political influence or pure personal ideology of the Justices. Partly, of course, this is a matter of presentation. The pressure to avoid dissents and if possible come to unanimous decisions enforces the suppression of personal writing styles and opinions, which may nevertheless shape the outcome considerably. Partly, however, the comparative length (6–7 years on average) and rigour of German legal education with its two state exams on a wide range of fixed subjects and subsequent two-year training as law clerks in hierarchical institutions may also, in fact, contribute to the development of more strongly homogenized professional personalities that facilitate the suppression of individual opinions and preferences.

Appendix: 40 Leading Cases

1. KPD-Verbot, BVerfGE 5, 85
2. BVerfGE 6, 32
3. Lueth, BVerfge 7, 198
4. BVerfGE 7, 377
5. Rundfunkentscheidung, BVerfGE 12, 205
6. BVerfGE 20, 56
7. Abhörurteil, BVerfGE 30,1
8. BVerfGE 33, 303
9. Soraya, BVerfGE 34, 269
10. BVerfGE 35, 202
11. Grundlagenvertrag, BVerfGE 36, 1
12. BVerfGE 39, 1
13. Lebenslange Freiheitsstrafe, BVerfGE 45, 187
14. BVerfGE 47, 46
15. Kalkar I, BVerfGE 49, 89
16. BVerfGE 50, 290
17. Nassauskiesung, BVerfGE 58, 300
18. BVerfGE 62, 1
19. Volkszählung, BVerfGE 65, 1
20. BVerfGE 67, 100
21. Brokdorf, BVerfGE 69, 315
22. BVerfGE 80, 188
23. Ausländerwahlrecht I, BVerfGE 83, 37
24. BVerfGE 89, 155
25. Out-of-Area Auslandseinsätze, BVerfGE 90, 286

26. BVerfGE 93, 1
27. Mauerschützen, BVerfGE 95, 96
28. BVerfGE 106, 310
29. Wasserverband Lippe, BVerfGE 107, 59
30. BVerfGE 108, 282
31. Grosser Lauschangriff, BVerfGE 109, 279
32. BVerfGE 111, 307
33. Luftsicherheitsgesetz, BVerfGE 115, 118
34. BVerfGE 118, 277
35. Online-Durchsuchung, BVerfGE 120, 274
36. BVerfGE 123, 267
37. Wunsiedel, BVerfGE 124, 300
38. BVerfGE 128, 226
39. Privatisierung des Massregelvollzugs, BVerfGE 130, 76
40. BVerfGE 132, 1

10

The Constitutional Court of Hungary

ANDRÁS JAKAB AND JOHANNA FRÖHLICH

The present chapter aims to discover the features of judicial reasoning in the Hungarian Constitutional Court (HCC).[1] The nature of the HCC has changed very recently (over several steps, beginning November 2010). The changes included the introduction of a German-style constitutional complaint instead of the *actio popularis* and the curtailing of the competences of the HCC concerning tax and financial statutes, as well as changes to the political culture surrounding the HCC. Though the sample judgments underlying the main analysis were chosen from between 1990 and 2010, the last part of the chapter reflects on the constitutional changes which resulted in the new Hungarian Fundamental Law[2] that came into force in 2012.

A Legal, Political, Institutional and Academic Context

The Constitution was practically rewritten in 1989–90, but some parts and provisions continued to be the legacy of socialism. The first HCC (led by László Sólyom, 1990–8, during socialism a professor of private law) had to use this basis to build up the conceptual system (and case-law) of modern Hungarian constitutionalism (called the "invisible constitution", e.g. in Dec. 23/1990 (X.31) AB). It successfully managed to do so, but in the literature it was often accused of "activism" (meaning making arbitrary decisions which could not be anticipated from the text). The

[1] We are most grateful to Orsolya Salát for her help in analysing the 40 leading cases and for many useful suggestions and remarks; to Botond Bitskey for statistics about the case law of the HCC; further to Armin von Bogdandy, Tímea Drinóczi, Balázs D Tóth, Rainer Grote, Gábor Halmai, Giulio Itzcovich, Vanda Lamm, Béla Pokol, Pál Sonnevend, Zoltán Szente, Esther Vogel and the participants of the workshops on 8 August 2012 at the Max Planck Institute for Comparative Public Law and International Law (Heidelberg) and 7 January 2015 at the Hungarian Constitutional Court (Budapest) for their critical remarks and useful references.

[2] Contrary to the official translation, some scholarly works refer to it as Basic Law.

HCC was itself divided over its role and the methods of constitutional interpretation (text-positivist vs. activist: these designations existed only in the scholarly literature,[3] in the judgments they were never mentioned). The two approaches could not be characterised by any group identity or political affiliation; the difference was only methodological. They should also not be understood as strict schools, because sometimes elements from the two differing approaches were used by the same judge or author. The characteristics should thus be understood as Wittgensteinian family resemblances.[4] The elements of these two approaches turned up in judgments, in scholarly texts and in the political discourse as well, so it seemed best to place their analysis before all other enquiries into the legal, political, institutional and academic context.

Text-Positivism

As a preliminary remark, text-positivism should not be confused with legal positivism (Kelsen or Hart): text-positivism was not a school of legal theory, it was just an approach to interpretation with some implied (but often unreflected) theoretical presuppositions, also in some of the sample judgments. This style of reasoning had three elements: (I) methods of interpretation, especially (a) the rejection of objective teleological arguments, (b) the preference for subjective teleological arguments and (c) the rejection of harmonising arguments referring to international law; (II) the preferred rank list of substantive arguments and (III) a general approach towards doctrinal-conceptual sophistication.

Ad (I). (a)-(b) The most important feature of this approach was the strong reliance on the text (this explains the designation "text-positivism") and the explicit rejection of the objective teleological method. To put it bluntly: "If it is not written explicitly, then it is not law". Consequently, if the text of the Constitution did not explicitly say anything (or if it says contradictory things) about a question, then that question cannot be decided.

This method of interpretation was a legacy of socialism. If we want to know why socialist legal scholars disfavoured the (objective) teleological

[3] In Western languages see e.g. Kim Lane Scheppele, "The New Hungarian Constitutional Court. After Solyom, Retreat into Formalism?" (1999) 8 *East European Constitutional Review* 81; András Jakab, "Wissenschaft und Lehre des Verfassungsrechts in Ungarn" in Armin von Bogdandy, Pedro Cruz Villalón and Peter M. Huber (eds), *Ius Publicum Europaeum*, vol 2 (CF Müller 2007) 773–801.

[4] Ludwig Wittgenstein, *Philosophische Untersuchungen* (3rd edn Suhrkamp 1982) I. § 66–7.

interpretation,[5] the leading legal scholar of Hungarian socialism, Imre Szabó, has an answer for us.[6] He identifies the true essence and the fatal flaw of the (objective) teleological approach: it detaches a law from the will of the legislator and elevates a purpose which was not determined by the legislator but simply assumed or derived, to a principle of interpretation. However, the sole purpose of legal interpretation, according to Szabó, is to ascertain, as far as possible, the original actual will of the legislator. Thus, according to this approach, teleological interpretation should *only* take place within the parameters of historical interpretation (i.e., only the subjective teleological interpretation is acceptable)[7] and therefore cannot be counted as an independent method of interpretation.

Seventeen years later, Szabó wrote the following: "Interpretation is always only declarative," and "One may not read anything into the text of the statute that is not already there."[8] A few pages further, he evaluated the objective teleological method: "the method – which later became completely dissociated from the historical method and, along with the purposive interpretation, introduced a sort of legal opportunism, that is, it gave a law a purpose that corresponded to the nature of a given case – this method reduced the law to a mere means to reach any arbitrarily desired end. This . . . methodological element, the so-called teleological interpretation, must be rejected . . . "[9]

We see, then, that the strongest objection to the objective teleological method was its departure from the original will of the legislator and its tendency to allow too great a discretionary scope in interpreting the law. Setting aside the ideological component, one could consider this an argument stating that the objective teleological method leads to legal uncertainty. Under the circumstances of the period, however, this point of view seems rather to have been an expression of the antipathy of both socialism and any "usual" dictatorship for unchecked creativity. Socialism wanted to turn the application of law into a predictable machine for the

[5] Before the Second World War, recognition of the objective teleological method was characteristic, if not exclusive. See Imre Szabó, *A jogszabályok értelmezése* ([The Interpretation of Legal Rules] KJK 1960) 103–09 (listing further references). But practically every author recognised it under some designation or another (for example, the "particular, logical method").

[6] Szabó (n 5) 97–109, esp. 104–09.

[7] Szabó (n 5) 105. His point of view corresponded fully with the opinion of the Soviet literature at the time. See *ibid.* 106 n 10 (citing further references).

[8] Imre Szabó, *Jogelmélet* ([Legal Theory] KJK 1977) 259 (authors' translation).

[9] Szabó (n 8) 261 (authors' translation).

processing of statutes.[10] Imre Szabó contributed to this phenomenon – probably more consciously than unconsciously.[11] On the other hand, adherence to the actual text was the strongest protection against party-political influence during socialism, thus it also gained a certain moral-professional standing.

Following the collapse of socialism, the concept of teleological interpretation began to regain (lost) ground in the legal literature, and as we are going to see from the numbers also in the interpretive practice of the HCC. But some of the quoted arguments (also from judgments of the sample) show signs of the previous approach.[12] Especially symptomatic were the deferential arguments which stated that they could not solve the case because "it is not in the text". Arguments relying on the subjective purpose were also characteristic, and the fact that in the second half of the period the number of such references increased supports the commonly held believe that changes in the personnel of the HCC resulted in a return to this old methodology.[13]

(c) Another feature of this traditional approach was its state-centred nature. Sovereignty was perceived as international independence which also applied against international human rights treaties (a necessary doctrine in every dictatorship, also in Eastern European countries during socialism). When the activist era ended at the HCC in 1998 (change of personnel), the references to international law dropped significantly

[10] Cf. Imre Szabó, *A jogelmélet alapjai* ([Fundamentals of Legal Theory] Akadémiai 1971) 184. The elimination of creativity was largely successful because the Hungarian judiciary avoided (and still avoids) speculative conceptual derivations. For Hungarian judges, the law is only what is "written in the text" (textualism). See Béla Pokol, *A jog elmélete* ([Theory of Law] Rejtjel 2001) 284 (discussing Hungarian courts' staunch loyalty to text).

[11] Like consolidating dictatorships in general, socialism also had certain characteristics which resembled the rule of law (or similar principles) to some degree. See Roger Scruton, "Totalitarianism and the Rule of Law" in Ellen Frankel Paul (ed), *Totalitarianism at the Crossroads* (Transaction 1990) 171–213 (analysing the phenomenon thoroughly). A good example of the phenomenon is "socialist legality," meaning roughly "legal certainty within the framework of a socialist dictatorship" (with emphasis on dictatorship). The term is fundamentally hypocritical, since its function is to legitimate lawlessness, if and when it is in the interest of the dictatorship of the proletariat. See Friedrich-Christian Schroeder, "Wandlungen und Konstanten der "sozialistischen Gesetzlichkeit"" (1989) 6 *Recht in Ost und West* 358.

[12] In ordinary courts it is considerably stronger. On the textualist interpretation as a legacy of socialism in the whole of Eastern Europe, see Zdeněk Kühn, "Formalism and Anti-Formalism in Judicial Reasoning" in Bjarne Melkevik (ed), *Standing Tall: hommages à Csaba Varga* (Pázmány 2012) 226–7 with further references.

[13] Scheppele (n 3).

(until that point, the majority of the sample judgments contained such references, after the change only 25 per cent).

Ad (II). Amongst the substantive arguments, democracy was the strongest, and separation of powers and protection of fundamental rights were the weakest.[14] This is a legacy of Marxist-Leninist constitutional doctrine, too, in which democracy had a much higher value than the protection of fundamental rights and which explicitly rejected the idea of separation of powers (principles of "unity of powers" and "democratic centralism").[15]

Ad (III). Activists also claimed that text-positivists were not particularly creative and did not see doctrinal-conceptual issues. Constitutional issues were conceptualised as procedural problems; the substantive problems often remained in the background.[16] This also seems to be a socialist legacy. During socialism, *Verfassungsdogmatik* was unnecessary, as (political) conflicts were never decided on the basis of the Constitution, but through the decisions of the socialist party. There was no constitutional court which could have applied it, and ordinary courts perceived the Constitution as only a political declaration (and it was only a political declaration).[17] To build up a systematic and sophisticated *Verfassungsdogmatik* under these circumstances would have been a futile exercise. Constitutional lawyers instead spent their time on comparative law or history of law (or on writing propaganda-like analyses of the Constitution, but with more ideological elements than conceptual sophistication). If a word in the Constitution was unclear, then statutes (!) were used to

[14] See e.g. the concurring opinion by Judge László Kiss in Dec. 4/1999 (III.31) AB stating that "the function and the competences of the Parliament *cannot be limited* because of the requirement . . . of democratic functioning" [Italics ours]. For a detailed critique of this statement, see András Jakab and Miklós Hollán, "Socialism's Legacy in Contemporary Law and Legal Scholarship: The Case of Hungary" (2004) 2–3 *Journal of East European Law (Columbia University)* 95, esp. 104–8. József Petrétei, *Alkotmányjog I.* ([Constitutional Law] Dialóg Campus 2002) 83–94 analyses the basic principles of Hungarian constitutional law. These are: sovereignty, democracy, the rule of law and market economy. They partly overlap, but the protection of fundamental rights is not included in any of them.

[15] See Georg Brunner, "Das Staatsrecht der Deutschen Demokratischen Republik" in Josef Isensee and Paul Kirchhof (eds), *Handbuch des Staatsrechts* vol. 1 (3rd edn. CF Müller 2003) para. 25–27 for a discussion of these principles concerning East Germany.

[16] For a criticism of this proceduralism, see Scheppele (n 3) with further references.

[17] It was not by chance that since the 1950s no (book-format, article-by-article) commentary of the Constitution had been published. The only function of the short commentaries in the '50s was to legitimatise the regime and not to help to decide political conflicts. But for legitimating you do not need a commentary. A commentary is needed only where conflicts are decided on the basis of law.

define it: the Constitution was thus not perceived as a limit on but rather as a recommendation to the legislature.

In the first decade, text-positivism was the usual approach in Hungarian legal scholarship (at the HCC it was only a minority opinion, though) and criticised the HCC (especially its first president, László Sólyom, 1990–8) for deciding according to an activist approach. In the second decade of the period, both at the HCC and in the literature, a balance of the two approaches could be seen, but the actual theses of the first decade survived even after their representatives left, because these were already engraved in precedents and text-positivists also considered HCC precedents as binding later interpretations.

Activism

Activism is not (or originally was not) a self-designation, but rather an accusation by text-positivists,[18] although later it was also accepted by activist authors themselves.[19] This approach can be characterised by (I) preferred methods of interpretation, (II) favourite substantive arguments and (III) the attempt to build a sophisticated *Verfassungsdogmatik*.

Ad (I) and (II). The most preferred methods were the objective teleological and the harmonising methods, but the non-legal argumentation method was also accepted in this approach. The Constitution was perceived as a comprehensive and coherent document which provided an answer to every possible question (even if the answers were sometimes just implied ones, if you were creative enough then you could find them). General principles of constitutional law were especially used for building harmonising arguments, but referring to a "value system" behind the Constitution,[20] also non-legal arguments. The favourite substantive arguments were the rule of law, democracy and human dignity.

The disappearance of non-legal arguments and the clear drop in the number of references to international law in the second half of the analysed period shows that changes in the personnel of the HCC did have some

[18] Very rarely, also used as a self-designation, see András Mink, "Interview with László Sólyom" (1997) 6.1 *East European Constitutional Review* 72.

[19] Gábor Halmai, "The Hungarian Approach to Constitutional Review: The End of Activism?" in Wojciech Sadurski (ed), *Constitutional Justice, East and West: Democratic Legitimacy and Constitutional Courts in Post-Communist Europe, in a Comparative Perspective* (Kluwer Law International 2002) 189–212.

[20] See, e.g., Gábor Attila Tóth, *Túl a szövegen. Értekezés a magyar alkotmányról* ([Beyond the Text. A Study on the Hungarian Constitution] Osiris 2009) 186–207.

effect on the style of reasoning, even though many of the other elements (both structural and substantive, except "human dignity" which clearly became less frequent) seemed to have survived the first-generation activist judges and are still pervasive today (often in the form of precedents quoted by the new judges but containing the old arguments).

Ad (III). The main task of constitutional scholarship and one of the tasks of the HCC was seen by the activists to be the building of a sophisticated *Verfassungsdogmatik*. A detailed conceptual system (which goes beyond the actual text of the Constitution) was seen as necessary in order to be able to solve cases and to do it in a flexible but predictable manner. This resulted in long (doctrinal) *obiter dicta* of the judgments which were probably often meant to teach both outsiders and the staff of the HCC.

1 Legal and Political Culture as Context for Constitutional Reasoning

Most of the lawyers who were working during the period between 1990 and 2010 were educated during socialism, and accordingly, the theses of text-positivists were the commonplaces they believed in. Many judges seriously thought that they were just the "mouthpiece of the legislator" (they even proudly quoted Montesquieu in order to show Western education). Many of them also cynically added that they could not do justice but just apply the law (in a textualist manner). They did not pay much attention to the HCC, as they considered it an issue for the legislator to deal with HCC judgments (this perception fitted well to the lack of constitutional complaint against judgments of ordinary courts).

Politicians kept changing their positions according to their political situations. In opposition, they were always huge supporters of the HCC, encouraging it to make creative and activist decisions (and the HCC usually chose to decide all hot issues, sometimes against all the political elite and even against public opinion), whereas on government they referred to it as anti-democratic. But in general, politicians were rather anti-HCC, on the one hand because politicians everywhere in the world tend to dislike limits on their power, and on the other hand because they were also educated during socialism and were indoctrinated with an anti-HCC standing. Hungarian politicians saw democracy as hierarchically superior to fundamental rights and also saw law as an instrument of social engineering in the hands of politicians (as it was seen during socialism), and not as a means of promoting justice. The HCC itself was seen as instrumental for them, and not as a value in itself.

The 1949/89 Constitution itself had little respect as such (even though the basic values of constitutionalism became a standard part of political discourse), partly because of its dubious origins. It had the dark year of 1949 in its title, and its main parts were adopted by an illegitimate body (the last communist parliament in 1989). No government rebelled actively against any judgment of the HCC; after some mourning about the anti-democratic activism of the HCC the bitter pills were swallowed (i.e. they accepted that an important statute was annulled) but the implementation of some of its judgments establishing an unconstitutional omission were ignored (i.e. no new statute was adopted).

Political parties did not really have any coherent political philosophies (or if they did, then they handled these in a very opportunistic way, keeping silent about them in certain situations, most likely just using them as rhetorical elements without actually internalising the content). Consequently, we could not establish any specific approach in the public discourse as to the nature of law and as to the nature of the political community. The social problems were pressing, but again, no social collapse or the like threatened; thus the HCC generally did not consider it its task to deal with these issues. Corruption (especially party financing) was also a major issue, but the HCC did not (care to or dare to) stretch its competences to deal with it.

2 *The Court and Constitutional Litigation*

According to the Constitution (Act XX of 1949 as revised and restated by Act XXXI of 1989) and to Act XXXII of 1989 on the Constitutional Court (ACC),[21] the HCC had the following competences:[22]

a) the ex ante examination for unconstitutionality of statutes adopted but not yet promulgated, and of provisions of the rules of procedure of Parliament and of international treaties;
b) the ex post examination for unconstitutionality of laws, as well as normative decisions and normative orders;

[21] During the first 20 years of the existence of the HCC (1990–2010), only a few changes were made to the constitutional and ACC rules on the HCC. If no other reference has been made, then the legal situation is the one directly preceding the curtailment of the competences of the HCC in November 2010. For more details see Kriszta Kovács and Gábor Attila Tóth, "Hungary's Constitutional Transformation" (2011) 7.2 *European Constitutional Law Review* 183. For more details on the HCC and for a translation of some of the important judgments of the first decade see László Sólyom and Georg Brunner (eds), *Constitutional Judiciary in a New Democracy. The Hungarian Constitutional Court* (University of Michigan Press 2000); Gábor Spuller, *Das Verfassungsgericht der Republik Ungarn* (Peter Lang 1998).

[22] Some other statutes conferred further competences on the HCC in the area of referenda and university autonomy.

c) the examination of conflicts between international treaties and laws, as well as normative decisions and normative orders;
d) judgment on constitutional complaints lodged for the violation of rights guaranteed by the Constitution;
e) the elimination of unconstitutionality by omission;
f) the elimination of conflicts of competence between state organs, local governments and other state organs, or between local governments;
g) the interpretation of provisions of the Constitution.

As a main rule, the abstract ex post review of laws based on *actio popularis* (i.e. a type of procedure in which anybody can challenge any statute by claiming that it is unconstitutional without having to show any direct personal interest and without having to have a concrete case either) dominated the work of the HCC (9.000 out of 15.000 cases).[23] Thus, in the majority of the procedures, anybody (even foreigners) could launch a procedure without showing any personal interest: a short letter stating the unconstitutionality (also naming the exact provision of the Constitution and the exact provisions of the law wished to be annulled). Ordinary courts also had standing to file a case upon noting the unconstitutionality of a law or any statutory instrument applicable in the judgment of a case while suspending that case (only the HCC could annul laws). The HCC did not have the power to annul judicial decisions, only the law upon which they (the judicial decisions) were based (and following such an annulment, the ordinary courts themselves had to redo their procedures according to their rules of procedure, but the HCC could not order this). In theory, individual complaint existed as a competence, but it practically died out as it did not provide any advantage over the abstract *actio popularis* review and was actually more difficult to file (i.e. strict deadline, and a legitimate interest had to be shown).[24] The HCC did not have any discretion to pick from the complaints and had to respond to all of them (obviously unfounded complaints could be *a limine* rejected without reaching the judges, but even they had to be answered). The combination of *actio popularis* on the one hand, and the lack of discretionary power on

[23] We are grateful to the Secretariat of the HCC for the (unpublished) data of the HCC (on file with the authors). Only cases which were not *a limine* rejected were counted.

[24] From 1999 onwards, there was a possibility of redoing the whole ordinary court procedure, if the original judgment had been based on a law or statutory instrument which was later annulled by the HCC. But this was always a separate procedure which had to be launched by the parties (incl. the Prosecution Service), and the HCC itself could not annul any individual judicial decision.

the other hand, led to the HCC being seriously overloaded. This resulted in delays of several years (there was no deadline in any of the procedures of the HCC).

As a politically very important but rather rare competence, the HCC could also realise the *ex ante* (or preventive) examination of statutes adopted but not yet promulgated for unconstitutionality, and of provisions of the rules of procedure of Parliament and of international treaties. This procedure was initiated by the President of the Republic.

International treaties as such could not be reviewed, but the internal legal acts implementing them (Hungary was a dualist country) could (Dec. 4/1997 (I.22) AB). If the implementing act was higher or the same in ranking as the conflicting other norm, then the other norm had to be annulled. If the implementing norm was lower in rank (typically: conflict between the Constitution and an international treaty implemented in a statute), then normally the HCC gave the affected law-maker some time to rewrite one of the norms. If this did not happen, then the implementing norm (but not the international treaty itself) was quashed.

As already mentioned, there was no review of decisions of ordinary courts on their constitutionality. The HCC tried, however, to acquire the power to review the decisions of ordinary courts through three methods. One of them was the so called "living law" doctrine (Dec. 57/1991 (XI.8) AB). According to this doctrine, which was borrowed from the Italian doctrine (*diritto vivente*), statutes have the meanings that courts attribute to them.[25] Therefore if unconstitutional case-law existed on the basis of a statute, then the statute was unconstitutional and had to be quashed. There was also a more statute-friendly method for ensuring constitutionality of judicial case-law: the HCC sometimes defined the constitutional interpretation of a statute, i.e. chose from different possible interpretations the one which was constitutional (Dec. 38/1993 (VI.11) AB). If the courts did not follow this decision, there was still the power to quash the statute itself. And finally, the Supreme Court had the power to issue "decisions for the unity of jurisprudence" (*jogegységi határozat*), i.e. abstract norms about the interpretation of statutes to be used by lower courts. The HCC claimed to have the power to quash these decisions, and in fact it did so (the first time in Dec. 42/2005 (XI.14) AB).

Another interesting power that the Hungarian CC possessed was the ability to declare that a state organ had made an "unconstitutional

[25] For more information on this doctrine see Antonio Ruggeri and Antonino Spadaro, *Lineamenti di giustizia costituzionale* (Giapichelli 2004) 134.

omission", which meant that it had failed to make a necessary law or statutory instrument; resulting in an unconstitutional situation (this procedure could also be launched *ex officio*). And finally, the competence to "interpret the provisions of the Constitution" has to be mentioned: If there was a concrete constitutional conflict (without such a concrete question, the decision would result in an academic monograph), then the HCC could provide an official interpretation of the relevant provision of the Constitution to be used in the conflict.

In addition, some other, but less important competences were regulated by Act XXXII of 1989 on the Constitutional Court and by other statutes (especially the constitutionality of referendum questions). The registration and dissolution of parties and the election cases were dealt with by the ordinary courts and not by the HCC.

There were no oral arguments at the HCC, and decisions had to be made on the basis of written submissions. Formally, there were no opposing parties, only the initiator of the procedure and the law. It was usual practice, however, to ask for the opinion of the government (more precisely: of the ministry of justice). Rarely, written expert opinions were also asked for (either on questions of law or on questions of fact). There were no specific (constitutional/statutory) rules about the admissibility of proof/argument in the court.

The HCC published all cases *which reached a judge.* Those which were *a limine* rejected (by the secretariat of the HCC) for being "obviously unfounded" were not published. The number of cases concluded each year ranged from 934 (2003) to 2.178 (1991), the average being around 1.300 cases. Approximately half of them were decided (*a limine* rejected) by the secretariat of the HCC. A quarter of the cases (around 350 cases per year) were actually decided either by the President of the HCC (if the petitioner persistently repeated or upheld his/her petition despite the secretariat's rejection, then the President of the HCC rejected it) or by a panel of judges (panels of 3 judges or the full chamber of 11 judges). Only these (thus a quarter) of the decided cases reached a judge, and were consequently published. The general rule for publication was to publish the judgments in the official journal of the HCC *(Alkotmánybírósági Közlöny)* and then the yearbook of the HCC *(Az Alkotmánybíróság Határozatai)*, but the most important judgments were *also* published in the Official Gazette *(Magyar Közlöny)*. The remaining cases were concluded only in an administrative sense, because they were merged with other cases.[26]

[26] The data stem from the website of the HCC: http://mkab.hu/letoltesek/statisztika_ossz.pdf.

The number of judgments peaked in 1991 (probably to be explained by the novelty of the institution which everybody wanted to try in the frame of the *actio popularis*) and also at the end of the examined period (probably best explained by the general economic and political crisis, in which it seemed to be a last hope). The internal proportions also changed: the percentage of cases which were reaching judges grew, whereas the number of rejections by the secretariat decreased. The reason for this was twofold: on the one hand, the public probably learned how to use the institution and the average quality of the petitions rose; on the other hand, (unfortunate) procedural rules made it necessary for the judges to deal with certain cases even if these were obviously unfounded (especially referendum cases).

3 *The Judges*

Until the entry into force of the new constitution in 2011, the HCC had 11 (if the Parliament failed to elect new judges, then sometimes in fact less) members who were elected by a two thirds majority of the Parliament for 9 years (re-electable once). According to the majority opinion of Hungarian scholars and judges, the HCC was not part of the judicature and also not simply a "negative law-maker", but rather a separate and independent branch of power. It also had a separate chapter in the Constitution, and the text mentioned "members" of the HCC (for the sake of simplicity, we will use the term "judge", though), and not judges (signalling that it was not a court in the traditional sense). The election of the members was highly politicised, but for procedural reasons a consensus between opposition and government was necessary. The necessary consensus meant that those constitutional law professors who could be categorised as belonging clearly to one political side or another could not be elected, or two of them had to be elected at the same time. Throughout this period, most of the HCC judges were university professors; the preconditions for election specifically mentioned the scholarly route as one of the alternative options.[27]

[27] Art. 5 ACC (1) Hungarian citizens with a law degree who have reached the age of 45 years and who have no criminal record may be elected as Members of the Constitutional Court. (2) The Parliament elects the Members of the Constitutional Court among learned theoretical jurists (university professors of law or "Doctors of State and Juridical Sciences" [of the Hungarian Academy of Sciences, i.e. a title corresponding to the German *Habilitation*]) and lawyers with at least twenty years of professional experience. Such professional experience must be acquired in a position demanding a degree in "state and juridical sciences". (3) Members of the Government or employees of political parties, as

4 *Legal Scholarship and Constitutional Reasoning*

Hungarian legal scholarship was never deferential at all towards the HCC. As a matter of fact, amongst evaluating articles, the majority were always rather critical. Law professors (if both alive and Hungarian) did not receive any references in the 40 leading cases sample, but the HCC was most likely aware of the vast majority of criticism, so it might have influenced the HCC in a hidden manner. The majority of judges have always been law professors (who continued teaching during their mandate), and this is very likely to have contributed to such influences. As a means of more direct influence, some law professors used the possibility of *actio popularis* and submitted petitions to the HCC.

In general, being a judge at the HCC had greater prestige than being a law professor (the salary was almost three times higher). Most law professors considered it to be the highest job they could ever reach. But there were also a (very) few (to the authors of the present study: two) known instances where an offer to become an HCC judge was rejected by an established law professor.

B Arguments in Constitutional Reasoning

The distribution of the 40 leading cases shows that during the 20 years, after a short learning period in the first 2 years, the number of leading cases rose for the next 3 years, and then sank constantly (with minor waves, but with an obvious tendency). The reason for this was probably that the older the case, the bigger the probability that it could gain quotes in the literature.[28] In the beginning phase there were more unresolved questions, thus the decisions were more likely to be surprising, i.e. their information value for the subsequent discourse was higher.

well as high ranking officials of state administration who served in such capacity during the four years before the election may not become Members of the Constitutional Court.

[28] One possible explanation could also be that the HCC itself was more likely to quote its older judgments in order to show that it was coherent and not arbitrary. This explanation is, however, ruled out, as the self-quotes and the reputation in the literature differed so much, as we established with the help of software designed specifically for the CONREASON project by Opten Kft. in order to see the number of self-quotes by the HCC. See András Jakab, Arthur Dyevre and Giulio Itzcovich, “CONREASON – The Comparative Constitutional Reasoning Project. Methodological Dilemmas and Project Design” *MTA Law Working Papers* 2015/9. http://jog.tk.mta.hu/uploads/files/mtalwp/2015_09_jakab.pdf 7.

5 *The Structure of Constitutional Arguments*

In the overwhelming majority of the judgments (31 of 40), we only found one-line-conclusive-structure arguments.

In only a few (8 of 40) judgments did we find a parallel conclusive structure. This type of argument was used, however, for only the main question of the cases, explaining why a law was unconstitutional, e.g., in 35/1994 (VI.24) AB: "[the statute] contravenes not only Art. 70A, but also Art 9(1) of the Constitution". Thus, several equal reasons were listed and any of them would have been enough to annul the statute, but the HCC "overkilled" it (probably in order to emphasise rhetorically the main point for those who might doubt it) by listing more than one reason. For intermediary steps in the reasoning it was used even less frequently.

We only found one example for the parallel, individually inconclusive, but together conclusive argument, when the opinion presents a range of relevant considerations, none of which is really conclusive, yet taken together they indicate a certain solution. In 36/2000 (X.27) AB, the existence of a general right to personal freedom was justified by referring to many different (explicit) fundamental rights of the Constitution.

6 *Types of Arguments in Constitutional Reasoning*

Petitions were summarised at the beginning of the judgments of the HCC (whether the summaries were correct is difficult to determine, as petitions of private persons were not public, unless the petitioner himself/herself published it). We did not analyse these parts, as these did not represent the reasoning of the HCC, but rather the reasoning of the petitioners. Those arguments which were used to interpret statutes or statutory instruments (i.e. infra-constitutional norms) were not considered either, as the focus of the research was *constitutional* reasoning at the HCC. We included in the analysis, however, the concurring and dissenting opinions, as they did form part of the reasoning culture of the HCC.

Analogies

We only found one case of analogy. In Dec. 4/1993 (II.12) AB the HCC argued that "The Constitution . . . guarantees free communication and freedom of expression independently from its content. This also applies to the freedom of religion." Even on this occasion, the analogy was rather just hinted at or implied, and not explicit. We can say that analogy in the sense that it was used in this research (i.e. applying a norm to a situation which actually does not fall under its scope, but for reasons of similarity of situations and for reasons of lack of precise detailed rules we still apply the norm) was basically non-existent in Hungarian constitutional reasoning.

Establishing/Debating the Text of the Constitution

We did not find any argument which dealt with doubts about how to establish the text of the Constitution. There seemed to be no problem establishing which norms were of constitutional rank and which were not.

Applicability of the Constitution

The question about the applicability of the Constitution only came up in a dissenting opinion in Dec. 4/1997 (I.22) AB, in which it was stated that the constitutional provision on constitutional review (Art. 32/A) could not be applied directly, but that its normative content was defined by other laws. The argument is weak (it basically questions constitutional review itself), and it did not appear again in our sample. Questions of primacy of EU law against the Constitution did not come up (even though the HCC could have discussed it in Dec. 30/1998 (VI.25) AB), state-centred arguments in a state of emergency are also unknown in Hungary,[29] and there has never been any explicit political question doctrine (even if objective teleological interpretation of constitutional competence provisions can play a similar function).

A special type of this applicability argument was when the court (or the dissenter) refused to use any method or argument and stated that the Constitution did not say anything about the issue or that it was contradictory (Dec. 23/1990 (X.31) AB) and consequently no decision could be taken. Examples of the former are Dec. 47/2007 (VII.3) AB which stated that "all efforts to establish exactly and exhaustively those reasons which the President of the Republic could use to justify to award an honour to a certain person, are not interpretations of the Constitution, but they are law-making, and consequently, outside the competence of the Constitutional Court"; or Dec. 64/1991 (XII.17) AB which contained that "the question whether the foetus is a legal subject cannot be decided through interpretation of the Constitution". Similar arguments were found in Dec. 38/1993 (VI.11) AB and in Dec. 8/1992 (I.30) AB.

[29] András Jakab, "German Constitutional Law and Doctrine on State of Emergency – Paradigms and Dilemmas of a Traditional (Continental) Discourse" (2006) 5 *German Law Journal* 453, esp. 475–6.

Ordinary Meaning of the Words of the Constitution or References to the "Wording of the Constitution" in General

This argument was found in 9 of the 40 judgments, making it a usual, rather than a dominant argument. There were three situations in which it was used: (1) when trying to find out the meaning of an individual word in the Constitution, (2) when trying to argue for a certain interpretation due to the phrasing of a sentence and (3) when trying to explain why the HCC could not do something (because it is just not in the text of the Constitution).

Ad 1. The meaning of an individual word can either be the everyday meaning or the technical-legal meaning. As a matter of fact, we mainly found examples for the latter one, e.g. in Dec. 23/1990 (X.31) AB when interpreting the word "arbitrary" from Art. 54(1) Constitution: "A punishment can qualify as arbitrary if it leaves too much discretion to the subjective decision of the judge." There was a similar situation and a similar style of reasoning in Dec. 4/1999 (III.31) AB when the word "decision" was interpreted from Art. 24(3) Constitution: "the 'opinion' or 'proposal' of a committee is obviously not a decision". A monolingual dictionary was even used once to determine the meaning of a legal term (*Magyar Értelmező Kéziszótár* in Dec. 4/1999 (III.31) AB)), but normally the judges preferred to use their own intuition as to the ordinary meaning of words. A grammatical type of argument was used in Dec. 49/2001 (XI.22) AB, in which the HCC argued that the expression "high courts" (*ítélőtáblák*) implied several courts because of the grammatical plural.

Ad 2. The general phrasing of a sentence can also give clues about its meaning. This was used by the HCC in Dec. 46/1994 (X.21) AB when stating that "both fundamental rights provisions . . . allow for limitations by statute" or in Dec. 34/1994 (VI.24) AB when inferring from the fact that "this right is phrased [in the Constitution] as subjective right". Here, you do not use a word singled out, but rather the word in its textual context.

Ad 3. And finally, in some cases the text of the Constitution was referred to as a limitation of the competences of the HCC: Something lacked in the text, something did *not* follow from the text. Examples are Dec. 48/1991 (IX.26) AB when stating that "an interpretation which does not follow directly from the text, which is thus an extensive interpretation, would actually mean a modification of the Constitution, which is, however, the competence of the Parliament"; Dec. 62/2003 (XII.15) AB when stating that "an opposing interpretation would mean the extension of the text of the Constitution" or Dec. 27/1998 (VI.16) AB when stating that "it does not follow from the use of words in the Constitution that . . . " This type of argument was basically a very simple deferential argument which also implied the rejection of the use of any other types of arguments and thus cut short the discussion of the issue.

Harmonising Arguments

(1) Domestic harmonising arguments can have the form of interpreting one constitutional provision in light of another, interpreting constitutional provisions in light of each other or using two constitutional provisions together to establish the constitutional standard. We found harmonising arguments in 32 of the 40 judgments, thus making it one of the three (quantitatively) most dominant arguments (along with precedents and objective teleological arguments). The method was explicitly mentioned in Dec. 23/1990 (X.31) AB when stating that "the whole of the Constitution is the basis [of the interpretation]" and in Dec. 48/1991 (IX.26) AB when stating that "we depart from the presupposition that the Constitution, like law in general, is a unified and coherent system" (formulated in a very similar way in Dec. 62/2003 (XII.15) AB).[30]

(2) International harmonising arguments use international law in order to interpret the Constitution. The method was explicitly mentioned in Dec. 30/1998 (VI.25) AB (explicitly about *favor conventionis*). We found such arguments in 17 of the 40 judgments. The overwhelming majority of these arguments referred to international human rights treaties (and their case law), especially to the European Convention on Human Rights (ECHR) and International Covenant on Civil and Political Rights, with a slight dominance of the ECHR.[31] Consequently, this type of argument was typically found in fundamental rights cases. Sometimes we only found vague references to "international treaties" without any concrete details in the reasoning, as in Dec. 38/1993 (VI.11) AB and Dec. 64/1991 (XII.17) AB. It is surprising that international law was also referred to in some cases in which it was obvious that Hungary was not bound by it, for example, the

[30] On one occasion we found a methodologically obviously flawed argument, when the HCC interpreted the Constitution in light of the then valid statutes (60/1994 (XII.24) AB), but we still marked it in the Excel table of the 40 leading cases (see Cambridge University Press companion website), as it was definitely a harmonising argument, and in this paper our purpose was not to critique the reasoning.

[31] An exception is the UN Convention on the Rights of the Child which is used as an aid for interpreting the Constitution in Dec. 21/1996 (V.17) AB.

ECHR before it was ratified by Hungary, even though the judgments did not mention its lack of binding force in Dec. 23/1990 (X.31) AB. In Dec. 36/2000 (X.27) AB, however, it was explicitly mentioned that Hungary was not bound by an international instrument, but that it was still used as an aid of interpretation. In yet another case (Dec. 20/2005 (V.26) AB), however, the HCC analysed in a very detailed manner how (and from when exactly) a Third Pillar EU instrument bound Hungary and, consequently, how it had to be used as an aid to interpret the Constitution. The use of international harmonising arguments became rarer in the second half of the period (whereas before 1998 more than half of the judgments contained such arguments, after that only 25 per cent of judgments did so). The reason might have been twofold: (a) On the one hand, this might have been caused by the change in the personnel of the HCC (see above activism vs. text-positivism). (b) On the other hand, frequent references to international law in the beginning phase could be explained by the lack of the own case-law of the HCC. Thus, with time, references to international law could be substituted with references to precedents.

Precedents (Former Own Cases)

This was the most widely used method (38 of 40). Only the first two cases did not contain references to former own cases, most likely because there were no cases to be quoted at all. Mostly, precedents were mentioned as individual cases (to be followed, or to be distinguished, which means a negative use of interpretation), but in a rhetorically stronger version, the HCC sometimes talked about the "permanent and coherent case law of the Constitutional Court" and mentioned a long list of cases in brackets (even though on one occasion they simply stated that there was a "permanent and coherent case law" on a certain legal issue, but no actual case was mentioned at all; see Dec. 17/1994 (III.29) AB).

Doctrinal Analysis of Legal Concepts or Principles

In 22 of the 40 judgments we found such arguments. This type of argument mainly seemed to appear when the HCC was trying to avoid giving any explanation: "the legal concept means this or that", just as a stipulation without any explanation, the style of mentioning such arguments was axiomatic (not showing any doubts). We could not help but sometimes ask ourselves in astonishment: "Where did you get this from?"

According to their exact topic, these arguments can be categorised into three groups: (1) abstract-general legal axioms about the whole legal order, (2) constitutional concepts and (3) criminal law concepts.

Ad 1. Examples of the abstract-general legal axioms concern the whole of the legal order. In Dec. 4/1993 (II.12) AB we find: "It is a principle which is accepted in different legal branches: legal declarations ought to be qualified or evaluated not according to their labelling, but according to their content". Even more general is Dec. 38/1993 (VI.11) AB when it states that "the unity of legal order requires [not having contradictions within the legal order]".

Ad 2. General constitutional concepts (democracy, the rule of law, sovereignty, constitution) are especially suited for this doctrinal type of argument, as lawyers have a general idea about them, objective teleological arguments would too easily lead to ideological quarrels, and harmonising arguments are also difficult to use for these concepts as normally these (explicitly not defined concepts) are used as aids to interpret the concrete provisions (and not the other way around). Examples include, *inter alia*, Dec. 11/1992 (III.5) AB when stating that "legal certainty is a fundamental element of the rule of law", Dec. 52/1997 (X.14) AB when stating that "it follows from the [principle of] rule of law that the constitutional organs have to co-operate" or Dec. 52/1997 (X.14) AB when stating that "it is a necessary conceptual element of direct democracy that the institution which is designed to implement it [i.e., the referendum – *the authors*] is under the influence of the affected, i.e. the citizen (or a certain number thereof)." And finally, a deferential doctrinal argument from Dec. 46/1994 (X.21) AB: "The Constitutional Court cannot review and annul any provision of the Constitution. If a provision has become part of the Constitution by the votes of two thirds of MPs, then it is conceptually impossible to establish unconstitutionality."

In some cases less abstract constitutional concepts received quite detailed definitions without the origins of those definitions being clarified. In Dec. 27/1998 (VI.16) AB the HCC stated that "The free mandate is the basis of the status of MPs. Free mandate means that the elected MP becomes independent . . . " The explanation of the concept was then continued over six lines. In Dec. 24/2000 (VII.6) AB yet another doctrinal thesis without any reference to its origin: "An unjustified delay qualifies as a breach of the duty to decide within reasonable time." And finally, a conceptual-doctrinal explanation from the area of fundamental rights: "exercising the right of self-determination 'in the name of someone' is . . . conceptually excluded" (Dec. 36/2000 (X.27) AB).

Ad 3. Some general ideas or concepts of criminal law were also used without their sources being explained. E.g. in Dec. 11/1992 (III.5) AB: "the state power to punish has to remain within the same limits at the time of the judgment, as what it was at the time of perpetration" or in Dec. 39/1997 (VII.1) AB: "The petitioner misunderstands the presumption of innocence. It is namely a procedural principle, and it is not an obstacle for disciplinary bodies of different instances to establish the statutory disciplinary punishments – even before the final judicial decision."

Linguistic-Logical Formulae Based on Silence

We found only a few arguments belonging to this category, and they had the form of *argumentum a contrario*. One type was when a the lack of a single word was the argument, as in the dissenting opinion in Dec. 4/1997 (I.22) AB which showed how a different text would justify the competence of the HCC: "If Art. 32/A contained the word 'all' [then the HCC would have the competence to review the acts implementing international treaties]." Another type was when the lack of a rule was the argument, as in Dec. 3/2004 (II.17) AB, in which the lack of subordination rules meant a certain legal status of independence: "The Constitution does not contain any provision about the subordination of the Prosecution Service to the Parliament or any other organ (e.g. Government or minister of justice) . . . Therefore, according to the current rules, the Prosecutor General is not subordinated to any other organ."

Teleological/Purposive Arguments Referring to the Purpose of the Text

Objective teleological arguments were very common (32 of the 40 judgments). They appeared (1) in different structures, (2) in different degrees of abstraction and (3) in different topics.

Ad 1. The most usual structure was when the argument explicitly stated the purpose behind the rule or the institution in general, and then followed the right interpretation accordingly. E.g. in Dec. 8/1992 (I.30) AB when stating that "this rule serves the continuous functioning of the state organisation" or in Dec. 36/1992 (VI.10) AB when stating that "the point [of this rule] is that none of the participants can decide on his or her own, thus he or she has to form a consensus with the others." In other judgments, however, the establishment of the purpose was not a separate step and was just be implied, as in Dec. 46/1994 (X.21) AB when stating that "the capacity of the army to function requires that, during their service, members of the armed forces do not participate in organisations which oppose the statutory task of the armed forces." Here, the "capacity of the army to function" was used in the reasoning without having before been established.

Sometimes the purpose was used in a positive way, i.e. stating the purpose and then concluding from it to the corresponding interpretation. E.g. in Dec. 64/1993 (XII.22) AB: "the establishment of the status of local authorities as property owners was a conscious decision, it was a consequence of the decision of the constitution-maker to establish a liberal democratic political system which is based on a multiparty system." At other times, however, it was used in a negative way, i.e. it was shown that a certain interpretation would contradict the purpose of the rule and therefore could not be selected. E.g. in Dec. 62/2003 (XII.15) AB "[this interpretation] would contravene the purpose and function of the competences of the President of the Republic, and also the system of division of powers which is based on balances and mutual control" or in Dec. 36/1992 (VI.10) "the enlargement of powers [of the President of Republic] cannot [result in] exercising political power without [political] responsibility".

This negative use could even have the form of *argumentum ad absurdum*, when not only the interpretation, but also the consequences of a certain interpretation were shown and then the interpretation was rejected because these consequences contradicted the purpose of the norm: "the deprivation of fundamental rights on the basis that these rights could be abused is as constitutionally unacceptable as imprisoning the majority of the population with the justification that the growth of criminality has to be stopped" (Dec. 35/1994 (VI.24) AB). Or in rhetorically less strong versions, but still having the structure of *argumentum ad absurdum*: "it will lead to draining the competence of the President of the Republic in Art. 26(2) Constitution, if there are no procedural rules guaranteeing the possibility of a discussion on the merits [of the bill which was rejected by the President of the Republic]" (Dec. 62/2003 (XII.15) AB).

Ad 2. Sometimes a very general purpose was established, like the "democratic functioning of the state organisation" in Dec. 47/2007 (VII.3) AB, in Dec. 36/1992 (VI.10) AB or in Dec. 48/1991 (IX.26) AB; the end of power concentration in Dec. 62/2003 (XII.15) AB ("The regime which was set up in 1989 ended the party-state-like concentration of power . . . "). The whole of these general purposes was called in Dec. 47/2007 (VII.3) AB the constitutional value system: "the constitutional value system is the sum of values which appear or which can be deduced from the Constitution". And an example of a fully fledged explicit argument in this style: "[the constitutional amendment] elevated the most important provisions on referenda to that of constitutional rank in order to express that the direct exercise of power by the people is of paramount importance" (Dec. 52/1997 (X.14) AB).

Other times, the established (or implied) purpose was less abstract, as in Dec. 24/2000 (VII.6) AB: "Smooth local governance requires . . . " or in Dec. 47/2007 (VII.3) AB "the scope of autonomous decisions by the President of the Republic is very narrow, exactly in order to protect the constitutional institution of the President of the Republic".

Ad 3. The topics in which objective teleological arguments were used were manifold. The topic could be state organisation, where the purpose of certain organs or institutions was established and then used in order to interpret a constitutional provision. The HCC was especially keen to speculate about its own purpose and function as the "guardian of the Constitution" in order to enlarge its own competences (Dec. 4/1997 (I.22) AB, Dec. 36/1992 (VI.10) AB, Dec. 42/2005 (XI.14) AB). In other judgments, the HCC used the insight that the purpose of qualified majority (organic) laws is to ensure political consensus (Dec. 4/1993 (II.12) AB, Dec. 1/1999 (II.24) AB). Or a fully fledged explicit objective teleological argument about the function of local governments: "The citizens elect the local council for the exercise of local autonomy, and therefore the competences of the local authorities lie with the local council" (Dec. 24/2000 (VII.6) AB).

But objective teleological arguments were also used for the interpretation of fundamental rights provisions. Democracy as such was mentioned as the purpose of freedom of expression in Dec. 36/1994 (VI.24) AB, the autonomy protection as the function of private property in Dec. 64/1993 (XII.22) AB and in Dec. 43/1995 (VI.30) AB.

We found some arguments which were at the borderline of objective teleological and subjective teleological arguments: they mentioned the "intention of the constitution maker", but if this intention was so abstract that no actual attempt was made to discover any original intent, then we counted them as objective teleological argument. E.g. in Dec. 3/2004 (II.17) AB, the judgment referred to the "intention of the constitutional maker", but only the texts of the amendments were used in order to discover it.

Teleological/Purposive Arguments Referring to the Purpose of the Constitution-Maker (Including Travaux Préparatoires)

Strangely, subjective teleological arguments appeared more frequently with the passing of time since the actual making of the constitution in 1989.[32] The lack of references in the beginning can most likely be explained by the fact that the *travaux préparatoires* did not reflect much of an understanding of constitutionalism, only very few people were reading Western legal literature and only two or three participated in the 1989 process (thus most of the debate was not led by them). The first occasion in our sample (but to our knowledge also in general) was the Dec. 4/1997 (I.22) AB, and then references became more frequent. We could not discover any plausible explanation as to why they began to be accepted in 1997.

A typical use was the reference to the ministerial explanation *(miniszteri indokolás)* of constitutional amendments. In Hungary, government bills have explanations attached to them which are written by ministerial bureaucrats in order to assist MPs when they vote (thus the official audience of these explanations is the Parliament, and not the general public, but they are available to the general public, and judges sometimes do refer to them). We found such references in Dec. 52/1997 (X.14) AB; Dec. 4/1999 (III.31) AB and Dec. 49/2001 (XI.22) AB.

On one occasion, the protocols of the opposition roundtable of 1989 were quoted. This happened in 1997, even though at that time the protocols had not been published yet,[33] (however, the president of the HCC had an example of the protocols at home, as he had been one of the participants of the roundtable). On another occasion the original (and later modified) drafts of the ministry of justice from 1989 were quoted in order to discover the meaning of the text of the constitution (Dec. 62/2003 (XII.15) AB).

Non-legal (Moral, Sociological, Economic) Arguments

Non-legal arguments appeared in very different topics, in fundamental rights, but also in state organisation issues (the balance was surprising for us, as we thought that fundamental rights suited this type of argument better). Some of these arguments were based on social sciences, like criminology (Dec. 23/1990 (X.31) AB on the use of the death penalty), administrative sciences (when defining "control" in Dec. 48/1991 (IX.26) AB), but natural sciences also appeared (an opinion by the Hungarian Society of Psychiatrists as the decisive (!) argument in a dissenting

[32] Some of the subjective teleological arguments did not refer back to 1989, but to the intention *(travaux préparatoires)* behind later constitutional amendments.

[33] They were published two to three years later in eight volumes, see András Bozóki (ed.), *A rendszerváltás forgatókönyve. A kerekasztal-tárgyalások 1989-ben* ([The Scenario of the Regime Change. The Roundtable Talks in 1989] Magvető [vols 1–4], Új Mandátum [vols 5–8] 1999–2000).

opinion for the acceptability of a statute in 36/2000 (X.27) AB; the question of biological components of homosexuality in Dec. 21/1996 (V.17) AB).

Moral arguments appeared in two forms, sometimes as social morality (the moral opinion of society), as in Dec. 21/1996 (V.17) AB about the growth of moral pluralism as an argument for the acceptability of homosexuality. But at other times, rather critical morality dominated, like in the abortion case ("human life as a value", "the moral value of humans" in Dec. 64/1991 (XII.17) AB), the death penalty case (human life as the "highest value" in Dec. 23/1990 (X.31) AB) and the lustration case (exposing lies is "a moral duty" according to Dec. 60/1994 (XII.24) AB). Critical morality was basically the moral intuition of the judges, or sometimes authors were quoted from the history of philosophy (such as Hobbes or Spinoza in Dec. 23/1990 (X.31) AB).

The most used non-legal argument was a reference to the "special historical circumstances" which justified (or which were special, but which still did not justify) a certain interpretation (Dec. 8/1992 (I.30) AB, Dec. 11/1992 (III.5) AB, Dec. 4/1993 (II.12) AB, Dec. 60/1994 (XII.24) AB, Dec. 35/1994 (VI.24) AB).

The most surprising result here was that non-legal arguments almost died out after 1996 (as opposed to subjective teleological arguments which appeared exactly at this time, without any apparent connection between the two tendencies). It seemed that in the beginning the HCC very much preferred these arguments, but later either for legitimacy concerns or because the results were already in precedents which could be quoted more easily, the HCC did not use them any more (or hardly ever). We found 10 judgments with non-legal arguments, and only one of them dates after 1996.

References to Scholarly Works

We found one reference to an ICCPR Commentary (by Manfred Nowak) which was used to interpret international law, which was in turn used to interpret the Constitution (Dec. 55/2001 (XI.29) AB). In another case, we found a reference to the principles of a future draft constitution (the principles were adopted in 1996 by the Parliament, but the actual new constitution which was supposed to be based on these principles was never adopted) in Dec. 62/2003 (XII.15) AB, and according to the introductory study[34] we qualified this reference as a scholarly reference. Although a

[34] András Jakab, "Constitutional Reasoning. A European Perspective on Judicial Reasoning in Constitutional Courts" (2013) 14 *German Law Journal* 1215.

few other scholarly references were found to assist in the interpretation of statutes,[35] we did not count them as we focussed on constitutional reasoning.

Out of the 40 judgments, we therefore only found two judgments in which references were made to legal scholarship in order to interpret the Constitution (but we did not find any references to contemporary Hungarian constitutional scholarship). The question is of course why such references were missing, if most of the judges were actually law professors (even if most of them were not constitutional law professors, but civil or criminal law professors). The reasons were probably manifold. On the one hand, it probably did not seem *legitimate* to rely on such works, on the other hand judges probably did not want to elevate outsiders to the same level as they were, and finally, the most relevant and usable genre, the scholarly commentary, was missing in Hungary until 2009 (commentaries of the Constitution were rather just copy-pasted collections of different parts of past judgments).[36]

References to Foreign (National) Law

There was a relatively strong presence of references to foreign national law (16 of the 40 judgments). As to their function, some of them were only mentioned for reasons of contrast, but most of the time they were mentioned in order to justify the choice of interpretation. Sometimes, however, no such role could be attributed to the reference to foreign law. The most blatant example for the last type is Dec. 60/1994 (XII.24) AB which explained in a very (!) detailed manner the German legal situation on lustration without actually using it in any way in the reasoning (it rather consciously ignored the German arguments; it did not even distinguish the Hungarian case from the German one). The function here was probably just to show that the HCC had very thoroughly considered its opinion.

As to their form, sometimes precise legal references were used, as in Dec. 35/1994 (VI.24) AB or in Dec. 23/1990 (X.31) AB which quoted US Supreme Court cases, in Dec. 4/1997 (I.22) AB quoting BVerfG decisions, in Dec. 4/1999 (III.31) AB quoting French and UK parliamentary standing rules, in Dec. 62/2003 (XII.15) AB quoting Romanian, Polish and British

[35] E.g., in Dec. 36/2000 (X.27) AB a reference to the works of the (deceased) law professor Szladits from 60 years before the judgment (i.e., from pre-socialist times).

[36] There were numerous critical case notes in different law journals (esp. *Fundamentum*), but a commentary is normally more helpful than a case note when deciding cases.

parliamentary standing rules and in Dec. 17/1994 (III.29) AB referring to the Swedish rules on the competence of ombudsmen.

At other times, however, we only found very vague phrases without concrete references, such as "in most European legal orders" in Dec. 21/1996 (V.17) AB, "based on many judgments of foreign constitutional courts" or "in modern constitutions and case laws of constitutional courts" in Dec. 64/1991 (XII.17) AB, "[the HCC] conducted a comparative research of the constitutions of constitutional democracies" in Dec. 11/1992 (III.5) AB, "as generally practised in the constitutional courts of the world" in Dec. 4/1997 (I.22) AB, "constitutions of democratic states" in Dec. 38/1993 (VI.11) AB or the "trend in the laws of European democratic countries" in 36/1994 (VI.24) AB.

Yet other times just a quote in a foreign language was mentioned without its origin being explained, such as Dec. 30/1992 (V.26) AB referring to the "clear and present danger" test.

On the basis of the explicit references, no clear geographic orientation could be discovered, but if we have a look at the general phrases, then "modern constitutions" or "general trends of Western democracies" basically almost always meant Germany (even if the German solution was actually unique, it was presented as "the" Western constitutional solution).[37] This was accordingly criticised in the literature.[38]

Other Methods/Arguments

References to Hungarian legal history were made relatively often (Dec. 48/1991 (IX.26) AB; Dec. 4/1999 (III.31) AB; Dec. 62/2003 (XII.15) AB; Dec. 3/2004 (II.17) AB; Dec. 20/2005 (V.26) AB; Dec. 42/2005 (XI.14) AB). The function in the reasoning was very similar to references to foreign

[37] On German constitutional influence in general see László Sólyom, "Aufbau und dogmatische Fundierung der ungarischen Verfassungsgerichtsbarkeit" (2000) *Osteuropa-Recht*. 230; Georg Brunner and Herbert Küpper, "Der Einfluß des deutschen Rechts auf die Transformation des ungarischen Rechts nach der Wende durch Humboldt-Stipendiaten. Das Beispiel Verfassungsgericht" in Holger Fischer (ed), *Wissenschaftsbeziehungen und ihr Beitrag zur Modernisierung. Das deutsch-ungarische Beispiel* (Oldenburg 2005), 421–49. The influence can be explained partly by a traditional (centuries old) intellectual orientation amongst Hungarian lawyers, partly by the similar constitutional situation (i.e. a post-dictatorial constitutional court) and partly by the generosity of German scholarship funds for visiting fellowships in Germany (DAAD, MPG and Humboldt Scholarships).

[38] Catherine Dupré, *Importing the Law in Post-Communist Transitions. The Hungarian Constitutional Court and the Right to Human Dignity* (Hart 2003), 171; Pokol Béla, "Aktivista alapjogász vagy parlamenti törvénybarát? A magyar alkotmánybíráskodásról" (1992) 5 *Társadalmi Szemle* 67.

national law: the court showed that its decision was well considered (i.e. well researched).

A methodologically flawed but nevertheless used argument was when the HCC inferred from the *fact* of a certain political practice (official honour awarding practice) that it was constitutionally *allowed* to continue this practice (Dec. 47/2007 (VII.3) AB). Finally, another argument (if we can qualify it as an argument at all) which is difficult to qualify was used in Dec. 21/1996 (V.17) AB which stated that there is no rule for such cases, but that the HCC could decide on a case-by-case basis.

Combined Arguments

Sometimes, different types of argument were interwoven. This occurred when the *telos* for the objective teleological argument was established by another argument, e.g. in Dec. 25/1999 (VII.7) AB when it is stated that "based on the comparative overview of constitution making processes . . . the function of referendum is almost exclusively the acceptance or the rejection of the adopted text of the constitution".

But the most frequent combined argument type was the use of proportionality tests in fundamental rights cases, which we qualified as doctrinal arguments (the test itself is a doctrinal figure) and teleological arguments (the application of proportionality necessarily implies teleological considerations).[39] Such arguments were found in e.g. Dec. 21/1996 (V.17) AB, Dec. 11/1992 (III.5) AB and Dec. 60/1994 (XII.24) AB.

Results

The Constitution did not contain any explicit reference to its own interpretation. As an indirect reference, Art. 7(1) mentioned that "The legal system of the Republic of Hungary accepts the generally recognised rules of international law, and shall harmonise the country's domestic law with the obligations assumed under international law", and *inter alia* one of our analysed judgments, Dec. 4/1997 (I.22) AB, considered it an obligation to interpret domestic law (including the Constitution) in conformity with international law.

Another indirect reference was Art. 8(2) stating that "[i]n the Republic of Hungary rules pertaining to fundamental rights and duties are determined by law; such law, however, may not restrict the core contents

[39] For the details of such qualifications, see András Jakab, "Re-Defining Principles as "Important Rules". A Critique of Robert Alexy" in Martin Borowski (ed), *On the Nature of Legal Principles* ([ARSP Beiheft 119], Steiner 2009), 145–159. Available also at http://ssrn.com/abstract=1918421.

[*Wesensgehalt – the authors*] of fundamental rights." This provision was seen as an obligation to interpret fundamental rights provisions in its light.

The methods of interpretation were thus basically freely chosen by the HCC (without a clear algorithm about the arguments to be chosen in specific situations or regarding specific topics), the most important ones being the references to precedents (38 of 40), the objective teleological arguments (32 of 40) and the harmonising (32 of 40) arguments. Other often-used arguments were the doctrinal-conceptual ones (22 of 40), the comparative law arguments (16 of 40) and the references to international law (17 of 40). All of the other types of arguments appeared in 10 or fewer of 40 (including non-legal, literal-textual and subjective teleological arguments). Some of the arguments were basically non-existent (in only 1 or 2 judgments), such as references to scholarly works, arguments based on silence, analogies, establishing/debating the text of the Constitution, and arguments about the applicability of the Constitution.

7 *The Weight of Arguments*

The weight of the arguments was entirely unclear; there were no explicit rules or generally accepted doctrines about this. It appears that judges only referred to methods which favoured their preferred outcomes; thus they never really measured the weights of the arguments against each other. Even when referring to foreign (national) law or to Hungarian legal history, it often remained unclear whether they were mentioned as decisive arguments, or only as auxiliary (secondary) arguments in order to make the decision more plausible and to place rhetorically more emphasis on the reasoning.

We could make only one observation: The permanent case law *(jurisprudence constante)* was stronger than just one decision (otherwise it would be unnecessary to quote many cases, but they did often quote a series of cases).

8 *Judicial Candour and Judicial Rhetoric*

There were quite a few non-legal arguments, and some of them were explicitly moral references. The value judgments were consequently relatively transparent.[10] We could not discover any significant correlation

[40] It was admitted even in interviews, see "A 'nehéz eseteknél' a bíró erkölcsi felfogása jut szerephez" [In hard cases the moral opinion will play a role. Interview with László Sólyom, the President of the HCC] (1997) 1 *Fundamentum* 31.

between the length of the opinions and the use of non-legal (including moral) arguments.

Majority opinions normally dealt with most of the arguments of the petitions (or at least those which were quoted at the beginning of the judgment). Opinions of legal scholars were, however, not dealt with explicitly (see above for the very few references to scholarly works), even though on the basis of the reasoning they were likely to be well known to the judges of the HCC (or at least to their clerks).

The language was quite technical and also at the same time very abstract (scholarly-professorial style). Some of the passages were even difficult for lawyers to understand if they were not specialists in constitutional law.

The target audience of the reasoning of the judgments was twofold. The primary audience was politicians (sitting in the legislature or in the government), but at the same time, because of the professorial style, judgments not only wanted to communicate the actual content but they also wanted to communicate the intellectual superiority of the judges over the politicians. The other (secondary) audience seemed to be the HCC itself: in a very detailed manner, concepts were explained with the likely purpose of making it clear to all judges (and their clerks) how cases should be decided in the future (building a *Verfassungsdogmatik*). Doctrinal explanations often went well beyond the actual case.

Ordinary judges were not part of the target audience, as there was no constitutional complaint against judicial decisions (thus judges were not forced to apply the decisions of the HCC; they just had the option of doing so by suspending procedures and initiating a concrete review, but neither the HCC nor the ordinary courts perceived it as an essential channel of communication). The academia was not an intended audience either, even though they were definitely aware of the different critical voices in the literature. Also, foreign courts were not perceived as audience: the HCC did not consider itself important enough to be listened to abroad.

9 *Length, Dissenting and Concurring Opinions*

As a trend, the length of the opinions grew during the period, which can probably be explained by the growing number of precedents (and the more and more sophisticated *Verfassungsdogmatik* based on these precedents) to which they had to react. The length did not show any strong correlation with the topic (only a weak one: fundamental rights judgments tended to be slightly shorter). It appears that judgments became longer when a new intake of judges arrived at the court (beginning of the period and then after 1998 when the 9 years mandate of the first judges expired). This may have been because the old judges wanted to teach their new fellows, or because the new judges felt the need to explain their positions to their fellow judges.

It was possible to submit dissenting or concurring opinions, and in the majority of cases (25 out of 40) there were dissenting or concurring opinions. We could not discover any specific factor though which could explain when and why dissenting or concurring opinions were submitted. The fact that there were no dissenting or concurring opinions does not mean, though, that these judgments were generally accepted later: the judgments on transitional justice (Dec. 11/1992 (III.5) AB) and Dec. 30/1992 (V.26) AB)) were some of the most criticised judgments of the HCC in the literature,[41] even though no separate opinions were submitted to them.

10 *Framing of Constitutional Issues*

Because of the possibility of *actio popularis*, petitioners were not forced to conceptualise their cases as fundamental rights issues. Thus, very general constitutional principles (especially "the rule of law" and "democracy") could play a relatively big role in all types of cases. This seemed constant throughout the whole period.

11 *Key Concepts*

The most popular arguments used by the HCC in its 40 most important judgments were references to "the rule of law" (29 of 40), "democracy" (27 of 40) and "proportionality" (21 of 40). The next group of relatively popular arguments mentioned *Wesensgehalt* (14 of 40), privacy (12 of 40), equality (12 of 40), human dignity (11 of 40) and the parliamentary form of government (11 of 40). The third (not-so-popular) group included freedom of expression (7 of 40), autonomy of local governments (6 of 40), references to "nation" (6 of 40) and the separation of church and state (4 of 40). Some arguments were basically non-existent, such as references to independence (or sovereignty, 2 of 40) or to the republican form of state

[41] E.g. Tamás Győrfi et al. "2. § – Alkotmányos alapelvek, ellenállási jog" [Art. 2 – Basic Constitutional Principles; Right of Resistance] in András Jakab (ed.), *Az Alkotmány kommentárja* ([Commentary on the [Hungarian] Constitution] 2nd edn. Századvég 2009), marginal numbers 130–139 with further references.

(1 of 40). Only one more substantive argument arose frequently, the right to life, which was mentioned in 5 of 40 judgments (Dec. 23/1990 (X.31) AB, Dec. 64/1991 (XII.17) AB, Dec. 46/1994 (X.21) AB, Dec. 36/2000 (X.27) AB, Dec. 47/2007 (VII.3) AB, and in many more uncounted cases in which only Art. 54 of the Constitution was quoted, but not because it contained the right to life, but because it also contained the right to human dignity). The rest of the arguments (*nullum crimen*, personal freedom, etc.) were rather unique and thus we did not count them.

We counted only the cases in which the argument was actually used, not just mentioned. E.g. the HCC often quoted Art. 2(1) of the Constitution which referred to "a democratic state based on the rule of law" also when it just wanted to use "the rule of law" in the reasoning: in such cases the mentioning of "democratic" was not counted. But we did also count those cases in which eventually, after an explanation or analysis of the concept, the HCC decided that a certain key concept did *not* contribute to the solution of the case.

"The rule of law" was used in the sample in the formal senses of legal certainty (especially clarity of legal rules) and primacy of the constitution, but also in the material sense of separation of powers. The rule of law did include, in the Hungarian constitutional understanding, the protection of fundamental rights (especially access to justice, *nullum crimen*), but in this sample it was used only rarely in that sense (rather, the actual fundamental rights were mentioned). One of the judgments explicitly rejected the idea that the rule of law would be based on (moral) justice (Dec. 11/1992 (III.5) AB: "The rule of law based on formal principles is to be preferred against justice which is always partial and subjective.")

"Democracy" included the social preconditions of democracy (pluralism of ideas, open public debates; see the cases where freedom of expression was also mentioned) and it did also include local democracy. In the Hungarian conceptualisation, only the national level had sovereignty (sub-state entities did not). The concept of nation in Hungarian legal terminology was not unified: sometimes it was ethnic, and sometimes it was civic.[42] In the sample, most of the arguments referred to the President of the Republic as a symbol of the "unity of the nation", where the nation was meant in the civic sense.[43]

[42] Helge Hornburg, "The Concept of Nation in the Hungarian Legal Order", in András Jakab, Péter Takács and Allan F Tatham (eds), *The Transformation of the Hungarian Legal Order 1985–2005* (Kluwer Law International 2007), 507.

[43] Virág Kovács, 29. § [A köztársasági elnök általános funkciója] (Art. 29 – The General Function of the President of the Republic), in: Jakab (n 42), para 16.

Both *Wesensgehalt* and proportionality were often mentioned but, if used as fundamental rights tests, they basically merged: "the necessary and unavoidable nature [of the measure] could not be proven, thus it breaches the essential core [*Wesensgehalt – the authors*] of the fundamental right" (Dec. 46/1994 (X.21) AB).[44]

Human dignity had two peculiarities (both developed in Dec. 23/1990 (X.31) AB).[45] On the one hand, it was stated that it cannot be separated from the right to life, as the two fundamental rights form a unity of illimitable rights. On the other hand, human dignity was said to have an "equality function", i.e. one of the consequences of human dignity is non-discrimination.

By procedural fundamental rights, presumption of innocence, access to justice and the usual rights of Art. 6 ECHR are meant. And finally, what we counted as "fed" (i.e., federal) arguments in the Table were arguments referring to the "autonomy of local governments" (Hungary is a unitary state).

From the above-mentioned constitutional concepts, the following were *explicitly* mentioned in the text of the Constitution (the Hungarian Constitution was one-layered, thus there were no *Ewigkeitsklausel* or alike): "the rule of law" (also "primacy of the constitution"), "democracy" (also "sovereignty of the people"), "republic", "separation of state and church", "nation", "autonomy of local governments", "*Wesensgehalt*", "human dignity", "equality", "non-discrimination", "access to justice", "fair trial", "presumption of innocence", "freedom of expression".

Concepts which were created by *Verfassungsdogmatik* (i.e. not mentioned in the text of the Constitution) were, however, the following: "legal certainty", "separation of powers", "parliamentary democracy", "proportionality", "procedural fundamental rights" (in general, particular rights were explicitly mentioned), "privacy" (in general, partial rights were explicitly mentioned).

All these concepts, if used, were used with normative force (either in order to interpret other provisions or to be applied on their own), not just as a rhetorical device. The only clear tendency we could discover was that the use of "human dignity" became rarer when the mandate of the first judges ended in 1998. Until that point, human dignity was also used in cases in which it was not entirely necessary, e.g. when another (more specific) fundamental right could have also been applied instead of

[44] For more details on the doctrine of fundamental rights tests in Hungary see Jakab and Sonnevend (n 51) 112–14.

[45] For details, see Dupré (n 38).

human dignity. The new judges seem to have preferred explicit concrete fundamental rights instead.

C Comparative Analysis

After the end of socialism, Hungary opted for the German constitutional model and its accessories in constitutional reasoning, such as dissenting opinions. The UK model with no formal constitutional guarantees seemed to be a dangerous option. The decentralized American constitutional review looked chaotic, and ordinary judges were servants of the *ancien régime* who could not be trusted to be guardians of the new democratic constitution. In the absence of strong democratic traditions, a very strong president looked too much like a dictator-to-be, so basically the choice was between a semi-parliamentary French system and the parliamentary German system; the unstable Italian parliamentary system looked less attractive, and there were no further major western democracies to look at. Some European post-dictatorial countries opted for the French model, but most chose the German model. The German constitutional system had been built up exactly as an intellectually sophisticated response to a former dictatorship. So, especially with its strong constitutional court, it seemed to fit such situations much more aptly than the French model, which originally was an answer to the incapacity of the executive branch to govern. The choice was partly motivated by the generous German scholarship policy, which meant that some of the talented constitutional lawyers from the new democracies had already spent several months or years at a German university or at the Max Planck Institute for Comparative Public Law and International Law in Heidelberg. Accordingly, they all had learned the democratic style of constitutional law from German literature. Once they had a position at the constitutional court of their home country, either as a judge or as an advisor to a judge, they implemented what they had experienced in Germany.

The main differences are the lack of explicit references to scholarship and the stronger use of international and foreign references in Hungary as opposed to the German practice. Reasons for the former can be the lower prestige of scholarship (even though still relatively high), in the beginning also the lack of relevant literature (even though in later years the lack of references to scholarly works does not apply any more). The contrast between Germany and Hungary is apparent in this respect, even though most judges at the HCC were academics themselves. The stronger use of international and foreign law can be explained by the usual arguments: at the beginning, in the absence of relevant Hungarian case law, references were used in order to strengthen the legitimacy of the reasoning. By the end of the period, the probability of references to foreign law considerably diminished in Hungary as well. In Germany the number of references to foreign legal material was 16, which corresponds to the Hungarian numbers in the period 1991–2010, but compared to the period 2012–13 it sank to only 11. Looking at the number of references to scholarly work, there is a striking difference: the German Constitutional Court reached a number of 37 references, whereas the HCC had only 2 references in the period 1991–2010 and 7 in the period 2012–13.

Some unwritten premises, implied presuppositions behind or major characteristics of the reasoning, differentiating the Hungarian style from others, seem to be the following: (1) The audience is politicians and the HCC itself (but not ordinary judges). (2) The rule of law does not include any element of justice. (3) Human dignity is connected to the right to life and it also justifies equality. (4) *Actio popularis* led to a conceptualisation where fundamental rights are less emphasised and general principles (the rule of law, democracy) are more emphasised. (5) In the majority of the cases one finds references either to international law or to foreign national laws (non-sovereigntist style of reasoning, references to "sovereignty in the sense of independence" are missing).

D Evaluation, Pathology and Criticism

Reasoning

The biggest problems with the reasoning seemed to be the following:[46]

(1) Some of the doctrinal figures appeared in the reasoning out of the blue. In the beginning phase, of course, there were no precedents to refer to. But references to (even foreign) legal scholarship or to foreign and international case-law would probably have been better than nothing. If such references were not possible, then it should have been made clear that the doctrinal figure was an invention of the HCC (e.g. the "unity of life and human dignity"), and the reasons for this should have been explained.

[46] For more details on critical points 3–6, see Zoltán Szente, "The Interpretive Practice of the Hungarian Constitutional Court – A Critical View" (2013) 14.8 *German Law Journal* 1591. Szente explains some of the argumentative mistakes with the party-political bias of the judges.

(2) The references to legal scholarship were very meagre. It is a waste of dialogue/resources and a sign of arrogance not to react to contemporary domestic constitutional scholarship, but to quote foreign authors and to quote non-legal authors.
(3) The weight of the arguments remained unclear. But this is most likely a usual feature of most constitutional courts.
(4) When referring to foreign law or to legal history, the HCC should have made it clear that these were not binding, but were being used only as an inventory of ideas (or in order to establish the *telos* of a certain institution).
(5) The usual objections against the use of comparative law could be brought also against the HCC: it remained unclear when and from which countries (why from those countries) the arguments came.[47] Sometimes contradicting conceptual elements were imported from different countries.[48]
(6) Sometimes, it remained unclear how one step followed from the previous one in an argumentation. Arguments were sometimes just mentioned, but not integrated in the whole of the reasoning of the judgment.
(7) And finally, a very technical issue: The HCC mostly referred to its own judgments via page numbers of its official yearbook (available on its website, but the early versions are in picture-format and consequently not electronically searchable). In the era of the internet, however, either the paragraphs of the judgments should have been numbered (as the ECJ does it), or clear numbered headings with texts should have been used. In this way, both search and referencing would have been easier. Luckily, since 1 January 2012, new judgments (when published in the gazette of the HCC, *Az Alkotmánybíróság határozatai*) have numbered paragraphs, and thus referring to them has become much easier.

[47] Zoltán Szente, "Unsystematic and Incoherent Borrowing of Law. The Use of Foreign Judicial Precedents in the Jurisprudence of Hungarian Constitutional Court, 1999–2010" in Tanja Groppi and Marie-Claire Ponthoreau (eds), *Constitutional Cross-fertilization. The Use of Foreign Precedents by Constitutional Judges* (Hart 2013), 253–72.

[48] E.g. mixing the German doctrine of human dignity (conceptually *absolute*, Kantian or Christian origins) with Dworkin (a concept based on comparison with others: "*same* concern and respect"). See Dec. 23/1990 (X.31) AB. Similarly also László Sólyom, "The Hungarian Constitutional Court and Social Change" (1994) 19 *Yale Journal of International Law* 222, esp. 229. The combination of the absolute *Unantastbarkeit* and the comparative "same concern and respect" was never explained or reflected upon.

As to positive features, the following could be mentioned:

(1) The pervasive use of the objective teleological method. According to the view of the present authors, this method is the key of legal interpretation in general, and also of constitutional interpretation.[49] Objective teleological argumentation avoids the dangers of formalism without descending into a fully fledged moral or political argumentation that might be perceived as inappropriate for a court of law.
(2) The wide use of foreign law and international law is a good method (especially in a small country) for avoiding the detachment of domestic discourse from international developments.
(3) Repeating the petitions at the beginning of the judgments makes the use of arguments more transparent.

The HCC in General

The HCC as an institution had positive effects on Hungarian political and legal culture. On the one hand, the institution of separate opinions contributed to leaving behind the socialist (Montesquieuean) view of judges: by showing that different interpretations are possible, it became more obvious that *reasons* had to be given for one interpretation being chosen over the others. On the other hand, it also made it clear that there are limits on politicians: they cannot do everything even if they are in government. This is a very important insight which is not at all obvious in a society after the end of a dictatorship. And finally, the HCC contributed to connecting Hungarian constitutional culture to Western values of constitutionalism.

The doctrinally unexplained decisions (see above) and the fact that these decisions sometimes were made against both public opinion and moral common sense (especially judgments on transitional justice) contributed to the legitimacy of criticising even the existence of the HCC openly.[50] Smarter compromises (or even agenda setting) could have

[49] András Jakab, "What Makes a Good Lawyer?" (2007) 2 *Zeitschrift für öffentliches Recht* 275, also available at http://ssrn.com/abstract=1918420.

[50] Most questions of transitional justice have nevertheless been solved in the meantime, except for the one of the former Hungarian *Stasi*-agents. This one, however, is unlikely to be solved in the near future (as opposed to most other post-communist EU member countries), as the biggest political parties all sabotage any attempt to reveal the list of former *Stasi*-agents. See http://www.komment.hu/tartalom/20120305-velemeny-ungvary-krisztian-ugynokaktak-nyilvanossaga-a-magyar-politika-csodje.html.

further strengthened its institutional standing and the ideas of constitutionalism in Hungarian society and public discourse.

E Postscript

Beginning in November 2010, the Hungarian constitutional system was transformed into a new regime.[51] The structure, procedure and powers of the HCC were notably changed, and – despite a major overlap in the text of the old Constitution and the new Fundamental Law – the constitutional text altered as well. In order to test the impressions about the changes, we decided to take a second sample, so we can compare the periods between 1990 and 2010, and between 2012 and 2013, respectively. We decided not to take into account the year 2011, as it was a transitory year in many respects which would have caused distortions in both time periods. Major constitutional changes took place in several steps as follows: the HCC's competence regarding statutes on financial, budgetary and tax matters was restricted (with effect of 20 November 2010); the number of judges at the HCC was raised from 11 to 15 (with effect of 1 September 2011) and instead of *actio popularis*, a German style of constitutional complaint system was introduced (with effect of 1 January 2012). The dominant competence of the HCC became the constitutional complaint (394 from 536 until the end of 2013)[52] and *a posteriori* norm control procedures were basically only initiated by the ombudsman.[53] It is also a relevant change that the HCC now has explicit deadlines[54] for constitutional complaint procedures, though only in the internal standing order and with the possibility to be prolonged by the chief justice of the HCC. The political climate has also been transformed: the governing parties had

[51] For more details see Pál Sonnevend, András Jakab and Lóránt Csink, "The Constitution as an Instrument of Everyday Party Politics: The Basic Law of Hungary" in Armin von Bogdandy and Pál Sonnevend (eds), *Constitutional Crisis in the European Constitutional Area* (Hart 2015) 33–109.

[52] See the statistics of HCC from all cases on 31 December 2013. http://mkab.hu/letoltesek/2013_12_en.pdf

[53] According to Art. 24 Abs. 2e) of the Fundamental Law, the HCC shall review any piece of legislation for conformity with the Fundamental Law at the proposal of the Government, one-fourth of the Members of Parliament, the President of the Curia, the Supreme Prosecutor or the Commissioner for Fundamental Rights. Excepting two cases coming from the Government, only the ombudsman took advantage of issuing an abstract norm control procedure, which was done 39 times.

[54] There are 120 days for the decision about the admissibility of the petition and an additional 180 days for the decision concerning its merits.

constitution-amending majority during the period 2012–13 and they regularly reversed judgments of the HCC; and in public statements the language used by politicians reflected a more open conflict between the government and the HCC than ever before.

All this considerably changed the actual work of the HCC. It is noticeable that the number of dissenting or concurring opinions rose from 25 to 35, but at the same time, the number of cases won against the state sank from 29 to 19. The simplest reason for this could be that the growing number of judges resulted in more separate opinions, which at the same time made it more difficult to find a compromise. Another, also plausible explanation is that facing numerous hard legal and constitutional problems because of the new Fundamental Law (including changes in the competences of the HCC), the fundamental differences between the judges could outcrop more easily. The combination of the rising number of separate opinions with the falling number of cases won against the state, however, makes the most plausible explanation the following: the new judges (i.e. those who were elected when the number of judges was raised from 11 to 15, and thereafter during the analysed period) seem to be more friendly with the governing parties and they took over the court despite a strong and explicit opposition by the old judges (as expressed in the separate opinions).[55]

As to the topics, cases concerning state organisation decreased significantly (from 16 to 3), but fundamental rights cases basically stagnated (increased from 18 to 22). The reason for this is the change of the *locus standi* rules of the HCC: in order for a complaint to be admitted, the petitioner must justify his or her personal interest concerning the rule in question, which mostly means to issue a fundamental rights case. The number of procedures regarding state organisation were high between 1990 and 2010 because of *actio popularis*, but under the Fundamental Law, only a handful of state organs can initiate a procedure without showing personal interest. So-called "other" cases that were neither about state organisation nor about fundamental rights significantly increased as well (from 11 to 20). In this last group we can mostly find cases concerning the question of the rule of law, legal certainty and the prohibition of

[55] For statistical analyses, with results similar to ours, see Zoltán Szente, "The Political Orientation of the Members of the Hungarian Constitutional Court between 2010 and 2014" (2016) 1 *Constitutional Studies* 123; Gábor Halmai, "In memoriam magyar alkotmánybíráskodás" [In Memoriam Hungarian Judicial Review] (2014) 1–2 *Fundamentum* 36.

retrospective legislation. The high number of such cases can be explained by the transitory situation based on the constitutional change.

The structure of the arguments fundamentally remained similar in 2012–13 as compared to the period between 1990 and 2010. We found that the arguments establishing or discussing the text of the constitution had great importance in the period 2012–13. Compared to the period between 1990 and 2010, when these arguments were entirely missing, under the new Fundamental Law there were four cases in which the debate about the text of the constitution emerged. The reasons for the emergence of this argument were the so-called "Transitory Provisions", a special act which was adopted in constitution-making process, but which was formally separated from the Fundamental Law. The HCC invalidated the Transitory Provisions on formal grounds, but the question of substantive and formal limits of constitution-amending powers also came up in other cases.[56]

Probably the most striking difference between the 1990–2010 and the 2012–13 period is the increase of the number of arguments on the applicability of constitutional law from 5 to 20. One reason for this is that admissibility became an issue regarding constitutional complaints (cf. end of *actio popularis*), where the HCC only admitted cases if they were not about simple legal interpretation but about "constitutional law issues of fundamental importance".[57] A second reason for the higher number of arguments about the applicability of constitutional law is that the HCC often referred to economic, social or political issues in determining whether a problem was of constitutional nature or not [Dec. 32/2012. (VII. 4.); Dec. 6/2013. (III. 1.)]. And a third reason is that the HCC seemed to use deference arguments about its own relationship both towards the legislature and the (ordinary) judiciary [Dec. 21/2013. (VII. 19.); Dec. 24/2013 (X. 4.)].

We can observe a significant rise in the number of arguments based on the ordinary meaning of words (from 9 to 17). One reason for this

[56] In Dec. 45/2012. (XII. 29.) the HCC was close to deriving a kind of eternity clause based on *ius cogens* on the one hand and the unified and homogeneous feature of the constitution on the other hand. After this decision, the Parliament adopted the Fourth amendment to the Fundamental Law, with which most of the annulled Transitory provisions were overridden. This amendment was challenged as well, but the HCC rejected the petition of the ombudsman in Dec. 12/2013. (V. 24.).

[57] See Art. 29 in Act CLI of 2011 on the Constitutional Court. By the end of 2013, from all the concluded cases (367), almost 200 were rejected because of their inadmissibility, and one of the most frequent grounds was the lack of fundamental importance.

concerns the applicability of former (pre-2012) decisions of the HCC: despite the fact that the HCC's rulings prior to 2012 were formally repealed,[58] the HCC decided[59] to use its earlier case law if the text of the constitutional rule had not been significantly changed. For this reason, the HCC very often analysed the wording of the Fundamental Law (and compared it to the text of the former Constitution) in order to justify the use of its previous decisions. Another reason for the increased number of textual interpretations could be again the deferential attitude of the HCC. Here, we have to notice that – notwithstanding the above-mentioned constitutional amendment – the precedent-based arguments remained the most frequent type of argument (35 in the period 2012–13). Mostly it meant pre-2012 judgments, which shows that the HCC tried to maintain its previous case law despite the formal repeal by the constitution-maker and despite some of the judges' explicit rejection of cases pre-2012 in their separate opinions.

Among the number of harmonising arguments there were no major changes: domestic harmonising arguments remained relevant (though decreased a bit, from 32 to 27) and the arguments of harmonising with international requirements were used a bit more often (from 17 to 20). The reason for the latter could be interpreted as an attempt by the HCC to strengthen the legitimacy of its decisions by referring to international and European level (mostly if they found against the government), and also as a cry for help in its struggle with the domestic constitution-maker (in separate opinions if the majority did not find against the government).

The second most frequently used argument was referring to principles and concepts (increased from 22 to 30). Contrarily, the number of objective teleological arguments was unexpectedly decreased (from 32 to 22) in spite of the explicit interpretative rule in Art. R in the Fundamental Law.[60]

The number of historical-intentional arguments referring to the (assumed) purpose of the constitution-makers doubled (from 5 to 10). As the HCC mostly used these arguments in order to reject the petitions, one possible explanation for the higher number could be that it fitted well

[58] This rule was adopted in the Fourth Amendment, and it is still in force in the Closing and miscellaneous provisions of the Fundamental Law.

[59] First, in Dec. 22/2012. (V. 11.) and in Dec. 13/2013. (VI. 17.).

[60] Art. R of the Fundamental Law introduced a special interpretative rule according to which "the provisions of the Fundamental Law shall be interpreted in accordance with their purposes, with the Avowal of National Faith [i.e. the preamble – *the authors*] contained therein, and with the achievements of our historical constitution."

the new deferential attitude of the HCC. Another reason could be that the adoption of the new constitution was (is) still very close, so the judges had vivid and direct impressions about the background motivations of the constitutional text.

Another major change is the rising number of non-legal arguments (from 11 during 1990–2010 to 26 in 2012–13). The decisions refer to social, demographic and budgetary considerations, several times explicitly to the global financial crisis [Dec. 23/2013. (IX. 25.); Dec. 26/2013. (X. 4.)]. Besides the argument on applicability, only non-legal arguments grew to such a great extent. This can be explained by the more value-laden text of the new Fundamental Law, or by the use of such arguments for deferential purposes or by the hard conflicts with the constitution-maker (and within the HCC itself) in which judges are more likely to refer to the underlying values.

Art. R determines the "achievements of the historical constitution" (whatever that exactly means) as an interpretative tool, and in some cases the HCC did indeed refer to legislative acts from before the Second World War, sometimes even to acts from the nineteenth century. As this type of historical reasoning was considered as "other", further remarkable growth could be observed in this group of arguments (from 7 to 20). Reference to the "spirit of the constitution", the comparative constitutional method and reference to time as a decisive factor were also counted to this "other" group of arguments (Dec. 43/2012. (XII. 20.); Dec. 36/2013. (XII. 5.)).

Reference to scholarly work and to foreign legal material did not change prominently, though it is worth mentioning that almost all the references to scholarly work – 7 cases in the analysed decisions – can be ascribed to one single judge (Béla Pokol).

As for the key concepts, "the rule of law" remained the most dominant concept, though decreased a bit (from 29 to 21) as – following from the new *locus standi* rule – issues have to be conceptualised in the language of rights. Proportionality, human rights, equality and basic procedural rights did not change significantly, but a small-scale decrease can be observed. What is striking, compared to the first period, is that references to state form, form of government, secularism, nation and federalism practically disappeared. The most plausible explanation for this can be the end of *actio popularis* which made admissibility for state organisation cases more difficult. Another (secondary) reason can be the short period of time passed after the entry into force of the new constitution, which did not generate suitable cases of this kind.

Appendix 1: 40 Leading Cases, 1990–2010

1. 23/1990 (X.31) AB
2. 48/1991 (IX.26) AB
3. 57/1991 (XI.8) AB
4. 64/1991 (XII.17) AB
5. 8/1992 (I.30) AB
6. 11/1992 (III.5) AB
7. 30/1992 (V.26) AB
8. 36/1992 (VI.10) AB
9. 37/1992 (VI.10) AB
10. 2/1993 (I.22) AB
11. 4/1993 (II.12) AB
12. 38/1993 (VI.11) AB
13. 64/1993 (XII.22) AB
14. 17/1994 (III.29) AB
15. 34/1994 (VI.24) AB
16. 35/1994 (VI.24) AB
17. 36/1994 (VI.24) AB
18. 46/1994 (X.21) AB
19. 60/1994 (XII.24) AB
20. 43/1995 (VI.30) AB
21. 21/1996 (V.17) AB
22. 4/1997 (I.22) AB
23. 39/1997 (VII.1) AB
24. 52/1997 (X.14) AB
25. 63/1997 (XII.12) AB
26. 27/1998 (VI.16) AB
27. 30/1998 (VI.25) AB
28. 1/1999 (II.24) AB
29. 4/1999 (III.31) AB
30. 25/1999 (VII.7) AB
31. 24/2000 (VII.6) AB
32. 36/2000 (X.27) AB
33. 49/2001 (XI.22) AB
34. 55/2001 (XI.29) AB
35. 62/2003 (XII.15) AB
36. 3/2004 (II.17) AB
37. 55/2004 (XII.13) AB

38. 20/2005 (V.26) AB
39. 42/2005 (XI.14) AB
40. 47/2007 (VII.3) AB

Appendix 2: 40 Leading Cases, 2012–2013

1. 22/2012 (V.11) AB
2. 31/2012 (VI.29) AB
3. 32/2012 (VII.4) AB
4. 33/2012 (VII.17) AB
5. 34/2012 (VII.17) AB
6. 38/2012 (XI.14) AB
7. 40/2012 (XII.6) AB
8. 42/2012 (XII.20) AB
9. 43/2012 (XII.20) AB
10. 45/2012 (XII.29) AB
11. 1/2013 (I.7) AB
12. 2/2013 (I.23) AB
13. 3/2013 (II.14) AB
14. 4/2013 (II.21) AB
15. 6/2013 (III.1) AB
16. 8/2013 (III.1) AB
17. 3076/2013 (III.27) AB
18. 10/2013 (IV.25) AB
19. 3104/2013 (V.17) AB
20. 12/2013 (V.24) AB
21. 13/2013 (VI.17) AB
22. 16/2013 (VI.20) AB
23. 17/2013 (VI.26) AB
24. 3132/2013 (VII.2) AB
25. 3133/2013 (VII.2) AB
26. 3142/2013 (VII.16) AB
27. 19/2013 (VII.19) AB
28. 21/2013 (VII.19) AB
29. 23/2013 (IX.25) AB
30. 24/2013 (X.4) AB
31. 25/2013 (X.4) AB
32. 26/2013. (X.4) AB

33. 29/2013 (X.17) AB
34. 30/2013 (X.28) AB
35. 31/2013 (X.28) AB
36. 3206/2013 (XI.18) AB
37. 3208/2013 (XI.18) AB
38. 32/2013 (XI.22) AB
39. 33/2013 (XI.22) AB
40. 36/2013 (XII.5) AB

11

The Supreme Court of Ireland

EOIN CAROLAN

A Legal, Political, Institutional and Academic Context

1 Legal and Political Culture as Context for Constitutional Reasoning

Ireland's early constitutional history was primarily characterised by internal and external disputes about the precise parameters of its post-colonial status.

From an external perspective, there was a lengthy period of constitutional ambiguity over the nature of its relationship with the United Kingdom. Ireland's War of Independence concluded with the establishment of an Irish Parliament (Oireachtas), an Irish "Free State" and the enactment of a Constitution for that State in 1922. At the same time, however, a Treaty had also been concluded with the United Kingdom government which contained a clause invalidating any provision of the Constitution which was inconsistent with that Treaty. Thus, there was a difference in interpretation over whether Ireland's autonomy of action was attributable to the Irish Constitution (the Irish point of view), or to the consent of the UK government (the UK point of view). Following the Balfour Declaration of 1926 and Statute of Westminster of 1931, renouncing Westminster's direct control over dominion affairs, the practical differences between these two perspectives became less significant.

In 1937, a new Constitution was adopted which went further than the 1922 Constitution had in terms of claiming Irish independence by, for example, replacing the Governor General with a President of Ireland and asserting a territorial claim over Northern Ireland. Ireland formally became a republic with the passing of the Republic of Ireland Act 1949.

Given the historical prominence of these tensions about the sovereignty and character of the state, it is perhaps surprising that they feature on relatively few occasions in the 40 cases selected for this survey. Both factors formed part of the Court's reasoning in considering the question of whether the royal prerogative survived independence in *Byrne v Ireland*,[1] while the independent and republican character of the state was invoked to support the courts' competence to exercise the (from the perspective of English common law orthodoxies) novel powers to invalidate legislation[2] and depart from previous precedent.[3] Otherwise, however, these factors have generally been considered in the distinct context of proceedings raising issues concerning Ireland's relationship with the European Union[4] or the role of the People as ultimate source of internal constitutional authority.[5]

Domestically the ambiguous nature of Irish independence under a Free State system led to a civil war between those opposed to the Treaty with the United Kingdom government and those in favour of it. Although the war lasted for a relatively short period of time, politically-inspired violence continued for several years. The assassination of the Minister for Justice in 1926 led to the introduction of repressive legislation which suspended the fundamental rights provisions of the 1922 Constitution. This had been a relatively liberal document, which sought to guarantee civil and political rights in a conscious break with the common law tradition of Parliamentary supremacy. However, a decision by the Oireachtas to extend its ability to amend the Constitution by ordinary legislation, and the use of that power to suspend or otherwise limit these provisions, meant that the rights guarantees proved largely ineffective. Ultimately, this "was an experiment which ended in failure."[6]

The 1937 Constitution thus combined a list of fundamental rights with a specific power of judicial review. The rights in question were primarily civil and political in nature but also included a right to education, as well as Directive Principles of Social Policy, the latter of which were stated to be non-cognisable by the courts. This is evidenced by the fact that 28 of the 40 cases considered, at least in part, issues of fundamental rights.

The Constitution also contained more conspicuously Catholic influences than its 1922 predecessor, including a religious Preamble[7] and

[1] [1972] IR 241 [2] *Buckley v AG* [1950 IR 67. [3] *AG v Ryan's Car Hire* [1965] IR 642.

[4] *Crotty v An Taoiseach* [1987] IR 713, *Pringle v Ireland* [2012] IESC 47.

[5] *McKenna v An Taoiseach (no. 2)* [1995] 2 IR 10; *Crotty v An Taoiseach* [1987] IR 713; *Re Article 26 and the Abortion Information Bill 1995* [1995] 1 IR 1.

[6] Donal Coffey, 'The Judiciary of the Irish Free State" (2011) *Dublin University Law Journal* 61, at 61.

[7] For discussion, see Mark Tushnet, "National Identity as a Constitutional Issue: The case of the Preamble to the Irish Constitution" in Eoin Carolan (ed), *The Constitution of Ireland: Perspectives and Prospects* (Bloomsbury 2012).

prohibitions on divorce and on blasphemy, as well as an acknowledgment of the special position of the Catholic Church (the last has since been removed). It has been suggested, however, that the nature and impact of these Catholic influences may be commonly overstated, with one leading commentator arguing that "[w]hat is more remarkable . . . is the extent to which that document also reflected secular . . . values of liberal democracy, respect for individual rights and the separation of Church and State and the extent to which it does not reflect Catholic teaching".[8] Leaving aside the question of the significance of rhetorical commitments in a constitutional text, the assessment that the religious provisions have had less impact in practice than commonly perceived is somewhat supported by the fact that reasoning about religion and secularism featured in only 5 of the 40 cases selected.

The 1937 Constitution remains in place. However, it has been amended on several occasions by a majority vote of the People in a referendum.

It seems plausible to conclude that certain aspects of the newly independent state's 1922 and 1937 Constitutions had a fundamental, if gradual, impact on the wider political and public culture insofar as it applies to constitutional reasoning. The inclusion of a textual commitment to fundamental rights, the conferral of the power to invalidate legislative acts on the judiciary, and the incorporation of plebiscitary mechanisms represented a deliberate and conscious rejection of British constitutional traditions of monarchy and parliamentary sovereignty. Over time, this facilitated a broader political and cultural shift from traditions premised on judicial deference to a sovereign Parliament to attitudes more associated with legal constitutionalism, judicial independence and the "respect which one great organ of the State owes to another" (*Buckley v AG*[9]).

While this evolution in Irish legal norms is often most associated with a greater willingness on the part of the courts to invalidate legislative or governmental acts, to regard this as solely a matter of judicial self-aggrandisement is a substantial overstatement.[10] It seems more reasonable to treat this cultural shift as one animated by underlying notions of the rule of law in a written constitutional system. Thus, while the courts have been prepared in reliance on their role as guardians of the Constitution

[8] Gerard Hogan, *The Origins of the Irish Constitution, 1928–1941* (Royal Irish Academy, 2012), at 215–16.

[9] [1950] IR 67 at 80.

[10] D. G. Morgan, "'Judicial-o-centric' separation of powers on the wane?" (2004) 39 *Irish Jurist* 142.

to scrutinise and invalidate actions of political actors in controversial areas such as foreign affairs,[11] expenditure on referenda (*McKenna*[12]) and parliamentary committees (*Re Haughey*;[13] *Maguire v Ardagh*[14]), they have also shown considerable – some have claimed undue[15] – restraint in enforcing constitutional rights against government bodies by reference to other rule-of-law-related principles such as the separation of powers[16] or relative institutional competences.[17]

In terms of the broader political and social culture, this has meant that there is little evidence of public concern about judicial activism in a constitutional context. This is also no doubt supported by the fact that a judicial decision to invalidate a government act will often strike a chord with at least some portion of the general public. More fundamentally, the fact that it is relatively easy to amend the Constitution to nullify the effect of a judicial decision, and that the decision to do so is one ultimately for the People rather than the political class, reduces the scope for long-term public disquiet over specific decisions of the Courts. The existence and regular exercise of this referendum power (33 times between 1937 and 2013) supports a relatively strong public perception of ownership of constitutional values. The consistent willingness of the voters to defeat proposed amendments, even amendments that were initially predicted to pass,[18] also speaks to a reluctance to disturb the constitutional status quo, as well as a certain suspicion of the objectives of the political class in proposing a specific amendment.

This distinction between the public and political attitude to constitutional reasoning is, in Irish terms, a relevant one to draw. While overt political criticism of constitutional decisions is relatively unusual, it seems fair to state that the political class would regard the judiciary as more activist than appropriate, especially when intervening in matters regarded by politicians as primarily their prerogative. The decisions in *McKenna*[19] on electoral expenditure and *Maguire*[20] on the powers of parliamentary committees, for example, have been the subject of ongoing if sotto voce public

[11] *Crotty v An Taoiseach* [1987] IR 713 [12] [1995] 2 IR 10.

[13] [1971] IR 217. [14] [2002] 1 IR 385.

[15] Brian Foley, "Diceyan Ghosts: Deference, rights, policy and spatial distinctions" (2006) 28 *Dublin University Law Journal* 77.

[16] *TD v Minister for Education* [2001] 4 IR 259. [17] *Pringle v Ireland* [2012] IESC 47.

[18] For a recent example, see the rejection of the proposed Thirtieth Amendment to the Constitution which is explained further in UCD Constitutional Studies Group, *A Guide to the Thirtieth Amendment*, available at https://www.ucd.ie/t4cms/Guide_to_the_30th_amendment.pdf.

[19] [1995] 2 IR 10. [20] [2002] 1 IR 385.

complaint from the political elite. However, as the defeat in 2011 of a referendum to effectively reverse *Maguire* demonstrated, there may be a substantial political challenge (and cost) in actively campaigning to persuade the public to endorse the view of the political class.

All of these factors mean that the Irish courts enjoy a considerable degree of practical and political independence in their constitutional reasoning. However, it would be wrong to rely on the judiciary's relative popularity when compared to politicians to overstate the degree of public faith in the judiciary as a stand-alone institution. While there is little evidence of public distrust in the strict context of constitutional reasoning, individual decisions, especially in the criminal context, can be the subject of very critical public and media comment. It should also be noted that there has been growing evidence in recent years of a perception on the part of some political figures that there may be political capital to be gained from conflict with the judiciary. The holding of an arguably unnecessary referendum to reduce judges' pay, the appearance in the media of details about a meeting between the Chief Justice and Taoiseach at which the question of judges' pensions was raised, and the Taoiseach's comment in defence of his (now former) Minister for Justice that he "is not liked by the Judiciary, not liked by the legal profession and he is not liked by the Gardai (police force) . . . but he has the courage to deal with the truth and to change it when it is necessary in the interests of our citizens"[21] support to varying degrees an impression of the government as defending the public interest against an implicitly remote or elitist judiciary.

The formation in 2011 of a representative body known as the Association of Judges of Ireland (AJI) was stated by its members to reflect a "concern that, in the absence of an independent judicial council established by statute, no satisfactory mechanism existed for the judiciary as a whole to convey its point of view on matters of concern to it, when appropriate, and in a manner consistent with the judicial function". This should also be seen against the backdrop of this more conflictual political environment, especially in respect of the debates at the time around reductions to judicial pay and pensions. As the AJI website put it:

> The background to the foundation of the AJI was the development, over the months that followed the change of government that occurred in March 2011, of a perceived difficult relationship between the judiciary and the executive, from the perspective of many members of the judiciary.[22]

[21] Dáil Debates, 26 March 2014. [22] http://aji.ie/ (accessed 31 March 2014)

This is a dynamic which may have long-term implications for the political and legal culture around judicial independence, the relationship between the judiciary and the political institutions of the State, and public perceptions of the judiciary – issues that may all, ultimately, impinge upon the space in which constitutional reasoning occurs.

2 *The Court and Constitutional Litigation*

The Concrete and Adversarial Structure of Litigation

Ireland's legal system operates on a traditional common law model, in accordance with which the parties are primarily responsible for the conduct and content of litigation. Constitutional litigation thus tends to be initiated by private parties, to be conducted on an adversarial basis, and can take a considerable period of time. The relative length of constitutional litigation is based in part on the fact that the will only address constitutional issues as a last resort where it is necessary to resolve the issues between the parties.

Ireland's Constitution has been accepted as having horizontal application with the result that some forms of constitutional litigation may take place between private parties alone. For example, a person may sue another for breach of constitutional rights,[23] or may contend that the purported application of private law principles to their situation should be modified to take account of constitutional principles. On occasions, the Attorney General (as the legal officer responsible for upholding the Constitution) may be invited to participate in proceedings between private parties, either by the parties or by the Court.

The Court applies doctrines of standing and jus tertii.[24] However, the rigours of this have been modified by the Court's willingness to allow a party to bring an action on others behalf where that other may not be able to do so,[25] and by the application of a principle that all citizens have an interest in ensuring that the Constitution is upheld.[26]

Where proceedings involve a challenge to legislation, the Attorney General must be notified[27] (even if the matter is between private parties) and will appear to defend the legislation. Applications have also been made on an increasingly regular basis by parties seeking to appear as amici curiae.

[23] *Meskell v CIE* [1973] IR 121. [24] *Cahill v Sutton* [1980] IR 269.
[25] *SPUC v Coogan* [1989] IR 734. [26] *Crotty v An Taoiseach* [1987] IR 713.
[27] Order 60, Rules of the Superior Courts.

In general, the Supreme Court has tended to respond positively to such applications, although they remain relatively infrequent.

The Article 26 Procedure for Abstract A Posteriori Review

Article 26 of the Constitution also provides for a form of pre-legislative screening in which the constitutionality of legislation can be tested prior to its enactment. This will occur when the President refuses to sign a proposed law on the basis that he or she believes it may be unconstitutional. The Bill is then referred to the Supreme Court which must, within 60 days, advise the President if the Bill is consistent with the Constitution. However, if the Supreme Court approves a Bill, the Constitution provides that it may never be challenged again. This is usually regarded as a deterrent to the use of the Article 26 procedure, with the consequence that it is infrequently invoked.

Article 26 proceedings are an exception to the fact-oriented character of Irish constitutional litigation. The absence of an individual litigant or litigant means that the court must undertake the unfamiliar exercise of assessing legislation in the abstract. This is addressed to some degree by the practice of generating an adversarial hearing by appointing different legal teams to challenge and to defend the proposed measure. That the Court's approach continues to be influenced by the common law technique of assessing the potential impact of the proposed legislation on individuals (albeit hypothetical) is illustrated by the Court's decision in *In re Article 26 and the Abortion Information Bill 1995* to appoint separate legal teams to represent the position of the hypothetical mother and the hypothetical unborn.[28]

The Supreme Court of Ireland as a "Constitutional Court"

While there is evidence that the possibility of a specific "constitutional court" was considered in the course of the drafting of the 1937 Constitution,[29] the decision was ultimately taken that constitutional litigation would remain within the ordinary courts. *Bunreacht na hEireann* (the Constitution of Ireland) reserves the jurisdiction to invalidate legislation as contrary to the provisions of the Constitution to the High and Supreme Courts alone, as the Superior Courts of Ireland. This means that

[28] [1995] 1 IR 1.

[29] Gerard Hogan, "John Hearne and the Plan for a Constitutional Court" (2011) 18.1 *Dublin University Law Journal* 75.

all proceedings in which the constitutional validity of legislation might be impugned (even as a residual or last-resort issue) have been initiated in the High Court with an automatic right of appeal to the Supreme Court.

One significant consequence of this for the nature of constitutional reasoning in Ireland is that constitutional questions are addressed in the course of litigation in which the court is also asked to address non-constitutional questions of law or fact. This has encouraged a continued emphasis in Irish constitutional reasoning on the necessity for judicial reasoning to be based on, and confined to, the facts proven before the court. This led to the articulation in a number of the court's most important early cases of various principles of judicial prudence or restraint, including the presumption of constitutionality,[30] the double-construction rule,[31] and relatively strict rules on standing and jus tertii.[32] Each of these principles seeks to ensure that a court will exercise its constitutional jurisdiction, especially the power to invalidate legislation, only where that has been demonstrated to be necessary to resolve the factual and legal issues before it.

That this approach is, in part, influenced by common law traditions seems evident from Henchy J.'s rationale for the limitations in *Cahill v Sutton*:

> While a cogent theoretical argument might be made for allowing any citizen, regardless of personal interest or injury, to bring proceedings to have a particular statutory provision declared unconstitutional, there are countervailing considerations which might make such an approach generally undesirable and not in the public interest. To allow one litigant to present and argue what is essentially another person's case would not be conducive to the administration of justice as a general rule. Without concrete personal circumstances pointing to a wrong suffered or threatened, a case tends to lack the force and urgency of reality. There is also the risk that the person whose case has been put forward unsuccessfully by another may be left with the grievance that his claim was wrongly or inadequately presented.[33]

A second consequence of the fact that constitutional litigation occurs almost exclusively in the two-tier ordinary superior court system is that the Supreme Court, in particular, has to combine the dual appellate functions of error correction and the principled development of the law. Given the significant growth in the volume and complexity of litigation in

[30] *East Donegal Co-op Ltd v AG* [1970] IR 317.
[31] *McDonald v Bord na gCon* [1965] IR 217.
[32] *Cahill v Sutton* [1980] IR 269. [33] *Cahill v Sutton* [1980] IR 269, 283.

Ireland in recent decades, the result has been a substantial increase in the workload of the Court. A 2006 report found that the Court received and processed substantially more appeals annually than any of its counterparts in common law jurisdictions.[34] The most recent figures show that the Court received 558 appeals in 2013, 605 in 2012 and 499 in 2011, disposing of 249, 202 and 190 respectively in the same periods.[35]

Constitutional litigation occupies a significant portion of the Court's caseload. Indeed, a substantial portion of the written judgments produced by the Court concern, at least in part, constitutional issues. However, the Court's capacity to focus on constitutional questions is constrained by the volume of appeals which it receives on an annual basis.

The 2006 report recommended the establishment of a Court of Appeal. A constitutional amendment to allow for the establishment of such a court was ratified by referendum in October 2013 with the Court of Appeal being established in October 2014. From that point, the Supreme Court will deal only with matters of general public importance and/or where the interests of justice require it to hear an appeal. Given these criteria, it seems likely that constitutional matters will be a substantial feature of the Court's caseload, such that it may begin to function more like a constitutional court.

3 *The Judges*

The Supreme Court is currently composed of a Chief Justice and 9 ordinary judges, together with the President of the High Court as an ex officio member. Until recently, the Court consisted of only 7 ordinary judges. The Court typically sits in panels of 3, 5 or, in exceptional cases, 7. The two most recent appointments were made to assist in clearing the Court's backlog prior to the creation of a Court of Appeal. The expectation is that the Court will revert to 7 ordinary members in the future.

Judges are appointed by the Government and must have previous experience as either practising barristers or solicitors. A committee recently called, on behalf of the judiciary, for the system of appointments to be "de-politicised" to remove the perception that appointments are made on the basis of political allegiance or connections.[36] Academics have on

[34] *Report of the Working Group on a Court of Appeal* (Courts Service 2006).

[35] Courts Service, *Annual Report 2013* at 33.

[36] Preliminary submission of the Judicial Appointments Review Committee to the Department of Justice (30 January 2014), available at: http://www.supremecourt.ie/SupremeCourt/sclibrary3.nsf/(WebFiles)/51E71A71B9961BD680257C70005CCE2D/$FILE/A%20Preliminary%20Submission%20of%20J.A.R.C.%2030.01.2014.pdf

occasion been appointed as judges, but only where they have also had the required 10 years' experience as legal practitioners.

With the exception of the Article 26 procedure where the Court, strictly speaking, provides its opinion to the President, there is no difference between a court's judgment and its decision. The decisions of the Supreme Court typically take a narrative form in which the courts introduce the proceedings, summarise the position and arguments of each party, make any necessary findings of fact and then proceed to explain the reasoning that has led the court to its legal conclusions. Each judge writes their own judgment, although it is more usual than not for some members of the Court to state that they agree with the judgment of one of their colleagues. Dissenting judgments are relatively common. Concurring judgments – in the strict sense of a judgment for which more than one judge takes authorial responsibility – are very rare but not unknown.

4 *Legal Scholarship and Constitutional Reasoning*

The study of constitutional reasoning forms a major part of Irish legal scholarship. A review of the recent output of the two leading peer-reviewed Irish journals (*The Irish Jurist* and the *Dublin University Law Journal*) which was conducted by the author for this report supports this assessment, demonstrating that articles dealing with issues relevant to domestic constitutional law comprise almost 50 per cent of the articles published each year.

For many decades, Irish law schools operated with very few full-time staff, with the consequence that many teaching staff were practising legal professionals. This meant that a number of judges, such as Mr. Justice Henchy, had worked on a part-time basis in the universities. The expansion of full-time faculty in the last 30 years has led to a greater distance between the academic and professional spheres. This is compounded by other ancillary factors, such as the pressure on professional academics to publish in international journals (which means the research is less likely to address domestic issues), and the rules requiring persons appointed as judges to have a minimum level of years as a practising barrister or solicitor. This has not, however, prevented academics such as Mr. Justice Hogan and Mr. Justice McMahon from being appointed to the judiciary where they also satisfied the rules regarding professional experience.

That is not to say that collaboration does not occur between the judiciary and legal academics. Judges frequently attend at and often chair sessions at academic conferences. Some universities operate a formal judge-in-residence programme, while others will invite judges to participate in events on a more ad hoc basis as they arise. Judges also publish articles on occasions in scholarly journals, although, for reasons of restraint, they generally do not address current or likely future issues of controversy.

What is more difficult to demonstrate is the influence of legal scholarship as a context for constitutional reasoning. As the figures for citation of scholarly work demonstrate, courts are willing to refer to scholarly material in their decisions but appear to do this on a relatively infrequent basis. That is particularly so when, as already observed, the majority of scholarly works cited are textbooks rather than articles in legal journals. This could be partly due to the omission of practitioners to rely on academic material in arguments. Whether this is due to a lack of familiarity with such material, a preference for primary materials in argument, or – which would be most relevant for the purposes of this piece – a perceived preference on the part of the judiciary for primary materials cannot be proved.

More broadly, it seems probable that legal scholarship may, over time, influence the general tenor or thrust of legal argument or reasoning in the courts. It has been speculated, for example, that it was the influence of the academy on a younger generation of lawyers and judges that ultimately led to the more enthusiastic embrace of the courts' judicial review powers after 1950.

The speed and force of this influence may be limited by the relatively small market for domestic scholarship which tends to encourage sporadic treatment of specific issues by one or two scholars rather than a sustained engagement on a single issue by several. Where a decision is viewed as sufficiently fundamental or controversial, however (such *as TD v Minister for Education*[37]), such deeper multi-scholar exchanges have occurred.[38]

In keeping with the relative prestige of judges and academics in the common law world, senior judicial salaries are higher than those paid to senior academics. Current pay scales for a university professor range from €96,000 to €136,000 (depending on factors such as the time of

[37] [2001] 4 IR 259.

[38] See, for example, Gerard Hogan, "Directive Principles, Socio-economic Rights and the Constitution" (2001) 36 *Irish Jurist* 174; Mark de Blacam, "Children, Constitutional Rights and the Separation of Powers" (2002) 37 *Irish Jurist* 113; Claire McHugh, "Socio-Economic Rights in Ireland: Lessons to be Learned from South Africa and India" (2003) 3.1 *Hibernian Law Journal* 109; Gerry Whyte, "The Role of the Supreme Court in Our Democracy: a response to Mr Justice Hardiman" (2006) 28 *Dublin University Law Journal* 1; Emma Keane, "Public Interest Litigaton, Socio-economic Rights and National Law" (2008) 26 *Irish Law Times* 62.

initial appointment and the length of time the post has been held) while an ordinary judge of the Supreme Court is paid €198,000.

B Arguments in Constitutional Reasoning

It is fair to say that the Irish courts have not confined themselves to a singular method of constitutional reasoning. Broadly speaking, the Supreme Court has endorsed a number of potential approaches to constitutional reasoning. The leading work on Irish constitutional law, *Kelly The Irish Constitution*, identifies five canons of constructions. These are:

(i) The literal approach.
(ii) A "broad" approach in which the words in the Constitution are given a more purposive reading.
(iii) A harmonious approach, in which the courts consider different provisions of the Constitution in an effort to identify an interpretation which is most consistent with the Constitution as a whole.
(iv) An historical approach, which involves an examination of how a term may have been understood or applied at the time of the Constitution's enactment.
(v) A natural law approach, which seeks to construe the Constitution in accordance with the principles of Thomistic natural law. This approach was based on a number of textual references in the Constitution which appear to imply an endorsement of natural law. However, it has largely fallen into disfavour in the course of the last 20 years.[39]

It has been suggested that the existence of multiple methods of interpretation is liable to generate uncertainty and confusion and facilitate subjective judicial rulings. Hogan and Whyte observe that the lack of methodological consistency on the part of the courts "gives rise to the suspicion that individual judges are willing to rely on any such approach as will offer adventitious support for a conclusion they have already reached".[40] This concern has been rejected by the Supreme Court. Hardiman J. expressed the view in *Sinnott v Minister for Education*[41] that:

> Tensions are said to exist between the methods of construction summarised in the use of adjectives such as 'historical', 'harmonious' and 'purposive'.

[39] See Gerard Hogan and Gerry Whyte (eds), *Kelly: The Irish Constitution* (4th ed, Butterworths 2003) at 3–38.

[40] See ibid, at 3. [41] [2001] 2 IR 545 at 688.

> In my view, much of this debate is otiose, because each of these words connotes an aspect of interpretation which legitimately forms part, but only part, of every exercise in constitutional construction.

Murray J. in Sinnott similarly stated that these methods were capable of co-existing but added that: "It is axiomatic that the point of departure in the interpretation of a legal instrument, be it a constitution or otherwise, is the text of that instrument, albeit having regard to the nature of the instrument and in the context of the instrument as a whole."[42]

This might be thought to indicate that the literal approach serves as the primary or principal method of interpretation. Such an analysis seems, however, overly simplistic for several reason.

First of all, while the courts' *dicta* tend to emphasise the importance of the constitutional text, the Court has shown itself to be prepared on numerous occasions to adopt a more purposive approach to constitutional construction. One of the most commonly cited summaries of this approach is the dicta of Henchy J. in his (dissenting) judgment in *D.P.P. v O'Shea*[43] to the effect that:

> I agree that if the relevant sub-section of the Constitution is looked at in isolation and is given a literal reading, it would lend itself to that interpretation. But I do not agree that such an approach is a correct method of constitutional interpretation. Any single constitutional right or power is but a component in an ensemble of interconnected and interacting provisions which must be brought into play as part of a larger composition, and which must be given such an integrated interpretation as will fit it harmoniously into the general constitutional order and modulation. It may be said of a constitution, more than of any other legal instrument, that "the letter killeth, but the spirit giveth life." No single constitutional provision (particularly one designed to safeguard personal liberty or the social order) may be isolated and construed with undeviating literalness.

This suggests a degree of eclecticism in the courts' understanding of how constitutional cases ought to be addressed, which may bespeak the residual influence of a common law outlook that regards abstract questions of reasoning or methodology to be subordinate to the primary obligation to determine the legal issues raised by the proceedings.

Secondly, the text of the Constitution is itself, relatively open-textured in many important respects such that many interpretive issues cannot be resolved by a strictly literalist approach. As Aileen Kavanagh has pointed out:"[T]he nature of the language in the Constitution is such that even

[42] [2001] 2 IR 545 at 679. [43] [1982] IR 384.

supposedly value-free linguistic analysis generates alternative interpretations. Not only is it legitimate to understand the Constitution by reference to principles not specified in it, it is unavoidable."[44]

Perhaps the best example of this is the doctrine of unenumerated rights, which was first articulated in the proceedings in *Ryan v A.G.*[45] The reasoning of the courts in this decision was founded on a literal interpretation of the phrase "in particular" in Article 40.3.2's statement that "The State shall, in particular, by its laws protect as best it may from unjust attack and, in the case of injustice done, vindicate the life, person, good name, and property rights of every citizen". This immediately followed a more general commitment under Article 40.3.1 to "defend and vindicate the personal rights of the citizen". In applying the ordinary meaning of the words "in particular", the courts concluded that Article 40.3.2 was a non-exhaustive identification of some of these "personal rights" which, by implication, left open the possibility that the Constitution protected other unenumerated personal rights.[46] By definition, the constitutional text was silent as to the content or nature of these rights. A literal or ordinary reading of the constitutional text accordingly led to the adoption of an important constitutional doctrine which required, for its ongoing application, the courts to apply other non-literal forms of interpretation.[47]

The same point can be made in respect of the courts' derivation of a doctrine of natural law from textual references to certain rights being "inalienable and imprescriptible ... antecedent and superior to all positive law."

Thirdly, the evidence of this survey does not support an assessment of the literal approach as the primary or principal method of interpretation. The fact that 13 of the 40 cases took account of the ordinary meaning of words confirms that the text of the Constitution remains an important factor in the courts' reasoning (even if this includes cases

44 Aileen Kavanagh, "The Quest for Legitimacy in Constitutional Interpretation" (1997) 32 *The Irish Jurist* 195, at 216.

45 [1965] IR 294.

46 For criticism of this interpretive reasoning, see Gerard Hogan, "Unenumerated Personal Rights: Ryan's Case Re-evaluated" (1990–1992) 25–27 *Irish Jurist* 95; and a response from Richard Humphreys, "Interpreting Natural Rights" (1993) 28 *Irish Jurist* 221.

47 Some of sources used are described and critically discussed in Siobhán Mullaly, "Searching for Foundations in Irish Constitutional Law" (1998) 33 *Irish Jurist* 333; and Aileen Kavanagh, "Natural Law, Christian Values and the Ideal of Justice" (2012) 48 *Irish Jurist* 71.

like *Ryan*[48] which invoked the text in support of an open-textured interpretation). By comparison, however, 23 of the cases involved domestic harmonising arguments – described in Kelly as "in logic, the first canon of construction"[49] – which suggests a general judicial preference for a form of constitutional reasoning which is based on or inspired by the constitutional text but not tied to a strictly literal interpretation of it.

5 *The Structure of Constitutional Arguments*

In keeping with the methodology of the project, the 40 cases have been identified as containing one of three structures of constitutional argument: one-line conclusive arguments; parallel conclusive arguments; and parallel, individually inconclusive, but together conclusive arguments.

There are a number of caveats to this exercise that might be borne in mind when interpreting the Irish results. The first is that this is necessarily in some cases a question of discretion, especially with regard to the distinction between the latter two categories. Secondly, the fact that a single method has been chosen does not mean that there are not elements of the other forms of argument in that decision. These points are both related to the third caveat, which is that that the discursive nature of Irish judgments – again reflecting English legal traditions – means that the weight of particular arguments in shaping the outcome of the decision may not always be clear. While courts sometimes identify a specific factor as critical in determining their conclusion, there are other instances where the relative influence of arguments to which the courts seems sympathetic may not be made explicit.

In this regard, there is a notable trend in Irish constitutional reasoning away from a predominant use of conclusive arguments in the early caselaw to a more recent preference for parallel arguments, whether conclusive or otherwise. With the exception of one Article 26 ruling (which, given the requirement of unanimity, are often more laconically reasoned), the other 13 cases in which the chain method was used pre-date 1994 and are typically much older than that. This may be attributed in part to changes in the practice of constitutional litigation in Ireland, such as greater complexity in the arguments submitted by the parties, the increased use of written submissions, the recruitment of some judicial research support in recent years, and enhanced accessibility of legal precedents (especially

48 [1965] IR 294.

49 See Hogan and Whyte (n 39), at 8.

comparative).[50] However, it is also noteworthy that there is evidence of parallel arguments in some of the older authorities. This suggests that differences in structure may be reflective of the extent to which the courts' consideration of parallel arguments – which are, after all, likely to be made in constitutional litigation that may turn on the courts' assessment of particular facts – is made explicit in the decision or is internalised in the production of a solitary conclusive argument.

6 *Types of Arguments in Constitutional Reasoning*

Introduction

Almost all of the forms of arguments identified in the materials for the project are evident to varying degrees in Irish constitutional jurisprudence. The main exceptions are arguments based on federalism and arguments based on the notion of a core concept of constitutional rights. The former are inapplicable to Ireland's unitary system, while the latter do not appear to have been considered by the Irish courts. In keeping with the courts' preference for domestic harmonising arguments, Irish constitutional law has generally eschewed claims that any particular constitutional right or value is pre-eminent or more core than others, with the possible exception of the right to life.[51]

Arguments based on establishing or discussing the text of the Constitution are also generally alien to Irish constitutional reasoning. This reflects the fact that there is a clearly enacted formal constitutional text, such that there is little, if any, room for doubt about whether a provision forms part of the constitutional text or otherwise. Even applications of unenumerated rights or principles tend to be based, as discussed above, on a written provision in the constitutional text.

The unusual character of the sole exception identified in the 40 cases underlines this point. *In re Article 26 and the Abortion Information Bill*[52] concerned, inter alia, the position of natural law under the Irish constitutional order. Specifically, an issue was raised as to whether the result of a referendum could be invalidated by the Supreme Court on the basis that it was contrary to natural law. The stark nature of this issue led the Court to declare – in apparent contradiction of earlier caselaw – that natural

[50] On which generally, see David J. Gerber, "Globalization and Legal Knowledge: Implications for Comparative Law" (2001) 75 *Tulane Law Review* 949.

[51] *People (DPP) v Shaw* [1982] IR 1. [52] [1995] 1 IR 1.

law did not enjoy any particular constitutional protection or status.[53] However, because this earlier caselaw had contained clear references to natural law, it was necessary for the Court to address such precedents and, therefore, to address the argument that it thereby formed part of the constitutional text.

The remainder of this section considers the nature and extent of the remaining arguments identified in the survey. In an effort to assist the reader, arguments that tend to be inter-linked in Irish constitutional reasoning are discussed together.

Applicability of Constitutional Law

The horizontal applicability of the Constitution[54] means that it is, in principle, broadly applicable to all issues that may arise before the courts. While it has been suggested that "the actual impact of this doctrine has been often muted by the adoption of a cautious approach towards developing private law remedies to reflect constitutional values",[55] the fact that the principle exists at all means that the argument that constitutional law may not be applicable to a particular act or omission is rarely canvassed.

Where arguments of this character appear, they might more strictly be described as arguments concerning the applicability of constitutional review by the judiciary. Arguments that certain issues are reserved to the political institutions of government were considered in the five cases identified under this heading in the survey. However, in most instances, these arguments were themselves based on certain provisions of the constitutional text. *Crotty v AG* is a good example in this regard. There, it was argued that Article 29 of the Constitution reserved powers in respect of international affairs to the executive branch of government, with the effect that the courts could not review a decision to conclude an international treaty with other European states. This was rejected by the majority of the Court. Hederman J.'s conclusion that the executive power could be subject to review on the basis that "[t]he State's organs . . . are the guardians of these powers – not the disposers of them" illustrates how broadly conceived the applicability of constitutional law is in Ireland.

[53] For a discussion of this aspect of the Court's opinion, see Adrian Twomey, "The Death of the Natural Law?" (1995) 13 *Irish Law Times* 270.

[54] *Meskell v CIE* [1973] IR 121.

[55] Colm O'Cinneide, "Taking Horizontal Effect Seriously: Private Law, Constitutional Rights and the European Convention on Human Rights" (2003) 4 *Hibernian Law Journal* 77. See also William Binchy, "Meskell, The Constitution and Tort Law" (2011) 33 *Dublin University Law Journal* 339.

The other instance in which this issue has arisen is in the specific context of Article 45 of the Constitution. This sets out certain Directive Principles of Social Policy which are stated to be non-cognisable by the courts. This has led to occasional arguments about whether or to what extent the courts are entitled to refer to or rely upon these principles.[56] While this was discussed in Article 26 and the Planning Development Bill,[57] the Court ultimately reserved its position on the matter.

Analogy and Precedent

In light of its common law and adversarial character, reasoning by reference to precedent and by analogy are widely used techniques in Irish law. The courts are culturally and professionally predisposed to the use of precedent and analogy in the constitutional context.

It is unsurprising, therefore, that precedent is the factor most commonly cited in the reasoning of the courts in the 40 cases surveyed. A roughly similar result might be expected from most equivalent samples of Irish decisions. One point to bear in mind is that precedent in this context includes the judicial citation of both binding and persuasive authorities. Strictly speaking, the Supreme Court is, of course, entitled to depart from any previous decision which it regards as having been wrongly decided.[58] The distinction between binding and persuasive precedent may be pertinent, however, to an evaluation of the degree of influence which precedent may have on the outcome of a given decision. This is particularly relevant given the frequency with which foreign and, especially English, precedents are considered by the Irish courts. These are merely persuasive, such that the Supreme Court is entitled to disregard them if it sees fit. This means that, while precedent is plainly an important factor in Irish judicial reasoning, it is also important not to overstate the extent to which the Supreme Court's reasoning in constitutional matters is determined rather than merely influenced by the citation of precedent.

The use of analogy is linked to the typically individual-oriented nature of Irish constitutional litigation. The fact that the Court is making a decision in respect of a specific individual or group of individuals means that its reasoning is often focused on that specific factual situation. Where the measure is of narrow scope, this does not require the use of analogy. Where, however, the measure impugned may have a more general applicability, the courts are more willing to make use of analogies. This

[56] See, for example, Hogan (n 38) 174; Keane (n 38) 62.

[57] [2000] 2 IR 321. [58] *AG v Ryan's Car Hire* [1965] IR 642.

is particularly so where the constitutional issue raised involves some consideration of, or balancing test with, the public interest.[59] This is true of arguably all of the 15 cases in which analogy was used in this survey.

Interpretive Arguments

As already discussed, the Irish courts typically favour an approach to constitutional interpretation which might reasonably be described as broadly textualist. While this often involves an assessment of the ordinary meaning of the words of the Constitution, this analysis will generally be conducted in light of a consideration of the text of the Constitution as a whole. This broad approach to interpretation means that arguments about the ordinary meaning of words (15) are common but, as far as this survey is concerned, less frequently used than both textual (25) and historical (17) forms of teleological reasoning. This attitude also explains the popularity of domestic harmonising arguments which are amongst the more commonly used forms of reasoning identified in this survey. They appear in 23 instances compared with 15 for more literalist arguments about the ordinary meaning of words.

This means, for example, that issues concerning the Constitution's institutional structures may be considered in light of the Constitution's commitment to individual rights (*Maguire v Ardagh*[60]) or democratic principles (*McKenna v An Taoiseach (no. 2)*[61]). Similarly, proceedings concerning the balancing of respective individual rights may be construed in a manner that promotes harmony with other more structural (*A. v Governor of Arbour Hill*[62]) or value-laden principles (*Northwestern Health Board v HW*[63]) in the constitutional text.

Linguistic formulas based on silence (10) have also been used. These tend to be applied in the context of the Court's analysis of the teleological purpose of the provision in question. The Court may assume that an omission to address a matter represented a deliberate decision on the part of the drafters. The courts' willingness to make use of these different techniques as appropriate is again based on a general conception of the Constitution as a coherent whole. The fact that certain provisions have subsequently been amended has not affected the popularity of this overall approach.

[59] See, in particular, *Heaney v Ireland* [1994] 3. IR 593; *People (DPP) v Shaw* [1982] IR 1, *State (Nicolaou) v An Bord Uchtála* [1966] IR 567; and, *Re Article 26 and the Planning and Development Bill 1999* [2000] 2 IR 321.

[60] [2002] 1 IR 385. [61] [1995] 2 IR 10. [62] [2006] IESC 45. [63] [2001] 3 IR 622.

The suggestion that the courts are committed to a broad but textualist approach to constitutional reasoning might appear to run counter to the large number of decisions (30) in which concepts or principles that do not appear in the constitutional text are considered. The frequency of this form of arguments must be considered, however, in light of the points made above about the open-textured nature of the Constitution. As already explained, certain of the Constitution's provisions can be construed as delineating the existence but not the content of broad concepts like natural law or unenumerated personal rights. This necessarily obliges the courts to develop their own interpretive criteria to guide proceedings in respect of such provisions. However, it is notable that in so doing the courts have often drawn on values which – while not expressly endorsed in a particular provision and thus technically not in the text – are arguably implicit within its overall framework. For example, in considering whether an asserted entitlement could be regarded as falling within the notion of the citizen's "personal rights", the courts in a number of cases based their conclusion on whether the right in question could be implied from the "Christian and democratic nature of the State".[64]

More generally, the courts' preference for a broadly harmonious approach to the constitutional order has also meant that they make reference in many instances to broad notions of public interest, even where that concept may not be expressly identified in the relevant constitutional provision under consideration (*A v Governor of Arbour Hill*[65]). Therefore, while it is correct to note that the courts do not rely on solely textualist forms of reasoning, the fact that many of the arguments in this category are based on concepts that do not expressly appear in the text but are arguably implicit within suggests that the extra-constitutional dimension of this reasoning should not be overstated. That the courts have confined themselves to textually implicit values in at least some instances of unavoidable interpretive freedom might be seen as confirming their inclination towards arguments that can be presented as consistent with the harmony of the constitutional whole.

By contrast to this preference for domestic harmonising arguments, the Irish courts make comparatively rare use of international harmonising arguments. This appears in only 4 of the 40 cases surveyed. Indeed, in 2 of these instances,[66] the courts were obliged by the nature of the case to address the question of international harmonisation because the issue

[64] *McGee v AG* [1974] IR 284. [65] [2006] IESC 45.

[66] *Crotty v An Taoiseach* [1987] IR 713; *Maher v Minister for Agriculture* [2001] 2 IR 139.

raised was how domestic constitutional law should respond to actions that were necessitated by Ireland's membership of what is now the European Union. It is notable that in other proceedings arising out of European Union membership,[67] the Court did not advert in its reasoning to any suggestion that domestic constitutional law should be shaped by considerations of international harmony. European Union membership provided the factual context for these proceedings, but the reasoning applied was based on domestic law alone.

This relatively low instance of international harmonising arguments may seem incongruous given the frequency with which the Irish courts refer to foreign legal material (31 of the 40 cases). As has already been suggested, however, the impression of a committed internationalist outlook that might be derived from these figures may be misleading given the prominence of English legal authorities amongst the foreign sources cited. That is not to say that the Court does not refer to other national or international courts. In this survey, references can be found, inter alia, to decisions from Canada, Australia, New Zealand, Germany, the ECHR, CJEU, Israel and South Africa, as well as to state courts from the US. However, English authorities dominate to a considerable degree.

In general, the Court retains a clear sense – based on the text of what is, after all, a Constitution with strongly nationalist influences – of the sovereign authority of Irish law. The Court has emphasised that, while it may and has previously had regard to international agreements as persuasive sources, they enjoy – at best – sub-constitutional status as a matter of Irish law. In *McD v L*[68], the Supreme Court overturned a High Court decision on the basis that it had sought to directly apply Article 8 of the European Convention on Human Rights by finding that a same-sex couple were a de facto family for the purposes of a guardianship application. Section 2 (1) of the European Convention on Human Rights Act 2003 provides that: "In interpreting and applying any statutory provision or rule of law, a court shall, in so far as is possible, subject to the rules of law relating to such interpretation and application, do so in a manner compatible with the State's obligations under the Convention provisions."

The Court held that:

> Those issues were determined as independent autonomous claims arising under Article 8. In my view the High Court had no jurisdiction to apply directly the provisions of the Convention in that manner. In considering and determining those issues the High Court was not exercising, or indeed

[67] *Pringle v Ireland* [2012] IESC 47. [68] [2009] IESC 81.

> purporting to exercise, a function pursuant to s. 2 of the Act and no issue had arisen under sections 3 or 5 of the Act. Accordingly there was no basis in law for applying Article 8 of the Convention to the status of PL and BM or any of the parties.

This reflected:

> The relationship between international treaties to which Ireland is a party and national law is imbued with the notion of dualism the effect of which finds expression in Article 29.6 of the Constitution. According to the concept of dualism, at national level national law always takes precedence over international law. At international level, as regards a state's obligations, international law takes precedence over its national or internal law which is why a state cannot generally rely on their own constitutional provisions as an excuse for not fulfilling international obligations which they have undertaken. Coming back to the national level the dualist approach means that international treaties to which a state is a party can only be given effect to in a national law to the extent that national law, rather than the international instrument itself, specifies.

Article 29.6 of the Constitution provides in very clear terms "No international agreement shall be part of the domestic law of the State save as may be determined by the Oireachtas." This is consistent with the sovereign legislative powers vested in the Oireachtas by Articles 6 and 15 of the Constitution. The Oireachtas, in turn, when determining whether, and to what extent, an international agreement shall be part of the domestic law of the State, is governed by the provisions of the Constitution.

This is not to take away from the fact that recourse may and has been had by the Irish courts to the caselaw of the European Court of Human Rights (ECtHR) for comparative law purposes when a court is considering the import of a right under domestic law where the right is the same or similar to one found in the Convention.[69]

Arguments Based on Structural Values and Principles

An influential category of arguments in Irish constitutional doctrine are those derived from aspects of the Constitution's structural and principled commitment to Ireland as "a sovereign, independent, democratic state" (Article 5) in which "[a]ll powers of government, legislative, executive and judicial, derive, under God, from the people, whose right it is to designate

[69] [2010] 2 IR 199, at 245–7. For analysis of this decision, see Maria Cahill, "McD v L and the incorporation of the European Convention on Human Rights" (2010) 46 *Irish Jurist* 221.

the rulers of the State and, in final appeal, to decide all questions of national policy, according to the requirements of the common good" (Article 6).

These principles manifest themselves in an overlapping family of arguments based on (in descending order of their appearance in the 40 cases) democracy, the form of government, the rule of law, sovereignty and the form of the state.

The recurring emphasis in this category of arguments tends to be upon the Constitution's commitment to popular sovereignty, as acknowledged in Article 6 and in the various constitutional provisions that provide for referenda on constitutional amendments or on questions of national importance.

The early references to popular sovereignty reflected the nationalist impulse that animated both the constitutional text and the values of Irish public life. It was in this context that arguments about the form of the state appear.[70] This sense of sovereignty as an assertion of external autonomy is well illustrated by the Court's approach to international affairs in *Crotty v An Taoiseach*,[71] where it was held that the entry into an agreement concerning very limited co-ordination of foreign affairs under the Single European Act was contrary to the Constitution (although the Court seems in the more recent *Pringle v Ireland*[72] case to have modified this strict interpretation of external sovereignty as control in fact).

These arguments more frequently take the form, especially in more recent decisions, of endorsing the People as the basic source of sovereign power.[73] In acknowledgement of this principle, the courts have attached particular significance to those occasions upon which the People as sovereign exercise their collective authority, whether by election or by referendum. This has led to the principle being invoked as a basis for the application of certain constitutionally-implied rules concerning the conduct of election or referendum campaigns in Ireland. The Court has held, for example, that the Constitution implicitly requires fairness in the broadcast coverage of referenda; prohibits the use of public monies to fund one side of a referendum campaign (*McKenna v An Taoiseach (no. 2)*;[74] requires a by-election to be held within a reasonable period of time;

[70] *Byrne v Ireland* [1972] IR 241; *Buckley v AG* [1950] IR 67.

[71] [1987] IR 713. [72] [2012] IESC 47.

[73] But see Colm O'Cinneide, "'The People are the Masters'. The Paradox of Constitutionalism and the Uncertain Status of Popular Sovereignty within the Irish Constitutional Order" (2012) 48 *Irish Jurist* 249.

[74] [1995] 2 IR 10.

and confers a particular level of protection on the media as the "eyes and ears of public opinion" in their coverage of public affairs such as the administration of justice.[75]

Individual Rights

The other group of factors surveyed which appear with a reasonable degree of frequency in the 40 cases are those relating to the protection of individual rights in the Irish Constitution.

The specific rights identified in the survey, namely privacy, equality and freedom of expression, appear relatively infrequently by comparison with the factors discussed above. This reflects, in part, the editorial choices made in selecting the 40 cases. However, it also probably speaks to the fact that each of these rights has, for various reasons specific to each one, not been the subject of as much litigation and/or judicial exposition as might be the case in other jurisdictions. Privacy, which appears in three of the cases, is not specifically recognised by the Constitution, so that it was only acknowledged as a right for the first time in the 1970s,[76] and even then only initially in the context of marital privacy.

Freedom of expression, meanwhile, is discussed on four occasions. While recent decisions have signalled a liberalisation in Irish constitutional law on freedom of expression,[77] the fact that the text of the Constitution included express limitations of the principle on the grounds of public order, morality, blasphemy and sedition meant that the right was for many decades comparatively under-developed.[78]

By comparison, equality is considered in a much larger number of these decisions (11). However, this category includes both proceedings in which equality is invoked as a free-standing right and proceedings where it is considered by the courts as an underlying constitutional value. The latter formulation of the principle has appeared in the Irish jurisprudence in the context of a judicial recognition of the broadly autonomy-oriented nature of the Constitution's conception of individual rights. In this regard, it is often referenced alongside related principles such as dignity or autonomy as part of the contextual background for the courts' reasoning. It may be relevant to observe that of the 9 and 11 cases in which dignity and equality appear, 5 are the same. This counsels against over-stating the role

[75] *Irish Times Ltd v Ireland* [1998] 1 IR 359.

[76] *McGee v AG* [1974] IR 284.

[77] *Irish Times Ltd v Ireland* [1998] 1 IR 359; Murphy v IRTC [1999] 1 IR 12.

[78] For a recent overview of the development of the right, see Carolan, Constitutionalising discourse (2014) 51 Irish Jurist 1.

of equality as a free-standing substantive entitlement. This is especially so given the fact that claims based on the Article 40.1 rights guarantee have long been hampered by a number of textual qualifications on the right which have made it, in practice, difficult to successfully invoke.[79]

This means that those factors more associated with the procedural aspects of judicial rights-reasoning may provide a more accurate proxy for the place of rights jurisprudence in Irish constitutional reasoning. This reflects the fact that judicially-created principles of constitutional justice (*McDonald v Bord na gCon (no. 2)*[80]) and fair procedures (*Re Haughey*[81]) were and remain amongst the most commonly litigated aspects of Irish constitutional practice. They are also amongst the principles most broadly applied by the courts, being held to cover criminal (*State (Healy) v Donoghue*[82]), parliamentary[83] (*Maguire v Ardagh*[84]; *Re Haughey*[85]), plebiscitary[86] (*McKenna*[87]) and administrative or regulatory[88] (*McDonald v Bord na gCon (no. 2)*[89]) procedures. This inclination towards proceduralisation of rights issues may also, in part, explain the popularity of the proportionality doctrine. In the roughly 25 years since its initial adoption by the Irish courts (*Re Heaney*[90]), it has become the primary method for assessing a case which involves either a conflict of constitutional rights or a balance between a constitutional right and a competing constitutional value (such as the common good). This is reflected in the fact that, even though it is a relatively new principle, it has been cited 9 times in the 14 cases decided since its endorsement.

Scholarly Work

Scholarly work is occasionally cited, but this is comparatively less frequent than in some other jurisdictions. While scholarly work was cited on occasions in these 40 cases, it should be borne in mind that the

[79] See Colm O'Cinneide, "Aspirations Unfulfilled: the Equality Right in Irish Law" (2010) 1.1 *Intercultural Human Rights Law Review* 41; Oran Doyle, *Constitutional Equality Law* (Round Hall 2004).

[80] [1965] IR 217. [81] [1971] IR 217 [82] [1976] IR 325.

[83] See John O'Dowd, "Knowing How Way Leads On to Way: Some Reflections on the Abbeylara Decision" (2003) 38 *Irish Jurist* 162.

[84] [2002] 1 IR 385. [85] [1971] IR 217

[86] See Bláthna Ruane, "Reflections on Procedural Rights in Constitutional Referenda" (2012) 48 *Irish Jurist* 1.

[87] [1995] 2 IR 10.

[88] Ailbhe O'Neill, "Fair Procedures – an Inviolable Constitutional Requirement?" (2011) 34 *Dublin University Law Journal* 319.

[89] [1965] IR 217. [90] Heaney v Ireland [1994] 3. IR 593.

majority of references were to the major textbooks on Irish constitutional law. Reference is most frequently made to Hogan & Whyte, *Kelly: The Irish Constitution* which is, while a prodigious scholarly effort, aimed as much at practitioners as at a scholarly audience. The limited impact of primarily academic-oriented work can, in be attributed to the small pool of Irish academic scholarship. There are relatively few academic journals in Ireland. In addition, there are a small number of universities, in which law schools also tend to be small by international standards. This is exacerbated by the tendency in recent years for universities to encourage academics to publish in international journals, many of which have limited interest in Irish constitutional issues. This all means that there may be few opportunities for the Court to identify and cite specifically relevant academic scholarship. The fact that the Court regularly cites textbooks suggests that it could be willing to refer to such scholarship if more of it was available to it, or was cited to it in argument by practitioners.

Non-legal Arguments

Non-legal reasoning appears rarely in the 40 cases reviewed. However, this is partly because the broad scope and content of the Irish constitutional framework means that arguments that might be regarded as non-legal in other jurisdictions have a constitutional basis within the Irish system. This is most evident in respect of the various Catholic elements of the text which have often provided a framework for discussion of religious or moral elements. For example, the Supreme Court in *State (Nicolaou) v An Bord Uchtála*[91] based its conclusions on what it viewed as the lesser moral capacity of an unmarried father, but was expressly entitled to do so by the text of the Article 40.1 equality provision.

Otherwise, non-legal reasons tend to be discussed by the Irish courts in the context of arguments that certain extra-legal facts constitute exceptional circumstances, of which account should be taken. These are usually argued to form some aspect of the public interest or common good of the measure being challenged before the courts.

7 *The Weight of Arguments*

The Court, as a general principle, does not formally regard any particular style of argument as having a particular a priori value.

[91] [1966] IR 567.

However, arguments may carry greater weight where they are drawn from a source which has a higher value within the legal system. Thus, arguments based on the constitutional text carry the greatest weight (assuming that the Court maintains its reluctance to draw upon natural law), whereas arguments based on the common law or foreign precedent have less value.

8 *Judicial Candour and Judicial Rhetoric*

It is inevitably difficult to provide an objective assessment of judicial candour given that an outsider cannot know whether or not the opinions and reasons expressed by the judges are, in fact, accurate. Nonetheless, there is little, if any, evidence to suggest that the reasons given by the Supreme Court are not accurate. Legal practice and tradition in Ireland places a high value on the common law principles associated with fidelity to precedent and to the legal text. While judges are clearly aware of their personal values, and of the impact these may have on their response to the issues raised before them, the techniques of reasoning and analysis applied in legal practice are intended to limit the impact of such values. There is little to suggest that judges see their position in legal realist terms as advancing a particular political perspective.

The language used in judgments varies in its technicality in accordance with the subject matter of the case, the arguments put by the parties, and the identity of the judges involved. Some judges write in a more eloquent and accessible style than others. Some use more rhetorical flourishes than others. On the whole, however, judgments are expressed in relatively accessible narrative terms, albeit with a tendency (not surprising given the background of the judges in legal practice) to use technical terms to describe particular legal concepts or approaches.

The Court's decisions have a general audience and are made freely available on the Courts' Service website. In recent years, the Supreme Court has also occasionally provided a short summary of its decision to journalists present in court where the case is one that may be of particular public interest or involve complex concepts. These summaries have no particular legal status.

9 *Length, Dissenting and Concurring Opinions*

Decisions of the Irish Supreme Court were formerly in the region of 20 to 40 pages of the Irish Reports but have tended in recent years to increase substantially in size. This seems attributable to a variety of factors, including the greater use in recent years of written submissions as well as oral argument, the greater accessibility of legal sources (especially from other jurisdictions), the greater sophistication and length of submissions by the parties, and the appointment of researchers to support the Court's work. On occasions, decisions have been very lengthy, numbering more than 100 pages. *TD v Minister for Education*[92] is, for example, 118 pages long. This occurs typically where a large number of legal issues have been raised before the Court. It is, again, partly attributable to the fact that the Irish Supreme Court has until recently been the first and only court of appeal and so generally lacks the capacity or entitlement to confine an appeal to particular points of public importance only.

There is an established tradition of dissenting judgments, many of which have subsequently been cited as the source of important principles or values. The right to individual privacy, for example, was first identified and articulated in the dissenting judgments of the minority of the Court in *Norris v A.G.*[93], which was a challenge to a pre-independence statute criminalising male homosexual conduct.

However, the Constitution has historically required that only one judgment be delivered in proceedings concerning the constitutionality of legislation. This rule, which was removed by referendum in October 2013, meant that it was impossible to identify whether a determination was a unanimous or majority judgment. This also meant that the decision had to be agreed by all members of the Court, such that the resulting judgment might not reflect the full reasoning of all individual members of the Court. It also frequently resulted in a situation where the Court would give a single judgment on the specific issue of the constitutionality of legislation and then deliver individual judgments on other issues raised during the proceedings. On occasions, these judgments could be shorter and more laconically reasoned than equivalent plenary proceedings. It is usually assumed that this indicates that the Court has found it more difficult to agree on a position on an issue or argument which would command unanimous support.

10 *Framing of Constitutional Issues*

The fact that the Supreme Court hears all appeals, and that an appeal raising constitutional issues may also involve other questions, makes this a difficult issue to address in general terms.

The Court is, once again, dependent in the first instance on the parties to frame the subject matter, content and scope of any constitutional

[92] [2001] 4 IR 259. [93] [1984] IR 35.

issues involved in the proceedings. Pleadings play an important role in this regard – it is possible (although not certain) that a constitutional dimension may not be considered by the Court if the party or parties have not included it in their pleadings.

Furthermore, the Court also applies a rule of practice that it will only consider the constitutionality of legislation as a last resort if it is not possible to determine the issues between the parties on other grounds. Thus, the framing and resolution of a constitutional question may depend on whether the parties included other grounds in their original proceedings.

11 Key Concepts

A number of concepts play a particularly important role in Irish constitutional jurisprudence. Several of these have already been considered at length in the earlier section on types of arguments in constitutional litigation. Domestic harmonising arguments, for example, are amongst the most important family of concepts in Irish constitutional reasoning given the way in which they provide a coherent overall framework for the courts' regular invocation of textualist, teleological, historical and precedent-based arguments. The way in which these concepts are framed in Irish constitutional jurisprudence tends, as explained, to implicitly accept the premise that the Constitution represented a cohesive statement of values and principles by its drafters.

Proportionality and popular sovereignty are other key and regularly-cited concepts that have been described at length in earlier section. Other key concepts that are worthy of comment but not explored in detail above are discussed in the remainder of this section.

1. Autonomy: Although the concept of autonomy has rarely been specifically invoked by the Court, the Court's interpretation of the fundamental rights provisions has tended to adopt an autonomy-oriented perspective which emphasise the necessity for individuals to have the freedom to make their own decisions. This is evidenced by the Court's endorsement of a Lockean conception of property rights, in its defence of the autonomy of the family against State intervention, and in the Court's consistent and very robust development of an implied constitutional right to fair procedures.
2. Implied constitutional rights: One of the most important doctrines of Irish constitutional law has been the notion of unenumerated constitutional rights. This was established in *Ryan v AG*[94] and holds,

[94] [1965] IR 294.

in effect, that the Article 40.3.1 guarantee of the "personal rights of the citizen" is not limited to those specifically referenced in that Article. This has subsequently been used to develop a host of rights, including the right to privacy, the right to bodily integrity, the right to earn a livelihood, the right to fair procedures, the right to die, the right to dissociate, and the right to communicate.

3. Separation of powers: The separation of powers is not explicitly enshrined in the constitutional text, but it has been embraced by the Court as a "high constitutional value". It has been applied both to prevent the political branches from assuming functions that may trespass on the rights of the citizen (*Maguire v Ardagh*[95]) and/or administration of justice (*Buckley v AG*[96]), and to require the application of judicial restraint when faced with proceedings involving matters that are adjudged to be more appropriately dealt with in the political arena. This was most controversially regarded by the majority in *TD v Minister for Education* as precluding the making of a mandatory order requiring the executive to construct a treatment centre where the failure to provide such a centre had been found to contravene the right to primary education of the child(ren) at issue.[97] The majority stated that such an order would involve the courts in performing the functions of the executive and should only be made in the most exceptional and limited of cases where there had been a clear disregard of the obligations imposed by the Constitution.

C Comparative Perspective

In considering the approach to constitutional reasoning adopted by the Irish courts from a comparative perspective, it is helpful to bear in mind the external influences that shaped the establishment and development of Irish constitutional jurisprudence. The specific history of the current 1937 Constitution has already been described. More generally, however, Ireland's institutional structures are most commonly regarded as an example of a so-called 'Washminster' system, in which certain elements of the traditional British and American constitutional systems are combined. For example, Ireland has retained the Westminster model of cabinet government whilst making provision for strong-form powers of judicial review. However, given Ireland's somewhat eclectic mixture of institutional features and constitutional influences, it is arguably misleading to

[95] [2002] 1 IR 385. [96] [1950] IR 67. [97] [2001] 4 IR 259.

place it neatly within conventional typologies of legal, political or Commonwealth constitutionalism.[98]

Recent research on the 1937 Constitution has, for example, demonstrated that this Anglo-centric conception of constitutional influences is unduly narrow and that the drafters, in fact, looked to a more diverse range of international sources than has traditionally been appreciated.[99] However, the close linguistic, geographical, professional and cultural links between Ireland and both the United Kingdom and the United States of America have meant that legal reasoning in these jurisdictions has had an ongoing influence on the development of Irish constitutional law. This meant that principles or provisions which may originally have been influenced by other considerations could on occasions be construed by lawyers and judges in light of English or American legal traditions.

For example, the powers of judicial review which were expressly conferred on the courts by both the 1922 and 1937 Constitutions remained unused for decades, a phenomenon attributed to the residual influence of British legal training and traditions. Writing extra-judicially in 1932, the then Chief Justice Hugh Kennedy observed that:

> Political and legal constitutional studies in this Country were in practice limited to the British Constitution and the working of the British Parliament. Professor Dicey's book became an evangel accepted reverently and without criticism or question in our schools (such as they were) of political philosophy and constitutional law.[100]

An example of the influence of US constitutional thought can be found in the interpretation of Article 15.2.1 of the Constitution, which reserves exclusive legislative power to the Oireachtas (Parliament), in *Cityview Press v ANCO*[101] as requiring the application of a non-delegation doctrine. This Article has been argued instead to have been intended as a clear exclusion of any claim which the British Parliament may have had to a

[98] Eoin Carolan, "Leaving Behind the Commonwealth Model of Rights Review: Ireland as an Example of Collaborative Constitutionalism" in John Bell and Marie-Luce Paris, eds., *Rights-Based Constitutional Review – Constitutional Courts in A Changing Landscape* (Edward Elgar, 2015).

[99] Gerard Hogan, *The Origins of the Irish Constitution 1928–1941* (RIA 2012).

[100] Hugh Kennedy, "Foreword" in Leo Kohn, *The Constitution of the Irish Free State* (George Allen & Unwin 1932), at xii–xiii. See also Ronan Keane, "Across the Cherokee Frontier of Irish Constitutional Jurisprudence: The Sinn Féin Funds Case: Buckley v Attorney General (1950)" in Eoin O'Dell (ed), *Leading Cases of the Twentieth Century* (Round Hall Sweet & Maxwell, 2000) 185, making a similar point about the judiciary's initial approach to the 1937 Constitution.

[101] *Cityview Press v ANCO* [1980] IR 381.

residual legislative power over Ireland.[102] The Supreme Court in *Cityview Press* cited both *Panama Refining Co. v Ryan*[103] and *Schechter (A.L.A.) Poultry Corporation v United States*[104] in support of its reasoning. Notably, the decision made no reference to the very specific political context of the Roosevelt-Court conflict in which these American decisions were originally delivered, or to the way in which US caselaw in subsequent decades tended to rhetorically endorse the doctrine while treating it in practice as an effective dead letter.[105]

This underlines the fact that, while the text of the 1922 and 1937 Constitutions may have drawn upon a wide range of constitutional sources, British and American legal thought has had – in comparison with other jurisdictions – greater relative influence on constitutional reasoning.

Nonetheless, there remain a number of features of the courts' constitutional jurisprudence that might be regarded as distinctive in comparative terms. The clear influence of natural law on the courts' approach to the identification and enforcement of constitutional rights over an extended period is one such feature, as is the related (and still valid) doctrine of unenumerated rights. The endorsement of a system of horizontal application[106] is another – and perhaps the most potentially influential – aspect of the courts' reasoning that has had significant implications for the scope, content and societal impact of the judiciary's powers to defend and vindicate constitutional rights when compared with other constitutional systems.

Appendix: 40 Leading Cases

1. *Byrne v Ireland [1972] IR 241*
2. *Buckley v Attorney General [1950] IR 67*
3. *Ryan v Attorney General [1965] IR 294*
4. *In re Haughey [1971] IR 217*
5. *East Donegal Co-op Ltd v. Attorney General [1970] IR 317*
6. *McDonald v Bord na gCon (no. 2) [1965] IR 217*

[102] D. G. Morgan, *The Separation of Powers in Irish Constitutional Law* (Round Hall 1997), 262–263. But see Hogan (n 1), 337–9.

[103] (1935) 293 U.S. 388.

[104] (1935) 295 U.S. 495.

[105] Aranson, Gellhorn and Robinson, "A Theory of Legislative Delegation" (1982) 68 *Cornell Law Review* 1; F. Farina, "Statutory Interpretation and the Balance of Power in the Administrative State" (1989) 89 *Columbia Law Review* 452.

[106] AS Butler, "Constitutional Rights in Private Litigation: A Critique and Comparative Analysis" 22 (1993) *Anglo-American Law Review* 1.

7. *Maher v Attorney General [1973] IR 140*
8. *Cityvew Press v ANCO 1[1980] IR 381*
9. *TD v Minister for Education [2001] 4 IR 259*
10. *Cahill v Sutton [1980 IR 269*
11. *SPUC v Coogan [1989] IR 734*
12. *Crotty v An Taoiseach [1987] IR 713*
13. *Pringle v Ireland [2013] 3 IR 1*
14. *McKenna v An Taoiseach (no. 2) [1995] 2 IR 10*
15. *A v Governor or Arbour Hill [2006] 4 IR 88*
16. *State (Nicolaou) v An Bord Uchtala [1966] IR 567*
17. *Heaney v Ireland [1994] 3 R 593*
18. *Crowley v Ireland [1980] IR 102*
19. *In re Article 26 and the Planning and Development Bill 1999 [2000] 2 IR 321*
20. *In re Article 26 and the Employment Equality Bill 1996 [1997] 2 IR 321*
21. *Iarnrod Eireann v Ireland [1996] 3 IR 321*
22. *McGee v Attorney General [1974] IR 284*
23. *Irish Times Ltd v Ireland [1998] 1 IR 359*
24. *Maher v Minister for Agriculture [2001] 1 IR 139*
25. *In re Article 26 and the Abortion Information Bill 1995 [1995] IR 1*
26. *People (DPP) v Shaw [1982] IR 1*
27. *Meskell v CIE [1973 IR 121*
28. *State (Quinn) v Ryan) [1965] IR 70*
29. *Northwestern Health Board v HW [2001] 3 IR 622*
30. *McD v L [2010] 2 IR 199*
31. *King v AG [1981] IR 233*
32. *State (Healy) v Donoghue [1976] IR 325*
33. *People (DPP) v Kenny [1992] 2 IR 141*
34. *Melling v Mathghamhna [1962] IR 1*
35. *People (DPP) v O'Shea [1982] IR 384*
36. *Tuohy v Courtney [1994] 3 IR 1*
37. *Meadows v Minister for Justice, Equality and Law Reform [2010] 2 IR 701*
38. *Maguire v Ardagh [2002] 1 IR 385*
39. *AG v Ryan's Car Hire 1[1965] IR 642*
40. *Murphy v IRTC [1999] 1 IR 29*

12

The Israeli Supreme Court

SUZIE NAVOT

A Legal, Political, Institutional and Academic Context

Introduction: Israel's Constitutional History – a Short Overview

Israel has no one document known as "The Constitution", and therefore, no specific "Constitutional Court".[1] The Supreme Court is the highest court in the State of Israel, and it plays two roles. It is the court of final resort for appeals against verdicts handed down by district courts, and thus rules on civil, administrative, and criminal matters. In addition, it sits as the High Court of Justice (HCJ) and hears petitions against state authorities and other tribunals, and since the constitutional revolution in the 1990s, it has had the power of judicial review of legislative norms that are inconsistent with "constitutional" norms.

Upon the establishment of the State, in 1948, Israel's Declaration of Independence determined that "the establishment of the elected, regular authorities of the State" would be "in accordance with the Constitution which shall be adopted by the Constituent Assembly . . . ". The Constituent Assembly was thus elected in January 1949 as both a constituent and a legislative body. The Constituent Assembly – later renamed "The First Knesset" – conducted extensive debates on the future constitution. But in the absence of consensus on the need for a constitution, its content and form, constitutional deliberations reached a deadlock. Before it dispersed, the First Knesset endorsed a "compromise" that became known as the "The Harrari Resolution".[2] In terms of comparative constitutional law, this compromise was unique: Israel would introduce a constitution "in

[1] I am grateful to Hadar Bar-Shalom and Adi Marom for their valuable research assistance.

[2] The Harrari Resolution reads: "The First Knesset charges the Constitution, Law, and Justice Committee with preparing a draft of the State Constitution. The Constitution will consist of separate chapters, each chapter constituting a Basic Law in its own. The chapters will be presented to the Knesset . . . and all of the chapters shall be consolidated into the State Constitution."

stages": the constitution would be composed of chapters, each comprising a single Basic Law unto itself. The upshot of the Harrari Resolution was that the initial decision to adopt a complete constitution for the State of Israel was deferred and replaced by the process of enacting a constitution chapter by chapter – a process that lead to the enactment of 13 basic laws, but was never completed and has yet to produce a full constitution.

By 1992, almost all of the basic laws that deal with government institutions in Israel had been adopted, but the proposal to pass a basic law dealing with human rights provoked great controversy in the Knesset. Therefore, another political compromise split the *Basic Law: Human Rights* into a number of separate basic laws. This process made it possible for the Knesset to agree and support the constitutional entrenchment of particular, consensual human rights, while leaving pending the discussion of "problematic" rights, such as freedom of religion, speech, and conscience; equality; etc.

Following this new "compromise", two basic laws dealing with human rights were enacted in 1992: *Basic Law: Human Dignity* and Liberty; and *Basic Law: Freedom of Occupation.* Both basic laws include a "limitation" clause, similar to the one found in the Canadian Charter of Rights and Freedoms. The basic laws on human rights of 1992 changed Israel's constitutional structure and were followed by a crucially important ruling handed down in 1995: the *Mizrahi Bank* decision.[3] In this monumental decision, the Supreme Court (sitting as the court of final resort for appeals, in a civil proceeding) declared that basic laws in Israel had a "supra-legal" constitutional status, and that the court is empowered to enforce the limitations they entail by judicial review of Knesset legislation, even if that power is not specifically mentioned in the basic laws. The basic laws on human rights and this Supreme Court decision were later known as the "constitutional revolution".

The constitutional revolution started a new era in Israel's constitutional law – a textual period, in which there allegedly exists a constitutional text. As the Supreme Court stated, the basic laws form the Israeli constitution. It is not a complete constitution, but rather a lame and restricted one. The constitutional revolution took Israel from the tradition of parliamentary sovereignty to a constitutional model and to the concept of judicial review of laws. This constitutional change is paramount in terms of judicial-reasoning – as we shall see in this report.

[3] CA 6821/93 *United Mizrahi Bank Ltd. v. Migdal Cooperative Village* (1995).

1 Legal and Political Culture as Context for Constitutional Reasoning

The failure to frame a constitution upon the establishment of the State had an immense influence on Israel's constitutional law. Many who disputed the content of the constitution in the early days are still with us today. The on-going struggle between secular and religious factions over issues such as human rights, the status and rights of minorities in Israel, the basic principles that should be anchored in the constitution, and who should safeguard them, as well as the issue of judicial review, are not just legacies of the past; they remain topical issues today. Present-day Israel lacks broad consensus on numerous arrangements, particularly those that pertain to state and religion issues. Despite the important constitutional move of 1992 and the transition from a Knesset with unlimited parliamentary sovereignty to a constitutional regime, the constitutionalisation of human rights is still plagued by the "decision not to decide". This being the case, the Supreme Court's influence over constitutional trends turns out to be decisive. The Court's great historical contribution has been to entrench some of liberalism's central values in Israel's state institutions, political culture and society.[4]

In the absence of an explicit constitutional norm, the acknowledgement of the Court's judicial review powers in 1995 was received with mixed political reactions. The Knesset did not react to the *Mizrahi Bank* verdict with new legislation; it did not rise to the challenge with which the Court presented it in that monumental verdict. The Court chose to leave an array of unresolved constitutional questions for the legislature, but the Knesset failed to answer them. This outcome appears to have been due to political reasons. Unable to resolve key political issues, in particular those concerning state and religion matters, the Knesset often found it convenient to defer them to the Supreme Court. Upon examination of the nearly 20 years of experience since the constitutional revolution, the Supreme Court's judicial review appears to have been and to have remained quite restrained. The Court has always taken into consideration institutional and cultural constraints. Therefore, whilst the adjudication has been extensive, the judicial intervention has always been rather limited. The Supreme Court has nullified some 12 laws (mainly specific sections) over the past 19 years, all following judicial rulings that these

[4] Menachem Mautner, "Constitutional Culture in a Culturally Polarized Country" (lecture, delivered at the Constitutional Culture Conference, Montreal, 6 May 2011), available at: www.tau.ac.il/law/mautner/luctuar/8.doc.

laws disproportionally impaired rights listed in the basic laws. The most important result of the expansion of the boundaries of judicial review is the impact on administrative and legislative behavior. The influence is expressed not necessarily in the main route of correcting injustices by operative court judgments. In many cases, the judicial influence is reflected in the fact that the authorities act in the "shadow" of the potential of judicial decision-making in the matter.

Recent decades have seen a shifting of power, mainly from elected politicians to unelected judges. In turn, the constitutional revolution and the change in the Court's position regarding the doctrines of justiciability and standing, the readiness of the Court to examine petitions on their merits, along with the difficulties of the political branch deciding on controversial issues, have all impacted the role of the Supreme Court. The Supreme Court has become a dominant and effective oversight body. In this capacity, a new, more expansive view of standing has proved a powerful mechanism for the Court to protect the rule of law and to ensure the legality of government authorities. Its decisions are followed, and largely quoted, by all ordinary courts.

2 The Court and Constitutional Litigation

The HCJ resulted from an historical, accidental, and unplanned process that created an unusual situation, in which certain complaints (administrative grievances of individuals harmed by government authorities) are filed directly with the Supreme Court. During the British Mandate, the lower courts (magistrates' and district courts) were presided over by local judges, Jews or Arabs, while the Supreme Court was exclusively composed of British judges. The policy was that local judges should handle ordinary civil and criminal issues, but disputes that pertain to the Mandate authorities should be heard, from beginning to end, by judges from the British establishment. Thus it was determined that the Supreme Court should address administrative disputes.

After Israel had been established, this structure was no longer needed, but the judicial situation did not change as the newly founded state decided to keep the Mandate's administrative and legal structures in place. Accordingly, the HCJ kept operating as it had done previously, only presided over by Israeli judges. Soon it became central to the development of justice and the basic principles of democracy – mainly the rule of law.

The procedures for judicial review of laws are not anchored in statute. Although the HCJ has been judicially reviewing laws for more than two decades, the very legitimacy and implementation of judicial review is the subject of a lively and often acrimonious political and public debate. As a result, the annulment of laws by the Supreme Court is particularly restrained.

Complaints against the government are filed directly with the HCJ, which serves as the first, last, and only instance of judicial review. Thus, when a citizen feels harmed by or has a grievance in relation to the government, he or she goes directly to the highest judicial body in the state. This is an almost entirely unique situation from a comparative perspective.

HCJ procedures differ from other courts. It does not hear oral testimonies, nor does it question witnesses. Its hearings are meant to provide an immediate remedy. According to the *Basic Law: The Judiciary*, the HCJ may extend "relief for the sake of justice" in every matter that is outside the jurisdiction of all other courts. The HCJ is explicitly authorised to issue *habeas corpus* and *mandamus*, ban orders of lawful holders of public positions, and even issue orders to other courts and to other bodies and individuals with judicial or semi-judicial powers. The boundaries of the HCJ's powers are broadly and vaguely defined, and the fact that it is easily accessible and its proceedings are simple and quick has turned the HCJ into the forum of main redress for civilians who feel offended by government action.

HCJ judges have extensively applied the "relief for the sake of justice" section, expanding the scope of their control of state authorities. Trends in HCJ's decisions in recent years indicate that, at least from the judges' point of view, the Court's jurisdiction has no boundaries. There is almost no record of the HCJ ever rejecting petitions because it was not authorised to discuss the issues raised in them. When it does reject petitions or refers them to another court, it does so only after exercising its discretion and stating that it does so because it would rather employ a cautious approach and self-restraint, despite having the power to discuss the issue.

The procedure for judicial review of the constitutionality of laws takes two basic forms:

1. Direct judicial review by the HCJ: Any person alleging a violation of his or her protected rights by a legislative norm may file a "direct" petition with the HCJ, challenging the constitutionality of that violation. Direct

petitions may be private – protesting the violation of a personal right, or public – where the petitioner represents a group and argues that harm has been suffered by an entire population sector. Initially, the HCJ would not acknowledge *actio popularis* petitions, but attempts were made in the early 1980s to persuade the Court to adjudicate "public" issues. Subsequently, the Court expanded the scope of its judicial review and eventually accepted *actio popularis* petitions. The HCJ has no filtering procedure and conducts no abstract judicial review. Since 1992, requests for judicial review of laws are also filed directly to the HCJ.

2. Indirect judicial review in all courts: In the absence of provisions to the contrary, theoretically, the power to examine the constitutionality of laws resides with any judge as part of the legal proceeding over which that judge presides. For example, in a criminal proceeding where the accused claims that his indictment is based on a law that violates the provisions of a basic law, the presiding judge may adjudicate the constitutionality of that law. This, however, has only happened once, when a magistrates' court judge invalidated a section of the *Income Tax Ordinance*.[5] This was the only (and exceptional) case of indirect judicial review by a magistrate's court. It is generally accepted that the only court authorised to nullify laws is the Supreme Court sitting as the HCJ. Therefore, petitions requesting judicial review are brought before it, and are discussed by an extended panel of 9 or 11 judges.

Petitions received by the HCJ that do not deal with judicial review of legislation are dealt with by a panel of three judges, unless decided otherwise, in which case they would be heard by a larger panel. However, the Court also often hands down decisions in which it declares the case to be dismissed immediately (*non suit*). With respect to the decision and remedies, the Court may strike down the law or certain articles in it. Sometimes, after concluding that a certain law is unconstitutional, the HCJ "suspends nullification", which postpones the verdict's application. This remedy prevents the formation of a "legislative vacuum" and gives

[5] MC (TA) 4696/01 *The State of Israel v. Hendelman* (Nevo, April 14, 2003). This decision was later criticised by the District Court: "Though this case was not presented before us, I wish to remark that the Magistrates Court should have exercised restraint and instead of hurriedly nullifying Section 236B1(b), it could have found a better solution for the alleged harm caused to the freedom of occupation right by appropriately interpreting the section;" par. 17 of Judge Shnitzer's verdict in DC (TA) 70597/04 *Hendelman v. The State of Israel* (Nevo, January 12, 2005).

the Knesset time to introduce a different legal arrangement. All decisions are published on the internet database of the Supreme Court and are available to the public.[6]

Standing and Justiciability

No ordinary or basic law prescribes preconditions that must be met before the HCJ can exercise its powers. Traditionally, however, the HCJ made the threshold requirement of "standing" a precondition for hearing a petition. Thus, only petitioners who were personally affected by a government act could file an appeal against it with the HCJ.[7]

Gradually, particularly since the 1980s, the HCJ has become more amenable when a public issue is deemed important, and has been willing to intervene even if the appellant has showed no personal damage.[8] This inevitably led to the creation of numerous public associations that file petitions with the HCJ whenever anything appears wrong to them. Justice Cheshin cynically described this in a verdict: "By way of exaggeration, we could say that today, people pick up a newspaper and, skimming through the items, find something they disapprove of and call to their friends: 'Let us make pilgrimage to the Supreme Court.' They then write the petition in the car."[9]

This trend has impacted Israeli society. Despite the fact that the HCJ did not have powers to oversee all government and legislative decisions granted by the constitution, the public has used the Court to obtain public policy decisions that could not be obtained through any other means. This phenomenon gradually enhanced and strengthened the Court's position as a key political player, which may be seen as creating a new balance of power between the branches of the State.

Since the 1980s, the Court's new approach has opened up judicial review of questions that used to be regarded as non-justiciable. For example, the HCJ has increased its involvement in internal Knesset affairs, political questions and military decisions, and has expanded the application of constitutional rules (such as the equality principle) to bodies that are not government agencies, including government-owned companies or

[6] Some of the decisions are translated into English and appear on the English version of the website: elyon1.court.gov.il/eng/home/index.html.

[7] HCJ 40/70 *Becker v. the Defense Minister* (1970).

[8] HCJ 428/86 *Barzilai v. Government of Israel* (1986).

[9] HCJ 2148/94 *Gelbert v. Hon. Supreme Court President* (1994).

semi-public bodies. HCJ decrees and verdicts are obeyed by all governmental bodies and public authorities. This is evident from the fact that it is very unusual for contempt of court sentences to be issued against such bodies. Nonetheless, some decisions are fiercely discussed in the public arena, also by politicians.

To quote Alexander Hamilton, HCJ judges have "no influence over either the sword or the purse",[10] only the public's trust in them. The HCJ judges' willingness to intervene in issues that would be viewed as unjustifiable in other countries, and the fact that it may judicially review legislation, coupled with its activist image, has placed the HCJ at the centre of Israel's public and political discourse in recent years.

The number of constitutional cases per year is unclear, due to the fact that the Supreme Court and the HCJ are one Court. Therefore, classifying a Supreme Court or an HCJ decision as "constitutional" is not an easy task in Israel. In the absence of a complete constitutional text and a constitutional court, it is almost impossible to present the specific number of constitutional cases per year. Addressing conflicts between citizens and government, the HCJ serves both as a High Court of Justice and as the state's administrative instance, which makes it hard to decide whether a given issue is constitutional or administrative in nature. More than 10,000 petitions/appeals are submitted to the Supreme Court every year.[11]

3 The Judges

Fifteen judges currently serve on the Supreme Court. Supreme Court rulings are final, but the *Courts Law* offers the Supreme Court President an option to schedule another hearing of a tried (civil, criminal, or HCJ) case with an extended panel when the issue at hand might have broad public or legal implications, or when the original verdict deviates from

[10] Alexander Hamilton, "No. 78: The Judiciary Department", in Jacob E. Cooke (ed.), *The Federalist Papers (1788)* (Wesleyan University Press 1961).

[11] For example, in 2011, 9,775 cases were filed to the Supreme Court, of which 3,903 major cases were discussed by a panel of three judges. Database that we got for another research from the Court's Director in 2009 showed the number of verdicts the Supreme Court handed down between 2002 and 2007. In 2002: 7,856 decisions were handed down, in 2003: 9,203 decisions; in 2004: 8,570 decisions; in 2005: 8,679 decisions; in 2006: 7,768 decisions and in 2007: 8,098 decisions. In 2012, 9,492 cases were filed. The work load of the Supreme Court must be examined not only according to the total number of cases filed and closed every year, but mainly by the number of "main" cases brought before a panel of three judges or more. In 2012, 3,781 main cases were submitted to the Supreme Court, 1,647 of which (43.56 per cent) were petitions to the High Court of Justice.

a previous ruling whose importance requires another hearing. In more exceptional cases, the president may order a retrial of criminal cases.

In Israel, the judiciary is an independent body that is not part of the political system. "Judges are not elected by and do not answer to the people the way that members of the legislature are and do. To be appointed, judges are not required to present a social platform that they intend to realise in the courtroom, and their term in office is not terminated when they fail to meet the people's expectations . . . Exercising judicial discretion, judges should not be viewed as 'representing' or 'accountable to' the people. Judges must stay 'above politics' and be constantly aware of that position."[12]

Judges for all courts, including for the Supreme Court, are selected by a Judges' Appointment Committee, appointed by the President of the State, and serve until they reach the age of 70. The Appointment Committee represents the concept of "the combination of powers" – a notion of "checks and balances" – rather than the separation of powers. The Committee comprises nine members: five of whom are not part of the political system (namely, three HCJ judges, including the President and the Vice President, and two representatives of the Israeli Bar Association) and four politicians (two members of the Knesset selected by the Knesset, and two cabinet members, including the Minister of Justice, who serves as the Committee Chairperson). Thus, the Committee represents all three branches of government. A candidate for appointment as judge must be selected by the majority of the Committee members (that is, at least five) and a Supreme Court candidate must secure the vote of at least seven Committee members.

In fact, past experience has shown that, thanks to its unique composition, the Committee makes decisions that are generally free of political considerations, and appoints judges who are both of high professional standards and free of political bias. It is the candidates' professional competence and not their political agenda that is evaluated. At present, Israel's judges are not appointed as sector representatives, although while evaluating a candidate's personal data, the Committee considers the "reflection principle", which means that it intends for the bulk of Israeli judges to reflect (or represent) the Israeli society as much as possible. Over the years, the Supreme Court judges have come to represent, though not

[12] Aharon Barak, *Parshanut Be'mishpat, Parshanut Hahakika (Interpretation in Law, II Statutory Interpretation* (Nevo 1993) 676–677. See also: Shimon Sheetrit, "Developments in Constitutional Law: Selected Topics" (1990) 24 *Israel Law Review* 368.

perfectly, the Israeli legal community. Most of them had served as district court judges before assuming the high post, while others served as Legal Advisors to the Government or State Attorneys, and two had been private lawyers. Over the years, law professors (from different fields of law) have also served as judges, but to a lesser extent. In that respect, the current (2014) bench now comprises 15 judges; only one of them is a law professor (recently appointed). This fact is particularly questionable given that the Court is not only an appeals Court but also Israel's Constitutional Court.

4 Legal Scholarship and Constitutional Reasoning

Israeli legal scholarship's writting about the HCJ cases is vast. It would be difficult to asses the ratio between deferential and critical, although perhaps the majority is critical towards the Court, mainly over judicial activism. Many scholars have argued that the Israeli Supreme Court was extremely activist in the 1980s and 1990s. Richard Posner wrote of the Supreme Court led by President Aharon Barak that:

> What Barak created out of whole cloth was a degree of judicial power undreamed of even by our most aggressive Supreme Court justices... A court can forbid the government to appoint an official who had committed a crime... or is otherwise ethically challenged and can order the dismissal of a cabinet minister because he faces criminal proceedings; that in the name of "human dignity" a court can compel the government to alleviate homelessness and poverty; and that a court can countermand military orders, decide "whether to prevent the release of a terrorist within the framework of a political 'package deal,'" and direct the government to move the security wall that keeps suicide bombers from entering Israel from the West Bank... In Barak's conception of the separation of powers, the judicial power is unlimited.[13]

Amnon Rubinstein, a renowned professor of constitutional law and Israel Prize laureate, wrote that "in fact, in many senses, under Barak's leadership, the Court has turned itself into an alternative government."[14] Following the academia's criticism, and perhaps personal changes in the Supreme Court, some argue that there is a decline in judicial activism in the last years.

The work of law professors does seem to have an impact on the Court. It can be seen by the number of references to scholarly work. These

[13] Richard Posner, "Enlightened Despot", *The New Republic* (23 April 2007), www.newrepublic.com/article/enlightened-despot [last accessed: May 11, 2014].

[14] Menachem Mautner, 'The Decline of Formalism and the Rise of Values in Israeli Law' (1993) 17 *Iyuney Mishpat* 503 (Hebrew). For the English version, see: Menachem Mautner, *Law and the Culture of Israel* (Oxford University Press 2011), 56.

references can sometimes be neutral (such as "*for further reading see . . .* "). However, the Court usually uses the academic work in order to strengthen an argument, and refers directly to the specific academic work, either agreeing or disagreeing with the scholar's view. As mentioned earlier, it must be stressed that unlike other constitutional courts, the large majority of Supreme Court judges are not law professors.

In general, being a judge in the Supreme Court seems to have a higher prestige than being a law professor (the salary in the Supreme Court is twice the salary of a law professor in a public university). Nowadays, we find law professors serving at the lower magistrate's court as well, and many law professors consider the Supreme Court as the highest of their aspirations. We know of only one law professor who rejected the post of a Supreme Court Judge.

Accepted Theories about Constitutional Reasoning

The "moto" of constitutional reasoning in general, and the role of a constituional judge, in particular, can be found in the follwing text:

> The judge is a partner in creating this system of law. The extent of this partnership varies with the type of law being created. In creating common law, the judge is a senior partner. In creating enacted law, the judge is a junior partner. Nonetheless, he is a partner and not merely an agent who carries out the orders of his principal. The second major task of the judge is to protect the constitution and democracy. In my opinion, every branch of government, including the judiciary, must use the power granted it to protect the constitution and democracy. The judiciary and each of its judges must safeguard both formal democracy, as expressed in legislative supremacy, and substantive democracy, as expressed in basic values and human rights.[15]

The idea reflected in this paragraph, as to the role of a judge, is well rooted in the HCJ reasoning. Therefore, the following characteristics may be outlined:

Broad, Objective and Generous Interpretation

Constitutional interpretation in Israel is guided by a purposive or "objective" interpretation. Aharon Barak's series of books on interpretation,

[15] Aharon Barak, "A Judge on Judging: The Role of a Supreme Court in a Democracy" (2002) 116 *Harvard Law Review* 19, 26.

mainly the book on Constitutional Interpretation,[16] is frequently cited in HCJ rulings, and it seems to be an accepted view. Barak's book states that a constitutional text should be interpreted with a broad perspective and with "generosity". It should not be approached "legalistically" but rather the judge should consider the nature of the text and the ways it establishes the Israeli way of life in the long run. According to Professor Barak, constitutional interpretation should follow the fundamental principles of the justice system: "The constitutional purpose that is the core of the constitutional text comprises the goals, principles, policy, and social purposes and interests that the constitutional text was meant to realize."[17]

Constitutional Reasoning and Judicial Activism

The Israeli Supreme Court is internationally known for its activism. Having operated without a constitutional framework since Israel was founded, it has developed numerous tools for intervention in government decisions. In the early years, still under the influence of the British tradition, Israeli constitutional reasoning was typically formalistic. The written word was of paramount importance and solutions for legal issues were mostly found in the texts of laws. The Court adhered to the strict separation of powers, particularly in its relationship with the Knesset. The absence of a formal, written constitution prevented the judicial review of laws, which left the Court with a merely interpretative role. Nonetheless, the HCJ became a central defender of democratic values very early on. In view of this, the Supreme Court's significant contribution to the protection of human rights is perhaps the most prominent and unique feature of Israel's constitutional law. Acting as the HCJ, the Supreme Court undertook to defend those rights and created what was to be known as the Bill of Judicial Rights – a set of human rights acknowledged and protected by HCJ verdicts – customary rights that feature only in HCJ adjudication, which, by virtue of *stare decisis*, have turned into binding legal norms in Israel. In this sense, it is important to recognise that rights protection has arisen from the decisions of the Supreme Court.

After the constitutional changes of 1992, judicial activism climaxed in the *Mizrahi Bank* affair,[18] in which the Court held that it has the power to judicially review laws. In addition, a new style of reasoning

[16] Aharon Barak, *Parshnaut Be'mishpat: Parshanut Hukatit (Interpretation in Law, III Constitutional Interpretation* (Nevo 1994).

[17] Ibid at 147. [18] Supra n 3.

evolved, addressing the laws' normative meaning. The earlier formalistic application of the law to the facts of each case was replaced by attempts to find balance between conflicting values. The new reasoning enhanced the importance of values in an attempt to attain just, moral, and value-based judicial results.[19]

B Arguments in Constitutional Reasoning

Introduction

Any discussion of the constructional reasoning of the HCJ in Israel would be incomplete without explaining the crucial impact of the writings of Professor Aharon Barak. Barak clearly played a central role in forming the foundations of constitutional interpretation in Israel. Having served on the HCJ bench for nearly 30 years, Barak presented a comprehensive view of the rules of constitutional interpretation in his publications, especially in his book on constitutional interpretation that is frequently cited in HCJ rulings.[20]

It is generally held that the interpretation of constitutional texts should follow the objective, purposive approach that is based on historic developments, on society's fundamental principles and primarily on the basic principles of the judicial system, such as the rule of law, the separation of powers, and human rights.[21] The attempt to apply these interpretative rules to basic laws is obstructed by a fundamental problem: the basic laws are not yet joined together as a constitution, they are incoherent and they are based more on rules and less on principles. Furthermore, until the constitutional revolution, the HCJ viewed basic laws as regular laws. In the last two decades, constitutional interpretation in Israel has focused on the basic laws on human rights, mainly because they include fundamental principles and clauses referring to their purpose.[22]

The clause outlining the fundamental principles in these basic laws states as follows: "Fundamental human rights in Israel are founded upon the recognition of the value of the human being, the sanctity of human life, and the principle that all persons are free; these rights shall be upheld in

[19] Mautner n 14. [20] Barak n 16.

[21] Aharon Barak, 'The Role of the Supreme Court in a Democratic Society', 51 (1995) *Hapraklit* 5, 6 (Hebrew).

[22] Referring to expressions such as "Jewish and democratic state," "human dignity," and "the values of the State of Israel," to mention but a few.

the spirit of the principles set forth in the Declaration of the Establishment of the State of Israel."[23]

This clause set forth the fundamental guiding principles of human rights in Israel and has played an interpretative role in understanding the scope of those rights, helping to shape the content and meaning of the rights stipulated in each basic law. These two basic laws further include a clause that stipulates their purpose. The purpose of these basic laws is "to anchor the values of the State of Israel as a Jewish and democratic state in basic laws." Thus, the basic assumption is that Israel's values are the values of a "Jewish and democratic" state. Though this clause features in basic laws on human rights, Professor Barak wrote: "It is only natural to assume that the State of Israel's values as a Jewish and democratic state are not limited only to the basic laws on human rights . . . A purposeful constitutional interpretation views constitutional instructions as uniform . . . The State of Israel's values as a Jewish and democratic state apply even beyond the confines of these basic laws."[24] Still, the expression "human dignity and liberty" was, and remains, the key for addressing aspects of human rights not explicitly protected in the constitution.

Since the enactment of *Basic Law: Human Dignity and Liberty*, judgments have yielded expanding constitutional interpretations of the "human dignity" phrase, acknowledging the constitutional status of rights that were not explicitly mentioned in this basic law, even if that acknowledgement is sometimes partial in the sense that only the aspects directly and practically associated with human dignity were accorded constitutional status. The rights in question here include freedom of expression, freedom of faith and worship, various rights in criminal proceedings and certain aspects of the right to equality. Granting constitutional status to those rights substantially changed Israeli constitutional law. The interpretative means by which rights that had not been explicitly listed are included in the human rights laws has been in effect for several years. Practically, this means that the Israeli Constitution is implicitly amended in a process that is mainly interpretative in nature.

5 The Structure of Constitutional Arguments

In most of the decisions analysed in this research, the Court first provides for the general principles relevant to the case, most of them deriving from earlier decisions, and it then applies these to the case at hand. Looking at

[23] Section 1 of *Basic Law: Freedom of Occupation*; Section. 1 of *Basic Law: Human Dignity and Liberty.*

[24] Barak n 16, at 309–10.

the 40 landmark judgments, it seems that the Court most often employs a "one line conclusive argument", which was found in the majority of cases (24 of 40). In 7 of 40 cases, we found "parallel conclusive" arguments, meaning a cumulative-parallel structure. In these cases the judges present several reasons for their decision, when it seems that one would have been enough to solve the question. In 9 of 40 cases we found parallel, individually inconclusive, but together conclusive reasoning, and in these cases the judges presented several relevant considerations; none seemed to be conclusive, but still all of them indicate a certain solution. For example, in the *Eisenberg*[25] case, when ruling in a petition against the appointment of a person with criminal past as a Ministry Director General, the Court stated that: "So far I have examined the first legal basis to the duty of a government authority to consider – when appointing a public servant – the applicant's criminal past . . . It seems to me that this duty derives from another source . . . " According to this statement, it is difficult to decide whether each reason would suffice to sustain the conclusion. We thought it was reasonable to assume that none of these arguments would have been sufficient in itself to ground the decision of the Court, especially taking into account that in this case the Court declared the existence of a new rule for all governmental agencies.

6 Types of Arguments in Constitutional Reasoning

Analogies We found 22 cases of 40 which included analogies. It should be mentioned that analogy is a method legally recognized as one of the sources a judge should use when dealing with *lacunae.* The Israeli law directs the court to fill in *lacunae* by way of analogy, among other sources. Analogy was used in different ways, to state an *a contrario* argument, to apply the same balancing test, to interpret a similar legal norm, etc. We only considered as analogy cases that expicitly metioned this way of reasoning. For example, in the *Miller* case,[26] Justice Dorner stated that: "In Israel, we have to borrow the criteria for dealing with rights, mutatis mutandis, from the limitation clause (Article 8 of the Basic Law) . . . Indeed, the limitation clause applies only to powers deriving from laws passed after the enactment of the Basic Law. But it is appropriate, by way of analogy, to apply the principles also to . . . " In the *Tal Law*[27] case, Justice Chechin stated that: "The most notable example so far has

[25] HCJ 6136/92 *Eisenberg v. Minister of Construction and Housing* (1993).
[26] HCJ 4541/94 *Miller v. Minister of Defence* (1995).
[27] HCJ 642701 *Movement for Quality in Government v. Knesset* (2006). (Hereinafter: *Tal Law* case).

been the *Yardor* case. In that case, the Court did not deal with the annulment of a law . . . , but the principles set in that case are appropriate – by direct analogy – for the judicial review of a Knesset law."

Establishing the Text of the Constitution We found 5 cases (of 40) dealing with the question whether norms were of constitutional status. The most important case (and by far, the most important case in Israel Constitutional law) is the aforementioned *Mizrahi Bank* case.[28]

Prior to the enactment of the basic laws on human rights and until the *Mizrahi Bank* judgment was handed down in 1995, the prevailing view was that Israel had no formal, written constitution. Until then, Israel was seen as having only a material constitution – a collection of binding principles and arrangements. The transition from a substantive to a formal constitution was based on limitation clauses in both basic laws on human rights. The *Mizrahi Bank* judgment determined that the limitation clause was intended to limit the Knesset's legislative power, and that Israel had a "formal" constitution. The question presented to the Supreme Court in the *Mizrahi Bank* case concerned the validity of a law enacted after the introduction of the basic laws of 1992. The facts of the case are incidental and were not the main focus of the Court's deliberations. Of relevance was the fact that petitioners argued that a new law infringed their right to property as guaranteed by *Basic Law: Human Dignity and Liberty*, and failed to meet the conditions of its limitations clause. It was the relationship between the allegedly infringing law and the basic law that raised a host of constitutional questions.

A nine-judge panel broached the broader issue of the normative status of basic laws in Israel and the impact of the new basic laws upon the legal system. The judgment was published in a separate volume, comprising 367 pages, dedicated primarily to the status of basic laws in general – both the new ones, enacted in 1992, and those concerning the various state institutions, enacted earlier.[29] The Court declared that the basic laws – considered until then regular laws – were of constitutional status, and therefore Israel had a "formal" constitution.

Applicability of the Constitution The Israeli constitutional cases dealt mainly with the question of whether a case is "justiciable", meaning,

[28] See n 2.

[29] Most of the judgment is *obiter dictum* because, as stated, there was no need to hold a constitutional discussion on the basic laws to solve the case at hand.

whether the Court may grant a remedy in a case which has political implications (something that may be close to the "political question doctrine"). Out of 13 cases discussing the applicability of the constitution, we found 12 cases in which the Court dealt with justiciability.

Pursuant to the traditional approach, an issue is deemed non-justiciable if the Court has no legal tools to address it and the task of its resolution is assigned to the political bodies in charge of the issue. Although the political nature of an act does not cancel out its legal nature, the legal nature of the executing body does impact on the nature of the rules applied by the Court.[30]

The HCJ decided that it has the power to supervise Knesset proceedings[31] and examine decisions by the Knesset Speaker and committees, as well as political coalition agreements;[32] but whether it actually does so, and the extent of its intervention, naturally depends on the body it audits. Dealing with the Knesset, for example, the Court exercises restraint.

Prima facie, the exercise of either doctrine – non-justiciability or judicial self-restraint – may ultimately produce the same result: the Court refrains from intervening. However, limiting this examination to outcomes could be misleading. Under the non-justiciability doctrine, the Court's non-intervention means that the decision itself is not examined on its merits. Yet, when a petition is rejected due to judicial self-restraint, the Court generally examines it on a substantive level, after which it decides not to intervene. This is a fine illustration of the approach endorsed in Israel. Acting within its own discretion, the Supreme Court may or may not intervene in political questions. The result is that the Court confirms decisions by government authorities after examining them on their merits. Thus, the Court is occasionally regarded as the body that grants the final "approval" of political decisions. Clearly, this lays the ground for, and offers an incentive to, filing appeals against almost every political decision, which is one of the explanations for the large number of cases dealing with this argument.

[30] Justice Barak, for example, addressed this issue as follows: "Conceivably, the decision to go to war or to make peace is not subject to normal rules governing administrative discretion. In these exceptional cases, petitions will be dismissed not because of the absence of a legal norm, but due to the absence of a prohibitive norm and the existence of a permitting norm; in other words, due to lack of grounds. The act is not non-justiciable, but rather justiciable and legal." HCJ 910/86 *Ressler v. the Defense Minister* (1988).

[31] HCJ 652/81 *Sarid v. Knesset Speaker* (1981).

[32] HCJ 5364/94 *Velner v. Labor Party* (1995).

Ordinary Meaning of Words of the Constitution or References to the "Wording of the Constitution" in General This argument was found in 11 of the 40 judgments. The situations in which it was used deal mainly with the ordinary meaning of the word "dignity" in *Basic Law: Human Dignity and Liberty*, and the need to "expand" the interpretation of this word in order to cover rights that are not included in the basic laws. The HCJ decided to interpret the meaning of human dignity broadly, so as to include such rights and protect them within the Basic Law.

In the *Adalah (family reunion)* affair,[33] it was argued that the law banning the reunion of Israeli Palestinians with their spouses from the Palestinian Authority violates their rights to equality and family life. These two rights are not included in the basic law on human dignity, but the appellants argued that they are "covered" by the constitutional right to human dignity. President Barak asserted that the right to human dignity is a "framework" right from which "daughter rights" could be derived, and that includes the right to family life.

Harmonising Arguments Fourteen of 40 cases included harmonizing arguments. We found both domestic harmonizing arguments (in 13 cases), in which the Court interprets the constitutional norms in light of other norms, as well as international harmonizing arguments (in 14 of 40), referring to international law.

In Israel, international law and domestic constitutional law operate in principle on two parallel levels, since Israel maintains a dual apparatus of absorbing international-justice norms.[34] For international norms to be implemented in the local justice system, they need to be introduced as laws by a legislative act, independently of and in addition to any endorsement of international treaties by the State of Israel. In Israel, international law is not used in order to interpret the Constitution. Nonetheless, the Court does refer to international law, and we find references to the Hague Convention (IV) respecting the Laws and Customs of War (1907); The Geneva Convention (IV) Relative to the Protection of Civil Persons in Time of War (1949) ("Israel honours the humanitarian provision of this Convention"), Inter-American Commission on Human Rights ("a similar approach as

[33] HCJ 7052/03 *Adalah Legal Centre for Arab Minority Rights in Israel v. Minister of Interior* (2006). (Hereinafter: *Adalah (family reunion)* case).

[34] Amihay Cohen, 'Unequal Partnership? The Introduction of International Law Rules into the Israeli Law by the HCJ: the Case of the Territories', (2007) 6 *Maazaney Mishpat* 157, 164 (Hebrew).

taken by the Inter–American Commission on Human Rights . . . "),[35] etc. Reference to the Family Reunification Evaluation Project (Final Report, The European Commission: Targeted Socio-Economic Research, Brussels 2004); The Convention for Protection of Human Rights and Fundamental Freedoms (1950), and the Universal Declaration on Human Rights (1948) are only some examples. In all these references, the Court shows that it is seeking to harmonize its decisions with these conventions. Even if the Israeli Court is not bound by some of the international conventions mentioned, the Court refers to them nonetheless as part of the reasoning, and in order to support the direction of the judge's interpretation.

As for the internal harmonizing, one special quote reveals the Court's approach to the importance of internal harmonizing: "The law is a creature in a living environment. The environment of the law is not just the other laws relating to the same matter. The environment of the law is a complex concept. It refers to the values, principles and interests that the legal system was meant to achieve."[36] This quote is largely used in order to justify the use of analogy from other norms on the need for harmony within the legal system. Another example of internal harmonizing was found in Justice Levi's opinion: "I believe that the solution to this difficulty is the constitutional principle of harmony . . . "[37]

Precedents The use of precedents is the most widely used method, and we found it in 40 of the 40 cases.[38] Israeli judges are obligated to follow the *stare decisis* principle. According to *Basic Law: The Judiciary*, the Supreme Court's decisions bind all lower courts, but not the Supreme Court itself – which may deviate from them. Still, though the Supreme Court is not obligated to adhere to its own rulings, it rarely deviates from its precedents because it holds judicial stability as a major value. The use of precedents is common in Israeli adjudication, and we seldom

[35] HCJ 769/02 *Public Committee Against Torture in Israel v. Government of Israel* (2006). (Hereinafter: *Preemptive killings* case).

[36] HCJ 58/68 *Shalit v. Minister of Interior* (1969), and also quoted in the *Eisenberg* case, *supra* n 23.

[37] HCJ 2605/05 *Academic Center for Law and Business v. Minister of Finance* (2009). (Hereinafter: *Privatization of prisons* case).

[38] The first case in the HCJ (HCJ 1/49 *Bejerano v. Minister of Police* (1949)) refers to precedents rendered by the courts in the land of Palestine under the British Mandate. Despite the fact that these are not "Israeli precedents" in the formal sense, as they were rendered before the establishment of the State, we decided to include this case as well, and therefore all Israeli Judgments include precedents.

find a case that does not refer to any previous Supreme Court decision. This is a practice that is firmly established. The reference to precedents includes extensive reference to case law, and also quotations of foreign case law. It may be interesting to point out that the decisions published by different law-editorials in electronic database form are usually edited, and at the beginning of the case there is a list of the legislation and other norms referred to in the case, as well as a list of the precedents (national and from other countries as well) that were quoted or mentioned in the case. Even before the electronic databases came into use, when judgments were published in books, these lists appeared at the beginning of each judgment. The lists are, sometimes, very long and can include dozens of cases. For example, the *Eisenberg* case includes 58 Israeli precedents and 2 American cases;[39] the *Miller* case includes 40 Israeli precedents, 15 American cases and 5 Canadian cases;[40] the *preemptive killings* case includes 59 Israeli cases, 4 European court cases, 5 American, 1 English, 5 International Courts cases and 1 Canadian;[41] the *privatization of prisons* case includes 105 Israeli precedents, 1 American, 2 English, 3 Canadian and 3 International Courts cases;[42] and the *Mizrahi Bank* case includes 77 Israeli cases, 3 Australian, 17 American, 5 English, 2 International courts, 2 German, 2 South African, 1 Indian and 3 Canadian cases.[43]

Doctrinal Analysis of Legal Concepts or Principles Legal concepts and principles are very widely used in Israeli constitutional cases. We found this type of argument in 40 of 40 cases. The first possible explanation for this particular finding is the lack of a constitutional text, at least prior to the constitutional revolution. In its capacity as the High Court of Justice, the crucial role that the Supreme Court has played in formulating Israel's constitutional law runs parallel to the development of the Knesset as the legislature. Thus, since very early on, the Israeli constitutional system relied upon constitutional principles and constitutional interpretation, mainly developed by the Supreme Court.

The concepts, values and principles used by the Court are difficult to categorize into sub-groups. We tried, at the beginning, to divide these arguments into two categories: one dealing with the specific values of the State of Israel, and the second category dealing with general constitutional values. But as the specific values of Israel include the democratic value, it made the categorisation almost impossible.

[39] See n 23. [40] See n 24. [41] See n 33. [42] See n 35. [43] See n 2.

We found several decisions referring to the values of Israel. Israel was defined as a "Jewish and Democratic state" in the 1992 basic laws. Constitutional interpretation in Israel has been focused on these two basic laws on human rights, mainly because they include fundamental principles and clauses referring to their purpose. The purpose of these basic laws, according to their text, is "to anchor the values of the State of Israel as a Jewish and democratic state."

Sometimes, a minimising definition is given by the Supreme Court to those values, in order to prevent, as much as possible, conflicts between Jewish and democratic values. For example, when the Court delivered its judgment in a petition to disqualify a political party because it negated the existence of the State of Israel as a Jewish and democratic state, the Court adopted a "narrow" interpretation of the term "Jewish" and a "slim" interpretation of the "democratic" concept so as to avoid denying the right to be elected as much as possible.[44]

General constitutional principles play a major role in Israel's constitutional reasoning. For example, the rule of law was expressed even in the earliest adjudication in Israel. Ruling in the 1949 *Bejerano*[45] affair, the HCJ established that in the absence of an explicit legal power to that effect, the Police Minister could not deny the freedom of occupation of those who filed others' car registration applications.

General constitutional concepts are also used in order to interpret concrete provisions. For example, when interpreting the immunity granted to Knesset members, President Barak described the purposes of immunity as measures designed to allow Israel's elected representatives to speak their minds freely, stressing the representation principle: "First of all, such protection is particularly essential for minority groups; second, immunity is vital as it is meant to guarantee the existence of a free market of views and ideas . . . ; third, in view of the above, immunity is essential for guaranteeing the democratic nature of the government."[46]

To conclude this section, the accepted view of the Israeli Court is that every norm "lives" and "breathes" within this normative world replete with values and principles, both Israel-specific and general. These values create a "normative umbrella" for the operation of the common law and a framework for interpreting all legal texts. Therefore, the Court's assumption is that every legal norm seeks to give effect to these values.

[44] See elections appeal EA 11208/02 *Central Elections Committee v Tibi (sixteenth Knesset)* (2003).

[45] See n 36.

[46] HCJ 11225/03 *Bishara v. Attorney-General* (2006).

Linguistic-Logical Formulae Based on Silence We found 9 of 40 cases belonging to this category. The lack of an explicit rule in a case may provide for an opportunity to solve the question by adapting principles of constitutional law. For example, in the *Poultry Growers Association* case,[47] the Court set out a test that allows for judicial review of a law due to its allegedly flawed enactment process. Although no rule exists allowing for judicial review of laws, the Court introduced new concepts regarding the fundamental principles of the legislative process that had not previously been discussed. According to the Court, there are four such principles which, when seriously harmed, might render the law null and void: (1) the majority ruling principle; (2) the formal equality principle; (3) the publicity principle; and (4) the participation principle. This case is regarded as a landmark case and acknowledges the possibility of judicial review of a law due to a flaw in the legislative process.

Teleological/Purposive Arguments Referring to the Purpose of the Text "[T]he Israeli law uses the theory of purposive interpretation. Our approach is that all legal text must be interpreted according to its purpose. From all the possible linguistic meanings, . . . the text should be given the interpretation that best realizes its intentions and aims. The purpose of the text deals with the values, the principles, the interests and the goals that the text was meant to achieve."[48]

Teleological arguments were found in 37 of 40 cases,[49] meaning that this is one of the most frequently employed arguments in constitutional cases. Constitutional interpretation in Israel is purposive. Concepts such as "the purpose of the law", "the spirit of the law", the rationale of the institution or the provision and even subjective teleological arguments such as "the legislator's intention" are very common. Aharon Barak's book on constitutional interpretation[50] states that a constitutional text should be interpreted with a broad perspective and "generosity". It should not

[47] HCJ 4885/03 *Poultry Growers Association v. Government of Israel* (2004).

[48] Aharon Barak, *Ekronot Klali'im shel Hamisphat BeParshnaut Be'mishpat* (General Principles of Law in Interpretation), in Shalom Lerner and Dafna Levinson-Zamir (eds), *Weissman Book* 1, 2 (The Harry and Michael Sacher Institute for Legislative Research and Comparative Law 2002) (Hebrew).

[49] We have included cases that deal with arguments referring to regular laws as well as basic laws. We left out two cases in which there was a purposive argument, but there was no text. For example, the case dealing with judicial review on internal parliamentary acts, where there is no constitutional provision allowing or prohibiting such an intervention (*Sarid* case, n 31). Also, the case dealing with judicial review of political party agreements contains a paragraph on purposive reasoning, but it was only mentioned as a principle, because there was no text to apply it to (*Velner* case, n 32).

[50] Barak n 15.

be approached "legalistically" or "pedantically," but rather judges should consider the nature of the text and the ways it establishes the Israeli way of life in the long run. The constitutional purpose needs to be based on the values and principles that the constitutional norm was meant to realise, and when these values and principles clash, judges must find the balance between them.

It is generally held that the interpretation of constitutional texts should follow the objective, purposive approach that is based on historic developments, on society's fundamental principles and primarily on the basic principles of the judicial system, such as the rule of law, the separation of powers, and human rights. If this is the basic premise for interpretation, the high prevalence of this kind of argument is easily explained.

(a) *Structure* The most usual structure is when the argument explicitly states the purpose behind the rule or the institution: "Indeed, in this respect, as in other cases, the purpose set at the base of the normative arrangement is decisive."

(b) *The Type of Cases: Institutional Constitutional Law or Human Rights Law* We found teleological arguments not only in institutional cases but also in cases dealing with human rights. For example, the Court determined that freedom of speech derives from democracy ("The principle of freedom of expression is closely bound up with the democratic process"[51]) – meaning that the rationale and purposes of freedom of speech are, among others, the search for truth and the safeguarding of democratic processes.

These findings are consistent with the findings concerning the use of principles and highlight the importance of purposive interpretation, as well as the judges' "point of departure" when dealing with a constitutional norm: the text deals with the values, the principles, the interests and the goals that it was meant to achieve.

Teleological/Purposive Arguments Referring to the Purpose of the Constitution-Maker

Subjective teleological arguments appear in 20 of 40 cases.[52] These findings are quite compatible with the findings in the previous section. The

[51] HCJ 73/53 *"Kol Ha'am" Co. LTD v. Minister of Interior* (1953).

[52] Most of these cases also include objective purposive arguments, and therefore appear in the previous section as well: we found 19 cases that contain both objective and subjective purposive arguments.

Israeli Supreme Court tends to rely on the objective purpose far more often than the on the subjective intention of the "founding fathers". The quote of Radbruch, claiming that "the law is wiser than its authors,"[53] is perhaps the "*moto*" in most constitutional cases. The subjective purposive arguments do not appear as a substitute for the objective teleological arguments, but rather as an addition, mainly in order to strengthen the solution reached by the judges, according to the objective purpose.

Some of the examples in which the constitution-makers' intent has been used are very interesting. First, in the monumental decision of *Mizrahi Bank*,[54] President Barak extensively described the discussions held in the Knesset Plenum (i.e. protocols of the Knesset, in which everything said by Knesset members is documented), in what seems to be an attempt to convince the reader that the Knesset was aware of its *pouvoir constituant* when voting on the basic laws. President Barak therefore concluded by stating that "the Knesset has given Israel a Constitution. These are the basic laws." Another example is the *Bar-On*[55] affair. Addressing a petition against a "provisional constitutional amendment," a seven-judge panel unanimously rejected the argument that challenged the constitutionality of amending a basic law. Their ruling, however, contained harsh remarks about the procedure chosen by the Knesset for this move. Nevertheless, the Court refused to judicially review the provisional basic law, and the protocols of the Knesset Committee were extensively quoted in order to reach the conclusion that the Knesset was aware of the meaning of their process:

> We discussed in detail the process in the Knesset Committee because the detailed professional hearing conducted, points out that the MK's were aware of the legislation of a temporary order . . . This fact should be taken into account when assessing the constitutionality of the law, since it may indicate that the Knesset understood that it was using its constituent authority and referred to the complexity of the matter.

Non-legal (Explicitly Moral, Sociological, Economic) Arguments

Non-legal arguments appeared in many of the cases (29 of 40 cases). Some cases contained more than one type of non-legal argument; therefore, we counted 29 cases, but referred to the arguments separately. That explains

[53] Gustav Radbruch, "Legal Philosophy", in *The Legal Philosophies of Lask, Radbruch and Dabin* (Harvard University Press 1950, trans. Kurt Wilk) 47, 141–2: "The interpreter may understand the law better than its creators understood it. The law may be wiser than its authors – indeed, it must be wiser than its authors."

[54] *Supra* n 2. [55] HCJ 4908/10 *Bar-On v. Israel Knesset* (2011).

the total number of arguments (37) being higher than the number of cases (29 of 40).

Israel adjudication has different types of non-legal arguments:[56]

(a) Security Considerations (11 of 29)

"Is it proper for judges to review the legality of the war on terrorism? Many... argue that courts should not become involved in these matters. Critics argue that judicial review undermines security, while others claim that judicial review unjustifiably legitimizes governments' actions against terrorism. Both arguments are unacceptable. Judicial review of the legality of the war on terrorism may make this war harder in the short run, but also fortifies and strengthens the people in the long run. The rule of law is a central element of national security..."[57]

The State of Israel has been embroiled in a grave security situation ever since its foundation. Some of its neighbour states have not yet accepted its presence in the region. The Israeli-Palestinian conflict, which has included terrorist attacks and curfews imposed on West Bank cities, inevitably arrived at the doorsteps of the HCJ. Many countries suffer from terror threats; even the United States had to deal with them following the 9/11 attacks. Terrorism defies democracy and challenges democratic states, while naturally some of the means available to fight terrorism are illegal and unjustifiable according to democratic standards. Democracies must make difficult and delicate decisions on ways to balance national security and human rights, while employing emergency means to counter the threats.

Time and again, the HCJ has rejected claims that issues it has addressed were non-justiciable or should not be measured by legal criteria. Each and every case was reviewed on its merits, as the Court has insisted for many years that a balance must be struck between often conflicting values, such as the need to protect the State and the security of its residents on the one hand, and the need to uphold human dignity and liberty on the other. Practically, the Court restricted the executive's choice of means and tools in its response to terrorism. Justice Barak put it plainly, in several cases, stating: "A democracy must actually fight terror 'with one hand tied behind its back' because the means that terrorists use cannot be employed by democracies."[58]

[56] In some cases we found more than one non-legal argument per case.

[57] Barak, *A Judge on Judging, supra* n 15, at p. 158.

[58] HCJ 5100/94 *Public Committee Against Torture v. Israel* (1999). (Hereinafter: *Interrogation and investigation methods* case.)

Out of 40 cases, 11 refer to security reasons. In all of them, security considerations were part of the judges' reasoning, and in all of them, security reasons were "balanced" with the possible harm to human rights. When dealing with the *GSS's* (General Security Service) *interrogation and investigation methods*,[59] the Court ruled that a balancing test is necessary for dealing with interrogation rules. The balancing process resulted in a set of rules for reasonable interrogation. These rules are based on preserving the suspects' humanity while observing the classic Israeli Defense Forces concept of "purity of arms" during the interrogation. According to the Court, they reflect reasonableness, common sense and fairness. Democratic states need such rules because illegal investigations harm not only the suspects' dignity but also that of the society. In the *preemptive killings* case,[60] the Court examined the legality of the targeted assassinations policy and outlined some rules for its implementation, but the petition against the practice was rejected: "The use of targeted assassinations must be proportional; that is, based on the balance between military benefits and the expected damage they might cause to innocent civilians."

(b) Moral Arguments (19 of 29)

Moral arguments appear in several forms. For example: social morality, the interests of the society, the social contract (Rousseau), the need for public trust in the institution, the public interest, the alleged harm on public feelings, the social importance of education, etc. One fine example of the "winds of change" in the moral opinion of society can be seen in the *Danielowitz* case.[61] A male El-Al flight attendant sued the Israeli airliner after it refused to issue a free airline ticket for his male partner, which was a traditional perk given to employees' spouses. This decision paved the way for additional judgments that upheld the rights of same-sex partners, particularly in relation to financial and property issues. Justice Dorner writes: "The French philosopher Michel Foucault has dealt with the impact of social norms – which reflect the accepted, the 'normal', and change from time to time and from one society to another – on the use of formal and transcendental laws . . . It seems to me that the case at hand cannot be resolved without considering the changes that have occurred in the norms of Israeli society concerning homosexuality."[62]

[59] Ibid. [60] *Supra* n 33. [61] HCJ 721/94 *El-Al Israel Airlines v. Danielowitz* (1994).
[62] Compare with the same type of argument in a similar case in the Hungarian report, p. 10.

Another completely different type of moral argument dealt with the moral rights of the Jewish people. For example, Justice Zilberg: "The Heritage, that we all – or almost all – are related to, is one of the cornerstones, on which our right to settle this land is based. We had been exiled from the land 1900 years ago, but we haven't been away from it for even one day. Our spiritual presence in this country was much more intense than the physical presence of all nations and peoples – who ruled or sat on it for 19 centuries . . . "[63]

(c) Economic Arguments (2 of 29)

Economic arguments were present in two cases. One of them is the *Miller*[64] case: Ms Miller filed a petition with the HCJ against the military practice of not letting women apply for pilots' courses. Justice Mazza wrote that budgetary considerations, which were presented as the reason why the IDF would not let women take pilots' courses (training women to be pilots costs more than training men because they serve relatively shorter periods), cannot take precedence, when the issue in question is a demand for the realisation of a fundamental right such as the right to equality: "In any event, when we are concerned with a claim to exercise a basic right – and such is the case before us – the relative weight of the budgetary considerations cannot be great, since 1 . . . the protection of human rights costs money, and a society that respects human rights must be prepared to bear the financial burden."

(d) Historical Circumstances (5 of 29)

Special historical circumstances appeared in 5 of the cases. Perhaps one of the most interesting is the case of *Yardor*,[65] dealing with the disqualification of a political party that negated the existence of the State of Israel as a Jewish state. President Agranat quotes Justice Zussman from a previous HCJ decision: "More than once throughout history, various fascist and totalitarian movements rose up against states with functioning democratic regimes, and used all the rights including the freedom of speech, press and assembly, which are granted to them by the state, in order to conduct their malicious activities in the virtue of those rights. Anyone who witnessed it in the times of the Weimar Republic will not forget the lesson."

[63] *Shalit* case, n 36. [64] See n 24.
[65] EA 1/65 *Yardor v. Central Election Committee (sixth Knesset)* (1965).

Reference to Scholarly Works

The Supreme Court makes extensive use of scholarly work, both Israeli and foreign precedents and references. Israeli constitutional scholarship is extensively quoted all through the judgments. We found that 32 of 40 cases cite scholarly works (books and articles). These are used in many different ways, mostly "for further reading", to accept or to reject the arguments in the scholarly work, to present the normative framework and the explanations, or just in order to enrich the judgment.

Reference to Foreign (National) Law

Reference to foreign law is highly frequent (37 of 40 judgments). The reference is both to foreign legal texts (constitutional and national norms) and to foreign legal precedents. In 15 of the 37 cases we also found reference to Jewish Law (non-binding) along with reference to other countries.[66] These results show a strong correlation with the reference to scholarly work. The Supreme Court of Israel makes extensive use of foreign law and foreign precedents.[67] Apparently, foreign law has always been extensively used in Israel because of, among other reasons, the great local impact of English law. That trend visibly changed in the early 1980s when American law became a stronger reference source, but use of foreign law as an important comparative source was and has remained an inseparable part of the Israeli adjudication. As President Barak said:

> Comparative law – whether international or local – is most important as it expands the interpretative horizon and field of vision. It has the power to instruct the interpreter as to the normative potential of other legal methods. It is limited because every legal system has its own institutions and typical ideology, and the way it treats the individual and the society is unique. Indeed, comparative law is like having an experienced friend. It is good to listen to their sound counsel, but it should not replace one's own decisions.[68]

[66] We referred to non-binding Jewish Law as "foreign law" because of its "comparative" purpose in such cases, but it is worth mentioning that there were no cases with reference to Jewish law only, meaning that all cases referring to Jewish Law (15 of 37 cases) also referred to precedents of different countries.

[67] For further reading see: Suzie Navot, "Israel: Creating a Constitution – The Use of Foreign Precedents by the Supreme Court (1994–2010)", in Tania Groppi and Marie-Claire Ponthoreau (eds.), *The Use of Foreign Precedents by Constitutional Judges* (Hart 2013) 129.

[68] HCJ 4128/02 *Adam, Teva v'Din an Israeli Association for Environmental Protection v. The Prime Minister* (2004).

Most of the references to foreign law were mentioned in order to justify the interpretation of the solution, but some of them were mentioned to emphasize *a contrario*. In one of the cases, the reference to foreign law (Article 21 of the German Constitution) was used to explain that "if this is the case in a country with a Constitution – in a country like ours without a formal constitution the more so."[69]

The use of purposive (objective) reasoning made it very easy for the Court to look at foreign sources for comparison, guidance, and inspiration. In addition, here we see a strong correlation between the use of foreign law and the use of teleological/purposive objective arguments. Foreign law and precedents from countries with long-standing democratic and human-rights oriented tradition serve as fertile soil for reference and a quite natural source of reliance.

Other Methods or Arguments

Only a few cases (6 of 40) referred to other methods or arguments. We categorized as "other methods of argument" cases where the Court used especially vague explanations, reflective reasoning or *a priori* (tautological) justification. Such cases are those where the judges refer to the test they are creating in the case and applying it at the same time: "We wish to set a flexible test that cannot be defined precisely; its scope and content shall be determined by the Court . . . "[70] Meaning that the Court proposes a flexible and vague test, because if the test is unclear, it would be up to the Court itself to decide whether to apply it or not. Other cases which were categorized here are the *Eisenberg* case,[71] where the Court said that the decision "ought" to be that way, because this is "what it should be", and the *Herut* case,[72] where the reason given is that it is a "legislative failure". An additional example is the *Shalit* case,[73] where the Court determined that "these things need no proof, it is obvious that a Jew remains a Jew."

The Weight of Arguments

The answer to the question on the weights of arguments is difficult. To quote from Aharon Barak's writings on the weight of principles:

69 *Yardor* case, n 63. 70 *Sarid* case, n 31. 71 See n 23.

72 HCJ 212/03 *Herut – The National Jewish Movement v. Chairman of the Central Elections Committee for the Sixteenth Knesset* (2003).

73 See n 34.

> How does the judge determine the 'weights' of the various fundamental principles? The answer to this question is difficult. Legal science has not yet developed a satisfactory 'theory of values,' and it is questionable whether such a theory could ever be developed. But it is certainly possible to say that a fundamental principle enshrined in a superior norm, such as a constitution, is of greater 'weight' than a fundamental principle enshrined in an inferior norm, such as a statute or common law.[74]

As discussed in previous chapters, the far most important accepted doctrine is the rule of purposive/objective interpretation of a constitutional norm. The result of 40 of 40 cases that include analysis of principles and values, and which deal mainly with the objective teleological argument referring to the purpose of the text rather than the text itself, is very clear and reveals the relative "weight" of this argument. President Barak, while writing about his role as a judge, explicitly referred to this type of interpretation as the "primary tool".[75] As Justice Chechin described it: "All of these – principles, values and tenets – are prima facie extra-legal, but they serve as an anchor for the law – for every law – and no law can be described without them. A law without that anchor is like a house without foundations; just as the latter will not last, so too a law which has only itself is like a castle in the air."[76]

Any of the 40 cases can serve as an example for the importance of this doctrine. Perhaps the cases dealing with the disqualification of political parties, the *Neiman* case[77] and the *Tibi* case,[78] serve as a nice illustration. In both cases, the principle reasoning and the objective purpose of the text were applied by the Court, even when the specific provisions of the text, as well as the purpose of the constitution-maker, were clear and against it. The background for both cases begins in 1985, when the Knesset introduced Section 7A of *Basic Law: The Knesset*, a provision that denies a party's right to participate in the Knesset elections if that party negates Israel's existence as a Jewish state and/or its democratic nature, or if it provokes racism. Although the clause that permits the disqualification of parties due to their "implicit goals" (not only their explicitly stated ones) is particularly broad, and although the phrase that refers to parties

[74] Barak, n 14, at 90.

[75] "The fundamental principles of the legal system constitute both a goal to which judges should aspire and a means through which they realize this goal. Indeed, in addition to being a source of interpretive guidance, fundamental principles constitute a primary tool that I need to realize my role as a judge." Ibid 84.

[76] Justice Cheshin in CA 7325/95 *Yediot Aharonot Ltd. v. Kraus* (1998).

[77] EA 1/88 *Neiman v. Central Election Committee (eleventh Knesset) (1988).*

[78] N 42.

that negate the democratic nature of the state is rather vague, the HCJ interpretation of that law has since been very narrow.

In 2000, the Knesset amended Section 7A and added a new cause for the disqualification: "Support of armed struggle by a hostile state or terrorist organization against the State of Israel." This amendment had a very clear purpose: the disqualification of certain Arab MKs that made a series of disputed statements that implicitly supported terror attacks. These remarks were the trigger for the new amendment. The new cause for disqualification was extensively discussed by a panel of 11 Supreme Court judges, when addressing the *Tibi* affair in early 2003.[79] A majority of seven judges decided to allow all the parties and candidates to participate in the elections. The majority opinion, delivered by President Barak, examined Israel's militant-democracy tools, but ruled that the right to vote and to stand for elections prevails, stating that, although the basic law allows for the disqualification of parties, the Supreme Court would not easily approve such disqualifications. According to the Supreme Court, "It is preferable that non-democratic pressures find expression within the legitimate frameworks of democracy and not outside it."[80]

8 Judicial Candour and Judicial Rhetoric

Judicial Candour Most of the Court's judgments are sincere and transparent as to the reasons, arguments, and considerations taken into account. In most of the judgments, the judges explicitly discuss different possible interpretations, while they explain their pros and cons. The judges also refer to each other's opinions (when dissenting or separate opinions are found). Some judgments include a genuine open dialogue within the panel itself, and even vivid discussions between them.

Counter-arguments The opinions present the arguments of both parties to the petition at hand in great detail. These include the facts of the case, as well as the precedents and the scholarly writing the parties cite, argued to be relevant to the case. In most cases the first part of the judgment contains the facts, and then the arguments of both parties, followed by what the Court usually names the "normative framework" of the case. This part deals with the constitutional frameworks and tends to disclose a high degree of generalisation. In this part the Court usually presents the guiding principles, the references to previous precedents and the reasoning.

[79] Ibid. [80] Justice Levi in the *Tibi* affair, ibid.

Technical Language The language of the constitutional cases is seldom technical. Because of the importance of constitutional cases in Israeli politics and for the Israeli public, many cases are written in a way that even the non-legal public can read and understand. In some cases, when there are difficult legal arguments and discussions within the case, the Court usually summarizes the problematic aspects of the case as if to make it easier for newspapers and websites editors to cite them and publish the *ratio decidendi* to the general public.

The style of the Court's reasoning is mostly neutral. Sometimes the Court expresses disapproval of certain behaviour, but still, it tries to keep the wording of the judgment objective. One example of the special narrative which can be found in most cases dealing with the fights against terrorism is the following paragraph, by President Barak:

> We are aware that this decision does not ease dealing with that reality. This is the destiny of democracy, as not all means are acceptable to it, and not all practices employed by its enemies are open before it. Although a democracy must often fight with one hand tied behind its back, it nonetheless has the upper hand. Preserving the Rule of Law and recognition of an individual's liberty constitutes an important component in its understanding of security. At the end of the day, they strengthen its spirit and its strength and allow it to overcome its difficulties.[81]

The Target Audience Supreme Court judgments have different audiences, depending on the case and on the constitutional question discussed. They are aimed at the general public, the legislative branch and the government, the academic field and the international community. Although the Court does not explain for whom it writes, there are still several factors that may help in understanding the different audiences. One factor is the Court's explicit address to the government, the legislator, the military commander or the parties.

Another factor is the translation of judgments. The relevant audience of the cases dealing with the fight against terrorism is the international community: international institutions, foreign judges and foreign academia. This can be learned by the fact that these cases are published in Hebrew and English on the same day. Not every Supreme Court decision is translated into English. But on the internet site of the Supreme Court, under the title "Judgements of the Supreme Court: Fighting Terrorism within

[81] *Interrogation and investigation methods* case, n 56.

the Law", one may find all cases dealing with this issue, in English.[82] For example, *the preemptive killings* case shows Israel's Supreme Court dialogue with the international community that closely monitors Israel's activities in the Occupied Territories.[83] It seems that, like many other security-related judgments delivered by President Barak during his term, this judicial document presents a sensitive statement of defence of Israel's constant war on terror.

Other judgments' main audience is the legislative branch, meaning politicians. These are mainly the cases dealing with judicial review. For example, the case in which the Court refused to judicially review a temporary basic law on a biennial budget clearly shows the dialogue between the Court and the Knesset: "The Knesset debates show that MKs are aware of the constitutional status of the basic laws and the restrictions arising from their legislative supremacy... The Knesset was aware of the problems of legislating by way of a temporary order... "[84] Within this dialogue, we also found remarks made by Supreme Court to the legislators, as to the need for amending the law ("We draw the legislator's attention to the undesired consequences ... "[85]).

In controversial issues, such as questions regarding the separation of State and religion, or the war against terror, we may clearly see the efforts of the Court to convince the general public. A nice example is the *Horev*[86] case, where the Court states:

> Long have I traveled down the treacherous road that is Bar-Ilan. The case before us is by no means simple. From a legal perspective, it is most difficult... The case before us is difficult from a social perspective. Attempts to reach an agreement and to strike a compromise have all failed. This being the case, the solution must be found in a judicial ruling, which is quite unfortunate. Nevertheless, in President Landau's words in Dawikat [case] 'as judges, this is our role and our duty'.

Degree of Generalization The degree of generalization is a direct result of the obective purpose in the interpretation of the constitution. If fundamental values are the premises for judicial interpretation, meaning that the interpretation is "dictated" by fundamental principles, then the judges' reasoning would result in a general rule, rather than a specific solution. Indeed, judicial arguments tend to be general, and usually develop rules

[82] See: elyon1.court.gov.il/VerdictsSearch/EnglishStaticVerdicts.html.
[83] *Supra* note 33. [84] *Bar-On* case, n 53. [85] *Velner* case, n 32.
[86] HCJ 5016/96 *Horev v. Minister of Transportation* (1997).

for future cases. The vast use of precedents also emphasises this approach. The degree of generalization is therefore very high, and judgments that concentrate on specific issues are rare, or even non-existent.

One excellent example is the early case of *Kol Ha'am* (1953),[87] whose verdict laid the foundations for the freedom of speech principle in Israel's constitutional law. The case started when the Minister of Interior decided to close a newspaper named *Kol Ha'am* (Hebrew: "The People's Voice") for 10 days, because it had published a series of articles against government policies. A 1919 Mandatory order that remained in effect was the source of the Minister's prerogative to close a newspaper "if it published material that is likely to threaten public order". The newspaper appealed to the HCJ, and the Court reversed the Minister's decision. Justice Agranat, future Supreme Court President, stated that the Minister's decision did not adequately consider the status of freedom of expression in Israel. The State of Israel is a democracy, Justice Agranat wrote, and democratic regimes cannot exist without freedom of speech. The judge remarked that the Minister of Interior should employ a "balancing test" and weigh state security interests against the freedom of expression, considering the latter's importance. That right, he stated, may be restricted only if it is "highly probable" that public order might be seriously and severely harmed. The introduction of the balancing test and the *Kol Ha'am* decision had a dramatic impact on the Israeli justice system. The judgment, and the balancing test, have been both extensively cited since then.

Another clear example can be found in the *Barzilai* case,[88] which also shows the candour of the Judge on the degree of generalization:

> When constitutional issues are examined, we must consider the meaning and their implications on the long run and therefore give proper weight to their influence on the character of the social or political framework in which they operate; if we adopt casuistic standards on constitutional issues and especially on matters of individual freedom and rights, we would miss the target.

Degree of Rhetoric The degree of rhetoric and the style are as different as the judges writing them and depend only on the judge. Each judge has his or her own language, either emotional or metaphoric, rich or technical. Nonetheless, an overview of the 40 cases reveals that the use of technical legal language is rare. Constitutional cases are sometimes intended to convince the various audiences, as discussed above. Therefore, the use

[87] See n 49. [88] See n 7.

of rich language, narratives, examples, foreign law and precedents, as well as religious sources, is common. Justice Chechin is an extraordinary example, and his emotional and colourful writting is well known. In the *Mizrahi Bank*[89] case he writes:

> Yet, with all my might I will oppose our recognition of the Knesset's authority to enact a constitution by force of a judicial ruling via a legal analysis of a document dating back 47 years, while relying on disputed concepts that have no firm roots in Israeli society. And where are the people? Should we not ask their opinion?[90]

Judges quote philosophers, writers, even quote poems and songs. Here is the first paragraph of Justice Cheshin's opinion in the case of *Adalah (family reunion)*[91] affair:

> When I got the opinion of my colleague President Barak, I gave him my hand and let him lead me through his path. And so we went on the way of basic principles, climbed mountains of human rights, passed through doctrines and descended to particular rules, and on our journey, we were accompanied, at all times, by justice, truth, honesty and common sense. Towards the end of the trip we embarked on a ship and arrived to an island in the middle of the ocean. We stepped down and there, on the dock, a venerable man greeted us warmly: 'Welcome'. 'Thank you and bless you' – we replied and added, 'We are from Israel, from the Supreme Court of Israel. And who are you, Sir'? – we asked. 'My name is Thomas, Thomas Moore. And some call me Thomas Moros'. 'Nice to meet you, and what is the place we are in? – we asked. 'You are in the State of Utopia' – replied the man, adding: 'The State of Utopia was established under a program outlined in a book I wrote and whose name is as the country: Utopia.' 'And by the way, – added the man – 'the word' utopia is in Greek, and the Hebrew translation is nowhere land'.
>
> 'Interesting, very interesting' – we said, 'and as jurists we ask you: what is the legal system in Utopia? Is it similar to the Israeli legal system?' (Our assumption was, of course, that the wise man knows the Israeli legal system).
>
> Mr. Moore smiled and replied: 'I'm sorry, but there are profound differences between the two legal systems, and it will be long before Israel reaches the level of Utopia. At this time you're fighting for your life, for the existence of the state, for the ability of the Jewish people to lead a community life as all other states. The laws of Utopia – in your situation as of today – are not for you. Not yet. Keep well, take care of yourselves, do your best, and live" – said the man and said no more. And I woke up and here's a dream.

[89] See n 2. [90] Ibid para. 63 of Justice Cheshin's decision.
[91] *Family reunion* case, n 31.

9 Length, Dissenting and Concurring Opinions

Israeli constitutional cases are quite long. The average number of pages in the 40 landmark cases is 69. The extensive use of precedents, foreign law, the discussion of the parties' arguments, the objective purposive reasoning – are all factors that influence the length of the cases.

We found that the length of the opinions grew over the years, with a peak in the 1990s, the decade of the *Mizrahi Bank* decision.[92] Until the 1990s, the average number of pages was less than 50, with two exceptions: the *Shalit* case,[93] dealing with the question of "who is a Jew", and the *Barzilai* case,[94] dealing with the President of the State's power of pardon.

There is a strong correlation between the length of the cases and the issues discussed in them. The more the issue is a controversial political question – the longer the judgment. In addition, due to the fact that separate opinions are allowed, the number of judges sitting on the bench may influence the length of the judgments.

For example, apart from the *Mizrahi Bank* case, which is of unusual length (367 pages), the longest cases dealt with the following questions and were handed down by the following numbers of judges:

- The *Adalah (family reunion)* case (11 judges) (281 pages) – dealt with an amendment to the *Citizenship Act*, which restricts the entry of residents of the West Bank and the Gaza Strip to the State of Israel. Among other things, restrictions were imposed on the reunion of married couples when one was an Israeli Arab and the other resides in Palestinian Authority territories.[95]
- The *Tal Law* affair (11 judges) (171 pages) – dealt with the constitutionality of the law that exempted *yeshiva* students from military service. The case is viewed as a significant "law and religion" case.[96]
- The *Tibi* case (11 judges) (110 pages) – dealt with the disqualification of political parties, and included discussions on security considerations and war against terror, as well as the tension between the Jewish character of the State and its democratic character.[97]
- The *Horev* case (7 judges) (172 pages) – dealt with the possibility to close a central road in Jerusalem on the *Sabbath*, also considered a "law and religion" case.[98]

As for separate opinions, Israeli case law allows for both dissenting and concurring opinions, and they are an inherent part of the judgment. Minority opinions were found in 19 of 40 cases. Sometimes minority

[92] See n 2. [93] See n 34. [94] See n 7. [95] See n 31.
[96] See n 25. [97] See n 42. [98] See n 84.

opinions become, in time, majority ones (in later cases dealing with similar questions).

We observed two kinds of dissenting opinions: in one group, a "material" dissenting opinion, meaning that the judge did not agree with the final decision or with the arguments and reasoning that lead to that decision. In the second group, we find "technical" dissenting opinions, meaning that the judge did not agree with the specific solution, but agreed to the arguments and the reasoning of the majority. A classic example for this are cases where there is a factual disagreement between the minority and the majority (e.g. whether it has actually been proven that the party supports terrorism), but the reasoning upon which both opinions are based is similar.

Another kind of separate opinion, yet not dissenting, was found among the majority opinions in some cases, when a judge reached the same conclusion regarding the solution of the specific case, but in a completely different way (separate concurring opinion).

10 Framing of Constitutional Issues

The framing of a constitutional issue is a difficult question, for several reasons. First, Israel does not have a separate Constitutional Court, and sometimes constitutional questions may appear in cases that are actually civil appeals or criminal appeals. However, most constitutional questions arise under the authority of the Supreme Court sitting as the High Court of Justice. Second, addressing conflicts between citizens and government, the HCJ serves as both a High Court of Justice and as the state's administrative instance, which sometimes makes it hard to decide whether a given issue is of constitutional or administrative nature.

We classified the constitutional cases in two categories: institutional judgments and human-rights judgments. Of the 40 cases, 21 were institutional (dealing with the different institutions of the State, the Knesset, government, elections, etc.) and 17 dealt with human rights. Two of 40 referred to other issues.

11 Key Concepts

Key concepts in Israeli cases can be divided into four groups:

Most Popular Arguments The most popular arguments used by the HCJ are "democracy" and "the rule of law" principle. In 33 of 40 cases we found references to democracy, and in 24 of 40 the Court referred to the different aspects of the rule of law. These findings are not difficult to explain. They perfectly support the objective purposive reasoning, according to which constitutional norms should be interpreted in the light of the basic principles of the legal system. As we have seen, these principles include the democratic principle, and since the early days of the State, the principle of the rule of law has been a main feature in Supreme Court rulings.

Relatively Popular and New Concepts The principle of "proportionality" was referred to in 13 of 40 cases. This figure may seem low, taking into account the importance of proportionality in Israeli constitutional law.[99] But this is a new term in Israeli adjudication. Therefore, it is not to be found in the judgments dating before 1992. Following the enactment of the basic laws on human rights in 1992, and the limitation clause according to which human rights may be harmed if this is done for appropriate reasons and if it is "proportionate", Israel's constitutional discourse has focused in recent years on proportionality. Since the constitutional revolution, every constitutional verdict that addresses the constitutionality of a law includes an analysis and a discussion of the issue of proportionality. Therefore, we found this term mentioned in all decisions dealing with human rights after 1992. The same applies to "human dignity", which is the core of the basic law on human rights: we found reference to human dignity in 15 of 40 cases.

Another popular argument used was the principle of "equality", which was found in 16 of 40 cases. The equality principle is a cornerstone of every democracy, and yet Israel is one of the few democracies that have not constitutionalised the right to equality, probably because this is the most problematic right in the Israeli context.[100] In the absence of a constitutional text on the equality principle, the Supreme Court has served as the body that has ordered government agencies to treat all citizens equally. In a series of judgments, the Court has established that "it ought to be assumed" that the purpose of all legislation is to promote and protect equality. We found the argument of equality in human rights cases, dealing with women's rights, minority rights and homosexual rights, as well as in institutional constitutional cases, when dealing with the principle of equality to stand for political elections.

We found that in many of the cases, the concepts of "equality" and "human dignity" appeared together, mainly after 1992. Since the

[99] See, for example: Aharon Barak, *Proportionality: Constitutional Rights and Their Limitations* (Cambridge University Press 2012).

[100] On account of religion and State issues (which create anomaly in areas of gender equality, obligatory military service and more), as well as the status of the Arab minority.

legislature failed to complete a constitutional bill of rights, the Court's interpretations expanded the right to dignity, allowing for judicial review of laws that disproportionally harm rights that are not listed in basic laws. New petitions filed with the HCJ asked the Court to invalidate laws that were inconsistent with unwritten rights, such as the right to equality. The Court established that the right to human dignity includes aspects of the right to equality.[101]

Not So Popular Many important arguments were not widely used. For example, freedom of expression, which is a most important right in Israel, was used only in 6 of 40 cases. We found reference to the concept of *Wesensgehalt*, meaning the essential core of human rights ("This protection is in the core of the right to human dignity"[102]) in 5 of 40 cases. The principle of "secularism" was found in 7 of 40 cases, mainly due to the fact that Israel is a Jewish and democratic state. For example, in the *Bavli* case,[103] the Court was requested to rule in favor of the democratic principle: "The HCJ does not accept the approach by which civil courts must follow Jewish law when addressing asset-sharing issues . . . "

Non-relevant or Almost Non-existent The Court dealt with the "form of government" in 4 of 40 cases, mainly enhancing the Israeli parliamentary system as opposed to other regimes such as the presidential regime. For example, in the *Barzilai* case,[104] when dealing with the authority to pardon convicted persons, which in Israel is one of the few powers granted to the President of the State, Justice Barak (dissenting) wrote that "under the Israel 'constitutional scheme', the Presidential power of pardon must not be construed as a paramount power, or as rivaling the powers of other State authorities, such as the police, the prosecution, the courts. It must be construed as a residual or a 'reserve' power to be exercised only after the other authorities concerned have exhausted their own powers, i.e. after conviction of the accused."

The principle of "sovereignty" was found in 2 cases of 40. In the case of *Adalah (family reunion)*,[105] while dealing with the sovereignty of a state to

[101] See, for instance: *Miller* case, *supra* note 24, regarding women's right to apply for pilots' course in the IDF; *Tal Law* case, *supra* note 25, regarding exemption of religious *yeshiva* students from obligatory military service; and HCJ 11163/03 *Supreme Monitoring Committee for Arab Affairs in Israel v. Prime Minister of Israel* (2006), regarding distribution of financial benefits to Jewish and Arab local authorities. It should be noted that other human rights have been "read into" the constitutional right of human dignity as well; For elaboration, see introduction.

[102] *Family reunion* case, n 31.

[103] HCJ 1000/92 *Bavli v. Great Rabbinical Court* (1994).

[104] See n 7.

[105] See n 31.

decide who will enter its borders, the Court determined: "The state is the one to decide who is eligible to immigrate to its territory." In addition, in the case dealing with the *privatization of prisons*,[106] the Court stated that at the constitutional level there is a "hard core" of governmental powers, which the executive branch may not transfer by the act of privatization. The Court considered imprisonment (and criminal procedure as a whole) as one of these core powers that can only be justified by the sovereignty of the State over its citizens.

The concept of "nation" was addressed by the Court in 2 cases of 40, mainly discussing the Jewish nation-State in the case of *Shalit*,[107] and dealing with the importance of the *Sabbath* for the Jewish nation, in the case of *Horev*,[108] while quoting *Ahad-Ha'am:* "He who feels in his heart a real connection with the life of the nation in all times, cannot possibly imagine the reality of the people of Israel without the Sabbath".[109]

"Basic procedural rights" were barely mentioned, and we found this argument in 2 of 40 cases. The main case where this argument arose was the *privatization of prisons*[110] case ("At all stages of the criminal process, from the criminal investigation, through the trial, sentencing and incarceration, a constant balance is needed between the use of government force required to enforce the law, and the protection of fundamental rights of the suspect, the accused and the convicted prisoner"). Finally, we found only 1 case of 40 dealing with "state form": the *Barzilai* case,[111] dealing with presidential pardon, in which the Court compared the power of pardon in a monarchy and in a republic.

The concept of "federalism" is almost irrelevant for Israel. Amongst the 40 leading cases of the sample, there were none which dealt with local autonomies either.

C Comparative Perspective

The constitutional reasoning of the Israeli Supreme Court discloses special characteristics, many of which are related to its special role in Israel's constitutional history, culture and society. The absence of a constitutional text impacted on Israeli constitutional reasoning in many ways. Generally, the interpretation of constitutional texts followed the objective-purposive approach, based on historical developments, on society's fundamental

[106] See n 35. [107] See n 34. [108] See n 84.

[109] The pen name of Asher Ginsberg, one of the foremost pre-state Zionist thinkers.

[110] See n 35. [111] See n 7.

principles such as the rule of law, on the separation of powers and on human rights.

Still, many of the applied key concepts in constitutional reasoning are similar to those applied in other countries. The use of the doctrine of proportionality is widespread and has become the primary method for assessing a case which involves a conflict of constitutional rights, in many countries within this project. The same can be argued as to the use of standards and tests such as "reasonableness" or "balancing" and as to the generous interpretation of the principle of equality. The comparison between constitutional courts shows that teleological interpretation, proportionality-based reviews and generous interpretive approaches developed by the judges themselves are quite common among different jurisdictions.

Evolution in constitutional discourse has also been seen in many different countries, new constitutional states as well as older ones (France). The phenomenon of judicial development of constitutional principles and rights in order to draw new rights or even duties imposed on governmental branches crosses legal families and legal systems. For example, the expanding of the concept of human dignity in order to include new rights – as we have seen in Israel's case law – has been similarly done in Italy concerning the interpretation of the equality principle, which allowed for development of the "reasonableness principle".

Judicial activism seems, at first glance, a typical Israeli feature in constitutional adjudication. However, the comparative approach shows that it may be the case in other countries as well (the Czech Republic).

The comparative perspective also shows that constitutional courts are writing more and more for different audiences (Australia, South Africa). Even in civil law jurisdictions, where traditionally constitutional courts did not include references or citations in their decisions (or very few, such as Italy), some changes are emerging. Such is the case in Taiwan, where the strong representation of former academics in the Taiwanese Court, as well as scholarly works, have influenced the Court's jurisprudence.

There is a widespread sense that despite the differences in legal cultures, in political theory and in judge selection systems, constitutional judges share a common language of principles, such as democracy, the rule of law, the principle of equality, proportionality and human dignity.

Furthermore, constitutional courts are turning more frequently to foreign jurisprudence for guidance and inspiration. The use of foreign law by almost all courts discussed in this project shows that constitutional judges are indeed engaging in a global judicial dialogue. The use of purposive (objective) reasoning makes it easy for the courts to look at foreign sources for comparison. It seems that there is a strong correlation between the use of foreign law and the use of teleological/purposive objective arguments. Academic scholars and jurists now speak in terms of a global community of courts or of a transnational judicial dialogue that unites judges around the world in a common global judicial enterprise.[112]

The use of foreign law is beneficial to judicial perspective in decision making, mainly in constitutional law. Foreign jurisdictions might have confronted similar problems and thus may provide insightful analysis or reasoning. Foreign law provides ideas, serves for comparison and for guidance, helps elaborate similar values and principles. Empirical comparative researches, as this one, may not only improve the quality of judges' particular decisions, help them frame their position and contribute to a "global jurisprudence". They may help also in the mapping and classification of the world of new constitutionalism, and in the creation of conceptual frameworks for comparative law.[113]

D Evaluation, Pathology and Criticism

The Supreme Court of Israel is not only a constitutional court, but also a dominant player in Israeli society. It seems that almost every political decision involves the Court. The lack of clear jurisdiction boundaries, the possibility to grant remedy "for the sake of justice", the non-existent standing precondition and the willingness of the Court to examine almost every case on the merits, have resulted in a social phenomenon which critics call the "judicialisation of politics", or the "constitutionalisation of public life".

Judicial reasoning has changed over the years. Since the 1980s, the Court has transitioned from its position as the protector of personal rights to the body whose task is to ensure the realisation of public values. New doctrines of standing – much more tolerant towards "public" actions – allowed for public petitioners and NGOs to present the Court with questions of human rights, Palestinian rights and minority rights. These were the issues that political institutions were unable to resolve, if not reluctant to deal with at all. This broad view of standing proved to be a powerful

[112] David S. Law and Wen-Chen Chang, "The Limits of Global Judicial Dialogue" (2011) 86 *Washington Law Review* 523.

[113] Ran Hirschl, "From Comparative Constitutional Law to Comparative Constitutional Studies: editorial" (2013) 11 *International Journal of Constitutional Law* 1, 2.

mechanism for the Court to protect the rule of law and the legality of government and to broaden the scope of constitutional issues.

Similarly, a new style of reasoning has evolved, addressing the laws' normative meaning. The earlier formalistic application of the law to the facts of each case was replaced by attempts to find a balance between conflicting values.[114] The new approach went hand in hand with the Supreme Court's use of reasonableness and proportionality as its primary instruments for the purpose of supervising the legislature, the government and administrative decisions. The purpose of the norm, not its language, has become paramount. Concepts such as "the purpose of the law", "the spirit of the law" and "the legislator's intention" replaced the dry legislative letter. Judges started indulging in more creativity in their judicial activities, feeling free to seek creative solutions in an attempt to attain moral and just results. The HCJ has expanded the scope of its intervention and even criticised the values and acts of public position holders. Thus, HCJ rulings started shaping policies and even determining general norms. There are many diverse examples of Israeli activist constitutional reasoning. Particularly prominent were cases that sought the enforcement of ethical norms in relation to public officials, mainly in the 1990s. In terms of comparative law, the Court's intervention in issues such as public ethics, government culture and proper administration is unique and largely criticised.

In fact, most of the key social decisions are still made by political institutions and not by the Supreme Court, although the latter is sometimes forced to engage in issues that the legislature avoids. In certain respects, the Court's very willingness to intervene weakens the political body it reviews. Though, theoretically, this willingness applies to a wide range of issues, reality has shown that the Court has actually intervened very little and Israeli politics is still conducted within government corridors. The same applies to judicial activism. The Supreme Court appeared activist when it overruled the decisions of other authorities, but alleging that it was actually engaged in activism would require a thorough inspection of its adjudication patterns, and no such study has been conducted. It is true that the Court is willing to examine every issue presented before it on its merits, but a detailed examination of its judicial control of government activities shows that it has almost always in practice confirmed government decisions, which has left the government with almost unlimited discretion.

[114] Mautner, *The Decline of Formalism*, n 13.

One possible line of criticism is directed at the Israeli composition of the Supreme Court. The Constitutional courts' compositions differ from supreme court of appeals in many jurisdictions. Israel has one Supreme Court that deals also with constitutional questions, following the Anglo-American heritage. There is room for further thoughts as to the fact that very few academics serve at the Supreme Court.

The formation of the State of Israel launched its path among nations without a written constitution or a bill of rights, referring directly to the British tradition of parliamentary sovereignty instead. The Israeli Parliament never completed the task of drafting and approving a constitution. It was the Supreme Court that stepped in and established the basic principles for the new state, as well as a solid base for the protection of human rights. Israel's constitutional history has demonstrated that the constitutional text is less important than its interpretation by judges.

Appendix: 40 Leading Cases

1. HCJ 1/49 Bejerano v. Minister of Police (1949).
2. HCJ 73/53 "Kol Ha'am" Co. LTD v. Minister of Interior (1953).
3. EA 1/65 Yardor v. Central Election Committee (sixth Knesset) (1965).
4. HCJ 98/69 Bergman v. Minister of Finance (1969).
5. HCJ 58/68 Shalit v. Minister of Interior (1969).
6. HCJ 652/81 Sarid v. Knesset Speaker (1981).
7. HCJ 428/86 Barzilai v. Government of Israel (1986).
8. HCJ 680/88 Schnitzer v. The Chief Military Censor (1989).
9. EA 1/88 Neiman v. Central Election Committee (eleventh Knesset) (1988).
10. HCJ 142/89 Laor v. Knesset Speaker (1990).
11. HCJ 6136/92 Eisenberg v. Minister of Construction and Housing (1993).
12. HCJ 3094/93 The Movement for Quality in Government v. State of Israel (1993).
13. HCJ 1000/92 Bavli v. Great Rabbinical Court (1994).
14. HCJ 721/94 El-Al Israel Airlines v. Danielowitz (1994).
15. HCJ 5364/94 Velner v. Labor Party (1995).
16. HCJ 1843/93 Pinhasi v. Knesset (1995).
17. HCJ 4541/94 Miller v. Minister of Defence (1995).
18. CA 6821/93 United Mizrahi Bank Ltd. v. Migdal Cooperative Village (1995).
19. HCJ 4676/94 Mitrael v. Knesset (1996).

20. HCJ 5016/96 Horev v. Minister of Transportation (1997).
21. HCJ 3267/97 Rubinstein v. Minister of Defense (1998).
22. HCJ 2671/98 Women's Lobby v. Minister of Labor and Social Affairs (1998).
23. HCJ 5100/94 Public Committee against Torture v. Israel (1999).
24. HCJ 6698/95 Ka'adan v. Israel Land Administration (2000).
25. HCJ 212/03 Herut – The National Jewish Movement v. Chairman of the Central Elections Committee for the Sixteenth Knesset (2003).
26. EA 11280/02 Central Election Committee v. Tibi (sixteenth Knesset) (2003).
27. EA 92/03 Mofaz v. Chairman of the Central Elections Committee for the Sixteenth Knesset (2003).
28. HCJ 4885/03 Israel Poultry Farmers Association Agricultural Cooperative Society Ltd v. Government of Israel (2004).
29. HCJ 5261/04 Fuchs v. Prime Minister of Israel (2004).
30. HCJ 11163/03 Supreme Monitoring Committee for Arabs Affairs in Israel v. Prime Minister of Israel (2006).
31. HCJ 11298/03 The Movement for Quality in Government v. Knesset Committee (2005).
32. HCJ 366/03 Commitment to Peace and Social Justice Society v. Minister of Finance (2005).
33. HCJ 11225/03 Bishara v. Attorney-General (2006).
34. HCJ 6427/02 Movement for Quality in Government v. Knesset (2006).
35. HCJ 7052/03 Adalah Legal Centre for Arab Minority Rights in Israel v. Minister of Interior (2006).
36. HCJ 769/02 Public Committee against Torture in Israel v. Government of Israel (2006).
37. HCJ 10203/03 "Hamifkad Haleumi" Ltd. V. Attorney General (2008).
38. HCJ 2605/05 Academic Center for Law and Business, Human Rights Division v. Minister of Finance (2009).
39. HCJ 4124/00 Yekutieli v. Minister of Religious Affairs (2010).
40. HCJ 4908/10 Bar-On v. Israel Knesset (2011).

13

The Constitutional Court of Italy[1]

TANIA GROPPI AND IRENE SPIGNO

A Legal, Political, Institutional and Academic Context

1 Legal and Political Culture as Context for Constitutional Reasoning

The Constitutional Court was introduced for the first time in Italy by the 1948 Constitution, enacted by the Constituent Assembly after the fall of the Fascist regime and the end of the Second World War. The Constitution established a "constitutional democracy", that is, a form of government in which sovereignty belongs to the people and is exercised within the limits established by a "rigid" Constitution, entrenched by a difficult amendment procedure.

Since the beginning of its activity, in 1956, the Court has played a crucial role in the implementation of the Constitution, acting in accordance with legal scholarship, and has contributed to the development on the part of ordinary courts of a new, open-minded attitude towards the newly-enacted Constitution.[2] Over the years, the Court has also displayed a high level of interpretative creativity and activism, which facilitated the evolution of the Italian legal system with a view to the establishment of a modern constitutional state in correspondence of the modernization of the Italian society.[3]

[1] The selection and analysis of the 40 leading cases is the result of the joint work of the authors. The report has been written by Tania Groppi (sections A, B except paragraphs "Non-legal Arguments", "References to Scholarly Work", "References to Foreign Law", "Length of Decisions", "Key Concepts", C) and by Irene Spigno (section B, paragraphs "Non-legal Arguments", "References to Scholarly Work", "References to Foreign Law", "Length of Decisions", "Key Concepts"). Translation by Gianluca Gentili, Lecturer, University of Sussex (UK).

[2] On the relationships between the Constitutional Court and ordinary courts, that, for the reasons developed in the text, are crucial for the comprehension of the Italian system of judicial review, see Elisabetta Lamarque, *Corte costituzionale e giudici nell'Italia repubblicana* (Laterza 2012).

[3] For an overview on the contribution of the Constitutional Court at the development of the Italian legal system, see Enzo Cheli, *Il giudice delle leggi* (Il Mulino 1996); see also Tania

In so doing, the Court has often reached beyond the text of the Constitution, becoming one of the players of its silent transformation. Despite the entrenchment of the Constitution, an important feature of Italian constitutionalism lies in that constitutional change has largely taken place informally – that is, outside of the rules established for the enactment of formal amendments – in a variety of forms: ordinary laws with constitutional effects (such as electoral laws or the Standing Orders of each Chamber of the Parliament); constitutional conventions and practices; European law, and, last but not least, decisions of the Constitutional Court.[4]

Many reasons concur in explaining this development – and are deeply connected with the specific features of Italy's constitutional culture and political system.

As for the constitutional culture, the most prominent Italian scholars since the beginning have endorsed a non-formalistic view of the Constitution. According to this view, the meaning of the Constitution reaches beyond the mere written text[5] to become the product of the political, social and economic groups that at different historical times and in various circumstances uphold the written text.[6] This has been the prevailing view throughout the life of the 1948 Italian Constitution,[7] together

Groppi, "The Constitutional Court of Italy: Towards a Multilevel System of Constitutional Review?" (2008) 3.2 *Journal of Comparative Law* 10. After the writing of this chapter, two important contributions on the Italian Constitutional Court were published. For the first time, a judge of the Court published his memoirs, once he left the Court at the end of his term, giving a unique insight into the institution: Sabino Cassese, *Dentro la Corte. Diario di un giudice costituzionale* (Il Mulino 2015). Recently, the first full account of the Court experience has been published in English: Vittoria Barsotti, Paolo G. Carozza, Marta Cartabia and Andrea Simonicini, *Italian Constitutional Justice in Global Context* (Oxford University Press 2016).

4 See Carlo Fusaro, "Italy" in Carlo Fusaro and Dawn Oliver (eds), *How Constitutions Change. A Comparative Study* (Hart 2011) 211–233; Tania Groppi, "Constitutional Revision in Italy. A Marginal Instrument for Constitutional Change" in Xenophon Contiades (ed), *Engineering Constitutional Change: A Comparative Perspective on Europe, Canada and USA* (Routledge 2012) 203–27.

5 The distinction between "*disposizione*" and "*norma*", or legal "provisions" and "norms", was introduced by Vezio Crisafulli, "Questioni in tema di interpretazione della Corte Costituzionale nei confronti con l'interpretazione giudiziaria" (1956) *Giurisprudenza costituzionale* 929, with regard to statutory interpretation.

6 The most influential book was Costantino Mortati, *La Costituzione in senso materiale* (Giuffrè 1939). The author, Costantino Mortati, later became a member of the Constituent Assembly and, further on, a judge of the Constitutional Court. He is considered the most influential Italian scholar in Constitutional Law.

7 See Augusto Barbera, "Ordinamento costituzionale e carte costituzionali" (2010) *Quaderni costituzionali* 311.

with a non-positivistic approach to constitutional interpretation,[8] which explains the important role played, over the years, by the creative interpretation of the Constitutional Court.

As for the political system, it should be noted that the 1948 Italian Constitution was the product of the political agreement reached between the various anti-fascist parties (the *Democrazia Cristiana*, DC – the Italian Catholic party; the left-wing parties – *Partito comunista* and *Partito socialista*; and some minor centrist parties). However, in May 1947, that is, even before the entry into force of the Constitution, this agreement collapsed, due to the beginning of the Cold War at the international level. This event determined two sets of consequences. First of all, many provisions of the Constitution remained without legal implementation. Second, in the absence of a large consensus, the prevailing opinion was that the procedure for constitutional revision could be resorted to only for minor changes. Thus, for major changes, other, informal, avenues developed eventually.

As a result of the aforementioned process, today the "living Constitution" in Italy is conceptually very far from the "written Constitution".[9] In this transformation, determined by the prevailing Italian constitutional culture, the Constitutional Court has played an important role.

2 *The Court and Constitutional Litigation*

The framers of the Italian Constitution rejected the few proposals aimed at the introduction of an American-style purely decentralized system of the judicial review of legislation and, in accordance with the dominant constitutional trends in post-war Europe (particularly as expressed by Hans Kelsen), they designed a system of centralized review, with the creation of an "ad hoc" organ of constitutional justice separate from the judiciary (art. 134–137).[10]

[8] This approach is well summarized in Gustavo Zagrebelsky, *Il diritto mite* (Einaudi 1992), a book that has deeply influenced the last two decades of Italian Constitutional Law history and has been translated into many languages (not including English).

[9] See Sergio Bartole, *Interpretazioni e trasformazioni della Costituzione repubblicana* (Il Mulino 2004) especially 241 ss.

[10] The debates in the Italian Constituent Assembly are summarized in Alessandro Pizzorusso, Vincenzo Vigoriti and G. L. Certoma, "The Constitutional Review of Legislation in Italy" (1983) 56 *Temple Law Quarterly* 503.

The Competences of the Constitutional Court

The functions of the Constitutional Court, as defined in article 134 of the Constitution, are those typical of constitutional tribunals.

The Court has the power:

(a) to adjudicate on the constitutionality of laws issued by the national and regional governments;
(b) to resolve conflicts between organs of the state, between the state and the regions, and between regions;
(c) to adjudicate crimes committed by the President of the Republic (high treason and attempts to overthrow the Constitution).

Article 2 of Constitutional Law no. 1 of 1953 added an additional function to those already listed in the Constitution:

(d) to adjudicate on the admissibility of requests for referendums to repeal laws, which may be promoted by 500,000 voters, or five regional councils, pursuant to article 75 of the Constitution.

Compared to other models of constitutional adjudication, especially those most recently established, these competences are notable for being apparently limited and minimalist.

On the one hand, the Italian Constitutional Court does not have some competences which are present in other constitutional systems, usually labeled as "political": for example, in many systems Constitutional Courts have powers connected to electoral issues, supervision of political parties and the declaration of incapacity of the President of the Republic.

On the other hand, with regard to the Court's main competence of reviewing the constitutionality of laws, several limitations arise from articles 134–137 of the Constitution, Constitutional Law no. 1 of 1948 and Law no. 87 of 1953. These limitations concern the means of triggering constitutional review and the object of review.

First of all, access to constitutional review is rather circumscribed: the Italian system offers only a posteriori, indirect, concrete review, which arises mainly out of a separate judicial proceeding ("a quo" proceeding). The keys that open the door to constitutional review are primarily in the hands of ordinary judges, who therefore perform the important function of "gatekeepers". The constitutional proceeding begins with a "certification order" whereby the judge suspends all proceedings and submits the question to the Constitutional Court. In that order, the judge must indicate the relevance and plausibility of the question, the law challenged, and the constitutional provision allegedly violated.

There is also an avenue of direct, abstract review, according to article 127 of the Constitution. The national government and the regional government may challenge, respectively, a regional or a national statute within 60 days of its publication. This way, direct review is only a tool for the guarantee of the constitutional separation of powers between national and regional governments. Neither private citizens nor parliamentary groups or local (sub-regional) governments can directly invoke the Court's jurisdiction.[11]

Secondly, the "object" of constitutional review is represented exclusively by laws. Delegated or administrative legislation is not reviewed by the Constitutional Court, but, conversely, by ordinary courts: those courts, however, cannot annul statutes, although they can annul or set aside secondary legislation.

Furthermore, the Court may not autonomously shy away from the "thema decidendum" (that is, the object and parameter of review) as identified in the application to the Court, as indicated in article 27 of Law no. 87 of 1953.

If we move from a simple list of the Court's functions to an analysis of the statistics about its activity, the limited nature of its powers becomes even clearer. Out of a total average of around 300 to 400 decisions per year in the last decade, the vast majority of the Court's activity is devoted to the constitutional review of legislation, which overshadows its other functions, in particular with regard to jurisdictional disputes between the state and the regions. This percentage has not changed over the years, although the total number of cases decided per year has been increasing, moving from the 100 to 200 of the first 20 years to the more than 1000 of the year 1988, when the Court adjudicated most of the pending questions previously delayed. After that date, the number stabilized around the current level.

Within the category of constitutional review of legislation, particular importance is assumed by concrete review, which has absorbed most of the Court's time during its almost 60 years of activity. However, the number of questions raised by ordinary judges has decreased in recent

[11] See Gianluca Gentili, "A Comparison of European Systems of Direct Access to Constitutional Judges: Exploring Advantages for the Italian Constitutional Court" (2012) 1 *Italian Journal of Public Law* 159.

decades, due to the "interpretation of the statutes in conformity with the Constitution"[12] and as a consequence of the fact that a number of controversies that could be brought to the Constitutional Court are rather decided in the European context, by the ECJ (European Court of Justice, now CJEU) or by the ECHR (European Court of Human Rights), both having competing jurisdiction in cases involving the protection of rights.

At the same time, the number of direct complaints (in the state-regions relationships) has increased, mainly as a consequence of the important constitutional revision of 2001 that affected most of the articles of the Constitution dealing with the state-regions relationship. In the last few years the majority of decisions[13] have concerned this latter competence.[14]

Constitutional Litigation

The powers of the Italian Constitutional Court and the process of constitutional review were regulated in the years immediately following the entry into force of the Constitution (the Court was established in 1956) and have not changed much since then.[15] The Constitutional Court does, however, enjoy a vast discretion in interpreting its procedure and practice, thus allowing it to modify the latter – by its rules of procedure or even on a case-by-case basis – in order to achieve a desired goal or to more fully implement constitutional values.

Within This Framework, Some Aspects Should Be Pointed Out In the concrete control, cases are only seldom argued orally. This usually happens in two sets of cases: when the parties appear before the Court, and where a dismissal of the challenge on procedural grounds is not an option. In these cases the parties appearing before the Court are not only the parties of the "a quo" judgment but also the national or regional government (according to the statute challenged): third parties, amici curiae etc. do not enjoy standing to participate in the process, despite the critical remarks

[12] See *infra* at para A 4. [13] Especially among the "*sentenze*": see *infra.*

[14] Data about the work of the Court may be found in Roberto Romboli (ed), *Aggiornamenti in tema di processo costituzionale* (Giappichelli from 1990 until 2012) and on the annual report of the President of the Court, published on the website of the Court: www.cortecostituzionale.it.

[15] See Const. Law 1/1948, Law 1/1953 and Law 87/1953. The rules of procedure of the Court, enacted in 1956, have been replaced in 2008.

of the scholarship towards this very restrictive Court's approach.[16] In the abstract review, conversely, cases are almost always orally argued: the parties are the national and the regional government. Conflicts are always orally argued. Independently from the possibility to argue orally, parties can always submit briefs to the Court, which are usually addressed in the "fact of the case" part of the judgments.[17] The Court can "ex officio" (on its own motion) ask for evidence or arguments, but this has happened rarely and in most cases it was just a device used in order to likely postpone complex decisions: most of the time, the Court acquires facts or other non-legal arguments informally.

Typology and Effects of Decisions

It is difficult to understand the legal reasoning of the Italian Constitutional Court without considering the typology of its decisions, especially in the constitutional review of legislation.[18]

From a formal point of view, there are two kinds of decisions: "sentenze" and "ordinanze". "Ordinanze" (orders) do not decide the question, but either play an interlocutory role or reject a question on procedural grounds. Usually they are motivated by lack of standing or other admissibility requirements. "Sentenze" (judgments) are longer and more motivated decisions about the question submitted. All the decisions of the Court are published in the *Official Journal.*

According to the constitutional and legislative provisions on Constitutional Court, there is a limited range of "sentenze": they can either accept or reject constitutional challenges, and these are known respectively as "sentenze di accoglimento" and "sentenze di rigetto".

The consequences of these two types of decisions, including their temporal effects, are rather straightforwardly defined by law and do not fall within the discretionary power of the Court.

Decisions that reject a constitutional challenge do not certify a law as constitutional; rather, they merely reject the specific challenge presented in the form in which it was raised. They are not universally binding, that

[16] See e.g. Vittorio Angiolini (ed), *Il contraddittorio nel giudizio sulle leggi* (Giappichelli 1998); Roberto Romboli (ed), *L'accesso alla giustizia costituzionale: caratteri, limiti, prospettive di un modello* (Jovene 2006).

[17] See *infra* at para. "The 40 Leading Cases: an Overview".

[18] See *amplius* Giancarlo Rolla and Tania Groppi, "Between Politics and the Law: The Development of Constitutional Review in Italy" in Wojchiech Sadurski (ed), *Constitutional Justice, East and West* (Kluwer Law International 2002) 143.

is, they are not effective "erga omnes". Thus, the same question can be raised again, on the same or different grounds; only the judge who has certified the question cannot raise it again in the same lawsuit. For this reason, such judgments are said to be effective only as between the parties, that is, "inter partes".

On the other hand, judgments that accept a constitutional challenge are universally binding and enjoy retroactive effect ("ex tunc"), in the sense that the statute declared unconstitutional can no longer be applied from the day after the judgment has been published. This retroactivity finds its limits in what are usually called "rapporti esauriti," which might be translated as "concluded relationships" or "res iudicata". For reasons of convenience and legal certainty, judgments do not affect situations that were already resolved by final judgments, claims that are barred by statutes of limitation, and the like. Yet, there is an exception to this rule where a final criminal conviction has been entered pursuant to the law now declared unconstitutional: the law provides that such a conviction and any related punishment should cease.

However, the Constitutional Court has, since the first years of its activity, developed a rich variety of judgments that arise from the need, recognized by the Constitutional Court, to consider the impact that its decisions have on the legal system as a whole and on other branches of government, particularly the Judiciary and the Parliament.

The need to establish a relationship with the ordinary courts, which are charged with the task of interpreting statutory law, led the Constitutional Court to develop "interpretative" decisions: with them the Court distinguishes between the text of constitutional provision and the underlying norm and either indicates to the certifying judge an alternative interpretation (norm) that is consistent with the Constitution, thus rejecting the constitutional challenge (i.e. a "sentenza interpretativa di rigetto"), or else judges the interpretation given by the certifying judge to be contrary to the Constitution and strikes down that specific norm, but not the text itself (i.e. a "sentenza interpretativa di accoglimento", rarely used nowadays).

Other types of decisions have instead affected the relationship between the Court and the Legislature.

An especially delicate issue has been the use of "additive" judgments, whereby the Court declares a statute unconstitutional not for what it provides but for what it fails to provide. This way, the Court manages to insert new rules into the legal system which cannot be found in any statutory text. With these judgments, the Constitutional Court transforms itself into a creator of legal rules, thereby playing a role that in the Italian system belongs almost exclusively to the Parliament.

3 *The Judges*

Requirement and Appointment

The Constitutional Court's composition reflects the effort to balance the need for legal knowledge and expertise (as any judicial body must do), against the acknowledgment of the unavoidably political nature of constitutional review:[19] 15 judges, chosen from among legal experts (magistrates from the higher courts, law professors and lawyers with more than 20 years of experience), one-third of whom are appointed by the President of the Republic, one-third by the Parliament in joint session, by three-fifths majority, and one-third by the upper echelons of the judiciary. The term of office is 9 years, and they cannot be re-appointed. Thus, the main feature of the judges is their legal expertise: mere politicians cannot be appointed, although it could happen that some former politicians are chosen, especially among lawyers.

The three categories have been present in almost equal proportion, although law professors have been slightly more numerous.[20] At the moment, 5 of the 13 judges are law professors, 2 are lawyers and 6 are magistrates.[21] Generally, the President of the Republic appoints scholars, whereas the Parliament elects both professors and lawyers, while the higher courts normally elect their own members.

The average age is high: the appointment at the Court is seen as the summit of a brilliant legal career. The age of retirement is not provided, and it is common that judges are appointed at 75, when professors and magistrates take compulsory retirement from their previous job. At the moment, the average age is 72.

In the Court's history, only three women have served as a Constitutional Court judges: at the moment, there is only one woman (a law professor).

[19] This balance has been pointed out by Gustavo Zagrebelsky, *La giustizia costituzionale* (Il Mulino 1988), which remains the most complete study on the Italian Constitutional Court.

[20] For some data, see Patrizia Pederzoli, *La Corte costituzionale* (Il Mulino 2008).

[21] At the moment (11 August 2014) the Court has 13 members, as the Parliament has not yet renewed 2 members.

Thus, judges are usually male legal experts in their 70s or 80s, with strong legal knowledge and little or no political background.

The Collegiality Principle and the Exclusion of Separate Opinions

One of the main features of proceedings in the Italian Constitutional Court is collegiality. All decisions are "decisions of the Court" and it is not possible to know the position of individual judges. A decision is usually written by a "rapporteur judge", appointed by the President of the Court in order to study the case and to propose a solution to the Court. Just in a handful of cases throughout the Court's history has the rapporteur asked the President to substitute another judge in writing the decision, as he was dissenting with the final outcome of the challenge. As a consequence, it is extremely difficult, almost impossible, to determine the effective influence of the personality and the legal culture of individual judges (others than the rapporteur) on the decisions.

The exclusion of dissenting (or concurring) opinions (and the related principles of secrecy of deliberation and collegiality) has been linked by scholars to the need to find a balance between politics and the law.[22] According to them, the principle of collegiality is a device protecting the Court from the pressures and interferences of politics, giving to the judges the opportunity to express their opinion freely, without having to justify their individual position outside of the Court. On the other hand, the prohibition on disclosing the individual opinions of the judges has been criticized because it may result in opaque, non-transparent motivation.[23]

Over the years some attempts to introduce dissenting opinions have been made by the Court itself, by its own rules on proceedings, but all have failed due to lack of consensus.

4 *Legal Scholarship and Constitutional Reasoning*

A close connection between the Court and legal scholarship has existed since the beginning of the Court's activity. Over time, the vast majority of the most qualified scholars (especially in the field of constitutional law) has been appointed to the Court; this is indeed the main professional

22 This is the point of view of Gustavo Zagrebelsky, *Principi e voti* (Einaudi 2005) 75 ss.

23 Costantino Mortati (ed), *Le opinioni dei giudici costituzionali e internazionali* (Giuffrè 1964); Adele Anzon (ed), *L'opinione dissenziente* (Giuffrè 1995); Saulle Panizza, *L'introduzione dell'opinione dissenziente nel sistema di giustizia costituzionale* (Giappichelli 1998).

ambition for most scholars, due to the prestige of the office and to the high salary, roughly four times that of a law professor.

Scholars devote special attention to the Court's decisions: one of the most influential Italian journals of constitutional law (*Giurisprudenza costituzionale*) was founded in the same year the Court was established (1956), and it is almost entirely devoted to commentaries on the judgments. Scholarship is not deferential to the Court and openly displays critical remarks. The Court, in turn, takes seriously into account these commentaries, which are collected by the Study Department and by judges' law clerks. We can assume that scholarship strongly contributes to the evolution of jurisprudence, although explicit quotations of authors are not permitted in judgments.[24]

As for constitutional interpretation, the absence, in the text of the Constitution, of any provision regarding its interpretation has generated extensive scholarly debate on the possibility for article 12 of the "Preleggi" ("Preliminary Rules to the Civil Code")[25] to be applied to cases of constitutional interpretation.[26] While the Constitutional Court has never made explicit reference to this article, it appears to have adopted a stance incompatible with the possibility of being bound by it. The Court has consistently avoided developing a hierarchy of interpretative methods, preferring a "case by case" approach:[27] this "swinging" attitude has been criticized by part of the scholarship, which has very often invited the

[24] As we will analyse further *infra* at para. "References to Scholarly Work".

[25] Article 12 states that "When applying the law, cannot be attributed to it other sense than the one made clear by the obvious meaning of the words based on connection between them, and by the intention of the legislature."

[26] The core of the debate – raised since the entry into force of the new Constitution: see Franco Pierandrei, "L'interpretazione della Costituzione", in *Studi in memoria di Luigi Rossi* (Giuffré 1952) 459 – lies on the specificity of constitutional interpretation with regard to statutory interpretation: in favor of this peculiarity see e.g. Giuseppe Ugo Rescigno, "Interpretazione costituzionale e positivismo giuridico" (2005) 1 *Diritto pubblico* 19; against it, see e.g. Riccardo Guastini, "Ancora sull'interpretazione costituzionale" (2005) 2 *Diritto pubblico* 457. On this debate, see Cesare Pinelli, "Il dibattito sull'interpretazione costituzionale tra teoria e giurisprudenza" in *Scritti in memoria di L. Paladin* (Jovene 2004) vol. 3 1671; Tatiana Guarnier, *Interpretazione costituzionale e diritto giurisprudenziale* (ES 2014) 3.

[27] See Franco Modugno, "Sulla specificità dell'interpretazione costituzionale" in id., *Scritti sull'interpretazione costituzionale* (ES 2008) 214; Alessandro Pace, "Interpretazione costituzionale e interpretazione per valori" in Gaetano Azzariti (ed), *Interpretazione costituzionale* (Giappichelli 2007) 109; Carlo Mezzanotte, "Tecniche argomentative e diritti fondamentali" in Sergio Panunzio (ed), *I costituzionalisti e la tutela dei diritti nelle corti europee* (Cedam 2007) 658.

Court to show more consideration for the text of the Constitution[28] and to embrace a more consistent approach to its own precedents.[29]

Despite these critical remarks, we can assume that some widely accepted theories about constitutional interpretation (interpretation in light of constitutional principles, or in light of constitutional values)[30] represent the main criteria inspiring the Court's reasoning and, although never explicitly mentioned in the judgments, they can be easily detected in the case law, especially in the rare decisions in which the Court made clear its doctrine of constitutional interpretation (e.g. Dec. 1/2013):

> The Constitution is grounded on principles, which are tightly interconnected and need to be balanced with each other, so that the task of judicial review must be conducted with regard to the constitutional system as a whole and not to individual provisions, considered alone. A fragmented interpretation of normative provisions – be them constitutional or statutory – runs the risk of leading to paradoxes, that would end up contradicting the provisions' very goals of constitutional protection.

This approach has been extended from the Constitutional Court to the ordinary courts, by the way of the doctrine of "interpretation in conformity with the Constitution", according to which, before referring a statute to the Constitutional Court, ordinary courts must try to give to it a constitutionally consistent interpretation, if necessary going beyond the text (otherwise the constitutional question is dismissed by the Court on procedural grounds).[31] As a result of these factors – and more generally as a consequence of an evolution in the legal culture, especially in the judiciary – there is nowadays a continuum, as far as constitutional interpretation is concerned, between the Constitutional Court and ordinary courts. The presence in the Constitutional Court of five judges of higher

[28] In this respect, see especially Alessandro Pace, "Metodi interpretativi e costituzionalismo" (2001) 1 *Quaderni costituzionali* 60; Gaetano Azzariti, "Interpretazione e teoria dei valori: tornare alla Costituzione" in Antonio Palazzo (ed), *L'interpretazione della legge alle soglie del XXI secolo* (ESI 2001) 240; Massimo Luciani, "Interpretazione costituzionale e testo della costituzione", in Azzariti (n 27) 49.

[29] Livio Paladin, *Le fonti del diritto* (Il Mulino 1996) 150.

[30] To quote just some of the more distinguished representatives of this approach (with nuances), see Antonio Baldassarre, "Costituzione e teoria dei valori" (1991) 4 *Politica del diritto* 654; Franco Modugno, "Interpretazione per valori e interpretazione costituzionale" in id. (n 27) 27 ss.; Gustavo Zagrebelsky n 8; Id., *La legge e la sua giustizia* (Il Mulino 2008).

[31] See Giusy Sorrenti, *L'interpretazione conforme a Costituzione* (Giuffrè 2006); Marilisa D'Amico and Barbara Randazzo (eds), *Interpretazione conforme e tecniche argomentative* (Giappichelli 2009).

courts and the fact that the large majority of the law clerks are ordinary judges (even from the Court of Cassation), often acting as part-time clerks while exercising judiciary functions, has further strengthened this tendency.

B Arguments in Constitutional Reasoning

The 40 Leading Cases: an Overview

In the analysis of the 40 decisions selected, the aforementioned different competences of the Court should be considered. Actually, the style of the motivations is not exactly the same: differences exist especially between the constitutional review of legislation and other competences, such as in conflicts or referendum cases, mainly due to the different institutional actors involved. Among the 40 decisions analyzed, 34 have been adopted in the constitutional review of legislation (28 in concrete review, 6 in abstract control), 4 in the resolution of conflicts between organs of the state, 1 in the resolution of conflicts between state and regions and 1 in the judgment on the admissibility of the abrogative referendum. As for the time, the distribution since 1956 shows that in the first decade (1956–65) we find only 3 judgments; in the second decade (1966–75) 5; in the third (1976–85) 5; in the fourth (1986–95) 5; in the fifth (1996–2005) 12; in the sixth (not exactly a decade yet), since 2006, 11. The reason for this is probably twofold: on one hand, the low number of decisions adopted during the first years; on the other, the tendency to avoid quoting and in favor of overruling older precedents issued by the Court itself, due to the perceived evolution of society as a whole (as far as fundamental rights are concerned) or to the change of the text of the Constitution (mainly with regard to regionalism issues).

In most decisions (27 of 39) the Court found the law (or the act, in conflicts cases), to be in violation of the Constitution, and consequently annulled the challenged provision(s). In the remaining decision (Dec. 16/1978), on the admissibility of abrogative referendum, the referendum was not admitted.

In the absence of separate opinions, the analysis has been limited to the Court's only opinion and, more specifically, to the "Conclusions on the point of law". We should point out that the "sentenze" are divided into two parts: the first part, "The facts of the case", is dedicated to summarizing the content of the petition and the arguments proposed by the parties in their written briefs; the second part, "Conclusions on the point of law" begins with some paragraphs dedicated to summarizing the petitions, in order to clarify the "thema decidendum". The following paragraphs contain the Court's reasons: our study has been focused on them.

5 *The Structure of Constitutional Arguments*

There is no dominant structure in constitutional reasoning. The chain structure (one-line conclusive argument) was prevalent in the first decades, and it remains present in more recent judgments (17 of 40), but the leg structure (parallel conclusive argument) (11 judgments) and the dialogic structure (parallel, individually inconclusive, but together conclusive argument) (12 judgments) are also present. Several reasons for this structure – and especially for the low level of chain (one-line conclusive arguments) judgments – can be detected.

First of all, the collegiality principle: the lack of separate opinions pushes the Court to take more inclusive and shared decisions. It is a well-known fact, also on the basis of the testimony of some judges,[32] that the usual technique of decision is to look for the broader consensus inside the Court, and that sometimes the decision is postponed until unanimity is reached. This approach obligates the author of the judgment to take into consideration all the opinions expressed in chambers by each judge, including those dissenting or concurring. One could guess that judgments with chain structured (one-line conclusive) arguments are unanimous.

Second, the structure of arguments seems likely to be influenced by the presence or the absence of parties: when the Court deals with many different arguments submitted by them, it usually prefers a dialogic structure (parallel, individually inconclusive, but together conclusive argument) or a leg-of-chair structure (parallel conclusive argument).

Finally, the individual personality of the judge authoring the decision is likely to influence the structure of arguments,[33] because there are judges (often with an academic background) more inclined to write longer and articulated motivations.

6 *Types of Arguments in Constitutional Reasoning*

Establishing the Text of the Constitution

We found eight judgments in which it is discussed what counts not exactly as constitutional text, but as "standard of review": that is, the provisions

[32] See Zagrebelsky n 8. [33] Pederzoli, n 20.

of the Constitution, constitutional laws or other sources referred to by them or on which they are based, which are claimed to have been violated.

Actually, the Italian Constitutional Court uses in its judgments not only the Constitution and the constitutional laws, enacted according to the special procedure provided for constitutional amendments (art.138), but also some other legal acts that do not enjoy constitutional status. These provisions are called (both by scholars and by the Court) "interposed rules": these rules supplement a constitutional principle, whilst always retaining a lower status, and it is necessary that they comply with the Constitution.

In Dec. 9/1959 the Court excludes that parliamentary rules could be used as principles in the constitutional control over legislative procedure, since they are enacted by each Chamber in its autonomy and the control over their compliance is in the hands of the President of each Chamber, and not of the Court.

In Dec. 7/1996, in which the constitutionality of the motion of no confidence to a single Minister was challenged, the Court uses as harmonizing argument also "the sources supplementing the Constitutional text, . . . especially parliamentary rules and common practice". These elements "supplement the written constitutional norms and define the role of constitutional bodies pursuant to unwritten principles and rules developed and established over time through the constant reiteration of consistent conducts (or, in any case, inspired by common criteria, applied to identical or similar cases): that is, in the form of fully developed constitutional conventions".

In Dec. 172/1999 the Court considers generally-recognized principles of international law as standards of review, according to art. 10.1 Const.

In Dec. 348/2007 the Court affirms that the international treaties supplement and make operative the principle contained in art. 117.1 Const., even if these do not acquire the force of constitutional law. This statement has been reaffirmed in Dec. 80/2011, in which the Court explicitly labelled the treaties as "interposed rules". The ECHR was applied also, as interposed legislation, in Dec. 138/2010, although to conclude that "the reference to national laws contained in art. 12 [of the ECHR], confirms the fact that the matter falls within the discretion of Parliament".

In Dec. 80/2010 the Court struck down a statute as in contrast with constitutional and international provisions, referring the latter to the UN Convention on the Rights of Persons with Disabilities.

In Dec. 102/2008 the Court reaffirmed its well-established jurisprudence according to which, in the abstract control, European Union law plays the role of "interposed rule", independently of whether or not it has a direct effect.

Applicability of the Constitution

The question about the applicability of the Constitution came up in 12 judgments, especially in the first years of activity of the Court, when the extension of its jurisdiction was at stake.

This is the case of probably the most famous decision of the Italian Constitutional Court: its first judgment, Dec. 1/1956, when the binding nature of constitutional provisions was discussed. Indeed, before the establishment of the Court, in the ordinary courts, especially the higher ones, an idea of the Constitution had prevailed according to which not all constitutional provisions would be immediately binding, but as containing mere "principles" and not full-fledged "rules" – some of them needed to be implemented by the legislator before they could be applied. Thus, the violation of one of those principles by a statute would not have determined the unconstitutionality of the latter, as the principles would have been only "programs", "guidelines" to be politically developed. Against this view, the Court affirmed the binding nature of all constitutional norms, specifying their binding character in relation not only to the government, but also to private parties, and reaffirmed its power to review any laws in contrast with the Constitution.

Another important issue concerns the possibility of the Court controlling compliance with the constitutional rules on legislative procedure: in Dec. 9/1959 (where it discussed the possibility of controlling the difference between the texts of a statute approved by the two Chambers) the Court affirmed its jurisdiction, although limited to the constitutional provisions, which are very short and synthetic on the matter, excluding the possibility of controlling compliance with parliamentary rules.

In Dec. 1146/1988 the Court affirmed the applicability of the Constitution in the review of constitutional laws, moving from the statement that

> The Italian Constitution expresses some principles that cannot be overthrown or modified in their core content, not even by constitutional amendments or other constitutional laws. These are not only the principles that the Constitution itself identifies as absolute limits to the amending power, such the Republican form of government (art. 139 Const.), but also those principles that, while not expressly included among those qualified as unamendable, are connected to the core of the highest values that lie at the very foundation of the Italian Constitution.

A more specific issue is dealt with in Dec. 102/2008, concerning the applicability of some articles of the Constitution to the special autonomous regions: these are regions that benefit from a more extensive autonomy, according to art. 116 of the Constitution. For those regions Constitutional Law no. 3/2001 provides that they would continue to benefit from the level of autonomy established by their special statutes, unless the new constitutional rules would be more favorable. In this case, the Court established that the new art. 119 of the Constitution, concerning the financial autonomy of regions, was less favorable than the rules contained in the special Statute of the Region Sardinia, and thus it could not be applied to this region.

The remaining judgments deal with two main issues: (a) the question of the primacy of EU law and (b) the question of legislative discretion.

(a) As for the primacy of the EU law, it is touched upon by Dec. 170/1984, 348/2007, 80/2011.

Since Dec. 170/1984, the Court, by overruling its precedents issued in the 1970s, considers that Community provisions "must have full binding effectiveness and direct application in all the Member States, without any requirement for the implementation or amendment of national laws, as instruments having the force and value of law in every state of the Community, in order to enter simultaneously into force everywhere and to achieve equal and uniform application in relation to all addressees". Thus, a question of constitutionality raised on the basis of the violation of a European provision cannot be judged by the Court, at least when the European rule produces direct effects, since it is up to the ordinary courts to solve the legal antinomy, by way of diffuse control. The abstract control is different, and the Court reaffirms its jurisdiction in any case in which a question of compatibility between a statute and EU law is raised in abstract control (Dec. 102/2008). This issue is considered also in Dec. 348/2007, when, conversely, the Court reaffirmed the applicability of the Constitution and its own jurisdiction in the case of violation of the ECHR, and in Dec. 80/2011, in which this approach is confirmed, despite the entry into force of the Lisbon Treaty, at least for matters that, as in that case, fall outside the EU competence.

(b) As for legislative discretion, this issue has been raised since Dec. 53/1958, in the context of a judgment based on equality principle, to circumscribe it as a control on the coherence of the legislation. In Dec. 15/1982 the issue was the constitutionality of the duration of preventive detention in the fight against terrorism. The Court expressly avoided considering whether preventive detention was in itself the best instrument to eradicate terrorism, as this evaluation is "prohibited for the judiciary, even for the Constitutional Court".

In Dec. 80/2010, conversely, the Court recognized that the discretion of the Legislature (in that case in the identification of measures to guarantee the rights of people with disabilities) is not absolute, as it finds a limitation in the respect of "an inviolable core of guarantees enjoyed by the people concerned".

In Dec. 138/2010 the Court dismissed the case of same-sex marriage: the issue was the lack of legal recognition for same-sex marriages within the Italian legal order. The Court, after assessing that the Constitution grants same-sex couples some form of legal recognition, adds that there are several possible solutions to this legislative vacuum, as displayed by a comparative overview. It, therefore, follows that it is for the Parliament (and not for the Court) to determine – exercising its full discretion – the forms of guarantee and recognition for same-sex unions.

Analogies

We did not find any case of analogy as the only instrument to fill a gap in the Constitution, although we did find four judgments in which some kind of analogical reasoning is developed, together with other arguments.

In two decisions it seems to be addressed to develop some kind of "non-written principles," by harmonizing some articles of the Constitution not directly affecting the issue.

In Dec. 15/1969 the Court declared unconstitutional a statute that provided the need for an authorization from the Minister of Justice to prosecute the crime of contempt of Constitutional Court, as in contrast with the independence of the Court, and stated that such authorization had to be given by the Court itself. In the absence of specific constitutional provisions on the topic, the Court made reference to many provisions on the immunity of the Court, considering their analogy with those on the immunity of the Parliament, from which is equally absent any provision for contempt, although it is universally accepted that the prosecution must be authorized by the Parliament.

In Dec. 496/2000 the Court declared unconstitutional a regional law that submitted to regional consultative referendum a proposal of revision of the Constitution to be presented to the Parliament by a regional Assembly. The Court examined the constitutional role of the abrogative referendum (art. 75), to conclude that as it cannot affect constitutional rules, the same can be said for a regional consultative referendum.

In the remaining two decisions, the Court rejects the analogical reasoning suggested by the parties.

In Dec. 106/2002 the Region Liguria tried to justify the recourse to the name "Parliament" for its regional Assembly (challenged by the state) on the ground of the analogy existing in the Constitution among the competences of the regional assemblies and the national Parliament. The Court indicated that the analogical argument cannot be applied, as the Constitution has explicitly mentioned the organs of the region.

Finally, in Dec. 1/2013, dealing with the wiretapping of the President of the Republic's telephone conversations, the Court excluded this possibility as the silence[34] of the Constitution on this issue cannot be considered a "lacuna" (gap) and cannot be filled by referring analogically to the provisions on the wiretapping of the Members of the Parliament.

Ordinary Meaning of Words of the Constitution or References to the "Wording of the Constitution" in General

References to the wording of the Constitution were found in 18 judgments, although the Court almost never relies on a pure textualist approach, which is explicitly excluded in the few decisions in which the Court tries to summarize its doctrine of constitutional interpretation.

We found only Dec. 422/1995, in which the Court decides the case mainly on the basis of textual interpretation: the law introducing "quotas" for women in the electoral law was struck down, since according to the wording of the Constitution (arts. 3 and 51), the equality principle mandates the irrelevance of gender in elections.

In most cases, the Court analyses, carefully or generally, the text of constitutional provisions, to either accept or reject an argument included in the petition, as a first step in the interpretation, before moving to a different argument.

For example, in Dec. 1/1956, the Court indicated that the distinction between freedom of expression and freedom of dissemination is not established in any provision of the Constitution; in Dec. 15/1969 that art. 137 textually affirms the independence of the Constitutional Court; in Dec. 164/1985 the Court distinguishes the first and the second clause of art. 52, in order to show that the defense of the country, and not military service, is a fundamental duty for every citizen. In Dec. 106/2002, on the use of the

[34] See *infra* at para. "Arguments from Silence".

word "Parliament" to indicate a regional Assembly, the Court begins with a textual approach (underlining that the Constitution names "*Consigli*" the regional Assemblies), but it adds that "the textual argument, although not completely irrelevant, cannot be considered crucial if it is not assessed in light of other arguments of constitutional interpretation" (in that case, historic-systematic ones).

Only a few decisions deal explicitly with the meaning of the words, and in most of them it is not discussed, but taken for granted: e.g. Dec. 15/1982 considers the meaning that the word "provided", used in art. 13 of the Constitution concerning the limitation to personal liberty, assumes in the legal language. Dec. 7/1996 refers to the fact that in the *travaux préparatoires* (preparatory works) the Constituent Assembly changed the word "personal" into "individual", referring to the responsibility of Ministers, "a change to which we cannot give only a lexical relevance, overlooking its purpose." Dec. 102/2008 refers to the meaning of the word "territory" in the Statute of Region Sardinia, considering that it includes also territorial waters. Dec. 138/2010 refers to the "social groups" recognized and guaranteed by art. 2 of the Constitution.

Harmonizing Arguments

(A) Domestic Harmonizing Arguments We found domestic harmonizing arguments in 23 judgments: this is one of the preferred arguments for the Italian Constitutional Court, that includes: (a) the logical-systematic interpretation, understood as the interpretation of one constitutional provision in the context of the entire constitutional law; (b) the interpretation in light of fundamental principles; (c) the interpretation of one constitutional provision together with another (combinato disposto, i.e. combined provisions); (d) the balancing among different constitutional principles; and (e) the interpretation of the constitution in light of ordinary legislation.

(a) The logical-systematic argument seems to be the argument preferred by the Italian Constitutional Court, which has very often explicitly stated its preference since Dec. 16/1978, in which the Court affirmed that "textual interpretation must be integrated, when necessary, by the logic-systematic interpretation". In that judgment the Court interpreted art. 75, which lists the statutes excluded from the abrogative referendum, in light of the entire Constitution, arguing that art. 75 should not be interpreted by itself.

In Dec. 7/1996 the Court argues that "in the interpretation of the Constitution, logic-systematic argument must be preferred", subsequently engaging itself in the interpretation of several articles of the Constitution to verify if the individual motion of no confidence can be considered an implicit element of the constitutional design.

(b) The interpretation in light of fundamental principles is quite common, especially by reference to art. 2, according to which "The Republic recognizes and guarantees the inviolable rights of the person". For example, in Dec. 27/1975, on abortion, the Court interprets art. 31 on the Constitution, on the protection of maternity in light of art. 2, to identify the guarantee of the fetus' rights; in Dec. 161/1985, on transsexualism, the Court interpreted the right to health in light of art. 2, to redefine the right to sexual identity. According to Dec. 223/1996, the prohibition of the death penalty is absolute, as a consequence of interpretation of art. 27 (that prohibits the death penalty) together with art. 2. In Dec. 172/1999 the Court refers to art. 2 – in order to interpret art. 52, on the duty of the defense of the country, as including the stateless – and to art. 11, according to which "Italy rejects war", to argue that the idea of the army has deeply changed and evolved over time.

(c) We found the interpretation of one constitutional provision together with another in Dec. 15/1969, declaring the unconstitutionality of the authorization of the Minister of Justice to prosecute the crime of contempt of Constitutional Court, in the absence of a specific constitutional provision on this topic.

(d) The balancing among different principles is a quite common interpretative strategy as far as fundamental rights are concerned: e.g. we found it in Dec. 27/1975 on abortion, where the Court balanced the "constitutionally-protected situation of the fetus" with the right to health of the mother, concluding that the absolute criminalization of abortion infringes this balance. According to Dec. 348/2007, the constitutional review of "interposed rules" "must always aim to establish a reasonable balance between the duties flowing from international law obligations, as imposed by art. 117(1) of the Constitution, and the safeguarding of the constitutionally protected interests contained in other articles of the Constitution." Dec. 138/2010, on same-sex marriage, argues that art. 3 on equality is not violated by the Civil Code that makes provision exclusively for marriage between a man and a woman, as this provision is grounded on the definition of marriage contained in art. 29 of the Constitution.

(e) The interpretation of the Constitution in light of ordinary legislation is conceptually mistaken, and we have not found it in the judgments, unless we consider in this category also the "legislative anachronism". In Dec. 508/2000 the Court carefully examined the evolution of the relationships between the state and the religious confessions, also making reference to legislation, to underline that the criminalization of the contempt of Catholic religion (as "religion of the State") is anachronistic. In two judgments we found this argument as additional: Dec. 80/2010 argues that the limitation of the education rights of students with disabilities is inconsistent not only with constitutional and international provisions, but also with the general legislative rules on the rights of people with disabilities. Dec. 223/2012 identifies the guarantee of the economic independence of the judiciary by the logic-systematic interpretation, making reference not only to constitutional provisions, but also to legislative general provisions on judges' salaries.

(B) International Harmonization Arguments The use of international law in order to interpret the Constitution is not explicitly accepted by the Court, which – as we examined above – since 2007, has considered international treaties as "interposed rules" when the petition claims that these have been violated (Dec. 348/2007, 80/2010, 138/2010, 80/2011; Dec. 170/1984 and 102/2008 deal only with EU law).

Despite this view, we found more or less vague references to international law with some kind of interpretative purpose in 5 other decisions (in total, 11 decisions). In Dec. 161/1985 the Court refers to a decision of the European Commission of Human Rights on transsexualism, to present the legislative evolution on this topic at the international level. A similar approach can be found also in Dec. 164/1985, quoting a resolution of the European Parliament on the right to refuse to serve in the armed military service, to point out the impossibility of striking down the entire law on conscientious objection. In Dec. 422/1995 the Court refers to a resolution of the European Parliament and two international conventions of the UN to illustrate that gender quotas in elections must be implemented by political parties in their internal rules and not by electoral law.

A more direct use of international law to interpret the Constitution can be found in Dec. 172/1999, which, to interpret the reference to "citizens" contained in art. 52.1 Const. in order to fulfil the duty of military service as falling also on stateless people, makes reference to international law (in specific, to a convention of the UN); and in Dec. 200/2012, which interprets the matter "competition protection" (art. 117. 2 lett. e)), as including also the competition "in markets" and "for markets", and makes reference to "the already well-established developments in European and international legal order".

Precedents

This is the most widely used method, used in 31 judgments.

Only a few decisions do not refer to precedents. Among them, the first judgment of the Court, Dec. 1/1956 and 8 more recent judgments concerning "new" issues (Dec. 27/1975, on abortion; Dec. 161/n.1985 on transsexualism; Dec. 13/1994, on the right to personal identity as right to name; Dec. 422/1995 on gender quotas in elections; Dec. 7/1996 on the motion of no confidence to a single Minister; Dec. 356/1996, that for the first time established the principle of "interpretation consistent to the Constitution" (constitutionally-oriented interpretation); Dec. 106/2002, on the use of the name "Parliament" to name regional assemblies; Dec. 138/2010, on same-sex marriage). In one of those judgments (Dec. 161/1985), we found a generic reference to the "permanent case-law" (on "atti dispotivi del proprio corpo", i.e. "individual rights over one's own body"), without making it clear if it is case law of the Constitutional Court or of the ordinary courts.

Mostly, precedents were mentioned as individual cases, but sometimes they are referred as "permanent and coherent case law of the Court", followed by a long list of references (Dec. 15/1982, on preventive detention; Dec. 289/1998, on parliamentary immunities; Dec. 348/2007 on the international treaties; Dec. 10/2010, on regional competences on social rights; Dec. 200/2012, on state competence on competition and market; Dec. 223/2012 on judges' salaries).

Precedents are not binding in the Italian legal system: this explains why we did not find any judgment that properly operates distinguishing from earlier cases. Rather, they are considered as having persuasive authority.[35] In most of the judgments, the Court refers to precedents established in similar cases in order to follow them (here the problem arises of whether the cases were really "similar", as it happened with Dec. 1146/1988, where

[35] Alessandro Pizzorusso, "Effetto di 'giudicato' ed effetto di 'precedente' delle sentenze della Corte costituzionale" (1966) *Giurisprudenza costituzionale* 1976; Adele Anzon, *Il valore del precedente nel giudizio sulle leggi* (Giuffé 1995).

the Court quoted several precedents on the special status of fundamental principles that did not refer to the control on constitutional laws, but on the State-Catholic Church Pacts, which do not enjoy constitutional status). Instead, in six judgments the Court overruled its precedents. In the first decades of its activity, overruling was justified for reasons of social changes that had taken place in the meantime: in Dec. 126/1968 the Court struck down the provision on the criminalization of female adultery, arguing on the intensity of social changes; in the Dec. 49/1971 on criminalization of dissemination of birth control practices, the Court added to the social changes also the fact that a previous interpretative decision was passed per incuriam.

Dec. 440/1995 declared the unconstitutionality of the crime of blasphemy due to legislative inactivity, following a previous 1973 reject judgment, in which the Court had warned the legislature to change the law.

In Dec. 348/2007, which establishes the status of "interposed rules" for international treaties, previously considered as having the same status of statutory law, the Court explains the change referring to the width of the constitutional revision of art. 117.1 of the Constitution that took place in 2001.

No adequate reasons for the overruling can be found in Dec. 16/1978, which identified in art. 75 new limits for the abrogative referendum that were not mentioned in previous decisions on the topic. In this case, the Court first tries to hide the overruling, as it explicitly affirms that the previous decisions were confirmed; later in the judgment, however, the Court strongly criticizes its own precedent.

Moreover, the important change in respect to EU law – and the acceptance of the *Simmenthal* doctrine of the ECJ, contained in Dec. 170/1984 – is not reasonably motivated: the Court only refers to the fact that "such conclusion, and arguments in favor of it, must be revised" and engages itself in a complex work of re-reading its precedents, also in light of the ECJ case law (that is generically quoted) and of the tendency existing in "all Member States (without exception)".

Doctrinal Analysis of Legal Concepts and Principles

We found this argument in 23 judgments. We consider in this category not only (a) the cases in which the Court avoids giving any explanation, limiting itself to a stipulation without any explanation, through an axiomatic reasoning, but also (b) the application of concepts and principles not present in the black letter of the Constitution but developed by the Court and by legal scholars.[36] Among those principles, we found: (b.1) the duty of "reasonableness of the legislature" and (b.2) the principle of interpreting all statutes in conformity with the Constitution, besides (b.3) other non-written principles.

(a) Since Dec. 1/1956 the Court has displayed its preference for axiomatic reasoning: in this judgment, discussing the limitation on freedom of expression in the absence of any textual reference in art. 21, it stated that "the concept of limitation is inscribed in the very concept of right". "Fundamental principles of our constitutional order" are always assumed, e.g. in Dec. 170/1984, or in Dec. 1146/1988, on the limits to constitutional revision, where the Court argued that "the Italian Constitution contains some fundamental principles that cannot be subverted or changed in their core content not even by laws of constitutional revision". We can give other examples. Dec. 13/1994: "it is certainly true that, among the rights that constitute the inviolable patrimony of the human person, art. 2 recognizes and guarantees also the right to personal identity", without any other argument to support this statement. Dec. 7/1996: "according to undisputed and common opinion, the confidence of the Parliament is the necessary prerequisite for the government to remain in office". Dec. 138/2010: "social groups must be deemed to include all forms of simple or complex communities that are capable of permitting and favoring the free development of the person through relationships." Dec. 496/2000: "the principle of participation of local communities in the decisions that concern themselves is a general principle intrinsic to the pluralistic democracy". Dec. 348/2007: "The requirement that the provisions which supplement the constitutional principle themselves respect the Constitution is absolute and inviolable in order to avoid falling into the paradox of a legislative provision being declared unconstitutional on the basis of another interposed provision, which in turn breaches the Constitution".

(b.1) The "reasonableness principle" has been developed by the Court by means of an evolving interpretation of the equality principle.

[36] See Antonino Spadaro, "Dalla Costituzione come 'atto' (puntuale nel tempo) alla Costituzione come 'processo' (storico). Ovvero della continua evoluzione del parametro costituzionale attraverso i giudizi di costituzionalità" (1998) *Quaderni costituzionali* 343; Giovanna Razzano, *Il parametro delle norme non scritte nella giurisprudenza costituzionale* (Giuffrè 2002).

From article 3 of the Constitution, according to which all citizens are equal before the law, a duty of reasonableness can be derived for the Legislature, so that it not only must regulate different situations differently, but also must avoid using arbitrary criteria. In order for a norm not to be unconstitutional, one must avoid contradictions between the goals of a law and the concrete normative rules, between the objective pursued and the legal tools used to achieve it. In sum, one must avoid irrational contradictions between the goals of the law and the content of its text (Dec. 15/1982; Dec. 361/1998; Dec. 172/1999; Dec. 102/2008; Dec. 80/2010; Dec. 200/2012).

(b.2) The principle of interpreting all statutes in conformity with the Constitution is for the first time expressly stated in Dec. 356/1996, according to which "statutes are not declared unconstitutional because it is possible to give them unconstitutional meanings (as some judges do), but because it is impossible to give them a constitutionally-consistent interpretation". We found this principle in several judgments (Dec. 23/2011; Dec. 200/2012; Dec. 1/2013).

(b.3) We found other non-written principles, such as "the rule of law" (Dec. 15/1969; Dec. 364/1988); "the fundamental principles of democratic coexistence" (Dec. 364/1988); "legal certainty" (Dec. 360/1996); the "constitutional principle of loyalty" in state-regions relationships (Dec. 303/2003) and in the relationships between powers of the state (Dec. 23/2011); and "trial publicity" (Dec. 80/2011).

Arguments from Silence

The Court makes reference to arguments from silence in seven decisions, always to consider that the lack of an explicit constitutional rule does not necessarily translate into the impossibility of finding, by way of constitutional interpretation, especially the logic-systematic one, a constitutional principle or rule applicable to the case.

In Dec. 1146/1988 the Court considers that the silence of the Constitution on the issue of review of constitutional laws cannot be interpreted as an exclusion of that control: the consequence would be a gap in the system of constitutional guarantees, concerning the more important legal norms.

In Dec. 7/1996 the Court considers that the silence of the Constitution on the individual motion of no confidence does not mean that this instrument falls outside the constitutional framework: the silence of the Constituent Assembly on the topic must be interpreted as the desire to leave open several possibilities for the implementation of the parliamentary form of government.

In Dec. 172/1999, on the possibility to extend the duty of military service to non-citizens, the Court considers that the fact that the constitutional provision at issue (art. 52) only refers to citizens does not exclude that the Parliament could extend the duty to non-citizens, under certain conditions. "The silence of the constitutional provision does not mean prohibition: one should interpret [the silence] as a gap of constitutional law, in which the Legislator can use its discretional power".

In Dec. 496/2000 the Court considers that regional Assemblies can submit constitutional revision proposals to the Parliament (art. 121 explicitly refers only to "bill to the Parliament"), as the Constitution is silent on the force of the act the proposal is directed to. Thus, also in this case, the silence of the text should not be interpreted as exclusion.

In Dec. 303/2003, the Court considers that the absence of "city planning" – that was explicitly listed in the text of the Constitution before the constitutional revision of 2001 – from the list of matters reserved for the state or of concurring legislation (according to art. 117, 2 and 3) does not mean that it was no longer included in the list, as a logic-systematic interpretation of the list displays that it should be considered as included in the "territory management" section.

In Dec. 223/2012 the Court excludes that the silence of the Constitution on the economic independence of the judiciary could be understood as the exclusion of this aspect from the conditions necessary to secure judicial independence.

Finally, in Dec. 1/2013, on the wiretapping of the President of the Republic's telephone conversations, the Court considers that the silence of the Constitution on the guarantee of the President's privacy of communications cannot be interpreted as an exclusion of such guarantee. Afterwards, the Court moves to the logic-systematic interpretation, dealing with constitutional rules on the position and role of the President in the Italian constitutional system.

Teleological/Purposive Arguments Referring to the Purpose of the Text

Objective teleological arguments are quite common (13 judgments), although less common than other arguments. Conversely, the teleological interpretation is without doubt the main argument referred to by the Court in interpreting ordinary legislation submitted to constitutional review.

In some cases, the argument consists of the "ratio" (rationale) of the constitutional provision as a result of the reformulation of the purpose of constitution-makers (subjective teleological arguments); therefore it is not easy to distinguish between the two categories.[37]

For example, Dec. 16/1978: "Indeed, it is consistent with the natural scope of the abrogative referendum (according to some important indications found in the proceedings of the Constituent Assembly), the need that the question to be submitted to the electors is simple and clear". Or Dec. 7/1996: "The express indication in the text of the Constitution of the functions of the Ministry of Justice, especially with regard to art. 110 and the organizational powers thereby presented, was mainly introduced in order to clearly identify – at a time when the *Consiglio Superiore della Magistratura* was also established – the powers of the Ministry of Justice."

Sometimes, the argument is used in its pure formulation, referring to the objective rationale of the constitutional provision: e.g. in the already quoted Dec. 16/1978, the Court established that, by excluding the law ratifying an international treaty from the possibility of subjection to abrogative referendum, the Constitution "aimed to avoid that, once the Treaty had become effective [in the Italian legal system], it would be deprived of its essential constitutional basis (pursuant to art. 80 Const.), thereby determining its disapplication and making the Italian Republic internationally responsible before the other Contracting Parties". This way, the Court decided that, beyond the wording of the Constitution, not only the "law ratifying", but also the "law executing" international treaties cannot be submitted to abrogative referendum. In Dec. 15/1982 the Court, interpreting the provision according to which "No punishment may be inflicted except by virtue of a law in force at the time the offence was committed" (prohibition against ex post facto laws), affirmed that "art. 25, clause 2, of the Constitution establishes a guarantee for the accused; it is also easy to understand that the true rationale of the provision is connected to a need of legal certainty".

37 See also Dec. 200/2006, not included in our selection, on a conflict between the President of the Republic (applicant) and the Minister of Justice (respondent) concerning the granting of a pardon to a convicted criminal. In that decision, the Court first focused on the purpose of the pardon, establishing – by referring to many historical arguments – that it has the scope "of mitigating or annulling a punishment on exceptional humanitarian grounds", then stated that "it is clear – in accordance with Article 87(11) of the Constitution – that the Head of State must be recognized as having the right to exercise this power, as a *super partes* institution", without any interference of the Minister of Justice.

This argument often appears in judgments related to articles of the Constitution that explicitly establish a purpose, such as art. 3 (prohibition against privileges and discriminations: Dec. 126/1968; removal of obstacles impeding women to reach certain results in terms of political participation: Dec. 422/1995) or art. 29 (unity of family: Dec.126/1968).

Most of the time a very general purpose appears, especially in judgments concerning state organizations, such as "the natural scope of the abrogative referendum": Dec. 16/1978; "the logic of the parliamentary form of government": Dec. 7/1996; "the parliamentary function, as activity free in its purpose and of general nature": Dec. 289/1998; "the unity and indivisibility of the Republic", which implies instruments to guarantee the unity and to make the division of competences between state and regions flexible: Dec. 303/2003; "the basic fundamental configuration of regionalism": Dec. 365/2007; "the constitutional role of the judiciary": Dec. 223/2012; and "the position and role of the President of the Republic in the Italian constitutional system": Dec. 1/2013.

Probably, we can include in this category the judgment that – declaring the unconstitutionality of the absolute irrelevance of "ignorantia legis" ("ignorance of the law") in order to discharge from a crime – refers to the "violation of the entire fundamental Charter and its fundamental principles", explicitly mentioning the democratic principle and the central position of the human person in the hierarchy of constitutional values (Dec. 364/1988).

Teleological/Purposive Arguments Referring to the Purpose of the Constitution-Makers

Subjective teleological arguments appear in 10 judgments, although in most cases these consist in extremely general references (such as "according to the proceedings of the Constituent Assembly . . . ": Dec. 16/1978, 15/1982, 106/2002), or in a short statement ("the Constituent Assembly, as it is well-known, after long and lively debates, was firm in excluding institutional arrangements that could be also generally, configured, as federal or even confederal": Dec. 365/1997), and only rarely does the Court examine directly and carefully the proceedings of the Constituent Assembly. In one case (Dec. 7/1996) the proceedings of the "Commissione Forti", a Commission established during the transitory period before the election of the Constituent Assembly, were also examined.

We did not find any case in which the proceedings concerning the procedure for constitutional revision were examined.

The arguments appear more frequently in more recent judgments (we could not find any reference before 1978): the reason could be that during the first two decades of the activity of the Court the style of reasoning was extremely brief and concise.[38]

In Dec. 422/1995 the text of art. 51 of the Constitution was compared to the draft project of the Constitution, to underline the inclusion, by amendment, of the explicit reference to gender equality in elections, stressing this way the "absolute equality" that justifies the unconstitutionality of gender quotas in electoral lists.

The project of the constitution and the subsequent amendments were examined also in Dec. 7/1996, on ministerial responsibility, to show that many references to the individual responsibility and individual no-confidence motion were present in the debate, although any reference was left out of the final text.

In Dec. 223/1996 the report of the Committee of 75 (an internal committee with the task to write the first draft of the project) to the Constituent Assembly is quoted, stating that "the prohibition of death penalty is a principle that can be qualified as 'Italian'".

In Dec. 223/2012 the proceedings of the Constituent Assembly are thoroughly quoted, by making reference to several sessions, sorted by date and time, in order to show that the silence of the Constitution on the economic independence of the judiciary should not be interpreted as if this principle were not included in the broad notion of judicial independence guaranteed by the Constitution.

Among the more detailed references, we found Dec. 364/1988, where for three pages the origin of art. 27.1 ("Criminal responsibility is personal") was investigated, by examining carefully the debates in the Constituent Assembly, the amendments proposed and rejected, and also the scholarship of the time, in order to detect the purpose of the provision, which was identified in the exclusion of the criminal responsibility in the absence of subjective element.

Anyway, the argument seems to be decisive only in Dec. 138/2010, according to which the "original" meaning of the word "marriage", referred to as the union of a man and a woman, deduced from the *travaux*

[38] Different findings – displaying a decline in the last decades – are presented by Luciana Pesole ("L'intenzione del legislatore costituente nell'interpretazione del parametro costituzionale", 133, 177) and Chiara Tripodina, ("L'argomento originalista in materia di diritti fondamentali", 229, 262), both in Felice Giuffrè and Ida Nicotra (eds), *Lavori preparatori e original intent nella giurisprudenza costituzionale* (Giappichelli 2008).

préparatoires (preparatory works), "cannot be set aside through interpretation, because to do so would not involve a simple re-reading of the system or the abandonment of a mere interpretative practice, but rather the implementation of a creative interpretation".[39]

Non-legal (Moral, Sociological, Economic) Arguments

Non-legal arguments are mentioned in 12 judgments. Usually each judgment contains only one type of non-legal argument, formulated in a very generic way, without any reference to the source of information of the Court and without use of the fact-finding provisions contained in the rules on Constitutional Court proceedings.

We found the following non-legal arguments:

(a) Terroristic emergency: Around the end of the 1970s, Italy faced a quite complicated situation with terroristic emergencies of both neo-fascist and communist origin. This was the framework in which the Court, with Dec. 15/1982, ruled that

> We have to admit that a state, in which terrorism sows death – also by the ruthless murder of innocent 'hostages' – and destruction, leading to uncertainty and, therefore, the need to entrust the safety of life and property in armed escorts and private police, is in a state of emergency; however, it must agree that the emergence, is a serious condition and certainly abnormal, but also essentially temporary. It follows that it legitimizes, yes, unusual measures, but that they lose legitimacy if unduly protracted.

(b) Historical considerations: with reference to gender equality in elections, the Court took into consideration the historical context in which the Constituent Assembly operated, a period in which legislative provisions excluded women from the majority of public offices (Dec. 422/1995). Some historical consideration, related to the period of time in which a specific legislative norm was approved, in comparison with the moment in which the Court is called to decide may be found in Dec. 126/1968, with specific reference to the crime of adultery perpetrated by a wife.

39 See Dec. 429/1992 as the only case in which the Court explicitly stated that "the reconstruction of the purpose of Constitution-makers, in a system with a rigid Constitution, is essential for carrying out the constitutional review of legislation". See Anna Poggi, "L'intenzione del costituente nella teoria dell'interpretazione costituzionale" (1997) 1 *Diritto pubblico* 153.

(c) Economic crisis: 3 of 40 decisions consider the economic crisis argument. A reference to the "economic downturn" is found in Dec. 348/2007 and to the "severity of the economic situation" in Dec. 223/2012. In Dec. 10/2010 the Court stated that the state's intervention in regions' competences in order to guarantee fundamental rights is characterized by the features of exceptionality and urgency due to the international economic and financial crisis that hit Italy in 2008 and 2009.

(d) Moral/Religious arguments: References to moral arguments can be found in Dec. 440/1995 declaring the unconstitutionality of the provision punishing blasphemy. Indeed, the Court considered that the practice prohibited by the challenged provision protects a value shared "by all religions that today characterize our national community, in which they have to live faiths, cultures and traditions".

(e) Social arguments: It is possible to trace a social argument in Dec. 49/1971, in which the Court, dealing with a case on the dissemination of birth control practices, considered that, due to the importance and social relevance of birth control, it was no longer possible to consider this practice as an offense to public morality, overruling its previous 1965 decision. Also in Dec.126/1968 the Court justifies the overruling by referring to the "actual social reality", in which the criminalization of female adultery, instead of supporting the unity of the family, can be destructive of the very unity.

We found a reference to the evolution of society also in Dec. 138/2010 on same-sex marriage, establishing that the concepts of family and marriage cannot be considered to have been "crystallized" with reference to the time when the Constitution entered into force, without taking into account, among other elements, also the evolution of society and customs.

(f) Scientific arguments: In Dec. 161/1985, on transsexualism, the Court referred to the medico-legal doctrine to define the meaning of "transsexual". In Dec. 185/1998 on cancer therapies, the Court referred generically to the evaluations made by technical-scientific bodies.

Reference to Scholarly Works

The Constitutional Court, like any court in Italy, is not allowed to quote scholarly work. As a matter of fact, according to art. 118, para. 3 of the "Implementing Provisions of the Civil Procedure Code" (to be applied also in Constitutional Court judgments, unless the Court decides to derogate it by its own special procedural rules), "In any case, any mention of legal scholarly work must be omitted". This is the reason behind the lack of any explicit reference to legal scholarship. However, there are a few cases in which the Court makes general references, as additional argument in constitutional interpretation, to "scholarship" (Dec. 15/82, 364/1988, 422/1995, 348/2007, 138/2010). We can only assume, without providing any evidence, that the scholarship lies behind the numerous decisions in which axiomatic arguments are used[40] and, more generally, that it constitutes the usual reference point for the Court.

References to Foreign Law

Reference to foreign law in Italian Constitutional Court judgments is not extensive (five decisions),[41] notwithstanding the Court's establishment since the 1980s of a specialized Comparative Law Department. Most of the references are also rather generic, referring to "choices taken and solutions followed in several countries": this is the case of Dec. 138/2010, on same-sex marriage, which refers to the different solutions adopted in different countries to indicate that there was not one compulsory solution to the problem, which remains within the boundaries of Legislator's discretion. In Dec. 172/1999, on the status of the stateless, we found a generic reference to the experience of other ECHR Member States where there are provisions similar to those present in the Italian legal order. Dec. 170/1984 contains a reference to the fact that the direct applicability of EC law is declared by ordinary courts in "all the legal orders of Members States" of the EU, including Germany.

We found more specific references to foreign legal materials in Dec. 303/2003, in which the Court, with regard to state-region competences, refers to German concurrent legislation (*konkurrierende Gesetzgebung*) and to the US Supremacy Clause as flexibility mechanisms to guarantee the unity of the legal order.

The only explicit reference to foreign precedents has been found in Dec. 161/1985, on transsexualism: the Court quotes some words from a 1978

[40] See *supra* at para. "Doctrinal Analysis of Legal Concepts and Principles".

[41] Recently this long-standing attitude – see Lucio Pegoraro, *La Corte costituzionale italiana e il diritto comparato: un'analisi comparatistica*(CLUEB 2007) – seems to be changing: in 2014 two important judgments (Dec.1/2014 on electoral law and Dec.170/2014 on the effects of sex change on previous marriage) contain several explicit references to *Bundesverfassungsgericht* decisions.

Bundesverfassungsgericht judgment in order to clarify, from the medical point of view, the issue at stake.

Other Methods/Arguments

We only found one argument. In Dec. 15/1982 the Court argues that art.25.2 of the Constitution, on the non-retroactivity of criminal law (prohibition against ex post facto laws), does not include criminal procedure law, referring also ("in addition" to its own precedents) to one judgment of the Court of Cassation.

7 *The Weight of the Arguments*

In the 40 judgments examined, the Italian Constitutional Court reveals its preference for some methods of constitutional interpretation: the reference to precedents is the most used argument (31 decisions), followed by the domestic harmonizing argument and the reference to principles not mentioned in the text of the Constitution (23 decisions each), by the ordinary meaning of the words (18 decisions), by the teleological textual argument (13 decisions), by non-legal arguments (12 decisions), by the international harmonizing argument (11 of 40) and by the teleological textual argument (10 decisions). Other arguments, such as reference to silence (7 decisions), to foreign legal materials (5 decisions) and to analogy (4 of 40), are almost absent. Scholarly works are not quoted at all, and indirect references can be found in only 5 decisions. The Court often combines different types of arguments, displaying a syncretistic approach to legal argumentation.

If we move from a quantitative to a qualitative analysis, by trying to evaluate the weight of arguments, the picture is slightly different. Although reference to precedents is frequently present, this does not seem to be the primary argument, but generally an additional one. On some occasions, precedents have been overruled without adequate reasons, and in many important decisions on new issues the Court does not seem concerned by the lack of precedents.

The main outcome of our research is that the Italian Constitutional Court is not concerned with the text of the Constitution. References to the wording of the Constitution are the necessary standpoint of many decisions, but this is only a starting point.

Textual interpretation is explicitly rejected by the Court, which has stated that "pure textual interpretation is always a primitive method, and even more so as far as constitutional interpretation is concerned"

(Dec. 1/2013). A similar attitude is displayed by the judgments on the silence of the Constitution that never translate into the impossibility of finding, by a different method, a constitutional principle or rule applicable to the case. The Court reads the Constitution as an open texture, to be supplemented by interpretation.

Similarly, the reference to the *travaux préparatoires* is not common and is usually considered a backup argument. Also, the Court displays a fluctuating attitude towards this material, e.g. by considering relevant both the absence and the presence of a provision in the preliminary draft of the Constitution, depending on the case at stake. The only exception is Dec. 138/2010, in which the Court states that

> it is true to say that the concepts of family and marriage cannot be considered to have been 'crystallized' with reference to the time when the Constitution entered into force, because they are endowed with the flexibility that is inherent in constitutional principles, and are therefore to be interpreted taking into account not only the transformations within the legal system, but also the evolution of society and customs. However, such an interpretation cannot go as far as to impinge upon the core of the provision at issue, modifying it in such a manner as to embrace situations and problems that were not considered at all when it was enacted.

Therefore, the core of the provision, that limits the evolutionary interpretation, seems in this case to have to be determined according to the "original intent" of the Constitution-makers.

With this exception, most of the cases are decided on the basis of either domestic harmonizing argument or by invoking principles not mentioned in the text of the Constitution. Only in 6 of 40 decisions are these arguments absent, and the cases are decided on the basis of the precedents (Dec. 53/1958 and 289/1998), social facts (Dec.126/1968 and 49/1971, in which precedents are overruled), textual interpretation (Dec. 422/1995) and legislative inactivity (Dec. 440/1995).

Domestic harmonizing arguments seem the primary arguments in fundamental rights judgments, together with the unwritten principle of "reasonableness". A special relevance holds in those cases the logic-systematic argument and the interpretation in light of constitutional principles, especially in light of art. 2.

In institutional cases, the primary argument seems to be the doctrinal analysis of legal concepts and principles, especially the reference to unwritten principles that are assumed by the Court without any explanation, displaying therefore an axiomatic reasoning.

Non-legal arguments (terroristic or economic emergency; historical considerations, social and scientific arguments) are generally present as additional arguments, and only in very few judgments are they presented as primary arguments (mainly, as we said, to overrule precedents).

The Court is reluctant to quote extra-systemic (non-EU) materials, although things have been changing in the last few years especially with regard to international law: international treaties, although not normally used as arguments in constitutional interpretation, can now integrate constitutional principles as "interposed legislation" in the Italian legal system. Explicit references to foreign materials are almost absent, even in judgments where extensive comparative work has be done by Italian scholars and where not many arguments are at stake (as in the judgment on the electoral quotas for women, Dec. 422/1995, whose reasoning, grounded on textual interpretation, has been considered particularly weak by the scholars), but we can guess that they exercise an important, implicit influence.

8 *Judicial Candour and Judicial Rhetoric*

The judgments of the Court do not display openly the value judgments underlying the decision. The attitude of the Court appears to be, if not secretive, certainly reserved, and the Court does not engage in open confrontations, either with parties of the judgment or with scholars.

The Court normally does not deal with all possible arguments in judgments that affirm a constitutional challenge, limiting itself to discussing the arguments on which the unconstitutionality of the statute is grounded. In the decisions where the Court rejects the challenge, the Court generally discusses briefly all the arguments submitted by the petitioner, not necessarily those submitted by the parties. In most decisions, arguments from legal scholars are not discussed, even implicitly, although there are a few judgments dealing with scholarship, without quoting the names of the authors (e.g. Dec. 364/1988).

The language is technical, perfectly understandable for lawyers, but not easily accessible to non-lawyers. It is not an abstract, scholarly professorial language, but a standard legal style, similar to that of the ordinary courts. Actually, the target audience of the reasoning are especially ordinary courts that are not only the main "gatekeepers" of the Constitutional Court, but also its main partners, since in the last decades the Court tried to decentralize its work maximally, involving ordinary judges more deeply in constitutional review than the European model of judicial review normally provides for, by way of the principle of constitutionally-oriented interpretation.[42]

The Court avoids generalization and tries to decide "one case at a time", concentrating on the very specific issue. Notwithstanding, obiter dicta are not absent, and they provide general conceptual principles for future cases.

The degree of rhetoric is very low, almost absent, unless in the few cases in which the target audience is the legislator, mainly as the Court asks this institution to legislate or addresses a case of legislative discretion. As we said for the structure of the arguments,[43] the author of the judgment plays an important role and judgments display relevant differences in style, according to the individual personality and background of the author.

9 *Length, Dissenting and Concurring Opinions*

Decisions issued by the Italian Constitutional Court are generally not very long. The average number of pages among the 40 selected cases is 17. Despite the extensive use of its own precedents and the quite lengthy descriptions of the parties' arguments, the Italian Constitutional Court usually does not resort to a long reasoning in deciding a case. However, during the first decades of its activity, judgments were shorter than those issued in more recent years and we experience a tendency towards longer decisions.

As already mentioned, dissenting and concurring opinions are not permitted.[44]

10 *Framing of Constitutional Issues*

There are no typical ways of characterizing constitutional issues; it depends on how constitutional review is triggered. In most cases concrete review deals with fundamental rights, whereas abstract review deals with institutional issues, although things have been changing since the constitutional revision of 2001. In recent years it has not been unusual to find fundamental rights issues raised by regions or by the government in the abstract review procedure. Irrespective of how cases are

[42] See *supra* at para. "The Weight of the Arguments".

[43] See *supra* at para. "The Structure of Constitutional Arguments".

[44] See *supra* at para. "The Collegiality Principle and the Exclusion of Separate Opinions".

conceptualized by the parties, the Court tends to reframe them in terms of "reasonableness".[45]

11 *Key Concepts*

The most popular concept invoked by the Italian Constitutional Court is "equality" (14 decisions).

Relatively popular concepts are "federalism" (7 decisions), "basic procedural rights" (7 decisions), "democracy" (6 decisions), and "sovereignty" (5 decisions). "Rule of law" (4 decisions), "form of government" (4 decisions), "core of constitutional rights or competences" (3 decisions), "secularism" (2 decisions), "proportionality" (2 decisions), "human dignity" (2 decisions), "freedom of expression" (3 decisions), "state form" (1 decision), "nation" (1 decision) and "privacy rights" (1 decision) are very rare arguments.

The Most Cited Concepts

It is not surprising that "equality" is the most frequently mentioned concept, representing one of the fundamental concepts of the Italian system of rights' guarantees. Leaving apart the cases in which equality is invoked as part of the test of reasonableness, since the very first years of the Court's activity equality has been used with specific regard to the advancement of human rights (Dec. 53/1958).

Subsequently, the principle of equality has been invoked with reference to gender (in this sense, Dec. 126/1968, female adultery; Dec. 422/1995, electoral quotas), religion (Dec. 440/1995 and 508/2000 – blasphemy and religious contempt), right to health (Dec. 185/1998 stating that the right to health cannot be dependent on personal economic conditions), social rights (Dec. 10/2010, according to which the legislator must relieve situations of extreme need) and same-sex marriage (Dec. 138/2010).

It has contributed to the advancement of the democratic system as well (see Dec. 364/1988 on inevitable ignorance) and other basic procedural rights, especially since the late 1980s.

It is also interesting to underline that since the second half of the 2000s, the principle of equality has been used more often in cases involving the organization of the state (see Dec. 102/2008, 10/2010, 23/2011).

[45] See *supra* at para. "Harmonizing Arguments".

Relatively Popular Concepts

Another popular key concept is "federalism", to be defined as the relationship between state and regions. In the very first years of the Court's activity, federalism was not a popular issue in constitutional case law (even before 1970 most regions were not effectively established), and it became more frequent after the 1999 and 2001 revisions of Title V of the Second Part of the Constitution (Dec. 496/2000; Dec. 106/2002; Dec. 365/2007). In recent years, there has been a strong revival of the principle of unity, beginning with Dec. 303/2003, which has been further enhanced by the legislation and jurisprudence issued during the economic crisis era (Dec. 10/2010).

It is no coincidence that one of the relatively popular key concepts refers to "basic procedural rights". In particular, with regard to the elements of the so-called due process (both as far as the reasonable length of judgments and the adversarial formation of the evidences are concerned), Dec. 361/1998 is at the origin of the constitutional revision of art. 111 of the Constitution, in which the principles of due process were expressly included in the text of the Constitution. Other relevant statements concern the legitimate impediment of the members of the Cabinet (Dec. 23/2011) and the wiretapping of the President of the Republic's telephone communications (Dec. 1/2013).

Within "democracy" we have included both references to the democratic state and popular sovereignty. Referendum is an instrument for the expression of popular sovereignty; therefore it is necessary that its questions be worded in a way that avoids coercing the choice of the voters (Dec. 16/1978); at the same time popular sovereignty is the foundation of democratic order, whose fundamental principles also include the publicity of judgments, especially criminal ones (Dec. 80/2011).

Democracy entails also that criminal punishment is not inflicted on those who are not in a position to be aware of the consequences of their conduct (Dec. 364/1988), while reference to pluralist democracy as an essential feature of the Italian Republic is argued in Dec. 422/1995. Pluralist democracy implies the involvement of local people in the key decisions that affect them (Dec. 496/2000). Finally, in the democratic state, constitutional immunities are not privileges granted *intuitu personae* (Dec. 1/2013).

"Sovereignty" is considered both from an internal and an external perspective. Dec. 365/2007 makes a clear distinction between sovereignty and autonomy, whereas Dec. 170/1984 concerns external sovereignty that is subjected to restrictions with regard to the relationship with the European

Union. The profound transformations of the principle of sovereignty as a result of the participation in the process of supranational integration have been highlighted in Dec. 106/2002 and in Dec. 348/2007, where the Court reiterated the difference between EU rules and ECHR standards.

Very Rare Concepts

The expression "rule of law" ("principio di legalità" or "Stato di diritto" in Italian) is not explicitly mentioned in the Constitutional text. However, there are some incidental references in the constitutional case law, in the form of the principle of legality or "riserva di legge" (Dec. 364/1988). The principle of legality is mentioned also with regard to the functions of the Constitutional Court (Dec. 15/1969) and the relationships between state and regions (Dec. 303/2003). Finally, a reference to the "democratic State based on rule of law" is included in Dec. 1/2013, when the immunity of the state organs is discussed.

Within the "form of government" category we included heterogeneous concepts. Constitutional jurisprudence has given a major contribution to the evolution of the form of government, recognizing the consistency with the Constitution of the individual motion of no confidence (Dec. 7/1996) as well as contributing to the balance of powers (Dec. 360/1996, 23/2011, 1/2013).

In Italy, as in Germany, constitutional jurisprudence has indicated the existence of a *Wesensgehalt*, a core content of rights, that cannot be limited. This core represents a limit to the legislative discretion (Dec. 80/2010) that resists also in times of economic crisis (Dec. 10/2010). As for the right to health, the core content includes, in cases of extreme therapeutic needs, the legitimate expectation to access specific treatments, even when these have not yet been completely assessed from a scientific and legal standpoint (Dec. 185/1998).

Only two cases deal with "secularism". In Italy the principle of secularism is not explicitly recognized by the Constitution but is the result of constitutional interpretation, built on the combined provisions of articles 3 and 8. The presence of this supreme principle characterizes the shape of the pluralistic state, within which different freedoms, faiths, cultures and traditions coexist (Dec. 440/1995 and 508/2000).

"Proportionality" is rare in Italian constitutional case law, and this circumstance can probably be explained by the fact that even if the Italian Constitutional Court is familiar with the proportionality reasoning, until recent cases[46] it has not developed a real test and uses proportionality as reasonableness.[47] Thus, proportionality is only incidentally quoted with reference to a legislative measure that is found to be not proportional (Dec. 23/2011), while with regard to state-regions relationships proportionality is invoked in order to evaluate the public interest underlying the assumption of regional functions by the state (Dec. 303/2003).

Although not expressly recognized in the text of the Italian Constitution, human dignity is interpreted essentially as the condition for the recognition of the value of every human being. The connection with an evolving legal culture more and more attentive to the values of the freedom and dignity of the human person, that is protected even in minority and abnormal situations emerges in Dec. 161/1985 concerning transsexualism, while in Dec. 10/2010 the reference is to the protection of the inalienable core of human dignity.

The only reference to the "state form", as a Republic, can be traced in Dec. 1146/1988, explicitly referring to the republican form of state as the only explicit limit to the constitutional amendment, according to art. 139. Similarly, a single reference was found to the concept of "nation", as, according to art. 67, the Parliament is the only place of national political representation (Dec. 106/2002).

Finally, we found references to the "freedom of expression" in three judgments, concerning public security issues (Dec. 1/1956), the diffusion of birth control practices (Dec. 49/1971) and conscientious objection to military service (Dec. 164/1985), while the only case on "privacy rights" deals with prerogatives of the President of the Republic (1/2013).

C Comparative Perspective and Final Remarks

The style of the judgments of the Italian Constitutional Court perfectly matches the model of judgment proper to civil law countries. The "reserved" attitude of the Court – which, as we have said, does not engage in an open confrontation with the parties of the judgment and does not admit intervention by third parties; the prohibition of explicit quotation

[46] Dec. 1/2014, on electoral law, not considered in this chapter as posterior to the selection of the 40 cases examined, represents one of the most important judgments of the Court's history and contains new statements on proportionality, among them a clear adoption of the proportionality test of the ECHR.

[47] See M. Cartabia, *I principi di ragionevolezza e proporzionalità nella giurisprudenza costituzionale italiana, intervento alla Conferenza trilaterale delle Corte costituzionali italiana, portoghese e spagnola*, Roma, 24/26–10–2013, 6, available on www.cortecostituzionale.it.

of scholarship; the absence of explicit reference to foreign precedents; the fact that separate opinions are not allowed and that the personal views of individual judges are kept secret; all of these are are elements distinguishing the Italian Constitutional Court from most of the other constitutional judges operating worldwide, with the sole exception, probably, of the French *Conseil constitutionnel.*

Despite this circumstance, in the reasoning of the Court's decisions it is routinely possible to identify many of the interpretative arguments employed by most constitutional judges, with which the Court has, over the years, developed a sort of "hidden" communication, especially with regard to the extensive use of standards and tests (e.g. "reasonableness" or "balancing") and the generous interpretation given to the principle of equality. More specifically, the Court – limiting its use of positivistic arguments, such as those concerned with the ordinary meaning of words and the purpose of Constitution-makers – has developed a wide array of interpretative approaches, grounded in the systematic interpretation in light of the constitutional principles and in balancing of rights. This attitude has promoted an idea of the Constitution as an "open texture", calling for a progressive interpretative approach akin to the "leaving tree" doctrine of the Canadian Supreme Court. This way, the Court has developed through its jurisprudence new rights and principles originally not included in the black letter of the Constitution, showing a level of judicial activism similar to judges in common law countries and contributing to distance the living Constitution from the written Constitution; a feature that has become typical of the Italian constitutional system.

This combination of a high degree of jurisprudential creativity and the lack of the transparency of the decisions (and, more generally, of the constitutional litigations) represents a special and often criticized feature of the Italian system of constitutional adjudication. Indeed, the high degree of interpretative discretion enjoyed by the Court may well turn into abuse, since the lack of transparency of decisions makes it more difficult for the "open community of the interpreters of the Constitution"[48] to control the work of the Court.

As of today, this risk remains purely prospective, and not effective, also because the Court has shown a substantial degree of prudence and the ability to engage with the other legal players of the living constitutional

[48] These are the words of Peter Häberle, *Die Verfassung des Pluralismus: Studien zur Verfassungstheorie der offenen Gesellschaft* (Konigstein-Ts 1980): this expression has become very popular in Italian scholarship.

law: scholars, ordinary judges, legislature, the entire political system and public opinion. However, unless the Court is able to show a higher degree of transparency and a more rigorous use of interpretative arguments, its legitimacy – while at the moment secure, especially in light of the current fragmentation of the Italian political scene and of the disrepute of the politicians – remains potentially at risk.

Appendix: 40 Leading Cases

1. Sentenza n. 1 anno 1956
2. Sentenza n. 53 anno 1958
3. Sentenza n. 9 del 1959
4. Sentenza n. 126 del 1968
5. Sentenza n. 15 del 1969
6. Sentenza n. 49 Anno 1971
7. Sentenza n. 27 Anno 1975
8. Sentenza n. 16 Anno 1978
9. Sentenza n. 15 Anno 1982
10. Sentenza n. 170 Anno 1984
11. Sentenza n. 161 del 1985
12. Sentenza n. 164 del 1985
13. Sentenza n. 364 del 1988
14. Sentenza n. 1146 del 1988
15. Sentenza n. 13 del 1994
16. Sentenza n. 422 Anno 1995
17. Sentenza n. 440 Anno 1995
18. Sentenza n. 7 Anno 1996
19. Sentenza n. 223 Anno 1996
20. Sentenza n. 356 Anno 1996
21. Sentenza n. 360 del 1996
22. Sentenza n. 185 del 1998
23. Sentenza n. 289 del 1998
24. Sentenza n. 361 del 1998
25. Sentenza n. 172 del 1999
26. Sentenza n. 496 Anno 2000
27. Sentenza n. 508 Anno 2000
28. Sentenza n. 106 Anno 2002
29. Sentenza n. 303 Anno 2003
30. Sentenza n. 348 Anno 2007
31. Sentenza n. 365 del 2007

32. Sentenza n. 102 del 2008
33. Sentenza n. 10 del 2010
34. Sentenza n. 80 del 2010
35. Sentenza n. 138 del 2010
36. Sentenza n. 23 Anno 2011
37. Sentenza n. 80 Anno 2011
38. Sentenza n. 200 Anno 2012
39. Sentenza n. 223 Anno 2012
40. Sentenza n. 1 Anno 2013

14

The Constitutional Court of South Africa

CHRISTA RAUTENBACH AND LOURENS DU PLESSIS

This contribution introduces and considers modes of reasoning that feature prominently in the jurisprudence of the Constitutional Court of South Africa (CCSA). Compared with that of similar adjudicative institutions elsewhere, the constitutional reasoning of the CCSA counts among that of systems still in – or just beyond – their infancy, but has nevertheless, over the past two decades, earned itself high praise among both its peers and expert observers worldwide. It has in particular been commended for some ground-breaking and courageous judgments which it handed down without casting either argumentative rigour or judicial self-restraint to the winds.

We have compiled a list of 40 cases which – at an apposite moment in time, and in the fertile soil of a circumstantial context conducive to the evolution of constitutional democracy – had the potential to become "leading cases".[1] What makes for a "leading case" is a question of methodology that will persist as long as informed opinions on the significance of CCSA judgments diverge. The absence of an unambiguous standard or yardstick to determine the inclusion or exclusion of cases on such a list can give rise to peripheral – as opposed to substantive and instructive – variations on the theme of comparativist constitutional reasoning. Ten of the judgments eventually selected for inclusion in our list of 40 were decided on because they had been handed down in the post-1994 – but pre-1997 – era of constitutional transition, with constitutional democracy – an idea whose time had by then finally arrived in South Africa – establishing itself. All of this started happening even with the transitional Constitution still in place.[2] We opted for the 10 judgments between 1994

[1] The 40 judgments analysed for the purpose of this project are cited in the text in an abbreviated form. The full citation is available at the end of this report in the appendix. Other cases, which are not included in the appendix, are cited in full.

[2] The title or "name" of the transitional constitution is the Constitution of the Republic of South Africa 200 of 1993. Hereinafter it will be referred to as the transitional Constitution, interim Constitution or the 1993 Constitution. It came into operation on 27 April 1994

and 1997 on account of their sustained standing as both trailblazing and founding constitutional precedents even after the commencement of the final Constitution on 4 February 1997, and to this very day. The principles of the transitional Constitution other than (and in addition to) those in Schedule 4[3] of that Constitution could, if the context and their content thus permits, be relied on to construe the final Constitution.[4]

The 30 remaining judgments have all been handed down since the final Constitution took effect.

A Legal, Political, Institutional and Academic Context

1 *Legal and Political Culture as Context for Constitutional Reasoning*

Before South Africa's first democratic Constitution took effect, South African courts were not authorised to test legislation and other government action or the common law against a higher norm of some sort. This was so because of the absence of a justiciable constitution that, as the highest law, would provide norms against which all forms of law and government action could be tested. South Africa's public law and in particular constitutional and administrative law were informed mainly by the English common law and a commitment to parliamentary sovereignty. English public law sits uncomfortably with a preference for constitutional (as opposed to parliamentary) sovereignty in order to safeguard democracy. This has shown not only in the practice of state governance, but also in adjudication. The high regard for legislative authority in common-law systems shows a wariness to entrust courts with extensive powers of review. Statute law is as a rule drafted in detail to avoid loopholes and to prevent misunderstanding the sovereign legislature. In civil-law legal systems, on the other hand, the wording of enacted law is characteristically

and was replaced by the final Constitution on 4 February 1997. The final Constitution was initially published as the Constitution of the Republic of South Africa 108 of 1996, but the Citation of Constitutional Laws Act 5 of 2005 amended the name of the Constitution to the "Constitution of the Republic of South Africa, 1996", thereby signalling the importance and superiority of the final Constitution. Hereafter the final Constitution will be referred to as the Constitution, the final Constitution or the 1996 Constitution.

[3] The principles in Schedule 4 were designed to effectually benchmark the certification of the 1996 Constitution – a process whose significance will be considered more fully at a later stage.

[4] In *National Coalition for Gay and Lesbian Equality v Minister of Justice* 1999 (1) SA 6 (CC) at para 15 the court accepted that the equality jurisprudence and analysis developed by the courts in relation to the equality clause in the 1993 Constitution is equally applicable to section 9 of the 1996 Constitution.

open-ended: "'[T]he expansive terms which are the universal language of constitutional texts' and which enumerate the fundamental rights of people in legal systems worldwide are commensurate with the characteristically broad and indeterminate manner in which enacted precepts in civil-law systems are phrased."[5]

Moving from a conventional common-law approach to a civil-law informed way of understanding and construing law requires definite changes of mind-set, and since 1994 South African jurists, especially those working with the interpretation of first the transitional and later the final Constitution, have found it necessary to make those changes. The two consecutive constitutional texts made provision to have their interpretation guided by foundational norms and values conducive to the settlement and perennial growth of constitutional democracy. Telling examples of this strategy can be found in section 35 of the transitional Constitution and section 39 of the final Constitution – both quoted below.

Interpretative Constitutional Provisions

Transitional Constitution: Section 35	**Final Constitution: Section 39**
(1) In interpreting the provisions of this Chapter a court of law shall promote the values which underlie an open and democratic society based on freedom and equality and shall, where applicable, have regard to public international law applicable to the protection of the rights entrenched in this Chapter, and may have regard to comparable foreign case law.	(1) When interpreting the Bill of Rights, a court, tribunal or forum (a) must promote the values that underlie an open and democratic society based on human dignity, equality and freedom; (b) must consider international law; and (c) may consider foreign law.
(2) No law which limits any of the rights entrenched in this Chapter, shall be constitutionally invalid solely by reason of the fact that the wording used prima facie exceeds the limits imposed in this Chapter, provided such a law is reasonably	(2) When interpreting any legislation, and when developing the common law or customary law, every court, tribunal or forum must promote the spirit, purport and objects of the Bill of Rights.

[5] Lourens Du Plessis, "Interpretation" in Stuart Woolman, Michael Bishop and Jason Brickhill (eds) *Constitutional Law of South Africa* (2nd ed, Juta 2012) at 32.7.

Transitional Constitution: Section 35	Final Constitution: Section 39
capable of a more restricted interpretation which does not exceed such limits, in which event such law shall be construed as having a meaning in accordance with the said more restricted interpretation. (3) In the interpretation of any law and the application and development of the common law and customary law, a court shall have due regard to the spirit, purport and objects of this Chapter.	(3) The Bill of Rights does not deny the existence of any other rights or freedoms that are recognised or conferred by common law, customary law or legislation, to the extent that they are consistent with the Bill.

Section 35 of the transitional Constitution and its subsequent equivalent, section 39 of the final Constitution, placed the interpretation of enacted law on a significantly new footing. The primacy of the "intention of the legislature" in interpretive endeavours has been exchanged for the "spirit, purport and objects of the Bill of Rights" as *Leitmotifs*. This tendency is also manifesting in an emerging preference for *purposive* or *teleological* to *literalist* interpretation.[6]

The prevailing (but by no means only) political culture is social democracy, subscribing to some basic tenets of classic liberalism, but then in the context of a developmental state, where a large number of the population are still socio-economically disadvantaged. Constitutionalism therefore does not only signify state abstention from interference with individual rights, but also active government intervention to introduce measures that will improve the position of the indigent majority of the population. Politics in South Africa still breathes a spirit of transition 21 years after the advent of the new dispensation, and the quest for transformation that has remained alive bears testimony to this.

The CCSA has produced numerous dicta acknowledging political culture as the context for constitutional reasoning.[7] Two judgments in our case sample may be referred to as examples. In *Makwanyane* Kentridge AJ declared: "it would be foolish to deny that the judicial process, especially in the field of constitutional adjudication, calls for value judgments in which extra-legal considerations may loom large."[8]

[6] See section 4 below. [7] Du Plessis (n 5) at 32.47. [8] At para 19.

In the *SARFU* case the CCSA had to deal with an application for recusal based on political bias. The Court acknowledged that "[a]bsolute neutrality on the part of a judicial officer can hardly if ever be achieved" and that "[i]t is appropriate for judges to bring their own life experience to the adjudication process", because: "In a multicultural, multilingual and multiracial country such as South Africa, it cannot reasonably be expected that judicial officers should share all the views and even the prejudices of those persons who appear before them."[9]

The CCSA is cautious, nonetheless, not to trade "political" views for "legal" ones without good reason. As aptly put by Sachs J in *Makwanyane*: "[o]ur function is to interpret the text of the Constitution as it stands... [W]hatever our personal views... might be, our response must be a purely legal one".[10]

There have been a few attempts to interfere with the independence of the judiciary, but so far none of these has proceeded beyond remaining veiled threats.[11] With the support and co-operation of the legislature and the executive, the CCSA has maintained high standards, and it is probably the most successful product of our constitutional democracy.

Methods of reasoning are different in the CCSA and other courts, but this is more and more becoming a matter of degree rather than substance or even style. The differences between interpretation of the Constitution and ordinary legislation are acknowledged from time to time by courts at every level. They are not debated very much, though. The dissimilarity is approached mostly from the angle of constitutional supremacy and longevity (which, in turn, calls for an expansive, open-ended constitutional text). From the perspective that text genre is an essential co-determinant of its interpretation, some scholars have pointed out that the Constitution and other statutes are generically closely related and therefore capable of being construed in very similar ways.[12]

The lower courts readily follow the CCSA's precedents and are also compelled to do so in accordance with the *stare decisis* rule.

In this contribution we focus mainly on the development of constitutional reasoning inspired and required by the Constitution. In keeping with the objectives of the CONREASON project we direct our attention

[9] At paras 42–43. [10] At para 349.

[11] Amy Gordon and David Bruce, *Transformation and the Independence of the Judiciary in South Africa* (The Centre for the Study of Violence and Reconciliation 2007) http://www.csvr.org.za/docs/transition/3.pdf (accessed on 28 October 2015) at 32.

[12] Du Plessis (n 5) at 32.2.

to the performance of the CCSA only, even though it is not just this court that has jurisdiction in constitutional matters.

2 *The Court and Constitutional Litigation*

The CCSA was first enacted into existence in 1994, by virtue of South Africa's transitional Constitution. The CCSA was destined to function as the country's highest court in constitutional matters[13] and as one of a number of post-apartheid legal and constitutional structures at the front cleaning up apartheid's refuse and contributing generously to the settlement and cultivation of a transformative legal and constitutional order.

The arguments for and against the establishment of a separate court dealing with constitutional matters are generally known.[14] Proponents of a separate court thought that in the wake of South Africa's turbulent apartheid past the existing court structures lacked legitimacy, and that the old-order judges were by and large ill-equipped to deal with the demands of a new constitutional dispensation based on the supremacy of a justiciable Constitution, constitutional values and the rule of law, and also introducing and entrenching fundamental rights. Opponents of the idea of a separate, specialist court for constitutional matters (with among them many judicial officers and legal practitioners) thought that, because of their legal training and experience, the existing judiciary would be quite up to the task of adjudicating constitutional and human rights issues. They contended for a highest court with two chambers, equal in status, and with one of its chambers dealing with constitutional matters to the highest level. The arguments for a separate court dealing with constitutional matters as a court of final instance won the day, and the existing CCSA came to into existence.

Nowadays the CCSA's activities and proceedings are regulated by the Constitution,[15] the Constitutional Court Complementary Act (the CCCA),[16] the Constitutional Court Rules (the CCR),[17] and practice

[13] It was established in terms of section 98 of the transitional Constitution. The final Constitution affirmed the continued existence of the Constitutional Court in section 166(a) read with item 16(2)(a) of Schedule 6 to the Constitution.

[14] Carole Lewis, "Reaching the Pinnacle: Principles, Policies and People for a Single Apex Court in South Africa" (2005) 21.4 *South African Journal of Human Rights* 509 at 510–12. She was appointed as a judge of the Supreme Court of Appeal in 2003.

[15] Constitution: Sections 166(a), 167, 172 and 173, generally.

[16] 13 of 1995.

[17] Regulation 1675 published in *Government Gazette* 25726 dated 31 October 2003. The rules contained in this regulation regulate matters relating to the proceedings of and before the SACC with effect from 1 December 2003.

directions issued by the Chief Justice (2010 Practice Directions).[18] The seat of the CCSA is Johannesburg and it has jurisdiction in all of the geographical areas of the Republic of South Africa.[19]

A Constitutional Court: The Question of Jurisdiction

Jakab describes a "constitutional court" as "the highest court of a legal order, whatever name they bear, which has as one of its tasks the adjudication of the validity of norms by reference to the constitution".[20]

On the face of it the CCSA appears to be a constitutional court mainly for three reasons: (a) it is named "Constitutional Court"; (b) it adjudicates mainly constitutional matters, and (c) it has exclusive jurisdiction in certain constitutional matters which are – or have more than but an average potential to become – contentious, since they authorise – and sometimes require – judicial intervention in the doings of parliament, the president and other organs of the executive, and they deal with amendments to the Constitution.[21]

The first characteristic is the most obvious; the official designation (or "name") of the CCSA is "The Constitutional Court of South Africa".[22] The second characteristic has become somewhat fuzzy, especially since 23 August 2013, when the CCSA's jurisdiction was extended to include not only constitutional matters but other legal matters of public importance as well. These amendments had the effect of establishing the CCSA as South Africa's apex court in all – and not just constitutional – matters.[23] The constitutional provision dealing with the jurisdiction of the CCSA is one of the provisions that have undergone considerable change since the commencement of the transitional Constitution. In order to understand and appreciate the most important changes, we provide an overview of the relevant sections of the provisions in the table below.

[18] Practice directions are defined in terms of rule 1 of the CCR as "directions given by the Chief Justice with regard to the procedures to be followed in the conduct and disposition of cases". The 2010 Practice Directions was issued in terms of rule 32 of the CCR. A copy of the directions is available at http://constitutionallyspeaking.co.za/practice-directions-from-the-chief-justice/.

[19] CCCA: Section 3.

[20] András Jakab, "Constitutional Reasoning. A European Perspective on Judicial Reasoning in Constitutional Courts" (2013) 14.8 *German Law Journal* 1215 at 1217.

[21] Constitution: Section 167(4).

[22] Constitution: Sections 166(a) and 167.

[23] For a detailed discussion, see I. M. Rautenbach and Siyambonga Heleba, "The Jurisdiction of the Constitutional Court in Non-Constitutional Matters in terms of the Constitution Seventeenth Amendment Act of 2012" (2013) 3 *TSAR* 405–18.

Constitutional Changes to the Jurisdiction of the CCSA since 1994

[A] Transitional Constitution 27 Apr 1994 to 3 Feb 1997	**[B] Final Constitution 4 Feb 1997 to 22 Aug 2013**	**[C] Final Constitution 23 Aug 2013 to current**
98(2) The Constitutional Court shall have jurisdiction in the Republic as the court of final instance over all matters relating to the interpretation, protection and enforcement of the provisions of this Constitution, including... (f) the determination of questions whether any matter falls within its jurisdiction.	167(3) The Constitutional Court- (a) is the highest court in all constitutional matters; (b) may decide only constitutional matters, and issues connected with decisions on constitutional matters; and (c) makes the final decision whether a matter is a constitutional matter or whether an issue is connected with a decision on a constitutional matter.	167(3) The Constitutional Court- (a) is the highest court of the Republic; and (b) may decide- (i) constitutional matters; and (ii) any other matter, if the Constitutional Court grants leave to appeal on the grounds that the matter raises an arguable point of law of general public importance which ought to be considered by that Court; and (c) makes the final decision whether a matter is within its jurisdiction.

The latest amendments (see column [C]) to the jurisdiction of the CCSA were a necessity because they do away with the illusionary distinction between constitutional and non-constitutional issues.[24] This distinction had been really problematic ever since the establishment of the CCSA.[25] In terms of section 167(3), the constitutional provision now

[24] Lewis (n 14) at 512–519.

[25] See also the discussion of Mathew Chaskalson, Gilbert Marcus and Michael Bishop, "Constitutional Litigation" in Stuart Woolman, Michael Bishop and Jason Brickhill (eds) *Constitutional Law of South Africa* (2nd ed, Juta 2012) at 3.2–3.3.

replaced (see column [B]), the CCSA had jurisdiction in (a) "constitutional matters"; and (b) "an issue . . . connected with a decision on a constitutional matter". An applicant thus had to show that an issue fell under either (a) or (b) in order to have access to the CCSA.[26] The replaced constitutional provisions and the (unfortunately still remaining) CCR made a distinction between constitutional and non-constitutional issues, but what the difference was, and still is, is not altogether clear, especially in the South African context where the Constitution is supreme law.[27] In *Van der Walt v Metcash Trading Limited*[28] Ngcobo J, alluded to this problem when he observed:[29]

> Whether one can speak of a non-constitutional issue in a constitutional democracy where the Constitution is the supreme law and all law and conduct has to conform to the Constitution is not free from doubt. However, as judges who swore to uphold the Constitution, we must accept that such distinction exists and try to make sense of that distinction.

Chaskalson P could not accept the contention that the common law is a body of law separate and distinct from the Constitution and stated:[30]

> There are not two systems of law, each dealing with the same subject matter, each having similar requirements, each operating in its own field with its own highest court. There is only one system of law. It is shaped by the Constitution which is the supreme law, and all law, including the common law, derives its force from the Constitution and is subject to constitutional control.

At a glance this dictum seems to indicate that all legal matters are rooted in the Constitution and are thus always and inevitably of a constitutional nature.[31] The distinction between constitutional and non-constitutional matters has, however, not been laid to rest. Nowadays litigation in the

[26] The amended section 167(3) must be read with rule 19(3)(b) of the CCR, which has not been amended or repealed yet. The rules contained in this regulation regulate matters relating to the proceedings of and before the Constitutional Court with effect from 1 December 2003, and if not soon amended will create confusion for applicants looking for respite in the Constitutional Court. As it stands, this rule requires from an applicant "a statement setting out clearly and succinctly the *constitutional matter* raised in the decision; and any other issues including issues that are alleged to be *connected with a decision on the constitutional matter*" (emphasis added). Since August 2013, an applicant would need to set out the "constitutional issue" and/or "point of law of general public importance".

[27] Constitution: Section 2. [28] 2002 (4) SA (CC). [29] At para 33.

[30] *Pharmaceutical Manufacturers of South Africa* at para 44.

[31] See also the viewpoint of Lewis JA (509–24), who is of the opinion that the distinction is illusory.

CCSA entails an investigation to determine (a) whether or not a matter is a constitutional issue,[32] and if not, (b) whether or not the matter raises important questions that, in the interest of justice, need to be dealt with by the CCSA.[33] For the purposes of this investigation, however, we have focused on the scope and meaning of the constitutional provisions only, and have not dealt with the interpretation of other legislation and common law rules by the CCSA.

The third characteristic of the CCSA is that it has exclusive jurisdiction in some decidedly political and constitutional matters. A certain measure of diplomacy and institutional respect for the other arms of government are required where exclusive jurisdiction prevails.[34] The CCSA is the only judicial organ which has the necessary political clout to hand down judgments of this kind. Examples of the CCSA's exclusive jurisdiction are the following:[35] deciding constitutional issues between organs of state in the national or provincial spheres of government; deciding on the constitutionality of any parliamentary or provincial bill; hearing applications for abstract review and deciding the constitutionality of such review; deciding on the constitutionality of any amendments to the Constitution; deciding if parliament or the president has failed to fulfil a constitutional obligation; and certifying a provincial constitution.

Competences of the CCSA: A Question of Standing

Section 38 of the Constitution stipulates at least three conditions for *locus standi* in constitutional matters.[36] The first is that a right must have been infringed or be threatened. Secondly, the CCSA must have the necessary jurisdiction to deal with a matter before it. Though the CCSA is a competent court for dealing with constitutional and other important issues, there are certain procedural requirements (excluding those where direct access is allowed)[37] which must be satisfied before the CCSA may hear a case.[38] Bear in mind that the CCSA finally determines whether

[32] Constitution: Section 167(3)(b)(i). [33] Constitution: Section 167(3)(b)(ii).

[34] Sebastian Seedorf "Jurisdiction" in Stuart Woolman, Michael Bishop and Jason Brickhill (eds) *Constitutional Law of South Africa* (2nd ed, Juta 2012) at 4.24.

[35] See Constitution: Section 167(4)(a)-(e).

[36] Cheryl Loots "Standing, Ripeness and Mootness" in Stuart Woolman, Michael Bishop and Jason Brickhill (eds) *Constitutional Law of South Africa* (2nd ed, Juta 2012) at chapter 7.

[37] Constitution: Section 167(6) read with section 8(b) of the CCCA 13 of 1995 and item 18 of the CCR.

[38] A discussion of these rules falls outside the scope of this chapter. For a detailed discussion, see Kate Hofmeyr "Rules and Procedure in Constitutional Matters" in Stuart Woolman,

or not it has the competence to hear a matter.[39] Thirdly, the person approaching the CCSA must belong to one or more of the categories of persons listed in section 38(a)-(e), which include the following: anyone acting in their own interest; anyone acting on behalf of another person who cannot act in their own name; anyone acting as a member of, or in the interest of, a group or class of persons; anyone acting in the public interest;[40] and an association acting in the interest of its members.

Generally speaking the CCSA has tended to construe provisions dealing with access to the CCSA generously in favour of parties claiming their rights. In the words of Chaskalson P:[41]

> Whilst it is important that this Court should not be required to deal with abstract or hypothetical issues, and should devote its scarce resources to issues that are properly before it, I can see no good reason for adopting a narrow approach to the issue of standing in constitutional cases. On the contrary, it is my view that we should rather adopt a broad approach to standing. This would be consistent with the mandate given to this Court to uphold the Constitution and would serve to ensure that constitutional rights enjoy the full measure of the protection to which they are entitled . . .

This *dictum* indicates that the three conditions for *locus standi* referred to above are not to be construed too strictly.

Proceedings in the CCSA

The CCSA does not have discretionary power to refuse to entertain a case and cannot make a selection of cases that it will hear to the exclusion of others. The Court has, however, in some instances used its discretion to hear a case that was moot[42] and in others heard more

Michael Bishop and Jason Brickhill (eds) *Constitutional Law of South Africa* (2nd ed, Juta 2012) at chapter 5.

39 Constitution: Section 176(3)(c).

40 In *Ferreira*, O'Regan J, who delivered a concurring but separate judgment, declared that the factors for determining if a person is genuinely acting in the public interest would include the following: "whether there is another reasonable and effective manner in which the challenge can be brought; the nature of the relief sought, and the extent to which it is of general and prospective application; and the range of persons or groups who may be directly or indirectly affected by any order made by the Court and the opportunity that those persons or groups have had to present evidence and argument to the Court." Her approach was followed in *Lawyers for Human Rights v Minister of Home Affairs* 2004 (4) SA 125 (CC).

41 *Ferreira* at para 165.

42 The question of mootness was dealt with in *MEC for Education*. Langa CJ spelled out the circumstances in which mootness will be dealt with – "With regard to mootness, this court has held that '(a) case is moot and therefore not justiciable if it no longer presents

than one case together where the issues that had to be decided were similar.[43]

The powers of other courts in constitutional matters are regulated by section 172 of the Constitution. It is competent and indeed obligatory for these courts to declare that law or conduct inconsistent with the Constitution is invalid to the extent of the inconsistency. A declaration of invalidity has the effect of striking down or amending impugned law or conduct. The CCSA must, however, confirm a full or partial declaration of invalidity by another, competent court. Only thereupon can a confirmation order, read with any other order initially sought, take effect.[44]

The CCSA is a court of record which normally does not function as a court of first instance.[45] Dealing with applications for direct access to the CCSA, the court has indicated that it would normally be inapposite for the CCSA to hear oral evidence in factual disputes,[46] hence its reluctance to do so. It is, however, customary for cases to be argued orally.[47]

The type of case with which the CCSA has to deal determines who the parties to the process will be. Three types of cases can be identified, namely those dealing with (a) exclusive jurisdiction, (b) confirmation of an order of invalidity or (c) an appeal or direct access. Seeking relief in terms of section 38 (human rights violations) would normally be dealt with by notice of motion with the party who alleges an infringement of rights as applicant and the person or organ of state alleged to be responsible for the infringement as respondent.

Amici curiae (friends of the court) frequently join the proceedings and make submissions, but may not present oral argument, although this is frequently done in practice. *Amici* are appointed in terms of rule 10

an existing or live controversy which should exist if the court is to avoid giving advisory opinions on abstract propositions of law'. Sunali is no longer at the school and the issue is therefore moot. This court has however held that it may be in the interests of justice to hear a matter even if it is moot if 'any order which [it] may make will have some practical effect either on the parties or on others'. The following factors have been held to be potentially relevant: the nature and extent of the practical effect that any possible order might have; the importance of the issue; the complexity of the issue; the fullness or otherwise of the argument advanced; and resolving disputes between different courts." Footnotes omitted.

43 The SACC heard three cases together, since they were all concerned with intestate succession in the context of customary law in *Bhe*. See also *Ferreira*, where the Court heard two referrals together because of their similarities.

44 Constitution: Section 172(2)(a) read with 8(1)(a) of the CCCA 13 of 1995 and rule 16 of the CCR.

45 CCCA: Section 2(1).

46 Ian Currie and Johan de Waal *The Bill of Rights Handbook* (6th ed, Juta 2013) at 130.

47 See rule 13 of the CCR, which regulates argument in the Court.

of the CCR. Their appointment depends on the consent of the parties and the permission of the Chief Justice.[48] An example of a judgment of considerable significance for cultural diversity in public schools is *MEC for Education*, where the CCSA was assisted by three *amici curiae*, namely the Governing Body Foundation, the Natal Tamil Vedic Society Trust, and the Freedom of Expression Institute. The participation of *amici curiae* in the proceedings is in the great majority of cases much more than just window-dressing. *Amici curiae* have through the years contributed to the high quality of many of the CCSA's judgments, because they often draw attention to issues useful to the CCSA. These issues are often supplementary to and different from those of the parties, but relevant nonetheless.

A case can be brought to the CCSA in various ways by way of application.[49] First, usually a case reaches the CCSA as an appeal against a decision of a court below, such as the Supreme Court of Appeal, a High Court (in a few cases) or a specialist court of appeal.[50] In all of these instances the CCSA acts as a court both of appeal and of final instance. The procedure for seeking leave to appeal to the CCSA is set out in rule 19 of the CCR, and if leave is granted, the procedure to be followed on appeal is set out in rule 20 of the CCR. Secondly, there are matters in which the CCSA acts as a court of first and final instance. Two categories exist. The first is where the Constitution expressly entitles the president, provincial premiers, members of parliament and members of provincial legislatures to bring certain matters within the exclusive jurisdiction of the CCSA[51] directly to the CCSA. The procedure to be followed in this instance is set out in rules 14,[52] 15,[53] 17[54] and 11.[55] The second category includes those

[48] Rule 10 of the CCR. *Institute for Security Studies: In re S v Basson* 2006 (6) SA 195 (CC) deals with the principles applicable to the appointed of *amicus curiae*. The process to be followed to be admitted as *amicus curiae* is also described by Max du Plessis, Glenn Penfold and Jason Brickhill, *Constitutional Litigation*(Juta 2013) at 53–4.

[49] The application procedure is set out in rule 11 of the CCR. There is also provision for urgent applications – see rule 12 of the CCR.

[50] Du Plessis, Penfold and Brickhill (n 48) at 61.

[51] Constitution: Section 167(4).

[52] Referral of a Bill by the president or a premier of a province in terms of sections 79(4)(b) or 121(2)(b) of the Constitution.

[53] Referral of a statute by the members of the National Assembly or a provincial legislature in terms of sections 80(1) and 122(1) of the Constitution.

[54] Certification of provincial constitutions in terms of sections 142 and 144(2) of the Constitution.

[55] Rule 11 is applicable in the case of disputes between organs of state in the national or provincial spheres, the constitutionality of constitutional amendments, and decisions that parliament or the president has failed to fulfil a constitutional obligation.

cases where a person brings a matter directly to the CCSA when it is in the interest of justice and with leave of the CCSA.[56] Rule 18 of the CCR sets out the procedure to be followed in this category of cases.

A third method of bringing a case to the CCSA is to initiate confirmation proceedings. This is done in terms of section 172(2)(a) of the Constitution, which stipulates that an order of invalidity by the Supreme Court of Appeal, a high court or court of similar status "has no force unless it is confirmed by the Constitutional Court". The process for confirmation orders is regulated by rule 16 of the CCR.

The written legal arguments that form part of the documentation in a case are not referred to as "heads of argument" but as "submissions", and their nature, use and function are regulated in terms of rule 13 of the CCR. In almost all cases the CCSA considers only the appeal record of the court *a quo*, but in exceptional circumstances it may consider new evidence on appeal on certain conditions contained in rule 31 of the CCR. New evidence is as a rule adduced by way of an exchange of written affidavits, but only if the CCSA had issued a direction to that effect.[57] As pointed out before, the CCSA is disinclined to hear oral evidence or examine witnesses. If the CCSA does require the presence of a witness, his or her attendance can be procured by using sections 10 and 11 of the CCSA.

CCSA hearings are open to the public and the press. The court itself is open to visitors and is frequented by both South African tourists and tourists from abroad.

3 *The Judges*

The CCSA consists of 11 judges: a chief justice, a deputy chief justice and 9 other judges.[58] A matter before the CCSA must be heard by at least 8 judges.[59] The 11 judges of the court are appointed by the president on the recommendation of a Judicial Service Commission consisting of, amongst others, the Chief Justice, other members of the judiciary, members of the legal profession and members of parliament.[60] Candidates appear before the Judicial Service Commission and are interviewed in public. They are not allowed to be members of Parliament, of government or of political

56 Constitution: Section 167(6)(a). For a discussion of the "interest of justice" requirement, see Du Plessis, Penfold and Brickhill (n 48) 83–90.

57 See, for example *Mayelane v Ngwenyama* 2013 (8) BCLR 918 (CC), where the court invited new evidence regarding the customary rules of the community.

58 Constitution: Section 167(1).

59 Constitution: Section 167(2).

60 Constitution: Sections 176–178.

parties.[61] They have a constitutional duty to be impartial and to uphold justice for all without fear, favour or prejudice.[62] They ordinarily serve for a non-renewable term of between 12 and 15 years. The majority of the judges were legal practitioners, but there are also some who were judges in other courts, and some legal academics. There used to be some prominent (ex-)political activists on the bench, but nowadays their numbers have declined.[63]

The workload of the CCSA seems to be reasonable and the judges are in a position to properly apply their minds to matters assigned to them. This contributes to a high standard of constitutional adjudication. In its first year of operation the CCSA handed down 14 judgments. The highest number of judgments handed down by the CCSA was 35 in 2011. From 1995 to 2013, the CCSA handed down a total number of 483 judgments.[64]

Judgments Handed Down from 1995 to 2013

1995	14	**2002**	32	**2008**	25
1996	27	**2003**	26	**2009**	33
1997	19	**2004**	22	**2010**	28
1998	21	**2005**	22	**2011**	35
1999	19	**2006**	26	**2012**	29
2000	29	**2007**	25	**2013**	25
2001	26				
TOTAL:	**483**				

At first glance, the statistics seem to indicate a workload considerably lighter than that of other jurisdictions dealt with in this project. There are a number of reasons for this. First of all, most constitutional matters can be and are already disposed of by other courts with constitutional jurisdiction, for example by the high courts or by the Supreme Court of Appeal, and it is not often necessary to proceed to the CCSA. Secondly, a judgment of the CCSA always stands a chance of becoming a leading case

61 See article 12 of the Judicial Code of Conduct (Reg 865 in *Government Gazette* dated 18 October 2012) adopted in terms of section 12 of the Judicial Service Commission Act 20 of 2008.

62 Constitution: Section 165.

63 Former political activists who served the court with distinction include Justices Albie Sachs, Zak Jacoob, Pius Langa, Yvonne Mokgoro, Dikgang Moseneke, Ismail Mohamed and Arthur Chaskalson.

64 The statistics for this chapter was collected at the end of 2013.

(which it often does), and the full bench of the CCSA is often called upon to reformulate the law on issues that had not been considered before. A judgment generally involves and requires the input of most of the judges. In keeping with the common law tradition, judgments of the CCSA may turn out to be rather voluminous and sometimes even long-winded. As a result of its lighter workload, the CCSA is able to deliberate longer and research its cases more extensively. Another less obvious reason is the fact that lawyers often prefer to litigate a case without making a constitutional point, thus negating the need to eventually proceed to the CCSA. There are speculations that the new status of the CCSA as apex court might increase its workflow in the future, and that judgments might become less comprehensive.[65]

So far the judges have taken their constitutional mandate to apply the Constitution and the law "impartially and without fear, favour or prejudice"[66] quite seriously, and in 30 judgments from our case sample the CCSA found against a statute or common law rule. The majority of the cases dealt with fundamental rights issues (37 cases), whilst only 19 dealt with state organisational issues and 15 with other issues. Most judgments include more than one topic. For example, a case would typically deal with fundamental rights issues, organisational issues and other issues. In *Bato Star Fishing* the CCSA had to evaluate an administrative decision of the *Minister of Environmental Affairs and Tourism*, involving the allocation of a fishing quota to fishermen, to determine if it was just in terms of the Constitution[67] and the Promotion of Administrative Justice Act.[68]

The CCSA's judgments are widely published in various formats and by a variety of publishers. Most notable are Jutastat (online and hard copy), LexisNexis (online and hard copy), Saflii[69] (online) and websites of the CCSA[70] and the government.

[65] Anon, "Creating an Apex Court in South Africa", *Legal Brief Today* (December 2012) http://www.legalbrief.co.za/article.php?story=20121205111259948 (accessed on 18 April 2014).

[66] Constitution: Section 165(2).

[67] Constitution: Section 33(1) "Everyone has the right to administrative action that is lawful, reasonable and procedurally fair."

[68] 3 of 2000. This Act was enacted to give effect to section 33(3) of the Constitution.

[69] The Southern African Legal Information Institute (SAFLII) publishes legal information for free public access which comprises case law and legislation from Southern Africa, including South Africa. The website is accessible at http://www.saflii.org/.

[70] The official website of the Court is accessible at http://www.constitutionalcourt.org.za/site/home.htm.

4 Legal Scholarship and Constitutional Reasoning

Academics played a leading role in preparing the way for a constitutional democracy by introducing the idea to an initially reluctant audience. Good quality publications were produced and some academics also assumed the role of activists. With the advent of the "new South Africa", legal academics – and especially constitutionalists – entered the mainstream of constitutional and human rights scholarship. Academics are generally polite towards judges, but politeness in this instance has not precluded vigorous and rigorous debate. Academics are definitely less deferential towards judges than during the apartheid era. The work of legal academics is taken note of and is assessed on individual merit. We do not have a system making for the presence of professors as judges on the bench, though since 1994 a handful of academics have been appointed to the CCSA and other higher courts. Judges enjoy high prestige – definitely more than law professors – and their salaries are not comparable since, on average, judges are paid at least 100 per cent more than professors, and they receive their salaries for life.

There is no coherent body of generally accepted doctrine informing all constitutional reasoning by the CCSA, and there is also no ranking of interpretive methods. Doctrine and methods are used in an *ad hoc* manner as opposed to consistent and systematic reliance on them. Some academics devote attention to theory, doctrine and method, and their work sometimes meets with judicial response. As a rule, judges generously recognise the authorities they use.

B Arguments in Constitutional Reasoning

5 The Structure of Constitutional Arguments

As pointed out already, South African law shows strong elements and accommodates remnants of the civil-law tradition in some areas, but when it comes to law-making through legislation and precedent, South African law has decisively and decidedly been common-law oriented. This means that case law plays a vital role in law-making and development, which in its turn makes for a dialogic mode of law-speak in legal and constitutional reasoning. Narrative plays a distinctive role, and in general the reasoning is neither overly deductive nor bent on instancing each and every case under its proper rules. It should therefore not come as a surprise if the 40 CCSA judgments we have selected will generally speaking probably tend to be more dialogic in nature than their "chain-like" (one-line conclusive structure) or "legs of a chair-like" (cumulative parallel structure) counterparts in other jurisdictions, although both of the latter two structures also feature in the discursive argumentation of the CCSA. We therefore emphasise that making a watertight distinction among the three structures of constitutional arguments just mentioned is not always feasible in discussing the judgments of the CCSA.

6 *Types of Arguments in Constitutional Reasoning*

The CCSA employs well-known and not so well-known arguments or strategies in its line of argumentation, in line with its counterparts elsewhere. The length of the CCSA's judgments makes it difficult to give exact numbers of the various strategies employed by the judges, and it is possible that we may have missed a few.

Analogies

We found nine judgments in which the CCSA employed analogical reasoning. In the majority of cases the court simply referred to other cases by way of analogy either by applying the other case or rejecting it. For example, in *Minister of Home Affairs* the CCSA had to consider the constitutionality of the Marriage Act,[71] which reflected the common law that did not allow same-sex marriages. Sachs J referred to legislative and jurisprudential developments which increasingly afforded recognition to same-sex relationships and argued as follows: "Similar reasoning was followed in *J*, which concerned the parental rights of permanent same-sex life partners in cases where one of the partners was artificially inseminated."[72]

In another case, *Fedsure Life Assurance Ltd*,[73] the CCSA drew an analogy between the powers of two structures in the local government sphere, namely the powers of the Transitional Metropolitan Council (TMC) and those of two substructures. Kriegler J reasoned as follows: "The fact that the TMC has such a power does not mean that Annexure B must be construed as denying a similar power to the substructures."[74]

The CCSA also applies analogical reasoning with regard to foreign law and precedents. A good example is *Zuma*, where Kentridge AJ considered the "rational connection" test by analogy with the two-stage approach

[71] 25 of 1961. [72] At para 58. Footnotes omitted.

[73] See also section 7 below where this case is referred to. [74] At para 139.

of the Canadian jurisprudence which he found to be helpful "not only because of their persuasive reasoning, but because s 1 of the [Canadian] Charter has a limitation clause analogous to s 33 of the South African Constitution."[75]

Analogy has also been used to bring forward the distinction between tacit and implied provisions of the Constitution. In *SA Association of Personal Injury Lawyers* Chaskalson P, for instance, held that, by analogy with the law of contract, unexpressed or implied provisions in the Constitution are valid and operative constitutional provisions. He found:[76]

> In the law of contract a distinction is drawn between tacit and implied terms. The former refers to terms that the parties intended but failed to express in the language of the contract, and the latter, to terms implied by law. The making of such a distinction in this judgment might be understood as endorsing the doctrine of original intent, which this Court has never done. I prefer, therefore, to refer to unexpressed terms as being "implied" or "implicit".

Establishing/Debating the Text of the Constitution

The CCSA does not often discuss what counts as constitutional text or what qualifies as constitutional norms. In the sample cases we found seven judgments which fall more or less in this category. Most eminent is *Certification of the Constitution*, where the CCSA was called upon to certify that the provisions of the final Constitution complied with the 34 Constitutional Principles[77] contained in the transitional Constitution.[78] In order to do so, it had to discuss the text of the final Constitution in detail before it could reach a final conclusion. Although the court did not concern itself with the question of whether or not the draft text of the Constitution before it was a constitutional text, it had to certify its compliance with the Constitutional Principles in the transitional Constitution and thus ultimately had to establish what constitutes "the text of the Constitution".

[75] At para 21. [76] At para 19. Footnotes omitted.

[77] The Constitutional Principles were a set of 34 provisions contained in Schedule 4 of the transitional Constitution. They represented principles which were agreed upon and adopted during the multi-party negotiating process to provide definitive guidelines for the drafting of the final Constitution.

[78] As pointed out by the Court (at para 1), "'judicial' certification of a constitution is unprecedented", but in this case made possible by section 71 of the transitional Constitution, to ensure that the final Constitution complied with the Constitutional Principles set out in Schedule 4 of the transitional Constitution.

The question of whether the Constitutional Principles contained in a Schedule to the transitional Constitution could be regarded as constitutional text formed the topic of discussion in another judgment of the CCSA, in *Executive Council*.[79] The Court found that these principles have a status other than the provisions of the Constitution themselves, regardless of the fact that they were contained in a schedule to the transitional Constitution, because they cannot be amended at all.[80]

The constitutional status of the epilogue to the transitional Constitution formed the subject matter in *AZAPO*. Mahomed DP came to the conclusion that it is indeed part of the constitutional text with "no lesser status than any other part of the Constitution".[81]

Confirmation for our viewpoint that conventional statutory interpretation and constitutional interpretation are not always distinguishable in a South African context is the last example, *viz.*: *Bato Star Fishing*, where the CCSA dealt with the question of whether or not the Promotion of Administrative Justice Act[82] can be regarded as constitutional text. It came to the conclusion that the Act gives effect to section 33 of the Constitution and "matters relating to the interpretation and application" of the Act will thus be constitutional matters.[83] Unlike section 33 of the Constitution, the text of the act itself is arguably not "constitutional text", and the latter is subordinate to the former.

Applicability of the Constitution

The South African Constitution is supreme law as provided by section 2 of the Constitution, which stipulates: "This Constitution is the supreme law of the Republic; law or conduct inconsistent with it is invalid, and the obligations imposed by it must be fulfilled."

In addition, section 8(1) of the Constitution makes the Bill of Rights applicable to "all law, and binds the legislature, the executive, the judiciary and all organs of state". The constitutional mandate of courts to promote the "spirit, purport and objects of the Bill of Rights" when interpreting any legislation or developing the common and customary law[84] is a further indication that constitutional law will almost always be applied by a court to a case at hand.[85]

[79] At paras 24–41. [80] At para 35. [81] At para 14.
[82] 3 of 2000. [83] At para 25. [84] Constitution: Section 39(2).
[85] For a detailed discussion of the application of both the transitional and final Constitutions, see Stuart Woolman "Application" in Stuart Woolman, Michael Bishop and Jason Brickhill (eds) *Constitutional Law of South Africa* (2nd ed, Juta 2012) at 31.1–31.161.

We have identified 26 judgments which dealt with the question of what constitutes constitutional law.

Ordinary Meaning of the Words of the Constitution: Literalism

The ordinary meaning of the words of the Constitution was referred to in 19 of the sample cases, but this is not in the least indicative of the fact that literalism still seems to be favoured by the CCSA. Most of the judgments that raise the issue of literalism do so in order to make the point that this approach to interpretation cannot play any decisive role in constitutional interpretation any more. In *Bato Star Fishing* Ngcobo J pointed out that

> [t]he emerging trend in statutory construction is to have regard to the context in which the words occur, even where the words to be construed are clear and unambiguous.[86]

In most of the judgments the quest for the ordinary meaning of words in the Constitution is merely a starting point in the judicial reasoning process. For example, in *De Lange* Ackermann J had to determine the meaning of the word "detention" in section 12(1)(b) of the Constitution.[87] His starting point was to find its grammatical meaning before deciding on its legal meaning, which is "determined by the context".[88]

Other judgments, however, reveal that nuanced versions of literalism are alive and kicking. Kentridge JA in *Zuma*, for example, maintained:[89]

> While we must always be conscious of the values underlying the Constitution, it is nonetheless our task to interpret a written instrument. I am well aware of the fallacy of supposing that general language must have a single 'objective' meaning. Nor is it easy to avoid the influence of one's personal intellectual and moral preconceptions. But it cannot be too strongly stressed that the Constitution does not mean whatever we might wish it to mean... [A] constitution is a legal instrument, the language of which must be respected. If the language used by the lawgiver is ignored in favour of a general resort to 'values' the result is not interpretation but divination.

He persisted in his view, albeit in the minority, in *Mhlungu* where he remarked that there were

[86] At para 90.

[87] This provision stipulates: "Everyone has the right to freedom and security of the person, which includes the right not to be detained without trial."

[88] At para 28. [89] At paras 17–18.

> limits to the principle that a Constitution should be construed generously so as to allow to all persons the full benefit of the rights conferred on them, and those limits are to be found in the language of the Constitution itself.[90]

The majority, on the other hand, agreed that a literal interpretation of section 241(8) of the transitional Constitution[91] involved "a very radical constitutional consequence because . . . it would deny to a substantial group of people the equal protection of fundamental rights guaranteed" in the transitional Constitution.[92]

Domestic Harmonising Arguments

At least 37 of the sample cases contain domestic harmonising arguments. The cases can loosely be grouped into at least eight categories. First, some judgments[93] make generic reference to the "values that underlie an open and democratic society based on human dignity, equality and freedom"[94] and the promotion of the "spirit, purport and objects of the Bill of Rights".[95] The second group deals with the harmonisation of the provisions contained in the Constitution itself.[96] A third group endeavours to harmonise the provisions of the Constitution and customary law.[97] The harmonisation of the provisions in the transitional and final Constitutions is dealt with in the fourth group.[98] The fifth group deals with the harmonisation of constitutional provisions with other ordinary statutes,[99] and the sixth group tries to harmonise competing fundamental

[90] At para 78.

[91] This provision stipulated: "All proceedings which immediately before the commencement of this Constitution were pending before any court of law, including any tribunal or reviewing authority established by or under law, exercising jurisdiction in accordance with the law then in force, shall be dealt with as if this Constitution had not been passed: Provided that if an appeal in such proceedings is noted or review proceedings with regard thereto are instituted after such commencement such proceedings shall be brought before the court having jurisdiction under this Constitution."

[92] At para 33.

[93] See *Alexkor* at para 51 ("the courts must have regard to the spirit, purport and objects of the Bill of Rights").

[94] Constitution: Section 39(1). [95] Constitution: Section 39(2).

[96] *Alexkor* at para 27 ("a purposive approach to the harmonising of s 167(3) and (7) and s 168(3)").

[97] *Alexkor* at para 53. In terms of section 211(3) of the Constitution, customary law must be applied by the courts *subject* to the Constitution. See Christa Rautenbach, "A Commentary on the Application of the Bill of Rights to Customary Law", 1999 *Obiter* 113–32 for a discussion of the constitutional status of customary law in South Africa.

[98] *De Lange* at para 85.

[99] *Christian Education* (the prohibition against corporal punishment in the South African Schools Act 84 of 1996 versus fundamental rights).

rights.[100] The seventh group deals with the harmonisation of the different levels of government (local, provincial and national)[101] and the last group is concerned with the harmonisation of the common law and constitutional law.[102]

International Harmonising Arguments

The Constitution recognises the place of international law in the South African legal order by declaring that courts must consider international law when interpreting the Bill of Rights.[103] In *Makwanyane* the court stated:[104]

> public international law would include non-binding as well as binding law. They may both be used under the section [35 of the interim Constitution] as tools of interpretation. International agreements and customary international law accordingly provide a framework within which [the Bill of Rights] can be evaluated and understood, and for that purpose, decisions of tribunals dealing with comparable instruments . . . may provide guidance as to the correct interpretation of particular provisions of [the Bill of Rights].

Arguably, section 39(1)(b) and its precursor (section 35 of the transitional Constitution) served as one of the stimuli for the growing acceptance and prominence of international law in South Africa in general.[105] Twenty-four of the sample cases utilised international law to interpret constitutional law, although in many of the cases mere lip service was paid to international law which hardly influenced the court's opinions.

[100] *ACDP* at para 18 (to reconcile the political rights of individuals participating in an election and the need for having well organised elections); *AZAPO* (the need to give victims of apartheid the opportunity to have their cases adjudicated is harmonised with the need for amnesty on certain conditions); *Bato Star Fishing* (the rights of those who previously benefited from the allocation of fish quotas are harmonised with those who were previously disadvantaged in the fishing industry).

[101] *Executive Council* (the constitutionality of presidential actions in respect of local government).

[102] *Lee* (development of the common law in line with constitutional imperatives).

[103] Constitution: Section 39(1)(b). South Africa follows a dualist approach to the incorporation of international law, which in essence requires the formal transformation of international law into domestic law. See John Dugard, *International Law: A South African Perspective* (Juta 2005) at 47–8.

[104] At para 35.

[105] Neville Botha, "The Coming of Age of Public International Law in South Africa" 18 (1992/3) *South African Yearbook of International Law* at 36.

Precedents (Former Own Cases)

The doctrine of *stare decisis* applies in South Africa and the CCSA, like all other courts, make extensive use of it. This is illustrated by the fact that all 40 of our sample cases considered earlier rulings of the Court.

Invokes Concepts or Principles Not Mentioned in the Text of the Constitution

At least 32 opinions refer to concepts or principles not mentioned in the text of the Constitution. They include, amongst others: indigenous title;[106] *uBuntu*;[107] constitutional duties;[108] horizontal application;[109] transformation (transformative constitutionalism);[110] rational connection;[111] separation of powers;[112] constitutional or founding values;[113] *stare decisis*;[114] public interest;[115] legality,[116] and presidential prerogatives.[117]

Arguments from Silence

We found 13 judgments which considered arguments from silence, although it is not always clear that a particular argument could undeniably be classified as such. A few examples are, firstly, *Alexkor*, where the CCSA held that there was nothing in the "events preceding the annexation of the Richtersveld or in the language of the Proclamation which suggests that annexation extinguished the land rights of the Richtersveld Community" and they thus remained intact.[118]

106 *Alexkor.*

107 *Bhe; MEC for Education; Metropolitan Municipality; Port Elizabeth Municipality.* See also the discussion of *uBuntu* under the heading "Key Concepts" at 11 below.

108 *Carmichele.*

109 *Christian Education; Modderklip Boerdery.*

110 *Daniels; Hassam; Metropolitan Municipality; Port Elizabeth Municipality; Makwanyana; Shilubana.*

111 *De Lange; Harksen; Metropolitan Municipality; National Coalition for Gay and Lesbian Equality; Lawrence; Soobramoney; Pharmaceutical Manufacturers Association of SA.*

112 *Doctors for Life; Ex Parte Minister of Safety and Security; Minister of Health; Ex Parte Minister of Safety and Security; Hugo; Modderklip Boerdery; Prince; Pharmaceutical Manufacturers Association of SA; Mohamed.*

113 *Fedsure Life Assurance; Harksen; Lee; Mazibuku; National Coalition for Gay and Lesbian Equality; Port Elizabeth Municipality; SARFU; Modderklip Boerdery; Prince; Lawrence; Shilubana; Soobramoney; Pharmaceutical Manufacturers Association of SA; Mohamed.*

114 *Ex Parte Minister of Safety and Security.*

115 *Ex Parte Minister of Safety and Security.*

116 *Metropolitan Municipality; Port Elizabeth Municipality; Pharmaceutical Manufacturers Association of SA; Mohamed.*

117 *Hugo.*

118 At para 67.

A second example is *De Lange*, where the CCSA found in favour of public service officers in circumstances where the Insolvency Act[119] was silent on their role in creditors' meetings:[120]

> There is nothing before us to show why these public service officers cannot legitimately be accommodated in the magisterial judiciary and used exclusively to preside over creditors' meetings or why, for that matter, specialist insolvency or bankruptcy courts cannot effectively be established under the Constitution in which their expertise can also be fully employed.

Thirdly, Ngcobo J in *Doctors for Life* held, with regard to section 80 of the Constitution,[121] that

> [t]here is nothing in the wording of s 80 that precludes this Court or any other Court from considering the validity of an Act of Parliament at the instance of the public.[122]

Teleological/Purposive Arguments Referring to the Purpose of the Text: Intentionalism qua Text

Teleological or purposive arguments referring to the purpose of the text of the Constitution were used in no fewer than 39 of the 40 cases we assessed. This is clear evidence that the literalist approach which had been the preferred approach of the South African courts before 1994 has been unseated once and for all.[123] The popularity of this approach can be illustrated with a few examples: *Alexkor* ("when one adopts a purposive approach to . . . ");[124] *ACDP* ("the statutory provisions viewed in the light of their purpose");[125] *AZAPO* ("[t]he purpose of schedule 4 to the Constitution");[126] *Bato Star Fishing* ("[t]he provisions of section 6 divulge a clear purpose");[127] *Bhe* ("[i]t . . . provides a contextual indicator of the purpose and intent of the overall scheme contemplated by s 23 and the regulations");[128] *Carmichele* ("The purpose of a referral under that provision is");[129] *Certification of the Constitution* ("[w]hat is envisaged by the CP [Constitutional Principles] is not access to information merely for the exercise or protection of a right, but for a wider purpose");[130] and *Daniels* ("[a]n important purpose of the statutes is to provide relief to a particularly vulnerable section of the population").[131]

119 24 of 1936. 120 At para 95.

121 Section 80 makes provision for the members of the national assembly to apply to the SACC for an order declaring that all or part of an act is unconstitutional but is silent on the issue of whether or not members of the public can do the same.

122 At para 64. 123 Du Plessis (n 5) at 32.52. 124 At para 27. 125 At para 25.

126 At para 13. 127 At para 25. 128 At para 67.

129 At para 19. 130 At para 83. 131 At para 22.

Teleological/Purposive Arguments Referring to the Purpose qua Intention of the Constitution-Maker

We found 20 cases where the CCSA referred to the purpose of the drafters of the Constitution. This does not, however, mean that a preferred method of interpretation is employed by the judges. In some cases the CCSA merely refers to the drafters of the Constitution in passing without attaching too much weight to what their intention was. In *Alexkor*, for example, the court commented as follows: "It must be assumed that . . . the drafters of the Constitution were aware of the general rule against retroactivity".[132]

In other examples the CCSA referred to a party's reliance on the history of relevant legislative instruments to infer a specific intention on the part of the drafters, but then rejected their contention.[133] However, the intention of the constitution-makers is not totally irrelevant as pointed out by Chaskalson P in *Makwanyane*:[134]

> Background evidence may, however, be useful to show why particular provisions were or were not included in the Constitution. It is neither necessary nor desirable at this stage in the development of our constitutional law to express any opinion on whether it might also be relevant for other purposes, nor to attempt to lay down general principles governing the admissibility of such evidence. It is sufficient to say that where the background material is clear, is not in dispute, and is relevant to showing why particular provisions were or were not included in the Constitution, it can be taken into account by a Court in interpreting the Constitution.

Non-legal (Political, Cultural, Moral, Sociological, Economic, Historical) Arguments

In the light of the fact that South Africa's notorious past was interspersed with human rights violations, it should come as no surprise that the CCSA refers to non-legal arguments in no fewer than 35 of the judgments we evaluated. Therefore, we agree with an observation in *Zuma* that the purposes of a country's constitution can be fully understood only if the country's legal history, traditions and usages are well known.[135]

References to Scholarly Works

Of the 40 judgments, 35 refer to scholarly writings. Judgments are published on the internet, often on the day that they were handed down, and subsequently in book form, mostly in a series of law reports. An academic

[132] At para 38. [133] *Fedsure Life Assurance* at para 143.
[134] At para 19. [135] At para 15.

style of referencing and footnoting is used. The judges of the CCSA are not slow or shy to give due recognition to the work of scholars with whom they agree or even disagree. They have access to a well-stocked library, research assistants and clerks who assist them in obtaining research materials for their judgments, and they refer to these materials in abundance in all their judgments.

References to Foreign (National) Law

South African judges have always used foreign precedents in support of their reasoning. It was to be expected that a newly established Constitutional Court would continue to do so, especially in the light of the section 39 mandate allowing them to do so. That the CCSA has so far cited foreign precedents quite extensively in its adjudication of constitutional issues is also evident from the 33 sample cases that refer to foreign law.[136] This comparative exercise is performed without the CCSA sacrificing its independence or sovereignty, and also whilst bearing a caveat in *Makwanyane* in mind:[137]

> In dealing with comparative law, we must bear in mind that we are required to construe the South African Constitution, and not an international instrument or the constitution of some foreign country, and that this has to be done with due regard to our legal system, our history and circumstances, and the structure and language of our own Constitution. We can derive assistance from public international law and foreign case law, but we are in no way bound to follow it.

The judges primarily consider circumstances in open and democratic societies and they do not hesitate to recognise both the differences and commonalities between the South African legal system and other jurisdictions, or those of the issues before them and analogous foreign issues. These features, in a nutshell, have been described in *National Coalition for Gay and Lesbian Equality v Minister of Home Affairs* as follows:[138]

[136] For a detailed discussion based on empirical results, see Christa Rautenbach C "South Africa: Teaching an 'Old Dog' New Tricks? An Empirical Study of the Use of Foreign Precedents by the South African Constitutional Court (1995–2010)" in T. Groppi and M-C. Ponthoreau (eds) *The Use of Foreign Precedents by Constitutional Judges* (Hart 2013) 185–209; Christa Rautenbach and Lourens du Plessis "In the Name of Comparative Constitutional Jurisprudence: The Consideration of German Precedents by South African Constitutional Court Judges" (2013) (14)8 *German Law Journal* at 1539–78.

[137] At para 39. [138] 2000 (2) SA 1 (CC) at para 48.

> In referring to these [foreign] judgments from the highest courts of other jurisdictions I do not overlook the different nature of their histories, legal systems and constitutional contexts nor that, in the last two cases, the issue was one essentially of statutory construction and not constitutional invalidity. Nevertheless, these judgments give expression to norms and values in other open and democratic societies based on human dignity, equality and freedom which, in my view, give clear expression to the growing concern for, understanding of, and sensitivity towards human diversity in general and to gays and lesbians and their relationships in particular. This is an important source from which to illuminate our understanding of the Constitution and the promotion of its informing norms.

Other Methods/Arguments

We identified other methods or arguments in the court's reasoning in at least 32 of the sample cases. Three of these stand out. First, reference to history is made quite often to illustrate why the CCSA has taken a certain stance in a case.

> The Constitution is located in a history which involves a transition from a society based on division, injustice and exclusion from the democratic process to one which respects the dignity of all citizens, and includes all in the process of governance. As such, the process of interpreting the Constitution must recognise the context in which we find ourselves and the Constitution's goal of a society based on democratic values, social justice and fundamental human rights. This spirit of transition and transformation characterises the constitutional enterprise as a whole.[139]

Secondly, the concept of "transformative constitutionalism"[140] has found considerable resonance in the jurisprudence of the CCSA. In *Hassam* this process was explained as follows:[141]

> In assessing the constitutional validity of the impugned legislative provisions in this case, regard must also be had to the diversity of our society which provides a blueprint for our constitutional order and influences the interpretation of our supreme law – the Constitution – which in turn shapes ordinary law. The interpretive approach enunciated by this court will ensure the achievement of the progressive realisation of our "transformative constitutionalism".

[139] Quoted with approval in *Bato Star Fishing* at para 91.

[140] The concept was used for the first time by Karl Klare, "Legal Culture and Transformative Constitutionalism" (1998) 14 *South African Journal on Human Rights* at 146–88.

[141] *Hassam* at para 27–28.

Thirdly, the founding values of the Constitution[142] (human dignity, equality, human rights and freedoms) continue to play a very important role in the reasoning of the CCSA.

7 *The Weight of Arguments*

Since the CCSA is required to be independent and to apply the law "impartially and without fear, favour or prejudice"[143] it is reluctant to attach relative weights to various doctrines or strategies. However, there are circumstances that may result in the CCSA prioritising certain strategies over others. The following are examples:

- The founding values (human dignity, equality, non-racialism and non-sexism, supremacy of the Constitution and the rule of law, universal adult suffrage and political rights related thereto) in section 1 of the Constitution demands special respect, as is evidenced by the fact that a special majority is needed to amend this section (75 per cent instead of the usual 66 per cent for other provisions of the Constitution).[144]
- The pressures coming from the requirement of *stare decisis* may have the effect of establishing certain patterns of dealing with rights, and these patterns may in some instances be hierarchical. In all 40 cases the judges considered their own previous judgments or those of other judges of especially higher courts.
- International law holds a special place in the constitutional reasoning of the CCSA – including as an interpretive aid.[145]
- Initially, during the first years of its existence, the CCSA held foreign law in great esteem and the Constitution indeed authorises its use. This changed somewhat as the CCSA began to develop its own constitutional jurisprudence.
- The notions of *stare decisis, ratio decidendi* and *obiter dicta* play an important role in the weight of arguments. What counts as binding in a South African high court's judgment is the *ratio decidendi*, while *obiter dicta* have persuasive force which can back up all that is *ratio decidendi.* There is a perception that arguments in commercial areas of the law are

142 Constitution: Section 1. 143 Constitution: Section 165(2).

144 Constitution: Section 74(1)(a).

145 For a general discussion of the Constitutional Court's use of international law, see Erika De Wet, "The 'Friendly but Cautious' Reception of International Law in the Jurisprudence of the South African Constitutional Court: Some Critical Remarks" 28 (2005) *Fordham International Law Review* at 1529.

more technical and "black-letter" oriented than the soft law arguments in constitutional law. We do not have any statistical evidence to back up such a perception or the opposite.

8 *Judicial Candour and Judicial Rhetoric*

The CCSA's judges readily acknowledge that their reasoning is influenced by inarticulate premises (and undisclosed prejudices), but they are nothing loath to pass value judgments, candidly, freely and openly. In most instances this does not affect the rigour of their reasoning. There is no evidence indicating a correlation between the length of an opinion and the judges' degree of candour.

The CCSA regularly has to deal with arguments coming from all the audiences mentioned in section 4 above. Noteworthy is the fact that the judges do not neglect considering scholarly opinions and do not hesitate to involve themselves in non-legal arguments. Thirty-five of the judgments we assessed explicitly mention scholarly literature, but the weight attached to academic viewpoints varies to a great extent from case to case.

The degree of technicality of the language used by the judges of the CCSA varies considerably. There are certain technical matters in the Constitution which call for technical precision; for example, *Mazibuko*, where the CCSA had to deal with issues involved in the administration of water supply by a local government. In cases dealing with life's everyday situations in the private sphere, the CCSA's opinions are much less technical and more understandable for non-lawyers.[146]

The target audience at which judgments are aimed includes courts and judges, parties to the proceedings, lawyers, politicians, the general public, law students and legal academics. There is a tendency for judges and experts in the constitutional field to take cognisance of the work of their peers worldwide, thereby contributing to creating a phenomenon dubbed "global judicial dialogue".[147] South African judges are part of this movement.

[146] Such as the constitutionality of school rules preventing the wearing of a Hindu nose stud (*MEC for Education*); the recognition of same-sex marriages (*Minister of Home Affairs*); and the status of monogamous and polygynous Muslim marriages in South Africa (*Daniels* and *Hassam*).

[147] See the contributions published in T. Groppi and M-C. Ponthoreau (eds) *The Use of Foreign Precedents by Constitutional Judges* (Hart 2013) and also the special edition of 14.8 (2013) *German Law Journal*, accessible at http://www.germanlawjournal.com/index.php?pageID=2&vol=14&no=8.

The judgments of the CCSA are, as a rule, not overly generalist. Much depends on the issue at hand. The CCSA, as apex court, is of course the judicial authority developing general conceptual frameworks and/or principles for future cases.

Some judges more than others are inclined to resort to rhetoric, especially in cases where political, socio-economic, cultural, religious and other similar controversies come up for adjudication. Our analysis of the sample cases reveals that at least 35 judgments considered non-legal arguments dealing with those types of considerations. There is quite a measure of political and emotive language in the text of judgments, but we do not regard these judgments as legally irrelevant. The CCSA was created to ensure the building of a new legal order as depicted in the first part of the Preamble to the Constitution, and therefore its judgments are interspersed with judicial candour and rhetoric:

> We, the people of South Africa,
> Recognise the injustices of our past;
> Honour those who suffered for justice and freedom in our land;
> Respect those who have worked to build and develop our country; and
> Believe that South Africa belongs to all who live in it, united in our diversity.
> We therefore, through our freely elected representatives, adopt this Constitution as the supreme law of the Republic so as to-
> Heal the divisions of the past and establish a society based on democratic values, social justice and fundamental human rights;
> Lay the foundations for a democratic and open society in which government is based on the will of the people and every citizen is equally protected by law;
> Improve the quality of life of all citizens and free the potential of each person; and
> Build a united and democratic South Africa able to take its rightful place as a sovereign state in the family of nations . . .

The approach of the CCSA to keep itself busy with both the text and the spirit of the Constitution has been described by another author as the court's success in undertaking its mandate as depicted in the interpretation clause of the Constitution[148] "while maintaining sensitivity to the more subjective elements of South Africa's social, economic and political reality".[149]

[148] Transitional Constitution: section 35; Final Constitution: section 39.

[149] Hoyt Webb, "The Constitutional Court of South Africa: Rights Interpretation and Comparative Constitutional Law" (1998) 1 *University of Pennsylvania Journal of Constitutional Law* 205 at 210–11.

9 *Length, Dissenting and Concurring Opinions*

The judges of the CCSA are renowned (perhaps even notorious) for delivering dissenting, concurring and separate opinions, as illustrated by 21 of the sample cases we evaluated. The decisions of the CCSA are reached by a majority vote. Each judge is entitled to indicate his or her conclusion on the outcome of the case, which is published in a written document. The possibilities are legion. A judge may publish, along with the main judgment, a separate concurring judgment if he or she agrees with the outcome of a case but on different grounds, or may wish to emphasise a special aspect of the matter. Other judges may concur with a separate judgment. A dissenting judgment will be published if a judge disagrees with the main judgment. Other judges may concur with the dissenting judgment. All the different types of judgments are presented in the same format and are published.

In *Makwanyane*[150] the CCSA handed down a unanimous decision by mouth of Chaskalson P. In addition to this, every one of the 11 judges also handed down separate judgments. All the judges agreed on the end result, namely that the law allowing for capital punishment is unconstitutional, but they used the opportunity to voice their own opinions in addition to the joint opinion of the CCSA. It would seem that the urgency of the issue and the controversy it caused compelled the judges to do this.

Examples also exist where the judges in one case concurred on certain issues, but dissented on others. In *Fedsure Life Assurance Ltd* the CCSA had to decide whether resolutions adopted by a local government and which resulted in the uneven increase of property taxes of people living in historically white areas were constitutional.[151] The 10 judges who adjudicated the matter were unanimous on the issue that the Supreme Court of Appeal did not have jurisdiction to hear matters of a constitutional nature in terms of the transitional Constitution,[152] that resolutions of local

[150] The Court declared the death penalty unconstitutional in South Africa.

[151] Goldstein J in the court *a quo* in *Fedsure Life Assurance Ltd v Greater Johannesburg Transitional Metropolitan Council* 1997 (5) BCLR 657 (W), held that the resolutions allowing for uneven rates were not unlawful. The aggrieved parties appealed to the Supreme Court of Appeal (in *Fedsure Life Assurance Ltd v Greater Johannesburg Transitional Metropolitan Council* 1998 (2) SA 1115 (SCA)) but the Court was of the opinion that it was precluded from hearing the appeal because of the constitutional issues raised and referred two issues to the Constitutional Court. First, were the resolutions constitutional and, if so, did the Supreme Court of Appeal have jurisdiction to adjudicate the matter?

[152] Albeit only under the transitional Constitution. The final Constitution removed this jurisdictional bar.

government were not "administrative action" but "legislative action", and that the property taxes imposed on the ratepayers were lawful. They were, however, evenly divided[153] on the issue of the lawfulness of the levies imposed by the Greater Johannesburg Transitional Metropolitan Council on the substructures of certain historically White areas. The CCSA stated the following:[154]

> As we are evenly divided on this issue, there is not a majority in favour of reversing Goldstein J's refusal to declare the levy and subsidies inconsistent with the Constitution. That makes it unnecessary for us to consider the effect which an unlawful levy might have on the lawfulness of the subsidies paid by the TMC[155] to the WMS[156] and SMS.[157]

This case exemplifies the developmental role equality plays in the making of a just society formerly divided by chronic socio-economic discrimination. The redress of the situation begets controversy. In deciding these matters, courts must inevitably break new ground and often without the backing of precedent. That is one factor accounting for the divergence of opinion among the CCSA's judges in *Fedsure Life Assurance Ltd* and other similar cases.

10 *Framing of Constitutional Issues*

There are no typical ways of characterising constitutional issues. How one does so depends on the nature of the dispute and the choices made by the parties.[158] In addition, the framing of issues is often a problem of interpretation. It is sometimes difficult to distinguish between conventional statutory and constitutional interpretation, especially if a statute has been enacted to give specific content and effect to certain constitutional rights. One such example is the Labour Relations Act (LRA),[159] which was enacted to give fuller effect to section 27[160] of the transitional Constitution.[161] In *National Education Health and Allied Workers Union v*

153 Chaskalson P, O'Regan J and Goldstone J delivered a joint judgment (concurred in by Ackermann J and Madala J), whilst Kriegler J delivered a dissenting judgment concurred in by Langa DP, Mokgoro J, Sachs J and Yacoob J.
154 *Fedsure Life Assurance Ltd* at para 79.
155 Greater Johannesburg Transitional Metropolitan Council.
156 Western Metropolitan Substructure (local government structure).
157 Southern Metropolitan Substructure (local government structure).
158 *The Pharmaceutical Manufacturers Association of SA.* 159 66 of 1995.
160 Corresponding with section 23 in the final Constitution.
161 The relevant sections in both the transitional and final Constitutions state that "everyone has a right to fair labour practices".

University of Cape Town[162] the CCSA held that "the proper interpretation and application of the LRA will raise a constitutional issue. This is because the legislature is under an obligation to "respect, protect, promote and fulfil the rights in the Bill of Rights"[163] and also "in the case of a statute such as the one in issue in this application which has been enacted to give content to a constitutional right, the proper interpretation of the statute . . . is itself a constitutional matter".[164]

A similar conclusion was reached in *Alexkor* regarding the Restitution of Land Rights Act (RLRA),[165] which was enacted in terms of section 28[166] of the transitional Constitution.[167] The CCSA held that the RLRA was enacted to give content to the section 25(7) constitutional right[168] and as a result the interpretation and application of section 2(1)(d) of the RLRA[169] are constitutional matters over which it has jurisdiction. In our research we have coined the phrase "subsidiary constitutional legislation" to describe this kind of legislation that gives specific effect to and amplifies constitutional legislation.[170]

In *Mankayi v Anglogold Ashanti Ltd*[171] Khampepe J pointed out that:

> The key question whether the threshold requirement for jurisdiction has been satisfied in an application for leave is dependent upon the constitutional character of the issue. This Court has recognised that, in a system of constitutional supremacy, it is inappropriate to construe the concept of what is a constitutional matter narrowly.[172]

She then continues to give examples of matters raising constitutional issues. Among these examples are the following: the interpretation, application and upholding of the Constitution itself; the development of the

[162] 2003 (3) SA 1 (CC). [163] Ibid, at para 14. [164] Ibid, at para 15. [165] 22 of 1994.

[166] Corresponding with section 25 of the final Constitution.

[167] Both of the relevant sections in the transitional and final Constitutions deal with property rights and the deprivation of those rights, albeit with important differences which are not relevant to this discussion. For a detailed discussion, see Theunis Roux, "Property" in Stu Woolman, Michael Bishop and Jason Brickhill (eds), *Constitutional Law of South Africa* (2nd ed, Juta 2012) at chapter 46.

[168] This provision stipulates as follows: "A person or community dispossessed of property after 19 June 1913 as a result of past racially discriminatory laws or practices is entitled, to the extent provided by an Act of Parliament, either to restitution of that property or to equitable redress."

[169] This provision prescribes the circumstances under which individuals or communities will be entitled to the restitution of land.

[170] Lourens Du Plessis, "The Status and Role of Legislation in South Africa as a Constitutional Democracy: Some Exploratory Explorations" (2011) 14.4 *Potchefstroom Electronic Law Journal* 92 at 95.

[171] 2011 (3) SA 237 (CC). [172] At para 10.

common law in accordance with the spirit, purport and objects of the Bill of Rights; the interpretation of a statute in accordance with the spirit, purport and objects of the Bill of Rights; the interpretation of statutes enacted to give content to the Constitution as illustrated by the two case law examples above; and executive and administrative action that conflicts with the Constitution.[173] In the same judgment Froneman J, delivering a concurring but separate judgment, leaves no doubt when he states that:

> In terms of the provisions of section 39(2) of the Constitution, a court must, when interpreting any legislation, promote the spirit, purport and objects of the Bill of Rights. This constitutional injunction makes it impossible to interpret any legislation other than through the prism of the Bill of Rights. *Statutory interpretation is thus inevitably a constitutional matter.* It is a legal issue which necessarily involves the evaluation of social and policy choices reflected in legislation.[174]

The interpretation of statutes and issues connected with it are almost always constitutional matters, but there are important differences between the interpretation of the supreme Constitution and ordinary statutes. One should, however, not forget that both result from the activities of authorised law makers and have important constitutional consequences.[175] An example of legislation enacted to give effect (and content) to the constitutional right of equality is the Promotion of Equality and Prevention of Unfair Discrimination Act (PEPUDA).[176] In *MEC for Education*[177] the CCSA reiterated that if a litigant brought his or her claim in terms of PEPUDA, he or she cannot circumvent the Act by relying on the constitutional right directly. This does not mean that the Constitution loses its relevance when PEPUDA is applicable. Section 39(2) of the Constitution makes it clear that any legislation, thus including PEPUDA, must be interpreted to promote the "spirit, purport and objects of the Bill of Rights".

A very important development in the framing of constitutional issues is the case of *Pharmaceutical Manufacturers Association of SA*,[178] where it was held that any issue dealing with the exercise of public power is a

[173] At para 11. [174] At para 118. Emphasis added.

[175] The principles upon which a constitutional bill of fundamental rights should be interpreted were dealt with in the first reported case of the Constitutional Court in *Zuma* at para 13 *et seq.*

[176] 4 of 2000. This Act was enacted in terms of section 9(4) of the Constitution, which provides: "... National legislation must be enacted to prevent or prohibit unfair discrimination".

[177] At para 40. [178] At para 44.

constitutional issue. Furthermore, it was unequivocally stated that there are not two systems of law (common law and constitutional law) applying to the review of the exercise of public power, but only one system shaped under and deriving its force from the Constitution.

In South African constitutional law there also exists a form of judicial or adjudicative subsidiarity.[179] This version of subsidiarity is concerned with the apportionment of power and responsibility to adjudicating fora in order to deal with the interpretation and application of the Constitution in particular instances.[180] This is especially relevant in the context of jurisdiction, where a distinction is drawn between common law rules and constitutional issues. In *Amod v Multilateral Motor Vehicle Accident Fund*,[181] for example, the CCSA held that the Supreme Court of Appeal was the more appropriate forum to develop the common law as contemplated in section 35(3) of the transitional Constitution.[182] This, however, is an issue of competency or jurisdiction, and not so much of the constitutional character of the matter.

11 Key Concepts

In analysing the results of the case sample, the following comments regarding the key concepts identified by the project overview can be made. At least 17 cases invoked the "rule of law".[183] The CCSA has held that the doctrine of legality is incidental to the rule of law,[184] and so is *stare decisis*.[185] The acceptance of the "rule of law" is an important development in South African constitutional law, where the parliamentary sovereignty that prevailed pre-1994 was one of the main origins of human rights abuses.

At least 27 cases invoked the concept of democracy, but the majority of these cases did so in generic terms in accordance with the provisions of the Constitution that states that South Africa is "one, sovereign, democratic state";[186] "the Bill of Rights is a cornerstone of democracy";[187] and when interpreting the Bill of Rights, the "values that underlie an open and democratic society" must be promoted.[188] The concept of sovereignty is

[179] Other examples include *Carmichele* and *S v Bierman* 2002 (5) SA 243 (CC) para 7.

[180] Du Plessis (n 5) at 32.146.

[181] 1998 (4) SA 735 (CC).

[182] See section 2 above for the wording of this provision.

[183] See section 4 above.

[184] *Fedsure Life Assurance Ltd* at paras 56–59 and confirmed in *Pharmaceutical Manufacturers Association of SA* at para 17.

[185] *Daniels* at para 94.

[186] Constitution: Section 1.

[187] Constitution: Section 8.

[188] Constitution: Section 39(1)(a).

invoked in only 6 of the cases and does not seem to be problematic in the South African context. There is only a single judgment that refers to the "form of state" in South Africa;[189] one that refers to "secularism",[190] one that refers to "nation",[191] and only one that refers to "federalism".[192] "Proportionality" is mentioned in at least 26 of the sample judgments.

The German guarantee of not negating the essential content of a right when limiting it was written into the transitional Constitution but it soon proved to be a concept without the possibility of becoming part of South African constitutional jurisprudence.[193] It was, therefore, not included in the text of the final Constitution and subsequently fell into disuse. There are 9 judgments nonetheless which consider the *Wesensgehaltsgarantie* or something directly or indirectly similar.

"Human dignity" is a founding value of the Constitution and it informs a number of other rights such as equality and freedom rights. It is invoked in no fewer than 18 judgments of the sample investigated. "Equality" is by far the most adjudicated right in South Africa. It is invoked in 30 of the judgments of the CCSA. Although "basic procedural rights" are important, only 10 of the sample cases mention these rights. "Freedom of expression" has been invoked in only 11 of the sample cases and the right to "privacy" in only 5 of the sample cases. The Constitution confirms that the Bill of Rights does not establish a *numerus clausus* of rights and that "other rights and freedoms that are recognised or conferred by common law, customary law or legislation" continue to exist, but subject to the Bill of Rights.[194]

Further key concepts which are very much "South African" are "constitutional values" as guiding lights. The notion of "transformative constitutionalism" also has a close relationship with the development of constitutional thinking in South Africa. *uBuntu* is a value which has earned itself the appellation "key concept" as well. It is of African origin and has many meanings, which has caused it to become a topic of many debates. In essence it refers to the key values of group solidarity, namely compassion, respect, human dignity, conformity to basic norms, and collectivity. It entered the legal discourse of the judiciary in 1995 in *Makwanyane* where Langa J explained its meaning as follows:[195]

[189] *Certification of the Constitution* at para 8.

[190] *Lawrence* at para 95 *et seq.*

[191] *National Coalition* at para 135 (only generically: "our future as a nation").

[192] *Certification of the Constitution* at para 287 *et seq.*

[193] Section 33(1) provided for the limitation of a right, provided that such a limitation "shall not negate the essential content of that right".

[194] Constitution: Section 39(3).

[195] At para 224.

> The concept is of some relevance to the values we need to uphold. It is a culture which places some emphasis on communality and on the interdependence of the members of a community. It recognises a person's status as a human being, entitled to unconditional respect, dignity, value and acceptance from the members of the community such person happens to be part of. It also entails the converse, however. The person has a corresponding duty to give the same respect, dignity, value and acceptance to each member of that community. More importantly, it regulates the exercise of rights by the emphasis it lays on sharing and co-responsibility and the mutual enjoyment of rights by all.

Some key concepts are spelt out in the constitutional text; others can be determined through a fairly straightforward interpretive process. Then there is also at least one concept, the use of which has consciously been avoided, namely *Wesensgehalt*. Whether a key concept will be used in an operative manner or as a rhetorical device will be determined by the issue at hand. The frequency of the use of most of these concepts has increased in the course of the first 20 years of constitutional democracy in South Africa. This was a process of growth rather than a sudden expansion.

C Comparative Perspective

A revision and reassessment of *Leitmotivs* animating and shepherding the construction of law in general and constitution-related interpretation in particular have inspired many fundamental (and directional) changes in post-1994 South African law – especially constitutional and human-rights law. This development has also brought with it a treasure trove of unprecedented versions of constitutional reasoning.

A decisively significant *Leitmotiv* emerged from and lent direction to South Africa's distinctive socio-political and -economic transition, invigorated by the quest for a metamorphosed South Africa. This *Leitmotiv* goes by the name of "transformative constitutionalism".[196] In none of the other jurisdictions included in this study have we encountered any specific reference to this forceful wind of change making for an atmosphere conducive to dynamic and up-to-date constitutional reasoning. This does not, however, mean that *Leitmotivs* are absent from the constitutional reasoning in these other jurisdictions. Their visible and tangible presence in the South African context is probably due to their proximity in time to the genesis and early development of a transformative new constitutional

[196] See section B.4 at "other methods/arguments" above.

state unshackled from more than three and a half centuries of injustice and oppression. Transformative constitutionalism provides courts with reasons and navigates them to steer clear of conventional interpretative literalism and formalism in the interpretation of the Constitution and all other law. It has also opened the judiciary's eyes to the significance of dialogic constitutional reasoning. An animated and eloquent common-law style of writing judgments has entered and established itself in the constitutional sphere.

Another distinctive feature of the South African Constitution and constitutional jurisprudence, interlinked with the decided presence of *Leitmotivs* and their role in constitutional reasoning, is a perennial concern and care for the founding values of the Constitution (human dignity, equality, non-racialism, non-sexism, supremacy of the Constitution, rule of law, universal adult suffrage and political rights) which enjoy prominence in almost all the decisions of the CCSA.[197] The CCSA cannot escape the fact that it is also responsible for dispensing justice in an African setting and therefore its utilisation of African values (such as *uBuntu*) in its reasoning is another feature that distinguishes it from most of its counterparts globally.

And, the South African judiciary has increasingly been taking leave from the myth and practice of not being allowed to consider and comment on "non-legal matters", such as ethical, socio-political, economic, cultural and policy issues in general, lest we forsake the esteem that jurists are expected to enjoy because of their ability to negotiate issues involving controversies with Stoic composure. At least three jurisdictions included in this project also make ample use of non-legal arguments in their reasoning, namely the Israeli Supreme Court, the Constitutional Court of the Czech Republic and the US Supreme Court.

Finally, the justices of the CCSA have used foreign precedents as extra-textual aids to assist in the process of constitutional interpretation to the full extent.[198] Statistics confirm that since its inception in 1994 the CCSA has been considering foreign precedents on an on-going basis. This may be explained partly by the fact that the newly established CCSA under a newly adopted Constitution was called upon to develop, through its jurisprudence, a sound foundation for the interpretation and application of that Constitution in the almost complete absence of domestic

[197] Ibid.

[198] See also the discussion of Laurie W. H. Ackermann, "Constitutional Comparativism in South Africa" (2006) 123 *South African Law Journal* 497.

precedent. On the other hand, it may also be in line with the global trend of constitutional judges to communicate with one another, as illustrated by some of the other country reports.

Against this background, four hypotheses formulated by the project designers have to be considered. Firstly, there is no such thing as a universal *Verfassungsdogmatik* as clearly illustrated by the results put forward by the country reports, though there are certainly many tangent points in the way constitutional judges do their reasoning. Secondly, there is no direct evidence that bigger or economically strong countries are less likely to use foreign law. Only two other country reports, besides that of the CCSA, reveal a high incidence of foreign case citations, namely the Constitutional Court of the Czech Republic and the Israeli Supreme Court. It is telling that South Africa, the Czech Republic and Israel are all countries with turbulent pasts on the road to transformation, albeit for differing reasons. Thirdly, there is also no evidence that purposive arguments are more likely to be used in the case of older constitutions which are more difficult to amend. The South African Constitution is a case in point. It is a fairly young Constitution but purposive arguments are, where feasible, the Court's preferred method anyway. Fourthly and lastly, there is no evidence that academics on the CCSA bench hand down more detailed and abstract judgments. Although the CCSA judges have an academic style of referencing and use footnotes, there is no consistent difference between the judgments of academics and practitioners on the bench.

None of us is aware of instances where judges of the CCSA, especially, have manipulated constitutional language. We advise observers to take note of the many innovative and exemplary characteristics of the Constitution and the way in which they have been implemented so far, but we would advise caution when it comes to the point of wanting to borrow too directly from "the real stuff". A constitution is not primarily designed for export purposes – and South Africa's Constitution is no exception.

D Evaluation, Pathology and Criticism

As repeatedly intimated before, the CCSA is held in high repute back home, but sometimes even more so in the global village known as "the world". This apparently favourable state of affairs can, however, not be allowed to lull its admirers into a state of complacency. Agility and unpretentiousness in constitutional business are never misplaced, since constitutional democracy can be surprisingly fragile and transient. In South Africa we have over the past five years been witnessing disquieting attempts by politicians at the very highest level of government to thwart and weaken constitutional democracy, because it has come to stand in the way of their own selfish political and material gain. Probably the most positive and encouraging observation in these circumstances is that our democratic institutions have, generally speaking, not failed the people beyond redemption. The judiciary in particular is not loath to keep the clockwork of checks and balances ticking in an attempt to procure competent and accountable government, punctually and fastidiously, but also with appropriate self-restraint. The courts and the CCSA in particular have handed down quite a number of world-class judgments.

All things considered, it would be unfair, presumptuous and cynical to proclaim South Africa a failed state. Its exemplary Constitution is very much intact. Nowhere within the legal and constitutional system are there unwanted pathologies that persist. (The same can unfortunately not always be said of the executive and the legislature.) There is agreement over a wide front that considerable progress has been made to alleviate the plight of the majority of the people in South Africa somewhat. There are, however, unfortunately also still too many flies in the ointment of governance that contribute generously and dangerously to – and could prepare the way for – possible failure.

There are many possible ports of entry accessible to anyone desirous to learn more about the advent of two decades of constitutional democracy in South Africa, and the history immediately preceding it. The inimitability of South African law as a hybrid, the historical reasons for this, and the curious combination of the elements and features of a legal patrimony from all over the world (dare one say?) but especially from Roman-Dutch law with its civil-law orientation, English law as epitome of common law, and customary law as the indigenous law of original first-nation populations, all constitute possible ports of entry to the knowledge and understanding of law in South Africa, including constitutional law, which of course loomed large in negotiations about the future of South Africa during the 1990s.

Discount, for the time being, the possibility that, unbeknown to Europeans, there could have been fusions of many of the legal systems of first nations (or elements of these systems) within the territory of present-day South Africa – all of that over a period of about 20 centuries. Roman-Dutch law was never abolished by the British authorities in the Cape and remained the principal source of private and criminal law. Commercial law and public law became anglicised, because English was dominant in business and in government (including the administration of justice). As far as the making and development of law by legislatures was concerned, common-law structures and procedures prevailed. Most of the private law and criminal law were of Roman-Dutch and thus civil law–like origin. Of considerable consequence was the fact that *stare decisis* was adopted and used by the courts to adapt and to a limited extent even "make" law. It thus came to pass that common-law adjudicative strategies were often invoked to implement and develop Roman-Dutch law. Many of the judges had very little knowledge of Roman-Dutch law and they often applied English law by mistake, thinking that it was Roman-Dutch law. In this way English law influenced Roman-Dutch law quite extensively.

Although common law and civil law may seem to be incompatible in many ways, the "blending process" in South Africa worked reasonably well. With the advent of constitutional democracy some resistance came from more traditionalist and conservative factions of the population in all walks of life. These included members of the judiciary, practising lawyers and legal academics. The mainstream resistance manifested as a reluctance to part with the common law in areas where it was quite possible to use the Constitution instead. The Constitution was thus perceived as a *correctio* of the common law and not as the supreme or highest law, capable of trumping (and often required to trump) all other law. With the CCSA at the helm, the courts nowadays assume that a feasible balance between reliance on the Constitution and common law must honour the Constitution's highest authority. This has brought about some far-reaching amendments of the common law and the constitutional case law in particular.

Another significant development is that indigenous law – in spite of clearly being subject to the authority of the Constitution – is increasingly being treated as a kind of common law, a fact which has enhanced its status and authority. In the South African mix of legal systems, indigenous law previously clearly enjoyed a lower status than common law.

Repressive apartheid law used to be an ingredient of the South African legal hybrid, but has by now largely (though not completely) been left behind, hopefully to wither away with the last remnants of the very apartheid crime against humanity itself. An appropriate response to the demise of apartheid law could just be: *Nie wieder!*

Appendix: 40 Leading Cases

1. *African Christian Democratic Party (ACDP) v The Electoral Commission* 2006 (3) SA 305 (CC)

2. *Alexkor Ltd v The Richtersveld Community* 2004 (5) SA 460 (CC)
3. *Azanian Peoples Organisation (AZAPO) v President of the Republic of South Africa* 1996 (4) SA 672 (CC)
4. *Bato Star Fishing (Pty) Ltd v Minister of Environmental Affairs and Tourism* 2004 (4) SA 490 (CC)
5. *Bhe v Magistrate, Khayelitsha; Shibi v Sithole; SA Human Rights Commission v President of the RSA* 2005 (1) SA 580 (CC)
6. *Carmichele v Minister of Safety and Security* 2001 (4) SA 938 (CC)
7. *Certification of the Constitution of the Republic of South Africa, 1996, In re: Ex parte Chairperson of the Constitutional Assembly* 1996 1996 (4) SA 744 (CC)
8. *Christian Education SA v Minister of Education* 2000 (4) SA 757 (CC)
9. *Daniels v Campbell* 2004 (5) SA 331 (CC)
10. *De Lange v Smuts* 1998 (3) SA 785 (CC)
11. *Doctors for Life v Speaker of the National Assembly* 2006 (12) BCLR 1399 (2006 (6) SA 416) (CC)
12. *Ex Parte Minister of Safety and Security: In Re: S v Walters* 2002 (4) SA 613 (CC)
13. *Executive Council, Western Cape Legislature v President of the RSA* 1995 (4) SA 877 (CC)
14. *Fedsure Life Assurance Ltd v Greater Johannesburg Transitional Metropolitan Council* 1999 (1) SA 374 (CC)
15. *Ferreira v Levin NO; Vryenhoek v Powell NO* 1996 (1) SA 984 (CC)
16. *First National Bank of SA Ltd t/a Wesbank v Commissioner, South African Revenue Service; First National Bank of SA Ltd t/a Wesbank v Minister of Finance* 2002 (4) SA 768 (CC)
17. *Government of the RSA v Grootboom* 2001 (1) SA 46 (CC)
18. *Harksen v Lane* 1998 (1) SA 300 (CC)
19. *Hassam v Jacobs* 2009 (5) SA 572 (CC)
20. *Lee v Minister of Correctional Services* 2013 (2) SA 144 (CC)
21. *Mazibuko v City of Johannesburg* 2010 (4) SA 1 (CC)
22. *MEC for Education KwaZulu Natal v Pillay* 2008 (1) SA 474 (CC)
23. *Metropolitan Municipality v Blue Moonlight Properties 39 (Pty) Ltd* 2012 (2) SA 104 (CC)
24. *Minister of Health v Treatment Action Campaign* 2002 (5) SA 721 (CC)
25. *Minister of Home Affairs v Fourie; Lesbian and Gay Equality Project v Minister of Home Affairs* 2006 (1) SA 524 (CC)
26. *Mohamed v President of the RSA* 2001 (3) SA 893 (CC)
27. *National Coalition for Gay and Lesbian Equality v Minister of Justice* 1999 (1) SA 6 (CC)

28. *Pharmaceutical Manufacturers Association of SA: In re Ex parte President of the RSA* 2000 (2) SA 674 (CC)
29. *Port Elizabeth Municipality v Various Occupiers* 2005 (1) SA 217 (CC)
30. *President of the RSA v Hugo* 1997 (4) SA 1 (CC)
31. *President of the RSA v Modderklip Boerdery (Pty) Ltd* 2005 (5) SA 3 (CC)
32. *President of the RSA v SA Rugby Football Union (SARFU)* 1999 (4) SA 147 (CC)
33. *Prince v President, Cape Law Society* 2002 (2) SA 794 (CC)
34. *S v Lawrence; S v Negal; S v Solberg* 1997 (4) SA 1176 (CC)
35. *S v Makwanyane* 1995 (3) SA 391 (CC)
36. *S v Mhlungu* 1995 (3) SA 867 (CC)
37. *S v Zuma* 1995 (2) SA 642 (CC)
38. *SA Association of Personal Injury Lawyers v Heath* 2001 (1) SA 883 (CC)
39. *Shilubana v Nwamitwa* 2009 (2) SA 66 (CC)
40. *Soobramoney v Minister of Health, KwaZulu-Natal* 1998 (1) SA 765 (CC)

15

The Spanish Constitutional Court

MARIAN AHUMADA RUIZ

A Legal, Political, Institutional and Academic Context

1 Legal and Political Culture as Context for Constitutional Reasoning

The approval of the Spanish Constitution on 27 December 1978 marked a real "new beginning" for the country after 40 years of dictatorship: the Spanish people regained sovereignty and founded a constitutional democracy. With the new regime of rights, freedoms and democracy Spanish society sought peace and prosperity, but also wanted to break with the international isolation to which the regime of General Franco had been doomed, to finally be aligned with the advanced societies of democratic nations. The vision of a "modern" Spain was, for all intents and purposes, a Spain fully integrated into Europe.[1]

The establishment of the Spanish Constitution (SC) was inspired by the experience of Germany, Italy, France and the first wave of constitution writing after the Second World War. Even though it lacks the revolutionary spirit of the Portuguese constitution, made two years earlier, it is a transformative and aspirational constitution with an important social imprint clearly visible in the part dedicated to fundamental rights and duties. The fruit of the highly revered "consensus" designed to regulate the transition to democracy, the Constitution is future-oriented and contains the basic design of the society and the government as it should be. The constitutional provisions contain rules, principles, and values, prescriptions which sometimes are very precise, sometimes general, vague or rhetorical. Next to provisions that recognize rights or establish duties, that create constitutional organs and institutions and confer competences,

[1] Art. 93 of the Constitution was designed for this purpose. The Act of Accession of Spain to the European Communities was signed on 12 June 1985. The effective joining took place in 1986, together with Portugal. Greece had already joined the EEC in 1981. In this way, still in the atmosphere of the cold war, the EEC supported the process of democratization of these countries coming out of the last military dictatorships in the south of Europe.

that regulate processes, we find also norms which establish tasks and state goals that guide the direction of public action. There are clear statements, ambiguities, silences and some inconsistencies. In sum, the inevitable imperfections of any human endeavor, but also the seal of any collective work. The Constitution bears testimony to a number of incomplete agreements behind mandates to the legislator. Indeed, following a strategy well studied by political scientists, in many cases the constituents moved with the agreements in the most general level by referring to a later time, and in Parliament, the battle over the details. Some fundamental aspects of the design of the constitutional system were not conclusively resolved in the Constitution, as notably happened with regard to many questions of territorial organization and the distribution of power between the central government and the regions (Autonomous Communities), which were not even formed at the time of the adoption of the Constitution[2].

All chronicles of the constituent process coincide in highlighting that if there was anything on which there was agreement from the outset, it was on the desirability of having a Constitutional Court. The Constitutional Court is regulated in Title IX of the Constitution, in title apart from the one dedicated to the Judiciary. The reasons for establishing the Constitutional Court are varied, but given our subject here, we are particularly interested in one of them. There is, as is well known, a whole catalog of reasons, political and legal, to justify the preference for the European style of centralized constitutional review.[3] A technical and practical reason was already put in the forefront by Hans Kelsen: in soils of civil law, where the system of judicial stare decisis and binding precedent does not apply, it is more suitable to entrust the task of overlooking the normative supremacy of the Constitution and monitoring compliance by public powers to a single specialized court and avoid the legal uncertainty resulting from attributing to all judges the competence to decide in each case the

2 An account of the constitution-making process is Francisco Rubio Llorente's "Writing of the Constitution of Spain" in Robert A. Goldwin and Art Kaufman (eds), *Constitution-makers on Constitution Making: the Experience of Eight Nations* (American Enterprise Institute for Public Policy Research 1988) 239–65. On incomplete agreements and deferral of conflicting matters, see generally Stephen Holmes, "Gag rules or the politics of omission" in Jon Elster and Rune Slagstad (eds), *Constitutionalism and Democracy* (Cambridge University Press 1988) 19–58; and Cass R. Sunstein, "Incompletely Theorized Agreements in Constitutional Law", University of Chicago Public Law & Legal Theory Working Paper No. 147, 2007, 1–28. In his *Verfassungslehre* Carl Schmitt had explained the presence and meaning of "delaying commitments" in the Weimar Constitution.

3 A good overview of the issue in Victor Ferreres Comella, *Constitutional Courts and Democratic Values. A European Perspective* (Yale University Press 2009).

constitutionality of the laws to be applied.[4] It does not seem, nevertheless, that the fundamental reason for Spanish constituents was elaborately theoretical. On the one hand, the Constitution replicated European models – mainly, the German one – and the Constitutional Court itself was part of this model. On the other hand, the institution was not unknown in Spanish constitutional history, although it is true that the history of the republican Court of Constitutional Guarantees was brief (1933–9) and anything but glorious. But along with this, and above all, was the not negligible advantage of solving in one shot, by means of the creation of a Constitutional Court, with new judges appointed ad hoc, the problem of what to do with judges trained in Francoist legality and, more particularly, what to do with the Supreme Court, some of whose members seemed hostile towards the liberal constitutional project.[5] In the constitutional regulation of the composition of the Constitutional Court it is provided that judges, prosecutors, lawyers, civil servants and law professors with over 15 years of practice can be appointed to this body. It is significant that in the first composition of the Constitutional Court, 9 of its 12 members were prestigious university professors.

The main big tasks of the first epoch for the Constitutional court can be summed up this way. First of all, it had to guide ordinary judges in the task of demolishing pieces of the pre-constitutional legal order inconsistent with the Constitution. At the same time, the Court had to establish standards for the interpretation of prior law in harmony with the new Constitution, whenever it was possible, in order to avoid legislation gaps. Thus, the new parliament, which had before itself an enormous legislative task with a good number of priority areas, was given more time and a little leeway. Secondly, the Court had to defend the normativity of the Constitution and make clear that it was not a programmatic norm – contrary to the assumption of the Supreme Court and some higher courts as late as in 1982, four years after the entry into force of the Constitution![6] The affirmation of the essential content of the fundamental rights, with independence of its legislative development, is a direct derivation of this premise and appears in the very first judgments of the Court.[7] In the third place, and for all the cases, the Court, acting

4 Hans Kelsen, "Judicial Review of Legislation: A Comparative Study of the Austrian and the American Constitution" (1942) 4 *The Journal of Politics* 185.

5 The factor of distrust in the judiciary is aptly highlighted in Pablo Pérez Tremps, *Tribunal Constitucional y Poder Judicial* (Centro de Estudios Constitucionales 1985).

6 See STC 80/1982, FJ 1.

7 STC 11/1981 and especially STC 15/1982.

as supreme interpreter of the Constitution, had to fix the constitutional doctrine with regard to any controversial constitutional question.

The Court of the first epoch was involved in the intense work of constitutional pedagogics. Its judgments have a distinctive formative and discursive flair. They abound in the general considerations on constitutional law and the function of constitutional justice.[8] Concepts are cleared up, new doctrinal categories are introduced (normally imported from the German and Italian constitutional law and case law). The connection – already foreseen in art. 10.2 SC – between "constitutional law on fundamental rights" and international instruments on human rights as well as the relation with the jurisprudence of the European Court of Human rights was also established at that time.

There is probably nothing so characteristic of the Spanish constitutional commentary during this first period as the concern, or even the obsession to affirm the normativity of the Constitution. Let us stress that the point was not constitutional supremacy, but the value of the constitution as a legal rule, its legally binding character. That concern, indeed, had ingrained itself in the Constitution, with an oddly redundant article 9.1 which establishes the obligation of all citizens and authorities to comply with the Constitution ("and the rest of the legal order"). The explanation of this collective concern is to be sought in the specific constitutional history of Spain because, after all, the country had a long experience with constitutions that have never been followed and that were replaced without ever having succeeded in unfolding all their effects. However, and here began the doctrinal complication, the emphasis on "the constitution as a legal rule"[9] was accompanied by the emphasis on the "legal peculiarities of the constitution as a legal rule".[10] All this is to stress that the

[8] A prime example in STC 17/1981 whose legal grounds consist of a "lesson" on one of the constitutional procedures (the certified question of unconstitutionality) and an interesting digression on the relationship between the judiciary and the Constitutional Court. The holding of the judgment is the least (the Tribunal finds no need to rule on the constitutionality of the law in question). The judgment is significant for its doctrine, since, by not deciding on the merits, it lacks the effectiveness of res judicata.

[9] This is the title of a famous and enormously influential book by Eduardo García de Enterría, *La constitución como norma jurídica y el Tribunal Constitucional* (Civitas 1981). Francisco Rubio Llorente had introduced the same issue in 'La Constitución como fuente del Derecho' in AA.VV., *La Constitución Española y las fuentes del derecho* (DGCE/IEF 1979) vol. I, 51–74.

[10] Also a title of a pointed and widely cited law review article by Alejandro Nieto: "Peculiaridades jurídicas de la norma constitucional" (1983) 1 *Revista de Administración Pública* 371.

peculiarities of the Constitution should not be detrimental to its effectiveness, although they ought to alter in a significant way the mode and manner of its interpretation (and most likely, its application). In sum: as a norm, the Constitution called for a legal interpretation, but [as a peculiar norm] not of the kind that ordinary courts were familiar with, which was an additional reason in support of a specialized constitutional jurisdiction. Unlike what happened in the field of more traditional branches of law, constitutional law did not have at that time a robust doctrinal reference. This gives an idea of the central role and enormous responsibility of the Constitutional Court when faced with the task of constitutional interpretation in the beginning.[11]

A strong tradition of studies on the theory of legal interpretation has existed in Spain, both in the field of the more generalist law, namely civil law, and in the area of the theory and philosophy of law. The interest of civil law scholars goes far back in time and their collective doctrinal enterprise somehow took shape in the Preliminary Title of the Spanish nineteenth-century Civil Code after a reform introduced in 1974. The appropriateness of including in the Code a legal provision on the rules of interpretation has been discussed, and their actual effectiveness has also proved controversial. But the interesting thing is to address the reasons for this regulation. Limiting the freedom and discretion of the interpreter by way of unifying the interpretation criteria, setting those ones conventionally accepted by academic doctrine, appears to be the most plausible reason behind it. On this basis, art. 3.1 of the Civil Code stipulates that "Rules shall be construed according to the proper meaning of their wording and in connection with the context, with their historical and legislative background and with the social reality of the time in which they are to be applied, mainly attending to their spirit and purpose". What we find is the Savigny legacy with the addition of the teleological and evolutionary (or sociological) criteria. The provision is consistent with the Spanish civil law legal culture and tradition, which favors the objective approach (attentive to the *ratio legis* more than to the *legislatoris voluntas*) and establishes a preference for the textualist or literal interpretation. The principle of the completeness of the legal order, associated with the nineteenth-century dogma of the rational legislator, is behind the regulation of analogy in art. 4.1 as a technique to fill gaps in the law: "Where the

[11] "The Court will assume before our people no small responsibility. In a fundamental part, the fate of our Constitution and the possibility of definitive rooting of democracy and freedom in our land will be in its hands", Eduardo García de Enterría (n 9) 207.

relevant rules fail to contemplate a specific case, but do regulate another similar one in which the same ratio is perceived, the latter rule shall be applied by analogy".

Whether these rules, criteria and approaches for legal interpretation are equally accurate for constitutional interpretation – that was the issue when the Constitutional Court came into operation, and that it largely remains now with an experienced Court.

As we will see in the next part of this study, the Court has made use of all the classical criteria of interpretation. It has also incorporated those specific principles of interpretation of the Constitution, first discussed in a Congress of the German Association of Professors of Public Law in 1961, and later canonized by the German doctrine: the principles of the unity of constitution, of practical concordance and of functional correctness.[12]

The examination of constitutional jurisprudence shows the absence of a pattern of use leading up to a rationalization or hypothesis regarding the methodological preferences of the Court on constitutional interpretation.[13] The inevitable conclusion is that the plurality of methods and criteria, attached to the absence of patterns of use, has the effect

[12] References to this Congress, the relevant contributions to it by Horst Ehmke or Hans Peter Schneider and the subsequent doctrinal development of the canons of interpretation, e.g. by Konrad Hesse, are in Peter Häberle, "Methoden und Prinzipien der Verfassungsinterpretation – ein Problemkatalog" (2000) 12 *Revue européenne de droit public* 867. The reception in Spain, and many Latin American countries, of this doctrinal construction took place mainly through Konrad Hesse's work, early translated by Pedro Cruz Villalón. See Konrad Hesse, *Escritos de Derecho Constitucional* (Centro de Estudios Constitucionales 1983; new enlarged edition in 2011 by P. Cruz Villalón and M. Azpitarte Sánchez).

[13] Two pioneering works – with origins in doctoral dissertations – which attempted a comprehensive and systematic analysis of the methods and criteria of interpretation employed by the Spanish Constitutional Court deserve mention. Both were published in the mid-1980s: Enrique Alonso García, *La interpretación de la Constitución* (Centro de Estudios Constitucionales 1984) and Francisco Javier Ezquiaga Ganuzas, *La argumentación en la justicia constitucional española* (Instituto Vasco de Administración Pública 1987). The Spanish legal literature on constitutional interpretation is now rich with remarkable contributions; however, there were no subsequent updates or followers of the Herculean enterprise of exhaustive analysis of constitutional case law. Representative works on the general subject of constitutional intepretation are: Manuel Aragón Reyes, "La interpretación de la Constitución y el carácter objetivado del control jurisdiccional", 17 *Revista Española de Derecho Constitucional* 1986, 85. Manuel Atienza, 'Constitución y argumentación", XXIV *Anuario de Filosofía del Derecho*, 2007, 199. Maria Luisa Balaguer Callejón, *Interpretación de la Constitución y Ordenamiento Jurídico*, (Tecnos 1997). Raúl Canosa Usera, *Interpretación constitucional y fórmula política*, (Centro de Estudios Constitucionales, 1988). Angel Carrasco Perera, "El juicio de razonabilidad en la justicia constitucional", 11 *Revista Española de Derecho Constitucional*, 1984, 39. Pedro Cruz Villalón, "*¿Reserva de Constitución?*", 9 *Revista Española de Derecho Constitucional*, 1983, 185. Francisco Javier Díaz Revorio,

of amplifying the freedom of the interpreter, who, potentially at least, can choose either method, one or the other criterion, depending on the interpretive results offered – a problem soon highlighted by a distinguished Spanish constitutional scholar.[14]

There is still a complementary avenue of analysis. Examination to the Court pronouncements on meta-interpretational matters – its understanding of the role of the interpreter of the Constitution, of its own position as the supreme interpreter of the Constitution, and its relationship with other actors (specifically, the legislator) – provides another viewpoint that leads to interesting if not clearer results in terms of articulation of methods or criteria of interpretation. We see high oscillation amplitude, from statements justifying the greatest restraint and modest role for the judicial interpreter[15] (and correlative great deference towards the legislator[16]), to statements enthroning the supreme interpreter and claiming reserved domains of interpretation, exclusive for the Constitutional Court.[17] In the end, what we find is a genuine concern on the part

Valores superiores e interpretación constitucional (Centro de Estudios Políticos y Constitucionales, 1997). Javier Jiménez Campo, "Interpretación Constitucional", in: *Enciclopedia Jurídica Básica* III (Civitas, 1995) 3685–3690. Juan José Moreso, *La indeterminación del Derecho y la interpretación de la Constitución* (Centro de Estudios Constitucionales, 1997). Luis Prieto Sanchís, "Notas sobre la interpretación constitucional", 9 *Revista del Centro de Estudios Constitucionales* 1991, 175. Tomas Requena López, *Sobre la función, los medios y los límites de la interpretación de la Constitución* (Comares, 2001). Francisco Rubio Llorente, "Problemas de la interpretación constitucional", in this author's collected works: *La Forma del Poder* III (Centro de Estudios Políticos y Constitucionales, 2012).

[14] Ignacio de Otto Pardo, "La posición del Tribunal Constitucional a partir de la doctrina de la interpretación constitucional" in AA.VV., *El Tribunal Constitucional* (IEF 1981), 1934–50. According to this author the only foreseeable remedy to this situation would come under the guise of a Theory of the Constitution which would provide the principles and guides orienting constitutional interpretation.

[15] E.g. STC 11/1981, FJ 7: "The Constitution is a framework of coincidences sufficiently broad to provide room for political options of extremely different kinds. The work of interpreting the Constitution does not necessarily consist of closing the door on options or variants imposing one of them in an authoritarian manner. This conclusion should only be reached when the unanimous nature of the interpretation is imposed by the play of interpretive criteria."

[16] *Ibid.* "It therefore corresponds to ordinary legislature which is the representative at any given time of popular sovereignty, to create a regulation of the conditions of exercise of the right, which will be more restrictive or open, in accordance with the political guidelines which have motivated it, provided it does not go beyond the limits imposed by specific constitutional norms and the generic restriction of art. 53 SC [respect for the essential content of the right]."

[17] In a rather cryptic way: STC 76/1983, FJ 4: "It corresponds to the Constitutional Court, in its role as supreme interpreter of the Constitution, guarding the permanent distinction between objectivation of constituent power and performance of the constituted

of the Court, persistent over time, to retain intact its power of creation of constitutional doctrine through interpretation:

> The Constitutional Court, as the supreme interpreter of the Constitution, is the only body with jurisdiction to determine the authentic – and indisputable – definition of the constitutional principles and categories. No other infra-constitutional ruler, due to their very nature, can act as an extended or newly arisen constituent power by formalizing one of the various meanings of a constitutional category. That task corresponds exclusively to the Constitutional Court and is likewise, always, an elemental principle of constitutional guarantee and defense: the principle that, in the event of a violation and in the lack of any express reform, allows the meaning to be adapted to that period in history.[18]

If at any time this power were to ally with a consistent practice of constitutional stare decisis, the effect would be the generation of constitutional common law, that is, judge-made constitutional law supreme in character.

2 *The Court and Constitutional Litigation*

According to the Constitution, the Constitutional Court has jurisdiction over the whole Spanish territory and is competent to hear three main types of cases: (a) constitutional review of legislation (including statutes and other norms of the same hierarchy and legal force), (b) resolution of conflicts and (c) application for protection (*amparo*) of constitutionally guaranteed fundamental rights. The law regulating the Court (Organic Law 2/1979 on the Constitutional Court, of 3 October 1979), which is also law of constitutional procedure, has added to the jurisdiction provided for in the Constitution two new types of proceedings: the process in defense of local autonomy and a warranty procedure of the constitutional jurisdiction against acts or decisions deemed to be detrimental to it. Constitutional jurisdiction is an exclusive, original and final jurisdiction. There is no further appeal.

powers . . . [t]he ordinary legislator cannot dictate merely interpretative rules, whose sole purpose is to define the one-way interpretation, among several possible, to be attached to a particular concept or precept of the Constitution, thus reducing the possibilities or alternatives of the Constitution to a single one, the legislator is in fact fulfilling the constituent's work and placing itself functionally on the same plane, crossing in doing so the dividing line between the constituent power and constituted power."

[18] STC 31/2010, FJ 57

Constitutional review of legislation (a) is carried out through three different types of procedures: (a.1) preventive or ex ante review of constitutionality, with respect to international treaties and Statutes of Autonomy; (a.2) abstract control of constitutionality by direct appeal; and (a.3) concrete control of constitutionality by certified questions of constitutionality brought before the court by ordinary judges. As previously noted, it is important to emphasize that the control of constitutionality before the Constitutional Court is aimed solely at the control of laws and regulations having the force of Parliamentary Acts (statutes, legislative decrees, decree-laws), international treaties in force and standing orders of legislative bodies (both Houses of central Parliament and legislative assemblies of the Autonomous Communities). Ordinary courts are competent to decide by themselves constitutional issues involving all other regulations.[19]

Through (b) conflicts jurisdiction, the Court resolves the so-called (b.1) "horizontal" conflicts, i.e. between organs of the State (legislative Houses, Government, General Council of the Judiciary) and conflicts of jurisdiction between the State and the Autonomous Communities or between Autonomous Communities (b.2). Conflicts can be positive (State and Regions claim jurisdiction on a matter) or negative (when both State and Regions refuse to act adducing lack of competence on a particular matter).

Finally, in (c) *amparo* procedure, the Court resolves individual complaints against acts said to be in violation of fundamental rights and liberties (recognized in arts. 14–29 SC plus conscientious objection to military service of art. 30.2 SC).

The standing to initiate the constitutional proceeding depends on the type of process. There is nothing similar to an *actio popularis.* In fact, individuals (natural or legal persons) cannot challenge laws before the Constitutional Court. The competence to file an abstract review of constitutionality is conferred to the President of the Government, the Ombudsperson, 50 deputies or 50 senators, and the legislative assemblies or governments of Autonomous regions. All of them have also standing to apply for the *ex ante* control of Statutes of Autonomy. Preventive control of International Treaties is on demand of the central government or any

[19] Ordinary courts are always competent to decide the applicable law to solve the cases in their jurisdiction (*iura novit curia*). This implies that they are also competent to decide if pre-constitutional law, including statutes, is still in force or has been derogated by the Constitution. See *infra* at 6 (*Applicability of the Constitution*).

of the two Houses of Parliament. Concrete review happens always at the request of a judicial body.[20] Conflicts of jurisdiction between the State and Autonomous Communities or between the latter can be brought by the central or autonomous governments claiming title over of the competence. Negative conflicts may also be brought by interested natural or legal persons. In the case of the *amparo*, the person (natural or legal) directly affected or, on behalf of her, the Ombudsperson or the Public Prosecutor Office has standing to lodge an appeal for constitutional protection.

The regulation concerning persons who can intervene in constitutional proceedings is highly restrictive. The starting point is that subjective interests are not aired in the constitutional processes, but the public interest in the guarantee of the Constitution; therefore, save what is established for *amparo* proceedings, intervention is usually reserved to institutional persons and bodies which represent and defend public interests. Even in the certification procedure, the intervention before the Constitutional Court of litigants in the judicial process *a quo* (where the constitutional question was raised) is very limited.[21] Nor is there a figure similar to the *amicus curiae.*

In all proceedings before the Constitutional Court there is an admission process. The Court checks that applications meet requirements of form, time and manner as established by law. In *amparo* proceedings, due to a chronic problem of overabundance of applications (many of them trivial), the screening procedure is particularly strict and has unique elements. Since the 2007 reform, the law allows the Court to make a selection of *amparo* petitions based on their "special constitutional significance" ("*especial transcendencia constitucional*"), regardless of the plausibility or severity of the denounced injury. The law leaves ample room for the Court to decide in each case whether this requirement is met. Aware of the difficulty for *amparo* plaintiffs which have to deal with such an indeterminate requirement, the Court specified in STC 155/2009, FJ 2 the kind of cases considered to have "special constitutional significance". In *Arribas Anton*

[20] According to art. 163 SC: "If a judicial body considers, in some action, that a regulation with the status of law which is applicable thereto, and upon the validity of which the judgment depends, may be contrary to the Constitution, it may bring the matter before the Constitutional Court in the circumstances, manner and subject to the consequences to be laid down by law, which shall in no case be suspensive".

[21] Only after a reform introduced in 2007 in the Law of the Constitutional Court, are litigants in the original lawsuit allowed to introduce a brief before the Constitutional Court. The reform was aimed to conform to the recommendation of the Strasbourg Court in *Ruiz Mateos v. Spain*, decided 23 June 1993.

v. Spain, decided 20 January 2015, the Strasbourg Court found that subjecting the admissibility of an *amparo* petition to the existence of objective criteria and to a requirement of justification by the appellant of its special constitutional significance was neither disproportionate nor in breach of the right of access to the Constitutional Court.

The procedure before the Constitutional Court is written. Although the law of the Court opens the possibility of oral argument (art. 85.3), there have been very few occasions in which such a possibility has been carried out, and always in *amparo* cases. In addition to the documents filed by the parties in the procedure, the Court may request reports from institutions and experts and it is also possible to introduce evidence. Nonetheless, the Constitutional Court is neither a "court of facts", nor a technical supervisory body, or a pure appeals tribunal in charge of reviewing the correctness of judicial decisions below.[22]

Resolutions are adopted by the full court (Plenary meeting of 12 members) or by the Chambers (there are two Chambers composed of 6 members each). Decisions of admissibility are normally issued by the four Sections (3 members each). The full court is in charge of all proceedings within the Court's jurisdiction, although *amparo* proceedings are normally decided by the Chambers.

Decisions on the merits take the form of a judgment (*sentencia*). When deciding the initial rejection, withdrawal and lapse, the Court issues a reasoned order (auto). In the *amparo* proceedings, decisions of admissibility are adopted by non-reasoned order (*providencia*), which in the case of rejection shall specify the requirements' breach. All judgments and some reasoned and non-reasoned orders are published in the "Official State Gazette"[23] and are also accessible at the Constitutional Court

[22] "Constitutional review is not a review of legislative technique, nor is this Court allowed to review and rectify interpretations corresponding to ordinary judges" stated the Court in STC 109/1987, FJ 3. The Court does not rule on issues other than those laid down in the application. Even if an *amparo* petition can be addressed against a judicial ruling or omission, art. 44.1b) of the law of the Court warns that the Constitutional Court in no circumstances will adjudicate the facts that led to the proceedings in which the denounced violation of right occurred; and art. 54 cautions that the role of the Court shall consist solely in determining whether the applicant's rights or freedoms have been violated and in preserving or restoring those rights or freedoms and that "it shall refrain from further comment on the actions of the judicial bodies".

[23] Since 1 January 2009 the State Official Gazette is an electronic publication (www.boe.es), thus easily accessible for the general public. At the webpage of the Constitutional Court (www.tribunalconstitucional.es) it is possible to find, along with other institutional

website. According to the Constitution, constitutional judgments have res judicata effect and no appeal may be brought against them. Judgments declaring the unconstitutionality and, generally, all those judgments not limited to the guaranteeing of a right have general (*erga omnes*) effect and shall be fully binding on all persons.

Within the scope of constitutional review of legislation, the court has developed over time, just as have other constitutional courts, a typology of judgments to fit the nuances of unconstitutionality in different circumstances. The law of the Court (art. 38) does not consider more than the alternative "unconstitutional / not unconstitutional" and specifies that "where the judgment declares the unconstitutionality, it shall also declare the nullity of the contested provision". In the constitutional case law, however, we are to find judgments of unconstitutionality without nullity, with deferred nullity, with deferred nullity plus a term-limit for the lawmaker to produce a new rule in conformity with the Constitution; interpretative judgments declaring that the law is not unconstitutional if interpreted in a certain way (or alternatively, if it is not interpreted in a certain way) or declaring a certain interpretation unconstitutional but not the written text; and judgments declaring that although the statute is "still constitutional" the legislator is to better adjust it to the rule of the constitution.

On average – and leaving aside the anomalous period between 2006 and 2010 – the Court issues more than 200 judgments per year, around 300 reasoned orders and no fewer than 7000 non-reasoned orders of inadmissibility for *amparo* applications. Although the number of *amparo* petitions decreased after the 2007 reform of the law of the Court (in the previous year, 2006, the Court registered 11,471 *amparo* petitions) the volume is still huge (7203 out of the total 7369 new cases in the Court in 2015) and burdens the activity of the Tribunal in all aspects. Along with constitutional review of legislation judgments (163 in 2015) the *amparo* judgments are the second large group (98 in 2015) followed at a distance by conflict of jurisdiction cases (7 in 2015). However, we must not lose sight of the fact that at present, an important number of constitutional review cases involve a controversy over competences.[24]

information, all reasoned decisions (judgments and orders) issued, and a selection of judgments translated.

[24] All data mentioned here are extracted from the Annual Reports of the Constitutional Court edited by the General Secretary of the Constitutional Court and accessible at the Court's webpage.

A graphic comparison of Court case-load between years 2010–2014 (left column: number of cases) shows that the docket of pending cases is persistent and overwhelming:

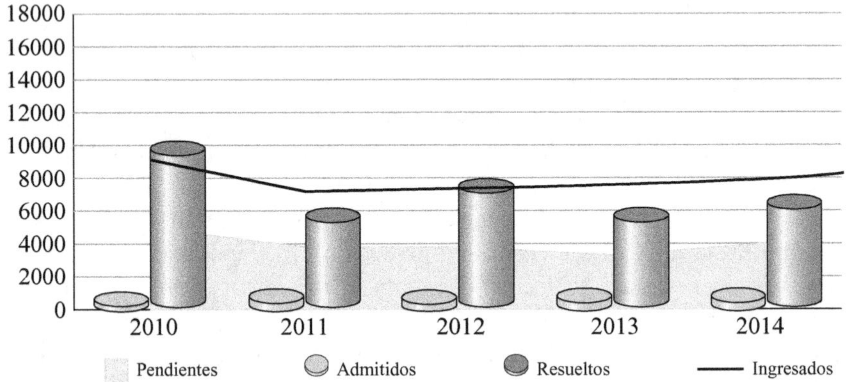

Grey area – pending cases / cylinder on the left for each year – admitted / cylinder on the right for each year – decided / black line – lodged.
Source: Annual Report 2014. Spanish Constitutional Court

3 *The Judges*

The Constitutional Court is composed of 12 judges appointed by the King on the proposal of the Congress (4 judges); of the Senate, after consultation with the legislative assemblies of the Autonomous Communities (4 judges); of the General Council of the Judiciary (2 judges) and of the Government (2 judges). They are appointed for a period of 9 years, at the end of which they cannot be immediately re-elected.[25] The renewal of judges is not all at once, but in blocks of 4 judges every three years.[26] Immediately after each renewal, the members of the Court elect one of their own to serve as its President, for a period of three years, which is renewable. A Vice-President is elected at the same meeting.

The Constitution requires that the judges of the Court be chosen from among "Judges and Prosecutors, University professors, public officials and lawyers, all of whom must be jurists of recognized standing with

[25] Reappointment could take place in a non-consecutive renewal.

[26] In recent times, however, Congress and Senate have revealed unable to provide for a timely appointment of judges, producing a serious disorder in the cycle of renewals that a 2010 law reform tried to remedy. Art. 16 of the Law of the Court as amended establishes that "in case of a delay in the renewal by thirds, the time delay in the renewal shall be reduced from the term of office of those appointed".

at least fifteen years' experience in the professional exercise" (art. 159 SC). University professors were a majority in the first Court and their presence remains important, although since the 1990s the number of judges from the judicial career has been on the rise. In contrast, other legal professions have had minor presence (there have been few lawyers and a single public prosecutor so far). The system of incompatibilities prevents members of the Tribunal from being active politicians, but there have been Constitutional Court judges with previous political experience. The Constitution provides that they cannot occupy "leadership positions" in political parties or trade unions. However, it has been discussed whether they should renounce membership of these organizations, as it is the case for ordinary judges.[27]

4 *Legal Scholarship and Constitutional Reasoning*

The constitutional case law has always been subject to scholarly attention. In the early years of the Court – which, as we have reported, were also the early years of the Constitution – its pronouncements were essential not only for the study of the Constitution, but to the doctrinal development of Constitutional Law on central aspects (sources of law, fundamental rights and, above all, territorial organization and distribution of competences). Constitutional case law was also a guide for interpretation "in harmony with the constitution" of the entire legal system, giving rise to the phenomenon commonly known as the "constitutionalization of the legal order". Indeed, beyond the realm of Spanish Constitutional Law "under construction", constitutional jurisprudence induced substantial changes in the approach of more traditional branches of law, very prominently in criminal law, labor law, administrative law and procedural law.

Nevertheless, the centrality of the constitutional jurisprudence in the early stages did not lead, opposite to what might be imagined, to an even more radical shift in the legal culture, that is, the transition from a "law of professors" to a "law of judges" (constitutional judges, of course). For

[27] The discussion was the issue of a series of Constitutional Court resolutions (starting with ATC 180/2013), deciding several requests to recuse the then President of the Court after it appeared in the news that he had kept contributing as paying affiliate member to the "Partido Popular" (at the time, in Government), after being appointed constitutional judge. As a ground to dismiss, the Court referred to the constitutional prescription that only precludes occupying leading positions in these organizations. Two members of the Court disagreed. Non-active political membership appears to be the accepted unwritten convention.

even if a sustained trend of "judicialization of the legal system" was at that time put into motion, it cannot be overlooked that constitutional judgments were always of quite unique quality. Not merely because of their special binding force, as established by the constitution, but above all because they were truly atypical, very different in tone and fabric of ordinary judicial pronouncements, including those of the Supreme Court. After all, most of the judges of the first Constitutional Court were reputed scholars who, in their role of constitutional judges, kept on writing as scholars. Years later, one of the members of the first Tribunal recognized that those judgments looked more like law review articles than like judicial pronouncements.[28]

There is no doubt that legal academia contributed to the consolidation of the constitutional jurisdiction and its doctrine. Although some voices warned against a blind following of constitutional doctrine and lack of critical attitude, the criticisms that some commentators have addressed to French or German constitutional law professors – lamenting their excessive submission to constitutional case law[29] – do not seem applicable to the Spanish case. In any event, the current situation is very different. The *auctoritas* of the Spanish Constitutional Court as an institution is not generally controverted, but the constitutional jurisprudence has long ceased to have the central role that it played in the first stage. Constitutional experience and a notable scientific production have fueled an independent academic debate, which no longer looks to the Court for guidance. On the contrary, it aims to influence the Court's decisions. Nor is the Court the professorial collegial body of the early days, and issues to be decided, even when they are novel and attract attention from the media, are rarely seminal in the way many of the first period were. The existence of an important doctrinal corpus on the most varied matters, the abundance of bibliographic references, and the easy accessibility of information on the case law of other constitutional courts facilitate the work of research of the Court, but also diminish the degree of acceptable originality in judicial reasoning. The decisions of the court are more exposed to criticism than they ever were in the past.

[28] Francisco Rubio Llorente, "El Tribunal Constitucional" in *La forma del poder. Estudios sobre la Constitución* (Centro de Estudios Políticos y Constitucionales 2012), vol. III, 1405.

[29] See Bernhard Schlink, "German Constitutional Culture in Transition" (1992–1993) 14 *Cardozo Law Review* 730 and Martin Shapiro, "The Success of Judicial Review and Democracy" in Martin Shapiro and Alec Stone Sweet, *On Law, Politics and Judicialization* (Oxford University Press 2002) 170–6.

Even if the Court does not exert the doctrinal influence it had in the beginning, an appointment as a judge of the Court remains prestigious. And it is a well-paid position: the assigned public salary is one of the highest in the Administration (certainly superior to that of the Prime Minister). In the General State Budget for 2016[30] it is set to €130,564.38 per year for the President, and €111,625.38 for each of the associate Judges.

B Arguments in Constitutional Reasoning

The commentary and analysis regarding the arguments in the constitutional judgments that follow covers a set of 40 judgments selected for their relevance in teaching constitutional law. A large majority of these decisions are "first impression" cases, in which the Constitutional Court establishes a doctrine and sets a guideline for the future. What makes these judgments important is not that they theorize on juridical arguments, nor that they are impeccably reasoned, but rather the approach they employ, the means by which they confront a new constitutional dispute, and the solution they offer. Some of these judgments are widely considered exemplary; others, by contrast, are highly controversial, and some could even be considered as belonging to an "anti-canon". In many cases, their singularity is what makes them so atypical. More than half of these judgments (23) belong to what we could call the foundational period of the Court, from 1981 to 1992, the year in which the last justices from the first Court finished their terms. It is difficult to choose among all the decisions of this era, as so many are relevant. The first Court created doctrine in practically every case it resolved at a time in which there was so much to be done.[31] The basic criterion to select the later judgments was to opt for those cases which have obtained special notoriety in order to highlight particularly controversial issues or those cases which have contributed in a singular way to establish doctrine which served to resolve later controversies.

5 *The Structure of Constitutional Arguments*

A large majority (29) of the decisions fit generally into the framework of linear argumentation which we call a one-line conclusive argument. This framework easily accommodates the traditional Euro-continental

[30] Law 48/2015, of October 29, on the state budget for the year 2016.

[31] The experts who gave their opinion on the judgments selected focused on this period when suggesting some alternative judgment.

understanding of the judgment as syllogism, in which the conclusion follows "logically" from a process of subsumption, a process which involves the previous and essential steps of determining the premises in such a way that in circumscribing the issue being presented before the judge (the minor premise), and establishing the relevant and applicable law to the case (the major premise), the legal solution (conclusion) becomes apparent. It is true that this image for judgments has been heavily criticized, being considered too simple and unrealistic. Even so it remains part of the juridical culture, at least formally, probably because it reinforces the notion of the judgment as a markedly technical and coherent decision, in which neither purely subjective preferences nor arbitrary imposition play a part. The Spanish Constitutional Court in *grosso modo* draws on this notion when it examines the sufficient grounding of the decisions by ordinary judges to determine whether the right to a "judicial" decision has been violated under the terms of the Constitution,

> ... given the impossibility of creating Law as a system of pure logic, this Court has joined, to the requisite of formal coherence in reasoning, a requisite that reasoning itself, from a legal perspective, cannot be labeled unreasonable. To that end ... judgments cannot be considered grounded and reasoned if, at first glance and without great intellectual and argumentative effort, it can be established that they draw on nonexistent or manifestly erroneous premises or the development of the argument falls into logical failures of such magnitude that the conclusions reached cannot be considered based on any of the reasons alluded to.[32]

Without needing to evaluate whether it is correct to apply the notion of the syllogism to the case of constitutional judgments,[33] there is no doubt that they are, as ordinary judgments, grounded in legal reasoning by the means of which the Court resolves the constitutional complaint in the terms posed by the application. "The Constitutional Court by its very nature and by the rule of Law", reads the early STC 5/1981, FJ 6, "is required to justify its decisions in response to the allegations of the parties by

[32] STC 224/2003, 15 December, FJ 4. In this decision, the Constitutional Court ruled that a violation of the right to a grounded judicial decision had occurred (art 24.1 SC) upon observing that in the case presented to it, the judge had committed a "logic flaw manifest in the argumentation" as it lacked "the minor premise of the syllogism".

[33] With regard to the process of control of constitutionality, a dissenting vote of STC 247/2007 refers to the technique of the "syllogism of constitutionality" as the appropriate structure for reasoning, while at the same time criticizing the abandoning of such a structure in the specific case, in which the Court proceeded with an interpretation in accordance with the Constitution.

interpreting the constitutional and legal precepts whose constitutionality is in dispute". In an unusual case resolved by STC 133/2013, the Court ruled that it may even examine the sufficiency of grounding of one of its own decisions to reject a petition.[34]

The interpretation of the Constitution is, thus, instrumental, inserted into the legal grounds as a prior step (the determination of the premises) in deciding if a challenged law is unconstitutional, or if an alleged fundamental right has been violated, or if the reproach of incompetence is founded or not. The accumulation or convergence of arguments is present in a small number of the judgments examined (6 and 6, respectively). Significantly, the dialogic discursive structure (i.e., the use of parallel, individually inconclusive, but together conclusive arguments) is characteristic of decisions on issues which polarize public opinion (ideologies in schools, abortion, same-sex marriage[35]) or in which the elaboration of theory is controversial (the relationship between a national and European constitutions or the constitutional nature and function of the Statutes of the Autonomous Communities[36]).

6 *Types of Arguments in Constitutional Reasoning*

Establishing/Debating the Text of the Constitution None of the judgments examined question the Constitution as it has been handed down.

Applicability of the Constitution As previously mentioned, among the most important undertakings of the Court was the assurance of the normativity of the Constitution, its status as an immediately effective, as opposed to a merely programmatic, law. The regulatory effects of the Constitution, and their impact on prior (pre-constitutional) law, is an issue central to STC 4/1981, in which the Court ruled on the effect of the Constitution as *lex suprema*, but also as *lex posterior* which derogates

[34] In STC 133/2013, the Constitutional Court ruled on an *amparo* petition filed by former justices of the same Court against the judgment by the Supreme Court (Civil Chamber) which sentenced them to pay damages as a result of the designation of strict liability for incurring in forbidden *non liquet* (refusing to issue a judicial decision). In reversing the Supreme Court decision, the full bench of the Constitutional Court concluded that, contrary to the erroneous appraisal by the Supreme Court, the constitutional justices had reached the decision in question basing themselves entirely on the Law and that, conversely, it was the judgment of the Supreme Court which contained flawed grounding stemming from a clear error in its premises.

[35] SSTC 5/1981, 53/1985, 198/2012.

[36] DTC 1/2004 and STC 31/2010.

all prior laws which oppose it (without waiting for a declaration of unconstitutionality by the Constitutional Court). The reasoning of the Court aims to guarantee the effectiveness of the Constitution, and the solution it offers illustrates its interest in preventing "shyness" on the part of ordinary judges from hindering the unfolding of the legal effects of the Constitution in the face of pre-constitutional law. After alluding to the alternatives offered by the Italian and German experience, the Court opted for an intermediate solution recognizing the judges' competence to evaluate and proclaim the derogation of pre-constitutional law contrary to the Constitution, but at the same time opening up the possibility, in unclear cases, for judges to raise the question of constitutionality to resolve (with *erga omnes* effects) the issue of possible incompatibility of pre-constitutional law with the Constitution.

In Spanish jurisdiction, there is nothing resembling "political question doctrine". The Constitutional Court must decide all of the applications admitted. Nevertheless, the question of the applicability of the Constitution is directly linked, in some cases, to determining the scope of the Court's competence. In both STC 292/2000 and STC 134/2000, the Court detailed how the canon of constitutionality was to be built for the case in order to distinguish its operation from other control parameters used to measure the compatibility of national law with EU law or international law. The issue of determining the scope of constitutional control is also central in STC 214/1999 regarding the scope of review by the Constitutional Court of ordinary courts' judicial performance, drawn on the premise that the Constitution "does not guarantee judicial correctness". The nature of the "pouvoir estatuant" (the power to make the Statute of Autonomy) and its legal submission to the Constitution are among the various big issues dealt with in STC 31/2010.

Analogies As András Jakab reminds us, analogy is not a means of interpretation in and of itself, but rather a rule for the application of law that allows for the filling of legal gaps.[37] As such, art. 4.1 of the Spanish Civil Code states that "where the relevant rules fail to contemplate a specific case, but do regulate another similar one in which the same ratio is perceived, the latter rule shall be applied by analogy". The Spanish Constitutional Court has resorted to this technique on various occasions, usually to solve constitutional disputes pursuant to the Constitution where there is no specific constitutional rule and to maintain similarity to regulated

[37] András Jakab, "Judicial Reasoning in Constitutional Courts: A European Perspective" (2013) 8 *German Law Journal* 1220.

cases. In some cases, this argument has allowed the Court to incorporate content in a more permanent way, literally "writing in". With respect to these cases, we can speak of the interpretive value of analogy *sensu stricto*. For instance, in STC 31/1984, the Constitutional Court used this argument to conclude that article 35.1 of the Spanish Constitution (on the right and duty to work), at including expressly the principle of equal pay for equal work without gender discrimination, included the same guarantee for the case of age difference; and in STC 23/1983, against the literal reading of the constitutional precept which seems to circumscribe the content of trade union freedom, the Constitutional Court applied an extensive interpretation which allows for the addition of content through analogy:

> as detailed and concrete as the wording of art 28.1 SC regarding the content of the trade union freedom may be, it must not be considered exhaustive or restrictive, but rather merely an example, with the consequence that the express listing of concrete rights which comprise generic trade union freedom does not exhaust, in the least, the total and global content of said freedom.[38]

In four of the decisions selected, analogy is a central aspect of the reasoning. In them, the Court has had to determine if there was an "equal legal relationship" from the point of view of the Constitution, and whether, as a consequence, the "same ratio" justifies equal legal treatment. The contribution of these cases to the interpretation of the Constitution is indirect, but it strengthens the effects of the Constitutional precepts by generating the doctrine which allows ordinary judges to fill relative legal gaps making use of the so-called *secundum Constitutionem* analogy.[39]

Ordinary Meaning of the Words of the Constitution or Reference to the "Wording of the Constitution" in General This argument repeats in over half of the cases selected. One might imagine that this follows a tradition of preference for a literal interpretation when interpreting laws, and codes in particular. Indeed, however you characterize the singularity

[38] The wording of art. 28.1 of the Constitution is as follows: "Trade union freedom includes the right to set up trade unions and to join the union of one's choice, as well as the right of trade unions to form confederations and to found international trade union organizations, or to become members thereof." Francisco Javier Ezquiaga Ganuzas refers to both cases of the use of analogy as a technique for constitutional interpretation in *La argumentación en la justicia constitucional y otros problemas de aplicación e interpretación del derecho* (México 2006) 34.

[39] Thereon, Javier Jiménez Campo, "Analogía '*secundum constitutionem*'" (1992) *Revista del Centro de Estudios Constitucionales* 9.

of the Constitutional interpretation, the Court has made the maxim its own that the "text" is the starting point and the limit of all interpretation. Nevertheless, the frequency of this argument is not indicative of its weight, which is relative. While in some decisions it seems to be the touchstone of argument,[40] in others it seems to be an argument the Court has not hesitated to discard as "misleading".[41]

Harmonizing Arguments Interpretation consistent with other elements of the domestic legal order is entirely habitual (31 cases). Along with the early adoption of the principle of constitutional unity in order to avoid inconsistent interpretations of constitutional precepts, the Court has drawn on the idea that the Constitution was not founded in a vacuum but rather in a preexisting legal system and therefore integrates as its own those principles rooted in the legal culture, provided they are compatible with constitutional provisions, principles and values.[42] Tellingly, it was by invoking long-established principles that the Court recognized the constitutional character of the *ne bis in idem* doctrine (*double jeopardy*), which is now an unwritten clause in the text of the Constitution.[43]

It is also usual (16 cases) that the Court relies on the interpretation of European laws and case law to support its interpretive choice. The latest evolution of the case law of the Court seems aimed at establishing a link between the guarantee of fundamental rights and the correct application of European law.[44]

Precedents (Former Own Cases) At this point in time, the citing of past decisions is not only ongoing and unavoidable, but also ritual. There is no doubt that the Court utilizes its established doctrine to solve cases; however, that is not to say that it ascribes to "stare decisis" in the same

[40] STC 72/1984, FJ 6: "Respect for the Constitution which art. 9 imposes on all public authorities makes it necessary that an interpretation which leads to a result other than that which is literally in the text on the Constitution is only conceivable when there is ambiguity or when the ambiguity is derived from the systematic coherence or connection between constitutional precepts".

[41] STC 18/1982, FFJJ 2 and 3: "There is a need that, on this occasion, we try to establish criteria which can serve to demarcate the line between the concepts of 'legislation' and 'execution' which art 149.1.7 of the Constitution uses... First of all, it is necessary to eschew mere literal interpretations; both the concept of 'legislation' and of 'execution' are broad enough to illustrate the need to reject an interpretation which simply assumes 'legislation' to mean the set of norms laws possessing the force of law and 'execution' to mean the set of specific implementation acts in a given area".

[42] STC 341/1993, FJ 8. [43] Anchored in art. 25.1 SC. See, STC 2/1981, FJ 4.

[44] On this precise line of evolvement, the recent STC 232/2015.

way as common law.[45] The citing of "precedents" does not always follow a clear order and, except in specific cases, the overabundance of references to former own cases obscures the identification of the "leading case" or the cases which make up the chain of precedents. Given that in the early years the doctrine of the Court was just taking shape, the selection of judgments illustrates how, starting in 1987, the reference to doctrine and previous decisions becomes a pattern.

Doctrinal Analysis of Legal Concepts or Principles Arguments based on dogmatic categories or concepts and the invoking of principles not expressly laid forth in the Constitution to support the grounds are entirely commonplace (33 cases). On the one hand, the Court takes into account and adopts concepts embraced by legal culture and tradition, generally without altering the accepted sense, albeit adapting them when necessary to what the Constitution requires. The Court did not have to explain references to good faith, *ne bis in idem*, retroactivity in bonus; or the principles of taxativity, of legal certainty, of legality, of legitimate expectation; the accusatory principle; or *pro actione* rule, among others. Occasionally re-interpretation has proven controversial.[46] Some of the concepts and principles have been imported and are typical in the practice of the constitutional jurisdictions (interpretation pursuant to the Constitution, the preservation of the law, the principle of democracy, of federal loyalty or comity, of militant democracy, of reasonableness, of proportionality, of weighting). It is in relation to territorial organization, and due to the lack of definition in the Constitution of the territorial model, that the Court has developed its most relevant doctrine (the concept of the "block of constitutionality", of autonomy, the categorization of competences as shared, concurrent or exclusive, the determination of basic State competences). Curiously, the Court has understood that the elaboration of these doctrinal categories and principles as applied to the definition of the territorial model is an exclusive competence of the Constitutional Court and cannot be "codified".[47] In other areas, the elaboration of doctrine has

[45] The considerations by Jan Komárek in "Reasoning with Previous Decisions: Beyond the Doctrine of Precedent" (2013) 61 *American Journal of Comparative Law* 149, are appropriate to the case.

[46] Revision of the notion of "prescription" in the area of criminal law has been a source of conflict between the Supreme and the Constitutional Court. See the dissenting opinion of Judge Rodríguez Arribas to STC 59/2010.

[47] Thereon, the considerations included in FJ 58 of STC 31/2010: "the definition of what are the legislative, regulatory and executive powers contained within the

been in collaboration with the legislature: the concept of "special constitutional significance", a central element in the present-day *amparo*, is a legal label whose content was clarified by the Constitutional Court, as shown in STC 155/2009, FJ 2.

Arguments from Silence In the building of its argument, it is not odd – it can be detected in 15 of the judgments selected – for the Court to pose the prior question as to how to interpret the fact that Constitution "says nothing" regarding some aspect relevant to an issue submitted to the Court for judgment – in other words, how to read "constitutional silence". In many cases, this approach does not go beyond a mere rhetorical resource, but on some occasions, the Court has solved the *quid* by applying interpretive logic which could be considered a variation on the systematic interpretation of the Constitution. A good example of this type of reasoning can be found in STC 114/1984 where the Court, in an *amparo* on the secrecy of communications, asked itself as to the proper legal treatment of evidence illegally obtained, in the absence of any provision in that regard.[48] In STC 103/2008, on the possibility of calling for a referendum in an Autonomous Community in an exercise of a hypothetical "right to decide", the Court held that in the face of the lack of an express constitutional provision, the possibility of interpreting that an implicit competence belongs to the Autonomous Community was excluded.[49] In STC 198/2012, on the constitutionality of the law regulating the marriage of people of the same sex, constitutional silence conditioned the whole argument, from the starting point that "the [legislative] option [adopted] was not excluded by the constitutional founders".

Teleological/Purposive Arguments Referring to the Purpose of the Text It is widely believed that teleological reasoning is the "natural" method for constitutional interpretation.[50] Irrespective of whether or not this

competences . . . These powers shall always and only be those that derive from the interpretation of the Constitution which is reserved to this Court, and . . . its content and scope shall only be those that may result from the evolution of this case-law."

48 "Despite lacking an express legal provision which establishes the procedural interdiction of the evidence acquired illegally, it is necessary to recognize that the preferential position of the fundamental rights in regulation and the confirmation of said rights as 'inviolable' (art. 10.1 of the Constitution), makes it impossible to admit evidence obtained in violation of a fundamental right or liberty to the procedure" (FJ 4).

49 "We should state, therefore, that in our constitutional system in matters of referenda there is no implicit jurisdiction or authority" (FJ 3).

50 There was an early insistence on the convenience of favoring this method of interpretation, both to ensure loyalty to the constitutional project and to remedy errors and lapses in the

is the case, it is clearly a frequent resource (31 cases of 40) in Spanish Constitutional case law. The resource of finalistic interpretation seems particularly appropriate in the case of guarantees of the constitutional rights and of all of the constitutional prescriptions which, in some way, set aims or orientation for the public powers. Finalistic interpretation of constitutional precepts implies that the interpretation of a legal precept in accordance with the Constitution will, therefore, adhere to it, as is very well reflected in STC 237/2005 (in which the Constitutional Court concluded that a restrictive interpretation, a "teleological reduction" of the law, harms the constitutional hermeneutical principle intrinsic in the guarantee of the *pro actione* principle).

Teleological/Purposive Arguments Referring to the Purpose of the Constitution-Maker (Including Travaux Préparatoires) In contrast to the previous argument, reference to *travaux préparatoires*, debates and, in general, constitutional interpretation grounded on the allegation of will or intention of the Constitution-maker is not a frequently used resource and, with few exceptions (4 cases), is not an argument of significant weight.[51] Even though in STC 53/1985 – in which the Court examines the constitutionality of the legislation decriminalizing abortion in certain circumstances – the Court considers it appropriate, given the "proximity in time", to take into account the debate of the Constitution-maker, the truth is that neither in the time nearer the drafting of the Constitution, nor after, has the Court identified loyalty to the Constitution as loyalty to the intention (*voluntas*) of its drafters. In fact, STC 198/2012 called for an evolving or progressive interpretation drawn on the fact that the Constitution must be read in light of modern-day issues and not be anchored to the view of those who wrote it.

Non-legal (Moral, Sociological, Economic) Arguments We have identified the presence of this type of argument in at least 11 of the cases; however, we must not forget that attention to these extra-legal considerations is often critical to the interpretation of constitutional rights and

text. Francisco Rubio Llorente, *La Constitución como Fuente del Derecho* (IEF 1979) 73–4; and Francisco Rubio Llorente and Manuel Aragón Reyes, "Enunciados aparentemente vacíos en la regulación constitucional del control de constitucionalidad" (1979) 7 *Revista de Estudios Políticos* 161.

[51] On its relative value the obiter consideration in STC 5/1981, FJ 9: "it is clear from parliamentary debates on this issue, *which comprise significant element of any interpretation, although they may not determine it*, that the constitutional legislature of 1978 wished . . . "

guarantees to such an extent that the very Constitution demands it.[52] Right from the start the use of the sociological argument is frequent and is very common on equality cases. Furthermore, attention to economic factors and data is also usual. The use of moral arguments is less common and more problematic when it is used in limiting the exercise of rights and freedoms or in evaluating the legitimacy of action by public authorities. The Spanish Constitution does not contain any express reference to morals as a limit to the exercise of rights[53]; thus, moral arguments are invariably a subject of criticism, even more so when not overtly recognized as such by the Court – as in STC 120/1990 and 214/1990. Representative in this respect is the dissenting vote by Judge Rubio Llorente in STC 53/1985, who laments the abandon of juridical rigor and the inclusion of ethical and value considerations in the Court's reasoning.

References to Scholarly Works Unlike what is regular in courts in common law countries, Spanish courts do not include references to authors and scholarly works in their judgments. In this regard, the Constitutional Court is no exception. Even in decisions in which the doctrinal influence of specific authors can be perceived, in the published text there is no trace of authors or their works. An example of the extent of the rigidity of this style of rule is STC 199/2013 in which the Court ruled on the probative value, in a criminal procedure, of the information resulting from a DNA sample from the suspect, taken without judicial authorization. The Court alludes to the US Supreme Court decision in *Maryland v. King* to support its argument; however, in the Spanish transcription of the American decision, the quotes and academic references present in the original text have been removed.[54]

We have identified two cases in the selection– SSTC 5/1981 and 15/1982 – representative of the exception to the rule of non-citation.

[52] For example, art. 16.3 SC addresses public authorities to take into account the religious beliefs of Spanish society.

[53] In STC 62/1982, FJ 3 the Court seems to suggest that morals have become a limit to freedom of expression, given their presence in the ECHR and thereby in the Constitution through the gate of art. 10.2 SC.

[54] The original fragment in *Maryland v. King*, 569 U.S. ··· (2013) reads: "the CODIS loci come from noncoding parts of the DNA that do not reveal the genetic traits of the arrestee. While science can always progress further, and those progressions may have Fourth Amendment consequences, alleles at the CODIS loci 'are not at present revealing information beyond identification.' Katsanis & Wagner, Characterization of the Standard and Recommended CODIS Markers, 58 J. Forensic Sci. S169, S171 (2013)". The transcription can be found in FJ 10 of STC 199/2013.

In both cases, there are express references to scholarly doctrine, though not to any specific author, as an authoritative argument for interpreting constitutional content. In STC 5/1981, the Court relies on "unanimous scholarly doctrine" to assert that freedom of association also encompasses the right to non-association, though this is not specifically set forth in the Constitution. In STC 15/1982, the Court expressly invokes "scholarly doctrine" to identify the content and scope of conscientious objection as a constitutional right and its link to ideological freedom. In both cases, given that the appeal to scholarly doctrine is generic, the argument does not seem to stray far from the use of concepts of doctrinal origin.[55]

References to Foreign (National) Law From the beginning, references to foreign law, with varying degrees of specificity, have been the norm (appearing in 23 judgments), thus illustrating the importance of comparative law on constitutional case law, and backs the well-known statement by Peter Häberle in order to consider comparative method as the "fifth" method of legal interpretation.[56] The abundance of foreign references is also an academic reflex, a professorial feature, not alien to the composition of the Court and the impact of the legal scholars who serve on it.

Some Concluding Remarks on the Types of Arguments in Constitutional Reasoning Often a judgment will combine more than one of the arguments we have examined here separately. Whether to strengthen the interpretive conclusion or to reveal constitutional ambiguity, the use of various methods in combination, despite any idea to the contrary, does not limit the interpreter's discretional space. In fact, the accumulation of interpretative arguments in the judgments we have characterized as discursive or dialogic in structure is taken as an indication of weakness in

[55] More exceptional, the mention of specific authors in the long separate opinion by Judge Tomás y Valiente to STC 5/1981, who in an openly professorial tone includes a quote from Kelsen and an express reference to the creation of the concept of institutional guarantee according to Carl Schmitt. The mention of authors fulfills a rhetorical function and is not central to the grounds. The rhetoric of mentioning authors and authorities can also be found, for instance, in the individual opinions of Judge Rodríguez-Zapata in SSTC 12/2008 (with reference to Kelsen) and 247/2007 (which includes a parade of names: Jacques Derrida, Charles Evans Hughes, and László Sólyom [wrongly spelt in the judgment as László Sóliom]).

[56] Peter Häberle, "Methoden und Prinzipien der Verfassungsinterpretation – ein Problemkatalog" (2000) 12 *Revue européenne de droit public* 867.

the conclusion, as denounced in several votes accompanying STC 53/1985 (abortion) and 198/2012 (same-sex marriage).

Of the judgments selected, none makes use of any method or argument other than those previously mentioned. Constitutional case law does, however, offer examples of the exceptional use of other methods, such as the noteworthy case of STC 126/1997 in which the Court embarked on a historical inquiry into the constitutionality of a medieval regulation which awarded preference to males over females in the succession of titles of nobility. After the long historical excursus, the Court concluded that the rule, in context, did not cause any effects on the right to equality as enshrined in the Constitution. The decision provoked one of the rare instances of legislative overruling.[57]

Lastly, it is worthwhile to draw attention to the only "imperative" criterion for interpretation required by the Constitution itself in art. 10.2, according to which: "the principles relating to the fundamental rights and liberties recognized by the Constitution shall be interpreted in conformity with the Universal Declaration of Human Rights and the international treaties and agreements thereon ratified by Spain".[58]

7 *The Weight of Arguments*

Unlike what occurs in other fields of Spanish law in which there is a convention as to the order or priority of use of interpretational criteria, an examination of constitutional case law yields no such convention. The Constitutional Court makes use of all the classical criteria of interpretation, under the terms set forth in Civil Code art. 3.1, without setting an order or general preference for use, but it does not see itself as confined by said limits, as proven by the discussion present in STC 198/2012 with regard to the "evolving interpretation" of the Constitution. Sporadic allusions to the text as a limit to interpretation do not describe an implicit preference for the literal method but are, instead, meant to serve as a reminders of the limits on the interpreter, who cannot attempt to reform the Constitution through interpretation.

It seems proper to highlight the special importance systematic interpretation has in the articulation of Constitutional doctrine. Systematic

[57] Law 33/2006, 30 October, on the equality between men and women in the succession of titles of nobility.

[58] In STC 198/2012 FJ 2 b the Court clarifies that noncompliance with this constitutional directive does not automatically imply a violation of the concerned right by "misinterpretation".

interpretation, inseparable from the principle of Constitutional unity resolutely adopted by the Constitutional Court, makes possible a coherent reading of the Constitutional regulation *ratione materiae*; the Court refers to the "economic Constitution",[59] the "territorial Constitution"[60] and the "system" of rights and guarantees,[61] and in each of these categories it has identified specific principles.

As previously noted, the ongoing referencing in constitutional judgments of earlier decisions must not be confused with the implementation of something similar to a *stare decisis* system in constitutional case law. The profusion of citations of prior judgments – which today makes reading some judgments a painful experience – instead of making the argument more solid and the construction of the doctrine more coherent, actually has the opposite effect of impoverishing the argument, a fact that has been denounced repeatedly in dissenting votes.

8 *Judicial Candor and Judicial Rhetoric*

The Court has been categorical in asserting that "ideological and political preferences are legitimate for the legislator and for the appellant as citizen, but they should not enter in the least into our reasoning".[62] As a result of this premise, the tone of dissenting votes is rather combative and takes on an accusatory tone when what it criticizes is, precisely, arguments it considers to be inspired for or serving ethical or ideological preferences.[63] The Court is not a representative body and its members are not chosen for their personal virtue[64] but rather, as the Constitution stipulates, for their prestige as legal professionals. In this way, the Court's authority rests exclusively on its nature as a specialized technical body.

59 STC 134/2011 60 STC 31/2010

61 On the indispensable nature of systematic interpretation in determining limits to rights, STC 11/1981 FJ 7 and STC 292/2000, FJ 11, among many others, all of which appeal to the demands of the principle of Constitutional unity.

62 STC 94/1998, FJ 2

63 "As in the Plenary Session of the Court, I must express my worry and consternation at the passing of this decision whose technical standard departs from the requisite of reasoned grounds in conformity with the basic rules of the Constitutional method. Instead of dealing with the problem under examination from a strict legal perspective as in Constitutional jurisdiction, this decision seems to be the result of a previously established position which does not manage to hide the shadow of the ideology that guides it", Dissenting Vote of Vice-President Justice Asua in STC 145/2015.

64 Dissenting Vote of Rubio Llorente in STC 53/1985.

There is no single guideline regarding the treatment of the different arguments which may appear in constitutional conflicts. The Court is not obliged to rule on all of the possible arguments and objections raised or imaginable. In general, it will focus on reasons alleged by the one who presented the legal challenge, who initiated the constitutional procedure, of whom special effort is demanded in argumentation to avoid trivial challenges or those lacking minimal grounds. When justifying the decision, however, it is not bound by the juridical arguments made by the parties, or by the way in which the constitutional problem is presented. Nothing stops the Court from dealing with doctrinal controversies in order to resolve constitutional cases.[65]

The language used in constitutional judgments is technical. Nonetheless, except when dealing with legal aspects where more sophisticated jargon prevails – and setting apart the whole bulk of convoluted case law on conflicts of competence – it is accessible to an educated audience. Judgments are universally binding, though the grounds are usually directed at a specialized audience: lawyers, judges, attorneys, the administration, the legislator, autonomic authorities, and, naturally, law professors. For some issues which generate great public interest, it is possible to imagine that the Court, aware of the impact of the decision, would include considerations directed toward public opinion. In general, however, the degree of rhetoric is low, even in concurring and dissenting votes where the style depends on the personality of each judge.

With respect to the degree of generalization, the Court tends to frame the issues within the broader context and from time to time will summarize its case law.

9 *Length, Dissenting and Concurring Opinions*

Normally, the length of the judgment is in direct relation to the complexity of the constitutional challenge contained in the initial writing or application, though the novelty and importance of the issue also play a part. Internal discrepancies, brought to light in the deliberation, may require the integration of different points of view into the grounds, complicating the line of argumentation. In general, the abstract control which allows for challenges to entire laws, article by article, attending to different grounds for unconstitutionality – and which, should the situation arise, could be

[65] As an example, reflections on the controversial doctrine regarding the figure of the "continuing offense" in STC 89/1983, FJ 3.

accumulated with others filed against the same law – is the one which has led to the most lengthy judgments. Among them, the one that stands out is the decision which resolves the challenge made to the law reforming the Statute of Autonomy of Catalonia, STC 31/2010, which took up nearly 500 pages in the small font of the Official State Gazette (BOE). In comparison, appeals for the protection of rights (*amparos*), which tend to be more circumscribed, produce shorter judgments, though there are significant exceptions. The shortest decisions are those of referral and rejection, where the Court does not rule "on the merits" of the case.

The Constitution recognizes the possibility to issue concurring and dissenting votes, which, at the time of its introduction, meant a radical novelty in the judicial tradition. The practice of concurring and dissenting votes has been common since the beginning. The votes must be announced during the deliberation and are joined to the judgment. In practice, the individual votes are written afterwards, which explains why judgments do not make mention of the precise arguments that appear in the separate opinions.

10 *Framing of Constitutional Issues*

The formal characterization of constitutional questions is determined by the procedure through which the question reaches the Court. Depending on the constitutional procedure opened, the Court will rule on the constitutionality of a challenged norm or on the violation of a fundamental right, or on the title over a competence. Constitutional proceedings are of "limited cognition": the Court cannot resolve more than the constitutional issue specifically posed by the actors, according to what is established by the law of the Court. Hence, a pronouncement on a constitutional question by the Constitutional Court is never a byproduct of a lawsuit but the solemn resolution of the sole and exclusive *thema decidendi* of a constitutional proceeding.

11 *Key Concepts*

Reference to the essential content of rights and guarantees (*Wesensgehalt*) or to those core powers that characterize an entitlement over a competence in dispute is recurrent in the pronouncements of the Constitutional Court (present in 33 of the selected judgments). There is nothing strange about the constant calls to "core content", since this is a concept written in the Constitution and central to the definition of fundamental rights and guarantees (in particular, against the legislator[66]). The Court stated in its first decisions an interpretation of the concept that has remained until today a "well established doctrine".[67] The insistence therefore has nothing to do with the need to clarify concepts, but with a decision-making technique (or, better, a formal rite) according to which the Court, before examining the denounced injury of a right, proceeds to the determination of its substance.[68] Similarly, in conflict jurisdiction the Court, before deciding on the holder of the disputed competence, will define its core and scope[69].

Although the above is by far the most widely used concept in the selection of sentences, the number of references to proportionality (17), equality (16), democracy (14) and the rule of law (14) is also remarkable. The use of *proportionality* as a canon of constitutionality is present from the early days of constitutional jurisprudence, although in the beginning, until the second half of the 1990s, in a rather intuitive fashion and with a somewhat confusing association with the idea of reasonableness. Typical examples of this first use are found in SSTC 161/1987[70] and 120/1990. Subsequently, a series of judgments, clearly following German inspiration, of 1995 and 1996 set the definitive characterization of the test of proportionality, which includes three consecutive "sub-tests": adequacy,

66 Art. 53.1 SC: The exercise of such rights and liberties, which shall be protected in accordance with the provisions of Article 161, 1a), may be regulated only by law which shall, in any case, respect their essential content.

67 The leading case for this doctrine is STC 11/1981, FJ 8: "In order to approach the idea of 'essential content' . . . there are two possible courses of action. The first is . . . to make use of what is generally called legal nature or the means of perceiving or configuring each right [generalized ideas and convictions usually admitted among legal professionals, judges and in general, specialists in law] . . . The second . . . consists in attempting to seek what a significant tradition has called legally protected interests as a nucleus and core of subjective rights". According to these directions a right is violated whenever it is "denaturalized" or made "impracticable".

68 Examples of this technique, among many others, in STC 37/1987 (property right), 161/1987 (conscientious objection), STC 120/1990, (right to life and hunger strike), STC 91/2000 (guarantees of due process and extradition), 236/2007 (foreigners fundamental rights), STC 235/2007 (criminalization of genocide denial and freedom of speech), STC 198/2012 (constitutional guarantee of marriage).

69 Examples of this way of proceeding STC 13/1992 (political and financial autonomy of the Autonomous Communities and spending power) and, with a thorough analysis of subject matter competences, STC 31/2010.

70 FJ 4 (on the temporal limitation on the exercise of conscientious objection to military service) "the legislature could certainly not put arbitrary conditions to the exercise of the right by the objector violating of the prohibition of arbitrariness contained in art. 9.3 of the Constitution, but can establish reasonable and proportionate conditions for the protection of the interests affected".

necessity and ponderation or proportionality *sensu stricto*.[71] In its practical application, the test of proportionality is more flexible than its characterization suggests. It is ubiquitous: although its natural place remains as the guarantee of rights – where its application is more or less orthodox – it is used in all constitutional procedures. Criticism of the extensive use of the test of proportionality emphasizes that *ad hoc* decisions, conditioned by the circumstances, make the precise enunciation of standards difficult, while increasing the perceived discretion of the Court.[72] In any case, it is not the only test of constitutionality but it shares the limelight with the test of reasonableness and its variants, commonly applied in cases of judicial due process and equality.

The constitutional litigation regarding *equality and non-discrimination* is plentiful. In the *amparo* jurisdiction, according to statistics of the 2015 Court Annual report, the denounced infringement of the rights of art. 14 SC (equality and non-discrimination) is present in 14 per cent of the complaints and is the second most invoked right, only behind the ubiquitous call to the right to effective judicial protection (judicial due process), which is to be found in more than 75 per cent of the demands. Respecting constitutional review of legislation the alleged violation of art. 14 SC or any equality clause contained in other articles of the Constitution (e.g., in arts. 1.1, 9.2, 23.2, 31.1, 32.1, 68.1, 139.1, 149.1.1 SC) is a main motive for constitutional challenges. In any case, what is important about equality cases is not their abundance, but their qualitative importance. The affirmation of equality and non-discrimination is the foundation of a doctrine that has been crucial in adapting pre-constitutional law to the Constitution, in the advancement of civil rights and in the transformation of Spanish society into a fairer order. It is not surprising that many of these judgments occur in the area of labor law and private law and that the construction of the doctrine has been particularly incisive in relation to gender equality. Among the selected judgments are some path-breaking

[71] FJ 8: For example, STC 61/1997, FJ 17 contains the reference to the statements hereinafter set for the doctrine of the proportionality test: "from the abstract evaluation of the rule in question does not follow the conclusion that there is an absolute and obvious lack of proportionality of the measure – the only perspective to be considered here (SSTC 66/1995, 55/1996 and 207/1996) –, given the different circumstances in each case." Other examples applying the three-step test in subsequent case law, in STC 12/2008 FFJJ 5, 6 and 7 (mandatory gender-balanced lists of candidates) or STC 45/2009 FFJJ 7 and 8 (aggravated punishment for gender violence).

[72] Generally, on the evolution and development of this cannon in the constitutional case law, vid. Markus González Beilfuss, *El Principio de Proporcionalidad en la Jurisprudencia del Tribunal Constitucional* (Thomson- Aranzadi 2015).

pronouncements on the building of equality case law: that is the case with the notorious SSTC 103/1983, 145/1991, 222/1992, and 12/2008 (most controversial has been the STC 45/2009). In SSTC 144/1988 and 247/2007 the potential and scope of equality as an instrument that limits the discretion of government is apparent.[73]

Reference to *democracy* never happens in isolation but in connection with other principles or rights. Beyond the cases in which the Court refers in a more or less generic way to democracy as a political, social or legal context on which it is to project the analysis of the constitutional controversy, we find statements about what democracy demands in accordance with our Constitution or the precise characteristics of Spanish democracy, that play a decisive role in the justification of the final decision (e.g., in STC 10/1983). Of particular interest are those cases which highlight the basic tension between constitutionalism and democracy, cases in which the Court examines the ultimate consequences of the duty of compliance with the Constitution and adherence to constitutional principles and values. All this is usually set in connection with the open possibility in Spain to carry out a "total" constitutional reform. This type of approach is to be found in STC 235/2007 and, above all, in SSTC 48/2003 and 103/2008. The blunt statement that ours is not a "militant democracy" system does not hide fluctuations in the line of reflection from the initial STC 101/1983 (overruled in 1990).

As for the concept of *rule of law*, it is a concept-umbrella, capacious for a variety of principles from different sources which converge in the "formal" definition of the rule-of-law State (*Estado de Derecho*). The legality principle, legal certainty, legal security, predictability, non-retroactivity, non-arbitrariness, protection of legitimate expectation, acquire a special meaning against the background of "rule-of-law constitutionalism" (*Estado constitucional de Derecho*). In essence, what is implied by the rule of law is well expressed in STC 161/1987, in which the Court, analyzing certain restrictions on the exercise of conscientious objection, states: "Conscientious objection in general, that is, the right to be exempted from compliance with the constitutional and legal duties considered to be in contradiction to one's convictions, is not recognized and cannot

[73] In STC 144/1988 the Court clarifies the doctrinal distinction between equality in the law (limit for the legislature) and equal application of the law (limit on the performance of administrative bodies and judges). In STC 247/2007, especially FJ 13, the Court addresses the issue of equality as a limit for the Statute-maker which cannot introduce a regulation of rights that somehow alters the basic principle of equality of Spaniards in all the country.

imaginably be recognized in our Law or any Law, as it would mean the very negation of the idea of the State." The special legitimacy of laws founded on the Constitution, in contrast with pre-constitutional laws, is the subject of STC 17/1981. Attention to the limits for the national rule of law in the European context stimulates another interesting approach to the issue in the STC 91/2000 and DTC 1/2004 (preventive check of constitutional compatibility of the Lisbon Treaty)[74]. The STC 45/1989 provides a very representative example of the Constitutional Court building of a consequentialist argument from the appeal for legal certainty (paradoxically, to justify the "non-applicability" of a legal rule which contained the obligation to declare null and void all legal precepts deemed unconstitutional[75]).

References to *human dignity* (12), *basic procedural rights* (12), *federalism* (11) and *sovereignty* (10) are less abundant in the set of judgments. With regard to the *dignity of the human person* – which art. 10.1 SC considers "foundation of political order and the social peace" – it should be noted that, differently to what is the case in the German system, it is not a right but a premise of the rights system. The modest number of references to *basic procedural rights* and *federalism* simply shows that the vast majority of the selected constitutional decisions come from a certain area of Court activity (review of legislation). In *amparo* jurisdiction the invocation of due process of law is ubiquitous. Similarly, the federalism concepts family (autonomy, autonomous regions, decentralization) is omnipresent in the conflicts of competence proceedings before the Court.

Finally, none of the decisions makes reference to the *form of the State*, not involved until the present in constitutional disputes. The reference to *form of government* (in the manner of appeals to the principles of parliamentary democracy or representative democracy) plays some role in the argument in 7 cases. The concept of *nation* (6) has not had regular presence in the constitutional set of arguments. However, the present

[74] The doctrine of the existence of absolute rights with "ad extra" binding force, that is, binding for foreign authorities was sketched in STC 91/2000 (and caused some difficulties on the implementation in Spain of the European arrest warrant as shows the "*Melloni* case" decided in STC 26/2014). In DTC 1/2004 the Court examined the question of how to accommodate the assertion of constitutional supremacy, the pillar of the constitutional rule of law, with the acceptance of the primacy of European law and the possibility of a European constitutional law superimposed to national constitutional law.

[75] Art.39.1 Law of the Constitutional Court: "Where the judgment declares the unconstitutionality, it shall also declare null and void the contested provisions... " In STC 45/1989 the Court declared some of the challenged prescriptions unconstitutional but not invalid (void) and established a limited prospective effect for the nullity effectively declared.

political scenario, with the radical demands of Catalan nationalism – some of them challenged before the Constitutional Court – predicts that this state of affairs is in the throes of change. A single sentence makes mention of *secularism* – "There shall be no State religion", states art. 16.3 SC – and only 8 cases deal with the concepts of *privacy* and *freedom of expression*. Surely in the big picture this proportion is not far from accurate. Although cases of freedom of expression and privacy are not the most numerous in *amparo* jurisdiction, they have been sufficient for the Court to develop a nuanced doctrine, which continues to evolve, and is not alien to developments in European jurisprudence[76].

C Constitutional Reasoning from a Comparative Perspective

To perceive the differences between the style of the Spanish Constitutional Court decisions and those typical of common law courts does not require much effort. As is usual in civil law courts, factual background and legal arguments are separated and, commonly, the first points in the legal reasoning deal with procedural matters. The reasoning is, however, complete and explanatory, in this sense, in marked contrast with the French judicial tradition. Even so, usually most of that reasoning is dedicated, depending on the type of proceeding (constitutional review, conflict of jurisdiction or *amparo*), to explaining the process of determination of the constitutional parameter, or to the identification of the applicable standard or doctrine, rather than to the justification of the conclusion as such. Thus, the image that the conclusion "is given" remains. Rarely has the Court overtly acknowledged that an alteration of previous doctrine happened. Judicial overruling usually happens *sub silentio*.

Although the decisions of the Spanish Constitutional Court are not strictly *per curiam* (as French or Italian ones are), neither do they correspond in their characteristics to those of a pure system of *seriatim* judicial opinions, in the English tradition. The constitutional judgment is always a "Court judgment", not a reasoned opinion by one Judge speaking for the Court with other judges joining, in the manner of the American Supreme Court practice. Therefore, even if the possibility of issuing separate opinions alters the dynamics of discussion and deliberation inside the Court, individual opinions do not count when setting constitutional doctrine.

[76] Even when the Court follows its own path, as in STC 235/2007 (declaring against freedom of speech the criminalization of behavior consisting in denying, without other qualification, a crime of genocide).

Unlike the German Court, the Spanish Constitutional Court gives no information in the judgment about the number of judges supporting the decision; thus, formally, a decision without published separate opinions is a unanimous decision. The reasoning never enters into discussion or dialogue with the arguments in dissenting or concurring opinions.[77]

The Spanish Constitutional Court is mindful of the doctrine of other constitutional courts and of European supranational jurisdictions. Constitutional borrowing commonly occurs in the area of constitutional rights and the interpretation of constitutional categories and concepts. The case law around the construction of the "State of Autonomies" has, however, led to a development and categorization that is highly idiosyncratic – difficult to understand for any foreign observer, who will probably be surprised by the recurrence of conflicts of competence.

Appendix: 40 Leading Cases

1. STC 4/1981, de 2 de febrero de 1981
2. STC 5/1981, de 13 de febrero de 1981
3. STC 17/1981, de 1 de junio de 1981
4. STC 15/1982, de 23 de abril de 1982
5. STC 10/1983, de 21 de febrero de 1983
6. STC 76/1983, de 5 de agosto de 1983
7. STC 101/1983, de 18 de noviembre de 1983
8. STC 103/1983, de 22 de noviembre de 1983
9. STC 111/1983, de 2 de diciembre de 1983
10. STC 114/1984, de 29 de noviembre de 1984
11. STC 53/1985, de 11 de abril de 1985
12. STC 82/1986, de 26 de junio de 1986
13. STC 37/1987, de 26 de marzo de 1987
14. STC 161/1987, de 27 de octubre de 1987
15. STC 144/1988, de 12 de julio de 1988
16. STC 45/1989, de 20 de febrero de 1989
17. STC 120/1990, de 27 de junio de 1990
18. STC 145/1991, de 1 de julio de 1991
19. STC 214/1991, de 11 de noviembre de 1991

[77] On the issue of Court majorities and the binding character of constitutional doctrine (with attention to situations of evenly divided court and plurality decisions), Marian Ahumada Ruiz, "La regla de la mayoría y la formulación de doctrina constitucional" (2000) 20 *Revista Española de Derecho Constitucional* 155.

20. STC 245/1991, de 16 de diciembre de 1991
21. STC 13/1992, de 6 de febrero de 1992
22. DTC 1/1992, de 1 de julio de 1992
23. STC 222/1992, de 11 de diciembre de 1992
24. STC 61/1997, de 20 de marzo de 1997
25. STC 214/1999, de 29 de noviembre de 1999
26. STC 91/2000, de 30 de marzo de 2000
27. STC 292/2000, de 30 de noviembre de 2000
28. STC 48/2003, de 12 de marzo de 2003
29. DTC 1/2004, de 13 de diciembre de 2004
30. STC 237/2005, de 26 de septiembre de 2005
31. STC 235/2007, de 7 de noviembre de 2007
32. STC 236/2007, de 7 de noviembre de 2007
33. STC 247/2007, de 12 de diciembre de 2007
34. STC 12/2008, de 29 de enero de 2008
35. STC 103/2008, de 11 de septiembre de 2008
36. STC 45/2009, de 19 de febrero de 2009
37. STC 155/2009, de 25 de junio de 2009
38. STC 31/2010, de 28 de junio de 2010
39. STC 134/2011, de 20 de julio de 2011
40. STC 198/2012, de 6 de noviembre de 2012

16

The Constitutional Court of Taiwan

WEN-CHEN CHANG

A Legal, Political, Institutional and Academic Context

1 Legal and Political Culture as Context for Constitutional Reasoning

In line with the third wave of democratization,[1] Taiwan has successfully transformed into a strong constitutional democracy with effective judicial review since the late 1980s.[2] The Constitution – entitled the Republic of China Constitution – promulgated in 1947 was not fully implemented until the lifting of the Martial Law Decree in 1987 and the suspension of the Temporary Provisions in 1991. The Martial Law Decree and Temporary Provisions were imposed because of the relocation of the Nationalist government from Mainland China to Taiwan and the ensuing war between the Nationalist government and the Chinese Communist Party on the Mainland. The Temporary Provisions substantially expanded presidential powers in disregard of the parliamentary system adopted in the Constitution, and suspended representative elections at the national level, permitting elections only at city and county levels. The Martial Law Decree along with other government measures restricted important civil and political rights, such as the right to organize a political party and the right to free speech, assembly and association. Although the courts including the Constitutional Court (also known as the Council of Grand Justices)[3] were maintained, they hardly provided for effective checks with

[1] Samuel P. Huntington, *The Third Wave: Democratization in the Late Twentieth Century* (U of Oklahoma P 1991); Bruce Ackerman, *The Future of Liberal Revolution* (Yale University Press 1992).

[2] Tom Ginsburg, *Judicial Review in New Democracies: Constitutional Courts in Asian Cases* (Cambridge University Press 2003); Wen-Chen Chang, "The Role of Judicial Review in Consolidating Democracy: The Case of Taiwan" (2005) 2.2 *Asia Law Review* 73, 74 ff; J. Yeh and W. C. Chang, "The Emergence of East Asian Constitutionalism: Features in Comparison" 59 (2011) *American Journal of Comparative Law* 805, 806 ff.

[3] The Constitutional Court was known as the Council of Grand Justices due to its Organic Act entitled "the Act of the Council of Grand Justices". In 1993, however, the Organic

the exercise of government powers or ensured strong guarantees of fundamental rights and freedoms.

The process of political liberalization and democratization eventually started in the late 1980s. The opposition party was formed in 1986. With the lifting of the Martial Law Decree in 1987, the guarantees of civil and political rights were gradually secured. The abolition of the Temporary Provisions in 1991 brought the return of constitutional rule, and in the meantime, constitutional revisions aimed at suiting the needs of a new democratic environment were undertaken seven times between 1991 and 2005.[4] Consequently, the first election of national representatives in Taiwan was held in 1990 and the first presidential election in 1996. The Nationalist party lost the presidential election to the opposition party in 2000, marking the first peaceful regime change in Taiwan, but soon returned to power in 2008. In the parliament, the Nationalist party continued to hold the majority, but at times met with strong challenges from the alliance of opposition parties. All in all, the Nationalist party continued to be the dominant political force in Taiwan, with the exception of the eight years between 2000 and 2008 in which a divided government was formed as the opposition party held the presidency while the Nationalist party dominated only the parliament.

The reform target of constitutional revisions in the 1990s and 2000s was primarily on the arrangements of government institutions. This was because the Constitution promulgated in 1947 was designed for Mainland China but not for Taiwan, and because the parliamentary system plus the five-power scheme stipulated in the Constitution was not suitable to the emerging power structure of democratic Taiwan. These rounds of incremental constitutional reform eventually created a semi-presidential system, in which a directly elected president appoints a prime minister heading the executive (also known as the Executive Yuan) answerable to the parliament (also known as the Legislative Yuan). Aside from the judiciary (also known as the Judicial Yuan), there are two other constitutional institutions: one independently administers examinations and matters regarding civil servants (also known as the Examination Yuan) and the other independently exercises the power of impeachment, censure and audit (also known as the Control Yuan).[5] Such a complex structure of

Act was substantially amended and the title changed to "the Constitutional Interpretation Procedure Act".

[4] JR Yeh, "Constitutional Reform and Democratization in Taiwan: 1945–2000" in P. Chow (ed), *Taiwan's Modernization in Global Perspective* (Praeger 2002).

[5] Ginsburg (n 2) 116 f; Yeh and Chang (n 2) 822 f.

government powers has easily generated institutional conflicts and power struggles that demanded for judicial resolution. It is thus no surprise that ever since the democratization, the Constitutional Court has been involved with a considerable number of disputes on power conflicts, some of which were quite politicized.[6]

Notably, as the target of constitution reforms was exclusively on institutional arrangements, no new rights or freedoms were added to the existing constitutional list. Yet, the Constitution promulgated in 1947 contains only a very brief list of rights and freedom. Quite a few fundamental rights and freedoms that are included in nearly all other constitutions are not provided. For example, human dignity, right of personality, right of reputation, right of privacy, right of marriage, due process, and indigenous rights are not explicitly guaranteed. Discontented with constitutional reforms, individuals and human rights groups have turned to the courts – especially the Constitutional Court – for judicial construction of new rights.[7] It has been witnessed that in articulating those unwritten rights and freedoms, the Constitutional Court has begun referring to foreign or international laws, especially to rights that are enshrined in core international human rights conventions.[8]

2 *The Court and Constitutional Litigation*

The 1947 Constitution provides in art. 79 that the Grand Justices appointed by the President with legislative confirmation shall have the power to interpret the Constitution and provide for uniform interpretations of laws and regulations. There is no other constitutional provision specifying the details regarding the organization or jurisdictions of the Grand Justices.

In 1948, the Grand Justices began functioning in accordance with the rules they made on their own. Constitutional or uniform interpretations

[6] Jiunn-Rong Yeh, "Presidential Politics and the Judicial Facilitation of Dialogue between Political Actors in New Asian Democracies: Comparing the South Korean and Taiwanese Experiences" 8 (2010) *International Journal of Constitutional Law* 911; Wen-Chen Chang, "Strategic judicial responses in politically charged cases: East Asian experiences" (2010) 8 *International Journal of Constitutional Law* 885 (comparing the experiences of Taiwan and South Korea).

[7] Wen-Chen Chang, "Public-Interest Litigation in Taiwan: Strategy for Law and Policy Reforms in Course of Democratization", in Po Jen Yap and Holning Lau (eds), *Public Interest Litigation in Asia* (Routledge 2010), 136–60.

[8] Wen-Chen Chang, "The Convergence of Constitutions and International Human Rights: Taiwan and South Korea in Comparison", (2011) 36 *North Carolina Journal of International Law and Commercial Regulations* 593.

rendered by the Grand Justices were termed as Judicial Yuan Interpretations with a sequential number abbreviated as J.Y. Interpretation No. 1, J.Y. Interpretation No. 2, etc. In 1958, the "Organic Act Regarding the Council of Grand Justice" was promulgated by the legislature, providing statutory details for jurisdictions and procedures of constitutional adjudication. It was due to this Organic Act that the organization of the Grand Justices was known as "the Council of Grand Justices". In 1993, however, this Organic Act was substantially amended and renamed "the Constitutional Interpretation Procedure Act". Since then, the Constitutional Court or the Grand Justices of the Constitutional Court became the official title.

As the Council or the Constitutional Court, the Grand Justices have – since 1948 – sat separately from other final courts of appeal, and exercised an exclusive power to review and invalidate laws that contravene the Constitution. It should be noted, however, that the exclusive power of review and invalidation is exercised on statutes. The Constitutional Court has made clear in its own decisions – J.Y. Interpretation Nos. 137 and 216 – that judges may still review administrative regulations adopted by government agencies and refuse to apply them in concrete cases if found inconsistent with the Constitution and laws.[9] While judges may refuse to apply unconstitutional administrative regulations, only the Grand Justices has the power to make a binding declaration on unconstitutionality of administrative regulations and directly invalidate them.

The jurisdictions of Taiwan's Constitutional Court are similar to other specialized constitutional courts in Europe and elsewhere. Article 79 of the Constitution authorizes the Constitutional Court to exercise two main powers, providing: (1) uniform interpretation of laws and regulations and (2) constitutional interpretations. The Constitutional Court's function to provide for uniform interpretations of laws and regulations was important in the early operation of the judiciary, but has become far less so in recent decades. At present, the jurisdiction over uniform interpretations constitutes only 2 per cent of the Constitutional Court's caseload, down from approximately 20 per cent in the 1960s and 1970s, and 50 per cent in the 1950s.[10]

The primary function of the Constitutional Court is to provide for constitutional interpretations on matters concerning (1) doubts or ambiguities in the application of the Constitution, (2) the constitutionality of statutes or regulations, and (3) the constitutionality of laws and

[9] J.Y. Interpretation No. 137 (14 December 1973), J.Y. Interpretation No. 216 (19 June 1987).

[10] See Chang, "The Role of Judicial Review", 77 f (Table 1).

regulations promulgated by local governments.[11] Requests for the above interpretations may be brought by central and local government agencies, one third of the total legislators, or individuals – including natural and legal persons or political parties – who have exhausted all available legal remedies and believe that his or her constitutionally protected right has been injured because of unconstitutional statutes or regulations applied to his or her case.[12] In addition, the Constitutional Court decided in J.Y. Interpretation No. 371 that if a judge in trying a case finds that the statute applicable to the case is unconstitutional, he or she may suspend the proceeding and petition to the Constitutional Court for a decision on the constitutionality of the disputed provision.[13] It should be mentioned that the Constitutional Court is also empowered to adjudicate over the impeachment of the President and Vice President and to decide on the dissolution of unconstitutional political parties. Yet, the Constitutional Court has not yet received any cases in these jurisdictions.[14]

The Constitutional Court exercises "abstract" review in constitutionality or unconstitutionality of laws and regulations. Even in cases where the request for review is brought up by individuals who have exhausted all available judicial proceedings or referred by judges who are currently presiding over the cases, the Constitutional Court cannot directly decide on those concrete cases. This is different from the power of other constitutional courts, such as the German Constitutional Court, in deciding individual constitutional complaints where the Court may vacate judicial decisions or provide for direct remedies.[15] In Taiwan, the Constitutional Court can only declare constitutionality or unconstitutionality of impugned statutes or regulations, and following upon an unconstitutional declaration, individuals may request a retrial or make an extraordinary appeal.[16] Over the years, the Constitutional Court has developed a variety of declarations regarding constitutionality or unconstitutionality of impugned statutes or regulations. Aside from direct invalidation of an unconstitutional statute, the Constitutional Court may declare a statute unconstitutional but sustain its effect for a certain period of time until further revision. The Constitutional Court may also make an

[11] Art. 4 of the Constitutional Interpretation Act.

[12] Art. 7 of the Constitutional Interpretation Act.

[13] J.Y. Interpretation No. 371 (20 January 1995). [14] Ibid at 77.

[15] D. P. Kommers, *The Constitutional Jurisprudence of the Federal Republic of Germany* (2nd ed., Duke University Press 1997) 15.

[16] J.Y. Interpretation No. 185 (27 January 1984). An English translation is available at www.judicial.gov.tw/constitutionalcourt/en/p03_01.asp?expno=185.

unconstitutional declaration of an impugned statute without any invalidation. It is also possible for the Constitutional Court to sustain constitutionality of an impugned statute while providing a warning on potential constitutional violations.[17]

Requests for interpretations of the Constitutional Court are first sent to a panel of three Grand Justices for an initial review, making suggestions for dismissal or acceptance. Final decisions of dismissal or acceptance require a majority vote of all Grand Justices.[18] A two-thirds quorum is required for the Constitutional Court to render interpretations regarding constitutionality of statutes, whereas a simple majority is sufficient in deciding the constitutionality of administrative regulations or judicial precedents and in rendering uniform interpretations of statutes and administrative regulations.[19]

In the first 10 years (1948–58) of the Constitutional Court, constitutional or uniform interpretations were written in only one or two paragraphs without detailed reasoning being given. No concurring or dissenting opinions were allowed to be issued back then. Beginning in 1958, "dissenting" opinions signed by individual Grand Justices were permitted to be issued separately. However, at this time, "dissenting" opinions actually included both those dissenting from the ruling and those dissenting from the reasoning, the latter of which should have been characterized as concurring opinions. Only after 1987 was the issuance of concurring and dissenting opinions institutionalized.[20] Since the 1980s, not only has the issuance of concurring and dissenting opinions increased steadily, the length of majority opinions, particularly the reasoning part, has also considerably expanded.

With the effective functioning of the Constitutional Court, its caseload has– quite expectedly – increased sharply. In the 1990s, the Constitutional Court received on average about 250 requests per year for interpretations. In the 2000s, the number has doubled to 500 or even 600 requests

[17] For comparative analyses on these different types of constitutional declarations, *see* W-C. Chang et al, *Constitutionalism in Asia: Cases and Materials* (Hart 2014) 443–61.

[18] See art. 10 of the 1993 Constitutional Interpretation Procedural Act, www.judicial.gov.tw/constitutionalcourt/en/p07_2.asp?lawno=73.

[19] See art. 14 of the 1993 Constitutional Interpretation Procedural Act, www.judicial.gov.tw/constitutionalcourt/en/p07_2.asp?lawno=73. This was reduced from three-quarters in deciding the constitutionality of statutes and two-thirds in deciding the constitutionality of administrative rules and judicial precedents and in rendering unified interpretations, stipulated by the 1958 Act Regarding the Council of Grand Justices.

[20] Ginsburg (n 2) 128 (Table 5.4).

per year.[21] The Constitutional Court has rendered on average 20 to 30 interpretations per year, and in those interpretations issued, the ratio of unconstitutional declarations has since the 1990s remained as high as 30 per cent or 40 per cent.[22]

3 *The Judges*

The 1947 Constitution does not specify the number of Grand Justices to be appointed. It was the Organic Act of the Judicial Yuan enacted in 1947 that provided the number of Grand Justices to be 17 with a renewable term of 9 years.[23] The constitutional revision, however, stipulated that beginning in 2003, the Constitutional Court would be composed of 15 Grand Justices with a non-renewable term of 8 years by staggered appointments.[24] Hence, between 1948 and 2003, the Constitutional Court had six terms of Grand Justices, each with a term of nine years. In 2003, to implement staggered appointments in accordance with the constitutional revision, 8 Grand Justices were appointed only for four years while 7 were appointed for eight years. Since 2003, the staggered appointment of Grand Justices with a non-renewable term of 8 years has been maintained.

The qualifications of Grand Justices were stipulated in the 1947 Organic Act of the Judicial Yuan and have remained since. Five categories of eligibility are set forth, and no single category is supposed to make up more than one third of the Constitutional Court. These five categories include a candidate who (1) has served as a judge of the Supreme Court for more than 10 years with a distinguished record; (2) has served as a member of the legislature for more than 9 years with distinguished contributions; (3) has been a professor of a major field of law at a university for more than 10 years and has authored publications in a specialised field; (4) has served at the International Court of Justice, or has published authoritative works in the field of public or comparative law; or (5) is a person highly reputed in the field of legal research with political experience.[25]

Notwithstanding the five categories of eligibility, the vast majority of those appointed to the Constitutional Court have been either law professors or career judges with prior experience in the Supreme Court or the

[21] Statistical information on the caseload of the Constitutional Court is available at www judicial.gov.tw/constitutionalcourt/p05.asp

[22] Yeh and Chang (n 2) 808.

[23] Article 3 of the Organic Act of the Judicial Yuan.

[24] See art. 5 of the Additional Articles of the ROC Constitution. An English translation is available at english.president.gov.tw/Default.aspx?tabid=1036#05.

[25] Article 4 of The Organic Act of the Judicial Yuan.

Ministry of Justice. In the past, more career judges were appointed than law professors. Since the 1990s, however, at least half of the Grand Justices appointed have been law professors. Currently, the Constitutional Court consists of 9 law professors, 5 career judges, and only 1 former private attorney.[26] Partly because of the strong representation of former academics in the Constitutional Court, Grand Justices have possessed impressive educational credentials and considerable advanced training in comparative laws.[27] For instance, in the present Constitutional Court, among 15 justices, 8 have doctorates from Germany, 1 from the United States, and 1 has a master's degree from Japan and 1 a master's degree from the United States. Only 4 of 15 do not have foreign degrees, and among these 4, 3 have a local doctorate.

4 *Legal Scholarship and Constitutional Reasoning*

The legal system in Taiwan has been shaped by the legacies of tradition, colonization and modernization. Taiwan was ceded to Japan in 1895 by the Chinese empire as a result of the Sino-Japanese War. During this colonial period, the legal system of Japan, modeled on European legal systems, was introduced to Taiwan, replacing traditional Chinese codes and local customs.[28] After the Japanese government surrendered in World War II, the nationalist government of the Republic of China regained Taiwan in 1945, and subsequently retreated to Taiwan because of their defeat by the Communist Party on the Mainland. Like the legal system in Japan, the legal and constitutional system established by the Republic of China on the Mainland was modeled on Western – primarily European – legal systems. Hence, the transition of Taiwan from Japan to the Republic of China has not brought significant changes to the legal system.

After World War II, Taiwan's legal system continued to be influenced by Japanese and European legal systems. Many lawyers went to Japan to study law. In the 1960s and 1970s, as German and other European scholarships became available, lawyers turned to study laws in European countries, mostly in Germany.[29] In recent years, however, perhaps due to the global competitiveness of American law, particularly in the area of

[26] The list of current justices (and their CVs) is available at www.judicial.gov.tw/constitutionalcourt/en/p01_03.asp.

[27] David S. Law and Wen-Chen Chang, "The Limits of Global Judicial Dialogue" (2011) 86 *Washington Law Review* 523ff.

[28] T-S. Wang, *Legal Reform in Taiwan under Japanese Colonial Rule (1895–1945): The Reception of Western Law* (University of Washington Press 2000) 157–9.

[29] Law and Chang (n 27) 571–2.

international trade, lawyers began studying law in the United States and other common law countries. This trend of lawyers studying abroad has remained since. Take, for example, the educational backgrounds of full-time faculty members at the National Taiwan University College of Law, the top law school in Taiwan. Among 45 full-time faculty members, 18 have doctorates from Germany, 10 from the United States, 7 from Japan, 5 from the United Kingdom and 1 from France. Only 4 of 45 hold local doctorates.[30] Also, as mentioned above, the current Constitutional Court has 9 doctorates, 8 from Germany and 1 from the United States.

Expectedly, the influence of foreign and comparative laws on both legal practice and jurisprudence has been strong in Taiwan. Interestingly, however, notwithstanding the strong influence of foreign and comparative laws, direct and explicit references to foreign or comparative law have been rare in judicial decisions. This is in part due to the custom of the civil law system in which judicial decisions usually do not include references or citations, and in part due to the fact that comparative legal analyses have been integrated into local scholarships and courts may feel no need to make further comparative analyses.[31] Similar to judgments made by lower courts, majority opinions of the Constitutional Court are shorter in length with very few direct or explicit references to comparative or international law or legal scholarship. However, separate – concurring or dissenting – opinions are written in a variety of styles reflecting personal styles of individual justices. Some opinions are quite lengthy, others are not; some are written with very few references, others may even be read like a scholarly article or a section in a treatise.

Overall, the style of constitutional reasoning held by Taiwan's Constitutional Court typically involves doctrinal analyses of legal concepts that may be borrowed from or inspired by comparative or international sources. In recent years, the Constitutional Court has also begun relying to a greater degree on its own interpretations as "precedents", despite the fact that there is no applicability in the principle of stare decisis.

B Arguments in Constitutional Reasoning

The 40 judgments in this research are selected from more than 700 interpretations made by Taiwan's Constitutional Court from 1948 to May

[30] http://www.law.ntu.edu.tw/main.php?mod=custom_page&site_id=0&page_id=47

[31] Wen-Chen Chang and Jiunn-Rong Yeh, "Judges as Discursive Agent: The Use of Foreign Precedents by the Constitutional Court of Taiwan" in Tania Groppi and Marie-Claire Ponthoreau (eds), *The Use of Foreign Precedents by Constitutional Judges* (Hart 2013), 373–92.

2013.[32] Because the Constitutional Court began functioning more effectively after the democratization in the late 1980s, most judgments selected were made in the 1990s and 2000s. Among these 40 judgments, 23 are concerned with fundamental rights issues and 19 with state organization issues. There are 4 judgments involving both fundamental rights and state organization issues. On the nature of judgments, among these 40 selected interpretations, 6 judgments are involved with the interpretation of constitutional provisions, and 34 judgments are concerned with constitutionality of laws or rules. Among the 34 judgments, 21 judgments find (at least partially) against the law or rule challenged. In one judgment, constitutional amendments were declared unconstitutional and rendered null and void.[33]

As mentioned earlier, the issuance of separate opinions was not permitted until 1958. Among the 40 judgments selected, 39 judgments were made after 1958, of which 31 came with separate opinions while 8 were made without any separate opinions issued. Because the style of majority opinions departs quite substantially from that of separate opinions, this research analyses both in terms of their respective types and styles of arguments.

5 *The Structure of Constitutional Arguments*

The arguments in most opinions – including majority and separate opinions – of the selected judgments (29 of 40) rely on chain structures (one-line conclusive arguments). The second most popular (27 of 40) is the dialogic method (parallel, individually inconclusive, but together conclusive structure) in that the judgments present a range of relevant considerations, none of which is conclusive. Only 8 judgments may be categorized as legs of a chair (parallel conclusive) arguments: J.Y. Interpretation Nos. 582, 584, 585, 649, 656, 666, 689 and 690.

A close examination of the structure of reasoning in majority opinions confirms the prevalence of one-line conclusive arguments (19 of 40) and parallel, individually inconclusive, but together conclusive arguments (15 of 40). Only 6 majority opinions are categorized as parallel conclusive arguments: J.Y. Interpretation Nos. 582, 584, 585, 649, 689 and 690.

Chain Structure (One-Line Conclusive Arguments)

One-line conclusive arguments are most popular in the opinions, especially majority opinions. As majority opinions tend to be brief and short,

[32] By the end of May 2013, the Constitutional Court has issued altogether 709 interpretations.
[33] J.Y. Interpretation No. 499 (24 April 2000).

one-line conclusive arguments have been preferred even in cases involving complex situations or even constitutional crises. For example, in J.Y. Interpretation No. 31, the Constitutional Court was faced with the de facto difficulty in which the second-term national representatives could not be elected from Mainland China because of the relocation of the government to Taiwan. Based on the argument of exceptional constitutional crisis, the Constitutional Court decided that the first-term national representatives should remain in office till the election of the second term.[34] Another recent example of using one-line conclusive arguments is the majority opinion of J.Y. Interpretation No. 708, in which the Constitutional Court dealt with an unconstitutional challenge on the deportation proceedings of illegal immigrants. The Constitutional Court decided that substantive and procedural protections of physical freedoms prescribed in Article 8 of the Constitution should be extended to foreigners and thus found the deportation without judicial hearing unconstitutional.[35]

Dialogic Structure (Parallel, Individually Inconclusive, but Together Conclusive Arguments)

The first judgment presenting a dialogic structure (parallel, individually inconclusive, but together conclusive arguments) is J.Y. Interpretation No. 242.[36] In this judgment, the Constitutional Court was requested to make an exception for the invalidation of second marriage under the Civil Code. Because of the relocation of the national government from Mainland China to Taiwan and the ensuing war between both sides, some of those who had left families on the Mainland married again in Taiwan. Whether the second marriage was legal and whether the spouses of the first marriage could revoke the second marriage became a difficult issue in the late 1980s when travels and communications became available again. Considering the right of marriage, family lives and human relations to be national crises at the time, the Constitutional Court decided to make exception to the prohibition in the Civil Code and sustained the legality of those second marriages.

Another example of dialogical structure reasoning is in the majority opinion of J.Y. Interpretation No. 261.[37] In this decision, the Constitutional Court was faced with a constitutional impasse in that the first-term national representatives had stayed in power for nearly four decades,

34 J.Y. Interpretation No. 31 (29 January 1954).
35 J.Y. Interpretation No. 708 (6 February 2013).
36 J.Y. Interpretation No. 242 (23 June 1989).
37 J.Y. Interpretation No. 261 (21 June 1990).

but a second national election that included the people on the Mainland was still impossible. Having considered the principle of democracy and periodic election, exceptional situations between the Mainland and Taiwan, the sustainability of constitutionalism and constitutional institutions, the Constitutional Court – without overruling J.Y. Interpretation No. 31 – decided to have a second election. A more recent example is J.Y. Interpretation No. 550, in which the Constitutional Court was asked whether local governments were obligated to finance the national health insurance system.[38] The Constitutional Court reasoned that according to constitutional provisions involving power divisions between central and local governments, a national health insurance system should be established and implemented by the cooperation of both. At the same time, however, the principle of local autonomy including financial autonomy was also guaranteed by the Constitution. Hence, the Constitutional Court decided that while local governments were obligated to finance the national health insurance system, they should be also entitled to participate in the decision-making process when the central government devised and implemented the system.

Legs of a Chair (Parallel Conclusive Arguments)

The only 8 judgments in the 40 selected judgments that can be categorized as relying on parallel conclusive arguments (legs of a chair) are J.Y. Interpretation Nos. 582, 584, 585, 649, 656, 666, 689 and 690.

In J.Y. Interpretation No. 582, the Constitutional Court was confronted with a challenge to the constitutionality of a judicial precedent in which criminal defendants were not permitted to cross-examine the statements made by co-defendants as witness.[39] The Constitutional Court found the challenged judicial precedent unconstitutional on two parallel grounds: the right to sue guaranteed by Article 16 of the Constitution and due process in the administration of criminal justice system embodied in Article 8 of the Constitution. Both grounds established the same conclusion that criminal defendants should be provided with the opportunity to cross-examine co-defendants as witness.

Another example of legs-of-a-chair argument is J.Y. Interpretation No. 585 involving a challenge to the constitutionality of a statute that created an independent commission to investigate a gun-shot incident in

[38] J.Y. Interpretation No. 550 (4 October 2002).

[39] J.Y. Interpretation No. 582 (23 July 2004).

a presidential election.[40] The Constitutional Court sustained the statute in part while invalidating it in another part. According to the Constitutional Court, the legislature may exercise the power of investigation and entrust this power to a legislative committee. At the same time, the executive also enjoys executive privilege inherent in its own powers. Hence, such an investigative committee can be constitutionally in existence only if it is a parliamentary committee without overt interference with the executive. The legs-of-a-chair argument appeared most recently in J.Y. Interpretation No. 690, in which the Constitutional Court reviewed the constitutionality of compulsory quarantine under the Communicable Disease Control Act. Having examined the protection of physical freedom guaranteed by Article 8 of the Constitution and legal clarity based upon the principle of the rule of law, the Constitutional Court found the impugned process still constitutional.[41]

6 *Types of Arguments in Constitutional Reasoning*

There is no self-reference in the Constitution about how to interpret constitutional provisions. Nevertheless, Article 13 of the Constitutional Interpretation Procedure Act privileges a historical method, stating that "In case of rendering an interpretation, the Justices shall refer to materials concerning the enactment and amendments of the Constitution, and the legislative history of a statute or regulation."

Analogies

None of the 40 judgments uses analogies in the reasoning. One possible explanation is that the Constitutional Court reviews the constitutionality of laws in the abstract. It is the law itself – rather than the case involved – that is the objective of constitutional review. Thus, the method of analogy rarely occurs in constitutional reasoning.

Establishing/Debating the Text of the Constitution

The question of what counts as a constitutional text rarely occurs to Taiwan's Constitutional Court. None of the majority opinions in the 40 selected judgments made any inquiry on this issue.

[40] J.Y. Interpretation No. 585 (15 December 2004).
[41] J.Y. Interpretation No. 690 (30 September 2011).

However, the two individual opinions of J.Y. Interpretation No. 709 entertained the question of whether the rights enshrined in the International Covenant on Civil and Political Rights (ICCPR) and the International Covenant on Economic, Social and Cultural Rights (ICESCR) should become part of the constitutionally protected rights and be accorded constitutional status.[42] The Republic of China government in Taiwan had signed both ICCPR and ICESCR in 1967 before it was expelled from the United Nations in 1971 and its seat taken by the People's Republic of China government on the Mainland. In March 2009, under pressure from human rights groups and the general public, the government finally ratified both Covenants, and the legislature also passed an Implementation Act to accord all rights enshrined in the two Covenants the status of law and make these rights directly applicable in the domestic legal system.[43] Yet, because of the universal nature and the paramount importance of the rights guaranteed in the two Covenants, a heated debate has taken place on whether these rights should be elevated to constitutional status.

J.Y. Interpretation No. 709 was involved with the constitutionality of several provisions in the Urban Renewal Act. The right to adequate housing guaranteed by Article 11 of the ICESCR was briefly referred to in the majority opinion. Yet, the majority opinion remains completely silent on the status of this right or other rights enshrined in the two Covenants. The concurring opinion issued by Justice Chun-Sheng Chen interpreted the majority's silence on the status of the Covenants rights as refusing to accord constitutional status with these rights and excluding the Covenants as constitutional sources. However, the opinion concurring in part and dissenting in part issued by Justice Chang-fa Lo strongly argued that the rights enshrined in the two Covenants were universal in nature and should be accorded constitutional status and directly applied by the Constitutional Court. In my view, the majority's silence on the constitutional status of the Covenants rights was not yet a rejection but a sign of ongoing heated debate among the Grand Justices.

Applicability of the Constitution

The issue of the applicability of the Constitution occurs only in 5 cases – including J.Y. Interpretation Nos. 328, 419, 499, 520, and 632 –of the

[42] J.Y. Interpretation No. 709 (26 April 2014).

[43] Wen-Chen Chang, "An Isolated Nation with Global-minded Citizens: Bottom-up Transnational Constitutionalism in Taiwan" (2009) 4.3 *National Taiwan University Law Review* 203, 222–33.

40 selected judgments. In 3 cases, J.Y. Interpretation Nos. 328, 419, and 499, the discussions appear in the majority opinions involving national territory, separation of powers and unconstitutional constitutional amendment.

J.Y. Interpretation No. 328 dealt with a controversial issue regarding the scope of national territory. In response, the Constitutional Court states that "national territory" is a "purely political question" and "is not subject to judicial review according to the constitutional principle of separation of powers".[44] By invoking the doctrine of political question, the Constitutional Court avoided an extremely sensitive issue regarding the relationship between Taiwan and Mainland China. Another case on constitutional applicability is J.Y. Interpretation No. 419, which was concerned with the timing of the premier's resignation after a presidential election. Based upon a parliamentary system, the Constitution stipulates the premier's resignation only after parliamentary elections. A popularly-elected presidency, however, was adopted in the constitutional amendment of 1994. After the first presidential election in 1996, whether the premier should resign after a presidential election was disputed. In J.Y. Interpretation No. 419, the Constitutional Court decided that premier's resignation after a presidential election is only "a matter of courtesy in deference to the newly elected president but not an obligation under the Constitution" and thus "how such a resignation should be handled falls within presidential discretion, not subject to constitutional review."[45]

J.Y. Interpretation No. 499 was the first case for the Constitutional Court to consider the constitutionality of constitutional amendment.[46] The question on constitutional applicability became inevitable, and the Constitutional Court affirmed unequivocally such applicability. In view of the majority opinion, "the primary function of interpreting law is to resolve overlaps or conflicts of rules, including doubts resulting from defects or gaps created by contradictory rules enacted at different times", and hence, the inquiry of "whether conflicts or contradictions may have occurred between the amendments to the Constitution and the Constitution itself" should fall within the interpretive powers vested in the Constitutional Court. Consequently, the Constitutional Court in this case provided for procedural and substantial constraints to constitutional amendments and even invalidated the impugned constitutional amendment of 1999.

44 J.Y. Interpretation No. 328 (26 November 1993).
45 J.Y. Interpretation No. 419 (31 December 1996).
46 J.Y. Interpretation No. 499 (24 March 2000).

The other two individual opinions that discuss constitutional applicability are J.Y. Interpretation Nos. 520 and 632. In J.Y. Interpretation No. 520, the executive's unilateral suspension of the fourth nuclear power plant was challenged before the Constitutional Court. Although the majority resolved the case by recognizing and balancing between the executive's power to implement (or not implement) government projects and the legislative's budgetary power in taking such decisions, 3 individual opinions – 1 concurring in part and 2 dissenting in part – insisted that the Constitutional Court should have dismissed the petition, as the dispute was purely political between the executive and legislative branches and better left to be resolved by them.[47] In J.Y. Interpretation No. 632, the Constitutional Court found a legislative inaction unconstitutional in that the legislative majority boycotted the appointment of members to the Control Yuan, functionally equivalent to ombudsmen, by not exercising the consenting power for several years. However, a dissenting opinion lamented the majority's decision, arguing that the dispute should have been left for political – rather than legal – resolution.

Ordinary Meaning of the Words of the Constitution

None of the majority opinions in the 40 selected judgments utilizes the method in interpreting ordinary meaning of the words in the Constitution. In the 3 individual opinions of J.Y. Interpretation Nos. 342, 550 and 708, however, this method was entertained.

In J.Y. Interpretation No. 342, Justice Chien-Hua Yang in his dissenting opinion argued that according to the ordinary meaning of "decide by resolution" in Article 63 of the Constitution,[48] the law-making of the legislature is "decided by resolution" and thus should not be subject to judicial review. J.Y. Interpretation No. 550 was concerned with the question of whether local governments should finance the national health insurance program. One dissenting opinion considered the wordings of "national", "central" and "local" governments in various constitutional provisions, arguing that the national health insurance program should be financed only by the central government.[49] J.Y. Interpretation No. 708

[47] J.Y. Interpretation No. 520 (15 January 2001).

[48] Article 63 of the Constitution provides: "The Legislative Yuan shall have the power to decide by resolution upon statutory or budgetary bills or bills concerning martial law, amnesty, declaration of war, conclusion of peace or treaties, and other important affairs of the State."

[49] J.Y. Interpretation No. 550 (4 October 2002).

was concerned with the constitutionality of deportation proceedings for illegal immigrants.[50] One opinion of concurring in part and dissenting in part relied upon the ordinary meaning of words in Article 8 of the Constitution,[51] arguing that as "personal freedom should be guaranteed to the individuals", this should include foreign individuals.

Domestic Harmonising Arguments

Domestic harmonising arguments are quite common, appearing in 14 majority opinions of 40 selected judgments. Individual opinions included, such arguments are seen in 16 of the 40 selected judgments. Domestic harmonisation has been undertaken in three categories of cases: when considering the balance of different constitutional rights (J.Y. Interpretation Nos. 509, 582, 649, 656, 666, 689 and 709), when entertaining separation of powers and finding the power scopes and limitations of different branches (J.Y. Interpretation Nos. 419, 499, 520, 530, 550, 585, 601), and perhaps quite exceptionally, when considering extraordinary constitutional situations (J.Y. Interpretation Nos. 31 and 261).

J.Y. Interpretation No. 509 represents a typical case in which domestic harmonisation takes place in balancing different constitutional rights. This case was concerned with criminal defamation, in which the Constitutional Court considered both freedom of speech protected by Article 11 of the Constitution and right of reputation by Article 22 and struck a delicate balance between the two rights.[52] In the second category of cases in which domestic harmonisation is utilised to balance powers of different branches, J.Y. Interpretation No. 520 represented the balance between the executive and legislative powers and J.Y. Interpretation No. 550 represented the balance between the central and local governments.[53] The last category of cases in domestic harmonisation may be quite rare and exceptional. In J.Y. Interpretation Nos. 31 and 261, the Constitutional Court had to strike a balance between constitutional provisions in which the second-term representatives must be elected from Mainland China, constitutional principles of democracy and periodic elections, and constitutional reality that the government was relocated to Taiwan.[54]

50 J.Y. Interpretation No. 708 (6 February 2013).
51 Article 8(1) of the Constitution: "Personal freedom shall be guaranteed to the individuals."
52 J.Y. Interpretation No. 509 (7 July 2000).
53 J.Y. Interpretation No. 520 (15 January 2001); J.Y. Interpretation No. 550 (4 October 2002).
54 J.Y. Interpretation No. 31 (29 January 1954); J.Y. Interpretation No. 261 (21 June 1990).

International Harmonising Arguments

International harmonising arguments do not appear as often as domestic harmonising arguments in the judgments of Taiwan's Constitutional Court. This is because the Republic of China (Taiwan) government was expelled from its seat in the United Nations in 1971 and has since been isolated from the international community. As mentioned earlier, in recent years, the government – under the pressure of human rights groups and the civil society – began unilateral accession to and voluntary compliance with some core international human rights conventions. The ratifications, accessions or implementations of the ICCPR, ICESCR, and the Convention on the Elimination of All Forms of Discrimination against Women (CEDAW), the Convention on the Rights of the Child (CRC) and the Convention on the Rights of Persons with Disability (CRPD) are representative examples.[55]

International harmonising arguments appear in 4 majority opinions of the 40 selected judgments, which are J.Y. Interpretation Nos. 392, 582, 690 and 709. Individual opinions included, 7 of the 40 selected judgments include international harmonisation, which include J.Y. Interpretation Nos. 392, 550, 582, 666, 690, 708 and 709.

J.Y. Interpretation Nos. 392 and 582 were both concerned with the rights of criminal defendants.[56] In both judgments, the protection of personal freedom and the guarantee of due process enshrined in the ICCPR as well as in the European Convention for the Protection of Human Rights and Fundamental Freedoms were discussed extensively for harmonising with related domestic constitutional provisions. In J.Y. Interpretation No. 690 on the constitutionality of compulsory quarantine, the relevant measures and expert opinions of the World Health Organization were given substantial weight in balancing with domestic constitutional and legal provisions.[57] In J.Y. Interpretation No. 709, albeit not expressly provided for in the Constitution, the right to adequate housing guaranteed in the ICESCR was referred to when the Constitutional Court considered the constitutionality of the Urban Renewal Act.[58]

In J.Y. Interpretation Nos. 666 and 708, international harmonisation was witnessed in individual opinions. In the former case concerning

[55] Wen-Chen Chang (n 8).

[56] J.Y. Interpretation No. 392 (22 December 1995); J.Y. Interpretation No. 582 (23 July 2004).

[57] J.Y. Interpretation No. 690 (30 September 2011).

[58] J.Y. Interpretation No. 709 (26 April 2013).

the criminalization of prostitution, one concurring opinion referred to the CEDAW, arguing that the principle of substantive equality and the prohibition of intersectional discrimination in the CEDAW should be applicable.[59] In the latter case on deportation proceedings of illegal immigrants, a few individual opinions referred to the guarantee of personal freedom, including the ones of foreigners by the ICCPR along with other key international human rights instruments.[60]

Precedents

Precedent-based arguments are quite popular in the judgments of Taiwan's Constitutional Court. In the majority opinions, 26 of the 40 selected judgments refer to precedents. Individual opinions included, 30 of the 40 selected judgments employ such arguments.

Notably, the Constitutional Court has thus far never overruled any previous interpretations. The reference to past interpretations primarily functions in two ways. First and most typically, the reference to precedents is made when the Court deals with the same or similar issues and decides to follow the precedents. The examples include J.Y. Interpretation No. 251 that referred to J.Y. Interpretation No. 166 as both dealt with the constitutionality of police detention,[61] and J.Y. Interpretation No. 585 that cited J.Y. Interpretation No. 325, as the power of parliamentary investigation was involved in both cases.[62] Such precedent-based arguments are frequently invoked in interpretations involving the same rights or freedoms.

Second, on fewer occasions, precedents are invoked to make adjustments to present situations. The most important example is J.Y. Interpretation No. 261 that referred to J.Y. Interpretation No. 31. The two interpretations dealt with the same constitutional dilemma, in which the first-term national representatives had overstayed in office because the second-term representatives could not be elected from the Chinese mainland due to the government's relocation from the Chinese Mainland to Taiwan. While J.Y. Interpretation No. 31 permitted the continuation in office, J.Y. Interpretation No. 261 ordered the first-term national representatives to leave office by a set deadline. Interestingly, however,

[59] J.Y. Interpretation No. 666 (6 November 2009).

[60] J.Y. Interpretation No. 708 (6 February 2013).

[61] J.Y. Interpretation No. 166 (6 November 1980); J.Y. Interpretation No. 251 (19 January 1990).

[62] J.Y. Interpretation No. 325 (23 July 1993); J.Y. Interpretation No. 585 (15 December 2004).

J.Y. Interpretation No. 261 did not overrule J.Y. Interpretation No. 31. Rather, J.Y. Interpretation No. 261 referred to J.Y. Interpretation No. 31 for support, contending that "neither J.Y. Interpretation No. 31, nor the Constitution was intended to allow the first-term national representatives to continue exercising their powers indefinitely."[63]

Doctrinal Analysis of Legal Concepts or Principles

Doctrinal analysis of legal concepts or principles that are not mentioned in the Constitution is the most popular method employed by the Constitutional Court. Of the 40 selected judgments, 31 majority opinions employ such a method. With individual opinions counted, 34 of the 40 judgments adopt such a method. The reasons for such a predominant reliance on doctrinal analyses of legal concepts or principles are mainly twofold. The first is due to the old age and concise nature of the ROC Constitution. The second is due to the scholarly backgrounds of justices.

First, the ROC Constitution that became effective in 1947 and consisted of 175 provisions is not as elaborate as other constitutions made or amended in the 1990s or 2000s. The list of fundamental rights and freedoms guaranteed by Chapter 2 of the Constitution from Articles 7 to 24 is particularly brief. Quite a number of contemporarily recognised rights and freedoms are not guaranteed. For example, right of marriage, right of privacy, right of reputation, freedom of contract, indigenous rights, rights of disabled persons or prohibition on discriminations against the disabled, press freedom or equal access to media, right of access to information, and human dignity, among many others, are not guaranteed in the Constitution. Key constitutional concepts regarding individual rights or state organizations such as due process, rule of law, legal clarity or legal certainty, the separation of powers, checks and balances, the principle of proportionality, or the non-delegation doctrine are also not expressly written or mentioned in the Constitution. Although there were seven rounds of constitutional revisions in the process of democratization during the 1990s and the 2000s, those amendments targeted only the institutional designs of state organizations such as the changes from an indirectly elected presidency to a directly elected presidency and from a parliamentary government system to a semi-presidential government system. Not a single provision concerning the rights and freedoms of individuals was

[63] J.Y. Interpretation No. 261 (21 June 1990); J.Y. Interpretation No. 31 (29 January 1954).

added or revised. There is, thus, a strong need for judicial articulation of rights or freedoms that are not enumerated in the Constitution and of key constitutional concepts or principles.[64]

An example is J.Y. Interpretation No. 603, in which the constitutionality of the Household Registration Act requiring applicants for a new identity card to submit fingerprints was challenged before the Constitutional Court. Although the right of privacy is not expressly guaranteed in the Constitution, the Constitutional Court nevertheless established that "To preserve human dignity and to respect the free development of personality are the core values of the constitutional structure of free democracy" and hence "the right of privacy should be considered as an indispensable fundamental right."[65] Based upon the preservation of human dignity and the respect of free development in personality, the Constitutional Court has articulated quite a number of unenumerated rights including right to personality,[66] right to reputation,[67] right to bear one's own name,[68] sexual freedom[69] and freedom of contract,[70] among others.

Similar lines of reasoning are presented in the developments of the principle of proportionality and the principle of non-delegation doctrine or statutory reservation (*Gesetzesvorbehalt*). Article 23 of the Constitution states that "All the freedoms and rights enumerated in the preceding Articles shall not be restricted *by law* except by such *as may be necessary* to prevent infringement upon the freedoms of other persons, to avert an imminent crisis, to maintain social order or to advance public welfare."[71] In light of this provision, the Constitutional Court in J.Y. Interpretation No. 443 has elaborated a complex set of rules in which the restrictions of some rights must be stipulated in statutes while others may be delegated by administrative regulations and still others may require no delegations at all. According to the Constitutional Court,

> the range of freedoms and rights of the people stipulated in the Constitution is very broad . . . Nevertheless, not every freedom and right is protected in the same way in the Constitution. The physical freedom of the people is stipulated in detail in Article 8 of the Constitution, in which those rights reserved in the Constitution shall not be limited even by the legislative

64 Wen-Chen Chang (n 8).
65 J.Y. Interpretation No. 603 (28 September 2005), Reasoning, [1].
66 J.Y. Interpretation No. 587 (30 December 2004).
67 J.Y. Interpretation No. 656 (3 April 2009).
68 J.Y. Interpretation No. 399 (22 March 1996).
69 J.Y. Interpretation No. 554 (27 December 2002).
70 J.Y. Interpretation No. 576 (23 April 2004).
71 Emphases are added by the author.

> authority, whereas freedom and rights under Articles 7, 9–18, 21 and 22 may be limited by the law upon meeting the conditions stipulated in Article 23 of the Constitution. The determination of which freedom or right shall be regulated by law or by rules authorized by the law shall depend on regulated intensity. Reasonable deviation is allowed considering the party to be regulated, the content of the regulation, or the limitations to be made on the interests or freedom . . . For policies concerning benefit to the people, the law governing such policies may be constructed more loosely compared to laws governing limitations on people's rights. Nevertheless, in the case where such policies are related to major public interests, they shall be made by law or rules authorized by law.[72]

The Constitutional Court articulates the principle of proportionality for the first time in J.Y. Interpretation No. 476, which was concerned with the constitutionality of special criminal laws on drugs that may impose even the death penalty. According to the Constitutional Court,

> these special criminal laws should not be deemed improper if their purposes aim to conform to the nationals' expectations and the affection of the laws. In addition, these special criminal laws should be deemed consistent with the principle of proportionality under Article 23 of the Constitution if the methods used to achieve such purposes are necessary to correct and prevent mistakes and are also reasonable actions to take even though they restrict the people's fundamental rights.[73]

Another example is the articulation of the principle of the separation of powers. While the Constitution stipulates and allocates different powers to different branches, it nevertheless does not contain any provisions articulating the principle of separation of powers. In J.Y. Interpretation No. 613, when dealing with the constitutionality of the creation of an independent regulatory commission, the Constitutional Court for the first time elaborates:

> the principle of separation of powers, as a fundamental constitutional principle, signifies not only the division of powers whereby all state affairs are assigned to various state organs with the right organizations, systems and functions so as to enable state decisions to be made more appropriately, but also suggests the checks and balances of powers whereby powers are mutually containing and restraining so as to avoid infringement upon the people's freedoms and rights due to unrestrained misuse of the powers. However, there are still some limits on the checks and balances of powers. There should be no violation of an unambiguous constitutional provision,

[72] J.Y. Interpretation No. 443 (26 December 1997).
[73] J.Y. Interpretation No. 476 (29 January 1999).

> nor should there be any encroachment upon the core areas of the powers of various constitutional organs or restriction of the exercise of powers by other constitutional organs or breach of the politics of accountability.[74]

There are many other similar examples of doctrinal analyses of constitutional concepts or principles in the interpretations of Taiwan's Constitutional Court. Aside from the first – and foremost – reason, the second reason explaining such a heavy reliance on doctrinal articulation is the scholarly background of the justices. As stated above, as a tradition, half of the Grand Justices on Taiwan's Constitutional Court have been law professors. There should be no surprise that these former law professors have brought their scholarly thinking and writing styles into the Constitutional Court. Even more importantly, as stated above, most of the Grand Justices – including both former career judges and former law professors – received advanced legal training abroad. It is only natural for them to apply what they have learned elsewhere in their own reasoning styles. Doctrinal principles these justices have learned elsewhere have contributed significantly to the jurisprudence of the Constitutional Court, which naturally embodies comparative laws with or without explicit references or citations.[75]

Arguments from Silence

Arguments from silence are rarely used by the Constitutional Court. Only 2 majority opinions in J.Y. Interpretation Nos. 328 and 632 and 2 individual opinions in J.Y. Interpretation Nos. 530 and 708 invoked such arguments. J.Y. Interpretation No. 328 was concerned with the scope of territory of the Republic of China. The majority opinion skillfully avoided answering this constitutional controversy by arguing that "Instead of enumerating the components, Article 4 of the Constitution provides that the national territory of the Republic of China is determined according to its existing national boundaries" and that such a silence on enumeration should indicate that "The delimitation of national territory according to its history is a significant political question and thus it is beyond the reach of judicial review."[76]

J.Y. Interpretation No. 632 was concerned with the issue of whether it was constitutional for the legislature not to exercise its consenting power over the appointment of the members to the Control Yuan, functionally equivalent to ombudsmen. The majority opinion noted that "neither the

[74] J.Y. Interpretation No. 613 (21 July 2006). [75] Law and Chang (n 27) 571–2.
[76] J.Y. Interpretation No. 328 (26 November 1993).

Constitution, nor any law provides an adequate mechanism to resolve the present issue and maintain the normal operations of the Control Yuan when the term has expired before succeeding candidates can be inaugurated." As a result of such silence, the Constitutional Court decided to provide a remedy by itself, stating that "[u]ntil the Constitution or law can be amended to address this issue, the normal operations of constitutional governance will continue to depend more on a constitutional agency having decision-making power over personnel administration issues to faithfully carry out its duties to fill the vacancies and to prevent such governance from being impacted" and that "the Constitution does not allow for the event in which either the president or the legislature fails to nominate or consent to the nomination of candidates so that the Control Yuan cannot exercise its power or function".[77]

Teleological/Purposive Arguments Referring to the Purpose of the Text

This type of argument is quite common in the interpretations of Taiwan's Constitutional Court. It is used in 29 majority opinions of the 40 selected judgments and, individual opinions included, 32 of the 40 judgments. It is interesting to note that when invoking teleological/purposive arguments, the opinions always referred to the text. In other words, text-based arguments are strongly connected to teleological and purposive arguments.

The other interesting finding is the connection between purposive arguments and the result of judgments. When the majority opinions invoked purposive readings of constitutional provisions, the case dispositions tend to be against the impugned laws. In the 29 judgments that invoked purposive arguments, 16 judgments ruled against the challenged laws and 10 judgments maintained them, while the remaining 3 judgments did not rule on constitutionality.

Teleological/Purposive Arguments Referring to the Purpose of the Constitution-Maker (Including Travaux Préparatoires)

Arguments based on the purpose of constitutional framers are not frequently used. They are used in 6 majority opinions of the 40 selected judgments, and, individual opinions included, 10 of the 40 judgments. It is noteworthy that the 6 majority opinions that referred to the purpose

[77] J.Y. Interpretation No. 632 (15 August 2007).

of constitutional framers were all concerned with the issues of state organizations or separation of powers, including J.Y. Interpretation Nos. 261, 328, 392, 419, 499 and 632.

For example, in J.Y. Interpretation No. 392, the question of whether prosecutors should exercise the power of detention was placed before the Constitutional Court. Having relied on the intent of framers in drafting Article 8 of the Constitution that resembles the system of habeas corpus, the majority opinion decided that prosecutors are not courts, and that the power of detention should be vested only in courts.[78] In J.Y. Interpretation No. 419, the question of whether the Vice President may concurrently serve as Premier was brought to the Constitutional Court. Again, the majority opinion relied on the record of constitution making to argue that constitutional framers did not intend to prohibit such concurrence in office.[79]

Non-legal (Moral, Sociological, Economic) Arguments

Non-legal arguments are rarely considered in the opinions. Only 3 majority opinions of the selected 40 judgments relied on such arguments. Individual opinions included, non-legal arguments appear in 6 of the selected 40 judgments.

As discussed earlier, J.Y. Interpretation No. 242 was concerned with the legality of a second marriage concluded after the spouses of the first marriage were separated because of warfare and the government's relocation from Mainland China to Taiwan in 1949. In the decision, the majority opinion considered such an exceptional situation, the influences of separation on "family life", "human relations" and "social order" and eventually decided to make an exception to the Civil Code to recognize the legality of the second marriage.[80]

J.Y. Interpretation No. 649 was concerned with the constitutionality of the Physically and Mentally Disabled Citizens Protection Act that gave an exclusive right to vision-impaired individuals for the practice of the massage business.[81] Such a business advantage provided for vision-impaired individuals was challenged as unequal treatment. The majority opinion considered sociological factors such as the "difficulties in learning and education" faced by those suffering from vision impairment, and "the

[78] J.Y. Interpretation No. 392 (22 December 1995).
[79] J.Y. Interpretation No. 419 (31 December 1996).
[80] J.Y. Interpretation No. 242 (23 June 1989).
[81] J.Y. Interpretation No. 649 (31 October 1998).

reality that vision-impaired individuals have traditionally been dependent upon massage business for their livelihood."[82] Nevertheless, the majority opinion still found such an exclusive business advantage for only vision-impaired individuals to be in violation of equal protection, right to work and the principle of proportionality. In view of the majority, "anyone interested in massage business should have been eligible to engage in the occupation after receiving corresponding training and qualification review" and "by only permitting the vision-impaired to be able to conduct such business", the impugned law "has resulted in the non-vision impaired transferring to other occupation or losing their jobs, and a multi-facet competitive environment for consumers to choose not being able to form", which is "not in parity with the interest to protect the right of employment for the vision-impaired."[83]

The other majority opinion that considered sociological and economic arguments is J.Y. Interpretation No. 666.[84] In this interpretation, the provision of the Social Order Maintenance Act that imposed administrative penalties on those providing sex for financial gains was challenged. Although the penalties were imposed on both men and women who provided sexual service, the Constitutional Court decided to review the impugned provision on the ground of sexual equality due to the social reality that the predominant number of those who engaged in sexual service were "the socially and economically disadvantaged females".[85] In view of the majority opinion, "in light of the fact that the gender of [sexual service providers] is more likely to be female, [the disputed provision] virtually amounts to a control that only targets and punishes those females participating in sexual transactions," and "their already miserable situations are often further aggravated by the penalties of the disputed provision."[86]

It is perhaps not a surprise that the Constitutional Court considers sociological or economic factors mostly in equality cases. When considering beyond formal equality, the Constitutional Court must take into consideration a complex range of social and economic structural factors in order to argue on the grounds of substantive equality. The other 3 interpretations in which individual opinions considered sociological or economic

[82] J.Y. Interpretation No. 649, Reasoning [2].
[83] J.Y. Interpretation No. 649, Reasoning, [5].
[84] J.Y. Interpretation No. 666 (6 November 2009).
[85] J.Y. Interpretation No. 666, Reasoning, [3].
[86] J.Y. Interpretation No. 666, Reasoning, [3].

factors are J.Y. Interpretation Nos. 584, 656 and 708. J.Y. Interpretation No. 584 was concerned with discrimination against those who had been convicted of certain offences on their right of occupation.[87] J.Y. Interpretation No. 656 was concerned with the constitutionality of judicially imposed apologies in the context of defamation.[88] In J.Y. Interpretation No. 708, the deportation proceedings of illegal immigrants were challenged as violating foreigners' right to physical freedom and due process guarantees.[89] Although these cases are not all about equal protections, they tend to invite judicial considerations on further social and economic factors concerning particular classes of citizens.

References to Scholarly Works

A significant disparity exists in referencing scholarly works between majority and individual opinions. There are only 2 majority opinions in the 40 selected judgments that made reference to scholarly works, whereas there are 25 of the 40 judgments in which individual opinions referenced scholarly works. Similar disparity is also witnessed in referencing foreign laws, which are discussed in the next section.

The disparity in referencing scholarly works between majority and separate opinions is no surprise given the tradition of civil law system in which judgments tend to be rather brief without lengthy references or citations.[90] Similar to the courts of the civil law system, Taiwan's Constitutional Court deems majority opinions as the opinions of the court, which must be signed by all justices regardless of their respective concurring or dissenting positions. In practice, majority opinions are discussed – paragraph by paragraph – by all justices. In other words, not only must the arguments of majority opinions win the majority of the court, but also the styles must be acceptable. Unlike separate opinions in which justices may embrace their individual styles in writing and arguing, majority opinions are usually compromises in both argument and style, presenting the court as a collective.

It is important to note that fewer references to scholarly works or foreign laws do not mean that majority opinions embody less academic views or comparative laws. On the contrary, as discussed above, Taiwan's

87 J.Y. Interpretation No. 584 (17 September 2004).

88 J.Y. Interpretation No. 656 (3 April 2009).

89 J.Y. Interpretation No. 708 (6 February 2013).

90 Tania Groppi and Marie-Claire Ponthoreau, 'Conclusion', in Tania Groppi and Marie-Claire Ponthoreau (eds), *The Use of Foreign Precedents by Constitutional Judges* (Hart 2013) 412.

legal community as well as the jurisprudence of the Constitutional Court has been heavily influenced by academic views and comparative laws. The composition of the Constitutional Court – in which half of the justices are former academics – and foreign educational credentials of the justices clearly indicate its comparative influences.[91]

The only 2 interpretations in which scholarly works are referred to are J.Y. Interpretation Nos. 419 and 499. J.Y. Interpretation No. 419 was concerned with the question of whether the Vice President could concurrently serve as the Premier. In illustrating the history of presidential powers with the development of modern parliamentary democracy, the majority opinion referred to two books – *Der Hüter der Verfassung* (The Guardian of the Constitution) and *Verfassungslehre* (Constitutional Lecture) – by Carl Schmitt and *Die Parlamentarischen Regierungssysteme in Europa* (The Parliamentary System in Europe) by Klaus von Beyme.[92] In J.Y. Interpretation No.499, the Constitutional Court reviewed the constitutionality of the constitutional amendments of 1999. In arguing the interpretive powers of the courts regarding conflicts of rules, the majority opinion referred to two scholarly works – one by Karl Larenz on *Methodenlehre der Rechtswissenschaft* (Methodology Lectures of Jurisprudence) and the other by Emillo Betti on *Allgemeine Auslegungslehre als Methodik der Geisteswissenschaften* (General Interpretation Lecture on Method of Human Science).[93] Because there are more justices who received doctorates in Germany than those who did so elsewhere, it is not surprising that these two majority opinions referred to German scholarship. In contrast, scholarly works referred to in separate opinions are far more diverse, including both domestic and foreign scholarship.

References to Foreign (National) Law

Similar to the finding in referencing scholarly works, references to foreign law are fewer in majority opinions but far more in individual opinions. In the 40 selected judgments, only 7 majority opinions referred to foreign law, and if individual opinions are included, 26 of the 40 selected judgments made reference to foreign law. My research elsewhere has shown that most references to foreign law were provided by the justices of scholarly backgrounds, and that there is a linkage between foreign references and foreign educations received by justices. In other words, justices receiving

[91] Law and Chang (n 27), 563ff. [92] J.Y. Interpretation No. 419, Reasoning, [4] I [8].
[93] J.Y. Interpretation No. 499, Reasoning, [3].

doctorates from Germany are more likely to make references to German laws, and justices receiving doctorates from the United States are more likely to refer to American laws.[94]

The 7 majority opinions that made references to foreign law are mostly concerned with high-profile issues on state organizations or separation of powers. They include J.Y. Interpretation No. 342 on legislative filibuster,[95] J.Y. Interpretation No. 419 on concurrence in offices of the Vice President and Premier,[96] J.Y. Interpretation No. 499 on unconstitutional constitutional amendments[97] and J.Y. Interpretation No. 632 on legislative inaction in confirmation. The other three are concerned with judicial powers and the administration of the judicial system, including J.Y. Interpretation No. 392 on the power of prosecutors,[98] J.Y. Interpretation No. 582 on criminal due process[99] and J.Y. Interpretation No. 665 on the judicial administration of case assignments.[100] Among these foreign jurisdictions cited, Germany, Japan, the United States and France are, as might be expected, the most popularly cited jurisdictions. However, depending upon the issues concerned, less known jurisdictions such as Costa Rica, Panama and Switzerland were also referenced in J.Y. Interpretation No. 419 when discussing institutional variations on whether a vice president may be or may be not permitted to concurrently serve in other positions.[101]

Other Methods/Arguments

As stated earlier, Article 13 of the Constitutional Interpretation Procedure Act advices the Constitutional Court to consider "the legislative history of a statute or regulation" when rendering interpretations. Indeed, the reliance on legislative history is a discernible method in the interpretations of the Constitutional Court. Of the 40 selected judgments, 2 majority opinions in J.Y. Interpretation Nos. 582 and 689 and 2 separate opinions in J.Y. Interpretation Nos. 603 and 644 consider legislative history of the disputed statutes.

94 Chang and Yeh (n 31), 373–92.

95 J.Y. Interpretation No. 342, Reasoning, [2].

96 J.Y. Interpretation No. 419, Reasoning, [7].

97 J.Y. Interpretation No.499, Reasoning, [3].

98 J.Y. Interpretation No.392, Reasoning, [10].

99 J.Y. Interpretation No.582, Reasoning, [2].

100 J.Y. Interpretation No. 665, Reasoning, [3].

101 J.Y. Interpretation No. 419, Reasoning, [7].

J.Y. Interpretation No. 582 was concerned with the constitutionality of a judicial precedent that restricted the right of a criminal defendant to cross-examine the statements made by another co-defendant as witness. In invalidating the impugned precedent, the majority opinion considered the legislative history of the Code of Criminal Procedures to articulate the guarantee of a criminal defendant's procedural rights in criminal proceedings.[102]

In J.Y. Interpretation No. 689, the Constitutional Court reviewed the constitutionality of Article 89, Paragraph 2 of the Social Order Maintenance Act that criminalized the act of stalking by a journalist. In sustaining the impugned provision, the majority struck a delicate balance between press freedom and right of privacy. In so doing, it re-visited the legislative history of the impugned provision, finding that "this provision was based on Article 77, Paragraph 1 of the Act Governing the Punishment of Police Offences which was promulgated on September 3, 1943 by the Republic Government, implemented on October 1 in the same year, and repealed on June 29, 1991. The Provision at issue purports to prohibit stalking or tailing others, including women, to protect people's freedom of movement. In addition, the Provision at issue also aims to protect an individual's bodily and mental security, individual's autonomy over his personal information and freedom from unwarranted intrusion in public spheres."[103]

7 *The Weight of Arguments*

As analysed above, most popular types of arguments in the interpretations of Taiwan's Constitutional Court are doctrinal analyses of concepts and principles not mentioned in the Constitution, teleological/textual arguments, precedent-based arguments and domestic harmonising arguments. Among these popular types of arguments, the most weighty are really doctrinal analyses of concepts and principles not mentioned in the Constitution and teleological/textual arguments. Although precedent-based arguments appear many times in the opinions, they do not function so much as arguments but rather as internal citations or references for the Constitutional Court itself.

Also quite weighty are the methods of referencing foreign law and the harmonisation with international law. As stated above, although there

[102] J.Y. Interpretation No. 582 (23 July 2004), Reasoning, [4].
[103] J.Y. Interpretation No. 689 (29 July 2011), Reasoning, [6].

have not been many references to foreign or international laws in majority or individual opinions, this does not mean that these foreign or international laws have not influenced the thinking or judging of the Constitutional Court. By training, Grand Justices – especially those appointed from scholarly backgrounds – are quite familiar with comparative and international laws, as are their law clerks, who are usually recent law graduates educated from local law schools where comparative law is a dominant approach. Elsewhere I have found – through interviews – that the Constitutional Court usually requests law clerks to prepare for all relevant comparative or international legal sources before beginning case discussions.[104]

8 *Judicial Candour and Judicial Rhetoric*

Most decisions of the Constitutional Court are indeed open and responsive to a range of arguments and considerations. Dialogues, debates or even mutual references may be seen at times between or among concurring or dissenting opinions. However, there is no such dialogue in majority opinions with separate opinions. As stated earlier, majority opinions are seen as the opinions of the court, and must be discussed and voted upon among all justices. It is extremely rare – if not impossible – to revise majority opinions after completion. Concurring or dissenting opinions are written after the completion of majority opinions, and thus there is no way for majority opinions to respond to separate opinions.

The language in the interpretations of Taiwan's Constitutional Court is usually filled with difficult legal terminology. This is quite expected, as doctrinal analyses or teleological/textual methods are most popular types of arguments. When opinions make a great deal of reference to scholarly works or to foreign and international legal materials, they may even be read like scholarly pieces rather than court judgments. It is especially so in the styles of individual opinions written by justices of scholarly background, and the intended audience of those opinions seems to be the legal community rather than the general public.

A few majority or separate opinions do show – in varying degrees – an awareness of social contexts. For example, in J.Y. Interpretation No. 584 concerning occupational restrictions to those convicted of certain crimes, both majority and separate opinions have acknowledged societal

[104] Law and Chang (n 27) 563ff.

concerns with public safety as well as the vulnerability, economic disadvantage and even discrimination against those with criminal records.[105] In J.Y. Interpretation No. 649, which was concerned with the privilege of the vision-impaired in the massage business, nearly all of the opinions considered a wide range of social and economic disadvantages of those vision-impaired and historical and cultural contingencies about their monopoly in the massage business.[106] In J.Y. Interpretation No. 666 in which the criminalization of prostitutes was under scrutiny, both majority and separate opinions have discussed quite extensively the relevant social and economic factors especially affecting the business of female prostitutes.[107] When majority or separate opinions employ arguments or rhetoric that better responds to social contexts, these opinions tend to receive more media coverage and are known to the general public.

9 *Length, Dissenting and Concurring Opinions*

The Length of the Opinions

In general, majority opinions are not lengthy, but over the years, they have become lengthier. The length of separate opinions written by individual judges varies. Some are extremely lengthy, especially those providing a thorough doctrinal analysis with detailed references.

It should be noted that before 1958, the Constitutional Court only issued majority opinions, which did not separate holdings from reasoning but contained only several paragraph of holdings. After 1958, holdings were separated from reasoning, and the issuance of dissenting opinions was allowed. Among the 40 selected judgments, only one judgment, J.Y. Interpretation No. 31, was made before 1985, and hence it is the only judgment without opinions.

Among the 40 selected judgments, the shortest majority opinion is J.Y. Interpretation No. 86, which was concerned with the organization of the judiciary and included 170 words. The longest majority opinion is J.Y. Interpretation No. 419, with 14,143 words. The average length of majority opinions in these 40 selected judgments is 3679 words.

There is a clear correlation between the length of majority opinions and the holding of oral arguments. Although the Constitutional Court may hold oral arguments, it rarely does so except for high-profile cases. The

[105] J.Y. Interpretation No. 584, Reasoning, para. 2.
[106] J.Y. Interpretation No. 649, Reasoning, para. 3.
[107] J.Y. Interpretation No. 666, Reasoning, para. 3.

4 lengthy majority opinions in the 40 selected judgments are those with oral arguments, including J.Y. Interpretation No. 392 (11,141 words), J.Y. Interpretation No. 419 (14,143 words), J.Y. Interpretation No. 445 (13,056 words) and J.Y. Interpretation No. 585 (11,666 words). With the holding of oral arguments, majority opinions must list the proceedings and arguments that relevant parties have put forward before the Constitutional Court, which naturally makes these opinions lengthier.

It is also interesting to note that in the 40 selected judgments, lengthier opinions tend to be those concerned with separation of power. In addition, the use of multiple types of arguments may naturally affect the length of opinions. The lengthier majority opinions in the 40 selected judgments are also those that employ multiple types of arguments. For example, in J.Y. Interpretation No. 392 (11,141 words), multiple types of arguments were employed, including harmonisation with international law, precedent-based argument, doctrinal analyses of concepts and principles, teleological/textual argument, teleological/historical argument, and reference to foreign law.[108] J.Y. Interpretation No. 419 (14,143 words) adopts multiple styles of arguments including domestic harmonisation, precedent-based argument, teleological/textual argument, teleological/historical argument, reference to scholarly works, and reference to foreign law.[109] Yet, as these opinions were also written with the holding of oral arguments, it is not clear without further study which factor is more relevant to the length of majority opinions.

Case No.	Words	Case No.	Words	Case No.	Words	Case No.	Words
31	172	**384**	2136	**530**	2441	**632**	2392
86	170	**392**	11141	**543**	1270	**644**	1682
162	518	**419**	14143	**550**	1674	**649**	2119
216	712	**435**	717	**582**	5401	**656**	1283
242	488	**443**	890	**584**	2266	**665**	5122
251	438	**445**	13056	**585**	11666	**666**	1040
261	1168	**490**	1546	**601**	7965	**689**	5701
328	205	**499**	9492	**603**	6912	**690**	3236
342	1642	**509**	966	**613**	6115	**708**	2637
365	896	**520**	3995	**627**	4932	**709**	6821
On the Average: 3679 words							

[108] As discussed in various sections above.

[109] As discussed in various sections above.

Dissenting or Concurring Opinions

In the past, not many interpretations of the Constitutional Court were issued with separate opinions. The recent years, however, have witnessed a rise in the number of separate opinions signed. In the 40 selected judgments, the average number of separate opinions per judgment is 3.25. Before J.Y. Interpretation No. 392, which was made in 1995, there was no interpretation issued with more than 3 separate opinions. However, interpretations were often issued with 3 or more separate opinions afterwards.

In the 40 selected judgments, the interpretations with the largest number of separate opinions signed are J.Y. Interpretation Nos. 689 and 709, both of which featured fundamental rights. J.Y. Interpretation No. 689 is a case concerning the criminalization of journalists' stalking.[110] J.Y. Interpretation No. 709 examined the Urban Renewal Act in terms of due process.[111] As these two interpretations are also the most recent ones, it is hard to conclude whether rights discourses themselves invite more individual opinions.

It is also interesting to note that prior to J.Y. Interpretation No. 499 rendered in 2000, there were more dissenting opinions issued than concurring opinions. However, afterwards, more concurring opinions seem to have been issued than dissenting opinions. It is not yet clear whether this difference would also be indicated if all cases, rather than a representative sample, were considered, and further research is certainly required before any conclusive findings can be offered.

10 *Framing of Constitutional Issues*

The Constitutional Court usually frames constitutional issues based upon separation of powers or individual rights. Such framing usually reflects who the petitioner is, as petitions by government agencies are often concerned with separation of powers while individual petitioners must claim their constitutionally protected rights are infringed.

It is important to note that the Constitutional Court is not bound to deal with the issues addressed by petitioners. In J.Y. Interpretation No. 445, the Constitutional Court made it clear that "the scope of constitutional interpretation is not limited to the purport of a petition."[112]

[110] J.Y. Interpretation No. 689 (29 July 2011).
[111] J.Y. Interpretation No. 709 (26 April 2013).
[112] J.Y. Interpretation No. 445, Reasoning, para. 8.

The Constitutional Court is at its own discretion to address other issues that are "substantially related" or "substantially cited and invoked" rather than those placed forward by petitioners.[113] In this decision, the Constitutional Court reviewed and even invalidated several provisions in the Assembly and Parade Act which the petitioners had not challenged. In J.Y. Interpretation No. 582, the Constitutional Court decided to review precedents that were not explicitly referred to in the cases concerning petitioners. In so doing, the Constitutional Court stated that all of the relevant precedents that had been relied upon – explicitly or not – as the basis for the final decision would all fall within the scope of interpretation as well.[114]

In cases concerning both liberty and equality, whether to frame such cases as liberty or equality or both is entirely within the discretionary power of the Constitutional Court. Thus far, the Constitutional Court has not shown any discernible pattern. For example, in J.Y. Interpretation No. 649 concerning the law privileging vision-impaired individuals in the practice of massage, the Constitutional Court reviewed on the grounds of both the right to work and equal protection.[115] In J.Y. Interpretation No. 584, however, facing occupational restrictions on those convicted of certain crimes, the Constitutional Court dealt only with the issue of the right to work.[116] In J.Y. Interpretation No. 666, in which the penalization of prostitutes was examined, the Constitutional Court reviewed only on the ground of sex discrimination, as most prostitutes were female, but did not consider the right to work.[117]

11 Key Concepts

As the following table shows, some of the most frequently mentioned concepts in the 40 selected judgments are the rule of law, the principle of proportionality, basic procedural rights, a core of constitutional rights or competences, and democracy. Other than these concepts, the right of privacy, the freedom of expression, and equality are also quite frequently mentioned. Less frequently mentioned are the concepts of the form of government, sovereignty, federalism and secularism. It seems that more concepts related to rights than to state organizations are mentioned.

113 *Id.* 114 J.Y. Interpretation No. 582, Reasoning, para. 1.
115 J.Y. Interpretation No. 649 (31 October 2008).
116 J.Y. Interpretation No. 584 (17 September 2004).
117 J.Y. Interpretation No. 666 (6 November 2009).

It is also interesting to note that the discussion of certain concepts seems more likely to result in unconstitutional declarations. For example, 10 of the 13 majority opinions featuring basic procedural rights found the impugned rules unconstitutional. In addition, 8 of the 12 majority opinions that mentioned the core of constitutional rights or competences also considered the complained statutes unconstitutional. Yet, whether this is a conclusive finding requires further study as it is merely inferred from the limited number of selected judgments.

Most mentioned concepts in the selected 40 judgments

Concepts	Times Mentioned in Majority Opinions	Times Mentioned in Judgments
The rule of law	27	30
Proportionality	16	19
Basic procedural rights	13	15
Core of constitutional rights or competences	12	15
Democracy	12	15

C Comparative Perspective

Taiwan has a long-standing constitutional court in and beyond Asia. The Constitutional Court has begun to function since the democratization and constitutional reforms of the 1990s. Similar to its counterparts in the civil law system, Taiwan's Constitutional Court frequently employs teleological/textual arguments and develops doctrinal analyses of concepts and principles that are not mentioned in the Constitution. Other types of arguments such as domestic harmonisation, international harmonisation and precedent-based arguments appear quite often in the opinions of the Constitutional Court as well. It is also noteworthy that multiple types of arguments are usually employed in high-profile cases, which may correlate with the length of opinions. Yet, the length of opinions relates strongly to the holding of oral arguments.

Although explicit or direct references to foreign law or harmonisation with international law do not as frequently appear in the opinions as in other jurisdictions, the jurisprudence of Taiwan's Constitutional Court is no less comparative or international. The comparative or international nature of Taiwan's Constitutional Court is manifest in the composition of the Grand Justices and their highly learned backgrounds. As a tradition, half of the justices are appointed from the ranks of law professors, and the majority of justices, including both legal scholars and career judges, usually have had advanced legal training abroad. The foreign-trained talents and comparative law approaches they embody have become distinctive features in the development of Taiwan's legal system, especially compared to other civil law systems, and there is no exception to the Constitutional Court and the jurisprudence developed by its own docket.

Appendix: Forty Leading Cases

1. *J.Y. Interpretation No. 31*
2. *J.Y. Interpretation No. 86*
3. *J.Y. Interpretation No. 162*
4. *J.Y. Interpretation No. 216*
5. *J.Y. Interpretation No. 242*
6. *J.Y. Interpretation No. 251*
7. *J.Y. Interpretation No. 261*
8. *J.Y. Interpretation No. 328*
9. *J.Y. Interpretation No. 342*
10. *J.Y. Interpretation No. 365*
11. *J.Y. Interpretation No. 384*
12. *J.Y. Interpretation No. 392*
13. *J.Y. Interpretation No. 419*
14. *J.Y. Interpretation No. 435*
15. *J.Y. Interpretation No. 443*
16. *J.Y. Interpretation No. 445*
17. *J.Y. Interpretation No. 490*
18. *J.Y. Interpretation No. 499*
19. *J.Y. Interpretation No. 509*
20. *J.Y. Interpretation No. 520*
21. *J.Y. Interpretation No. 530*
22. *J.Y. Interpretation No. 543*
23. *J.Y. Interpretation No. 550*
24. *J.Y. Interpretation No. 582*
25. *J.Y. Interpretation No. 584*
26. *J.Y. Interpretation No. 585*
27. *J.Y. Interpretation No. 601*
28. *J.Y. Interpretation No. 603*
29. *J.Y. Interpretation No. 613*

30. *J.Y. Interpretation No. 627*
31. *J.Y. Interpretation No. 632*
32. *J.Y. Interpretation No. 644*
33. *J.Y. Interpretation No. 649*
34. *J.Y. Interpretation No. 656*
35. *J.Y. Interpretation No. 665*
36. *J.Y. Interpretation No. 666*
37. *J.Y. Interpretation No. 689*
38. *J.Y. Interpretation No. 690*
39. *J.Y. Interpretation No. 708*
40. *J.Y. Interpretation No. 709*

17

The Supreme Court (House of Lords) of the United Kingdom

TAMAS GYORFI

The aim of the present paper is to analyse the reasoning behind the landmark constitutional decisions delivered by the UK Supreme Court (UKSC) and its predecessor, the House of Lords (UKHL, from 1948, the Appellate Committee of the House of Lords),[1] between 1876 and 2012.[2] The paper outlines the institutional background of constitutional adjudication, and then summarises the main findings of the research by putting the raw data of the accompanying table into context. It then offers a brief explanation for some of these findings. Finally, by identifying the distinctive features of constitutional reasoning in the UK, it puts the findings into comparative perspective.

A Legal, Political, Institutional and Academic Context

1 Legal and Political Culture as Context for Constitutional Reasoning

The Lack of a Codified Constitution

The United Kingdom is one of the very few states that does not have a codified constitution. This poses many challenges regarding how the conceptual framework of this comparative project can be applied to it. Therefore, this paper has devoted a relatively large amount of space to a discussion of these methodological challenges in order to put the findings of the research into a proper context.

[1] The author would like to thank Mátyás Bódig, Angus Campbell, Greg Gordon, Heather Green, András Jakab, Aileen Kavanagh, Adam Perry and Robert Taylor for their helpful comments on earlier drafts.

[2] Unless indicated otherwise, "the court" and "UKSC" will refer both to the Supreme Court and the House of Lords, and the term "judges" refers both to the Law Lords of the House of Lords and the Justices of the Supreme Court.

The lack of a codified constitution is usually explained by both historical and conceptual reasons.[3] The development of the constitution was decisively shaped by the mid-seventeenth-century conflicts between Parliament and the Crown, and the settlement which followed the Revolution of 1688. Wicks states that:

> The constitution, and the way in which individuals are governed under it, has undergone some radical transformations since the seventeenth century – the growth in the executive, the role of the Prime Minister, union with Scotland, democratic suffrage and the increasing influence of international and European obligations – and yet the contemporary relations between Crown and Parliament, between individual and government still rest upon foundations of this seventeenth-century revolution settlement.[4]

This means that the foundations of the British constitution were laid down well before the idea that constitutions could be made by deliberate human decisions became widespread. However, since the settlement of 1688 the British constitution has developed in an incremental way, without major interruptions. Therefore, Britain has lacked the constitutional moment that gave birth to most codified constitutions.

The settlement between the Crown and Parliament also laid down the foundations of parliamentary supremacy that has become the cornerstone of the British constitution. This is the principle that Parliament's law-making power is not subject to legal limits and that no court can declare any statute enacted by Parliament to be void. According to the orthodox understanding of the doctrine, there is no *formal* distinction between "ordinary statutes" and "constitutional statutes"; all Acts of Parliament have equal legal status. The lack of formal hierarchy between constitutional statutes and ordinary statutes is also reflected in the legislative process, since all Acts of Parliament are amended or repealed using the same procedure.

The Pool of Constitutional Cases

The first challenge for this paper is to determine the domain of constitutional law. Codified constitutions provide commentators with a formal criterion to identify "constitutional cases". The lack of a codified constitution implies that no similar formal criterion can be applied here. Instead, a substantive concept of the constitution has been relied upon. As a guide,

[3] Vernon Bogdanor, *The New British Constitution* (Hart 2009) 10.

[4] Elizabeth Wicks, *The Evolution of a Constitution: Eight Key Moments in British Constitutional History* (Hart 2006) 11.

the working definition given by the House of Lords Select Committee on the Constitution has been used: "The set of laws, rules and practices that create the basic institutions of the state, and its component and related parts, and stipulate the powers of those institutions and the relationship between the different institutions and between those institutions and the individual."[5]

Three comments are necessary here. First, although all standard British textbooks on public law deal with the mechanisms of human rights protection, substantive human rights issues are usually discussed under the heading of human rights and not public law. Similarly, electronic databases apply separate subject headings to human rights cases and constitutional law cases. Although this distinction is convenient and useful for some purposes, the broad definition of constitution applied here does not justify the exclusion of substantive human rights cases from the pool of constitutional decisions.

Second, public law itself can be conveniently divided into constitutional and administrative law and some of the decisions selected for the purpose of this analysis would be very likely classified as administrative rather than constitutional law cases in the light of this distinction. However, the substantive definition of constitution applied here suggests that these cases are clearly of high constitutional importance and should also qualify as constitutional cases for the purposes of this research. For instance, although the so-called *GCHQ* case[6] technically belongs to administrative law, few would deny that it has profoundly influenced the relationship between the judiciary and the executive on the one hand, and the government and the individual on the other. As this case illustrates, administrative law is underpinned by key constitutional principles.

Third, the selection also includes some cases that revolved around disputes between individuals or private organisations. Their inclusion in the pool of constitutional cases is justified by the fact that they have substantially contributed to the doctrinal development of constitutional rights.[7]

The evolutionary character of the British constitution has raised a further methodological question for the selection of cases. As there have

[5] House of Lords, Select Committee on Constitution, First Report, para 20, <www.publications.parliament.uk/pa/ld200102/ldselect/ldconst/11/1103.htm>. In the discussion that follows, the constitution is shorthand for the rules that qualify under this definition.

[6] *Council of Civil Service Unions v Minister for the Civil Service* [1985] 1 AC 374.

[7] See e.g. *Campbell v MGN* [2004] UKHL 22; [2004] 2 AC 457.

been no sudden interruptions in British constitutional history since the seventeenth century, how is it possible to draw a non-arbitrary line in constitutional history for the purposes of case selection? Although the evolutionary development of the British constitution could possibly justify going back until the seventeenth century, this possibility was rejected. Since the aim of this project is to compare the jurisprudence of Constitutional and Supreme Courts, it was important to identify the court whose position was roughly comparable to its counterparts in other jurisdictions. The ability of the House of Lords (the High Court of Parliament before the fourteenth century) to consider judicial appeals went back to the twelfth century, but it was not a professional court that could be usefully compared to present-day Constitutional and Supreme Courts until the nineteenth century. Although the professionalisation of the judicial activity of the House of Lords was a gradual process, the Appellate Jurisdiction Act 1876 can be justly considered to be the most important milestone in this process. Therefore, it seems to be the most sensible starting date for the purposes of case selection.[8] This choice is also supported by another argument: modern case reporting goes back to roughly the same date,[9] and without the consistent quality of case reporting it is difficult to draw general conclusions about constitutional reasoning.

In the selection of landmark cases, three considerations were taken into account: (1) whether the case was extensively cited or analysed by textbooks on public law and human rights;[10] (2) how often the case was

[8] For a general overview about the Judicial House of Lords, see Louis Blom-Cooper, Brice Dickson and Gavin Drewry, *The Judicial House of Lords: 1876–2009* (Oxford University Press 2009).

[9] The Council for Law Reporting was established in 1865.

[10] We have relied primarily on Joanne Coles, *Key Cases: Constitutional and Administrative Law* (Routledge 2013); Helen Fenwick, Gavin Phillipson and Alexander Williams, *Text, Cases and Materials on Public Law and Human Rights* (3rd ed, Routledge 2010); Peter Halstead, *Key Cases Human Rights* (Routledge 2013); David Hoffman and John Rowe, *Human Rights in the UK: An Introduction to the Human Rights Act 1998* (4th edition, Pearson 2013); Richard Stone, *Textbook on Civil Liberties and Human Rights* (9th edition, Oxford University Press 2012); Andrew Le Sueur, Maurice Sunkin and Jo Murkens, *Public Law: Text, Cases, and Materials* (2nd ed, Oxford University Press 2013); Adam Tomkins and Colin Turpin, *British Government and the Constitution Text and Materials* (7th edition, Cambridge University Press 2012); Lisa Webley and Harriet Samuels, *Complete Public Law* (2nd ed, Oxford University Press 2012). For older cases David Pollard, *Constitutional and Administrative Law: Text with Materials* (2nd ed, Butterworths 1997); Owen Hood Phillips, *O. Hood Phillips' Leading Cases in Constitutional and Administrative Law* (6th ed by Paul Jackson, Sweet & Maxwell 1988) have been also consulted.

cited by other cases;[11] and (3) how often the case was cited by journal articles.[12]

The Changing Constitutional Landscape of Britain

The above considerations delimit the subject matter and the temporal coverage of the selection but do not say much about how the nature of constitutional litigation has changed within the period under discussion. A brief overview of these changes, however, is necessary to understand the institutional context of constitutional reasoning.

Although the label "uncodified" identifies one important feature of the British constitution, it does not fully capture the nature thereof and does not aid in understanding how the constitution has changed since the 1960s. As King points out, written constitutions "are never, ever coextensive with all of a country's most important rules regulating the relations between different parts of government and those between the government and the people".[13] To a large extent, the relationship between the most important political institutions in the UK either was defined by the political practices of these institutions or was regulated by constitutional conventions rather than by judicially enforceable legal rules before the 1960s. That is why there is some truth in the claim that the United Kingdom has a *political constitution.* John Griffith, who coined this term, notes that "the constitution of the United Kingdom lives on, changing from day to day for the constitution is no more and no less than what happens. Everything that happens is constitutional. And if nothing happened that would be constitutional also."[14] Judges had a small and relatively passive role in this constitutional setup. Important constitutional cases within this period began to appear only after the First World War. The most high-profile cases before 1960 focused on the emergency powers of the government and the royal prerogative.[15] "Judicial passivity" reached its peak in the 1950s. In 1953, the House of Lords heard only 19 cases and

[11] The Justcite online research platform was relied upon: <www.justcite.com>.

[12] Two databases have been relied upon: Westlaw and Justcite. For a variety of reasons, this method builds into the selection process a bias towards more recent cases. Therefore, this criterion was used primarily to choose cases from more recent case law.

[13] Anthony King, *Does the United Kingdom Still Have a Constitution?* (Sweet & Maxwell 2001) 3.

[14] J. A. G. Griffith, "The Political Constitution" (1979) 42 *MLR* 1, 19.

[15] Brigid Hadfield, "Constitutional Law" in Blom-Cooper et al. (n 8) 500–1.

almost half of them concerned tax law.[16] When they had to decide constitutional cases, judges adopted a formalistic approach and proved to be highly deferential to the elected branches.[17]

However, since the 1960s the constitutional landscape has changed dramatically and ever more aspects of government activity have become regulated by legal rules and have been subjected to judicial scrutiny. Some of these developments have been incremental and relatively slow, while others, especially the constitutional reforms of the Labour government after New Labour's landslide victory in 1997, reflected a more large-scale attempt to reshape the constitutional structure.[18] For the purposes of this paper, four developments have had special significance.

Firstly, since the 1960s courts have gradually expanded the scope and increased the intensity of judicial review.[19] The growth of judicial review has rebalanced the relationship between the judiciary and the executive.[20] Although this judicial assertiveness indicates a significant turn in the jurisprudence of the modern House of Lords, we should not forget that the judicial control of executive action has had a long tradition in English (and later British) constitutional law.[21]

Secondly, since the coming into force of the European Communities Act 1972 (ECA), British laws must be compatible with European Community (and later European Union) law. The 1972 Act, for the first time since the 1688 settlement, elevated a source of law above the Acts of Parliament. Although judges managed to avoid head-on collision with the legislature for almost 20 years, the second *Factortame* decision[22] made it clear that they are ready to disapply Acts of Parliament to implement Community law.

16 Robert Bocking Stevens, *The English Judges: Their Role in the Changing Constitution* ([Rev ed], Hart 2005) 27.

17 Ibid 26.

18 Whether there is a coherent constitutional vision behind these attempts is open to debate.

19 Judicial review is used to decide whether a public body has acted illegally, irrationally or unfairly.

20 The increasing number of judicial review applications over this period reflects accurately the scope and significance of this constitutional change: in 1968 there were only 87 judicial review applications, in 1985 the number was 1169 and in 2011 the number was 2511. The last number does not include immigration-related applications. With immigration-related cases the same number is 11200. <www.theguardian.com/news/datablog/2012/nov/19/judicial-review-statistics#data>.

21 See e.g. *Prohibitions del Roy* [1607] EWHC KB J23, 77 ER 1342, 12 Co.Rep. 64; *Case of Proclamations* [1610] EWHC KB J22, 77 ER 1352, (1611) 12 Co Rep 74; *Entick v Carrington* [1765] EWHC KB J98, 95 ER 807.

22 *R v Secretary of State for Transport, ex p Factortame Ltd (No.2)* [1991] 1 AC 603.

Thirdly, the Human Rights Act 1998 (HRA) incorporated the European Convention on Human Rights (ECHR) into domestic law (hence the academic literature prefers the term "Convention rights" to constitutional or fundamental rights). The HRA imposes a duty on judges to interpret domestic law in a Convention-compatible way, "so far as it is possible",[23] and authorises them to make a declaration of incompatibility if such an interpretation is not possible.[24] Although judges cannot strike down the Acts of Parliament under the HRA, the Act increased further the possibility of judicial scrutiny over legislation.

Finally, devolution has reconfigured the relationship between the constituent parts of the United Kingdom and legalised much of these relationships. By the three Devolution Acts: the Scotland Act 1998, the Government of Wales Act 1998 and the Northern Ireland Act 1998, the British Parliament established (or reinstated) devolved administrations and transferred wide-ranging power to them.

The aforementioned changes have reshaped the constitutional structure so dramatically that it does not seem far-fetched to speak about a New British constitution.[25] The United Kingdom is gradually moving away from the orthodox understanding of parliamentary supremacy.[26] However, the future of the constitution is very much in flux: after the Scottish referendum on independence, the relationship of the different parts of the United Kingdom is being reconsidered, and a referendum on the European Union might lead to a British exit from the EU.

It is important to spell out a couple of implications of these tectonic changes, since they are directly relevant to constitutional reasoning. First, due to the cumulative effect of these developments, the judges' constitutional role has undergone a significant change; they have moved from the periphery of the constitutional landscape to adopt a more central and certainly more visible role. Although the Constitutional Reform Act 2005 (CRA), which abolished the UKHL and replaced it with the UKSC, has not changed significantly the powers of the court, this change has had great symbolic significance. The Appellate Committee of the House of

[23] Human Rights Act 1998 s 3(1). [24] Human Rights Act 1998 s 4.

[25] See Bogdanor (n 3). A few other reforms have also contributed to the transformation of the British constitutional landscape but they are less relevant for the constitutional reasoning of the courts. These changes include the growing significance of referendums, the reform of the House of Lords, the direct election of mayors and the constitutional implications of a new coalition government.

[26] This paper falls short of claiming that the present institutional setup of the UK is not compatible with any plausible interpretations of the doctrine.

Lords, as the name suggests, was a committee of the upper chamber of the Parliament and the Law Lords were members of the legislature. In addition, the office of the Lord Chancellor combined executive, legislative and judicial functions, and the Lord Chancellor himself personified the fusion of the three branches of the government. He was a government minister who sat occasionally as a judge in the Appellate Committee. The 2005 Act ceased this fusion and symbolically elevated the judiciary to a co-equal branch of the government. Some commentators predict that this newly-gained independence will transform the self-image of the court and will make judges even more assertive.[27]

Second, the aforementioned constitutional changes have also affected the volume of constitutional litigation and the composition of the court's case-load. Since the 1960s, the proportion of public law cases has risen significantly. A statistical analysis that addressed the impact of the HRA on the UKHL pointed out that the since the 1998 Act came into force, the ratio of human rights and other rights-related cases increased from 20 to 40 per cent of the petitions given leave, and the court has "a far more pronounced public law profile than it had pre-HRA".[28] This explains the paradox that, although the British constitution has evolved without major interruptions for centuries, the selection for this paper includes only three cases which were decided before 1960, and more than half of the cases originate from the twenty-first century.

Third, as Cross's treatise on statutory interpretation suggests, "the approach of the courts varies according to the judges' perception of their constitutional role at any given period".[29] Before the 1960s, the British legal culture and its dominant approach to statutory interpretation was highly formalistic.[30] Risking an overgeneralisation, it could be argued that the constitutional changes sketched above also substantially shaped the general style of statutory interpretation and resulted in a more purposive approach. Lord Griffiths's often quoted opinion in *Pepper v Hart* captures well the direction of this change:

[27] See e.g. Kate Malleson, "Diversity in the Judiciary: The Case for Positive Action" (2009) 36 *Journal of Law and Society* 376.

[28] Sangeeta Shah and Thomas Poole, "The Impact of the Human Rights Act on the House of Lords" [2009] *Public Law* 347, 361. This evidence is also supported by Alan Paterson's research. See Alan Paterson: *Final Judgment: The Last Law Lords and the Supreme Court* (Hart 2013) 17.

[29] George Engle, J. S. Bell and Rupert Cross, *Cross: Statutory Interpretation* (3rd ed, Oxford University Press 1995) 10.

[30] P. S. Atiyah and R. S. Summers, *Form and Substance in Anglo-American Law: A Comparative Study in Legal Reasoning, Legal Theory, and Legal Institutions* (Oxford University Press 1994).

> The days have long passed when the courts adopted a strict constructionist view of interpretation which required them to adopt the literal meaning of the language. The courts now adopt a purposive approach which seeks to give effect to the true purpose of legislation and are prepared to look at much extraneous material that bears upon the background against which the legislation was enacted.[31]

Lord Reid's remarks on judicial law-making shed light on an other aspect of this change:

> There was a time when it was thought almost indecent to suggest that judges make law – they only declare it . . . But we do not believe in fairy tales any more. So we must accept the fact that for better or worse judges do make law, and tackle the question how do they approach their task and how should they approach it.[32]

Finally, ever since the reforms have challenged the fundamental principles and assumptions of the constitutional structure, they have invited theoretical reflection. The justification for more intensive judicial review; the debates about the challenge posed by the EU to parliamentary supremacy; the incorporation of Convention rights into domestic law; and the introduction of a new form of constitutional review, have all generated sustained academic interest. These have made public law a flourishing academic discipline and produced voluminous amounts of literature on the subject.[33] Judicial decisions in the UK are subject to detailed, high-quality and critical analysis.[34]

2 *The Court and Constitutional Litigation*

Jurisdiction

The UKSC, like its predecessor, the UKHL, is the final court of appeal for all civil cases in the UK and for criminal cases from England, Wales and Northern Ireland. However, before the establishment of the UKSC, "devolution cases" were heard by the Judicial Committee of the Privy

[31] *Pepper v Hart* [1993] AC 593, at 617.

[32] Lord Reid, "The Judge as Law Maker" (1972) 12 *Journal of the Society of Public Teachers of Law* 22.

[33] Although the increasing number of constitutional law/human rights related articles in the Westlaw database is a very rough indicator of this growth, the trend seems to be reasonably clear: in the 1980s, there were 505/782 such articles; in the 1990s, the respective numbers were 3325/6951; in the 2000s the same numbers were 6504/31225.

[34] For up-to-date academic reflection on constitutional issues, see the UK Constitutional Law Association's blog <http://ukconstitutionallaw.org>.

Council (JCPC). Compared to their constitutional significance, devolution cases are therefore under-represented in the case selection. Since the UKSC came into existence, these cases have also been heard by it.

The Powers of the Court

The UKSC is not a specialised constitutional court but is in fact the highest appeal court in the country. Constitutional issues are, therefore, as a general rule, raised in the context of actual cases.[35]

The generalist nature of the court implies that a case can raise both constitutional and non-constitutional questions; many cases in the selection made are therefore not "pure constitutional cases". The powers of the court also reflect its constitutional status and are more similar to other appeal courts than to specialised constitutional courts.

However, these powers are, in many respects, comparable to those of constitutional courts. In judicial review cases, the court has to decide whether a public body has acted illegally, or irrationally, or unfairly because the correct procedure was not followed, and it can quash such acts. The court can also strike down the Acts of devolved legislation in "devolution cases", disapply the Acts of Parliament if they violate EU law and make a declaration of incompatibility if an Act of Parliament cannot be interpreted in a Convention-compatible way. Since the case selection includes many human rights cases, one power of the court is in need of a more in-depth analysis. Section 3 of the HRA imposes an interpretative duty on courts (not only courts but also other bodies exercising public functions) and requires judges to interpret legal provisions in a Convention-compatible way "so far as it is possible". If the natural interpretation of a legal provision would result in the violation of Convention rights, the court can deviate even from the unambiguous meaning of the relevant rule, and can remove the incompatibility by way of interpretation. This power is in many respects comparable to the power of certain constitutional courts that can determine the constitution-compliant interpretation of a legal provision, if the provision is not unconstitutional on its face but can be also applied in unconstitutional ways.

[35] However, the Supreme Court can also be asked to scrutinise Bills of the Scottish Parliament (under section 33 of the Scotland Act 1998), Bills of the Northern Ireland Assembly (under section 11 of the Northern Ireland Act 1998) and Bills of the National Assembly for Wales (under section 112 of the Government of Wales Act 2006).

Procedure, Reporting and Caseload

The UKSC hears appeals on "arguable points of law of general significance". This criterion shows that the justices of the court have wide discretion in the selection of cases. In nearly all cases (except for Scotland) a "permission to appeal" (PTA) is required. This permission can be granted either by the court that is appealed from, or if this court refuses permission, by the UKSC.[36] Applications for PTA are generally decided by a panel of three justices. Intervention by third parties can be also granted. Supreme Court hearings are open to the public and the press, and the court itself is open to visitors. Most of the proceedings of the Supreme Court are filmed and are sometimes broadcast on TV and radio news networks. The surge in the number of extrajudicial speeches is also a good indicator of the growing public visibility of the new Supreme Court.[37]

UKSC judgments are widely published in various formats and by a variety of publishers. Most notable is *Appeal Cases* (AC), which is a subseries of *Law Reports*, the *Weekly Law Reports* (WLR), the *All England Law Reports* (All ER), *Westlaw UK*, *Lexis*, *Bailii* (the website of the British and Irish Legal Information Institute) and the website of the UKSC.

Since 2009, the UKSC has received between 228 and 259 PTA applications annually; has granted between 64 and 86 applications; has heard 69 to 120 cases; and has given 56 to 115 opinions.[38] As the UKSC has 12 justices, but the court usually sits in a panel of 5, there is a certain division of labour among the judges; the way the cases are assigned to them takes into consideration their areas of expertise. This suggests that certain judges have a greater role in constitutional cases and can influence the development of law more profoundly than others. An empirical analysis, focusing on the judges' involvement in human rights cases, has pointed out that there are "marked differences in the number of human rights cases heard by different judges".[39]

3 The Judges

The 1876 Act enabled the sovereign to appoint several Lords of Appeal in Ordinary (LAOs) to life peerages. The "Law Lords", as they were

[36] Today, in 90 per cent of cases the permission is granted by the UKSC. Thirty years ago, the proportion of such cases was around 30 per cent. See Paterson (n 28) 209.

[37] See <http://supremecourt.uk/news/speeches.html>.

[38] The figures were taken from the volumes of the *Supreme Court Annual Report and Accounts*.

[39] Thomas Poole and Sangeeta Shah, "The Law Lords and Human Rights" (2011) 74 *MLR* 79, 95.

commonly called, were professional salaried judges who were appointed specifically to consider appeals. They were originally drawn from men of 15 years' standing at the English or Irish bar or the Scottish Faculty of Advocates (barristers), or from the holders of high judicial office. It is important to note that the 1876 Act did not formally exclude lay persons from the decision-making process. Originally, only 2 Law Lords were appointed and the court sat as a panel of 3. This number gradually increased, and immediately before the UKHL was replaced by the UKSC the number of Law Lords was 12 and the court usually heard cases as a panel of 5. The UKSC also consists of 12 members (to be more precise, the full-time equivalent number of judges of the Court at any time cannot be more than 12);[40] 11 of the 12 former Law Lords became Justices of the Supreme Court in 2009. A person is qualified to be appointed if he has (a) held high judicial office for a period of at least 2 years; (b) satisfied the judicial-appointment eligibility condition on a 15 year basis; or (c) been a qualifying practitioner for a period of at least 15 years.[41]

Although the formal eligibility requirements for becoming a Law Lord were, especially recently, not particularly restrictive, the upper judiciary of the UK was considered sociologically far more homogeneous than the judiciaries of other democracies. The typical Law Lord was a white male from an upper-middle class family, educated in a private school. In addition, although the position was formally open to solicitors, the senior judges were almost exclusively drawn from barristers, in particular, from a couple of commercial barrister chambers in London. The judges of the Court of Appeal have typically been promoted from being judges of the High Court and the Law Lords were typically promoted from the Court of Appeal.[42] Although the Law Lords were officially appointed by the Queen on the advice of the Prime Minister after a consultation with the Lord Chancellor, the Lord Chancellor's consultation with senior judges about prospective candidates has played a decisive role in producing a socially and professionally highly homogeneous judiciary.[43] Political affiliation also played an important role in judicial appointments before the Second World War. However, since then the process has been considerably depoliticised and the common view is that the British judiciary, unlike

[40] Constitutional Reform Act 2005 s 23(2). [41] Constitutional Reform Act 2005 s 25(1).

[42] Kate Malleson, "Appointments to the House of Lords: Who Goes Upstairs" in Bloom-Cooper et al. (n 8) 115.

[43] Ibid 117–118; Lizzie Barmes and Kate Malleson, "The Legal Profession as Gatekeeper to the Judiciary: Design Faults in Measures to Enhance Diversity" (2011) 74 *MLR* 245.

many other Constitutional and Supreme Courts, is not sharply divided along ideological lines.

The CRA, among other things, aimed to make the selection of judges more open and transparent, produce a more diverse judiciary, and further depoliticise the appointment process. Judicial vacancies are now advertised and the criteria for appointment are clearly specified. The 2005 Act has also established an independent Judicial Appointments Commission for England and Wales and similar bodies for Scotland and Northern Ireland to make the judiciary more independent and prevent cronyism. Supreme Court Justices are recommended by an ad-hoc selection commission, consisting of at least five members (at least one lay member, at least one judge of the Court and at least one member of each of the three territorial judicial appointments commissions).[44] The 2005 Act decreased the role of the Lord Chancellor in the process and made the role of the Prime Minister nominal.

Nevertheless, the CRA and more recent reforms introduced by the Crime and Court Act 2013 have not managed to increase judicial diversity considerably.[45] The increased role and the higher public profile of the court makes the lack of judicial diversity even more pressing and raises the question of whether the government and the selection commission should take more positive action to increase diversity.[46]

The higher public profile of judges has also raised the issue of whether Parliament should be involved in judicial appointments and scrutinise the views of nominees. The dominant view in the UK is against the hearings (both pre-appointment and post-appointment) for judges.[47]

4 *Legal Scholarship and Constitutional Reasoning*

The received wisdom about the legal systems of the UK, primarily about England, is that legal scholars play a very marginal role compared to judges

[44] Constitutional Reform Act 2005 s 27.

[45] For a plausible explanation, see Barmes and Malleson (n 43) and Graham Gee and Kate Malleson, "Judicial Appointments, Diversity and the Equal Merit Provision" UK Const. L. Blog (6th May 2014) (available at: <http://ukconstitutionallaw.org>).

[46] See the Report of the Advisory Panel on Judicial Diversity <www.judiciary.gov.uk/wp-content/uploads/JCO/Documents/Reports/advisory-panel-judicial-diversity-2010.pdf>.

[47] See The House of Lords Select Committee on the Constitution, Judicial Appointments, 25th Report, Session 2010–2012, paras 39–48 <www.publications.parliament.uk/pa/ld201012/ldselect/ldconst/272/272.pdf>.

and legislators.[48] To qualify this general claim somewhat, judges do not attach considerable weight to the scholarly writings of living authors. However, Bankowski and MacCormick noted already in 1991 that "there is at present a growing tendency among English judges to cite in their opinions articles in learned journals, monographs and so on".[49]

B Arguments in Constitutional Reasoning

5 *The Structure of Constitutional Arguments*

Since the UKSC is not a specialised constitutional court, and a case can raise both constitutional and non-constitutional issues, it is important to distinguish from the outset between the disposition of a case and the decision on a constitutional issue. The fact that an appellant wins a constitutional argument does not necessarily mean that the appeal is upheld, since the constitutional issue might have been only one aspect of a complex case. As the research focuses on constitutional reasoning, in answering to Q4 (see Appendix B in the present volume) this paper indicates how the court decided the constitutional issue, not how it disposed of the case. In addition, in two cases, the question was not applicable because the legal dispute took place between private individuals or organisations. Finally, the relevant cell of the table was left blank in two cases where the court has found an incompatibility with Convention rights, but could remove it by using its interpretative power under Section 3(1) of the HRA.

The distinction between the disposition of a case and the constitutional issue also has important implications for how the structure of the constitutional argument was determined for the purposes of the present research. Again, the analysis focused on the reasoning that is related to the constitutional issue, as opposed to the reasoning of the whole opinion. It can happen that the constitutional reasoning is built on a "one-line conclusive argument" ("chain structure"), but the judge also supports the conclusion of her decision by another, non-constitutional argument. For the purposes of this analysis, this additional argument does not make the

[48] R. C. van Caenegem, *Judges, Legislators and Professors: Chapters in European Legal History* (Reprint ed, Cambridge University Press 1992).

[49] Zenon Bankowski and Neil MacCormick, "Statutory Interpretation in the United Kingdom" in Neil MacCormick and Robert S Summers, *Interpreting Statutes: A Comparative Study* (Dartmouth 1991) 379. For an up-to-date evaluation of the dialogue between Supreme Court Justices and academics, see Paterson (n 28) 213–21.

structure of the argument "parallel conclusive" ("legs of a chair"), since the additional argument is not related to the constitutional issue.

On the other hand, when the judge's position on the constitutional issue is based on a "one-line conclusive argument", but an intermediary step in this reasoning is supported by parallel arguments (either individually conclusive or not), the structure was coded for the purposes of this research as a parallel argument.

In most cases (22 out of 40) the conclusion of the opinion was supported by a "one-line conclusive argument". However, it was not uncommon (15 cases out of 40) for judges to develop alternative lines of arguments that would have been individually sufficient to justify the conclusion or an intermediary premise of the reasoning.

Whether judges are able or feel compelled to develop alternative arguments to support their conclusions on the constitutional issue depends on the context of the individual case; it would be difficult to generalise from these cases. However, it is worth highlighting two scenarios where the doctrinal framework invites these kinds of parallel arguments.

First, even if prior to 1998 the UK did not have a comprehensive Bill of Rights that was comparable to the HRA, the protection of individual rights had a very long tradition that goes back arguably to the Magna Carta of 1215. In the British constitutional discourse, these rights were traditionally called civil liberties. Furthermore, the emergence of robust judicial review imposed further limits on executive power. The HRA, by providing an additional layer of protection, did not replace but rather supplemented civil liberties and the traditional form of judicial review under the common law. As a consequence, it can happen that the individual's interests are protected both by civil liberties under the common law and the HRA, or the same act of a public authority is unlawful under both traditional judicial review and the HRA. This layered protection is particularly conducive to alternative constitutional challenges and explains why, in some of these cases, judges develop parallel arguments.[50]

Second, constitutional reasoning in human rights cases can be conveniently broken down into two stages.[51] In the first stage, the court focuses on the question of whether the right-holder's rights were interfered with by the government. If the court answers the question in the affirmative,

[50] For an example, see Lord Hope's opinion in *R v DPP, ex p Kebilene* [2000] 2 AC 326, at 376.

[51] Stephen Gardbaum, "Limiting Constitutional Rights" (2007) 54 *UCLA Law Review* 789.

it goes on to scrutinise whether the government was successful in justifying the interference. It follows that a judge can reject the individual's claim on two grounds: (1) he/she believes that the right in question was not interfered with; (2) he/she believes that the interference is justified. However, he/she can choose to develop both arguments, and this strategy seems especially sensible if other judges disagree with (1).[52]

Only three cases have been found where the reasoning or a part of it is based on "parallel, individually inconclusive, but together conclusive arguments" (dialogic structure), and two of them address the same issue. Section 6 of the HRA imposes a duty on public authorities to respect human rights. Non-governmental bodies that have public functions are considered "hybrid public authorities". However, the pertinent cases do not provide a single test to determine that a body is a hybrid public authority. Instead, they have identified a series of considerations that are individually inconclusive, but taken together are sufficient to classify the body in question.[53] But even in these cases, the parallel structure is meant to establish only an intermediary step in the reasoning and is part of a "one-line conclusive argument".

6 *Types of Arguments in Constitutional Reasoning*

Establishing the Text of the Constitution

Although the UK does not have a codified constitution, this argument can be, in principle, relevant for interpretation if there are doubts about the text of those laws that form the constitution. However, in none of the cases was this argument actually used.

Applicability of the Constitution

Similar to the previous argument, the question of applicability can, in principle, be also applied to the uncodified constitution of the UK. There were four cases that raised such questions and three of them were related to the same historical circumstances. The HRA was enacted in 1998 but the Act only came into force in 2000. The three cases originated from this transitional period and revolved around the different aspects

[52] For illustrations, see *Campbell v MGN Ltd* [2004] UKHL 22; [2004] 2 AC 457 [28] (Lord Nicholls); *R (Countryside Alliance) v Attorney General* [2007] UKHL 52; [2008] 1 AC 719 [15] (Lord Hoffman); *R (Begum) v Denbigh High School Governors* [2006] UKHL 15; [2007] 1 AC 100 [25] (Lord Bingham).

[53] *Aston Cantlow v Wallbank* [2003] UKHL 37; [2004] 1 AC 546 [12] (Lord Nicholls); *YL v Birmingham City Council* [2007] UKHL 27; [2008] 1 AC 95 [61]-[72] (Lady Hale).

of the applicability of the HRA.[54] In the fourth case, where the validity of the Hunting Act 2004 and the Parliament Act 1949 was challenged, some judges explicitly addressed the question of whether the issue was justiciable.[55]

Analogies

Analogical reasoning in general is a pervasive feature of common law systems. However, this research gives analogy a narrow definition: only those cases qualify where the court applied a norm to a situation that actually did not fall under the scope of the norm. In applying this narrow definition, only two cases were found where analogies figure in the argument.[56] Even in one of these two cases the analogy used is very limited since it proposes to apply a doctrinal solution based on the right to respect for the home to the right to family life, and both rights are protected by the same article (Article 8) of the ECHR.

Ordinary Meaning of the Words of the Constitution or References to the "Wording of the Constitution" in General

Almost half of the cases (19) considered explicitly the ordinary meaning of the words or referred to the wording of the constitution. However, it is important to emphasise that this number does not necessarily do justice to the importance of linguistic considerations in constitutional reasoning. The lack of explicit references may well mean that the meaning of the constitutional text is clear and uncontroversial. On the other hand, the lack of linguistic arguments can also mean that the issue cannot be solved by those arguments.[57] For instance, hardly any linguistic arguments were found about the meaning of substantive human rights provisions.

Harmonising Arguments

The purpose of statutory interpretation is to construct the meaning of words used in the statute. It is a well established rule of interpretation in the UK that judges must give primacy to the ordinary or literal meaning

[54] *R v DPP, ex p Kebilene* [2000] 2 AC 326; *Porter v Magill* [2001] UKHL 67; [2002] 2 AC 357; *R v Lambert* [2001] UKHL 37, [2002] 2 AC 545.

[55] *Jackson v Attorney General* [2005] UKHL 56; [2006] 1 AC 262 [111] (Lord Hope), [169] (Lord Carswell).

[56] *R v DPP, ex p Kebilene* [2000] 2 AC 326, at 369 (Lord Steyn); *Huang v Secretary of State for the Home Department* [2007] UKHL 11; [2007] 2 AC 167 [17].

[57] Aileen Kavanagh, "The Elusive Divide between Interpretation and Legislation under the Human Rights Act 1998" (2004) 24 *Oxford Journal of Legal Studies* 259, 263–4.

of words. However, literal interpretation does not imply that the meaning of words has to be determined acontextually. On the contrary, ordinary meaning is understood as the ordinary meaning of words in the given context. As a consequence, the considerations of harmonisation not only come into play after the ordinary meaning of words is established but also figure in the determination of ordinary meaning.[58] However, context is very often assumed rather than articulated and therefore these considerations do not always qualify as arguments.

In addition to establishing the ordinary meaning of words, harmonising arguments can also help judges to choose between possible ordinary meanings. In such cases, the role of harmonising arguments is to ensure the coherence of the legal system. Since coherence can be aimed at or established in different ways and at different levels of generality, harmonising arguments can take more than one form. For instance, an interpretation can be coherent with the more immediate legal environment of a rule, but incoherent with the underlying principles of a certain field of law. Accordingly, some of the cases under consideration refer to the context of the whole Act,[59] or the structure of the Act,[60] while others refer to a more general context.[61] In some cases, harmonising arguments are in place to ensure the consistent use of certain concepts,[62] while in others they are there to ensure that the rules serve the same underlying purpose or principles.[63] Altogether, 15 cases were identified where judges made harmonising considerations quite explicit.

As far as the mere numbers are concerned, harmonisation with the requirements of international law plays an even greater role in the jurisprudence of the court than domestic harmonising arguments (26 cases). The growing significance of "international harmonising arguments" shows an accurate imprint of the changing character of the British constitution. Of the 40 landmark cases, the first 8 cases did not look to the requirements of international law. Although the ECHR was mentioned in *Derbyshire County Council v Times Newspapers Ltd*, Lord Keith felt

[58] Engle et al. (n29) 32.

[59] *Jackson v Attorney General* [2005] UKHL 56; [2006] 1 AC 262 [6] (Lord Bingham).

[60] *Attorney General v De Keyser's Royal Hotel* [1920] AC 508, at 529 (Lord Dunedin).

[61] See e.g. *Aston Cantlow v Wallbank* [2003] UKHL 37; [2004] 1 A.C. 546 [42] (Lord Hope), reading the HRA in light of the Scotland Act 1998 and Northern Ireland Act 1998.

[62] For example, see Lord Atkin's long list of statutes that use the term "reasonable cause for suspicion" in the same way. *Liversidge v Anderson* [1942] AC 206, at 229–231.

[63] For an example, in *Countryside Alliance* Lady Hale was interpreting the purpose of Article 11 of the ECHR in the light of Article 10. *R (Countryside Alliance) v Attorney General* [2007] UKHL 52; [2008] 1 AC 719 [118].

it important to emphasise that he had reached his conclusion without relying upon the Convention.[64]

The first case on our list that relies on such an argument is the so-called *Spycatcher* case[65] that revolved around freedom of expression. In his speech, Lord Goff observed that there was no inconsistency between English law and Article 10 of the ECHR and added that, "in any event, I conceive it to be my duty, when I am free to do so, to interpret the law in accordance with the obligations of the Crown under this treaty".[66] Between 1988, when the *Spycatcher* case was decided, and 2000, when the HRA came into force, the picture became more mixed since 6 out of 10 decisions utilised "international harmonisation arguments". The *Brind* case from 1991 is particularly interesting in this respect. Although the court referred extensively to the ECHR, and reinforced that there was a presumption that Parliament intended to legislate in conformity with the international obligations of the UK, the court also made clear that this presumption could not override the unambiguous words of a statute, since that would amount to a covert incorporation of the ECHR.[67] The upshot is that although the court referred extensively to the ECHR, the Convention did not figure in the reasoning that supported the conclusion of the decision.

Since 2000, the overwhelming majority of the cases selected make use of international harmonising arguments. The explanation of this phenomenon is quite straightforward: the proportion of human rights cases has increased and Section 2(1) of the HRA requires the courts to "take into account" the jurisprudence of the ECtHR. Although the wording of the HRA suggests that the jurisprudence of the Strasbourg court is only one of the relevant considerations, in reality the ECtHR's interpretation creates a very strong presumption: "courts should, in the absence of some special circumstances, follow any clear and constant jurisprudence of the Strasbourg court".[68]

Two implications of this position have to be spelled out. First, it is not contested that although the ECtHR's interpretation is a weighty consideration, it is not absolutely binding. British courts can deviate even from the constant jurisprudence of the ECtHR if they have compelling reasons to

64 *Derbyshire County Council v Times Newspapers Ltd* [1993] AC 534, at 551.

65 *Attorney General v Guardian Newspapers Ltd (No 2)* [1990] 1 AC 109.

66 Ibid, at 283.

67 *R v Secretary of State for the Home Department, ex p Brind* [1991] 1 AC 696.

68 *R (Ullah) v Special Adjudicator* [2004] UKHL 26; [2004] 2 AC 323 [20] (Lord Bingham).

do so. That is the case, for instance, if the jurisprudence of the Strasbourg court lacks clarity, if the ECtHR did not take into consideration relevant arguments, or if since the decision significant social changes have taken place.[69] Second, the above position leaves open whether British courts can go further than the Strasbourg court and give protection in the absence of Strasbourg jurisprudence, or whether they should protect Convention rights when "the Strasbourg court has declared a question to be within the national margin of appreciation". The dominant position seems to be that the court has to come up with its own independent interpretation when the question is within the national margin of appreciation,[70] but otherwise it does not have to go further than the Strasbourg court. Lord Bingham has concisely summarised the underlying justification for this practice:

> [The] Convention is an international instrument, the correct interpretation of which can be authoritatively expounded only by the Strasbourg court. From this it follows that a national court subject to a duty such as that imposed by section 2 should not without strong reason dilute or weaken the effect of the Strasbourg case law. It is indeed unlawful under section 6 of the 1998 Act for a public authority, including a court, to act in a way which is incompatible with a Convention right. It is of course open to member states to provide for rights more generous than those guaranteed by the Convention, but such provision should not be the product of interpretation of the Convention by national courts, since the meaning of the Convention should be uniform throughout the states party to it. The duty of national courts is to keep pace with the Strasbourg jurisprudence as it evolves over time: no more, but certainly no less.[71]

Precedents (Former Own Cases)

As can be expected in the case of a common law system, precedents play a crucial role in constitutional reasoning in the UK. Precedents figured in the reasoning of all the selected cases. Similar to harmonising arguments, precedents are very often used not independent of or as rivals to linguistic arguments when the meaning is ambiguous, but in order to determine the ordinary meaning of the words.

[69] See e.g. *R v Horncastle* [2010] 2 AC 373. For a detailed analysis of these reasons, see Aileen Kavanagh, *Constitutional Review under the UK Human Rights Act* (Cambridge University Press 2009) 150–2.

[70] *In re G (Adoption: Unmarried Couple)* [2008] UKHL 38, [2009] 1 AC 173, at 174.

[71] *R (Ullah) v Special Adjudicator* [2004] UKHL 26; [2004] 2 AC 323 [20] (Lord Bingham).

Doctrinal Analysis of Legal Concepts or Principles

Judges refer to concepts and principles that are not part of the statute law in virtually all the cases. However, only a subset of these concepts gains a more or less fixed meaning and becomes part of the judges' more permanent conceptual toolkit. In addition, some doctrinal inventions are not part of the statutory text but are very closely related to the interpretation of certain categories of the text. For instance, the distinction between "core public authority" and "hybrid public authority" is not part of the HRA; nevertheless, these categories are directly linked to the interpretation of Section 6 of the 1998 Act. For the purposes of the present research, the focus has been on those doctrines that are not related so intimately to the text of constitutional statutes. The conclusion is that, even by following this quite narrow definition of doctrinal concepts and principles, they are almost ubiquitous in constitutional reasoning: 29 cases out of 40 refer to such doctrinal principles and categories, and others might have classified even more concepts as doctrinal ones if the category was used less restrictively.

Without aiming to provide a general and neat typology, it is convenient to divide these concepts and principles into four categories.

1. Overarching constitutional principles, such as parliamentary supremacy, the rule of law or separation of powers, whose legal status does not derive from any specific enactment, but rather from the fact that they serve to rationalise and justify legal rules and legal institutions.
2. Doctrinal concepts and distinctions that were invented or utilised to solve particular cases. As an illustration, see the distinction between domestic and foreign cases;[72] between administrative and judicial decisions;[73] or between policy decisions and the determination of rights.[74]
3. Doctrinal categories that are recurrently used to structure the argument of the court, like proportionality, or the margin of appreciation.
4. Interpretive presumptions that allocate the burden of justification, such as the Crown is not bound by a statute unless specially

[72] *R (Ullah) v Special Adjudicator* [2004] UKHL 26; [2004] 2 AC 323 [9] (Lord Bingham).

[73] *R (Alconbury) v Secretary of State for the Environment* [2001] UKHL 23; [2003] 2 AC 295 [139] (Lord Clyde). Ibid at [90] (Lord Hoffmann).

[74] Ibid at [90] (Lord Hoffmann).

mentioned;[75] the Crown can do no wrong;[76] the presumption of liberty;[77] or the principle of legality.[78]

Linguistic-Logical Formulae Based on Silence

The analysis of leading constitutional cases shows that the argument based on silence plays only a marginal role in the UK. Only four cases were found where the argument takes this form. The clearest example of such an argument can be found in Lord Nicholls's opinion in *Jackson*:

> Section 5, which was added by amendment at a late stage in the passage of the Parliament Bill, really introduces another exception by defining "Public Bill" as not including any Bill for confirming a Provisional Order. The effect of sections 2(1) and 5 is therefore to exclude expressly from the scope of the term "Public Bill" any Money Bill, or any Bill containing a provision to extend the maximum duration of Parliament beyond five years or any Bill for confirming a Provisional Order. Expressio unius exclusio alterius or exclusio unius inclusio alterius. Since Parliament has expressly excluded these three types of Bill from the scope of section 2(1), in the absence of any indication to the contrary, I would read that provision as applying to a Public Bill to amend section 2(1) itself.[79]

Teleological/Purposive Arguments Referring to the Purpose of the Text

The teleological approach has been part of the British judges' intellectual toolkit at least since 1584 when the Barons of the Exchequer first gave an authoritative formulation of the so-called mischief rule in *Heydon's* case.[80] This canon of interpretation requires judges to interpret the relevant legal provisions in the light of the mischief or the defect the statute intended to remedy. Although from the eighteenth century a more literal approach became dominant in general, the cases selected testify that the purposive approach has been of crucial importance in high-profile constitutional cases; well-identifiable purposive arguments could be found in 35 cases.[81] If Lord Griffiths's view, cited above, on the growing

[75] *Attorney General v De Keyser's Royal Hotel* [1920] AC 508, at 526 (Lord Dunedin).

[76] Ibid at 532 (Lord Atkinson); *M v Home Office* [1994] 1 AC 377, at 407 (Lord Templeman).

[77] *Liversidge v Anderson* [1942] AC 206, at 218 (Viscount Maugham).

[78] *R v Secretary of State for the Home Department Ex p. Simms* [2000] 2 AC 115, at 130 (Lord Steyn).

[79] *Jackson v Attorney General* [2005] UKHL 56; [2006] 1 AC 262 [61].

[80] (1584) 3 Co Rep 7a, 7b.

[81] The purposive approach is sometimes technically distinguished from and claimed to be more limited than the mischief rule. However, this does not change the fact that both are teleological methods.

significance of purposive interpretation is taken at face value, the frequent incidence of purposive arguments in this sample is far from surprising, since the preponderance of the cases originates from the post-1990 period. However, since purposive arguments figure in the reasoning of the court quite consistently during the whole period, a better explanation seems to be that most of the high-profile constitutional cases address issues that simply cannot be resolved by semantic arguments alone or raise questions of principles that invite purposive arguments even where semantic arguments are also available.

Teleological/Purposive Arguments Referring to the Purpose of the Constitution-Maker (Including Travaux Préparatoires)

One of the most interesting types of argument is the one that refers to the intention of Parliament. The challenge is that "the intention of the legislature" is not one type of argument but a figure of speech that can be a shorthand for different types of arguments.[82] However, the cases themselves rarely spell out which argument "the intention of the legislature" refers to. Ten cases have been identified where this figure of speech could refer to either the meaning that it is reasonable to attribute to Parliament from the effect of the statutory words it has enacted (objective purpose) or to Parliament's intended meaning (subjective purpose). In some of these cases, the most natural interpretation would be the subjective interpretation. For instance, in *Countryside Alliance* Lady Hale noted that "when the Convention was written it would not have crossed anyone's mind that there might be a prima facie right to hunt wild animals with dogs".[83] The reference to the state of mind of the framers very strongly indicates the subjective concept of intention.

However, these references to Parliamentary intention should be read with reservations and should be interpreted against the backdrop of the general assumptions about statutory interpretation. The dominant view is captured by Lord Reid's often quoted passage in *Black-Clawson International Ltd v Papierwerke Waldhof-Aschaffenburg AG*: "We often say that we are looking for the intention of Parliament, but that is not quite accurate. We are seeking the meaning of the words which Parliament used."[84] This position suggests that the subjective intention in itself has no constitutional relevance. Even when external aids to the interpretation, like the ministerial statement in the Parliamentary debate, are admissible, they

[82] Bankowski and MacCormick (n 49) 386–7.

[83] *R (Countryside Alliance) v Attorney General* [2007] UKHL 52; [2008] 1 AC 719 [124].

[84] [1975] AC 591, at 613.

are used to reconstruct not the frame of mind of the legislators (whatever it means), but the meaning of words that Parliament used.

Having said that, 6 of the 10 cases explicitly refer to the reports of the parliamentary debates (Hansard). Before 1992, there existed a general ban on the use of Hansard to elucidate the meaning of legal provisions. *Pepper v Hart*, (one of our 40 cases) relaxed this exclusionary rule provided that three conditions are met: "(a) legislation was ambiguous or obscure or led to absurdity, (b) the material relied upon consisted of one or more statements by a Minister or other promoter of the Bill together if necessary with such other Parliamentary material as was necessary to understand such statements and their effect and (c) the statements relied upon were clear."[85]

However, there is some disagreement about the exact scope of these exceptions and judges now seem to be extremely reluctant to rely on such materials. For instance, it is disputed whether ministerial statements can be referred to in order to identify the reasons of policy as opposed to being used to construct the meaning of words.[86] It must also be added that reference to Hansard as such is not inadmissible if it is used to reconstruct the legislative history or identify the mischief the statute wanted to remedy. For instance, in *Jackson* Lord Bingham drew heavily on Hansard[87] but could consistently claim that he had reached his conclusion without reliance on statements made in the course of parliamentary debate. This was only possible because the parliamentary report was used to reconstruct the legislative history and not to determine the meaning of the words. The latter would have been inadmissible under *Pepper v Hart* because the words of the statute were neither ambiguous nor obscure nor did they lead to absurdity.

Non-legal (Moral, Sociological, Economic) Arguments

Appealing to evaluative (moral and political) considerations and making empirical assumptions are a pervasive feature of constitutional reasoning; almost all legal opinions would be incomplete without such premises. However, judges relatively rarely subject their empirical assumptions to sustained analysis and most of their moral and political arguments

85 [1993] AC 593, at 594.

86 See *R (on the application of Spath Holme Ltd) v Secretary of State for the Environment, Transport and the Regions* [2001] 2 AC 349, at 398 (Lord Nicholls) and at 407 (Lord Hope).

87 *Jackson v Attorney General* [2005] UKHL 56; [2006] 1 AC 262 [20].

are filtered through doctrinal categories. There are at least two points where evaluative arguments systematically enter into constitutional reasoning: the first one is when judges establish the purpose of legal rules or legal institutions; the second when they engage in proportionality analysis. However, for the purposes of this research, this category has been narrowly constructed: purposive arguments constitute a separate category and proportionality analysis, in itself, was not classified as a non-legal argument. The arguments were classified under this rubric only where judges made non-legal considerations quite explicit in their reasoning.

Even when the category of non-legal arguments was constructed narrowly, there were still 16 cases that invoked such considerations. Generalising from these cases, four subcategories of non-legal arguments can be usefully distinguished.

1. There were 8 cases in which judges referred quite explicitly to policy arguments. The clearest example of such policy arguments can be found in *Pepper v Hart*, where the increased cost of litigation was perhaps the most formidable argument against relaxing the ban on using the parliamentary reports to identify the intent of the legislature.[88]
2. In two cases that raised the issue of parliamentary supremacy, judges opened up legal reasoning to the background principles of political philosophy. It is worth citing Lord Hope's opinion in *AXA General Insurance Ltd, Petitioners* to illustrate this use of non-legal arguments: "The fact is that, as a challenge to primary legislation at common law was simply impossible while the only legislature was the sovereign Parliament of the United Kingdom at Westminster, we are in this case in uncharted territory. The issue has to be addressed as one of principle."[89] In *Jackson*, considering the consequences of rival interpretations, Lord Steyn also openly addressed fundamental justificatory questions and contrasted this approach with "strict legalism".[90]
3. Two cases were found where judges felt it necessary to make the empirical assumptions of their decisions explicit. In one case, the reference is quite short but absolutely essential for the conclusion of the opinion.[91] By contrast, Baroness Hale's analysis about the significance of the dress

88 [1993] AC 593, at 615 (Lord Mackay). 89 [2011] UKSC 46; [2012] 1 AC 868 [48].

90 [2005] UKHL 56; [2006] 1 AC 262 [100]-[102].

91 *R v Secretary of State for the Home Department Ex p. Simms* [2000] 2 AC 115, at 128 (Lord Steyn).

code in Muslim society and for Muslim women is much more reflective and supported by many academic references.[92]

4. Finally, in three cases the decisions refer to what Hart aptly calls "positive morality"[93]: public sentiment;[94] the increased social acceptance of different sexual orientations;[95] and the domestic legal and cultural values and traditions.[96]

References to Scholarly Works

The selected constitutional cases show that judges cite scholarly works quite often. Of the 40 cases, only four did not make a single reference to academic literature. Altogether, 227 such references were found. This means that, on average, judges alluded to academic opinion 5.7 times in every decision.[97]

The earlier decisions tended to cite such classical authors as Blackstone, Dicey, Holdsworth, Pollock, Maitland and Vattel. Unsurprisingly, Albert Venn Dicey is the most important authority in these decisions.[98] However, more recent decisions refer extensively to contemporary authors. In particular, three textbooks were consulted by judges in these opinions: Clayton and Tomlinson's *The Law of Human Rights*;[99] David Feldman's *Civil Liberties and Human Rights in England and Wales*;[100] and Wade's *Administrative Law*.[101]

In some cases, judges also refer to non-legal academic literature in order to better understand the historical or socio-economic context. Lord Bingham's opinion in *Jackson*[102] and Lady Hale's opinion in *Begum*[103] provide

[92] *R (Begum) v Denbigh High School Governors* [2006] UKHL 15; [2007] 1 AC 100 [93]-[95].

[93] H. L. A. Hart, *Law, Liberty and Morality* (Oxford University Press 1968) 20.

[94] *Burmah Oil Co (Burma Trading) Ltd v Lord Advocate* [1965] AC 75, at 127 (Viscount Radcliffe).

[95] *Bellinger v Bellinger* [2003] UKHL 21; [2003] 2 AC 467 [20] (Lord Nicholls).

[96] *R v Lambert (Steven)* [2001] UKHL 37; [2002] 2 AC 545 [195] (Lord Hutton).

[97] The top three decisions are: 1. *Burmah Oil Co Ltd v Lord Advocate* [1965] AC 75 (30 references); *Jackson v Attorney General* [2005] UKHL 56; [2006] 1 AC 262 (28 references); *R v A* [2001] UKHL 25; [2002] 1 AC 45 (21 references).

[98] He is cited 15 times in 6 decisions.

[99] Richard Clayton and Hugh Tomlinson, *The Law of Human Rights* (2nd ed, Oxford University Press 2009).

[100] David Feldman, *Civil Liberties and Human Rights in England and Wales* (2nd ed, Oxford University Press 2002).

[101] William Wade and Christopher Forsyth, *Administrative Law* (10th ed, Oxford University Press 2009).

[102] *Jackson v Attorney General* [2005] UKHL 56; [2006] 1 AC 262, especially [9]-[20].

[103] *R (Begum) v Denbigh High School Governors* [2006] UKHL 15; [2007] 1 AC 100 [94]-[95].

good illustrations. Among the references to academic literature, two cases deserve special mention. *Aston Cantlow v Wallbank* is the only case where reference is made to contemporary continental legal scholarship written in a language other than English.[104] The other is Lord Walker's opinion in the *Prolife Alliance* decision where he does not simply allude to contemporary academic literature but critically engages with Richard Edwards' article on deference.[105]

References to Foreign (National) Law

Foreign law is extensively cited in the jurisprudence of the court. Of the 40 cases, there were only 6 that did not refer to foreign law in some form. However, the concept of foreign law is in need of some clarification in the UK context.

Firstly, the UK itself consists of three legal systems: England and Wales, Northern Ireland and Scotland. In some contexts, it might be useful for the court to compare the different legal solutions of these three legal systems. One case was found where this "internal comparison" played an important role in the reasoning. In *R (Anderson) v Secretary of State for the Home Department*[106] it was argued that the involvement of the Secretary of State in the sentencing process was incompatible with the claimant's right to a fair hearing by an independent and impartial tribunal under Article 6(1) of the Convention. Since the relevant laws of Scotland and Northern Ireland were different from English law, the UKHL had taken into account the different practices of the other two legal systems.

Second, the UKSC often refers to the jurisprudence of the Judicial Committee of the Privy Council (JCPC). The JCPC is the final appeal court for the UK Overseas Territories and Crown Dependencies and for a couple of independent Commonwealth countries.[107] This means that when the UKSC refers to the decisions of the JCPC, it refers to the decisions of a UK court (consisting of very much the same judges), but since the JCPC applies the substantive law of the territory where the appeal originates from, these were also coded as references to foreign law in this research. There were 12 cases where the court referred to foreign law in this sense. Some of these cases raised constitutional questions of fundamental importance. In *Jackson*, for instance, the question was raised about

[104] *Aston Cantlow v Wallbank* [2003] UKHL 37; [2004] 1 AC 546 [62] (Lord Hope).
[105] [2003] UKHL 23; [2004] 1 AC 185 [143]-[144].
[106] [2002] UKHL 46; [2003] 1 AC 837.
[107] The other powers of the JCPC are irrelevant for our purposes.

whether the Parliament Act 1911 was analogous to the establishment of colonial legislatures by the imperial Parliament.[108]

As far as foreign law in the strict sense is concerned, the court's main points of reference are, quite predictably, the Commonwealth countries and the United States. In the selected cases, the court referred most frequently to the law of Canada (12 cases), New Zealand (10), the United States (9), Australia (8) and South Africa (7). In many of these cases, the court provided a detailed and in-depth analysis of the relevant case law of these countries. By contrast, only two references to French law were found. It is also telling that both of them are quite cursory and indirect: in one case the court's information derived from a Canadian judgment;[109] in the other case it came from Wade's textbook on Administrative Law.[110]

Although it can be safely predicted that references to Commonwealth jurisdictions will continue to dominate in the jurisprudence of the UKSC, the sample cases suggest that the references to continental jurisdictions are likely to increase. Applying the HRA, the court has already occasionally referred to the domestic laws of other countries that were challenged before the ECtHR, or to how the institutions of other countries interpret the European Convention.[111]

Other Methods/Arguments

There are arguments that do not easily fit into the above categories.[112] According to our research, there were 21 cases where the court appealed to such arguments. Since this is a catch-all category that is defined in a negative way, it is difficult to generalise from these cases. Nevertheless, two arguments deserve special attention: deference and political practice.

There are at least 10 cases that refer to the idea of deference (whether they use the term or not). Deference, strictly speaking, is not a method of interpretation since it is not about what a legal provision means. Rather, this argument is about the question of institutional capacities, i.e., which institution is better suited to determine the meaning of the text or establish

[108] *Jackson v Attorney General* [2005] UKHL 56; [2006] 1 AC 262 [174] (Lord Carswell).

[109] *Campbell v MGN Ltd* [2004] UKHL 22; [2004] 2 AC 457 [154] (Lady Hale).

[110] *R (Alconbury) v Secretary of State for the Environment* [2001] UKHL 23; [2003] 2 AC 295 [53] (Lord Slynn).

[111] This practice explains an unexpected reference, for instance, to the law of Bosnia-Herzegovina. See *R (Ullah) v Special Adjudicator* [2004] UKHL 26; [2004] 2 AC 323 [23] (Lord Bingham).

[112] However, it is particularly difficult to distinguish them, on the one hand, from concepts and principles that are not part of the constitution and, on the other hand, from non-legal arguments.

an intermediary premise in the reasoning. As Kavanagh says, when judges defer to the other branches of government, they "assign varying degrees of weight to the judgments of the elected branches, out of respect for their superior expertise, competence or democratic legitimacy".[113] This idea is discussed extensively in *Kebilene* by Lord Hope[114] in *Prolife Alliance* by Lord Hoffmann,[115] and in *A v Secretary* by Lord Bingham.[116] It also plays a central role in *Huang*[117] and is at the centre of academic discussions about the interpretation of the HRA.[118] As Jeffrey Jowell notes: "It is becoming clearer by the day, that the most difficult question for the courts in the interpretation of the Human Rights Act 1998 (HRA) is the extent to which they should defer to Parliament and other institutions of government on matters relating to the public interest."[119]

The other type of reason worth mentioning is the argument from actual political practice. Although this argument does not occur very often, it says much about the archaeology of the British constitution. The idea of political constitution where there is no sharp dividing line between the existing political practice and the constitution as the source of normative requirements has already been alluded to. This idea has special significance in those cases where the court was asked to define the limits of prerogative powers. This is well illustrated by the speech of Lord Reid in *Burmah Oil*: "What we have to determine in this case is whether or when,

113 Aileen Kavanagh, "Defending Deference in Public Law and Constitutional Theory" (2010) 126 *Law Quarterly Review* 222, 223.

114 *R v DPP, ex p Kebilene* [2000] 2 AC 326, at 380–1.

115 *R (ProLife Alliance) v BBC* [2003] UKHL 23; [2004] 1 AC 185 [74]-[77].

116 *A v Secretary of State for the Home Department* [2004] UKHL 56; [2005] 2 AC 68 [42].

117 *Huang v Secretary of State for the Home Department* [2007] UKHL 11; [2007] 2 AC 167.

118 See T. R. S. Allan, "Human Rights and Judicial Review: A Critique of "Due Deference"" (2006) 65 *Cambridge Law Journal* 671; "Deference, Defiance, and Doctrine: Defining the Limits of Judicial Review" (2010) 60 *The University of Toronto Law Journal* 41; A. D. P. Brady, *Proportionality and Deference under the UK Human Rights Act: An Institutionally Sensitive Approach* (Cambridge University Press 2012); Richard Clayton, "Judicial Deference and "Democratic Dialogue": The Legitimacy of Judicial Intervention under the Human Rights Act 1998" (2004) *Public Law* 33; Richard A. Edwards, "Judicial Deference under the Human Rights Act" (2002) 65 *MLR* 859; Jeff A. King, "Institutional Approaches to Judicial Restraint" (2008) 28 *Oxford Journal of Legal Studies* 409; Francesca Klug, "Judicial Deference under the Human Rights Act 1998" (2003) *European Human Rights Law Review* 125; Lord Steyn, "Deference: A Tangled Story" (2005) *Public Law* 346; Alison L. Young, "In Defence of Due Deference" (2009) 72 *MLR* 554; Alison L. Young, "Deference, Dialogue and the Search for Legitimacy" (2010) 30 *OJLS* 815; Alison L. Young, "Ghaidan v Godin-Mendoza: Avoiding the Deference Trap" (2005) *Public Law* 23.

119 Jeffrey Jowell, "Judicial Deference: Servility, Civility or Institutional Capacity?" (2003) *Public Law* 592, 592.

in a case not covered by any statute, property can be taken by virtue of the prerogative without compensation . . . I would think the proper approach is a historical one: how was it used in former times and how has it been used in modern times?"[120]

References were also made to actual political practice in *Jackson*, but the argument here revolved around the foundations of parliamentary sovereignty. Lord Hope concluded his speech with the following argument: "[The] restrictions on the exercise of the power of the House of Lords that the 1949 Act purported to make have been so widely recognised and relied upon that these restrictions are, today, a political fact. It is no longer open to the courts, if it ever was, to say that that Act was not authorised by section 2(1) of the 1911 Act."[121]

7 *The Weight of Arguments*

This research has recorded the incidence of each type of constitutional argument discussed above. However, the mere number of arguments is not always informative enough. As can be expected, precedents are crucially important in a common law system. On the other hand, there are some types of argument that are hardly used. These facts do not tell us very much about the distinctive features of constitutional reasoning in the UK. However, if the numbers are put into proper context, we can draw some informative conclusions on the basis of these findings. Firstly, the high number of objective teleological arguments (35) coupled with the relatively high incidence of non-legal arguments on the one hand, and the relatively low number of linguistic arguments (19) on the other, lends support to the view that the questions that are raised by landmark constitutional cases very often cannot be solved by linguistic arguments.[122] Secondly, although it is not uncommon for courts to appeal to Parliamentary intention, putting these cases into a proper context shows that reference to subjective intention is a disfavoured argument in the UK even after *Pepper v Hart.* Thirdly, the growing number of international harmonisation arguments fits well with, and can be explained by, the changing constitutional landscape of the UK. Fourthly, the increased incidence of references to contemporary academic writings indicates a shift in how judges have been engaging with legal academia in the last few

[120] *Burmah Oil Co Ltd v Lord Advocate* [1965] AC 75 101.

[121] *Jackson v Attorney General* [2005] UKHL 56; [2006] 1 AC 262 [128].

[122] Kavanagh (n 57) 263–4.

decades. Finally, many constitutional lawyers argue that today there exists a *global* judicial dialogue about the requirements of constitutionalism. The detailed analysis of the use of foreign law shows very clearly that this dialogue is somewhat limited by linguistic barriers and the differences in legal culture; UKSC judges draw inspiration predominantly from other common law countries.

Although the relative incidence of constitutional arguments makes possible some generalisations, it does not inform us about the weight of the different arguments. Therefore, it is important to put the raw numbers into proper context and address the question of whether there are priority rules between the different types of arguments. According to one of the most acclaimed treatises on statutory interpretation, the dominant approach of British judges can be summarised in five basic rules.[123] For the purposes of this paper, the first two rules are of special importance. In a simplified form the two rules run as follows: (1) the judge must give effect to the ordinary meaning in the general context of the statute; (2) if the judge considers that the application of the words in their ordinary sense would produce a result which is contrary to the purpose of the statute, he/she may apply them in any secondary meaning which they are capable of bearing.[124] Although as general rules of statutory interpretation these rules are still important, in the light of this paper a couple of qualifications must be made.

First, as we have already mentioned, there are many constitutional disputes that cannot be resolved by linguistic arguments. For instance, hardly any linguistic arguments were found about the meaning of substantive human rights provisions. Purposive arguments do not come into play after the primary ordinary meaning of words is determined, as the priority rules above suggest, but are inescapable even at the first stage of the reasoning, where the primary ordinary meaning is established.

Second, in human rights adjudication the primary meaning of words is very often not determined by the court's own purposive considerations, but by international harmonising arguments. Since by giving effect to Section 2(1) of the HRA the court attaches significant weight to the jurisprudence of the ECtHR, most of the time the interpretation of the Strasbourg court will determine the "true meaning" of Convention rights. Even where the jurisprudence of the ECtHR is less than clear, the court often tries to predict what the Strasbourg court would decide instead of

[123] Engle et al. (n 29) 49. [124] Ibid.

developing a distinctive British jurisprudence.[125] As this research focuses on the UKSC, it is not necessary to address the question of what lower courts are required to do when domestic precedents conflict with a later decision of the ECtHR. As far as the UKSC is concerned, it seems to be ready to depart from its own previous judgments if later Strasbourg rulings conflict with them.[126]

Third, Section 3(1) of the HRA, imposing an interpretative duty on courts, changes how *other laws* must be interpreted in the light of Convention rights and qualifies the general primacy of literal interpretation.[127] As a consequence of Section 3(1), judges can deviate even from the unambiguous meaning of the text. As Lord Nicholls put it in *Ghaidan v Godin-Mendoza*:

> But once it is accepted that section 3 may require legislation to bear a meaning which departs from the unambiguous meaning the legislation would otherwise bear, it becomes impossible to suppose Parliament intended that the operation of section 3 should depend critically upon the particular form of words adopted by the parliamentary draftsman in the statutory provision under consideration. That would make the application of section 3 something of a semantic lottery. If the draftsman chose to express the concept being enacted in one form of words, section 3 would be available to achieve Convention-compliance. If he chose a different form of words, section 3 would be impotent.[128]

When concluding this section, it is important to add that the main "interpretive debates" in the UK do not seem to revolve around the suitability of the above argument types or their priority. Although it is possible to distinguish between an activist and a minimalist approach to constitutional reasoning,[129] the dividing line is hardly between the proponents of literal and purposive interpretation. Rather, the most important interpretive debates seem to gravitate around three issues, the first is a general question for constitutional law, the second and third issues are specific to human rights adjudication. First, there is a lot of discussion on the

[125] See Hickman's important distinction between predictive and normative reasoning. Tom Hickman, *Public Law After the Human Rights Act* (Hart 2010) 39.

[126] *Manchester City Council v Pinnock* (Nos 1 and 2) [2010] UKSC 45, [2011] 2 AC 104 [45]-[50].

[127] *R v A* [2001] UKHL 25; [2002] 1 AC 45 [44] (Lord Steyn).

[128] [2004] UKHL 30; [2004] 2 AC 557 [31].

[129] Helen Fenwick, Roger Masterman and Gavin Phillipson, "The Human Rights Act in Contemporary Context" in Helen Fenwick, Roger Masterman and Gavin Phillipson (eds), *Judicial Reasoning under the UK Human Rights Act* (Cambridge University Press 2011) 9.

proper intensity of judicial review and on the related question of judicial deference. Second, there is a voluminous amount of literature on Section 3(1) of the HRA and the desirable division of labour between Section 3 and Section 4. Much of this debate addresses the question of the extent to which judges can bend or stretch the language in order to remove an incompatibility with Convention rights. Third, there is an important debate about the status of the HRA. Hickman formulates the issue thus: "There is, then, a tension at the very heart of the Act between the creation of new domestic rights and the provision of a remedy in domestic law for rights that exist on the international plane."[130] Although this debate goes far beyond the method of proper constitutional interpretation, its implications for constitutional reasoning can be easily understood; the two approaches would give slightly different weight to the judgments of the Strasbourg court. The first approach tends to use the Stasbourg case law as the source of broad principles, while the second one tends to use them as binding precedents.[131]

8 *Judicial Candour and Judicial Rhetoric*

Making general claims about the motivation of judges requires an extensive analytical machinery that cannot be discussed within the confines of this country report. Without systematic empirical studies that cover the whole period under discussion, any suggestions that British judges are motivated by factors other than the reasons they offer would be based on speculation or anecdotal evidence.[132]

As far as judicial rhetoric is concerned, the most characteristic feature of British judgments, especially if they are compared to US Supreme Court decisions, is that even when judges disagree, the style of opinions is courteous and polite, rather than confrontational. As a consequence, whenever judges use a more confrontational style, the sharp contrast with the rest of the decisions makes these opinions very salient. Perhaps the

[130] Hickman (n 125) 27.

[131] For an overview, see Roger Masterman, "Aspiration or foundation? The status of the Strasbourg jurisprudence and the "Convention rights" in domestic law" in Fenwick, Masterman and Phillipson (n 129).

[132] For studies that aim to reveal the background motivation of judges, see David Robertson, *Judicial Discretion in the House of Lords* (Clarendon 1998); Chris Hanretty, "The Decisions and Ideal Points of British Law Lords" (2013) 43 *British Journal of Political Science* 703; Rachel J. Cahill-O'Callaghan, "The Influence of Personal Values on Legal Judgments" (2013) 40 *Journal of Law and Society* 596. It is important to note however, that none of these papers cover the whole period between 1876 and 2012.

most famous dissenting speech was given by Lord Atkin in *Liversidge v Anderson*, and one could argue that the style of the opinion contributed as much to its fame as the quality of the argument. The central argument revolved around the interpretation of the following provision: "If the Secretary of State has reasonable cause to believe any person to be of hostile origin or associations". The majority argued that: "A has a reasonable cause" means that "A thinks that he has a reasonable cause". In his dissent, Lord Atkin characterised this position as follows:

> I know of only one authority which might justify the suggested method of construction: "'When I use a word,' Humpty Dumpty said in rather a scornful tone, 'it means just what I choose it to mean, neither more nor less.' 'The question is,' said Alice, 'whether you can make words mean so many different things.' 'The question is,' said Humpty Dumpty, 'which is to be master – that's all.'" ("Through the Looking Glass," c. vi.) After all this long discussion the question is whether the words "If a man has" can mean "If a man thinks he has." I am of opinion that they cannot, and that the case should be decided accordingly.[133]

9 *Length, Dissenting and Concurring Opinions*

The decision-making of the court can be simultaneously characterised by a certain kind of methodological individualism and a considerable measure of substantive unity. Methodological individualism[134] is manifested in three features of UKSC judgments.

1. A typical judgment consists of the opinions (in the case of the UKHL these were officially called speeches) of individual judges and is not presented as the opinion of the court.[135] As a general rule, each judge makes a statement about his/her position on the disposition of the case. When the judge does not give independent arguments for his/her position, he/she almost invariably uses the following formula: "My Lords, I have had the advantage of reading in draft the speech prepared by my noble and learned friend, XY, and for the reasons he/she gives, I, too, would allow/dismiss the appeal." This sends the message that even

[133] Liversidge v Anderson [1942] AC 206, at 145.

[134] The term "individualism" is borrowed from Louis Blom-Cooper, "Style of Judgments" in Blom-Cooper et al. (n 8) 245.

[135] This is usually called the *seriatim* approach to judgment giving.

if the judge does not give independent arguments, his/her position is the outcome of individual rather than collective reflection.[136]

2. However, methodological individualism goes beyond the way judicial decisions are presented. It also implies that judges most often do support their position with reasoned arguments. In our 40 cases, if each judge who was involved in the decision-making process had delivered a reasoned opinion, they would have written a total of 216 opinions. In reality, 188 reasoned opinions were delivered in the 40 cases. This means that on average each judge supported his/her vote with a reasoned opinion in 87 per cent of the cases, which seems to be an extremely high number from a comparative perspective.
3. This picture could be further refined if we distinguished different forms of concurring opinions. A concurring opinion can develop a full argument that spells out all the steps of the reasoning that lead to the disposition of a case. On the other hand, concurring opinions could be limited to one or a few intermediary premises of a full argument, without intending to deal with all steps that are necessary to dispose of the case. The first can be called a *parallel* concurring opinion and the second one a *supplementary* concurring opinion. Our point is that when the judges of the court deliver concurring opinions, they most often develop a parallel argument and do not simply supplement the reasoning of their colleagues. This feature of the judicial decision-making procedure gives a further illustration of the individual responsibility of judges.

Turning from the individual opinions to the judgments of the court, and drawing on Poole and Shah's research, three types of judgments will be distinguished.[137] A judgment is termed "unanimous" if there is one main opinion and the other judges agree with the disposition of the case, but their opinions do not contain reasons that support the conclusion. A judgment is called "unanimous by concurring" if each judge agrees with the disposition of the case, and at least two opinions contain reasons that support the decision. Finally, a judgment is called "majority over dissent'" if there is at least one dissenting opinion. It is important to note that this methodology conceals some fundamental

[136] The speeches of the Law Lords were published in the law reports in the order of seniority. By contrast, in the practice of the Supreme Court the opinion that is published first in the law report tends to be the lead judgment that sets out the facts of the case.

[137] Poole and Shah (n39) 83–87.

constitutional disagreements, since not all constitutional disagreements lead to differences in the disposition of the case.[138]

Among our 40 cases, there was only one where the decision was presented as the opinion of the court and there was one unanimous decision (taken together they amount to 5 per cent of all cases). The majority of decisions (25 cases, 62.5 per cent) were unanimous by concurrence, and 13 judgments (32.5 per cent) were decided by majority over dissent. Of these 13 cases, there were 6 split decisions (15 per cent). Since our selection focused on high-profile constitutional cases, the number of concurring opinions is significantly higher than the average and these numbers do not reflect accurately the changing attitudes of judges to opinion-writing.[139] However, the relatively low number of split decisions suggests that the high degree of methodological individualism is not necessarily coupled with sharp substantive disagreements. This might have a lot to do with the extremely homogeneous nature of the British judiciary, the depoliticised appointment process and the small size of the panel. However, the hypothesis set out in this paper is that the relative unity among judges can, to some extent, be explained by the strong influence of the Strasbourg court. Judges who would disagree on substantive human rights issues can more easily agree on what the Strasbourg court actually decided.

The methodological individualism of the court goes a long way towards explaining the prolixity of judgments. However, "the more pronounced public law profile" (Shah and Poole) of the court could also contribute to the fact that judgments have, as a general rule, become longer in recent decades. According to this explanation, public law issues affect not just the litigant parties but also the wider public, and the change of the audience requires judges to make more comprehensive judgments.[140]

10 *Framing of Constitutional Issues*

There are no typical ways of characterising constitutional issues; the framing of the issue depends on the nature of the dispute. However, the coexistence of more traditional civil liberties protected under common law

[138] See e.g. *Pepper v Hart* [1993] AC 593. In a technical sense, Lord Mackay wrote a concurring opinion, even if he disagreed with the other Law Lords on the fundamental constitutional issue.

[139] Alan Paterson's research points out that the Supreme Court makes conscious efforts to decrease the number of concurring and dissenting opinions. He also provides an excellent overview of how judicial attitudes to multiple judgments have been changing over time. See Paterson (n 28) 97–122.

[140] Blom-Cooper (n 134) 159–63.

and human rights protected by the HRA implies that some issues can be framed in two different ways or give rise to alternative arguments. The same applies to the coexistence of the HRA and traditional judicial review under the common law.

11 Key Concepts

Rule of Law

Of the key concepts, the selected cases invoked most often the rule of law or its cognate terms (24 cases). Most frequently, the court referred directly to the rule of law; less often to predictability or legal certainty; and on two occasions the emphasis was on legitimate expectations.[141]

Democracy

Democracy was mentioned in 21 cases. Out of these cases, 9 were directly related to freedom of speech or freedom of assembly, and 2 cases revolved around parliamentary procedure. In the rest of the cases, the mention of democracy was less expected and was more loosely related to the subject matter of the decision.

Sovereignty

Of our 40 cases, 15 invoked the concept of sovereignty. It is important to emphasise that in many legal systems the idea of sovereignty is related either to the external aspect of sovereignty (the sovereignty of the state), or to the subject of the constituent power. By contrast, in the UK context, in the overwhelming majority of cases where sovereignty is an issue, the concept refers to the idea of parliamentary sovereignty, and only a couple of cases mention the sovereignty of the state. This was rather predictable since one of the general themes that underlie many of the recent constitutional reforms is the challenge to the traditional understanding of parliamentary sovereignty.

State Form

Only three cases were found where the monarchical form of the state had some relevance, and these cases are all related to the idea of the royal prerogative.

[141] *Council of Civil Service Unions v Minister for the Civil Service* [1985] 1 AC. 374; *R v DPP, ex p Kebilene* [2000] 2 AC 326.

System of Government

The system of government does not play an important role in any of the cases in the sample. This can be explained by the fact that most of the rules that govern the relationship between the Crown, the Executive and Parliament are political rather than legal in nature. In addition, the UK government is based on the interdependence rather than the separation of executive and legislative powers and that gives less chance for conflict between the two branches.

Secularism

The relationship between the church and the state is addressed only in one decision. Perhaps unexpectedly, this is not the one that is related to freedom of religion. *Aston Cantlow* revolved around the concept of public authority in the HRA, and the court addressed the question of whether the established Church of England can be considered a public authority for the purposes of the HRA.

Nation

References to the nation are also almost non-existent. In many countries, constituent power is located in the nation and the nation is the source of all political authority. This idea does not fit with the UK constitutional tradition. The nation is mentioned only in one case and in a very different legal context.

Devolution

The United Kingdom is a unitary state, but devolution (transferring powers to the Welsh and Northern Ireland assemblies in Cardiff and Belfast, and the Scottish Parliament in Edinburgh) has been one of the most important developments in the UK's recent constitutional history. However, it was the JCPC and not the UKHL that had jurisdiction in devolution cases before 2009. This explains the almost complete lack of references to the concept of devolution. *AXA General Insurance Ltd, Petitioners*,[142] the only case that refers to devolution, was decided in 2011 by the new Supreme Court.

Proportionality

Proportionality is one of the most important terms of modern constitutional adjudication, and the number of cases that invoke the concept (20)

[142] [2011] UKSC 46; [2012] 1 AC 868.

testifies to its importance. Its emergence in UK case law illustrates nicely the trajectory of British constitutional law. It is not mentioned at all in our cases before the 1980s; the term appears first in the *GCHQ* case in Lord Diplock's speech,[143] but the idea of finding a balance between fairness and national security is also central to the case as a whole. Between 1985 and 2000, the number of references to proportionality increased, and from 2000 most human rights cases refer to the concept. What requires explanation is not the reference to proportionality in such cases but rather the lack of it. There are two explanations for this. First, the proportionality analysis is unnecessary because (a) the right in question is not engaged at all; (b) the right is absolute and cannot be limited; and (c) the limitation does not have a legitimate aim or is not prescribed by law.[144] Second, the court applies not the proportionality analysis, but a more contextual version of it.[145]

Core of Constitutional Rights

The ECHR does not have a clause that is comparable to Article 19(2) of the German Basic Law that protects the essential content *(Wesengehalt)* of fundamental rights, so the almost complete lack of this concept in British case law is not surprising. However, there is one context where the court used very similar terminology. In *Ullah*, the court argued that when a contracting state removes a person from its territory and this person was foreseeably at risk of some kind of ill-treatment, an issue can be raised if the "actual or threatened treatment would amount to a flagrant denial or gross violation of the relevant right".[146] This means that there is a real risk of a flagrant violation of the very essence of the right.[147]

Human Dignity

The ECHR is built on the idea of human dignity. However, unlike many national constitutions, it does not guarantee a subjective right to dignity. Therefore, it could be expected that the court does not invoke this concept very often. Altogether, there were four references to this concept, and two of them were related to the limits of freedom of expression.

143 *Council of Civil Service Unions v Minister for the Civil Service* [1985] 1 AC 374, at 410.

144 See e.g. *Bellinger v Bellinger* [2003] 2 AC 467; For a very nice syllogistic reasoning without proportionality analysis, see R (Anderson) v Secretary of State for the Home Department [2002] UKHL 46; [2003] 1 AC 837 [20]-[31] (Lord Bingham).

145 *R (Ullah) v Special Adjudicator* [2004] UKHL 26; [2004] 2 AC 323.

146 Ibid at 324. 147 Ibid [50] (Lord Steyn).

Equality

Equality is referred to in 9 cases; the majority of them relate to the alleged violations of Article 14 of the Convention.

Fifteen cases invoke *basic procedural rights*, 13 invoke *freedom of expression* and 11 invoke the *right to privacy*. Although the difference between the number of these references is not very substantial, their distribution is quite telling. Of the 15 references to basic procedural rights, 6 predate the coming into force of the HRA and 9 originate from the post-2000 period. The respective numbers in relation to freedom of expression are 7 and 6. By contrast, of the 11 references to the right to privacy, only 1 predates the HRA. These numbers indicate that procedural rights and freedom of expression were, using the British constitutional terminology, traditional civil liberties protected by the common law, while the right to privacy did not enjoy the same protection and its constitutional significance can be traced back to the HRA.

C Comparative Analysis

The above analysis has already alluded to some of the distinctive features of constitutional reasoning in the UK. Those findings of the research that seem to be the most important for the purposes of comparative analysis are highlighted here again.

1. Although one could argue that constitutional interpretation is just a special form of statutory interpretation and there is no qualitative difference between the two enterprises, in many legal systems constitutional reasoning has its own distinctive style, compared to ordinary statutory interpretation. In those systems, centralised constitutional courts, unlike their decentralised counterparts, often recruit their members from the ranks of legal academics; their decision-making process also often differs from ordinary adjudication (e.g. they are allowed to publish dissenting opinions); and specialisation in (or monopoly over) constitutional issues is also a contributing factor. The UK constitutional system is remarkable for the "continuity" between constitutional reasoning and ordinary statutory interpretation. Although there are many other countries where there is a strong continuity between these two enterprises due to the lack of a specialised constitutional court, in the UK, the lack of a codified constitution blurs the above distinction even further.

2. Almost all constitutional courts are influenced to some extent by the jurisprudence of other courts. However, in some cases this influence is considerably stronger than in others. Constitutional courts in Europe in some sense all work under the supervision of the ECtHR, since the jurisprudence of this court, through various channels, has infiltrated virtually all European legal systems. Some constitutional courts, like the Czech one, decided to interpret their own domestic constitutions in the light of the jurisprudence of the ECtHR. In other cases, the constitution itself prescribed the method of Convention-friendly interpretation.[148] Still other countries, such as Finland, have explicitly modelled their own domestic bill of rights on the ECHR. However, in the UK the role of international harmonising arguments is even stronger because the HRA's provisions on substantive rights are virtually coextensive with those of the Convention, and the lack of a separate textual identity permits less room for the UK courts to manoeuvre.
3. As the analysis has already indicated, appealing to the subjective intention of the legislature is a disfavoured argument in the UK, and ministerial statements in parliamentary debates are admissible only in exceptional cases. This sharply contrasts the UK with some other constitutional democracies.[149]
4. Another point worth reiterating here is that although the UKSC often uses foreign law as an inspiration, the references of the court are very much limited by linguistic barriers and by the legal tradition the UK belongs to.
5. Perhaps the voting records and the style of decision-making are even more distinctive features of the constitutional reasoning of the UKSC than the type of arguments that are used by the court. The combination of methodological individualism and the lack of sharp ideological disagreements along party political lines on substantive issues makes the UKSC markedly different from both some centralised constitutional courts and the US Supreme Court. To highlight these differences, it is worth emphasising that 87 per cent of the votes of British judges were

[148] Article 10 para. 2 of the Spanish constitution; Article 16 para. 2 of the Portuguese constitution. For a detailed analysis of the relationship between the jurisprudence of the ECtHR and domestic law, see Catherine Van de Heyning, "Constitutional Courts as Guardians of Fundamental Rights. The Constitutionalisation of the Convention through Domestic Constitutional Adjudication" in Patricia Popelier, Armen Mazmanyan and Wouter Vandenbruwaene (eds), *The Role of Constitutional Courts in Multilevel Governance* (Intersentia 2013) 21.

[149] For instance, in the USA 27 cases referred to the intention of the framers.

supported by a reasoned opinion in our sample cases while the respective number in the United States is only 48 per cent. These numbers show that the British judiciary is more individualistic in its judgment-giving practice than the American. On the other hand, it is much less divided than its American counterpart. We used three criteria to determine the dividedness of the court: (a) the proportion of "majority over dissent" judgments, (b) the proportion of dissenting votes and (c) the proportion of split decisions. The UKSC proved to be consistently less divided according to these criteria than the Supreme Court of the USA. The respective numbers were (a) 32.5 per cent (UK) – 67.5 per cent (USA); (b) 8.8 per cent (UK) – 22.1 per cent (USA) and (c) 15 per cent (UK) – 25 per cent (USA).

6. As far as the key concepts of public law are concerned, the most salient feature of the UK constitutional discourse, exemplified by the cases from the sample, is the central role of parliamentary sovereignty and the corresponding lack of references to popular sovereignty (as well as the related concepts of constituent power, the people, or the nation). In reconstructing the conceptual history of popular sovereignty in the UK, Loughlin points out that constitutional discourse after the 1688 settlement has gradually conflated "the constituent power of the people with that of the constituted authority of the commons".[150]

Appendix: 40 Leading Cases

1. A v Secretary of State for the Home Department [2004] UKHL 56; [2005] 2 A.C. 68
2. Anisminic Ltd v Foreign Compensation Commission [1969] 2 A.C. 147
3. Aston Cantlow and Wilmcote with Billesley Parochial Church Council v Wallbank [2003] UKHL 37; [2004] 1 A.C. 546
4. Attorney General v De Keyser's Royal Hotel [1920] A.C. 508
5. Attorney General v Guardian Newspapers Ltd (No 2) [1990] 1 A.C. 109
6. AXA General Insurance Ltd, Petitioners [2011] UKSC 46; [2012] 1 A.C. 868

150 Martin Loughlin, "Constituent Power Subverted: From English Constitutional Argument to British Constitutional Practice" in Martin Loughlin and Neil Walker, *The Paradox of Constitutionalism: Constituent Power and Constitutional Form* (Oxford University Press 2007) 43.

7. Bellinger v Bellinger [2003] 2 AC 467
8. British Railways Board v Pickin [1974] AC 765
9. Burmah Oil Co (Burma Trading) Ltd v Lord Advocate [1965] A.C. 75
10. Campbell v Mirror Group Newspapers Ltd [2004] UKHL 22; [2004] 2 A.C. 457
11. Council of Civil Service Unions v Minister for the Civil Service [1985] AC. 374
12. Derbyshire County Council v Times Newspapers Ltd [1993] A.C. 534
13. Ghaidan v Godin-Mendoza [2004] UKHL 30; [2004] 2 A.C. 557
14. Huang v Secretary of State for the Home Department [2007] UKHL 11; [2007] 2 A.C. 167
15. Jackson v Attorney General [2005] UKHL 56; [2006] 1 A.C. 262
16. Kay v Lambeth LBC [2006] UKHL 10; [2006] 2 A.C. 465
17. Liversidge v Anderson [1942] A.C. 206
18. M v Home Office [1994] 1 A.C. 377
19. Pepper (Inspector of Taxes) v Hart [1993] A.C. 593
20. Porter v Magill [2001] UKHL 67; [2002] 2 A.C. 357
21. R. v A (Complainant's Sexual History) [2001] UKHL 25; [2002] 1 A.C. 45
22. R. v DPP, ex p Kebilene [2000] 2 A.C. 326
23. R. v Halliday, ex p Zadig [1917] A.C. 260
24. R. v Lambert (Steven) [2001] UKHL 37; [2002] 2 A.C. 545
25. R. v Secretary of State for the Home Department, ex p Brind [1991] 1 A.C. 696
26. R. v Secretary of State for the Home Department, ex p Fire Brigades Union [1995] 2 AC 513
27. R. v Secretary of State for the Home Department Ex p. Simms [2000] 2 AC 115
28. R. v Secretary of State for Transport, ex p Factortame Ltd (No.2) [1991] 1 A.C. 603
29. R. (Anderson) v Secretary of State for the Home Department [2002] UKHL 46; [2003] 1 A.C. 837
30. R. (Begum) v Denbigh High School Governors [2006] UKHL 15; [2007] 1 AC 100
31. R. (Countryside Alliance) v Attorney General [2007] UKHL 52; [2008] 1 A.C. 719
32. R. (Daly) v Secretary of State for the Home Department [2001] UKHL 26; [2001] 2 A.C. 532
33. R. (Alconbury) v Secretary of State for the Environment [2001] UKHL 23; [2003] 2 A.C. 295

34. R. (Laporte) v Chief Constable of Gloucestershire [2006] UKHL 55, [2007] 2 AC 105
35. R. (ProLife Alliance) v BBC [2003] UKHL 23; [2004] 1 A.C. 185
36. R. (Ullah) v Special Adjudicator [2004] UKHL 26; [2004] 2 A.C. 323
37. RB (Algeria) v Secretary of State for the Home Department [2009] UKHL 10; [2010] 2 A.C. 110
38. Reynolds v Times Newspapers Ltd [2001] 2 A.C. 127
39. Ridge v Baldwin [1964] A.C. 40
40. YL v Birmingham City Council [2007] UKHL 27; [2008] 1 A.C. 95

18

The Supreme Court of the United States

HOWARD SCHWEBER AND JENNIFER L. BROOKHART

A Legal, Political, Institutional, and Academic Context

1 *Legal and Political Culture as Context for Constitutional Reasoning*

The American Revolution has been famously described as "politically radical but legally conservative," a description that captures the tendency of revolutionary leaders to insist that they sought restoration of the "rights of Englishmen" rather than a new regime.[1] Unlike the French Revolution, the American Revolution was not followed by a wholesale rewriting of legal principles. Instead, the traditions of English common law were accepted as the basis for private and public law principles. Every state had a "reception statute" acknowledging the authority of the common law except insofar as it was altered by positive legislation, and state courts did not hesitate to appeal to English precedents or Blackstone's *Commentaries* as an authoritative source.

The legal conservatism of the American regime was further reinforced throughout the creation and adoption of the Constitution. Far from a purely idealistic blueprint for a utopian society, the creation of the Constitution was in large part prompted by concerns over the ability of the national government to pay its debts and threats to property rights from the rise of populist sentiments within the states. During debates over drafting, ratification, and the addition of a Bill of Rights other concerns emerged, but the descriptions of limited national powers and protected individual rights bore the marks of the concerns of the time, and particularly debates over the proper relationship between the state and federal governments.

Issues of federal-state relations continued to dominate constitutional debates through the nineteenth century. It was only after the Civil War,

[1] Beverly Zweiben, *How Blackstone Lost the Colonies: English Law, Colonial Lawyers, and the American Revolution* (Garland 1990); Hendrik Hartog, "Law" in Hartog (ed), *Law in the American Revolution and the Revolution in the Law* (NYU Press 1981).

with the adoption of the XIVth Amendment, that rights issues came to the fore. From the 1870s until the 1930s, the Court played a conservative and intermittently obstructionist role, limiting the authority of Congress and adopting relatively weak interpretations of rights except for the property rights of employers. In the early 1930s, in particular, the Court struck down a number of the initiatives of President Franklin Roosevelt's New Deal. In the context of the Great Depression and an industrialized economy, the Court's insistence on applying nineteenth-century doctrines of limited national powers and few substantive rights became intolerable. Beginning in the 1930s – the year usually referenced is 1937 – the justices reversed course and established the principle that, where regulation of economic behavior was concerned, any "rational basis" for state action would suffice.[2] On the rights side, this is also the beginning of a shift from discussions of general principles of "liberty" to the idea that the XIVth Amendment incorporated specific guarantees of the Bill of Rights against the states. The first cases to introduce this idea involved freedom of expression and criminal procedure, with a critical expression of the guiding principles appearing in *Palko v. Connecticut* (1937).[3]

After World War II, the emergence of an immensely powerful and capable national state was an inescapable element of the constitutional landscape. At the same time, the experiences of the wartime years prompted rethinking of the legitimacy of racial discrimination in particular. By the late 1950s, with the arrival of Chief Justice Earl Warren to the bench, the Court launched into a unique period of promoting rights protections, preventing states from engaging in discriminatory treatment, and requiring due process in criminal cases.

In the 1980s, a political backlash to the liberalism of the preceding two decades became evident in the revival of Southern political fortunes and the emergence of new, powerful conservative voting coalitions. Similarly, in the Court a new emphasis on originalism, empowerment of states, and conservative judicial thinking emerged. The cases decided in the 1980s and 1990s did not undo the Rights Revolution, much less return the federal government to the status and authority it had in the 1920s, but in case after case a narrow Court majority scaled back Congress' most ambitious attempts to enforce the XIVth Amendment and gave signs of losing patience with the infinitely expansive interpretation of federal authority that had dominated the preceding period. New theories of state

[2] *United States v. Carolene Products Co.*, 304 U.S. 144 (1938). [3] 302 U.S. 319.

sovereignty appeared, and once again precedents thought to be long-settled were called into question. Issues of protecting religious minorities were challenged by members of majority religious groups seeking constitutional protections for their right to influence policy and ensure their public recognition, states and localities successfully challenged measures that had been imposed to remedy past racial discrimination, and protections for the always controversial right to abortion were rolled back.

As we move beyond the first decade of the twenty-first century, the state of the American polity is best described as divided. Studies have shown that the current Congress is ideologically more divided, and the right end of the spectrum more extreme, than at any time in modern history. The electorate, too, is increasingly polarized and regionalized. Both the liberalism that emerged in the 1960s and 1970s and the responding conservatism of the 1980s and 1990s remain central fixtures in American political and social thought. Constitutional thinking on the Court reflects the same polarization; members of the Court in recent years have displayed widely varying philosophies, interpretive approaches, and historical understandings when confronting fundamental constitutional questions.

2 *The Court and Constitutional Litigation*

The American Constitution says relatively little about the structure of the judiciary. The bulk of judicial structure, jurisdiction, and rules of litigation come from statutory law, little of which has changed since the early twentieth century. In broad strokes, the United States' judiciary system comprises two parallel systems – the federal and the state. For each, cases may begin at either the district (federal) or trial (state) level or for some issues at a specialized court. From there, cases may be appealed to an intermediary court: federal circuit court or state intermediary appellate court. If the case originated in state court, it may then be appealed to the state supreme court.[4] Only from there or a federal circuit court can a case be appealed to the Supreme Court, although the Supreme Court retains original jurisdiction in a few instances, such as when "Ambassadors, other public Ministers and Consuls, and . . . a State shall be Party".[5] In fact, when

[4] Drawn from Figure A-1, "Getting to the U.S. Supreme Court," in Howard Gillman, Mark A. Graber and Keith E. Whittington, *American Constitutionalism, vol. 1. Structures of Government* (Oxford University Press 2013) 731.

[5] U.S. Constitution, Article III, § 2.

a state is party to the suit, the Supreme Court has exclusive jurisdiction over the case.[6] In all other cases – that is, cases which are appealed – the Supreme Court has discretionary authority to choose which cases to place on its own docket. What follows is a brief summary of how cases and judges get to the Supreme Court.

Jurisdiction

The Supreme Court declared its authority to review and nullify federal laws on constitutional grounds in the early case of *Marbury v. Madison* (1803).[7] Lower courts, too, can annul statutes on constitutional grounds, although such annulments can be appealed to a higher court. In order to be heard by a federal court a case must be justiciable, meaning (1) that the parties are not seeking an advisory opinion, (2) that the issues in the case are neither unripe nor moot, and (3) that the resolution of the case does not require judgment on a political question.

The rule against advisory opinions derives from the constitutional grant of authority to the federal courts to adjudicate "cases" and "controversies".[8] Thus, the courts may not issue opinions that are merely "advisory," meaning that they respond to hypothetical questions or requests for advice in the drafting of legislation. The tradition of avoiding advisory opinion goes back to the first Chief Justice, John Jay, who declined President George Washington's request for advice on a matter of foreign policy.[9] Additionally, the requirement for an actual "case or controversy" provides the backbone of standing. In order to bring a case to court, a plaintiff must show that she has sustained or will sustain direct harm and that this harm is capable of redress.[10] Disagreement with a government policy – including a claim that such a policy is unconstitutional – is not sufficient grounds for standing.[11] There is one arguable exception: a taxpayer may bring a suit to challenge government expenditures that violate the Establishment Clause of the Ist Amendment.[12] In other cases, however, the undifferentiated claim of a taxpayer that his or her taxes are being used in an unconstitutional way is not sufficient to grant standing.[13]

[6] 25 U.S. Code, section 1251. [7] 5 U.S. 137. [8] U.S. Constitution, Article 1II, § 2.

[9] Letter from John Jay to George Washington (8 August 1793).

[10] *Valley Forge Christian College v. Americans United for Separation of Church and State*, 454 U.S. 464, 472 (1982); *Lujan v. Defenders of Wildlife*, 504 U.S. 555, 560–61 (1992).

[11] *County of Riverside v. McLaughlin* 500 U.S. 44 (1991), *Northeastern Florida Chapter of the Associated General Contractors v. City of Jacksonville*, 508 U.S. 656 (1993), *Lujan v. Defenders of Wildlife*, 504 U.S. 555 (1992).

[12] *Flast v. Cohen*, 392 U.S. 83, 99 (1968). [13] *Frothingham v. Mellon*, 262 U.S. 447 (1923).

Nor will the courts hear unripe cases: that is, cases where harm to the plaintiff has not yet been threatened or where not all judicial alternatives have been exhausted. Conversely, a moot issue is one in which matter at issue has been resolved or the potential for harm has been removed, such as in the case of college entrance or abortion.[14] However, the Court may take up an otherwise "moot" case if it involves a situation that is likely to recur, thus presenting an issue "capable of repetition, yet evading review."[15]

It is important to note that in addition to constitutional limitations on standing, the U.S. Supreme Court has also chosen to adopt "prudential" rules limiting access to federal courts. For example, standing may be denied "to avoid deciding questions of broad social import where no individual rights would be vindicated and to limit access to the federal courts to those litigants best suited to assert a particular claim."[16] More generally, the court has identified three criteria for determining whether prudential standing should be found: (1) that the claim of injury to an individual's interests falls within the "zone" of the constitutional or statutory protection being asserted; (2) that the claimant is not attempting to litigate a generalized grievance shared by a large group of individuals as opposed to a specific claim of their own; and (3) that the claimant is not attempting to assert the interest of a third party rather than their own.[17]

Finally, the Court generally refuses to hear or decide political questions, preferring to leave such matters to the political branches – Congress and the presidency. This principle goes back to *Marbury v. Madison* (1803), where Chief Justice Marshall argued that it would be impossible for the Court to assert an authority to review the processes of executive appointments:

> The province of the Court is solely to decide on the rights of individuals, not to inquire how the Executive or Executive officers perform duties in which they have a discretion. Questions in their nature political or which are, by the Constitution and the laws, submitted to the Executive, can never be made in this court.[18]

The fullest modern explication of the political question doctrine appears in *Baker v. Carr* (1962). In a highly contested decision featuring six

[14] *Arizonans for Official English v. Arizona*, 520 U.S. 43 (1997), *Hicklin v. Orbeck*, 437 U.S. 518 (1978).

[15] *Roe v. Wade*, 410 U.S. 113 (1973).

[16] *Gladstone Realtors v. Village of Bellwood*, 441 U.S. 91, 99–100 (1979).

[17] *United States v. Richardson*, 418 U.S. 166 (1974).

[18] *Marbury v. Madison*, 5 U.S. 137, 166, 170 (1803).

separate opinions, the Court determined that the process of drawing electoral districts was subject to judicial review as a justiciable, non-political question. Justice Brennan, writing for the Court, identified six factors to be considered in determining whether a matter presented a political question, the first of which he identified as a case of a "political question": "Textually demonstrable constitutional commitment of the issue to a coordinate political department."[19] Consistent with this principle, the Supreme Court refuses to hear cases on issues it sees as the exclusive domain of one of the other branches.[20]

The majority of cases that are heard by the Supreme Court arrive by route of a writ of *certiorari* (discretionary appeal). Since the Judiciary Act of 1925, the Supreme Court has almost complete discretion to choose which cases to place on its docket. The Court exercises this discretion broadly, hearing less than 1 percent of appealed decisions.[21] Rule 10 of the Court indicates the kinds of situations under which the Court is likely to take up an appeal: when lower courts have issued conflicting decisions on the same important matter of federal law, or when a lower court has issued an opinion on an important question of federal law that the Supreme Court has not yet settled, or when the decision of a lower court conflicts with Supreme Court precedent.[22] In particular, the Court takes up cases where lower courts reached different determinations on the same question, such that action by the Supreme Court is necessary to ensure consistent application of a legal principle across all geographical judicial districts.

There are few specific rules governing the kinds of argument or evidence that can be brought in support of a constitutional claim. In general, constitutional claims are treated as "questions of law" rather than "questions of fact," on the common law principle that trial courts decide issues of fact and appeals are brought only on purely legal questions. Thus in earlier cases we see references to cases brought "on writ of error" to the lower court. Rules of the Supreme Court of the United States Rule 24(1)(i) says that briefs shall contain "[t]he argument, exhibiting clearly the points

[19] *Baker v. Carr*, 369 U.S. 186, 217 (1962).

[20] *See, e.g.*, *Oetjen v. Central Leather Co.*, 246 U.S. 297 (1918, executive authority over foreign relations); *Nixon v. United States*, 506 U.S. 224 (1993, congressional impeachment proceedings).

[21] "Frequently Asked Questions (FAQ)" (The Supreme Court of the United States) <http://www.supremecourt.gov/faq.aspx> accessed on 30 April 2014.

[22] "Rule 10, "'Considerations Governing Review of Certiorari'" in *2013 Rules of the Supreme Court of the United States*.

of fact and of law presented and citing the authorities and statutes relied on," while Rule 28 states that "[o]ral argument should emphasize and clarify the written arguments in the briefs on the merits." Since there are no testifying witnesses or presentation of evidence, ordinary rules governing the admissibility of evidence do not apply, and since the Supreme Court has the unique authority to revisit previously settled questions of constitutional law, there is no obligation on the part of the attorneys arguing a case to conform their arguments to existing precedent.

Caseload and Litigation

The number of cases decided by the Supreme Court has declined considerably over time. In addition to the Judiciary Act of 1925, which granted discretionary docket control to the Supreme Court except in cases of original jurisdiction, the 1988 Supreme Court Case Selection Act reduced the number of mandatory cases on the Court's docket by eliminating appeals as of right from state court decisions to the Supreme Court. Because of the confluence of these two Acts, the Supreme Court has been hearing and deciding steadily fewer cases (a decrease from 250 to 80 cases a year, although the number of cases was similarly low before 1860).[23] Nearly all *certiorari* petitions are denied without comment. The few cases that are taken on by the Court then go through the process of brief filing, oral arguments, conference discussion, and decision publication. The parties to a case file legal briefs with the Court summarizing their arguments; third parties may also file *amicus curiae* briefs, when granted permission by the Court under Rule 5 and when that brief "brings to the attention of the Court relevant matter not already brought to its attention by the parties."[24] Cases are always orally argued, although each side of the case is restricted to no more than a half-hour of oral argument, during which justices frequently ask questions. Like the number of cases, the length of oral argument has contracted dramatically over the years. Time for oral arguments was unrestrained until 1849, when it was restricted to two hours per side. It was reduced again in 1925 to one hour and finally in 1970 to the current half-hour per side.[25] After oral argument, justices

[23] Drawn from Figure A-2, "Number of Supreme Court Cases with Separate Opinions," in Gilman et al. (n 4) 732.

[24] "Rule 37, 'Brief of an *Amicus Curia*'" in *2013 Rules of the Supreme Court of the United States*.

[25] Matt Morrison, "U.S. Supreme Court Oral Arguments," Cornell University Law Library. <http://www.lawschool.cornell.edu/library/whatwedo/researchguides/supreme-court-oral.cfm> accessed on 30 April 2014.

discuss the case in conference and while writing the Opinion of the Court (assigned by the most senior member of the majority, often the Chief Justice). The Opinion of the Court is always published, first as a slip opinion and later in the United States Reports, although in reality, opinions are usually posted to the Court's website the morning the decision is announced.

3 *The Judges*

Like structure, jurisdiction, and many points of litigation, the Constitution leaves it to Congress to set the size of the Supreme Court. The first Congress set the number of justices to 6 in the Judiciary Act of 1789. As the nation grew throughout the nineteenth century, the Court experienced a similar expansion, correlating to the number of judicial circuit courts: first to 7 justices in 1807, 9 in 1837, and 10 in 1863.[26] However, the Judicial Circuits Act of 1866 provided for the gradual reduction of the size of the Supreme Court from 10 to 7, and thereafter the Judiciary Act of 1869 set the number of justices of the Supreme Court at 9, where it has remained since.

The Constitution dictates that the justices serve lifetime terms, on condition of good behavior; a sitting justice may retire or die while in office, but may only be removed from office through a process of impeachment.[27] Upon a vacancy, the President nominates and the Senate confirms an individual to fill the position. Since the Constitution sets no qualifications for the office of Supreme Court justice, the President and Senate can presumably choose anyone they wish. However, the vast majority of all Supreme Court justices have had extensive legal background, and all justices have had legal training of some kind. From 1789 to 1959, 96 percent of appointed justices had a primary career in law, although some were active in both the legal and political realms. Only four justices during that time period did not serve as lawyers; instead, they were occupied as law school educators and administrators.[28] Since 1959, the trend has been to appoint Federal Circuit (appellate) Court judges to the highest

[26] 'The Supreme Court of the United States and the Federal Judiciary' in *History of the Federal Judiciary* (Federal Judiciary Center) <http://www.fjc.gov/history/home.nsf/page/courts_supreme.html> accessed on 30 April 2014.

[27] The Constitution of the United States of America. Article III, section 1.

[28] John R. Schmidhauser, 'The Justices of the Supreme Court: A Collective Portrait' (1959) 3.1 *Midwest Journal of Political Science* 1.

court.[29] Although many justices have been selected from the legal profession, there are quite significant shifts in the particular kind of law they practiced. In the early years of the United States, roughly 1789–1861, most justices (60 to 85 percent of the appointees) had previously served in a political capacity, as politicians at the local, state, or national level. Corporate lawyers were appointed to the Court at their highest numbers around the turn of the century (29 percent). Academic appointments were mostly the result of nominations by Franklin Roosevelt in the 1930s and 40s (19 percent). Perhaps most interestingly, appointees who had prior judicial experience surged in number during the latter halves of both the nineteenth (45 percent) and twentieth centuries (100 percent).[30] Thus, one could say that while legal training is a *de facto* prerequisite for service on the Supreme Court of the United States, the particulars of the legal careers have changed dramatically over time.

Scholars of the appointment process have proposed that the President and Senators value two, often competing, qualities in a judicial candidate: qualifications and ideology.[31] Thus, a nominee who is both well qualified and close in ideology to the majority of Senators should be confirmed with relative ease. However, when nominees are relatively less qualified or ideologically distant from the majority of the Senate, confirmation votes may depend on a range of political factors. According to Jonathan Day, the variables that have the greatest impact include "the party of the President in relation to the Senator's party, the popularity of a President, the type of nomination (chief or associate justice), the previous justice's ideology in relation to the nominee's ideology, and specific characteristics of the nominee (qualifications, age, and experience)".[32]

The influence of ideology on the senatorial confirmation has been increasing over the last half-century, at least according to research by

[29] Lee Epstein, Jack Knight and Andrew D. Martin, 'The Norm of Prior Judicial Experience and its Consequences for Career Diversity on the U.S. Supreme Court'(2003 91.4 *California Law Review* 903.

[30] For further detail, please see Table 11, "Categories of Lawyers Appointed to the Supreme Court Classified by Numbers and by Percentages in Six Historical Periods," in Schmidhauser (n 28) 34.

[31] Charles M. Cameron, Albert D. Cover and Jeffery A. Segal, "Senate Voting on Supreme Court Nominees: A Neoinstitutional Model" (1990) 84.2 *The American Political Science Review* 525.

[32] Jonathan P. Day, "The Conditional Nature of Ideology's Influence on Supreme Court Confirmation Votes" (Annual Meeting of the Midwest Political Science Association, Chicago, IL, March 2007).

Epstein et al., who argue that this trend began in the 1960s.[33] Interestingly, this trend toward an emphasis on ideology for Supreme Court justices appears to mirror the trend toward nominees with judicial backgrounds in the Circuit Court. This trend has meant that, as a percentage of nominations, fewer Circuit Court judges have been confirmed since the 1980s (60 percent instead of 90 percent).[34] That is, since Senators care more about the ideology of Supreme Court justices, and since Supreme Court nominees are increasingly chosen from among the ranks of Circuit Court judges, Senators are increasingly particular about the ideology of Circuit Court nominees. In addition, the trend toward nominating and confirming Circuit Court judges to the Supreme Court ensures a judicial background with a wealth of examples from which to divine judicial ideology, from which Senators believe they can predict how a justice will decide cases.

4 *Legal Scholarship and Constitutional Reasoning*

In early cases, referring to scholarly work was a fairly common practice; particularly, references to Blackstone to establish English precedent were widespread. For example, Justice Bradley cites Blackstone in *Slaughterhouse Cases* (1873) to establish the proposition that the right to property is reckoned as fundamental.[35] Interestingly, commentators have noted that in recent decades the Supreme Court has paid less and less attention to academic writing and the justices produce significantly less legal scholarship than at least some of their predecessors. There may be several reasons for this development: the political partisanship that has entered into the confirmation process means that an extensive academic paper trail provides ammunition for the opposing party; the legal academy is less and less concerned with traditional legal doctrine as opposed to deconstructions of judicial decision-making or highly theoretical arguments; and, justices are increasingly drawn exclusively from the federal bench rather than from politics or academia (the current Roberts Court is the first one in which all the members were previously federal judges). Some of the justices, in particular, are highly resistant to the idea that their

33 Lee Epstein, Rene Lindstadt, Jeffery A. Segal and Chad Westerland "The Changing Dynamics of Senate Voting on Supreme Court Nominees" (2006) 68.2 *The Journal of Politics* 296.

34 Drawn from Figure 11–2, "Percentage of Federal Circuit Court Nominations Not Confirmed, 1945–2008" in Gillman et al. (n 4) 634.

35 82 U.S. 36.

decision-making should be influenced by developments in legal philosophy or global trends in legal development, a position that reinforces the tendency to reason hermetically within the canon of constitutional jurisprudence.

B Arguments in Constitutional Reasoning

"Great cases... make bad law," wrote Oliver Wendell Holmes, Jr. "For great cases are called great, not by reason of their importance... but because of some accident of immediate overwhelming interest which appeals to the feelings and distorts the judgment."[36]

Holmes' admonition reminds us that the 40 leading cases (see Appendix) are not a representative sample of constitutional reasoning. They may, however, be taken to be a roughly representative sample of the reasoning that goes on in the kinds of cases that Holmes feared would make "bad law": those that press hardest against the limitations of existing understandings of constitutional law. Whether these are occasions to be regretted or celebrated, Holmes' observation contains the interesting assumption that constitutional judgments ought to conform to the norms of ordinary legal reasoning in the first place.

In comparison with those that we find in other systems, particularly those that feature Kelsenian "constitutional courts," arguments in U.S. constitutional law are noteworthy for their emphasis on legalistic forms of reasoning. Likely this is because in the United States the Supreme Court hears non-constitutional private and public law cases as well as constitutional cases due to the Constitution's dual grant of jurisdiction ("diversity" cases as well as cases "arising under" the Constitution and federal law).[37] Moreover, at the time of the Court's founding, the idea of constitutional law as a source of judicially enforceable higher law was novel and in sharp contrast to the British tradition of Parliamentary supremacy. As a result, the Court would sensibly gravitate toward a style of reasoning borrowed from traditional forms of legal reasoning. In fact, however, the very earliest cases (*Chisholm v. Georgia* (1793), *Calder v. Bull* (1798)) reflect broadly philosophical arguments and appeals to political principles.[38] It was only after *Marbury v. Madison* in 1803 that the Court, under the leadership of John Marshall, sharply distinguished political from legal questions,

[36] *Northern Securities Co. v. United States*, 193 U.S. 197 (1904) (Holmes, J., dissenting).
[37] U.S. Constitution, Article III, § 2.
[38] *Chisholm v. Georgia*, 2 U.S. 419 (1793); *Calder v. Bull*, 3 U.S. 386 (1798).

insisting that its authority to interpret the Constitution extended only to legal questions. It is generally understood by historians that Marshall was motivated by prudential political concerns about preserving the authority of the Court.[39] That concern with preserving the legitimacy of the Court has been both explicitly invoked and implicitly worked to push constitutional lawyers and judges toward traditional modes of legal argumentation as well as promoting prudential doctrines of abstention, limited standing, and constitutional applicability.

The equation of constitutional reasoning with legal reasoning helps explain why no case among the 40 leading cases set deals with the problem of establishing the text of the Constitution. The U.S. Constitution is a single written document. Whatever temptation there might have been at various points to grant constitutional status to additional documents such as the Declaration of Independence has been countered by legal principles such as the "four corners" rule for the interpretation of contracts. In general, the pervasiveness of legal reasoning in constitutional argument is an outstanding feature of American constitutionalism.

Nonetheless, among the 40 leading cases, we continue to see appeals to extra-legal principles drawn from non-legal sources: foreign law, founding documents, scholarship and research, and political philosophy. The last arises particularly where the meaning of the term "liberty" in the XIVth Amendment is concerned. There is also a notable line of modern cases, not included in the 40 leading cases list, that appeal to background principles to find sovereign immunity for states under the XIth Amendment in contexts outside the scope of the words of the text. For example, while the XIth Amendment speaks of states being immune from suit in federal court, the Court has found immunity to extend to state courts as well, and, where the XIth Amendment speaks only of suits brought in federal court against a state by a citizen of another state, the Court has found that immunity also extends to suits brought in state courts and suits by a citizen of the same state.[40]

Another notable feature of US Supreme Court constitutional argumentation is the proliferation of opinions: the 40 cases reviewed feature 151 separate opinions. It is frequently the case that a minority opinion, whether dissenting or concurring, will be written in a style different from that of the majority opinion. It is plausible, indeed, that when justices know their opinions do not have direct precedential value, they feel liberated to diverge from strictly legal reasoning. Furthermore, the practice

[39] 5 U.S. 137. [40] *Alden v. Maine*, 527 U.S. 706 (1999).

of dissenting and concurring opinions featuring the names of individual justices encourages the practice of writing opinions in order to build up a reputation for a particular judicial philosophy over time, to appeal to a public constituency, or to secure a place in posterity, all of which further encourage justices to step out from under the limitations of traditional legalistic argument.

5 *The Structure of Constitutional Arguments*

Almost all of the opinions analyzed are easily identifiable as employing one-line conclusive reasoning (application of a single line of reasoning moving from one principle to the next to arrive at an ultimate conclusion, or "chain structure"), consistent with the idea that traditional norms of legal argumentation should inform constitutional reasoning. There are only two opinions that exhibits "dialogic" reasoning (drawing on multiple observations no one of which is taken to be conclusive but which in combination are found to favor an outcome): Justice Brennan's opinion declaring the death penalty unconstitutional in *Furman v. Georgia* (1972)[41] and Justice Douglas' famous (or infamous) discussion of the "penumbras and emanations" of various constitutional provisions that provides the basis for his discovery of a generalizable right to privacy in *Griswold v. Connecticut* (1965).[42] Of these two, only Douglas' was an opinion for the majority, and the case featured three separate concurring opinions written in the one-line conclusive style. There are only six opinions in which one or more of the opinions demonstrates "legs of a chair" style reasoning (multiple adequate constitutional ground supporting a single outcome), and none of these opinions is the majority opinion of the case. The most recent use of parallel conclusive reasoning is in *United States v. Carolene Products* (1938), in which, upholding Congress' authority to regulate dairy products shipped interstate, Justice Stone wrote: "[W]e might rest our decision wholly on the presumption of constitutionality. But affirmative evidence also sustains the statute. In twenty years evidence has steadily accumulated of the danger to the public health from the general consumption of foods" of the kind regulated under the law at issue.[43] This is also the first case clearly to assess proportionality (see below), a determination that is intrinsically more fact-driven than those

[41] 408 U.S. 238. [42] 381 U.S. 479.
[43] *United States v. Carolene Products* 304 U.S. 144, 148 (1938).

involved in other types of constitutional decision-making, and thus more likely to utilize parallel conclusive reasoning.

There are some arguments that are difficult to classify. In particular, the persistent tendency to appeal to various forms of originalism or past practice creates forms of argument that do not readily fit into one category or another. In American constitutional jurisprudence, originalism is an entire category of analysis and discussion all by itself. Originalism can take at least three distinct variants in the 40 leading cases list: "original intent" (an appeal to the subjective intentions of specific authors), "original understanding" (an appeal to the publicly shared understanding of a concept at the time of ratification), or "legal originalism" (an appeal to the technical legal understanding of a term or concept at the time of ratification).

Original intent is best captured by teleological/purposive arguments (see below). In these instances, justices appeal to the purpose behind a particular textual position, sometimes overlapping with arguments about the overall purpose of the Constitution-makers (variously "the Founders," "the drafter," or "the people" at the time of ratification). To illustrate, in in the majority opinion in *Slaughterhouse Cases* (1873), Justice Miller writes of the Privileges and Immunities Clause of the XIVth Amendment[44]:

> The constitutional provision there alluded to did not create those rights, which it called privileges and immunities of citizens of the States. It threw around them in that clause no security for the citizen of the State in which they were claimed or exercised. Nor did it profess to control the power of the State governments over the rights of its own citizens. Its sole purpose was to declare to the several States that, whatever those rights, as you grant or establish them to your own citizens, or as you limit or qualify or impose restrictions on their exercise, the same, neither more nor less, shall be the measure of the rights of citizens of other States within your jurisdiction.

In the dissenting opinion of that same case, Justice Bradley appeals to the understanding of "the people" at the time of the founding, which goes beyond the meaning of the text to a more general sense of the purpose to be achieved: "In my judgment, it was the intention of the people of this country in adopting that amendment to provide National security against violation by the States of the fundamental rights of the citizen."[45] Often this kind of argument is cloaked in originalist appeals to the deep wisdom

[44] "No State shall make or enforce any law which shall abridge the privileges or immunities of citizens of the United States." U.S. Constitution, Amendment XIV, § 1.

[45] *Slaughterhouse Cases*, 82 U.S. 36, 121 (1873, Bradley J., dissenting).

of the constitutional design, contrasted unfavorably with the political mood of the historical moment.[46] In particular, arguments of this kind are frequently presented in the context of a description of the overall structure of the Constitution, as in appeals to principles of separation of powers or the limits of the authority of one or another branch.[47] Unfortunately, the other forms of originalism have less clear cases. "Teleological argument – historical" in fact comes close to a theory in the literature known as "New Originalism" that appeals to a jurisprudence of what might be called original purposes.[48] In almost every case justices offer appeals to originalism as support of a linear series of logically progressive propositions.

6 *Types of Arguments in Constitutional Reasoning*

Case Disposition

Often, the Court announces major principles or rights protections while denying the actual claim being litigated. Examples in the set include *Marbury v. Madison* (1803, establishing judicial review of federal actions while denying a remedy for lack of subject matter jurisdiction),[49] and *Palko v. Connecticut* (1937, establishing a standard for applying rights contained in the Bill of Rights to the states while concluding that the specific right at issue did not qualify for such application).[50] In more recent years, however, this phenomenon disappears from the 40 leading cases. In addition, while in some cases the Court will decide on an outcome, in many others the case is remanded for reconsideration by a lower court in accordance with a newly announced rule. These distinctions – between determination of outcome and remand, and between a successful claim in a case and the successful promotion of a constitutional theory – are not reflected in the coding of the 40 leading cases.

General Topic

The distinction between powers of government and rights and liberties is normal in U.S. constitutional thinking – indeed, it is the standard division between two semesters of a university or law school course on the topic of constitutional law. In practice, however, the two categories overlap.

46 *Ex Parte Milligan* 71 U.S. 2, 120 (1866).
47 *United States v. Lopez*, 514 U.S. 549 (1995).
48 Keith Whittington, *Constitutional Interpretation* (University of Kansas Press 1999); Jack Balkin, *Living Originalism* (Belknap 2011).
49 5 U.S. 137.
50 302 U.S. 319.

For example, in *Barron v. Baltimore* (1823) the Court declared that the rights guarantees of the Bill of Rights did not apply to the states.[51] This could be either a statement about the limits of rights or about the design of the constitutional polity. In *Dred Scott v. Sanford* (1857) one question was whether a free person of African descent whose ancestors had been brought to the United States as slaves was a "citizen" entitled to file suit in a federal court.[52] This question, too, could be interpreted as falling into either category. Questions involving both the powers of government and the rights of individuals during wartime occur in *Ex Parte Milligan* (1866, whether a military authority could try civilians in military courts in an area removed from actual fighting)[53] and *Korematsu v. United States* (1944, whether the military authorities could issue orders of exclusion that ultimately led to the detention without trial of hundreds of thousands of Japanese and Americans of Japanese descent).[54] Both cases are classified as concerning fundamental rights, but in both cases the question at issue could equally be described as concerned with the extent of government power during an emergency or the right of each citizen to due process of law.

Applicability Discussed

The term "applicability" is arguably imprecise, as the issue is often more described as a question of judicial enforceability rather than the applicability of the Constitution itself. This is the case with respect to the "political question doctrine." It is important to recognize, however, that in every case the assertion of a political question is presented as reasons for a court to decline to rule on a question that is addressed by the Constitution and is within the court's constitutional jurisdiction. In other words, the claim is not that the Constitution does not apply but rather that the courts should not be the institution to apply it.

Perhaps the most dramatic example of a judicially discovered reason for courts to refrain from enforcing a provision of the U.S. Constitution concerns the IXth Amendment.[55] The IXth Amendment was added to the original Bill of Rights by James Madison in order to address fears that the process of enumerating rights would result in a narrow conception of what rights were protected by the Constitution. Nonetheless, and despite the fact that the IXth Amendment is the only provision in the Constitution

[51] 32 U.S. 243. [52] 60 U.S. 393. [53] 71 U.S. 2. [54] 323 U.S. 214.

[55] "The enumeration in the Constitution, of certain rights, shall not be construed to deny or disparage others retained by the people." U.S. Constitution, Amendment IX.

that contains explicit instructions about how the text is to be interpreted ("shall not be construed"), the Supreme Court has consistently refused to recognize a constitutionally protected right based on that portion of the text. No case has ever been decided on the basis of the IXth Amendment, although it is mentioned in Justice Douglas' majority opinion and is the basis for Justice Goldberg's concurring opinion in *Griswold v. Connecticut* (1965).[56]

Analogies

Analogic reasoning – as a staple of Anglo-American common law reasoning – frequently occurs in constitutional arguments, particularly those that attempt to resolve constitutional questions in the manner of traditional legal analysis. Analogic reasoning appears in half of the 40 leading cases, most likely because cases that are considered "leading" are those that examine new questions. It is reasonable to assume that a larger list of less controversial cases would feature more examples of this sort of reasoning.

Ordinary Meaning of Words of the Constitution or References to the "Wording of the Constitution" in General

Appeals to ordinary meaning or dictionary definitions of terms are common in opinions that feature "textualist," "strict constructionist," or "original understanding" approaches to constitutional interpretation. These are relatively modern modes of analysis; in early periods, parsing particular words and phrases in the manner of lawyers reviewing a contract was considered inappropriate for constitutional interpretation.[57]

Harmonizing Arguments – Domestic Law

The need to harmonize a constitutional provision at issue with other sections of the Constitution or with a federal statutory scheme is commonplace in American constitutional law – particularly, as justices may interpret one phrase in light of its use in a separate part of the Constitution. For example, in *Martin v. Hunter's Lessee* (1816), Justice Story writes:

[56] 381 U.S. 479.

[57] Justice Black, dissent in *Katz v United States*, 389 U.S. 347 (1967): "In interpreting the Bill of Rights, I willingly go as far as a liberal construction of the language takes me, but I simply cannot in good conscience give a meaning to words which they have never before been thought to have and which they certainly do not have in common ordinary usage."

> The same expression, "shall be vested," occurs in other parts of the Constitution . . . The second article declares that "the executive power shall be vested in a President of the United States of America." Could Congress vest it in any other person, or is it to await their good pleasure whether it is to vest at all? It is apparent that such a construction, in either case, would be utterly inadmissible. Why, then, is it entitled to a better support in reference to the judicial department?[58]

Indeed, the perception of a need to reconcile such tensions often motivates the Supreme Court to grant *certiorari* in a case in the first instance. In analyzing the 40 leading cases, harmonizing arguments directed toward domestic law are found in 22 of 40 cases.

Harmonizing Arguments – International Law

Although there are a number of cases in which references to "foreign" legal materials appear,[59] there are very few cases in the sample of 40 leading cases in which the Court saw fit to reconcile their interpretation of the Constitution with international law. The exceptions involve early appeals to the "law of nations" to resolve questions about the meaning of state sovereignty,[60] and cases in which the treaty obligations of the United States were taken into account in determining the scope of governmental power.[61] One interesting case in this regard is *Furman v. Georgia* (1972).[62] In *Furman*, Justice Douglass relied on "evolving standards of decency" to conclude that the death penalty was in violation of the VIIth Amendment's prohibition on "cruel and unusual punishment".[63] In subsequent cases, that has become accepted as the test for VIIIth Amendment violations, and internationally shared standards are often invoked to determine the meaning of "decency." In *Furman*, however, while foreign legal materials were referenced as background, there was no attempt to argue that U.S. constitutional law should be made consistent with international legal practice (although not with any specific international law). Similarly, in both *Lawrence v. Texas* (2003)[64] and *Roper v. Sims* (2005)[65]

[58] *Martin v. Hunter's Lessee*, 14 U.S. 304, 329–30.

[59] One particular problem is the classification of British cases. For purposes of this study, British cases and statutes are treated as "foreign" if they occurred subsequent to American independence, but not if they occurred during the colonial period.

[60] *Chisholm v.* Georgia 2 U.S. 419 (1793); *Prigg v. Pennsylvania*, 41 U.S. 539 (1842); *Dred Scott v. Sanford*, 60 U.S. 393 (1857).

[61] *Youngstown Sheet and Tube Co. v. Sawyer*, 343 U.S. 579 (1952)

[62] 408 U.S. 238.

[63] "Excessive bail shall not be required, nor excessive fines imposed, nor cruel and unusual punishments inflicted." U.S. Constitution, Amendment VIII.

[64] 539 U.S. 558.

[65] *Roper v. Simmons*, 543 U.S. 551 (2005).

Justice Anthony Kennedy appealed to international legal norms and practices regarding, respectively, homosexuality and the execution of juveniles. In *Roper*, in particular, Kennedy's observation of "the stark reality that the United States is the only country in the world that continues to give official sanction to the juvenile death penalty" drew a stinging rejoinder from Justice Antonin Scalia, who wrote "the basic premise of the Court's argument – that American law should conform to the laws of the rest of the world – ought to be rejected out of hand."[66] In fact, however, it is not at all clear what role the appeal to international practices played in Kennedy's analysis, including whether his comments were mere *obiter dicta* or reflected an independent reason for reaching his conclusion.

Precedents

In common law, the concept of precedent developed as a core principle since the early modern period when the practice of recording written decisions became widespread in England.[67] Respect for precedent is explicitly invoked in the form of the principle of *stare decisis*, most clearly articulated in the case of *Planned Parenthood of Southeastern Pennsylvania v. Casey* (1992), in which the Court declined to overrule *Roe v. Wade* (1972):[68]

> The obligation to follow precedent begins with necessity, and a contrary necessity marks its outer limit... [W]e recognize that no judicial system could do society's work if it eyes each issue afresh in every case that raised it. Indeed, the very concept of the rule of law underlying our own Constitution requires such continuity over time that a respect for precedent is, by definition, indispensable.

As a result,

> when this Court re-examines a prior holding, its judgment is customarily informed by a series of prudential and pragmatic considerations designed to test the consistency of overruling a prior decision with the ideal of the rule of law and to gauge the respective costs of reaffirming and overruling a prior case.[69]

66 Justice O'Connor, although joining Scalia in dissenting from the majority decision, was at pains to note that in the context of the VIIIth Amendment, "Over the course of nearly half a century, the Court has consistently referred to foreign and international law as relevant to its assessment of evolving standards of decency." In *Roper* (n 65) 605.

67 Richard J. Ross, 'The Commoning of the Common Law: The Renaissance Debate over Printing English Law, 1520–1640' (1998) 146 *University of Pennsylvania Law Review* 323.

68 410 U.S. 113.

69 *Casey*, 505 U.S. at 854–55 (citations omitted).

Stare decisis may serve less as a mode of constitutional interpretation than a meta-constitutional principle that guides the courts in their work, along with other prudential checks on the exercise of jurisdiction. Nonetheless, given the tendency of the U.S. Supreme Court justices to present their constitutional arguments in legal terms, they will seek to invoke precedent where it is plausibly available. Therefore it is surprising that in 8 of the 40 leading cases there were no appeals to precedent in any of the opinions. In early cases, there simply were no precedents on which to draw. Moreover, many issues faced by the Court in its early years were literally unprecedented, as they involved determinations about the distribution of roles and authority under the new Constitution. Thus, there are no appeals to (American) precedents in *Chisholm v. Georgia* (1793),[70] *Marbury v. Madison* (1803),[71] *Fletcher v. Peck* (1810),[72] *Gibbons v. Ogden* (1824),[73] or *Barron v. Baltimore* (1833).[74] It is perhaps also unsurprising that there is no attempt to rely on precedent (as opposed to rejecting precedents) in *Brown v. Board of Education* (1954)[75] in light of the prior historical unwillingness of the Court to confront racial discrimination.

Invokes Concept or Principle Not Mentioned in the Text

Of the 40 leading cases, only one did not feature at least one opinion that drew on principles or concepts external to the constitutional text. The one exceptional case was *Barron v. Baltimore* (1833) in which Chief Justice Marshall wrote the only opinion in the case holding that the Vth Amendment does not apply to actions by a state government.[76] In every other case, either a majority, concurring, or dissenting opinion drew on principles and concepts from sources external to the text. For deviations from the constitutional text, see sections on non-legal arguments, references to scholarly work, and references to foreign legal arguments.

Arguments from Silence

In looking for this element of constitutional argumentation we did not count iterations of the proposition that the national government has enumerated powers so that any power not explicitly granted to that government is outside its authority. On the other hand, we find a genuine argument from silence where a justice insists that only enumerated rights are protected by the Constitution, such that the absence of a reference in the text to a particular right is an indication that no such constitutionally

[70] 2 U.S. 419. [71] 5 U.S. 137. [72] 10 U.S. 87. [73] 22 U.S. 1.
[74] 32 U.S. 243. [75] 347 U.S. 483. [76] 32 U.S. 243.

protected right exists. Black's dissenting opinion in *Katz v. United States* (1967) gives a good illustration of this type of argument:

> There can be no doubt that the Framers were aware of this practice, and if they had desired to outlaw or restrict the use of evidence obtained by eavesdropping, I believe that they would have used the appropriate language to do so in the Fourth Amendment. They certainly would not have left such a task to the ingenuity of language-stretching judges.[77]

In addition, a fairly common historical argument from silence claims that a practice has been engaged in without objection over a long period of time, and that this lack of prior objection proves the practice was not considered offensive to the Constitution. Examples include Justice Scalia's dissenting opinion in *United States v. Virginia* (no historical objection to maintenance of a public male-only institution of higher learning) and Justice Rehnquist's dissenting opinion in *Roe v. Wade* (1973):

> By the time of the adoption of the Fourteenth Amendment in 1868, there were at least thirty-six laws enacted by state or territorial legislatures limiting abortion. While many States have amended or updated their laws, twenty-one of the laws on the books in 1868 remain in effect today . . . The only conclusion possible from this history is that the drafters did not intend to have the Fourteenth Amendment withdraw from the States the power to legislate with respect to this matter.[78]

Similarly, Justice Burger in his dissenting opinion in *Furman v. Georgia* (1972) pointed to the fact that capital punishment had been an established practice for a long time without objection to indicate that it did not constitute an "unusual" punishment.[79] Finally, in *Ex Parte Milligan* (1866), declaring that the Constitution does not permit trial by military tribunal in times of emergency when *habeas corpus* has been suspended, we find,

> The Constitution goes no further. It does not say, after a writ of habeas corpus is denied a citizen, that he shall be tried otherwise than by the course of the common law; if it had intended this result, it was easy, by the use of direct words, to have accomplished it.[80]

Applying these criteria, arguments from silence appear in at least one opinion in 15 of the 40 leading cases.

[77] 389 U.S. 347. [78] 410 U.S. 113. [79] 408 U.S. 238, 379. [80] 71 U.S. 2, 126.

Teleological/Purposive Arguments Referring to the Purpose of a Textual Provision

See discussion of originalism as a structure of constitutional argument (Section B5, above).

Teleological/Purposive Arguments Referring to the Purpose of the Constitution-Maker

See discussion of originalism as a structure of constitutional argument (Section B5, above).

Non-legal Arguments

Arguments that reach beyond legal principles to political philosophy, economics, or security are remarkably common in light of the insistence by many justices that the Constitution is a purely legal instrument. Economic realities are emphasized in *West Coast Hotel v. Parrish* (1937)[81] to explain the Court's shift toward permitting governmental intervention in economic relations, while political philosophical principles appear frequently in discussions of state sovereignty as in *Chisholm v. Georgia* (1793),[82] *Martin v. Hunter's Lessee* (1816),[83] *Dred Scott v. Sandford* (1857),[84] and *Prigg v. Pennsylvania* (1842),[85] or as the basis for finding unenumerated rights as in *Calder v. Bull* (1798)[86] and *Lawrence v. Texas* (2003).[87] Altogether, arguments of this kind were found in 28 of the 40 leading cases. Appearance of these types of arguments in support of state sovereignty concentrate in earlier cases, an artifact of the data set. In numerous modern cases, justices, attempting to explain why states retain special prerogatives despite textual commitments of authority to the federal government, have appealed to extra-legal principles based on states' history as sovereign entities (see section on "Sovereignty" below).

References to Scholarly Work

For a full discussion, see section A4 above. Arguments containing these references appear in 15 of the 40 leading cases. This number does not include places where justices referred to scholarly works in order to establish empirical rather than legal propositions, such as the famous discussion of sociologist Kenneth Clarke's "doll study' in *Brown v. Board of Education* (1954) which established the harmful effects of segregated schools.[88]

[81] 300 U.S. 379. [82] 2 U.S. 419. [83] 14 U.S. 304. [84] 60 U.S. 393.
[85] 41 U.S. 539. [86] 3 U.S. 386. [87] 539 U.S. 558. [88] 347 U.S. 483

References to Foreign Legal Material

Almost all references to "foreign" legal material involved the citation of post-independence English legal material. These were treated as "foreign" because subsequent to independence no decision of an English court could have any precedential value for an American court. This was a difficult category to analyze because of the status of the United States as an ex-colonial state. In a few other cases there were discussions of obligations under international law (see above). There is no case in which an American justice argued that foreign law or precedent was binding on the U.S. government or courts and no case in which foreign law was used as the only support for an argument.[89]

Other Methods/Arguments

In general, the categories provided in this typology are fairly exhaustive. However, these are not criteria specifically developed for U.S. constitutional reasoning, nor that of any other particular country. As a result, it is inevitable that there will be patterns of constitutional argumentation that do not readily fit into any of the categories. One example is originalism, noted above in Section B5 and in this Section in regard to teleological/purposive argumentation.

A closely related form of argument is one that relies on long practice, or "settled usage." In the words of Justice Brennan, "the existence from the beginning of the Nation's life of a practice, [while] not conclusive of its constitutionality . . . is a fact of considerable import" (*Walz v. Tax Comm'n of New York City* (1970)).[90] Many of the 40 leading cases are marked by the willingness of the Supreme Court to overturn longstanding practices, whether these involve public prayers, school segregation, or laws regulating sexual conduct. In many cases, however, dissenting justices pointed to the fact of a long history to argue that the practice at issue was constitutional or that the Court was overreaching its mandate.

7 *The Weight of Arguments*

To a remarkable degree, the justices seem to treat all forms of argument equally. Although in particular historical periods there may have been a

[89] Ryan C. Black, Ryan J. Owens and Jennifer L. Brookhart, 'We Are the World: The Supreme Court's Use of Foreign Sources of Law' (2015) *British Journal of Political Science* 1

[90] 397 U.S. 664, 681.

preference for one or another approach, in the modern era individual justices employ every conceivable mode of argumentation. Prudential considerations carry the same mandatory weight as constitutional structures, meta-principles – such as stare decisis – and theories of judicial restraint. Indeed, these alternatives can outweigh contrary arguments based on extrapolations from the text or precedent. Justices frequently pronounce allegiance to approaches that should privilege one set of sources over another, but in practice all justices to one degree or another deviate from their stated principles. Thus is it that no members of the Court, past or present, seem particularly troubled by the fact that the Ist Amendment's protection of "speech" extends to expressive conduct, that there is no textual authority for the creation of an Air Force, or that the phrases "separation of powers" and "state sovereignty" do not appear in the words of the text but are rather derived by implication from the historical debates and overall structure of the document. All of which suggests that the relative weight that is given to different forms of argument is a matter of convention and individual approach rather than anything that can be ascribed to the system of constitutional argumentation.

8 *Judicial Candour and Judicial Rhetoric*

As noted, the rhetoric of judicial opinions is resolutely legalistic, with occasional departures into political philosophy or historical exegesis. Technical legal arguments are less common in the 40 leading cases than in the overall body of U.S. Supreme Court decisions. The cases in the set are precisely those in which, for one reason or another, the justices see fit to depart from ordinary legalistic rhetoric, and consequently they are the most likely to feature broadly framed, non-technical arguments. By contrast, the run-of-the-mill Supreme Court case is likely to comprise a lengthy recitation of highly technical legal arguments and counter-arguments. The tradition of multiple, signed opinions and the deep divisions in the American polity ensure that there will be no shortage of the latter.

The question of judicial candour has vexed political scientists and legal scholars for generations. When asked, judges invariably insist that their decisions are drawn entirely from legal principles.[91] Scholars who study the Court are not always convinced, and suggest three models for

[91] David O'Brien, *Judges on Judging: Views from the Bench* (CQ Press 2012).

understanding the candour of judicial decision-making: legal, attitudinal, and strategic. (These models are discussed at length in Section D: Evaluation, Pathology, and Criticism.)

Even if one rejects the descriptions of wholesale dissembling found in the attitudinal and strategic models, there are particular cases in which the justices' sincerity is difficult to credit, as when a novel theory of standing is presented to justify declining to hear a highly controversial case in which the expected outcome is a 4–4 tie (due to a recusal).[92] And inevitably, the more controversial the case, the more likely it is that those who are dissatisfied with the outcome will accuse the majority of a hidden agenda.

These speculations on the "real" agenda of Supreme Court justices feeds speculation about who is the "real" audience. Given the nature of U.S. constitutional decision-making, and particularly the way the "case or controversy" requirement precludes the clear presentation of complete theories, opinions are frequently read as signaling devices intended to prompt the federal appeals court to bring up new issues or avoid a line of argument in future cases. Separately, to the extent that one conceives of Supreme Court decision-making as a more or less hidden exercise in political partisanship, one would expect that the public and other branches of government are the intended audience – as is clearly the case to a greater degree in the 40 leading cases than in ordinary litigation.

Finally, the degree of rhetoric that is employed in these opinions is entirely idiosyncratic. Some justices employ flowing and flowery rhetoric, while others prefer to employ plain, often deceptively simple formulations. There is a tradition of collegiality in the tone of opinion writing, which is encouraged by the conference procedures and the need to attract others to form a majority;[93] in recent years, however, that tradition seems to be in decline.[94]

[92] *Elk Grove Unified School Dist. v. Newdow* 542 U.S. 1 (2004, atheist parent challenging recitation in school of Pledge of Allegiance due to inclusion of the words "under god").

[93] Forrest Maltzman, James F. Spriggs II and Paul J. Wahlbeck, *Crafting Law on the Supreme Court: The Collegial Game* (Cambridge University Press 2000)

[94] Justice Scalia, in modern times, has established something of a reputation for a sarcastic and insulting tone that is more ordinarily associated with the editorial pages of local newspapers than with legal scholarship, as in his description of an opposing argument as "terminal silliness" (*Romer v. Evans*, 517 U.S. 620, 638 (1996)), "beyond absurd," (*Lee v. Wiesman*, 505 U.S. 577, 637 (1992)) or "entirely irrational" (*Austin v. Michigan Chamber of Commerce*, 494 U.S. 652, 684 (1990)). Justice Kennedy has demonstrated a penchant for occasional forays into philosophical and even poetic language, as evidenced in his majority opinion in *Lawrence v. Texas*, 539 U.S. 558 (2003).

9 *Length, Dissenting, and Concurring Opinions*

As was noted in the introductory section, the 40 leading cases tend to be rather long, and feature an average of four opinions for each case. The exceptions are those few cases in which the Court spoke with one voice: in *Cooper v. Aaron* (1958) the Court produced a single *per curiam* opinion in which all the justices joined in a deliberate demonstration of the unity of their position that state courts were bound to follow federal judicial decrees mandating desegregation of schools.[95] In *Brown v. Board of Education* (1954), there was a single opinion, written by Chief Justice Warren, in which all the justices joined.[96] These cases are extraordinary for the unity of judicial opinion, however, a fact that reflects the centrality of the twentieth-century judicial project of eradicating formal racial discrimination. Aside from these two, the only cases in the 40 leading cases set that do not feature concurring or dissenting opinions are *Marbury v. Madison* (1803, establishing judicial review of federal actions),[97] *McCulloch v. Maryland* (1819, establishing the supremacy of federal authority over that of states), and *Barron v. Baltimore* (1833, Bill of Rights held not applicable to the states).[98] The prevalence of multiple opinions is a marked characteristic of U.S. constitutional decision-writing.

Looking at the judgments in the 40 leading cases set, there is no obvious correlation between length and subject matter, except that cases involving the extent of congressional power tend to feature long opinions because the analysis is so dependent on specific empirical findings. More systematic research on the structure of Supreme Court opinions has found some correlations. For instance, while the median length of opinions has increased since 1970, the interquartile range of total majority opinion length began to increase as early as the 1950s.[99] The data also suggest that smaller majorities (say of 5 or 6 justices, instead of 8 or 9) write longer opinions, probably in an effort to appeal to diverse opinions and to address dissenting arguments. The same logic holds true for cases in which there is a great deal of bargaining among justices, as measured by number of conference memoranda. As one would expect, more salient and more complex cases also have longer opinions, as do opinions that overturn precedent. Conversely, however, if a justice is working on multiple opinion drafts at a given time, the resulting opinions tend to be shorter.

[95] 358 U.S. 1. [96] 347 U.S. 483. [97] 5 U.S. 137. [98] 32 U.S. 243.

[99] Ryan C. Black and James F. Spriggs, II, "An Empirical Analysis of the Length of U.S. Supreme Court Opinions" (2008) 45 *Huston Law Review* 621.

Significantly, the research does not find that opinion length varies consistently with the individual writing the opinion, by case topic, or by political context.

Correlating strongly with the increased length of majority opinions, the number of dissenting and concurring opinions has also risen in recent years.[100] Researchers have found that the occurrence of dissenting opinions does not depend on case type, but rather on the policy preferences of individual justices. That is, when the ideology of the justices is divided in such a way that there are at least two distinct groups, one is likely to dissent to the other's opinions. With the rise in ideologically divisions among the members of the Court, the number of dissents and concurrences has also increased.

10 Framing of Constitutional Issues

The issues that form the frame for constitutional arguments in the U.S. Supreme Court can be categorized into seven groups: limits of federal powers, authorities of each branch, federalism and state prerogatives, the role of the courts, equality rights, procedural rights, and substantive rights. Each of these may be divided into various subdivisions. In particular, questions of federal authority break down into questions about the role of courts, congressional power to regulate commerce, and executive authority over regulatory, security, and foreign affairs. In addition, the categories often overlap or come into conflict, as in arguments that even where a power has been granted to Congress or the federal courts, it may not be exercised in a way that infringes on states' sovereign prerogatives, or the assertion of a right to use the federal courts to challenge state religious establishments. In many cases, the framing of the issue is potentially dispositive of the outcome, and justices sometimes disagree about how the case before them should be framed.

Historically, different frames of constitutional issues have dominated different time periods. For example, from the late nineteenth century through the 1930s, justices eschewed reliance on textual analysis in favor of a broad understanding of background principles and relied on the concept of "liberty" and limitations of governmental authority rather than on what Ronald Dworkin calls the "rights as trumps" model. From the 1930s through the end of the 1970s, in a response to historical conditions,

[100] Drawn from Figure A-2, "Number of Supreme Court Cases with Separate Opinions" in Gillman et al. (n 4) 732.

there was a move toward a focus on the text and, for the Warren and Burger Courts, toward a recognition of "rights" as overriding exceptions to grants of governmental authority. In the 1980s, the Court emphasized originalism, in contrast to the framing of preceding decades. This promotion (or revival) of originalism – including specific litmus tests to be applied to judicial candidates in the appointments process – was an explicit element of an ideological movement to reshape the role of the judiciary in response to the liberal interventions of the Warren Court. These frames may or may not lead to different conclusions. As noted in the discussion of judicial sincerity, justices may select frames that support predetermined outcomes; alternatively, accepted frames of constitutional analysis may unequally burden or privilege certain kinds of claims.

11 Key Concepts

Rule of Law

Appeals to the "rule of law" primarily occur where justices are accusing their fellows of misusing the authority of the Court to overstep:

> As a member of this Court, I am not justified in writing my private notions of policy into the Constitution, no matter how deeply I may cherish them or how mischievous I may deem their disregard. The duty of a judge who must decide which of two claims before the Court shall prevail . . . is not that of the ordinary person. It can never be emphasized too much that one's own opinion about the wisdom or evil of a law should be excluded altogether when one is doing one's duty on the bench.[101]

The issue also appears in rare cases under a question of whether an emergency situation justifies suspension of normal due process.[102]

Democracy

There are no judgments in the 40 leading cases set in which justices explicitly invoke the principle of democracy in the way that term is used in a European context. There are four cases, however, in which popular sovereignty, the rule of the people, or the needs of a democratic system (for a free press) are invoked. There are also a great number of cases in which justices argue that a limited role for the judiciary is explained, in part, by the idea that too great an interference with the discretion of the

[101] *West Virginia Bd. of Educ. v. Barnette*, 319 U.S. 624, 647 (1943).

[102] See, e.g., *Ex Parte Milligan*, 71 U.S. 2 (1866) and *Korematsu v. United States*, 323 U.S. 214 (1944).

legislature would represent a usurpation of democratic decision-making. These cases, however, were not marked as falling into this category in the analysis of the 40 leading cases, as the argument is one analytical step removed from a direct appeal to "democracy."

Sovereignty

References to the concept of sovereignty appear in six cases, all pre–Civil War. During that antebellum period, states periodically attempted to assert the proposition that they were independent and equal to the federal government. After the Civil War, this concept disappears from the judgments in the 40 leading cases set, although it does appear in other cases of constitutional discourse.

State Form (Republic, Monarchy)

Although there are some cases – particularly early cases – in which the Court discusses "republican principles" or similar concepts, these arguments invoke shared philosophical commitments rather than the form of the national state.

Government Form (Parliamentary, Presidential)

This concept does not appear in any of the 40 leading cases. References to a related idea do appear in arguments about separation of powers where justices propose that the specific arrangement of the branches of government dictates an overall structure that precludes certain forms of interbranch cooperation.[103] Arguments over the form of the U.S. government also figure into discussion of "political questions" and the role of the courts, especially arguments about which matters are available for judicial consideration:

> Deciding whether a matter has in any measure been committed by the Constitution to another branch of government, or whether the action of that branch exceeds whatever authority has been committed, is itself a delicate exercise in constitutional interpretation and is a responsibility of this Court as ultimate interpreter of the Constitution.[104]

103 See, e.g., *INS v. Chadha*, 462 U.S. 919 (1983, striking down immigration law that permitted legislative veto); *Morrison v. Olsen*, 487 U.S. 654 (1988, striking down Independent Counsel Act permitting Congress to request Justice Department to appoint special prosecutor).

104 *Baker v. Carr*, 369 U.S. 186, 211 (1962).

Secularism (Separation of Church and State)

Separation of church and state is a core principle in Ist Amendment jurisprudence focusing on the Establishment and Free Exercise Clauses.[105] Secularism appears in only 3 of the 40 cases in the set, but there are many more such cases in U.S. constitutional jurisprudence.

Nation (Concept of "Nation" or "Nationality")

This concept does not appear in the 40 judgments set. This may reflect the understanding that the United States had no organic, pre-constitutional identity as a "nation" but was rather a creation of political will and positive law. Although there are frequent references in both legal and non-legal discourse to an "American people," there is no notion of a "nation" in any kind of Romantic sense.

Federalism

The federalist system of the United States appears as a background principle for arguments about enumerated powers or the limited of federal authority in 10 of the 40 leading cases; however, this generalized reference did not satisfy the criterion of federalism for the purposes of this project – that is, federalism as the relationship between federal and state courts or conflict between federal and state laws.

Proportionality (or Means-and-Ends)

The concept of proportionality appears in American constitutional arguments in a more limited form than in other jurisdictions. Rather than a universal standard, "proportionality" appears as a test under a variety of guises when a higher than ordinary level of judicial scrutiny has already been invoked. Thus laws or government actions that infringe on "fundamental rights" (particularly Ist Amendment rights) and those that employ "suspect" classifications may be declared unconstitutional by virtue of their "overbreadth," "overinclusive" character, or means which "sweep unnecessarily broadly".[106] More formally, the idea that the government's actions must be proportional to the harm to be remedied or the interest to be furthered is captured in the comparison of means to ends

105 "Congress shall make no law respecting an establishment of religion or prohibiting the free exercise thereof . . . " U.S. Constitution, Amendment I.

106 *Griswold v. Connecticut* 381 U.S. 479, 485 (1965); *see also Butler v. Michigan*, 352 U.S. 380, 383 (1957) (Justice Frankfurter describing a law prohibiting sale to adults of material deemed harmful to children "to burn the house to roast the pig").

when the Court calls for "strict" or "heightened" scrutiny. A law subject to such heightened constitutional scrutiny "cannot be upheld unless it is supported by sufficiently important state interests and is closely tailored to effectuate only those interests".[107] Where non-fundamental rights or "neutral" classifications are involved, however, the Court usually refrains from imposing any but the most cursory analysis of proportionality. A law or government action will be upheld unless it "passes the bounds of reason and assumes the character of a merely arbitrary fiat."[108]

The issue of proportionality is raised more explicitly when the Court reviews Congress' exercise of its authority under the XIVth Amendment, section 5, to enact "remedial" legislation to counter the effects of discrimination by the States. In that situation, the Court applies an explicit evaluation of the proportionality of the law in response to the rights violation that it claims to correct. In Justice Kennedy's words, in situations of this kind, "There must be a congruence and proportionality between the injury to be prevented or remedied and the means adopted to that end. Lacking such a connection, legislation may become substantive in operation and effect."[109] Overall, analysis of this kind was found in 9 of 40 cases in the set, all in the modern era.

Wesensgehalt, or Core of Constitutional Rights or Competences

The term *Wesensgehalt* is understood in the sense in which it appears in the German case *Regarding the Luftsicherheitsgesetz.*[110] In that case, the German high court ruled that a law authorizing the shooting down of hijacked aircraft violated the fundamental principle expressed in the guarantee of "human dignity" that no individual may be treated as an instrument of state ends. In this same sense, there are a few cases in which justices have been moved to argue that the question before them involves a core principle of U.S. constitutionalism. Perhaps unsurprisingly, of the 8 cases in the 40 cases set in which appears arguments of this kind, 3 are the first chronologically: *Chisholm v. Georgia* (1793) (Justice Wilson, "do the people of the United States form a Nation?" appealing to fundamental principles of popular sovereignty),[111] *Calder v. Bull* (1798) (Justice Chase

[107] *Zablocki v Redhail*, 434 U.S. 374, 388 (1978).

[108] *Euclid v Ambler Realty*, 272 US 365, 388 (1926).

[109] *City of Boerne v. Flores* 521 U.S. 507, 519 (1997).

[110] German Constitutional Court, Judgment of 15 February 2006, 1 BvR 357/05, BVerfGE 115, 118.

[111] 2 U.S. 419.

appealing to the "great first principles of the social compact"),[112] and *Marbury v. Madison* (1803) (Justice Marshall declaring that "The very essence of civil certainly consists in the right of every individual to claim the protection of the laws whenever he receives an injury").[113]

Human Dignity

Although human dignity may be implicit in many formulations of rights under the U.S. Constitution, there are only 3 cases in the 40 cases set in which one or more justices explicitly appealed to this basic value: *Heart of Atlanta Motel* (1964, upholding Congress' authority to order the desegregation of private businesses engaged in interstate commerce)[114]; *Furman v. Georgia* (1972, death penalty ruled unconstitutional),[115] and *Lawrence v. Texas* (2003, criminalization of intimate homosexual conduct violates privacy rights).[116]

Equality

Equality is a central concern of the Equal Protection Clause of the XIVth Amendment, under which cases usually concern legislation that treats people differently based on race or gender. The concept appears in other constitutional arguments, however, notably in early forms of substantive due process analysis that struck down preferential (or "class") legislation and in arguments about the equality of states or the equal legal status of state residents and visitors. Equality appears as a theme in constitutional arguments in 13 of 40 cases in the set.

Basic Procedural Rights

Basic procedural rights – in U.S. Constitutional terms, "procedural due process" and related matters – stand at the center of U.S. Constitutional law. No fewer than three of the first eight Amendments in the Bill of Rights deal with the matter of procedural rights. However, only 4 cases dealing with this concept appear in the 40 leading cases set: *Miranda v. Arizona* (1966, establishing the right to have an attorney present during question and to be informed of relevant rights prior to questioning)[117]; *Palko v. Connecticut* (1938, considering whether the right to a grand jury in the Vth Amendment applies to state proceedings)[118]; *Prigg v. Pennsylvania* (1842, whether a slaveowner has a right to an order from a court in a

[112] 3 U.S. 386, 388. [113] 5 U.S. 137, 163. [114] 379 U.S. 241.
[115] 408 U.S. 238. [116] 539 U.S. 558. [117] 384 U.S. 436. [118] 302 U.S. 319.

free state compelling local authorities to assist in the recapture of an escaped slave)[119]; and *Marbury v. Madison* (1803, whether a person who has been denied an appointment to which his right has "vested" is entitled to a court order ("writ of mandamus") compelling government officials to perform their duties).[120] Thereafter, the main category of procedural rights involves criminal proceedings, but the Court has also established constitutionally required procedures in the context of denial of welfare benefits.[121]

Freedom of Expression

Like procedural rights, freedom of expression is a core principle of the Constitution, found in the Ist Amendment, and consequently appears in numerous cases. It is a matter of the selection process that the concept appears in only 6 of the 40 cases in the set.

Privacy Rights

Privacy rights are a central concern of modern substantive due process jurisprudence, beginning in the 1960s with *Griswold v. Connecticut* (1962)[122] and running through *Lawrence v. Texas* (2003).[123] Versions of a constitutionally enforceable division between private and public matters go back as far as *Pierce v. Society of Sisters* (1925, holding that a state cannot force all children to attend public school)[124] and *Munn v. Illinois* (1877, holding that regulatory authority extends only to property "clothed with a public purpose").[125] But it was in the 1960s, under the Warren Court, that a full-fledged jurisprudence of privacy rights begins to emerge.

Other Fundamental Rights

The largest category of rights recognized as fundamental by the U.S. Supreme Court but not explicitly identified in this study is property and contract rights. One particular example is the right to compensation for public condemnation of land, including regulations that have the effect of depriving land of all commercial value, but several of the cases in the set have to do with the assertion of constitutionally guaranteed property rights of one kind or another.

[119] 41 U.S. 539. [120] 5 U.S. 137.

[121] *Goldberg v. Kelly*, 397 U.S. 254 (1970); *Matthews v. Edlridge* 424 U.S. 319 (1976).

[122] 381 U.S. 479. [123] 539 U.S. 558. [124] 268 U.S. 510. [125] 94 U.S. 113.

C Comparative Perspective

As the oldest written constitution of its kind, the U.S. Constitution was highly influential on constitutional design in other countries in the decades after World War II, although that influence has declined in recent years.[126] Nevertheless the U.S. model retains distinctive features. First, the courts have extremely broad powers of substantive judicial review, powers that have extended to striking down state and federal laws and assuming direct control over the operation of local school districts. Second, and relatedly, the U.S. Supreme Court is not purely a constitutional court; it is the highest court of appeal for all questions raised under federal law and state law cases involving parties from multiple states. As a result, the Supreme Court hears cases in all areas of law. Moreover, the rule against "advisory opinions", combined with a strong tradition of separation of powers, precludes the justices from working cooperatively with the legislature or the executive to craft laws that will withstand constitutional challenge. Instead, the Court occupies a position that is sometimes adversarial and sometimes strategically cooperative with respect to the other branches of the federal government and to the states.

In addition, the depth of disagreement among justices of the U.S. Supreme Court is at times far greater than that observed in most other court systems. Justices disagree vehemently about basic questions: how the Constitution ought to be interpreted, the function of the judiciary in relation to other branches or officials of government, the nature of American federalism and the locus of national sovereignty, and the nature and sources of American law. Part of this is because the U.S. Constitution is a relatively short document in which key provisions are written in what Justice Robert H. Jackson called "majestic generalities,"[127] which permit multiple interpretations. Questions of national identity, fundamental, shared commitments, and the basic purposes and functions of government are deeply contested in American politics, a cultural phenomenon which inevitably finds its way into the range of constitutional understandings displayed in constitutional arguments. These observations, in turn, point to another interesting aspect of American constitutionalism. As the results of this study demonstrate, American constitutional argumentation is noteworthy for its variety. Debates over modes of constitutional

[126] David S. Law and Mila Versteeg, "The Declining Influence of the United States Constitution" (2012) 87.3 *New York University Law Review* 762.

[127] *West Virginia St. Bd. of Educ. v. Barnette*, 319 U.S. 624, 639 (1943).

reasoning or major issues in constitutional law that appear to be settled at one point in history are reopened for renewed discussion at a later date, and individual justices actively seek to stake out intellectual territory by distinguishing themselves from their colleagues. As a result, lawyers have reason to attempt even apparently "off the wall"[128] arguments or approaches to constitutional reasoning, as there is always the possibility that one or more justices will seize the opportunity to blaze a new trail or revisit one that has been previously closed off.[129]

D Evaluation, Pathology, and Criticism

The pathologies of American constitutional jurisprudence often fall into pairs: for each moment of failure caused by excess in one direction, there are moments caused by the reverse excess. These pairs of pathological tendencies arise from tensions inherent in the role of the Court.

The Constitution is both an instrument that empowers popular self-rule and a higher law statement of inviolable rights; the first pair of jurisprudential pathologies arises from the fact that the Court enforces both principles. Once appointed, justices remain in office for "life or good behavior."[130] This distance is supposed to insulate the Court from political pressure so that it can stand as a check on majoritarian tyranny. That is, the process of appointing justices is removed from popular self-rule while the justices often act as enforcers of minority rights. In asserting that role, however, the Court runs into what Alexander Bickel described as "countermajoritarian difficulty," the challenge of justifying limitations on majority rule in a democratic system.[131] The need for the Court to take on this countermajoritarian role can lead to pathologies in judicial

[128] *See* Jack M. Balkin, "From Off the Wall to On the Wall: How the Mandate Challenge Went Mainstream" (*The Atlantic*, 4 June 2012). <http://www.theatlantic.com/national/archive/2012/06/from-off-the-wall-to-on-the-wall-how-the-mandate-challenge-went-mainstream/258040/> accessed on 27 April, 2014.

[129] *See, e.g.*, *McDonald v. Chicago*, 13 S.Ct. 3020, 3084 (2010) (Thomas J. accepting the invitation of lawyers to reconsider the precedent of the *Slaughterhouse Cases* 83 U.S. 76 (1873)).

[130] Constitution, Article III, § 1. Congress can impeach a justice for poor behavior, ill-defined. However, only one Supreme Court justice, Samuel Chase in 1804, was ever impeached, in his case on partisan grounds. Chase was acquitted, and no other Supreme Court justice has ever been faced with impeachment charges, although a number of lower court judges have.

[131] Alexander J. Bickel, *The Least Dangerous Branch: The Supreme Court at the Bar of Politics* (Yale University Press 1962).

decision-making in either of two opposing ways. Justices who are unduly concerned with their public standing or that of their institution may allow themselves to be swayed by the will of the majority and fail to uphold the rights of minorities and individuals. Conversely, Justices may go too far in reading their own values into the constitutional text in an exercise of "judicial activism," thus impermissibly invading the province of the democratically elected legislature. Justices are frequently criticized for both tendencies.

A second pair of pathologies arises from the tension between deciding particular cases and announcing constitutional rules. On the one hand, justices are sometimes accused of excessive formalism, memorably mocked by Anatole France's declaration that "the law in its majestic equality forbids the rich as well as the poor to sleep under bridges . . . "[132] Conversely, on other occasions justices may be accused of bending or ignoring legal rules in order to achieve a satisfactory outcome in the particular case before them, a possibility that inheres in the practice of considering constitutional questions in the context of the adjudication of particular "cases or controversies." Again, both of these potential failings have been asserted in criticisms of judicial decisions and opinion-writing.

In addition to these potential pathologies in constitutional decision-making, a lively debate surrounds the question of how to explain judicial outcomes. There are three basic explanatory models for judicial decision-making, each of which implies a certain level of judicial candor. The "legal model" takes the justices at their word; constraining legal principles can explain judicial opinions.[133] When asked, justices and lower court judges usually insist that their best understanding of the law is the only basis for their decision-making.[134] However, most scholars are reluctant to accept this explanation as entirely satisfactory, either because legal doctrine is underterminative or because judicial decision-making is employed as a cover for political or policy preferences.[135] Yet another theory proposes

[132] Quoted at *Hill v. Colorado*, 530 U.S. 703, 744 (2000) (Justice Scalia).

[133] On the legal model, see, e.g., Jeffrey A. Segal, "Predicting Supreme Court Cases Probabilistically: The Search and Seizure Cases, 1962–1981" (1984) 78 *American Political Science Review* 891; Lee Epstein and Joseph F. Koblyka, *The Supreme Court and Legal Change* (University of North Carolina Press 1992).

[134] David O'Brien, *Judges on Judging* (2nd ed, CQ Press 2003).

[135] An early version of this argument appeared in the form of Legal Realism. William Fisher III, Morton J. Horwitz and Thomas A. Reed (eds), *American Legal Realism* (Oxford University Press 1993). The current version of this thesis in political science is "judicial behaviorism," described in Jeffrey Siegel and Harold Spaeth, *The Supreme Court and the Attitudinal Model Revisited* (Cambridge University Press 2002). A different, neo-Marxian

that in some cases Supreme Court decision-making is best explained as an exercise in strategic institutional positioning, both internally among the justices and with respect to the other branches of government.[136] Regardless of the correlations between judicial votes, nominating-president's ideology, and other patterns suggestive of non-legal decision-making, scholars cannot know for certain why justices decide the way they do, especially when decisions come cloaked in the language of constitutional reasoning.

Appendix: 40 Leading Cases

1. *Chisholm v. Georgia, 2 U.S. 419 (1793)*
2. *Calder v. Bull, 3 U.S. 386 (1798)*
3. *Marbury v. Madison, 5 U.S. 137 (1803)*
4. *Fletcher v. Peck, 10 U.S. 87 (1810)*
5. *Martin v. Hunter's Lessee, 14 U.S. 304 (1816)*
6. *McCulloch v. Maryland, 17 U.S. 316 (1819)*
7. *Gibbons v. Ogden, 22 U.S. 1 (1824)*
8. *Barron v. Baltimore, 32 U.S. 243 (1833)*
9. *Prigg v. Pennsylvania, 41 U.S. 539 (1842)*
10. *Dred Scott v. Sandford, 60 U.S. 393 (1857)*
11. *Ex Parte Milligan, 71 U.S. 2 (1866)*
12. *Slaughterhouse Cases, 83 U.S. 36 (1873)*
13. *Civil Rights Cases, 109 U.S. 3 (1883)*
14. *Plessy v. Ferguson, 163 U.S. 537 (1896)*
15. *Lochner v. New York, 198 U.S. 45 (1905)*
16. *Gitlow v. New York, 268 U.S. 625 (1925)*
17. *West Coast Hotel v. Parrish, 300 U.S. 379 (1937)*
18. *Palko v. Connecticut, 302 U.S. 319 (1937)*
19. *United States v. Carolene Products, 304 U.S. 144 (1938)*
20. *West Virginia State Board of Education v. Barnette, 319 U.S. 624 (1943)*
21. *Korematsu v. United States, 323 U.S. 214 (1944)*

version of a similar claim is propounded by writers in the Critical Legal Studies school. Roberto Mangabeira Unger, *The Critical Legal Studies Movement* (Harvard University Press 1986).

[136] Barry Friedman, *The Will of the People: How Public Opinion Has Influenced the Supreme Court and Shaped the Meaning of the Constitution* (Farrar, Straus & Giroux 2009); Keith Whittington, *Political Foundations of Judicial Supremacy: The Presidency, the Supreme Court, and Constitutional Leadership in U.S. History* (Princeton University Press 2009); Lee Epstein and Jack Knight, *The Choices Justices Make.* (CQ Press 1997).

22. *Youngstown Sheet & Tube Co. v. Sawyer, 343 U.S. 579 (1952)*
23. *Brown v. Board of Education, 347 U.S. 483 (1954)*
24. *Cooper v. Aaron, 358 U.S. 1 (1958)*
25. *Baker v. Carr, 369 U.S. 186 (1962)*
26. *Abington School District v. Schempp, 374 U.S. 203 (1963)*
27. *Heart of Atlanta Motel, Inc. v. Unites States, 379 U.S. 241 (1964)*
28. *New York Times v. Sullivan, 376 U.S. 254 (1964)*
29. *Miranda v. Arizona, 384 U.S. 436 (1966)*
30. *Katz v. United States, 389 U.S. 347 (1967)*
31. *Brandenburg v. Ohio, 395 U.S. 444 (1969)*
32. *Griswold v. Connecticut, 381 U.S. 479 (1965)*
33. *Furman v. Georgia, 408 U.S. 238 (1972)*
34. *Roe v. Wade, 410 U.S. 119 (1973)*
35. *Moore v. East Cleveland, 431 U.S. 494 (1977)*
36. *Regents of Univ. Cal v. Bakke, 438 U.S. 265 (1978)*
37. *Lee v. Weisman, 505 U.S. 577 (1992)*
38. *United States v. Lopez, 514 U.S. 549 (1995)*
39. *United States v. Virginia, 518 U.S. 515 (1996)*
40. *Lawrence v. Texas, 539 U.S. 558 (2003)*

CONCLUSION

ANDRÁS JAKAB, ARTHUR DYEVRE AND GIULIO ITZCOVICH

I Patterns and Variability in Constitutional Reasoning

What does the study of great cases tell us about the manner in which constitutional judges justify and communicate their decisions? To be sure, summarising the content and findings of 18 chapters of comparative reporting is no easy task. Each chapter offered an in-depth analysis of a court's constitutional reasoning on the basis of a comprehensive investigation of its 40 most canonical decisions. At least on the face of things, it looks as if we would have made our job much easier had we – as with most classic comparative studies of judicial reasoning[1] – confined our inquiry to just a handful of institutions. However, the dataset we assembled with the help of our contributors aids mitigate this problem. As explained in the introductory section, in addition to his or her written report, each contributor took the trouble to encode information on the reasoning employed by the court in its 40 landmark cases in a spreadsheet. For every landmark judgment, she thus coded the presence of language discussing the purpose of constitutional provisions, precedents, proportionality, etc. Each opinion characteristic was numbered from Q1 to Q37 according to the question it answered. Save for Q5 (general topic addressed by the opinion) and Q7 (argumentation structure), all opinion characteristics were coded as dichotomous variables (yes/no). Although the data-collection procedure and coding scheme we employed are far from perfect and certainly not error-free, the CONREASON Dataset greatly facilitates aggregate analysis. Putting numbers on variations makes the identification of patterns of resemblance and divergence across analytical categories considerably easier. Consider the use of scholarship in judicial discourse. Poring over the chapters of this book, it is hard to get an immediate sense of the frequency of this argument form across the 18 courts (19 including

[1] See e.g. Jeffrey Goldsworthy (ed), *Interpreting Constitutions: A Comparative Study* (Oxford University Press 2006); Mitchel de S. Lasser, *Judicial Deliberations: A Comparative Analysis of Judicial Transparency and Legitimacy* (Oxford University Press 2004).

the post-2010 Hungarian Constitutional Court) and 760 landmark judgments. Yet, using the measures coded in the CONREASON Dataset, we can see that the average proportion of leading judgments citing scholarly work is 47.5 per cent. In other words, a court, on average, makes reference to scholarship in 19 of its 40 leading judgments.

Of course, one does not need a degree in advanced statistics to know that the mean does not represent a robust measure of the central tendency of a distribution, as its value may be disproportionately influenced by extreme observations. A mean of 47.5 per cent can result from few courts mentioning scholarship in all their opinions and other courts ignoring this practice, just as it can result from all courts using this argument type with the same regularity. A more effective way to appraise the structure and variability of a collection of data-points consists in constructing a box-and-whiskers plot.[2] Such a plot characterises the distribution of a variable using the median along with the first, second and third quartile. Plotted in Figure 1 are variations in the incidence of 17 opinion characteristics pertaining to topical and argumentative structure, sources of constitutional law and interpretive methods, in the courts' leading judgments. For each opinion characteristic, the band in the middle of the box indicates the middle of the distribution, the median. The area within the box, below and above the median, represents the second and third quartile. (The area within the box thus accounts for 50 per cent of the courts.) Below the box is the area corresponding to the (first) lower quartile and above the box to the (fourth) upper quartile. The whiskers show how the data spread within the lower and upper quartile, while the dots denote the outliers.

Though lawyers and legal scholars may not be familiar with this approach to data visualisation, Figure 1 provides a good overview of the cross-court variability for the argumentative categories displayed. Among other things, the plot reveals that the category Q20, i.e. reference to scholarship, exhibits greater variability than, for instance, variable Q18, which measures the proportion of decisions referring to the framers' intent. The median for citation to scholarly work is 52.5 per cent, but the other observations are widely spread out around this value. The proportion of opinions mentioning one form of scholarship or another varies between zero and 92.5 per cent. The second and third quartile, accounting for half

[2] On the advantages of box plots over other data visualisation techniques see Martin Krzywinski and Naomi Altman, "Points of Significance: Visualizing Samples with Box Plots" 11 (2014) *Nature Methods* 119.

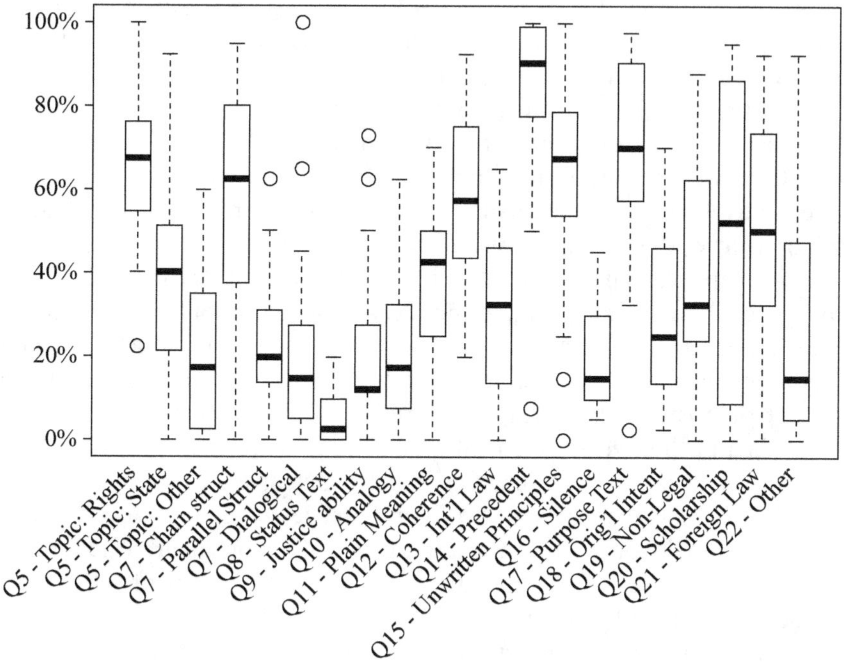

Figure 1 General Opinion Characteristics as Proportion of Courts' Leading Judgments[3]

the observations, span the 10 to 80 per cent range. This means that the incidence of this argument type differs considerably from court to court. While less frequent (median value = 25 per cent), opinions considering arguments from original intent (historical-intentional interpretation) are also subject to a lower degree of cross-court fluctuation. Most courts, it turns out, wind up in the 2 to 40 per cent range corresponding to the first, second and third quartile.

Precedent-based arguments (Q14) appear to occur with both high frequency and great regularity across courts and landmark rulings, except for one outlier, the French Constitutional Council, represented by the small dot at the bottom of the panel. The French Constitutional Council is also an outlier when it comes to purposive interpretation (Q17). Elaborations on the purpose of the constitutional text seem fairly common in salient cases, with three fourth of the courts considering the argument form in more than 60 per cent of their decisions. Yet the Constitutional Council

[3] N = 19.

does not consider this form of teleological interpretation in any of its 40 leading judgments. More surprising is that the Council, despite the activism it has displayed in expanding its remit and review powers since the 1970s, appears to make greater efforts to tether its pronouncements to a piece of constitutional text than other courts. While subject to significant cross-court variations, "unwritten" constitutional principles (Q15) are relatively frequent (median = 65 per cent), yet only 6 of the 40 Council opinions (15 per cent) consider this argument type. Only the ECtHR takes greater care not to base its interpretations on "extra-Convention principles", but always refers to the text and structure of the Convention, the Convention's object and purpose, or precedents in which a certain principle has been recognised. The other dots in Figure 1 are the High Court of Australia with respect to rights (Q5); the Supreme Court of Canada and the Czech Constitutional Court for the proportion of decisions containing legs-of-a-chair (parallel-conclusive) reasoning (Q7); the South African Constitutional Court and, to a lesser extent, the Taiwanese Constitutional Court with regard to the use of dialogical argumentation; and the ECtHR and the South African Constitutional Court for the share of decisions considering justiciability arguments (Q9).

What about the use of generic constitutional concepts and doctrines such as the "rule of law" and "proportionality"? Figure 2 shows how the proportion with which these arguments occur in leading judgments varies across courts. The fact that, compared to Figure 1, arguments in this category generally occur less frequently in landmark rulings – only two variables, "rule of law" (Q24) and "proportionality" (Q37) have a median above 40 per cent – suggests that these arguments have a more contingent character. This is hardly surprising. One would normally expect formal, issue-independent characteristics to recur more frequently than substantive ones. More surprising perhaps is that so few leading judgments consider secularism and the form assumed by either the government (parliamentary, president) or the state (monarchy, republic).

Among the more frequent items of constitutional reasoning, we see significant differences in patterns of variability. Courts vary wildly in their propensity to consider "democracy" (Q24), for instance, with the proportion ranging from 0 (French Constitutional Council) to over 80 per cent (Israeli Supreme Court). Considerations pertaining to "equality" (Q34), by contrast, occur with greater regularity across courts. This is reflected in most courts being close to the median. The plot, however, shows two outliers. One, in the upper part of the plot, is the South African Constitutional Court, which considers equality more frequently than any other court. The other, near the bottom of the panel and on the opposite

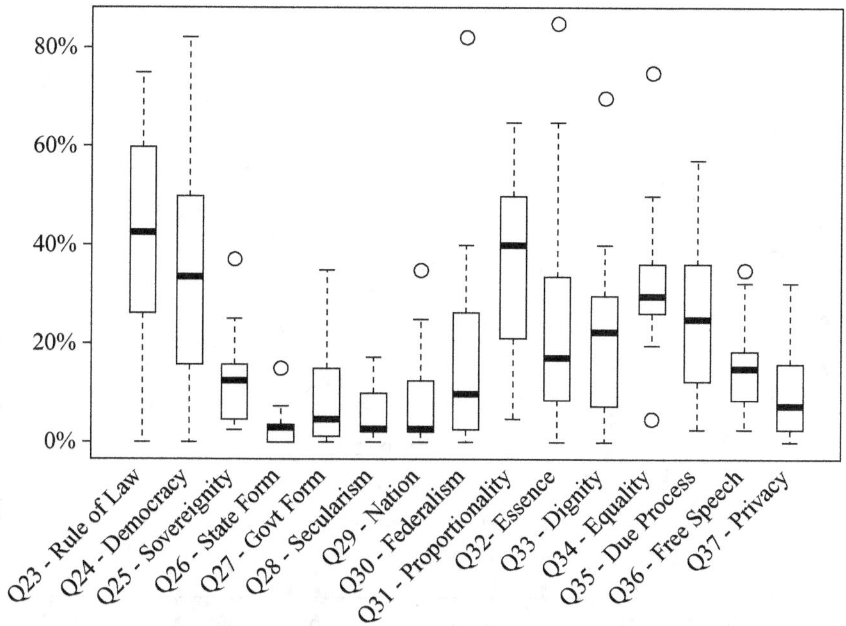

Figure 2 Key Concepts and Generic Doctrines as Proportion of Courts' Leading Judgments[4]

side of the distribution, is the High Court of Australia, which considers equality the least of all courts. Interestingly, the South African Court is also an outlier in its marked fondness for "human dignity" (Q33). Staying with outliers, the court whose opinions are most likely to mention "sovereignty" (Q25) is the UK Supreme Court, which, as highlighted by Tamas Gyorfi's report, is easily explained by the centrality of the doctrine of parliamentary sovereignty in British constitutionalism. In similar fashion, because references to "subsidiarity" and the "margin of appreciation" in ECtHR decisions were coded as federalist arguments (Q30), the ECtHR comes out far ahead of other courts in federal jurisdictions such as the High Court of Australia and the US Supreme Court. The Spanish Constitutional Tribunal, meanwhile, stands out for the frequency with which its opinions elaborate on the "core content" of constitutional rights and competences (Q32).[5] Finally, the German Constitutional Court has

[4] N = 19.

[5] In the chapter on the Spanish Court, Marian Ahumada Ruiz linked the recurrence of this notion in judicial discourse to the constitutional charter, which expressly secures the "essential content" of rights against legislative encroachments.

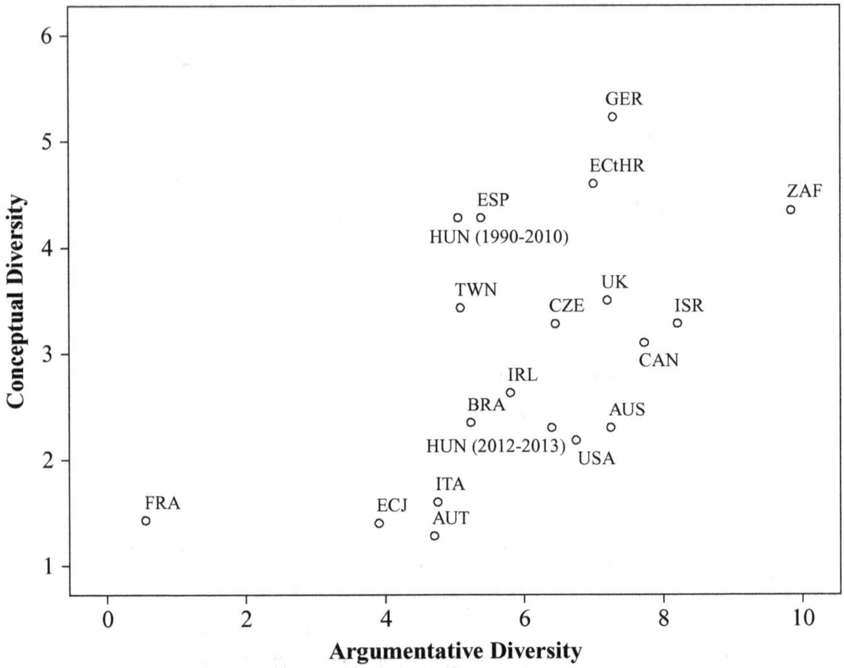

Figure 3 Argumentative Diversity and Conceptual Diversity in the Courts' Leading Judgments[6]

the highest proportion of leading judgments considering "free speech" (Q36).

Not only do courts differ in regard to the type of arguments and key concepts on which they rely, but they also diverge in regard to the range, variety and diversity of the reasons they adduce for their rulings. Some courts draw on a restrictive repertoire of arguments and concepts, which then tend to recur frequently in their opinions. Others make use of a rich and diverse set of justifications, styles and argument forms, resulting in greater variability across decisions. Figure 3 shows how the average numbers of arguments (Q8–Q22) and key concepts (Q23–Q37) differ in the courts' leading cases. Not surprisingly, the French Constitutional Council comes out as a clear outlier. This reflects the terse, rigidly formalistic reasoning characteristic of French constitutional discourse. On average, a French leading judgment contains less than two generic

[6] N = 19.

concepts and instantiates less than one general argument type. Somewhat similar, but less extreme, are the Austrian Constitutional Court, the Italian Constitutional Court and the ECJ. At the other end of the spectrum are the German Constitutional Court, the ECtHR and South Africa with reasoning styles embracing a large set of arguments and key concepts.

Argumentative variations across courts and argumentative variations across cases within the same court may call for distinct explanations. While we cannot rule out the possibility that they are, to some extent, an artefact of our case selection procedure, we may speculate that divergences in patterns of argumentation and conceptual sophistication among courts result from differences in legal tradition; historical background; linguistic peculiarities of the constitutional charter and institutional set-up. We further elaborate on these explanations below.

These factors, however, cannot serve as an adequate basis for explaining variations across decisions issued by the same tribunal, as they usually remain constant across cases. Most courts in our study consider plain meaning arguments in some of their landmark rulings. Yet constitutional judges do not appear very consistent in the way they use this argument form. No court considers it in all its leading judgments. Instead, what happens is that plain meaning is considered in some judgments, but completely ignored in others, without the judges explaining why. The same goes for other canons of interpretation such as coherence (Q12) and original intent (Q18). Some courts, including the German, South African and Czech constitutional courts, along with the ECtHR, appear to be relatively systematic in their reliance on purposive/teleological interpretation (Q17), which they consider in virtually all their leading judgments. But this is by no means the case for all courts: half the courts consider this argument form in somewhere between 2.5 and 70 per cent of their leading judgments, i.e. with a significant cross-judgment variability. This suggests that constitutional reasoning does not always obey a systematic judicial philosophy but relies on a good deal of cherry-picking. Rather than rigidly observing the commands of a particular theory of interpretation, constitutional opinion-writers often simply pick the argument or set of arguments that best suits the result they want to achieve and ignore or play down considerations pointing in the opposite direction. In other words, constitutional argumentation, as least as far the actual practices of the courts are concerned, is not an exercise in scientific exposition but a distinctively rhetorical enterprise.

II Relativising the Common Law vs. Civil Law Distinction

Given the prominent place enjoyed by the Common Law vs. Civil Law distinction in the comparative law literature, we might want to ask how this distinction squares with the data we have collected. Do constitutional tribunals neatly divide up into a Common Law and a Civil Law constitutional reasoning style? Scholars, of course, differ in what they identify as the defining traits of the two traditions. Yet one view, seemingly prevalent in the Anglophone literature, suggests that Common Law judicial reasoning differs from Civil Law legal reasoning in four respect. First, codified rules are supposed to have greater traction in Civil Law jurisdictions than in Common Law systems.[7] For the same reason, Civil Law constitutional reasoning is supposed to be more deductive; Common Law constitutional reasoning more inductive.[8] Second, because Common Law is associated with judge-made law, whereas Civil Law is associated with codified legislation, precedents are believed to matter less in the latter.[9] Third, Common Law judges are thought to be more candid than their Civil Law counterparts in acknowledging the role played by policy arguments and non-legal considerations and, more generally, in admitting that judges do, indeed, make law in the course of settling disputes.[10] Civil Law judicial reasoning,

[7] See Thomas Lundmark, *Charting the Divide between Common and Civil Law* (Oxford University Press 2012) 101; Christian Kirchner, "The Difficult Reception of Law and Economics in Germany" (1991) 11 *International Review of Law and Economics* 277, 284. The presumption that codification makes Civil Law courts both less independent from the other branches and less responsive to fluctuations in the economic cycle underpins the claim made by law and finance economists that Common Law legal systems are more efficient and enjoy higher growth rates, see Thorsten Beck et al., "Law and Finance: Why Does Legal Origin Matter?" (2003) 31 *Journal of Comparative Economics* 653. These economists argue that, unlike most of their Civil Law counterparts, Common Law courts are "obsessed with facts and deciding concrete cases, rather than adhering to the logical principles of codified law", *Id.* at 660.

[8] Roscoe Pound, *The Spirit of the Common Law* (Marshall Jones 1921) 170, and "What Is the Common Law" (1937) 4 *University of Chicago Law Review* 176, 186.

[9] John Henry Merryman, *The Civil Law Tradition: An Introduction to the Legal Systems of Western Europe and Latin America* (Stanford University Press 1985) 26 ("One often hears it said, sometimes by people who should know better, that civil law systems are codified statutory systems, whereas the common law is uncodified and is based in large part on judicial decisions"). While recognising that it oversimplifies the difference between Common Law and Civil Law systems, Merryman goes on to argue that it expresses "an important set of basic differences between the two traditions", *Id.* In the same spirit, Justice Scalia links his textualist approach to constitutional interpretation to Civil Law mode of judicial decision making, see Antonin Scalia, *A Matter of Interpretation: Federal Courts and the Law: Federal Courts and the Law* (Princeton University Press 1998) 3.

[10] Lundmark (n 7); John Philip Dawson, *The Oracles of the Law* (University of Michigan Law School 1968); Kirchner (n 4) 282.

by contrast, is conceived of as articulating a strictly legalistic, formalist conception of judicial decision making, which denies that judges play any role at all in developing the law. Finally, Common Law judges are commonly viewed as practicing a more discursive style of judicial reasoning, which allows the individual judge to make his voice heard. With Civil Law opinion-writing, meanwhile, the received view associates a more oracular, impersonal style, where the voice of the individual judge remains hidden behind the collective "court".[11]

Four of our 18 courts are ordinarily viewed as belonging to "classic" Common Law systems: the UK Supreme Court, the United States Supreme Court, the High Court of Australia and the Supreme Court of Ireland.[12] Ten belong to Civil Law jurisdictions: the Austrian Constitutional Court, the Supreme Federal Tribunal of Brazil, the Constitutional Council of France, the German Federal Constitutional Court, the Italian Constitutional Court, the Hungarian Constitutional Court, the Czech Constitutional Court, the Spanish Constitutional Tribunal and the Taiwanese Constitutional Court.[13] Three courts belong to "Mixed" systems with both Common Law and Civil Law influences: the South African Constitutional Court, the Israeli Supreme Court and the Supreme Court of Canada. On top of these domestic courts come two supranational tribunals, the ECtHR and the ECJ, which have been subject to varying influences but are not associated with a specific legal tradition. Provided these classifications are correct, the foregoing chapters of this book along with the empirical measurements from the CONREASON Dataset suggest that there is a grain of truth in the received view of the Common Law/Civil Law divide. Consistent with previous studies,[14] we find that constitutional opinions from Common Law jurisdictions make more frequent use of precedent-based arguments than do constitutional opinions from Civil Law systems. The chart in Figure 4 shows that 93 per cent of Common Law constitutional opinions in great cases cite some precedent, a figure that rises to 99 per cent for opinions from Mixed systems. For Civil Law constitutional courts, by contrast, the proportion of leading judgments containing reference to previous decisions is 75 per cent. The difference,

[11] Tania Groppi and Marie-Claire Ponthoreau (eds), *The Use of Foreign Precedents by Constitutional Judges* (Hart 2013) 413; Lasser (n 1); Kirchner (n 7) 282.

[12] See Central Intelligence Agency, The World Factbook, https://www.cia.gov/library/publications/the-world-factbook/fields/2100.html (last visited December 28, 2015); Juriglobe, World Legal Systems, http://www.juriglobe.ca/eng/sys-juri/index-alpha.php (last visited December 28, 2015).

[13] Central Intelligence Agency (n 12); Juriglobe (n 12).

[14] Groppi and Ponthoreau (n 11).

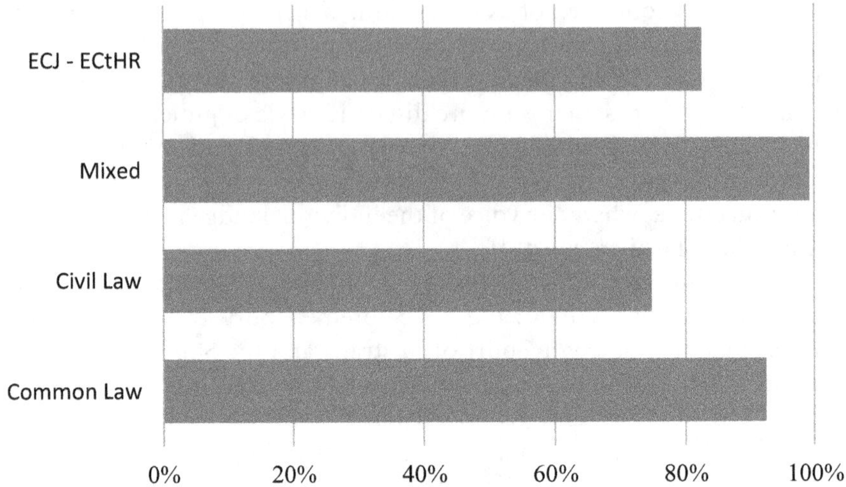

Figure 4 Average Proportion of Leading Judgments Citing Precedents (Q14)[15]

though, fails to meet standard cut-offs of statistical significance.[16] The two supranational courts, meanwhile, fall somewhere between Civil Law and Common Law constitutional courts.

Arguably, variations in tone, mood and diction are harder to capture by a single metric. Yet the contributions assembled in the present book confirm the existence of important stylistic differences between Common Law and Mixed systems, on the one hand, and Civil Law systems, on the other. Especially arresting is the contrast between the rigidly formalistic, impersonal tone of French Constitutional Council opinions and the free-flowing, conversational style of the opinions penned by US and Israeli constitutional judges. As Arthur Dyevre observes in the chapter on the Constitutional Council, the sort of flowery rhetoric and sarcastic tone

[15] $N = 19$. The graph displays average proportions. First, we calculated the proportion of judgments that contain reference to precedents for each of the 19 courts. Then, after classifying courts into four groups (ECJ/ECtHR, Mixed, Civil Law, Common Law), we plotted the average of each group.

[16] $F = 1.242$, $p > 0.1$. Short explanation for lawyers: The p value (calculated from the test statistic F) indicates that performing this analysis on 1000 different samples, we would conclude that there is a connection between the two variables more than 10 per cent of the time even if the differences between legal traditions were purely random. The standard, commonly accepted cut-off for the probability of this type of error in the statistical literature is $0.05 = 5$ per cent. Thus, p-values above this threshold indicate a non-significant relationship. This being said, the lack of statistical significance in the present case may very well stem from our small sample size.

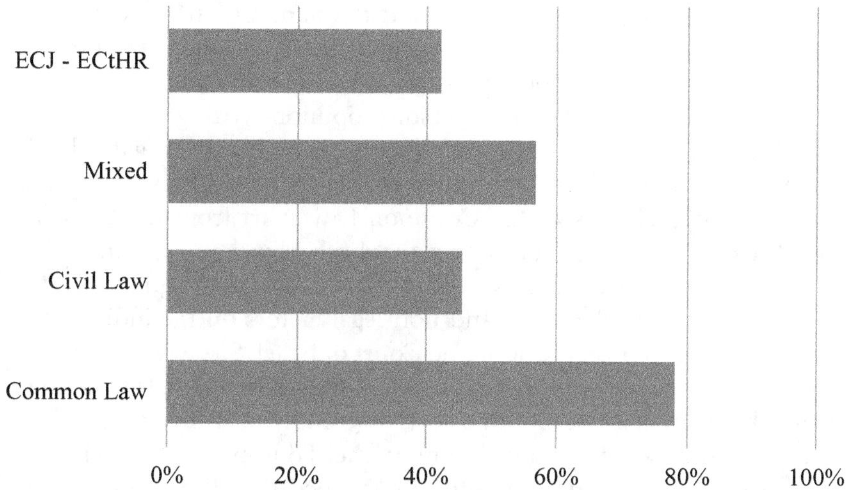

Figure 5 Average Proportion of Leading Judgments with Concurrence or Dissent (Q3)[17]

encountered in some US Supreme Court opinions appears just outlandish from a French Civil Law perspective. In the same manner, the magisterial tone characteristic of constitutional opinion-writing on the German, Hungarian, French, Italian and Czech constitutional courts is at variance with the practice of Israeli Supreme Court judges to cite songs and poems, along with writers and philosophers. Generally speaking, Common Law and Mixed constitutional reasoning tend to make more frequent use of metaphors and other literary figures of speech and to employ everyday language rather than dry, technical language. Also facilitating the expression of the judge's individual voice and style in Common Law and Mixed constitutional reasoning is the frequency of separate opinions. As shown in Figure 5, concurrences and dissents are more prevalent in Common Law and Mixed judgments. Rather than indicating an aversion to dissent on the part of Civil Law judges, these figures are more readily explained by the fact that constitutional courts in Austria, Italy and France ban the publication of separate opinions. If we remove these courts, the proportion of landmark decisions featuring a concurrence or a dissent rises to 66 per cent. The same goes for supranational courts. The ECJ bans dissents. But 32 out of 40 (80 per cent) leading ECtHR rulings come with one or more separate opinions.

[17] N = 19.

While preserving the fiction of judicial unanimity, bans on dissents prevent the individual judge from using the pen to advance his own interests – including personal prestige and fame. This, in turn, works to hinder the emergence of a more personal opinion-writing style.

There are other aspects of constitutional reasoning investigated by the present book that seem to support the conventional wisdom on the characteristics supposed to set the Common Law apart from the Civil Law world. We do, indeed, find evidence that both Mixed and Common Law courts show greater candour when it comes to acknowledging the influence of policy considerations and non-legal factors on the judicial process. In the Chapter on the Supreme Court of Israel, Suzie Navot presents some fascinating morsels of constitutional reasoning where Israeli judges expressly consider the economic costs of complying with human rights standards and variously quote from Michel Foucault and Jean-Jacques Rousseau. US Supreme Court decisions, too, occasionally recite economic arguments. An illustration offered by Howard Schweber and Jennifer Brookhart in the Chapter on the US Supreme Court is *West Coast Hotel v. Parrish*, the 1937 decision that ended the political showdown between the Supreme Court and the Roosevelt administration. In a remarkable display of openness, the majority opinion of Chief Justice Hughes emphasised the economic realities that New Deal policies sought to address. This modicum of judicial candour contrasts with the reluctance of constitutional judges in the Civil Law world to adduce justifications for their decisions that may imply that courts are doing more than just applying pre-existing legal rules. However controversial the issue, German constitutional discourse is not distinctly prone to policy arguments, as Michaela Hailbronner and Stefan Martini report in the chapter on the German Federal Constitutional Court, because policy arguments are framed in a distinctively legal terms.[18]

In order to get a better sense of how courts diverge in that regard, we asked our contributors to compile information on the use of "non-legal" arguments in the leading judgments set. To be sure, operationalising such a concept is an exercise fraught with difficulties and we do not regard our approach as unassailable. We deliberately chose not to tie our definition

[18] This finding is consistent with the observation made by other authors. Of German court opinions, Lundmark (n 4) 102, for example, says: "The almost total absence of policy arguments in the judgments of German courts, even in the judgments of the German Federal Constitutional Court, is striking from the viewpoint of a common lawyer. Even decisions on controversial and political topics such as abortion are written very formalistically, which gives the impression that judges are operating in a political vacuum."

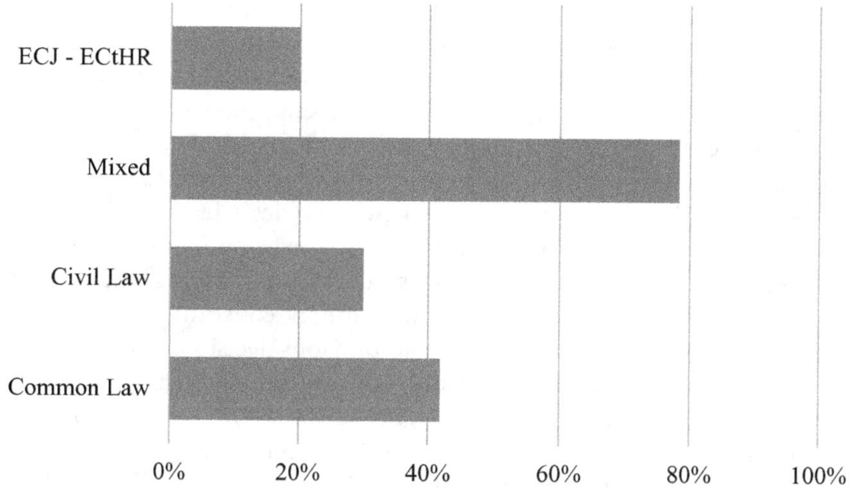

Figure 6 Average Proportion of Leading Judgments Considering "Non-legal" Arguments (Q19)[19]

to a specific theory of law. Nor did we anchor it in an explicit theory of constitutional interpretation. Instead, contributors were instructed to count an argument as "non-legal" only when it was *explicitly* presented as moral, economic or sociological in the sense of being grounded in reasons external to the law.[20] Surely, these instructions still required the contributors to make some judgment calls, which warrants taking the results with a grain of salt. This said, though, the data we have gathered show patterns that are broadly consistent with the claim, central to the received view, that the Common Law tradition – broadly defined to include Mixed legal systems – is more transparent as regards the policy-making function of constitutional judges. As Figure 6 illustrates, non-legal arguments (Q19) are more frequent in Common Law and Mixed opinions than in Civil Law ones. Breaking down the results by court, we find that appeal to non-legal reasons is especially prevalent in the opinions of the supreme courts of Canada (consideration of non-legal arguments in 30 opinions out of 40), the United States (28) and Israel (29), as well as in those of the Constitutional Court of South Africa (35).

[19] N = 19.

[20] This definition entails that the category "non-legal" (Q19) is not necessarily congruent with the category "principle not found in the Constitution" (Q15) – a fact confirmed by the smallish correlation ($r = 0.36$) between the two items.

Nevertheless, while there seems to be a grain of truth in the received view, both the qualitative reports and the quantitative data offer plenty of reasons to nuance what continues to be regarded as the conventional wisdom in comparative constitutional scholarship. Start with precedents. Though precedent-based arguments are more frequently considered in Common Law opinions, references to previous decisions are hardly absent from constitutional reasoning in Civil Law countries. Clearly, while somewhat less frequent than in Common Law and Mixed opinions, precedent-based arguments represent nonetheless a very common argument form in Civil Law jurisdictions – at least in landmark constitutional cases. In fact, save for France, where reference to previous decisions is found only in 3 opinions, our dataset shows that constitutional judges in jurisdictions traditionally regarded as belonging to the Civil Law tradition cite precedents in more than 75 per cent of their opinions. The importance of this argument form is further illustrated by the fact that all 40 leading judgments of the German Federal Constitutional Court in our sample consider some precedent-based argument.

Another aspect of the received view which the present inquiry challenges is the notion that textual arguments have more traction in Civil Law jurisdictions. This notion tends to overlook the spread of "textualist", "strict constructionist" and "original understanding" approaches to constitutional interpretation in the United States. This evolution explains why US Supreme Court opinions frequently feature dictionary definitions together with careful parsing of the Constitution's words and sentences. Yet US constitutional judges are not alone in the Common Law world in stressing the written word when expounding the constitutional charter. Judges on the High Court of Australia, too, tend to emphasise the ordinary (or plain) meaning of the constitutional document as their default method of interpretation. Standing in marked contrast to these two Common Law courts is the looser attitude towards what may otherwise appear to be clear constitutional language found in France, Germany, Hungary, Italy and Brazil. Meanwhile, constitutional judges in Taiwan – which is also ordinarily held to belong to the Civil Law tradition – do sometimes invoke textualist arguments in landmark cases but, as Wen-Chen Chang reports in her study of the Taiwanese Constitutional Court, they seem more inclined to do so in dissent than in the majority. In the CONREASON Dataset, we actually find a greater proportion of Mixed and classic Common Law opinions expressly dealing with the meaning of words and expressions occurring in the constitutional document (Figure 7). The

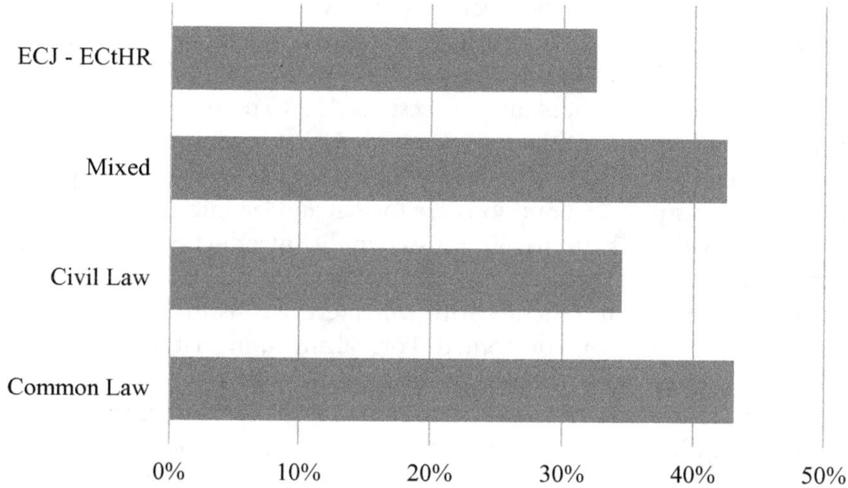

Figure 7 Average Proportion of Leading Judgments Considering Arguments from Plain Meaning (Q11)[21]

difference, however, is small and fails to meet standard cut-offs of statistical significance.[22]

Also challenged by what this book reveals of the courts' actual practices is the greater candidness of Common Law constitutional reasoning. Although both Mixed and Common Law opinions in our sample make, on average, more frequent use of "non-legal" arguments, the difference with Civil Law countries is easily exaggerated. At any rate, it is wrong to equate Civil Law constitutional argumentation with legal formalism and Common Law with legal realism. In fact, judges in all the jurisdictions considered in this book – with perhaps the exception of Israel – appear to be wary of being exposed as policy-makers lest this prompt attacks of judicial activism. In the chapter on the US Supreme Court, Howard Schweber and Jennifer Brookhart observe that, save for occasional departures into political philosophy and historical exegesis, the rhetoric of US constitutional law is resolutely legalistic. If anything, the rhetoric of legalism permeates the opinions issued by the High Court of Australia, the Irish Supreme Court and the UK Supreme Court to an even greater extent. This fact is all the more remarkable because landmark cases are typically the cases where constitutional judges push the limits

[21] N = 19. [22] $F = 0.301, p > 0.1$.

of the law to establish new doctrines and where policy considerations are arguably the most relevant. In sum, formalism remains the official model of judicial decision-making, and this seems to hold true irrespective of stylistic divergences in other respects. Few are more vocal in their invocation of formalism than US Supreme Court Justice Antonin Scalia. And yet the opinions he has authored are just as flowery and irreverent as French constitutional opinions are formal and laconic. This finding is consonant with the hypothesis discussed in the Introduction that formalism represents the judges' chief strategy when it comes to addressing the counter-majoritarian difficulty with which every constitutional tribunal is, one way or another, confronted. Formalism is, in that sense, part of what has been termed "generic constitutional law."[23]

Returning to the Civil Law vs. Common Law divide: rather than going over each individual variable in our Leading Judgments dataset to determine whether it correlates with the classification, a more effective method to assess the validity of this distinction consists in examining aggregate patterns across opinion attributes without making any prior assumption about the relevance of legal traditions. The appropriate statistical technique for this task is called "cluster analysis". In brief, cluster analysis is a statistical procedure used to group a set of objects on the basis of their attributes and in such a way that objects in the same group are more similar to each other than to objects in other groups. As the name suggests, cluster analysis algorithms are designed to help researchers identify how objects "cluster" together on the basis of a given list of attributes. In our case, the objects are the 19 courts in the CONREASON Dataset, while the attributes are the corresponding opinion characteristics collated by our contributors. We must appreciate the fact, however, that the 36 opinion characteristics listed in Figures 1 and 2 above are not all relevant for such an analysis. The primary reason is that some of these indicators measure characteristics which appear too specific to reflect underlying cross-court differences in argumentation style. This holds for the variables capturing key concepts and generic constitutional doctrines (Q23 to Q37 in Figure 2) such as "privacy", "human dignity", "sovereignty", "democracy", "proportionality" and "rule of law". Indeed, it is hard to see how these variables can possibly relate to traditional classifications of legal families in any way that may properly be called systematic. For this reason, the only indicators that come into consideration are those that are

[23] See David S. Law, "Generic Constitutional Law" (2004) 89 *Minnesota Law Review* 652 and the discussion in the Introduction to this volume.

Table 1 *General Opinion Attributes Included in Cluster Analysis*

Opinion Attributes	Mean	SD	Min.	Max.
One-line conclusive argumentation structure (Q7)	23.21	10.51	0	38
Cumulative-parallel argumentation structure (Q7)	9.53	7.10	0	25
Dialogic argumentation structure (Q7)	8.84	9.87	0	40
Consider constitutional status of text (Q8)	2.21	2.50	0	8
Justiciability argument (Q9)	8.95	7.62	0	29
Analogical argument (Q10)	8.74	7.97	0	25
Plain meaning (Q11)	14.95	7.11	0	28
Domestic coherence argument (Q12)	23.26	7.89	8	36
Precedent-based argument (Q14)	33.26	8.79	3	40
Consider principle not found in constitutional text (Q15)	24.53	10.40	0	40
Argument from silence (Q16)	8.05	4.97	2	18
Teleological-textual argument (Q17)	27.74	9.77	1	39
Teleological-historical (intentional) argument (Q18)	11.63	8.49	1	28
Non-legal argument (Q19)	15.63	9.97	0	35
Reference to scholarship (Q20)	19	14.42	0	38
Reference to foreign legal material (Q21)	20.26	10.60	0	37
Other argument or method (Q22)	10.32	11.22	0	37

sufficiently general to capture structural argumentative differences among courts. Thus for the purpose of cluster analysis we retained only the opinion characteristics Q7 to Q12 and Q14 to Q22 listed in Table 1. We do not include topic (Q5) because we see no reason why a court's propensity to cast its rulings as human rights or separation of powers issues should be assumed to relate to the Common Law vs. Civil Law distinction. Nor do we include treaty-conform interpretation of the constitution (Q13) because we believe that this indicator may be influenced by regional factors. EU membership and the accompanying growth of EU law, for instance, may induce European constitutional judges to consider this form of harmonising argument more frequently.[24] Table 1 provides the average number

[24] Courts in EU member countries use this type of argument more frequently. Yet there is no significant connection between EU membership and the rate at which courts consider the

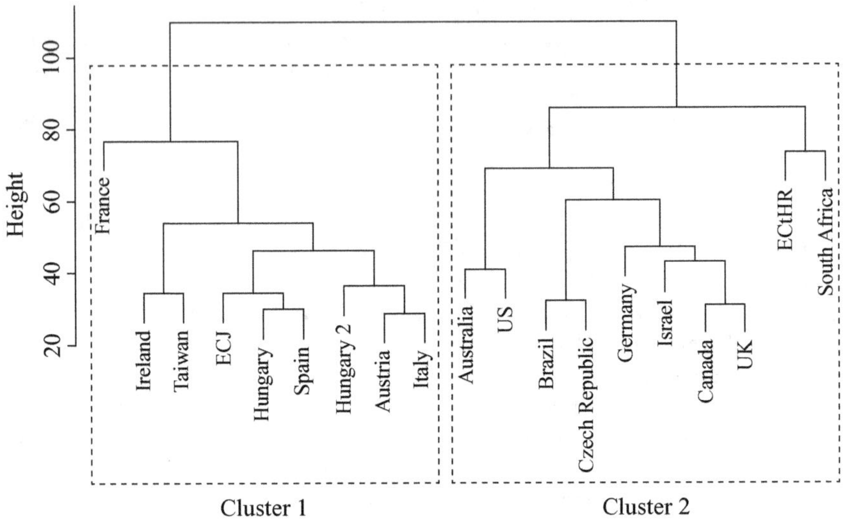

Figure 8 Cluster Analysis of General Opinion Characteristics

of opinions per court featuring the corresponding attribute, alongside the standard deviation and the maximum and minimum value.

How do the courts cluster together based on these characteristics? The results are depicted in Figure 8 in the form of a tree diagram (dendrogram).[25] Such a dendrogram can be thought of as a sort of family

harmonising argument in their leading judgments ($F = 1.012$, $p > 0.1$). Including Q13 as a clustering variable had no effect on cluster membership either.

25 To construct the cluster, we employed the hclust function in R; we used the Ward method (implemented as "ward.D2" in R) and cut the tree in 2 (as our goal was to determine if our courts divide into two clusters, civil law and common law). Ward's minimum variance method is an agglomerative hierarchical clustering procedure in which the total within-cluster variance is minimised. The analysis starts out with N clusters, and continues until there is only one cluster left. During the analysis, we experimented with other methods such as the complete linkage or the single linkage method (implemented as "single", "complete", "average", "median", "centroid" in R). All algorithms identified France, South Africa and the ECtHR as outliers (and very often as separate clusters). As to the rest of the courts, results are strikingly similar. As Ward's method created very intuitive results, and at the same time visualises outlying cases rather well, we decided to include this version into our analysis. Nevertheless, we should note that choosing a different algorithm would not change the results substantially. We are aware that in a related methodological context, latent class analysis, Anton K. Formann, *Die Latent-Class-Analyse: Einführung in die Theorie und Anwendung* (Beltz 1984) recommends a minimum sample size of 2^m, where m equals the number of clustering variables, as a rule of thumb. Nevertheless, this is only a rule of thumb: there is no hard and fast rule about the number of dimensions analysed

tree, with more distant parents separated by longer branches. Just as close family relatives share more genes whereas distant relatives share less, the degree of "parentage" between two courts is a function of the proportion of opinion characteristics they happen to share. Specifically, the degree of family resemblance between two courts is indicated by the height at which their branch points join: the greater the height, the greater the difference.[26]

Figure 8 highlights two broad clusters. In Cluster 1 we find a sub-group of 5 relatively close-knit European constitutional courts (Italian Constitutional Court, Austrian Constitutional Court, Hungarian Constitutional Court 2012–13, Spanish Constitutional Tribunal, Hungarian Constitutional Court 1990–2010) along with the ECJ. The closest relatives to courts in this sub-group are then the Irish Supreme Court and the Constitutional Court of Taiwan. The isolated position of the French Constitutional Council, meanwhile, reflects its outlier character within Cluster 1. Compared to Cluster 1, Cluster 2 is somewhat more heterogeneous (branch points join at a greater height). It encompasses four sub-groups. One comprises the British, Canadian and Israeli supreme courts together with the German Constitutional Court. Most closely related to this sub-group are the Brazilian Supreme Federal Tribunal and the Czech Constitutional Court and, to a lesser degree, the US Supreme Court and the High Court of Australia. Most dissimilar from these three sub-groups within Cluster 2 are the ECtHR and the South African Constitutional Court on the upper-right branch of the dendrogram.

Readily noticeable in Figure 8 is that all Mixed courts and all Common Law courts, with the exception of the Irish Supreme Court, constellate in Cluster 2. That courts from Mixed systems wind up in the same cluster as most Common Law courts implies, as do Figure 4, 5, 6 and 7 above, that these courts are closer to the Common Law than to the Civil Law tradition. Equally consistent with common classifications of the world's legal systems is that all courts in Cluster 1 – with the notable exception of

in *cluster analysis* in relation to the minimum amount of objects, and the methodological literature provides plenty of examples departing from the 2^m rule. See e.g. H. Charles Romesburg, *Cluster Analysis for Researchers* (Lulu 2004) 34–37; http://www.stata.com/manuals14/mvclusterlinkage.pdf. In any case, there is no mathematical theorem that would rule out our analysis.

[26] The branches of courts with identical opinion characteristics would thus join at a height of zero. Just to avoid misunderstandings: the fact that Italy and Australia seem to be near to each other on the diagram does not imply any proximity. Proximity is expressed only through the branches of the tree.

the Irish Court – are ordinarily associated with the Civil Law tradition. The Civil Law vs. Common Law dichotomy would thus appear to be able to account for a good deal of the observed argumentative variance in constitutional reasoning. This impression is further reinforced by the fact that the courts whose argumentation style comparativists tend to regard as most typical of the Civil Law tradition – such as the French Constitutional Council,[27] the Italian Constitutional Court and even the ECJ[28] – concentrate in Cluster 1. Moreover, all courts in Cluster 2 allow separate opinions – a feature habitually associated with the Common Law – whereas all the courts that enforce a ban on separate opinions are in Cluster 1.

Even so, cluster analysis also highlights patterns that are hard to reconcile with orthodox legal typologies. For one thing, Cluster 1 and Cluster 2 are far from perfectly congruent with the Common Law vs. Civil Law classification. Cluster 2, in particular, includes three Civil Law courts (the German Constitutional Court, the Brazilian Supreme Federal Court Tribunal and the Czech Constitutional Court). This implies that, at least in landmark cases, the form of constitutional reasoning practiced by these Civil Law courts has more in common with constitutional reasoning on Mixed and Common Law courts like the UK Supreme Court, the Israeli Supreme Court, the Canadian Supreme Court or even the US Supreme Court than with constitutional argumentation in Civil Law countries like Italy, France or Austria. Second, we would not expect to find the Irish Supreme Court in the company of Taiwanese, Hungarian and Italian constitutional judges, if the Common Law vs. Civil Law typology were actually able to account for all the inter-court variability across the 18 indicators in Table 1. Nor would we expect to find the ECtHR in Cluster 2, as the Strasbourg Court is not habitually understood to belong to the Common Law family.

These seemingly inconsistent patterns suggest that it might be instructive to take a closer look at how they result from the variables listed in Table 1. It turns out that, barring the one-line conclusive – or chain-like – argumentation structure, which is more frequent in Cluster 1 opinions, all the variables are positively correlated with Cluster 2. Put differently, 17 of the 18 opinion characteristics occur more often in Cluster 2 opinions than in Cluster 1 opinions.[29] Some variables, though, make a stronger

[27] See Lasser (n 1) and the discussion in the introductory section. [28] *Id.*

[29] One might argue that high correlation between clustering variables may distort the results in a way that the same underlying concept is taken into account multiple times, see David

contribution to the cluster classification. This holds true, in particular, for reference to scholarly materials (Q20), non-legal considerations (Q19), precedent-based arguments (Q14), analogical reasoning (Q10), teleological-textual argumentation (Q17) and citations to foreign legal materials (Q21). Two of these characteristics – namely, precedent and non-legal reasoning – bear a direct connection to prevailing representations of Common Law legal reasoning. But the connection with Common Law reasoning is less evident for the other four. In the Introduction to this volume, though, we put forward an alternative classification of argumentation styles, which differentiates courts depending on the degree of institutionalisation and ritualisation of judicial communication. According to this classification, judicial communication on Cluster 1 courts must conform to a rigid, highly ritualised template. This template requires opinion-writers to employ only stereotyped, impersonal and technical language. It may also prohibit dissents, as is the case with the ECJ and the French and Italian constitutional tribunals. The effect of such a rigid template is to hamper the individual judge's argumentative creativity and to favour a conservative and predictable style of constitutional reasoning – which, by the way, may often be an effective public relations strategy.[30] The resulting opinions thus tend to deploy a smaller and less diverse repertoire of arguments. The position ascribed to the French Constitutional Council by cluster analysis is consistent with the notion that it represents an extreme illustration of this argumentation style. French constitutional opinions, even in salient cases, tend to be relatively terse and extremely formalistic. They invariably follow a syllogistic structure which is there to suggest that judicial decision making is nothing but applied formal logic. As a result, French constitutional opinions instantiate few of the

J. Ketchen, Jr. and Christopher L. Shook, "The Application of Cluster Analysis in Strategic Management Research: An Analysis and Critique" (1996) 17 *Strategic Management Journal* 441. Indeed, there is definitely some interrelatedness among variables. Excluding variables – one at a time – that are highly correlated with other factors, we find that Ireland and Taiwan very often move from Cluster 1 to Cluster 2. In the case of Taiwan, this seems like a plausible alternative categorisation, as its legal system is primarily under German and secondarily under US influence (see Wen-Chen Chang's report in the present volume), and both the German Federal Constitutional Court and the US Supreme Court are in Cluster 2. In the Irish case, the historical legacy of the British rule, the usual common law categorisation, and the linguistic proximity (with the easier influence of foreign laws and doctrines) can plausibly explain why it might be placed in the same cluster as the UK, the US, Canada, Australia, South Africa and Israel.

30 Lee Epstein et al., *The Behavior of Federal Judges: A Theoretical and Empirical Study of Rational Choice* (Harvard University Press 2013) 315.

arguments comprised in our typology. In contrast to courts in Cluster 1, courts in Cluster 2 illustrate the flexible argumentative template. Thanks to looser constraints on judicial communication, constitutional judges enjoy more leeway to choose, combine and develop a richer set of argument types. Moreover, the absence of ban on separate opinions not only allows the individual judge to consider arguments ignored by the judges in the majority, but also creates an incentive for the majority to embrace a larger set of arguments in anticipation of dissent. Constitutional reasoning on most Mixed and Common Law constitutional courts seems to fit this characterisation. Yet this richer and more discursive mode of judicial reasoning is by no means exclusive to these countries and may also be said to characterise the landmark decisions of the Brazilian Supreme Federal Tribunal, the German Federal Constitutional Court, the Czech Constitutional Court and the ECtHR.

These findings can be interpreted in two ways. The first is that the Common Law vs. Civil Law opposition may not be as clear-cut as some of the comparative literature seemingly implies, at least in the case of landmark constitutional cases. But another, equally plausible explanation is that courts outside the Common Law world are influenced by Common Law-style constitutional reasoning and have come to espouse some of the argumentative practices traditionally associated with a Common Law writing style. The demarcation line between Common Law and Civil Law modes of argumentation is thus blurring as a result of the diffusion of Common Law norms of judicial communication. To investigate this hypothesis further, we now move on to discuss the evolution of constitutional reasoning over time.

III Global Trends in Constitutional Reasoning: Towards Generic Constitutional Reasoning?

Given that the distribution of cases in our dataset is temporally skewed – with most judgments rendered in the period 1980–2010 – we should be especially cautious when trying to draw conclusions over temporal trends. In any case, the temporal imbalance along with the fact that few courts existed prior to 1950 justify restricting the analysis to decade-by-decade evolution for the period 1951 to 2010. Starting again with precedents, (Q14), we can see from Figure 9 that more recent constitutional opinions cite precedents with greater frequency. Importantly, Figure 9 suggests that constitutional judges in Civil Law countries are converging towards Common Law practices as far as reasoning is concerned. Giulio Itzcovich

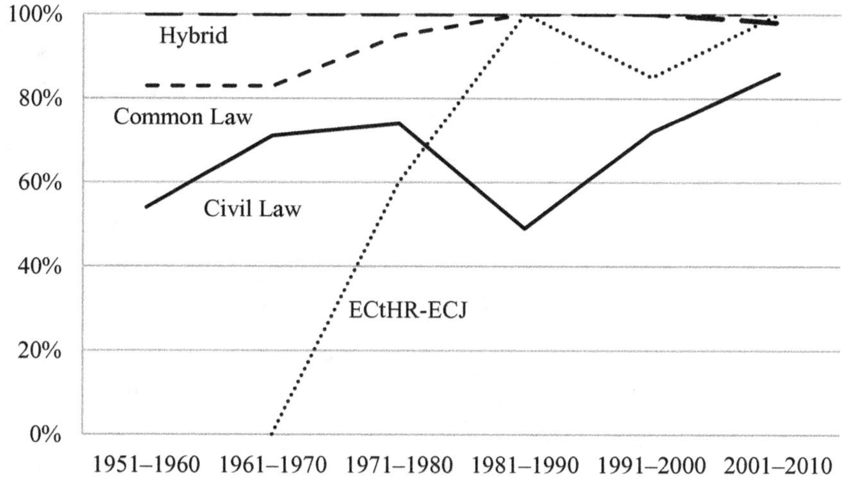

Figure 9 Proportion of Leading Judgments Featuring Precedent-Based Arguments, 1951–2010 (Q14)[31]

in the chapter devoted to the Court of Justice pointed to a similar evolution in the practice of the European Court. Rare in early years, reliance on this argument form is now firmly established in the case law of the European Court. These findings support the common-lawisation hypothesis. It is also true that, as Ireland and the United Kingdom joined the European Union, the Court of Justice had incentives to adjust to its new audience. Part of the explanation for the increased popularity of precedents as constitutional argument could be more mundane, though. Indeed, a new judicial body will initially have few precedents to cite. As Janneke Gerards notes in her report, ECtHR judges had no previous ruling to refer to when they drafted the first decision of the Court. As decisions accumulate and the pools of precedents grows, though, relating a new case to earlier ones becomes easier.

Are there any other indications of the emergence of a generic style of constitutional argumentation? One of the most tangible signs of global convergence is the place of fundamental rights in constitutional adjudication. As highlighted in the Introduction, there is a close connection between the rise of judicial power and the spread of rights rhetoric. To assess the pervasiveness of rights rhetoric in great cases, we coded information on the general topic addressed in each judgment (Q5). When the

[31] N = 647.

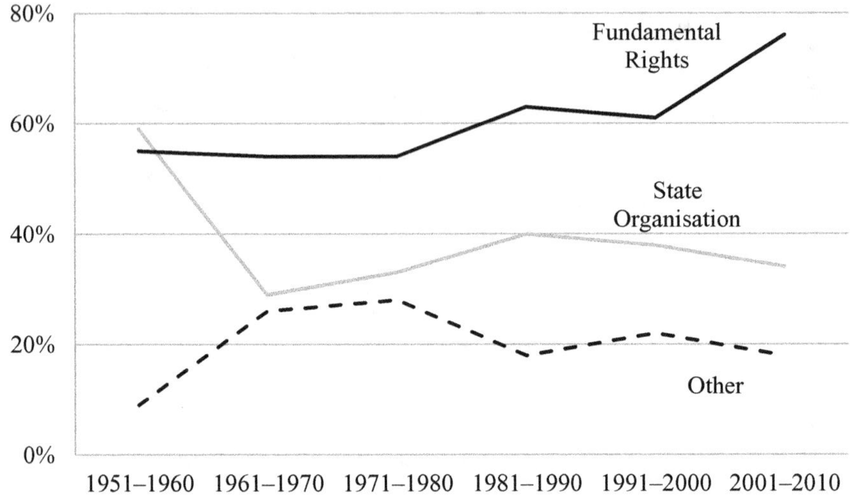

Figure 10 Proportion of Leading Judgments, General Topic, 1951–2010 (Q5)[32]

ruling framed the issue as a rights question, the decision was coded as "fundamental rights". When the issue was characterised as pertaining to federalism or the separation of powers, it was coded "state organisation". Cases that did not fit any of these two categories were then classified as "other". Figure 10 illustrates the results. Because some rulings consider both fundamental rights and state organisation issues, the overall count exceeds 100 per cent. Even so, the results confirm the centrality of rights rhetoric in the leading judgments analysed in this book. Nearly two-thirds of the opinions address fundamental rights issues. The proportion is even higher in the 2000s, and Figure 10 suggests an upward trend. Save for the High Court of Australia, the ubiquity of rights considerations in landmark rulings is observed across all courts. For the European Court of Human Rights, the figure attains 100 per cent, which is hardly surprising given that the Court's jurisdiction is restricted to claims of violations of Convention rights.

The heightened emphasis on rights in constitutional reasoning is presumably driven by multiple factors. Often opinion-writers may be simply responding to the arguments put forward by the parties. Yet litigation strategies tend to anticipate the outcome of the judicial process. Litigants file suits and frame their constitutional claims based on what they believe is

[32] N = 647.

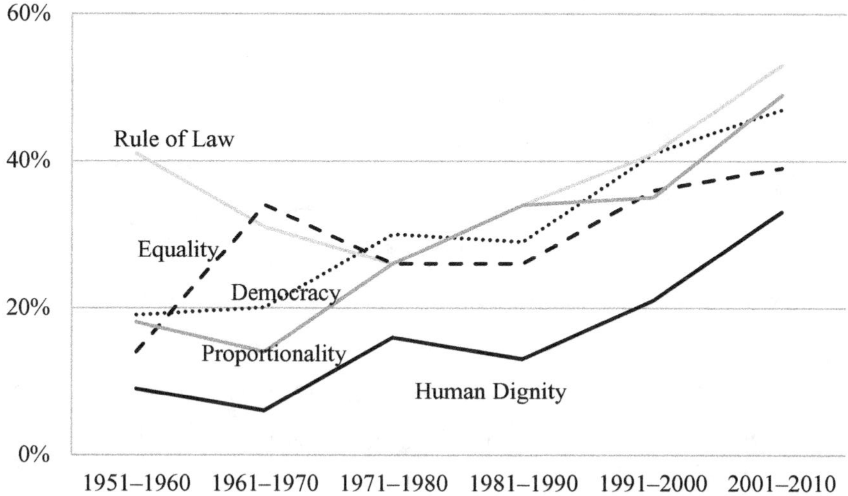

Figure 11 Proportion of Leading Judgments Mentioning Democracy (Q24), Rule of Law (Q23), Equality (Q34), Proportionality (Q31) and Human Dignity (Q33)[33]

likely to elicit the desired judicial response. So if judicial discourse emphasises rights, litigants will interpret this as a cue that demands framed as rights claims are likely to fare well in the judicial arena. If some rights-litigation eventually succeeds, this will create a feedback loop, whereby greater judicial emphasis on rights leads to more rights litigation, leading to even greater emphasis on rights in judicial discourse, leading to yet more rights litigation, and so on. As for why judges might want to emphasise rights in the first place, we saw in the Introduction that the rhetoric of rights not only has the advantage of flexibility but also enables courts to project the image of champions of both freedom and the rule of law.

Judicial preference for flexibility had also led us to predict that constitutional courts would be keen adopters of the proportionality test. Figure 11 confirms this intuition. Similar motives would seem to explain the rising popularity of "equality" and "human dignity". Ditto for "rule of law" and "democracy".

Taken together, Figures 9, 10 and 11 suggest that, to the extent that salient judgments offer any indication of the global evolution of constitutional reasoning, precedents, broad rights and proportionality along with

[33] N = 647.

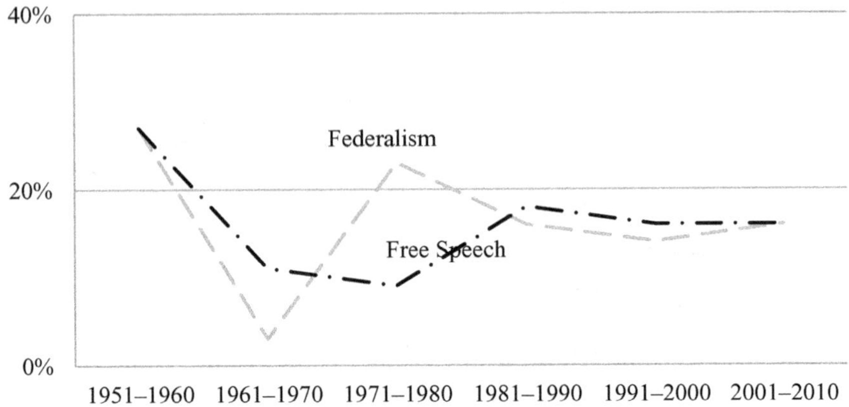

Figure 12 Proportion of Leading Judgments Mentioning Federalism (Q30) and Free Speech (Q36)[34]

general, indeterminate principles such as equality and human dignity are emerging as important elements of the generic phraseology of constitutional dispute resolution. The growing popularity enjoyed by these generic concepts is even more striking when compared with the other two key concepts that have at some point over the six decades figured among the four most popular, namely "federalism" and "free speech", which appear somewhat less indeterminate than "human dignity", "proportionality, "rule of law", "democracy" and "equality". Figure 12 suggests that these have lost traction among constitutional opinion-writers, if not in absolute then at least in relative terms.

Lending further support to the judicial self-empowerment hypothesis are the diverging trajectories of canons of constitutional interpretation like purposive (aka objective teleological) interpretation, original intent and ordinary meaning. While ordinary meaning and original intent, two canons mostly regarded as more constraining for judges, have lost popularity, purposive teleological interpretation, which is commonly thought to afford judges greater latitude, has gained momentum, as shown in Figure 13. These patterns seem to buttress the view that constitutional judges have grown less deferential and more activist over time. According to this, the evolution of constitutional reasoning reflects the fact of expanding judicial power, as judges resort to less constraining modes of argumentation to justify their activist policy pronouncements. To be sure,

[34] N = 647.

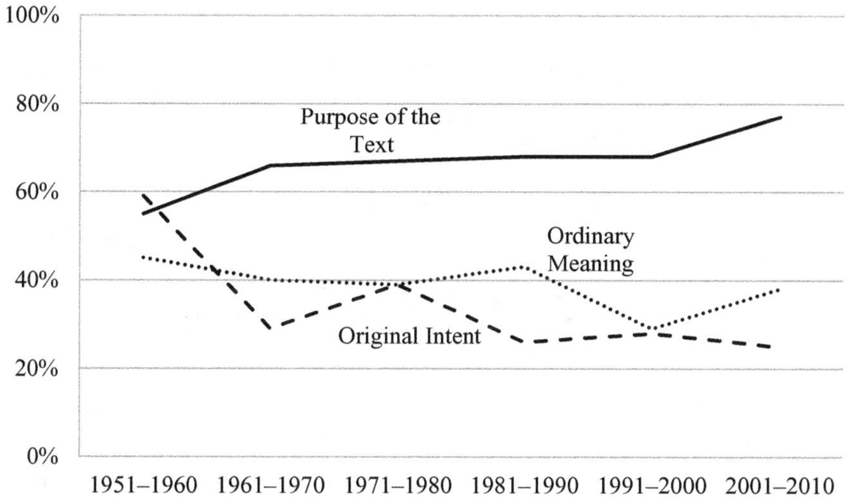

Figure 13 Proportion of Leading Judgments Referring to Original Intent (Q18), Ordinary Meaning (Q11) and Purpose of the Text (Q17)[35]

alternative explanations can be thought of to account for this evolution. It can be argued, for example, that the pattern illustrated in Figure 13 merely reflects the ageing of constitutions. As constitutions get older and face new issues which the framers could not possibly envisage, the argument goes, original intent and ordinary meaning become less relevant as methods of constitutional construction. Yet this argument is hard to reconcile with the fact that many of the courts analysed in this book are expounding relatively young constitutional charters. The new constitutional dispensation of the South African Constitution came into effect in 1994, first in terms of the 1993 Constitution, followed by the final Constitution in 1996; that of the Czech Republic in 1993; Brazil's Constitution was promulgated in 1988; Canada's Charter of Rights and Freedoms in 1982; and Spain's Constitution in 1978. Nor are the French, German and Italian constitutions exactly old documents, dating back, as they do, to the post-war period. So if the hypothesis that the incidence of these interpretive canons correlates with the age of constitutions were true, we would in fact expect the opposite trend.

Another interesting trend is the growing argumentative and conceptual diversity of leading judgments. Figure 14 plots our measure of

[35] N = 647.

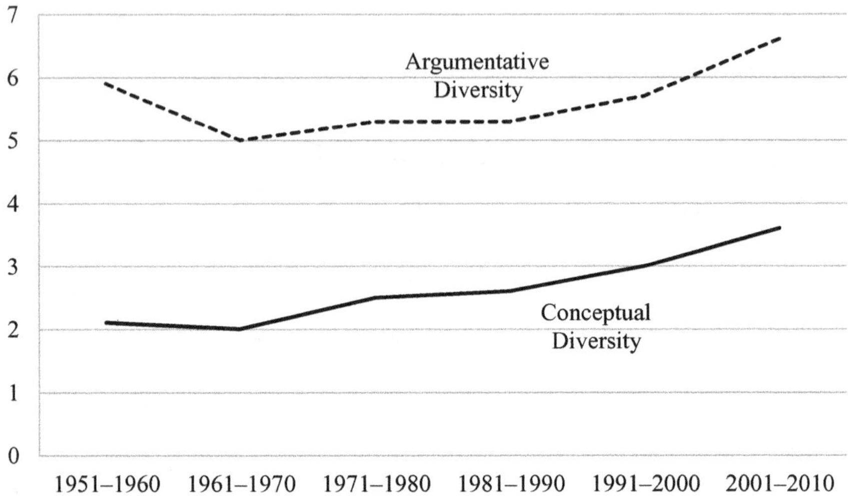

Figure 14 Argumentative (Q8–Q22) and Conceptual Diversity (Q23–Q37) in Leading Judgments[36]

argumentative diversity, defined as the average number of argument types (Q8–Q22) instantiated in landmark constitutional judgments, and conceptual diversity, defined as the average number of key concepts (Q23–Q37) over the 1951–2010 period. Again, this pattern can be accounted for by the judges' desire for flexibility. The ability to avail themselves from a larger repertoire of arguments offers judges greater freedom to choose and justify the outcome they regard as optimal. It would thus seem that more cherry-picking is going on in more recent rulings.

We find yet more evidence for the narrative of greater judicial freedom and heightened activism when we look at the basic structure of judicial reasoning. Depicted in Figure 15 is the incidence of the one-line conclusive (or chain-like) argumentation structure against that of the dialogical and parallel-conclusive structure. Because it requires judges to state clearly the one, main reason justifying a particular conclusion, the one-line conclusive structure is arguably the most constraining of the three basic modes of reasoning. Yet, although it is still the most popular one, we see that its popularity has declined. This decline stands in contrast to the growing frequency of judgments adopting the more malleable, and possible more opaque, dialogical structure.

[36] N = 647.

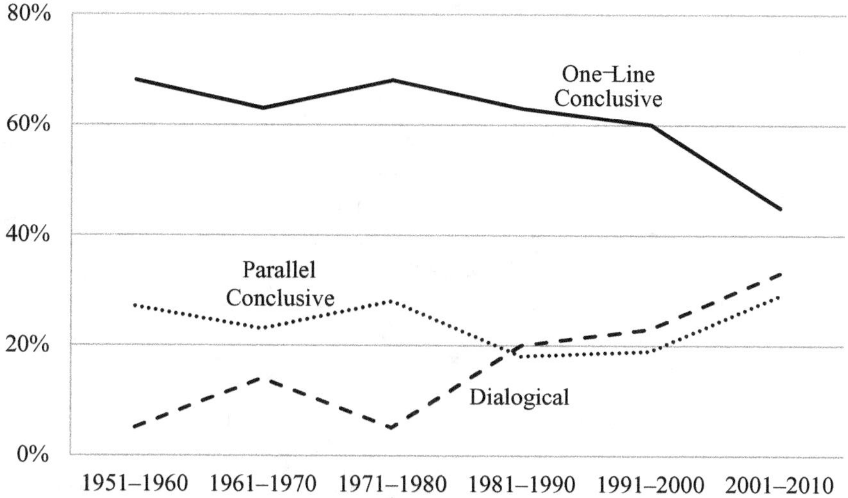

Figure 15 Proportion of Leading Judgments Using Only One-Line Conclusive Arguments, Parallel Conclusive Arguments and Dialogical Arguments (Q7)[37]

As for the channel through which the argumentation practices diffuse, scholars, as we saw in the Introduction, have stressed the emergence of transjudicial networks as important forums for judges to exchange insights on how best to solve similar problems.[38] Citations to foreign precedents and foreign legal materials are taken to represent a key indicator of the increasing significance of transnational judicial dialogue for the diffusion of constitutional ideas. As with previous studies,[39] we also found an upward trend towards more frequent reference to foreign legal materials, foreign judicial decisions included. The trend plotted in Figure 16 holds for both Civil and Common Law constitutional reasoning. Another diffusion channel discussed in the comparative literature is the top-down

[37] N = 647. Basically all judgments contained one-line conclusive (chain) structures, but some of them also contained parallel conclusive (legs of a chair) or parallel inconclusive but together conclusive (dialogical) structures. Only judgments which contained *only* chain structures were categorised as such. For more details on the coding of argumentative structures see Appendix.

[38] See Anne-Marie Slaughter, *A New World Order* (Princeton University Press 2005); Alec Stone Sweet and Jud Mathews, 'Proportionality Balancing and Global Constitutionalism' (2008) 47 *Columbia Journal of Transnational Law* 73; See Anne-Marie Slaughter, *A New World Order* (Princeton University Press 2005); Michal Bobek, *Comparative Reasoning in European Supreme Courts* (Oxford University Press 2013) 47–50.

[39] Groppi and Ponthoreau (n 11).

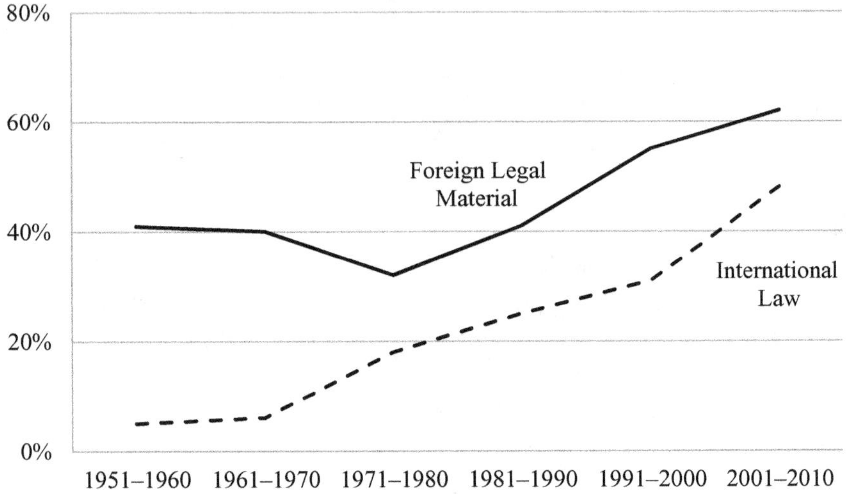

Figure 16 Proportion of Leading Judgments Considering Foreign Legal Material (Q21) and International Law (Q23)[40]

pressure created by the multiplication of international legal regimes and the expanding influence of supranational courts.[41] Consistent with this explanation, Figure 16 documents a marked upward trend in the share of leading judgments referring to international law. While top-down pressure may sometimes lead a domestic constitutional court to adopt norms and standards promoted by international law, embracing international law and citing international law instruments (even in cases where these are not binding) may also be part of a deliberate strategy to bolster its legitimacy at home.[42] In fact, the same dynamics, whereby domestic constitutional judges appeal to the legitimacy of established and reputed

[40] N = 647.

[41] Mark Tushnet, 'The Inevitable Globalization of Constitutional Law', 49 (2008) *Virginia Journal of International Law* 985; Rosalind Dixon and Eric A. Posner, 'The Limits of Constitutional Convergence' (2010) 11 *Chicago Journal of International Law* 399.

[42] See e.g. Alec Stone Sweet, 'Sur la constitutionnalisation de la Convention européenne des droits de l'homme' (2009) 20 *Revue trimestrielle des droits de l'homme* 923; Peter M Huber, 'Offene Staatlichkeit: Vergleich' in Armin von Bogdandy et al. (eds), *Ius Publicum Europaeum II* (Müller 2008) 403–459; Anne Peters, 'The Constitutionalisation of International Organisations' in Neil Walker and Stephen Tierney (eds), *Europe's Constitutional Mosaic* (Hart 2011) 253–86; Gwendolyn Sasse, 'The Council of Europe as a Norm Entrepreneur: The Political Strengths of a Weak International Institution' *ibid.* 171–204.

institutions to reinforce their position in their political system, may explain the rising popularity of foreign law.[43]

IV Global Evolutions with Local Particularities: "Glocal" Constitutional Law

Despite the diffusion of common practices and generic argumentation frameworks such as rights and proportionality, local particularities continue to abound. Courts are subject to country-specific constraints variously arising from the particular wording of the constitutional charter, the constellation of political forces, the prevailing conceptions of acceptable judicial conduct, the legacy of traumatic historical events or even from the judges' varying degree of ability and creativity when it comes to crafting persuasive arguments. For all these reasons, global convergence cannot but continue to co-exist with myriad local singularities. Comparative constitutional scholars generally rule out full-scale convergence and agree that constitutional systems will retain many of their particularities.[44] Yet some authors speak not merely of local singularities or variations but go on to characterise countries like Australia and the United States as being committed to "constitutional exceptionalism".[45] Is such a characterisation justified in light of our study? If we consider Australia, it is true that Australian constitutional reasoning appears to be, in some respects, exceptional. This holds, above all, for the High Court of Australia's reluctance to resort to the rhetoric of rights. Whereas over two-thirds of the leading judgments investigated in the present book contain some rights language, only 22.5 per cent of Australian leading constitutional rulings do. Similarly, Australian constitutional judges shun equality, which they consider significantly less often (5 per cent of cases) than their peers in other jurisdictions (with mean = 30 per cent and median = 32.5 per cent). Cheryl Saunders and Adrienne Stone in the chapter devoted to the High Court argued that the diminished place of rights rhetoric in Australian constitutional reasoning stems from the absence of a written

[43] See esp. Eyal Benvenisti, 'Reclaiming Democracy: The Strategic Uses of Foreign and International Law by National Courts' (2008) 102 *American Journal of International Law* 241.

[44] See Law (n 23); Tushnet (n 40); Dixon and Posner (n 40).

[45] Tushnet (n 40); Lorraine Weinrib, "The Postwar Paradigm and American Exceptionalism" in Sujit Choudhry (ed), *The Migration of Constitutional Ideas* (Cambridge University Press 2007) 83.

bill of rights combined with the Court's orientation towards formalist legal methods, under the rubric of "Australian legalism". Unlike the Court of Justice, the French Constitutional Council or the Israel Supreme Court, the High Court has been disinclined to create rights by judicial fiat. For that reason, constitutional litigation has focused on federalism and separation of power issues rather than rights. Of the Court's 40 leading judgments, 37 (92.5 per cent) are framed partly or entirely as either separation of power or federalism issues, the highest proportion of all courts. This represents evidence that that the constitutional text has a real constraining effect on the behaviour of Australian constitutional judges, even in high-profile cases. No other court investigated in the present book displays the same consistent adherence to textualism. Some US Supreme Court justices, most notably Antonin Scalia, are vocal supporters of textualism. But it is almost certainly wrong to say that this approach to constitutional interpretation holds sway in US constitutional reasoning. The Austrian Constitutional Court used to practice a form of textualism very similar to the Australian brand. In the 1970s, however, Austrian constitutional judges moved away from this approach to embrace a more flexible argumentation style, as Konrad Lachmayer explains in his report on the Austrian Court. So, to the extent that we regard a focus on rights litigation combined with a loose approach to constitutional construction as the dominant paradigm of global constitutionalism, we do find some evidence to sustain the claim of Australian exceptionalism.

Yet talk of "exceptionalism" is easily misleading, because every court may be, in some respect, exceptional. A court's practices will inevitably depart from those of most other courts on one or more aspects of constitutional reasoning, which renders the label of "exceptionalism" meaningless. Consider the South African Constitutional Court. From a statistical standpoint, it is the most consistent outlier on the measures of opinion content we compiled for this project. For obvious historical reasons, the South African Court is the judicial body that most frequently elaborates on equality in its leading judgments (75 per cent of leading judgments) – making it the exact counterpoint to the High Court of Australia. In their contribution, Christa Rautenbach and Lourens Du Plessis emphasised the central place equality occupies in South African constitutional discourse, where it is seen as instrumental to "the making of a just society formerly divided by chronic socio-economic discrimination". For related reasons, the South African Court is also particularly keen to invoke human dignity (18 cases, i.e. 45 per cent). It is also the only court in our study whose leading judgments were all coded as dialogical in structure.

Moreover, although not strictly an outlier on these measures, the South African Constitutional Court is the court that has the highest proportion of opinions discussing arguments from coherence (Q12) and non-legal considerations (Q19). Yet in other respects, such as the share of decisions devoted to rights issues or the frequency with which it discusses textualist arguments, the South African Court is fairly close to the median.

Another judicial body with a credible claim to exceptionalism is the French Constitutional Council. Compared to those issued by the other courts, the decisions delivered by the Council tend to contain fewer and less varied arguments. Among the 40 landmark Council rulings studied in this book, we do not find a single one dealing with the definition of a word or phrase appearing in the documents which the Council has elevated to constitutional status. Nor do we find any reference to scholarly works or foreign legal materials. Meanwhile, though not nonexistent, references to the framers' intent (2.5 per cent compared to an average of 30.6 per cent), to the purpose of constitutional provision (2.5 per cent against 73.1 per cent) or to domestic harmonising arguments (20 per cent against 60.3 per cent) are significantly less frequent than in the decisions of other courts. But talk of exceptionalism may yet again mask more complex dynamics. The analysis offered in this book shows that, despite the constraints of the French, French constitutional judges are not entirely immune to the pull of global constitutional convergence. French constitutional opinions have become significantly longer over time and have begun to develop a broader repertoire of arguments – an evolution that we also observe in salient cases. On that score, the book demonstrates that the comparativists who lump together the Council together with the other two French supreme courts – the *Conseil d'Etat* and the *Cour de cassation* – miss significant shifts in the Council's argumentative practices. What is more, the cavalier manner with which the Council treats the constitutional text is hardly exceptional in contemporary constitutionalism. If anything, the opposite is true, as shown by the discussion of the Australian case. Nor does the focus on rights adjudication (77.5 per cent of landmark cases) set the Constitutional Council apart from constitutional courts in the rest of the world.

We could easily carry on detailing other aspects of constitutional reasoning where one or the other court appears to stand out from its peers. The German Constitutional Court has the highest proportion of landmark cases dealing with freedom of speech (35 per cent, as opposed to the average 6.05 per cent). This reflects the importance of landmark rulings such as the *Lüth* decision, in which the German Court famously held that freedom of expression, as protected by the Basic Law, included the right to call for the boycott of a film-director who had gained fame during the Nazi period. Also, the German Court is only second to the Supreme Court of Canada when it comes citing academic writings. Compared to other constitutional courts (except for the Canadian Supreme Court), German leading constitutional decisions are twice as likely to mention scholarly works (92.5 per cent, as opposed to the average 47.5 per cent). Unlike in Canadian constitutional discourse, though, the scholarship that finds its way into German constitutional opinions seems to be almost exclusively of the doctrinal sort. The authority thus attributed to the work of legal scholars appears to stem from the comparatively high status enjoyed by legal scholarship in Germany as well as from the composition of the Court – where law professors tend to dominate, at least in recent decades.

This implies that exceptionalism, like many other things, is, at least in part, in the eye of the beholder. Depending on the facet of constitutional reasoning we choose to stress, a different court will come out as exceptional. Hence, rather than global convergence with pockets of exceptionalism, glocalisation[46] – by which we mean the intersection of global trends with local, particularising tendencies – may provide a more accurate description of the evolution and current state of constitutional reasoning. Glocal constitutionalism is shaped by competing forces pulling judicial practices in opposite directions. At the global level, human rights treaties, supranational courts, transnational human rights NGOs and transjudicial networks favour convergence towards common approaches and generic standards. But at the domestic level, many combinations of idiosyncratic constitutional provisions, hostile judges and unsympathetic audiences may hamper the adoption of argumentation frameworks and modes of judicial communication developed elsewhere.

V The Future of Constitutional Reasoning Research

The aim of this book was to bring comparative constitutional reasoning research to a new level by systematically documenting the actual practices of constitutional judges. We hope to have demonstrated how a mixed methods research design blending qualitative analysis with a more quantitative approach can sharpen our understanding of judicial argumentation

[46] On the concept in general see Roland Robertson, 'Glocalization: Time-Space and Homogeneity-Heterogeneity' in Mike Featherstone, Scott Lash and Roland Robertson (eds), *Global Modernities* (SAGE 1995) 25–44.

across constitutional systems. We are confident that our study represents an important contribution to the literature on constitutional reasoning. But we must also acknowledge its limitations. These arise, in part, from the fact that our study is limited to the 40 leading constitutional judgments of 19 courts. Owing to our focus on great cases, we cannot assume that our findings are true for constitutional reasoning general (but we do think that our results are generalisable to "leading cases" of constitutional courts). Oliver Wendell Holmes argued that great cases tend to distort our perception of the law. But one need not agree with the great American judge to admit that great cases might not be representative of constitutional reasoning at large. The systematic analysis of non-salient cases may reveal different patterns. Necessity is often the mother of innovation, and the controversial nature of great cases may induce constitutional judges to embrace argumentation strategies they would not entertain in routine cases. Constitutional reasoning in routine opinions may take on a more stereotypical form. Differences between Common Law and Civil Law courts could prove more marked. Or perhaps not. But the question will not be settled unless scholars seriously begin to investigate constitutional reasoning in this class of cases. As for the geographical coverage of our study, although our 18 judicial bodies figure among the world's most powerful and influential constitutional courts, they represent only a fraction of the constitutional courts currently in operation around the world.

Some limitations are more methodological in character. The method we used to identify the leading judgments is not unassailable either. As mentioned in the Introduction, there cannot be perfect intersubjective agreement on what constitutes a leading judgment. Some will lament the absence of cases they regard as essential and criticise the inclusion of decisions they deem less so. Nor should we believe the quantitative data we have collected to be entirely error-free. We gave detailed instructions to our contributors, and we did our best to ensure their uniform implementation. Yet each contributor individually coded the data for his or her court, and we could not conduct inter-coder reliability tests. So, despite our constant attention, we cannot be fully certain that all our contributors have interpreted our concepts and definitions in the same consistent manner throughout the analysis and coding process. Lastly, the typology of constitutional arguments deployed in this book and the theory of judicial communication that underpins it are in need of further elaborations. For many lawyers distinguishing among chain-like, legs-of-a-chair and dialogical reasoning structures may be straightforward enough. But in order to delve deeper into the structure of judicial reason-giving, a more fine-grained analytical framework may be required. One place to look for inspiration is the rich literature on argumentation drawing from philosophy, formal logic and psychology.[47]

Aware of these limitations, however, our hope is that future researchers will pick up the baton where we have left it. There are many descriptive questions which remained unanswered about comparative constitutional reasoning, but for which we probably need bigger samples and a somewhat different questionnaire.[48] Our insights fit to theories of strategic judicial behaviour – an explanatory model which is by its nature simplifying, like every model, and which we could not *prove* here either, of course, but we could corroborate this model with our data. We also saw how recent changes in constitutional reasoning can be described with glocalisation. And we also managed to relativise the common law/civil law distinction in constitutional reasoning. But naming a few of our conclusions would probably not do justice to our efforts. This volume is not only about constitutional reasoning itself, it is at least that much about *demonstrating* how quantitative (or mixed) methods can be useful when analysing a classical doctrinal topic such as constitutional reasoning.

Quantification does not necessarily make arguments more plausible, but it does make them more transparent, they can be falsified (instead of the struggle of anecdotal evidence of legal academia), the full dataset is freely available and methodology is far more explicit in this volume than it is usually the case in comparative constitutional law. Quantitative methods also make general trends easier to discover, and maps easier to draw if there are numerous factors to be considered at the same time (which would otherwise be difficult to overview at the same time and weigh with traditional qualitative methods). Establishing time trends, as we did above, would not have been possible without some statistical

[47] Douglas Walton et al., *Argumentation Schemes* (Cambridge University Press 2008); Keith J. Holyoak and Robert G. Morrison, *The Oxford Handbook of Thinking and Reasoning* (Oxford University Press 2013); Frans H. van Eemeren et al., *Handbook of Argumentation Theory* (Springer 2014); Stephen Toulmin, *The Uses of Argument* (Cambridge University Press 1958).

[48] Just to give a few ideas: is there any correlation between the style of reasoning, on the one hand, and judicial independence, rule of law (as measured by rule of law indexes), GDP or size of a country, on the other hand? Are the general patterns of change in the style of reasoning time similar in every country, or are there any outliers? If so, how could this be explained? Does the growing length of judgments (we did not measure the length of judgments in this project) explain the growing argumentative diversity? How do leading cases differ from average cases in their style of reasoning?

analysis. Many of the results were also formerly well-known or at least suspected (e.g. the overwhelming popularity of purposive arguments), and we could confirm these with novel methods and novel arguments. But we also had "discoveries" in a true sense, which actually surprised us, such as the character of reasoning in mixed jurisdictions (being *not* the middle way between common law and civil law, but rather the extreme value) – something that would have been far more difficult with traditional legal methods.

We are aware of many of the limitations of our research, as mentioned above, but we are confident that the present volume is the most comprehensive and methodologically most advanced comparative analysis of constitutional reasoning so far. We hope future researchers will use our findings to further refine the theory, improve the methodology and broaden the geographical coverage of empirical constitutional reasoning research to further illuminate judicial practices.

APPENDIX

A Questionnaire for the Country Reports[1]

Each Country Report is meant to provide a description of the argumentative practices of the court under consideration on the basis of an in-depth analysis of the court's 40 leading judgments (the 'canon' of the court that is normally considered to be the most important, e.g. because it is the core teaching material in university courses on constitutional law). Authors can refer to cases outside of the 40 leading judgments, if this seems necessary in order to explain the wider context or to show contrasts. The present Guidelines are there to ensure comparability across the Country Reports. Hence it is crucial for the comparative analysis and the validity of the research results that the authors read the Guidelines carefully and follow them strictly in writing their Country Report.

The answers should form a full-text, self-contained essay. Care should be taken to avoid repetitions and to present the answers in the order that appears most relevant and appropriate. Accompanying the Guidelines, a Table is a separate file in Excel format which each author should complete in light of his/her analysis of the 40 judgments sample. One of the functions of the Table is to 'relieve' the texts of the Country Reports of too many details (i.e., to store some of the details in the Table instead of in the actual text) in order to make the texts easier to read. We strongly recommend that authors read the sample Country Report on the Hungarian Constitutional Court before drafting their Country Report.

As far as possible, questions should be answered in the order given below. Authors may change the structure of the questionnaire and alter the order of sections and paragraphs, but only to the extent that is necessary to improve the readability and logical coherence of the reports. While new paragraphs and subparagraphs can certainly be added, please do

[1] Updated and edited version for the purposes of the present publication. The original questionnaire and codebook have been amended in light of the results of the Heidelberg Workshop (15 February 2013) and the Budapest Workshop (7–8 February 2014).

not change the titles of the sections and paragraphs of the questionnaire, unless absolutely necessary, as consistency in the use of the titles facilitates comparison.

Please remember that with a view to publication, Country Reports should not be in excess of 15,000 words. Unfortunately this is an external and non-negotiable constraint. Given the research question and design of our project, providing examples of constitutional reasoning is, of course, fully apposite. However, long literal quotations and detailed case discussions are likely to result in reports exceeding the word limit. Please bear in mind that the priority is to ensure maximum comparability across the reports. This means that the priority is to answer the questions listed in the Guidelines. Finally, note that while the 'Comparative Perspective' and the 'Evaluation, Pathology and Criticism' sections are to be included in the 15,000 words limit, the latter is optional.

Should doubt arise regarding the meaning of a particular question or about any other matter related to the Comparative Constitutional Reasoning Project, please contact us: conreason@mpil.de.[2]

A Legal, Political, Institutional and Academic Context

The exposition of the institutional context should not be overly detailed and should be limited to those general aspects or characteristic features that allow for a meaningful comparison with other experiences. With regard to those legal systems where a clear-cut distinction between ordinary statutory law and constitutional provisions is missing and where the identification of the constitution cannot be made with reference to well-established, uncontroversial criteria, the authors of the reports should justify the choices they have made to identify the constitution and/or the criteria they followed in selecting the cases – the first section, 'Legal, Political, Institutional and Academic Context', is the place where this can be done.

1 Legal and Political Culture as Context for Constitutional Reasoning

1.1 The prevailing legal and political culture, including traditional conceptions of the nature of law and the proper role of courts; the

[2] For further details about the present terminology and conceptual-doctrinal frame see the study by András Jakab, 'Constitutional Reasoning. A European Perspective on Judicial Reasoning in Constitutional Courts' (2013) 8 *German Law Journal* 1215–78.

attitudes and reactions of the other branches of government towards perceived judicial 'activism'; and the extent to which judges have felt compelled to 'stretch' their constitutional authority in order to deal with problems such as corruption, oppression, and injustice. What are the typical implied political philosophical presuppositions (the existence of a pre-legal state or human rights as natural rights)? What are the usual spoken or unspoken premises about the purpose of the political community and of its constitution?

1.2 Are methods of legal reasoning different in ordinary courts? How far do the literature of your system and the judgments themselves consider the extent to which constitutions differ from statutes, and require different methods of interpretation? If there are such differences in practice and/or they are analysed in the literature, how are these differences explained? Is it by the intended longevity of constitutions, their inclusion of broad, abstract terms, or the difficulty of amending them? Do ordinary courts follow the judgments of the constitutional court?

2 The Court and Constitutional Litigation

2.1 What are the relevant competences (e.g. *a priori* or *a posteriori* abstract review, individual complaint etc.) of the court? Who has standing (MPs, ombudsman, ordinary courts, individuals . . .) to bring a case and under what circumstances can the court choose among the cases brought? Does the court have any discretionary power to refuse to review a case? In every report it should be clear what kind of decision the constitutional court can make, i.e., whether it can strike down legislation, refuse the application of laws *in concreto*, issue declaratory judgments and if so what kind of declarations.

2.2 Do other courts have the competence to annul statutes?

2.3 Are cases (always, frequently, never) orally argued? Who are the parties to the procedure?

2.4 Are there any specific (constitutional/statutory) rules about the admissibility of proof/argument in the court? How often are they used? Please provide examples.

2.5 What is the workload of the court (number of cases decided per year, incl. a limine rejections for formal reasons or for being obviously unfounded)? How has it varied throughout the years? Are all of decided cases published (what is the percentage of published vs. unpublished cases)?

2.6 What kind of judgments does the court adopt as to their legal nature? Is there a commonly accepted typology of constitutional judgments? (e.g., judgments on admissibility/on the merits, 'interpretative judgments', 'warning decisions', etc)

3 The Judges

3.1 How many members does the court have? How are the judges selected? Are they elected/appointed for life or for a shorter period?
3.2 Are the judges academics, politicians, judges or other practitioners? Has the ratio of these four groups changed significantly over time?

4 Legal Scholarship and Constitutional Reasoning

4.1 Is legal scholarship critical/deferential towards the court? Are the works of law professors (who are not sitting on the court) perceived to have an impact on the way the court argues or on the court's jurisprudence?
4.2 How do you see the prestige of a constitutional court judge compared to that of a constitutional law professor in your system? Can you compare the salaries?
4.3 Are there any generally (or at least widely) accepted theories about constitutional reasoning, constitutional interpretation or legal interpretation (including the ranking of interpretive methods) in general in the country under consideration? If yes, please outline them (2 pages max.). Are these theories explicitly mentioned in the judgments?

B Arguments in Constitutional Reasoning

For this part of the Country Report the authors are required to base their analysis on the 40 Leading Judgments of the Court.[3] Each author should strive to identify the 40 judgments that are perceived, in the legal community broadly defined (i.e. encompassing judges, law professors and practitioners), as being the Court's most influential ever (both in the scholarly discourse and in legal practice). Authors should also include the separate (dissenting and concurring) opinions of the judgments in the analysis. Note that the Excel Table as Appendix is attached in a separate file.

[3] Authors can, of course, refer to cases outside of the 40 leading judgments, if this seems necessary in order to explain the wider context or to show contrasts.

5 The Structure of Constitutional Arguments

What is the usual structure of arguments? What is your assessment of the frequency of use of the following argumentative structures in judicial opinions on constitutional matters:[4]

- 'one-line conclusive arguments': We mean a self-standing structure, in which every premise is presented as a necessary component of the argument.
- 'parallel conclusive arguments': We mean a cumulative parallel structure, in which distinct, autonomous considerations lead to the same conclusion.
- 'parallel, individually inconclusive, but together conclusive arguments': The various considerations brought up by the opinion are neither presented as necessary nor as sufficient to entail the conclusion, but as elements bearing, at least, some relevance for the issue at hand.

Note that results can change depending on the level of generality. The three types of structure are in a more-or-less relationship as to their structural clarity, i.e., the 'one-line conclusive arguments' is the clearest structure and the 'parallel, individually inconclusive, but together conclusive arguments' is the most opaque one. Consequently, if several of them turn up in the same judgment then you should tick the box according to the most complicated one. I.e., if you find both a chain (one-line conclusive argument) structure (which is most likely to be in every judgment) and a legs-of-a-chair (parallel conclusive) argument, then you should only tick the box in the Excel Table for the latter one.

6 Types of Arguments in Constitutional Reasoning

6.1 Which of the following arguments are used (or explicitly rejected) in the 40 opinions?[5] Please do not consider those arguments which are used to interpret statutes or regulations (i.e. infra-constitutional norms). Please fill in the Excel Table of the 40 Leading Judgments on the use of the following arguments:

Analogies,
Establishing/Debating the text of the Constitution,

[4] In the early stage of the project, based on Jakab (n 2), we used the terms "chain structure", "legs of a chair structure" and "dialogic (discoursive) structure", but in order to have terms which cannot be misunderstood, we decided to use the above different terminology. Abreviations in the Excel Table (C, L, D) are based on the old terminology.

[5] See above Jakab (n 2).

Applicability of the Constitution (e.g., political question doctrine, primacy of EU law against the Constitution, state-centred arguments in a state of emergency),
Ordinary meaning of the words of the Constitution or reference to the 'wording of the Constitution' in general,
Harmonising arguments (separate domestic harmonising and international/EU harmonising arguments)
Precedents (former own cases),
Doctrinal analysis of legal concepts or principles,
Arguments from silence,
Teleological/purposive arguments referring to the purpose of the text,
Teleological/purposive arguments referring to the purpose of the Constitution-maker (incl. *travaux préparatoires*),
Non-legal (moral, sociological, economic) arguments,
References to scholarly works,
References to foreign (national) law,
Other methods/arguments (explain in the text especially these arguments).

Please also mark those judgments with 'yes' where a certain argument was considered but eventually rejected (e.g. if the opinion distinguishes the case at hand from former precedents, it does count as an 'argument from precedent'). However, do not mark 'yes' if the argument type is rejected altogether as irrelevant or inappropriate (e.g. the argument 'we do not consider here moral arguments because it is a court of law' does not count as a non-legal argument).

6.2 What are the typical situations in which these arguments are resorted to?
6.3 Is there any self-reference in the Constitution about how to interpret its provisions?

7 The Weight of Arguments

The rate at which an argument type recurs in the case law of a court tells us relatively little about its function in given opinions. Just as widely used expressions may prove operatively inert, routine references to past rulings do not necessarily imply that the court is bound by its prior decisions. Consequently, authors should use their written reports to correct the misrepresentation that may possibly arise from the strictly quantitative method employed in the Excel Tables.

7.1 Are there any specific doctrines on the relative weight of the above arguments (methods)? If yes, please give illustrations.

7.2 Is it possible to categorise arguments as auxiliary/secondary (offering only a backup or additional argument for the result which has already been derived from another argument) as opposed to main or primary arguments? Does the weight of a specific argument (e.g., literal, purposive argument or reference to precedents) differ depending on the specific area of constitutional law (human rights vs. allocation of authority among governmental institutions)?

8 Judicial Candour and Judicial Rhetoric

The question here pertains to the difference you are able to discern between the reasons the judges publicly adduce for their decisions and their real motives. Authors should indicate in their written reports to what extent they believe the judges to be straightforward about the factors affecting the court's decision-making process. Authors should also indicate the extent to which judges acknowledge internal disagreement within the Court.

8.1 Judges make value judgments in the course of adjudicating cases, but to what extent are these value judgments acknowledged in their opinions? Do you see a correlation between opinion length and the judges' degree of candour?

8.2 Do the opinions deal with possible counter-arguments (and/or the arguments of the parties, if there are parties to the procedure; and/or from legal scholars, even if not referring to them explicitly)?

8.3 How technical is the language used by the opinion writers? Is it understandable for non-lawyers and/or for lawyers not specialised in constitutional law?

8.4 Who are the target audience of the reasoning of the judgment? Courts? Parties in the proceedings? Lawyers? Politicians? General public? Law students? Academic constitutional lawyers? Judges of the same court? Foreign or international courts (aiming at judicial dialogue)? Please weigh the relevance of the audiences.

8.5 What is the degree of generalisation? Do judgments concentrate on the very specific issue to be decided or are they trying to develop a general conceptual frame and/or principles for future cases?

8.6 What is the degree of rhetoric? Do you find (legally irrelevant) political and/or emotional language in the text of judgments?

9. Length, dissenting and concurring opinions

9.1 Does the length of the opinions show any correlation with the topic? Has it been growing by time or not? Are there any other factors influencing it (e.g. changes in political power, changes in constitutional text, changes in the personnel of the court)?

9.2 Is it possible to submit dissenting or concurring opinions? If yes, then how often does this happen? On what does it depend, whether there are dissenting and concurring opinions to a judgments? Are there any factors (the nature of the topic, changes in political power, changes in constitutional text, changes in the personnel of the court) that make it more it likely?

10 Framing of Constitutional Issues

Framing is fundamentally about the language or phraseology used to characterise an issue. One question is whether constitutional cases are primarily framed (or conceptualised) as being about fundamental rights or, rather, about separation of powers, federalism or legislative procedure. This may, of course, depend in part on the arguments raised by the parties to the case. But litigants themselves may be tuning their rhetoric to the predilection the Court has shown for certain frames in previous rulings.

10.1 Can you see any typical ways of characterising constitutional issues (e.g. as competence conflict rather than as fundamental rights issue)?

10.2 Have there been changes over time in the way constitutional cases are conceptualised?

11 Key Concepts

11.1 Taking a broader look at the Court's jurisprudence and argumentative practices, how frequently, if ever, does it make use of the following concepts (please give a definition only where a constitutional lawyer with a general basic knowledge of comparative law might be surprised: the purpose is not to analyse any concept, but only to avoid misunderstandings when comparing with other countries):

- 'the rule of law' (incl. 'separation of powers', 'primacy of the constitution' or 'legal certainty'; does it include moral justice and access to justice?),
- 'democracy' (incl. sovereignty of the people; does it include local democracy?),
- 'sovereignty' ('international independence', 'state' or 'statehood', do sub-state entities have sovereignty?),

- state form ('republic' or 'monarchy'),
- form of government (presidential or parliamentary)
- 'secularism' (or the separation of state and church),
- 'nation' (civic, ethnic or a mixture?),
- 'federalism' (or 'regionalism', 'autonomous regions', 'devolution', 'autonomy of local governments', 'subsidiarity),
- proportionality (test),
- *Wesensgehalt* (of competences or of fundamental rights),
- 'human dignity',
- 'equality' (or non-discrimination),
- procedural basic rights (incl. 'due process' and 'presumption of innocence', but excl. procedure of law making),
- 'freedom of expression',
- 'privacy' (right to privacy, data protection),
- further fundamental rights.

11.2 Are there any further key concepts widely used by the Court? If yes, which ones and how are they defined? Are there are other peculiarities in constitutional terminology which could be surprising to foreign constitutional lawyers (max. 1 page)?

11.3 Are the key constitutional concepts spelled out in the constitutional text(s) (respectively in the text of the founding treaty)? Are the key concepts somehow derived from higher ranked constitutional provisions (*Ewigkeitsklausel* or alike)?

11.4 Are they used in an operative manner in the sense of triggering specific legal consequences, or are they essentially deployed as rhetorical device? Has the frequency of use of any of these concepts changed throughout the years? If yes, what would be the most plausible explanation?

C *Comparative Perspective*

12 Constitutional Reasoning from a Comparative Perspective

Authors should write this part after having read the first drafts of the other country reports, thus after our February 2014 Heidelberg workshop.

1 Can you see any major differences in the applied key concepts, typical arguments etc. as compared to the other countries as seen in the country reports? How can this be explained?

2 Please also consider: (1) the possible correlation between procedural aspects of constitutional review and the style of reasoning,

(2) differences in political theory in the countries (relative roles of courts and legislature), (3) differences in legal culture, including legal theory, (4) differences in personnel (including training and background) for explaining the differences in constitutional reasoning.

3 Hypotheses that could be tested (examples): (1) 'Without a full posterior constitutional review and a great amount of cases, the conceptual sophistication in constitutional law (*Verfassungsdogmatik*) remains underdeveloped' (2) 'The bigger and/or economically stronger the country, the more likely is the rejection of the use of foreign law' (3) 'The older the Constitution is and the more difficult it is to amend it, the more likely the judges are to use purposive arguments instead of literal arguments' (4) 'The more academics are sitting in a court, the longer and more detailed the judgments / the more abstract the judgments / the more references to academic literature'

4 As a conclusion, list a handful of important general unwritten premises (implied presuppositions) that you think a foreign lawyer needs to know in order to understand a judgment of your constitutional court. E.g. 'the Constitution says something about every single legal case', 'constitutional law should only be considered, if it is an important political issue'.

D Optional Questions: Evaluation, Pathology and Criticism

13 Evaluation, Pathology and Criticism

13.1 What features of the argumentative practices of the constitutional court in your country do you consider to be pathological? Highly subject to criticism? For example, do judges manipulate constitutional language? Do they make bad arguments of a given type? What else? Or the opposite: do you see any exemplary elements which other countries should consider to borrow? How common are these?

13.2 The authors are invited to conclude their chapters with some overall critical observations, on issues such as whether the courts have been either too legalistic or too creative, and the contribution they have made to their societies.

B Explanations of the 40 Leading Judgments Excel Table (Codebook)

The present codebook should be read together with the questionnaire of the country reports. The Excel Tables will not be printed in the book, but they will be placed on a companion website of Cambridge University Press with the purpose that (1) our research results can be verified, (2) the results can also be used by other scholars throughout the world.

Please also mark those judgments with 'yes' where a certain argument was considered but eventually rejected (e.g. if the opinion distinguishes the case at hand from former precedents, it does count as an 'argument from precedent'). However, do not mark 'yes' if the argument type is rejected altogether as irrelevant or inappropriate (e.g. the argument 'we do not consider here moral arguments because it is a court of law' does not count as a non-legal argument).

You should only consider *constitutional* interpretation. As a first step we would suggest that in those legal orders where there is no formal constitution (the UK), the textual analysis of 'constitutional' ('cardinal', 'basic', 'fundamental') statutes should be seen as textual arguments. But authors can contact us, if this conceptualisation is problematic in their system for some reason. If a case brought before a constitutional (or supreme) court deals exclusively with the interpretation of ordinary legislation, then these arguments are not relevant – or, at least, not directly relevant – for this Project. As regards the interpretation of a statute in light of the constitution, we are only interested in the arguments establishing the meaning of the constitution, as opposed to how these arguments bear on the meaning of ordinary legislation.

Please try to classify the arguments as one from our list. If – despite your efforts – it does not seem possible, then there is a special box in the 40-judgments table (Q22), and you can explain in your report why it did not fit into any of our categories.

We would like to minimise missing values (or 'not applicable', 'na' values). We would like to have uniform data (with one exception: 'not applicable' is used for one type of question, if – because of the nature of the procedure – it does not make sense to inquire what the case disposition was, i.e. whether the state won or not). Beyond that, the questions are 'is there an argument of type-x in this judgment?', and the answer is either 'yes' or 'no' (whether the 'no' can be explained by the fact that it was not even possible to have such an argument for some reason, can be explained in the report itself, but in the schedule we just want a 'yes' or 'no'). Otherwise we might run into very difficult problems of deciding whether we deal with a 'no' or with a 'not applicable'.

You should equally consider majority and minority (dissenting or concurring) opinions: it does not matter whether the argument turned up in the majority or in the minority opinion. We only consider whether a type of argument came up in the reasoning, not how many times it did. Because of repetitions and half-repetitions it would be difficult and very time-consuming to quantify the frequency within the judgments.

If we consider an argument as borderline between two types of arguments, then we shall make a mark for both categories. If a judgment quoted an argument from another judgment, then the quoted argument also qualified on its own (and not just as a 'precedent-argument').

Q1: Reference of the decision?

> Please give the official reference of the decision in original language, except for languages using non-Latin alphabet, in which case reference in English should be provided.

Q2: Year?

> Specify year the decision was rendered.

Q3: Dissenting or concurring opinion in the case?

> Please indicate Yes or No. If irrelevant (separate opinions not allowed), leave blank.

Q4: Case disposition?

> Please indicate (Yes or No) whether the Court found (at least partially) against the law/decision/act (of the government) challenged. If the judgment is prescribes a binding interpretation (of a statute or of the Constitution), then the box should be left blank. If the Court establishes an 'unconstitutional omission' (if that is possible in your legal order), then it counts as a 'Yes'. Admissibility decisions can also be categorised as 'yes' (admissibility granted) or as 'no' (admissibility denied). If the case is only about an interim relief, then an interim relief against the law/decision/act also qualifies as a yes.

Q5: General topic?

> Please specify: Fundamental Rights (F), State Organisation (S), or Other (O). You can also indicate a combination of the general topics, if there were several in one single judgments, e.g. 'F, S', 'F, S, O'.

Q6: Concrete issue?

> Please characterise the issue at hand, using your own words.

Q7: Structure of argument?

> Please specify: 'one-line conclusive arguments' (C), Also 'one-line conclusive arguments' (L), 'parallel conclusive arguments' (D).[6]

[6] The abbreviations C, L and D stem from a former terminology of the project. See above the remarks to Point 5 of the Questionnaire.

- 'one-line conclusive arguments' (C): We mean a self-standing structure, in which every premise is presented as a necessary component of the argument.
- 'parallel conclusive arguments' (L): We mean a cumulative parallel structure, in which distinct, autonomous considerations lead to the same conclusion.
- 'parallel, individually inconclusive, but together conclusive arguments' (D): The various considerations brought up by the opinion are neither presented as necessary nor as sufficient to entail the conclusion, but as elements bearing, at least, some relevance for the issue at hand.

If both C and L structures are present in the same judgment, then mark it as L. If you notice a D structure, then mark the judgment with D even if there are also L and C structures. The structure of a judgment that contains only one argument (or which just simply states the interpretation without explaining why the court chose it) is a C.

Q8: Establishing or discussing the text of the constitution?

Please indicate (Yes or No) whether the opinion explicitly discusses what counts as constitutional text. Establishing the text is different from establishing the content of the constitution. The latter refers to the meaning and interpretation of what is already identified as a *constitutional* text. Prior to that is the question of what counts as a constitutional text. This is the question the present category is intended to capture. It includes all segments of an opinion in which the constitutional status of legal sources is considered (e.g. what is considered to be a standard of review).

Q9: Is the applicability of constitutional law discussed?

Please indicate (Yes or No) whether the opinion explicitly considers whether constitutional law can be applied by the Court to the case at hand (e.g. because/despite political question doctrine). Does the opinion consider the applicability of constitutional law to the case at hand? This question may notably arise in connection with political question doctrines and state of emergency situations or, in EU member states, in relation to the primacy of EU law over domestic constitutional law, or when the Court holds that the case is not governed by the constitution, but by some other legal source. Deferential arguments, stating that no constitutional answer can be found to the question, should also be noted here. This category covers considerations as to the applicability *ratione materiae* of the constitution, the binding force, as well as to the enforceability and justiciability of the constitution. Illustrations are statements such as 'the case at hand has no constitutional relevance', 'the case falls within the discretion of the legislator [or other non-judicial institution]', 'a Constitution has to bind all state organs', etc.

Q10: Analogy?

Please indicate whether the opinion features any instance(s) of analogical reasoning. For the purposes of our research, analogy is an argument that is presented as filling a gap (lacuna) in the constitution and is used to solve a case that is not explicitly regulated by the constitution by using a constitutional provision that regulates similar cases. If the court categorically says that 'analogy as such is always an invalid argument' then you should *not* count it. But if the court simply rejects the use of analogy in a certain case without rejecting the genre of this argument in general, then you should count it.

Q11: Ordinary meaning of words?

Please indicate (Yes or No) whether the opinion explicitly considers the ordinary meaning of the text of the constitution.

Q12: Domestic harmonising arguments?

Please indicate (Yes or No) whether the opinion seeks to conciliate different constitutional requirements with one another. In case harmonising involves international law, it shold be categorised under Q13 (with the separation of Q12 and Q13, we aimed at acquiring information also about the openness towards international law). Please do not consider interpretation of statutes in light of the constitution *(verfassungskonforme Auslegung)*, as that is not about the interpretation of the constitution but about the interpretation of statues which we are not dealing with.

Q13: Harmonising with international law requirements?

Please indicate (Yes or No) whether the opinion seeks to interpret constitutional law in light of international law (including EU law, if applicable).

Q14: Precedent-based arguments?

Please indicate (Yes or No) whether the opinion considers previous rulings of the court. Please also mark it with 'Yes' if the court distinguished the present case from the former one, and therefore they did not apply it.

Q15: Invokes concept or principle not mentioned in the text of the constitution?

Please indicate Yes or No. The application of concepts and principles (incl. different constitutional tests for fundamental rights restrictions) developed by courts or by legal scholars.

Q16: Arguments from silence?

Please indicate (Yes or No) whether the opinion considers argument from silence.

Q17: Teleological (textual) arguments?

Indicate (Yes or No) whether the opinion invokes or considers the supposed purpose of the constitutional text or part thereof. This kind of teleological argument (often called 'objective teleological argument') refers to the purpose of the text rather than to the purpose of its authors.

Q18: Teleological (historical-intentional) arguments?

Indicate (Yes or No) whether the opinion invokes or considers the purpose of the constitution-makers. This type of teleological argument (often called 'subjective teleological argument') equates the purpose of a constitutional provision with the purpose pursued by the constitution-makers. It may take the form of a reference to the travaux préparatoires.

Q19: Non-legal arguments?

Please indicate (Yes or No) whether the opinion explicitly considers economic, sociological or moral arguments. The present project does not want to contribute to the endless debate about the concept of law, so we are using a rather practical and simple test on what counts as 'non-legal'. For the purposes of the present research, non-legal arguments are explicitly moral, economic and sociological arguments (i.e. arguments that are explictly grounded on considerations external to the law) about the interpretation of the constitution.

There is a significant degree of overlap between legal and other forms of discourse. This fact is particularly evident in the realm of constitutional law and with terms such as 'sovereignty', 'human dignity', 'democracy', etc. Generally speaking, though, the fact that an expression is also used in moral or political discourse does not automatically make it non-legal. Though explicit mention in the constitutional text is not a necessary condition for legalness, it should in principle be sufficient. So if a specific constitutional rule mentions 'public morality' or 'budgetary stability' then the explanation of these concepts is legal. Also, the explanation of the facts of a case does not qualify as a non-legal argument: we are looking only for arguments which justify a certain interpretation of a constitutional rule.

We also remind you that the court should not be regarded as having recourse to a non-legal argument when a non-legal argument is rejected as invalid, irrelevant or inappropriate. If, for example, the court observes 'we do not consider here moral arguments because it is a court of law', this does not count as a non-legal argument.

The proportionality analysis is an interesting issue because it explicitly requires courts to balance rights against public morals or safety etc. We would still suggest that this should not be categorised as a non-legal argument. Because if we say that this is a non-legal argument we will end up including too much in the 'non-legal' category. Similarly, many constitutions explicitly refer to public morals and safety and health or 'human dignity' and therefore require the courts to interpret them and protect them. But again, if we included these concepts which are commonly contained in written constitutions, the category of non-legal arguments would become too broad and it would be misleading.

Q20: Reference to scholarly work?

Please indicate (Yes or No) whether the opinion explicitly mentions academic literature. Unnamed, generic references to the 'dominant doctrine', 'authoritative doctrine', etc., should also be qualified as references to scholarly works. On the other hand, the use of concepts and theories known to have scholarly origins should not count as 'references to scholarly works' if no explicit references to legal scholarship are made. Nuances in the use of scholarly arguments that are not captured by the Table can, and should, be discussed in your written report.

Q21: Reference to foreign legal material?

Please indicate Yes or No. A vague reference to 'foreign laws' or an expression such as 'after having analysed the results of comparative law' does qualify as a comparative law argument in the Excel Table. By contrast, simply quoting a foreign concept (even if it is used in a foreign language, e.g. German words like *Drittwirkung* in a Spanish judgment) should not count as a reference to foreign law. Nuances in the use of both foreign law arguments that are not captured by the Table can, and should, be discussed in your written report.

Q22: Other types of argument or method?

Please indicate Yes or No. Including references to domestic legal history, if you cannot qualify it as some kind of teleological argument.

Q23: The rule of law invoked as argument?

Please indicate (Yes or No) whether the opinion invokes the rule of law or a similar concept. This refers to the rule of law (or similar concept such as 'Rechtsstaat', 'Etat de droit' . . .) and includes principles the concept is generally taken to imply: the separation of powers, the supremacy of the constitution, access to justice and legal certainty (if these are considered to be part of the rule of law in the legal order you are analysing).

Q24: Democracy?

Please indicate (Yes or No) whether the opinion invokes democracy. Reference to the concept of democracy may also come in the form of phrases such as 'sovereignty of the people' or 'government of the people'.

Q25: Sovereignty?

Please indicate (Yes or No) whether the opinion invokes sovereignty.

Q26: State form?

Please indicate (Yes or No) whether the opinion invokes arguments related to the form of the state (republic, monarchy.).

Q27: Government form?

Please indicate (Yes or No) whether the opinion invokes arguments related to the government form (parliamentary, presidential).

Q28: Secularism?

Please indicate (Yes or No) whether the opinion invokes arguments related to the separation of state and religion. This includes references to 'secularism', the separation of church and state and state neutrality in religious affairs.

Q29: Nation?

Please indicate (Yes or No) whether the opinion invokes the concept of nation.

Q30: Federalism?

Please indicate (Yes or No) whether the opinion invokes federalism (including 'regionalism', 'autonomous regions', 'devolution', 'autonomy of local governments', 'subsidiarity').

Q31: Proportionality?

Please indicate (Yes or No) whether the opinion invokes proportionality or similar means-end test.

Q32: Core of constitutional rights or competences?

Please indicate (Yes or No) whether the opinion considers doctrines referring to the core content *(Wesensgehalt)* of either fundamental rights or of competences.

Q33: Human dignity?

Please indicate (Yes or No) whether the opinion explicitly invokes the concept of human dignity.

Q34: Equality?

Please indicate (Yes or No) whether the opinion invokes equality. This includes references to non-discrimination.

Q35: Basic procedural rights?

Please indicate (Yes or No) whether the opinion invokes basic procedural rights. This includes references to procedural due process, right to effective judicial review, adversarial principle, rights of the defence, right to be heard, ne bis in idem, principle of the legality of criminal offences and penalties, presumption of innocence, but excludes references to the legislative process and parliamentary procedures.

Q36: Freedom of expression?

Please indicate (Yes or No) whether the opinion invokes freedom of expression rights. This includes reference to freedom of speech and freedom of the press.

Q37: Privacy rights?

Please indicate (Yes or No) whether the opinion invokes the right to privacy. This includes references to data protection.

C Sample Judgment Questions

Please attach a typical judgment (possibly one of the 40) in English, which shows the typical length (incl. dissenting or concurring opinions) and the typical arguments. If the judgments of your court are not available in English and if you are unable to acquire the translation of a fitting judgment, we can provide for translation.

The Sample Judgments will not be printed in the book, but they will be placed on a companion website of Cambridge University Press with the purpose that (1) our research results can be verified, (2) the results can also be used by other scholars throughout the world.

On the basis of your judgment, explain also the usual structure and elements in a note following the judgment. What do the published judgments contain? Describe shortly:

(a) Case name and any other identification?
(b) Name of the deciding court? Name of the judges? A reference to in whose name the judgment is declared ('In the name of the Republic', 'In the name of the law', etc.)?
(c) The final decision, concrete order/decision and the *ratio decidendi* (holding) of the judgment?
(d) Statement of facts (how detailed, approximately what portion of a judgment)?
(e) Discussion of procedural background (incl. prior decisions of lower courts) in this very case?
(f) General statement of legal issue or issues?
(g) Reason or reasons for the ruling?
(h) Dissenting or concurring opinions?
(i) Summary of arguments by counsel/petitioner?
(j) Opinion by legal officials other than judges, e.g., secretary of court?

If the published judgment does not contain one or more of the above, are these generally discoverable from other sources? Explain.

Note on the Classification of Certain Arguments from US Constitutional Case Law[7]

1 How do I classify arguments used by American-style originalism (the meaning of terms must be understood as they were understood at the time of enactment)?

[7] We are grateful to Howard Schweber for bringing up the questions and for suggesting the majority of the answers to them.

American originalism has three sub-types:

1.1 Textualism or original understanding: words mean today what they meant in everyday language at the time of enactment. This would be qualified in our terminology as 'The Ordinary or (Legal or Non-Legal) Technical Meaning of the Words'.

1.2 Original intent: words mean what the drafters of the Constitution wanted them to mean. This would be qualified in our terminology as 'Relying on the Intention of the Constitution-Maker (Subjective Teleological Arguments)'. A typical example of this is where a judge appeals to Madison writing in the Federalist Papers.

1.3 Original legal understanding: This looks to original legal/technical meanings, based on references to statutes, common law principles, and past English practices. This is particularly common in the early cases – so in Fletcher v. Peck (1810) it was the meaning of 'contract', in Calder v. Bull (1798) it was the meaning of 'ex post facto', and in Chisholm v. Georgia (1793) it was the traditional understanding of sovereign immunity. The sources referred to included Blackstone's Commentaries, common law principles, Charles II's debt problems in English courts, and citations to Coke's commentaries and old English cases . . . none of which are exactly the same as either the intent of the authors or the common understanding. So these are appeals to earlier legal authorities to define a constitutionally relevant term, not to either the presumed intentions of the drafters or to ordinary language. This happens in modern cases as well, although not as frequently. These could be classified as follows:

1.3.1 If the original legal understanding is determined by statutes that were in force in the US at the time of the enactment of the Constitution, then it is a 'domestic harmonising argument', similar to the Austrian *Versteinerungstheorie* (if the statutes were not in force in the US, but only in the UK, then it was foreign law, thus it is a 'comparative law' argument). No English statutes could be in force in the US at the time of ratification, so we would have to be talking about a separately adopted American piece of legislation. Any appeal to an English statute would clearly be a case of foreign legal authority.

1.3.2 If the original legal understanding is determined by judicial decisions or by references to 'common law': see the answer below at 2.

1.3.3 Blackstone's Commentaries and Coke's commentaries: scholarly works.

2 How do I classify references to old English cases (i.e. cases from the time before US independence) and references to 'common law'? Here are five (made up) examples in order to answer this question and similar ones: (a) 'The phrase 'ex post facto' in the Constitution will be understood as it is explained in the English case of Smith v. Jones (1750).' (b) 'The phrase 'ex post facto' in the Constitution will be understood as it is explained in the American case of Smith v. Jones (1795) which was not specifically about the interpretation of the Constitution'. (c) 'The phrase 'ex post facto' in the Constitution will be understood as it is explained in the American case of Smith v. Jones (1830) which already interpreted these words of the Constitution'. (d) 'The phrase 'ex post facto' in the Constitution will be understood as it is understood in common law cases in our jurisdictions'. (e) 'The ideas of fundamental fairness are to be understood in terms of 'traditional common law principles'.'

(a) Smith v. Jones (1750 UK) – foreign law ('comparative law argument')

References to old English cases seem to be references to foreign law (i.e. 'comparative law' argument and not 'precedent' argument), because by the time of ratification (i.e. after the independence) American courts considered themselves in practice no longer to be bound to by English precedents. A counterargument against this approach could be that the States all had reception statutes that said that English common law remained in force unless and until replaced by legislation, thus – so the counterargument – the 1750 English case in example (a) appears to be a binding precedent. But in practice, from early on American courts (state and federal) demonstrated a willingness to innovate, meaning that in practice English precedents were only used as starting points and/or persuasive precedents. The American judges knew perfectly well that they were appealing to precedents from a nation not their own.

(b) Smith v. Jones (1795 US, not specifically on the interpretation of the Constitution) – 'domestic harmonising argument'

American common law is a separate and potentially divergent system from American constitutional law, so by appealing to an American common law precedent the Court is ensuring that the two systems remain consistent.

(c) Smith v. Jones (1830 US, interpreting the US Constitution) – 'precedent'

Straightforward case.

(d) common law specific rule, no case cited – 'domestic harmonising argument'

The reason is that the citation of common law deals with fixing the definition of a specific legal term. Again, just like in example (b), the goal is to ensure that the use of the term in a constitutional setting will not diverge from established usage in a different legal source, thus extending the idea of *ejusdem generis* across the two sets of legal rules. Although there is no citation to a specific case, there is citation to a very specific 'rule' defining an equally specific concept. It would be the same if the Court said 'understood as it is understood in our statutes' without citing a particular statute. We are particularly inclined toward this interpretation because in the lawyers' briefs there were always numerous citations to cases and/or statutes – these briefs were appended to the case reports in the early years, so it may be that the justices' failure to cite specific reference was based on the assumption that anyone who was curious could go back a few paragraphs. This is also consistent with a tradition in American constitutional law of treating common law rules as 'the law of the land' (e.g. Hurtado v. California 1884). That is, common law is a species of 'law' no less than statutory law.

(e) common law general principle, whether or not cases are cited – 'concept or principle outside the constitution'

Even if the justices (or lawyers) have cited cases, the appeal is to a broad concept ('fundamental fairness') rather than to a specific definition or rule in the Constitution. If there were no cases cited, only a reference to a general principle of common law in order to interpret the Constitution, also then it is a 'concept or principle outside the Constitution'.

3 **If an interpretation is justified on the grounds that it accords with 'the law of nations', then it is an argument 'harmonising with international law'. Is this correct?**

Yes, this is correct.

4 **One form of argument that turns up with some regularity is one that goes 'we have been doing this for a long time without controversy, so it must be okay'. How would you classify this?**

It might be 'precedent', 'silence' or 'principle outside the Constitution', depending on the exact formulation in the judgment. If none of these categories fit to the concrete judgment, then – as a last resort – you can use the 'other type of argument' (Q22), but please try to use this category as sparingly as possible.

5 **'Establishing or discussing the text': In American cases, every case starts with the text. I know that's not necessarily true in others – is this just an artefact of the American system that every case will be checked 'yes' for that one, or should I be applying a more discriminating understanding of the term in this context?**

We meant this category for (probably very rare) cases where the actual text of the Constitution could not easily be established, because e.g. there were so many modifications (maybe not explicit ones). We are aware of only one Hungarian case where the constitutional amendment determined about itself that it will be in force only for 4 years and then it 'deletes itself', but they drafted it so poorly that some scholars thought that the section in question was still in force after 8 years. At the end of the day, the Constitutional Court had to decide what the actual text of the Constitution is.

The mere statement of the text of the Constitution does not suffice for this category of argument.

How do I categorise an argument which states that 'you have to follow a precedent because of the *stare decisis* principle, no matter whether you agree with the precedent or not'?

This is actually not an argument about the interpretation of the Constitution. It is only about which method should be used to interpret the Constitution, thus it remains on a meta-level of interpretation (an argument about the use of arguments, but not about the actual interpretation). This argument, consequently, remains outside of the scope of the categories in the Excel Table, and you should not tick any of the boxes in the table. You can mention the use of this argument in the essay part of the country report.

How do I categorise an argument which states that 'it is wiser for the Court to take this position to preserve its legitimacy or to avoid getting involved in a messy situation'?

This seems to be a non legal argument (Q19).

How do I categorise arguments referring to the 'fundamental principles of sovereignty' and to the 'republican principle'? Are these non-legal arguments?

If the judgment contains political philosophical, moral or anthropological explanations, then these should be categorised as non-legal arguments. But a mere reference to a concept which also has political philosophical, moral or anthropological components (e.g., democracy, the rule of law) does not qualify as a non-legal argument. If these concepts are mentioned in the Constitution and they are used in order to interpret other articles of the Constitution, then it is a 'domestic harmonising argument'. In any case, these concepts should be noted in the table in Q23–Q26, respectively.

Note on the Classification of Certain Arguments from Israeli Constitutional Case Law

'Security reasons / considerations' or military reasons arise in numerous Israeli cases being a country with different security problem, with a continuous need for measures to fight terrorism etc. How would you categorise these arguments?

(a) If the argument goes as follows: 'This article of the Constitution has to be interpreted in light of such and such security considerations' then it is a case of Q19 (non-legal argument).
(b) If the argument goes as follows: 'The constitution does not apply (notwithstanding any explicit provisions) because common sense says that we do not bind ourselves in the fight against terrorism' then it is a case of Q9 ('applicability of the constitution').

'Concepts and principles outside the Constitution' would refer to legal arguments that are not mentioned in the text of a Constitution (e.g. 'separation of powers' was not mentioned in the Hungarian Constitution, but the Constitutional Court regularly referred to it). In your case it does not apply.

We try to avoid categorising anything as 'other type (Q22)' argument, this is rather just a last resort if all else fails.

INDEX

For EU product safety concerns, contact us at Calle de José Abascal, 56–1°,
28003 Madrid, Spain or eugpsr@cambridge.org.

www.ingramcontent.com/pod-product-compliance
Lightning Source LLC
LaVergne TN
LVHW052202200926
848481LV00001B/14
9781107449763